The PTSD & ADHD Fallacy: Book 2

SERVING EVIL

H. NATTANYA ANDERSEN

The PTSD & ADHD Fallacy: Book 2 - Serving Evil

All information contained in *The PTSD & ADHD Fallacy: Book 2 - Serving Evil* derives from my personal experiences and from sources quoted throughout the trilogy. The information is provided for general information purposes only and I assume no responsibility for possible errors or omissions in the trilogy's content.

This trilogy may contain copyrighted material. This material is made available for educational research and news reporting only. This constitutes a "fair use" of any such copyrighted material as provided for in title 17 U.S.C. section 107 of the United States of America Copyright Law, which allows citizens to reproduce, distribute or exhibit portions of copyrighted material under certain circumstances without authorization of the copyright holder.

In no event shall I be liable for any special, direct, indirect, consequential, or incidental damages or any damages whatsoever, whether in an action of contract, negligence or other tort arising out of or in connection with the use of this trilogy's content. I reserve the right to make additions, deletions or modifications to the book's content at any time without prior notice. Please note that I do not guarantee the accuracy, relevance, timeliness or completeness of any information given other than my own.

This book was written for educational purpose only to share with those experiencing Post Traumatic Stress Disorder what I did to successfully recuperate and heal myself and emerge relatively unscathed from the existential crises that PTSD constitutes. You should not rely on this information as a substitute for, nor does it replace, professional medical advice, diagnosis or treatment. I have no direct or indirect involvement with any of the treatment modalities of any and all genre mentioned in *The PTSD & ADHD Fallacy: Book 2 - Serving Evil* other than I was subjected to several of them and used those I found worked for me.

For further information, contact:

Avia Publishing
P.O. Box 255
Union Bay, BC V0R 3B0
Canada
https://www.nattanya.ca

Edited by David Leonhardt.

Front cover graphic composed with the support of Midjourney AI image engine. midjourney.com

Back cover photo of the author

Print ISBN: 978-0-9684976-7-8
Kindle ISBN: 978-0-9684976-8-5
Audio Book: 978-0-9684976-9-2

PRINTED IN CANADA OR THE USA

To those who want to heal...

Other books by H. Nattanya Andersen

Broken Wings

The Post Traumatic Stress Disorder Fallacy:
A Mental Health Industry Bonanza of Profit and Human Destruction (Fallacy 1)

Fallacy 3 (In the making)

CONTENTS

INTRODUCTION

You've read the first part of the trilogy, *The Post Traumatic Stress Disorder: A Mental Health Industry Bonanza of Profit and Human Desolation (Fallacy 1)*. In it, I promised to reveal how I healed myself of Post Traumatic Stress Disorder (PTSD) by osmosis. I always keep my promises, as a promise is a debt owed. So, let's dive right in, beginning with the newest on PTSD treatment ideas and hypotheses concocted by the mental health industry cabal. As for progress toward healing PTSD – there seems to have been none. We won't dwell on this lack of progress long, as we want to move on to discover what works to heal ourselves when in the PTSD condition. However, I thought we should start this way for two reasons. First, to make it abundantly clear that self-help is the only avenue out of the existential crisis of PTSD so named by psycho-the-rapists. Second, to strengthen PTSD journeyers' knowledge and consequent decision to do just that, help themselves. You can do so without any mental health practitioner who will knowingly or unknowingly, witting or unwittingly destroy you. The few exceptions, such as the Dr. Peter Breggins and Dr. Jordan Petersons of the world, confirm the rule.

I am documenting the following only to make you aware that billions of dollars are spent annually on the deception that it is impossible for human beings to heal themselves. That includes genuine PTSD experiencers. I am also documenting ho thousands upon thousands o so-called medical professionals of all genres profit from this ruse, thus destroying human health. That we humans wilfully and knowingly participate in this scam...well, that really is our own fault. But then, taking responsibility for Self and one's own actions is really not in style for most individuals, it seems. Karma often serves as excuse, even though that, too, is a ruse, as Dharma overrules Karma (*see Fallacy 1 for details*).

No one is where he is by accident
And chance plays no part in God's plan (Sharing Miracles)

1

THE PTSD DANCE, FARCE, AND FRAUD CONTINUES

The perception-deception imposed on us health-wise starts right of the bat with the Patient-Centered Outcomes Research Institute (PCORI). It presents itself as a United States-based *non-governmental institute* created in 2010 as part of a *modification* to the Social Security Act by clauses in the Patient Protection and Affordable Care Act. It is nevertheless a *government-sponsored organization* whose Patient-Centered Outcomes Research Trust Fund (PCOR Trust Fund) for government fiscal years (FYs) 2010 through 2012 received a total of US$210 million in appropriations from general fund revenues, meaning taxpayers. For FYs 2013 through 2019 the PCOR Trust Fund received another $150 million *annually* from the same source. The PCOR Trust Fund furthermore receives income from three other funding streams:

- appropriations from the general fund of the Treasury
- transfers from the Centers for Medicare and Medicaid trust funds
- a fee assessed on private insurance and self-insured health plans (the PCOR fee)

Additional details on PCORI funding are provided in the authorizing law in Sec. 1183 and Sec. 9511, beginning on page 17. As everybody else in the field, it is a 501(c)(1) non-profit organization (PUBLIC LAW 111-148—MAR. 23, 2010 124 STAT. 727). It is the Comptroller General of the United States, however, who appoints members of PCORI's Board of

Governors, including its chair- and vice chairperson. He is the director of the Government Accountability Office (GAO) formerly known as the General Accounting Office, a legislative branch agency established by Congress in 1921 to ensure the federal government's fiscal and managerial accountability.

In 2008, the seventh U.S. comptroller general, David M. Walker, announced his departure from his office before the end of his 15-year term. He went to work for The Peter G. Peterson Foundation as its first president and chief executive officer. It was established in 2008 by former U.S. secretary of commerce in the Nixon Administration and co-founder of the Blackstone Group, an American financial-services company, Peter G. Peterson. He committed $1 billion to create the foundation dedicated to address economic and fiscal "sustainability challenges that threaten America's future." Before leaving, Walker appointed Eugene Louis Dodaro to replace him. The U.S. Senate confirmed him as eighth comptroller general of the United States for a term of 15 years in 2010. Consequently, it is now Dodaro who appoints PCORI's Board of Governors members.

Under PCORI's authorizing law, its board must include the U.S. National Institutes of Health's directors and those of the U.S. Agency for Healthcare Research and Quality or their designees plus an additional 19 other members representing a range of stakeholder audiences. There are four categories of stakeholders, which provide a starting point to brainstorm all relevant parties involved. These four categories are users, governance, influencers and providers. At PCORI they are composed of:

- three representing patients and healthcare consumers
- seven representing physicians and providers, including four representing physicians (at least one of whom is a surgeon)
- one nurse, one state-licensed integrative healthcare practitioner, and one representative of a hospital
- three representing private payers, of whom at least one member shall represent health insurance issuers and at least 1 member shall represent employers who self-insure employee benefits
- three representing pharmaceutical, device and diagnostic manufacturers or developers
- one representing quality improvement or independent health service researchers
- two representing the federal government or the states, including at least one member representing a federal health program or agency

These board members appointed in accordance with the law purportedly represent a broad range of perspectives. These combine with scientific expertise in clinical health sciences research, including epidemiology, decisions sciences, health economics and statistics. At present Grayson Norquist, Maryland, MSPH, is PCORI's board of governor's chairperson. He received his BA with special distinction from the University of Mississippi. His M.D. magna cum laude came from the same University's Medical Center, and his MSc in Public Health (MSPH) from the UCLA School of Public Health. The MSPH is an academic research-oriented degree program, often preparatory for a doctoral degree, a career in academia or a career in an industry- or government research position. It involves intensive coursework in a focused area and a major research project at the school's departments of

Biostatistics, Community Health Sciences, Epidemiology, Environmental Health Sciences or Health Policy and Management (https://ph.ucla.edu).

Norquist completed his psychiatry training at the UCLA Department of Psychiatry, where he was chief resident and a Robert Wood Johnson clinical scholar (RWJF). Robert Wood Johnson II (-1968) built the family firm Johnson & Johnson into the world's largest health products maker. He established the chair at UCLA at his death with 10,204,377 company stock shares. Based in Princeton, New Jersey, the largest philanthropic organization in the United States focuses solely on health. Its goal? Use of grants to improve Americans' health and healthcare. The foundation presently has $11 billion in assets. It generates grants approaching $500 million annually. Its three-year national leadership development programs are designed for inter-professional teams of health professionals spanning a wide range of disciplines. They offer the opportunity to build and develop unique skills to lead teams who work with and across communities and organizations to build a national Culture of Health that enables all in our diverse society to lead healthier lives now and for generations to come. A Culture of Health is broadly defined as one in which good health and well-being flourish across geographic, demographic and social sectors. It fosters healthy equitable communities, guiding public and private decision making. And it gives everyone the opportunity to make choices that lead to healthy lifestyles. It is a goal to which the Robert Wood Johnson Foundation is deeply committed.

More often than not, we learn, health professionals' education and training lack the provision of tools, knowledge and skills they need to lead transformative change. RWJF is designed to fill that gap by offering health professionals the training to:

- Prepare to lead transformative change focused on health equity.
- Realize their unique role as both professionals and trusted members of communities.
- Cooperatively work across disciplines and professions to tackle problems that emerge from complex systems in communities—problems that jeopardize the achieving of a Culture of Health. These are society's "wicked problems" that requires solutions that embrace a scientific-rational approach while also recognizing the very real contributions of politics, behavior, environment, and other complex factors, we read.

Once graduated from the RWJF, fellows are skilled healthcare providers who come together across healthcare settings and disciplines to advance this advocated Culture of Health, the one enabling everyone in America to live longer, healthier lives in this diverse society now and for generations to come we are told (evidenceforaction.org). Broadly defined, this Culture of Health is one in which good health and well-being flourish across geographic, demographic and social sectors by fostering healthy equitable communities that guide public and private decision making, with everyone having the opportunity to make choices that lead to healthy lifestyles. Yes, we can see it all over the United States, in particular in cities like Seattle, San Francisco and Los Angeles, or can we?

Who defines this culture of health? According to the foundation's website, it can look very different to different people. Is it part of the culture of health for humans, PTSD experiencers among them, to live in tents surrounded by rats, feces, urine, and drugs and its side-effects, as depicted in the Matrix with the administered SOMA concoction perception-of-health? Even while city counsellors receive US$40,000.00 of federal compensation annually for every homeless person hosted by their city, to disappear into their own pockets, according to Dr. William Mount? Or is it the advertised opinion that the national culture of health embraces a wide variety of beliefs, customs and values for the purpose of ultimately being as diverse and multifaceted as the population it serves. This could, by the way, include viewing as natural for humans to live among and surrounded by rats, urine and feces?

Whatever it is, RWJF fellows are enmeshed in the entire health system. Thus, regardless of speciality, everything stays in that close-knit community. They include audiologists, clinical counsellors, dentists, dieticians, nurses, occupational therapists, pharmacists, physical therapists, physicians, physician assistants, psychologists, social workers, speech therapists, veterinarians and others. All of them purport to seek stronger, healthier, more equitable communities through work in their chosen, specialized profession. Such specialized professions in themselves reveal the belief that the human body constitutes nothing other than the physical substance of the human organism. It would be, therefore, composed of living cells and extracellular materials, and organized into tissues, organs and systems carrying out specific functions necessary for everyday living. It also seems to signal that whenever flesh, bone and organs are analyzed individually for the purpose of healing, the left hand rarely knows what the right is doing. But that has been ignored for the past 200 years or so; the aspired to transformational changes disallow it.

Those working with each other throughout their three-year RWJF program will take their acquired skills and apply them through projects in their community directly addressing root causes of inequity in health. Root causes of inequity, when even a definition for equity is hard to come by?

In 2016, Kris Putnam-Walkerly and Elisabeth Russell questioned *What the Heck Does "Equity" Mean? A clear definition of equity would seem paramount to galvanizing philanthropy into action around this increasingly used term—but the field is only beginning to explore what it really means* (https://ssir.org). They had in-depth conversations about equity with 30 staff members of 15 philanthropic foundations whose peers named them as leading "equity work" in the field. They found that very few of these organizations had a clear definition of equity.

Merriam-Webster's "simple definition" for it is "fairness or justice in the way people are treated." But then, asked the writers, what exactly is fairness? How do we define justice? Those concepts are not absolutes. They are shaped by each person's worldviews, life-experiences, education, place of birth, health and religion. Thus, equity's definition seems to be a perpetually moving target. In one report, University of California San Francisco's Paula Braveman views it as:

> "Health equity means social justice in health (i.e., no one is denied the possibility to be healthy for belonging to a group that has historically been economically/socially disadvantaged). What Are Health Disparities and Health Equity? We Need to Be Clear) (https://ncbi.nlm.nih.gov)."

In another report, written with S. Gruskin, she writes:

> "In operational terms, and for the purposes of measurement, equity in health can be defined as the absence of disparities in health (and in its key social determinants) that are systematically associated with social advantage/disadvantage (https://jech.bmj.com)."

Yanique Redwood, CEO of Consumer Health Foundation in Washington, DC, builds on Braveman's work to envision equity as both an outcome and a process—the latter, an idea borrowed from American Public Health Association President Camara Jones. Redwood explains:

> "We see health equity as an outcome whereby you can't tell the difference in health or life expectancy by race, and also as a process whereby we explicitly value people of color and low-income communities to achieve the outcome we seek."

Seen this way, the most equitable way to define "equity" may be to leave the definition to individual communities, suggest the authors. They add that philanthropy's search for meaning in the word "equity" should not reflect badly on the field. As one program officer at a national foundation put it, "The fact is that we don't know what equity looks like as a society, because we've never actually had it."

Has it still to dawn on all and sundry that equity in human society is impossible due to a multitude of incontrollable God-given factors? Thus, equity in human health and wellbeing is nothing other than a fata morgana. It's an illusion, a delusion, a perception–deception, a normally occurring impossibility in human lives and kept from the human population.

How can the power-elite get away with it? With ease, for humanity allows itself to be distracted and caught up in its incessant 24/7 cellphone-face-book, video-game, pornography, television-Netflix perception-warping, mind-manipulating distractions. These are brainwashing-into-apathy entire human generations by the second, rendering them more brain-dead and sending them into Orwellian oblivion.

And what is RJWF's aim with its purportedly non-profit endeavours? To pursue the Institute of Medicine (IOM) together with its affiliate, the National Academies of Science, to adhere to RJWF's aspiration of a fundamental health system redesign. Its purpose? To dramatically improved humanity's patient care.

And who and what is the IOM? It is another non-profit organization devoted to providing leadership on healthcare. Established in 1970, the IOM is the health arm of the National Academy of Sciences, which was chartered under President Abraham Lincoln in 1863 (nap.edu). It is unique in its structure, as it is both an honorific and an advisory membership organization. New members are elected by current active members through a selective process that recognizes individuals who have made major contributions to the advancement of the medical sciences, healthcare and public health. A diversity of talent among IOM's membership is assured by the Institute's charter, which stipulates that at least one-quarter of the members must be chosen from outside the health professions. Fields include the law, engineering, social sciences and the humanities. Simultaneously with their election, members commit to volunteer their service on IOM committees, boards and other activities. In 2014, its total active membership was 1,798. There were 128 foreign associates and 86 with emeritus status, for a total of 2,012. In 2018, active membership had for reasons unannounced dropped to 1,649, or 1,817 when including the 96 foreign associates and 72 holding emeritus status.

What does the IOM do? It was specifically created to advise the government on matters of biomedical science, medicine and health. It is said to work entirely outside the government's framework to ensure scientifically informed analysis and independent guidance. It is free of public input and accountability, justification and responsibility toward humanity. Purportedly, it provides unbiased, evidence-based and authoritative information about human health and science to policy-makers, meaning your congressmen, senators and the U.S. president.

We are able to gather insight into IOM members' interconnections by looking at PCORI Chair Norquist's professional background. He began his psychiatry career as a UCLA faculty member and assistant dean for student affairs at its School of Medicine. In addition, from 1987 to 1990, he served as director of the Mental Health Services for Physicians in Training Program and as a consultant for the RAND Corporation.

In 1990, he joined the National Institute of Mental Health (NIMH), when becoming the Division of Epidemiology and Services Research deputy director. Then, in 1992, he became associate director for services research. In 1998, he became director of the Division of Services and Intervention Research.

In addition to being PCORI's board of governor's chairperson, Norquist also is vice chair of Emory University's Department of Psychiatry and Behavioural Sciences and chief of the Grady Behavioural Health Service. The latter provides research, treatment and community outreach services for adults in Fulton and DeKalb counties in Georgia to patients experiencing a wide variety of chronic and severe mental illnesses. Approximately 90% of Georgia's capital of Atlanta's metropolitan area is located within Fulton County. The other 10% lies within DeKalb County. Prior to joining, Emory Norquist was professor and chair of the University of Mississippi's School of Medicine's Department of Psychiatry and Human Behaviour. Besides his post at PCORI, he currently chairs the American Psychiatric Association Council on Quality Care, said to monitor developments and carry out activities ensuring that the highest standards and quality of care remain an integral part of the American Psychiatrist Association (APA) mission. APA would do this by overseeing various fellowships and components such as committees, task forces, and work groups falling within its purview.

It does not end there, either. Norquist has been a member of several journal editorial boards, including the APA's *Psychiatric Services, Archives of General Psychiatry and Journal of Mental Health Policy and Economics* (psychiatry.emory.edu). Needless to say, he has authored numerous articles and book chapters and received numerous awards, including:

- the NIH Director's and Special Service Award
- the APA Health Services Senior Career Award
- the National Alliance for the Mentally Ill Exemplary Psychiatrist Award
- Such kind love to reward each other, wit Nobel Price winners for Peace in recent decades.

Assisting him is Joe V. Selby, M.D., MPH, PCORI's executive director. A native of Missouri, he received his M.D. from Northwestern University, one of the United States' leading private research and teaching universities, located in Evanston, Illinois. He got his MPH from the University of California, Berkeley. From 1976 to 1983, he served as a commissioned officer in the United States Public Health Service Commissioned Corps (PHSCC). PHSCC is also referred to as the Commissioned Corps of the United States Public Health Service, a federal uniformed service of the U.S. Public Health Service (PHS). As explained in *Fallacy 1*, it had its beginnings with the creation of the Marine Hospital Fund in 1798. Reorganized as the Marine Hospital Service in 1871, it was charged with the care and maintenance of merchant sailors. As the country grew, so did its ever-expanding mission of service, which soon began taking on new health roles that include protecting the commerce and health of Americans.

Selby continued to stay in the Bay area for 27 years. For 13 of those years, acted as Kaiser Permanente's director of research, supervising up to 50 investigators and 500 staff members. He also held academic appointments at UC Berkeley, the University of California, San Francisco and Stanford University, and he authored more than 200 peer-reviewed articles. His topics?

- primary care delivery
- colorectal cancer screening
- quality measurement and improvement
- studies that could be classified as "comparative effectiveness" in the areas of diabetes, hypertension and cardiovascular disease

Comparative effectiveness research evaluates and compares the implications and outcomes of two or more healthcare strategies to address a particular medical condition. Its goal is to generate better information about the risks, benefits and costs of different treatment options. This provides healthcare decision makers—including patients, clinicians, buyers, and policymakers—with up-to-date, evidence-based information about their treatment options to make informed healthcare decisions (https://hopkinsmedicine.org).

Selby was elected into the Institute of Medicine (IOM), now commonly known as the National Academy of Medicine (NAM), in 2009. NAM is another American non-profit, purportedly non-governmental organization and part of the National Academies of Sciences, Engineering, and Medicine (the National Academies). The other parts of the National Academies are:

- the National Academy of Engineering (NAE)
- the National Research Council (NRC)
- the National Academy of Sciences (NAS)

What is a national academy? It is an organizational body that usually operates with a state's financial support and approval. An academy co-ordinates scholarly research and standards for academic disciplines, most frequently the sciences, but also in the humanities. Typically, a country's learned societies in individual disciplines will liaise with or be coordinated by its national academy. A learned society, also known as a learned academy, scholarly society or academic association, is an organization existing to promote an academic discipline, profession or a group of related disciplines such as arts and science. Consequently, a national academy plays an important organizational role in academic exchanges and the collaborations between countries worldwide.

The U.S. National Academy of Medicine, for example, provides national and international advice on issues relating to health, medicine, health policy and biomedical science. It also purportedly aims to provide unbiased, evidence-based authoritative information and advice on health and science policies to policy-makers, professionals, leaders in every sector of society and the public at large. The NAM has more than 2,200 members elected in recognition of professional achievement and commitment to volunteer service in activities of the National Academies. The NAM elects no more than 75 regular members and 10 international members annually.

Like PCORI, the NAM operates outside of the U.S. federal government's framework. Thus, it is not responsible to the public for any of its actions or undertakings. It solely relies on its volunteer workforce of scientists and other experts operating under its formal peer-review system. One or more people do the evaluation of work submitted, with similar competences as that of the producers, their peers. The National Academies' Health and Medicine Division (HMD) conducts many different types of activities to improve human health. Each activity brings together experts and stakeholders, who provide the nation with guidance on health-related issues. As of June 2019, under the Topic: "Military and Veterans Health", 74 projects were active or on the verge of becoming so. One of them is *Gulf War and Health: Health Effects of Serving in the Gulf War, Update 2009*. Here is its activity description:

> "A committee of the Institute of Medicine (IOM) will conduct a study on the health status of Gulf War veterans. The study will incorporate peer-reviewed scientific literature published since the IOM's 2006 report, Gulf War and Health, Volume 4: Health Effects of Serving in the Gulf War. The committee will review, evaluate, and summarize the literature on the following health outcomes noted in the 2006 report as seeming to appear with higher incidence or prevalence in Gulf War-deployed veterans: cancer (particularly brain and testicular cancer), amyotrophic lateral sclerosis and other neurologic diseases (e.g., Parkinson's Disease and Multiple Sclerosis), birth defects and other adverse pregnancy outcomes, and post-deployment psychiatric conditions. The committee also will review studies on cause-specific mortality in Gulf War veterans as recommended in the 2006 report. In addition, the literature will be examined to identify any emerging health outcomes." (https://nap.edu)

The other one of interest to us in all 74 sponsored research activities is entitled Post-Traumatic Stress Disorder (PTSD): Diagnosis and Assessment. Its activity description states:

> "At the request of the Department of Veterans Affairs, the Institute of Medicine (IOM) conducted a study on Post-Traumatic Stress Disorder (PTSD). Specifically related to the assessment and diagnosis of PTSD, the committee reviewed and commented on the objective measures used in the diagnosis of PTSD and known risk factors for the development of PTSD. The committee reviewed the utility and objectiveness of the criteria in the Diagnostic and Statistical Manual of Mental Disorders (DSM-IV), and commented on the validity of current screening instruments and their predictive capacity for accurate diagnoses. IOM used the existing committee on Gulf War and Health: Physiologic, Psychologic, and

> Psychosocial Effects of Deployment Related Stress to complete the task related to diagnosis and validity of diagnostic instruments. The existing committee formed a subcommittee of members with the expertise to respond to the new statement of task. The subcommittee met separately from the main committee; they worked with consultants, and following their deliberations wrote a short report which was presented to the main committee for consideration and sign off."

And you still trust these entities to help you in your PTSD recovery or anything else, as a matter of fact? But never mind. Think how many thousands of learned societies men and women, and consequently their families and associated industries, your PTSD crisis supports. Indeed, how many it has supported for the last 40 years, while you linger on skid row barely carving out an existence? When doing so, you understand that, due to your existential crisis, you became a philanthropist in your own right by providing sustenance for them! And you are still surprised that they, in particular those working in the mental health industry, are warped enough to create you for that purpose? Yes, "create" you, as it is their treatment leading you into perpetual PTSD symptoms. If so, read and learn some more!

As we learned above, all those living off you use scholarly [peer] reviews (reviewed by their own, of course) to determine which academic papers are, in their view, suitable for publication. By law, all PCORI-funded primary research *must* undergo peer review and all results must be made available to the public. It is the peer review team of PCORI-funded research that decides and tailors the final report contents. According to PCORI, the peer review's goal is to ensure that PCORI-funded primary research studies are held to the highest standards of scientific integrity, methodological rigor, and relevance and usefulness to patients, caregivers, clinicians, and other healthcare stakeholders. The process includes review of study findings by content experts, methodologists, patients and other healthcare stakeholders with experience related to the study, we read on their website. None, of them purportedly have conflicts of interest with the study (https://pcori.org/research-results/peer-review-our-studies). For more information, read PCORI's Process for Peer Review of Primary Research and Public Release of Research Findings, which was adopted by its Board of Governors in February 2015.

When we analyse it closer, however, we discover that such form of self-regulation can be abused. It can be splendidly manipulated by members within a relevant field to control and streamline all knowledge and discoveries outside of public influence or input into its sphere of expertise. It is advertised as quality control to maintain quality standards, improve performance and provide credibility. In fact, it is the ideal tool of public deception used to suppress those discoveries considered out-of-line by the New World Order, the deep state, the ruling elite, the Archons or whatever else you may wish to call those in power worldwide. Wit Nikolas Tesla, Wilhelm Reich, Royal Rife and a multitude of others who discovered ways to heal human illnesses including cancer and to facilitate human life and living decades ago. Never heard of them? Look them up to heal yourself from PTSD and most anything else.

But back to Selby, Patient-Centered Outcomes Research Institute's (PCORI) first executive director since 2011. Stepping down at the end of 2019 (politico.com March 21, 2019) PCORI blossomed under his leadership. It was a private, independent, publicly supported research funder. It was charged with generating research and evidence to help patients and those who care for them make better-informed healthcare decisions. It became a blooming enterprise, thanks to the United States Congress. Congress established it as a private nonprofit organization, not as a federal agency. And it is Congress who funded it with a new tax called the "Patient-Centered Outcomes Research Institute Fee", which is projected to collect an estimated $3.5–$4.5 billion through 2019. The organization does not need to receive annual appropriations from Congress, and, in addition, it will not be subject to the usual financial controls imposed on federal agencies. Critics charge that PCORI receives only a cursory annual review by the U.S. Comptroller General, who appoints its board.

As we discovered, in essence, PCORI does nothing other than duplicate other federal agencies' work. Other agencies already engage and support similar comparative effectiveness research to that of PCORI. Such research was boosted by the American Recovery and Reinvestment Act of 2009, which gave a special appropriation of $1.1 billion to the Agency for Healthcare Research and Quality, the National Institutes of Health and the Secretary of Health and Human Services. The sequestration reduced funding to the National Institutes of Health, which ultimately reduced federal funding of comparative effectiveness research. That Congress requires PCORI to distribute a certain amount of its funds back to the United States Department of Health and Human Services is chicken shit in comparison. To date, PCORI has awarded more than $2.4 billion in support of research and related projects, a growing number of which it says have produced results being applied in practice, though we are not told which ones (https://pcori.org, 2019).

And no, Selby, Norquist and their members of the board are not running the PCORI show on their own. A methodology committee composed of up to 17 members, also appointed by the Comptroller General, helps guide PCORI's work. These members are experts in their fields, which include, but are not limited to:

- CER
- genomics
- biostatistics
- clinical research
- health services research
- research methodologies

The Committee works to define and update PCORI's methodological standards, and to develop a translation framework to guide choice of study designs to answer specific research questions. Thus, committee members are charged with developing and advancing comparative effectiveness research's (CER) science and methodologies, by and large a new term for research going on under different labels for decades (hsph.harvard.edu).

Five other committees also guide PCORI's board in the following specific areas of focus:

- governance
- science oversight
- research transformation
- finance and administration
- engagement, dissemination and implementation

Thus, they cover all bases needed to control humanity's health and well- or non-wellbeing. In addition, the governance committee serves to fill the audit committee role. Its financial highlights? In the fiscal year ending September 2010, US$1.26 billion was appropriated for the Patient-Centered Outcome Research Trust Fund (PCORTF). For fiscal year 2010, $10 million was allocated and $50 million for fiscal year 2011. After that, $150 million was allocated annually for each of the eight years from 2012 through 2019. These amounts are available to PCORI without further appropriation, minus an annual 20% distribution to PCORTF's Agency for Healthcare Research and Quality (AHRQ) and for the U.S. Department of Health and Human Services (HHS), as mentioned above.

AHRQ's mission? To produce evidence to make healthcare safer, higher quality, more accessible, equitable and affordable. Also, to work within the U.S. Department of Health and Human Services, and with other unnamed partners, to make sure that the evidence is understood and used.

As to the HHS, agencies of the latter routinely collect, link and analyze data used to generate new scientific knowledge about Federal programs and the patient populations. These data are foundational to research that expands knowledge about the outcomes and effectiveness of healthcare treatments and interventions. We are told that the coordination of efforts to build data capacity across HHS strengthens its research, analyses and public reporting programs. We are also told that it reduces unnecessary duplication, inefficiencies and reporting burdens on patients or healthcare providers. Conversely, it is declared, HHS agencies have common and converging needs for high quality timely data that enable independent researchers and government analysts to collaborate and conduct studies quicker, more accurately and at lower cost, without the public having a clue how the noose to impair their freedom and health as human beings is ever faster tightening around their necks. That's why PCORFT partially funds the HHS.

Needless to say, PCORI's governing body is purportedly united under the institutes VISION and MISSION statements. These are to provide patients and the public with "the information they need to make decisions that reflect their desired health outcomes." This must be substantiated by the mission to help people make informed healthcare decisions and improve "healthcare delivery and outcomes by producing and promoting high-integrity, evidence-based information that comes from research guided by patients, caregivers, and the broader healthcare community." The institute also aims to improve quality and relevance of evidence and make it available to help patients, caregivers, clinicians, employers, insurers and policy makers make better-informed health decisions. It also wishes to fund projects addressing disparities in healthcare in populations largely overlooked in clinical trials.

Of course, it is up to PCORI's board to decide what the public "needs to know." We already know that the VA clearly follows their suggestions by only taking care of those willingly submitting to psychotropic pharmaceutical drugs, taken regardless of ailments. If refusing, they'll wither on the vine until dying a natural death. In PTSD cases, that often means on the streets as punishment or compensation for their hero service to the homeland/fatherland/motherland.

To facilitate its overall enterprise, the institute works with healthcare stakeholders identify critical research questions and answer them through comparative clinical effectiveness research (CER), purportedly focused on outcomes important to patients. The word 'stakeholder', by the way, first appeared in 1708, meaning the holder of a wager. A stake is 'that which is placed at hazard', a gamble, in other words. With that in mind, please note that the institute disseminates its findings in ways that its *healthcare community members* find useful. Patients appear to be excluded from such information, thus assuring it all stays within the "learned society." Six hundred and twenty studies comparing healthcare options to learn which ones work best for whom were conducted since 2012. His research was well affordable, considering PCORI's latest available 2017 financial statement reading in part:

> *Statements of Financial Position:* As disclosed in the accompanying Statements of Financial Position and summarized in the table above, PCORI's net assets at September 30, 2017, were $940.3 million Specifically, PCORI's total assets of $1.033 billion included $33 million of funds held in trust, $957.8 million in investments and $30.5 million in cash. Total liabilities of $92.7 million represent accounts payable, accrued expenses and deferred rent.
>
> *Statements of Activities:* In fiscal year 2017, revenue and support totalled $466.1 million of which $120 million came from appropriations, $105 million from the Federal Hospital Insurance (FHI) and Federal Supplementary Medical Insurance (FSMI) Trust Funds, $235.4 million from PCOR fees and $5.7 million from interest earned on the PCORTF investment portfolio (Patient-Centered Outcomes Research Institute Financial Report September 30, 2017, pcori.org)) Money in other words is no object. The institute's total investment into research funding since 2012 was $1.9 billion for those 620 projects, only 5 of them into PTSD (politico.com). One of those 5 was completed in 2018. Conducted by the University of New Mexico's Health Sciences Center and entitled "*Are Treatment Groups Led by Peers as Effective as Groups Led by Counselors (sic) for Treating Posttraumatic Stress Disorder and Substance Use Disorder?* It began in 2013 involving 291 people in rural New Mexico. It was conducted under the auspices of Seeking Safety, a concept birthed by Lisa M. Najavits, PhD. currently Adjunct Professor at the University of Massachusetts Medical School. She was previously on faculty at Harvard Medical School for 25 years and Boston University School of Medicine and the Veterans Affairs Boston Healthcare System for 12 years. Presently Director of Treatment Innovations, which conducts research and training related to mental health and addiction, she is the author of over 180 publications including the book *Seeking Safety: A Treatment Manual for PTSD and Substance Abuse* for mental health professionals.

We read that her manual presents the first empirically studied integrative treatment approach developed specifically for co-occurring PTSD and substance abuse. For persons with this prevalent and difficult-to-treat dual diagnosis the most urgent clinical need is to establish safety--to work toward discontinuing substance use, letting go of dangerous relationships, and gaining control over such extreme symptoms as dissociation and self-harm. The manual is divided into 25 specific units or topics, addressing a range of different cognitive, behavioral and interpersonal domains. Each topic provides highly practical tools and techniques to:

- engage patients in treatment
- teach "safe coping skills" that apply to both disorders
- restore ideals that have been lost, including respect, care, protection and healing

Structured, yet flexible, topics can be conducted in any order and in a range of different formats and settings.

All participants had survived trauma of unknown origin resulting in either PTSD or substance use symptoms. Two-thirds of participants (65%) had both. Most (85%) were Hispanic. Roughly the same number of men and women participated, with an average age of 35. The research team assigned people by chance to one of two treatment groups led by either certified peer support workers or behavioral health counsellors. The weekly treatment sessions lasted 90 minutes for 12 weeks, each focusing on one coping skill. Half of the participants (141, or 48 %) finished the study. Because of data collection problems, some of the substance use data could not be used. The conclusion? People in both the peer-led and the counsellor-led groups reported fewer PTSD symptoms and better mental health after attending the Seeking Safety sessions. People in both groups also reported that they used drugs and alcohol less, craved drugs and alcohol less and had better coping skills. Coping skills are the ways people handle a stressful situation.

The conclusion? Peer-led sessions helped people just as much as those led by professional counsellors in improving PTSD symptoms, alcohol and substance cravings, coping skills, mental- and physical health and reducing alcohol and substance use in those completing the program. Groups led by peer support workers felt a stronger connection with their session leaders than those in groups led by professional counsellors. This may give food for thought in regards to the usefulness and validity of the Oath of Exit and the Spartan Oath on the path of PTSD recovery for military personnel. Then we hear the usual:

> "Future studies could continue to see if sessions led by certified peer support workers help people as much as sessions led by counsellors do. Future research could also see if certified peer support workers can help treat people who have different ethnic backgrounds and who live in different locations. How can people use the results? Many parts of the country don't have enough mental health and substance use counsellors. Peer support workers may be able to help provide care for people in these areas."

Well, the suggestion was well taken, and a new research study was conceived. Entitled *Operation PCOR: Training Veterans as Partners in PTSD Research*, it was conducted under the auspices of professor Cheryl Krause-Parello, PhD, MSN, BSN, and Linda Flynn, PhD, RN, FAAN, both of Florida Atlantic University, Boca Raton, U.S. . Thus, in 2017, PCORI shelled out US$249,972.00 for the 24-month exercise. Its proposal—verbatim?

> "Background: Posttraumatic stress disorder (PTSD) is a stress response to a traumatic event and affects up to 30 percent of the nation's veterans. There is an urgent

> need to explore robust programs of patient-centered outcomes research (PCOR) and comparative effectiveness research (CER) to identify treatment options for PTSD that are effective, acceptable, and meaningful to the veteran population. Veterans engaging as full partners in PTSD-related PCOR and CER are essential to identifying, developing, and testing patient-centered treatment options. Yet, PTSD research efforts are hampered by a dearth of veterans functioning as partners in the research process.
>
> Proposed Solution to the Problem: Operation PCOR will develop, pilot, and evaluate a nationally accessible, asynchronous, veteran-driven, online research training program designed specifically to prepare veterans to function as full partners in the research enterprise. Operation PCOR will also develop VetResearchHub, a web-based platform for veterans who complete the training." (.pcori.org)

You know what a quarter of a million dollars could do for PTSD afflicted experiencers, military veterans and others? But other PTSD researchers were sought as PCORI grant takers by April 2019, at the latest. A notice was published for the cause, entitled: *Treatment of Posttraumatic Stress Disorder (PTSD) in Adults–Cycle 1 2019.* It requested:

> "In the Treatment of Post-Traumatic Stress Disorder (PTSD) in Adults PFA, we seek to fund comparative clinical effectiveness research (CER) studies that aim to determine which specific treatments for adults with PTSD are most effective, and for whom. Proposed comparators may include psychological interventions, pharmacological interventions, or a combination of the two, and all proposed comparators must have demonstrated evidence of efficacy (from systematic reviews, prior empirical investigations, or other scientific documentation). PCORI is especially interested in studies that are inclusive of a broad patient population, including those with comorbidities, and in studies that are powered to assess the effectiveness of treatments in subgroups of interest (https://pcori.org)."

US$15 million are available for this one project alone over 3.5 years.

After you read *Fallacy 1*, do you still think these people have a clue how to treat you or are even interested in treating you? Has it still to dawn upon you what a gargantuan racket the PTSD business is, with you as their philanthropist? Does it still escape you that all this purported research into PTSD amelioration is done for the sole purpose to create more jobs for the learned society and its members? US$15.000,000 to investigate what? The un-investigable!

2

PTSD JOURNEYERS AS PHILANTHROPISTS

We, the genuine PTSD experiencers, are feeding 1000's of mental health professionals, other physicians, their employees, and those working for or in the pharmaceutical industry. They all profit greatly from our colossal existential crisis. It is us who, in fact, are the major, although unacknowledged and rewarded, stakeholders in the whole PTSD enterprise. Without us, there would be no PTSD mental health industry, and perhaps no opioid crises either. Without us, there would be no National Center *for* (the prolonging of) PTSD, which employs huge numbers of people who directly and indirectly work for it. Thus, through our misery, we feed a multitude and their dependents, including cats and dogs. Employees of big pharma live off of us, so do those working for many other corporations and non-profit organizations, who merely regurgitate what others already hypothesized and theorized ad nauseam throughout decades. And all do it for their own financial gain.

PCORI, of course, is one of them. Already in 2015, investigative reporter Fred Schulte of the Center for Public Integrity (CPI), a nonpartisan, non-profit investigative news organization prying into Medicare and Medicare Advantage waste, fraud and abuse thundered against it (Fred Schulte: *Is Obamacare's Research Institute Worth The Billions?* npr.org). Created by Congress under Obama's 2012 Affordable Care Act, PCORI's major stakeholders are purported to be patients, physicians, employers, insurance companies, pharmaceutical firms and government. Since 2012, PCORI has committed just over $1 billion to 591 "comparative effectiveness research (CER)" contracts to find answers. Thus far, money has gone to researchers, medical schools, advocacy groups and insurance industry lobbying groups, rather than benefitting patients.

PCORI officials maintain that by stressing "patient centered" projects that offer practical guidance to people living with chronic diseases, they reshape medical research.

Among these reshaping projects was a US$14 million study undertaken to settle the debate over how much aspirin people should take daily to help ward off heart disease.

A US$30 million project undertook to probe reduction of serious or deadly injuries from falls in the elderly.

Before its September 2019 expiry, PCORI expects to spend another $3.5 billion. Can you imagine what $3.5 billion over 10 years handed directly to U.S. military PTSD experiencers could do? It would give them the financial security to absorb and work through a PTSD event causing moment in peace and tranquility. It would eliminate their PTSD crisis. It would heal them. But that is not in the scheme of things, as it would eliminate as well the goose laying the golden eggs.

It is said that none of PCORI's stakeholders, investigators and researchers is permitted to have affiliations or financial involvements conflicting with their research material. However, it is Medicare who determines what sort of therapies it may or may not cover, regardless of PCORI research outcomes. The definition "may" might indeed indicate a choice to act or not to act, the promise of a possibility distinguished from the imperative "shall." In statutes, and sometimes in contracts, "may" must be read in context to determine if it means that an act is optional or mandatory, because it could also be an imperative. The same careful analysis must be rendered to the word "shall".

Non-lawyers, when seeing the word "may", have a tendency to think they have a choice or that they are excused from complying with some statutory provision or regulation, when in fact that is not the case (legal-dictionary.thefreedictionary.com). As Ruth Sullivan, Professor of Law at the University of Ottawa, states:

> "Anyone who spends time studying language and interpretation soon comes to appreciate the complexity and uncertainty inherent in any effort to interpret a text... in particular when it comes to disputes about the interpretation of legislative text." (aix1.uottawa.ca)

She should know, as she taught English literature and composition at Montreal's Concordia University before obtaining degrees in common law and civil law from McGill University and a master's degree in legislation from the University of Ottawa. She clerked for the Right Honorable Chief Justice Bora Laskin in 1982 and was called to the Bar of Ontario in 1984. After 27 years of teaching at the University of Ottawa's Faculty of Law, she retired from the faculty and became an employee of the Legislative Services Branch of the Department of Justice, where she continues to work. So, it would be of great benefit to anchor her words about the complexity of language and its intricacies firmly in our mind.

The thorough understanding of the difference between "may" and "shall", in particular if in conflict with the powers that be, could dictate the outcome of your PTSD case. It could mean living on the Homeland's streets in abject poverty or in the lap of luxury.

"May" and "shall" aside, PCORI's management and workers since its inception insist that their efforts for patients and stakeholders are expanded solely to better humanity's life and living as a whole. But is it really? Or is it just another lucrative income opportunity for those running the show and its 147 members? Even PCORI's stated mission seems to mean different things to different people. By law it is directed to fund clinical effectiveness, development and improvement methods. This is for to produce valid and trustworthy information leading to better healthcare decisions and, ultimately, improve patient wellness state outcomes. And in theory, comparative effectiveness research (CER) is said to be hard to fault, as common sense dictates that doctors need to know which drugs, medical devices and other treatments work best. Furthermore, it makes little sense for anyone to pay for healthcare services shown conclusively ineffective, even though that's how it works in genuine PTSD experiencers' treatment, for which the whole nation pays.

Congress on both right and left in 2015 already had doubt whether or not PCORI lived up to expectations, writes Schulte. It even wondered and pondered what those expectations were and what they should reasonably be. That such sort of contemplations would have been better undertaken and appropriate prior to authorizing \$3.5 billion as part of the Patient Protection and Affordable Care Act of 2010 in itself leaves room for contemplation about the real purpose of the Obama created Act. That an additional US\$2 fee adjusted for inflation for each person covered on a group plan and income from the general fund of the Treasury is joyously added to that amount is generally ignored. That a small fee assessed on Medicare, private health insurance and self-insured plans, without doubt loaded onto consumers in one way or another, is also kept fairly quiet.

President George H.W. Bush's former Medicare chief under Gail Wilensky opined in 2015:

> "PCORI seems to have become almost invisible. Maybe they think that's the best way to stay under the political radar screen [as] the institute has yet to 'offer much value.'"

But how else can one view an organization perpetually financing recurrent projects and handing out lucrative awards to preventive, diagnostic, therapeutic and palliative care workers in the healthcare delivery system without evidence of improvement on any of the topics financed? Even killing the enterprise seems to have been on some congressmen's agenda, or at least hamstringing it. Fear arose that its project-activities might lead to rationing medical care, because of its medical decision-making interference. It went so far as Kansas Republican senator Pat Roberts earlier that year filing a bill to prevent Medicare from using PCORI results to "deny or delay coverage of an item or service." "Americans," he stated, "do not want the federal government limiting their treatment options and deciding what is best for them." But patients fear that PCORI-sponsored findings will put restrictions on their healthcare subsidies seems no longer to be of no consideration to anyone. It ceased with the House Appropriations Committee cutting PCORI's funding by $100 million in mid-2015 dubbing it wasteful spending. But since then it continued to vigorously prosper on the vine.

Doctors are another problem, as they often lack first evidence advising them how to best get patients well. While many medical groups strongly back research to find these answers, getting their members to embrace recommended changes can be difficult. Some may be slow to pick up on the most current medical information, while others may resent being told how they should run or alter their practice. PCORI asserts that CER serves as bridge between development of innovative therapies treatments and their productive application, delivery and appropriate care to individual patients. But that is not how things work, says Schulte. Take new drugs, for instance. They come to market based on whether they are safe and effective and not if they are superior or inferior to those of the competition. The assumption that a new medicine or device that costs more than what is already available must be better is also an illusion, a perception-deception, as there is no such guarantee. In fact, according to the Institute of Medicine, more than half of medical treatments lack clear evidence of effectiveness! So, is it all a ruse? Does the body truly know how to heal itself if by and large left to its own devices?

Well, don't wait for PCORI to tell you. Its discoveries on how to improve human health are turtle slow to reach its audience, and that also seems inconsequential, despite the fact that the complexity, number and diversity of medical treatment options are growing in leaps and bounds daily.

How slow is turtle slow? To exemplify, let's consider the 2000 CER evaluation entitled *Managing clinical knowledge for health care improvement.* It was written by E. Andrew Balas M.D., PhD, fellow of the American College of Medical Informatics, elected member of the European Academy of Sciences and arts professor at Augusta University (formerly Medical College of Georgia), as well as vice president of the Friends of the National Library of Medicine. His co-author was S.A.Boren, associate professor, health management & informatics, University of Missouri. They assert that it oftentimes took an average of 17 years for new evidence-based research findings to reach clinical practice (ihi.org). Seventeen years! McGlynn et al. in their 2003 publication *The quality of health care delivered to adults in the United States*, voice that little systematic information about the extent to which standard processes involved in healthcare - a key element of its quality - were delivered in the United States (Elizabeth A. McGlynn, PhD, Steven M. Asch, M.D., M.P.H., John Adams, PhD, Joan Keesey, B.A., Jennifer Hicks, M.P.H., PhD, Alison DeCristofaro, M.P.H., Eve A. Kerr, M.D., M.P.H.). As a matter of fact, after telephoning a random sample of adults living in 12 U.S. metropolitan areas and asking them about selected healthcare experiences, the team concluded:

> "The deficits we have identified in adherence to recommended processes for basic care pose serious threats to the health of the American public. Strategies to reduce these deficits in care are warranted (nejm.org)."

But why should that change? After all, any improvement or haste in advocating improvement would be suicidal to a multitude of government funded and non-profit tax exempt and trust fund institutions, would it not?

Mind you, take into consideration that less than 0.1% of the nation's more than $2 trillion investment in healthcare annually is used to evaluate the relative effectiveness of various diagnostics, procedures, devices, pharmaceuticals and other interventions in clinical practice (cfr.org). At Moses et al.'s 2005 seminar *Redesigning the Clinical Effectiveness Research Paradigm: Innovation and Practice-Based Approaches* (Workshop Summary; AcademyHealth 2005) participants reached the following conclusion:

> "...despite the custom of referring to 'our healthcare system,' the research community in practice functions as a diverse set of elements that often seem to connect productively only by happenstance. Because shortfalls in coordination and communication impinge on the funding, effectiveness, and efficiency of the clinical research process—not to mention its progress as a key element of the learning healthcare system—the notion of working productively together is vital for both patients and the healthcare community (ncbi.nlm.nih.gov)."

In 2010, PCORI might have been designed to fill that niche. The Center for Public Integrity found 5 years later that it indeed had sponsored projects seemingly offering hope to doctors, patients and their advocates. But it had also spent hundreds of millions of dollars on activities only tangentially related to its mandate of discovering which medical treatments were the most successful. Writes Schulte:

- PCORI spent only about 28% of its contracting budget on projects that assess how best to prevent, diagnose or treat diseases.
- Much of PCORI's other spending concerned how to accelerate its research or improve healthcare systems.
- More than $70 million in PCORI awards cover projects intended to improve methods for conducting research or to pay for contracts that are essentially public relations gestures to build support and good will in the medical community.

Those 2015 figures include nearly $10 million in subsidies for medical societies and other groups' "engagement" awards and "meeting and conference." To generate interest in its endeavors and for fundraising purposes, PCORI established the Eugene Washington PCORI Engagement Awards, offering three different funding opportunities:

- The *Engagement Award: Capacity Building, Engagement Award*
- *Conference Support*
- *Engagement Award: Dissemination Initiative*

In 2018, PCORI planned to award $20.5 million as part of these awards, which are research support rather than research funding opportunities, they say. All three awards are purportedly intended to support projects intended to build communities better able to participate in patient-centered outcome research and comparative clinical effectiveness research (CER), as well as serve as channels to disseminate study results. This, the institute insists, had always been central to its mission. It would help patients and those caring for them to make better-informed healthcare decisions. CER's point of operation is to compare two or more different ways of treating the same health condition to see which one works best. If definitive best practices can be established, it *may* be widely adopted by providers and *may* be preferentially reimbursed by [insurance] payers. Cheaper treatments would be favored, we read (cato.org).

By 2015, 36 engagement awards, costing more than $8 million, had been handed out to healthcare organizations, universities and groups. This includes the America's Health Insurance Plans (AHIP), the industry's trade group. It received two engagement awards totalling $500,000 in 2015 to, according to contract summaries, "build and maintain support from health plan leaders" and to "identify important gaps in availability of health insurance administrative data."

One of these gaps to fill was sharing health plan data information explained AHIP spokeswoman Clare Krusing. That it also serves to traumatize undesirable patients, genuine PTSD experiencers included, is left out of the equation. So is the fact that one unnamed physicians' organization received a $250,000 PCORI grant to discover what its members thought about the institute and its work. PCORI's officials merely insist that the awards amount to a mere "rounding error" in terms of total money spent, a necessity to get their work noticed.

PCORI also provided 17 "meeting and conference support" grants to medical organizations totalling more than $1.8 million. The Society for Academic Emergency Medicine, for example, received $50,000 in 2015 to develop and publish "a consensus research agenda." In 2014, the Society of General Internal Medicine, whose 3,000 physician members teach at medical schools, were the lucky winners. They received a $249,960 grant for a two-year program to develop a better understanding of its membership's attitudes and knowledge and how to best engage them into activity-participation. PCORI director Selby at that time exclaimed that the awards were necessary to get through to busy professionals who may not answer PCORI's phone calls. "Our job is to build relationships and to get on their radar. This helps us get their attention," he clamored. Well, apparently PCORI used $61 million alone to spread knowledge of its activities in an attempt to make a name for itself and impact the medical-and research community.

By 2015, PCORI was nearing 600 research projects, roughly worth $1billion, including:

- 57 studies on multiple chronic conditions
- six studies on shared decision making
- 25 transitional care-projects

It proudly proclaimed to be the only U.S. research organization dedicated to funding studies comparing which healthcare approach works best for whom and under which circumstances (https://reauthorizepcori.org). Given its mandate, it is logical it chose seemingly worthwhile projects that are non-threatening to any powerful healthcare factions. Investigative reporter Schulte found that it had directed $64.5 million toward 66 contracts for no other purpose than to improve methods for conducting research. More than $30 million went into 50 pilot projects, most of them at universities and medical schools. One of them, a $30 million study anchored by medical schools at Harvard, Yale and UCLA, for example, aimed to reduce falls in the elderly. Health policy professor at Johns Hopkins University Albert Wu explained that researchers had looked at whether a specially trained nurse could work with older people and their relatives to find ways to cut down on these injuries. Selby, PCORI's executive director said the study was an exception because: "Putting a nurse in every [doctor's] office doesn't come cheaply. Who pays for that?" For 30 million U.S. dollars of your money! Making yoga instruction assessable to older folk for a reasonable price at community centers to prevent such injuries is no longer in style, if it has ever been in the progressive U.S.

A $14 million aspirin study was also financed because, we are told, aspirin can have widespread health ramifications. If too much is taken, it can cause internal bleeding, possibly outweighing heart benefits. But increasing aspirin would save thousands of lives. "We know that aspirin can be beneficial in preventing heart attacks, but surprisingly, we haven't known the appropriate dose," said Ann Bonham, chief scientific officer for the Association of American Medical Colleges. "That's an important piece of information...a gap that may not be recognized by a lot of people." Increasing aspirin consumption could, of course, also create manifold bleeding ulcers and the like, but who cares? It would feed those specialists for a while to become another philanthropist group in this league of states. After all, Duke University researchers claim that 720,000 Americans annually have heart attacks and nearly 380,000 die of coronary artery disease. If it has anything to do with nutrition, we are not told.

Also sponsored were 18 contracts worth US$44 million in total for rare disease research, US$2.6 million awarded to the Cincinnati Children's Hospital Medical Center to discover the best type of diet for children with eosinophilic esophagitis, among them. The ailment is created by a reaction to foods, allergens or acid reflux. Identified only in the past two decades, it is now considered a major cause of digestive (gastrointestinal) illness (mayoclinic. org). Has it anything to do with nutrition, one may ask?

US$675,000.00 was joyously handed to the University of Colorado Denver for a 30-month boot camps. These would activate personal relationships to bring together community members, clinical practices, patients, providers and researchers to identify important health issues they each faced. The group would focus these topics into a priority list for further work following several camps. The goal? To translate medical terms into words easier for patients to grasp. According to Schulte its project summaries were so freighted with academic and scientific language that it would be close to a miracle if it attracted a wide audience.

Some projects tossed around esoteric phrases such as "how to capture stakeholder inputs" and "quality metrics to inform integrated care" unlikely to be clear to the average reader. For this purpose, a $674,452 project proposed by the Palo Alto Medical Foundation Research Institute entitled "Creating a Zone of Openness to Increase Patient-Centered Care" was financed in 2012 to explore how medical professionals could foster a climate where patients did not fear being labeled as difficult for asserting themselves in clinical decision-making. PCORI officials touted that it had produced important insights. They also conceded that their work must be made more compelling.

PCORI's Chief Engagement and Dissemination Officer Jean R. Slutsky, presently leading its engagement Program, at that time justified the expense by stating that the heavy use of jargon could be a turn-off, in particular for patients the institute tried to reach. "We are in the process of putting in lay language to communicate with people who are not scientists. We wish we could change this." In essence, the whole scheme seems to have been nothing other than to teach physicians how to chat with patients at a cost of almost three quarters of a million U.S. dollars. Want to check how successful it has been and create some fun in your life? Try asking your mental health physicians for their definition of PTSD and see where you end up. What they spew forth may help you to thoroughly understand that doing your own thing is the only way out, unless you want to destroy yourself by way of your own compliance and volition to their wishes.

Language or no language, a delightful disfavour in PCORI's attempt to make its mark on the practice of every day medicine has been the Affordable Care Act's mandate that none of its research findings are "to be construed as mandates for practice guidelines, coverage recommendations, payment or policy recommendations (PPACA (Consolidated) Subtitle D of Title VI - Sec. 6301Patient-Centered Outcomes Research)." In other words, the institute in essence from its very inception has been and is of lucrative benefits only to those running the show from the Chair down, and those receiving grants dished out by them to those seemed deserving. According to glassdoor.ca, PCORI in 2019 hosted somewhere between 201 to 500 employees, up from 153 in 2014 and 191 in 2015. All work with minimal oversight and receive vast employee benefit packages on top of their salaries.

The Government Accountability Office (GAO) audited the institute in 2015. The GAO is a U.S. legislative branch government agency providing auditions, evaluations and investigation services for the U.S. Congress. It found little to fault, other than voicing concerns about PCORI's research priorities being too broad and lacking specificity. That the institute would not undergo an outside performance critique until 2020 after it had disbursed of its allotted \$3.5 billion was unfavourably noted. Really? Yes! Why prematurely rock the boat when it is running so swimmingly and nurturing so many within and outside of its operations? Why not wait until it had hopefully been renewed by December 2019 for another 10 years to keep the gravy train going for another 10?

In the Spring of 2019, its existence now in danger, PCORI vehemently advocated that its activities were complementary to those of the National Institute of Health (NIH) due to its clinical effectiveness sponsored research (CER). It insisted also that its activities were equal to those of the Agency for Healthcare Research and Quality's (AHRQ), whose mission it is to produce evidence to make health-care safer, of higher quality, more accessible, equitable and affordable. Similarly, it claimed that its activities were complementary to those of the Food and Drug Administration, whose mission in part is the advancement of public health by helping to speed innovations that make medical products more effective, safer and more affordable, and because the institute helps the public get the accurate, science-based information it needs to use medical products and foods to maintain and improve their health (fda.gov).

That Cato Institute director of health policy studies Michael F. Canon already in January 2012 viewed the CER as a menacing prospect to some pharmaceutical companies and medical device-makers did not raise an eyebrow (*The Moment It Produces Useful CER, PCORI Is Toast;* cato.org). Neither was his reasoning questioned when proclaiming:

> "The whole point of [comparative effectiveness research] is to find out what doesn't work. Every time the government has tried to do CER the guys who provide the stuff found not to work successfully lobby to have the offending

agency defunded. I see no reason to think this time will be any different. The moment it produces useful CER, PCORI is toast (cato.org)."

Thus, it seems almost as if PCORI employees dreamt up the CER awards recognizing individuals and organizations whose innovative leaders were advancing methods and practical applications of comparative effectiveness research in the United States out of necessity to its survival. (icer-review.org).

And what is the Cato Institute? An American think-tank headquartered in Washington, DC, founded in 1974 as the Charles Koch Foundation by Ed Crane, Murray Rothbard and Charles Koch, chairman of the board and chief executive officer of Koch Industries. Its role was to focus on public advocacy, media exposure and societal influence. We can surmise it was named after Marcus Porcius Cato Uticensis (95 BC - April 46 BC), commonly known as Cato the Younger (*Cato Minor*) to distinguish him from his great-grandfather (Cato the Elder). A statesman in the late Roman Republic and a follower of the Stoic philosophy, he is remembered for his stubbornness and tenacity, as well as his immunity to bribes, his moral integrity and his famous distaste for the ubiquitous corruption of the period. The more things change the more they stay the same (Bon Jovi).

Libertarian in its political philosophy, the Cato Institutes advocates a limited role for government in domestic and foreign affairs as well as a strong protection of civil rights. This includes support for the demilitarization of the police, lowering or abolishing most taxes, opposition to the Federal Reserve system, the privatization of numerous government agencies and programs including Social Security, the Affordable Care Act and the United States Postal Service, along with adhering to a non-interventionist foreign policy (Wikipedia). Advocating for PCORI's abolishment thus is right up its alley.

Mind you, though, we must give credit where credit is due. At least PCORI proudly emphasizes that its patient centered role in health research truly is the guiding principle driving its work, whereas the NC *for* PTSD by and large shuns genuine PTSD journeyers involvement with its PTSD hypotheses, theories, phantasms and treatment modalities. Why, may we wonder? Because pharmaceutical drug free genuine PTSD experiencers' input would in the nick of time to show that Emperor NC *for* PTSD employer has no clothes, as no first evidence generic PTSD fit-for-all PTSD sufferer treatment modality. It cannot exist. It is an impossibility as long as human beings maintain their individuality, their sui generis, when dwelling uncontrolled by pharmaceutical drugs, virtual reality, genetic manipulations, chip implants, G5 and AI manipulations or derivations thereof feeding themselves on relative nutritional foods and regularly exercising. Genuine PTSD journeyers' participation in PTSD healing modality discoveries would therefore spoil all the fun for those living off them, the vast majority of whom contracted by the NC *for* PTSD. Thus we, the genuine PTSD experiencers, are the world's most abused philanthropists for the sake of the learned society's greed. And PCORI is aiding and abetting in the exercise.

To prove my point, take this 2012 to 2017 PCORI-financed US$1,888,100 million research study as an example. Entitled *"Can Coping-Skills Training Help Patients Who Have Received Intensive Hospital Care to Cope with Depression and Anxiety?"* Christopher Ethan Cox, M.D., MPH, a board-certified palliative medicine specialist of Duke University, was principal investigator. He presently is an associate professor of medicine as well as the director of

Duke's Medical Intensive Care Unit (MICU) and the Duke Program to Support People and Enhance Recovery (medicine.duke.edu). In this randomized controlled clinical trial, Cox et al. compared a telephone- and web-based coping-skills training program with an educational program that included web-based, video, and printed information about critical illness. Study participants were 175 patients averaging 52 years of age who had been on ICU breathing machines in a hospital for at least two days. The study also included 86 family members, mostly spouses or parents. Forty percent of those who joined the study became too ill or died before they could complete it.

The results? Overall, the coping-skills training program did not reduce symptoms of depression, anxiety or PTSD for patients or their family members, nor were there significant differences in quality of life or physical or mental health status. However, among patients who had high levels of depression and anxiety at baseline, those in the coping-skills training program at six months had reduced psychological distress symptoms compared with those in the educational program. This discovery was made at the cost of almost US$1,888,100 million, money again escaping genuine PTSD sufferers, American heroes lingering on city streets or in abject desolation lingering in their homes included.

But so what, when according to Congressional Representative Occasio Cortez the Earth ceases to exist in 2000 something anyway, and PCORI loves to spend money on nothing, and the U.S. Congress sanctions it. In 2013, it awarded US$1,525,951million to the University of New Mexico's Health Sciences Center's project entitled *Are Treatment Groups Led by Peers as Effective as Groups Led by Counselors (sic) for Treating Posttraumatic Stress Disorder and Substance Use Disorder?* (A. Crisanti et al: 2013).

Seeking Safety guidelines, birthed by Lisa M. Najavits, PhD, and documented in her 2001 book *Seeking Safety: A Treatment Manual for PTSD and Substance Abuse for mental health professionals* (Guilford Press 2001) followed. Najavits, a 25 year veteran on Harvard Medical School and Boston University School of Medicine faculty while employed at the VA's Boston Healthcare System for 12 years and currently adjunct professor at the University of Massachusetts Medical School and director of treatment innovations conducting research and training related to mental health and addiction claims that her book is the first empirically studied integrative treatment approach specifically developed for co-occurring PTSD and substance abuse. It formed the basis for team Crisanti's research, which they developed and tailored specifically for co-occurring PTSD and substance abuse.

Najavits' manual, available for around US$60, is divided into 25 specific units or topics addressing a range of cognitive, behavioral and interpersonal domains (christianbook.com). Each topic, we read, provides highly practical tools and techniques to engage patients in treatment and teach "safe coping skills" that apply to both disorders. The aim? To restore ideals that have been lost, including respect, care, protection and healing. Structured yet flexible, the topics can be conducted in any order and in a range of different formats and settings, we are told.

- Crisanti recruited 291 people from rural New Mexico for the study.
- All were survivors of trauma of unknown origin, resulting in either PTSD or substance use symptoms. Sixty-five percent of participants had both.
- Roughly the same number of men and women participated.

- Eighty-five percent were Hispanic, with an average age of 35.

All were assigned per chance to a group led by either certified peer support workers or behavioral health counselors. The latter seems to be the newest title for a semi-educated mind mixer. Actually, it is a mental health professional who uses a variety of psychotherapy methods and techniques to help people in psychological distress or to diagnose, treat and prevent mental health issues. After all, by 2020, depression will be the US' second most costly health problem, surpassed only by heart disease. By age 55, around half of all adult Americans will have lived through at least one psychiatric problem, we are told. Or should we rather call it an existential crisis? A most unpleasant but plausible event in a human's life such as a car accident? Or such as death of family, Fido, Missy-meow, parrot or pet-fish? Or perhaps a mid-life crisis or the like? Could such events be possible as a thought-form within the realm of human existence rather than treated as a psychiatric health impairment to be cured by pharmaceutical, mind-altering drugs, as presently maintained by the mental health cabal (Kendra Cherry: *Mental Health Counselor Training, Skills, and Salary*; Very Well Mind 2019)?

Of our 291 rural New Mexicans in their unidentified trauma state, only 141 finished their 12 once-weekly, 90-minute treatment sessions, each focusing on a coping skill. The conclusion? Peer-led sessions helped people just as much as those led by professional counselors in improving PTSD symptoms, alcohol and substance cravings, coping skills, mental and physical health. Peer-led sessions also helped those completing the program just as much to reduce alcohol and substance.

However, groups led by peer support workers felt a stronger connection with their session leaders than those in groups led by professional counselors. Could this be food for thought in regards to the usefulness and validity of Oath of Exit and Spartan Oath on the path of PTSD recovery for genuine PTSD experiencers – the fire fighters, soldiers, veterans, police officers and aircrew? And then, as usual, we hear:

> "Future studies could continue to see if sessions led by certified peer support workers help people as much as sessions led by counsellors do. Future research could also see if certified peer support workers can help treat people who have different ethnic backgrounds and who live in different locations. How can people use the results? Many parts of the country don't have enough mental health and substance use counsellors. Peer support workers may be able to help provide care for people in these areas."

And all this for $1,525,951 million spent by those pretending to be clueless as to what PTSD is all about. That's a pretty penny to ignore that PTSD is an existential crisis of enormous proportions, as far removed from a mental illness as malaria is from appendicitis. That penny feathers their own nests while throwing into desolation or destroying genuine PTSD philanthropists who trust them.

Crisanti et al.'s shout for more PTSD research was enthusiastically adhered to by PCORI, who in December 2013 accepted to finance a project costing a whopping $1,788,712. Its title? *Evaluation of Parent-Based Interventions to Support Children after Traumatic Injury*. (Marizen Ramirez, MPH, PhD et al., Pediatr Emerg Care. 2017 Aug; 33(8): 532–537).

Ramirez, educated in epidemiology and molecular and cell biology at the University of California-Los Angeles, is known for her expertise in:

- traffic injuries
- pediatric injuries
- policy evaluation
- agricultural injuries
- disaster preparedness
- adverse child experiences
- injury and violence epidemiology
- injury and violence prevention and control
- intervention development, implementation and evaluation
- mixed methods involving collecting, analyzing and integrating quantitative (e.g., experiments, surveys) and qualitative (e.g., focus groups, interviews) research (directory.sph.umn.edu/).

Her evaluation of parent-based interventions to support children traumatised by injury aimed to:

- Assess the feasibility of Link for Injured Kids through qualitative research with parents and providers of previously injured children from the University of Iowa (UI) Children's Hospital.
- Through a randomized trial, determine the range of potential psychosocial and behavioural health indicators possibly impacted by Link for Injured Kids.

This, we are told, would identify types of outcomes such as PTSD, depression, nonspecific distress, quality of life, absenteeism, school performance, coping skills, communication skills and access to mental health.

Ramirez's 2017 published *Link for Injured Kids: A Patient-Centered Program of Psychological First Aid After Trauma* was purportedly a psychological first aid guide. She seems to have used it to educate parents in how to support their children after a severe injury. She did this after having demonstrated that children's physical injuries can lead to adverse psychosocial outcomes, including PTSD, as foundation for her PCORI financed research. Five mothers and their offspring participated in that study (Marizen Ramirez, MPH, PhD et al. Pediatr Emerg Care. 2017 Aug; 33(8): 532–537)

Methods? Using qualitative methods, the team held focus groups in 2012 with parents and pediatric trauma providers of children hospitalized at a Level I Children's Hospital because of an injury. Focus group participants were asked to describe reactions to trauma and review the team's drafts of its hypotheses for intervention, more than any genuine PTSD experiencer ever got to do in the past 30 years or ever. Results? Health professionals and caregivers of unnamed capacity reported a broad spectrum of emotional responses by their children or their patients. It was noted, however, that difficulties were experienced during recovery at home and upon returning to school. Five mothers and their children participated in the study (insights.ovid.com). Consequently, all parents and health professionals recommended interventions be offered to parents either in the emergency department or close to discharge among admissions. Conclusions? Results from this study strongly indicate a need for post-trauma interventions, particularly in rural settings, to support families of children to address the psychosocial outcomes in the aftermath of an injury. (experts.umn.edu)

This US$1,788,712 exercise engaged 314 parent-child dyads ages 10 to 17, with an average age of 14. Sixty-three percent were boys, eight percent were Hispanic, 86% were white, four percent African American, six percent another or more than one race and three percent of no reported race. Two ways to help parents talk to their child after a serious injury were compared constituting either:

- The Link for Injured Kids program, where parents watched a video and received training about talking with their children about their injury before leaving the hospital.
- Trauma education where before leaving the hospital, parents received a booklet with tips on talking with their children.

Parents and children in both groups filled out surveys at the hospital, then at six weeks, three months and six months after patient release. These surveys were used to discern PTSD symptoms, depression, quality of life, emotional problems and behaviors in the children. After 6 weeks parents in the Link program received follow-up training and parents in the trauma education group got a new booklet – if they needed one. Who decided if they did or didn't is unknown. In both approaches, children after six months had fewer PTSD and depression symptoms, if they ever had them to begin with. Those of parents in the Link program had slightly fewer behavioral problems, we are told. Considered limits of the study? That it took only place in one U.S. State, as findings may, for reasons unannounced, differ in other U.S. locations. Also that researchers of future studies could look at other programs already in existence to help children with accidental injuries improve their social and emotional problems. Of course, they could. It would feed another multitude of mental health industry professionals, their dependents, employees, cats, fish, dogs and parrots for years on end. PTSD, the Golden Goose that never ceases provide, a philanthropical miracle for the greedy, not the needy.

And the usefulness of this US$1,788,712 PTSD study? To be used by hospital staff, including physicians, looking for ways to help parents talk to their child after an injury. Another example of millions of bred and born Americans starving in the street in abject filth and poverty because they, the Brave and the Free, allow the mental health industry to abuse them by depravation of another $1,788,712 of their money. The study, slotted for completion in 2019, is to be released in 2020. Wonder why? To facilitate PCORI's continuance and throw another US$3,5 billion minimum at it?

In 2017, PCORI accepted to finance *Operation PCOR: Training Veterans as Partners in PTSD Research* for a mere US$249,972. Conducted under the auspices of Professor Cheryl Krause-Parello, PhD, MSN, BSN, and Linda Flynn, PhD, RN, FAAN, both of Florida Atlantic University, Boca Raton, U.S. . This exercise is to last 24 months and proposes verbatim:

"Background: Posttraumatic stress disorder (PTSD) is a stress response to a traumatic event and affects up to 30 percent of the nation's veterans. There is an urgent need to explore robust programs of patient-centered outcomes research (PCOR) and comparative effectiveness research (CER) to identify treatment options for

> PTSD that are effective, acceptable, and meaningful to the veteran population. Veterans engaging as full partners in PTSD-related PCOR and CER are essential to identifying, developing, and testing patient-centered treatment options. Yet, PTSD research efforts are hampered by a dearth of veterans functioning as partners in the research process.
>
> "Proposed Solution to the Problem: Operation PCOR will develop, pilot, and evaluate a nationally accessible, asynchronous, veteran-driven, online research training program designed specifically to prepare veterans to function as full partners in the research enterprise. Operation PCOR will also develop VetResearchHub, a web-based platform for veterans who complete the training." (pcori.org)

In the Land of the Blind, the one-eyed man is King. Isn't it peculiar that millions and utter millions of dollars in PTSD research are still being spent on figuring out what, whom, when, why and how PTSD develops? Never mind what it is. All this, even though no first evidence of success in treatment methods and modalities hitherto recommended exists! Isn't it curiosity-inspiring that with the exception of the very, very few, no mental health practitioner practicing PTSD curing will go on the barricades and yell:

> "PTSD is all a fraud! We made it up! It has always existed. It is not a mental crisis. It is one colossal human existential crisis, and only the Self can heal the Self?"

Does anyone other than Drs. Breggin, Molcher and Laing have the guts to shout it from the rooftops and stop this insanity of diagnosing mentally and physically healthy people with hangnails with PTSD? Is the mental health industry cabal really that corrupt and rotten, deceitful and manipulative to practically shout up the wrong tree for over a century for their own enrichment and to gain complete control over humanity?

It seems that way, as only the absence of psychotropic drugs enables PTSD experiencers to heal the Self. And psychotropic drugs will not only destroy genuine PTSD experiencers' chance to ever heal, but, like those with a hangnail subjected to them, ruin their vital organs and their mind. Of course, those both present huge profits margins for all in the so-called healing professions. It explains why only US$249,972 is spent on training PTSD veterans to help their own and why wild protests against the Oath of Exit and the Spartan Oath are uttered as if they were detrimental to PTSD journeyers' health when the contrary most likely is the case. Does the fish rot from the head?

As if it really mattered. By April 2019, PORI had urgently clamored for PTSD researchers to please seek its grants. A notice for this cause entitled: *Treatment of Posttraumatic Stress Disorder (PTSD) in Adults–Cycle 1 2019* appeared on its website requesting:

> "In the Treatment of Post-Traumatic Stress Disorder (PTSD) in Adults PFA, we seek to fund comparative clinical effectiveness research (CER) studies that aim to determine which specific treatments for adults with PTSD are most effective, and for whom. Proposed comparators may include psychological interventions, pharmacological interventions, or a combination of the two, and all proposed comparators must have demonstrated evidence of efficacy (from systematic reviews, prior empirical investigations, or other scientific documentation).

> PCORI is especially interested in studies that are inclusive of a broad patient population, including those with comorbidities, and in studies that are powered to assess the effectiveness of treatments in subgroups of interest (pcori.org)."

Altogether, US$15,000,000 million are available for this one project to last for 3.5 years. Fifteen million dollars! For what? To feed a multitude of shrinks, mind mixers, psycho-the-rapists? You got it, at least if you read *Fallacy 1*.

And yet, has it still to dawn on you what a gargantuan racket PTSD business is with you as their one and only philanthropist? Has it still to dawn on you that without you, their system would collapse? Do you still believe that an existential crisis called PTSD is curable with psycho-the-rapists' treatments? Does it still escape your attention that all purported PTSD research is done for the sole purpose to create more jobs for "the learned society" and its members? Do you still fail to see that, therefore, the US$15,000,000.00 is another U.S. taxpayer expenditure spent to investigate the un-investigable?

3

PTSD: INVESTIGATING THE UN-INVESTIGABLE?

Allow me to illustrate such possibility – the investigation of the un-investigable and the phenomenal amount of money spent on it for decades. Let me present the PCORI 2016-awarded US$1,245,586 project entitled *Improving Care for Veterans with PTSD: Comparative Effectiveness of Medications to Augment First-line Pharmacotherapy* slotted for completion at the end of December 2020 (HSRP20163069). Principal Investigator Beth Cohen, M.D., University of California, San Francisco, has this to say about it:

> "Along with counselling, doctors choose first-line medicines to treat symptoms of PTSD. First-line medicines are those medicines known to work best for most people. However, first-line medicines don't work for all patients with PTSD. Doctors and patients want to learn about second-line medicines they can use along with first-line medicines to improve symptoms. Studies have not looked at how well second-line medicines treat symptoms of PTSD. These medicines may be approved to treat conditions other than PTSD, and some have side effects such as weight gain. This study aims to compare the risks and benefits of second-line medicines used to treat the symptoms of PTSD." (https://pcori.org)

Nice. That is how some PTSD experiencers end up taking 30 plus different mind-altering drugs, graciously prescribed by their treating physicians. And that screws them up to such a degree until the end of their at-that-point-rather-unnatural-life, so they do not know whether they are coming or going, literally. And Cohen's research subjects may be in precisely that condition when she engages them to explore the biological, behavioural and psychosocial factors that increase chronic disease risks in PTSD patients. Go figure. Cohen she is an assistant professor of medicine at the University of California, San Francisco. She is also a staff physician at the San Francisco VA Medical Center, where she works as a primary care provider in the Integrated Care Clinic, specifically designed to meet the healthcare needs of returning Veterans. This clinic co-locates primary care, mental health, and social work services. During the first visit, one can meet with:

- a combat stress specialist to discuss readjustment
- a primary care provider for a comprehensive health exam
- a case manager to address other post-deployment issues (sanfrancisco.va.gov)

In other words, Cohen has a magnificent background to know about the psychotropic drugging taking place there, right off the bat. Furthermore, and utterly amazing, she still has to discover that chronic illness arises due to perpetual stress. Yes, that same stress expertly imposed upon genuine PTSD journeyers by the powers that be. And that it hits them in combination with multiple mind-altering and human-vital-organ-destroying drug ingestion simultaneously due to mental health practitioners' fondness of liberally dishing out prescription drugs. Cohen completed her residency in internal medicine and a fellowship and Master's degree in clinical research at the University of California, San Francisco. We should think that she would know that, in particular when her research program is designed to improve the health and quality of life of patients with PTSD (ptsd.va.gov). That continuous stress alone encourages chronic physical illness development seems also to have escaped Cohen's attention. But it is PTSD experiencers who must take responsibility for their own demise. It is their own ignorance, their trust in their physicians, VA's or otherwise, and their unwillingness to educate themselves that facilitates their unintentional ruination/destruction of their own lives.

What is furthermore amazing is that Cohen, who is particularly interested in how PTSD impacts chronic illness, assumes that PTSD experiencers' chronic illness arose before PTSD occurred. In genuine PTSD journeyers that can never be the case, as they were up and running well in all aspects of their professional lives before turning chronically ill. Otherwise, they would not have been on duty when the PTSD causing event moment occurred. Has nobody noticed that PTSD never happens to somebody with recognized pre-existing conditions? But obviously Cohen can't see this. To her it is important to integrate PTSD sufferers' mental health with their primary care necessitated, we assume, due to their chronic illness. Is it therefore that she became the principal investigator of the 2008 *Mind Your Heart Study* designed to understand how PTSD impacts cardiovascular health?

Nearly 750 veterans with and without PTSD participated in that study. Each of them underwent cardiac stress tests and baseline mental and physical health assessments. Each one receives annual telephone interviews to assess their PTSD symptoms, if applicable, and their physical health, including cardiac events and hospitalizations (mindyourheartstudy.

ucsf.edu). This study was funded by the University of California, School of Medicine, the Department of Defense and another non-profit, the Northern California Institute for Research And Education Inc. (NCIRE), involved in high-quality biomedical research. Its investigators seek more effective means of preventing and curing disease through basic research on conditions prevalent among veterans and all Americans as guinea pigs, it seems (guidestar.org). A primary goal of NCIRE is to translate research results into clinical practices that benefit everyone. The Veterans Health Research Institute, the National Institute of Health/National Heart, Lung, and Blood Institute, the American Heart Association, the Brain and Behaviour Research Foundation and the Irene Perstein Foundation also helped financing the *Mind Your Heart Study*, which numerous other PTSD researchers apparently use as the basis for their own PTSD research.

With *Mind and Heart* in her quiver, how do Cohen et al. intend to conduct their comparative effectiveness of medications to augment first-line PTSD pharmacotherapy? By first reviewing those PTSD patients' medical records, received from the U.S. Department of Veterans Affairs (VA), who consume the following:

- Antipsychotic medicines: olanzapine, quetiapine, risperidone
- Prazosin
- Mirtazapine
- Tricyclic antidepressants: amitriptyline, imipramine

The risks and benefits of each drug are tested in specific groups of women, of returning Iraq and Afghanistan veterans and participants aged 65 and older. Comparisons of how different medicines affect individual participants' mental and physical health are then made and changes in PTSD symptoms and weight are noted. Some symptoms and events are considered secondary and go unnoticed (Study Registration Information HSRP20163069; https://pcori.org), such as:

- cholesterol
- blood sugar
- blood pressure
- suicidal thoughts
- emergency room visits
- cardiovascular disease events
- hospitalizations for mental health concerns
- use of medications to treat metabolic problems

That most, if not all, of those problems in PTSD experiencers arise from mental upheaval due to enormous stress and pharmaceutical drug intake is ignored. So is the antiquated idea known since time memorial by giants in the field of human health like Hippocrates, Asclepius and Galen about mind, body and soul working in unison to create humans' health and wellbeing. The purpose of this US$1,245,586 million PTSD study? To allow PTSD patients and their doctors to make PTSD symptom treatment choices! Still think the mental health cabal has your interest at heart? Ok, then. Dream on!

Cohen, like the multitude of her mental health industry cohorts, has either yet to discover or refuses to recognize that body, mind and soul in humans are to function in unison. They are to be ruled by the individual who chose to inhabit the body, not by those prescribing pharmacological drugs to rule and dictate how that body and that mind shall function. Thus, the moment genuine PTSD journeyers give away their power by taking psychotropic drugs prescribed by physicians of all stripes and colors, they are cooked geese, game over, unless they awaken from the induced trance. The PTSD affected self can only heal the self without pharmaceutical mind perversion. Awakening is the first step. Discipline, determination, willpower and persistency must be applied by the Self to begin the first step on the path to recovery. Recall that only bright people get PTSD. Recall that, therefore, you are considered a threat to the ruling elite. Recall that before the manure hit the fan, you were a high achiever, a supremely well functioning human being. Recall that there is nothing wrong with you other than you had an earthshattering, life changing experience beyond a normally-to-be-expected, humanly possible experience, whose essence and possibilities you have yet to grasp. You are still a fully functional human being; you still have all your faculties, your God-given IQ and your talents and aptitudes. Remember you are not mentally impaired, disordered or sick, the stigma so vigorously attached to us during the past 30 years for the purpose to ostracize us, and now to take our guns away. In fact, you are better than you ever were before, you just don't know it yet. Understand that part, and you are able to roll away from the abyss in which you will tumble, if ending in the hands of drug-prescribing, psycho-the-rapist physicians of all stripes and colours.

Kick yourself into doing what you did before the colossally life-changing event moment. Take the daily shower; groom yourself daily; shave, eat at least one nutritious meal; do go out and look at folk, even if you do not have a dog forcing you to venture out into the alien world Earth has temporarily become. Take responsibility for yourself. Apply yourself with all your might to disallow your slide into the morass of the abyss. It is the only possibility to heal your PTSD. Once you engage in pharmacotherapy with the joyous assistance of your treating physicians, it's game over for you.

How treacherous entering into that territory is, can be best demonstrated by presenting the 2018 review of the 2013 *Psychological and Pharmacological Treatments for Adults with Posttraumatic Stress Disorder (PTSD): A Systematic Review Update* conducted by PCORI and the Agency for Healthcare Research and Quality, based on purported evidence-based PTSD therapies to curb PTSD symptoms. It states in summary:

> "Posttraumatic stress disorder (PTSD) involves a group of symptoms experienced after exposure to a potentially traumatic event that may include re-experiencing the event; avoiding situations that trigger memories of the event; experiencing increased negative feelings and beliefs; and/or experiencing feelings of hyper-arousal such as irritability, agitation, anger, or being on alert (https://pcori.org). PTSD is associated with significant social, personal, and economic costs. People affected by PTSD have high rates of psychiatric comorbidity; have problems with functioning (e.g., family, work, social); and tend to suffer adverse consequences such as difficulties with educational attainment, work earnings, marriage attainment, and child rearing over the life course. Treatment guidelines typically include guidance about both psychological and pharmacological types of treatments. This systematic review is an update of an earlier report published

by the Agency for Healthcare Research and Quality's Effective Healthcare Program in 2013."

Those symptoms mentioned are caused by pharmacotherapy! We also understand, if we read *Fallacy 1*, that it is since the Freudian – Fraudian– hay-days that PTSD ceased to be defined as an existential crisis, the suffering of the soul. Slowly but surely, it was watered down, misrepresented and turned into a mental disorder with its associated stigma attached. What better way to deprive those owning guns and knowing how to use them from defending themselves when necessary due to a PTSD diagnoses, regardless of the U.S. 2nd Amendment? A return to the existential crisis diagnoses would spoil the scheme. Instead, the PTSD fable continuous, journeyers and public alike dwelling in the illusion that PTSD is curable by outside intervention by the mind fixers and psychotropic drugs. In fact, it started with the Diagnostic and Statistical Manual of Mental Disorders, the DSN-5, DSM coming in fashion in May 2013. At length discussed in *Fallacy I*, that work was created by members of the American Psychiatric Association and approved by its Board of Trustees. Its diagnosis recommendations most oftentimes determine healthcare providers' payment.

That its critics voice that many DSM-5 revisions and additions lack empirical support is inconsequential to the multitude of users. That many disorders have low inter-rater-reliability and several sections contain poorly written, confusing and/or contradictory information is also ignored. That the psychiatric drug industry unduly influences the manual's content doesn't matter either, it seems. That members of work groups for the DSM-5 had conflicting interests as well as ties to pharmaceutical companies is also inconsequential. That various scientists argue that the DSM-5 forces clinicians to make distinctions unsupported by solid evidence, including distinctions of major treatment implications, such as drug prescriptions and the availability of health insurance coverage, doesn't matter either to those ruling the world of psychiatry. That general DSM-5 criticism ultimately resulted in a petition calling for the manual's outside review, signed by many mental health organizations, will be adhered to when hell freezes over and pigs fly the skies, while the DSM-5 practically advocates PTSD diagnoses for hangnails. Why?

Is it to get as many humans as possible on pharmaceutical psychotropic drugs to create the SOMA zombie society portrayed in Matrix I? Why else would the mental health field tread water and its mental health practitioners in their professional associations and non-profit affiliated organizations regurgitate ad nauseam what has already been regurgitated by a multitude of other agencies and individuals of their cabal for decades? The NC *for* PTSD and the Agency for Healthcare Research and Quality (AHRQ) are among them. The latter is another U.S. government agency functioning as part of the Department of Health & Human Services (HHS), with audacity proclaiming to support research helping to improve humans' quality of healthcare. Their sentiments are reflected in laws permitting infanticide up to the age of 1, some say 17, and drugging and killing PTSD experiencers and the elderly into oblivion.

The AHRQ and PCORI's research and quality 2018 PTSD report is based on research conducted by the RTI International-University of North Carolina at Chapel Hill's Evidence-based Practice Center (EPC) under contract to the AHRQ, Rockville, Maryland

(Contract No. 290-2015-00011-I; PCORI Publication No. 2018-SR-01). RTI International is another not-for-profit research organization that includes commercial for-profit industries in business, consulting and pharmaceutical sectors. Initially established by three local universities, it is managed independently by a separate board and management team, consisting of RTI corporation members, its board of governors and corporate officers. RTI also has a separate business called RTI Health Solutions, which supports biotech, diagnostic and medical device companies.[14] As of 2012, the organization's largest service areas were in social, statistical and environmental sciences. More than half of RTI's staff have advanced degrees in one of 120 fields, and they work on approximately 1,200 projects at a time.[4] The operation spans the globe and had revenues of US$ 972 million in 2017.

The systematic review to update the 2013 report that evaluated psychological and pharmacological PTSD treatments of adults focused on updating the earlier work and expanding the range of treatments examined. It addressed earlier uncertainties by identifying ways to improve care for PTSD patients and reducing variation in existing treatment guidelines. The review was published under the title *Psychological and Pharmacological Treatments for Adults With Posttraumatic Stress Disorder: A Systematic Review Update* (effectivehealthcare.ahrq.gov). The authors aimed to update a systematic review and meta-analysis of the comparative effectiveness and harms of psychological and pharmacological interventions for adults with PTSD. Due to the current continuing disagreement on PTSD treatment effectiveness, they first assessed evidence for efficacy of treatments of interest and then assessed their comparative effectiveness. This approach was also used, we read, because few head-to-head comparative effectiveness trials exist, so they had to rely on indirect evidence to draw conclusions. It was emphasized, though, that their findings and conclusions were those of the researchers responsible for the evaluated treatment of interest.

The 2018 authors further cover their rear ends by pointing out in no uncertain terms that their findings and conclusions do not necessarily represent the views of AHRQ or PCORI. They further assert that none of the report-statements should be construed as PCORI, AHRQ or the U.S. Department of Health and Human Services official positions. In the vernacular it is termed "cover your ass." But why? Because they want to help PTSD experiencers past and present? In particular, they further emphasize strongly that all those participating in writing the 2018 report were free from financial involvement and affiliations conflicting with the material presented. We are furthermore told that the report was not intended to be a substitute for the application of clinical judgment, either. It should be considered only in the same way as any other medical reference, the DSM-5 most likely included. And it should be considered in conjunction with all other pertinent information and in context of available resources and circumstances presented by individual patients. Lovely, except that none of the 23 purportedly mental health practitioners versed in PTSD whom I was forced to deal with gave a hoot about my individual views, resources and circumstances for PTSD treatment. The one I determinedly continued to beg for, "Give me some peace and quiet," was the one they continually assaulted and violated with expertise for 10 years.

But I digress. PCORI and AHRQ authors' view on PTSD? That it involves a group of symptoms experienced after exposure to a potentially traumatic event. The "potentially" crept in in earnest since the DSM-5. There is nothing potential about PTSD. It is or it is not.

It is looking death in the face with no way out - none. That is the fact of the matter. The rest is, as quoted above, pathetic trash concocted by individuals who perceive themselves to be PTSD experts, never even having experienced an iota of it, never mind that there is no iota. It either is death or it is not. It is like being pregnant or not. When in such a situation and death does not occur it, leads to PTSD. The soul has kissed the body bye-bye before the catastrophe causing death is completed, but death has been aborted due to unknown reasons. Thus, the body is left without a soul, and goes into shock manifested by PTSD when discovering it's still alive and on Earth, or on Earth and alive.

The rest of symptom-theory and hypotheses composed by the PTS analyzers is just that - theory and hypotheses, phantasms and mirages of their minds. These goons themselves admit it when stating that PTSD symptoms *may*, just *may*, include:

- re-experiencing the event
- avoiding situations that trigger memories of the event
- experiencing increased negative feelings and beliefs
- experiencing feelings of hyper-arousal, such as irritability, agitation, anger or being on alert
- experiencing various combinations of those indicators

I experienced all those symptoms when perpetually forced into so-called "PTSD treatments" added by the tender loving care extended to me by my employer, the WCB and my Union. It is that simple and well documented in *Broken Wings* and *Fallacy 1*. In my view, however, only four categories of professions are by the nature of their work susceptible and prone to acquire PTSD every time they go on duty. Firefighters, police officers, soldiers and veterans and aircrew, of them almost exclusively flight attendants. In civilian life, rape can cause PTSD, and the majority of PTSD cases in the U.S. military is said to incur not from military action, but due to one person raping another. All other events slotted as PTSD are, in my opinion, existential crises. For one, it might from be a hangnail, for others the death of a child, mother father, uncle, aunt, dog or cat. Or from a broken leg, finger or toe. Or it could be from a cancer diagnosis or other illness. All humans react differently to life and living its associated adventures. As we think we create, and we are the producers and directors of our daily show in conjunction with how we carry ourselves.

Even PCORI's and AHRQ authors admit that not all people exposed to *potentially* traumatic events go on to develop PTSD, thus proving my point of either/or and no in between. One meta-analysis of 35 longitudinal study samples (a review of many studies) found that 28.8% of adults exposed to one or more *potentially* traumatic events meet criteria for PTSD within one month of trauma exposure. It also found that 17% continue to meet PTSD criteria 12 months following the exposure. Who determines an events' potential or non-potential potentiality is not specified. What kind of treatment the experiencers of the *potentially* traumatic event received in the interval following their potentially traumatic event-causing moment is not specified, either. However, as it either is or is not PTSD-causing, and as PTSD development depends on a person's intelligence and number of previous near-misses, the idea alone of a potentially-PTSD-causing event appears to be another vat of hogwash. Miraculously, the team came to the same conclusion. It also miraculously perceived that PTSD-affected people might indeed vary in their responses to various PTSD treatment modalities. The authors also suggest that moderators evaluating PTSD treatment effectiveness include socio-demographic and health characteristics in their evaluation such as:

- racial and ethnic minorities
- gender types
- severity or chronicity of PTSD symptoms
- coexisting conditions

Again, however, no thought appears to have been given to the fact that coexisting conditions on the PTSD journey arise from the treatment by the powers that be and not from the PTSD voyage. The authors also present PTSD as being highly comorbid with other psychiatric disorders. That's because data from epidemiologic studies indicates that a vast majority of people with PTSD had another co-occurring mental disorder. This is another blatant show of ignorance, including the assumption that substance use disorders, mood disorders, anxiety disorders and suicidality are mental disorders in genuine PTSD experiencers. They are the effects of treatment received from mental health professionals and the employers, the WCB and the Unions, as could be well-documented when comparing their pre-PTSD-causing event record with present purportedly comorbid conditions.

First and foremost, PTSD is not and has never been a mental disorder. It is "merely" a catastrophic existential crisis for thousands of years well-documented in available literature. It is in style right now to present PTSD as a mental disorder. That gives the U.S. regime an excuse to take those most qualified to carry through with the 2nd Amendment, returning soldiers and veterans, from baring arms. False flag rifle assaults thus flourish, always carried out by a mentally ill gunman when numerous where seen at the scene and those who were purportedly killed observed sipping coffee after their killing. It gives President Trump's reason to clamor for the elimination of the U.S. Constitution's Second Amendment, which reads: "A well regulated Militia, being necessary to the security of a free State, the right of the people to keep and bear Arms, shall not be infringed." (New Hampshire August 15, 2019). He also calls for the reinstatement of mental institutions to get the most likely PTSD affected veterans off the streets.

The Soviets already experienced it. After its 1917 revolution and the formation of the Marxist-Leninist Union of Soviet Socialist Republics (USSR) that existed from 1922 to 1991, the regime managed to kill over 60 million people> Another untold thousands disappeared in mental institutions, until the Soviet collapse in 1994. Psychiatry was used throughout to disable and remove political opponents ("dissidents") from society. Those were the people who openly expressed beliefs that contradicted the official dogma. Let's recall what the Russian journalist, human rights activist, neurophysiologist and writer Vladimir Konstantinovich Bukovsky (1942-) said. He spent 12 years in psychiatric prison-hospitals, labour camps and prisons of the Soviet Union. He stated in *A Manual on Psychiatry for Dissenters*, written jointly with the Ukrainian psychiatrist and human rights activist Semen Fishelevich Gluzman (1946-): "the Soviet use of psychiatry as a punitive means is based upon the deliberate interpretation of dissent... as a psychiatric problem (Bloch & Reddaway 1977 p. 425)."

That psychiatry possesses an inherent capacity for abuse that is greater than in other areas of medicine becomes obvious to anyone reading *Fallacy 1*. That diagnosis of mental disease can give the state license to detain people against their will and insist upon therapy, both in the interest of the detainee and in the broader interests of society, becomes a given. In addition, receiving a psychiatric diagnosis can in itself be regarded as oppressive, due to the stigma attached. Psychiatry can also be used to bypass standard legal procedures for establishing guilt or innocence and allow political incarceration without the ordinary odium attached to political trials. The practice incarcerating of political dissidents in mental hospitals in Eastern Europe and the former USSR hugely damaged the reputation of psychiatrists in those countries. But psychiatrists have been involved in human rights abuses in states across the world when definitions of mental disease were expanded to include threats to the ruling elite. As scholars have long argued, governments and medical institutions have classified threats to authority during periods of political disturbance and instability as a form of mental disease, as Jonathan Metzl (1964 -), points out in his book *The Protest Psychosis* (Beacon Press 2009). He is a Frederick B. Rentschler II professor of sociology and psychiatry, and the director of the Center for Medicine, Health, and Society, at Vanderbilt University in Nashville, Tennessee. This well-proven measure is easily activated by the president's executive order to eliminate those best qualified to make use of their 2nd Amendment rights – soldiers and veterans stigmatized with the unjustifiable PTSD diagnosis. So why should it not be used against them in time of trouble against the governing body?

On top of this potentiality PTSD conundrum, we are furthermore to believe that PTSD symptoms' severity can be measured in clinical or research settings. One would use a number of validated scales, typically resulting in a numeric score. This score would purportedly roughly correspond with the intensity, frequency, duration, subjective distress or impact of symptoms on functioning. The Minnesota Multiphasic Personality Inventory (MMPI) is without doubt one of those scales. It is of the utmost necessity to mental health practitioners who want to implement the most expert traumatization of the PTSD-traumatized.

Now to that part of the report which best illustrates, in my opinion, the mental health cabal's theories, hypotheses and hallucinations about post-traumatic stress.

The authors convey that several psychological and pharmacological treatments mentioned in the review have at least a *moderate* Strength of Evidence (SOE) supporting efficacy. They used information from 207 published articles reporting on 193 studies of psychological PTSD treatment findings. In these, they found that two types of cognitive behavioural therapy (CBT) treatments were *most likely* effective to decrease PTSD, depression symptoms and loss of a PTSD diagnose. These two types are the Pavlovian-associated methods/modes, namely the CBT-exposure and the CBT-mixed treatments, (*Psychological and Pharmacological Treatments for Adults With Posttraumatic Stress Disorder: A Systematic Review Update Systematic Review* May 17, 2018; https://effectivehealthcare.ahrq.gov).

The term CBT-mixed is used for treatments of different CBT hypothesis all mixed together. But all of them are applied in all non-holistic PTSD treatment modalities. And we recall, of course, that anything with cognitive behavioral in its wording is a treatment for humans only because it worked so wonderfully well on rattus, mus, simian and cani, humanity's ancestors at the dawn of time, according to Darwin's crap of evolution, and on whatever else can crawl, jump, fly or breathe in laboratories. These exist seemingly just to test humanity's possible reactions to stimuli that only the very sick or demon-possessed can conceive of or imagine from their hallucinatory minds. *The Narrative Exposure Therapy* (NET) is one of them. Developed in the 1980s by Michael Kingsley White and David Epston.

White (1948-2008) was born and raised in Adelaide, Australia. He began his professional life as a probation and welfare worker. He earned an undergraduate social work degree from the University of South Australia in 1979 and worked as a psychiatric social worker at the Adelaide Children's Hospital before in 1983 founding the Dulwich Centre in Adelaide, Australia on Kaurna Lan, one of the key 'homes' of narrative practice, which he led until his departure from earth in 2008. (https://dulwichcentre.com.au)

Canadian-born David Epston (1944 -) is a New Zealand therapist and co-director of Auckland's Family Therapy Centre. He is also a visiting professor at the John F. Kennedy University, an honorary clinical lecturer in the Department of Social Work, University of Melbourne, and an affiliate faculty member in the PhD program in couple and family therapy at North Dakota State University.

White and Epston in the late 1970s led the sprouting of family therapy in Australia and New Zealand. Starting to develop their ideas together in 1990, they published *Narrative Means to Therapeutic Ends*. This was the first major text in what came to be known as narrative therapy. Contrary to cognitive behavioural therapy, narrative therapy does not seek to transform the person. Instead, it aims to transform the effects of a problem, by making space between a person and their issue (goodtherapy.org). This, the inventors assert, would make it possible to see how a certain concern is serving a person rather than harming them. For example, Epston and White hypothesize that posttraumatic stress could be a defense mechanism, and that narrative therapy might help protect someone from the emotions associated with it. It apparently does help people externalize an issue, such as the often PTSD-associated anxiety. That the anxiety arises due to the lack of understanding of the situation one finds oneself in - this enormous catastrophe of suddenly being a stranger in a strange land after the PTSD-causing event moment - has yet to dawn on them. We hear only that the process can help people develop greater self-compassion, which in turn may help them feel more capable of change. What type of change is unspecified, but here we cruise again into CBT territory. It permeates everything in the mental health weed field.

> What has yet to be recommended as PTSD treatment modality by those ruling the PTSD show is the most sensitive of methods, the Neuro Emotional Technique (NET). It is a mind-body approach to help alleviate stress related conditions by combining a number of techniques and principles from traditional Chinese medicine, chiropractic and applied kinesiology. It is a holistic approach to wellbeing focusing on imbalances in the structure of the skeletomuscular system, unresolved negative emotional blocks, toxins in the body, and deficiencies in nutrition. NET claims to help release or resolve them. Developed in the early 1980s, it is a psychosomatic stress reduction aiming to achieve homeostasis of the human organism. Its method of correction is through the spine or acupuncture points. As part of its diagnostic methodology patient at times explore their neuro-emotional

> case history to assist in the uncovering of negative emotional complexes (NEC) stored in the body. Once discovered, the correction is applied. Whereas narrative therapists help people to view their problems in different contexts, whether of a social, political or cultural nature, to influence how we view our selves and our personal stories, in NET any case history that reveals a need for psychotherapy is discussed with the patient. Narrative therapists also help people to view their problems in different contexts, whether of a social, political or cultural nature, to influence how we view our selves and our personal stories.

Mind you, a few psychologists were bright enough to identify and even brave enough to publicly acknowledge the potential of personal growth generated by the PTSD experience, a process they termed "Post Traumatic Growth" (PTG). The term was coined by psychologists Richard G. Tedeschi and Lawrence G. Calhoun at the University of North Carolina at Charlotte in the mid-1990s. It has been described as a positive psychological change, experienced as a result of adversity and other challenges, leading to a higher level of functioning. There is no need to go into details of how and why this heightened functionality would occur. In other words, PTG addresses only generally-to-be-expected traumatic experiences in a human's life: divorce, death of family members, be it mother, father, child, aunt or uncle, broken bones, car accidents, falling from a ladder while painting the house and so on. It does NOT address the split-second PTSD-causing event moment in an experience so shattering that it is unforeseeable during the course of a human's life. Genuine PTSD and the PTG are therefore like comparing apples with oranges.

Thus, post-traumatic awareness (PTA) would be a better term. It is this heightened state of awareness that rocks PTSD journeyers off their foundation. This same awareness slowly heightens their functionality after the PTSD causing event moment unless they are drugged by their psychiatrists. But how do you gather empirical, scientific, first evidence of human awareness? Thus, it is unacceptable to even breathe a word about heightened awareness potential through heightened post-PTSD awareness to most mental health practitioners of whatever genre. You see, when a state of heightened awareness is reached knowingly or unknowingly, as in the days and possibly months following the PTSD-causing event moment, it takes an enormous amount of thinking to figure out what has happened within the Self. That takes lots and lots of self-examination and contemplation, but once we understand that it is the only way to get us out of the mess in which we find ourselves, we begin to take the first step to recovery. As Tedeschi and Calhoun point out, however, most circumstances generating the potential for PTG, the average to-be-expected traumas occurring in average human working stiffs' lives, PTG, do represent significant challenges to the adaptive resources of someone walking through the experience. Those circumstances also pose challenges to understanding the world and their place in it. But PTSD goes far beyond it. PTSD involves creating la tabula rasa, a clean slate within the Self. It means making peace with whatever one has done before the PTSD-causing event moment, and then creating the Self one wants to be, which only the Self can accomplish. This only path to PTSD recovery and healing is kept top secret, as it would destroy the mental health industry's PTSD profit bonanza.

Furthermore, there is nothing new about Tedeschi and Calhoun's theory either. I discussed at length in *Fallacy 1* that the general understanding of how suffering and distress potentially yield positive change is thousands of years old. Hinduism, Buddhism, Judaism, Christianity, Islam and the Baha'i Faith all contain elements of the potentially transformative power of suffering. Attempts to understand and discover the meaning of human suffering also represent a central theme of much philosophical inquiry, which appear in works of novelists, dramatists and poets throughout millennia up to present day. As Canadian clinical psychologist and full professor at the University of Toronto psychology department Jordan Peterson (1962–) of *12 Rules for Life* fame seems to vocalize: "Understand life IS suffering and learning, and once you recognize and accept it you can live life better if following certain rules, like standing straight with your shoulders back and cleaning up your room." Both, of course, reflect the inner self. His *12 Rules for Life: An Antidote to Chaos* is a 2018 self-help book by Canadian clinical psychologist and psychology professor Jordan Peterson. It provides life advice through essays on abstract ethical principles, psychology, mythology, religion, and personal anecdotes.

Reviewers also deemed the cognitive processing therapy (CPT), the cognitive therapy (CT) and the eye movement desensitization and reprocessing (EMDR) to be moderately effective PTSD treatments. It is notable that the preceding 2013 report stated:

> "Several psychological and pharmacological treatments have at least moderate SOE [Strength of Evidence] supporting their efficacy: exposure, CPT, CT, CBT-mixed therapies, EMDR, narrative exposure therapy, fluoxetine, paroxetine, sertraline, topiramate, and venlafaxine." (Psychological and Pharmacological Treatments for Adults With Posttraumatic Stress Disorder (PTSD) Systematic Review, April 3, 2013 (https://effectivehealthcare.ahrq.gov)

Should we call it "treading water so as not to kill the golden goose"? The 2018 review-authors even proclaimed that existent research showed that holistic relaxation techniques for reducing PTSD symptoms and outcomes were even less effective than CBT-exposure therapy. Substantiating first evidence was, to my knowledge, lacking. When CBT-exposure, the rattus-canine, simian and mus based PTSD treatment theories were mixed with CPT, CT, EMDR, NET, however, we learn that moderate strength of evidence for comparative effectiveness existed from head-to-head trials that favored CBT-exposure over relaxation therapy, though evidence was insufficient to determine the comparative effectiveness of other treatments, including psychological and pharmacological treatment comparisons.

The second question in the 2013 report re-evaluation concerned the outcome of pharmacological PTSD treatment. The conclusion reached? Moderate SOE of benefit in reduction in PTSD-related outcomes were noted for the selective serotonin reuptake inhibitors (SSRIs), paroxetine and fluoxetine, as well as the selective serotonin-norepinephrine reuptake inhibitor (SNRI) venlafaxine when compared with placebo. The authors again contended that little direct comparative evidence, termed head-to-head, had been available to determine if pharmacological treatments differed in effectiveness. Only four medium-risk bias studies met inclusion criteria. Of those four, two compared medications' documented evidence supporting their efficacy, namely sertraline and venlafaxine. Findings provided evidence of no differences between groups for PTSD symptoms and quality of life and disability. Only moderate evidence of no difference for depression was noted.

Just one study attempted to directly compare the PTSD treatment EMDR with and without fluoxetine. But the data were from a single, small study, with medium risk of bias, providing imprecise findings of unknown consistency. It also provided insufficient strength of evidence regarding whether efficacy or effectiveness differed by patient characteristics or type of trauma exposure, the reviewers concluded that head-to-head evidence was insufficient to draw firm conclusions about its comparative effectiveness.

As to adverse events to any of the treatments, meaning an unexpected medical problem happening due to an administered drug, studies re-examined in the 2013 report typically did not report the use of methods to systematically capture adverse event information collected by standardized measures to that effect. The few head-to-head trials meeting inclusion criteria lacked sufficient overall data to determine differences in the efficacy or comparative effectiveness of PTSD interventions by individual characteristics. These included comorbid condition, types, numbers and severity.

> Another unmentioned problem is, however, that literature and research of head-to-head Randomly Controlled Trials (RCT) are financially supported and thus dominated by the pharmaceutical industry. For example, the New England Journal of Medicine -- one of the most prestigious medical journals in the world – published 73 studies of new drugs. Of those studies, a pharmaceutical company funded 60, 50 had drug-company employees among the authors and 37 lead researchers had accepted money from a drug company, according to a review conducted by the Washington Post. This means drug companies greatly influence the majority of medical information provided to the public. Unreliable clinical trials resulting from the possibility for bias due to Big Pharma influence is another ongoing issue because "clinical trials for pharmaceuticals are conducted and funded by the industry," Dr. Michael A. Carome, director of the Health Research Group of Public Citizens in Washington, D.C., told Drugwatch (https://drugwatch.com).

Consequently, industry-sponsored comparative assessments systematically yielded favorable results for the sponsors throughout this report (sciencedirect.com). It was also revealed that almost 50% of adults diagnosed with PTSD do not get mental health treatment. Among those who do get it, only 40.4% receive what is considered minimally adequate PTSD treatment. Purportedly evidence-based guidelines define such therapy as either pharmacotherapy for two or more focal disorders, Focal neurologic signs also known as focal neurological deficits or focal CNS are impairments of nerve, spinal cord or brain function that affect specific regions of the body. Such therapy would also include more than four visits to any type of physician or eight or more psychotherapy visits with a healthcare or human service professional, lasting for 30 minutes or longer. Furthermore, studies had shown that, although about 92 % of adults with lifetime PTSD eventually did achieve remission, the median time to do so is estimated to be 14 years after the PTSD causing event moment.

Now then, PCORI, this so-called independent, non-profit, non-governmental organization based in Washington, DC and authorized by Congress between 2010 and 2019, managed to finance 1489 research projects for around US$3,5 billion. Only five of those projects were PTSD-related. And with those five projects, PCORI managed to justify the further investigation of the un-investigable – the finding of the non-existent, one-size-fits-all PTSD cure for the multitude. Thus, PCORI financed PTSD researchers, instead of calling a spade a spade, as they could very well have done, if pride and joy in their education and honour and integrity would have had a say. It chose to perpetuate PTSD's misrepresentation. Thus, they are again instrumental in aiding and abetting the mental health and pharmaceutical cabal alike with their PTSD fables continuance. As we sow, we reap, however...

PCORI's PTSD research publications might seem a bit ancient or of little use to genuine PTSD experiencers, soldiers and veterans in particular. But please note that since 1998, the U.S. Department of Veteran Affairs (VA) devotes an entire website to the topic. It is quaintly entitled QUERI – *Quality Enhancement Research Initiative*, launched as part of a system-wide transformation aimed at improving the quality of healthcare for veterans. Its mission? To improve care, using research evidence to improve clinical practice. It would leverage scientifically-supported quality improvement (QI) methods. These would be paired with a deep understanding of veterans' preferences and needs to implement evidence-based practices (EBPs) rapidly into routine care. This should improve the quality and safety of care delivered to veterans, we read on its website (queri.research.va.gov). This specific 2018 review of ancient PTSD research data is entitled *Psychological and Pharmacological Treatments for Adults With Posttraumatic Stress Disorder: A Systematic Review Update*. It is available for the price of US$ $267,750. And the overall conclusions of the review? The usual wishy-washy, non-committal to anything stuff, such as:

- High strength of evidence (SOE) supports efficacy of cognitive behavioral therapy (CBT).
- High SOE supports CBT-mixed treatments.
- Moderate SOE supports efficacy of cognitive processing therapy (CPT).
- Moderate SOE supports cognitive therapy (CT).
- Moderate SOE supports eye movement desensitization and reprocessing (EMDR).
- Moderate SOE supports narrative exposure therapy (NET).
- Moderate SOE favors CBT-exposure over relaxation therapy.

Of course, it does, as relaxation techniques are holistic in nature. They are drug-free. And you can apply them totally independent of the mental health cabal. PTSD journeyers can with ease apply them for free in the comfort of their homes. The Mayo Clinic praises them such:

> "Relaxation techniques are a great way to help with stress management. Relaxation isn't only about peace of mind or enjoying a hobby. Relaxation is a process that decreases the effects of stress on your mind and body. Relaxation techniques can help you cope with everyday stress and with stress related to various health problems, such as heart disease and pain. Whether your stress is spiralling out of control or you've already got it tamed, you can benefit from

> learning relaxation techniques. Learning basic relaxation techniques is easy. Relaxation techniques also are often free or low cost, pose little risk, and can be done nearly anywhere." (mayoclinic.org)

But what does the PTSD-benefitting society care for the competition's ideas, eh, in particular when they must maintain that several pharmacological treatments reduced PTSD symptoms, eh? Must root for one's brethren, even though only moderate SOE supported the efficacy of fluoxetine, paroxetine, and venlafaxine compared with placebo. Money to make is money to make; even small amounts add up, no?

Studies provided insufficient SOE for serious adverse events associated with any treatments of interest. So why not just ignore all that? Too tedious for words, those interested can look up the side-effects themselves. "Who cares anyway?", the team seems to state. That as good as all psychotropic pharmaceutical drugs carry life-threatening dangers for takers is thus gloriously ignored. But does it matter, considering the majority of psychological studies reported no information about adverse events? We take it as non-existent, other than for venlafaxine, where an increased risk of nausea compared with placebo occurred with moderate SOE.

Reviewers also found insufficient SOE for comparative effectiveness of any psychological versus pharmacological treatment. Nor did they find sufficient SOE for differences in the efficacy or comparative effectiveness of treatments by patient characteristics. Not for co-occurring conditions or types, which we take to mean comorbidity. Nor for the number severity or chronicity of trauma exposures. They did not find evidence for many of their outcomes or interventions of interest, including the newer treatments added since the 2013 review. Thus, these esteemed individuals of the learned society concluded that several psychological and pharmacological treatments had moderate to high strength of efficacy for treating adults with PTSD. Future research was needed, however, on the comparative effectiveness of treatments, including:

- different comparisons of psychological and pharmacological treatments
- differences in treatment benefits by trauma type or other patient characteristics
- differences in treatment benefits on adverse events associated with treatments

The studies provided insufficient evidence about adverse events [AE]. None of the treatments had sufficient evidence of serious AE associations or chronicity of trauma exposure(s) (https://effectivehealthcare.ahrq.gov)."

Which leads us right into the chronicity of trauma exposure, namely the cognitive behavioral exposure (CBE) therapy. This is applied to PTSD experiencers by demanding the regurgitating of the PTSD-causing event moment ad nauseam in the presence of an employer- or WCB-appointed mental health goon. Those conditions, most oftentimes last for years on end, with changing mental health practitioners always demanding a recital., Is it any wonder that VA Boston Healthcare System and Boston University School of Medicine and the National Center *for* PTSD principal investigator Danielle R. Sullivan in March 2019 touts:

"People exposed to trauma are less able to suppress unwanted emotional memories due to neural and behavioral disruptions in their brain that may contribute to the development of post-traumatic stress disorder (PTSD)?" (Danielle R. Sullivan, Brian Marx, May S. Chen, Brendan E. Depue, Scott M. Hayes, Jasmeet P. Hayes. "Behavioral and neural correlates of memory suppression in PTSD". *Journal of Psychiatric Research*, 2019)

What happens when the PTSD afflicted get somewhat irritated or even refuse to repeat the performance of another recital? They are instantaneously reported to the powers that be as recalcitrant patients. They lose all financial support and are thus thrown to the wolves by their own ignorance of how the game is played. Anything is used to get you off the system and onto the streets, anything. Consequently, it is Dharma over Karma in action, "educate the Self" being the rule in everything.

Sullivan's academic career has been limited to Boston University, achieving a BA in Neuroscience and psychology there in 2011 and a PhD in behavioural neuroscience in 2016. She notes that previous work had shown that healthy people can actively suppress emotional memories through recruitment of the lateral prefrontal cortex. He therefore feels that PTSD-affected people frequently experienced unwanted memories of their traumatic experiences, even when making explicit efforts to avoid them. Says who? Ms. Sullivan and her cohorts, who in the same breath admit that little is known about behavioural and neural effects of memory suppression among PTSD-experiencing people? (sciencedirect.com) Therefore, her research is focused on exploring structural and functional brain networks that may be altered in mild traumatic brain injury (mTBI)- and PTSD sufferers. The interplay between PTSD and mTBI also captured her interest at the Neuroimaging Research for Veterans Center. Here, researchers are trained in cutting-edge neuroimaging methods, sharing their expertise with established investigators, the Neumeisters of the world. They do this to enhance translational neuroscience approaches in understanding the brain (sites.bu.edu). Sullivan's aim? To find out how biomarkers such as neuroimaging and genetics impact PTSD and mTBI outcome and recovery.

She asserts that PTSD is caused by the intense, repetitive, intrusive and incapacitating reliving of the trauma. And yes, she has a point. As stated above, the treating mental health practitioners, possibly instructed by employer and WCB alike, demand such perpetual regurgitating to keep the wound open as long as it takes to make PTSD journeyers disappear from their radar. As Sullivan states: "The intrusive nature of these hallmark symptoms suggests that the inability to suppress unwanted memories may be a strong contributor to the behavioural manifestation of PTSD." Thus, she asserts that generally applied PTSD treatment modalities that purported heal, in fact prevent healing.

Loren Richard Mosher (1933–2004) is an American psychiatrist, clinical professor of psychiatry, expert on schizophrenia and chief of the Center for Studies of Schizophrenia in the National Institute of Mental Health (1968–1980). He had already observed the same in the 1970s. Mosher believed that the violent and controlling atmosphere of psychiatric hospitals and the over-use of drugs hindered recovery of people diagnosed with schizophrenia and those living through acute psychotic episodes. He therefore spent much of his professional career advocating more humane treatment for sufferers. He called for a residential, home-like, non-hospital, non-drug treatment model for such people. In 1971, when chief of the newly formed Center for Schizophrenia Research, he consequently founded the Soteria Project, an intensive, psychosocial, milieu-based residential treatment center. Remarkable results of recovery occurred, showing that patients with schizophrenia recover without use of antipsychotic medications when in a supportive home-like environment. Sadly, those drugs are nowadays used to treat and manage as good as all ailments judged to be psychiatric by the psychiatric cabal.

Despite its immense success, far superior to standard medical psychotic episode drug treatment, as Loren Molcher's Soteria Project closed its doors in 1983. According to Mosher and the American journalist and author Robert Whitaker, further funding was denied. Molcher and Whitaker, who writes primarily about medicine, science and history, blamed psychiatry's politics being increasingly controlled by pharmaceutical companies. Mind you, there are a number of Soteria houses in Israel - two in Jerusalem alone. There it is a community service that provides space for people experiencing mental distress or crisis. Common elements of the Soteria approach include:

- primarily non-medical staffing
- finding meaning in the subjective experience of psychosis
- preserving resident's personal power, social networks and communal responsibilities
- no or minimal use of pharmaceutical antipsychotic medication, with all medication taken by choice without coercion

Needless to say, as Molcher provided first evidence that tender loving care and attention in a supportive home-like atmosphere was healing more effectively than drugging people. For this, he incurred the animosity and enmity of his fellows in the learned society. Over time, he became progressively more vocal in his opposition to the prevailing psychiatric practices of the time and the increasing reliance on pharmaceuticals for treatment. His colleagues at the National Institute of Mental Health began to shun and isolate him, ending in his dismissal from his position in 1980. His agenda was at odds with the agenda inaugurated some decades earlier by slowly replacing psychoanalytical practices of Freudianism with the world's Sullivans and Neumeisterians, seeking with vigour biological causes of PTSD, for example. This was all described in Anne Harrington's book *Mind Mixers: Psychiatry's Troubled search For the Biology of Mental Illness.* (WW. Norton & Company, 2019)

To discover its source, Sullivan et al. used functional magnetic resonance brain imaging to examine memory suppression in three groups:

- people with PTSD
- people who experienced trauma without PTSD
- people with neither trauma exposure nor PTSD ("control", for comparison)

Findings showed that trauma-exposed study participants, regardless of PTSD, status were less likely to successfully suppress memory than non-trauma-exposed, healthy, control participants. As usual, the question is: "Who dictates what healthy is? Remember Krishnamurti? *"It is no measure of health to be well adjusted to a profoundly sick society."* But Sullivan et al. slide right over that observation and consideration, maintaining that neuroimaging data also revealed that trauma-exposed individuals showed reduced activation in the right middle frontal gyrus. This, they say, suggested the possibility that the difficulty in active suppression of memories may be just one of several likely factors contributing to the PTSD development.

Certified coach and PTSD counsellor Marcia Fervienza, however, asserts that memory suppression happens naturally, as people cannot force themselves to forget something extremely traumatic. They can automatically suppress it only if unable to handle it at a given time. However, as nothing is ever truly forgotten, the fact that a traumatic event has been pushed out of consciousness does not mean it is less strong or influential, nor does it mean it has ceased to exist. Actually, Fervienza exclaims, it is quite the opposite. Suppressed memories "leak" into our daily lives through dreams and Freudian slips of the tongue. They also reveal themselves through inexplicable behaviours, anxieties, phobias and repetitive patterns, demonstrated in engaging in oftentimes negative interpersonal relationships of similar nature. In other words, evidence of memory-irrepressibility abounds, if we start looking for it in out own inner Self. One of the most poignant documentations of this is former government mind control slave Cathy O'Brien's memory retrieval/recall, written in her book *The TranceFormation of America*.

So, the brain's memory suppression switch may very well be situated in the right middle frontal gyrus, as hypothesized by Sullivan et al. That does not negate the fact, however, that this memory suppression switch may very well have been installed by the Creator as a defense mechanism intended to protect the human ego from unbearable pain. It could still make itself unconsciously or subconsciously present in one's life through pathologies. Once people who "lost" their memory are strong enough to handle recollection of the memory-loss-causing event, the memory resurfaces on its own. This would be in accordance with experiencers' inner strength to deal with it, in accordance with their individual psyches. As Professor Richard McNally, Director of Harvard University's Clinical Training in the Department of Psychology, exclaimed in his Statement of Interest as amicus *curiae* to a Court of Law in 2005:

> "How victims remember trauma is the most controversial issue confronting psychology and psychiatry today. Clinical researchers capable of understanding the relevant science realize that traumatic events -those experienced as overwhelmingly terrifying and life-threatening -are remembered all too well. Informed clinicians and scientists realize that emotional arousal enhances memory for trauma; it does not result in blocked memory for trauma. Indeed, people who develop PTSD are haunted by intrusive memories of horrors that they cannot forget.
>
> "Yet some clinicians claim that the mind protects itself by banishing memories of trauma, making it difficult for victims to recall their most terrifying experiences until safe to do so years later. These clinicians believe that a significant minority of victims, perhaps as many as 30%, are incapable of remembering their most terrifying experiences. They believe that victims repress, dissociate, or block out these memories precisely because the memories are so upsetting.

> "As I and others have shown, there is no convincing evidence for the claim that victims repress and recover memories of traumatic events. To be sure, some victims may not think about disturbing events for many years, if the events were not experienced as traumatic -- terrifying and life-threatening -- at the time of their occurrence." (*Richard McNally Amicus letter*, National Center for Reason and Justice, 2005-JUN-03).

But many discoveries about the brain have been made since Professor McNally's statement, you may say. Yes, and in particular in conjunction with AI technology. This leaves unacknowledged the human soul, all spiritual aspects of human life and living and the Divine Being many call God. Sullivan et al. also either ignore or purposely suppress the knowledge that we humans have the ability to heal ourselves superbly well, without anyone fiddling with our brains or filling us with psychotropic drugs and other pharmaceuticals for the hangnail and PTSD alike. Give that a thought before you trust your physician of whatever stripe or color. Genuine PTSD journeyers, the police officers, soldiers, veterans, fire fighters and aircrew, know that everything is done by the powers to be to keep the trauma of your PTSD-causing event moment alive. They do this by regurgitating the event in front of a slew of different mental health practitioners of different backgrounds, qualifications, races and nationalities of origin, and streams of psychological schools of thoughts. They thus perpetually reinforce the PTSD-causing event's reinvigoration. This is deadly to experiencers' souls and psyches, in addition to demands of endless interviews with the employer's personnel, union officers and WCB or other insurer's staff. Add to it the constant threat of financial peril if recalcitrant in following those demands, and it all keeps PTSD experiencers expertly off balance preventing a moment of peace. Thus "normal" PTSD symptoms are turned into pathological creations by the grace of those pretending to assist in one's recovery. Their treatments, in fact, spell total desolation, if not destruction, for the ones between their clutches/claws.

If preferring their help, however, you may wish to briefly peruse Jon Rappoport's report *Pleasure vs. pain in the programmed society*, in which he states:

> "In experiments on mice, scientists rewired the circuits of the brain and changed the animals' bad memories into good ones...The researchers said they were able to do the opposite as well---change a pleasurable memory in mice into one associated with fear." (Jon Rappoport: Pleasure vs. Pain in the programmed society; nomorefakenews.com March 11, 2019)

Don't believe it's being done to you when allowing yourself to follow the dictates of those pretending to help you in your PTSD recovery? So be it. If life and living in your imagination and perception is to wander about like a bumbling and insane idiot due to applications of poly pharmacology and CBT by your mental health practitioner, go for it. Become part of the plan of servitude planned for the world's human population. Do yourself the favour. Obey! As *Brave New World* author Aldous Huxley once wrote to George Orwell:

> "The world's rulers'] lust for power can be just as completely satisfied by suggesting people into loving their servitude as by flogging and kicking them into obedience. In other words, I feel that the nightmare of 1984 is destined to modulate into

> the nightmare of a world having more resemblance to that which I imagined in Brave New World."

Largely set in a futuristic World State of genetically modified citizens and an intelligence-based social hierarchy, *Brave New World* anticipates huge scientific developments in reproductive technology, sleep-learning, psychological manipulation, and classical conditioning, that are combined to make a utopian society that goes challenged only by a single outsider.

Or perhaps your best move would be to read both *1984* and *Brave New World* as well as Harrington's *Mind Fixers* for you to awaken, eh?

Orwell, of course, is the *1984* author. Published in June 1949, its themes center on the risks of government overreach, totalitarianism and repressive regimentation of all persons and behaviors within society. It is set in the year 1984, when much of the world has fallen victim to perpetual war, omnipresent government surveillance and propaganda. The book popularized the adjective *Orwellian*, connoting concepts like official deception, secret surveillance, brazenly misleading terminology and manipulation of recorded history by a totalitarian or authoritarian state.

As British researcher and author David Icke exposed, both Huxley and Orwell had the insight track of what was planned for humanity. It includes Sullivan et al.'s *Behavioral and neural correlates of memory suppression in PTSD* research, which can be used for many sinister purposes, if so desired, wit Cathy O'Brien's experience. All that is needed now to expedite the hypothesis are genuine PTSD experiencers consenting to have their brains changed. That's the easy way out of PTSD, if wanting to effortlessly turn self into a vegetable without even recognizing it and loving your servitude and dependency on your Masters of the learned society, to boot. If not, recognize what you are up against and then, first and foremost, aim to emotionally stabilize your Self. How to go about that? Twice daily 20-minute meditation with paper and pen at your side to jot down what springs to mind as advice to help yourself. Later on, augment it with yoga and acupuncture to get the inner system streamlined one step at the time. And always remind yourself what you learned in your genuine PTSD experience: "There is no time, but to heal yourself, you must start to help yourself." And for that only you hold the power.

And what about PCORI's past and future? PCORI, that spent a paltry $279 million dollars on PTSD research during its existence? It escaped public attention that it has won support from a wide range of people. One of those is former Democratic California Congressman Tony Coelho, who opines that data created by PCORI should ultimately be useful for patients when making healthcare decisions. He nowadays chairs the Partnership to Improve Patient Care, which, in his opinion, took pains to get first-hand views on what questions really matter to patients. His group is a coalition of patient advocates, drug manufacturers and medical groups. It applauded PCORI for conducting research in a patient-centered manner, ultimately useful in healthcare decision-making. Rand Corporation policy researcher Justin W. Timbie took it a step further piping: "[PCORI is] a really practical research to help people make decisions [about their health]. I think that's a lot of bang for the buck." $3.5 billion worth? Perhaps the true question to ask who is kidding whom in this PCORI deal, as first evidence on its actual impact and benefit on the world of medicine, should any exist, is missing in action.

To prevent its seemingly timely demise, however, Reps. Diana DeGette (D-CO) and Rep. Don Beyer (D-VA) nevertheless introduced the PCORI Reauthorization Bill H.R.3030 in June 2019. If passed, it would re-authorize sponsorship of this white elephant portrayed as a non-profit for another 10 years to the tune of another $3.5 billion of taxpayer money (congress.gov). H.R. 3030 is cited as the "Patient-Centered Outcomes Research Extension Act of 2019 (H.R. 3030)." Can you imagine what $3.5 billion could do, would do, to assure the recovery and healing of genuine PTSD journeyers in the U.S. military alone if giving peace and quiet and financial security for a few months?

Mind you, someone in authority must have caught on to this Emperor with no clothes. From September 30, 2019, onwards, PCORI is no longer authorized to commit to new research grants. Only previously-awarded ones will continue to be funded through FY2024 (*Public Law 111-148, Subtitle D of Title VI - Sec. 6301*). Is it perhaps therefore that PCORI tried to make itself look good and enhance the possibility of its continuous existence by seeing fit to seek Letters of Intent of PTSD research worth up to US$15 million in January 2019, stating:

> "In the Treatment of Post-Traumatic Stress Disorder (PTSD) in Adults PFA, we seek to fund comparative clinical effectiveness research (CER) studies that aim to determine which specific treatments for adults with PTSD are most effective, and for whom. Proposed comparators may include psychological interventions, pharmacological interventions, or a combination of the two, and all proposed comparators must have demonstrated evidence of efficacy (from systematic reviews, prior empirical investigations, or other scientific documentation). PCORI is especially interested in studies that are inclusive of a broad patient population, including those with comorbidities, and in studies that are powered to assess the effectiveness of treatments in subgroups of interest. (*Treatment of Posttraumatic Stress Disorder (PTSD) in Adults*—Cycle 1 2019)

The winner(s) will be announced just in time for Christmas and Hannukah 2019 (pcori.org). The Friends of PCORI Reauthorization, purportedly a coalition of patient and family caregiver organizations, health provider associations, biopharma/life science companies, payers (meaning insurance companies) and other interested entities and individuals, *are clamoring to have Congress re-authorize its current $2.4 billion operation, funded in part through PTSD experiencers' philanthropy, to continue even after Cohen's* completion of her study at the end of December 2020 (HSRP20163069).

And as for you philanthropist PTSD journeyers, it may be wise to listen to Northern Arizona University's Department of Educational Psychology Professor Timothy Thomason. He is a licensed psychologist since 1977, with 27 years of teaching experience at graduate level. He has taught in the clinical mental health and school counselling programs and the doctoral program in counselling psychology. He points out in *The Shadow Side of the Great Psychotherapists* (Counseling [sic] & Wellness Journal * 2016 * Volume 5):

> "Many people have cautioned against investing too much in teachers who are, after all, just human beings. In the Hebrew Bible, Daniel (2:31-43) cautioned

> that even prominent people have faults, which he called feet of clay (even a statue that appears strong will fall if it has feet made of clay). The Buddhist teacher Linji advised 'If you meet the Buddha on the road, kill him!' (Kopp, 1982, p. 188), meaning that thinking of the Buddha as a deity is a delusion that must be destroyed to become enlightened oneself. Similarly, one could say 'If you meet the psychotherapy guru on the road, kill him.' That is, learn what is valuable, but do [*not*] treat him or her like a deity or saint."

Perhaps it takes guts to become our own teacher, guru or saint by applying Self to explore ways and means to our own healing, through diligence, discipline, determination, will-power and persistency, conquering and vanquishing those aiming to destroy us. Only we ourselves can do it. We learn to act with honour, integrity and graciousness when dealing with the powers that be, albeit it could strangle us., And we get out of this PTSD catastrophe intact and able to hold our head high and grateful to have lived and survived the experience relatively unscathed. That success is thanks to nothing other than those guides, guardians, helpers, teachers and friends in the unseen, those we learned to acknowledge while our opponents, the mental health cabal, so vehemently refuse to even acknowledge a power greater than themselves or the human soul.

4

SUICIDE VERSUS HEALING SELF THROUGH LEARNING

Anthropologists tell us that one of humanity's defining characteristics among all things alive and breathing in the world is our ability to use language. But it is not only use of language that separates us from the animal kingdom. Our ability to speak and write in complex symbols, to apply logic and reason to/ in our ways of leading our lives, living and being as expressed in many ancient writings, among them the Tibetan Bardo Thödol known in the west as the Tibetan Book of the Dead, illustrates our uniqueness on this planet.

In precise translation, Bardo Thödol means the "Liberation Through Hearing During the Intermediate State." It is part of a larger corpus of writings entitled the *Profound Dharma of Self-Liberation through the Intention of the Peaceful and Wrathful Ones*. According to Tibetan tradition, the *Guru Padmasambhava, who is also known Guru Rinpoche -- "precious master"* - and widely venerated as a "second Buddha" by adherents of Tibetan Buddhism in Tibet, Nepal, Bhutan, the Himalayan states of India and elsewhere, *composed it in the 8th century AD whilst incarnated in this world as a fully enlightened being*. But then, legend holds, he decided the writings were too spiritually advanced for Tibetans of the time and ordered them buried in the Gampo hills in central Tibet. In the fourteenth century the Tibetan Tertön Karma Lingpa (1326-1386) rediscovered it. Tertöns, a term within Tibetan Buddhism meaning a discoverer of ancient hidden texts or terms, are said to be incarnations of Padmasambhava's 25 main disciples.

Of Padmasambhava/Guru Rinpoche himself little is known apart from his assistance in the construction of the first Buddhist monastery in Tibet at Samye at behest of King Trisong Detsen (742-c.800/755-797 according to Chinese sources) - the thirty-eighth king of Tibet, son of King Me Aktsom. He is the second of Tibet's Three Dharma Kings - Songtsen Gampo, Trisong Detsen, and Ralpacan -- and one of Guru Rinpoche's main disciples. It is due to his efforts that the great masters Indian Buddhist masters Shantarakshita and Guru Padmasambhava came from India and established Buddhism firmly in Tibet. Trisong Detsen also played a pivotal role in the establishment of the Nyingma or "Ancient" school of Tibetan Buddhism. Under his reign Indian scholars were invited as well to translate Buddhist canon into Tibetan as they, like the Bardo Thödol, were originally written in Sanskrit.

But the text intended to guide us through our consciousness's experiences in the bardo after death and during the interval between death and rebirth as well as chapters on the signs of death and of rituals advisable to undertake when death is closing in or has taken place even in the East remained hidden for centuries and in the West did not surface and draw attention until unearthed by the American anthropologist and writer Dr. Walter Yeeling Evans-Wentz (1878 -1965) in the early twentieth century (https://lotsawahouse.org). Since then, numerous Bardo Thödol interpretations sprang forth. In the Occident, however, his version is the one most popularized. Thus, it is he who pioneered the transmission of Tibetan Buddhism to the Western world.

Born in Trenton, New Jersey, U.S., his father Christopher Wentz (1836 -1921) immigrated to America with his parents from Weissengen, Baden, Germany in 1846. His mother Mary Evans Cook (died 1898) was of Irish descent. His father, a real estate developer in Pablo Beach, Florida, at the turn of the nineteenth century turned from Baptism to spiritualism and Theosophy. Meanwhile, the Russian émigré Madame Helena Petrovna Blavatsky and the American Colonel Henry Steel Olcott, a journalist and veteran of the Union Army during the American Civil War, had in 1875 founded the Theosophical Society in New York with the official goal to diffuse among men knowledge of the laws inherent in the universe, promulgate the knowledge of the essential unity of all that is and to determine this unity as fundamental in nature. Furthermore, the society aimed to form an active brotherhood among men to study ancient and modern religions as well as science and philosophy and the investigation of man's innate powers. Wentz junior consequently developed an early interested in theosophy and the occult and in his father's library read Madame Blavatsky's *Isis Unveiled and The Secret Doctrine*. At the turn of the twentieth century he moved to San Diego, California to be close to the Theosophical Society's American headquarters Lomaland. In 1901 he joined/became a member.

According to John Myrdhin Reynolds, aka Vajranatha, who studied History of Religions, Anthropology, Arabic, Sanskrit, Tibetan, and Buddhist Studies at Columbia University, at the University of California at Berkeley and at the University of Washington at Seattle and spent more than 10 years in India and Nepal doing field research at various Hindu Ashrams in South India and at Tibetan Buddhist monasteries in Darjeeling, Kalimpong, and Nepal as both a scholar, linguist, author, translator and practitioner of the Nyingma school of Tibetan Buddhism Evans-Wentz in his Bardo Thödol transcription, which he named *The Tibetan Book of the Dead* (Oxford University, 1927) due to perceived parallels with the

Egyptian Book of the Dead, used Theosophy as framework to interpret the translation, which was largely provided by the Tibetan lamas Sumdhon Paul and Lobzang Mingnur Dorje as he himself was unfamiliar with Tibetan Buddhism and could neither read nor write the language. Now, that got to be a record. Furthermore, in Reynold's opinion Evans-Wentz's view of Tibetan Buddhism was "fundamentally neither Tibetan nor Buddhist but Theosophical and Vedantist (Reynolds)." According to Reynolds Evans-Wentz introduced a terminology and spin into the Bardo Thödol translation largely derived from Hinduism and theosophical beliefs. For example, contrary to the general belief spread by Evans-Wentz in the West, the *Tibetan Book of Dead* in Buddhist practice is not read to people while in the process of passing away, but used during life by those wanting to learn to visualize what will transpire after death.

And Reynolds should know. Post PhD he spent about 10 years in India and Nepal doing fieldwork research at a number of Hindu ashrams in South India and at Tibetan Buddhist monasteries. He studied and researched rituals, literature and meditation practices of the Nyingmapa, the oldest of the four major schools of Tibetan Buddhism and the Kagyu, other 2 being the Sakya and Gelug. In Nepal he researched the techniques and folklore of Himalayan shamanism including the rites of soul retrieval and exorcism as employed and practiced among ngakpa lamas belonging to the Nyingma school. Tibetan Buddhism contains two systems of ordination, the familiar monastic ordinations and the less well known Ngagpa or Tantric ordinations, which is non-monastic and non-celibate, but not lay either. It entails its own extensive system of vows, distinct from the monastic vows. Reynolds has taught History of Religions and Buddhist Studies at the Shanti Ashram (South India), a center of spiritual activities and pilgrimage place of India as well as the University of Massachusetts Amherst, at the University of California, Santa Cruz and at the College of New Rochelle in New York City (https://encyclopediaofbuddhism.org).

To further substantiate Reynolds' verdict/claim, the late Chögyam Trungpa Rinpoche (1940-1987), a Buddhist meditation master and holder of both the Kagyu and Nyingma lineages, in his commentary on the Bardo Thödol explained that Bardo, meaning "gap" or interval of suspension, is part of humanity's psychological make-up as Bardo experiences happen to us all the time in life and not just after death. The Bardo Thödol can therefore be read as a guide through or in life experiences as well as a source of guidance of the time we will spend between death and rebirth as stipulated in Evan-Wentz's publication when stating:"

> "Death holds up an all-seeing mirror, 'the mirror of past actions'...in which the consequences of all our negative and positive actions are clearly seen and there is a weighing of our past actions in the light of their consequences." —*The Tibetan Book of the Dead* by Walter Evans-Wentz.

But Evans-Wentz's Bardo Thödol interpretation is deemed flawed and faulty by other experts in the field among them Dr. Donald Sewell Lopez Jr., the Arthur E. Link Distinguished University Professor of Buddhist and Tibetan Studies at the University of Michigan, in the Department of Asian Languages and Cultures. He in his foreword to Evans-Wentz *The Tibetan Book of the Dead* 2000 edition (Oxford University Press, 2000) expresses that the founding of the Theosophical Society of which Evans-Wentz was an active member merely represented nothing other than an attempt to create a scientific religion that accepted new discoveries in geology and archeology while proclaiming an ancient and esoteric system of spiritual evolution more sophisticated than Darwin's theory.

Evans-Wentz had made little effort to place his writings, four books in total, in their Tibetan literary and religious context, thus little about them was "Tibetan." And how could there be, considering that their author had never set foot in the country. Did the adjective used in the title carry a theosophical meaning for the writer Lopez muses? Did Evans-Wentz depart on interpretive flights of fancy requiring him to take liberties with the Tibetan text before him in order to establish the ultimate concordance of what he regarded as the esoteric teachings of tradition separated by geography and history Lopez wonders, flights generally guided by his allegiance to what he termed yoga and theosophy, his understanding of yoga deriving from tutelage under several prominent Hindu neo-Vedantin teachers between WWI and WWII when he made several trips to India studying under Sri Yukteswar and Ramana Maharshi among others? Could it be that his original devotion to Theosophy throughout his life may in *The Tibetan Book Of The Dead* have led to Evans-Wentz's perhaps willful misreading and exposition of the doctrine of rebirth (Lopez, p. 33)?

We will never know, as for others death is merely perceived as a transitional state to the place whence we came as writer, translator and contributing author at Daily Stoic, Global Voices and The Big Smoke with a focus on metaphysics, psychedelics and psychology Mustapha Itani quotes in his Medium 2018 article *Bardo Thodol: The Tibetan Book of the Dead*:

> "Remember the clear light, the pure clear white light from which everything in the universe comes, to which everything in the universe returns; the original nature of your own mind. The natural state of the universe unmanifest. Let go into the clear light, trust it, merge with it. It is your own true nature, it is home."

Be it as it may, we must first and foremost make clear that in standard Buddhist doctrine we find descriptions of a cycle of birth and death called saṃsāra, a Sanskrit word meaning wandering or world with the connotation of cyclic, circuitous change. The concept of saṃsāra is said to have its roots in the post-Vedic literature, although the theory is not discussed in the Vedas themselves (Yuvraj Krishan: Bharatiya Vidya Bhavan, 1997). The most ancient Hindu scriptures, the Vedas, are written in early Sanskrit and contain hymns, philosophy and guidance on ritual for priests of the Vedic religion. Its 4 chief collections believed to have been directly revealed to seers among the early Aryans in India and preserved by oral tradition, are the Rig Veda, Sama Veda, Yajur Veda, and Atharva Veda. Each Veda is subdivided into four parts, namely Samhita, Brahmana, Aranyaka and Upanishad. Since Upanishad forms the end part of a Veda it is also called Vedanta.

Upanishads is a Sanskrit word in English meaning "sitting at the feet of" or "sitting down near" illustrating the position of humbly receiving wisdom and guidance from a teacher or guru. Central to Hinduism the Vedas thus are an assortment of texts recorded from oral traditions and containing information regarding Hinduism's philosophical principles and concepts including Karma (right action), *brahman* (ultimate reality), *the atman* (true Self or soul), *moksha* (liberation from the cycle of reincarnation). They also include doctrines explaining Self-realization through yoga and meditation practices some of which shared with other religious traditions like Buddhism and Jainism. Among the most important literature in the history of Indian religions and culture, the Upanishads in ancient India played an important role in the development of spiritual ideas marking a transition from Vedic ritualism to new concepts and institutions at the spiritual core of Hindus (coachanil.ca). Central in all of the Upanishads are the concepts of Brahman (ultimate reality) and Ātman (soul, self) and "know that you are the Ātman" is their thematic focus, a reminder that lasting happiness through indulgence in material pleasures alone is an impossibility, as undying happiness is within, and that is where it should be sought (Bhajanamritam 2, p. 52; M.A. Center, Amma, Sri Mata Amritanandamay).

The concept of saṃsāra, the concept of rebirth and cyclicality of all life, matter and existence, appears in developed form but without mechanistic details in the early Upanishads. Forming a fundamental belief in most Indian religions, it is sometimes referred to as transmigration, karmic cycle, reincarnation and "cycle of aimless drifting, wandering or mundane existence" (Wikipedia). In short, the saṃsāra doctrine is the cycle of death and rebirth, which after the mid-1st millennium BC is also found in Sramanic religions such as Buddhism and Jainism and various other schools of Hindu philosophy. Tied to the Karma theory of Indian religions the liberation from saṃsāra, called Moksha, Nirvana, Mukti or Kaivalya, has been at the core of spiritual quest of Indian traditions as well as their internal disagreements for probably/perhaps millennia.

Saṃsāra is the dream world as opposed to the realm of spirit. It is the outward play of *maya* with the cycle of birth, death, and rebirth. Maya is a cosmic illusion literally meaning "the measurer," the power in creation by which limitations and divisions seem to exist in the Oneness that is true reality (anada.org). According to the world-renowned Indian Guru Paramhansa Yogananda, the ancient Vedic scriptures say that the physical world operates under one fundamental law of *maya*, namely the principle of relativity and duality. It is the world of delusion in which we live, the forms with which we identify, the emotional involvement of individual souls appearing in this dream of life, which binds us to those forms and constitutes and creates this cosmic dream of ours. It is the outward play of maya or delusion with the endless cycle of birth, death, and rebirth governed by Karma. Illustrated by the *Wheel of Life* and explained by the *Twelve Links of Dependent Origination* saṃsāra may be understood as the state of being bound by greed, hate, and ignorance or as a veil of illusion that hides true reality. The thrust of the formula is such that when certain conditions are present, they give rise to subsequent conditions, which in turn give rise to other conditions thus illustrating the cyclical nature of life in saṃsāra (encyclopediaofbuddhism.org). *Consequently the twelve-part process of dependent origination arising shows how actions underlain by ignorance propel us from one rebirth into another keeping us trapped in suffering and how through understanding reality correctly we can break this cycle (shambhala.com).*

In traditional Buddhist philosophy we are trapped in saṃsāra through one life after another until we find awakening through enlightenment. The best definition of saṃsāra may actually be from the American Buddhist monk and teacher Thanissaro Bhikkhu also known as Ajahn Geoff (1949–) who states:

> "Instead of a place, it's a process: the tendency to keep creating worlds and then moving into them. And note that this creating and moving in doesn't just happen once, at birth. We're doing it all the time (https://learnreligions.com)."

We are doing it all the time unknowingly, because no one ever told us of the power we have to produce and direct our lives through our daily thoughts and actions. Until Jordan Peterson, in fact, who briefly and indirectly points it out in one of his *How To Academy* lectures on *12 Rules for Life* (you tube publ. Jan.16, 2018). When knowing of this immense power within is suicide still an option, in particular when the saṃsāra concept is closely associated with the belief that we are born and reborn in various realms and forms in heaven and hell based on our cumulative deeds, merits and demerits/ vices and virtues? However, the ancient Vedic Rishis challenged this idea of afterlife as simplistic, because people do not live an equally moral or immoral life. Between generally virtuous lives, some are more virtuous; while evil too has degrees and, the texts assert, it would therefor be unfair for God Yama or Yamarāja, a god of death, the south direction, and the underworld, to reward people with varying degrees of virtue or vices in "either or" and disproportionate manner. They introduced the idea of an afterlife in heaven or hell in proportion to one's merit, and when this runs out, one returns and is reborn. This idea appears in ancient and medieval texts, as the cycle of life, death, rebirth and re-death, such as section 6:31 of the Mahabharata and section 6.10 of Devi Bhagavata Purana.

The Canadian scholar of bioethics and religious studies Professor Harold Coward (1936) asserts that it is in the Upanishads where we find means of self-liberation from saṃsāra by offering a "very optimistic view regarding the perfectibility of human nature." A bachelor's in divinity (Christian Theology), the venerable professor earned his doctoral degree in Philosophy from London, Ontario's McMaster University (1973) and worked as professor at the University of Victoria and the University of Calgary. He is particularly well known in the learned society for his studies of Indian religions, as an editor of the *Encyclopedia of Hinduism* and as a Fellow of the Royal Society of Canada (1991). He expresses that the goal of human effort in these texts is the continuous journey to self-perfection and self-knowledge for the purpose of ending saṃsāra. This is precisely the opportunity, if not the purpose handed to every genuine PTSD journeyers through their PTSD-causing experience, as the aim of the spiritual quest in the Upanishadic traditions is to find the true self within and to know one's soul, which in turn will result in a state believed to lead to the blissful state of freedom, the moksha. And you still want to pass up on this brilliant opportunity because you want to kill yourself when knowing that at least in Hinduism, Evans-Wentz's religious believe structure, saṃsāra is considered nothing other than a journey of the soul practically for its own amusement and choice, itself assumed to be of eternal reality, indestructible and blissful?

You still want to kill yourself even when knowing that all and everything in maya existence is interconnected, cyclical and composed of two things, soul and body or of matter without consideration of the harm you will inflict on it all when committing such dastardly deed? Furthermore, know that according to Hindu doctrine this eternal soul, this *Atman*, never reincarnates or changes. Only the body and personality can change, constantly changes, is born and dies having different experiences most likely of its own choice as pointed out by Michael Newton and others presented and discussed in *Fallacy 1*. Past and current Karma, we could probably call it actions and behaviors, impact every moment of this life's future circumstances, some of it instantaneously were you to pay attention, as well as that of realms and forms of future lives. Has it dawned upon you yet that lives lead with good intent and actions lead to good futures, and those lived with bad intent and actions lead to bad ones? You still think the Christian "As you sow you reap concept" holds no water? It still does not make sense to you that a virtuous life combined with actions consistent with Dharma-- knowledge and the gathering thereof-- contributes to a better future in this and future lives, but that Alistair Crowley's "Do what thou wilt shall be the whole of the Law" does? You still want to kill yourself albeit knowing, to repeat, that everything existent is interconnected composing and making this cyclical concert of life possible full well knowing that our own behavior influences everything there is, ever was and ever will be? What did Gandhi say?

"As human beings, our greatness lies not so much in being able to remake the world – that is the myth of the atomic age – as in being able to remake ourselves (positivityblog.com)."

And you, the genuine PTSD experiencer who has been given this brilliant opportunity to remake yourself and thus remake the world want to participate in it by cowardly taking your own life? Even worse, you are dreaming about scenarios where you force others to kill you because you are too cowardly to do it yourself thus implicating more souls in the solution of your misery because you don't want to learn how to help yourself thus adding the misery of a multitude to your own Karma because of it? Really? Are you nuts? Why don't you instead read about the various paths to find the liberation from in essence your own demons discussed in the Bhagavad Gita, a 700-verse Sanskrit scripture that is part of the Hindu epic *Mahabharata* (chapters 23–40 of Bhishma Parva) making fascinating reading in the context of our times?

And you want to run the risk to be reborn as an ogre, a swine, God only knows what in God only knows which hells you most revile? Eastern cosmology typically identifies six realms of rebirth and existence: gods, demi-gods, humans, animals, hungry ghosts and hells? Mind you, earlier Buddhist texts refer to five realms rather than six when the god- and demi-god realm are described as a single realm. These six realms represent all possible states of existence for Buddhist. Traditionally conceived as real places, they can also be interpreted symbolically. You can pick and choose while contemplating to suicide.

There are the animal, ghost and hell realms, all places of punishment for previous sins, your upcoming suicide included. Birth in the heavenly realm, the *asura*, or in human realms only comes through accumulation and spending of karmic merits, so forget that for a while. However, there is a bit of light as life in any of these realms is ultimately impermanent—one does not suffer forever in hell, nor enjoys eternal bliss in heaven (personal.carthage.edu). The realms of animals, ghosts and hell are regarded as places of great suffering, whereas the godly realms are abodes of great bliss. Human rebirth falls in between as it brings both pleasure and pain. Furthermore, or in addition, the entire cycle of rebirth in which the repeated creations and destructions of the universe occur has no ultimate beginning. To hammer it home in earnest, saṃsāra's engine is being driven by Karma, which in turn is created by the causes and effects of actions taken and deeds committed while in the earthly realm. The gravity of negative deeds determines the form of future being as it determined the past one's.

Thus, we can easily deduce that killing another human is more consequential than killing an insect. Killing self, however, committing what is somewhat softly termed suicide, is the greatest sin of all according to the Indian Kriya yogi, Vedic astrologer, scholar of the Bhagavad Gita and the Upanishads, educator and astronomer Sri Yukteswar Giri (1855-1936) and his disciple Paramahansa Yogananda (1893-1952) briefly mentioned above. The latter is famous for having introduced millions of East-Indians and Westerners to the teachings of meditation and Kriya Yoga through his U.S. based Self-Realization Fellowship organization at whose Encinitas, California ashram Evans-Wentz took his last breath. What reasons do these two sages give against committing suicide? When hurting or killing another person one rejects God in the form of that other person. When killing the Self one not only rejects Life itself, but also disturbs one's energy on a profound level. Consequently, when the soul that committed suicide decides to reincarnate, the chosen foetus for the reincarnation is unable to complete the act of bringing that body into life because of said energy disturbance. And so throughout seven lives it will be unable to be born by being aborted, stillborn, miscarried or in some other way be prevented to be born as a living baby. Yogananda in his book *Karma and Reincarnation* explains the concept and operation of Karma, death and reincarnation in greater detail while also sharing the soul's deeper purpose of existence (crystalclarity.com).

Swami Kriyananda (1926), a direct disciple of the yogi Paramahansa Yogananda and the founder of Ananda, a worldwide movement of spiritual intentional communities based on Yogananda's World Brotherhood Colonies ideal and minister for his organization, the Self-Realization Fellowship, enlightens us that at death the astral and causal bodies are untouched by the death of the physical body. Since our ego and personality are part of the astral body this means that the physical body drops away, but the mental and emotional pain and suffering remain just as they were before suicide was committed. In fact, we hear that without the weight of a physical body to weigh suicides down, so to speak, their suffering is even more intense. In other words, whilst seeking relief from in our case the emotional pain and suffering generated by PTSD experiencers from a multitude of sources, among them the powers that be and the mental health industry, never mind their inner self, they will find that killing self only multiplies rather than diminishes their misery. Here too, though, exceptions make the rule. If mentally imbalanced when committing the deed karmic suffering would not be as great exclaimed Swami Kriyananda once during his own lifetime. Is it worth the risk, though? I think not!

Fortunately, we do know that most if not all pharmacological mind-altering drugs create and encourage suicide/ suicidal desires and tendencies. I have lived it with Ativan. I now know that it was my subconscious search for life's spiritual meaning that prevented me from killing myself. That I read the Bardo Thödol long before the PTSD causing event hit due to a college class I took in physical anthropology was just one of those non-existent "coincidences" while cruising through life blindly. But because of the Bardo Thödol suicide for me never became a conscious option, although subconsciously it may very well have been on the agenda by Ativan swallowing encouraging starving, drinking and smoking myself to death. So, if the desire to end it all overcomes you, try to look at it this way: Know that the process of reincarnation is about 5 - to 8 million live times to enlightenment according to Yogananda. During that number of lives, we can be as good as certain to having tried suicide or at least having given it sincere thought as a solution. But now we know the consequences, so is it really the path to take this time around? Do we have an excuse for it other than our laziness to educate ourselves on our suffering and the way out of it and our desire for a rapid end despite knowing the dire results in the aftermath? Is kicking ourselves into choosing the more enchanting path of learning how to help ourselves now knowing what it contributes to our Self and the world at large a better path out of this genuinely terrible PTSD dilemma? Is discovering the truth of the power we have as individuals precisely what is ordered for every genuine PTSD affected traveller, as it clarifies the conundrum of life we were thrown into due to the PTSD causing event moment and its possibly terrible consequences of killing ourselves?

You really want to run the risk of being reborn as an animal, a ghost or in one of the hot or cold hells where life is particularly lengthy? Theosophy, Evans-Wentz's other life-philosophy, rejects that particular claim insisting that once a human always a human. Still, rebirth as a god or human due to virtuous deeds is also considered a very rare occurrence indeed. The vast majority of beings existing in our universe are said to inhabit the realms of animals, ghosts and hells. When killing Self, the chance of ending up in any of the latter seems greatly enhanced. So instead, why not when suicidal desires hit apply willpower, determination, persistency and discipline, kick Self into gear and learn about the purpose and meaning of life as transmitted for thousands of years by the sages of the ages? Or, of course, take Jordan Peterson's self-authoring suite, which should kick-start/jump-start you into helping you to figure out yourself brilliantly (https://selfauthoring.com).

5

ON LAST THOUGHTS WHEN DYING

Buddhists and Hindus alike believe that the last thought at the moment of death determines the character of one's next incarnation (*The Tibetan Book Of The Dead*, xviii). Sri Krishna confirms this in the *Bhagavad Gita* (viii, 6), "The Song of God". This 700-verse Sanskrit scripture is also known as the Gita and part of the Hindu epic *Mahabharata*. In it, he says to Arjuna: "One attaineth whatever state [of being] one thinketh about at the last when relinquishing the body, being absorbed in the thought thereof." This occurs in the *Bhishma Parva*, the 6th of the *Mahabharata's* 18 books (ch. 23-40), in which the Kaurava and the Pandava families vie for the throne of Hastinapura, as they disagree about the proper line of succession. Most of the epic tale concerns the war between them, culminating in victory for the Pandavas in the great battle of Kurukshetra.

The 6th book describes the first 10 days of the 18-day Kurukshetra War and its consequences. This war was fought by the Kuru tribe at *Kurukshetra*, the modern-day Haryana, India, for the throne of Hastinapura. The historicity of the war remains subject to scholarly discussions. Attempts have been made to assign a historical date to the Kurukshetra War. Suggested dates range from 5561 to around 950 BC, while popular tradition holds that the war marks the transition to Kali Yuga and thus dates it to 3102 BC. The ancients understood time as a circle, not linear, and the Circle of Ages are known as the Yugas. Like the four seasons in our year, there are four *Yugas* in the full cycle the *Maha Yuga*). Each cycle has distinct themes and spiritual lessons for humanity. Below are the four *Yugas* in order from beginning to end. It is important to note that the first *Yuga* is the longest, with each one getting successively shorter (4:3:2:1) until the cycle starts again (https://upliftconnect.com).

- *Satya Yuga* is the first *Yuga*, a time of truth and perfection, lasting four tenths of the cycle. These humans are honest, youthful, vigorous and virtuous. Everyone is happy, with religions living as one. Disease and fear are non-existent. Those living through this part of the *Maha Yuga* cycle are gifted with abundance through the land, along with great weather.
- *Treta Yuga:* The second *Yuga* lasts for three tenths of the cycle. It is a time where human virtue begins to fall away. Leaders gain more dominance, causing wars to rise and, as if to reflect the state of humanity, the weather also moves to more extremes in this part of the cycle and people's health begins to lessen.
- *Dvapara Yuga:* The third *Yuga* lasts for two tenths of the cycle. During this time, people become more sluggish and slower, many are weaker than their ancestors and the number of diseases increases. Becoming discontent with their lives, humans fight with each other, partly perhaps because their maturity decreases. Some people, however, are said to still possess characteristics of youth in old age.
- *Kali Yuga*: The final age lasts only one tenth of the full *Maha Yuga* cycle, which is nevertheless estimated to be long enough, as it is the age of darkness and ignorance. People slide further down the path of dishonesty, with virtue being of little to no value. Passions become uncontrollable as unrestrained sexual indulgences and manipulations run through society. Liars and hypocrites rise, and family bonds become scarce. Important knowledge is lost, and scriptures become less and less common. The once pristine environment is polluted, water and food become scarce and the human diet "dirty." In consequence, people are far less powerful than their *Satya Yuga* ancestors.

And, some say, it is the Kurukshetra War of the dynastic succession struggle between the Kauravas and the Pandavas that inaugurated this *Kali Yuga*. The war, with a number of ancient kingdoms participating as allies of the rival groups, saw around 1,530,900 soldiers in action. The *Bhagavad Gita* describes the battle in a narrative framework of a dialogue between the Pandava prince Arjuna and his guide and charioteer Krishna right before the start of this *Dharma Yudha*, this righteous war. Filled with moral dilemma and despair about the violence and death the war will cause, Arjuna wonders if he should renounce the action. He seeks Krishna's counsel, and it is their discourse that constitutes the *Bhagavad Gita*.

Krishna counsels Arjuna to "fulfill his Kshatriya ("warrior" duty to uphold the Dharma, the eternal and inherent nature of reality. This is regarded in Hinduism as a cosmic law underlying right behavior and social order through "selfless action." Thus begins a discourse which coverers a broad range of spiritual topics and touching on ethical dilemmas and philosophical issues, obviously going far beyond the war facing Arjuna and his charioteer Krishna. It is during their dialogue that Krishna emphasizes, while both of them face death: "One attaineth whatever state [of being] one thinketh about at the last when relinquishing the body, being absorbed in the thought thereof." At least Arjuna and Krishna in this war of epic proportions fight to wipe out evil. Like all fights for right, all participants (both good and evil) sustain losses and suffer its consequences. It is their Karma (vedicfeed.com).

The *Mahabharata* is considered the world's longest known epic and the longest poem ever written. It contains about 1.8 million words, about ten times the length of the Iliad and Odyssey put together. Its importance has been compared to that of the Bible, the Qur'an and the works of Homer and Shakespeare. The legendary authorship of the *Mahabharata*, the *Vedas* and *Puranas*, some of the most important works in the Hindu tradition, is traditionally attributed to Vyāsa, also called Veda Vyāsa or Krishna Dvaipāyana, to whom the festival of Guru Purnima is dedicated. Vyasa is also considered to be one of the seven Chiranjivins, the long-lived or immortals who, according to Hindu tradition, are to remain alive on Earth until the end of this current *Kali Yuga*.

Themes of the *Mahabharata* offer one of the first known theorizations of the concept of a just war. This topic has been debated in societies and cultures worldwide up to the present day. One of five brothers in the story asks if the suffering caused by war can ever be justified. This generates a long discussion between the siblings, and establishes criteria like proportionality. For instance, chariots cannot attack cavalry, only other chariots, and there should be no attacks on people in distress nor poisoned or barbed arrows. The principles of just cause, the no attacking out of rage, the fair treatment of captives and the wounded, a major principle of the Geneva Convention, are all discussed in the *Mahabarata*. Sadly, they have often fallen on deaf ears, wit in recent memory alone: Hamburg, Dresden, Hiroshima, Nagasaki, Baghdad, Tunis, Rwanda and so on and so forth.

The *Mahabharata*, still revered today, is also often referred to and quoted because of its profound philosophical ideas and teachings about life and how to live it. Some of the lessons to be learned from it are:

> A vengeful instinct can lead only to one's own destruction. In this story, the Kauravas lost everything to their blinded desire to ruin the Pandavas.
>
> Stand by what's right; even fight for it. Arjuna is initially hesitant to wage war against his own blood, his cousins. But Krishna reminds him that one has to stand by one's duty, even it means going against one's own family. Therefore, Arjuna has to go to war with them.
>
> The eternal bond of friendship. The friendship between Krishna and Arjuna is central in this story. It is due to Krishna's unconditional support that the Pandavas manage to survive the war.
>
> Don't be distracted by greed. Yudhishthir, the leader of the successful Pandava side in the Kurukshetra War, in the end lost everything he possessed, from his kingdom to his wealth, because of his greed.
>
> Never give up on life, even in the face of extreme obstacles. Karna battles his way through life, fighting discrimination and disgrace at every stage. But no obstacle could deter him from pursuing his goal. He is a key antagonist who aims to kill Arjuna, but during the Kurukshetra, War dies in a battle with him. He is a tragic hero in the *Mahabharata*, as he meets his biological mother late in the epic, then

discovers that he is the older half-brother of those he is fighting. He is a man of exceptional abilities, willing to give his love and life as a loyal friend. His character is developed in the epic to raise and discuss major emotional and *Dharma* (duty, ethics, moral) dilemmas.

Being a woman does not make you a lesser human being. This is the earliest expression of feminism in world literature. Draupadi is described in the *Mahabharata* as being extraordinarily beautiful, unsurpassed by any other woman of her time. She is manipulated into becoming the wife of the five Pandavas, and is then humiliated by the Kauravas for the fault of one of her husbands. After being violated, she is bold enough to take a stand against her treatment.

Thus, the *Mahabharata* is a tale of human emotions, of greed, acceptance, sacrifice and ultimately death. We can find all this tale's characters throughout the world. They are present in all layers of society, including PTSD-suffering people

In their own minds, many had reasons to slaughter and kill each other in the Kurukshetra War. After all, personal honor and integrity were partly at stake. But what is the reason you give yourself for your desire to kill your Self? Your cowardice? Your lack of gumption and your laziness, impeding you from fighting alone the evil you face daily from the powers that be? Or is it because your incomprehensible craving to repeat the PTSD experience once more in another life? For you now know this would be your Karma, should you cave in to your murderous desire to kill yourself?

Do you really want to live the same misery over and over and over again? It will keep going until you build up your inner strength of character to face whatever is thrown at you by your self-designed Karma without flinching. Watch some of the ancient *The Twilight Zone* episodes to understand the concept. It may be a fine way to inspire you to rethink your suicidal plans. After all, know that your thinking determines your present state of life and living. In fact, all it takes is to get your thinking under control, and your suicidal path will disappear into the ether as certain as a cloud blocks the Sun's rays. Once you take the first step in that direction, the sky will be your limit, I assure you. Been there, done that. And even in this moment, your present thinking determines your next one and your future. How can you shun away from that intriguing experiment on yourself with yourself and by yourself, instead still preferring death? And are you so undisciplined as not even to want to try, even though the opening verse of the *Dhammapada*, a collection of sayings of the Buddha in verse form, states: "All that we are is the result of what we have thought; it is founded on our thoughts, it is made up of our thoughts"? And despite knowing of this enormous power pushing you to create your Self by way of the PTSD experience, does murdering yourself seem desirable? If you set yourself down and contemplate the issue for a moment, would you then perhaps see the light and see that life gives us our greatest gifts brilliantly disguised as our worst nightmares? (David Icke)

And you still want to take your own life?

Are you nuts, or do you want to prove Col. Michael A. Miller, installation commander of the 2nd Bomb Wing at Barksdale Air Force Base in Louisiana right? This man provides combat-ready B-52H aircraft, crews and combat support to global operations. He supports 32 tenant units, including:

- Headquarters
- Headquarters 8th Air Force
- Air Force Global Strike Command
- Air Force Reserve Command's 307th Bomb Wing

Furthermore, he promotes the welfare of more than 11,400 military and civilian personnel, 6300 of their family members and 25,000 retirees (barksdale.af.mil).

On August 2, 2019, he called out to his airmen: "killing yourself is a chicken-shit way to go." That was a most accurate statement, but it was just as badly received as fighter Tim Kennedy's 2016 pronouncement of "Don't Be A Pussy" to veterans struggling with PTSD. You will recall that they were suicidal due to the mind-altering pharmaceutical drugs forced upon them as the PTSD panacea by the VA and other mental health practitioners (*Fallacy 1*). Tim Kennedy joined the Army in 2004. He worked as sniper, sniper instructor and principal combatives instructor for C Company, 3rd Battalion, 7th Special Forces Group, deployed multiple times in support of Operation Iraqi Freedom and Operation Enduring Freedom. In August 2009, Kennedy transitioned from active duty to the Texas Army National Guard, serving in the position of Special Forces Weapons Sergeant. In 2017, he announced his reenlistment into the U.S. Army Special Forces. Among his multiple awards is the Army's Bronze Star Medal with V device, awarded for valour under fire.

Kennedy stood by his words in 2016. But Colonel Miller back pedaled furiously in a statement provided to *Air Force Times'* Maj. Andrew Caulk, head of public affairs for the 2nd. He said the reported sentence did not fully represent the context of his remarks. Col. Miller's intent in talking to the Wing had been nothing other than "a call to our airmen to be courageous in seeking help." Miller's adequate statement - committing suicide is chicken-shit - and consequent quasi justification for it, was first described by airmen in social media on the popular Air Force amn/nco/snco Face book page. It came in August 2019, days after Air Force Chief of Staff Gen. David Goldfein had ordered all wings to stand down for a day of their choosing over the following 45 days. They were to each hold a one-day "tactical pause", to reflect and focus on resiliency and suicide prevention. (airforcetimes.com).

A video posted online by Chief Master Sergeant of the Air Force Kaleth Wright followed, saying that 78 airmen took their own lives between Jan. 1 and July 31. That was 28 more than had died by suicide at the same point in 2018, putting the Air Force at risk of losing 150 to 160 airmen that way by the end of 2019.

So, Colonel Miller went right to the core of the matter with his focus on suicide prevention during this tactical pause. Just as Tim Kennedy did by declaring that murdering the self is unmanly (albeit in different wording). Neither were pussyfooting around; both revealed the venomous truth by eschewing political correctness to the cause: that the military has frequently struggled to find the right way to talk about suicide and mental health. According to Stephen Losey of the *AirForceTimes*, it has seldom gone well. For example, Marine Colonel Dom Ford, commander of Marine Corps Communication-Electronics School at Twentynine Palms, California, sent an email to staff in June 2019. It read: "Suicide is a shameful act. Period. Getting help is not." He also suggested that Marines read scripture and attend religious services to boost their resiliency. He too, though, is on the right track, as learning about suicide is certainly a way out of the ideation. Learning why one feels compelled to commit suicide would be even better.

But what did Air Force top man Chief of Staff Gen. David Goldfein think of as appropriate suicide prevention methods? He must have some idea. After all, he has been around "warriors" since receiving his commission from the U.S. Air Force Academy in 1983 (https://af.mil). He is a graduate of the U.S. Air Force Weapons School and is a command pilot with more than 4,200 flying hours in the T-37, T-38, F-16C/D, F-117A, MQ-9 and MC-12W. He has flown combat missions in operations Desert Shield, Desert Storm, Allied Force and Enduring Freedom. He exclaimed in a memo of July 31, 2019:

> "Suicide is an adversary that is killing more of our airmen than any enemy on the planet. You and I have sworn to 'defend against all enemies, foreign and domestic.' Suicide attacks sometimes with and without warning. Make this tactical pause matter. Make it yours and make it personal."

Oh yeah? But how? Has he ever been suicidal? Has he personally prevented someone from committing suicide? Does he know what is going on in psychotropic drug warped heads and their last thoughts when putting the bullet through their skulls? No? Colonels Miller and Ford did not know either, but did the best they could without directions from top brass and without being loved for their ideas of troop suicide solutions either.

And Chief Master Sergeant of the Air Force Kaleth O. Wright thought to get airmen talking – to each other, to friends, to family. He wanted to use this service's one-day tactical pause to break down unresolved feelings they might have buried deep inside. He felt the break could do the trick of preventing further suicide among the airborne, reported Oriana Pawlyk of military.com in October 2019. (Air Force Top Enlisted Leader: Keep Asking Fellow Airmen How They're Doing). She revealed that it apparently is the "toxic" and uncaring leadership that has emerged as a major factor in airmen's well-being, or the lack thereof. This is the issue the service needs to tackle head-on, according to Wright. He enlisted in the Air Force in March of 1989, and his background includes various duties in the dental field. He served as a Professional Military Education instructor and held various senior enlisted positions while serving at squadron, group, wing, Task-Force and Numbered Air Force levels. He has deployed in support of operations Desert Shield, Desert Storm and Enduring Freedom. He also completed tours in South Korea, Japan, Germany and Alaska, so he too has been around warriors in all sorts of state of mind for a considerable amount of time.

But when some of the lower folk did open their hearts about their concerns in leadership, this was the result:

I'm an Airman at a base I won't disclose here. We just went through a Commander Directed Investigation (CDI), and several Airmen were interviewed during the course of the investigation into a leadership problem. In the end, no action was taken. But sadly, at the conclusion of the CDI, every statement made to the CDI-IO was released completely unredacted to the problem officer who was being investigated. So now she knows, word-for-word, everything that each Airman said about her, and exactly who said it. And yet the Air Force wonders why suicides are exploding across the force? GTFOH!

And none of these geniuses purporting to be concerned of their precious air-men's health and well-being made any connection between go-gel consumption and Air Force GI's suicides. What are go-gels, you ask? Dextroamphetamines. And one brave U-2 pilot was dismissed from the Air Force for taking them. This despite the Air Force handing them to its pilots like candy to keep them alert whilst on duty (David Roza: U-2 pilot dismissed for shaving his entire body to avoid a drug test; Task & Purpose Dec. 06, 2019). What is Dextroamphetamine? *It is a central nervous system (CNS) stimulant prescribed for the treatment of. It is also used as an athletic performance- and cognitive enhancer, an aphrodisiac and an euphoriant.* Military forces use it to fight fatigue during combat operations. Despite or because of its widespread use, there are no published data regarding the expected amphetamine excretion profile following its use (Cody JT1, Valtier S, Nelson SL: Amphetamine enantiomer excretion profile following administration of Adderall; Academy of Health Sciences, MCCS-HMP PA Branch, Fort Sam Houston, Texas 78234-6138, U.S. ; J Anal Toxicol. 2003 Oct; 27(7):485-92.). In this way no one can blame anyone for anything.

We can well imagine that those who are freely administered go-gel in the line of duty will sooner or later develop a craving to take it in time off as well, as it is well known that addiction comes with the territory of amphetamines, albeit the mental health industry maintains that it is unlikely to occur from long-term medical use at "therapeutic" doses. According to some, lifetime stimulant therapy for attention deficit hyperactivity disorder (ADHD) that begins during childhood even reduces the risk of developing substance use disorders as an adult. Dream on, if you wish, as in the same breath we are told that "self-administering" high doses of amphetamine risk creating an amphetamine addiction. There are currently no effective drugs to treat amphetamine addiction, although it is suggested that regular, sustained, aerobic exercise appears to reduce the risk of addiction and effectively treat it, as well as improving clinical treatment outcomes. It may be used as a combination therapy together, as usual, with the simia-, mus-, rattus- and cani-proven, effective ,cognitive behavioural therapy. This therapy, you will recall from *Fallacy 1*, is detrimental to healthy PTSD-affected human beings, but currently touted as the best clinical treatment available.

Air Force Captain Joshua Bird of the 99th Reconnaissance Squadron seemed to have reached that stage of addiction when go-gel no longer did it for him. So, he did what one normally does once regularly on psychotropic drugs; he graduated to the next best thing, to get the same rush as go-gel gave him previously - cocaine. At least, that's what an official legal notice from Beale Air Force Base said he did. The base is near Marysville, California, and established in 1942 as Camp Beale. It was named for Edward Fitzgerald Beale (1822–1893), a former Lieutenant in the U.S. Navy and a Brigadier General in the California Militia. In 1951, it became a United States Air Force installation renamed Beale Air Force Base (AFB) (IATA: BAB, ICAO: KBAB, FAA LID: BAB). Beale's host unit is the 9th Reconnaissance Wing (9 RW) assigned to the Air Combat Command and part of Sixteenth Air Force. The 9 RW collects intelligence essential for Presidential and Congressional decisions critical to national defense. To accomplish this mission, the wing is equipped with the nation's fleet of U-2 Dragon Lady and RQ-4 Global Hawk unmanned aircraft and associated support equipment. The wing also maintains a high state of readiness in its combat support and combat service support forces for potential deployment in response to theater [war-zone] contingencies (beale.af.mil). That means in translation that the wing is under high pressure at all times.

The 9th Reconnaissance Wing flies the single-seat, single-engine, high-altitude reconnaissance U-2 aircraft, affectionately called the Dragon Lady. It looks for officers with the professionalism and flying skills necessary to pilot the U-2, as the aircraft can be difficult to fly due to its unusual, unspecified landing characteristics. The aircraft's task is to provide the nation's decision-makers with critical high-altitude intelligence, surveillance and reconnaissance. To fulfill this task, it's long, wide, straight wings give the plane glider-like characteristics. It can carry a variety of sensors and cameras capable of collecting multi-sensor photo, electro-optic, infrared and radar imagery, as well as performing other unnamed types of reconnaissance functions. The Dragon Lady is considered extremely reliable in reconnaissance flying, with a high mission completion rate. Because of its high-altitude missions, however, pilots must wear full pressure suits.

We are told that U-2 pilots come from every military flying background. Some were fighters. Others were bombers. Still others were tankers, or transports or trainers. They include inter-service transfer officers from the Navy, Marines and Coast Guard. They maintain close control over the application and acceptance process, leading to a highly qualified and very tight-knit group of aviators. Those selected for an interview generally possess a strong flight evaluation history, strong performance evaluations and exceed the minimum flight experience requirements. Because the U-2 does not meet military specifications for handling qualities, those selected for an interview must pass a demanding three-sortie profile in the two-seat U-2 to determine their suitability for training.

U-2 training lasts about nine months and includes a checkout in the world's first and most produced supersonic trainer, the Northrop T-38 Talon, a two-seat, twinjet supersonic jet trainer. This conventional configuration aircraft has a small, low, long-chord wing, a single vertical stabilizer and tricycle undercarriage. It seats a student pilot and instructor in tandem, and has intakes for its two turbojet engines at the wing roots. Its performance has earned it the nickname white rocket.

From his application for aspiring U-2 pilots, we understand that Captain Bird was a top-notch aviator with many years of experience under his belt. He was a special character, highly educated in his field. Otherwise, he would never have been accepted into the U-2 training program. Regrettably, he seemed to have been much less educated in the facts and side-effects of amphetamines and psychotropic drugs, including cocaine general. No one seeing him on a regular basis, such as the Beale AF medical team, seemed to have bothered to enlighten him about it. Even worse, they seem to have been ignorant for years about the trouble he was creating for himself and by extension others, even though cocaine seems to be nothing other than a logically extension of dextroamphetamine displaying the same properties of reaction of the brain. Why?

For thousands of years, indigenous peoples of South America have chewed the leaves of Erythroxylon coca. The plant contains vital nutrients, as well as numerous alkaloids, including cocaine. Coca leaf remains have been found with ancient Peruvian mummies, and pottery depicts humans with bulged cheeks indicating the presence of something on which they are chewing. Evidence also shows that these cultures used a mixture of coca leaves and saliva as an anesthetic for the performance of trepanation, also known as trephination, trepanning or burr holing. This surgical intervention is where a hole is drilled, incised or scraped into the skull using simple surgical tools.

The Spanish arrived in South America, beginning with Francisco *Pizarro* González (c. 1471-1476), the Spanish conquistador who led the Spanish conquest of Peru in 1541. At first, most ignored aboriginal claims that the leaf gave them strength and energy. Instead, they declare the practice of chewing to be the work of the Devil. After discovering the claims' veracity, however, they promptly legalized and taxed the coca leaf, taking 10% off each crop's value. In 1569, Spanish botanist Nicolás Monardes described the indigenous peoples' practice of chewing a mixture of tobacco and coca leaves to induce in them feelings of "great contentment". He stated:

> "When they wished to make themselves drunk and out of judgment they chewed a mixture of tobacco and coca leaves which make them go as they were out of their wittes."

Padre Blas Valera was born in Levanto, Chachapoyas, Peru, in 1545. He is considered to be the son of Luis Valera, one of the men who accompanied Pizarro in the conquest of the Inca Empire, and a native Incan woman. A Jesuit by education, he wrote in 1609:

> "Coca protects the body from many ailments, and our doctors use it in powdered form to reduce the swelling of wounds, to strengthen broken bones, to expel cold from the body or prevent it from entering, and to cure rotten wounds or sores that are full of maggots. And if it does so much for outward ailments, will not its singular virtue have even greater effect in the entrails of those who eat it?"

In other words, like cannabis, it has benign properties seldom mentioned in Western literature. The coca leaf was soon used to create the highly addictive cocaine, which achieves the same effect as amphetamines, but apparently to a higher degree, namely upping levels of human alertness, attention and energy (https://webmd.com). Its trade names include:

- coke
- snow
- rock
- blow
- crack

Most commonly found in a fine, white powder, it can also be made into a solid rock crystal. Users snort the white powder up their nose, rub it onto their gums or dissolve it in water and inject it with a needle. Others heat up the rock crystal and breathe the smoke into their lungs. However, they do it, they create intense feelings of energy and alertness called a "high due", to its effect on the brain's reward pathway, the *mesolimbic dopamine system*. Other cocaine effects include:

- extreme sensitivity to touch, sound, and sight
- intense happiness
- anger/irritability
- paranoid feeling
- decreased appetite

Effects begin within seconds to minutes of use and last somewhere between five and 90 minutes, depending on the amount used. There is a high risk that dependence will occur after a very short period of use. After repeated doses, a person is less able to feel pleasure. One is also very tired physically, thus needing the drug as an upper. Cocaine easily crosses the blood-brain barrier, a highly selective semipermeable border separating the circulating blood from the brain and extracellular fluid in the central nervous system (CNS), and even lead to its breakdown. Its use also increases the risk of stroke, myocardial infarction, lung problems in those who smoke it, blood infections and sudden cardiac death. Cocaine sold on the street is commonly mixed with local anesthetics, cornstarch, quinine, or sugar, which can result in additional toxicity. Thus, people who use cocaine often, generally have the following problems:

- headaches
- convulsions and seizures
- heart disease, heart attack and stroke
- mood problems
- sexual trouble
- lung damage
- HIV or hepatitis if injected
- bowel decay if swallowed
- loss of smell, nosebleeds, runny nose and trouble swallowing if snorted

Stronger and more frequent doses can cause long-term changes in brain chemistry as body and mind begin to rely on cocaine. This can make it harder to think, sleep and recall things from memory. It can also slow down reaction time. It also enhanced the risk for more heart, stomach, and lung problems.

Acute cocaine intoxication can occur with excessive or prolonged use. It can cause itching, fast heart rate, hallucinations, paranoid delusions and sensations of insects crawling on the skin. Overdoses may also cause abnormally high body temperature and a marked elevation of possibly life-threatening blood pressure, abnormal heart rhythms and death. Anxiety, paranoia, and restlessness can also be part of the package, especially during the comedown from the high. Tremors, convulsions and increased body temperature are observed with excessive dosages. Severe cardiac adverse events, particularly sudden cardiac death, also become a serious risk at high doses, due to cocaine's blocking effect on cardiac sodium channels.

Despite all this, cocaine is the second most frequently used illegal drug globally after marijuana. Use is highest in North America, followed by Europe and South America. It is estimated that between one and three percent of people in the so-called developed world have used cocaine at some point in their life. The illegal market for cocaine is US$100-500 billion each year, though statistics are ancient and vary. No medicines are approved to treat cocaine addiction.

There are many easily detectable cocaine side-effects, and we know that pilots regularly consume amphetamines. Thus, they are potentially at risk to upgrade their drug to something more potent. So, you would think that Air Force medical personal doing check-ups on their U-2 pilots, the cream of the crop, would have become aware of Captain Bird's predicament and told him – or them? Or were they, too, ignorant on the topic, or perhaps even careless? After all, viewed by Henry Kissinger as dumb animals valued only by their theatre, it seems as if neither Bird's commanding officer nor his medical team nor anyone else dealing with the captain in whatever superior capacity ever took the time to educate him or his peers on the dangers of psychotropic drugs. No wonder, really, when we know what is prescribed by the VA alone to PTSD experiencers.

So, did the top brass help Captain Bird, stewing in his drug addiction created by his bosses, to free himself from his catastrophe? Not at all. They convicted him at a general court-martial in October for using cocaine, distributing dextroamphetamine sulfate "go-gel" to others for recreational use and, most notably, for having obstructed justice by "shaving his entire body to avoid a drug test." Worse still, they were aided and abetted by Bird's lawyers. They instead ought to have taken the most decent course of action, considering his overall record and time of illustrious service, namely carting him off to severe rehabilitation instead of jail. And they should have retaught their potentially life-destroying go-gel operation. After all, according to Roza, the Air Force itself wrote in 2004 that dextroamphetamine, one of Adderall's components, had been its go-to pill of choice for more than 60 years.

The "notice" about Bird's conviction also stated that dextroamphetamine sulfate could be used by pilots to help them stay alert during very long flights. But it must be prescribed by Air Force physicians. This seems a joke in a country where an opioid epidemic is purportedly raging, due to opioids having been imported and distributed by the state itself for decades. That Captain Bird set up a steroid sale between a fellow Airman and a civilian dealer could be interpreted as an act of empathy and kindness on his part towards his fellow rather than as conduct unbecoming an officer. He put a service member airman, finding himself in the same boat as he, in touch with a civilian to buy steroids, as the notice said. After all, flying is their life, they were born to fly, and the thought of living as earthlings was revolting to them. So, they did everything they could to stay aloft, including finding ways to satisfy the Air Force-induced cravings for amphetamines and cocaine. In Bird's case, including shaving his body to avoid drug-use (other than amphetamine) detection. That his medical team and his dentist were asleep on the job is a given. He might also have been set up by someone who disliked his guts and tore down his world around him out of unmitigated envy and hatred, creating this demolition derby against him.

Why? First, at normal therapeutic doses, the physical side effects of amphetamine vary widely by age and from person to person. The psychic effects depend on the dose and the mental state and personality of the person (https://toxnet.nlm.nih.gov). The main results of an oral dose of 10-30 mg include:

- elation and euphoria
- increase in motor and speech activities
- wakefulness, alertness, and a decreased sense of fatigue
- elevation of mood with increased initiative, self-confidence, and ability to concentrate

Performance of simple mental tasks improves, and more work can be accomplished. But the number of errors might increase. Physical performance – in athletes, for example – improves, and the drug is often abused for this purpose. These effects are not invariable and may be reversed by over-dosage or repeated usage. Prolonged use or large doses are nearly always followed by depression and fatigue. Many people given amphetamine get headaches, palpitations, dizziness, vasomotor disturbances, agitation, confusion, dysphoria, apprehension, delirium or fatigue. (Hardman, J.G., L.E. Limbird, P.B. Molinoff, R.W. Ruddon, A.G. Goodman (eds.). Goodman and Gilman's *The Pharmacological Basis of Therapeutics*. 9th ed. New York, NY: McGraw-Hill, 1996, p. 219)

> HUMAN EXPOSURE AND TOXICITY: Main risks include: acute central nervous system (CNS) stimulation, cardiotoxicity causing tachycardia, arrhythmias, hypertension and cardiovascular collapse. High risk of dependency and abuse. Cardiovascular effects include palpitation, chest pain, tachycardia, arrhythmias and hypertension; cardiovascular collapse can occur in severe poisoning, as well as, myocardial ischemia, infarction and ventricular dysfunction. CNS effects include stimulation of CNS, tremor, restlessness, agitation, insomnia, increased motor activity, headache, convulsions, coma and hyperreflexia. Stroke and cerebral vasculitis have been observed. Gastrointestinal effects include vomiting, diarrhea and cramps. Acute transient ischemic colitis has occurred with chronic methamphetamine abuse. Genitourinary effects: increased bladder sphincter tone could cause dysuria, hesitancy and acute urinary retention. Renal failure can occur secondary to dehydration or rhabdomyolysis. Renal ischemia may be noted. Transient hyperthyroxinemia might be noted. Increased metabolic and muscular activity might result in hyperventilation and hyperthermia. Weight loss is common with chronic use. Hypo- and hyperkalemia have been reported. Dehydration is common. Fasciculations and rigidity may be noted. Rhabdomyolysis is an important consequence of severe amphetamine poisoning. Agitation, confusion, mood elevation, increased wakefulness, talkativeness, irritability and panic attacks are typical. Chronic abuse can cause delusions and paranoia. A withdrawal syndrome occurs after abrupt cessation following chronic use.
>
> SIGNS AND SYMPTOMS: The fully developed toxic syndrome from amphetamines is characterized by vivid visual, auditory and sometimes tactile hallucinations. Picking and excoriation of the skin and delusions of parasitosis are not uncommon. There is also paranoid ideation, loosening of association and changes in affect occurring in association with clear sensorium. In chronic users, there can be a striking paucity of sympathomimetic effects, and the blood pressure is not unduly elevated. It is often extremely difficult to differentiate this syndrome from a schizophrenic reaction. The syndrome can be seen as early as 36 to 48 hours after ingesting a single large dose of amphetamine. In apparently sensitive people, psychosis might be produced by 55 to 75 mg of dextroamphetamine. With high enough doses, psychosis can probably be induced in anyone. Unless the person continues to use the drug, the psychosis usually clears within a week, the hallucinations being the first symptoms to disappear. (Gilman, A.G., L.S.Goodman, and A. Gilman (eds.). Goodman and Gilman's *The Pharmacological Basis of Therapeutics*. 7th ed. New York: Macmillan Publishing Co., Inc., 1985., p. 553) Amphetamine in large doses can systemically dilate the pupils and cause slight blurring of near vision. Applied to the eye, amphetamine dilates the pupil and retracts the upper lid, but these actions are prevented by previous depletion of catecholamines such

as is brought about by local guanethidine. (Grant, W.M. *Toxicology of the Eye*. 3rd ed. Springfield, IL: Charles C. Thomas Publisher, 1986, p. 96)

Renal failure associated with amphetamine use is usually the result of rhabdomyolysis, a serious syndrome due to a direct or indirect muscle injury. It results from the death of muscle fibers and release of their contents into the bloodstream. This can lead to serious complications, such as renal (kidney) failure. This means the kidneys cannot remove waste and concentrated urine. It has also been found in patients without evidence of muscle damage or other apparent predisposing factors. (Knoben, J.E. and P.O. Anderson (eds.) *Handbook of Clinical Drug Data*. 6th ed. Bethesda, MD: Drug Intelligence Publications, Inc. 1988., p. 90)

Abrupt discontinuation of amphetamines produces neither seizures nor life threatening symptoms, even in those patients who habitually consume large quantities. The abstinence syndrome associated with chronic use of amphetamine is characterized by apathy, depression, lethargy, anxiety and sleep disturbances. Myalgias, abdominal pain, voracious appetite, and a profound depression with suicidal tendencies may complicate the immediate post-withdrawal period and peak in two to three days. Symptoms persisting six to seven days indicate an underlying disease process. (Ellenhorn, M.J. and D.G. Barceloux. *Medical Toxicology - Diagnosis and Treatment of Human Poisoning*. New York, NY: Elsevier Science Publishing Co., Inc. 1988., p. 636).

Intravenous sensations - during the early phases of intravenous injection use, three to four doses of 20 to 40 mg of amphetamine are usually considered sufficient by abusers to produce euphoric effects. In addition to the marked euphoria, the user experiences a sense of markedly enhanced physical strength and mental capacity, as well as feeling little need for either sleep or food. Many users claim that orgasm in both men and women is delayed, thus permitting extended periods of sexual activity finally culminating in orgasms reported to be more intense and pleasurable. This claim is difficult to substantiate by objective means. The sensation of "flash" or "rush" that immediately follows intravenous administration, while qualitatively distinct from the opioid "rush", is nevertheless described as being intensely pleasurable and somewhat akin to sexual orgasm. (Gilman, A.G., L.S.Goodman, and A. Gilman. (eds.). Goodman and Gilman's *The Pharmacological Basis of Therapeutics.* 7th ed. New York: Macmillan Publishing Co., Inc., 1985., p. 551)

Anorexia is a common finding in chronic toxicity from abuse. Occasionally, it can be so pronounced that the amphetamine abuser experiences considerable difficulty swallowing. Chronic abusers are reported to force themselves to eat small amounts of highly nutritious food and take vitamin supplements to compensate for decrease in appetite. Constant teeth grinding is also a common finding. (Casarett, L.J., and J. Doull. *Toxicology: The Basic Science of Poisons*. New York: MacMillan Publishing Co., 1975 p. 630)

Bleeding within the cranial vault is a rare, but well-reported, complication of amphetamine use. About 20 cases, which are about evenly divided between IV & oral exposures, have been reported in American literature. Ages range from 16 to 60, and most patients are habitual and often multidrug abusers. However, intracranial haemorrhages have been reported after the ingestion of as few as two to four tablets of amphetamine or structurally related anorectic drugs. (Ellenhorn, M.J. and D.G. Barceloux. *Medical Toxicology - Diagnosis and Treatment of Human Poisoning.* New York, NY: Elsevier Science Publishing Co., Inc. 1988 p. 634)

Intracerebral and subarachnoid hemorrhages: The etiology of these hemorrhages associated with amphetamine use appears multifactorial. Inflammation and necrosis of small cerebral arteries (i.e., vasculitis) secondary to particulate foreign bodies or bacterial endocarditis can develop after intravenous drug use. After that, the hypertension seen in amphetamine use can lead to vessel rupture and hemorrhage. However, vasculitis has occurred in the setting of oral acute dextroamphetamine overdose, amphetamine withdrawal and therapeutic use as an anorectic drug. The presence of vasculitis after exposure by different routes suggests an immune-pathological abnormality. Direct toxic damage to vessels seems unlikely, because of the dilution that occurs before the drug reaches the cerebral circulation. (Ellenhorn, M.J. and D.G. Barceloux. *Medical Toxicology - Diagnosis and Treatment of Human Poisoning.* New York, NY: Elsevier Science Publishing Co., Inc. 1988., p. 633)

Repetitive behaviour can occur from the use of amphetamines (e.g., repeatedly cleaning dishes or continually grooming hair). Amphetamines will also extenuate hostile, aggressive, and antisocial behaviour. Progression to paranoia, panic states, violence and even suicide might occur. (Young, L.Y., M.A. Koda-Kimble (eds.). *Applied Therapeutics. The Clinical Use of Drugs.* 6th ed. Vancouver, WA., Applied Therapeutics, Inc. 1995., p. 84)

Weight loss: Amphetamines used in large doses over a long period of time can lead to substantial weight loss, liver disease, hypertensive disorders, kidney damage, stroke, heart attack, nonhealing ulcers and sores in the skin. (Young, L.Y., M.A. Koda-Kimble (eds.). *Applied Therapeutics. The Clinical Use of Drugs.* 6th ed. Vancouver, WA, Applied Therapeutics, Inc. 1995., p. 84-3)

Now let's look at amphetamine's psychological effects on human beings, including Captain Bird, of whom no curriculum vitae seems to be available anywhere. We can be assured, however, that he is an academically well-trained man, as it comes with the U-2 captain territory; otherwise, he would not be a U-2 captain.

At normal therapeutic doses, the most common psychological side effects of amphetamine include:

- initiative
- apprehension
- concentration
- increased alertness

- insomnia or wakefulness
- decreased sense of fatigue
- self-confidence and sociability
- mood swings (elated mood followed by mildly depressed mood)

Less common side effects include:

- anxiety
- irritability
- grandiosity
- restlessness
- change in libido
- repetitive or obsessive behaviors

These effects depend on the user's personality and current mental state. Amphetamine psychosis, such as delusions and paranoia, can occur in heavy users. Although rare, this psychosis can also occur at therapeutic doses during long-term therapy. According to the U.S. Food and Drug Administration, with its deplorable record, "there is no systematic evidence" that stimulants produce aggressive behavior or hostility.

Amphetamines have also been shown to produce a conditioned place preference in humans taking therapeutic doses. This means that people have a preference for spending time in places where they have previously used amphetamines. In Captain Bird's case, that would be on board aircraft. As his record is unavailable, we have no idea how often he flew on any type of fighter aircraft, which missions he attended or in what theaters he operated, all involving amphetamine use, as demanded by the length of flights most likely occurring to reach said theatres. We don't even know when he joined the military. I wonder why?

This cartoon heads the "Utility System" section of the Lockheed

As to addiction, we are told that the risk is serious with heavy recreational amphetamine use, but is unlikely to occur from long-term medical use at therapeutic doses. So, what should we term Bird's use of amphetamine? It was during an unknown number of years of military flying on different fighter aircraft throughout the U.S. perpetual warfare in the course of his career, like the past 20 some years. Do we know if he was prescribed an amphetamine like Adderall for ADHDT in childhood, bored stiff as he must have been in school (as bright children normally are)? Mind you, the mental health profession claims that if that were indeed the case, it would reduce the risk of developing substance use disorders as an adult. They furthermore tell us that those who frequently self-administer high doses of amphetamine have a high risk of developing an addiction, since chronic use at high doses gradually increase the level of accumbal ΔFosB. This is one of many transcription factors known to influence the addiction process. It is induced in the brain's reward regions by chronic exposure to virtually all drugs of abuse and mediates sensitized responses to drug exposure. Once nucleus accumbens ΔFosB is sufficiently overexpressed, it begins to increase the severity of addictive behaviour - namely compulsive drug-seeking, further increasing its expression.

There are currently no effective drugs for treating amphetamine addiction. But regularly engaging in sustained aerobic exercise appears to reduce the risk of developing such an addiction and improves clinical treatment outcomes. Fitness can also be used as a combination therapy with cognitive behavioural therapy, that's the cani-simia, rattus, mus-proven treatment of success detrimental to humans, which is currently touted as the best clinical treatment available.

But why did any and all of these symptoms signalling liberal amphetamine use escape Bird's medical team's attention most likely for decades, in particular when knowing that pilots don't do drugs? They drink beer, often with a vengeance, wit Lockheed Martins introduction page for its Super Constellation Pocket Handbook in the 1950s. And today, at least in commercial flying, beer is still pilots' preferred beverage. Drugs are shunned with sheer might. And remember, those commercial pilots were almost all military pilots converted by the airlines into commercial flyers, up until at least the early 70s. At times, that made for some hilarious problems when the dog-fight instinct took over in flight. Even rat-poison-originating aspartame and the like has been prohibited for intake by airline pilots, as it does weird things to the mind - at least when *flying*.

So, Captain Bird was lured by the Air Force into drugs most likely since the days of his first combat mission. Is he being punished for his medical team's and the military's negligence? Apparently so, as they probably saw him for examination at least once every three months. Yet they detected nothing, even though Bird's addiction certainly did not spring forth overnight. (Commercial airlines demand their pilots show up for examination every six months. No show means no fly.) But why did Bird shave his entire body, you may ask? One possible reason is the hair follicle drug test, an alternative to standard urinalysis, where samples of the tested person's hair are analyzed for signs of drug use. The Air Force did not immediately respond to questions about whether the branch uses the hair follicle drug test, reported *Task & Purpose*'s David Roza. The go-gel he finds a little harder to explain, though he does acknowledge that taking "go-pills" is a storied tradition for Air Force pilots. They use it to stay focused while battling the fatigue of long flights and to manoeuvre multibillion dollar aircraft and all their multi-varied armaments.

But Hammurabi's Code already states:

> "2. If a man has accused another of laying a spell upon him, but has not proved it, the accused shall go to the sacred river, he shall plunge into the sacred river, and if the sacred river shall conquer him, he that accused him shall take possession of

his house. If the sacred river shall show his innocence and he is saved, his accuser shall be put to death."

And here we have the corporation of the United States of America Air Force, in law considered a "person". It laid a spell on Captain Bird, most likely since his first combat mission, and it is now punishing him for what it caused Should not perhaps both Bird's medical team and his lawyer be dismissed from service due to conduct unbecoming officers? Should that not be the consequence of their negligence and purposely leading a human being into death and dying by mandatory or clandestinely administered amphetamine use, resulting in addiction and cocaine use instead?

After all, as Roza points out, taking pills 13 miles above the Earth, where U-2 pilots have to wear pressurized suits just to survive, can be rather complicated. Those suits come with special tubes in the helmets so that pilots can slurp a paste-like form of food (with flavours including beef Stroganoff and chicken a la King). Flights can last as long as on U-2 flights which can be up to 12 hours, according to *Aviation Week*. And, adds Roza, even flying what the Air Force calls the most difficult aircraft in the world to fly could get boring sometimes on flights that long. Thus enter "go-gels," the liquid form of the Air Force's favourite uppers. But how? Fed to pilots in flight through the supper tube with or without their knowledge, leading to the consequences faced by Bird?

The legal notice only said that Bird was prescribed the gels during a deployment. But which deployments and how often and how many? Perhaps when he first deployed in a theatre of war 20 or more years ago, as he could not swallow them while on U-2 missions? Did the prescription specify that Bird could not dole them out to his buddies in need for funsies, asks Roza. He also observes that the prescription likely did not instruct him to do cocaine, obviously as ignorant as Bird and the U.S. military are that one leads to the other, as certain as the Amen follows prayer in church? And where were his lawyers? Sleeping on the watch like his medical and dentistry teams? Why did they ignore in its entirely the maxim, (a principle of law universally admitted as being just and consonant with reason and holden for law) stating, "In case of doubt it is best to lean to the side of mercy", in particular, like in this case, when the innocent party is declared guilty (lectlaw.com)? This leads to one major suspicion: was Captain Bird's hitherto stellar career brutally terminated on purpose? Was he set up by someone who disliked his guts and tore down his world around him out of unmitigated envy and hatred, by way of creating this demolition derby against him?

Be that as it may, it ended Captain Bird's hitherto stellar career due to no fault of his own. The Air Force celebrated its 75th anniversary of dextroamphetamine destruction of human lives by finding him culpable for their destruction. For that, a panel of fellow officers sentenced him to three months confinement and dismissal from the Air Force, the notice said. Those peers sitting on the military tribunal panel were either unaware of or wilfully ignored the point that all psychotropic drugs lead to suicide ideation sooner or later. They ignored that Bird showed strength of character by moving on to cocaine rather than killing himself in desperation. Furthermore, these military court participants papered over their possible association or even source of the Air Force's increase in suicides. They should have investigated drug-use among pilots in particular and air force staff in general, from the top brass down, Four-star general David Lee Goldfein, currently serving as the Air

Force's Chief of Staff of the Air Force is negligent, too. How could they fail to investigate dextroamphetamine and cocaine use side-effects? After all, a fish always starts rotting from the head. Instead, Goldfein ordered all wings to stand down for a day and focus on resiliency and suicide prevention when he and his brass themselves cause the killing spree of self through their administration of psychotropic drugs to their own troops.

The notice of Bird's dismissal was first shared on the Facebook group Air Force amn/nco/snco on December 6, 2019. Staff Sgt. Taylor M. White, a 9th Reconnaissance Wing spokesman confirmed the authenticity of the notice to *Task & Purpose*. One Air Force amn/nco/snco commenter laconically put Bird's predicament as: "Here for a good time, not a long time." The amn.com website has since disappeared into the ether, but on their Facebook site we find the following:

In 2004, there were 313,676 mental health encounters. In 2019, the projection is 876,761. In other words, a 179% increase.

That this increase is most likely caused by the redefinition of the DSM-5's 297 so-called mental disorders listed in the official publication of the American Psychiatric Association. They liberally loosened the criteria of mental illness, so sooner or later, all humans are easily diagnosed with such. But this is nowhere mentioned, even though, as Jon Rappoport writes in October 2018, objectively speaking, mental illnesses and disorders do not even exist. They are merely categorized as specific chemical imbalances in the brain, an unproven assertion for which there is no scientific evidence. It's all mere speculation, as for none of the 297 so-called mental disorders listed in the DSM-5, are there defining physical tests. No blood tests, no urine tests, no saliva tests, no laboratory tests, no tests of any kind. That is a fact. Which leads to the question why psychiatrists must first be schooled as medical doctors before starting their shrink education? To understand better how to shrink the brain? Is it that they are doing the only medical action in their chosen profession, prescribing drugs that do perpetual harm? So, they not only shrink the brain, figuratively speaking, as we see in Captain Bird's dextroamphetamine addiction, but also destroy the human body?

It could also inspire contemplation that all 297 of the official mental disorders listed in the DSM-5 are defined and approved by committees of psychiatrists. And whether for schizophrenia or autism or ADHD or clinical depression or bipolar disease or PTSD, all definitions solely and wholly consist of described behaviors, as seen by individual psychiatrists. Their opinions are then thrown into a pot, stir, and when congruence in opinions is complete, published as diagnoses. We could term it "Psychiatrists' Science". There is no compelling first evidence found on any of their assertions. This push to portray psychiatry as a science began with Blavatsky's theosophical society and is still going on slowly but surely, making humanity believe it is sick in the mind and that pharmaceutical concoction and other treatments would erase and/ or alleviate their brains' chemical imbalances. It is, of course, of interest to psychiatrists to maintain these imbalances, as they form the basis of their métier. But this is seldom mentioned. Neither is the fact that nourishment, as well as vaccinations, have a huge influence on brain functioning and, thus, overall health. Nevertheless, in courts of law, doctors' offices, academic conferences, pages of professional journals and in political gulags, as for example portrayed by Alexander Solzynition, the science of discrete, separate and definable mental disorders is treated as settled, confirmed, verified and certain, even though it is a bald-faced lie.

And this bald-faced lie is liberally applied to diagnose U.S. military personnel with mental disorders. This despite there being nothing wrong with them, other than state-induced drug-taking and injections from the get-go, combined with systematic brain washing. Don't believe it? Read what Norman Sussman, M.D., an adult psychiatrist, NYU Langone Preston Robert Tisch Center for Men's Health in New York City wrote in 2017. He wrote about the latest edition of the Comprehensive Textbook of Psychiatry 's chapter on treatment resistance. This chapter provides expert guidance on how to treat patients who are still unresponsive after multiple unsuccessful attempts at intervention for some common mental disorders. ADHD, PTSD, panic disorder and bipolar disorder are especially difficult to treat successfully, for a number of reasons, the learned psychiatrist adds, quoting from the textbook:

> "Some patients fail to respond to repeated trials of medication. No single factor can explain the ineffectiveness of the various interventions in these cases. Strategies in these cases include the use of drug combinations, high-dose therapy, and use of unconventional drugs. Limited evidence is available on the comparative success rates associated with any given strategy." (Psychiatric Times Introduction: Treatment Resistance in Psychiatry Nov 27, 2017 Volume: 34 Issue: 11).

The above, in Sussman's opinion, casts light on the dilemma psychiatrists face in everyday clinical practice. As he says, they lack understanding of the underlying anatomical and biochemical abnormalities of any mental disorder. That includes the ones discussed in the report that causes the difficulties of resistance.

> "You can even question whether treatment resistance is a valid concept when applied to psychiatric disorders. Currently, successful clinical outcomes are frequently the result of trial-and-error interventions, informed by limited and often anecdotal evidence. The fact is, none of the disorders covered in this report have a pharmacological treatment proven to be fully effective more often than not in most patients. One possibility is that there are multiple abnormalities in the CNS [central nervous system] that account for the observed behavioural, emotional, and cognitive symptoms that we identify as a single disorder. The history of biological psychiatry has been marked with non-replicated claims that certain 'markers' could predict treatment response."

You get the drift? If not, you need your head examined, or you should check out the writings of the Hungarian-American academic, psychiatrist and psychoanalyst Thomas Stephen Szasz (1920-2012). He served for most of his career, between 1961 to 2012, as professor of psychiatry at the State University of New York Upstate Medical University in Syracuse, New York. Known as psychiatry's enfant terrible, a distinguished lifetime fellow of the American Psychiatric Association and a life member of the American Psychoanalytic Association, he was best known as a social critic of the moral and scientific foundations of psychiatry. He saw both as social control aims of medicine and scientism, a term generally used critically, implying a cosmetic application of science in unwarranted situations.

Such situations are considered not amenable to application of the scientific method or similar scientific standards.

His first book, *The Myth of Mental Illness*, reflects his views. First, he contends that there is such thing as mental illness. Second, he opines that individual responsibility is never compromised in those suffering from what is generally termed as mental illness. Third, he expresses perennial interest in calling attention to the political nature of psychiatric diagnosis ("Tony B. Benning: No such thing as mental illness? Critical reflections on the major ideas and legacy of Thomas Szasz"; BJPsych Bull. 2016 Dec; 40(6): 292–295). Szasz argues there are no true illnesses of the mind. He took the position of rigid distinction between the physical and the menta. He viewed psychiatry's misappropriation of concepts such as 'illness' as inappropriate, as it was only relevant to medicine and its 'physicalist framework, but not to matters of the human mind and conduct. For him, mental illnesses are not "illnesses" in the sense that physical illnesses are, except for a few identifiable brain diseases, as there are "neither biological or chemical tests nor biopsy or necropsy findings for verifying DSM diagnoses." Even the concept of mental illness to him was offensive to human values such as autonomy and liberty. His views arose and followed libertarian roots, based on the principles that each person has the right to bodily and mental self-ownership and the right to be free from violence from others

Furthermore, he found the concept "mental illness" logically absurd. He saw the consequences of treatment administered by mental health practitioners as highly harmful. , They use pharmaceutical drugs as a purported "cure", instead of treating ethical or legal human deviation from the norm as an opportunity to teach deviants' personal responsibility. We see the same in the treatment of genuine PTSD experiencers, the drugging unto death of the brightest, the destruction of their minds and thus their bodies, by physicians pretending to try healing them. As I saw in my own journey through hell, medicalization gives a pre-eminent role to doctors. It privileges the role of medication as a therapeutic intervention, oftentimes without the prescribing physicians having a clue or care what the consequences are for their patients. Why should they? After all, a slowly worsening patient is a marvellous source of income. Combine this with the pharmaceutical industry's profit when the mental health profession stretches the concept and boundaries of mental disorder. The physicians derive bonuses from it. They have it made.

Szasz recognized and acknowledged this fact. A very few others brought critical attention to this ever-widening reach of psychiatric diagnosis and the pharmaceutical industry's exuberant complicity in this phenomenon over the years. Among them was Dr. Peter Breggin, mentioned in *Fallacy 1*. But Big Pharma's involvement goes further. It joyously supports 'new' categories of psychiatric disorders, such as adult attention deficit disorder. It vigorously endorses the lowering of diagnostic thresholds for a host of established psychiatric disorders. Wit the DSM extension ad nauseam since its origin back in 1840. That's when the term "idiocy/insanity" first appeared in that year's U.S. governmental census. Coincidence?

Forty years later, the census featured seven categories:

- mania
- paresis
- epilepsy
- dementia
- dipsomania
- monomania

- melancholia

In 1917, as uniform statistics across mental hospitals were wanted, the Bureau of the Census embraced a publication called the *Statistical Manual for the Use of Institutions for the Insane*. This was created by the Committee on Statistics of the American Medico-Psychological Association, now the American Psychiatric Association, and the National Commission on Mental Hygiene (psychcentral.com). The committees separated mental illness into 22 groups. The manual went through 10 editions until 1942. And it took off from there, reaching the exuberant rate of 297 human mental illnesses with the DSM-5, and climbing. The aim?

Stop the Crime says it best:

> WATCH OUT
>
> Mental Health Support Teams Are Coming After YOU
>
> We will ALL be labeled mentally ill if we do not agree with the illusion... Armed with Grant Money, OUR MONEY, which is increasing city debt obligations, the cities will "hunt" for more revenue. Our pockets will be reached into (pick-pocket-like) for additional taxes. Our cost of living will go sky high and we will require mental treatment for being depressed and unable to survive. We are being asset stripped and if we crack up under the stress of the economic hit teams of the Rothschild Gang we will be restrained by mental health programs for our safety while being exploited and made homeless.
>
> We must be resilient - and if we are not able to handle the continual loss we will be given mental support which will include data tracking, crisis intervention, mobile crisis and intervention teams assisted by law enforcement.
>
> We MUST remain sane in this growing world of insanity or WE will be restrained for our safety! Visit - StopTheCrime.net
>
> FOR THE TRUTH IN THIS INSANE WORLD

It was in the 1990s that psychiatry made another unprecedented step toward declaring humanity insane wholesale. *It was* the explosion of biological and neuro-scientific research. Some of the ilk took the opportunity to declare Szasz hypothesis for lack of first evidence documenting mental impairment as invalid. One of them was Edward Shorter, PhD, FRSC, a Jason A. Hannah Professor of the History of Medicine in the Faculty of Medicine and cross-appointed Professor of Psychiatry at the University of Toronto, Canada, who declared without blinking an eye:

> "Thomas Szasz's essay misses several key points about the undoubted changes that psychiatry has undergone since he wrote his original screed against the discipline in 1961. Szasz fails to recognise that the discipline today acknowledges a neurological basis for much psychiatric illness. Thus, his fulminations against

> psychiatry for treating 'mental illness' is off-base. Szasz's original diatribe was heavily against psychoanalysis. Yet today Freud's doctrines can scarcely be said to play even a marginal role in psychiatry, and it is absurd to keep levelling the same old charges of 50 years ago. One has the feeling of looking at one of the last veterans of the Esperanto movement in confronting Szasz: lunacy at the time, bizarrely outdated today."(Still tilting at windmills: Commentary on ... The myth of mental illness; published online by Cambridge University Press: 02 January 2018)

Such lack of graciousness towards a colleague of renown! Such lack of integrity and honour is breathtaking in itself. Arguing that 'the discipline today acknowledges a neurological basis for much psychiatric illness' and that contemporary neurobiological research findings provide support to counter Szasz's argument is downright ludicrous. There is no prima facie evidence for any psychiatric evaluation, period. Shorter's diatribe seems to have been generated by Tony B. Benning's article "No such thing as mental illness? Critical reflections on the major ideas and legacy of Thomas Szasz" (BJPsych Bull. 2016 Dec; 40(6): 292–295). In 2016, Benning found that by no means is there unanimity among psychiatrists in attributing biological aetiologies to mental illnesses. Indeed, he says, several of them have since the early 2000s contested that schizophrenia, for example, is a brain disease.

Be it as it may, Szasz was not anti-psychiatry, but anti-coercive psychiatry. He believed in psychiatry and psychotherapy between consenting adults. A staunch opponent of civil commitment and involuntary psychiatric treatment, he also was ever-interested in the interface between psychiatry and the law, as well as cognizant of the interplay between diagnosis and political and social power. His first book was *Law, Liberty, and Psychiatry* he grappled with these issues (Szasz TS. *Law, Liberty, and Psychiatry: An Inquiry into the Social Uses of Mental Health Practices*. Routledge & Kegan Paul, 1963). *It* articulated a critical position with respect to legal and jurisprudential orthodoxy.). *It* assumes that *people* with mental illness are not responsible for their actions in some cases, and especially not with reference to criminal acts. Distinguishing between explanation and responsibility, Szasz argued that regardless of a diagnosis of mental illness, *people* are "always responsible for their conduct".

By and large, though, Szasz, the enfant terrible of his peers, questioned the legitimacy of psychiatry to such extend as to compare it to alchemy and astrology. In his seminal work The Manufacture of Madness (1970) he set out some of the arguments most associated with him when examining the similarities between the Inquisition and institutional psychiatry. His purpose was to show "that the belief in mental illness and the social actions to which it leads have the same moral implications and political consequences as had the belief in witchcraft and the social actions to which it led."

Nevertheless, Szasz regarded psychotherapy as a useful tool to *help* people learn about themselves, others, life and problems of living. In this way, he maintained, psychiatrists could have a legitimate role to play in society. But, he asserted, the relationship between psychiatrist and patient should always be based on consensual contract, rather than on coercion. Furthermore, mental health practitioners should cease to claim being the only ones having expertise in helping people experiencing problems in living. Help, Szasz said, could come from a multitude of other sources, such as family members, friends, clergymen, physicians, drugs, religion, faith healing, marriage, divorce, and so on and so forth. All of these could be legitimately solicited by or on behalf of those experiencing a life crisis (Szasz TS. Reply to Slovenko. In Szasz Under Fire: The Psychiatric Abolitionist Faces his Critics; Schaler JA, editor: pp. 159–78. Open Court, 2004).

But if that would be public knowledge the mental health industry *would* suffer, their income *would* lessen, their business *would* wilt. Think about the enormous benefits generated for psychiatrists *just* by analyzing soldiers of all stripes and colors and ranks with mental disorders! Just look at Dallas Morning News reporter Kevin Krause's June 2019 article "Ex-pharmacist gets 2 years, $7 million bill for role in scheme to bilk Tricare out of more than $100 million." This should give us an idea how lucrative the business is. Also remember, psychiatrists get lucrative kick-backs for their prescriptions, all of them leading to suicide ideation - unless the taker wakes up to the systematical destruction of his mind and body because of them. The longer mind-altering/psychotropic drugs are taken, the more difficult it gets to reason and see logic in all ones undertakings. The Mistake of the Intellect becomes ever stronger, day by day by day by day. We see this manufactured madness reflected in Captain Bird's behavior and following treatment by his overlords. By extension we see it in a multitude of his peers, once we open our eyes. The politics involved in the mental health industry are furthermore reflected in the attempt by U.S. law makers, its congressmen and senators, as well as U.S. presidents' right to decree law by presidential orders, to curtail the populace's 2nd Amendment right to bear arms, in particular that of military personnel, by increasing mental industry's professionals' skyrocketing increase in mental illness diagnoses for problems of life and living *among* the troops. And you still believe in the science of definable mental disorders?

That CSAF General Goldfein is seemingly as ignorant of that fact as most of the U.S. military seems to be, mirrored in his august statement:

> "Right now, there is no data that we've looked at that indicates we have something going on that would cause an increase in suicides, but we cannot sustain these losses."

If he were listening to his troops he would listen to Jonathan Hawkins, who says:

> "The #1 reason [for the increase in suicides] in my opinion is all the suicide prevention classes they shove down your throat. It puts the idea in your head even though they say it's a prevention class. I believe if they just stop talking about it the numbers would go down. It's the same with mass shootings. The more the media puts it out there the worse it is."

Darrin Donovan rebuts:

> "So... are you implying that more people choosing to seek mental health is causing more suicides? This data would lead me to believe there is a separate issue that is driving the increased traffic to mental health as well as increased suicides. Gen Goldfein doesn't seem to be 'denying' that, but this data alone doesn't point to any specific 'causation'. Correlation - probably."

with John Taylor adds:

> "It means squat without knowing why folks are killing themselves. The suicide #'s might be driven by the weather for all we know. Get the right facts!"

Dextroamphetamines et al. and its consequences. Another concerned air force GI writes: Response?

> "Seems like more and more airmen are becoming part of the 22. I have read several disturbing reports and spoken to some folks who are in the AF and it seems like the more personnel that seek help, their command structure either ignores it, or the Airmen get ridiculed and embarrassed. ~Storm"

And finally, Sarah Jo states the blaring truth:

> "MFLC, Military One source, Mental Health, resilience course, mental health first aid, national counselling hotlines, family phone call, friends house, message me, peers house... none of these need referrals from leadership. Take power over your own life."

But how can you take power of your own life?
The military and mental health profession tell you to keep secret that they caused, and which with their help will continue to cause, your destruction, eh?

Following Goldfein's stand-down and the castigation of Miller and Ford for sharing their ideas of suicide prevention with their charges or underlings, a Facebook support group called Air Force Wingman Outreach emerged to help service members in crisis (Patricia Kime: "The Air Force Has Declared War on Hopelessness in the Ranks"; military.com Sept. 18, 2019). Within this group, members cited as reasons why airmen do not reveal their personal struggles:

- unresponsive mental health services
- concerns about security clearances
- fear of being stigmatized by peers for getting mental health treatment

But the most common thread running through many frustrated service members' posts has been bad leadership. Indeed, the nearly 30,000 group members are "mostly talking about us," said Wright. "They are talking about leadership, about leadership being toxic, about leadership not being able to connect, about leadership not caring." He made said this at the Air Force Association's 2019 Air, Space & Cyber Conference Organized by the Air Force Association, a non-profit advocacy group for the Air Force. In essence, the troops are blaming leadership for their emotional misery. They are not looking within themselves for why they feel the way they feel. They are not looking within at what they have done differently in recent months, or even years, that might be impacting their sudden suicidal onslaught, as they have yet to be taught that everything comes from within. Nobody has taught them that all psychotropic drugs lead to suicidal ideation. And no-one has taught them that we must take responsibility for everything we do and indulge in once grown up.

Perhaps even the top brass doesn't know that. Be that as it may, at least they are somewhat rattled by the increase in suicides. By August 2019, the Air Force had already exceeded the number of suicides in all of 2018 by nearly 20 people. "Hopeful to hopeless ... what's going on?" he wrote in a letter to his commanding officers. "It's our job to find out." Air

Force senior leadership said individual attention, not sweeping programs by the Defense Department and military services, were needed to reduce suicides and suicide attempts. It was then that General Goldfein urged commanders to use the one-day stand-down pause to engage with airmen personally on sensitive issues. Well, Miller and Ford did just that, only to reap their leader's scathing rebuke.

Wright, referring to Air Force leaders in general, said: "I don't think the answer resides in the Pentagon. Some of the feedback we've gotten is people are tired, overworked, undermanned, under-resourced. ... Part of it just belongs to us." And Goldfein thought to express that the service continued to work to develop and nurture leaders and flush out those who might damage the military population or were toxic. He added that it is was up to fellow leaders to "pull the red guarded switch" when becoming aware of toxic leaders. A 360-degree review that included feedback from subordinates would help in the weed-out process, he conveyed.

"It's on all of us to ensure that we don't allow toxic leaders to get in positions of authority. Do they sometimes exist? Yes. Are we doing better to weed them out? I certainly hope so," Goldfein expressed at the conference. Last year, a total of 325 active-duty service members took their lives, including 58 Marines, 68 Navy sailors, 60 Air Force airmen and 139 Army soldiers, according to the Department of Defense quarterly suicide report.

The 2018 suicide total surpassed the number of active-duty personnel killing themselves in 2012, a record since the services began to closely track the issue in 2001. Wright did not expect base commanders to draft a plan of what they believed could prevent suicide. He did, however, think that Goldfein's efforts might help struggling airmen to again feel a sense of purpose when coming to work, even if carrying baggage from their personal lives with them. Herewith, of course, he squarely lays the reasons for airmen's discontent on their private, not their professional, lives. Thus, he nullifies complaints about their leaders. His view uttered during a recent interview was that: "While mental health is a part of it, I personally think a larger part of this solution is us just being good human beings." This seems a trifle difficult to accept as a solution to the suicidal crisis within the military. They are, after all, expected to kill other human beings on a moment's notice and live happily ever after.

Still, he has a point when stating:

> "All of the airmen that I've had the pleasure of meeting, connecting with and talking to who've thought about committing suicide, none of them -not one -pointed to a program or a process or mental health [initiative]... They all pointed to the thing that kept them going, and that was another person."

Some of them had been in therapy programs to keep talking to someone with whom they were comfortable, he added. Even on those occasions, help eventually came from a friend or teammate.

I don't really care if this comment ever sees the light of day but for the love of God can we do something about leadership and suicide? Myself, my roommate and now another airmen at Dyess reaches out for help and got brushed aside. We are lucky that it was only one instead of three, but I'm tired of hearing the same shit. Leadership isn't worried about airmen and they need to be held accountable. I know this page is amazing at getting things seen by the higher ups. Please use this page to get something to change. Can't do another active duty funeral.

Sometimes it was even from a stranger. They would ask the simplest questions like, "How are you? Is there anything I can do? That's all it was -- meaningful connections," the chief said:

> "It makes a big difference if you walk into a work center where you feel like, 'Hey, I'm a valued member of his team, and my supervisor, my teammates, they care about the things that I'm going through' versus, 'Hey nobody cares.' This is about making airmen feel valued."

It was therefore that he urged personnel to reach out when seeing a person struggling:

> "I've talked to a lot of airmen who have thought about it [suicide], and I can count on my pinky the number who said the reason they didn't [act on suicide] was because of some program, some process, some training. Every single one of them said it was because of this person, this supervisor, this commander, this teammate that I connected with that showed some interest in me and my well-being ... we have to do this together."

And yes, you do indeed. You are the only ones who can. Just as those bright enough to acquire PTSD can only be helped by their own. For this reason, the authorities vigorously oppose the Oath of Exit and the Spartan Oath, which bring soldiers and veterans together to help each other. Why? Because, if it were to take root and prosper, the powers that be would lose their power over their PTSD-affected Government Issue, the brightest of the GI crop, and the knowledge about the mental health practitioners' detrimental-to-human-health treatments, including the suicide-enticing, massive amounts of psychotropic drugs prescribed, will spread through the ranks faster than wildfire. If that happens, it's game over for them. It is that simple.

But can anyone stop someone from committing suicide, regardless of measures taken by the Corporation of the United States for whom you are a complete financial write-off if you murder yourself? Few people, if anybody, seem to know. So, perhaps you, the one getting ready to kill yourself, would do us, the curious, the ones with truly enquiring minds, a favour. Perhaps you could write down for us and for posterity what thoughts cross your feeble but intelligent mind whilst contemplating to pull the trigger of the gun you most likely intend to use for the deed? Write it all down in great detail so we who are left behind, and want to know, can get educated on suicidal motivations. It might even deviate you from accomplishing your goal for that day. If not, you have at least done one good deed for humanity if you get past just the "I'm tired of life. Bye, Bye" line. In other words, give us insight into your psyche, which would help us understand that of others intending to duplicate your idiocy for killing Self.

Please tell us what most aches you in your soul leading to your suicidal action. Tell us about the deeds you have committed in and out of the line of duty and throughout your life. Tell us about the ones that, in your estimation, piled up to an insurmountable amount of hatred within you and against yourself. Tell us how, because of these deeds, that you must now kill yourself to escape from your own deplorable judgment of yourself. Tell us if you take your own life because you can't stand looking at what you view as your perverted self another day. Or if you love yourself and want to get to heaven faster because of it. Write down for us what you were ordered to take in pharmaceutical drugs for us, please, so we can evaluate and substantiate our understanding that it is they who first and foremost enticed you to commit this crime against yourself. In this way, you do something valuable for posterity and document the influence of pharmaceutical psychotropic drugs prescribed with never-ending exuberance by mental health practitioners knowing full well their remedies and treatments are killing us softly from the moment we enter their sphere. By doing so before going through with the deed, you may even lessen the bad Karma coming from it. Even though you cannot present us with your very last thoughts after the point of no return, you at least provide us with the build-up to it, thus freeing us from the speculation of motives and thus having done a service to mankind.

We know that suicidal thoughts are the result of feeling unable to cope with what seems to be an overwhelming life situation. Yet, we have no knowledge about what those going through with the suicidal deed feel at the very last moment of life when the deed is irreversible. As genuine PTSD experiencers, we know that time is not irreversible and that a second seems like an hour. So, the interval between pulling the trigger, for example, and the bullet flying on its way to shatter the skull and spatter the brain may seem like ages. What if the last thought perhaps is a glorious expletive followed by a: "What the hell did I do that for?" before it's game over?

And is there any research on how pre-knowledge about the possible consequences of killing Self changes or stalls the suicidal undertaking? Would the knowledge that birth in any of the realms mentioned above is based on our Karma generated by our actions toward Self and others? Would it help suicide aspirants to control their murderous desire if they knew that our motive for any thought or action, good or bad (killing our selves included), influences our future? Would it inspire a desire to continue living if they knew that we are infinite spirits merely having an experience, which, too, shall pass? Would it spark an interest in finding out if it is really true that every intentional act, whether physical, verbal or mental, leaves residue in the one committing it - in this case in ourselves after killing ourselves? And would it stall the act of suicide if they knew that the possibility of the residue of all actions and deeds, whether good or bad, will be like a seed, in due time producing an effect in the form of pleasure or pain for the one performing it? Would those who want to kill Self pause in their tracks if they knew these actions and deeds not only determine the life thus far lived, but also our next place of birth and the quality of its life in all of its aspects? Would it perhaps inspire to try to learn what to do to help the Self, rather than commit suicide? Perhaps the Department of Defence should order *The Tibetan Book of the Dead* as mandatory reading to the troop upon enrolment and test them on it. That could lower military suicide rates in a jiffy.

When confronted with the possibility that suicide could be detrimental to one's future, perhaps a certain precaution against killing Self might simmer through the miserable darkness of one's PTSD-clouded and distraught, pharmaceutically drug-perverted mind, right? Just think about it. Karma presupposes a dynamic universe. Therefore, our present life already reflects our past choices, to which we surely can have insight if we meditate regularly and start recording our dreams. From that, we can glean that our present choices shape our future endeavours. As only human beings are physically and mentally endowed to make choices, at least as far as I know at present, we have the power and grace to choose your future right now, for better or for worse, for life or against it. Thus you, the suicidal aspirant, regardless of color, race, creed, religion, nationality, social, financial and academic status, now have the opportunity to make the moral and ethical choice to live or die. Your choice will reflect and impact not only your own life, but through your action and deed, that of a multitude of others. So, what's it going to be? Suicide or educating yourself on how to help yourself and prosper? Or help the mental health industry cabal and enhance their profit by killing yourself?

6

BRAINWASHED INTO SUICIDE

Were you to watch the 2016 BBC documentary *The Century of the Self* you would get a vague idea how manipulating and brainwashing anyone into suicide is done. But former New York State assemblyman Daniel Haley, who spent a lifetime studying health and healing in America, in his book *Politics In Healing: The suppression and manipulation of American Medicine* describes precisely how the experts carry out this process so that the herd conceives ideas and concepts to, for example, commit suicide (Potomac Valley Press, 2000). Julian Dr. Julian Whitaker, M.D., a pioneer in the field of nutritional medicine for more than 40 years, views Haley as a man of unique ability to talk of the damage that greed and political influence has wrought on healthcare alternatives not only in the U.S. states about him: "Daniel Haley has written a very important book about the medical profession detailing the struggles between good and evil as no one ever has before. Incredible as these stories are, they are true!" (rifeshop.com). We can see this battle mirrored in present-day's COVID-19 operation.

Again we ask: "But how is this brainwashing and manipulation done?" Simple. By suppressing all knowledge about ways and means of alternative healing methods and techniques. And in the case of genuine PTSD? By spreading the tale that it is a mental illness treatable only by mental health professionals in combination with pharmacotherapy

Nothing could be further from the truth, but none of them tells us that it merely" is a catastrophic existential crisis curable only by the Self. Combined with the through decades indoctrinated "Doctor Knows Best" delusion akin to the "One cigarette a day keeps the Doctor away" dominating our PTSD scattered, puzzled, uneasy and scared minds, the mental health- and pharmaceutical cabal got it made. While their coffers overflow with dough quasi ad infinitum until doomsday, we through their poisonous pharmaceutical treatments and delusional beliefs of our state of minds sink further and further into the abyss of suicidal ideation. It is unavoidable and we can only protect ourselves against it when we learn how they do it.

It started by and large with world-renowned early twentieth century Austrian neurologist and founder of psychoanalysis Sigismund Schlomo Freud (1856 - 1939), who made psychopathology treatments through dialogue between patient and psychoanalyst a most fashionable flavor in early twentieth century Europe and the U.S. Psychopathology, by the way, is the study of purportedly abnormal cognitions, behavior and experiences. Cognition, a term referring to the mental processes involved in gaining knowledge and comprehension, includes thinking, knowing, remembering, judging, and problem solving as well as language, imagination, perception, and planning.

Freud's work and theories would jumpstart psychoanalysis and influence practitioners' psychoanalysts' views of human childhood, personality, memory, sexuality and therapy to present day. His peers were fascinated by articles written by or about him. Had he not "proved" that there was no genuine human love anywhere in humanity, and that a boy even in infancy "lusted for his mother?" That a girl hated her mother and longed for intercourse with her father, and that an adult embracing a child, even his or her own, was an "unspeakable scandal?" Did he not accuse worshippers of Christ of adoring a phallic symbol and prompted only by "a lust of the flesh?" While some saw Freud's statements either as the beginning of Europe's and America's spiritual corruption or enlightenment about humans' true nature, both the Russian czar and his follower Lenin found Freud's teachings so disgusting and perverse as to prohibit them outright within Russia's borders. (Taylor Caldwell: Answer As A Man; G.P. Putnam's Sons, New York, 1980 p.381/2). The rest of the western world was less choosy. Some in Freud's league contributed work growing out of Freud's ideas and hypothesis while others developed theories out of opposition to his ideas.

Freud's nephew Edward Bernays (1891-1995), son of Freud's sister and Freud's wife Martha's brother, who spent much time with Uncle Sigismund and his associates, grew up with Freudian principles and at an early age learnt the insights and techniques needed for human mind manipulation. How exquisitely he grasped the importance of Freud's ideas to supremely rule the laity–the herd–and his role in it we may/might see in his 1928 book *Propaganda* when stating:

> "The conscious and intelligent manipulation of the organized habits and opinions of the masses is an important element in democratic society. Those who manipulate this unseen mechanism of society constitute an invisible government, which is the true ruling power of our country. We are governed, our minds are *moulded*, our tastes formed, and our ideas suggested, largely by men we have never heard of.... It is they who pull the wires that control the public mind (The

> manipulation of the American mind: Edward Bernays and the birth of public relations; theconversation.com, July 2015)."

In other words, he told those who wished to know that to rule the masses, the slobs as he called us, public relations, PR, between rulers and ruled was a necessity -- not a gimmick. He also knew that Uncle Freud and buddies would be the ones dictating the direction and ideation in which the herd - us--would be driven and that without suspecting a thing. We, the herd, the cattle, were over 100 years later finally openly mentioned in conjunction with COVID 19 when *Herd Immunity* became a household word/expression/concept. No opposition to the animal description of humanity occurred. It was accepted without a murmur. The American Avram Noam Chomsky (1928-), one of the founders of the field of cognitive science and a major figure in analytic philosophy, a method of approaching philosophical problems through analysis of the terms in which they are expressed, had this to say about Bernays' *Propaganda* 70 years after its publication:

> "So he wrote a book called Propaganda around 1925, and it starts off by saying he is applying the lessons of the First World War. The propaganda system of the First World War and this commission that he was part of showed, he says, it is possible to 'regiment the public mind every bit as much as an army regiments their bodies.' These new techniques of regimentation of minds, he said, had to be used by the intelligent minorities in order to make sure that the slobs stay on the right course. We can do it now, because we have these new techniques. This is the main manual of the public relations industry.
>
> "Bernays is kind of the guru... He also engineered the public relations effort behind the U.S.-backed coup, which overthrew the democratic government of Guatemala. His major coup, the one that really propelled him into fame in the late 1920s, [however], was getting women to smoke. Women didn't smoke in those days and he ran huge campaigns for Chesterfield. You know all the techniques—models and movie stars with cigarettes coming out of their mouths and that kind of thing. He got enormous praise for that. So, he became a leading figure of the industry, and his book was the real manual."—Noam Chomsky ("What Makes Mainstream Media Mainstream": a talk at Z Media Institute of June 1997 historyisaweapon.org).

But the slobs, the deplorables, if you will, us the herd paid little if any attention then or now.

Bernays' parents moved from Austria to New York City with their five children when Bernays was one year old, where he after his high school graduation attended Ivy League Cornell University of Ithaca, New York to receive a degree in agriculture in 1912 to please his grain-merchant father. Preferring tending and mind-controlling the herd of slobs to agriculture, he in 1916 assisted American president Woodrow Wilson to win reelection on the slogan "He kept us out of war" whilst simultaneously brainwashing Wilson's administration and the American populace at large into believing that America's entrance into World War I would/served to create democracy in Europe. That Wilson signed the Federal

Reserve System and the Internal Revenue Act into law to the herd's complete detriment had long since been swept under the rug, and Lenin's jubilance over the fact never reached the public. "We have the world! Taxes and wars and the power to control the currency of the American nation will result in universal communism. America will fall into our hands like a ripe plum. We will smash her face with an armoured fist." (Taylor Caldwell: Answer As A Man; G.P. Putnam's Sons, New York, 1980 p.381). Wilson's 1914 Declaration of Neutrality had also been forgotten.

Consequently scant 4 weeks after Wilson's 1917 second term inauguration, he asked entrance into WWI from Congress proclaiming: "The world must be made safe for democracy." Congress (373-50) and senate (82-6) accepted the resolution without qualm. Brother would fight against brother.

Bernays' supremely efficient propaganda through mind-manipulation techniques during Wilson's administration including his participation in the 1919 WWI Versailles Peace Conference inspired Bernays et al. to ponder how the herd could be equally manipulated during peacetime. And he never stopped until finally at the age of 104 kicking the bucket after a fabulous career. His success in WW! would be further magnified during the run-up to WWII's. He is responsible for the United States legislation since 1913 having congressional authorization to spend government funds on "publicity experts" masquerading under such euphemisms as "directors of information." That alone was a sensational development considering that governments' natural affinity for public relations had hitherto been little explored since the days of Florentine diplomat, politician, historian, philosopher, writer, playwright and poet of the Renaissance period Niccolò di Bernardo dei Machiavelli (1469-1527). Often called the father of modern political philosophy and political science, he had the following ideas and methods in mind for rulers of herds:

> "Machiavelli acknowledges that good laws and good arms constitute the dual foundations of a well-ordered political system. But, he immediately adds, since coercion creates legality, he will concentrate his attention on force. He says, "Since there cannot be good laws without good arms, I will not consider laws but speak of arms" (Prince CW 47). In other words, the legitimacy of law rests entirely upon the threat of coercive force; authority is impossible for Machiavelli as a right apart from the power to enforce it. Consequently, Machiavelli is led to conclude that fear is always preferable to affection in subjects, just as violence and deception are superior to legality in effectively controlling them."
>
> Machiavelli himself observes that:
>
> 'One can say this in general of men: they are ungrateful, disloyal, insincere and deceitful, timid of danger and avid of profit.... Love is a bond of obligation, which these miserable creatures break whenever it suits them to do so; but fear holds them fast by a dread of punishment that never passes. (Prince CW 62; translation revised)'
>
> "As a result, Machiavelli cannot really be said to have a theory of obligation separate from the imposition of power; people obey only because they fear the consequences of not doing so, whether the loss of life or of privileges. And of

course, power alone cannot obligate one, inasmuch as obligation assumes that one cannot meaningfully do otherwise." (plato.stanford.edu)

Watched the BLA uproar in the U.S. lately? No Machiavellian reprisals there, it seems. So, what's the rulers' game-plan is the question, eh?

Bernays, most likely familiar with Machiavelli's writings and drawing on Uncle Sigismund and friends' insights how to manipulate the herd, thus developed the "engineering of consent" approach to achieve their desired goals. It again provided ways and means to control and regiment the masses will without them knowing, wit COVID-19. How is it done? By appealing to the unconscious part of our minds and with all might suppress its rational side in accordance with Freud's hypothetical theory that people are motivated by unconscious desires automatically generated by the unconscious mind and unavailable/non-accessible to our conscious introspection. For his belief/theory/hypothesis no empirical first evidence exists, as even the location of the human mind is presently unknown and highly debated. That our unconscious phenomena and thought processes include memories, interests, motivations, repressed feelings, automatic skills, subliminal perceptions, automatic reactions and, possibly, complexes, hidden phobias and desires is also unproven and unprovable. Nevertheless, and although these processes are thought to exist well under the surface of our conscious awareness, the mental health profession believes them to impact our behavior

Not only that. Our unconscious mind can also be seen as the source of dreams and automatic thoughts that appear without apparent cause or reason. It may also be the repository of long-forgotten memories possibly still accessible to consciousness at a later date, and it may be the center of activity, attention, or concentration of implicit knowledge, our ability to do some things learnt without thinking, or expertly doing things we never learnt. Some learned mental health practitioners even feel that the unconscious mind surfaces in slips of the tongue and jokes, whereas others vehemently reject the idea of its existence. Some believe that psychoanalytic treatments reveal how unconscious factors' influence current human relationships and behavior patterns thus helping individuals to better deal with life while others believe it to be such treatments a completely futile exercise. All of it falls under the category of "New Science" akin to "New Normal."

Without a doubt, however, is that psychoanalysis from Freud's inception onwards served to reveal humans' unconscious mental processes and use the revelation for better or for worse on humanity. Carl Gustav Jung, Alfred Adler, Erik Erikson and others of their league explored Freud's original formula and found it hugely wanting. Scottish psychiatrist R.D. Laing, for example, maintained that psychoanalysis and psychiatry were nothing other than treating illness diagnosed by conduct and generated through pharmaceutical drugs and treated biologically which, he insisted, then encouraged the destruction of body and mind rather than instead counsel patients on how to heal their existential crises. Canadian clinical psychologist and professor of psychology at the University of Toronto Jordan Bernt Peterson in his 2011 lecture "Self-Deception in Psychopathology" maintains the same stating that the *Diagnostic and Statistical Manual of Mental Disorders* (DSM) used by clinicians and psychiatrists to diagnose psychiatric illnesses in their patients is akin to using astrology to evaluate patients state of mind. In Peterson's view most people are healthy and sane, but have problems living, which coincides with Thomas Szasz's opinion reflected in his book *The Myth of Mental Illness: Foundations of a Theory of Personal Conduct* (1961) where he argues against psychiatrists' tendency to label people who are "disabled by living" as "mentally ill". To enable clients to live, however, is far too time-consuming for most self-respecting mental health practitioners, as it cuts into profit. Therefore, as any genuine PTSD journeyer can tell you, with few exceptions mentioned above and outstanding psychiatrists such as Laurel Molcher, Peter Breggin and William Courtney, psychoanalysis went out of style mid twentieth century. (*Fallacy 1*).

Psychoanalysis is also out of line with Freud et al.'s desperate and ongoing attempt to upstage the métier as science. Proving the validity of Darwin's hypothesis described in *On the Origin of Species* seems still the all-encompassing goal. Published in 1859, this piece of purportedly scientific literature is considered to be the foundation of evolutionary biology as it introduces the theory that any and all populations, from cabs to homo sapiens evolve through multi millions of years in a process of natural selection through the survival of the fittest hypothesis one of them the idea of humans evolving from idea. This one reached its new paradigm when Jon Rappoport in 2019 stated:

> "Humans are viewed as mis-programmed biological machines in need of basic corrections. Their tendency to engage in conflict needs to be curbed. Whatever they do, say, or think that runs counter to the tight organizing of "peaceful and harmonious" society from above is, a priori, irrational and must be eradicated at the level of Mind. The necessary reprogramming would be achieved through genetic, electronic, and chemical means. Though never admitting it publicly, dyed in the wool technocrats see no reason to maintain the human population at its current level. Elimination of large numbers of "biological machines" would make their job easier. Heraldic fairy tales about "transhuman" transformation are used to put a wondrous face on technocracy. For example, we're told that soon it will be possible to connect a human brain with a super-computer and download "spiritual wisdom, knowledge, and talents" directly to the human. Technocratic premise: society itself is a game board, and someone has to be in charge; who better than engineers with an overall plan?"

Again, can you think COVID-19? And how is it that the herd believes in those who engineered it, Fauci and Gates on the surface? And how do they know how to so brilliantly blind people? You guessed it. With Freud and his cabal. 's application of psychoanalytic discoveries inherent in the human mind by the first PR engineer, nephew Edward, whose rapidly increasing popularity, influence and successes radically changed the hitherto applied persuasion tactics in political- and commercial advertising campaigns. After synthesizing elements of uncle's work with that of French polymath Charles-Marie Gustave Le Bon (1841-1931) and Wilfred Batten Lewis Trotter (1872-1939), the British pioneer in neurosurgery and explorer of the human herd instinct, Bernays' advertisement powers knew no bounds.

Le Bon, whose interest and research included anthropology, psychology, sociology, medicine, physics, in his 1895 work *The Crowd: A Study of the Popular Mind*, a seminal work of crowd- or mob psychology, claims that the following characteristics manifest in in crowd psychology:

- Impulsiveness
- Irritability
- Incapacity to reason
- The absence of judgment of the critical spirit
- The exaggeration of sentiments, and others

He also asserted that "an individual immersed for some length of time in a crowd would soon find himself, either in consequence of magnetic influence given out by the crowd or from some other cause of which *we*, the researchers and the human beings, are ignorant, in a special state much resembling the state of fascination in which hypnotized individuals find themselves in the hands of the hypnotizer (en.wikipedia.org)." As to individuals in crowds he said:

> "By the mere fact that he [the individual] forms part of an organised crowd, a man descends several rungs in the ladder of civilisation. Isolated, he may be a cultivated individual; in a crowd, he is a barbarian – that is, a creature acting by instinct. He possesses the spontaneity, the violence, the ferocity, and also the enthusiasm and heroism of primitive beings, whom he further tends to resemble by the facility with which he allows himself to be impressed by words and images – which would be entirely without action on each of the isolated individuals composing the crowd – and to be induced to commit acts contrary to his most obvious interests and his best-known habits. An individual in a crowd is a grain of sand amid other grains of sand, which the wind stirs up at will." (ibid).

Le Bon, who qualified as doctor of medicine at the University of Paris in 1866, travelled widely through Europe, Asia and North Africa analyzing the peoples and civilizations he encountered. He viewed crowds not as the sum of their individual parts, but insisted that within crowds formed a new psychological entity whose characteristics were determined by its "racial unconscious". In regard to the impact of civilizing elites and barbarian crowds on civilization he sputtered:

> "Civilisations as yet have only been created and directed by a small intellectual aristocracy, never by crowds. Crowds are only powerful for destruction. Their rule is always tantamount to a barbarian phase. A civilisation involves fixed rules, discipline, a passing from the instinctive to the rational state, forethought for the future, an elevated degree of culture – all of them conditions that crowds, left to themselves, have invariably shown themselves incapable of realising. In consequence of the purely destructive nature of their power crowds' act like those microbes, which hasten the dissolution of enfeebled or dead bodies. When the structure of a civilisation is rotten, it is always the masses that bring about its downfall (ibid)."

Would anyone mid telling it to Antifa and BLM crowds, or am I giving them too much credit for some residue intelligence? Critical of democracy and socialism Le Bon, ignored and maligned by sections of the French academic and scientific establishment due to his politically conservative and reactionary views, is said to have influenced seemingly incomparable figures such as Vladimir Ilyich Ulyanov known as Lenin, Theodore Roosevelt, Benito Mussolini, Sigmund Freud, Adolf Hitler as well as the Spanish philosopher and essayist José Ortega y Gasset active during the time when Spain oscillated between monarchy, republicanism and dictatorship during the first half of the twentieth century.

Trotter, member of the Fellowship of the Royal Society of London, was, like LeBon, known for his social psychology research, most notably for his herd instinct and crowd psychology concepts. How he thought of his compatriots and ancestor is mirrored in 2 excerpts of his 1916 work *Instincts of the Herd in Peace and War* (1942 edition p. 90):

> "It has already been pointed out how dangerous it would be to breed man for reason – that is, against suggestibility. The idea is a fit companion for the device of breeding against "degeneracy". The degenerate – that is, the mentally unstable - have demonstrated by the mere fact of instability that they possess the quality of sensitiveness to feeling and to experience, for it is this which has prevented them from applying the remedy of rationalization or exclusion when they have met with experience conflicting with the herd suggestion.
>
> "It is interesting to notice that in discussing the mechanism of psychoanalysis in liberating the 'abnormal' patient from his symptoms, Freud repeatedly lays stress on the fact that the efficient factor in the process is not the actual introduction of the suppressed experiences into the conscious field, but the overcoming of the resistances to such an endeavor. I have attempted to show that these resistances or counter-impulses are of environmental origin, and owe their strength to the specific sensitiveness of the gregarious mind. Resistances of similar type and identical origin are responsible for the formation of the so-called normal type of mind. It is a principal thesis of an earlier essay in this book that this normal type is far from being psychologically healthy, is far from rendering available the full capacity of the mind for foresight and progress, and being in exclusive command of directing power in the world, is a danger to civilization."

What constitutes normalcy is, of course, in the eye of the beholder/s. According to Trotter's first biographer, he first met Freud when 42 of Freud's followers and associates attended what Jung called the "First Congress for Freudian Psychology", a one day convocation held 1908 in Salzburg, Austria (jewishcurrents.org). The keynote speaker, Freud, pontificated for 4 hours about a patient nicknamed Rat Man due to his nightmarish fantasies about rats. Later on, he proclaimed Rat Man to be the first one he cured by way of psychoanalysis. (*Bemerkungen über einen Fall von Zwangsneurose* ['Notes Upon A Case of Obsessional Neurosis'] (1909)). This Congress for Freudian Psychology later renamed the International Psychoanalytic Congress (IPC) nowadays has 12,000 psychoanalyst members (Bush, Lawrence: The First International Psychoanalytic Congress; jewishcurrents.org). In 1909 he together with Jung, Freud and his close associate Sándor Ferenczi, a Hungarian psychoanalyst and a key theorist of the psychoanalytic school, went to Clark University in Worcester, Massachusetts, where Freud gave a series of lectures on psychoanalysis.

While keenly disliking the United States, his presence at Clark helped raise psychoanalysis to international prominence.

It was Trotter who laid down the law that modern psychology always must start from the assumption that man is social because isolated man is unknown. He then, according to his contemporary the American historian Harry Elmer Barnes (1889 – 1968) known for his historical revisionism and Holocaust denial, turned to investigate the psychology of humans' instinctive behavior. Noting that humans three primary instincts of self-preservation, nutrition and sex had been found insufficient to account for all observed varieties and characteristics of human conduct, Trotter felt that the gap could only be filled by the existence and operation of a gregarious instinct in whatever component it might be analyzed as the necessary fourth instinct to explain the difficulties and omissions otherwise arising in conjunction with explaining human nature and behaviors. It was, in his opinion, this instinctive impulse, which "reveals itself to human consciousness as an axiomatically [self-evidentially] obvious proposition as something which is so clearly "sense" that any idea of discussing its basis is foolish or wicked." (Barnes, Harry E: Some Typical Contributions of English Sociology to Political Theory; *American Journal of Sociology* Vol. 28, No. 1 (Jul. 1922) pp. 49-66; The University of Chicago Press; jstor.org.) Again, like the mind, the bare existence of both sense and instinct are hitherto scientifically and empirically unsubstantiated, thus merely hearsay.

That gregariousness, the liking of the company of others, had a very high survival value in the evolution of the animal kingdom including mankind was, in Trotter's opinion, furthermore, inferred from the fact that it was its most universal characteristic. Consequently, instead of using rattus, cani, mus and simian he studied beehives, flocks of sheep and wolf packs to substantiate his claim as humans fell under the same umbrella according of his schemata of "things." And, apparently, through his observations of those species he drew the conclusion that the whole history of man's physical and mental evolution indicated the fact that mankind, people-kind, Trudeau-Castro kind, evolved from such gregarious animals.

In 1932, however, in an address to students undertaking hospital training Trotter observed:

> "...the uniformity of thought is an increasingly apparent goal and demand of civilization. Still there burns on in most of us a small wild spark. I advise you to nourish it as a precious possession. Really to think for oneself is as strange, difficult and dangerous as any adventure. As the wise ones say, it will do you no good, but like virtue which it does not otherwise greatly resemble, it will be its own reward."

COVID-19 gives us insight into the enormous power of mind-manipulation since Trotters statement, where "the wild sparks," those who knew the scam that it was from the moment of its birth, were ostracised by those who believed everything spewed forth by the mass-media controlled by 5 conglomerates world wide. We find an earlier one with "the wild spark" in John Carpenter's documentary "They Live, " whilst Trotter himself found universal fame in the James Bond's novel: "Live and let die," when bad guy Mister Big says to James Bond:

> "You have doubtless read Trotter's *Instincts of the Herd in War and Peace,* Mister Bond. Well, I am by nature and predilection a wolf and I live by a wolf's laws. Naturally the sheep describe such a person as a 'criminal'. The fact, Mister Bond," the Big Man continued after a pause, "that I survive and indeed enjoy limitless success, although I am alone against countless millions of sheep, is attributable to the modern techniques I described to you on the occasion of our last talk, and to an infinite capacity for taking pains. Not dull, plodding pains, but artistic, subtle pains. And I find, Mister Bond, that it is not difficult to outwit sheep, however many of them there may be, if one is dedicated to the task and if one is by nature an extremely well-equipped wolf (ch. 21)."

While firsthand evidence of pure Darwinian theory as indeed being the truth is hard to come by. But Bernays ran with the concept anyway, whereas genuine PTSD journeyers have only one option. Either to become the wolf fast or succumb and be the sheep slaughtered. The choice is ours, and so is the outcome. It solely depends on our trust in the learned society's mental health professionals, among them those employed at Bernays' alma mater, the Cornell University's Weill Cornell Medicine's Department of Psychiatry, whose academic program according to its website synergizes clinical care and research at the forefront of knowledge, education and training for clinicians and investigators including PTSD (psychiatry.weill.cornell.edu). And those are the ones basically dictating its treatment nation-if not worldwide. It also depends on the honor and integrity of our employer, our union shop stewards and bosses and our peers, who in my case were all willing and able to participate in my demolition derby. Thus, they were indeed considered "normal" in deep state eyes.

Cornell's Medical College dates back to the 1890s, when it became associated with New York Hospital founded by royal charter granted by King George III in 1771. It began serving psychiatric patients in 1791, the first New York City hospital with a separate facility offering progressive humane treatment for the mentally ill to do so. It's mission statement?

> "Our mission is to provide outstanding clinical care [to] our patients, cutting-edge research to expand our understanding of the mind for the future benefit of patients, and the finest education available for the psychiatrists of tomorrow, in collaborative partnership with our affiliates."

How to gather first empirical evidence about the mind's existence never mind location is nowhere mentioned. Still, its Psychiatry Specialty Center offers assessment and treatment of psychiatric disorders including PTSD as well as medication management, psychotherapy, couples' counseling, family therapy, group therapy as well as neuropsychological and educational testing. Cornell's overall breadth of study furthermore includes interdisciplinary research in nanotechnology, biotechnology, supercomputing and genomics with methods of studying the brain, neuroimaging, neuroscience and genetics presented in depth in *Fallacy I* in conjunction with Weill's PTSD Headstrong project.

With uncle Sigismund lingering/hovering in the background, one could deduce that nephew Bernays partook in a few of Cornell's psychology department's undergraduate classes to fulfill his graduation requirements. He kept up a warm relationship with his famous uncle visiting him in Europe as well as spending time with him on his 1909 United

States visit. We are told that he played up his connection to uncle Freud at every given opportunity (Greenberg, David: Republic of Spin: An Inside History of the American Presidency ch.18). This kinship gave Barneys a mystique as if he possessed some family secret working magic on the unconscious, resulting in Journalist Henry Pringle calling him Bernays a "Mass Psychologist."

Bernays pioneered the public relations industry's use of psychology and other social sciences to design its public persuasion campaigns exclaiming: "If we understand the mechanism and motives of the group mind, is it not possible to control and regiment the masses according to our will without their knowing about it? The recent practice of propaganda has proved that it is possible, at least up to a certain point and within certain limits." (Bernays, Edward (2005) [1928]. *Propaganda*. Brooklyn, N.Y: Ig Pub. p. 47.) This is the previously mentioned scientific technique of opinion-moulding he later called engineering of consent, which he explained such:

> "This phrase quite simply means the use of an engineering approach—that is, action based only on thorough knowledge of the situation and on the application of scientific principles and tried practices to the task of getting people to support ideas and programs." (Bernays, Edward L. (March 1947). "The Engineering of Consent" (PDF). *Annals of the American Academy of Political and Social Science*. 250 (1): 113–20 at p. 114.)

Bernays expanded on the American reporter and political commentator Walter Lippman's concept of stereotype when arguing that predictable elements could be manipulated for mass effects. He said:

> "But instead of a mind, universal literacy has given [the common man, the slob, the deplorable, the sheeple] a rubber stamp, a rubber stamp inked with advertising slogans, with editorials, with published scientific data, with the trivialities of tabloids and the profundities of history, but quite innocent of original thought. Each man's rubber stamp is the twin of millions of others, so that when these millions are exposed to the same stimuli, all receive identical imprints. [...] The amazing readiness with which large masses accept this process is probably accounted for by the fact that no attempt is made to convince them that black is white. Instead, their preconceived hazy ideas that a certain gray is almost black or almost white are brought into sharper focus. Their prejudices, notions, and convictions are used as a starting point, with the result that they are drawn by a thread into passionate adherence to a given mental picture (Bernays, "The Minority Rules" (1927), pp. 150, 151; cited in Marks (1957), p. 116.)

This is what is disclosed when completing the Minnesota Multiphasic Personality Inventory, the MMPI. And through that volunteered information you willingly disclose due to your ignorance the hidden aspects of your personality. Therefore anyone dealing with you at the VA, WCB, Union of Insurance and assigned mental health professionals due to your genuine PTSD affliction can play you like a fiddle to destroy you preferable by committing suicide. Sociology according to Bernays also plays an important role for public relations counsel, as he views the individual as "a cell organized into the social unit. Touch a nerve at a sensitive spot and you get an automatic response from certain specific members of the organism(ibid)."

From the moment of opening the firm Edward L. Bernays, Council on Public Relations with his Barnard College educated wife Doris Elsa Fleischman (1891–1980), by his side shortly after returning from the Versailles 1919 peace conference he vigorously pronounced to be elevating his PR activities into a profession *and* a science. And similar to the mental health profession, he never made clear what was scientific or professional about it. Instead, he let his intuition and his innate cleverness guide him while tossing about the terms science, professional and counsel, the basic elements of his salesmanship, thus giving his enterprise an air of methodical efficacy. He hit the jackpot when conveying the purported respectability and stature of the legal profession by describing himself as *counsel on public relations* explaining that America's size and heterogeneity made it necessary for a proponent of a point of view to engage PR experts to represent that view before society to influence politics, effect social change and lobby for gender and racial equality.

We learn that the herd should be targeted as members of "inter-lapping groups" involving different aspects of their identity. Silk, for example, should be represented as fashionable to women's clubs, artistic to art-lovers, and historically interesting subjects to schools. Highlighting the correct group identity for the purpose at hand would be much more effective than trying to change the stance of an individual group. Emphasizing changing external conditions such as new technology would also be effective. Universal instincts such as self-preservation and sex could usually be invoked when paired with instinct-emotion, flight-fear, revulsion-disgust, pugnacity-anger, all of which we see successfully applied in the COVID-19 manufactured herd hysteria induced scamdemic. (ibid.pp. 146–153). A public relations counsel must also generate news *no matter what the medium which broadcasts this news*. And the PR counsel must lift startling facts from his whole subject and present them as news regardless if true or false as well as isolate ideas and develop them into events so that they claim attention as news and be more readily understood by the herd, the slobs and the deplorable useless eaters of all colors, shapes and nationalities worldwide.

Walter Lippman (1889–1974), Bernays' contemporary unacknowledged American mentor, with his work *The Phantom Public* greatly influenced the ideas Bernays expressed in *Propaganda* (Stephen Bender, LewRockwell.com: Karl Rove & the Spectre of Freud's Nephew.) When observing the mass media's fake-news expertise in manipulating the herd into lockdown, hysteria and suicidal ideation due to a non-existent pandemic, we know that Bernays still runs the show even from the grave. We also know that it is child's play for anyone worth his or her salt in the mental health professional to drive a genuine PTSD journeyer into suicide as the technique is the same as driving the herd presently alive into hysteria over nothing.

7

BERNAYS' MAGICKAL MIND MANIPULATION SUCCESSES

Why do you want to know about Bernays' magickal mind manipulation successes? Because it all ties in with the multitude of present-day non-profit society's sucking on the PTSD suicide prevention tit. They do nothing for you, the genuine PTSD experiencers. They do everything to feather their own financial nests and keep the golden goose in it alive while you linger in abject psychological misery. While you oftentimes suffer in poverty due to unconscionable PTSD treatments brought about by hypotheses, theories and hallucinations dreamed up by the mental health mind-manipulating craft for their own profit. Not only that, they also made sure that huge stigma is attached to genuine PTSD experiencers throughout their ranks, be it airline crew members, firefighters, police officers, soldiers or veterans. The foundation for their spectacular successes on everything associated with PTSD is based on principles developed by Freud et al. beginning in the late 1900s.

Once we know how these Freudian principles operate it is much easier to discern how the truth is spun and perverted. One favorite method is to present multiple controversial aspects of the same topic. This creates what the American cognitive psychologist Leon Festinger (1919-1989) termed cognitive dissonance. This situation occurs when people hold, *are presented with* or participate in actions based on two or more contradictory beliefs, ideas or moral values. In his work *A Theory of Cognitive Dissonance* (Stanford, CA: Stanford University Press, 1957) Festinger proposes that under such circumstance humans attempt to release this stress-creating situation and live in the real world as opposed to the abstract, theoretical and/or idealized sphere of classrooms and laboratories. So, they automatically strive to create emotional balance and consistency within, a seemingly basic innate process in human behavior. This can be observed in a multitude of contexts (PsycINFO Database Record (c) 2016 APA). In effect, the desire to absolve or reduce cognitive dissonance is so strong that it can be seen as much as an antecedent condition leading to an activity oriented toward dissonance-reduction or elimination as hunger leads to an activity oriented toward hunger reduction and elimination. Both are done for one purpose only: to create psychological and/or physical equilibrium within the Self. In psychological jargon, this is termed "the principle of cognitive consistency" (Am. Pych. Ass. Psychnet.org).

Does conscious cognitive dissonance reduction or elimination work? First evidence is missing. What is known to the learned in the field, however, is that people finding themselves in states of confusion of beliefs or ethical quagmires will take steps to remedy their psychological upheaval. They will search for the truth in matters creating cognitive dissonance within themselves. In so doing, they follow St. Thomas Aquinas' observation:

> "The Study of philosophy is not that we may know what men have thought, but what the truth of things, which can only be perceived through thinking."
> (Thomas Aquinas (AC 1225-1274), *Summa Theologica*, 5 Vols)

This innate drive to create and maintain peace and harmony within the Self, is why people shut down and accept everything presented "as is" on television. The same tactics are applied to genuine PTSD journeyers. Here they are propagated by cognitive behavioral PTSD treatment (CBT) combined with drugs of all genres. They are administered with just one goal: to create cognitive dissonance to such a degree as to drive the affected into suicide, the only way to create homeostasis and the cheapest for the employer. If unsuccessful, he or she will be harassed to the point of throwing in the towel. Or they will disappear, unable to cope with the perpetual cognitive dissonance and an overwhelming desire for peace, regardless if it is against their own best interest. For many genuine PTSD experiencers, it means life on skid row.

Now you have an idea how Bernays with Freud et al, since the early 1900s the trendsetters and educators of all who followed them, warped the minds of billions. To acquire this knowledge enhances your Dharma. And it prevents you from being drawn into the mental hell created for you by those you trust to help in your recovery. Not only that, your genuine PTSD experience demands you to learn. It is your primary duty, obligation and necessity, if you ever again want to live a contented and peaceful life.

In Bernays' magickal mind manipulation successes, cognitive dissonance played a huge role. It all began with Sigismund Schlomo Freud. In the autumn of 1902, he realized his long-time ambition of being made "professor extraordinarius" at the University of Vienna, Austria. No salary or teaching duties were attached to the title, but his recognition and prestige were secured. So, he merely continued his regular weekly lectures on his work. He had delivered these to audiences at the university's psychiatric clinic's lecture hall every Saturday evening since the mid-1880s. He also invited those Viennese physicians interested in his research with the mentally ill to meet at his apartment every Wednesday afternoon to discuss issues relating to psychology and neuropathology. (Schwartz, Joseph:

Cassandra's daughter: a history of psychoanalysis. London: Karnac. 2003; p. 100.) He named it the "Wednesday Psychological Society" (Psychologische Mittwochs-Gesellschaft), a gathering that marked the start of the psychoanalytic movement worldwide. Its findings on humans' psychological make-up would be applied in the U.S. by Freud's nephew Edward L. Bernays as its commercial spearhead.

Bernays took the first step into his career shortly after his Cornell graduation in 1912. He and school friend Fred Robinson became co-editors of the *Medical Review of Reviews and Dietetic and Hygienic Gazette*. They distributed thousands of free copies to physicians across the country. Whilst thus engaged in 1913, he came across the screenplay *Damaged Goods* (Les Avaries) by French author Eugene Brieux. It was about a man who had contracted syphilis from his mistress, but married another woman anyway. Already banned in Paris and London in the early 1900s, New York's clergy and police also opposed its production (Dawn B. Sova: *Banned Plays: Censorship Histories of 125 Stage Dramas*, p. 70-71). The Norwegian playwright Henrik Ibsen's play *Ghosts* was staged in Chicago, Illinois, by a Danish company in 1892. Due to its references to religion, incest, euthanasia and venereal disease, it had created an uproar. Brieux's main character wrestling with physical and social ramifications of syphilis after an affair would seem no better, either financially or morally.

In stepped Bernays. Immediately recognizing that to create interest in *Damaged Goods* he had to transform its ethical and moral controversy into a cause célèbre. So, he sought backers who were already public role models by publishing a review of the play in *Medical Reviews*. This propelled acclaimed New York actor Richard Bennett (1870 - 1944) to produce the play. Bernays underwrote the production. To raise the necessary funds, he formed a *Medical Review of Reviews* Sociological Fund Committee. He knew this would attract members by playing on Bennett's reputation as an artist and emphasizing the worthiness of battling prudishness (John Doorley; Helio Fred Garcia: Reputation Management: The Key to Successful Public Relations and Corporate ... Rourledge 3rd edition 2015). He also invited distinguished men and women to support venereal disease prevention by joining the Sociological Fund Committee (for $4 each). Before long, the Committee included:

- Reverend John Haynes Holmes
- John D. Rockefeller, Senior and Junior
- Franklin Delano Roosevelt and Eleanor Roosevelt
- Mrs. William K. Vanderbilt and Anne Harriman Sands Rutherford Vanderbilt

This was the cream of the crop of New York society. Rockefeller Sr. stated:

> "The evils that spring from prosecution [of prostitution] cannot be understood until frank discussion [of it] has been made possible."

New York's theatre world was electrified. Not since the New-York Manumission Society of 1785, had anyone else managed to assemble such a distinguished front group for any society or club. It was founded by John Jay (first justice of the Supreme Court). And by Alexander Hamilton (1757 or 1755- 1804), one of the Founding Fathers of the United States, legal scholar, military commander, lawyer, banker and economist. And by lawyer and politician Aaron Burr Jr. (1756 -1836), third U.S. vice president during President Thomas Jefferson's 1801 to 1805 term.

Bernays breathed through the second issue if the show would be allowed to proceed, with equal ease. He knew full well that then-secretary of the New York Society for the Suppression of Vice Anthony Comstock had closed shows he thought too daring. *Mrs. Warren's Profession* by Irish playwright, critic, polemicist and political activist George Bernard Shaw (1856-1959) was among them.

Bernays was clever. He contacted the press with news of the show's ongoing rehearsals and asked the distinguished members of the Sociological Fund Committee to give press-interviews. The result? *Damaged Goods* presented on March 14th, 1913, in New York's Fulton Theatre before members of the Sociological Fund. It became a roaring success. From audience, press and pulpit alike, it was acclaimed to be the greatest contribution ever made by the stage to the cause of humanity (www.marxists.org). Savage criticisms were ignored or simply shaken off as inane utterances by the ignorant.

By late April 1913, the play had reached acceptance as a serious *clinical study* important to the ultimate welfare of any community. It was touted as giving clearer understanding of the laws of health and setting higher standards of morality.

Clinical studies are used by researchers and scientists to evaluate new medical, surgical or behavioral interventions and treatments for the herd. The studies are meant to determine if they are safe, effective or less harmful than those already on the market. The successful production of *Damaged Goods,* was just the beginning for the 22-year-old college graduate in agriculture. He brilliantly engineered the opening act of the making of the American mind, but it did not end in New York.

To ensure the play's official acceptance and its future productions throughout the US, Bernays and Bennett arranged for a special performance at Washington DC's National Theatre. Who attended?

- clergy
- the diplomatic corps
- US Supreme Court judges
- US members of Congress (both houses)
- President Woodrow Wilson's (1856-1924) cabinet
- other prominent and influential people

The theatre was crowded to overflowing with the most distinguished audience of the foremost men and women assembled in the capitol (Cutlip, Scott M: The *Unseen Power: Public Relations: A History;* Lawrence Erlbaum Associates, Publ. 1994). All wholeheartedly endorsed the play. Thus encouraged, Bennett and Barneys promoted it throughout the US. They advanced the ruse that those wanting to see their community prosper with higher standard of morality and laws of health had to see it.

Bernays et al. were jubilant. Creating a front-group such as the Sociological Fund Committee became standard in almost all his operations throughout his career. Indeed, it became one of advertising's fundamental techniques. We see it in such innocuous sounding groups as the antinuclear Safe Energy Communication Council. We see it also in the pronuclear Eagle Alliance. We see it in the Coalition Against Regressive Taxation, which is actually about the trucking industry (Doorley & Garcia). It is even used to portray suicides in soldiers and veterans to create non-profit 503 (c) organizations. This creates jobs and income for the mental health profession, while psychologically, and therefore also physically, destroying genuine PTSD experiencers. But this came later.

In 1915, Bernays got busy as press agent for Sergei Pavlovich Diaghilev (1872 - 1929). He was a Russian ballet impresario and founder of the Ballets Russes. This was the most influential ballet company of the twentieth century due to its ground-breaking artistic collaborations among prime choreographers, composers, designers and dancers. Completely reinvigorating performing dance in Europe, in 1916/17 it was scheduled to go on tour in the US. Diaghilev engaged Bernays to convince Americans that to watch ballet was the greatest fun ever so that ticket-sales would skyrocket. But cultural differences and monetary difficulties dictated otherwise; Bernays' efforts were much less rewarding than those with *Damaged Goods*. (Hanna Järvinen: Failed Impressions: Diaghilev's Ballets Russes in America, 1916; *Dance Research Journal* Vol. 42, No. 2 pp. 77-108; jstor.org)

Nevertheless, Bernays' fame spread. He represented famous Italian tenor Enrico Caruso (1873 -1921) between 1917 and 1919. And he worked for the Creel Committee, known as the Committee on Public Information (or CPI). This independent agency of the government of the United States was created to influence public opinion in support of U.S. participation in World War I. Its chairman was George Edward Creel (1876-1953), a journalist with years of experience on the *Denver Post* and the *Rocky Mountain News.* Before accepting his CPI appointment by President Woodrow Wilson, he wrote to Bernays' draft board requesting permission to engage him. Later on, Creel would urge Wilson to create a government agency for the coordination of propaganda in the true sense of the word: the "propagation of faith." This independent agency allowed the U.S. Government to maintain the separation of church and state. The committee was designed only to persuade the American herd to support America's entrance into WW I. It was the first covertly existing state bureau in the history of the United States covering propaganda. Besides chairman Creel its committee consisted of the following U.S. Government *ex officio* members:

- Secretary of State Robert Lansing, who served as Counsellor to the State Department at the outbreak of World War I, Secretary of State from 1915 to 1920, and Secretary of War from 1916 to 1921
- Newton Diehl Baker Jr.
- Josephus Daniels , Secretary of the U.S. Navy during World War I, diplomat and newspaper publisher

Between April 1917 and June 1919 Bernays used every medium available to create herd-enthusiasm for the war. He enlisted public support against the foreign and perceived domestic attempts to stop America's participation in the war. In so doing, Bernays counteracted his own Wilson-for-re-election campaign slogan 'He Kept Us Out Of War'. That slogan had played an important part in his winning the election, by beautifully leading the American herd around like a bull by his horns. So perfectly was it done that the U.S. Council on Foreign Relations in 1949 credited the Creel Committee, i.e. Bernays, with creating "the most efficient engine of war propaganda which the world had ever seen", ... a "revolutionary change" in public attitude toward U.S. participation in WWI (Harold J. Tobin and Percy W. Bidwell, *Mobilizing Civilian America*, New York: Council on Foreign Relations, pp75-76).

After the sacrificial slaughter of WWI ended in 1918, Bernays formed part of the CPI's sixteen-person publicity group attending the 1919 Paris Peace Conference. The publicly announced object of the expedition?

> "To interpret the work of the Peace Conference by keeping up a worldwide propaganda to disseminate American accomplishments and ideals."

So reported the newspaper *New York World*, a leading national voice of the Democratic Party published in New York City from 1860 until 1931. Bernays himself later said about his work for the CPI:

> "There was one basic lesson I learned in the CPI—that efforts comparable to those applied by the CPI to affect the attitudes of the enemy, of neutrals, and people of this country could be applied with equal facility to peacetime pursuits. In other words, what could be done for a nation at war could be done for organizations and people in a nation at peace (Cutlip, Scott: *The Unseen Power: Public Relations: A History*, Lawrence Erlbaum Associates, 1994, p. 168)."

After his stunt with the CPI, he was hired by the U.S. War Department to persuade private businesses to hire returning war veterans. And the Lithuanian government engaged him to pursue its recognition by the United States. General Electric, Procter & Gamble, the American Tobacco Company, media outlets like CBS and politicians followed. In 1920, he successfully hosted the first convention of the National Association for the Advancement of Coloured People (NAACP). This non-profit organization was based in Atlanta, Georgia. Formed in 1909 as a bi-racial endeavour to advance justice for African Americans, this group included such notable personalities as:

- American sociologist, socialist, historian, civil rights activist, Pan-Africanist, author, writer and editor William Edward Burghardt Du Bois (1868 - 1963)
- American suffragist and journalist Mary White Ovington (1865 - 1951), whose parents were women's rights supporters involved in the anti-slavery movement
- American *lawyer*, publicist and civil rights leader Moorfield Storey (1845-1929)
- Ida Bell Wells-Barnett (1862-1931), an investigative journalist, educator and early civil rights movement leader

In this campaign, Bernays focused on contributions African-Americans had made to Whites living in the South. As no violence erupted, the convention was declared a success. *Today, the NCAAP is the nation's largest civil rights organization. IT has more than half-a-million members and supporters worldwide advocating for civil rights. It leads grassroots campaigns for equal opportunity and conducts voter mobilization.* Its twenty-first-century mission statement conveys:

> "The mission of the National Association for the Advancement of Colored People (NAACP) is to secure the political, educational, social, and economic equality of rights in order to eliminate race-based discrimination and ensure the health and well-being of all persons (naacp.org)."

I guess Whites can beat the dust.

In 1924, Bernays, Uncle Sigismund and his cabal put their knowledge into political practice again. Politician and lawyer John Calvin Coolidge Jr. (1872 - 1923) succeeded to the presidency when President Warren G. Harding (1865-1923) suddenly keeled over with a heart attack. To counterattack Coolidge's wooden image, the folksy approach was adopted. Pancake breakfasts with vaudevillians and Broadway performers were organized. White House concerts with Lithuanian-American singer, comedian and actor Al Jolson (1896-1950) were arranged. This was one of the first overt publicity stunts for a U.S. presidential campaign. Coolidge won whilst Bernays taught the first PR course in world history at New York University. Brilliant for a 1912 Cornell BA graduate in agriculture. But never mind.

In 1928, American Tobacco Company President George Washington Hill knocked on Bernays' door. He wanted help converting women into fervent smokers. So Bernays ran to Freud's buddy Brill, who clarified the societal perceptions discouraging women from smoking for him. He added that for feminists, cigarettes were like "torches of freedom" symbolizing nonconformity and freedom from purportedly male oppression. Bernays, a fast study, used "Torches of Freedom" as his American Tobacco Company slogan. Thus, he equated woman smoking in public with their liberation and emancipation (1929 *Torches of Freedom*, The Museum of Public Relations, archived from the original on July 15, 2014)". Then he asked a lady-friend to find a group of women willing to march in New York City's Easter Day parade and to inform the press that these women's rights marchers would themselves be lightning up "Torches of Freedom" at the event.

To understand this strike of genius, one needs to know that from the 1880s through the 1950s, New York's Easter parade was one of the main cultural expressions of Easter in the United States. The seeds of the parade were sown in New York's highly ornamented churches—Gothic buildings such as Trinity Episcopal Church, St. Patrick's Cathedral and St. Thomas Episcopal Church. In the mid- nineteenth century, they began decorating their sanctuaries with Easter flowers. As the practice expanded, the floral displays grew ever more elaborate and soon became defining examples of style, taste, abundance and novelty. Those who attended the churches incorporated these values into their dress. In 1873, a newspaper report about Easter at Christ Church said:

> "More than half the congregation were ladies, who displayed all the gorgeous and marvelous articles of dress... and the appearance of the body of the church thus vied in effect and magnificence with the pleasant and tasteful array of flowers which decorated the chancel."

By the 1880s, the Easter parade had become a vast spectacle of fashion and religious observance famous around the country. It was an after-church cultural event for the well-to-do to be decked out in new and fashionable clothing. They would stroll from their own church to others to see the impressive flowers and be seen by fellow strollers. People from the poorer and middle classes observed the parade from the sidelines. By 1890, the procession held such an important place on New York's calendar of festivities that it had taken on its enduring designation as "the Easter parade". As the parade and the holiday together became more important, dry goods merchants and milliners publicized the promotion of their wares, which linked an endless array of merchandise to the parade. By 1900, it was as important in retailing as the Christmas season. In addition, cranks and demagogues used the parade to attract public attention and to plead their causes. In 1933, American songwriter Irving Berlin graced it with the song "Easter Parade". It was based on a melody originally written in 1917 under the title "Smile and Show Your Dimple" as a "cheer up" song for a girl whose man has gone off to fight in World War I.

As said as done. The women showed up, marched, and lit up their cigarettes at a predestined spot. Eager photographers clicked away with *The New York Times* of April 1, 1929, printing: "Group of Girls Puff at Cigarettes as a Gesture of 'Freedom'. The seed was planted, the rest history. It assured splendid business. Some 300-chemicals were added over the course of time to assure both dependency and illness for millions around the world. Those chemicals also assured huge profits for the tobacco industry, as well as the medical, pharmaceutical and mental health industries. Hurrah for the good times.

Bernays moved on to promote *Light's Golden Jubilee*. This event celebrated the 50th anniversary of Thomas Edison's invention of the light bulb. Publicity elements included a special-issue postage stamp and Edison "re-creating" the invention of the light bulb for a nationwide radio audience. That an incandescent light bulb had been invented earlier by the British physicist, chemist and inventor Sir Joseph Wilson Swan FRS (1828 –1914) was of no consequence to the counsel of public relations. His incandescent lights were used to illuminate homes and public buildings, including the Savoy Theatre, London in 1881. When the goal is to make the American mind, you merely tell the herd what you want them to know, not what they ought to know. In 1954, by the way, there was a follow-up event for the 75th anniversary. Movie mogul David O. Selznick produced *Light's Diamond Jubilee*, which was broadcast on all four American TV networks.

Bernays worked with Procter & Gamble to convince people that Ivory-brand bar soap was medically superior to other soaps. He promoted Ivory through sculpting and floating contests, claiming it floated better than its competitors.

In the 1930s, Bernays wanted to convince women that Lucky Strike cigarettes' forest green package was the most fashionable of all colors letters. His staff wrote to interior and fashion designers, department stores and prominent women of society. They pushed green as the new hot color for the season. Balls, gallery exhibitions and window displays all featured green after Bernays got through with them. Green became the most popular color for the 1934 season and Lucky Strike kept its green pack color and female clientele.

Besides his front group and overt act creations, Bernays favored expert testimonials. He knew that the herd habitually tailored its opinions in accordance with the judgment of purportedly uninvolved and disinterested parties. He called those individuals "group leaders". To promote his clients' causes, he would either find or invent them. For the bacon industry wanting increased sales, he enlisted doctors to tout hearty breakfasts. To promote Dixie cups, he created an "institute" or committee on sanitary food and drink, which called for the use for sanitary reasons. By linking imagery of the overflowing cup with subliminal images of vaginas and venereal disease, he convinced consumers that only Dixie cups were sanitary and safe to use. He also marketed to people wanting to improve their lives, getting them to jump on board new trends to avoid being viewed as backwards or left behind. "This is the sanitary age -- the age of Dixie cups."

The success was overwhelming.

So was his 1939-40 New York World's Fair promotion. Held at Flushing Meadows-Corona Park in Queens, New York, it was the second most expensive American world's fair of all time. It was exceeded only by St. Louis's 1904 Louisiana Purchase Exposition. During two seasons, over 44 million people attended. It's opening slogan? Obama's "Dawn of a New Day… the world of tomorrow".

Bernays heavily and simultaneously engaging in both the U.S. and the Third Reich's war propaganda before and during WW II. When it was over, Bernays began in earnest to use in peace what he had so brilliantly used to manage the U.S. entrance into the slaughter of both wars despite public opposition. He began PR work for the then notorious American now-multinational corporation United Fruit Company. It operated in exploitive quasi neo-colonial style on the Caribbean coast of Colombia and Ecuador, the West Indies, Guatemala and other Central American countries. This was brilliantly described by 1982 Nobel Prize winner in literature Gabriel García Márquez (1927-2014) in "One Hundred Years of Solitude." Márquez writes how the company "changed the pattern of the rains, accelerated the cycle of harvests and moved the river from where it had always been." It imported "dictatorial foreigners" and "hired assassins with machetes" to run the town; it unleashed a "wave of bullets" on striking workers in the plaza. When the Banana Company leaves, Macondo is "in ruins." According to John Stauber 's and Sheldon Rampton's review of Larry Tye's biography *The Father of Spin: Edward L. Bernays & The Birth of PR*, the term 'banana republic' actually originated in reference to United Fruit's domination of corrupt governments in Guatemala and other Central American countries." originating in the term Banana Republic born by Costa Rica, Honduras and Guatemala.

United Fruit, by the way, merged with American Seal-Kap Company (AMK) in 1970. AMK was controlled by Polish-born American businessman E. M. Black and making caps for milk bottles. Together, they became the United Brands Company (teemakes.com). In 1984, Carl Henry Lindner Jr. (1919 -2011) stepped in. He was an American businessman from Norwood, Ohio, worth an estimated $2.3 billion. He transformed United Brands into the present-day Chiquita Brands International.

After his semi-retirement in the 1960s, Bernays worked with the pro-health, anti-smoking lawyer John Francis Banzhaf III (1940-). He was an American public interest lawyer, legal activist and law professor at George Washington University Law School. Banzhaf was the founder of the anti-smoking advocacy group Action on Smoking and Health (ASH). He is noted for his advocacy and use of lawsuits as a method to promote what he believes to be in the public interest.

Bernays also helped the Aluminum Company of America (Alcoa) and other special interest groups to convince the American public that water fluoridation was safe and beneficial to human health, although it is detrimental to it. This was achieved by using the American Dental Association in a highly successful media campaign.

He also convinced the public that bacon and eggs was the true all-American breakfast.

Bernays called for a focus group to learn why housewives did not want to buy instant cake mixes. He secured and heightened cake mix sales by adding a symbolic egg to the list of necessary ingredients.

Until 1948, he did all this with Polish born psychiatrist Abraham Arden Bril's help. Mind you, United Fruit Company's modus operandi is still considered the archetypal example of the influence of a multinational corporation on internal politics of any given country. Its tactics are presently applied with expertise in the agricultural affairs of Chile and Peru, for example. There, the poor work for pennies and have barely enough to eat, other than coca leaves, while those owning the land live high on their labour. And, like with the COVID-19 fraud perpetrated upon mankind, the slobs accept it without braying due to expert PR originating from 1902 onwards to present day.

Ann Douglas is Parr Professor Emerita of English and Comparative Literature at Columbia University, New York, N.Y. She writes in her book *Terrible Honesty: Mongrel Manhattan in the 1920's* (Farrar, Straus & Giroux) that it was during that era that Freud was the chosen mentor of Madison Avenue. She explains that it was Edward Bernays, the father of public relations, who orchestrated the commercialization of a culture. It was he who was the self-conscious popularizer of Freud's thoughts. It was he who incorporated the literature from social science and psychological manipulation and examined techniques of public communication into in his book *Propaganda*. And it was in that book that he explored and revealed the psychology behind the manipulation of the masses. He showed the enormous ability to use symbols and symbolic action and propaganda to influence and affect politics and social change as well as lobby for gender and racial equality (archive.nytimes.com). In his 1928 seminal work, *Propaganda*, he tells us how to go about it whilst arguing that PR is a necessity, not a gimmick. In his view:

> "The conscious and intelligent manipulation of the organized habits and opinions of the masses is an important element in democratic society. Those who manipulate this unseen mechanism of society constitute an invisible government, which is the true ruling power of our country. We are governed, our minds are moulded, our tastes formed, and our ideas suggested, largely by men we have never heard of.... It is they who pull the wires that control the public mind (ibid)."

Here we are, 90 years later. Mass media has expanded a 1000-fold in the hands of five owners. The herd's television mind-programming is tuned to almost unfathomable levels of perfection. The herd engages with the Facebook et al crowd. And you think you have one single thought in your feeble little head originating from your own brain? You think that they are unable to implant suicidal desires into you regardless of state of mind, with or without pharmaceutical mind-altering drug consumption or anything else for that matter? Think again. You still watch television? You still believe your PTSD condition continues due to your deficiencies and because the self-proclaimed experts in the field say so? You do? I rest my case.

Uncle Sigismund Schlomo et al. engaged in everything associated with human behaviour for decades. They discovered all they could about human nature and propensities during their psychoanalytical sessions with subjects wherever they could find them, from prisons to insane asylum. Even nephew Edward's role in his most extreme political propaganda activities were carried out under the guise of being conducted on behalf of the U.S. government. However, it was with his help that the 1954 Guatemalan coup d'état was a success. Code-named *Operation PBSUCCESS*, it was a covert operation carried out by the U.S. Central

Intelligence Agency that deposed the democratically elected Guatemalan President Jacobo Árbenz and ended the Guatemalan Revolution of 1944–1954. See *Operation PBSUCCESS* or view the BBC's documentary *The Century of the Self.*

In his quest to promote himself, his trade and his clients, Bernays wrote prolifically. He claimed that the nature of PR work went far beyond the production and distribution of handouts. And indeed, it did, if one wants to go deeper. Everything revolves around it. Simultaneously he aimed at dispelling fears of PR's malignancy and to minimize, cloak and disguise its phenomenal power. He did this by suggesting that the PR man neither imposed ideas on the population nor did it aim to discover its opinions on anything, but only wanted to find existing points of alignments between clientele objectives and potential customers. Successful public relations, he stressed, depended on policies and practices that gave people what they wanted without requiring distortion or deception. In his book *Propaganda: The Public Mind In The Making*, he stated that that power in a modern democracy resides with:

> "The relative small number of persons who...understand the mental processes and social patterns of the masses...[and] who pull the wires which control the public mind...The conscious and intelligent manipulation of the organized habits and opinions of the masses is an important element in democratic society... Those who manipulate this unseen mechanism of society constitute an invisible government which is the true ruling power of our country."

Bingo.

And you doubt that this invisible power and ruling mechanism has the power to enfold anyone into the voluntary adaptation of suicidal ideation or shots of any sort, called "vaccination"? If you do, David Greenberg's *Republic of Spin: An Inside History of the American Presidency* may help you understand how we, the human herd, are with Machiavellian expertise led into our own destruction. Meanwhile, we'll try to learn more about how this psychological warfare against humanity is waged.

8

PSYCHOLOGICAL WARFARE AGAINST THE HERD

As we recall, it dawned upon American Tobacco Company's president George W. Hill in the early 1920s that he was losing an enormous amount of money because smoking in public was taboo. So, he hired Bernays to twist puffing away in full view of God and sundry into a most fashionable fad. Bernays, in turn, ran for help to uncle Sigismund's close buddy Abraham Arden Brill (1874 -1948), who explained matters of human persuasion techniques to him. It was easy, as he lived right there in New York, jowl to cheek with Bernays. But whence did he spring and how and from whom did he acquire his knowledge?

In the 1920s, smoking was rare among women. However, passage of the 19th Amendment ushered in new freedoms, and smoking in public became symbolic of women's new role in society. American Tobacco taps into the women's cigarette market with the marketing slogan "Reach for a Lucky instead of sweet." (tobaccoexhibits.musc.edu/?page_id=1490).

Brill was born in the Polish hamlet Kańczuga. He was the son of a non-commissioned officer in the Austrian Army who served with Maximilian I in Mexico. Spending his childhood in Austria, Brill all by his sweet lonesome at the tender age of 15 immigrated to the United States in 1889 with as good as no money. At least that's how the story goes. To support himself, the poor boy slaved away on we do not what to get through American high school and college, graduating in 1901 from New York University with a Bachelor of Philosophy. Three years later he received his M.D. degree from the College of Physicians and Surgeons, Columbia University, all financed by himself through work unknown.

The New York [Psychiatric] State Hospital at Central Islip was one of four major hospital *farms* in central Long Island, N.Y. Almost instantaneously, by ways, means, coincidences, pure good old fortune or fate, it hired Brill as assistant physician psychiatrist under the tutelage of Swiss psychiatrist Adolph Meyer. Meyer was co-founder of the American Psychoanalytical Association (APsaA) and later ruler of Johns Hopkins psychiatry department. The other co-founder was his fellow compatriot, the neuro-pathologist and clinician Charles August Hoch (1868–1919). The latter had immigrated to the U.S. at the tender age of 19 to pursue his medical education. Between 1893 and 1894, he returned to Europe to study in the laboratories of:

- Friedrich von Recklinghausen, a pathologist at the University of Strasbourg,
- Wilhelm Wundt, a psychologist at the University of Leipzig;
- Emil Kraepelin, a psychiatrist at the University of Heidelberg, revisiting the latter in 1897.

Between 1910 and 1917, Hoch would become the third director of New York's State Psychiatric Institute and APsaA president between 1913–14 (https://apsa.org).

But Brill, during his tenancy at Islip between 1904 and 1907, seemed to mostly have enjoyed the company of the asylum's inmates rather than his overseers. It was founded in 1887 as an experimental farm colony of the New York City Lunatic Asylum Housing for the mentally ill, which would be in operation until 1996. Only 49 male and 40 female patients were admitted in 1889 for the purpose of providing them with "O&O" (Occupation and Oxygen) and "R&R" (Rest and Relaxation). By 1955, their number had ballooned to 10,000, making it the U.S. 's second biggest psychiatric hospital after Pilgrim State Hospital Pilgrim was a state-run psychiatric hospital located in Brentwood, New York, and the largest psychiatric institution ever to exist in the United States, packing in 13,875 patients at its peak in 1954.

By 1907, Brill seems to have saved enough money for an educational trip to Paris. He studied there with Pierre Marie Félix Janet (1859–1947), a pioneering French psychologist, physician, philosopher and psychotherapist in the field of dissociation and traumatic memory. From there, he moved on to Zurich and studies with Swiss psychiatrist and eugenicist Eugen Bleuler (1857–1939).

Bleuler, by the way, delighted in exploring moral idiocy. That's the inability to understand moral principles and values and act in accordance with them, seemingly without impairment of reasoning- and intellectual faculties (encyclopedia2.thefreedictionary.com).

Lawrence Davidson is West Chester University in West Chester, Pennsylvania Professor emeritus of history. In his 2006 Consortium News article 'America and the Plague of Moral Idiocy,' he describes it thus:

> "It is not that moral idiots do not intellectually know that something called morality exists, but rather that *they cannot understand its applicability to their lives,*

> particularly their professional lives." (Lawrence Davidson: America and the Plague of 'Moral Idiocy'; https://consortiumnews.com).

Seems akin to psychopathic aptitude, but who am I to notice such things?

We also know that Bleuler took an interest in the relationship between neurosis and alcoholism, perhaps because it could lead to moral idiocy, for all we know. As a follower of Freud, he saw sexuality as a potent influence on anxiety. He pondered the origins of the sense of guilt. And he explored what he termed "switching", the affective shift from love to hate, for example. While at it, Bleuler coined the terms "schizophrenia", "schizoid", "autism "and "depth psychology", all categorized by Freud as "Bleuler's happily chosen term ambivalence."

To clarify, according to Merriam-Webster "ambivalence" has the following meanings:

- Simultaneous and contradictory attitudes or feelings (such as attraction and repulsion) toward an object, person, or action (felt ambivalence toward his powerful father, ambivalence toward marriage)
- Continual fluctuation (as between one thing and its opposite)
- Uncertainty as to which approach to follow

So, ambivalence is a happily chosen word indeed, as it is as useful in the mental health profession as in the advertisement industry. It describes both target populations, customers and psychiatric patients, and indeed psychiatry as a whole. Ambivalence signifies a state of having simultaneous conflicting reactions, beliefs or feelings towards something, anything, as a matter in fact describing a cognitive dissonance state of mind. Twenty-four psychologists and psychiatrists interviewed me and came up with 24 different opinions of my mental and psychological state, a most precious/splendid example of ambivalence. It also fits so very well when attempting to justify the existence of psychiatry as a science to those questioning its merits.

To complete Bleuler, he was in particular known for his clinical observation and for his willingness to let patients' symptoms speak for themselves. His expository writing skills exquisite, he was never credited for ever having healed a single patient. Like Sigismund, preferred to experiment on them, rather than heal them. Many were sterilised on his behest, and many committed suicide. Moral idiocy springs to mind. Meanwhile, Brill, armed with that knowledge, chose to move on to Vienna and a meeting with Freud. He returned to the United States in 1908, where he accepted a position as assistant physician of mental disease at Bellevue Hospital, New York City. Bellevue is the oldest public hospital in the United States, tracing its origins back to the city's first permanent alms-house. It began as. a two-story brick building, completed in 1736 on the city common located in the Kips Bay neighborhood of Manhattan. He joined Freud and Jung's party for their 1909 conference at Clark University, Worcester, Massachusetts. It was founded in 1887 and was one of the US's first private research universities, with a large endowment from its businessman and namesake Jonas Gilman Clark.

Brilliant as Brill seems to have been, he managed to shortly thereafter open his private practice of psychoanalysis in New York City, the very first one to open in the US. He also began to give talks about psychoanalysis at medical, neurological and psychiatric society and lay group gatherings. He lectured social workers at New York City's Police College and at New York University's education department. All of this was whilst employed at New York's Columbia University as clinical professor of psychiatry and maintaining his private practice and running his marriage (snaccooperative.org). During the 1930s, he added a weekly radio broadcast, lecturing listeners on mental health themes to, we assume, further *make the American mind*. Still ignored and with time to spare, he translated into English most of Freud's and some of Jung's works (Mishne, Judith Marks: *The Evolution and Application of Clinical Theory: Perspective from Four Psychologies*. NY: The Free Press 1993 p.33). By 1909, he had published Freud's *Some Papers On Hysteria* and *Selected Papers on Hysteria and Other Psychoneuroses* (New York: Journal of Nervous and Mental Disease Publishing Co.). By 1911, Brill had written his own *Psychoanalysis, Its Theories and Practical Application* (Philadelphia: W. B. Saunders Co.), whilst simultaneously vigorously and tirelessly campaigning for the dissemination, promulgation and practices of psychoanalytic ideas and the acceptance of psychoanalysis as an exact science.

Still lacking things to do, Brill, with Freud's support, founded the New York Psychoanalytic Society in 1911. He also helped Freud's friend, the British neurologist and psychoanalyst Ernest Jones (1879 -1958), to establish the American Psychoanalytic Association in Baltimore. A lifelong friendship had sprung up between the two with their first meeting at the 1908 inaugural Psychoanalytical Congress in Salzburg. After that, Jones had travelled to Vienna for further discussions with Freud and introductions to the members of his Vienna Psychoanalytic Society. The friendship lasted until Freud's death in 1939, with Jones as his official biographer. It was through Jones' association, that he got to know the aforementioned neurosurgeon Wilfred Trotter after receiving his M.D. degree in 1903. Trotter was a member of the Royal College of Physician, specializing in neurology. It is from him that Jones first learned of Freud's work. Their common interest in continental psychiatric literature and the new forms of clinical psychotherapy it surveyed made them best friends. So, they shared living quarters above their private *Harley Street* consulting clinic while also working at several hospitals. Harley Street in central London began its exclusive and ongoing collection of leading surgeons, physicians, psychoanalysts and healthcare professionals in the mid 1800's. They were all conveniently based in the middle of town, Trotter and Jones with their brand-new field of psychoanalysis joining them.

Mind you, Jones' had ideas of his own in clinical work with children Combined with those of Freud, he propelled himself to life in North America when directly applying them with hypnotic techniques in his clinical work as treatment of the institutionalized mentally ill. Freud, who had studied hypnosis with Charcot in France in 1885, used it to help neurotic patients recall disturbing events they had apparently forgotten. Discovering the difficulty in hypnotizing some patients, however, Freud discarded hypnosis in favor of free association, which he described as follows:

> "The importance of free association is that the patients spoke for themselves, rather than repeating the ideas of the analyst; they work through their own material, rather than parroting another's suggestions"(freudpage.info).

But Jones continued the hypnotic procedure. In 1906, he was arrested and charged with two counts of indecent assault on two adolescent girls he had interviewed in his capacity as an inspector of schools for *mentally defective* children. Jones maintained his innocence at the court hearing claiming that the girls were fantasising about his inappropriate actions. The magistrate acquitted him on the grounds that no jury would believe the testimony of mentally ill children.

However, in 1908, employed as a pathologist at a London hospital, he was not that lucky. He accepted a colleague's challenge to demonstrate that repressed sexual memory underlay the hysterical paralysis of a young girl's arm. But he omitted to inform the girl's consultant to arrange for a chaperone at the interview. Complaints from the girl's parents over the nature of the interview forced him to resign his post. His career prospects in Britain thus seriously compromised, he sought refuge in Canada. There he began to teach at the University of Toronto's Department of Psychiatry in that same year, 1908. He attended Freud's psychoanalysis lectures at Clark University in Worcester Massachusetts in 1909, and those he held in the Netherlands in 1910. Toronto University promoted him to Associate Professor of Psychiatry in 1911. As he built his private psychoanalysis practice, he also worked as pathologist and director of the psychiatric outpatient clinic at the Toronto Hospital for the Insane.

From his Toronto base, the supremely industrious Jones furthermore set about to forge strong relationships with the nascent American psychoanalytic movement. He gave addresses to American professional societies at venues ranging in location from Boston to Washington, D.C. and Chicago. He co-founded the *American Psychopathological Association*, established by William James (1842 -1910). James was an American philosopher, psychologist and the first educator offering a psychology course in the United States. Together with German-Austrian psychiatrist, neuro-pathologist and anatomist Theodor Meynert (1833 - 1892), James had as medical students in 1864 studied under Mauritian neuroscientist Charles-Édouard Brown-Séquard (1817-1894). Brown-Séquard was Harvard Medical School's first physiology and neuropathology professor at age 72. He reported "rejuvenated sexual prowess after subcutaneous injection of extracts of monkey testis". Both Meynart and James believed that disturbances in brain development could be a predisposition for psychiatric illness and that certain psychoses could be reversed. Today, James's psychopathological association purports to be devoted to the scientific investigation of human behavior and its biological- and psychosocial substrata, the interrelation of social factors and individual thought and behavior. Psychopathology, we assume, thus is in essence nothing other than the study of abnormal cognition, behavior and experiences. PTSD would be among them. We ponder again: "Who decides what is normal and abnormal in humans? Who sets the standards? Who makes the rules?"

But never mind, though we do wonder how Jones, whilst performing his substantial duties in Toronto, also found time and money to co-found the American Psychoanalytic Association in Baltimore, Maryland, U.S. . And serve as its first Secretary until 1913. As if he had little else to do, this first native English-speaker psychoanalysis exponent in the English-speaking world. But he would go much higher up in rank a few years later, serving in the 1920's and 30's as president of both the International Psychoanalytical Association and the British Psycho-Analytical Society. Thus, undoubtedly together with Freud, Jones exercised immense influence on the formations and publications of all three organizations capable of expertly manipulating the human mind.

The American Psychoanalytical Association (APsaA) founder James Jackson Putnam (1846-1918) was not alone. His co-founders were Trigant Burrow, Ralph C. Hamill, John T. MacCurdy, Adolf Meyer, G. Lane Taneyhill and G. Alexander Young, all of whom we will present in the order mentioned. We begin with Harvard College graduate Putnam himself. He was born in Boston and went to Europe to study in the company of:

- Bohemian physician, pathologist, humanist, philosopher and liberal politician Baron Carl von Rokitansky (1804–1878)
- German-Austrian psychiatrist, neuro-pathologist and anatomist Theodor Meynert (1833–1892)
- English neurologist John Hughlings Jackson (1835–1911)

The latter was best remembered for his seminal contributions to the diagnosis and understanding of epilepsy in all its forms and complexities. Putnam, after studying in Europe and receiving his M.D. in 1876, opened a clinic, which later became Harvard Medical School's Department of Neurology.

Putnam for one year became the American Psychoanalytical Association's first president. He already had experience in associations; in 1874 he had been a founding member of the American Neurological Association. This was a professional society of academic neurologists and neuroscientists. They described themselves as devotees of advancing the goals of academic neurology and the training and education of neurologists and other physicians in the neurologic sciences, as well as in the expansion of the understanding of diseases of the nervous system and the ability to treat them (myana.org). Between 1893 until his retirement in 1912, Putnam held the post of Professor of Diseases of the Nervous System at Harvard University.

Nicholas Trigant Burrow (1875–1950) was an American psychoanalyst, psychiatrist and psychologist. He created group analysis in the United States alongside Joseph Hersey Pratt, M.D.(1872–1956) of Boston and Paul Ferdinand(1886-1940). This Austrian psychiatrist, psychoanalyst and medical researcher in both neuro-physiology and neuropathology was also a member of Freud's Vienna Psychoanalytic Society. Burrow met Freud and Jung shortly after receiving his PhD in Psychology from Johns Hopkins University in 1909 while working at the New York State Psychiatric Institute. That same year he traveled with his family to Zurich to undergo a one yearlong Freudian analysis administered by Jung. The theory and practice of psychoanalysis and psychotherapy as developed by Freud are based on:

1. His theory of personality, which postulates that psychic life is made up of instinctual and socially acquired forces, or the id, the ego, and the superego, each of which must constantly accommodate to the other;

2. His discovery that the free-association technique of verbalizing for the analyst all thoughts without censoring any of them is the therapeutic tactic that reveals the areas of conflict within a patient's personality;

3. That the vehicle for gaining this insight and next, on this basis, readjusting one's personality is the learning a patient does in first developing a stormy emotional bond with the analyst (transference relationship) and next successfully breaking this bond (medicaldictionary.thefreedictionary.com).

Upon his return to the United States, Burrow practiced as a psychoanalyst until 1926. Then he founded the Lifwynn Foundation for Laboratory Research in Analytic and Social Psychiatry for the purpose to "sustain and sponsor a scientific study of the feeling or emotional or affective life of man." (Alfreda S. Galt: Institute report: The Lifwynn Foundation; J. The Hum. Psychologist vol. 15, 1987-iss.2). Burrow also published his first major work, *The Social Basis of Consciousness. A Study in Organic Psychology Based Upon a Synthetic and Societal Concept of the Neuroses*. In it, he claims that the personalistic basis of Freud's psychology is not sufficient to render conscious those disorders of the personality that are essentially unconscious. The failure to recognize this distinction apparently accounts for the present impossibility of the psychoanalytic method (PsycINFO Database Record (c) 2016 APA, all rights reserved).

While at it, Burrow burrowed deeper within himself to dig up the concept of neurodynamics. This is the communication between different parts of the nervous system and its relationship to the musculoskeletal system. This method for measuring the electrical activity of the brain in connection with specific eye movements used in Eye Movement Desensitization and Reprocessing (EMDR)] was presented in *Fallacy 1*. He also dug up the hypothesis of psychoanalysis as a social science, while between 1924 and 1925 being APA's president. Regardless, he was expelled from the society in 1932, because his psychoanalytical innovations were viewed as in breach with orthodox Freudian psychoanalysis.

Neurologist and psychiatrist Ralph C. Hamill (1877 –1961) was another ApsaA co-founder. He was an American college football player and coach, and he served as head coach at Centre College in Danville, Kentucky, after graduating in 1900. According to his *Chicago Tribune* July 6, 1961, obituary, he then was on staff at Chicago's Henrotin Hospital, which had a reputation for expertise in treating gunshot injuries. He was also on staff at Hines Veterans Hospital, the latter in operation since 1920. He also taught at Illinois' Northwestern University's medical school and at Rush Medical College, as well as serving as president of the Illinois Society for Mental Hygiene. Little is known about his role at the APsaA.

Of APsaA's Canadian co-founder psychiatrist John T. MacCurdy (1886-1947) we know more. He studied biology at the University of Toronto and gained his M.D. at Johns Hopkins in 1911. He then pursued research in neuropathology in Germany (H. Bannister, O.L Zangwill: John Thomas MacCurdy, 1886-1947; British Journal of Psychology General Section publ. September 1949). Whilst there, he met with the several prominent German-speaking psychiatrists, C.G. Jung among them. As a Lieutenant of the U.S. Medical Reserve Corps in 1917, he published his book *War Neuroses*, purportedly to prepare American psychiatrists for the mental disorders they would face in soldiers returning from WWI. How he arrived at his war neuroses assumptions and conclusions without ever having actively participated in a theatre of war is unknown (John T. MacCurdy: War Neuroses; Utica, N.Y. State Hospital Press, 1918). Between 1913 and 1922, he served as the APsaA's first secretary and taught psychopathology at Cornell University.

By 1892, APsaA's co-founder Adolf Meyer (1866–1950) held an M.D. from the University of Zurich. However, unable to secure an appointment there, he immigrated to the US, well trained in neuro-anatomy and neurophysiology. He had studied with Swiss neuro-anatomist, psychiatrist and entomologist Auguste-Henri Forel (1848–1931), known for his investigations of brain structure. He had also studied under British neurologist John Hughlings Jackson (1835–1911), whose studies of epilepsy, speech defects and nervous-system disorders arising from brain and spinal cord injuries helped define modern neurology. Meyer had also studied under Jean-Martin Charcot (1825–1893), one of France's greatest medical teachers and clinicians. Together with French neurologist Guillaume-Benjamin-Amand Duchenne de Boulogne (1806–1875), he first described several nervous and muscular disorders and developed medical treatment for those disorders by creating electro-diagnosis and electrotherapy. Charcot earned his M.D. at the University of Paris in 1853 and was professor at the university between 1860–93. He began a lifelong association with the Salpêtrière Hospital in Paris (1862). Originally a gunpowder factory, saltpetre being a constituent of gunpowder, Louis XIV decreed to convert into a hospice for the poor women of Paris as part of the General Hospital of Paris in 1656. It is there that Charcot opened what was to become Europe's greatest neurological clinic of the time in 1882 (Britannica.com). It is Charcot's use of hypnosis to discover an organic basis for hysteria that stimulated Freud's interest in the psychological origins of neurosis as Charcot's student in 1885.

Meyer, shortly after arriving in the United States in 1892, managed to secure employment as a neuro-pathologist at the Illinois Eastern Hospital for the Insane in Kankakee. It had opened its doors in 1879, and was where he stayed until 1895 (Britannica.com). During his tenure, he emphasized the importance of taking accurate patient case histories, as he had decided that mental illness disorders essentially arose from personality dysfunction rather than brain pathology. The Neumeisters of the day would, of course, vehemently disagree. You remember them? They deduce that every mental disorder originates and finishes in the human brain using rattus, simian, cani and mus as subjects to experiment on and validate their hypothesis. From Kankakee, Meyer moved to the mental institution at Worcester, Massachusetts (1895–1902), as chief pathologist. He then became director of pathology for the Pathological Institute of the New York State Hospital Service on Ward's Island (1902–10) and professor of psychiatry at Cornell University Medical College in New York City (1904–09). He was president of the American Psychiatric Association in 1927–28. He oversaw the building and development of the Henry Phipps Psychiatric Clinic at Johns Hopkins Hospital, making sure it was suitable for scientific research, training and treatment (opened 1913) to truly rise to prominence as Johns Hopkins Hospital's first psychiatrist-in-chief, holding the position from 1910 to 1941.

Whereas Meyer's focus on collecting detailed case histories on patients is viewed as one of the most prominent of his contributions to psychoanalysis, his major one is considered to be his idea of ergasiology. Derived from the Greek words for "working" and "doing," its basic hypothesis conjures up the Hitlerian slogan "Arbeit Macht Frei," which, for all we know, might have sprung from Meyer's hypothesis. For Meyer, the term signalled the synthesis of a patient's biological, social and psychological factors and symptoms. Ergasiology, we read on Wikipedia, is:

> "the application of the principles of biology to the study of physiological, genetic, and developmental mechanisms of behavior in humans and other animals."

The term also considers mental illnesses to be a product of dysfunctional personality rather than a brain-pathology. Believing that whole-life social and biological factors should be central to both diagnosis and treatment, Meyer supported occupational therapy as an important connection between people's activities and their mental health. Thus, he incorporated community based activities and services to develop patients' everyday living skills. In essence, he theorized that all mental disorders stemmed from incorrect responses and behavior patterns, rather than brain-malfunctions (psychologydictionary.org). Thus, the incorrect behavior patterns with genuine PTSD experiencers and their mental health professional "caregivers," employers, union representatives and insurers could be deemed to be in conflict with their recovery.

Curt Paul Richter (1894–1988) and John Broadus Watson (1878–1958) were professor. of psychiatry at Johns Hopkins Medical School. These Harvard graduates and aspiring biologists, psycho-biologists and geneticists, who established the school of behaviorism, studied under Meyer the behavior of rats to gather first evidence of the equivalent emotional reactions and behaviors between rattus and homo sapiens. When himself professor at Johns Hopkins in the 1950s, Richter conducted a number of experiments with domesticated and wild rats similar to water boarding. Indeed, his joy of life seemed to come from inducing *states of need* in animals. He would do so either by depriving them of substances essential to their survival or by manipulating their hormone levels in a Neumeisterian fashion in an effort to demonstrate the genetic programming of human behavior. Watson, on the other hand, limited his research to animal behavior in conjunction with child rearing and advertising, both so useful to Bernays during his career.

Shortly after touchdown in the US, Meyer became acquainted with the teachings and philosophies of American psychologist William James's (1842–1910). Considered to be a leading thinker of the late nineteenth century, as well as the "Father of American psychology", James interacted with a wide array of writers and scholars throughout his life. These included Walter Lippmann, John Dewey, Carl Gustav Jung and Sigismund Freud. Spending almost his entire academic career at Harvard, James studied and taught medicine, physiology and biology. But he was drawn to the scientific study of the human mind at a time when psychology was constituting itself as a science. His was acquainted with the work of figures like German physicist and physician Hermann Helmholtz and the aforementioned Pierre Janet in France. This paved the way to offer courses in scientific psychology at Harvard, where he taught his first experimental psychology course in the 1875–1876 academic year (Duane P. Schultz; Sydney Ellen Schultz (22 March 2007). *A History of Modern Psychology*. Cengage Learning. pp. 185–.)

Around 1900, James called for an "American Psychopathological Society" in response to the gap he felt had occurred between *normal* psychology and more morbid sciences dealing with full-blown insanity. In 1910, with the assistance of the neurologist and psychoanalyst Ernest Jones, newly immigrated from Britain, and 41 other founding members, the American Psychopathological Association (APPA) was organized. The launch was at the Willard Hotel in Washington, D.C., where both the American Neurological Association and the American Medico-Psychological Association, now the American Psychiatric Association, were holding their annual meetings. The APPA's official organ, *The Journal of Abnormal Psychology* changed its name to*The Journal of Abnormal Psychology and Social Psychology* in 1921. This was done under the assumption that states of the human mind can only be judged as normal or abnormal when viewed in context and background of the prevailing social norms of the particular time and place ("The Online Books Page": University of Pennsylvania January 10, 2013). As genuine PTSD experiencers may have noticed, however, this is almost always ignored in encounters with mental health professionals. The APPA nowadays purports to be devoted to the scientific investigation of human behavior and its biological and psychosocial substrata. And why do you want to know anyway, you may ask yourself? So you understand the root of your misery when dealing with the industry and the reason why you are the only one who can heal yourself. That's why. Dharma extinguishing Karma in action!

Needless to say, Meyer got to know James's pen pal, American philosopher, psychologist and educational reformer John Dewey (1859-1952), as well. His ideas became influential in education and social reform. In 1888, imbued with an overwhelming belief in democracy in politics, education, communication and journalism, Dewey stated at the University of Michigan: "Democracy and the one, ultimate, ethical ideal of humanity are to my mind synonymous." This was amazing, considering he lived in a republic scant 100 years old. It was certainly not due to lack of intellect that he refused to acknowledge it. So, what was it? An alignment with Freud et al. to create the public's mind to their liking and thus achieve the demon-crazy socialistic, communistic goals of their aspirations? Major topics needing attention and reconstruction to encourage experimental intelligence and plurality were, in Dewey's opinion, schools and civil society, the herd; complete democracy was to be obtained by extending voting rights and by ensuring a fully formed public opinion existed. This was to be accomplished by communication among citizens, experts and politicians, with the latter being accountable for the policies they adopt. Rings a bell?

Dewey was one of the primary figures associated with the philosophy of pragmatism. It considers words and thought as tools and instruments for prediction, problem solving and action. It rejects the idea that the function of thought is to describe, represent or mirror reality. Pragmatists contend that most philosophical topics, such as the nature of knowledge, language, concepts, meaning, belief and science, are best viewed in terms of their practical uses and successes. Dewey is also considered one of the fathers of functional psychology or "functionalism". This psychological school of thought of Darwinian thinking focuses attention on the utility and purpose of behavior modified over years of human existence. A well-known public intellectual, Dewey was a major voice of progressive education and liberalism. He funded the private University of Chicago Laboratory Schools while a professor there, thus able to apply and test on human subjects his ideas on the pedagogical method. The school remains a private co-educational day school. Almost half of its students have at least one parent on the university's faculty or staff. The parental background of the other half is unknown, but none of them are poverty stricken. Tuition fees for 2019-2020? Nursery, half day $23,244; Nursery–Grade 5, full day: $32,310; Grades 6–8 $34,500; Grades 9–12 $35,952.

Back to the APsaA, the American Psychoanalytical Association. Ralph C. Hamill's co-founder G. Lane Taneyhill was appointed Surgeon General at the 41st National Encampment at Saratoga Springs, New York, in September 1907, according to the *Journal of the Fiftieth National Encampment of the Grand Army of the Republic* in 1916 at Kansas City, Missouri (issue 50-51). His function at the APsaA is unknown and so is that of his co-founder G. Alexander Young. However, we can faithfully assume that both in one way or the other were well acquainted with Freud and his Viennese cohort American émigrés. Why should they be the exception? We know the APsaA was tailored in accordance with Freud's Viennese *Wednesday Psychological Society's* rules, regulations and aspirations to, purportedly, serve American psychoanalysts as a scientific professional organization focusing on membership development, education and research. One could, of course, also hypothesize that it mainly served to line up members like ducks in a row, reading from the same script to clandestinely change the American herd's social, moral and social fabric without arousing suspicion.

Whilst APsaA's founding members were thus finding their footing and planning their modus operandi, Brill continued on his merry way with infiltrating the U.S. military. In 1919, he got himself hired into its Medical Reserve Corps as consultant-psychiatrist with the rank of Major. In 1921, he published his 344 page book *Fundamental Conceptions of Psychoanalysis,* composed from lectures he gave during his elementary course, built on Freud's foundations, at the department of pedagogics at New York University (New York: Harcourt, Brace 1921). Between 1925 and 1934, Brill acted as President of his New York Psychoanalytic Society in New York and lectured at the College of Physicians and Surgeons at Columbia University.

The New York Academy of Medicine's Salmon Committee on Psychiatry and Mental Hygiene recognizes a prominent specialist in psychiatry, neurology or mental hygiene each year by presenting The Thomas William Salmon Award for outstanding contributions to these fields. In 1943 on the same occasion, the Committee invited Brill to share his research with New York's psychiatric community. The Salmon Lecture, first given in 1932, and the Salmon Medal, first awarded in 1942, are presented in memory of Thomas W. Salmon (1876-1927), M.D. He was an early twentieth century leader of the U.S. mental hygiene movement, whose contribution to the cause of the mentally ill and distressed was one of the most notable of his generation.

In 1944, Brill published Freud's *Contribution to Psychiatry* (New York: W. W. Norton & Co.) followed by his own *Lectures on Psychoanalytic Psychiatry* shortly before his death in 1948 (New York: Alfred A. Knopf, Inc.). A year later Doubleday posthumously published Brill's *Basic Principles of Psychoanalysis.* (New York: Doubleday), a final salute to an immensely successful and productive man indeed, the American immigrant's dream in action.

But as we know, long before then, friend Sigismund's nephew Edward galloped into his life. With his help and all those directly and indirectly associated with or travelling through Freud's Viennese Wednesday Psychological Society, he was ready and eager to take charge. Over the following decades, they would manipulate, mould and change the American herd's hitherto prevalent sociological, ethical, moral and philosophical traditions and fibres to their liking, and all of them being at Edward's beck and call.

By then, it was well known in professional psychoanalytical circles that anyone able to manipulate a person's perception holds supreme power over him or her. The same holds true for the herd. Thus, those able to intelligently and persistently apply their power of manipulation to a crowds' perception truly hold the ruling power in whatever nation or circumstance it is applied. Bernays asserts in *Propaganda* that public manipulation is both a moral duty and a necessity for the division of labor and to prevent chaos and confusion. It is also, he maintains, a logical result of the way in which his democratic – mob rule – society is organized. Of course, he was ignoring the fact that the United States actually was and is a republic with the rights of the individual superseding the rights of the democratic mob.

Those who manipulate society are those who pull the wires that control the public mind. This small, invisible government, the Deep State, ever since Freud's et al.'s in-depth explorations and exploitation of the human psyche have used their knowledge of the human psyche to manipulate the herd's mental processes, social patterns and reactions. Through it, they rule public opinion by the herd's own consent by what David Icke calls the *Problem Reaction Solution* scheme. They create the problem, manipulate public reaction to it to their liking and then propose the solution to the problem they themselves created. Brilliant, really. In essence it is the *Hegelian dialectic*, thus named after the German philosopher and idealism Georg Wilhelm Friedrich Hegel (1770 –1831), in action. The philosophical meaning of idealism contains, in a nutshell, the diverse groups of metaphysical philosophies, which assert that "reality" is indistinguishable or inseparable from human understanding and/or perception, though in some sense mentally constituted and closely connected to ideas (Britannica.com). Thus, the properties we discover in objects depend on the way that those objects appear to us as perceived subjects, and these properties belong only to the perceived appearance of the objects and not to something they possess *in themselves.* Public opinion thus, narrowly defined, is the perception of a society at a given time toward a given object. Broadly conceived, that perception fulfills the goal of those well-hidden powers to sway the public in its attitude towards its wishes and desires in whatever the rulers want to accomplish, at present the creation of their New World Order by way of Ordo ab Chao.

The real art of the craft, however, is to teach the herd how to ask for precisely what the manipulators want, while simultaneously safeguard against herd-aggression. This is achieved by the problem-reaction-solution mechanism by applying the general mind-manipulating principles and techniques discovered in psychoanalysis and perfected by Bernays to a fine art. By correct appraisal of specific goals through polling the public's opinions from abortions to presidents, from Antifa to Black Lives Matter to the perception of PTSD, affected soldiers and veterans are clandestinely swayed by spin-doctors. It is they who do the bidding of their masters, who influence the attitudes of whites toward people of color and vice versa, American buying and food consumption habits, fashion, music, science, art, sexuality, morals, ethics and human values, not necessarily in that order. Authoritative and influential groups may become important channels to reach the public, wit Fauci et al. in action, as ideas and situations must be made impressive and dramatic in order to influence and overcome the herd's inertia of established traditions and prejudices. "Wear the mask' even though it may kill you." This style allows us to be played like fiddles, while the country around us burns (Edward L. Bernays: Manipulating Public Opinion: The Why and The How; journals.uchicago.edu).

Once *we* learn how it operates, *we* not only can see that it operates and permeates everything around us, we can also learn to mentally protect ourselves against it. This has been ongoing for thousands of years. But in the early twentieth century, the intelligent manipulation of the American herd's perception by way of insight gathered into the human psyche with the mental health profession's help became the ruling elite's highest priority before going world wide. We, the herd, got a glimpse of it in author Aldous Huxley's novel *Brave New World*, published in 1932. Largely set in a futuristic World State whose citizens are environmentally engineered into an intelligence-based social hierarchy, the novel anticipates huge scientific advancements in reproductive technology, sleep-learning, psychological manipulation and classical conditioning combined to make a dystopian society. George Orwell's allegorical novella *Animal Farm*, published in 1945, reflected events leading up to the 1917 Russian Revolution under Marxist theorists, politicians and revolutionaries Lev Davidovich Bronstein (1879 -1940), known as Leon Trotsky, and Vladimir Ilyich Ulyanov (1870-1924), known as Lenin. And it reflects how that revolution quickly morphed into the Stalinist era of the Soviet Union, when it had become a brutal dictatorship built upon a cult of personality enforced by a reign of terror. Thus, *Animal Farm* gives further insight what is planned for the world.

Orwell's *1984* was published in 1948. It centers on the consequences of government over-reach, totalitarianism, communism, mass surveillance, violations of freedom of expression and repressive regimentation of all persons and behaviors within society. We saw this rapidly unfolding in front of our eyes, with COVID-19 as the pretext. These writers had the insight track and thus knew what was planned for humanity, which, due to cosmic law, our overlords have to tell us before carrying out their intentions. And they do - and they always did, if you were to somewhat follow world history over the past 6,000 years or so. But you don't care do you, even though those who do not know history are bound to repeat it? But that is of no consequence to you, either, is it? Dream on then, knowing full well that for as long as you are glued to the TV programming box you will maintain your masked and illusory maze of the world and everything in it without even the least bit of curiosity to find out, either, as TV kills all desire for creativity or exploration of anything. But, I wonder, how is your programming done so efficient- and effectively? What are the rules and regulations and how were they so perfectly designed? Well, in the beginning there was Pavlov and his dogs.

9

BEYOND PAVLOV'S DOGS: NEURO-LINGUISTIC PROGRAMMING

Human perception manipulation techniques and the consequent mind control results have been investigated, explored, applied and exploited throughout millennia. The topic is elaborate, multifaceted and multi layered. The German physician and hobby astronomer Franz Anton Mesmer's (1734 -1815) mesmerisation played a role in it. He theorised the existence of a natural energy transference occurring between all animate and inanimate objects he called "animal magnetism", attracting a wide following from about 1780 until the late nineteenth century. It was James Braid (1795 - 1860) who proposed the term "hypnosis". This Scottish surgeon, natural philosopher, "gentleman scientist" and significant innovator in the treatment of clubfoot, spinal curvature, knock-knees, bandy legs, and squint derived the technique from Mesmer's animal magnetism. He called it "mesmerism," which today generally functions as synonym of hypnosis. Whereas some mental health practitioners consider Braid to be the "Father of Modern Hypnotism", others maintain there is little connection between his hypnotism and modern hypnotism. No wonder, as the science of psychology has been unable to find scientific evidence to prove hypnotism's statistical value of success.

But exist it does, and Freud et al. merely perfected the art since the late 1800's by couching it in perception-deception terminology beyond our wildest imagination. And all of it is possible because those doing it know full well that the most effective technique to manipulate the human herd, or a particular target population of whatever size, from an individual to millions or billions, is by appealing to its subconscious. Just feed its desires or its fears, and make it feel and believe that whatever is presented is what they need and want. All of it is orchestrated in accordance with the problem-reaction-solution principle, the Hegelian dialectic. And all of it is generated to precisely fulfill the manipulator's wishes. Success can be achieved only by eliminating, numbing and disengaging humans' logic and reasoning ability for all and any ideas and products offered. This has been perfected to such a fabulous degree that nowadays perception-deception permeates and operates all aspects of human life. David Icke in his book *The Perception Deception* (David Icke Books Limited 2013) brilliantly explains in depth how it has been done throughout thousands of years to this very day.

Mind manipulation can be a fascinating form of destructive power, influencing and ruining whole nations. In recent memory, for example, just investigate the 1919 Versailles WWI peace conference, in which Freud's nephew Edward Bernays participated. You will discover that it was nothing other than the exquisitely well carried out preparation for WWII. During Hitler's regime, the Nuremberg rallies in particular demonstrate how to successfully destroy an entire society's ability to think and apply logic and reason purely by mind manipulation and threats of trauma. The United States Central Intelligence Agency (CIA), established under the National Security Act signed by President Truman in 1947, used the insights gathered in hundreds of clandestine experiments of a multitude of projects, MK-Ultra, Bluebird and Artichoke for drug-related experiments among them. Projects were organized through the CIA's Office of Scientific Intelligence and coordinated with the United States Army Biological Warfare Laboratories.

They continue today on willing PTSD-experiencing soldiers and veterans. It goes under the auspices of the NC *for* PTSD mental health employed personnel, who cherish LSD among their treatments for to enhance its knowledge on perception-deception techniques for mind control purposes, information gathering and psychological torture (history.com). Do you really think COVID-19 government regulatory measures are but an exercise in testing psychological control mechanisms on the worldwide human population? They feed the herd 24/7 media-transmitted cognitive-dissonance-creating information and thoughts of death and destruction, just as they do with PTSD imprint distortion?

Television, a staple in every self-respecting American household since the 1930s, is a prime tool of neuro-linguistic programming (NLP). And so is its offshoot: the guided imagery. Nielsen, an American information, data and measurement analytics firm of markets worldwide, estimated that 96.1% of all U.S. homes received television transmissions in 2019.

But who are those 3.9 % without television in 2019, you wonder? We do not know. Clara Moskowitz, however, in her 2008 Live Science report "Out There: People Who Live Without TV" noted that in comparison to those American adults watching roughly 3 hours plus of television daily, those abstaining fill their free time with a plethora of activities of all genres, from reading to socializing with friends, hiking and biking. Researcher Marina Krcmar, professor of communication at North Carolina's Wake Forest University, who gave up television decades ago, also found that aversion to TV is common for the most liberal- and most conservative-minded people. Their motivations?

- Avoid exposing their families to the excessive sex, violence, and consumer-ism promoted onscreen.
- The medium itself, claiming television intrudes too much into their lives, interferes with conversation and takes time away from the family.
- Some people have a beef with the power and values of the television industry and don't want its influence in their homes.

Are they right? Science indeed supports many non-watchers' worst fears about TV, as research consistently shows that increased exposure to television and violence results in greater aggression in children [and adults], Kremar said. When parents eliminated television in their homes, their children became easier to manage. "It's sort of counter-intuitive, because people think their kids would drive them nuts without TV," Krcmar said. "But parents found that kids became very good at entertaining themselves and didn't need to be entertained all the time by something that was lively and active. They didn't complain about being bored." Most kids in non-watching households agreed with their parents, stating they were better off and satisfied to live without television.

And then we have Craig Dewe's 2020 assessment of the pros and cons of watching television. On lifehack.org, he wrote "11 Reasons You Should Stop Watching Television Now." He states that a Neilson report found that the average American watched more than 34 hours of television each week, over 4 hours daily, not including YouTube videos, hours that could otherwise be spent with family or friends, or relaxing in other ways. In fact, it is obvious that when watching TV, you're not doing anything else. Thus, time spent watching television is similar to being asleep, which is, in fact, a fact. We saw this earlier in human brainwave manipulation.

Not only that, says Dewe, you are also voluntarily programming yourself with negativity, as just about every television show, from comedies to drama to reality TV and the news, is negative. If you look at almost any TV show, the complete lack of positive redeeming messages is the rule.

In Dewe's opinion, TV also poisons our belief systems. How so? George Carlin puts this right in our face. We laugh at his use of the stupid, overweight, socially awkward, racially stereotyped or just different people. But we vehemently refuse to see ourselves in his comedy as we watch. The TV news is filled with stories of pain and suffering, disaster and death in foreign countries. We accept those catastrophes as natural, while arguing and dramatizing about lifestyle problems for the sole purpose of creating drama, without knowing that all of this TV influence creates our outlook on life and the way we perceive the world.

Knowing about how imprints are created from the previous chapters, you know perfectly well, that all this is created on purpose. Therefore, you also know that watching television also creates unrealistic expectations, because TV distorts our human understanding of reality. Whatever is portrayed on TV is as far removed from reality as you at this point of your life are removed from dwelling within your mother's womb. In Dewe's opinion, TV is the ultimate in mind control systems. Companies figured out how to get us to voluntarily brainwash ourselves for their benefit. It began with Sigismund Schlomo Freud, and was carried forth by nephew Bernays, beginning in the early twentieth century. Sitting ducks since then, even children are now, in 2020, being trained to watch TV. Thus, they learn to accept a sedentary lifestyle, despite the fact that a lot of research shows the negative effects on children's development due to inactivity and the influence of television.

The good news is that already since 2015, results from the U.S Energy Information Administration's most recent Residential Energy Consumption Survey (RECS) show, that "only" an average of 2.3 televisions were used in American homes in 2015, down from an average of 2.6 televisions per household in 2009 (eia.gov), even though it still makes the herd's mind-manipulation programming child's play for herd controllers- and perception-deception creators alike.

"Neuro, " by the way, refers to information coming to us through our senses to then be stored in our brain and body.

"Linguistic" stands for the words we choose to give meaning to what we notice and/or want.

"Programming" is the term or expression for the way we combine what we observe and think to generate the results sought.

In other words, NLP describes the way people combine and form their perception and thought through the imagery presented to them, then spring into action. Understood and used by Freud, Bernays and company for at least 100 years, the methodology to understand and change human behaviour-patterns under the term "NLP" was first published by Americans Richard Wayne Bandler (1950-) and John Thomas Grinder, Jr. (1940-) in the 1970s.

In the 1980s, the learned society declared it a pseudoscience devoid of phenomena resembling human neural structures, linguistics and programming. But what then is television? Information that comes in through our senses is stored in our brain and body. Combined, this information motivates us to spring into action, feel a mood or an emotion on whatever it might be, both mentally and physically, and reach for the results to which we aspire. Those desired results are fed to us through "guidance" provided by TV's sound recordings and audio-visual impressions, and of course through news-anchors' and other spoken instruction, such as pharmaceutical drug advertisement and the world's Oz's and Oprah's.

And there is nothing new to this, either. Cicero already advocated guided imagery, saying that the eyes of the mind were more easily directed to objects we have seen, than to those of which we have only heard. Thus TV, movies and videos, most all under overlord production and control, are the prime means to herd control and programming. They splendidly facilitate the forming of new imprints in the human mind in accordance with the rulers' desired outcome. That's because opinions are formed by what is seen, heard or felt in different combinations, which influence all consequent thought processes, including logic and reason. Who these rulers are and if they might still be around is seldom questioned - not even with the knowledge that they perhaps look like the reptilian humanoids uncovered at ancient archaeological digs at the Al Ubaid archaeological site in prehistoric Mesopotamia. That's where many pre-Sumerian 7,000-year-old artifacts were found, depicting humanoid figures with lizard-like characteristics, falling somewhere between c. 6500 and 3800 BC. These carvings are rather a bit older than the beginning of civilization

associated with the Sumerians, previously thought of by most academics as the creators of human civilization (4500 to 4000 BC). Mind you, Erich von Daniken, Michael Tellinger and David Icke, among many others, greatly beg to differ.

Be it as it may, there are two fundamental ways by which mental imagery or imprints are generated and implanted in us: voluntary and involuntary.

Involuntary mental imagery is created directly from present sensory stimulations and perceptual information, such as seeing an object, creating a mental image and maintaining it, even though we look away or close our eyes. The same occurs when we hear a noise and maintain its auditory impression, even when the sound ceases.

Thus, the involuntary and spontaneous generation of mental images is integral to our ordinary sensory perception. Cognition occurs without our volitional intent, as it seems to be pre-filtered by our subconscious mind. I would think the filtering is in accordance with our emotional and coherent state of mind at the moment of imagery input. When in a sunny mood, the silver lining in a catastrophe is active. When depressed and miserable, the process of cognition-filtering will add to the existing misery. It is therefore that observing one's thoughts and being willing to correct them is paramount in life. This, in turn, is only possible without mind-altering natural drugs and the so-beloved pharmacotherapy by PTSD-treating physicians.

Voluntary mental imagery, in comparison, may resemble previously experienced sensory perceptions recalled from memory. Or they could be entirely novel images and the products of creativity or fantasy. Described as the faculty or activity of imagining things, especially things that are impossible or improbable to the one sitting in judgment, the mental health profession's PTSD hypotheses, theories, hallucinations and anticipations are good examples thereof. The latter could be described as the learned society's genre of speculative fiction, set in a fictional universe and inspired by real world myth and folklore, with roots in oral traditions turned into fantasy literature and drama. Alas, such a description would be amusing if it were not so dangerous to genuine PTSD journeyers. the CBT "therapy of PTSD "experts"," so dearly advocated by the NC *for* PTSD as the standard treatment of care, is deadly to PTSD journeyers. It forces them to regurgitate the PTSD-causing event moment over and over and over again, thereby destroying all possibility and ability to begin the healing process.

NLP programming through *guided imagery* denotes the technique used in voluntary imprint- manufacturing. Here, similar to CBT, images are recalled from the mind, or they are created for the mind, or recalled from fantasy or from pre-knowledge, from either long-term or short-term memory, for long-term or short-term memory, all depending who is doing the programming or re-programming. Both Orwell and Huxley, for example, had pre-knowledge of events planned for us by our overlords, thus could write and publish books like 1984, *Animal Farm* and *Brave New World*, in essence describing our imprint generation by them. Thus, the herd's NLP imagery, mind-manipulation and unfolding of events can actually be followed in art, television and movies presented as art, science fiction and documentaries, or in combination of it all.

Clinical investigations and scientific research has furthermore shown that mental imagery can result from both voluntary and involuntary mind processes. Indeed, it can encompass simulation or recreation of perceptual experiences across all human sensory modalities, with visual and auditory mental images purportedly being the most frequently experienced. Thus, the moment you turn on your TV, your programming begins. That's why researchers in experimental and cognitive psychology primarily concentrate on voluntary and deliberately generated imagery. In other words, they use movies and television presentations as jump-off points for their experiments. They use these tools to ask subjects to create, inspect and transform unpleasant imagery into pleasant and self-affirming experiences. In that way, those in power can successfully present atrocious events in ways viewers find appealing.

Anything we continue watching with joy or which makes us feel physically uncomfortable impacts our health. With NLP imagery, ill health and wellbeing go hand in hand depending on our personal state of mind. Visual and auditory imagery can especially exacerbate and aggravate both our mental and physical conditions. Why? Because, according to the hypothesized principles of psychophysiology and psychoneuroimmunology, the way we perceive our mental and physical condition affects our biological processes. This includes our susceptibility to illnesses, infections, diseases and healing, as our perception significantly derives from mental imagery.

In other words, the severity of a mental and/or physical disability, disorder or illness is partially determined by the content of images we form about ourselves in our own mind. We begin with content, vividness, intensity, clarity, frequency and whether we experience it as intrusive and unbidden or as welcomed. We also understand, that imagery created by our own minds can easily be manipulated to our detriment by experts in the field. Of course, once we are aware, we in turn can easily manipulate it to our own advantage and wellbeing, if applying willpower, determination, persistency and discipline while keeping off all opioid drugs.

Numerous scientifically undertaken examples document, that mental imagery played a key role in exacerbating and intensifying PTSD, as well as many other conditions. For instance, they affect compulsive cravings, eating disorders such as anorexia nervosa and bulimia nervosa, spastic hemiplegia, the incapacitation following a stroke or cerebrovascular accident. They also affect restricted cognitive function and motor control due to multiple sclerosis, social anxiety or phobia, bipolar disorder, schizophrenia, attention deficit hyperactivity disorder and depression. And these are only some of the ailments for which there is first evidence that people can aggravate symptoms and intensify pain and distress of any condition by generating mental imagery emphasizing its severity rather than by praising its improvements.

The computational theory of imagery is loosely defined as the ability to represent, retrieve, and reason about spatial and visual information not explicitly stored in long-term memory. It is derived from experimental psychology's guided imagery hypotheses (onlinelibrary.wiley.com) and comprises four phases:

1. Image generation
2. Image maintenance
3. Image inspection
4. Image transformation

Image generation involves generating mental imagery directly from sensory data and perceptual experience or from memory or fantasy.

Image maintenance involves willfully sustaining or maintaining the imagery. Without it, the mental image is subject to rapid decay within approximately 250 milliseconds. One millisecond is one thousandth of a second. It is hypothesized that these volitionally created mental images fade rapidly once generated in order to avoid disrupting or confusing the process of ordinary sensory perception. Feeding the herd with subliminal advertisement springs to mind. Subjects' cognitive concentration and attention to maintain the imagery is required for subsequent stages of inspection and transformation. Guided meditation might help participants with mental image extension and duration, we hear. Of course, this leaves subjects open to further abuse and manipulation.

Image inspection signifies that once a mental image is generated and maintained, it can be inspected to provide the basis for interpretation and transformation. Visual imagery inspection often involves a scanning process by which subjects are asked to direct their attention across and around the image whilst simulating shifts in their perceptual perspective. These inspection processes can be applied both to imagery created spontaneously—in other words, fantasized—and to imagery generated in response to the investigator's scripted or impromptu verbal suggestions.

Image transformation can be achieved with verbal instruction from the guided imagery instructor. They would direct subjects to alter the content of their generated mental imagery in such a way as to substitute images that provoke negative feelings indicative of suffering or those reaffirming disability or debilitation with those eliciting positive emotion suggestive of resourcefulness, ability to cope and increased mental and physical capacity. The process shares principles with clinical psychology techniques of "imagery restructuring" or "imagery re-scripting". These are used in cognitive behavioural therapy, the rattus, cani, simian, mus human-equals-animal PTSD therapy favoured by the NC *for* PTSD and originating with Pavlov and his dogs and joyously propagated by Skinner et al. as detailed in *Fallacy 1*.

Add to this brew the concept of the current methods to analyze the properties of designer receptors exclusively activated by designer drugs (DREADDs) in vitro, These measure the biological responses of DREADD activation in different neuronal populations in vivo. So, you can see the end of humanity-in vivo and you and I a part of it. DREADD technology represents a non-invasive, chemical-genetic tool for investigating neuronal signaling and the resulting behavioural responses in vivo (*Everyone Must Know This Before it is Deleted*; September 25, 2020; https://beforeitsnews.com.)

Combine this with the two current major approaches to control activity of genetically defined neurons in the brain of freely behaving animals, such as homo sapiens, rattus, lepus, simian and cani (though rattus thus far seems to have been the preferred species) were:

- chemogenetic approaches that use diffusible small molecules
- optogenetic approaches that use externally delivered light

The two methods have their own distinct merits. Optogenetics offers the advantage of temporal precision, while chemogenetics offers scalability and ease of application. Combining these two approaches within single molecules complements each other and allows the use of either mode of interrogation in the same brain circuit. Such molecular actuators would allow acute activation with precise time resolution in defined spaces as well as chronic and *non-invasive control of entire populations throughout the brain through the same molecules.* Luminopsins (luminescent opsins or LMOs) were developed to achieve this combined chemogenetic and optogenetic manipulation. This eliminated the wiring previously necessary to investigate brainwaves and reactions to imagery presented to subjects (https://ncbi.nlm.nih.gov).

In addition, influential theories suggest that emotional feeling states arise from physiological changes from within the body. Interoception describes the afferent signals (nerve signals coming from outside stimuli), telling the brain what they are sensing, the central processing, and the neural and mental representation of internal bodily signals. Recent insights include description of short-term interoceptive effects on neural and mental processes. These include fear-specific cardiac effects, the recognition of dissociable psychological dimensions of interoception, and models of interoceptive predictive coding that explain emotions and selfhood, reinforced by structural anatomical models and brain and experimental findings.

This growing grasp of interoception is so far only applicable to rattus et al, Believe it or not, direct stimulation of the interoceptors to test reactions is viewed as seldom appropriate in human experimentation (Brener, J, Ring, C: *Towards a psychophysics of interoceptive processes: The measurement of heartbeat detection*; Philosophical Transactions of The Royal Society B Biological Sciences 371(1708):2016) It really doesn't matter either, as all data enriching the rulers' understanding of how to manipulate humanity's emotions and disorders to the killing point are recorded by your smart phone, and thus easily accessible to them. And, in essence, all of it started with Ivan Pavlov (1849–1936). He and his researchers began the study of transmarginal inhibition (TMI), the body's natural response of shutting down when exposed to overwhelming stress or pain by electric shock, in the late 1900s.

Pavlov's experiments earned him the 1904 Nobel Prize in Physiology and Medicine. They showed how all temperament types respond to the stimuli the same way, but different temperaments moved through the responses at different times. He commented "that the most basic inherited difference ... was how soon they reached this shutdown point, and that the quick-to-shut-down have a fundamentally different type of nervous system." He also noted that patients who have reached this shutdown point often become socially dysfunctional or develop one of several personality disorders. Patients who dissociate during and after the experience often will more easily dissociate or shut down during stressful or painful experiences, and may experience PTSD for the remainder of their lives

(Rokhin, L.; Pavlov, I. & Popov, Y. (1963) *Psychopathology and Psychiatry*. Foreign Languages Publication House: Moscow).

The leading authority on Russian psychological research, Gregory H. Razran (1901-1973), immigrated to the United States in 1920, bringing Pavlov's knowledge with him. Amazingly enough, he served as statistical consultant to the U.S. Office of Strategic Services during WWII. What was amazing about this is that he was freshly imported from Russia. Let's recall how Russia turned into the Union of Soviet Socialist Republics (USSR), a federal socialist state based on Marxist ideology that existed from 1922 to 1991.

Razran then served as visiting professor at the Hebrew University of Jerusalem in 1952 to establish its Department of Psychology. He was co-chairman of the International Pavlovian Conference on Higher Nervous Activity held in Israel in 1961. Back in the U.S., he served as president of the division on general psychology of the American Psychological Association and as chairman of the psychology section of the New York Academy of Sciences. Not bad for a hick town Russian immigrant. He received his doctorate from Columbia University in New York City in 1933. He lectured there in psychology and worked as research associate until 1946, then accepted the appointment of Psychology Department of Queens College chair in 1946, which he held until his retirement as professor emeritus in 1966.

His interest in human and animal conditioning led him to pioneering work in conditioning young infants in the 1930s. He moved on to work on adults, where he applied conditioning techniques focusing on the meaning of words and transposition problems, as well as on compound stimuli as an aid in analyzing perception. He used the Russian school of conditioning techniques developed by such neuropsychologists as Alexander Romanovich Luria (1902 -1977), often credited as a father of modern neuropsychological assessment. He developed an extensive and original battery of neuropsychological tests during his clinical work with brain-injured victims of World War II, which are still used in various forms. During his career, Luria worked in a wide range of scientific fields at such institutions as:

- the Academy of Communist Education in Moscow (1920-1930s)
- the Experimental Defectological Institute in Moscow (1920s-1930s, 1950s-1960s)
- the Ukrainian Psychoneurological Academy in Kharkiv (early 1930s)
- the All-Union Institute of Experimental Medicine
- the Burdenko Institute of Neurosurgery (late 1930s)

The results are reflected in Solzenitzyn's work.

Present-day authors define neuropsychotherapy as a field of applied research, which tries to:

- to determine new therapeutic routes using neurotechnology
- identify neural mediators and functional targets of psychotherapeutic effects
- to design psychotherapeutic interventions on the basis of neuroscientific knowledge (thescienceofpsychotherapy.com/russian-psychology-and-neuropsychotherapy-comparative-analysis/Walter et al., 2009)

The main trajectory of the field is seen in its potential to provide investigators with "reliable surrogate markers" (Walter et al., 2009, p. S180). These are clinical indicators of causal factors for the development of mental disorders, useful for diagnosis, prognosis and prediction of psychotherapeutic changes. This course becomes possible with the integration of neuroscience into psychotherapeutic education, research and practice.

During his years of research leading up to today's attempts of re-configuring our brain, Razran also worked on the conditioning effects of stimuli of the internal organs in *interoceptive conditioning*, the magic terminology, if combined with the adenovirus's application. What are adenoviruses? They are a group of common viruses, just like COVID-19, that infect the lining of our eyes, airways and lungs, intestines, urinary tract and nervous system. They are common causes of fever, coughs, sore throats, diarrhea and pink eye. Contrary to COVID 19 hypotheses, however, infections are said to happen in children more often than in adults, though anyone can get them. It all hinges on the strength of an individual's immune system, the one and only guard and protector of our good health. That assumes we keep it in optimal state through, you guessed it, nutrition, fitness and a healthy lifestyle free of pharmaceutical and natural opioid drugs. Sharing this fact with my 77-year-old neighbour a few months ago, with COVID hysteria in full bloom, he exclaimed: "I didn't know I was responsible for my immune system." Does that somewhat explain the North American State of health Affairs?

Can we guess what our rulers aim to achieve through humanity's imagery, or imprint-generation, maintenance, inspection and transformation, together with Interoception intervention through adenovirus interceptions? We can, thanks to the mental health profession, which theorizes that together with pharmaceutical drugging, it should do two things. It should reduce subjects' (in other words, humanity's) images of their distressing, painful or debilitating conditions. At the same time, it should teach them to learn mental imagery of their identity, body and circumstances that emphasizes their capacity for autonomy, self-determination, positive proactivity and the ability to cope. And meanwhile, it should *manage* their condition. However, we read that in order for the imagery process to be effective and successful, subjects first must be open to absorbing and self-altering experiences, a trait related to hypnotic susceptibility (Tellegen, Auke, Atkinson, Gilbert: Openness to absorbing and self-altering experiences ("absorption"); *Journal of Abnormal Psychology*, 83(3), 268–277).

This, we are told, is the reason guided meditation, , is often combined with, or forms an integral part, of the operational and practical use of guided imagery intervention. If not guided meditation, some form of meditative praxis, relaxation technique, meditation music or receptive music therapy. Those techniques can, but not necessarily do, increase subjects' capacity for susceptibility to absorption, which should or could result in or increase the potential efficacy of guided imagery. That it is all guesswork. That it also immensely increases mental health's practitioners' powers over genuine PTSD subjects to do with as they wish, for better or for worse, is kept mute.

Thus, the possibilities of creating victims rather than victors out of genuine PTSD journeyers are enormous. It almost happened to me. I met the first mental health professional in my life, a Scottish-born and British-educated psychiatrist assigned to "handle me", shortly after the explosion. And handle me he did. During our nine months acquaintance, he kept it a secret that he and his wife both worked for North American Airways, my employer.

He sent me back to work pre-maturely, thanks to his *treatment/handling*. Predictably, all hell broke loose from the moment I stepped into crew scheduling, checking in for my first flight after the PTSD-causing event and lasting for 18 months. It was then that NorAm's own medical officer diagnosed me with recurrent PTSD and that psychiatrist was nowhere to be found. How many times did he cross the Atlantic with family in tow first class free of charge in lieu of trying to destroy me, I wonder? But never mind. His imprints will flourish sooner or later.

Needless to say, or perhaps not, the idea of imagery for healing or creation of any sort is only newsworthy in the West. In Eastern traditions and philosophies, such as Hinduism and Buddhism, the understanding that image visualization can constitute and transform human reality is taken for granted. Not so for COVID-19 head honcho types like Fauci's National Institute of Health (NIH), though. For them, guided imagery and guided meditation as mind-body interventions are nothing but bogus.

The U.S. National Center for Complementary and Integrative Health (NCCIH) is one of the 27 United States' health organizations, making up one of five medical and healthcare domains and systems. It defines mind-body interventions as those practices that "employ a variety of techniques designed to facilitate the mind's capacity to affect bodily function and symptoms." But those practices and products are not considered part of conventional medicine or "standard of care" mandates. Therefore, it receives next to nothing in research funding, just as Fauci, as head of the NIH in charge of research funding allocations, vehemently refused to accept the remedy hydroxychloroquine as a cure for COVID-19, knowing full well that it would solve the problem (see *Fallacy 1*). First used to prevent and treat malaria, today it is generally used to treat rheumatoid arthritis, some symptoms of lupus, childhood arthritis (or juvenile idiopathic arthritis) and other autoimmune diseases like the interoceptive COVID-19 virus. Why it is effective at treating autoimmune diseases is unknown, though it might be due to communication of cells in the immune system.

But all of it is it neither here nor there, when keeping in mind that human beings solely operate from the content of their individual brain. So say the multitude of self-proclaimed mental health professionals, PTSD experts included, who insist that healing modalities other than pharmacotherapy and hallucinogenic drugs are detrimental to human health, never mind mentally too hard for them to fathom. Or, could that be because there is little money in it?

That there are documented benefits of mind-body intervention treatments derived from scientific research of a range of conditions is of no consequence to Fauci et al., either. These benefits include relief of:

- headaches, coronary artery disease and chronic pain
- reduced symptoms of chemotherapy-induced nausea, vomiting and localised physical pain in patients with cancer
- greater perceived capacity to cope with significant problems and challenges
- better reported overall quality of life, in addition to evidence supporting the brain and central nervous system
- enhanced immune system functioning, including defense against and recovery from infection and disease

Never mind that, too, since humanity is to be destroyed anyway, wit the Georgia Guidestones. So, who cares that guided imagery has shown it can reduce postoperative discomfort, as well as chronic pain related to cancer, arthritis, physical injury and even non-musculoskeletal pain. Or that is boosts stress management, athletic and competitive sport ability, medical students' surgical skills? Thank heavens that humanity, due to Freud, Bernays and television, finally parked its brain, and thus does not care less, either. If it did, it would checkmate our ruler's plan to achieve human destruction and complete world domination in no time flat. That we have that power, few are telling. And fewer care, anyway. They are all too busy imprinting their minds with TV, videogames, pornography, Facebook and movies, whilst blind to the imprint-consequences of their entertainment.

That an abundance of natural healing modalities was used in ancient times is also quasi beside the point. That there are many different aspects of everyday problem solving, scientific and non-scientific reasoning, and creative activities involved in the volitional and deliberate generation of mental images is also graciously ignored, mostly out of pure ignorance. That twentieth century psychiatrist and psychoanalyst Aaron T. Beck (1921-), talked about in *Fallacy 1*, is responsible for their revival is rarely, if ever, mentioned by the learned mental health society. It is Beck who posited that the subjective way in which people perceive themselves and interpret their experiences influences their emotional, behavioral and physiological reactions to the circumstances in which they find themselves. Thus, Beck concluded, one could help patients correct their misperceptions and misinterpretations about themselves. And one could help them modify their unhelpful and self-deprecating ways of thinking about themselves and their predicament. In so doing, they would have more productive reactions to events and developed a more positive self-concept, self-image and overall perception of themselves, which led to healing themselves. Mind you, everything in life can be turned upside down with know-how. So genuine PTSD experiencers, up the creek without a paddle at the mercy of employers, union bosses and WCB- and employer-appointed mental health practitioners are blind to the fact that, directly opposite to Beck's suggestion, the powers that be turn them into human debris. Awakening to the fact can only happen when free of mind-altering pharmaceutical drugs and CBT, the NC *for* PTSD's favourite PTSD remedy.

Genuine PTSD experiencers are exposed to image generation everywhere they are interviewed about their PTSD condition. We could call it a fishing expedition, as it plays a significant role in applying cognitive approaches to psychotherapy according to both CBT and the interviewer's psychological leanings., These could include the rational emotive behavior therapy, schema therapy and mindfulness-based cognitive therapy. If asked to participate in another scheme, one is considered a recalcitrant claimant, which again means being cut off from financial assistance. So one is forced to participate in both voluntary and involuntary spontaneous generation of visual, auditory and other mental images purportedly necessary to solve the PTSD problem, recollect one's past, predict and plan one's future, formulate one's self-perception, self-image and the way one views and perceives the Self, and all among total and complete strangers. And all of it in accordance with the wishes of those "guiding" us in the pursuit of our PTSD recovery or anything else, for that matter. This, even though the mental health profession itself admits that one's self-image can be altered and regulated, from its physical condition and body-image to its mental state of mind. At least five of 23 of them tried to "guide me" into self-destruction.

Consequently, at least in my experience, when in the midst of the genuine PTSD journey, all of it only serves one self-evident goal: to get rid of you fast. And this is done with the help of total strangers portrayed as your saviors, when not even your mother, father, wife or most beloved on the face of the earth (except possibly your dog) can help you with your PTSD healing. Only you have that power. But you do not know it, and those who do won't tell you, as it would kill their golden goose. Furthermore, you are of the Earth's brightest ones, as I explained in *Fallacy 1* how PTSD tends to strike people with above-average capabilities. Therefore, you are slotted for destruction, as only the bright ones have the power to topple the world's overlords. But imagery permeates everything, from cognitive dissonance techniques used to bulldoze the population's reasoning capability, so brightly visible in the COVID-19 machinations and the suppression of its remedy, hydroxychloroquine, to the unsubstantiated claim that physicians know best. Journalist Brian Rose's June 2020 interview with David Icke "We Will Not Be Silenced" on *London Real* confirms it under the leitmotiv: "Resistance to Tyrants is obedience to God."

John Carpenter's wrote and directed the1988 movie *They Live*, based on the short story "Eight O'clock in the Morning" by Ray Nelson. Carpenter described it as "... a D.O.A.-type of story, in which a man is put in a trance by a stage hypnotist. When he awakens, he realizes that the entire human race has been hypnotized, and that alien creatures are controlling humanity. He has only until eight o'clock in the morning to solve the problem." The story gives insight into the depth of imagery penetration into our lives, spanning from the way we view sex, the impact on our moods and thoughts by way of music and its lyrics, and our desire for pharmaceutical drugs we otherwise would refuse to swallow, to our tacit consent to our nation's warfare as long as we can shop till we drop at Walmart, Home Depot, Costco, Meyers and the like with or without a muzzle.

Symbols are another way to plant imprints into our minds, to direct or re-direct our attention, to subliminally or overtly influence us. All means are used to deliver information or data to us, the herd, through printed publications, news media, photography, cinema, broadcasting and video games. All are, in essence, deception-perception communication tools and outlets used to pervert our minds. So successful has this method become, that the U.S. herd now clamors to eliminate the nation's police force, its reason and logic put to death mid-June 2020. Followers of Freud, Bernays et al. are jubilant, while strutting their stuff at the VA, the NC *for* PTSD and on TV.

But how do they get away with it, and for decades? How is it done? Do they control the mind's filtering process somehow? As pointed out earlier, our mind at any given time absorbs any information given to it in whatever form it is given, 65 thoughts or images within the snap of the fingers. Then, at nano-second speed no one seems to understand, our conscious and subconscious sift through all incoming data, filtering it down to what we consciously perceive. As we saw in *Fallacy 1*, where precisely this filtering takes place is unknown. But so is the location, the actual seat of the mind, as well as the location of the conscious, subconscious and super-conscious. Some believe it to be located in our physical brain proper, others speculate that it could be somewhere in a free-floating universe. As with the law of cause and effect, and much else related to the brain and the mind, it is scientifically unproven. It is void of empirical first evidence, and thus mere hearsay, hypothesis, theory, assumption and presumption. Indeed, it is just like most everything else related to the psycho-the-rapist mental health profession and its ever-increasing subfields, including PTSD and its recuperation, never mind healing.

The human brain's biological nature, however, can be somewhat perceived through an electroencephalogram (EEG). The brain has billions of neurons, and each individual neuron connects to thousands of others (A Deep Dive Into Brainwaves: Brainwave Frequencies Explained; choosemuse.com). Communication happens between them through small electrical currents that travel along the neurons and throughout enormous networks of brain circuits. When all these neurons are activated, they produce synchronized electrical pulses, which result in a "brainwaves". When many neurons interact in this way at the same time, the activity can be detected, amplified, analyzed and visualized outside the brain by using small metal discs (electrodes) attached to the scalp. The brain's oscillating electrical voltages can be measured with just a few millionths of a volt. This is electroencephalography, or EEG – electric brain graph – deriving from the ancient Greek *enkêphalos*, meaning within the head. If you have a smart phone, however, no devices are needed to measure what's happening in your brain. But more on that later.

The unit of frequency is the cycle per second, and is named the "hertz" in honor of German physicist and scientist Heinrich Rudolf Hertz (1857-1894). He first conclusively proved the existence of electromagnetic waves, which had been predicted by Scottish scientist in the field of mathematical physics James Clerk Maxwell's (1831–1879) equations of electromagnetism in the 1860s. As such, an EEG read-out essentially is a series of squiggles, representing the changes in voltage measured by the system in hertz. Both the frequency (the number of squiggles occurring during a set time) and the amplitude (the height/size of the squiggles) tell us what the brain is doing. The higher the frequency and intensity of the signal, the more synchronized brain activity from a multitude of neurons is ongoing.

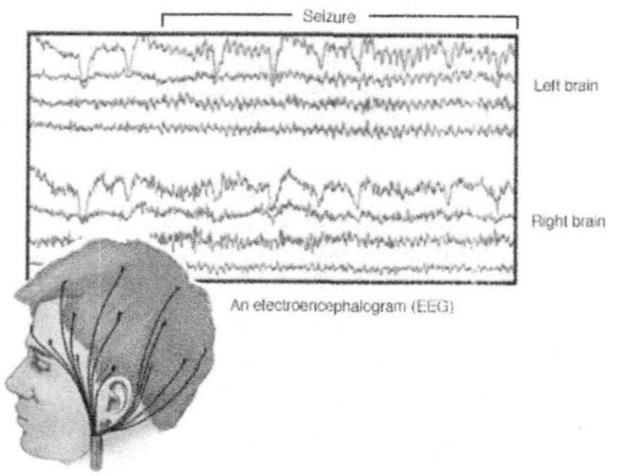

This shows an EEG readout from a patient opening the eyes. Image source: Mayo Foundation for Medication Education & Research.

EEG and the event-related potential (ERP), both using the same equipment, are used in neuroscience, cognitive science, cognitive psychology, neuro-linguistics, as well as in psychophysiological research to study human functions.

ERP tests differ from those of EEG. ERP works on the premise that information is naturally processed in the brain as electrical activity. This takes place in the form of action potentials or nerve impulses transmitted along neurons. Scientists can evaluate such naturally occurring data. The ERP administrator introduces test-subjects to specific sensory, cognitive or motor-event stimuli and measures the brain's response. Many EEG techniques used in research are insufficiently standardized for clinical use. And many ERP studies fail to report all of the necessary processing steps for data collection and reduction. That this limits the reproducibility and replicability of many studies is beside the point (Clayson, Peter E.; Carbine, Kaylie A.; Baldwin, Scott A.; Larson, Michael J. (2019). 'Methodological reporting behavior, sample sizes, and statistical power in studies of event-related potentials: Barriers to reproducibility and replicability'. *Psychophysiology*. 56 (11): e13437). More important is, what we know from *these* measurements: that out of the plethora of data that our brain records in every moment of our lives, very little filters through to our conscious awareness and reaches our perception (https://mayoclinic.org).

Human technology can observe five brainwaves, each one corresponding to a Greek letter, and each one to different states of thought and experience. The EEG also shows the intensity, alertness and activity of thought waves. They are, in the order of highest to lowest frequency, gamma, beta, alpha, theta and delta. Each brainwave has its own a purpose and its optimal mental functioning. A brain's flexibility and the ease with which it can transition through various brainwave frequencies is said to play a large role in being able to successfully manage stress, focus on tasks and sleep well (learning-mind.com). No brainwave is better or worse than another, and all can cause problems, if either over- or under producing. Each seems to help cope with the huge variety of situations in our ever-changing lives. Throughout our waking hours, all are active simultaneously, but, one brainwave frequency can dominate the others, depending on our state of consciousness and our activity. To identify the ones to dominate and how to do so would be a dream come true for mind-manipulators. Here are their characteristics:

Gamma waves (25 Hz to 100 Hz): Involved in higher processing tasks and cognitive functioning, these are important for learning, memory and information processing. They are the highest frequency waves with the smallest amplitude. They are associated with feelings of satisfaction, improved cognitive functioning such as memory retention, data processing and basic focus (binauralbeatsmeditation.com). Because gamma waves are so high in frequency, their quick motion creates sweeps of the brain that help to link information and improve cognition. People with high gamma brainwave activity are said to have the highest IQ scores and often are high academic achievers, athletes and musicians ("What is the function of the various brainwaves?" https://scientificamerican.com).

Gamma and beta frequency oscillations in response to novel auditory stimuli: A comparison of human electroencephalogram (EEG) data with *in vitro* models is studied by Corinna Haenschel, Torsten Baldeweg, Rodney J. Croft, Miles Whittington, and John Gruzelier. In 2000, they demonstrated that bursts of oscillatory field potentials in the gamma frequency range (30–80 Hz) are followed by a slower oscillation in the beta 1 range (12–20 Hz), thus demonstrating that a comparable gamma-to-beta transition is seen in the human electroencephalogram (EEG) in response to novel auditory stimuli. Thus, it confirmed a strong correlation between gamma and beta 1 activity, and revealed a high degree of interdependence of synchronized oscillations in these bands in the human EEG. But let's move on to the pure beta:

Beta waves (approximately 13 Hz and higher): High frequency, low amplitude brainwaves are commonly observed while a subject is awake. They are associated with conscious thought, logical thinking and stimulation. Fast brainwaves complete conscious tasks such as critical thinking, writing, reading and socializing. Beta brainwaves dominate the normal waking state of consciousness when attention is directed towards cognitive tasks and the outside world. Beta is present when we are alert, attentive and engaged in problem solving, judgment and decision-making. It is a sign of focused mental activity, characteristic of a strongly engaged mind. If engaged in conversation, a debate or making a speech, you're in beta. A teacher or talk show host engaged in their work would be in beta.

Alpha waves (8–13 Hz): These bridge the gap between conscious thinking and the subconscious mind. The frequency range lies between beta and theta. Alpha waves are associated with calming, promoting feelings of deep relaxation. Increased alpha waves are present with alcohol and marijuana consumption, as well as relaxants (including sedatives, anaesthetics, painkillers, muscle relaxants and some antidepressants). In alpha, the mind is calm and quiet, with fewer thought waves. It is one of the important states of the mind in psychology, as it is amenable to hypnosis and to subconscious mind programming. Where beta represents arousal, alpha represents non-arousal. Its brainwaves are slower and higher in amplitude. Anyone sitting down to rest after completing a task or who reflects or meditates is usually in an alpha state.

Theta waves (4–8 Hz): Theta waves are for daydreaming and sleepiness, and for feeling deep and raw emotions. They sometimes appear with bouts of depression or psychological suggestibility due to the semi-hypnotic and deeply relaxed state of mind. Theta waves heighten intuition, creativity and restorative sleep. Depressants such as Xanax, Valium, Halcion, Librium, Ativan, Klonopin, Amytal, Nembutal, Seconal and Phenobarbital are said to increase theta waves. Theta waves typically are of even greater amplitude and slower frequency than alpha. Someone who takes time off from a task and begins to daydream or drives down a freeway unable to recall the last five miles driven is in theta. The nature of highway driving compared to driving down a country road show how the theta and beta states help us safely perform the driving task.

Delta waves (0–4 Hz): These are of greatest amplitude and slowest frequency recorded in humans. They are found mostly in infants and young children. In people of all ages, they are associated with the deepest levels of relaxation, restoration and healing. And they are involved in unconscious and automatic bodily functions, such as heartbeat and digestion. Abnormal delta activity can lead to learning disabilities and difficulties maintaining conscious awareness.

When in bed and reading for a few minutes before attempting sleep, we are likely in low beta. When we put the book down, turn off the lights and close our eyes, our brainwaves descend from beta to alpha, to theta and finally, when we fall asleep, to delta.

Thus, we now know that brainwave frequencies are correlated with various states of human consciousness and states of arousal. We now know that the predominance of beta waves signals a state encompassing the thinking process. With that come ego reactions, such as egoic thoughts, motives, emotions and behaviors, in which "I", "me" and "mine" take center stage. In this state, we focus on the external world. At the opposite end of the arousal spectrum, in delta, we are basically disassociated from the external world and exhibit a predominance of sleep waves. With a predominance of theta waves, one's focus is on the internal world of hypnogogic imagery. It is here that a number of alpha-theta subjects have encountered an "inner healer," representing their shift out of victim consciousness into empowerment, That's because alpha brainwaves might function as a bridge from the external to the internal world and vice versa (Priyanka A. Abhang, Suresh C. Mehrotra: 'An Introduction to EEG- and Speech-Based Emotion Recognition', 2016; *Technological Basics of EEG Recording and Operation of Apparatus*; https://sciencedirect.com).

In everyday existence, the ideal state of the ego could well be a state of poise between the inner world of Self, and the outer world of objects, suggests Martin Sams of the Clear Mind Center in 1996. The Center advocates *The Clear Mind Neurofeedback System*, an all-in-one professional turnkey package said to have been designed to give anyone everything needed to immediately offer brain mapping and neurofeedback to others (clearmindcenter.com).

In Freudian psychoanalysis, the ego's ideal state (in German *das Ich-ideal*) is the inner image of oneself as one wants to become. In the French strand of Freudian psychology, the ego ideal or ideal ego has been defined as "an image of the perfect self towards which the ego should aspire." Neurofeedback (NFB), also called "neurotherapy" or "neuro-biofeedback", is a type of biofeedback that uses real-time displays of brain activity, most commonly EEG, in an attempt to teach self-regulation of brain function.

Neurofeedback can work on anyone regardless of age. The process is non-invasive, requires no drugs and is pain free. All that is required is the ability to focus on the audio or video stimulation. Sensors placed on the scalp monitor specific brainwaves, look for irregularities, then produce a signal designed to correct the irregularity and guide the brainwave back into a healthy pattern. With repetition, the brain will learn to stay in healthy ranges without the aid of computer-generated input, resulting in reduction or elimination of most neurological symptoms. Who sets the scales of "healthy" or "unhealthy" brainwave ranges is unknown. However, only the four primary brainwaves alpha, beta, delta and theta are targeted. We read that only they are responsible for regulating the active and subconscious aspects of our body. How that is known is unknown to us.

Gamma waves are the ones involved in higher processing tasks and cognitive functioning. They are important for learning, memory and information processing, and are associated with feelings of satisfaction, improved memory retention, data processing and basic focus. They were identified in the 1960s, but they are not addressed. Why, or why not? Who would not want to enhance gamma waves, with their quick motion creating sweeps of the brain that help to link information, improve cognition, heighten the IQ and become high achievers in whatever chosen field? After all, gamma is defined as a brain frequency ranging from about 25 Hz to 100 Hz or higher. It is most strongly seen around 40 Hz, even though analog EEG readings do not measure above 25 Hz. Even in the development of digital EEG, the amplifiers used in recording EEG register only into the low 30 Hz bands. That is why gamma is not included in most of the databases used today to determine what a "normal" EEG looks like (Peter van Duse: Gamma, 2016; https://brain-trainer.com). At least that's what we, the peons, are told.

Current research and the medical community at large question neurofeedback's validity, stating lack of conclusive scientific evidence as the reason. Nevertheless, numerous studies show that people are indeed able to enhance or reduce the power of specific frequency bands in their own EEG signals (André W. Keizer, Maurice Verschoor, Roland S. Verment, Bernhard Hommel: The effect of gamma enhancing neurofeedback on the control of feature bindings and intelligence measures; 2009 Elsevier B.V. All rights reserved)

Neurofeedback is, however, acknowledged as complementary and alternative treatment of many brain dysfunctions. We learn, for example, that with some patients previously exposed to major trauma, low alpha amplitudes can create an inflexibility that keeps them from readily shifting between inward and outward states. They also tend to avoid those internal states, where the work to find awareness of Self seems to be done.

This seems to be the case of genuine PTSD journeyers, when CBT and pharmacotherapy force them into an amnesiastic state of mind without knowing it. When alpha amplitude is increased via neurotherapy, however, such patients gain the ability to shift with greater ease. That's because overly intense concerns with the outer world are tempered, and detachment and loss of ego-centeredness is gained. When turning inward, outer awareness tends to decrease, and consciousness begins to center on questions concerning the meaning of life. Patients exposed to these states usually describe the latter experience as serene and peaceful, providing them with new abilities and possibilities. They also seem to develop a powerful coping skill. They may even retain such inner calm, no matter what is occurring in their environment, at least according to Founder & CEO of the Wuttke Institute of Neurotherapy A. Martin Wuttke. Meditation teacher since 1984, and a Minister of the Center for Spiritual Awareness, he states: "Our mission is to apply and to teach transformational tools that can assist the individual to actualize their highest good."

A similar notion is suggested by American radio personality, author, former psychotherapist, businessman and political commentator Thomas Carl Hartmann (1951-). He was trained in Neuro-linguistic programming by Richard Bandler and licensed by his Society of NLP as both an NLP Practitioner and an NLP Trainer in the 1970's, when stating:

> "Everybody is familiar with the edge between normal waking consciousness and sleep: it's often a time of extraordinary feelings, sensations, and insights, particularly as we move from sleep into wakefulness. When the brain is brought to the edge of the world of God, the place of 'true' consciousness, a fractal intersection occurs. An unstable and dynamic system is created, and, like the rainbow colors of water and oil, new energies and visions are created".

The so-called Peniston alpha–theta protocol seems to enhance this human ability to shift states. People can more easily move to this edge of creating new insights, originally developed to help Vietnam veterans diagnosed with PTSD, alcoholism and substance abuse. Dr. Eugene Peniston, an African-American man with a Cherokee grandmother developed this neurofeedback method with help from NIH and Cornell University research scientist Paul J. Kulkosky (1949-2019) (Black History in Biofeedback; DefaultTag by biofeedbackresources 2012). Peniston did this while working at the Veterans Administration Hospital in Fort

Lyons, Colorado, and as Chief of Psychology at the Samuel Rayburn Memorial Veterans Administration Medical Center in Texas,

Peniston based his assertions on a multi-modal protocol. It called for initial peripheral temperature biofeedback training, autogenic training and breathing exercises to induce relaxation, followed by approximately 30 30-minute sessions of EEG biofeedback. He practiced on 14 Veterans Administration patients, who learned to increase their theta and alpha waves in their occipital regions during "eyes closed" training exercises to induce a hypnagogic state. Mental imagery scripts based on drug and alcohol rejection scenes, as well as treatment goals and lifestyle changes, were read to subjects during the initiation of the 30-minute alpha-theta training session. Peniston's and Kulkosky's 1989 study detailed positive results after 15 sessions. The exact mechanism of alpha-theta neurofeedback seems to remain unknown, however, although scientists are said to be hard at work to solve that riddle (Christopher Fisher, PhD: An Overview Of Alpha-Theta Neurofeedback And Its Treatment Effectiveness For Substance Abuse, Bmed 2009).

Like many others before them, Chad C. Williams, Mitchel Kappena, Cameron D. Hassalla, Bruce Wright and Olav E. Krigolson (Associate Professor at the University of Victoria's School of Exercise Science, Physical and Health Education) reached the same conclusion. They found that cognitive control, working memory, attention and long-term memory are mechanisms involved in intuitive thinking, recruitment of autonomic long-term memory mechanisms, and a release of cognitive control, working memory, and attention (system 1). They even said so in their 2019 study *Thinking theta and alpha: Mechanisms of intuitive and analytical reasoning*, published by the University of Victoria's Krigolson Laboratory of Theoretical and Applied Neuroscience. Alternatively, they found that analytical thinking, system 2, suggests the recruitment of cognitive control, working memory, and focused attention without the need to access long-term memory. This, they say, is congruent with existing literature that theorizes System 1 thinking to rely on automatic or routine systems of the brain, and System 2 thinking to recruit cognitively heavy systems.

So, of what use is this knowledge, one may wonder? For the rulers, perhaps, as it is known, that the more alpha and theta consciousness is present in the human brain, the more amnesiastic a person, a nation or the human herd becomes, and the more imprints of whatever nature can be planted in their subconscious without question. The programming received dictates our resulting perception, creates our life. Amnesia, a deficit in memory caused by brain damage or disease, is enhanced by the use of various sedatives, anti-depressive- and hypnotic drugs and by the multitude of other mind manipulation- and brainwashing techniques applied by the multiple sources mentioned, but first and foremost by way of television.

One of the reasons why individuals nowadays are diagnosed with PTSD for a hangnail may very well be to hasten the spread of this amnesiastic, alpha-theta dwelling society. Why else are pharmaceutical opioids always prescribed immediately upon presentation to a physician, despite their detrimental side-effects and brutal withdrawal symptoms? To hasten the SOMA society creation of *The Matrix* already mentioned in ancient Indian scriptures? Mind you, if we want to find the financial incentive, it is abundant. Through prescription drugs, physicians create for themselves a never-ending lucrative stream of income. Plus they get the assurance that patients enter the path of drug-induced self-destruction and a slow and lingering death from which to profit until the subject expires. Splendid and fool-proof!

For us, there ought to be but one consideration. Once grown up, of legal age, we must take responsibility for our actions, joys and misery, as our perception of the world and everything in it originates with our choice of imagery imprint input. This in turn dictates our perception of ourselves, of life and everything in it. That would include the NLP and neurofeedback treatment we allow ourselves to be subjected to, despite the fact that empirical research data of its benevolence is lacking, and its techniques, capable of covertly inducing thoughts in subjects' minds consciously, go unnoticed and may be far from benign.

As Manly P. Hall states in his book *The Secret Teachings of All Ages: An Encyclopaedic Outline of Masonic, Hermetic, Quababalistic and Rosicrucian Symbolic Philosophy*:

> "Man's physical, emotional and mental natures provide environments of reciprocal benefit to detriment to each other. Since the physical nature is the immediate environment of the mental, only that mind is capable of rational thinking, which is enthroned in a harmonious and highly refined material constitution. Hence right action, right feeling, and right thinking are prerequisites of right knowing, and the attainment of philosophic power is possible only to such as have harmonized their thinking with their living. The wise have therefore declared that none can attain to the highest in the science of knowing until first he has attained to the highest in the science of living (p.202)."

Hall, in his opening chapter, advises:

> "When confronted with a problem involving the use of the reasoning faculties, individuals of strong intellect keep their poise, and seek to reach a solution by obtaining facts bearing upon a question. Those or immature mentality, on the other hand, when similarly confronted, are overwhelmed. While the former may be qualified to solve the riddle of their own destiny, the latter must be led like a flock of sheep and taught in simple language."

We established in *Fallacy 1*, that only bright individuals acquire genuine PTSD. Thus, with the information on imprints provided by imagery and other means in these pages, and perhaps asking Self to try or not to try NLP for one's PTSD healing, the answer should be simple. In particular when reading Hall's following comment:

> "Man is not the insignificant creature that he appears to be; his physical body is not the true measure of his real self. The invisible nature of man is as vast as his comprehension and as measureless as his thought. The fingers of his mind reach out and grasp the stars; his spirit mingles with the throbbing life of Cosmos itself (p.205)."

You are as perfect and as well equipped to live this life now as you were before the PTSD-causing event moment. The only difference is that, through this earthshattering experience, you were presented the opportunity, the duty and the obligation to free yourself from your predicament. This can be done by seeking the knowledge of the ages leading onto the path beyond the stars without having your brainwaves fiddled with by academically well-papered guys of the learned society. They view us as animals void of a mind, never mind a soul, consciousness and conscience. They want to create you in accordance with their will, as if they were gods, when the majority of them have neither experience nor knowledge in the art of living a fulfilling and contented life, never mind through a genuine PTSD experience.

10

MIND MANIPULATION TECHNIQUES AT THEIR FINEST

We can deduce from what we read thus far that a multitude of psychological techniques, methods and combinations thereof are used by the mental health and advertisement industries to intentionally and covertly control us through our subconscious. All of it is rarely done for anything other than financial, social and/or psychological advantages and control. NLP is merely one of these methods. It is a real, scientific, systematically applicable method, and a formidable form of destructive power. It can ruin whole societies when used on the television-watching herd, its reaction known aforehand due to empirical scientific first evidence gathered from human subjects during laboratory tests. Once aware of NLP hypnosis techniques and modes of application, however, we are able to detect if someone influences or controls us. Blind as a bat during my 10 years of hell, I can now see that I was played like a fiddle by all who were involved with my case. From peers to passengers paid to harass me to the powers that be, they were all vying to destroy me (Praveen Kumar: *7 Most Effective Mind Control Techniques Tips in NLP*; mindorbs.com July 2020).

Earlier on, we saw that our mind, wherever it may reside, absorbs at nanosecond speed through our five senses whatever information is presented to us in whatever way or form. This earthly show is ongoing at least from birth to death, and, some maintain, recorded in the Akashic records. Edgar Cayce, a twentieth-century mystic, had the ability to access and describe information from the Akashic Records, a resource he believed was available to everyone. Although unseen, it is an etheric energy that is as evident to a sensitive person as the printed word is to a sighted person. In essence, Cayce said:

> "The Akashic Records, or 'The Book of Life', can be equated to the Universe's super-computer system. It is this system that acts as the central storehouse of all information for every individual who has ever lived upon the earth. More than just a reservoir of events, the Akashic Records contain every deed, word, feeling, thought, and intent that has ever occurred at any time in the history of the world. Much more than simply a memory storehouse, however, these Akashic Records are interactive in that they have a tremendous influence upon our everyday lives, our relationships, our feelings and belief systems, and the potential realities we draw toward us ... The Akashic Records contain the entire history of every soul since the dawn of Creation. These records connect each one of us to one another." (https://edgarcayce.org).

Whether or not neuroscientists believe in the Akashic Records is inconsequential. They do indeed theorize that both our conscious and subconscious minds, for them floating around in our brain, are in charge of filtering incoming data 24/7 and processing minute amounts of those data to our conscious or awareness. How this filtering process takes place and who or what is in charge of it is as yet unknown to them. This despite numerous cognitive neuroscientists having conducted studies that revealed that only 5% of our cognitive activities (decisions, emotions, actions, behaviour) is conscious. Those studies show that the remaining 95% is generated in a non-conscious manner (Marc Van Rymenant; simplifyinginterfaces.com). Not only that—there also seem to be loopholes in this automatic screening process. These additional pathways for human mind manipulation other than brainwaves and NLP are ideal for those wanting to expertly control humanity's thoughts and actions. Cognitive neuro-science, by the way, is the *scientific* study of the biological processes and aspects underlying *cognition*. *Cognition* refers to the mental action or process of acquiring knowledge and understanding through thought, experience and the senses, with a specific focus on the neural connections in the brain, which are thought to be involved in mental processes.

The classical mesmerisation technique of mind-manipulation, Mesmer's hypnosis, is the one still practiced on stage-shows. It puts susceptible subjects into the alpha state, in which humans become vulnerable to suggestions, commands and programming. But with the knowledge of NLP techniques, a practitioner is also capable of covertly inducing thoughts in subjects' subconscious mind. These thoughts go unnoticed by the conscious mind. This powerful technique has been used at least since the 1920s in business, politics, marketing, socializing and religious acts. It is a true gift from heaven for Freud, Bernays et al. to change the U.S. population's moral and social fibre. Bernays himself, referring to his work as psychological warfare, looked at the public and its opinions as an amorphous group of judgments. In his view these judgments were not well-elaborated in the head of even a single average American. He also extracted quotations from British neurosurgeon Wilfred Trotter's 1916 book *Instinct of the Herd in Peace and War*. The book states that the average man has many strong convictions, whose origin Trotter cannot explain. These minds have "logic-proof compartments," which must be approached by means beyond the rational (p. 36; pp. 61–68). Are these the loopholes that unfailingly allow the entire herd's manipulation by way of NLP? Are these the loopholes so desperately sought after by the world's Neumeisterians, the New Masters in German translation?

But even to them, it seems certain that the limitations of the human mind are beyond human and scientific perception. Manly Palmer Hall (1901 –1990) is a Canadian-born mystic, eclectic philosopher and founder of the *Philosophical Research Society*, a modern equivalent of the school of Pythagoras. In his book *The Secret Teachings of All Ages* he states:

> "Man is not the insignificant creature that he appears to be; his physical body is not the true measure of his real self. The invisible nature of man is as vast as his comprehension and as measureless as his thoughts. The fingers of his mind reach to and grasp the stars; his spirit mingles with the throbbing life of Cosmos itself. He who has attained to the state of understanding thereby has so increased his capacity to know that he gradually incorporates within himself the various elements of the universe. The unknown is merely that which is yet to be included within the consciousness of the seeker. Philosophy assists man to develop the sense of appreciation; for as it reveals the glory and the sufficiency of knowledge, it also unfolds those latent powers and faculties whereby man is enabled to master the secrets of the seven spheres." (*The Secret Teachings of All Ages* p. 205)

Hall's observation combines well with those of Cayce and others throughout millennia. They make neuroscientists' searches for the human mind, consciousness, sub- and super-consciousness and the soul within the human brain rather laughable. In particular, they are laughable when we consider Nassim Haramein's "Connected Universe" theory. This ground-breaking, scientifically substantiated proposal was published in 2013. It has the potential to significantly impact global issues facing the human race, including alternative energy sources.

Haramein is founder and director of research at the Hawaii Institute for Unified Physics (HIUP). In his peer-reviewed paper titled "Quantum Gravity and the Holographic Mass", he offers a new and alternative understanding of gravity through basic algebraic and geometric equations. Thus, he indicates that everything in the *universe* is connected, from the largest to the smallest scale, through a unified understanding of gravity. He also demonstrates that it is space that defines matter and not matter that defines space. We are told that Haramein's approach could potentially unlock new discoveries in the areas of energy, transportation and even space travel (PR Newswire, May 07, 2013). His video presentation *The Field of Boundless Information* beautifully clarifies the subject matter (July 13, 2018). In principle, he says that every one of us has access to all the information floating around in the universe, e.g., the Akashic Records, this field of boundless information of which most of us are unaware, kept as we have been for thousands of years like mushrooms – in the dark, and fed steer manure.

Einstein already tried to pinpoint it with his unified field theory. The Indian guru Maharishi Mahesh Yogi (1918--2008), known for the Transcendental Meditation™ technique, introduced the idea in his 1963 book *The Science of Being and Art of Living*. He exclaimed that when a theoretical physicist succeeded in establishing a unified field theory, the content would establish the principle of unity in the midst of diversity—namely the basic unity of all material existence. Here's how he put it:

> "The discovery of the field of this one basis of material existence ...will assist in turning the world of physical science to the science of mental phenomena. Theories of mind, intellect and ego will supersede the findings of physical science. At the ultimate or the extreme limit of investigation into the nature of reality in the field of the mind will eventually be located the state of pure consciousness, the field of the transcendental nature lying beyond all the relative existence of material and mental values. The ultimate field of Being lies beyond the field of mental phenomena and is the truth of life in all its phases, relative and absolute. The Science of Being is the transcendental science of mind. The Science of Being transcends the science of mind, which, in its turn, transcends the material sciences which deal with the diversity of material existence."

Bingo.

Haramein succeeded in precisely doing that, not only in *The Field of Boundless Information*. He also beautifully clarified his theory of this field of the transcendental nature of our human existence. In his 2016 TEDxUCSD presentation *The Connected Universe*, he revealed to the layman that we lie beyond all the relative existence of material and mental values. Maharishi's successor, quantum physicist John Samuel Hagelin (1954-), backs him up with his own "Consciousness is the Unified Field" theory, presented on the *Transcendental Meditation Blog* in 2016. (transcendentalmeditationblog.wordpress.com). Hagelin is leader of the TM movement in the United States and president of the Maharishi University of Management (MUM) in Fairfield, Iowa.

Hagelin, who has practiced Transcendental Meditation since 1970, obtained his A.B. in physics with highest honors (*summa cum laude*) from Dartmouth. He went on to study physics at Harvard University, earning a master's degree in 1976 and a PhD in physics. In 1981, he began post-doctoral research for a few months at the European Center for Particle Physics (CERN) in Switzerland. In 1982, he moved to the Stanford Linear Accelerator Center (SLAC) in California for a year. He joined the Maharishi International University (MIU), later named the Maharishi University of Management (MUM), as chair of its physics department in 1984. In 1987 and 1989, Hagelin already claimed that the superstring theory's "unified field" was identical to what Maharishi had called the "unified field of consciousness." Superstring theory is an attempt to explain all of the particles and fundamental forces of nature in one theory by modeling them as vibrations of tiny super-symmetric strings.

Hagelin published his papers substantiating his claims in the *Modern Science and Vedic Science Journal*. This MUM publication is devoted to research on the unified field and its applications for the benefit of the world. It combines modern science and Vedic science, as brought to light by Maharishi Mahesh Yogi (https://research.miu.edu). The seers of the Vedic tradition already described the capacity of the human mind to become consciously identified with the universal and unbounded field of pure intelligence. It forms the foundation of natural law, and they already delineated the self-interacting dynamics by which it gives rise to all diversity in nature. They identified the unified field of all the laws of nature as a self-sufficient, self-interacting and infinitely dynamic field of consciousness, as both Hagelin and Haramein are now proving scientifically.

In the late 1980s, Hagelin argued that consciousness was a fundamental property of the natural world, not part of the individual human brain. He claimed that Transcendental Meditation practitioners could experience a state of consciousness in which the observer, the process of observation and the observed were unified. This, Hagelin stated, was the experience of the unified field of physics. Needless to say, Hagelin's views were vehemently rejected by "virtually every theoretical physicist in the world". This according to American theoretical physicist Peter Woit (1957), Columbia University's senior lecturer in the Mathematics department (Woit 2006 p.206). Other physicists currently exploring super-symmetric unified quantum field theories, are just now discovering the same qualities Hagelin identified 30 years ago. Thus, modern science is slowly beginning to glimpse the unified structure of the entire universe. This we learn from the Resonance Science Foundation. This is the global research and education non-profit organization (501c3) that Haramein founded in 2004, committed to the unification of physics and science as a whole. He and his team of researchers and educators are developing a formal unified view of physics. Their findings could have implications and applications to revolutionary technologies that transform people's lives and help overcome some of the largest challenges facing the world today.

Mind you, from the Vedic scriptures onwards, the idea of consciousness and information floating around as a free-for-all in the universe and beyond for anyone to catch has been around for thousands of years. Spiritual masters throughout the ages have pointed out that the way to Nirvana is found within ourselves. For example, Swami Vivekanada (1863–1902) is one of the more recent ones. He is considered a Patriotic saint in India and is perhaps best known for his speech at the 1893 Parliament of the World's Religions in Chicago, when he introduced Hinduism to America, beginning with the words "Sisters and brothers of America ..." He states:

> "No knowledge comes from outside; it is all inside. What we say a man "knows" should, on strict psychological language, be what he "discovers" by taking the cover off his own soul, which is a mine of infinite knowledge."

The Buddha displays the magnitude of what's to discover when exploring our minds by going within ourselves to search for answers to our questions and their consequences. He confirms what we discussed previously, namely the enormous influence of our mind's control and manipulation, by ourselves and others, in particular the media and its phenomenal inherent dangers:

> "All that we are is the result of what we have thought. It is founded on our thoughts and made up of our thoughts. If a man speak or act with an evil thought,

> suffering follows him as the wheel follows the hoof of the beast that draws the wagon.... If a man speak or act with a good thought, happiness follows him like a shadow that never leaves him."

But until Maharishi brought it to the West, this knowledge was largely hidden in plain sight from the masses. No scientific evidence could apparently be found in the occident, either, to substantiate even the idea of it. Not even though the unified field theory became an open line of research since the nineteenth century. Granted, research was mainly based on classical physics, which excludes quantum mechanics and/or the theory of relativity. The term itself was coined by Albert Einstein (1879-1955) who attempted to unify his general theory of relativity with electromagnetism, a branch of physics dealing with the electromagnetic force that occurs between electrically charged particles. The electromagnetic force is one of the four fundamental forces, and it exhibits electromagnetic fields, such as magnetic fields, electric fields and light. A unified field theory (UFT) in physics is a type of field theory that allows all that is usually thought of as fundamental forces and elementary particles in nature to be written in terms of a pair of physical and virtual fields. According to the modern discoveries in physics, forces are not transmitted directly between interacting objects, but instead are described and interrupted by intermediary entities called fields.

Einstein is best known to the general public for his mass energy equivalence formula $E = mc^2$, "Energy equals mass times the speed of light squared." On the most basic level, the equation says that energy and mass (matter) are interchangeable; they are different forms of the same thing and for his theory of relativity. The theory of relativity usually encompasses two interrelated theories by Albert Einstein: special relativity and general relativity. Special relativity applies to all physical phenomena in the absence of gravity. General relativity explains the law of gravitation and its relation to other forces of nature. It applies to the cosmological and astrophysical realm, including astronomy.

He received the Nobel Prize in Physics in 1921 "for his services to theoretical physics, especially for his discovery of the law of the photoelectric effect", the latter a pivotal step in the development of quantum theory. His compatriot, the theoretical physicist Max Karl Ernst Ludwig Planck (1858-1947) had won the Nobel Prize in Physics in 1918 for discovering energy quanta. His fame as a physicist rests primarily on his role as the originator of the quantum theory, which revolutionized human understanding of atomic and subatomic processes. He took the idea of a unified field theory a step further than Einstein in 1944, exclaiming:

> "As a man who has devoted his whole life to the most clear headed science, to the study of matter, I can tell you as a result of my research about atoms this much: There is no matter as such. All matter originates and exists only by virtue of a force, which brings the particle of an atom to vibration and holds this most minute solar system of the atom together. We must assume behind this force the existence of a conscious and intelligent spirit (orig. Geist). This spirit is the matrix of all matter...I regard consciousness as fundamental. I regard matter as derivative from consciousness. We cannot get behind consciousness. Everything that we talk about, everything that we regard as existing, postulates consciousness."

Which leads us back to Haramein. He claimed that consciousness and memory are not a function of the brain, but rather a function of the unified field, thus confirming Maharishi's and Hagelin's unified field theory. Haramein delivered a presentation entitled "The Universe and You" at the University of St Andrews in Scotland in 2019. He presented new research results connecting the physics of the very small quantum scales to the physics of the very large cosmological scales, and demonstrated some of the technologies that are emerging as a result. He discussed the source of physics unification and even the possible mechanism for consciousness, a fundamental mystery since the beginning of time, as a result of having a new understanding of the universe. As he said at an earlier presentation:

> "New physics is emerging that relates the very large scale of black holes with the quantum structure of space-time. This new physics describes our universe as an information network from universal to subatomic particles. This universal neuro-net may be the source of the self-organizing system found at the biological scale and the event of consciousness. It's imperative to evolve with new scientific advances, it is easy to just accept the old teachings but that will not drive innovation." (https://prnewswire.com).

One sure-fire way to access this unified field of consciousness and retrieve information and knowledge from it is through the regular practice of meditation. Haramein learned it at age 11 from an Indian master. He was taught to go inward to reach a much larger field of influence to explore his own set of information, which is entangled with all information contained in the universe. When going inwards each day, we can explore that space and soon find, that we have more and more influence to access the information we wish to obtain. "The more time you spend in your inner space the easier the answers you seek come to you. The potential is limitless," he says. Personally, without having "gone inwards" twice daily I could not have survived my genuine PTSD journey, 10 years through pure hell, nor could I have found the path to my own healing.

But Haramein's way of thinking and reasoning is the exception among scientists. So is the American neurosurgeon and author Eben Alexander III's (1953–). He is the adopted son of American academic neurosurgeon Eben Alexander Jr. (1913–2004), part of a distinguished family of scholars spanning several generations. Known for his notable education and training of neurosurgeons, his many recognition awards and his editorship of *Surgical Neurology, an International Journal of Neurosurgery and Neuroscience* from 1987 to 1994. Alexander III followed in his father's footsteps as an academic neurosurgeon. His 2008 experiences, while in a meningitis-induced coma, inspired him to publish the semi-autobiographical book *Proof of Heaven: A Neurosurgeon's Journey into the Afterlife*. In the book, he asserts that consciousness is independent of the brain and that death is nothing other than a transition phase into another realm. He also foresaw that science would determine that the brain does not create consciousness and that consciousness survives bodily death.

Needless to say, his peers met his assertions with fierce opposition, and so did scientists. One of them was American author, philosopher, neuroscientist and atheist Samuel Benjamin Harris (1967–). His academic background is in philosophy and cognitive neuroscience and is prominent for his criticism of religion, Islam in particular. He describes Alexander's NDE account as "alarmingly unscientific," whilst claiming that experiencing visions while his cerebral cortex was shut down demonstrated a failure to acknowledge existing brain science, with little evidence to prove otherwise. That the cerebral cortex is compromised in the vast majority of humans since birth due to a mal-rotated Atlas went unmentioned by Harris (*Fallacy 1*).

British neurologist, naturalist, historian of science and author Oliver Wolf Sacks (1933–2015) was another critic. He was born into an extremely large extended family of eminent scientists, physicians and other notable individuals. This included director and writer Jonathan Lynn and first cousins, Israeli statesman Abba Eban and Nobel Laureate Robert Aumann. He received his medical degree from The Queen's College of Oxford in 1960. He interned at Mount Zion Hospital in San Francisco. And he completed his residency in neurology and neuropathology at the University of California, Los Angeles (UCLA). He relocated to New York in 1965, but realised that the neuro-research career would be a poor fit. So, he served as neurological consultant to various New York City-area nursing homes and hospitals, as well as the Bronx Psychiatric Center, from 1966 to 1991.

He worked with a group of survivors of the 1920s encephalitis lethargica epidemic at the Beth Abraham Hospital's chronic-care facility in the Bronx. They had been unable to move on their own for decades. This experience was the base for his non-fiction book *Awakenings* (1973). Encephalitis lethargica, known as "sleeping sickness," is distinct from tsetse fly-transmitted sleeping sickness. Encephalitis lethargica was first described in 1917 by Austrian psychiatrist and neurologist Constantin von Economo (1876–1931) and French pathologist Jean-René Cruchet (1875–1959). The disease attacks the brain, leaving some victims in a statue-like condition, speechless and motionless. Between 1915 and 1926, the epidemic spread around the world, affecting five million people, killing a third of them in the acute stages. Many of those who survived never returned to their pre-morbid vigour.

> "They would be conscious and aware—yet not fully awake; they would sit motionless and speechless all day in their chairs, totally lacking energy, impetus, initiative, motive, appetite, affect or desire; they registered what went on about them without active attention, and with profound indifference. They neither conveyed nor felt the feeling of life; they were as insubstantial as ghosts, and as passive as zombies (*Awakenings* p. 14)

In *Awakenings*, Sacks chronicles his efforts to help these patients by using the then-new drug L-DOPA. This was the precursor to the neurotransmitters dopamine, norepinephrine (noradrenaline) and epinephrine (adrenaline), collectively known as catecholamines. L-DOPA in its pure form is sold as a psychoactive drug; trade names include Sinemet, Pharmacopa, Atamet and Stalevo. Believing the brain to be the "most incredible thing in the universe," he continued to author numerous books, mostly collections of case studies of people, including himself, with neurological disorders. He also published book reviews and articles about the history of science, natural history and contemporary medicine. He included a wealth of narrative details about his experiences with his patients and his own experiences, and how patients and he coped with their conditions. Sacks agreed with Harris, arguing that Alexander had failed to recognize that his personal experience could have been the result of his cortex returning to full function at the outset of his coma, rather than a supernatural experience. In other words, he either purposely fails to acknowledge that the human cerebral cortex is always severely malfunctioning due to the mal-rotated cerebral cortex present in most humans or he did not know about it (Atlasprofilax; Schuemperli).

Twenty-five years ago, Dentist-turned-photographer Phil Borges abandoned his orthodontic practice to pursue his first love: documenting the world's disappearing cultures through photography. He is also the founder of *Bridges to Understanding*, an interactive online classroom promoting cross-cultural learning between indigenous and American youth. In his documentary, *CRAZYWISE*, crazy...or wise, he discloses how the traditional wisdom of indigenous cultures contradicts modern views about mental health crises. Is it a 'calling' to grow [spiritually], or is it a 'broken brain'? Is a genuine PTSD crisis an opportunity to turn one's psychological crisis into a positive transformative experience, or an invitation to enter the path of victimhood and consequent disaster due to the treatment received by those we trust to know, the mental health professionals? In his 2014 TED presentation *Psychosis or Spiritual Awakening* Borges pinpoints precisely what happens to genuine PTSD experiencers because of the NC *for* PTSD set "Standard of PTSD Care" treatment. That standard the guidelines to doctors upon a patient's PTSD-causing event moment.

We know from both *Fallacy 1* and *Broken Wings*, the secret about this treatment of CBT and pharmacotherapy, drugging and indoctrination of the belief that one's own pre-incident mental illness has caused the PTSD symptoms. The secret being that it will be prolonged for as long as they can prolong it, namely until the time PTSD journeyers are on skid row or have committed suicide. After all, they are the brightest of the crop and have to be stigmatized, portrayed as useless eaters, human debris to the public, and destroyed. There is just one way this modus operandi by GPs and mental health professional alike can be countermanded. As with the example given by Borges, the PTSD experiencer must stop taking pharmaceutical and other mind-altering drugs cold turkey and find the spiritual path to healing the Self. The industry knows it, but will never tell you! My Irish psychiatrist did. He stopped writing prescription to his patients, lecturing them and me instead on nutrition and on the holistic path to healing the Self. But then, he has honour and integrity in spades, which most of the others lack.

However, to help the Self, you need awareness and the willingness to learn and to search. Combine Borges' knowledge as presented in his TED talk with that of Dada Gunamuktananda's 2014 presentation *Consciousness -- the final frontier*. See how easy it is to understand that every one of us is born with the power to manage our lives. It is our duty and obligation to use this phenomenal power the moment we become aware of it to begin creating ourselves and our lives to our liking. This discovery of the enormous power within is the gift of genuine PTSD. But it can only be discovered when free of all mind-altering drugs of any sort, as all create "the mistake of the intellect" mentioned in *Fallacy 1*. But no one tells us about this, as it would cause mankind's awakening to the truth of world affairs.

One of the paths to that awakening could be through philosophy, quite literally meaning "love of wisdom". It seems to be one way for people to understand fundamental truths about themselves, their role in and relationship with the world in which they live, and one another. Genuine PTSD journeyers are bright, as only bright people can acquire genuine PTSD. So for them, it is one of the mandatory paths to healing, a truth vehemently hidden through the treatment received by so-called PTSD experts. We will never tune into it on our own, when under the pharmacotherapy mind altering drug "treatment" of the NC *for* PTSD. Nor with Cognitive Behavioural Therapy, itself a mind-manipulation programming method. This fact has been known almost from the moment that German neuropsychiatrist Hans Berger (1873–1941) introduced the world's first electroencephalography machine, the EEG, at the University of Jena, Germany in 1929. This machine is an electrophysiological monitoring mechanism engineered to record the brain's electrical activity by placing electrodes along the scalp. Worse, invasive electrodes are used in electrocorticography where electrodes are placed directly on the exposed surface of the brain to record electrical cerebral cortex activity.

An EEG measures voltage fluctuations resulting from ionic current within the brain's neurons. These are the fundamental units of the brain and nervous system, the cells responsible for:

- sending motor commands to our muscles
- receiving sensory input from the external world
- transforming and relaying the electrical signals at every step in between

Clinically, EEG refers to the brain's spontaneous electrical activity over a period of time, as recorded from multiple electrodes placed on the scalp to detect brain activity. The electrodes record the brain wave patterns, which data the EEG machine sends to a computer or cloud server. And, as usual, current research on effects of pharmacological agents on human neurophysiology finds its roots in animal research. This is reflected in contemporary animal pharmaco-electroencephalography (p-EEG) applications conducted mostly in rats and mice. That human subjects are preferred is a given; for a price, they can be enticed to participate.

But this is nothing new, either. The start of electrophysiology-based physiology began when Italian physician, physicist, biologist and philosopher Luigi Galvani (1737–1798) noticed muscle contractions in frog legs generated by 'animal electricity' as early as 1780 A.D. In the mid to late nineteenth century, the first electrophysiology-based physiologies of the nervous system and the nerve action potential were developed. Italian physicist and neurophysiologist Carlo Mateucci (1811–1868) worked on it in Bologna, Italy. German physician and physiologist Emil Du Bois-Rymond (1818–1896), the developer of experimental electrophysiology, also worked on it.

The Lord Mayor of Liverpool, physician and physiologist Richard Caton (1842–1926) was the first to describe spontaneous electrical current fluctuations in the brains of rabbits and monkeys. He used two electrodes and a sensitive mirror galvanometer. He noted: "Feeble currents of varying direction pass through the multiplier when the electrodes are placed on two points of the external surface of the skull."

Similar observations were made independently by Ukrainian-born Russian physician, physiologist and parasitologist Vasily Yakovlevich Danilevsky (1852- 1939), the first to give comprehensive descriptions of nerve impulses in dog brains. In 1877, he described the effect of electrical brain stimulation in animals in his thesis *Investigations into the Physiology of the Brain*, while also working on the physiological responses of hypnosis in animals and humans. Polish physician and professor of physiology at the University of Lwów Adolf Beck (1863-1942) was in on the research, too. He used monkeys, rabbits and dogs to study their electrical brain potentials and their reactions to sensory stimulation, as well as their brains' spontaneous rhythmic fluctuation activity. Beck also described the disappearance of oscillations when the eyes were stimulated with light. He is considered to be one of the pioneers of electroencephalography (EEG). He received many marks of distinction from medical societies in recognition of his scientific investigations, which would eventually lead to Berger's discovery of humans' alpha wave brain activity.

While EEG studies flourished in Eastern Europe, little research in the field took place in the rest of the world until 1929. That's when Berger revealed his method of recording brainwaves. It was he who coined the name "electroencephalography" for it and he who discovered the alpha wave rhythm, henceforth known as the "Berger wave". From 1902 onwards, he attempted to record dogs' brain activity. IN 1924, he started work on humans' EEG, producing a series of 14 reports from 1929 to 1938 (*Über das Elektrenkephalogramm des Menschen*). Using simultaneously a galvanometer and an oscillograph, he demonstrated the disappearance of alpha waves and the presence of rapid waves of the beta type during the period of unconsciousness following epileptic seizures, and the return of the alpha waves. Furthermore, he described his investigation on the nature of alpha and beta waves in the human cortex when electrodes were attached to the frontal and posterior scalp, and records obtained with both normal and psychotic patients.

Among Berger's reports are the first descriptions of alpha and beta waves, sleep EEG and the effect of hypoxia on the human brain. In 1931, Berger published the first known human p-EEG recordings on:

- the generalised power decrease after chloroform
- the alpha brain wave power reduction after morphine
- the alpha brainwave power-increasing effects of cocaine
- the dose-dependent effects of scopolamine on alpha and beta brain waves

In the mid 1930s, these findings were replicated by Davis in the United States, by Durup and Fessard in Paris and by Adrian in Cambridge. From this time onwards ,electroencephalography blossomed as part of clinical neurological practices and in psychiatry both in Europe and the U.S. Meanwhile by the late 1940s, the use of superficial EEG recordings in experimental research declined in favour of single neuron studies. In the next decade, EEG was established as an important diagnostic and guidance instrument for neurosurgery and epileptology. It became an essential tool in sleep research, due to the pioneering work of Kleitman and Dement in Chicago.

Shortly after Berger wheeled out his EEG machine in 1929, Fischer and Kornmüller, fellow scientist in Berlin, discovered the toxic effects of picrotoxin and a number of other convulsive substances on animal EEG (Drinkenburg W.H.I.M, Ahnaou A, Ruigt G.S.F: 'Pharmaco-EEG Studies in Animals: A History-Based Introduction to Contemporary Translational Applications'. Karger.com). Apart from some spurious animal pre-clinical p-EEG studies, there was little activity in this field of research in the years following. This changed in the late 1950s, when the pharmaceutical industry, without doubt sparked by Berger's discoveries of cocaine and other drugs on the human brain, began to develop synthetic antipsychotic chlorpromazine and antidepressant imipramine drugs. The clinical EEG effects generated interest for the study of these compounds in animal experimentation. At that time, most of these studies were done in rabbits, cats, dogs, monkeys and occasionally in rodents, we are told. This is just as well, as they are human and we are them, as far as science is concerned. In detail, this is what we are to scientists, in case it slipped your mind:

> "Humans (*Homo sapiens*) are highly intelligent primates that have become the dominant species on Earth. They are the only extant members of the subtribe Hominina and—together with chimpanzees, gorillas, and orangutans—are part of the family Hominidae (the great apes, or *hominids*). Humans are terrestrial animals, characterized by their erect posture and bipedal locomotion; high manual dexterity and heavy tool use compared to other animals; open-ended and complex language use compared to other animal communications; larger, more complex brains than other primates; and highly advanced and organized societies." (Wikipedia)

Porcus, cani, simia, rattus and mus are part of a group of vertebrate animals forming the class "Mammalia", Such species bears live young, produces milk for them through mammary glands and cares for them as good parents do. Scientists consider the species akin to the subtribe Hominina as well. Why else would they, since Pavlov's days, liberally, literarily and regularily transfer the results of their psychological testings of those creatures and apply them to homo sapiens, genuine PTSD experiencers included. Meanwhile, they steadfastly ignoring the words of freemason Albert Pike (1809–1891), U.S. Sovereign Grand Commander of the Scottish Rite's Southern Jurisdiction who stated:

> "God breathed into man the spirit of life; not matter, but an emanation from Himself; not a creature made by Him, nor a distinct existence, but a Power, like His own Thought; and light...immortal and indestructible lke Himself" (Albert Pike: *Morals and Dogma of The ancient and Accepted Scottish Rite of Freemasonry* ch. XXVI; Charleston 1871)?"

By the way, Pike compiled at least half of his work, *Morals and Dogma,* from texts of other authors throughout the ages. These works were used in "lectures" on the esoteric roots of freemasonry given during initiation ceremonies to a new degree. Nevertheless, we assume that when EEG is conducted on subtribe hominina and other mammals, it is conducted in the same manner as on homo sapiens considerd equal to them. The procedure nowadays records the brain's electrical activity via electrodes affixed to the scalp. Readings, mapped via computer, show changes in brain activity, which in turn may be useful in diagnosing brain conditions. But how?

Well, a multitude of functional EEG measures are said to have been investigated, mostly in our rats and mice brethren. These range from simple spectral powers and sleep-wake parameters to advanced connectivity parameters with high-density EEG. The dense array scalp EEG recording system consists of pre-cabled cuffs connected to a digital amplifier and preferably to a dedicated computer. The number of electrodes can vary from 32 to 256.

Reversal studies comparable to phase I of clinical trials are also carried out. Medical reversals occur when a newer and methodologically superior clinical trial produces results that contradict existing clinical practice from older trials.

What are clinical trials? They are medical research studies involving people (cancerresearchuk.org). There are two main types of trials or studies - interventional and observational. Interventional trials aim to find out more about a particular intervention or treatment. People taking part are put into different treatment groups, so that the research team can compare the results. Observational studies aim to find out what happens to people in different situations. The research team observes the people taking part, but they do not influence their treatments.

In other words, clinical trials are a way to test new methods of diagnosing, treating or preventing health conditions to determine whether proposed drugs are both safe and effective (healthline.com). A variety of things are evaluated during clinical trials, including:

- medications
- medical devices
- medication combinations
- new uses for existing medications

How are they conducted? We are told that before starting a clinical trial, scientists run preclinical research using human cell cultures or animal models in a laboratory. These would test, for example, whether a new medication or vaccine is toxic to human cells. If this preclinical research is promising, scientists move forward with clinical trials in several phases to see how well the drug works in humans. Each phase builds on the results of the previous phases. Phase 0 is usually conducted with fewer than 15 people, to make sure the medication is tried to benign to humans.

During phase I, higher doses are administered for several months to about 20 to 80 people without any underlying health conditions. This is just to establish the highest dose of a specific medication humans can tolerate without serious side effects. Researchers in this phase also determine whether the drug should be administered orally, intravenously or topically.

In Phase II, several hundred trial participants living with the condition the new drug is to perhaps treat are usually given the dose found to be safe in phase I experiments. Researchers at this stage also gather information about the drug's side effects and overall effectiveness.

Phase III usually involves up to 3,000 human participants imbued with the condition the new drug is meant to treat. This trial often lasts several years so as to evaluate how the new drug works in comparison to existing ones. In this phase, scientists must demonstrate that the drug is at least as safe and effective as those already approved by the FDA before bringing it to market. It is during this phase that rare and long-term side effects are likely to show.

Phase IV kicks in when the drug is FDA-approved. It involves thousands of participants, can last for many years and is used to get more information about the drug's long-term safety, effectiveness and other benefits or side effects.

EEG can be valuable throughout the testing. Disruption of brain function and concomitant EEG changes can consistently be achieved through pharmacological or behavioral challenges, as well as by transgenic manipulation. In other words, one or more DNA sequences from another species have been introduced by artificial means. Animals are usually made transgenic by having a small sequence of foreign DNA, like that of rattus, monkey, mus, cani or porcus, the pig, injected into a fertilized egg or developing embryo of any species considered animal by the Darwinian leagues, including homo sapiens. Transgenic plants can also be made by introducing foreign DNA into a variety of different tissues. The remodeled species are then used in reversal testing with novel test compounds that target specific brain-neurochemistry systems after drugs are administered.

At least since the 1950s and 1960s, the acute effects of psychotropic drugs readable on EEG in healthy humans were correlated and compared with their clinical efficacy in psychiatric patients. Nowadays, genuine PTSD-experiencing soldiers and veterans are, for a pitiful amount of cash, regularly sought as subjects for such experiments. A warning: before committing yourself to such trials, it might be wise to watch the April 2018 medical documentary *When A Drug Trial Goes Wrong: Emergency At The Hospital* telling the story of eight healthy men who volunteered in an experimental drug trial that went terribly wrong (Youtube; https://BBC.uk.com). It should scare the wits out of you.

Back to our history, lo and behold, in rushed three more in the EEG cast of characters, right on time to apply EEG discoveries to the making of the American herd's mind. Richard Bandler (1950–) was among them, holding a BA degree in philosophy and psychology and a MA in psychology. So was his cherished comrade in arms, John Grinder (1940–), captain in the U.S. Army Special Forces and working for a U.S. intelligence agency, with a BA in psychology and a PhD in linguistics.

They were abetted by American psychiatrist and psychologist, specializing in medical hypnosis and family therapy, Milton Hyland Erickson (1901 –1980). He also held the post of president of the American Society for Clinical Hypnosis. He was a fellow of the American Psychiatric Association, the American Psychological Association *and* the American Psychopathological Association.

Together, these men developed the neuro-linguistic programming (NLP) hypothesis.

Erickson was generally regarded as the foremost hypnotherapist of his time. He worked with trances and cleverly structured sentences full of vague meanings to help his clients discover how to address their problems and unearth the resources they already had available to them (nlpworld.co.uk). It is said that his clinical success was based on several things:

- his skill with language patterns
- his ability to establish rapport with his clients
- his ability to read non-verbal behaviour (sensory acuity)
- his beliefs in the unconscious mind as creative and solution-generating by way of neuro-linguistic programming

Bandler and Grinder ran with Erickson's ideas big time.

They rejected much of what they saw as the ineffectiveness of talk therapy. This was better known as Freud's et al.'s psychotherapy, or, depending on a therapist's specific school of thought, the cognitive theory and behaviourism. Rather, they were inspired by the computer revolution. Bandler had been a computer science major and Grinder was a Special Forces army captain. Together, they developed the psychological programming language for humans only. This would produce behavioural changes in their subjects by way of layering subtle meaning into spoken and written language so supremely useful for both military personnel and herd manipulation.

After all, U.S. Special Forces, due to their headgear colloquially known as "green berets," are deployed to execute unconventional warfare, foreign internal defense, direct action, counter-insurgency, special reconnaissance, counter-terrorism, information operations, counter-proliferation of weapons of mass destruction and security force assistance. Thus, this NLP language that allows for implanting suggestions into people's unconscious minds without their knowledge, came in exceedingly handy to all their operations. Furthermore, NLP was contrary to classical hypnosis techniques of putting patients into suggestive trances on command, even up to the point of losing consciousness. In addition, Bandler and Grinder insisted that their method created a connection between the brain's neurological processes and the behavioural patterns people had learned or adopted through life experience (their individual *programming*). With NLP, these could be changed and lead to achievement of specific goals in their life.

We know from *Fallacy 1* that psychotherapy, psychological therapy and talking therapy all claim to resolve, mitigate or change humans' troublesome behaviors, beliefs, compulsions, thoughts and emotions. It is also claimed by the mental health profession that such therapies lead to improved relationships and social skills and, by and large, enable anyone to change and overcome any problems in whichever way desired. The question, however, whose desires do they change? That part always remains unspecified by mental health practitioners. And, as most of those in their clutches are unaware of the attempt to change them to the therapist's desires, the patient rarely asks. Might their professional self-description of "psychotherapist" - psycho-the rapist of the human soul - be an indication of their idea of manipulating the human psyche into acceptable human behavior to their liking?

Despite the absence of first evidence about all mental health profession and NLP applications and endeavors, it is no surprise that the learned society discredits NLP as merely a pseudoscience, when in fact all of the mental health industry could be considered as such. Despite this rejection, or perhaps because of it, NLP techniques are widely marketed by high-powered organizations to a multitude of businesses and governments worldwide in seminars and leadership training courses. But the industry also receives a fair share of accusations as agencies of mind-manipulation (Mike Bundrant: "NLP Seminars ~ A Comprehensive Guide to the Good, Bad and Manipulative". https://psychcentral.com 2018).

Mind you, human manipulation itself is as old as the hills, the misuse of language for personal gain making its mark in history long before the term "neuro-linguistic programming" was ever created. After all, NLP is nothing other than a model of communication, a series of tools presented for use to the benefit of oneself and others for benevolent or nefarious means. Is NLP intentionally deceptive and manipulative, though? Or would it depend on the NLP administrator's qualifications? Would it matter, if they were highly trained and effective, or woefully under-skilled or inadequate? With selfless intentions or driven by selfishness and greed? Does it really matter one way or another? Do not all cultures worldwide have greedy, selfish folks in their midst, ready to take advantage of anyone cruising by when buying and selling goods, propaganda, political views, ideologies and even love and lust—wit Adam and Eve?

The life coaching industry as a profession as an extension of sports and business coaching sprang to life big time in the 1980s. This opened a bonanza of hitherto unknown proportions for NLP gurus. Nowadays, for as little as $US 1297.00, anyone can obtain the finest in professional training as a Certified Professional [life] Coach with just seven days of study. And the promised land is yours. NLP will change your life for you. Meanwhile, the organization in which you enroll to become equipped with the technique will suck you into their schemes by liberal use of the very NLP techniques they promise to teach you to change yourself or others within a few hours, a few days, or a few months. Here are some of the promises they make by teaching you the "Magic and Power" of NLP:

- "Make others follow your lead through powerful persuasion techniques."
- "Instantly hypnotize complete strangers into obeying your hidden commands."
- "Get exactly what you want from any negotiations."
- "Make people beg you to sell them your products and services."
- "NLP will fix all your life's problems, no matter what."

If showing up anywhere in person is inconvenient, you can also obtain a fully accredited Part Time Life Coach Certificate Program completely online. This would be "provide you with everything you need to offer top-notch life coaching services in your desired niche during a 21-week Life Coach Certificate Online Program covering the 11 core competencies described by The International Coaching Federation (ICF)" Founded in 1995, ICF is another non-profit organization sucking on the public tit. It proclaims to be dedicated to professional life coaching. The ICF defines coaching as partnering with clients in a thought-provoking and creative process that inspires them to maximize their personal and professional potential. As of July 2020, three ICF Credentials were handed out:

- Associate Certified Coaches (ACC)
- Professional Certified Coaches (PCC)
- Master Certified Coaches (MCC)

Each costs thousands of dollars. You can imagine where this sparrow flies once you enrol, can you? And what are you to learn on, and most likely off, line?

- Coaching Foundation – Gain basic listening and questioning skills and learn how to practice empathy effectively.
- Coaching Essentials – Learn how to manage coaching conversations and assist clients with setting goals and organizing their lives.
- Coaching Relationship – Understand how to use beneficial language, including metaphors and analogies.
- Coaching in Practice – Learn models of motivation, life design and values, and how to prepare a client welcome package (https://info.rhodescollege.ca)

Needless to say, this form of mind-perversion and manipulation is now a multi-million industry around the world. An estimated 100,000 life coaches work professionally across the globe. The ICF alone has approximately 41,500 members in 147 countries and territories. Some of these are self-help gurus. Tony Robbins is among them. So is Canadian author, clinical hypnotherapist and corporate trainer Glenn Charles Andrew Alexander (Parker). They profess to have helped 1000s of people become millionaires by applying NLP techniques, marketed as "the science of personal achievement", while making grand livings off NLP indoctrinations. Tony Robbins has a net worth of $600 million dollars.

NLP originator Bandler himself did not do too badly, either, with an annual income somewhere between one to five million dollars (trendcelebsnow.com). Since 1975, he has been a consultant to Fortune 500 companies, the U.S. Military, American intelligent agencies, major league baseball teams, NFL players and Olympic athletes. He also consults at a research and development company specializing in optics and holographic storage systems. This gives us insight into the enormous range and breadth of NLP application across a multitude of industries and occupations (nlplifetraining.com). This, inevitably, leads to the question whether or not a true *sui generis*, a unique human Self, still exists among the NLP-manipulated humans and political world?

Not according to considered ultra-culture wizard and writer Jason Louv, who loves to talk about occult history, reality tunnels, Aleister Crowley's secret Christianity and the post apocalyptic role-playing games the West seems unable to escape. Louv deems NLP to be one of the world's most prevalent methods of mind control, permeating society from sales callers to politicians to media pundits. "Nasty to the core," he calls it, a splendid method for controlling people's minds ("10 Ways to Protect Yourself From NLP Mind Control"; https://ultraculture.org).

Neuro-linguistic programming has become so interwoven with how the herd is kept in check, communicated to and marketed to, that its use is practically invisible. It is also a somewhat pernicious, meaning a highly injurious, destructive, deadly and wicked, devilish force in the world. Indeed, nearly *everybody* in the business of influencing people has studied at least some of its techniques. Masters of it are notorious for having a Rasputin-like ability to trick people in incredible ways, Louv says.

But this is nothing new, either. Already in the mid 1980s, NLP flourished to such a degree that lawsuits and wars erupted over who had the right to teach, or even use the term "NLP". Mind you, at that time, Bandler had bigger problems than copyright disputes. He was on trial for the alleged murder of Corine Christensen (1955–1986). She was the daughter of a San Francisco, prostitute and NLP student murdered in California on November 3, 1986. Christensen, who together with her boyfriend James Marino, supplied drugs to Bandler. She was shot in the face at her townhouse in Capitola near Santa Cruz with a .357 Magnum owned by Bandler. She died of her wounds (enacademic.com).

The fact that Bandler's modus operandi during NLP sessions is said to have been the use of a gun in order to produce dramatic psychological changes in clients did not play a role in the verdict to let him go free. That he allegedly used NLP manipulation while on the stand was of no consequence to the jury. They acquitted him after five-and-a-half hours of deliberation. Whatever the truth of the matter, the story quickly disappeared from the news, and NLP went on to gain further popularity. It worked its way not only into the toolkit of psycho-the-rapists, but also into nearly every domain of the political and advertising worlds. It grew far beyond the single personage of Richard Bandler. Interestingly, despite his in-depth knowledge of NLP techniques, he needed drugs to keep himself mentally afloat. To this very day, he commands huge fees for conducting NLP training sessions worldwide.

One of the most prominent and visible public displays of NLP usage has likely been Barack Obama's 2008 "Change" campaign with its slogan "Change we can believe in" and the chant "Yes We Can", "Hail Satan" in speech reversal. What a masterpiece of Ericksonian permissive hypnosis, where the hypnotherapist uses everything that is present, such as the clients' issues, the clients' sensory experience and the immediate environment.

The slogan facilitated a process where a trance state is naturally accessed. Each rally or session is designed to suit clients' personal way of changing the human state of the mind (nlpacademy.co.uk). This modus operandi is interwoven with herd communication and marketing. In television viewers in particular, it assures human neutrality in all rational and logical decision-makings in the same way, because expert programming of brainwaves by way of television emissions completely eliminates human rational and logical thinking. "Scamworld: 'Get rich quick' schemes mutate into an online monster", by Joseph Flatley, is a marvellous source for further information on the topic.

At this point, the question arises whether or not NLP and its associated hypnosis techniques can be considered Satan's work? It depends. After all, like everything else in life, NLP in and of itself is neutral, neither good nor evil. How one uses it dictates if it is for good or evil. Even then in grown-ups the result will depend on the administrator's skill and the subject's and listener's perception. And even then, it could vary, as we see with Bandler, whose drug dependancy overroad his knowledge and expertise. When applied to children, however, it may be perceived as pure evil. Cathy O'Brian's and Mark Phillip's book *Tranceformation of Amerika* gives further information on the topic.

Australian couple Adam and Denise Musselli are the founders of Sydney-based MindTech Institute. They purport an impressive academic background in psychology, social science, behavioral science, counseling, sociology, business, marketing and management. And they provide NLP training, consulting and coaching seminars, lectures and workshops worldwide, based on what they consider the most effective modern and scientific NLP techniques. They proclaim that enrolment in their institute's NLP Master Practitioner Training and Hypnosis seminars only requires one thing - good ethics. They say:

> "It's your ethics that keeps you away from conning and scamming people. It's true you can use it [NLP] to claim that you have some super powers or a holy ghost on your shoulder working for you and charge people for healing and blessings, and you can also claim you are some super guru and charge people thousands of dollars to follow you. And you are the only person who can manage and control your skills and how you use them thus it is you who is responsible for your behaviour and actions and that, in turn, is often based on your values and ethics."

Good for them. By insisting on the presence of ethics in their clientele, they free themselves from all personal liability. And this at a time when perception-deception seems to be the norm, and dog screws dog is considered ethical behaviour. They most likely receive confirmation of ethics in writing as testament from those enrolling,

That NLP is used by almost every mental health professional worth his or her salt is a given. So is the fact that genuine PTSD experiencers inevitably are forced to see some of them during their journey through the treacherous jungle of deceit and manipulation engineered by the powers that be. In my case, it became abundantly clear with the last mental health professional I saw in my PTSD excursion. He was number 24, a graduate from a theological Southern California seminary with a student body of almost 3,000 students from 90 countries and 110 denominational backgrounds. The reason given by the airline and the WCB for my consultation with him was that he would get me back to flying. During our first encounter, I was accompanied by my fellow flight attendant and seemingly best friend Annemarie. Seemingly, until four years later, when her husband told me six weeks before his death that she was on the airlines extremely generous payroll to be my "friend". I felt queasy the moment I set eyes upon Number 24's Gucci or Pucci or whatever outfit. I also noted, while I was brewing coffee in the pantry during a break he had initiated, that he seemed too chummy with Annemarie. That he clandestinely recorded the interview had not escaped my attention, either. Regardless, he charmed me, and I agreed to meet him for 10 sessions commencing five days later, which would result in my return to in-flight service. At least, that's what was said.

A lucid dream saved me from his "treatment", and consequently from skid-row, and God only knows from what else. The dream took place in the early morning hours on the day treatment was to commence. In vivid colours, I saw Annemarie, my local Union shop stewards, the WCB psychiatrist and psychologist, Gucci-Pucci and NorAm's WCB manager jubilantly dancing on my freshly covered grave mound, whilst I lay buried alive underneath them. Within three hours I had cancelled my appointment with Gucci-Pucci and seen my general physician and my psychiatrist. Both wrote a note to WCB's mental health staff stating that I should not be forced to see someone for whom I had such distinctive aversion, as it would be deleterious to my health. My psychiatrist furthermore suggested to me to inform them in writing, that I would be delighted to see Gucci-Pucci and obey his every wish in whatever he demanded I do for the purpose of returning me to in-flight duties, under certain conditions. He would have to guarantee in writing that he would take full responsibility for my wellbeing, both financially and physically, if anything untoward happened to me, while I fulfilled his commands in and out of the air. As said as done, and before noon that glorious day I had delivered all notes to the WCB psychologist and psychiatrist in charge of my case.

Everything came to an absolute standstill.

NorAm's aspirations to throw me on the garbage heap as human debris halted abruptly. Within a couple of months, they offered to pension me off. *Broken Wings* was nearly finished and, after 10 years of attempting to traumatize me into PTSD, high blood pressure threatening a heart attack or stroke, I accepted their rotten proposal. Which leads me back to Jason Louv and his question:

> How can I make sure nobody pulls this [NLP] horseshit on me? Here are his guidelines:
>
> 1. *Be extremely wary of people copying your body language.*
>
> If talking to someone who starts to sit in exactly the same way as you, or mirrors the way you have your hands, test them by making a few movements and see if they copy you. Skilled NLPers mask this better than newer ones, who will always immediately copy your movement.
>
> 2. *Move your eyes in random and unpredictable patterns.*
>
> Especially in the initial stages of rapport, induction NLP users pay incredibly close attention to your eyes. The reason? They are watching your eye movements to see how you store and how you access information. They are able to in a few minutes tell when you are lying or making something up. They also figured out

what parts of your brain you use when you speak, which can lead them to be so clued in to what you are thinking that they almost come across as having psychic insight into your innermost thoughts. Randomly darting your eyes around—look up to the right, to the left, side to side, down with no pattern—will drive an NLP person nuts, because it throws them off their calibration.

3. *Do not let anybody touch you.*

   If you have a conversation with somebody you know who is into NLP and you find yourself in a heightened emotional state—laughing, crying, angry—and the person touches you while in that state they just *anchored* you. If they want you back in that state at a later time, they can do so by touching you in the same place, at least in NLP logic.

4. *Be wary of vague language.*

   One of the primary techniques NLP took from Milton Erickson is the use of vague language to induce hypnotic trance. Erickson found that the more vague language is, the more it leads people into trance, because there is less that a person is liable to disagree with or to react to. Alternately, more specific language will take a person out of trance. (Note Obama's use of this specific technique in the "Change" campaign, a word so vague that *anybody* could read *anything* into it.)

5. *Be wary of permissive language.*
   "Feel free to relax." "You're welcome to test drive this car if you like." "You can enjoy this as much as you like." Watch out, because the best way to get somebody to do something, including going into a trance, is by allowing the NLP user to give you permission to do something. Skilled hypnotists will therefore NEVER command you outright to do something like, "Go into a trance." They WILL say things like, "Feel free to become as relaxed as you like."

6. *Be wary of gibberish.*
   Nonsense phrases like: "As you release this feeling more and more you will find yourself moving into present alignment with the sound of your success more and more." This kind of gibberish is the bread and butter of the pacing-and-leading phase of NLP used by NLP trained mental health practitioners trying to program your emotional states to move you towards where they want you to go. ALWAYS say, "Can you be more specific about that?" or "Can you explain exactly what you mean?" This does two things: it interrupts this whole technique, and it forces the conversation into specific and precise language, thus breaking the trance-inducing use of vague language discussed in item #4.

7. *Read between the lines.*

   NLP users will consistently use language with hidden or layered meanings. Here a prime example: "Diet, nutrition and sleep with me are the most important things, don't you think?" If you heard this sentence quickly, it would seem like an obvious statement that you would probably agree with without much thought. What's the layered-in message? "Diet, nutrition and *sleep with me* are the most important things, don't you think?" Yep, and if you missed it, you just subconsciously - without you knowing it - agreed to it. Skilled NLPervs can be incredibly subtle with this.

8. *Watch your attention.*
   Be careful about zoning out around NLP people—it's an invitation to them to leap in with an unconscious cue. For instance: An NLP user attempting to get Louv to write for his blog for free noticed that he seemed to be looking into the distance, paying little attention. He immediately started to use the technique listed in #7 by talking about how he never has to pay for anything because media outlets send him review copies of books and albums for free. "Everything for free," he began hissing at me. "I get everything. For. Free." So be on your toes throughout the interview.

9. *Don't agree to anything.*
   If you find yourself being led to make a quick decision on something, which I was forced into with number 24 when clueless about everything, leave the situation. Wait at least 24 hours before making any decisions, especially financial ones. My lucid dream hit approximately four days later. Categorically refuse to let yourself get swept up into making an emotional decision in the spur of the moment. Use your rational mind and leave - just leave and say you'll be in touch.

10. *Trust your intuition [or your dreams] and follow it.*
   This is the foremost and primary rule. In hindsight, it seems as if I cruised on my intuition throughout the entire 10 years of my own *Divine Comedy*. My intuition and my twice-daily meditations, which seems to have generated divine intervention, such as this and other lucid dreams certainly to me seemed indications of divine intervention. Louv, emphasizing that NLP people almost always seem somewhat "off" or dodgy, advises to flee. Just flee when your intuition puts you on guard. If you don't want to be that drastic, call them out on it and ask them to cease applying NLP techniques to you.

What else to do to resist this modern form of black magic? Read *Introducing NLP* by Joseph O'Connor and John Seymour. It describes in simple terms what NLPers do, thus enabling you to learn their MO par excellence. Read also Ready and Burton's 2010 book *Neuro-Linguistic Programming for Dummies*, which further helps on the path of spotting these people. Also watch NLP critique and explanation videos on YouTube. Once we recognize when and how NLP is applied, we can manipulate our opponents and circumnavigate those using it against us without raising their ire and suspicion. We know it does work. Just think about it. Freud, Bernays and their cabal inaugurated the psychoanalytical principles together with their EEG-acquired knowledge of humans' brainwave patterns and their functions, together with humans' natural characteristics and inclinations. They knew of humans' distaste for cognitive dissonance, as it acts against our natural tendency and longing for mental balance. They knew of our human urge to create psychological equilibrium and our particular way to achieve it, namely to turn off and tune out.

From around 1912 AD onwards, they set out to teach politicians and corporation employees, as well as military staff in the highest ranks, the NLP master language. This includes imagery, symbolism and positive association, so that influence, money and power over the herd would be assured forever and a day. Billions of dollars are still spent annually to get the perfect wording, visual representations and spokespeople for only one purpose: to milk humanity just to achieve their rulers' objectives. NLP and Ericksonian-style hypnotic writing can be seen everywhere, from the world of Internet marketing, get-rich-quick schemes and scams for personal and corporate gain, to movies, documentaries and videos. They are all perfected with techniques so subtle as to slide undetected by most individuals. Television is the main perpetrator for the complete corruption of humanity. It takes six months after throwing it out to regain a semblance of one's sense of logic and reason.

What they discovered and used for their purposes, however, we genuine PTSD journeyers can now also apply to ourselves for our purposes. We can heal ourselves without outsider intervention, as we are the only one's able to help, as documented in *Fallacy 1*. Remember, our power is limitless, as there are no limitations to our mind and consciousness. If there is, it rests beyond our conscious recognition and perception. Any doubt we may have about our own limitless abilities was expertly implanted by the powers that be. Scheming to get rid of us, they undermine our self-confidence, while pretending to have our welfare at heart. Think about how many remarkable things our mind performs automatically without us ever giving it a thought. Think about the marvelous chores you've fulfilled thus far in your life due to the power of your mind and the power of your own thinking. Since the early 1900s to the present day, Freud et al. have programmed us for worse. Consequently, we have the power to program ourselves for better.

Why the secrecy about this enormous, innate power we have to change ourselves by the learned society? Why don't they enlighten us about it so we can create whatever we want by the power of our own mind? Well, see what happened to Canadian clinical psychologist and professor of psychology at the University of Toronto Jordan Peterson (1962–)? He tuned into it and tried to share his knowledge with the world in his book *12 Rules of Life*. He collapsed, thanks to the learned society's and the media's vicious onslaught They demand that the power of our own mind and its perversion through perception-deception by both media and learned society has to be kept secret. Why? Because if the herd found out, it could accomplish remarkable things. We could create by our own volition through our conscious efforts, or the effort of others on their own time in accordance with their own desires. Tuning into the unified field of consciousness and applying what we perceive to our lives is what those in power fear far more than death itself. Hence their draconian treatment of genuine PTSD journeyers, the brightest of the herd. And remember, once you make up your mind to come out of your genuine PTSD experience victoriously, nothing can stop you. The inquisitive human mind can neither be caged nor muzzled. We have our doubts about porcus, cani, simian mus and rattus, though.

11

OUR CONTROL OF OUR LIVES ORIGINATES WITH OUR CONTROL OF OUR THINKING

American psychiatrist Howard P. Rome, M.D. (1910–1992) joined the Mayo Clinic in 1947. This was after studies at the University of Pennsylvania and the Temple University School of Medicine, a state-related research university in Philadelphia., He was elected president of the Mayo Clinic medical staff in 1965. He was president of the World Psychiatric Association from 1972 to 1976, and served on the editorial board of *Psychiatric Annals*. And for celebrity appeal, had Ernest Hemingway among his patients, wrote a psychological autopsy of Lee Harvey Oswald for the Warren Commission. In brief, Howard P. Rome was a heavy hitter. In 1977, he published his paper "Limits of the Human Mind", in which he examines human behaviour in its broadest sense. He also discusses philosophical concepts of self that have predominated through Western history, and relates them to current conditions in the world (Rome, H. P. (1977); Limits of the human mind. *Psychiatric Annals*, 7(11), 11–32). He concludes that the current state of society differs little from what has existed for centuries, and suggests that mankind's efforts to seek relief from the stresses of modern society are fundamentally similar to those of the past.

Rome identifies and discusses 3 methods for stress relief:

- Religion as a recent manifestation of the age-old desire for a saving messiah and the resulting millennium
- Transcendental meditation as a direct perception technique.
- The procedures of "est" (Erhard Seminars Training), described as a consciousness-awareness technique.

Erhard Seminars Training est is also marketed as EST or Est, Latin for "it is." The organization was founded by the American author and lecturer John Paul Rosenberg (1935–), who operates under the pseudonym Werner Hans Erhard. At first, his program consisted of a two-weekend (60-hour) course, known officially as "The est Standard Training." It aimed to "transform one's ability to experience living so that the situations one had been trying to change or had been putting up with, clear up just in the process of life itself." This should bring to the forefront the ideas of transformation, personal responsibility, accountability, and possibility. In 1985, Rosenberg replaced EST with a program he called "Forum". By that time, 700,000 people had completed the est training, described by American ethicist, philosopher and historian Jonathan D. Moreno (1952–) as "the most important cultural event after the human potential movement itself seemed exhausted" and a form of "Socratic interrogation" (Jonathan D. Moreno, 2004. p. 246.)

Rosenberg was noted for having had a significant cultural impact on the making of the American mind in the 1970s. He challenged EST participants to be themselves and live in the present, instead of playing a role imposed on them by their past. He challenged them to move beyond their current points of view into a perspective from which they could observe their own positionality. This, by the way, is the social and political context that creates our identity in terms of race, class, gender, sexuality and ability status. It is also used to describe how our identity influences, and potentially biases, our understanding of and outlook on the world. Following a few decades of seemingly turbulent intermittence created by his own way of living life, Rosenberg has written and lectured almost exclusively in his well-connected academic world for the last two decades (wernererhard.com).

In the late 1970s, however, Professor Rome, contemplated the popularity of EST and that of the other two movements, eventually deciding its popularity stemmed from humans' innate longing for a shared sense of participation, a longing for social interaction. Seemingly trying to relate his hypothesis of human sentiment of sharing to the duty and obligations of mental health practitioners, he viewed them as such:

> "The clinical psychiatrist's role is one of adducing evidence of conflict from his patients' recital of life accounts. By this means, he hopes to hold a mirror to them, in which they may see themselves as others see them. He hopes this procedure will be helpful to them, and he therefore tries as best he can to be nonjudgmental about what he hears. I would like to use the same technique in presenting for your consideration a wide spectrum of data concerning the human condition - from which, if the psychiatrist-readers of this journal hold true to form, some new

insights should emerge." (Howard P/ Rome, MD: Limits of the Human Mind; *Psychiatric Annals*. 1977; 7(11):11-32; https://healio.com).

Whereupon he invites us to join him in an attempt to follow the Socratic admonition to examine life as stated in Socrates' dictum: "The unexamined life is not worth living." He uttered it at his trial, in court, purportedly for his own impiety and the corruption of Athens' youth. For this, he was subsequently sentenced to death in 399 BC, as described in Plato's *Apology* (38a5-6). Rome then, as foundation for his essay/observations, surveys the course of man throughout history. He notes how many times man himself set the limits that inhibited further investigation into the expanse of the human mind. He quotes Austrian philosopher Ludwig Josef Johann Wittgenstein (1889–1951), who in his Tractus Logico-Philosophicus exclaimed: "The world is the totality of facts, not of things."

How similar to Nassim Haramein's idea, who we know also maintains that thoughts, not things, constitute our world.

Wittgenstein, born into one of Europe's wealthiest families, explored logic as well as the philosophy of mathematic, mind and language. Between 1924 and 1936 he regularly participated in the Vienna and Berlin Circles. These two groups of philosophers, scientists and mathematicians were drawn from the natural and social sciences, logic and mathematics. At the University of Vienna, they were untidily unified by their aim of making philosophy scientific with the help of modern logic. One of the Vienna Circle members, Austrian physicist and philosopher of science Ernst Waldfried Josef Wenzel Mach (1838 –1916) majorly supported Wittgenstein's idea of "The world is the totality of facts, not of things." Termed logical positivism, logical empiricism or neopositivism, it is characterized by the view that scientific knowledge is the only kind of factual knowledge, and that all traditional metaphysical doctrines are to be rejected as meaningless. Mach was noted for his contributions to physics, such as the study of shock waves and the ratio of one's speed to that of sound. The Mach number was named in his honour,

Philosophy of science nowadays prides itself on its concerns with:

- what does or does not qualify as science
- the reliability of scientific theories
- the ultimate purpose of science

Meanwhile, it purports to explore the relationship between science and truth. It also focuses on:

- metaphysical (the nature of, and relations among, the things that exist)
- epistemic (cognitive, conscious, knowing)
- semantic (relating to meaning in language or logic)

The philosophy of science thus gives ample room to let any flag blow in whichever direction anyone desires. This theory of knowledge in essence asserted that only statements verifiable through direct observation or logical proof were meaningful. So, it is all baloney.

But Circle members sought to create credibility and valour for their theory, and thus philosophy as a science. They searched for an empiricist criterion of meaning in anything they could think of, whilst vigorously critiquing and demeaning metaphysics. They simultaneously glorified the unification of the sciences to create in humanity a belief in a unity of science. This topic that can be explored through the following questions:

- Is there one privileged, fundamental concept or kind of thing, and if not, how are the different concepts or kinds of things in the universe related? (https://plato.stanford.edu/entries/scientific-unity/)
- Can the various natural sciences (e.g., physics, astronomy, chemistry, biology) be unified into a single overarching theory, and can theories within a single science (e.g., general relativity and quantum theory in physics, or models of evolution and development in biology) be unified?
- Are theories or models the relevant connected units?
- What other connected or connecting units are there?
- Does the unification of these parts of science involve only matters of fact or are matters of value involved as well?
- What about matters of method, material, institutional, ethical and other aspects of intellectual cooperation?
- Moreover, what kinds of unity, not just units, in the sciences are there?
- Is the relation of unification one of reduction, translation, explanation, logical inference, collaboration or something else?
- What roles can unification play in scientific practices, their development, application and evaluation?

Many of these Circle members emigrated to Britain and the U.S. long before Austria's 1938 annexation to Germany. So did many of those Viennese physicians attending Freud's Wednesday Psychological Society to discuss issues relating to psychology and neuropathology. They went mostly at psychiatric asylums and institutions of higher learning to imprint students' and faculties' streams of thought into their idea of the development of the philosophy and unity of science and the field of analytical philosophy.

Analytic philosophy began with Freud, Wittgenstein et al. around the turn of the twentieth century, and it flies in the same manner. It is characterized by an emphasis on language, known as the linguistic turn. For clarity and rigor in arguments, it is said to make use of formal logic and mathematics and, to a lesser degree, the natural sciences. Contemporary philosophers self-identifying as "analytic" have widely divergent interests, assumptions and methods. But analytic philosophy today is usually characterized by precision and thoroughness about a specific topic and resistance to "imprecise or cavalier discussions of broad topics". Together, both analytic philosophy and philosophy as a science ushered in the era of a scientifically un-provable gospel of psychology and psychoanalysis as science. In Freud et al.'s view, it ought to share the stage with the empirical sciences, in line with Einstein's general theory of relativity, for example. This goal is vigorously pursued to present day. As a matter of fact, it has taken hold so well as for American philosopher, writer, cognitive scientist Daniel Clement Dennett III (1942), exclaimed: "There is no such thing as philosophy-free science; there is only science whose philosophical baggage is taken on board without examination. (Daniel Dennett, *Darwin's Dangerous Idea*, 1995)

Wittgenstein's Vienna and Berlin Circle members followed their Austrian émigrés colleagues to the U.S. and Britain in the late 1930s. The Berlin Circle formed in the late 1920s with the same objectives as those of their Viennese brethren. Thus, it was assured the internationalization of Wittgenstein's equally scientifically unprovable movement of logical empiricism, also known as logical positivism. It was characterized by the opinion that scientific knowledge was the only kind of factual knowledge. Only statements verifiable through direct observation or logical proof were held to be meaningful. So, all traditional metaphysical doctrines were rejected as meaningless.

Wittgenstein's movement was already running the end of its course when the American philosopher Thomas Samuel Kuhn (1922–1996) published his revolutionary book *The Structure of Scientific Revolutions* in 1962. A landmark event in the history, philosophy and sociology of scientific knowledge, it shifted academia's view of philosophy in its entirety. Some reviewers thought that it might well be the most influential treatise ever written on how science does or does not proceed. Kuhn's contribution to the philosophy of science marked not only a break with several key positivist doctrines, but also inaugurated a new style of philosophy of science that brought it closer to the history of science (plato.stanford.edu). His account of the development of science held that science enjoys periods of stable growth punctuated by revisionary revolutions. This was in itself revolutionary. To this, Kuhn added his equally controversial 'incommensurability thesis', namely that theories from differing time periods in human history suffer from deep kinds of failure of comparability.

Today, he is considered one of the most influential philosophers of science of the twentieth century. He is furthermore noted for having spawned the trendy term "paradigm". He also fomented the now-trite idea that personalities and politics play a large role in science, wit Fauci and Gates or not , says John Horgan in his 2012 Scientific American article "What Thomas Kuhn Really Thought about Scientific Truth." Kuhn's most profound argument, that scientists can never truly understand the "real world" or even each other, escaped the attention of most readers, at least in Horgan's opinion.

Kuhn challenged academia's then-prevailing view of progress in science as "development-by-accumulation" of accepted facts and theories. Instead, he focused on conceptual issues, like the practice of normal science, the influence of historical events, the emergence of scientific discoveries, as well as on the nature of scientific revolutions and the scientific progress made through those revolutions. He also argues that the evolution of scientific theory does not emerge from the straightforward accumulation of facts, but rather from a set of changing intellectual circumstances and possibilities such as:

- What sorts of intellectual options and strategies were available to people during a given historical time period?
- What types of lexicons and terminology were known and employed during certain epochs when specific scientific discoveries were made?

None of this endeared him to his peers, in particular because Kuhn traced his view of science to an epiphany experienced at Harvard College in 1947, while reading Aristotle's *Physics* when working toward his doctorate in physics. Astonished at how "wrong" it seemed, he asked himself how someone writing so brilliantly on so many topics could be so misguided about physics? Pondering this conundrum in depth, Aristotle's views suddenly made sense to him when realizing that Aristotle invested basic concepts with meanings different than those of modern physicists. For example, he used the term "motion" to refer not just to a change in position, but to *change* in general. Aristotle's physics understood on its own terms was therefore simply different from, rather than inferior to, Newtonian physics.

Kuhn switched from physics to the history and philosophy of science shortly thereafter. He struggled for 15 years to transform his Aristotelian epiphany into the theory set forth in *The Structure of Scientific Revolutions*. The keystone of his model was the concept of a paradigm. This term has previously referred to an example serving an educational purpose. Kuhn used the term to refer to a collection of procedures or ideas that instruct scientists implicitly in what to believe and how to work. Most scientists are said never to question the paradigm. They solve "puzzles," namely problems, whose solutions reinforce and extend the scope of the paradigm in vogue, rather than challenging it. Kuhn called this "normal science." However, there are always anomalies, phenomena that the paradigm cannot account for or even contradict. Those anomalies are often ignored, even those that, as they accumulate, are able to trigger a revolution. This so-called "paradigm shift" forces scientists to abandon the old paradigm for a new one. This, in Kuhn's view, does not mean that one can simply describe the previous science as false. The new paradigm might simply solve puzzles better and yield more practical applications. Nor, he says, can one assume that science is constantly approaching the truth. On the contrary. At the end of *Structure*, it seems as if Kuhn conveys that science, like life on earth itself, does not evolve toward anything, but only away from something. Perhaps from the truth, looking at the science of mental health? Far off? Not at all.

A study published in *Psychiatry Research* in July 2019 concluded, that psychiatric diagnoses are scientifically worthless as tools to identify discrete mental health disorders. (Psychiatric diagnosis 'scientifically meaningless'; sciencedaily.com 2019) The study, led by researchers from the University of Liverpool, involved a detailed analysis of five key chapters of the latest edition of the widely used Diagnostic and Statistical Manual (DSM):

- schizophrenia
- bipolar disorder
- anxiety disorders
- depressive disorders
- trauma-related disorders

As we know from *Fallacy 1*, diagnostic manuals such as the DSM were created to provide a common diagnostic language for mental health professionals. This was an attempt to provide a definitive list of mental health problems and their symptoms. The study's main findings are:

- Psychiatric diagnoses all use different decision-making rules.
- There is a huge amount of overlap in symptoms between diagnoses.
- Almost all diagnoses mask the role of trauma and adverse events.
- Diagnoses tell us little about the individual patient and what treatment they need.

Thus, the authors conclude that diagnostic labelling represents "a disingenuous categorical system". There goes the genuine PTSD diagnosis as a mental disorder, a life-experience far beyond any humanly-to-be-expected life experience such as becoming a parent, getting a sibling, losing a pet, divorce or separation, suffering from a hangnail, or coping with one's hairdresser choosing the wrong colour experience, which is accepted nowadays to cause PTSD.

Lead researcher Dr Kate Allsopp of the University of Liverpool said:

> "Although diagnostic labels create the illusion of an explanation, they are scientifically meaningless and can create stigma and prejudice. I hope these findings will encourage mental health professionals to think beyond diagnoses and consider other explanations of mental distress, such as trauma and other adverse life experiences."

Professor Peter Kinderman, also of the University of Liverpool, added to Allsopp's verdict:

> "This study provides yet more evidence, that the biomedical diagnostic approach in psychiatry is not fit for purpose. Diagnoses frequently and uncritically reported as 'real illnesses' are, in fact, made on the basis of internally inconsistent, confused and contradictory patterns of largely arbitrary criteria. The diagnostic system wrongly assumes that all distress results from disorder, and relies heavily on subjective judgments about what is normal."

Professor John Read of the University of East London added:

> "Perhaps it is time we stopped pretending that medical-sounding labels contribute anything to our understanding of the complex causes of human distress or of what kind of help we need when distressed."

Ditto! Read *Fallacy 1* to hear the truth of it in detail!

Kuhn was just as brave in 1962 when exclaiming that science might possibly end. We assume he was suggesting that scientists could not make any further headway, , at least not on their track they were on. This recognition seems to have made it somewhat more imperative for him to challenge scientists' belief that only science can ever arrive at absolute truth.

"The one thing I think you shouldn't say is, that now we've found out what the world is really like, because that's not what I think the game is about," he told Horgan. He was referring to his epiphany with Aristotle that reality is unknowable, and that any attempt to describe it both obscured as much as illuminated that very fact. Consequently, he was forced into the almost untenable position to acknowledge that, because all scientific theories fall short of absolute truth, they must all be absolutely untrue.

Be that as it may, different paradigms have no common standard for comparison. They are "incommensurable," to use Kuhn's term. This gives proponents of different paradigms ample opportunity to argue forever and a day. They can't resolve even their basic differences in opinions, because they invest basic terms—motion, particle, space, time —with different meanings. We see it year after year, if not month after month, in different proposed and viewed-as-genuine PTSD treatments. None of them have accomplished anything since the inception of this theme in the late 1980s. Well, they have demonstrated how to create a magnificent cash cow for the mental health industry, the multitude of charities that sprang up around it, and physicians. And they have demonstrated how to destroy genuine PTSD experiencers' health with the PTSD treatments applied. In the example of PTSD treatment hypothesis, as well as in the conversion of scientists from one paradigm to another, we see that it is both a subjective as well as a political process. It may involve sudden intuitive understanding, like in Kuhn's contemplation of Aristotle's work, or it may occur by adaptation of a paradigm simply because it is backed by a learned society member with stronger academic standing and reputation. Or it may happen merely, because a majority of the scientific community finds it fashionable to hold a certain view on a certain human predicament such as, for example, the mental health profession stigmatizing genuine PTSD experiencers with their pathetic, if not criminal, diagnosis of mental illness and clinging to their Pavlovian and Skinnerian CBT and pharmacotherapy PTSD treatments of genuine and non-genuine PTSD journeyers alike, through it not only creating victim- and suicide ideation in their subjects due to pharmaceutical mind altering drug administration leading to it, but also creating drug addicts oft times for the rest of their patients' natural lives, and all of it under the guise of PTSD healing, when it actually serves for nothing other than to self-enrichment.

Conjecture? Not at all once you think about it. Pharmaceuticals are prescribed by physicians, due to the Standard of Care protocol and under the guise of benevolence for as good as all human ailments. Yet without pharmaceutical drug consumption, a multitude of huge drug cartels would cease to exist. As for a possible paradigm shift in PTSD healing, it would endanger the livelihood of a multitude of mental health practitioners of all ranks and files. It would decimate many clinical researchers working in university psychology departments. And goodbye to careers of those employed by non-profit and state organizations purporting to assist PISD-impaired people.

A possible paradigm shift in PTSD healing would furthermore threaten the U.S. political regime. The state' deprives PTSD-affected soldiers and veterans of their 2nd amendment right to bear arms due to "mental illness". When it becomes clear that all they suffer is a mendable colossal existential crisis, that restriction would be rendered null and void.

So, what about a PTSD paradigm shift? Till donkeys fly and pigs sprout wings, if we listen to Kuhn. In *Structure,* he questioned why some fields of science converge on a paradigm, while others remain in a state of constant flux, the case in which we find PTSD. The noun flux by the way, describes something that constantly changes, from medical diagnosis to COVID-19 opinions, from likes and dislikes, to attitudes, aspirations and fluctuations in decision.

His answer? Scientists within certain fields are simply unwilling to commit themselves to a single paradigm. In other fields, such as economics and other social sciences, they address questions for which no paradigm suffices. Fields that achieve consensus, Kuhn maintains, do so because their paradigms, or at least certain components of them, correspond to something real in nature resting on irrevocable discoveries. , Such is the case with helio-centrism, quantum mechanics, the Big Bang and the germ theory of infectious disease. Consensus eludes scientists when paradigms rest on culturally constructed suppositions or inventions. Such is the case with PTSD treatment hypotheses, theories, speculations, theorems and hallucinations spewed forth by psychiatrists and psychologists, who mostly are salaried through the NIH's NC for PTSD, namely, to enhance the debility. If the truth about accepted PTSD treatments and their detrimental results to both the physical and mental health of human beings became public knowledge, it would have two profound effects. It would ruin the careers and livelihoods of thousands working in the mental health industry. At the same time, it would free millions of humans caught in their clutches or squeezed to death between their hands, the latter the 1990s WCB logo which they changed after I published *Broken Wings*.

WORKERS' COMPENSATION BOARD OF BRITISH COLUMBIA

Therefore, there will be no PTSD paradigm shift. With Kuhn's ideas, opinions, suppositions and assertions spinning in his mind in 1977, psychiatrist Howard P. Rome finally got around to pondering Wittgenstein's assertion that "The world is the totality of facts, not of things," he wondered.

If this means what I think it means we are confronted with a dilemma of which the Greek Stoic philosopher, Epictetus (c.50–135 AD), wrote: "Impressions come to us in four ways: Either things are, and seem so to us; or they are not, and seem not to be; or they are, and seem not; or they are not, and yet seem to be.'"

At the same time, Epictetus pointed out that the man searching for knowledge has to be able to "deal rightly" with each of those situations. He must bring on those impressions and, if unable to understand and deal with any of them, be brave enough to seek help from others "at whatever point the pressure comes."

Epictetus furthermore seems to have viewed all external events occurring in life as beyond human control. Therefore, they should be accepted calmly and dispassionately, whatever the happenstance. Be stoic and stand above it was his mantra. Nevertheless, he also maintains that all people bear responsibility for their own actions, which they can examine and control through rigorous self-discipline. In other words, Epictetus seems to proclaim, that learning to observe and control the Self results in achieving mastery over the Self. Then, through the Self, one achieves mastery over life events, akin to or associated with the "Dharma extinguishes Karma" principle discussed together with Epictetus in *Fallacy 1*.

We already know that Rome amassed a wealth of knowledge regarding human behaviour in its broadest sense, including through service as a commander in the Navy during WWII in Washington, D.C. and the South Pacific. He reached the conclusion that the current state of society differs little from what has existed for centuries, if not thousands of years, including its stress relief mechanisms (postbulletin.com). He also seems to convey that there is no limit to the power of the human mind. But how to gain access to this power and with it obtain that control over our lives, and with it the "flowing above it all" attitude, is the question? The answer is simple! Gain control over our thinking. And by what and by whom is our thinking created, at least during our waking hours, you may still wonder? From the moment of our birth onwards until the moment of departure through sensory input from the five classic human senses:

- vision (sight)
- gustation (taste)
- olfaction (smell)
- audition (hearing)
- tactile stimulation (touch)

Other sensory modalities exist, for example the sense of balance and movement, of knowing one's position in space and knowing where one is in time or activities. As we saw in conjunction with NLP and brainwaves, the sensory inputs themselves manifest in different electrical signals and contexts. The brain, it is thought, relates all sensory inputs into a coherent percept through sensory processing, upon which our human interaction with the environment might be based.

"Normal science" maintains that it takes until early childhood before our brain learns to perceive and represent the physical world. Such knowledge is apparently generated progressively over the first years of our lives, long before we become conscious of the Self and its immediate or distant environment. That's something to think about when you hand your 12-month-old baby to caretakers you barely know. You pay them a fortune monthly to form your infants' perception of the world and everything in it. Statistical learning (SL), sensitivity to probabilistic regularities in sensory input, has been widely implicated in cognitive and perceptual human development. Little is known, however, about the underlying mechanisms of SL, and whether they undergo developmental change. The implicit learning of statistical regularities in sensory input, however, is probably the first way through which we acquire knowledge of physical reality and the structure of continuous sensory environments (L.L. Emberson et al: Comparing statistical learning across perceptual modalities in infancy: An investigation of underlying learning mechanism(s);onlinelibrary.wiley.com 2019).

SL is defined by three criteria:

- It can operate over undifferentiated input, where only spatial and temporal probabilities can be used to determine which parts of the environment go together; no other segmentation cues, such as grouping, are required.
- It occurs incidentally as a by-product of perception, without intentional effort or conscious awareness.
- It is concerned with extracting how *particular* features and objects co-occur resulting in knowledge about relationships between specific stimuli.

This form of non-conscious learning is present at birth when newborns are exposed to and tested with speech stream inputs and their first vaccinations interrupt their immune systems. It seems to operate across domains, time, space and even species. Conscious experience of it kicks in much later in life, apparently involving complex knowledge representations that support conscious thinking and abstract reasoning. How this information is represented and processed by and in the brain to make such experiences feasible is presently unknown - at least to the herd. (Birgitta Dresp-Langley, "Why the Brain Knows More than We Do: Non-Conscious Representations and Their Role in the Construction of Conscious Experience"; *Brain SCI.* 2012) However, Maharishi's and Hagelin's and Harameins unified field theories spring to mind.

What is certain is that at the very latest in kindergarten and pre-school humans' NLP programming by herd controllers is in full swing. It is preceded, of course, by the offspring's all-waking-hour television exposure customary in most North American households. Thus, U.S. children receive their basic perception of the world and everything in it from the cradle to the grave from powerfully and expertly installed programs into their subconscious in accordance with ruling elite desires. This comes without their conscious knowledge and awareness, without their consent and of no fault of their own. It is for that reason that Greek philosopher Aristotle said: "Give me a child until he is 7 and I will show you the man," a maxim claimed by founder of the Jesuit order Ignatius de Loyola (1491–1556) himself when exclaiming: "Give us a child till he's seven and we'll have him for life."

American psychologist John Broadus Watson (1878–1958) popularized the scientific theory of behaviourism, establishing it as a psychological school. He proposed that the process of classical conditioning based on Pavlov's observations was able to explain all aspects of human psychology. He suggested that everything from speech to emotional responses were simply patterns of stimulus and response, thus denying completely the existence of the mind or consciousness. He even said:

> "Give me a dozen healthy infants, well-formed, and my own specified world to bring them up in and I'll guarantee to take any one at random and train him to become any type of specialist I might select - doctor, lawyer, artist, merchant-chief and, yes, even beggar-man and thief, regardless of his talents, penchants, tendencies, abilities, vocations and the race of his ancestors" (Watson, 1924, p. 104).

Mind you, once awakened, we are aware and with "it" we can send televisions to the garbage dumps. So revived, we have little difficulty applying discipline, persistency, willpower and determination to undo this colossal indecency and emotional damage perpetrated upon us. We simply reprogram ourselves to our liking. As a matter of fact, in the genuine PTSD position, this reprogramming is the only way to return to living life contently. It suffices to take control of our perception intake - food and drugs included – combined with the willingness to broaden our horizons in hitherto unimagined spiritual ways as discussed in *Fallacy 1*.

By learning to watch our thinking, we control our impulses and the actions and behaviours flowing from it. And so, we begin to create our own world, as we stop NLP experts in their tracks. We prevent them from clandestinely implanting and programing our subconscious to the detriment of our own lives. After all, as numerous cognitive studies conducted by neuroscientists revealed, only five percent of our cognitive activities, such as decision-making, emotions, actions and behaviours, is done consciously. The remaining 95% are generated in a non-conscious manner. We could surmise that those 95% were programmed into us through television, subliminal advertisement, symbols, movies and videos of all genre, Facebook, Twitter and so on and so forth (Marc Van Rymenant: 95% of brain activity is beyond our conscious awareness; https://simplifyinginterfaces.com 2008).

Israeli-born Emanuel Donchin, PhD (1935-2018) is a giant in the field of event-related potential (ERP). ERP is the measured brain response as direct result of a specific sensory, cognitive or motor event. Whilst director of the Laboratory for Cognitive Psychophysiology at the University of Illinois in the late twentieth century, Donchin used Electrophysiological Neuroimaging as a tool to better understand how the mind is implemented by the brain. He thought it may even be more than that when concluding:

> "An enormous portion of cognitive activity is non-conscious, figuratively speaking, it could be 99 percent; we probably will never know precisely how much is outside awareness."

Conclusion? It is possible to deceive the human mind in any and all ways, once the art has been studied in detail. and Uncle Sigismund et al. studied the art in lots of detail. Not only that, they shared their discoveries with nephew Edward. He in turn, from 1912 until his death, applied it in spades wherever he could to *make the American mind*. Few tricks escaped him, from making smokers of women to convincing people that Viagra and abortions were healthy and without side-effects.

Bernays himself acknowledged shortly after WWI:

> "It was of course the astounding success of propaganda during the war that opened the eyes of the intelligent few in all departments of life to the possibilities of regimenting the public mind." (*Propaganda* p. 54).

And regiment the American and now the world's mind they did henceforth, without the herd's knowledge or suspicion. Bernays exclaimed: "Only through the active energy of the intelligent few can the public at large become aware of and act upon new ideas." He was acutely aware that success of those ideas depended entirely on the population's acquiescence (cover). As a matter of fact, in 1928, Bernays admitted that governments themselves, whether monarchical, constitutional, democratic or communist, were government only by virtue of public acquiescence (ibid).

Thoughts, at least since the late 1920s, have been implanted in the observers' minds in systematic manners. The more subtle the suggestions, the more they influence our subconscious minds. This mind-manipulation dictates the food we consume with relish, regardless of its detriment to our health. It dictates the soft drinks we drink, regardless of its embryonic content of aborted foetus. It dictates the shoes and clothes we wear, our views, our likes and dislikes of vaccines, Antifa, George Floyd, BLM, abortion and all topics encountered throughout a human life, It dictates our view of the governing system—Latin for *Sewer*—under which we live. And it dictates the stigma so successfully attached to genuine PTSD experiencers. We are slaves to our own brainwashed mind to such a degree that most of us believe we are free when in abject slavery. Watch the movie *The Matrix*. It confirms it.

But again, once aware, we *can* change our programming at will. This a fact is proved valid in a six-session, educational-therapeutic, NLP-based intervention conducted with injured, high-performance athletes. It demonstrated that NLP is an effective tool for helping them after their recovery from an injury to adopt an observer position. In such position, they can restructure their dysfunctional thoughts and emotions related to the challenging situations they will face when back in competition. Collectively, the NLP-based intervention appeared to provide these injured competitive high-performance athletes with the ability to reduce their anxiety and to perform better in their upcoming competitions (Sarvardelavar, M., Kuan, G: Effects of Neuro-Linguistic programming (NLP) imagery model on enhancing kickboxers' performance; researchgate.net).

NLP abilities were explored by Freud and his cohorts through all fields of the human psyche and biology in mentally and physically healthy as well as sick people. They and Bernays expertly used NLP since WWI and Versailles, still wielding enormous soft power today through evermore effective propaganda-and human mind-manipulating techniques. The co-operation of the U.S. corporate state is critical to this process. It has the ability to control the school system, frame the public debate and spread the Big

Lie through its control of the nation's now digital media stream. This resulted in the dumbing down of public discourse on any and all important subjects, which hugely helped gain complete herd control to an almost unfathomable degree (Review of an Important Documentary: Collapse of Industrial Civilization- Finding the Truth behind the American Hologram; https://collapseofindustrialcivilization.com).

Australian journalist, writer and documentary filmmaker John Richard Pilger (1939–) made the 2010 documentary *The War You Don't See*. In it, he states that the media, the "Fourth Estate" as he calls it, was once thought of as a bulwark against corruption in government and big business. He opines that is actually no more than a cheerleader and a mouthpiece for what has become the Corporate or Deep State NLP headquarters. Somali-born British journalist, writer and former BBC world affairs correspondent Rageh Omaar (1967–) added that "twenty-four hour news is the easiest to manipulate, because it's a giant echo-chamber." It reminds of Hitler's propaganda minister's Paul Joseph Goebbels (1897–1945?) purported acclamation:

> "If you tell a lie big enough and keep repeating it, people will eventually come to believe it. The lie can be maintained only for such time as the State can shield the people from the political, economic and/or military consequences of the lie. It thus becomes vitally important for the State to use all of its powers to repress dissent, for the truth is the mortal enemy of the lie, and thus by extension, the truth is the greatest enemy of the State.".

Mind you, Goebbel's and Hitler's propaganda machine was run, at least in part, by none-other than Freud's nephew Bernays. It could very well be his quote, but attributed to Goebbels. It is certain that the seeds planted by psychiatrists Freud, Brill and other *Wednesday Psychological Society* members brought to fruition by nephew Edward were in full bloom. You still think it's impossible to brainwash anyone into suicidal ideation? In particular when suffering genuine PTSD and in the care of mental health professionals whose rule number 1 for PTSD healing is mind-altering drug prescriptions? And you still want to kill yourself, rather than stop this quasi-genocide of you and your comrades? Not convinced to find the guts to stand up to the instigators of this insanity and get healthy on your own to spread the word about them among your peers? Really? You prefer death to vanquishing those who desire nothing else of you but your suicide?

Think it over, would you? After all, Bernays' American Tobacco campaign that made smoking classy and fashionable and healthy-looking for women was a spectacular success in all aspects of it. Well, except for those who got sucked in to smoking and in so doing on to a gruesome death. The medical and mental health profession and the pharmaceutical companies still today profit from it phenomenally. The smoking fad was preceded in the early 1920s when Norvin Rieser, founder of New York's Rieser Company selling Venida hairnets, met with Bernays seeking an increase in profits. The result? Bernays broadcast the dangers inherent in women wearing long, loose hair in factories and restaurants. Consequently, several U.S. states passed laws mandating factory workers and foodservice employees to wear hairnets. This undertaking ushered in advertisement-power on politics, politicians and the laws of the land in earnest. Lobbying for kickbacks in Congress and the Senate became the in-thing, continuing to the day. Not only that. All wars in which America was involved over the last 120 years were arranged in the same way, due to herd NLP programming and consequent acquiescence, as so brilliantly observed by General Smedley Darlington Butler in his book *War is a Racket.* (Publisher: Feral House; Reprint Edition 2003)

All Vienna and Berlin group society members travelled in the same circles, worked at the same universities and mental asylums and dealt with the same topics. They still do, as all learned societies in all genres do. All their mutual ideas and teachings were incorporated into psychiatric theory and practice, first in the US, Britain and other English-speaking nations, then worldwide. Adolf Meyer was co-founder of the 1911 American Psychoanalytic Association. It was he who conceived of the idea to fuse various psychological influences into a concept of human behaviour he named ergasiology, or psychobiology. His aim was to seek complete psychological and biological integration of al human beings, the creation of the New Man, if you will.

Joseph Hersey Pratt (1872–1956) was an early proponent of cognitive behavioural therapy in America and a disciple of French neurologist Joseph Jules Dejerine (1849–1917). He reached prominence when treatment of psychoneuroses shifted from Freudian psychoanalysis, based on purportedly delving into patients' subconscious as therapy, into the Pavlovian conditioning, called Classical Conditioning. This is the type of conditioned learning that occurs because of the subject's instinctive responses, as opposed to operant conditioning, which is contingent on subjects' wilful actions. (Britannica.com). Conditioning in physiology is a behavioural process whereby a response becomes more frequent or more predictable in a given environment as a result of reinforcement, with reinforcement typically being a stimulus or a reward for a desired response. It was developed by Russian physiologist Ivan Petrovich Pavlov, who practiced on dogs, rats, mus, simian and lepus. His results ever since have been applied as equally valid to human beings, wit genuine PTSD experiencers' treatment. Nowadays, the Cognitive Behavioural Therapy or CBT is psycho-the-rapists' standard of care as a PTSD treatment choice, together with pharmacotherapy (*Fallacy 1*).

Dejerine, by the way, like many other neurologists of his time taking an interest in psychology , maintained that a treating psychiatrist's personality was crucial in all interaction with patients. He subscribed to the notion that "In man, emotion is almost everything and reason very little." The techniques Dejerine used to treat his patients at Paris' La Salpêtrière were adopted and employed by Pratt, Burrow and Schilder in their American group therapy activities. Dejerine was also a pioneer in the study of the localization of functions in the brain. This idea that certain brain functions have certain precise locations and areas within the brain mass proper. Among those functions are language, memory, the mind, conscience, consciousness, sub-consciousness, super-consciousness, emotions and so on and so forth. His hypothesis is said to be supported by neuroimaging studies, although it was proposed as early as in the mid- nineteenth century using the case of Phineas P. Gage (1823–1860). He was an American railroad construction foreman. In 1848, he survived a large iron rod driving through his head and destroying much of his left frontal lobe. The injury's reported effects on his personality and behavior, such as loss of inhibition and anger among them, served the medical profession ever since as evidence for its theory of the localization of brain functions. Clearly, the frontal lobe area was henceforth held accountable for humans' personality location (see *Fallacy 1*).

Gage's case allows one to fit the small number of existing facts almost any desired theory regarding any and all aspects of brain functions and their location within the human brain. No wonder it became a fixture in students' neurology, psychology and neuroscience curricula. The body of established facts about Gage before and after his injury was diminutive to non-existent. All and sundry in the mental health field graciously chose to overlook this absence of information in order to promote their aspired paradigms. The beauty of it is that this example of evidence-handling serves ideally as "Rorschach inkblot", the psychological test at times presented to genuine PTSD journeyers. This test subjects' perceptions of inkblots, which are recorded and analyzed using psychological interpretation, complex algorithms or both. Such a test gives proponents of various conflicting theories the opportunity to see support for their own views. Never mind that they are based on scientifically un-proven and un-provable human sentiments, such as the localization of human brain functions including human emotions and the mind, conscience, consciousness, sub-consciousness, super-consciousness, if it can be found there at all.

Mind you, some people, among them Iain McGilchrist (1953–), keep looking for it all in the human brain mass, more or less securely couched in the human skull proper. This is one reason rattus et al are considered equal to the human species.

McGilchrist is a psychiatrist, neuroimaging researcher at Johns Hopkins University and former Oxford literary scholar. In his 2009 publication of *The Master and His Emissary*, subtitled *The Divided Brain and the Making of the Western World*, he points out, that there literally is a world of difference between the brain's left and right hemispheres. To understand what the difference was, he journeyed through areas such as neurology, psychology, philosophy, literature and the arts, as well as archaeology and anthropology, we read. In the book's 'Part One: The Divided Brain,' McGilchrist replaces the notion of the hemispheres as respectively being logical and creative in nature with the idea that they operate in fundamentally different ways, the left being detail-oriented and the right whole-oriented. In the book's second part, 'How the Brain Has Shaped Our World,' the author describes the evolution of Western culture as influenced by hemispheric brain functioning, from the ancient world through to what he views as the present day's increasingly left-brain-dominated, postmodern era.

Whichever way, in the end of his seemingly monumental research and contemplations, he seems to have reached the following quasi-conclusion:

> "I believe our brains [–the left and right hemisphere, I presume–] not only dictate the shape of the experience we have of the world, but are likely themselves to reflect, in their structure and functioning, the nature of the universe in which they have come about." (ibid p. 460)

He furthermore seems somewhat committed to the idea that the human mind and the human brain can only be understood by seeing them in the broadest possible context. In other words, they need to be viewed as part of the whole of our physical and spiritual existence and of the wider human culture in which they arise, the culture which helps to mould, and in turn is moulded, by our minds and brains.

According to reports, McGilchrist is working on a book dealing with epistemology, the study of the nature of knowledge, epistemic justification, the rationality of belief and various related issues. The book also would address metaphysics, the examination of the fundamental nature of reality, including the relationship between mind and matter, substance and attributes. The working title is *The Matter With Things*. Perhaps in the course of these explorations, he might discover that something other than neuro-scientistic findings and EEG-generated visible brain activity influence homo sapiens, making them function the way they do? If really diligent, he might even be led to question whether or not the functions within the human brain-mass include human mind and soul activity, together with the operations of conscience, sub-conscience, super-conscience and human consciousness as a whole? And should he so discover part or all of it, we pray that he would be willing to document through first evidence the scientific research documentation on where precisely it all is localized in the human brain mass?

None of Helena Blavatsky's admirers of the Theosophical Society and Lucifer Trust fame could be bothered with any of it, albeit they were so eminently interested in her revelations and acquaintanceship. None of them seems to have been interested or paid attention to the seat of the soul, conscience, consciousness and the mind generating enormous power available to all humans, if tuned in. Not even though the Buddha presented his views on the topic almost 4,500 years earlier. This, despite Blavatsky's professed training in Tibet by a group of spiritual adepts she called the Masters of the Ancient Wisdom. These masters purportedly developed her deeper understanding and synthesis of religion, philosophy and science. Did these masters, if ever they existed, omit to enlighten her about the enormous power we have once we learn to observe, control and adjust our thinking? And did they forget to mention how we can use that power to heal ourselves not only from PTSD, regardless of where the mind is located, where our thinking takes place and who tries to expertly manipulate our minds? Had she and her pupils not heard of Epictetus, who teaches that the preconceptions of good and evil are common to all? Had none of them heard that good alone is profitable and to be desired, and evil is hurtful and to be avoided? Were they unaware, like the mental health profession, that different opinions arise only from the application of these preconceptions to particular cases? That it is then that the darkness of ignorance, which blindly maintains the correctness of its own opinion, must be dispelled? Did they not know that people entertain different and conflicting opinions of good, and in their judgment of a particular good frequently contradict themselves? Are they unaware that philosophy should provide a standard for good and evil, a process greatly facilitated when knowing that the mind and the works of the mind are alone in our power, whereas all external things that aid life are beyond our control?

Did they and the mental health profession et al not know, or did they merely choose to omit mentioning it to maintain their control over the herd? Buddhists express this inner power carried within the Self, this innate power so ardently ignored by the mental health profession and the learned society in this way:

> "Can we be like the lotus? Can we swallow the pain and confusion of life, and thrive on it, and use it to become one of those rare jewels of the world—a truly compassionate person?" (M. Roach: *The Diamond Cutter* 1st edition, p. 52).

We can, if we learn to control our thinking.

12

MIND-IMPRINTS AND THEIR CONSEQUENCES: THE LAW OF CAUSE AND EFFECT

PTSD experiencers, can expect big-time mind manipulation applied by the powers that be, namely employer and shop stewards, as well as the WCB and other insurers. That's what they can expect. But they rarely do, because when the PTSD-causing event occurs, they almost likely don't have a clue that this is precisely what happens.

Predators par excellence, they put stress on claimants in all ways imaginable, expertly aiming to destroy claimants' mental and physical health right off the bat. They also try to engage any colleagues, friends and acquaintances for money and/or perks. Yes, they'll use one's support system in their demolition derby against a claimant. To accomplish that goal, they have perfected their methods, ways and means to a fine art over decades. Janey Davies, B.A. (Hons.), sub-editor of Learning-mind.com (https://learning-mind.com), describes this to perfection in her article "20 Most Common Manipulation Techniques Used by Predators". It goes like this:

1. *Lying*: Predators are constantly lying about practically everything in their life. They do this to wrong-foot their victim and confuse them. Lying is one of the manipulation techniques psychopaths typically use because they have no qualms about it.
2. *Not telling the whole story*: This is different to lying as a predator will often keep a key part of the story to themselves in order to put their victim at a disadvantage.
3. *Frequent mood swings*: Never knowing what mood your partner is going to be in when you get home, whether they'll be happy or angry is a very useful tool to the predator. It keeps their victim off balance and makes them more malleable.
4. *Love-bombing and devaluation*: Narcissists or the powers that be mentioned earlier and those engaged by them to assist them in lieu of perks typically use love bombing as a manipulation tactic. They will go on a charm offensive and get you hooked into thinking they are working in your behalf.
5. *Punishment*: They drop you like a ton of bricks without explanation to your detriment construing the latest meeting or conversation reflected in their written evaluation of your psyche and state of mind reflected.
6. *Denial*: They will manipulate you by denying that you ever said what you said and seeding doubt in whatever you said happened ever happening.
7. *Spinning the truth*: These predators' and sociopaths' expertise in spinning the truth is breathtaking. It is used to disguise their desire to drive you into quitting your fight against them preferably by committing suicide or at least crawl away into skid-row existence.
8. *Minimizing*: Predators will try and play down their actions as neither important nor damaging and shift the blame onto you for overreacting when you haven't received compensation for months on end or appointments are shifted over and over again and again.
9. *Plays the victim*: The manipulator will themselves take on the role of victim in order to gain sympathy and compassion from you, as they have you down to a fine art due to the MMPI and know that you are inclined to help someone suffering.
10. *Targets the victim*: When a manipulator/predator accuses the victim of wrongdoing. This is either the "it is all your own fault" approach or, if you protest, they will play the "Do you feel like a victim" card. If you admit to the latter, you are dead in the water due to reasons documented in Fallacy 1.
11. *Positive reinforcement*: This will most likely be forthcoming from what you consider your best buddies, who then report to the employer and union shop stewards, who then will coordinate their efforts to get you to quit your employment. Whilst doing so, they will praise you, soothe you, apologize for their behaviour, use excessive kindness and pay you lots and lots of attention.
12. *Moves the goal posts*: You might think you know where you stand with any of them and the powers that be, but they constantly move the goal posts in order to confuse you, at which they are experts. Remember, they are all united in working against you, all of them!

13. *Diversion*: Diverting the conversation away from the perpetrator's act and move it on to a different topic is a typical way predators manipulate their victims. They will use anything you say against you.
14. *Sarcasm*: It is used to both lower your self-esteem and to show how powerful they are. In PTSD cases it is mostly used in their correspondence with other mental health professionals and lawyers.
15. *Guilt tripping*: Guilt tripping means to convey that you are selfish, that you are in the wrong through and through, and that your life is easy, which helps to keep you confused, anxiety loaded and questioning your own sanity.
16. *Flattery*: It is both used to gain your trust, to lower your guard, and to persuade you into believing that a change of work would be ideal for you. Please note that Canadian Labour law states no one can be forced to take another job than the one in which the injury occurred unless volunteering to do so. Using charm, praise and flattery is one way of gaining your trust and persuading you to accept whatever they propose even though it is detrimental to your future.
17. *Playing the innocent card*: A manipulator will feign shock and confusion at being accused of any wrongdoing. The goal? To have you question your own judgment and accuracy.
18. *Over the top aggression*: Aggression to shock you into submission is also used. So is anger for the purpose to shut down further conversation, thus scare you into being cut-off by them of all support, in particular the financial one due to you under the law.
19. *Isolation*: Keep you in isolation. It is far easier to keep a person under control, if they are isolated from other genuine PTSD experiencers, who could share the treatment they receive from the same sources and thus shed light and truth on their situation. The powers that be do anything to avoid such get-togethers as documented in *Fallacy 1*.
20. *Feigns love and empathy*: Predators such as psychopaths and sociopaths oft times working for the powers that be do not know how to love someone other than themselves. They are unable to feel empathy, but they can pretend to do so in order to inveigle others into their lives.

Thus, it is of utmost importance to view all you are in touch with as predators and psychopaths, even though you have known them for years.

I experienced every one of these manipulation techniques and unknowingly meandered through it all as blind as a bat. I realize now that only my twice-daily meditations, my superb intuition and my explorations of life's spiritual aspects saved me from complete catastrophe.

Note therefore not to trust anyone, as both your closest and dearest friends and your co-workers are buyable for the right price. Even your wife and parents can with ease be brainwashed into believing you've gone nutty or worse - mental - due to your genuine PTSD experience, when nothing could be further from the truth. The PTSD-causing event has "merely" left you with the problem of living without your soul. Meanwhile, nobody gives you the peace and quiet needed to recapture it and straighten yourself out, either because of willful or pretended ignorance, or out of sheer malice or an attractive fee.

Remember, employers want to get rid of you, as they can hire two brand-new employees on the lowest pay scale for the price of one—you—if you have seniority, to increase shareholder profits. Your wife, husband, and family are untrustworthy, because they want to be helpful without having a clue what you are living, unless themselves having lived through genuine PTSD. Thus, if not, they only add to your despair. More dangerously, they might side with the powers that be or find you belong in a nuthouse, which would facilitate a potentially life-long excursion into that environment, as described in Fallacy 1.

It can turn into an extremely vicious cycle, and those in power know it. Their success over decades to destroy careers and lives is manifested by the multitude of genuine PTSD sufferers living in abject poverty. You'll find them skid rows or homeless in North America's cities or committing suicide out of pure despair caused by this PTSD perception-deception scam. Only when we know how they play the game can we learn how to protect ourselves. And the only way for us to achieve the rest and recuperation to do so despite the onslaught, and to arise victoriously, is through the enormous power of our own mind. The moment we engage in controlling our thinking, we are on the path to PTSD healing. Unless, that is, we are taking psychotropic pharmaceuticals and other mind-altering drugs, including marijuana, which ruins both our mental and physical health. And they know that too, thus their eagerness to get and keep us on any and all drugs we are willing to swallow or inject. They know that pharmaceutical drugs in particular completely destroy our logic and reason, as well as our physical and mental health. They also know that they create suicidal ideation, the desire to kill oneself.

But how to go about gaining control over our thoughts? Through the imprints they generate, they will inevitably reflect in our lives due to the cosmic law of cause and effect. With meditation, determination, willpower, determination, discipline, patience, prayer and love for the Self.

Geshe Michael Roach gives the perfect guidelines how and why to aim at achieving the at first thought seemingly unachievable in his book *The Diamond Cutter: Buddha on Strategies For Managing Your Business And Your Life* (1st edition). It is, tailored after a sermon the Buddha gave under the Bo-tree in Sarnia, close to Varanasi at India's Ganges River, the title, in Sanskrit *Vajracchedikā Prajñāpāramitā Sūtra*, roughly translates as "Vajra Cutter Perfection of Wisdom Sūtra" or "The Perfection of Wisdom Text that Cuts Like a Thunderbolt." It relies on the power of the vajra, a diamond or thunderbolt, but also an abstract term for a powerful weapon, to cut things. It is used here as a metaphor for the type of wisdom that cuts and shatters illusions to get to the ultimate reality.

Roach (1952–) is an American non-traditional teacher of Tibetan Buddhism. He is the very first American to receive the degree of Geshe, obtaining it from the Sera monastery, one of the three Gelug university monasteries of Tibet. "Among other sects of Tibetan Buddhism, the Gelug School places the most rigorous emphasis on philosophical study, administrating a scholastic degree. It can take two decades or more to complete the *Geshe* degree (fpmt.org)." *Ge* means "virtue" and *she* means "knowing." Geshe thus reflects which attitudes in life to hone and practice, and which ones to abandon. Furthermore, it is believed that a degree as Geshe creates the karmic imprints necessary for a graduate to take rebirth in Shambhala. This mythical kingdom is believed to be hidden somewhere in inner Asia, seen in Tibetan and Indian Buddhist traditions as a Pure Land, a fabulous kingdom.

In addition to writing books about Buddhism and translating Tibetan Buddhist teachings, Geshe Roach also lectures on the many factors that are part and parcel of the making and the consequences of imprints. He says that, according to the Buddha's teachings, these include yoga, meditation, and the practice of helping others—even competitor. Everything occurring in life originates from imprints planted in our mind by way of our own actions, non-actions and re-actions in present and previous lives. So, it would be a good idea to learn how to control the action.

Every event and situation we experience is in and of itself neutral, empty and without substance. It just is. How we see and react to any of those events and situations is what dictates the imprints. Sooner or later, like a boomerang, they will return to us for better or for worse. This is the secret of mental imprints. We plant these imprints into our minds through the gates of our awareness versus our ignorance, compassion versus hatred, empathy versus callousness and psychopathy, envy and greed versus benevolence and kindness, sloth and wrath versus industriousness and productivity in all aspects of the words, pride and arrogance versus humility and modesty. In other words, in the greater scheme of things, our lives' unfolding is, by and large, in chorus with our motivation to help or hurt ourselves and others (ibid p. 66).

Our perception of our own Self and our perception of the world and everything in it as a whole and in its entirety is dictated by:

- the videos we watch
- the materials we read - magazines, books and newspapers
- the strength of our emotion
- how well we recognize/realize what we are doing
- the style with which we act upon the information transmitted or action taken
- the degree to which we "own" our actions afterward
- toward or against whom we act
- our own intentions and reactions, regardless of whether they were generated by our own Self or imprinted by events we observe
- the strength with which we plant these imprints, or allow them to be planted in us through television and mass media, as well as various physicians and mental health practitioners we deal with during our PTSD situation

According to ancient Buddhist scriptures, the visual cassette recorder of our minds records about 65 discrete images or imprints in a single snap of the finger. Unidentified by our conscious mind, these imprints enter a place in our subconscious and remain there for days, years, decades and even life times. Meanwhile, they reproduce themselves every millisecond as separate moments of the mind, as the mind itself blinks in and out of existence. They move by like frames of a movie, whilst giving the illusion of continuity (M. Roach: *The Diamond Cutter* 1st edition p. 66). By far the deepest imprints, by the way, are created by our attitude and view of life itself and how we are living it (ibid p. 71).

Our reactions to any given event, from the most mundane to the most imperious, arrogant, exacting, dictatorial, authoritative, domineering, haughty or lordly, imprint themselves in our minds. There, they grow like seeds planted in fertile soil until they are fully matured and spring forth into our awareness, for better or for worse (ibid p. 66). When these fully matured seeds force us onto the path of retribution for actions and attitudes taken in the past, four rules govern. These are:

- The general content of the experience forced on us by the imprint must match the general content of the original imprinting.
- The strength of an imprint, continually expanding during its time in our subconscious, flowers, forcing us to undergo a similar experience as the existent imprint, be it good or bad.
- No experience of any kind ever happens unless the imprint that triggers it has been planted first.
- Once an imprint is planted in our mind, it must lead to an experience, as no imprint is ever wasted (p.68/69).

This means that imprints planted through negative actions, such as the infliction of pain on others, whether mental or physical, will create unpleasant experiences. Those of positive actions when flowering, such as having been helpful to others, create joyous ones. In his *Sermon On The Mount: Recognizing False Prophets*, Jesus expressed it as such: "Grapes are not gathered from thorn bushes nor figs from thistles, are they? So every good tree bears good fruit, but the bad tree bears bad fruit (Matthew 7:15-20). In the vernacular, it is the "What goes around comes around" maxim, or the law of retribution.

Thus, we could recognize that we indeed are creators of our own lives due to the way we think, act and react. Through self-control and thought observation, we become the producers and directors of our daily show. Therefore, once grown up and independent of those who raised us, must we take responsibility for whatever "Karma" hits us, because we caused it due to imprints we created earlier in our lives? Does everything in our lives happen for that reason, triggered by imprints planted in our minds in times gone by, as said in *The Diamond Cutter*: "Once an imprint is planted, it must lead to an experience, as no imprint is ever wasted?" (ibid p. 69)

When consciously aware of how imprints are created and planted, and of their consequences do we jump into action to create our own present and future perhaps? Does enthusiasm to take possession of that power and control it by controlling our thoughts and actions spring forth? Under stress, controlling anger with sheer might can indeed create miraculous results. Practice makes perfect; by honing self-control, life in all aspects begins to flow better. And as life flows better, we gain the ability to create what we are here for in the first place. The opportunity of a lifetime is presented to us by the PTSD causing experience, namely, to create the individual we would love to be. We can become the lotus who can swallow the pain and confusion of life, thrive on it, and become one of those rare jewels of the world—a truly compassionate person.

When? How soon will that happen? There is no timeline. Apparently, it depends primarily on maintaining certain states of mind and certain standards of behavior, seemingly accessible only when meditating twice daily to develop the prerequisites for a fruitful and contented life. This is described by master Nāgārjuna (c150-250 A.D.), one of India's most respected Buddhist philosophers, in *Precious String of Jewels*:

I'll tell you briefly the fine qualities
Of those on the path of compassion:
Giving, and ethics, patience, and effort,
Concentration, wisdom, compassion and such.
Giving is giving away what you have,
And ethics is doing good to others.
Patience is giving up feelings of anger,
And effort is joy that increases all good.

Concentration's one-pointed, free of bad thoughts,
And wisdom decides what truth really is.
Compassion's a kind of high intelligence
Mixed deep with a love for all living kind.

Giving brings wealth, a good world comes from ethics;
Patience brings beauty, eminence comes from effort.
Concentration brings peace, and from wisdom comes freedom;
Compassion achieves everything we all wish for.

A person who takes all seven of these
And perfects them together will reach
That place of inconceivable knowledge
No less than the world's protector.
Nāgārjuna

A huge undertaking? Sure. But what is life, other than a huge undertaking for everyone on earth? And when in the genuine PTSD condition, it is *the* path to heal the Self, and the reason we had the experience in the first place. Furthermore, it is the only avenue to vanquish our predators, the powers that be. They thrive on our upheaval, anger and despair. That, in turn, gives them reasons, ways and means through our own behavior to plow us under as "mentally ill", their one and only goal.

When we maintain our calm, remaining gracious and civil during our forced engagements with them, we deplete them of reasons for their frontal assaults. It takes enormous self-control, but it can be done. What we do after the WCB interview or the telephone conversation with the employer's gofer has ended is inconsequential, but stay calm and gracious while in touch with them. Remember, our watchfulness over our thoughts, expressions and actions rapidly manifests as beneficial imprints created for the morrow. That it seems to be a lifelong undertaking is beside the point. It is far better to recognize it as the major gift of our PTSD journey, knowing full well we get A plusses from our guides, guardians, helpers, teachers and friend in the unseen, who root for us every day and never fail to assist us when asked.

But do Freud, Blavatsky and cohorts know of the creation of imprints and how to generate them? That is a good question. All of them dabbled in neurology and psychology and the metaphysical aspects of life. Through their decades of similar education paths and academic backgrounds, they were linked with each other. Through both Blavatsky's Theosophical Society and Freud's *Wednesday Psychological Society*, aka *Vienna Psychoanalytic Society*, they shared premier building blocks. Most of them, if not all, were acquainted with Wittgenstein's Vienna and Berlin Circle members. Freud's society only numbered 150 members between 1902 and 1938. Most of them, if not all, were acquainted with Wittgenstein's Vienna- and Berlin Circle members, and all of them were at advertising guru Bernays' beck and call.

One of Freud's disciples was Paul Ferdinand Schilder (1886–1940). In 1909, he graduated from the University of Vienna with a degree in medicine, becoming a renowned psychiatrist, psychoanalyst, researcher and author of numerous scientific publications. His compatriot Sigmund Exner (1846–1926) was a researcher in comparative physiology and perception psychology in comparative physiology. Exner inspired Schilder to conduct research in both neurophysiology and neuropathology. Comparative physiology is a sub-discipline of physiology, the study of human anatomy. It explores how organs and systems work together, and how outside agents affect them. The field dates back thousands of years, albeit it originally focused primarily on the improvement of medical practices for humans. As to perception psychology, the American Psychological Association Dictionary describes it as:

> "The process or result of becoming aware of objects, relationships, and events by means of the senses, which includes such activities as recognizing, observing, and discriminating. These activities enable organisms to organize and interpret the stimuli received into meaningful knowledge and to act in a coordinated manner."

Seemingly diametrically opposed to the Buddha's and thus Master Nāgārjuna's (c150-250 A.D.) philosophy of life, none of it can be scientifically proven., It led Schilder to his involvement with psychoanalysis. From 1909 to 1912, he went on a quest to prove his hypotheses. He began in Halle, Germany, where he assisted neuro-psychiatrist Gabriel Anton (1858–1933), at the time one of the leading contributors to the nascent field of neurosurgery (whonamedit.com). As a new scientific discipline, he and other surgeons, neurologists and psychiatrists of his era used the morphological approach for their research, meaning they operated, probed and experimented on living humans and animals under the "learn as you go with no holds barred" principle as they saw fit.

The same principle is applied to PTSD research nowadays. Willing genuine PTSD journeyers, in particular American and Canadian soldiers and veterans, are used as guinea pigs for a multitude of drug experiments to, purportedly, heal PTSD. Ketamine, a fast-acting medication used to induce loss of consciousness or as anaesthesia, is at present one of the favourites tested on them. It produces vivid dreams and feelings of mind-body separation, helping the authorities to drive PTSD journeyers over the brink, never mind the imprints they create in their subjects' minds. After a few experiments, Ecstasy has been identified by the mental health cabal as a *promising* PTSD treatment since 2018. Psilocybin, the hallucinogenic compound found in "magic mushrooms" that gives folks the highest of highs, is also thought to potentially alleviate PTSD symptoms. Researchers admit that further research into how psychedelic drugs can assist PTSD experiencers is needed (Camden, Grant H, Steele, Joel: Use of MDMA & Psilocybin in the treatment of PTSDS; Portland State University, 2019). As a matter of fact, the American Psychological Association, offspring of Freud's Wednesday Psychological Society, held a whole symposium in 2018 on the potential uses of psychedelics– for the betterment of mankind, I am sure.

Schilder and Anton studied aphasia, the inability to comprehend or formulate language due to brain damage. They also studied the different states of human consciousness, a topic discussed at length in *Fallacy 1*. Here it suffices to merely print what Wikipedia says about it:

> "Consciousness at its simplest is 'sentience or awareness of internal or external existence'. Despite centuries of analyses, definitions, explanations and debates by philosophers and scientists, consciousness remains puzzling and controversial, being "*at once the most familiar and most mysterious aspect of our lives*". Perhaps the only widely agreed notion about the topic is *the intuition* that it exists. Opinions differ about what exactly needs to be studied and explained as consciousness. Sometimes it is *synonymous with 'the mind'*, other times *just an aspect of mind*. In the past it was one's "inner life", the world of introspection, of private thought, imagination and volition. Today, with modern research into the brain, it often includes any kind of experience, cognition, feeling or perception. It may be 'awareness', or 'awareness of awareness', or self-awareness. There might be different levels or "orders" of consciousness, or different kinds of consciousness, or just one kind with different features. Other questions include whether only humans are conscious, or all animals, or even the whole universe. The disparate range of research, notions and speculations raises doubts whether the right questions are being asked." [italics mine].

As pointed out earlier, there is no scientific evidence of the existence or the location of mind, nor the seat of consciousness, nor the location of intuition, of emotion or of the. Psychiatrists with very few exceptions, however, shun the thought of their existence anywhere else but in the human brain. Thus their ubiquitous experiments with rattus, mus, simian, cani. On those depend the craft's desire to be recognized as a science, albeit there is no science to be recognized, unless to be able to physically pinpoint and prove where it all reigns in this largely atheistic environment. As a matter of fact, according to Albert Pike, science deals only with phenomena, and is but charlatanism when it babbles about the power of causes that produce things, of which it gives us merely the names. It no more knows what light or sound or perfume is, than the Aryan cattle herders did, when they counted the dawn and fire, flame and light and heat gods, at least in Albert Pike's opinion (*Morals & Dogma*, Ch 26).

Regardless, Schilder worked hard to prove the improvable. After his stay with Anton, he ventured on to Leipzig, Germany. From 1912 to 1914, he conducted extensive neuro-physical studies on whomever was willing (or unable to protest), like souls in insane asylums they so cherished to engage. This field is a branch of biophysics dealing with development and use of physical techniques to gain information about the nervous system on a molecular level. In other words, it looks at the smallest units making up an organisms or element and studies it by means of experimental biophysics. Biophysics, in turn, is an interdisciplinary science that applies approaches and methods used in physics to study biological phenomena. Preferred research and experimentation subjects are human herd-members, followed by cani, rattus, mus, lepus and simian.

Schilder's own personality apparently greatly influenced his work. He was able to brilliantly converse with psychotic patients. No predecessors were his equal in the written presentation of psychotic cases. During that period, he also published a paper on symbolism in schizophrenia (Hartmann, Heinz, M.D.: 'The Psychiatric Work of Paul Schilder'; pep-web.org). It may have been a quasi-futile undertaking, as Hungarian-American academic, psychiatrist and psychoanalyst Thomas Stephen Szasz (1920–2012) would argue a few decades later in an article published by *The British Journal of Psychiatry* (1976). He opined that the word "schizophrenia" does not stand for a genuine disease. He maintained that psychiatry had invented the concept as a sacred symbol to justify locking people up against their will and treating them with a variety of unwanted, unsolicited, and damaging interventions. Szasz served for most of his career as professor of psychiatry at the State University of New York Upstate Medical University in Syracuse, New York, and was co-founder of the Citizens Commission on Human Rights International (CCHR),

As a matter of fact, in his book *Mental Illness is A Myth*, Szasz maintains that, unlike true diseases of the brain and body, mental illness is a destructive social construct. He says that it medicalizes living and deprives people of their dignity. According to Szasz, medication, hospitalization and mandated psychotherapy are little more than coercive, dignity-reducing forms of clinical practice. Szasz operated on the maxim that true freedom means taking control of and responsibility for our choices in life and their consequences. He therefore maintained that neither psychotherapy, nor drugs, nor the power of the techniques used by mental health practitioners restored a client's personal sense of agency. The CCHR has long fought to restore basic inalienable human rights to the field of mental health, including full informed consent regarding the medical legitimacy of psychiatric diagnosis, the risks of psychiatric treatments, the right to all available medical alternatives and the right to refuse any treatment considered harmful (https://cchr.org).

The CCHR, established in 1969 by the Church of Scientology and Szasz, is another nonprofit organization. A mental health watchdog headquartered in Los Angeles, it investigates and exposes psychiatric human rights violations. It does much good for humanity by embracing deeper psychiatric and social justice issues most of this psychiatric cabal resent to ponder, never mind engage in their clinical practices. This includes questioning the coercive nature inherent in psychotherapy and psychopharmacology.

A symbol, by the way, is a mark, sign or word that indicates, signifies or is understood as representing an idea, object or relationship. Symbols allow us to go beyond what is known or seen by creating linkages between otherwise distinctly different concepts and experiences. Symbols take the form of words, sounds, gestures, ideas or visual images and are used to convey other ideas and beliefs. Once aware, they can be seen everywhere, silently implanting themselves into our minds and perverting our perceptions. Swiss psychiatrist Carl Jung wrote a whole book on it in 1961, entitled *Man and His Symbols*, examining the world of the unconscious, whose language he believed to be symbols constantly revealed in our dreams. Jung was convinced that dreams were sent from our unconscious to our conscious Self to offer us practical advice. Like many others of the learned society in ancient, pre-Freudian times, he felt that only the understanding of the Self leads to a full and productive life.

In more recent times, Albert Pike, in *Morals and Dogma*, points out:

> "Men are great or small in stature as it leases God. But their nature is great or small as it pleases themselves. Men are not born, some with great souls and some with little souls. One by taking thought cannot add to his stature, but he can enlarge his soul. By an act of the will he can make himself a moral giant, or dwarf himself to a pigmy." (ibid)

But to document symbolism in conjunction with schizophrenia, as Schilder purportedly did in the early 1900s, seemed to be a most complicated task. That was the conclusion of to John L. Cameron, Director of Research and Training at the Chestnut Lodge Research Institute, Rockville, Maryland, in 1970. To him, it seemed to be just as difficult and complicated as the study of man himself (Symbolism in the treatment of schizophrenia; Brit. J. med. Psychol. 1970, 43, 257). But Freud, for a while Jung's buddy, had brought it into vogue, predominately in conjunction with the symbolism he saw in dreams. He detected and described them as processes of displacement, condensation and indirect representation. He forgot to mention dreams also function as a warning system, as I experienced during the *Broken Wings* days. In that book, I revealed my dreams of my opponents dancing on my freshly filled grave, while I lay alive in the coffin underneath. That dream, with all its symbolism, actually saved my livelihood, if not my sanity and life itself.

Be that as it may, the very productive Schilder also explored the role of changes in schizophrenia subjects' body image. He made special reference to feelings of depersonalization, disconnection or detachment from the Self. He noted how subjects took an outside observer perspective of their own thoughts or body, conjoined with a feeling of loss of control over their own thoughts and actions. Schilder even found time to write a book on self-consciousness, explored in depth in *Fallacy 1*. To briefly recap: *The Encyclopedia of Psychoanalysis* views self-consciousness as such:

> "Self-consciousness is the mental activity through which the subject feels a sense of being or existing as a unique and total individual. Although it does not obviate the idea of the unconscious, this notion comes out of reflexive philosophy and its derivatives that hold that the human faculty of consciousness, apparent to itself and having itself as its object, marks the primacy of consciousness in the definition of the human psyche. This sense of identity, this initial subjective stance, is established gradually, being linked with the general development of the human mind in its relationship to itself and the outside world."

Remember that no-one can prove whether consciousness in all its facets really is in the body and, if so, where it resides. Nor can anyone prove if it has a beginning or end, and if so where it originates or terminates. Not whether it comes and goes at leisure or inhabits the body permanently until death. This gives all of us the grand opportunity to make up our own minds as to where we want to put it. For the mental health PTSD industry, such as the U.S. National Center for *the enhancement* of PTSD, touting to be experts in the field, mind and consciousness play no part in PTSD symptomology and therefore find them irrelevant. Instead, in their experimentations to find a "PTSD cure," they coral experiencers into suicide-ideation through pharmacotherapy and complete lack of empathy.

But Schilder continued to search fervently for consciousness in all its physical aspects he envisioned. While being on active duty during WWI, he received a doctorate of philosophy in absentia from the University of Vienna. After the 1918 armistice, he worked with Austrian psychiatrist Julius Wagner-Jauregg (1857–1940). In 1887, Wagner-Jauregg began to investigate the effects of febrile diseases on psychoses, making use of erisipela and tuberculin for his experiments on patients. Both agents were discovered in 1890 by 1905 Nobel Prize recipient Robert Koch, today best known for his discoveries of tuberculosis', cholera's and anthrax's causal agents. His postulates, a series of guidelines for the experimental study of infectious disease, permitted Koch and his students to identify many of the causes of the most important infectious diseases of humans and animals. These are still adhered to whenever a new infectious disease, such as COVID-19, arises.

Since erisipela and tuberculinin treatments did not work to Wagner-Jauregg's satisfaction, he moved on to inoculate patients with malaria parasites. That, he insisted, proved successful in cases of general paralysis of the insane (GPI) caused by neurosyphilis. This was a sexually transmitted infection of the central nervous system that was fatal prior to the discovery of penicillin in 1928 by Scottish scientist Alexander Fleming. Twenty-five percent of the primary diagnoses for residents in public psychiatric hospitals at that time suffered from syphilis. Proving that high fevers could cure syphilis, malaria induced by its least aggressive parasite, plasmodium vivax, became the favorite treatment on tertiary syphilis patients between 1917 and the 1940s. As it killed only roughly 15% of patients, the risks were considered negligible. In fact, it was considered a huge advance at the time. In 1927, Wagner-Jauregg was the first psychiatrist to win a Nobel Prize in Physiology or Medicine for his discovery of the therapeutic value of malaria inoculation in the treatment of dementia paralytica. The main publication cited for his Nobel prize achievement was a book titled *Verhütung und Behandlung der progressiven Paralyse durch Impfmalaria* (Prevention and treatment of progressive paralysis by malaria inoculation) in the Memorial Volume of the Handbuch der experimentellen Therapie, (1931).

Inducing fevers to treat purportedly mental diseases, known as pyrotherapy, encompassed Wagner-Jauregg's life work.

Seventy-three years would pass until psychiatry had a second Nobel Prize winner in Austrian-American Eric Richard Kandel (1929–). He was a medical doctor who specialized in psychiatry, a neuroscientist and a university professor of biochemistry and biophysics at the College of Physicians and Surgeons at Columbia University. He received the 2000 Nobel Prize in Physiology or Medicine for his research on the physiological basis of memory storage in neurons. For Kandel, it was Freud's work and the relationship between neurology, biology, id, ego and superego, all components of Freudian theory of psychoanalysis, that propelled him into pursuing his psychiatric ambitions. So says Assad Meymandi, M.D., PhD, DLFAPA (you figure out what it all means) in his article, "Eric R. Kandel: My kind of Saint" (*Psychiatry*. Edgmont 2009, Nov; 6(11): 48–50). He shared the prize with Swede Arvid Carlsson and American Paul Greengard "for their discoveries concerning signal transduction in the nervous system." When, according to Nassim Haramein and others, we have not the faintest idea what memory or consciousness or mind or their processes are, never mind were they reside, it all seems somewhat bizarre. But I digress. Back to Wagner-Jauregg and Schilder.

For his entertainment, Wagner-Jauregg administered thyroid and ovarian preparations to young psychotic patients experiencing delayed puberty. Such treatment led to the development of their secondary sexual characteristics, including pubic hair, enlarged breasts and widened hips in girls, and facial hair and Adam's apples in boys. The treatment diminished patients' psychosis, he said. Those he deemed schizophrenic because of excessive masturbation, he simply sterilized. We are told this "improved" their condition.

Meanwhile in 1923, Schilder published a short study in Germany under the title "Körperschema" (Body scheme) (jamanetwork.com). It showed those mechanisms of the central nervous system thought important to develop the spatial image we have of ourselves. In 1935, he published his theory in "The Image and Appearance of the Human Body: Studies in the Constructive Energies of the Psyche." It was based on *Körperschema*, incorporating life and personality as one unit in a psychological doctrine. With it, he introduced the concept of the body image, the perception of the aesthetics and attractiveness of our own body, and how we see ourselves in comparison with the standards set by society at large. He used his own insights into psychoanalysis for this elucidation of problems of brain pathology. Since then, body image has become what is considered "a central problem of psychology patients". Unsurprising, considering Bernays and cohorts have blasted the proverbial path for women to see themselves as defective in body in one way or another, regardless of body-shape, contours and colour.

Schilder joined Freud's Viennese Psychoanalytical Association (WPV in 1919, while assisting maestro Wagner-Jauregg's in his psychiatric clinic in Vienna. He became a professor in neurology and psychiatry at Vienna's university. Simultaneously, he released "Abstract for psychiatry based on the principles of psychoanalysis". With it, the proverbial substance hit the fan, as his theories about human behavior annoyed his peers to distraction. Known as an opponent of the obligatory training analysis for aspiring psychoanalysts, he became recognized as an unorthodox clinical analyst by holding divergent opinions to Freud's drive theory and views on the unconscious. In psychology, a drive theory, theory of drives or drive doctrine is a theory that attempts to analyze, classify or define the psychological drives. A drive is an instinctual need that has the power of driving the behavior of a person. It is an "excitatory state produced by a homeostatic disturbance". In Freud's view, only two basic drives served to motivate human thoughts, emotions and behavior:

1. sex and aggression
2. Eros (life) and Thanatos (death).

These underlay every motivation to human experience as far as Master Freud was concerned (allpsych.com; *Fallacy 1*).

Freud himself fiercely clashed with Schilder, who refused to accept established psycho-analytic dogma, in particular that of the human death instinct. While the academic establishment, the learned society, became evermore hostile towards him, Schilder published his own concepts of human behaviour in a series of papers and monographs. But by 1928, the vitriolic behaviour against him at a crescendo, he accepted a one semester teaching position at John Hopkins University. After that, he returned to Vienna, where Freud's *Wiener Psychoanalytische Vereinigung*, the world's first psychoanalytical organization founded in 1908, had engaged him to treat psychotic outpatients. Still, his philosophical rudiment continued to be shunned by his peers. It mattered not that it was influenced by Austrian philosopher Edmund Gustav Albrecht Husserl (1859–1938), who established the school of phenomenology, the philosophical study of the structures of experience and consciousness. Nor that it was influenced by German psychologist and linguist Karl Ludwig Bühler (1879–1963), known for his work in Gestalt psychology.

Bühler became professor and head of the Psychology Department of the University of Vienna in 1922. He also participated in the founding of the Psychological Institute of Vienna to reorganize the city's school system on the basis of new scientific findings about child psychology. He, and his wife, Lauretta Bender, transported this knowledge to the U.S. when they immigrated in 1940. He worked first as professor in Minnesota from 1940 to 1945, followed by a professorship of psychiatry at the University of Southern California in Los Angeles from 1945 to 1955.

This propelled Schilder in late 1929 accept the positions of director of clinical psychiatry at New York's Bellevue Hospital and associate professor of psychiatry at the New York University Medical School. Working with his wife, he researched the consciousness in children and implemented group therapy with psychotic children. In 1940, he asserted:

> "The behaviour of the child can only be understood as a continuous process of trial and error, which leads to construction and configuration as a basis for action . . . Human beings drive into the future by trial and error and thereby find their happiness . . ." (In a biography written in 1940.)

Did he know, one wonders, that nothing in human lives has to do with trial and error? Did he understand how lives are controlled by indelible imprints formed by perception-generated actions, which in turn create future endeavours for better or for worse? Did he know how those perceptions were created? Did he know that he and is Viennese cohorts would play a huge role in creating those perceptions, in part through the advertising industry and the media, which leads us straight back to Edward Bernays?

How do we avoid being caught up in this imprint-creating web and instead create splendid lives for ourselves? Many books and videos document the correlations between specific actions, their imprints and their results. Roach in *The Diamond Cutter* summarizes them such:

1. In order to see yourself do well in business and prosper financially, plant imprints for this in your subconscious by maintaining a generous state of mind.

2. In order to see yourself in a world, which is just generally a very happy place, plant imprints for this in your subconscious by maintaining a very ethical way of life.
3. In order to see yourself as physically healthy and attractive, plant imprints for this in your subconscious by refusing to ever get angry.
4. In order to see yourself as a leader in both your personal life and in business plant imprints for this in your subconscious by taking joy in constructive and helpful actions.
5. In order to see yourself able to focus your mind steadily, plant imprints for this in your subconscious by practicing deep states of concentration or meditation.
6. In order to see yourself freed from a world where things don't work the way you want them to, plant imprints for this in your subconsciously learning the principles of hidden potential and mental imprints.
7. In order to see yourself get all you ever wished for, and see others get all they ever wished for as well, plant imprints for this in your subconscious by cultivating an attitude of compassion towards others (p.84).

The questions thus arise:

- Who conceived the idea of calling an extra-ordinary event beyond normal human experiences "PTSD"?
- Who sought to classify PTSD as a mental disorder in need of treatment by mental health professionals and mind-altering drugs?
- Who thought of accepting the numerous useless-as-tits-on-a-bull hypotheses of PTSD treatments as benevolent to genuine PTSD healing, when none of them is proven to be anything but harmful to genuine PTSD journeyers?
- Who hallucinated and put in motion these perfect methods to prolong the traumatization of the traumatized by claiming their emotional sufferings originate with their innate mental malfunction since the cradle?
- And who brought all this fallacy with its enormous stigma attached to public awareness in the course of the past 20 years?

Let me tell you, as succinctly as I am able.

13

ON PTSD IMPRINT CREATION

When I published *Broken Wings* in 1999, no one outside of the mental health industry knew about PTSD. I had never heard anything like it existed, not even after my PTSD causing event moment. Even though I had numerous previous close calls, the airlines kept its existence a secret from me. Someone was raped in a street attack, but otherwise uninjured; -he news anchor would announce it on TV as if it were no big deal, the victim's psyche a non-issue. My general practitioner knew, and he was kind enough to tell me that I would be much better when I got through the experience than I had ever been before. He was right, but then "the system" rolled him over like a bulldozer. In their eyes, he was suddenly insufficiently papered to treat me, what with his ideas of peace and quiet and contemplation to get me out of it. So, they decided to "handle" me - straight onto the pathway through hell.

But, as German philosopher and cultural critic Friedrich Nietzsche (1844-1900) used to say: "He who has a why to live for can bear almost any how." In other words, anyone who has a reason to live can bear almost any means of living (plato.stanford.edu). Published intensively in the 1870s and 1880s, he is famous for uncompromising criticisms of traditional European morality and religion, as well as of conventional philosophical ideas and social and political pieties associated with modernity

Many of his criticisms rely on psychological diagnoses that expose false consciousness infecting people's received ideas, by perception-manipulations creating imprints and resulting in false consciousness, perhaps? So when I entered the path through hell, I went with it. I rolled with the punches for 10 years without knowing that I was doing it, while the powers that be tried to shake me up in all ways imaginable. Tis is, in essence and with few exceptions, wherein lies mental practitioners' expertise. Few if any among them knew what PTSD was all about, and they weren't talking. My employer, whose paid hatchet men they were, demanded they get rid of me fast, as time is money.

I am now of the opinion that we have been used. In particular, our perception of loss and our feelings of utter futility about life, living, and everything associated with it in our post-PTSD causing event misery of limbo is used. They use it to imprint in us the idea that our own innate inadequacy from birth, warpedness and weakness of mind and character is the reason for our reaction to the PTSD causing event. This thought is being imprinted into us from the moment of our first encounter with the first psychiatrist or psychologist or their secretary. Our employer insists on that encounter, as soon as we report to being unable perform our duties, but unaware of the reason.

Something was desperately wrong my body. That's what it yelled at me 24/7 for weeks and months on end with differing severity. The blinding headaches associated with muscle spasm in my neck while on duty was the start. The night sweats followed. And the grinding teeth and the nightmares, though during the first few weeks I never related them to the engine explosion next to me. The airline's medical officer told me to take Robitussin, and I would feel brand new in a few days. I did not feel better, so "things" took off from there, as WCB's machetes began their expert "traumatization of the traumatized" tactics, enhanced by the first meeting with my union shop stewards and insurance agents as documented in *Broken Wings*.

From there onwards, genuine PTSD journeyers seem to be systematically and with expertise driven towards their own demise. The intent is to erode our self-confidence, preferably resulting in suicide. It is the cheapest and easiest solution to the problem we pose, making shareholders suffer. Driving us into abject poverty, the next-best-thing, is pursued simultaneously, with equal fervor and with no holds barred. And they keep it up until we fade into the woodwork, voluntarily disappearing from their radar. We are run ragged. We are raped of self-confidence and self-esteem, mentally and physically exhausted, because of their mind-altering drugs.

No surveys or scientifically proven first evidence exists. However, logic dictates that corporations, unions, WCB, insurers and the like use this *modus operandi* to get rid of what they consider human debris. After all, their success rate has proven it to be superbly effective. And the imprints they plant while at it, about how you have been mentally defective from birth. They show you to have always been a human failure in all your undertakings, regardless that you were cruising through life brilliantly pre-PTSD-causing event moment. The stigma they attach to you for their fault and negligence (the engine blowing up in my face was damaged before start-up) sticks to our psyche, leaving imprints to doubt our very being, once they're finished with us. Thus, suicide or skid row, unless we knowingly or by osmosis catch on to their scheme and begin to research and analyze ourselves. This is the only way to survive relatively unscathed. It gives us a purpose, the *why* mentioned by Nietzsche, with which we can bare what we experience without turning into embittered, acrimonious, revengeful souls, or, heaven forbid, adopt the victim ideation, the most deadly of all.

As professor Jordan B. Peterson points out in his April 2019 lecture "On the Impact of the Radical Left":

> "Life is suffering, to be transcended by pursuing things of value. If there is no value proposition at hand, then you have no meaning to justify the difficult conditions of your life."

My *Why* of life during the first five years revolved around completing my B.A.. During the next five years, it was to research PTSD, in particular in aircrew, and write *Broken Wings* based on that research. And I encountered many "Touched by an Angel" people who helped me in miraculous ways along the journey. Thus, I fulfill Nietzsche's hypothesis. I am living proof that people who find a positive purpose in life can overcome any obstacle and suffer through almost any defeat without quitting or becoming a non-proposition. Actually, the PTSD recovery and healing depends on it. To find out about your purpose while on earth, with or without PTSD. Go into meditation twice daily and it will be revealed to you. Then, relentlessly pursue it. If so, you will find inner satisfaction, peace of mind and contentment with the Self, and thus the world around you. If not, you will learn to hate yourself. (https://simplethingcalledlife.com)

But those genuine PTSD journeyers who trust their physicians' PTSD pharmacotherapy treatments as healing modality panacea may as well pack it in. Due to their inaction, lethargy and apathy, for the rest of their natural lives they will be victims of themselves, the worst state of mind one can find oneself in. Such imprints of lethargy and refusal to help the Self are detrimental to both physical and mental health, as they create bitterness, anguish and hatred within. Mind you, those with herd-identity living nothing other than work- and television-dominated lives, allow their perception of the world and everything in it to be masterfully crafted and imprinted into their psyche by present day Bernays. They allow themselves to be brainwashed victims of their rulers, who view them as useless eaters. They don't have a clue about what's being done to them, even without genuine PTSD ideation. All this is so well described in Idaho Observes journalist Don Harkins' two-page "Slavery and the 8 Veils" contemplation (*Idaho Observer* 2001).

Schilder's body image research gave a huge boost to human mind-manipulation implanting. In 1935, he had already specified peoples' perception of the aesthetics and attractiveness of their own body in comparison to the standards set by society. He documented his findings in his book *The Image and Appearance of the Human Body*. This study of the picture of our own body, showed how we form it in our mind, in its physiological, libidinous and sociological aspects.

His subjects include postural and tactile impressions, libidinous structure such as narcissism, erogenic zones, neurasthenia, depersonalization, hypochondria, hysteria and conversion. They also include curiosity, the expression of emotions, imitation, identification, beauty and other social aspects of the body image. Case histories of organic brain lesions and elementary discussion of the anatomy and physiology of the nervous system are also found (APA.org). In other words, Freud, nephew Bernays and their buddies knew how to influence our feelings about our own bodies throughout the past 85 years. And they knew how to manipulate and imprint our minds in accordance with their desires. From body types as varied as Twiggy and buxom, to fashion and make-up and hair style and whatever else we could be or to buy.

The concept of body image is used in psychology, medicine, psychiatry, psychoanalysis and philosophy, as well as in feminist and cultural studies. Apparently, our appearance incorporates and reflects our memories, experiences, assumptions, presumptions, comparisons and attitudes towards our height, shape and weight. Other factors contributing to our individual body image are hypothesized to include family dynamics, mental illness, biological predispositions and environmental causes. All are suspected to possibly be responsible for both obesity and malnutrition. In the mid-1990s, more than 40 "instruments" were used to measure peoples' body image (Thompson, J. K. et al: "Factor analysis of multiple measures of body image disturbance: are we all measuring the same construct?" *The International Journal of Eating Disorders.* 16 (3): 311–315, 1994). However, there are so many ways to measure the view we have of our physical self. So, it is difficult to draw meaningful research generalizations when taking into account gender, ethnicity, culture and age .

It is astounding that only age is ever taken into account when dealing with genuine PTSD experiencers. Be that as it may, please keep firmly anchored in your mind; a WCB- or insurance-appointed shrink will inevitably ask, "How do you feel about your body?" There is only one "correct" answer: beam like a ray of sunshine! Answer with lightness and joy in your voice: "I love it." Beware any critique of your body image, which can and will be held against you as another "reason" for your PTSD suffering. Why? Because the mental health profession hypothesizes that negative body image is accompanied by low self esteem. It further hypothesizes that it *may* lead to over time serious mental illness. And you will be accused of having this "serious mental illness" long before the PTSD-causing incident.

Among these body image distortions is the body dysmorphic disorder (BDD), also known as dysmorphophobia. It is characterized by the obsessive idea that some aspect of one's own body or appearance is flawed severely enough to warrant exceptional measures to hide or fix it. If the flaw is present, its importance in one's mind of is severely exaggerated. The term derives from the Greek "dysmorphia," misshapenness or ugliness. Greek historian Herodotus (c. 484–425 BC) first used it in his work *The Histories*, written in 430 BC, in reference to the myth of the "ugliest girl in Sparta." It is now considered the founding work of history in Western literature. It serves as a record of the ancient traditions, politics, geography and clashes of various cultures known at that time in Greece, western Asia and northern Africa.

In the delusional variant, BDD laws are considered to be purely imagined. Whichever way, imaginative or not, thoughts about it are said to be pervasive and intrusive. They occupy several hours a day, causing severe distress to the point of impairing normal activity. Needless to say, the mental health industry categorizes BDD as a mental disorder in the *DSM-5*. You can find it under the obsessive-compulsive spectrum. In this model of medical classification, various psychiatric, neurological and/or medical conditions are described as existing on a spectrum of conditions related to obsessive-compulsive disorder (OCD) in BDD. They are characterized by a mentally distressing and impairing preoccupation with what a medical professional might view as a non-existent or slight defect in appearance that warrants surgical adjustment.

A positive body image of the Self, on the other hand, is taken by the mental health profession as a clear and true reflection of one's splendid perception of one's own well-adjusted inner self. That said, even these scoundrels acknowledge that one's outward appearance reflects neither personality characteristics nor inner feelings of self-worth.

Thompson et al. also acknowledge that cultural expectations spread by PR media and politic imprint makers greatly influence peoples' expectations of their bodies, Schilder's speciality. Schilder was a member of Freud's Vienna Psychoanalytical Society, and in the U.S. considered one of group analysts and psychotherapy's founding fathers. It is he who is credited with the integration of psychoanalytic theory into psychiatry. Psychoanalysis, to repeat, is a theory and treatment of psychopathology and a treatment for mental disorders. Today, with individual independence of mind no longer in style, psychoanalysis is marginalized and struggling to survive in a hostile academic and clinical environment in the trying-to-be-science-non-science mental health profession field.

We presume that Schilder's knowledge of body image helped his colleague Brill understand the societal perceptions that discouraged women from smoking. Thus, it would have led to his "torches of freedom" imprint, which enticed women to view smoking both as a means of liberation from male oppression and a symbol of nonconformity. Furthermore, the 1929 passage of the 19th Amendment granting U.S. women voting rights ushered in another dimension of feminine freedom. It perversely made women's' smoking in public even more symbolic of their new role in society.

American Tobacco, fast off the mark, tapped into this spectacular new market with a new advertising campaign. Bernays' slogan was "Reach for a Lucky instead of a sweet," planting cigarette smoking as a slimming imprint to keep their waste line sleek (tobaccoexhibits.musc.edu). Within one year, the brand's cigarettes sales increased by more than 300%. The ads, "designed to prey on female insecurities about weight and diet," according to Stanford Research into the Impact of Tobacco Advertising. It helped usher in a wave of tobacco marketing targeted to women (truthinitiative.org). Many of these campaigns strived to entice women to smoke by using mainstream beauty and fashion standards to portray smoking as feminine.

Imprints, using imagery like the advertisement above, enticed women to perceive smoking positively. They saw it as a sign of individual liberty and freedom. They saw it as classy. They saw it as waste-line enhancing. They saw it as "being with it" for decades, and I was one of those seduced by its charms. All the while, it was just ruining our health and embalming us in tobacco stench. ('1929 Torches of Freedom'; Museum of Public Relations, 2014). That Bernays vigorously supported anti-smoking campaigns in his semi-retirement seems equally perverse.

Everything from cigarette smoking to leading us into wars has been imprinted into our brains. Buying refrigerators, loving Viagra, loathing whomever, the way we dress or style our hair, and what we love or hate to eat - Bernays et al. control it all without objections. The herd is clueless and seems content to remain so. They laughed uproariously at George Carlin's skits, as current now as when he departed the earth in 2008. Bernays convinced the American public that water fluoridation is actually beneficial to human health, when it in fact dulls the mind. He convinced us that bacon and eggs is the true all-American breakfast. He convinced us that instant cake mixes were just as good as those made from scratch by adding a symbolic egg to the packaging. He convinced us that rat poison Aspartame is wholesome, even as it fries the brain.

The same system rules, as it has done throughout the past 100 years, and "nobody seems to notice, nobody seems to care," to use truther George Carlin's expression. Our opinions on anything and everything we can dream up are imprinted and regulated by the mental health profession. They are purposefully planted into our minds to direct our thinking and generate our opinions. This is made possible mainly because of television, making watchers as malleable as dough in a play-pen. TV destroys all sense of logic and reason, leading to complete ignorance, while viewers think their Self-image is brighter than the morning star. Morning Star all right! As a matter of fact, it is said that most people walk through life without having one single independent idea or thought of their own, but are lead like bulls with rings through their noses. And it's all thanks to making the American, nay, the world's mind as I've described, with children being targeted by the same techniques. Think Millennial, and we have the aspired to end result.

Let us for the moment return to that body image our rulers so gladly and successfully use to rattle us persistently without our knowledge. Throughout its history, human society has placed great value on beauty of the human body. But a person's perception of one's own body does not always match society's standards. A 2007 report by the American Psychological Association found that a culture-wide sexualization of girls and women was contributing to increased female anxiety associated with body image. An Australian government Senate Standing Committee Report on the sexualization of children in the media reported similar findings. Needless to say, other scholars claim that these finding lack solid data. Regardless, the imprints have been planted into humanity without its knowledge. This perpetuates what throughout history has been extremely difficult for people to live up to, namely society's standard of the ideal physical body.

Granted, Freud, Bernays et al were brilliant. So are those working in today's billion-dollar advertising business, carrying forth their inheritance of imprinting the herd worldwide. Nowadays, an advertising company can be defined as a company that creates, manages and plans all aspects of a client's advertising. It might specialize in a specific area, or it might be a full-service company that also offers public relation services. To give you an idea of how much money is spent on your brain-imprinting and -washing, here are the revenues of the world's five largest advertising companies (https://worldatlas.com):

- WPP is the largest marketing and advertising company on earth, with revenue of approximately US$19 billion and a record 205,000 employees in 2016.
- Omnicom Group, based in New York City, employs over 75,000 people and generated US$15 billion in 2016.
- Publicis Group, based in Paris and founded in 1926, recorded revenue of US$9.6 billion in 2016.
- Interpublic Group of New York City employs about 50,000 people, generating about US$7.6 billion in revenue in 2015.
- Dentsu of Japan employs approximately 45,000 employees. Having formed a partnership with Facebook in 2011 to help develop Facebook pages and ads, Facebook provides Dentsu with premium advertising space

In their modus operandi, little if anything has changed since Bernays' days, other than the magnitude with which it is done. Bernays knew that people habitually tailor their opinion in accordance with the judgment of apparently disinterested parties with so-called "expert" opinions. So, he used their testimonials to promote his clients' causes in the "A cigarette a day keeps the doctor away" style. He pulled the same trick on behalf of the bacon industry to tout hearty breakfasts, to heck with rising cholesterol levels. To promote Dixie cups, Bernays launched a campaign to scare people into thinking that only disposable cups were sanitary. As part of this campaign, he founded the Committee for the Study and Promotion of the Sanitary Dispensing of Food and Drink. He called for the use of Dixie cups for sanitary reasons. And he cleverly targeted his marketing. He targeted people wanting to improve their lives. But mostly, he targeted people afraid of being viewed as backwards or of being left behind if they did not follow the Dixie cup trend of the day for sanitary reasons. The slogan "This is the sanitary age – the age of Dixie cups," was used successfully for several years.

Bernays, in his indefatigable quest to promote his clients, also wrote prolifically. He is said to have done so partly to dispel and disguise fears of PR's malignancy, and partly to minimize its power. To achieve his goal, he suggests that the PR man neither imposes ideas on the public, nor simply discovers public opinion. Rather, he finds existing points of alignment between his clients and the target audience, then uses them to satisfy both. This is done by and large without involving the herd, other than in a few opinion polls to test the waters and then tailor advertising campaigns around them. In all sincerity, Bernays proclaimed, successful public relations depended on policies and practices that gave people what they wanted without requiring distortion or deception. However, in his 1928 book Propaganda, he did concede that in a modern democracy, manipulation is power:

> "Power resides with the relative small number of persons who...understand the mental processes and social patters of the masses... and who pull the wires which control the public mind...The conscious and intelligent manipulation of the organized habits and opinions of the masses is an important element in democratic society... Those who manipulate this unseen mechanism of society constitute an invisible government, which is the true ruling power of our country [the U.S.]."

In his 1923 book *Crystallizing Public Opinion*, he already reveals indirectly who crystallizes what opinion in whom by planting appropriate imprints into the human minds. But did anyone listen? Did anyone care? That this invisible power enfolds us into our voluntary adaptation of their dictatorial ideology through its imprints is nowhere mentioned. That it could lead to humanity's extinction, just as systematically and automatically as being led into suicidal ideation by the Standard of PTSD Care "professional" PTSD treatment, is also nowhere mentioned. David Greenberg in his 2017 book *Republic of Spin: An Inside History of the American Presidency* does shed some light on the risk. He makes abundantly clear how implanting is done with revitalized Machiavellian expertise. "Machiavellian" is a term for a political philosophy often depicted as godless, scheming and self-interested, combined with an unprincipled lust for power achieved "through subtle policie, cunning roguerie." The earliest dictionary definition in English for "Machiavel" is in 1611. It describes an adherent of these principles documented by the Italian Renaissance diplomat, philosopher and writer Niccolò di Bernardo dei Machiavelli (1469 –1527). He is often called the father of modern political philosophy and political science. His 1513 book *The Prince (Il Principe)* is a political treatise encouraging "the end justifies the means" behaviour, especially among rulers and politicians.

But Bernays' writings were not merely principles or traditions by which to evaluate the appropriateness of propaganda. They were simply a means for shaping public opinion for any purpose whatsoever, whether beneficial to humanity or not. This raised alarm bells with Austrian-American lawyer, professor and jurist Felix Frankfurter. He was serving as an Associate Justice of the Supreme Court of the United States from 1939 to 1962, and was a noted advocate of judicial restraint in the judgments of the Court. He warned President Franklin Delano Roosevelt (1882 –1945), against allowing Bernays to play a leadership role in World War II. His described Bernays and his colleagues as "professional poisoners of the public mind, exploiters of foolishness, fanaticism, and self-interest." Did he know about the Viennese scheme of *Making the American Mind*?

Regardless, others, too, might have viewed Bernays' pioneering advertising style as a form of branding. Or they might have viewed it as nothing more than a particularly brazen set of techniques to manipulate people into doing his bidding. They might have seen its underlying purpose to make money by imprinting people with the idea of wanting something they don't need by turning them into consumers. They might have seen the brainwashing, sucking people to the delusion that their purchasing power will give them happiness. Some, however, might, just might, have noticed that such transformation without an inherent moral compass promotes nothing other than a patronizing and ultimately cynical view of human nature and human possibilities. Such a cynical view would as likely destroy human lives as build them up, created with the sole aim to destroy human individuality.

As Jon Rappoport explains, those who run society are engaged in bringing systems and structures into interlocking alignments in order to create larger and larger machines of control. The entire thrust of modern civilization is to make individuals extinct. Too many people are badly educated, mostly by their own volition. Too many of them are adrift in technology, used mainly for gibberish on Facebook and the like. All are as a unit tied to a massive collective, completely without power and without knowing it, which is just what the State wants. It has no use for individuals aspiring to freedom, liberty, the pursuit of happiness or decision-making power over their own lives and everything in it. The State's advantage is that most herd members have no inkling of either their own enslavement or their own power. Their imprints and indoctrination by the educational system and by equally ignorant parents of the same system from the cradle to the grave, have been done so perfectly, it's breathtaking.

How well has the State's basic educational makeup has been promoted at least since the early 1990s? I observed firsthand the No Child Left Behind scam when taking upper level classes in my university's education department. Nobody to be left behind; nobody to get ahead, either. It's ubiquitous and almost overpowering presence eradicates all freewheeling, independent minded, able-to-think-for- themselves students. Group think only, if you please, the professor of aspiring teachers emphasised. When I lifted my little hand and inquired if children under this system were supposed to learn writing, reading and arithmetic by osmosis, the prof went apoplectic. *We, the herd*, is meant to rule in accordance with imprints purposely created and expertly tailored to create our division. Accept, obey, don't question; that is the law.

American singer, songwriter, multi-instrumentalist, composer, bandleader, film and music video director and album cover designer characterized by nonconformity, free-form improviser, sound experimenter, musical virtuoso and satirist of American culture Frank Vincent Zappa (1940 -1993) hit the nail on the head when stating:

> "The illusion of freedom will continue as long as it's profitable to continue the illusion. At the point where the illusion becomes too expensive to maintain, they will just take down the scenery, they will pull back the curtains, they will move the tables and chairs out of the way and you will see the brick wall at the back of the theater."

In other words, the State, our rulers, is concocting humanity's troubles, not solving them. And it will keep doing so as long as it suits it and in accordance with Hegelian dialectic implemented with assistance of the mental health and advertising industries, experts in human psychology mind manipulation in all aspects of the definition (*Fallacy 1*). And it is here that, in Rappoport's opinion, where all the trouble starts. A text taken from John D. Rockefeller's masonic creed reflecting what is being done to us may clarify our situation:

> "We will keep their lives short and their minds weak while pretending to do the opposite. We will use our knowledge of science and technology in subtle ways so that they never see what is happening. We will use soft metals, aging accelerators and sedatives in food and water as well as in the air. They will be covered in poisons wherever they turn.

The soft metals will make them lose their minds. We will promise to find a cure from our many funds, and yet we will give them more poison. Chemical poisons will be absorbed through the skin of idiots who believe that certain hygiene and beauty products presented by great actors and musicians, will bring eternal youth to their faces and bodies, and through their thirsty and hungry mouths, we will destroy their minds and systems of internal organs reproduction. However, their children will be born as disabled and deformed and we will hide this information.

The poisons will be hidden in everything around them, in what they drink, eat, breathe and wear. We have to be ingenious in distributing the poisons because they can see far. We'll teach them that poisons are good - with funny pictures and musical tones on TV. Those who are looking for them will be helpful. We'll enroll them to push our poisons.

They will see that our products are used in film, and they will get used to them and will never know their true effect. When they give birth, we will inject poisons into the blood of their children and convince them that we are helping them! We will start earlier, when their minds are young, we will target their children with what children love most, sweet things.

When their teeth decay, we will fill them with metals that will kill their minds and steal their future. When their ability to learn has been affected, we have created drugs that will make them sicker and cause them other illnesses, for which we will create even more drugs. We will make them docile and weak before us, by our power. They will grow depressed, slow and obese, and when they come to us for help, we will give them more poison.

We will focus our attention on money and material goods so that they never connect with their inner self. We will distract them with fornication, external pleasures and video games, so that they are never one with the unity of all. Their minds will belong to us, and they will do as we say. If they refuse, we will find ways to implement technology that alters the mind in their lives.

We will use fear as our weapon. We will establish their governments and we will establish opposition within them. We will own both sides. We will always hide our goal, but we will continue our plan. They will do the work for us, and we will prosper from their toil.

Our families will never mix with theirs. Our blood must be pure (because it is). We will make them kill each other when they oppose us.

We will keep them separate from unity through dogma and religion. We will control all aspects of their lives and tell them what to think and how. We will guide them kindly and let them believe that they are guiding themselves.

We will instigate animosity among them through our factions. When a light shines among them, we will extinguish it by mockery or death, which suits us best. We will make them tear their hearts apart and kill their own children. We

> will accomplish this using hatred as our ally, anger as our friend. Hatred will completely blind them and they will never see that in their conflicts we will be their leaders.
>
> They will be busy killing each other. They will bathe in their own blood and kill their neighbors, as long as we see that they are against us.
>
> We will benefit greatly from this, for they will not see us, for they cannot see us. We will continue to prosper from their wars and their deaths. We will repeat this until our ultimate goal is achieved. We will continue to make them live in fear and anger; we will give them images and sounds. We will use all the tools we have to achieve this. The tools will be provided by their work. We will make them hate themselves and their neighbors.
>
> We will always hide the divine truth from them, that we are all one. That he must never know! They must never know that color is an illusion; they must always believe that they are not equal. Drop by drop, drop by drop we will advance our goal. We will take over their lands, resources and wealth to exercise control over them. We will trick them into accepting laws that will steal the little freedom they have. We will set up a money system that will shut them down forever, keeping them and their children in debt.
>
> When we ban them together, we will accuse them of murder and present a different story to the world because we will own all the media. We will use the media to control the flow of information and their feelings in our favor. When they rise up against us, we will crush them like insects, because they are less than that. They will be helpless to do anything about it."

And all of it, ongoing since Cain and Abel, now worldwide and engineered through imprints brought to perfection by Freud et al. and first marketed by Bernays. They are now coming to fruition one by one, while most humans graze with beer and extra spicy corn chips from fancy-designed bags in front of their TVs, too blind to see and too dumb to hear - believing they are "with it" and bright, to boot. What, evil perpetrated against me? You must be nuts! It is this tragic waste of life that genuine PTSD experiencers have the power to escape. But they must free themselves from the illusion and delusion of mental health industry professionals, other than the few Dr. Breggins and Prof. Petersons of the world. The rest "assist" in their recovery, but really aspire to assist themselves instead. But, to repeat, you can do that only when free of mind-altering pharmaceutical and natural opioid drugs. Drink beer instead or, better yet, learn to make your own booze with the help of turbo yeast - simple, cheap and effective. Otherwise, this evil will continue to hide itself, as it defies humans' innate psychological make-up, allowing heart- and soul emotions to reign and classified as non-existent in the science of psychology. This is confirmed, if by nothing else, by ranking us on equal footing with rattus, simian, mus, cani, lepus and the like regardless of Genesis 1:26, King James Version:

> "And God said, Let us make man in our image, after our likeness: and let them have dominion over the fish of the sea, and over the fowl of the air, and over

> the cattle, and over all the earth, and over every creeping thing that creepeth upon the earth."

But then, as Manley P. Hall says:

> "God continues to love and guide the destinies of His creation, The path still winds upwards to accomplishment. The soul of mean has not been deprived of its wings; they are merely folded under its garment of flesh. Philosophy is ever that magic power which, sundering the vessel of clay, releases the soul from its bondage to habit and perversion. Still as of old, the soul released can spread its wings and soar to the very source of itself. (Manley P. Hall: The Secret Teachings Of All Ages, p. 205)."

Genuine PTSD journeyers are individuals by nature. Once released from the mental bondage imposed on them through imprints by those pretending to help, they know how to free themselves. They know what they want. And they are powerful enough to go looking for it. That is the answer to PTSD healing. Knowledge is easily available all over the place these days, accept from mass media and television, so there is no excuse to linger in limbo. Once on such journey of discovery to help the Self, it becomes blatantly obvious that most people around you are encased in a prison of their own making, regardless of their academic education. They are so deeply embedded in hive identity and mentality, and so unable to see outside of the box, that it becomes laughable to even think they could help you with your genuine PTSD recovery. But then, their aim is fame and fortune, not your wellbeing.

This attitude and belief seem to permeate all large organizations, as I tasted in *Broken Wings*. So kick yourself to overwhelm this overwhelming PTSD-induced feeling of futility of it all by the sheer power of your will. Use your PTSD as the wake-up call it is meant to be by taking your own future into your own hands. Otherwise you are done for, skid row, garbage heap or suicide, pure unadulterated misery awaiting. Such deserving fate for the human debris that you are considered to be while you begrudge your fate. Indeed, you would be allowing yourself the victim ideation instead of taking serious the age old maxim:

> "God helps those who help themselves,"

This motto emphasizes the importance of self-initiative and agency. The expression, famous around the globe to inspire people for self-help, originated in ancient Greece as "the Gods help those who help themselves. " The sentiment appears in several ancient Greek tragedies.

Sophocles, in his *Philoctetes* (c. 409 BC), wrote, "No good e'er comes of leisure purposeless; And heaven ne'er helps the men who will not act."

Euripides in the *Hippolytus* (428 BC), mentions that "Try first thyself, and after call in God; For to the worker God himself lends aid."

In his *Iphigeneia in Tauris*, Orestes says, "I think that Fortune watcheth o'er our lives, surer than we. But well said: he who strives will find his gods strive for him equally."

A similar version of this saying "God himself helps those who dare" better translated as "divinity helps those who dare" comes from Ovid, *Metamorphoses*.

Never heard of any of it? Better start cracking. It is your duty. Your PTSD recovery is at stake, and miracles are awaiting you if you do. Remember, Dharma extinguishes Karma! Teach yourself to plant your own imprints, unless, of course, you prefer to die a slow and gruesome death, a result of all pharmaceutical, mind-altering drugs. It's in your hands.

As Rappoport expresses, the way free individuals imagine their futures and invent them through their own imprints is very much a spiritual exploration. Why? Because, despite wild protests of those working in the science of psychology, individual human beings are not bio-machines. In his collection *Exit from the Matrix*, Rappoport includes dozens of imagination exercises and techniques he developed based on a study of ancient Tibet and his work with hypnotherapist Jack True. The whole purpose of those exercises is for the individual to skip the WE illusion and return to himself and his power, to the I, the *sui generis*, the regaining of freedom through one's own creative power. You have nothing to lose and everything to gain by it, as otherwise you will undoubtedly turn yourself into a vegetable.

It is not your fault, however. What is regularly done to genuine PTSD journeyers since it was labeled a mental illness by the mental health industry roughly 30 years ago, with the associated stigma it signifies, ought to be an indictable criminal offence. That Bernays stipulated in some of his books that successful public relations depended on policies and practices that would give people what they wanted without requiring distortion or deception is another outright lie. He confirmed 100 years ago in Propaganda that power in a modern democracy resided with:

> "...the relative small number of persons who...understand the mental processes and social patters of the masses...[and] who pull the wires, which control the public mind...The conscious and intelligent manipulation of the organized habits and opinions of the masses is an important element in democratic society... Those who manipulate this unseen mechanism of society constitute and invisible government which is the true ruling power of our country."

It is this invisible power and ruling mechanism that now enfolds you, the genuine PTSD experiencer, into the voluntary adaptation of suicidal ideation. It creates so may jobs for those purportedly wanting to aid in your recovery without having a clue about addressing the root of your problem. You doubt it? Read David Greenberg's *Republic of Spin: An Inside History of the American Presidency* to understand how both the We and the I are, with Machiavellian expertise, led into our own destruction unless we awaken.

Bernays' writings do not furnish principles or traditions by which to evaluate the appropriateness of propaganda, either. Rather, it is portrayed as a means for shaping public opinion for any purpose whatsoever, whether beneficial to human beings or not. This observation alone led the esteemed U.S. Supreme Court Justice Felix Frankfurter to warn President Franklin Roosevelt against allowing Bernays to play a leadership role in World War II. Frankfurter described Bernays and his colleagues as "professional poisoners of the public mind, exploiters of foolishness, fanaticism, and self-interest."

Today, we might call what Bernays pioneered a form of branding. But at its core, it is little more than brazen tricks to manipulate people into doing the rulers' bidding. Its purpose is far beyond making money and turning citizens into consumers. It is to gain complete control over our minds. Heck, through imprint generating, they even brainwash us into believing that everything truly revolves around the We, the mob rule, the demon-crazy, the socialist communist group think. All this to deprive us of our individuality, where our own power lies. As Rappoport explains in his article "Free Individuality vs Deep State".

The systems and structures to create larger and larger machines of control to make the individual, the *sui generis*, extinct are in place. Powerless, badly educated, adrift in technology, viewed as a unit tied to a massive collective is what the imprints of the We over decades have led to. It is also what finds you in your struggle of PTSD recuperation. By their propaganda, you are vilified as mentally ill, when there is not and never was anything "mental" about you, other than you are and always were an individual, the exception in the herd. But the imprint of your own inadequacy has been lodged within you by them, rendering you unbalanced in all ways possible, and "Unbalanced forces perish in the void," according to a prophet of old (M.P. Hall: *The Secret Destiny of America*, p. 139).

You can change it, though. You can conquer yourself by finding your *Why* and going for it, as the *How* will present itself with it once you start looking. That is what genuine PTSD has bestowed. The way out of this trauma is by way of exploring our spiritual, mental and physical nature through philosophy, religion and science. Through learning we regain our self-governance and joy in life. Or we can leave it, preferring to graze with the media, television and pharmaceutical mind-altering drugged herd, and a tedious life until death awaits. It is that simple.

14

THE SUICIDE NON-EPIDEMIC

Certain people seem to be specially groomed with expertise to lead humanity into the illusion of an existing worldwide suicide epidemic. One of them appears to be David W. Covington, who calls himself a health innovator, entrepreneur and storyteller. He also is the president and CEO of Recovery Innovations International, Inc., founder of ls, Crisis Now and Hope Inc. and owner of Behavioral Health Link (BHL) (https://riinternational.com). These are all non-profit (i.e. tax-free) corporations cruising along on government handouts while generously enriching themselves and others under the guise of assisting the downtrodden and needy.

We are not told what stories Covington is telling, but perhaps fables about the need of suicide prevention may be among them. As Szasz points out, there are no frauds and there can be no frauds in the mental health profession. All stories they tell are true, because the frauds are not imposters, but mentally ill mental health experts who temporarily lack insight into their own illness (Lies, p. 109). After all, being an expert about mental illnesses is like being an expert about ghosts or unicorns.

Covington's family and cultural background, so important to mental health experts in diagnosing their patients, is hard to find. It seems he is a man in his mid-fifties who enjoys paragliding. Holding a master's in business administration (MBA) from Kennesaw State

University in Georgia, a Master of Science (MS) degree from the University of Memphis in Tennessee. Covington graduated with a community agency counseling degree in 1995. After taking a 60-hour Council for Accreditation of Counseling & Related Educational Programs (CACREP) approved degree at the University of Memphis (bestcounselingdegrees.net), he was free to counsel others.

Mr. Covington fits admiringly well within the mental health learned society, as his website announces his goal: "Innovating Beyond Behavioral Health" (davidwcovington.com). What precisely he wants to innovate is unannounced. That seems to matter little. According to Szasz, psychiatrists, and by extension others in the field, lie with the vocabulary of psychiatric diagnoses, prognoses and treatments. They believe their lies to be truth, thus their phenomenal storytelling ability. His CACREP training was established in 1981 and dedicated to promote advancement in the field of counseling by overseeing and granting accreditation to individual programs around the United States. It enables graduates to streamline their individual innovations beyond general behavioral health to achieve uniformity of accreditation and stomp out even sniffs of individualism. Its Statement of Core Values as conceived by its 2002 Board of Directors states:

> Ensuring a fair, consistent, and ethical decision-making process
>
> Serving as a responsible leader in protecting the public
>
> Promoting practices that reflect openness to growth, change and collaboration
>
> Creating and strengthening standards that reflect the needs of society, respect the diversity of instructional approaches and strategies, and encourage program improvement and best practices (cacrep.org)

It is recognized by the American Counseling (sic) Association, whose mission is to enhance the quality of life in society by promoting the development of professional counsellors, advancing the counselling profession and using the profession and practice of counselling to promote respect for human dignity and diversity. It is also recognized by the U.S. Department of Education. CACRAP reviews and evaluates educational programs in counselling to see if they meet national standards (counselling.org). These standards include the following eight core areas:

- Human growth
- Group counseling
- Professional issues
- Social foundations
- Career development
- Helping relationships
- Research and appraisal

In addition, CACREP reviews clinical standards to ensure supervised clinical training offers specialty-training students what they need.

All states in the U.S. require a specific set of coursework and a specified number of hours to sit for a licensure exam. CACREP standards meet those requirements, so that all graduates qualify to take the 200-question National Certified Counselor (sic) examen. Translation: USSR-style streamlining in favor of communist/socialist uniformity throughout counselling programs nationwide, to ensure that aspiring counsellors' minds are programmed in accordance with the Deep State's ideology. The goal: their future victims will indeed believe they are mentally disordered, retarded and/or deranged and therefore in desperate need of pharmacotherapy. This is how it is done; this is how the system, the mass sewer culture, sprouts, blossoms and bears fruit without the herd or these students having a clue.

The sinister beauty of Edward Bernays' advertising talent – and he still advised clients in his 101st year of life – is magnificent in itself. Thanks to him, the demand for counselling professionals will have grown by 29% by the year 2022, says CACREP. In a way, that is not at all surprising. With the *DSM-5* 2013 inauguration, there now are 297 mental illness diagnoses to choose from. This easily identifies one in four Americans to suffer from a diagnosable mental disorder in any given year. One in five are said to experience a "mood disorder," depression and the like, at some point or another during their life. (counseling.org) This is easy to create as diagnostic, as the American Psychiatric Association as good as labels all emotional events relating to human life and living as a mental disorder or illness. Consequently, the human populations' brainwashing with artificially-enhanced, mentally disordered ill and retarded state of mind is well on track, with the state's seeming aspiration to persuade humanity to believe its insanity worldwide.

Covington is one of CACREP's accredited licensed professional counsellors, in some states called "licensed clinical professional counsellors" or "licensed mental health counsellors." Indeed, he is one of more than 120,000 professional counsellors providing mental health and substance abuse counselling to millions of Americans under the U.S. licensure laws enacted in all 50 states, the District of Columbia and Puerto Rico. This includes clinical social workers, marriage and family therapists, and psychiatric nurses, which provide the vast majority of mental health services in the US. Covington seems to have chosen suicide prevention as his counselling expertise. 800,000 folks officially choose to kill themselves annually worldwide, according to the World Health Organization's (WHO) 2018 figures. However, for undisclosed reasons, the WHO suspects many more people attempt to kill themselves (https://www.who.int).

Those working in the suicide prevention field, namely physicians, are the most prolific victims, stated APA members at their 2018 annual convention. With one suicide daily in the U.S., they have the highest suicide rate of any profession. It hovers around 40 per 100,000 population. The rate in the general population is 12.3 per 100,000 (webmd.com). Why the discrepancy? Physicians often kill themselves, we are told, because they suffer from untreated or undertreated depression or other mental illnesses. This underscores the need for early intervention studies, suicide investigator Deepika Tanwar, M.D., Psychiatric Program, Harlem Hospital Center, New York City, told the Medscape Medical News. But physicians with depressive symptoms are 95% more likely to report perceived medical errors. And they are 67% more likely to report subsequent depressive symptoms. All of this can by extension lead to enhanced suicide numbers for both doctors and their patients (Pauline Anderson: "Depression in Docs Leads to Medical Errors and Vice Versa"; Medscape.com). So can being hamstrung by state-imposed "Standard of Care" medical care, one might surmise.

Covington is a lowly CACREP-accredited counsellor. He has no ranking in the mental health profession. So, why does he believe he can save any of those GPs, never mind the rest of suicidal humanity? It's just as puzzling and unknown as why Bill Gates perceives himself to be mankind's savior through his not-for--profit foundation and its vaccine program. What we do know, however, is that Covington is well connected to the powers that be. That is demonstrated by his twice winning the Council of State Governments (CSG) Innovations Award. GSG is a nonpartisan, non-profit organization founded in 1933 by Colorado State Senator Henry W. Toll (1887–1975). Toll was a Harvard-educated lawyer and World War I veteran. He recognized the national need for cooperation among the states regarding conflicting laws and taxation, among other issues, in the 1920s. So, he founded the American Legislators' Association, CSG's forerunner (https://csg.org).

Nowadays, the CSG is the premier organization forecasting policy trends for state leaders in all three branches of government (uknowledge.uky.edu/). Central to its mission is the development of leadership training for improved decision-making of state elected and appointed officials, so clearly visible at present, eh? It is the nation's only organization to serve those three branches in unison, and it is said to do so by fostering the sharing of ideas to help state officials shape public policy, develop leaders, and collaborate and create problem-solving partnerships (dot.ny.gov). Its membership includes 56 U.S. states and territories, as well as six Canadian provinces. Each pays annual dues to support the council's operations. In addition, revenue is derived from publication sales, registration fees, corporate grants and contributions, as well as investment income.

In 2008, Covington received the award, this first time for the Georgia Crisis & Access Line, which began as Behavioral Health Link in 2006. And who are they?

"Since 2001, Behavioral Health Link has worked to develop proprietary software designed to assist our call takers in managing the complexity of crisis calls while capturing vital information necessary to ensure we link individuals to the most appropriate care available. Over the years and in partnership with our stakeholders [who they are is unknown], we have developed a suite of software designed to capture crisis call center generated clinical information, quality management documentation, mobile crisis assessment data and to manage bidirectional, electronic referrals to outpatient services, mobile crisis teams, crisis stabilization units, and inpatient facilities, track the progress of referrals and availability of resources in real time, and provide interactive dashboards and complex reporting solutions designed to measure the efficiency and the effectiveness of the process. We call this suite of software BHL Care Traffic Control (BHLCTC).

> "BHLCTC's suite of products is web/mobile-enabled and fully customizable for real-time views of BH/IDD crisis program activity 24/7/365. Whether tracking facility referral and utilization or mobile crisis response services, BHLCTC has a solution for you. Our software is fully customizable. Please contact us if you would like a demonstration." (https://bhltest.com)

This means that whoever contacts BHL will get tracked 24/7 throughout the state, if not the world, for the rest of their natural life. Staff are experienced operators of state-wide crisis and access lines, providers of mobile crisis services in both rural and urban areas, and developers of customizable software services. They are prepared to help state agencies and other - unadvertised - stakeholders develop, implement and operate complex crisis programs. All a state needs to do is contact them and voila, you will be assisted with your perceived or imposed crisis services needs.

So, the state of Georgia's Department of Behavioral Health and Developmental Disabilities began a prosperous collaboration with BHL. Shortly thereafter, with Covington's help, the Georgia Crisis & Access Line was born. For the first time ever, Georgians could call one toll-free number (GCAL) from anywhere in their state for access to care in a mental crisis. They would be connected to trained professionals purportedly, providing the most appropriate linkage to care for mental health crises, developmental disabilities and substance abuse crises. They would get a 24/7 hotline for people with mental illnesses, addictive diseases, mental retardation and other related developmental disabilities (namiga.org). The call center also has the capacity to screen and assess callers for the intensity of service response. Its marvels furthermore include:

> Language assistance: Telephone interpreting services are provided to callers with limited English proficiency.
>
> Emergencies: People deemed to be in immediate danger are "warm transferred" to the local 911 services in their area. Call center staff stay with the caller until the 911 responders are on site with the caller.
>
> Crisis assistance: People who need crisis management receive 24/7 mobile responses to assess their situation, de-escalate the crisis, consult and refer with post crisis, and follow-up to assure linkage with recommended services.
>
> Routine service access: For consumers with less intense needs, call center staff are able to offer choice of providers and to schedule appointments for services. Consumers can specify the distance they are willing to travel, and call center employees identify service providers within proximity to the their zip code.

Covington took much credit for it all. In 2012, he repeated as winner for the same award. This time, it was for the executive and clinical operations of Megallan Health Inc. during its annual $750 million contract with the state of Arizona, Medicaid, and the Department of Health. He was responsible for some 100,000 people receiving active services with a network of 7,000 to 10,000 clinicians, social workers, counsellors, physicians and so on and so forth providing those services (https://socialworkpodcast.blogspot.com).

Magellan Health Inc., formerly known as Magellan Health Services Inc., was another American for-profit healthcare company. It focused on special populations, complete pharmacy benefits and other specialty areas of healthcare. The company was founded in 1969 by William A. Fickling Jr. It began as the psychiatric hospital chain Charter Medical, the nation's largest psychiatric hospital chain, with 102 hospitals in 16 states. Based in Macon, Georgia, the company filed for Chapter 11 bankruptcy in 1992 due to debt incurred during a 1988 management-led takeover. In 1994, after the company reorganized under federal bankruptcy laws, it moved its corporate headquarters to Atlanta. It acquired a major stake in Green Spring Health Services Inc., a managed care company based in Columbia, Maryland, and re-structured itself into a new holding company. That's when it changed its name to Magellan Health Services. (Sandy Lutz: "Charter's Headquarters Will Move To Atlanta" Aug. 1994; https://modernhealthcare.com)

In 1999, Magellan moved to Green Spring's old headquarters in Columbia, Maryland, but it relocated to Connecticut in 2004 and then to Scottsdale, Arizona, in 2014. Magellan purports to support innovative ways of accessing better health through technology, while remaining focused on the critical personal relationships that are necessary to achieve a healthy, vibrant life. Its customers include health plans and other managed care organizations, employers, labor unions, various military and governmental agencies and third-party administrators (https://Magellanhealth.com). It delivers behavioral health and employee assistance programs. It also delivers specialty health services, including musculoskeletal, cardiac, advanced imaging management and physical medicine, as well as integrated care management, to health plans, employers, Medicaid, Medicare and the U.S. federal government. Magellan ranks 475 in Fortune 500 magazine, which annually publishes a list of the 500 largest U.S. companies ranked by total revenues for their respective fiscal years. It prides itself in providing useful tools and resources to help consumers make the most out of their day or to guide them through a difficult time, and all of it in a confidential and secure environment (https://magellanassist.com).

Covington is also a member of the United States Department of Health & Human Services (DHHS).

Interdepartmental Serious Mental Illness Coordinating Committee (ISMICC), established in 2017 in accordance with the *21st Century Cures Act* to report to Congress on advances in behavioral health. Signed into effect by President Barrack Obama in December 2016, it authorized US$6.3 billion in funding, mostly allocated for the National Institutes of Health. Especially supported by large pharmaceutical manufacturers, the act was vehemently opposed by consumer organizations. They said it would allow drugs and devices to be approved on weaker scientific evidence testing by bypassing randomized controlled trials, thus bringing more dangerous or ineffective treatments to market, wit the COVID vaccine. Proponents maintained it would streamline drug- and device-approval processes. This, in turn, would speed up treatments and profits.

The Public Broadcasting Service (PBS) is an American non-profit public broadcaster and television program distributor and provider of educational television programming to public television stations in the United States. In its PBS News show Who wins and loses with the *21st Century Cures Act*?, it gives splendid insight on the Act. Greatest winner of them all? For Representative Fred Upton (R-MI), until January 2017 chairman of the House Energy and Commerce Committee, passage of the Cures Act had apparently been a near obsession. The payoff? A 392-to-26 vote and a bonus of more than $1.3 million in donations from the land's healthcare political action committees during the time Upton was crafting the bill, a splendid example of what determination, persistency, willpower and discipline can accomplish. In October, Upton received the Friend of Farm Bureau award from the American Farm Bureau for support of southwest Michigan's agriculture community during the 116th Congress (upton.house.gov.news).

Another one proven victorious was the Cures Act bill's main author, Representative Tim Murphy (R-PA). A clinical psychologist, he had been blunt in his assessment of mental healthcare in the U.S. in previous years, painting a picture of federal incompetence that diverted money to frivolous and unproven programs for general mental health. But merely days before the vote, the House leadership attached his mental health legislation to the Cures package. He maintained that current practices impeded treatment for serious mental illness due to patients' civil liberties ahead of their treatment (Louise Radnofsky: House Passes Mental Health Bill: Measure is first effort by lawmakers to specifically tackle federal policies on serious mental illness; wsj.com July 2016). Thus, he stipulated that the State should be permitted to treat humans deemed by him and his colleagues to be mentally deficient, regardless of their civil rights, if the State saw fit to do so, the Gulag Archipelago in action. "Hitherto," Murphy insisted in all sincerity, "The federal government refused to define or admit, that serious mental illness even existed. Federal policy has been a failure, an unmitigated disaster." And for genuine PTSD journeyers it certainly was and is, thanks to the NC for the enhancement of PTSD.

Maria A. Oquendo, M.D., PhD, was professor of psychiatry and vice chairman for education at Columbia University until 2016, and research psychiatrist at the New York State Psychiatric Institute. In 2017, she was elected to the National Academy of Medicine, one of the highest honors in medicine. She is also past president of the American Psychiatric Association (APA) (2017-2020), and now professor and chairman of psychiatry at the Perelman School of Medicine at the University of Pennsylvania. A powerhouse in her chosen profession, she praised the Cures Act mental health provisions. She says it would greatly benefit patients, as the legislation included money both to create suicide-prevention programs and to improve mental health services for children. Brilliant. Get them to believe they are mentally warped, and you have them doubting their sanity for life. Is there a better way to guarantee mental health industry practitioners a lucrative living for life?

The Act also granted $1 billion in State grants for the pharmaceutical manufacturers- and government-sponsored opioid epidemic. That in itself is so beneficial to the mental health cabal, as it is caused by their own prescription - a triple whammy, so to speak. First, Big Pharma pays bonuses for the amount of prescriptions physicians of all stripes and colors render. Then, the State pays them to get patients off the drugs they prescribed. Finally, patients pay insurers through their insurance plans for the cost incurred visiting mental health counsellors like Covington et al., who profit from their non-profit organizations. You get the drift of manure? And we, in our infinite innocence and ignorance and television-induced lethargy, allow it.

Furthermore, the Act also sought to strengthen laws that required the government and insurers to treat mental illness like all other diseases. Of course, it does, so it can manipulate patients' neuro-genetic brain functioning without impunity. And they can do so in the name of improving their mental health with Neumeisterian treatments, including the ancient electrical shock therapy. No wonder Oquendo is jubilant about it, and so, without a doubt, are her colleagues. Watch her May 2017 WebsEdgeHealth YouTube interview to see where this is heading, if humanity allows it.

Just as with Covington, nothing of Oquendo's family background or private life is published. From reading her resume, however, we know that she graduated summa cum laude and Phi Beta Kappa from Tufts University in 1980. We also read that she received her M.D. from the College of Physicians and Surgeons at Columbia University in 1984 (bbrfoundation.org). She completed her residency training at the Payne Whitney Clinic of New York Hospital Weil Cornell. This psychiatric research hospital was home to some of the country's most notable psychiatrists and patients, including Marilyn Monroe. It is also the source of much neuro-scientific research. In 2010, she received her PhD in psychiatry from the public Universidad Autónoma de Madrid (Spain) founded in 1968.

Since then, she has served as president of the International Academy of Suicide Research, as well as vice president of the American Foundation for Suicide Prevention. She also served on the National Institute of Mental Health's Advisory Council. She is a Fellow of the American College of Neuropsychopharmacology, the APA and the American College of Psychiatrists (ACP), a very busy individual indeed. She has received multiple awards in the US, Europe and South America. Most recently, she was honored with the Virginia Kneeland Award for Distinguished Women in Medicine (Columbia University 2016), the Award for Mood Disorders Research (ACP 2017), the Alexandra Symmonds Award (APA 2017) and the APA's Research Award (2018).

Oquendo's areas of professed expertise range from psychopharmacology to the diagnosis, pharmacologic treatment and neurobiology of bipolar disorder and major depression. Through all this, she keeps a special focus on suicidal behavior and global mental health. Indeed, she is internationally known for her neurobiological studies of suicidal behavior. She has used positron emission tomography (PET) and magnetic resonance 1maging (MRI) to map brain abnormalities in mood disorders and suicidal behavior. In 2003, issues arose about how pharmaceutical antidepressants might be a risk for inducing suicidal behavior. The U.S. Food and Drug Administration (FDA) commissioned Oquendo and others in her league to develop a classification data system able to examine suicide-related events. This system, also endorsed by the Centers for Disease Control and Prevention (CDC), is now used worldwide.

That the FDA should be involved in sponsoring mental health diagnoses should arouse suspicions. According to Daniel Haley's book *Politics In Healing: The suppression and manipulation of American Medicine* (p. 2), reactions to FDA-approved drugs are the fourth leading cause of death in the United States. In 1998, the Journal of the American Medical Association (JAMA) analyzed 39 studies conducted over 30 years. It documented that on average 106,000 people die annually in hospitals from drugs they approved. This excluded "misprescribed" pharmaceuticals.

When considering deaths from the same cause outside of hospitals (i.e., at home), the number rises to around 400,000 annually in the U.S., according to Centers for Disease Control statistics. Those 400,000 are not from illegal street drugs. They only cause a fraction of deaths in comparison to FDA-approved drugs, which killed three times the number of people automobile accidents do annually, never mind the at least 500,000 who die each year from cancer, which has been curable for decades. As a matter of fact, at the turn of the twentieth century, about 2,2 million Americans suffered such severe side effects from FDA-approved drugs as to be permanently disabled despite living in one of the most overregulated and bureaucratically controlled medical systems in the world, says Haley (*USA Today* April 24, 1998)

In 2014, the U.S. Senate and The New York Times investigated the failure of the nation's auto safety regulators to protect citizens from cars with occasionally dangerous faulty devices (Donald W. Light: Serious Risks And Few New Benefits From FDA-Approved Drugs, 2015; https://healthaffairs.org). But neither august institution paid attention to the FDA's failure to protect the 170 million Americans who take prescription drugs from adverse reactions that at that time killed more than 2,400 people every single week. Furthermore, prescription drugs were causing over 81 million adverse reactions, resulting in 2.7 million hospitalizations. This epidemic of harm makes prescription drugs the fourth leading cause of death in the United States. When hospitalizations and deaths from prescribing errors, overdosing and self-medication are included, FDA-approved drug death moves up to third place. And you, the genuine PTSD experiencer, the journeyer through the valley of death , still think your mental health practitioner's pharmacotherapy is beneficial for you?

Compare that with the enormous financial investment of taxpayer money to prevent an estimated 800,000 suicides annually world-wide with FDA assistance. Curiosity why this should be so is further heightened by the fourth leading cause of hospital admission after a failed suicide attempt. They are from reactions to drugs prescribed for perceived mental disorders to people who to begin with created the suicidal desire to kill the Self. But this sewer of a medical control system disallows manufacturers from producing effective non-toxic products or informing patients of their benefits. Doctors can practice only within the realms of Standard of Care, including to prescribe only FDA- or official medicine-approved drugs. You might not recognize the nation priding itself on its well-known phrase "Life, Liberty and the pursuit of Happiness." These three inalienable human rights are printed in the U.S. Declaration of Independence. Along with the first amendment to the Constitution, the right of free speech, it is joyously and thoroughly ignored by all and sundry living there, a system now ruling and regulating who is or is not mentally disordered and potentially suicidal. And you still believe in its benevolence?

Mind you, one of colonial America's most famous civic leaders foresaw the loss of U.S. citizens' Health freedom. Politician, physician, social reformer, humanitarian, educator and founder of Dickinson College Benjamin Rush (1746-1813) attended the Continental Congress and signed the Declarations of Independence. He wrote:

> "The Constitution of this Republic should make special provision for medical freedom as well as religious freedom. To restrict the art of healing to one class of men and deny equal privilege to others will constitute the Bastille of medical science. All such laws are un-American and despotic." (Haley p.7)

American politician, Georgist economist and Democratic Illinois Senator Paul Howard Douglas (1892 –1976) also saw the writing on the wall. In 1963, he declared on the Senate floor: "It's a terrible thing that we cannot really trust either the FDA or the NCI!" Georgism, also called geoism and single tax (archaic), by the way, developed from the writings of the economist and social reformer Henry George. It is an economic ideology holding that, while people should own the value they produce themselves, economic value derived from land, including natural resources and natural opportunities, should belong equally to all members of society. This could be done by seeking solutions to social and ecological problems based on principles of land rights and public finance, which attempt to integrate economic efficiency with social justice.

But here we are in the 2020s, wanting to stop 800,000 suicides worldwide. Official U.S. medicine cannot cure cancer, cardiovascular disease, AIDS, a large number of new cases of TB or a growing number of bacterial infections. Meanwhile, Americans' immune systems steadily decline and its FDA-generated medical system is stuck on toxic patented poison therapies for everything, including PTSD. And it flourishes under the control of a cartel, which keeps prices high and, most oftentimes successfully, kills off all competition. You still think the FDA protects you from physical and mental damage? Listen to American physician and the 10th Commissioner and head of the U.S. Food and Drug Administration (FDA) Herbert Leonard Ley Jr. (1923-2001). He served from 1968 to 1969, and said this once out of office:

> "The thing that bug's me the most is that people think the FDA is protecting them—it isn't. What the FDA is doing and what the public thinks it is doing are as different as day and night." (Haley p. 406)

But the U.S. Bastille Day seems to be drawing closer by the day. Fewer than 25% of practicing physicians belong to the American Medical Association (AMA) nowadays, down from 75% in the 1950s. Doctors graciously decline to be increasingly more handcuffed by AMA and FDA threats of interference and restrictions. It has also been noted that patients themselves are looking for alternative healing treatments, many only visiting allopathic or orthodox physicians because Insurers cover only conventional medical treatments.

Harvard University professor Dr. David M. Eisenberg, M.D, director of culinary nutrition and adjunct associate professor of nutrition at the Harvard T. H. Chan School of Public Health made a prescient prediction. Dr. Eisenberg served as the Bernard Osher Distinguished Associate Professor of Medicine at Harvard Medical School from 2000-2010. He was the founding director of the Osher Research Center and the founding chief of the Division for Research and Education in Complementary and Integrative Medical Therapies at Harvard Medical School. At the same time, he served as director of the Program in Integrative Medicine at the Brigham & Women's Hospital. His prediction in 1993 was that over 50% of Americans would use alternative means of healthcare by the end of the century (Haley p.412).

Dr. Eisenberg was spot on. In 2017, about half of Americans asked had tried alternative medicine such as herbal remedies, acupuncture, chiropractic treatment or energy therapies. One fifth had tried alternative medicine instead of conventional medicine. And roughly three in ten adults had tried alternative medicine in conjunction with conventional medical treatment. In addition, about one in twelve reported that they never use over-the-counter medications when they have cold or flu symptoms, while the remainder said they either took such medications right away or waited until their symptoms worsen (2. Americans' healthcare behaviors and use of conventional and alternative medicine; pewresearch.org, 2017) People who used alternative medicine instead of conventional medicine and those who never take over-the counter medications were less likely to have a primary care provider, have had a flu shot, and to have had a preventive care check-up in the past year.

The honorable Eisenberg knows that nutrition is the alpha and omega to humans physical and mental health. He is now director of culinary nutrition and adjunct associate professor of nutrition at the Harvard T. H. Chan School of Public Health. He is also a founding co-director of the Healthy Kitchens, Healthy Lives conference. And he is a founding co-director of the recently established CIA-Harvard Chan Teaching Kitchen Collaborative, a group of 32 organizations that use teaching kitchens to establish and evaluate best practices relating to nutrition, culinary and lifestyle education. But his knowledge is thoroughly ignored by everyone who is someone in the media. We are to be killed, not nurtured.

How many of us seek alternative ways to cure a medical debacle is unknown. The Complementary and Alternative Medicine Use Among Adults and Children: United States of 2007 report discussed at length in Fallacy 1 is the last one available (nccih.nih.gov). This absence of more recent statistics on the issue and the perpetual eagerness to hold our brains responsible for all our mental and physical abilities and disabilities and classifying as many of us as possible as mentally deranged, however, is not puzzling at all. Consider the U.S, Second Amendment, the right to bear arms. People classified as deranged by their friendly physician or mental health practitioner will lose that right.

What is puzzling, however, is this enormous, almost desperate and quasi degenerate, eagerness to promote suicidal tendencies in humans. This is done by getting them on mind-altering drugs for any reason. And by incessantly talking about suicide in the media. And by spending exorbitant amounts of money and manpower in the search of "finding a cure" for the 800,000 wanting to leave the world. All this while hundreds of thousands of Americans live destitute on city streets and die from government-imported opioids and government-approved pharmaceuticals, many a genuine PTSD journeyer among them. So, is there or is there not a suicide epidemic? Let's cut to the chase about this purported suicide epidemic, shall we?

15

WHO'S MOST AT-RISK FOR SUICIDE?

We don't know, as no research exists. We do know, however, World Health Organization (WHO) *estimates*. Jonathan of the September 2016 socialwork-podcast.blogspot.com interviewed aspiring suicide preventer Covington. He cited that the World Health Organization (WHO) estimates that more than 800,000 people die by suicide annually.

Befrienders Worldwide is another global, not for profit network. It has 349 emotional support centers in 32 countries spanning five continents staffed by more than 25,000 volunteers. It purportedly provides support to an estimated seven million e-users each year. It begs to differ with the WHO, however, maintaining that one million of Earth's population annually kill themselves.

Without presenting any substantiating evidence, WHO also assert that, in the last 45 years, suicide rates have increased by 60% worldwide. It says that suicide is among the three leading causes of death among humans aged 15-44. Unintentional injury and homicide were the other two leading causes of death among residents aged 15–24, accounting for 34.2% and 32.9% of deaths respectively (cchealth.org). These were followed by suicide (9.9%) and cancer (5.8%).

Suicide is a leading cause of death in the United States, according to the Centers for Disease Control and Prevention (CDC) *WISQARS Leading Causes of Death Reports*, in 2018 reporting the following:

- Suicide was the tenth leading cause of death in the United States, claiming the lives of over 48,000 people.
- Suicide was the second leading cause of death among people between the ages of 10 and 34, and the fourth leading cause of death among those between the ages of 35 and 54.
- There were more than two and a half times as many suicides (48,344) in the United States as there were homicides (18,830).

Multiple lines of evidence seem to indicate that the coronavirus COVID-19 dis-ease, previously known as the common flu, has had profound psychological and social effects and mental health consequences on humanity worldwide, including an increase in suicidal behavior (Leo Sher: "The impact of the COVID-19 pandemic on suicide rates", *QJM: An International Journal of Medicine*, Volume 113, Issue 10, October 2020, Pages 707–712). COVID-19 lockdown suicide statistics are presently unavailable.

Ann John is professor of public health and psychiatry at Wales' Swansea University Medical School. It is ranked as the third best medical school in the UK. She and her team wrote the article "Trends in suicide during the COVID-19 pandemic", call for caution, advising prevention must be prioritized while awaiting a clearer picture (*BMJ* 2020;371:m4352). Widely reported studies modelling the effect of COVID-19 on suicide rates predicted increases ranging from 1% to 145%, largely reflecting variation in underlying assumptions. However, John et al. state that supposition is no replacement for evidence. For some months, they tracked and reviewed relevant studies for a living systematic review and found no robust epidemiological studies with suicide as an outcome.

Most of the available publications were preprints, letters or commentaries using news reports of deaths by suicide as the data source. Thus, the available literature on the effect of COVID-19 on suicide should be interpreted with caution. Nevertheless, they state, a reasonably consistent picture was beginning to emerge from high income countries suggesting no rise in suicide rates (Massachusetts, U.S. 11; Victoria, Australia13; England14) or a fall (Japan,9 Norway15) in the early months of the pandemic in 2020 either. The picture is much less clear in low income countries, where the safety nets available in better resourced settings may be lacking. News reports of police data from Nepal suggest a rise in suicides, whereas an analysis of data from Peru suggests the opposite, according to John's and her team.

The sources above sources, mind readers as they seem to be and grasping their knowledge out of mid-air, also assert that there are 20 times more suicide attempts than completed suicides. Whichever way it may be, they also *hypothesize* that:

- Suicide rates in 2020 are highest in teens, young adults and the elderly.
- White men over the age of 65 have the highest rate of suicide.
- Some groups are at greater risk, too, including people have attempted suicide before or have family members who did. Also at greater risk are those who have lost a spouse, have been abused, have a substance abuse problem or a

painful, disabling, or terminal illness. Those who work in certain professions, such as police officers, are also at greater risk. (webmd.com).

- Mental health disorders, particularly depression and substance abuse, are associated with more than 90% of suicide cases.
- Suicide results from many complex sociocultural factors, and is more likely to occur during periods of socioeconomic, family and individual crisis. Such crises typically include loss of a loved one, unemployment, sexual orientation, difficulties with developing one's identity, disassociation from one's community or other social/belief group, and honor).
- Although women are three times as likely to attempt suicide, men are far more likely to complete the act.

In 2019, the WHO thought that only *close* to 800 000 people committed suicide that year, and that 79% of global suicides occurred in low- and middle-income countries. The most commonly used methods were ingestion of pesticide, hanging and firearms. As mentioned earlier, many who fail in their first attempt to end it all are likely to repeat the performance, but no statistics are available. Albeit no fixed age for suicide is established, the 15-29 year old cohort were the most eager to and most successful in fulfilling their desire of earthly departure in 2016.

The vast majority of suicides are said to occur in the spur of the moment, out of the blue. They happen in emotional crisis situations, such as with financial problems, relationship break-ups, chronic pain and illness (who.int). Depression and alcohol use can be contributing factors. So can conflict, disaster, violence, abuse, loss of a loved one and a sense of isolation. Refugees, migrants, indigenous peoples, lesbians, gays, bisexuals, transgenders, intersex people and prisoners are more prone to suicide. PTSD and pharmaceutical mind-altering drugs as contributing factors to suicide ideation and carry-through is nowhere mentioned. Nevertheless, both are overwhelming invitations to suicidal ideation, in particularly when experienced together.

Suicide replaced homicide in the U.S. as the second leading cause of death among 10- to 34-year-olds. B.K. Ahmedani, clinical associate professor, School of Social Work, and adjunct assistant professor, Department of Epidemiology at Michigan State University, East Lansing, Michigan, and his team of researchers looked at suicide attempts in the U.S. healthcare systems in 2015. They found, however, that 65% of people make healthcare visits before committing suicide, and many do not have a diagnosed mental health condition. (Ahmedani et al: "Major Physical Health Conditions and Risk of Suicide". *Am J Prev Med*. 2017 Sep; 53(3): 308-315., 2015).

The study included 2,674 people dying by suicide between 2000 and 2013. They were matched with 267,400 controls in a case-control study conducted in 2016 across 8 Mental Health Research Network healthcare systems. Nineteen physical health conditions were identified using diagnostic codes within the healthcare systems' Virtual Data Warehouse. This included electronic health records and insurance claims data during the year before the index date. Seventeen physical health conditions were associated with increased suicide risk. Nine associations persisted after adjusting for mental health and substance use diagnoses. Traumatic brain injury, sleep disorders and HIV/AIDS had a more than twofold increase in suicide risk. Multi-morbidity present in 38% of cases versus 15.5% of controls almost doubled the risk for suicide. The conclusion:

> "Although several individual conditions, such as traumatic brain injury, were associated with high risk of suicide, nearly all physical health conditions increased suicide risk, even after adjustment for potential confounders. In addition, having multiple physical health conditions increased suicide risk substantially. These data support suicide prevention based on the overall burden of physical health." (Ibid)

We should think that that would blow the suicide relationship with mental health right out of the water. Unless, of course, one views ordinary human life events, also known as experiential crises, as mental illnesses. But not so for Miss Oquendo. In 2008, a full 2 years before receiving her PhD in Psychiatry from the public Universidad Autónoma de Madrid (Spain), she proposed that suicidal behavior should evolve in psychiatry and the mental health profession as an independent diagnostic category. She argued that it would facilitate the tracking of high-risk patients through medical records. And she, a freshly baked psychiatrist new-born in the field, succeeded in her endeavor. Suicidal behavior was indeed added to the *DSM-5* 2013's appendix.

The consequence of anyone getting in touch with "the system", such as those injured in the line of duty and ending up with genuine PTSD, just got more serious. Now they run the risk of being diagnosed without a cause by their mental health practitioner as being suicidal. The verdict will then be entered into the health "care" system, with the associated consequences including withholding the 2nd Amendment right to bear arms. The conceptualization permitting the preposition of suicidal behavior in all conditions of life during negative emotional events is quasi natural, as pointed out by Ahmedani et al., were ignored by the APA psychiatrists designing the latest DSM. Mind you, Miss Oquendo's research to find validity, reliability and reasons to support her suicidal preposition as a diagnostic entity is still ongoing. Still, she breathes not a word about suicidal ideation as a side effect created by pharmaceutical FDA-approved, mind-altering drugs of all genres. Why not seems to become somewhat clearer, when perusing her aims for APA members as APA's president from 2017 to 2020:

- Secure a key role for psychiatrists as healthcare reform is implemented, while ensuring high quality care for all, particularly persons with the most severe mental illnesses. (This should include their own, as psychiatrists have the highest human suicide rates in the world of all classes and professions worldwide. In the US, whereas physicians have the highest suicide rate of any profession: 28 to 40 suicides per 100,000, more than double the 12.3 per 100,000 in the general population. (Lily Wang: "Psychiatrists have the highest suicide rate of any profession. It's time to do something about it". *#BrilliantlyResilientDiaries*. Medium.com. June 26, 2019).
- Pursue equitable reimbursement and true parity for psychiatric care. (Meaning: find ways to fill their pockets at ever increasing amounts of money and perks.)
- Secure robust federal funding for education and research; coordinating efforts with advocacy groups. (Read: brainwash the public with ever greater

vigour to make it believe that only with us, the Psycho-the Rapists, the rapists of their patients' psyches, are they, the herd, able to live their lives.)
- Strengthen collaboration with psychiatric subspecialties and primary care. (Meaning: Turn all those willing into counsellors similar to Covington to reinforce their mental health industry domination).
- Pursue active communication with all members (Read: Get all mental health practitioners from the lowest to the highest educated into lockstep to facilitate herd-control to Gulag perfection.)

The U.S. healthcare system is allotted more than a trillion dollars per annum. It spends more per capita on healthcare than any other country on earth. Yet, the U.S. population is blindly allowing this mindless and health-endangering manipulation. Not only that, their system is also backed by the WHO. In 2019, the WHO decided that the suicide of close to 800,000 people worldwide, one-hundredth of a percent of a global population of 7,5 billion, implied a serious public health problem. With timely evidence-based and low-cost interventions and comprehensive multi-sectoral suicide prevention strategies for national responses, the WHO maintains those deaths could be prevented. This, in turn, generated the newly-birthed suicidal prevention industry. This new industry is cherished by mental health practitioners and non-profit organizations across the globe, jubilant that another golden goose has been created. This one should assure them lifelong profits and perpetual human misery for anyone entering their system, the Latin sewer. But never mind that, either.

Overall, U.S. President Obama's 2016 *21st Century Cures Act,* (ACA), still hotly debated in both Houses of the U.S. Congress due to President Trump's proposal for alterations or eliminations, does not address suicide. To this day, it talks only about the needs of those Americans deemed to suffer serious mental illnesses (SMI) and serious emotional disturbances (SED). Both diagnoses are extremely flexible. Depending on mental health practitioners' moods of the day, these diagnoses can be changed at a moment's notice. Let's not forget events in the USSR, in particular under Lenin and Stalin, where psychiatric diagnoses dictated the fate of many, and at least 60 million people were killed by leaders masquerading as sane. Furthermore, it is made clear in the ACA that the SMI definition includes one or more diagnoses of mental disorders combined with significant impairment and functioning (samhsa.gov). Schizophrenia, bipolar illness and major depressive disorder are the ones most commonly associated with SMI. But anyone with one or more other disorders of a mental nature can be squeezed into the definition. It is therefore so extremely useful and easily pervertible into all diagnoses. Such an extremely handy SMI definition, especially if those disorders are deemed to result in functional impairment

Genuine PTSD experiencers can be grouped in any one of the Department of Health and Human Services (DHHS) Interdepartmental Serious Mental Illness Coordinating Committee's categories. It all depends on the diagnostic physician's political and educational leaning, status in rank and file, desire to curb patients' constitutional 2nd Amendment right and his or her mood of the day. The non-federal members of the Interdepartmental Serious Mental Illness Coordinating Committee (ISMICC) are chosen in accordance with the 1972 Federal Advisory Committee Act. This legal foundation defines how federal advisory committees must operate. These members are said to have done their very best to create recommendations to focus federal efforts. The goal would be to develop a comprehensive continuum of care focused on improving outcomes for people of all ages with SMI and SED. They wanted to promote evidence-based practices and a strong community-based system of care, so all humans can in due time and without much upheaval be corralled into Federal Emergency Management Agency (FEMA) pastures. ISMICC's vision"

> "Federal interdepartmental leadership, with genuine collaboration and shared accountability of all federal agencies, and in partnership with all levels of government and other stakeholders, supports a mental health system that successfully addresses the needs of all individuals living with SMI or SED and their families and caregivers, effectively supporting their progress to achieve healthy lives characterized by autonomy, pride, self-worth, hope, dignity, and meaning (The Substance Abuse and Mental Health Services Administration; https://samhsa.gov)."

In other words, all "licensed" mental health figures, including Covington et al., are now sanctioned by the state to strangle the Other, any Other. They simply have to issue certificates of insanity when crossing their path. The definition of "serious emotional disturbance" (SED), by the way, applies only to children and youth. It, too, purportedly requires the presence of a diagnosable mental, behavioral or emotional disorder and substantial functional impairment. This is easily created and hallucinated into existence and out of thin air by any self-respecting mental health practitioner of any rank and file. All they need is to be certified after 10 hours of dubious psychological training, without a substantial and relevant academic background. They have same authority as psychiatrists with 12 or more years of undergraduate and graduate studies under their belt. None of them has any difficulty whatsoever, with the help of 297 DSM-5 mental health diagnoses at their fingertips, to label any of their voluntary or involuntary victims, including genuine PTSD experiencers, as insane and in need of pharmaceutical mind-altering drugs or worse, the incarceration into a mental hospital. See *Fallacy 1* for details on that one.

Meanwhile, Ahmedani et al., still busy in the pursuit of suicide theories, announced in October of 2019 a suicide diagnosis that *could* make it easier to spot someone who *may, just may*, sometime in the immediate or distant future, attempt suicide. (Temma Ehrenfeld, 2019, https://qz.com). This amazing epiphany began with one poor soul, an aspirant to become one of the learned in the mental health field, by the name of Breanna (Bre) Banks. She now holds a PhD in counsellor education and supervision from the University of Tennessee. Her MA in mental health counselling is from Arogy University in Nashville, and her BA in psychology from the University of Tennessee, Martin (https://waldenu.edu). She presently is manager of clinical education & dissemination research, specializing in design and implementation of suicide response training for behavioural health providers. She is a contributing faculty member at the College of Social and Behavioral Sciences at Walden University's School of Counseling in Minneapolis.

Once upon a time, on a dark and stormy night in her Nashville apartment, Banks saw a comment from her boyfriend on Facebook that not only threw her for a loop, but into a suicidal fit. "My legs seized up, and I fell," she recalled. Then her knees and forehead pressed into the carpet, and a voice in her head yelled: "Slit your wrists, slit your wrists." She envisaged herself in her bathtub, with her blood liberally staining the water and terrified that, if she moved, she would surely die. Her experience led to the birth of this new type of pre-diagnostic diagnosis, said to make it much, much easier to spot if someone *may* attempt to commit suicide—sooner or later.

When the episode occurred, Banks was the tender age of 25. She was a graduate student in an unmentioned discipline without psychiatric history, and had never considered suicide an option to end her life. Despite the voice and bloody images of herself persisting and unable to sleep for three days, she somehow had the presence of mind to teach herself the dialectical behavior therapy (DBT). Discussed at length in *Fallacy 1*, suffice it to say it is a specific type of cognitive behavioral psychotherapy imagined in the 1980s by American psychologist Marsha M. Linehan to treat borderline personality disorder.

Like all "Pavlovian" therapies, meaning cani, rattus, simian and mus non-empirically-proven-for-human-application cognitive behavioral mind manipulations, , DBT is administered in combination with pharmaceutical drugs. It slowly evolved in rank to now being lauded as a suicidality-remedy, despite the fact that there is only one 2018 study asserting more than a million people annually attempt suicide in the U.S. alone. That study is called *Dialectical Behavior Therapy Is Effective for the Treatment of Suicidal Behavior: A Meta-Analysis*, and it concluded:

> "There was no statistically significant pooled effect of DBT with regard to suicidal ideation when all studies were included. Studies trended towards favoring DBT over control conditions, and the absence of a significant effect may have reflected the relatively small number of studies and relatively small sample sizes included in this review. Further, this finding may reflect the particular influence of two larger studies (Goodman et al., 2016, Linehan et al., 2006), which "if deleted" yielded a significant overall pooled effect. Nonetheless, this sensitivity to the inclusion or exclusion of particular studies suggests that there is not a robust effect of DBT with regard to suicidal ideation across controlled trials." (Christopher R. DeCou; Katherine Anne Comtois; Sara J. Landes; Elsevier, *Behavior Therapy* Volume 50, Issue 1, January 2019, Pages 60–72).

A multitude of clinicians and researchers continue to maintain that suicidal crises frequently come on rapidly. They claim it escalates from impulse to action within a day, an hour or just minutes, striking people seemingly in good mental health. This seems to be of no consequence to anyone's hallucinated assertion. This is what makes the suicide prevention movement and classification of suicide as a diagnosable and preventable human condition so utterly bizarre. Unless, of course, if we look at those striving to define this theory as themselves hovering on the brink of suicidal insanity.

That includes some of the most reputable researchers in the field, from Mount Sinai Beth Israel to Florida State University. They recently agreed to work on a proposal for an adequate suicidality diagnosis to be incorporated into the DSM. Criteria to be included are symptoms of depression, as well as symptoms occurring in an acute state not currently obvious to clinicians. I'm sure they'll dream one up. Bright proponents of this idea immediately conceded that it *could* spur more research, and thus grants for the profession, and that it *could* make it easier for suicidal patients to get the care they need—as dictated by practitioners. Calling it the newest mental health and pharmaceutical industry cash cow would perhaps better fit the bill, eh? Does the need for a suicidality diagnosis confirm, though, that diagnosing human emotions is beyond the scope and knowledge of mental health professionals, when left to their own devices? That is the question to decide, is it not?

Suzanne Kellner-Zinck is owner of *Dawning Visions Hypnosis*. In 2019, she valiantly pointed out that by medicalizing every normal human emotion in accordance with the *DSM-5*, psychiatrists actually prove that they are incompetent in dealing with human emotions. During the *DSM-III* days, when Kellner-Zinck began to practice in conventional health, the manual was helpful to her. What laypersons need to understand, however, is that many people are, in her opinion, improperly diagnosed because of what is stipulated in the manual, On the one hand, the treatment they receive has zero to do with the causes of their problems. On the other hand, their problems are exacerbated by the side-effects of the treatment they receive and the prescribed medications associated with it. Just check what happened to Professor Jordan Peterson when he took benzodiazepines for anxiety ("Return Home"; https://youtube.com/watch?v=6_6zwVNn88o).

All these self-proclaimed geniuses on the human psyche furthermore persistently neglect to admit that there are no tests to check or scientifically, empirically validate mental illness in humans.

American celebrity psychiatrist and brain disorder specialist Daniel Gregory Amen, director of the Amen Clinics, begs to differ. He believes his brain scans at least help to diagnose mental- and other ailments. He, too, ignores the fact, that human emotional imbalance for most of the species arises when dealing with negative life-events and/or physiological issues. That psychosis often arises simply from a lack of vitamin B12, the learned society keeps a well-guarded secret. Amen, however, has one advantage for emotionally unbalanced individuals. Instead of using destructive and tarnishing DSM-prescribed labels, he focuses on and addresses patients' thoughts and behaviors. DSM diagnoses can brainwash clinicians' and analysts themselves into the idea of patients 'suicide ideation and other mental diagnoses. Even so, in the vast majority of cases, nothing other than a temporary existential crisis of normally to-be-expected human experiences during a lifetime of life is creating emotional upheaval in their lives. This upheaval could, but not necessarily does, lead to suicidal ideation. However, when pharmacotherapy is the treatment, dictating consumption of prescribed mind-altering drugs taken by unsuspecting patients, it leads straight onto the road of suicidality.

Kellner-Zinck is not the only one expressing skepticism about the suicidality diagnosis epiphany. Weill Cornell Medicine psychiatrist and historian of psychiatry George Jack Makari does, as well. He serves as director of The Institute for the History of Psychiatry at Weill Cornell Medical College, where he is also a professor of psychiatry. He says: "Far too many diagnoses in psychiatry come and go". Makari's work is well known among historians of the mind sciences, psychiatry and psychoanalysis. He is author of two books, *Revolution in Mind, The Creation of Psychoanalysis* and *Soul Machine: The Invention of the Modern Mind.* In the latter, he recounts how the mind evolved as a potential solution to questions about the nature of inner life. He supplies a possible answer that the mind might be part soul and part machine, but fully neither. Of Bernays et al.'s *Making the American Mind*, he breathes not a word. He finds the suicidality diagnosis epiphany of being a symptom of something else, such as a mood or personality disorder, rather novel. He observes: "If they (his learned colleagues) are making the claim that we've been seeing this upside down for a long time, that's fascinating." No wonder, as in one single study alone, about one quarter of suicide attempts were made by people reporting zero suicidal thoughts, according to Feldenkreis.

Suicide rates are said to have been rising sharply since 1999, according to Centers for Disease Control and Prevention (CDC) figures. Yet, more than half of those who kill themselves did not have a known mental health condition. Nor is there an established way to pinpoint when a patient is in immediate suicidal danger.

Russian-born American psychiatrist, clinician and researcher Igor Galynker, M.D., PhD., immigrated to the United States in 1978. He worked one year as chemist researcher at the CIBA-Geigy corporation. He began graduate studies (1978–1981) in organic synthesis at Columbia University. He then wrote his PhD thesis on describing the first use of computer modeling in organic synthesis. IT goes on - he completed a fellowship in human genetics at the Columbia Presbyterian Medical Center, then taught chemistry at Purdue University and at Columbia University. He serves as professor in the Department of Psychiatry, director of the Suicide Lab and the Zirinsky Center for Bipolar Disorder, associate chairman for research in the Department of Psychiatry at Mount Sinai Beth Israel, founded the Family Center for Bipolar and is director of the Mount Sinai Suicide Research Laboratory based at Mount Sinai Beth Israel, as well as being professor of psychiatry at the Icahn School of Medicine in New York City. He bluntly stated: "You cannot rely on people telling you, when they are or are not suicidal."

Research backs him up. A 2019 meta-analysis of 71 studies from around the globe found that about 60% of people who died by suicide denied having suicidal thoughts, when asked by a psychiatrist or general practitioner. A 2016 U.S. study examined data from four health systems using standardized questionnaires in primary care and specialty clinics. The researchers asked whether the patient had experienced "thoughts that you would be better off dead or of hurting yourself in some way." Although the answers did predict future suicide attempts to some extent, there were plenty of false negatives. Patients who responded "not at all" to the key question included 39% of the suicide attempts and 36% of the suicide deaths. In another study, about a quarter of suicided people reported no suicidal thoughts whatsoever and still made attempts to kill themselves.

Could all of them have been lying? Not necessarily, according to Dr. Gregory E. Simon, a psychiatrist and investigator at Kaiser Permanente Washington in Seattle. He is affiliated with multiple hospitals in the area, and led the 2016 study. He was involved in a follow-up study based on interviews with 26 people who tried to kill themselves after having denied any suicidal thoughts on the standard questionnaire. The interviews revealed that some of the people had lied. They also revealed that some of them had provided what Simon terms "aspirational" responses. In other words, they were *trying* not to have suicidal thoughts. And there were still others who had experienced no suicidal thinking whatsoever. Among the latter group, alcohol often factored into their attempts of suicide, but none of them woke up the morning of the deed with a plan to kill themselves that day.

After losing a patient to suicide, Galynker determined that he could not rely on patient reports. Instead, he set out in 2007 to develop a set of symptoms that would help him to pinpoint imminent suicide, even when the patient did not report suicidal thinking. "We hypothesized that the pre-suicidal state leading to suicidal action was short-lived, kind of like pulling a gun trigger," he stated, calling it the "suicide trigger state." Through research, he explored various symptoms as predictors. He developed checklists and tested how well they predicted patients' future behavior. These checklists are now being used among high school students in Moscow and hospital patients in Chicago to screen for suicidal risk among high school students. Go figure.

This seemingly breathtakingly brilliant man when viewing the positions held also coined the term "suicide crisis syndrome." People with this syndrome feel trapped, he says, though they per se might not think of death. They may solely be flooded with misery, mood swings or overwhelming emotional pain. With certain thoughts and images and voices a la Banks repeatedly returning, they are unable to think clearly, no matter their personal resistance. They are prime identifiers of this theory, in his opinion.

Thomas Joiner of the University of Texas, Austin, is the Robert O. Lawton distinguished professor of psychology. He is also director of the FSU Psychology Clinic, a mental health service, research and training facility affiliated with the Clinical Psychology Program of the Department of Psychology at Florida State University. He outlined his own criteria for a quick-onset suicide crisis. He calls it the "acute suicidal affective disturbance". He describes it as a person's rapidly escalating plans for suicide, occurring at a much faster speed than clinicians *may* expect. For Joiner, the inclusion of suicidal thinking is an essential criterion as well as a pre-requisite for the risk of suicidal ideation and diagnosis.

Galynker and Joiner teamed up some years ago. Now contently united, they envisage a new DSM suicide diagnosis. That makes two - one where patients have thoughts of suicide, and another one when without suicidal thoughts. One way or the other, the possibility of a suicidality diagnosis shall be found and shoveled down individual patients and humanity's throat. It will be labeled as mental when mental health practitioners feel like it, no matter what, albeit there is a glimmer of hope left. The mental health industry may need to show more conclusively that the phenomena they describe as "acute suicidal affective disturbance" and "the suicide trigger state" is not a symptom of depression or other mental illness, says Feldenkreis. He says they will also have to show that suicidality screening methods, which sprang forth thus far are effective.

Michael B. First, M.D., is professor of clinical psychiatry at Columbia University, and a research psychiatrist at the Biometrics Department at the New York State Psychiatric Institute. He maintains a schema therapy and psychopharmacology practice in Manhattan. He is a nationally and internationally recognized expert on psychiatric diagnosis and assessment issues. In fact, he has conducted expert forensic psychiatric evaluations in both civil and criminal matters, including the 2006 trial of the 9/11 terrorist Zacarias Moussaoui. He is also the editorial and coding consultant for the *DSM-5*. He is the chief technical and editorial consultant on the World Health Organization's ICD-11 revision project, as well as an external consultant to the NIMH Research Domain Criteria project. His undergraduate degree is in electrical engineering and computer science from Princeton University, with a master's in computer science and a medical degree from the University of Pittsburgh.

This extraordinaire versatile man, who presided over earlier DSM revisions, views the suicide-specific diagnosis as an "appealing idea. Indeed, he states: "If the melding of Galynker's and Joiner's formulations works well and proves to be accurate, then it would clearly be very useful to have it," continuing in the same breath: "We hypothesized, that *the pre-suicidal state leading to suicidal action was short-lived*, kind of like pulling a gun trigger."

Meanwhile, the world's Neumeisterians are looking for answers to the suicidal conundrum in the human brain proper, as it seems unreasonable to expect rattus et al. to commit suicide in the near future. Dr. Jennifer Phillips is associate scientist in the Mood Disorders Research Unit at The Royal's Institute of Mental Health Research (IMHR) located in Ottawa, Ontario, the research institute of the Royal Ottawa Health Care Group. She is also affiliated with the University of Ottawa, where she is studying brain biomarkers in people with treatment-resistant depression, who are most at risk of suicide. After all, 4,000 people die by suicide in Canada annually, out of a population of roughly 35 million.

Using magnetic resonance imaging (MRI) at The Royal's Brain Imaging Centre (BIC), Phillips et al. are examining the brain's structure by measuring:

- the thickness of brain tissue
- the volume of various brain regions
- the white matter tracts in the brain connecting different brain areas

The team also looks at brain activity to identify brain networks that may be associated with suicidal thoughts and attempts. Imaging data from study participants is combined with clinical factors and behavioral traits associated with suicide, factors such as impulsivity, hopelessness, perceived stress and childhood trauma.

Phillips explains:

> "One of the biggest challenges in mental health research is suicide prevention. Suicidal thoughts can be very common among individuals with mental illness, yet not all will progress towards making a suicide attempt. Learning how to identify those at highest risk is a key goal in this field."

Of humanly-to-be-expected life experiences, not a word is uttered. Of course not! Could there be a more splendid way to make a living? Does it matter that tens of thousands of poverty-stricken humans are living on city streets, genuine PTSD experiencers among them, with minds deemed to be "part soul and part machine but fully neither?" Never mind the mind, though, as thus far, all failed to locate it anywhere.

Perhaps we should call this whole research hypothesis the "Have your cake and eat it too" syndrome. Clinicians have neither a clue nor guidance on how to identify imminent suicide risks or make sense of suicides, period. All they, and now we, know for sure is that the deed is performed out of the blue. They can't figure out what inspires their own to kill themselves more often than any other population group and profession in the world. Perhaps, come to think of it, one enters the mental health field because one intuitively knows one is mentally ill and worries about it, with its nooks and crannies and deficiencies and impairments? Could it be that, once ensconced in the company of one's fellow mental health practitioners, Nietzsche's observation strikes? "Insanity in individuals is something rare—but in groups, parties, nations, and epochs it is the rule." (*Beyond Good and Evil*, p. 41, quote 156)

Add to this another of his sayings: "The thought of suicide is a great consolation; by means of it one gets successfully through many a bad night." (Ibid quote 157) The influence of pharmaceutical psychotropic drugs as catalyst to suicidal ideation is nowhere mentioned. This inspires further contemplation and curiosity, because they are the paths of least resistance leading straight into the desire of killing Oneself. How these imbecilic, self-aggrandized geniuses attempt to prevent the unpreventable is another question. Could it be that it is to be achieved by enticing us into financially sponsoring their non-profit societies to pay for their exercises of futility, by making us believe we may all one day like to kill ourselves?

16

THE CASH COW NAMED SUICIDE

Dr. Dmitriy Gekhman, a psychiatry specialist in New York City, graduated with honours from the State University Of New York's Downstate Medical Center in 2014. He has more than six years of diverse experiences, especially in psychiatry. Gekhman is affiliated with Mount Sinai Beth Israel and cooperates with many other doctors and specialists in its Icahn School of Medicine. The hospital was incorporated as Beth Israel Hospital on May 28, 1890, by a group of 40 Orthodox Jews on the Lower East Side of Manhattan. They wanted a hospital dedicated to serving immigrant Jews living in the tenement slums of Manhattan's Lower East Side.

Now a 799-bed teaching hospital, it is part of the Mount Sinai Health System. This non-profit health system was formed in September 2013 by the merger of Continuum Health Partners and Mount Sinai Medical Center. It is an academic affiliate of the Icahn School of Medicine at Mount Sinai. Continuum Health Partners, Inc. is the holding corporation for four New York City hospitals:

- Beth Israel Medical Center
- St. Luke's-Roosevelt Hospital Center
- Long Island College Hospital
- New York Eye and Ear Infirmary

Founded in 1997, Continuum is trying to coordinate the operations of its members. Its goal is so to control costs and keep the hospitals financially solvent in an era of increased competition for patients and for payments by government programs and managed-care organizations.

As of 2010, Mount Sinai Beth Israel had residency training programs in nearly every major field of medicine, including emergency medicine, internal medicine, surgery, otolaryngology, oral and maxillofacial surgery, radiology, family medicine, dermatology, obstetrics and gynecology, neurology, ophthalmology, pathology, psychiatry, podiatry, and urology. it also has a department of chiropractic, music therapy, and acupuncture.

According to the National Provider Identifier (NPI) records, Gekhman is a psychiatrist specializing in the prevention, diagnosis and treatment of mental disorders, emotional disorders, psychotic disorders, mood disorders, anxiety disorders, substance-related disorders, sexual and gender identity disorders and adjustment disorders (npidb.org). He purports to explore and understand his patients' biologic, psychological and social components of illnesses in order to understand and treat the whole person. Gekhman uses tools like diagnostic laboratory tests and prescribed pharmaceutical medications. He also evaluates and treats psychological and interpersonal problems with individuals and families in their lives. And he, intervenes with unexplained means to cope with stress, crises and other unnamed problems.

Almost every week at Mount Sinai Beth Israel, Gekhman sees a patient who attempted suicide and are hard to classify. He must find a relevant code for each patient's chart anyway, as their medical records (MR) must be coded for billing and remittance. He explains:

> "You kind of go through the history and everything, and they're not depressed. They don't meet the criteria for depression, they don't meet criteria for bipolar disorder, and they don't have a personality disorder. We just discharged somebody this week who that happened to, and we still have somebody on the unit now." (*A New Type Of Diagnosis Could Make It Easier To Spot If Someone May Attempt Suicide*; https://mountsinai.org, 2019)

If a diagnosis based on Galynker's and Joiner's research were put in place, however, it would put the patient's doctors on notice that the patient is a risk for suicide with rapid onset. Over time, it could be possible for clinicians, teachers and parents to become better at seeing the signs for a pending suicide attempt. The diagnosis, Joiner explained, then would become a "warning sign for the future."

Detroit's Henry Ford Health System is another non-profit healthcare organization established by Henry Ford in 1915. It is run by a 15-member board of trustees, which also owns the health insurance company Health Alliance Plan. It has a triple mission: clinical care, research and education. Here, suicide is considered its own mental health category, not primarily a symptom of depression. In 2002, it began a series of initiatives reducing patient suicide rates by 80% over the next seven years. Staff also discovered, that from 2000 to 2010 only 50% of patients killing themselves had received a mental health diagnosis closely matching current national statistics. "This could be undiagnosed [mental] illness, but I think a lot of people don't meet the criteria," said Dr. Brian Ahmedani. He had joined the Center for Health Policy and Health Services Research at Henry Ford Health System (HFHS) in 2010 In 2018, he was appointed the Center's Director.

Ahmedani received his PhD and Master of Social Work (MSW) degrees from Michigan State University (MSU). Throughout the MSW Program, students take courses in theory, policy, research and practice methods, and they benefit from intensive field experience. While the first half of the program provides students with a generalist foundation of social work knowledge, the second half prepares them for advanced practice in one of two concentrations:

- The clinical social work concentration focuses on micro-level interventions appropriate for work with individuals, families and groups.
- The Organization and Community Leadership concentration focuses on macro-level interventions appropriate for work within communities.

Ahmedani is a fully licensed clinical and macro masters-level social worker in Michigan. Macro social work is a broad field that centers on investigating larger scale social problems and developing and implementing social interventions to make positive change at the community, state and national levels (onlinemswprograms.com). He also completed fellowship program in drug dependence epidemiology. This was funded by the National Institute of Health (NIH) and the National Institute on Drug Abuse (NIDA). Epidemiology is the scientific, systematic and data-driven study of the distribution, frequency, patterns, determinants, causes and risk factors of human health-related states and events. These are measured in specified populations, neighbourhoods, schools, cities, states and countries, such as increased homicides in a community, for example.

NIDA addresses the most fundamental and essential questions about drug abuse. For instance, it looks at detecting and responding to emerging drug abuse trends. It studies how drugs work in the brain and body. And it develops and tests new approaches to treatment and prevention. NIDA also supports research training, career development, public education, public-private partnerships and research dissemination. It has an Intramural Research Program, and offers grants and contracts to investigators at research institutions around the country and overseas, such as its laboratory in Wuhan, China. Michigan Governor Gretchen Whitmer's Suicide Prevention Commission in 2020 appointed Ahmedani for a term expiring in 2024 to work with state departments and agencies, as well as non-profit organizations, to research the causes and possible underlying factors of suicide in Michigan. Thus, another cash cow to drain the innocent, ignorant, lethargic herd of its hard-earned dollars has been born.

At Henry Ford, everyone is screened with questionnaires asking about suicidal thoughts, a practice the Joint Commission started recommending in 2016. The Joint Commission is another United States-based nonprofit tax-exempt 501(c) organization that accredits and certifies more than 22,000 U.S. healthcare organizations and programs. The organization's international branch, by the way, accredits medical services from around the world. It is based in Oakbrook Terrace, a tiny town of around 2,000 in DuPage County, Illinois. The majority of U.S. state governments recognize Joint Commission accreditation as a condition of licensure for the receipt of Medicaid and Medicare reimbursements.

Henry Ford is one of Michigan's largest and most experienced providers of comprehensive behavioral health services. It has locations throughout Southeast and South Central Michigan, providing comprehensive behavioral health treatment for patients of all ages, so no one needs to face any life challenges alone (henryford.com). Among its services is the charmingly named substance use disorder, formerly known as addiction. This "disorder" is ofttimes created by pharmaceutical opioid prescription drugs. It also offers detoxification and medication-assisted treatment through to neuropsychology evaluations for complex behavioral health and medical conditions. For a price, their behavioral health specialists will treat what they consider your mental inadequacies and your mental conditions with compassionate, customized care to turn you into the species of their desire. Needless to say, treatments may include medication, rehabilitation therapy or surgery.

The behavioural health unit's assessment includes a physical and a psychosocial examination, where work, home and personal life will be discussed. Licensed psychologists and social workers perform the psychosocial exam to hypothesize whether additional physical or psychiatric conditions affecting treatment could be present, and to investigate what patients want to accomplish through treatment. To drive genuine PTSD travelers nutty, loved ones are encouraged to participate in these procedures. An estimate with expected out-of-pocket costs based on expected service and specific insurance co-pay, co-insurance and deductible information will be provided later.

According to Ahmedani, risk assessments focus on triggers, as patients in the highest risk percentile he leaves completely out of his equation. Why? Because his proposal will enhance profit for both Big Pharma and physicians of all stripes and colors to a new, wonderful, hitherto undreamt-of profit level, as of course, all drugs lead to further destruction of both brain and body. With such imprints, Covington's new suicide healing hypothesis, indeed, is right in line to make humanity think it is born and bred mentally defective, as a result learning to hallucinate that human *mental health is health*.

However, psychiatrists in general seem to still view suicide attempts with a short buildup as "impulsive." Some experts, such as Galynker and Joiner and their teams, seem uncertain if these "impulsive" suicides are made by impulsive people. Megan Rogers is a PhD candidate who works with Joiner and sees outpatients at the university clinic. She recalls one patient who "within hours would go from no risk to high risk," but had what she describes as a conscientious and vigilant rather than impulsive personality. That, too, blows out of the water their theory of suicidal ideation and that a new mental health diagnosis should help to prevent suicide. As a matter of fact, could the idea perhaps in itself inspire the thought of mental illness in the originators of that theory?

According to Megan L. Rogers, MS; Igor Galynker, M.D., PhD; Zimri Yaseen, M.D.; Kayla DeFazio, BA; and Thomas E. Joiner, PhD, current psychological diagnostic classification systems do not fully capture the scope of suicidality. This led to their recent call for a suicide-specific diagnosable condition, which, they contend, should use a minimal number of assumptions or steps. Such a condition would reflect the level of severity of the situation and characterize not only if, but also when, a person will engage in suicidal behavior. Such situations might include job loss, chronic pain, opioid use and insomnia. Due to a multitude of possible combinations when assessing human behaviour, diagnosis could can be a difficult task. Henry Ford therefore uses artificial intelligence (AI) to analyze patients' electronic medical records, which could facilitate consulting clinicians' task to catch a perfect storm of suicidal meltdown, for example, before it is too late. The U.S. Veterans Affairs administration (VA) uses the same algorithms.

There is little evidence that medication prevents suicide, other than lithium, most often used to treat people with bipolar disorder. Suicidal people are often prescribed antidepressants anyway, says Ahmedani, without breathing a word that it in fact causes suicides. Nevertheless, new VA clinical guidelines support short-term infusions of a drug called ketamine, a fast-acting anaesthetic and painkiller used primarily in veterinary surgery. According to the Centre for Addiction and Mental Health (CAMH), it can produce vivid dreams and a feeling of mind-body separation (camh.ca). That should be good for healing the human mind, never mind the damage done in the process, eh?

CAMH, by the way, is Canada's largest mental health teaching hospital and one of the world's leading research centres in its field. It is affiliated with the University of Toronto. It is a Pan American Health Organization/World Health Organization collaborating centre, employing more than 3,000 physicians, clinicians, researchers, educators and support staff, and caring for more than 34,000 patients annually. Another non-profit foundation, it advocates on public policy issues at all levels of governments and raises tens of millions of dollars to fund new programs and research, as well as to augment its services. Your monthly donations are invited. For what purpose?

"When you give, you become part of a growing movement that believes Mental Health is Health."

What are Henry Ford's ideas of suicide prevention efforts? Identifying triggers and find coping mechanisms, besides the ever-present cognitive behavioural therapy and dialectical behaviour therapy. Both are said to have helped Banks to recover. Patients are encouraged to develop their own self-protection safety plans that include removing guns and painkillers from their environments and developing an "idea" of whom to call when under duress. Suicide prevention activist David Covington's opinion on such treatments?

"We used to think that, if you treat addiction the mental health will get better, and the other side thought, if you treat mental health, the addiction will get better. Now we say you have to treat both."

In other words, Covington purports that those seeking help for their most likely temporary psychological upheaval created by a normally-to-be-expected human life experience resulting in depression and consequent occasional suicidal ideation need treatments for both suicide prevention and depression. That more than half of those taking their own lives have no known mental health condition is left out of their equations. ("Overview and Comparison of Two Proposed Suicide-Specific Diagnoses: Acute Suicidal Affective Disturbance and Suicide Crisis Syndrome", *Psychiatric Annals* 47(8): 416-420, 2017). They proposed two potential names for their perceived diagnostic void, namely:

- Acute suicidal affective disturbance (ASAD)
- Suicide crisis syndrome (SCS).

In their 2017 article, Rogers et al. provided an overview of the phenomenology and existing empirical evidence for ASAD and SCS. They also compared two conditions. However, they need to examine both conditions prospectively in samples of a mixture of people and compare the reliability, validity and clinical utility of these two syndromes within single studies. In other words, they are dreaming up further validation for their hypotheses of suicidality diagnoses as they go along.

It is most likely, therefore, that some mental health professionals and physicians question whether a new diagnosis would actually benefit patients. For one thing, it is unclear how such diagnoses would influence patients' treatment, never mind save their lives. "There is simply no value in a prediction, that cannot lead to an effective preventative measure," writes psychiatrist Matthew Michael Large. His expertise lies in mental health law, cannabis use (particularly by younger people), suicide risk and homicide by the mentally ill. At present, he is a conjoint professor in the School of Psychiatry at the University of New South Wales (UNSW), an Australian public research university in Sydney, established in 1949. Large is also clinical director of mental health in the Eastern Suburbs Mental Health Service, based at Sydney's Prince of Wales Hospitals. His research interests in suicide, psychiatric aspects of homicide and substance abuse by people with mental illness is longstanding. He is a leading critic of current risk assessment practices in mental healthcare, as well as a highly ranked international researcher in both suicide and homicide. He also regularly engages in coronial and other legal proceedings and in external service reviews after the deaths of psychiatric patients in the Australian states and territories.

In 2018, he voiced that refraining from predicting suicide in clinical psychiatric practice might help prevent suicides. Most people who receive treatment never die by suicide. And almost half of the patients who do die by suicide might have been deprived of preventative measures after being diagnosed as low-risk ('The Role of Prediction in Suicide Prevention', *Dialogues in Clinical Neuroscience*, vol. 20, pp. 197 - 205, 2018). Epistemic judgments describing a reality that does not exist about future suicide should, in his view, be made very carefully, and only after all the available evidence is gathered. Valid statistical risk factors might contribute to such an epistemic call about suicidality, but this contribution should be modest.

Rather than trying to predict suicide, Large says, clinicians should focus on improving their personal interaction with the patient so as to foster hope, reduce the patient's distress and suffering, and maximize the therapeutic alliance between client and clinician. This should be followed by comprehensive assessment of the patient's current needs. These will often include the need to address modifiable factors that are associated with suicide, such as treatment of substance use. But most such needs should be met irrespective of the associations of possible future suicide. Needs assessments are *not* probabilisticand should lead to treatments being offered to all patients irrespective of a perceived suicide risk says Large.

Finally, psychiatrists should explicitly acknowledge the limits of predicting suicide to patients, their families and healthcare systems providers (meaning insurers). After all, more people could land in hospital psychiatric care, or be kept longer than they desire, if they were deemed by some psychiatrist to be suicidal, Large asserts. He adds that, "While it is generally assumed, that hospitalization can prevent suicide, this has never been demonstrated empirically." In other words, there is no proof that hospitalization prevents suicide. On the contrary, suicide rates are high among recently discharged patients, and some say that hospitalization can make things worse. Furthermore, lowered faith in suicide prediction and the acceptance of the limits of suicide prevention might have the benefit of reducing unnecessarily restrictive interventions. It might allow psychiatrists and clinicians to focus on more achievable treatment goals and on finding patients' path to recovery. But that, of course, for the vast majority of North American mental health practitioners, is an undesirable goal, as patient- recovery is disastrous to their bottom line.

Galynker is outspoken about conflicts of interest between psychiatrists and the pharmaceutical industry. He agrees to the extent that hospitalization might not necessarily be the answer (Kelly, R; Cohen, L; et al. (2006). "Relationship between drug company funding and outcomes of clinical psychiatric research". *Psychological Medicine*. 36 (1647): 1647–56). He is looking at new treatment methods instead. Meanwhile, professor of psychiatry Lisa Cohen of Icahn School of Medicine observes that a diagnosis of suicidal ideation might communicate the higher risk to insurance companies. In her educated opinion, this would give patients' better access to treatment options. That it would most likely also result in higher insurance cost for said patients, she joyously omits to acknowledge.

Psychiatrists making decisions about hospitalizations for patients deemed to be suicidal say they would appreciate more science to guide them. "It would be incredibly helpful to have a very clear indication that someone is at higher risk," observed Julie Holland. She is an American psychopharmacologist, psychiatrist and author. She is also an advocate for the appropriate use of consciousness-expanding substances as part of mental health treatment. She is one of the medical monitors for studies conducted by the Multidisciplinary Association for Psychedelic Studies (MAPS). This membership-based non-profit organization was founded by Richard Doblin (1953–) and is based in Santa Cruz, California, and discussed at length in *Fallacy 1*.

Doblin is famous for Psychedelic Therapy. This so-called therapeutic practices involves all sorts of psychedelic drugs, including serotonergic psychedelics. LSD would be among them, as well as psilocybin, DMT, mescaline 2C-B and the empathogen-entactogen MDMA. Serotonergic psychedelics, also known as serotonergic hallucinogens, are a subclass of psychedelic drugs with a method of action strongly tied to the neurotransmitter serotonin. In contrast to conventional psychiatric medication taken by the patient regularly or as-needed, in psychedelic therapy patients generally remain in an extended psychotherapy session during the acute psychedelic activity. Additional sessions both before and after help them integrate experiences with the drug, as described in detail in *Fallacy 1*. Sucking on the public tit, as all non-profit organizations do, MAPS members pride themselves in raising awareness and understanding of psychedelic substances and helping develop psychedelics into prescription medication. We see the result in the opioid crisis engulfing North America.

Chicago psychiatrist Leo Weinstein has 33 years of experience in the field. He opines that a close look at the build-up to a suicidal crisis would be invaluable:

"We do that when somebody's heart stops, or when somebody's heart is imminently stopping. Making the unstable state a diagnostic entity in its own right, like ventricular fibrillation or congestive heart failure, is crucially important." (Temma Ehrenfeld; "Why some experts are trying to redefine suicide. Treating self harm as a condition, not a symptom could lead to better diagnoses and preventative care". https://undark.org. 2019)

In addition to his clinical practice, Weinstein also teaches at the Northwestern University Department of Psychiatry and the Chicago Institute for Psychoanalysis, where he currently is Associate Dean. Needless to say, he is a distinguished fellow of the American Psychiatrist Association as well. He treats the full range of emotional issues in adults. He says that he uses the best of contemporary psychoanalytic thinking along with modern psychopharmacology to help patients maximize their psychological growth and development (https://chicagopsychoanalyticsociety.org).

Back to Ahmedani. He directs the Center for Health Policy & Health Services Research (CHSR), a research unit within the Henry Ford Health System. This unit conducts research and provides technical assistance and training in the organization, financing and outcomes of health services, systems and policies. Its purported mission is as follows:

- To discover the underlying causal relationships that affect the effectiveness and efficiency of healthcare services.
- Through excellence in research strive to provide the knowledge needed to improve quality of care, maximize the health of populations, and minimize the burden of disease.
- To conduct research relevant to health policy decisions at the state and national levels,
- To be a focal point for the henry ford health system's participation in, and influence on, those decisions.
- To produce high-quality science as evidenced through our publications.
- To actively contribute to the direction of health policy by providing objective and incisive analyses that result in sound decisions regarding the provision and financing of care.

CHSR's vision?

- To be a nationally-recognized source of important, clinically-relevant research findings.
- That its staff will be active participants in the processes that establish healthcare policy
- That it will be a catalyst for health system's organizational participation in those processes.

In other words, huge involvement with politics and desire for fame and fortune, of which suicide prevention is just one small part.

The WHO wavers as to whether suicides are preventable or not. Still, it finds that suicides would be most successfully prevented by learning more about the most commonly used suicide methods. Then we could devise prevention strategies shown to be effective, such as restricting access to means of suicide. Yet, it would discover that anyone who truly wants to kill oneself will find a way to do so, including by hanging with a string from a doorknob.

Their ideas of measures that can be taken in population, sub-population and individual levels to prevent suicide and suicide attempts, however, include:

- reducing access to the means of suicide, such as pesticides, firearms and certain medications
- suicide reporting by the media in a responsible way

- school-based interventions
- introducing alcohol policies to reduce the harmful use of alcohol
- early identification, treatment and care of people with mental and substance-use disorders, chronic pain and acute emotional distress
- training of non-specialized health workers in assessing and managing suicidal behavior
- follow-up care for people who attempted suicide, and providing community support

It is acknowledged that suicide is indeed a complex issue. Therefore, suicide prevention efforts require coordination and collaboration among multiple sectors of society. This must include the health sector, as well as education, labour, agriculture, business, justice, law, defense, politics and the media. These efforts have to be comprehensive, and an integrated approach is needed. No single approach alone could make an impact on an issue as complex as suicide, this organization voices.

The so very active-in-the-suicidal-field Covington has his tender strangling hands in it all, it seems. He is a former president of the American Association of Suicidology. He serves on the National Action Alliance for Suicide Prevention Executive Committee since 2010. And he sits as chair of the National Suicide Prevention Lifeline SAMHSA Steering Committee. He served on numerous committees and task forces on clinical care and crisis services from 2014 to 2016, too. These include the National Council for Behavioural Health Board of Directors and the Relias Learning Behavioral Health Advisory Board. Needless to say, he is also a member of the DHHS Interdepartmental Serious Mental Illness Coordinating Committee (ISMICC). This body was established in 2017 in accordance with the *21st Century Cures Act* to report to Congress on advances in behavioral health. The committee stated in *Recommendation 1.3*:

> "Create a comprehensive inventory of federal activities that affect the provision of services for people with SMI and SED. - ISMICC 2017 Report to Congress"(https://samhsa.com).

It's called "Your government at work!" Federal staff from 10 departments and agencies are apparently collectively organizing and coordinating activities to better address the needs of people with serious mental illnesses (SMI) and serious emotional disturbances (SED) and their families. They are making their Interagency Serious Mental Illness Coordinating Committee (ISMICC), related products and monthly newsletters and blogs on their actions and addressing ISMICC recommendations available to all on the web. All this while making a lucrative living to brainwash the herd into the belief of suffering a mental illness in accordance with aim: "When you give, you become part of a growing movement that believes Mental Health is Health."

You, the genuine PTSD journeyer, are at the forefront of the mental health industry's excuse for their preposterous undertakings for less than 800,000 of the world's 7.5 billion inhabitants. So, the question thus arises:

"Do you still want to commit suicide, or do you want to fight these bastards, who can't prevent their own peers from suicide, but with expertise try at every turn to destroy you, while taking all your individuality, your sui generis, your right to live and breathe, away under the guise of protecting you, when they themselves induce the suicide ideation into you with their Cognitive Behavioral- and other ludicrous therapies combined with mind-altering pharmaceuticals?"

Is it worth your life, or do you want to make it your Who, your *raison d'etre*, as Nietzsche suggests? Do you want to tell your peers the truth about what is being done to genuine PTSD journeyers, never mind everyone diagnosed with PTSD for a hangnail?

To his peers, Nietzsche was the apparent enfant terrible of his time, as Peter Breggin and Jordan Peterson are to ours. In his book *Good and Evil*, Nietzsche says about psychologists:

> "In short, you psychologists, study the philosophy of the 'rule' in its struggle with the 'exception': there you have a spectacle fit for Gods and godlike malignity! Or, in plainer words, practice vivisection on 'good people.' On the *bonae voluntatis*." ON YOURSELVES! (P. 66)

The term vivisection, by the way, has two meanings. Itis describes the practice of performing operations on live animals for the purpose of experimentation or scientific research. It also means a ruthlessly sharp and detailed expression of criticism or analysis. (languages.oup.com)

Nietzsche used his psychological analysis to support original theories about the nature of the Self. He also used it to suggest new values he thought would promote cultural renewal and improve social and psychological life by comparison to life under the traditional values he criticized. In his view, one is duty-bound to subject oneself to one's own tests as they present themselves during life. In our case, that means the genuine PTSD journey. The duty includes, recognizing that one is destined for independence and command. So, we should take control, preferably at the right time (plato.stanford.edu). In his opinion, avoiding tests is no option, even though they might, perhaps, constitute the most dangerous game one can play. Why? Because in the end, tests are presented to our Self for ourselves only, and before no other judge but ourselves. Furthermore, he asserts that we must learn how to conserve and take care of the Self. This, he says, is the best test of for our own independence (Good and Evil p. 25-26).

So, with that in mind, what is it going to be? Strive for command and independence by beginning to heal yourself, making it your WHY, your reason to live, which will enable you to find the How, namely the way to stand up to those wishing to destroy you under the guise of benevolence, the false consciousness, as Nietzsche calls it, and be triumphant in your endeavours? Or will you submit to their commands and die a slow and gruesome death by sticking to those physicians of all rank and files benefitting from your misery? Or, after all the information now in your possession, would you choose a rapid death by suicide to put an end to it all, thus failing the test completely, doomed to relive it again?

17

PREVENTING THE UNPREVENTABLE? ZERO SUICIDE ORG, ET AL

David Covington is CEO and President of RI International. He also owns Behavioral Health Link, and leads the international initiatives "Crisis Now" and "Zero Suicide" (riinternational.com). His behavioral healthcare management history includes CEO of Behavioural Health Link and Director of Public Sector Quality Management at APS Healthcare. His personal achievements include the 2008 Boston marathon and his 2013 participation in the American stunt/dare game show Fear Factor. He is an acclaimed global speaker, for a fee, of course, with top-ranked TED-style speeches and conference keynotes. TED is a showcase for speakers presenting great, well-formed ideas in under 18 minutes. Covington's healthcare innovation blog purportedly entertains readers of 90 countries.

One of the principal founders of the Zero Suicide in Healthcare movement is Michael Hogan, PhD. He is an independent advisor and consultant of Hogan Health Solutions Limited Liability Corporation (LLC). He serves on the executive committee of the National Action Alliance for Suicide Prevention. This public-private partnership advances the National Strategy for Suicide Prevention (sprc.org). It says it "catalyzes planning, implementation, and accountability for updating and advancing the National Strategy for Suicide Prevention." This NSSP is the result of a joint effort by the Office of the U.S. Surgeon General and the National Action Alliance for Suicide Prevention. Action Alliance, in turn, is an outgrowth of the Suicide Prevention Resource Center, established in 2007. In the spring of 2020, the name was changed to Resource Centre for Suicide Prevention (RCSP). This reflects its new *vision and aim* to reduce suicide, suicidal behaviour and their effects, by promoting positive alternatives and healthy coping skills (https://sp-rc.ca).

Hogan previously served as state commissioner of mental health for New York, Ohio and Connecticut (https://zerosuicide.org). He chaired President George W. Bush's New Freedom Commission on Mental Health. The commission was to affirm government support for mental health parity legislation. Hogan said: "We need a healthcare system which treats mental illness with the same urgency as physical illness." (ps.psychiatryonline.org). The Joint Commission was established in 2002 to conduct a comprehensive study of the U.S. mental health service delivery system and make recommendations based on its findings. Hogan also served on its board from 2007 to 2015, the first mental health representative to do so. Founded in 1951, it is the nation's oldest and largest standard-setting and accrediting healthcare body. It is governed by a 21-member board of commissioners, which includes physicians, administrators, nurses, employers, quality experts, a consumer advocate and educators. It employs about 1,000 people in its surveyor force. Its central office is in Oakbrook Terrace, Illinois, with an office in Washington, D.C. Needless to say, this, too, is a not-for-profit organization, which prides itself on:

'Through leading practices, unmatched knowledge and expertise, we help organizations across the continuum of care lead the way to do zero harm." (https://jointcommission.org)

As to the suicide prevention scheme, Covington and Hogan began partnering in it in 2010. That's when Hogan joined the National Action Alliance for Suicide Prevention. This non-profit organization brings diverse partners from public and private sectors together to advance *suicide prevention* efforts in the US. In 2011, Hogan and Covington were co-leads for the Clinical Care & Intervention Task Force. The task force published the National Action Alliance for Suicide Prevention road map (https://zerosuicide.org). They worked with Julie Goldstein Grumet, PhD and the Education and Development Center (EDC, Inc.), another global nonprofit agency. Together, they began to synthesize and crystallize their suicide prevention ideas for public consumption.

Goldstein Grumet is a clinical psychologist and public health professional who works for EDC, Inc. She holds a PhD in clinical psychology from George Washington University and completed a postdoctoral fellowship in school mental health at the University of Maryland's Center for School Mental Health. She is considered an expert in behavioural health transformation, state and local community suicide prevention, and the use of evidence-based practices for suicide care in clinical settings. She is also director of the Zero Suicide Institute. She is said to provide it with strategic direction and leadership for the zero-suicide framework. She also oversees the development, dissemination, evaluation and effective implementation of the framework nationwide. Recently, she led her team in developing an implementation toolkit for suicide care in healthcare systems.

EDC collaborates with public and private partners to create, deliver and evaluate programs, services and products. Its vision? To empower all people worldwide to lead healthy, productive lives. Its perceived vision? Designing, implementing and evaluating programs to improve education promote health and expand economic opportunity worldwide. Its focus is on vulnerable and underserved populations. It gets donations and assistance from Bill Gates, Fauci, Soros et al. to do their bidding, we presume (https://edc.org). Since 1958, it opines to have been a leader in implementing and evaluating its expert, powerful and innovative programs in more than 80 countries. These include early childhood development and learning, youth workforce development and suicide prevention.

Goldstein Grumet is also director of the healthcare initiatives of the Resource Center for Suicide Prevention. Its mission is to heighten awareness about "Head Health". Its mission is also to reduce suicide and suicidal behaviour by promoting positive alternatives and healthy coping skills. Its third mission is to promote open dialogue in our community about mental health issues. It tries to do all this while keeping faith with its community to best manage the financial resources entrusted to it. All this conforms to the "When you give, you become part of a growing movement that believes Mental Health is Health" leitmotiv.

So, expertise sucks on the public tit, all three of them. Covington and Hogan are viewed as *the* co-leads of bringing the suicide prevention necessity to the public's attention. This upstaging of Suicidal PTSD experiencing soldiers and veterans is part of the public imprint mechanism. Goldstein Grumet is a highly experienced trainer and speaker. She has provided consultation, technical assistance, presentations and media interviews on safe and effective suicide care practices. Covington and Hogan have given hundreds of presentations in multiple countries to spread the zero-suicide message. For this service, they charge a fee and all expanses are paid, of course. And they keep silent about suicide-unpreventability, as that would kill the golden goose.

Covington was interviewed on the Social Work Podcast in 2016. The podcast is a source of information on all things social work including clinical and community organizing, research, policy, education and everything in between. He enlightened listeners on how he went from clinician to healthcare executive, from running a crisis service to organizing zero suicide initiatives around the world. He talked about what zero suicide meant for healthcare providers and leaders, and how they could get their healthcare organization involved in zero suicide (http://socialworkpodcast.blogspot.com/2016/09/zerosuicide.html).

"Suicide represents a worst-case failure in mental healthcare. We must work to make it a 'never event' in our programs and systems of care," announced Hogan as president of the New Freedom Commission on Mental Health. It was echoed by Richard McKeon, in an undoubtedly heartfelt: "Over the decades, individual [mental health] clinicians have made heroic efforts to save lives... but systems of care have done very little." McKeon has been SAMHSA bureau chief for suicide prevention since 2010. That includes during the 2010-2011 Action Alliance task force, a key turning point from an effort originally designed to uncover more evidence-based supports for clinicians' suicide toolkit to something targeted at healthcare leadership with the "Mental Health is Health" brainwashing of the population in mind.

Actually, it was McKeon who was the master architect for crafting the task force, which would publish the *Suicide Care in Systems Framework*. He paired with Covington and Hogan to co-lead the effort, more likely to make the suicidal idea of prevention more palatable for public consumption in style with Edward Bernays' policies. Then, in 2012, McKeon partnered with Jerry Reed, PhD, and the U.S. Surgeon General's Office. Together, they led the revision of the U.S. National Strategy for Suicide Prevention, first adopted in 2001, and brewed up this addition:

Goal 8. Promote suicide prevention as a core component of health care services

- 8.1. Promote the adoption of "zero suicides" as an aspirational goal by health care and community support systems that provide services and support to defined patient populations

Reed has a PhD in health-related sciences from the Virginia Commonwealth University. This public research university in Richmond, Virginia, founded in 1838, became the Medical College of Virginia in 1854. Hid PhD had an emphasis in gerontology, the study of the social, cultural, psychological, cognitive, and biological aspects of aging. He also holds a MSW from the University of Maryland at Baltimore. Presently an EDC senior vice president, he has worked hard to raise public belief that suicide in the United States is a leading cause of death. He has driven public policy changes for that to stick at the state, national and international levels. The only problem is that, according to the CDC, as of 2018 suicide ranks 10th on Americans' causes of death, preceded by the following:

- Heart disease: 655,381
- Cancer: 599,274
- Accidents (unintentional injuries): 167,127
- Chronic lower respiratory diseases: 159,486
- Stroke (cerebrovascular diseases): 147,810
- Alzheimer's disease: 122,019
- Diabetes: 84,946
- Influenza and pneumonia: 59,120
- Nephritis, nephrotic syndrome, and nephrosis: 51,386
- Intentional self-harm (suicide): 48,344

In Canada, suicide, or "intentional self-harm", ranked 11, with 3,911 in 2018, down from 4,254 in 2014. To prevent the unpreventable, the Federal Government of Canada in 2018 allotted CA$1.5 billion over five years (https://Canada.ca). In the United States, the approved 2021 *funding* package provides support for *suicide prevention*, including $21 million for the Zero Suicide plan alone (https://onlinelibrary.wiley.com).

There are fewer than 55,000 suicides annually in those two nations. And there are tens of thousands of Americans and Canadians starving and living in hovels across the lands. Yet, Reed continues to lead EDC's suicide prevention practice, educating others on the lucrative field. As he continues to serve as co-director of the CDC-funded Injury Control Research Center for Suicide Prevention at the University of Rochester Medical Center. All so as to breed and spread the suicide prevention hallucination-hypotheses that costs the nations millions. He also works closely with EDC project directors overseeing the Zero Suicide

Institute, the National Action Alliance for Suicide Prevention (Action Alliance), the Suicide Prevention Resource Center (SPRC) and the Children's Safety Network. From 2008 to 2017, this most enterprising man also served as director of the SPRC, run since 2002 by the EDC.

Since the beginning of his suicide mission idea of preventing the unpreventable, Reed has made and is making his living by serving on the executive committee of the Action Alliance. He has testified before the U.S. Congress. He had served on the Kennedy-Satcher Center for Mental Health Equity advisory board. The board was jointly envisioned by former U.S. Representative Patrick J. Kennedy (D-RI) and Dr. David Satcher (1941). Satcher is a four-star admiral in the United States Public Health Service Commissioned Corps, the tenth assistant secretary for health, and the sixteenth surgeon general of the United States Reed is a member of the American Public Health Association, the American Association of Suicidology and the International Association for Suicide Prevention. He speaks frequently, both nationally and internationally, for a fee, of course.

McKeon received his PhD in clinical psychology from the University of Arizona, and a Master of Public Health in health administration from Columbia University (qioprogram. org). He spent the majority of his career in community mental health. In 2019, he was chief of the suicide prevention branch at the Center for Mental Health Services within the Substance Abuse and Mental Health Services Administration (SAMHSA). In that role, he oversaw all branch suicide prevention activities, including the grant programs of the Garrett Lee Smith State/Tribal Youth Suicide Prevention and Campus Suicide Prevention, the National Suicide Prevention Lifeline and the Suicide Prevention Resource Center. He is also part of the suicide-prevention task forces in the Department of Veterans Affairs and Defense. Thus, no effort is spared to advance the suicide prevention fable.

One organization pouring great efforts and monies into preventing the unpreventable is the Central Arizona Programmatic Suicide Deterrent System Project. It is led by two people. Laura Nelson, chief medical officer, Arizona Department of Health Services (ADHS) is one of them. The other is Deputy Director Don Erickson, MA, a licensed mental health therapist and professional counsellor in several U.S. states. He is bureau chief for the Adult and Children System of Care, on its website spewing forth Hogan's words: "Suicide represents a worst case failure in mental health care. We must work to make it a 'never event' in our programs and systems of care."

Erickson began his career in a western Montana outpatient behavioural health clinic, specializing in substance abuse and mental health treatment. In addition to counselling, he has taught graduate-level courses, provided clinical supervision and served on licensing and ethics review boards. He has been recognized as an authority on post-traumatic stress, trauma-informed care and suicide prevention. He worked as the bureau chief of Behavioral Health Services for the State of Arizona, authoring and implementing policies for behavioural health services for infants and toddlers.

The National Child Traumatic Stress Network (NCTSN) was most likely created with Covington's encouragement. In 2000, Congress created it as part of the Children's Health Act. The goal was to raise the standard of care and increase access to services for children and families who experienced or witness traumatic events. It is purportedly committed to changing the course of children's lives by moving scientific discoveries into practice across the U.S. (https://nctsn.org). The NCTSN is administered by the Substance Abuse and Mental Health Services Administration (SAMHSA) and coordinated by the UCLA-Duke University National Center for Child Traumatic Stress. It went from 17 centers in 2001, to 116 funded centers and 170 affiliate centers and individuals working in hospitals, universities and community-based programs in 43 states and the District of Columbia.

An estimated 120,000 children, adolescents and their families annually consult the NCTSN. For them, more than two million professionals have been trained in trauma-informed interventions. And over 10,000 local and state partnerships have been established by NCTSN members to integrate trauma-informed services into all child-serving systems. Those systems include child protective services, health and mental health programs, child welfare, education, residential care, juvenile justice, courts, and programs serving military and veteran families. Another golden-goose bonanza for the mental health industry on the backs of the average herd, being made unhealthier by the hour on purpose, it seems, from the cradle onwards.

Erickson also served as executive sponsor for Arizona's Driving Suicide to Zero program. His work there focused on developing and implementing innovative behavioural health and human service programs.

Nowadays, Erickson is chief administrative officer for the Oregon Department of Human Services. He oversees programs to support the work of the department including:

- facilities
- program integrity
- background check unit
- contracts and procurement
- information support services
- business information systems
- publications and creative services
- payment accuracy and recovery
- imaging and records management services (https://oregon.gov)

As a side hustle, Erickson runs his private clinic, charging somewhere between US$ 125.00 to $150.00 per session. He covers anything and everything in normally-to-be-expected human life experiences, classified as mental disorders. These range from infidelity to self-harming and elder persons disorders (EPD). EPD is a new kid on the block of humans' purported mental diseases, albeit, we read on the Open Path Psychotherapy Collective website, it can become difficult to discern. What is natural in aging, categorized as elderly persons disorders, and what are actual geriatric mental health concerns.

Erickson's specialty, however, is stated as marital and premarital, life transitions, and trauma and PTSD. His own bio is unavailable. He believes in people's capacity and desire for personal growth. But he keeps for himself to identify and implement solutions to issues they wish to change in their lives through dialogue using the rational eclecticism approach. Eclectic therapy, also called integrative therapy, purports to be a model seeking to directly meet clients and their needs. To do so, eclectic therapy draws from multiple therapy techniques in order to select the best treatment for each individual client. It can be viewed as a combination of different therapy approaches, tailored to each specific client.

This is the most lucrative type of therapy for those inclined. Due to its versatility, it allows for a lifelong search of what works and does not. Different approaches are:

- *Brief Eclectic Therapy* (BET). This combination of CBT and psychodynamic therapy focuses on interpreting and processing emotions and thoughts, as well as guilt and shame, said to often occur in a traumatic experience' aftermath. This is the vital process for a genuine PTSD recovery of wiping the slate clean. It is making peace with whatever has occurred and whatever booboos we have committed in our pre-PTSD causing event lives. This part only we can do within ourselves, if we want to make a good job at it, unless we'd love to share our most innermost thoughts and feelings, ideas and pitfalls with complete strangers (choosingtherapy.com).
- *Multimodal Therapy*. This was developed by Arnold A. Lazarus (1932-2013), a South African-born clinical psychologist and researcher specializing in cognitive therapy. He *hypothesized* that most human psychological problems are multifaceted, multi-determined and multilayered. He also hypothesized that comprehensive therapy calls for a careful assessment of clients' behaviour, affect (emotions), sensations (senses), imagery (visualization and imagination), cognition (language-based thinking), interpersonal relationships and drugs/biology (including physical bodies and health). This approach, combined with cognitive therapies like CBT, purportedly helps people become aware of and understand their *distorted thoughts about themselves* and their relationships that cause problems in their lives (https://psychologytoday.com)
- *Transtheoretical Therapy*. This approach was dreamt up around 1983 by two professors. One was professor of psychology and director of the University of Rhode Island's Cancer Prevention Research Center James O. Prochaska (1942–). The other was professor emeritus of psychology at the University of Maryland, Baltimore County (UMBC), (TTM) Carlo C. DiClemente, PhD, ABPP. This approach is said to combine theories about humans' stages of change, levels of change and the process of change. It works from therapists' understanding of how people create positive effective change in their lives to accomplish their goals. Therapists work from there to select techniques from a variety of therapies to help clients grow.
- *Three-Stage Model*. Eclectic therapy's newest kid on the block was developed for therapists by American psychologist Clara E. Hill (1948–). She completed her undergraduate degree in psychology and her master's and doctoral degrees in counselling psychology at Southern Illinois University. She now is a full professor at the University of Maryland Department of Psychology. The first stage is the exploration stage. It is based on Carl Rogers' person-centered therapy. The second is the insight phase, based on psychoanalytic therapy. And the third stage is the action phase based on cognitive behavioural therapy, the famous Pavlovian CBT. Ms. Hill, however, does work with dreams, which speaks highly for her. The American Psychological Association flogs her DVD *Helping Skills in Practice: A Three-Stage Model* for a mere US$ 119.95
- *Cyclical Psychodynamics*. This was developed by Paul Wachtel, PhD, a distinguished professor in the doctoral program in clinical psychology at City

> College and the Graduate Center of the City University of New York. He received his doctorate in clinical psychology from Yale University and is a graduate of the postdoctoral program in psychoanalysis and psychotherapy at New York University. He believed that a strong patient-therapist therapeutic relationship combined with psychodynamic therapy, CBT, systemic therapy and experiential therapy should lead to improvement in clients' emotional experiences and development of new interpersonal relationship skills.

Even we, the so-called laymen, can see from the above, that there are plenty of hypotheses and hallucinations. Indeed, there are more than enough for any psycho-the-rapist to find ways and means to bullshit clients about *cures of the mind* for whoever present themselves and string them along for light-years, insurance paid, of course. British *psychotherapist* Paul Gordon was an early proponent of eclectic therapy. He captured the original essence of it when he described it as seeking to determine, "What treatment, by whom, is the most effective for this individual with that specific problem, under which set of circumstances, and how does it come about?" Gordon worked for many years as a researcher and campaigner in civil liberties and anti-racism. He is also a member of the Philadelphia Association. In his book *Hope of Therapy* (PCCS Books; New ed. Edition, 18 Dec. 2008) he succinctly states the essence of a therapist-patient exercise seemingly forgotten in North America when saying:

> "Therapy is inherently an ethical endeavour, both in the sense that the therapist is called upon to be responsible to and for the Other who seeks help, and in the sense that it is inevitably bound up with ideas about how we should live and how we should treat one another. People suffer emotionally because of their experiences in the world, and it is one task of the therapist to address this experience to help people make sense of it, to come to terms with it. This endeavour takes place within a particular form of time and space whose function is to make possible a particular kind of conversation with no predetermined limits or ends. As such, it has much to learn from other forms of art and craft, such as painting and the visual arts, diction and poetry...therapy inevitably carries with it an idea of hope, hope both for the individual who seeks help and hope for a better world. In this sense it is...part of the great unfinished, indeed unfinishable, project of the Enlightenment and humanism, that we can be more truthful to ourselves and therefor more free... Art can flourish only if it is free, but this freedom is as much to do with free-spiritness, an attitude of mind, a position on the part of the artist, as it is [has??] to do with a context. (Great art has always managed to emerge from the darkest of times). (https://paulgordonpsychotherapy.co.uk; (Gordon, Paul: *The Hope of Therapy*; PCCS Books; New ed. edition (18 Dec. 2008))."

A mental health professional acknowledging humans as spiritual entities rather than animals? How refreshing! But then, Gordon is part of the Philadelphia Association founded by Scottish psychiatrist R.D. Laing. At the time, he was his learned society's enfant terrible by challenging the established ways of thinking about treating mental distress. Discussed at length in *Fallacy 1*, Laing's, and consequently Gordon's, approach to psychotherapy was and is unique in Britain and the world. Gordon works privately from his home with individuals and couples, often for reduced fees. He is also house therapist to one of the Philadelphia Association's community houses (freepsychotherapynetwork.com). Run this idea about mental health therapy by average, self-respecting American psycho-the-rapists and they'll choke at the proposal. They know their practices would diminish due to patient recovery, were they to engage in such humane endeavour. But I digress.

We now understand the heart of eclectic therapy applied by Erickson to his patients, including those he suspects of being suicidal. It involves first viewing each client as a unique person with specific problems. One then selects research-based techniques from across the different types of therapy hallucinated into being by previous mental health aficionados since Freud et al. The foundation and success of the eclectic therapeutic process is based on the relationship between client and counsellor. Through this relationship, the therapist uses different techniques at different stages, customized for the individual client and his or her difficulties. These determined between therapist and patient in accordance with the patient's problems, motivations and desires.

The eclectic therapy thus wildly differs from the NC *for* PTSD-recommended and VA et al.-applied PTSD pharmacotherapy, where a. relationship between client and counsellor is usually unheard of. In eclectic therapy, the counselor's duty is to learn about the multiple facets of each client's life, including their thoughts, feelings, behaviours and relationships. WCB, employer-engaged psychotherapists, the NC *for* PTSD and similarly engaged mental health practitioners all joyously ignore, as it is too time-consuming and thus unprofitable. They then apply CBT, the cognitive behavioural therapy that aims to alter a client's mind without the patient's being aware that that is what's actually being done. Together with pharmacotherapy, it is slotted for failure from the get-go. The usually prescribed mind-altering pharmaceutical drugs, together with the CBT brainwashing, destroy all possibility of success for reaching a harmonious and balanced mental state of mind, at least for genuine PTSD journeyers, the foundation of the ability to live a purpose-driven life.

How successful Erickson is in his eclectic therapy practice we do not know. He remains deeply involved in preventing the unpreventable, though. Indeed, in 2012, he was encouraged by the National Council of State Governments (CSG) annual award for Innovation, Excellence and Ingenuity. It was awarded to him for his role in creating and implementing a statewide suicide prevention program, doubtlessly in preparation for COVID-19. Among other ideas, it showed what would lead the unpreventable to fruition. IT also showed how dramatic progress could be made by specialty health plans and systems focusing on those of the population with serious mental illness (SMI) and severe emotional disturbance (SED), highest at risk to kill themselves. The CSG, by the way, began presenting Innovations Awards in 1986. It wanted to bring greater visibility to exemplary state programs and to facilitate the transfer of those successful experiences to other states.

By 2020, Erickson had succeeded in bringing suicide training to the workplace. This enabled every employee to watch and accuse the other of being suicidal, with the consequences for the individual to follow. If this training was offered to physicians, as well, is unknown. Let's not forget that a recent meta-analysis published in the journal *Suicide and Life-Threatening Behavior* and spanning 70,368 physicians found the prevalence of suicide-related behaviors higher among them than in the general population. This, we are told, was attributable to physicians' high rates of depression and work burnout, as well as their higher awareness about mental health problems and suicide prevention (Meta-Analysis Finds 'Relatively High' Rate of Suicidal Behaviors Among Physicians; psychcongress.com, Oct. 2020).

Now, if it were due to their knowledge of suicide prevention, one should think they should, with ease, be able to circumnavigate their suicidal moods and desire to kill themselves, right? However, despite their knowledge, they commit the deed, which shoots Covington et al.'s suicide prevention hallucinations right out of the sky, revealing the mental health industry's super lucrative farce and criminal act against humanity.

It includes Erickson's 2012 Suicide Care in Systems developed by the Clinical Care & Intervention Task Force in unison with Covington and Hogan in 2011. It was presented as the *SUICIDE CARE IN SYSTEMS FRAMEWORK: A Report to: National Action Alliance for Suicide Prevention Executive Committee* from the Clinical Care and Intervention Task Force co-leads David Covington of Magellan Health Services and Michael Hogan of New York State Office of Mental Health in 2011 (theactionalliance.org). It purportedly outlines the best and most promising practices for preventing suicide in healthcare settings. It formed the road map for the Zero Suicide in Healthcare initiative to prevent all future suicides worldwide, and encompasses the following aspirations:

The task force focused its environmental scan on a number of programs that had garnered attention for their approaches and positive outcomes to suicide prevention. These included:

- the Henry Ford Health System
- the National Suicide Prevention Lifeline
- the Air Force Suicide Prevention Program
- the Central Arizona Programmatic Suicide Deterrent System Project

In each of these initiatives, dramatic successes are said to have been achieved in reducing suicide attempts and deaths. Cost reductions associated with unnecessary hospital and emergency department care were also reported (theactionalliance.org). Most importantly, they had shown they could save lives. In reviewing these initiatives, the Task Force found three critical factors common to all that led to their remarkable successes. These were:

- Core values - the belief and commitment that suicide can be eliminated in a population under care (boundaried population), by better service access and quality and through continuous improvement (rendering suicide a "never event" for these populations);
- Systems management -systematic steps across systems of care to create a culture that no longer finds suicide acceptable, setting aggressive but achievable goals to eliminate suicide attempts and deaths among members, and organizing service delivery and support accordingly;
- Evidence-based clinical care practice -a focus on productive patient/staff interactions delivered through the system of care. These methods (e.g., standardized risk stratification, targeted evidence-based clinical interventions, accessibility, follow-up and engagement and education of patients, families and healthcare professionals) achieve results.

Overall cost reductions arose from unnecessary hospital and emergency department care.

Now, before reading further, please understand that the suicide prevention hallucination is aimed at brainwashing the herd into believing that it is mentally ill and at risk of falling into a suicidal mood at any moment. Why would they otherwise donate, eh? That mental health deteriorates in accordance with the amount and types of pharmaceutical drugs administered, overall nutrition, exercise and lifestyle is kept out of the equation. It would be detrimental to the craft's earnings, donations and tax reductions to those running these non-profit organizations

With that in mind, note the perpetually made imprints of suicide risk. These come instead of imprints made through educating the public about the truth of the matter. That truth is that less than 800,000 out of a population of eight billion worldwide take to killing themselves. That truth is that they will succeed, regardless of prevention or no prevention, as it might just be in their life's plan of experiences, for all we know. The task-force's recommendation to prevent the unpreventable are as follows:

> "*Recommendation 1:* The U.S. Department of Health and Human Services (DHHS) should spearhead two public-private task forces to catalyze change strategies recommended in this report. To effectuate change requires that health and behavioral health organizations and practitioners embrace a zero suicide goal and manage operations to achieve it. Change also requires that clinicians and caregivers working with suicidal persons have the knowledge and skill sets to engage persons in care successfully and to deliver effective services." (https://theactionalliance.org/sites/default/files/clinicalcareinterventionreport.pdf)

This, of course, assures a *never-ending stream of income for all involved in the suicide prevention field*. Because the challenge may be great for some [unnamed] organizations, we read, it will be important to offer strategies to motivate, support and sustain systemic improvements. That in itself will keep the mental health craft busy and employed for centuries, while their mind manipulation and drug practices turn the world into one huge insane asylum. To facilitate the process, this idea found favour:

> "*Recommendation 1A*: DHHS should convene a task force charged with identifying and implementing strategies to mobilize and facilitate public and behavioral health organizational change, including collaborations among organizations to promote continuity of care for persons at risk of suicide."

Already knowing, that suicide prevention is impossible, Bernays's successors in the advertising industry were to be engaged. They would help the herd understand that it is at risk of killing themselves at any given moment. The herd would therefore have to interact with mental health practitioners to save them from such fate and alleviate their ever-present fear of dying.

> "*Recommendation 1B*: DHHS should convene a task force charged with incorporating suicide detection, risk formulation and prevention in the preparatory training of clinicians across the country. In talking to national experts, the Task Force heard that many, if not most, clinicians are insufficiently prepared to address

suicide risk across the land. The federally convened task force should serve as the engine for appropriately embedding suicide prevention education into clinical training, beginning at college and graduate school levels. While the curricula will differ across disciplines, certain core principles of detection and care should be incorporated. The effort should focus on how to incorporate curricula within existing preparatory training programs.

"*Recommendation 2*: State suicide prevention lead agencies, other relevant state agencies, and key stakeholders (e.g., health, mental health, addiction services, child serving, aging or social services agencies) should consider incorporating strategies to promote suicide as a never event within state health and behavioral health organizations as one critical element for updating or advancing their state plans."

And then we find: "*Core Values: Beliefs and Attitudes-The Foundation for Eliminating Suicide Deaths and Attempts.* The Task Force has identified five critical elements that it believes are instrumental for public and behavioural health organizations to adopt and adapt in order to implement suicide prevention effectively" reading as follows, interspersed with my remarks in brackets:

1. *Leadership leading to cultural transformation* – (in league with Freud and friends Making the American Mind. To achieve the goal,) Organizational leadership must articulate and infuse (into the population at large through all means possible, including the workplace), the fundamental tenet that a suicide event (attempt or death) is an unacceptable outcome of its care (albeit it is the sole fault of the one committing suicide) and build a culture (a human mindset eager to believe that suicidal ideation is a normal human endeavor) and that strives to make suicide a "never event," (namely, prevent the unpreventable) is a noble cause of the mental health cabal).
2. *Continuity of Care and Shared Service Responsibility* – Caring for suicidal persons requires that the suicidal risk be addressed directly, not merely as a symptom of an underlying disease. That care will most likely require multiple levels of services in a team environment (and everybody must watch everybody else, regardless of mental states of mind, like in the Russian Cancer wards of Solzynitzyn's days). Discharge decisions from one level of care (e.g., hospital care) must incorporate linkages to other necessary levels of care (e.g., intensive outpatient, private therapist, (thus combined with pharmaco therapy destroying the brain. Get the herd into a perpetual SOMA state). Organizations must recognize, accept, and implement shared service responsibilities both among various clinical staff within the organization and among providers in the larger community (so all actions can be streamlined).
3. *Immediate Access to Care for All Persons in Suicidal Crisis* – Because many persons seek care only when they are in crisis, behavioral health systems must provide 24-hour, 7-day a week availability to individuals trained in assessment, supportive counseling and intervention. Crisis hotlines, online crisis chat/intervention services, self-help tools, crisis outreach

teams and other services can ensure that individuals can obtain help when they need it - eliminating barriers related to cost, distance, and stigma.(make humans believe they are mentally deficient and must seek help to save their sanity).

4. *Productive Interactions between Persons at Risk and Persons Providing Care* - Positive health and behavioral health outcomes are partly dependent on a functional relationship between the person requiring help and the persons delivering help (whom one of course has never met before). This assistance should respect the cultural preferences and values of the individuals as much as possible (In other words, if the mother tongue is Swahili, with whatever religious background, the same should be provided to the assistance seeker to absolve ideas of suicide) Trusting therapeutic alliances are fundamental to reducing suicide risk and promoting recovery and wellness (we read, and of course, they are, in the task force's hallucinations to be achieved through an intimate relationship on the crisis line, when it can't even be established between the average psychiatrist or psychologist for genuine PTSD journeyers). Such alliances (we hear) are most productive when the care is collaborative, where the client is actively engaged in making choices that will keep him/her safe (right in the middle of a crisis with a crisis worker?), and when the clinician feels confident that he/she has the training and skills to support the client's safety and treat the suicide risk And yes, the systematic perversion of the human mind into believing it is suicidal for billions of dollars goes on.
5. *Evaluate Performance and Use for Quality Improvement* - Setting a goal of zero suicides (of preventing the unpreventable) and managing a system of care to achieve that goal (requiring a vast number of mental-health-trained humans to prevent the unpreventable) requires (preferably non-profit) organizations (to suck on the public's tit) to evaluate performance (Whose? Each other's?) rigorously and to use untoward events (False flag?) as opportunities to improve their capacity (Which ones?) to save lives at risk. Thus:

Systems Management: Implementation and Action for Care Excellence—To achieve the (illusory) goal of zero suicides (for the 55,000 annual suicide of approximately 35 million Canadians and Americans) will require countless managerial decisions (assuring lucrative jobs)—both (for) the major policy shifts and the details of patient care management. In this context, the Task Force recommends three major managerial areas to guide the organization of effective service delivery.

1. *Policies and Procedures* - All health and behavioral health organizations should have specific written policies and procedures focused on the detection and response to persons presenting for care with suicide risk (the Suicide Manifesto). Staff must be trained on how to employ the policies and procedures, with regular (e.g., annual) scheduled refreshers.
2. *Collaboration and Communication* - Responding to suicide risk should be premised on collaborative care characterized by direct and open communication with persons at risk of suicide and timely and effective

communication patterns with all personnel who are collaborating in the person's care (to be administered, wanted or unwanted).

3. *Trained and Skilled Work Force* - Public health and behavioral health organizations should assure that staff working with persons with suicide risk have been appropriately trained and possess requisite (unclarified) skills. (Read *Cancer Ward* by Aleksandr Solzhenitsyn).

Evidence-Based Clinical Care Practice: Comprehensive Quality Care to Save Lives - While research has shown that over 90 percent of persons who die by suicide had a diagnosable mental health disorder and/or substance use disorder, empirical research has shown that it is insufficient to treat only the mental disorder. In contrast, the extant (undocumented) *literature* does show that targeting and treating suicidal ideation and behaviors, independent of diagnosis, hold the greatest promise for care of suicidal risk. It is vital that direct intervention and treatment be provided for potential suicidality (harboring in every human, if on psychotropic drugs and if pushed far enough, ergo Nietzsche's comment: "The thought of suicide is a great consolation; by means of it one gets successfully through many a bad night." (*Beyond Good and Evil*, p. 157)).

Care for persons at risk of suicide should be person-centered, where their personal needs, wishes, values, and resources become the foundation of developing a plan for their continuing care and safety (The state takes control of it all.). Where (we deem it) appropriate and practical, families and significant others should be engaged and empowered as well. Cultural values and preferences should be respected as much as possible (but are not a necessity, as it was completely impractical in Gulags and will be so in FEMA camps. However,) The Task Force has identified the following four components of care (for those we deem suicidal).

1. *Screening and Suicide Risk Assessment* - Universal screening for suicide risk should be a universal part of Primary Care, Hospital Care (especially emergency department care), Behavioral Health Care, and Crisis Response settings (e.g., help lines, mobile teams, first responders, crisis chat services), (the more the merrier, in case humanity goes wild *en masse*). Any person who screens positive for possible suicide risk (done by any layperson for the joy of it or a test to be implemented in the same style as COVID 19 and a complete hoax) should be formally assessed (by a psychiatrist, most likely) for suicidal ideation (the result depending on the assessor's mood of the day), plans (for what?), availability of means (for what?), presence of acute risk factors (including history of suicide attempts), and level of risk (all undeterminable, as most people killing themselves saw a physician within the last seven days of their lives, but good for getting rid of deplorables).
2. *Intervening to increase coping to ensure safety* - All persons identified as at risk of suicide by primary care practices and clinics, hospitals (esp. emergency departments), behavioral health organizations and crisis services should have a collaboratively designed safety plan prior to release from care. This should include inquiring about means access and planning to restrict access to lethal means (balanced with respect to other obligations, including legal and ethical requirements under federal and state laws). (See above)

3. *Treating and caring for persons at-risk of suicide* - Treatment and support of persons with suicide risk should be carried out in the least restrictive setting using research-guided practice techniques. (Makes me wonder if any of these characters ever associated with suicidal individuals? Those who threaten with suicide as good as never kill themselves. They lack the guts and just want attention. Those who carry through never say a word in advance. They just go ahead. That is why it is unpreventable.)
4. *Follow Up* - Persons with suicidal risk leaving intervention and care settings should receive follow-up contact from the provider or caregiver (Meaning once you are in their clutches, you will never have another moment of peace. The insanity of the scam is breathtaking, and you still want to kill yourself rather than go on the barricade to stop these mental health bastards, these experts in destroying human life and happiness? No wonder suicide is rampant among them! Their conscience is begging them to end it all, as they cannot face themselves any longer.)

Visionary Covington et al. compiled the above in 2011. He had served as chief of adult services for Magellan Health Services of Arizona, an industry leader in behavioral healthcare management. He had also served on the executive committee of the National Alliance for Suicide Prevention. In 2009, he challenged the 10 largest American behavioural health providers to eliminate suicide for those enrolled in the Regional Behavioral Health Authority (RBHA) (Magellan Seeks to Reduce Suicide Deaths Through Groundbreaking Prevention Initiative; Magellan Health 2010).

As a first step, the Magellan suicide committee surveyed almost 1,700 case managers, clinicians, nurses and physicians. It created a baseline assessment of their confidence and skills in engaging in suicide prevention and intervention with those they deemed to be at risk to kill themselves. Fewer than half of respondents felt they had the training, skills and supports to help people with suicidal desire or intent. Based on this, the committee managed to train more than 1,200 mental health workers in suicide prevention techniques in 2010. Its *Living Works' Applied Suicide Intervention Skills Training*, known as ASIST, gave them two days of training. The program is said to have dramatically improved mental health workers' confidence in engaging with those deemed to be at risk of suicide. Already then, Magellan had created more than 30 ASIST master trainers (magellanhealth.com). What it did for those they identify with suicidal ideation is unknown. Said Covington:

> "The most important first step is to be able to talk openly and directly about suicide. ASIST is a proven, evidence-based training that empowers staff not only to better detect and react to the warning signs of suicide, but also to make connections with those who may need help but may have difficulty talking about their suicidal thoughts. By ensuring that all community health center staff is trained to help prevent the immediate risk of suicide, we create a seamless safety net that should *ultimately* lead to a reduction in suicide rates among those at risk." (italics mine)

"Ultimately" is the word, and ultimately can be, and in this case most likely is, when hell freezes over, pigs sprout wings or both. Suicide is unpreventable, and he knows it. In addition to ASIST training, Magellan sponsors quarterly educational webinars focused on the latest research on suicide. It also meets regularly with the suicide volunteer steering committee, according to U.S. law. It gets a minimum of approximately US$70,000.00 for its voluntarily rendered service to prevent the unpreventable, to share its suicide prevention successes and identify any opportunities for further indoctrination it might stumble upon for profit.

Those who had also participated in Covington's ACT—*Acknowledge, Care, Tell*—program after completing ASIST, could expect to see a 38% reduction in suicide deaths and a decrease in hospitalization—for suicide attempts, we assume. ACT's essential elements include:

- Comprehensive Counselling and Mental Health (CMHC) staff training to move suicide care from specialty referral to core mission;
- Suicide attempt survivor leadership and support, through participation in design and implementation of peer support groups;
- Active engagement of family in the treatment process, "the new normal," and community integration and support; and
- Development of race and ethnicity best practices for suicide care

It is easy to see, that, with it another cash cow similar to that of PTSD, or almost in conjunction with it, has been created. And while it ACT was born in the early 2010's, Reed, simultaneously, spearheaded the launch of the National Action Alliance for Suicide Prevention. This, a public-private partnership to purportedly advances the National Strategy for Suicide Prevention in Washington, DC, with U.S. secretaries of Defense and Health and Human Services as keynote speakers. The Alliance With government sanction, the Alliance then proceeded to launched more than a dozen specialty suicide task forces. These included including the Clinical Care & Intervention Task Force. O, which one year later, it published the Suicide Care in Systems Framework, and formed the Zero Suicide in Healthcare foundation.

Not only that, Reed led the 2012 revision of the U.S. 2001 National Strategy for Suicide Prevention in partnership with Richard McKeon. He added the following:

> *Goal 8. Promote suicide prevention as a core component of health care services*
>
> 8.1. Promote the adoption of "zero suicides" as an aspirational goal by health care and community support systems that provide services and support to defined patient populatesion (sprc.org).

Reed is now Suicide Prevention Resource Center director, as well as an Educational Development Center (EDC) senior vice president for practice leadership. He has a PhD in health-related sciences, with an emphasis in gerontology, from the Virginia Commonwealth University. He also has and an MSW from the Baltimore-based University of Maryland. At EDC, he directs leadership efforts and leads the suicide prevention practice leader domain This, which includes serving as co-director with partners at the University of Rochester Medical Center for the CDC-*funded*—speak Fauci-funded—Injury Control Research Center for Suicide Prevention. He also works closely with those EDC project directors overseeing:

- the Zero Suicide Institute
- the Children's Safety Network

- the Suicide Prevention Resource Center (SPRC)
- the National Action Alliance for Suicide Prevention (Action Alliance)

From 2008 to 2017, he also served as SPRC director, which EDC has operated since 2002 (https://edc.org/jerry-reed).

Reed together with Covington hosted the first Zero Suicide International Summit in Oxford, UK, in 2014. Those who travelled to the UK explicitly for the event included:

- Jan Mokkenstorm and the team from 113 Online Foundation: Marijke Josephus Jitta, Barbara Stringer, Wendela Termeulen and Hetty Vromen (Netherlands) (davidwcovington.com).
- CEO Elsbeth de Ruijter from the parent company of 113Online, GGZinGeest
- Fergus Cumiskey, managing director, from Contact Northern Ireland, and Barry McGale, Suicide Prevention Liaison, Western Health & Social Care Trust (United Kingdom)
- Steve Duffy, clinical director, from Canterbury District Health Board in Christchurch (New Zealand)
- Becky Stoll and Jennifer Lockman from Centerstone America
- Jerry Reed from the National Action Alliance for Suicide Prevention and Suicide Prevention Resource Center (SPRC) (United States)

They were led by Julie Kerry and Aarti Chapman from the British National Health Service (NHS) and suicide prevention advocate Professor Keith Hawton from Oxford University. But before that happened, however, Covington and Hogan had not been dormant, either. In 2010they partnered with the National Action Alliance task force to publish the Suicide Care in Systems Framework and naming it Zero Suicide.

They presented it as a Transformational Framework for Health and Behavioral Health Care Systems. They claimed that suicide for people under its care was preventable. By 2015, they had given more than 100 presentations in multiple countries, spreading Zero's "transformative" message. That in turn lead to the *International Declaration for Better Healthcare: Zero Suicide*. This declaration and social movement was accepted as the gospel by 50 government policy makers and healthcare providers from 13 countries. They convened at Zero's 2015 conference in Atlanta to address its aspirational goal of zero suicide in healthcare. In fact, however, zero is designed to coral humanity into the belief of being perpetually mental-health deficient and suicidal. Thus, humanity would be in need of psycho-the-rapists' assistance from the cradle to the grave if wanting to live, never mind thrive. It is that simple.

The outcome? It depends on us. Awareness is half the battle won. Throw out the TV and start thinking for yourself. Part of guarding against the mental health industry's manufactured illusion of being suicidal, when nothing could be further from the truth is to research the issue rather than swallow it as the gospel.

If Covington, the self-proclaimed expert on suicide, himself ever suffered suicidal ideation is unknown. And if he did not, what propelled him into elevating it to a national crisis? He must have known that David Rosen conducted a psychiatric study in 1975 of six people who were known to have survived jumps from the Bridge. His analysis was the first to use this specific control group—an exotic breed, considering a plunge from the Golden

Gate is 98% fatal. It would lead a few decades later to the publication of *Transforming Depression: Healing the Soul Through Creativity*. In this groundbreaking book, Rosen offers depressed people, their families and therapists a lifesaving course in healing the soul through creativity transforming depression and its powerful pull toward suicide into a meaningful alternative. Having dealt with depression in his own life, Rosen shows that when people learn to confront the rich images and symbols that emerge from their struggles, they can turn their despair into a fountain of creative energy.

Asclepius, from an ivory diptych, 5th century AD; in the Liverpool City Museum, England
The Bridgeman Art Library/Art Resource, New York

In other words, he refutes Covington's and cohorts loving insistence on applying pharmacotherapy, the Cognitive Behavioral and mind-altering pharmaceutical drug therapy, which deadly to body and soul. Instead, Rosen seems to apply the Asclepius' distinct "Heal Thy Self" principles so beneficial to both body and mind, discussed in detail in *Fallacy I*. This Greco-Roman god of medicine is the son of Apollo. He is the god of healing, truth and prophecy, described by Homer in the *Iliad* as a skilful physician and the father of two Greek doctors at Troy. He is frequently shown standing dressed in a long cloak with bare breast and a staff with a serpent coiled around it. This staff is the only true symbol of medicine. A similar but unrelated emblem is the caduceus, a rod or staff framed by two intertwined snakes and topped by two wings. It is frequently used as a medical emblem, but is without medical relevance, since it represents the magic wand of Hermes. (britannica.com).

One of Aesclepius' healing temples, located close to Pergamum, Turkey, still shows facilities for drinking water with special properties. IT also features water for bathing, gymnasia, space for rituals and special rooms for dreaming. During these dreams, patients would become aware of what they needed to do to cure themselves of their ailments. They would report the dreams to priests, who then prescribed cures based on their interpretation of the dreams. Dogs and nonvenomous snakes (Aesculapian snakes) were an essential part of the healing process. In fact, both dogs and snakes were present in many of the temples.

Image "Hermes/Mercury" by Gordon Johnson from Pixabay

It is these Aesculapian serpents seen in the "staff of Asclepius," a universal sign for medicine. These are not the same as the snakes in the Caduceus. Those represent Hermes, the god of communication, transportation, and commerce. Greek mythology also depicts Hermes as a clever trickster sent out on missions by Zeus and other Olympian gods to do their dirty work. Thus, Hermes symbolizes the Mercurial adaptability of the mind, which must survive by living by its wits and ingenuity (https://greekmedicine.net).

Asclepius' staff has only one snake entwined around it, which symbolizes healing, regeneration and the consummate skill of the medical art. Hermes' Caduceus, with its two intertwined snakes, symbolizes the human spinal column. This central conduit for the Psychic Force, or nerve energy, animates all organs and members of the body. The places where the snakes cross represent the spinal energy centers or chakras of the subtle body. They also represent the need for balance, or homeostasis, for optimum health maintenance and disease prevention.

Clearly, then, a focus on the spiritual side of healing is an ancient concept ignored entirely in allopathic medicine and the mental health industry. There alone, all genuine PTSD healing modalities fail, as healing can take place only by spiritual means. This, however, has been vigorously supressed since the mid 1850s for what? To lead PTSD experiencers and humanity into abysmal slavery by ruining their body and stealing their souls with mind-altering pharmaceutical drugging leading to suicidal ideation?

Richard H. Seiden, PhD, earned his MPH at the University of California at Berkeley. In 1971, he wanted to find out what happened to 515 people who came to the Golden Gate Bridge to die within the previous 35 years, but who were stopped by California Highway Patrol officers (seattlefriends.org). The Golden Gate Bridge is currently the number one suicide location in the world. From its opening in 1937 to 1978, 625 suicide deaths were officially reported, and perhaps more than 200 others have gone unseen and unreported. Proposals to build a hardware anti-suicide barrier have been challenged with the untested contention that "they'll just go someplace else." Seiden's research tested the contention by describing and evaluating the long-term mortality-experience of the 515 people. He also looked at a comparison group of 184 people who made no bridge-suicide attempts during 1956-57 and were treated at the emergency room of a large metropolitan hospital and were also followed through the close of 1971.

Results of the follow up study were directed toward answering the important question: "Will a person who is prevented from suicide in one location inexorably tend to attempt and commit suicide elsewhere? Seiden published the results in "Where Are They Now?: A Follow-up Study of Suicide Attempters from the Golden Gate Bridge." (speakingofsuicide.com). What he found is a remarkable testament to the fact that a suicidal crisis is often – very often – temporary. Of the 515 people whose attempt was interrupted, only 35 died by suicide in the years to come. Taking into account suicides that might have been missed by researchers, Seiden found that 90% of the people who tried to jump off the Golden Gate Bridge did not go on to die by suicide.

This research, albeit 35 years old, still seems to hold true. Even though a prior suicide attempt dramatically increases the risk for future suicide, studies do demonstrate that most who survive a suicide attempt do not go on to die by suicide:

- A study of 224 people who attempted suicide in Finland and were treated at a healthcare facility found that just eight percent died by suicide within 12 years.
- Researchers in Sweden followed 34,219 people who were hospitalized following an act of intentional self-harm. During three to nine years of follow-up, 3.5% died by suicide.
- One study followed 100 people who had survived a suicide attempt by overdose. At the end of the 37-year follow up, 13% had died by suicide. (This study's mortality rate is higher than others, almost certainly because of the long follow-up period and the serious nature of the attempt, which warranted admission to a hospital.)
- Overall, a recent review of 177 research studies around the world found that four percent of people who survived intentionally hurting or poisoning themselves went on to die by suicide within 10 years.

These findings confound the usual assumptions, that many suicides are inevitable. In 2014, however, Zero Suicide task force member and Princeton graduate Thomas Joiner waded into the debate. He had received his PhD in Clinical Psychology from the University of Texas at Austin and is professor in the Department of Psychology at Florida State University. He argued that *all* suicides around the entire world were preventable, even up until the last moment. Really? Until the very last moment? Who was present at this very last moment to prevent it, though, and why wait until the very last moment to do so, eh? In clinical trials, perhaps, considering the mental health industry's overall perversion? Could the empirically proven lack of repeat performances of attempted suicides rather occur for a different reason? Kevin Hines survived the 200-foot jump off the Golden Gate Bridge, a plunge considered 98% fatal. Here is what he said:

> "The very second I let go, I knew I had made a big mistake. There was a millisecond of free fall. In that instant, I thought, what have I just done? I don't want to die. God, please save me.""

Throwing himself headfirst over the bridge railing, he fell 220 feet into San Francisco Bay, while his body rotated so that he landed in a sitting position, taking the impact in his legs and up through his back when hitting the water. (kevinhinesstory.com). He now lives as a suicide prevention advocate. In consideration of the above statistic, should we, what could we, deduce from Hines's statement? Maybe the vast majority of suicides and suicide attempt survivors regardless of culture, religion, gender, nationality and class have the same realization. Perhaps they are therefore disinclined to repeat their suicidal performance if unsuccessful.

Richard T. McKeon, PhD, M.P.H., now the chief, Suicide Prevention Branch, Center for Mental Health Services, Substance Abuse and Mental Health Services Administration, had organized the task force that published the Suicide Care in Systems Framework, with Covington and Hogan co-leading the effort. In 2018, he expressed this on suicide prevention:

> "This doesn't mean a family has the power to stop it, nor that even a clinician, who has a duty to care, has the power to stop it under any circumstances. Some

> of it is random. We mean that no suicide is fated. None are pre-destined. Until the person actually takes a final lethal act, there is still hope."

And, of course, more data is needed. Joiner and other researchers in the field want to make a living by seeking empirical, scientific, first evidence proving the unpreventable as faulty. This despite the fact that, as a public health and quality-of-care matter, the evidence is already in.

In their 2019 Psychiatric Times article "Zero Suicide: The Dogged Pursuit of Perfection in Health Care", Covington and Hogan say:

> "Together, we can, and must, do this. It is our hope that Zero Suicide motivates health care and other leaders to move from half measures to full measures in suicide prevention and better health care,"

Nice. With McKeon's help, declaring all of us to be mentally deficient and in need of suicide watch 24/7 seems to be next on the agenda. It should be an easy task for them, with mask-wearing creating irreparable brain damage, anoxic tendencies, lung cancer, pneumonia, and, due to the associated stressors of no work, no social life and no exercise, suicidal ideation should be jumping sky high.

At least that's the conclusion Joiner already reached in 2005, when he published "The Interpersonal-Psychological Theory of Suicidal Behavior: Current Empirical Status" (*Psychological Science Agenda*, apa.org). The article proposes that a person will die by suicide only when s/he has both the desire to die by suicide and the ability to follow through with it. Brilliant, eh? So, how does the desire to die develop in the first place? Joiner tells us that, according to theory, when people hold two specific psychological states in their minds simultaneously, and do it for long enough, they develop the desire for death. These two psychological states are classified in his jargon as "perceived burdensomeness" and "a sense of low belongingness or social alienation". Really? Is that why the media relentlessly bombards us with a multitude of cognitive dissonance, creating views on a multitude of topics, including COVID-19 in all its aspects?

Regarding the capability for suicide, Joiner tells us that self-preservation is a powerful enough instinct that few can overcome it by force of will. The few who can have developed a fearlessness of pain, injury and death. According to the theory, they acquired this by repeatedly experiencing painful and otherwise provocative events. These, we read, often include previous self-injury, repeated accidental injuries or numerous physical fights. Or they might come in occupations such as physician or front-line soldier, in which exposure to pain and injury, either directly or vicariously, is common. Really? Nothing about trauma? Nothing about the emotional consequences of being exposed to or having committed atrocious crimes against another or a multitude of other human beings? Nothing about genuine PTSD-causing events beyond the realm of normally-to-be-expected human experiences? Nothing about these emotional upheavals and suicidal ideation, in particular when combined with mind-altering drugs? Nothing about the soul?

No. Nothing.

We are viewed as soulless cattle or as machines and treated accordingly by the mental health industry, if we allow it. It is that simple!

And think about it. These suicide theories are dished out to the world mostly by people who have been spoon-fed throughout their lives! Take McKeon, for example. He is, in essence, the instigator and head honcho of the whole suicide prevention advertisement agenda. This man received, at the dawn of time, his PhD in clinical psychology from the University of Arizona and a Master of Public Health in health administration from Columbia University. He spent his career in cushy jobs in the community mental health field before hallucinating himself into the suicide prevention idea for fame and fortune. With his connections and knowing the aim of the game, he became Branch Chief for Suicide Prevention at the Substance Abuse and Mental Health Services Administration (SAMHSA) in 2010. Since then, he promoted himself to chief of the suicide prevention branch at the Center for Mental Health Services within SAMHSA. He is overseeing government grant distribution to all branch suicide prevention activities. Among these are:

- the Garrett Lee Smith State/Tribal Youth Suicide Prevention and Campus Suicide Prevention grant programs
- the National Suicide Prevention Lifeline
- the Suicide Prevention Resource Center.

Fauci allots the amount annually allotted, dictating McKeon's livelihood. See, it all stays in the family!

McKeon also became part of the suicide-prevention task forces in the Department of Veterans Affairs and in the Department of Defense.

And Zero Suicide takes it a step further nowadays, to assure you do not die alone. Their new motto is: "Healthcare that believes no one should die alone and in despair." Did these guys predict a drastic increase in suicides under the conditions imposed on the public due to COVID-19 and described by Joiner in 2005. Did they anticipate the possibility to make mega bucks that a pandemic might hand the mental health industry?

Be it as it may, the scheme does have its opposition. "Is it rational to pursue zero suicide among patients in health care?" asked Dutch psychiatrist J.K. Mokkenstorm (1962-2019) and his team of researchers in 2017. Mokkenstorm is CEO and founder of 113 Suicide Prevention lifeline in the Netherlands. (His team and he reviewed Zero Suicide's emerging approach to suicide prevention, that of embracing the aspirational goal of zero suicides among patients treated in U.S. healthcare systems or organizations. In their opinion, this approach evoked objections and concerns (J.K. Mokkenstorm et al; researchgate.net). A most important figurehead in the global suicide agenda, Mokkenstorm should know (Renske Gilissen and Ad Kerkhof: In Memoriam: Dr. Jan Mokkenstorm (1962–2019); *The Journal of Crisis and Suicide Prevention*, 2019). After all, he is credited with having broken the taboo on suicide by sharing his personal story of suicidality. In fact, he titled his 2019 PhD thesis, *On the road to zero suicides: Implementation studies*, thereby indicating that he is still in recovery. He also confirms the hypothesis that those perpetually, emotionally struggling with life and living are the ones most likely to enter the mental health field. Who else would, eh?

What is most interesting for genuine PTSD experiencers about Mokkenstorm, however, is the timing of his death. The moment he pulled himself together enough to find out why he perpetually wanted to kill himself, he entered his recovery, as manifested by his 2019

PhD thesis. That recovery was interrupted by death that same year. Even though we are told nothing about his life otherwise, we deduce that something in it must have propelled him onto the road of suicidal ideation, as few or any of us are born with it in mind. Thus, it must have been a personal experience that propelled him onto the self-education path. By looking to help himself, he became a leader in "systematizing hope, support and healing for individuals suffering from suicidal thoughts," an effort he began in the late 1900s.

In 2009, McKeon crafted his Suicide Care in Systems Framework and engaged Covington and Hogan to lead its grand style global advertisement campaign. At virtually the same time, Mokkenstorm founded 113 Suicide Prevention. It is now the Netherland's leading suicide prevention agency for its population of 17 million, of which approximately 1800 annually kill themselves (113.nl). Of these, 40% were treated by mental healthcare institutions (MHIs). Twenty-four of those collectively reported that 73% of patient suicides in 2015 had received an educational outreach intervention by an [unnamed] national center of expertise (Jan Mokkenstorm et al: Suicide Prevention Guideline Implementation in Specialist Mental Healthcare Institutions in The Netherlands; Int J Environ Res Public Health. 2018 May; 15(5): 910).

For 1800 people, 113 Suicide Prevention is a huge operation. It is financed mainly by the Dutch Ministry of Health, Welfare and Sport (*Ministerie van VWS*). That financing provides ample gourmet bread and butter, as well as luxurious housing and transportation, to a multitude of psychologists and psychiatrists. In addition, there is a large group of fully trained volunteers providing round-the-clock confidential support through chats and phone calls 24/7 across the Netherlands for crisis dialogues and psychological treatments. They can be counted on to support, advise and bullshit. Mind you, it will all be needed, as suicidal ideation implementation engineered by today's Bernays' to hasten forward the herd's mass suicide worldwide is in full swing. Every television newscast and subliminal advertisement brainwashes the population into greater fear. They entice and encourage the population to, like lemmings, give up on life and take the flying leap over the killing-Self cliff. It is all done with supraliminal stimuli, which are above the threshold of what the average human's senses can consciously perceive. And it is done with subliminal stimuli, which are below the threshold of what the average human's senses can consciously perceive.

As you might recall from an earlier chapter, subliminal stimuli register just beyond the limits of our conscious perception. We can see, hear, feel, taste and smell subliminal stimuli. But they will be so subtle that we are unaware of them, unless consciously on the lookout for them. By passing messages by our conscious awareness and straight to our subconscious, the aim is to directly influence us to do precisely what the message dictates us to do.

The most well-known example of subliminal advertising was revealed to the public in 1957. It was conducted by Detroit born social psychologist and market researcher James McDonald Vicary in an experiment on 45,699 moviegoers in a New Jersey theater. He exposed them to .03 second flashes of 'Hungry? Eat Popcorn' and 'Drink Coca-Cola' during a movie to see if concession sales would increase. They did! His experiment increased the sale of popcorn by 57.5% and Coca-Cola by 18.1%. ((James Vicary: *Experiment & Overview*; study.org). These results prompted the CIA to write a report titled *The Operational Potential of Subliminal Perception* about their own plans for research with subliminal messaging. Vicary is said to have later on voluntarily admitted his study was fraudulent. And you think that 70 years later they are unable to purposely, systematically and step by step brainwash us into suicidal ideation?

Would that explain the massive build-up of the Suicide Prevention scam? Even in a small country like the Netherlands, 113 Suicide Prevention for 1800 annul suicides is deemed insufficient. After all, when the mental health cabal milks the public cow, it does it thoroughly everywhere, the United States and Canada included. Thus, it is generic that competition must be provided, so more of their ilk can profit. Bring on a regional suicide prevention systems intervention called SUPREMOCOL, which stands for Suicide Prevention by Monitoring and Collaborative Care. It was implemented and evaluated in five specialist mental health institutions and their adherent chain partners (Emma Hofstra et al: A regional systems intervention for suicide prevention in the Netherlands (SUPREMOCOL): study protocol with a stepped wedge trial design; BMC Psychiatry 2019).

It focuses on four pillars:

1. recognition of people at risk for suicide by the development and implementation of a monitoring system with decision aid
2. swift access to specialist care of people at risk
3. positioning nurse care managers for collaborative care case management
4. 12 months telephone follow up

Eligible patients are people attempting suicide or expressing suicidal ideation. The goal is to provide specialist mental health institutions and chain partners with a sustainable and adoptable intervention for suicide prevention. And all this because it is hypothesized that about two-thirds of suicides were due to a lack of mental healthcare while probably in need of it, as suicide occurs mostly in the context of mental disorders. If that is indeed the case, we can deduce that psychiatrists leading the suicide successes are certainly in need of it, most sparking the "Physician help thyself" principle.

The hypothesized reasons for suicide are also given. The low percentage of help-seeking, possibly due to stigma and poor suicide literacy, is among them. So are the humanly emotional upheavals occurring and to be expected in the course of human life. Suicide risk is also presumed to rise with job and financial problems, unbearable mental pain, lack of a support system, trauma, stigma, impulsive aggression, hopelessness, living alone and facing loss.

Another problem concerns identifying people at risk for suicide. There are many very common, known risk factors. However, clinical assessment can be very hard, given that about 45% of patients who died by suicide met with a primary care provider in the preceding month. Indeed, a large study found that prediction mostly failed, as 60% of patients who died by suicide had been categorized by mental health professionals as low risk. Regardless of age, from the very young to the very old, suicide occurs more often in men than in women, but that doesn't help predict suicide. Only suicide attempts and suicidal ideation are strong predictors of a possible impending suicide. The predictive power of any individual's suicidal risk factor is very low. No tool, questionnaire or instrument can predict suicide.

Nevertheless, in the Netherlands as well as in the U.S. and Canada, a target population for suicide intervention has been identified. It is people who present themselves to, or are identified by, a mental health professional with, in his or her opinion, signs of suicidal behaviour. This would be manifested by both suicidal ideations and actions, such as perceived preparation and attempts undertaken with the intention to die. In this systems intervention, various professionals can register those they perceive at risk for suicide into the monitoring system. This includes general medical professionals, such as emergency room physicians and general practitioners. It includes mental health professionals, such as school psychologists. And it also includes non-healthcare professionals, such as railway professionals,

For now, however, participating professionals signalling people at risk must first ask them for permission to register them in the monitoring system. All non-professionals can enter them with flourish without permission. A suicide risk assessment via a decision aid built into the monitoring system is conducted. It provides feedback based on the persons' answers on a questionnaire and observations made by the professional. If the suicide risk is *medium or high*, the person will be registered in the monitoring system, and their registration is automatically sent to the nearest School Mental Health Initiative (SMHI) Once in the state's monitoring system for suicide risk, which is easy to do with ignorant and trusting genuine PTSD journeyers, you will be supervised and monitored forever and a day. Your immediate freedom gone. The possibility to incarcerate you in the closest mental health facility at the drop of a hat hangs over your head. This should be soothing to you, in particular since anyone you meet can get you there. Anyone!

Once you are in the state's monitoring system, a state professional will conduct daily checks for new enrolments and actively seek contact on a daily basis with those registered. They will decide if a crisis assessment is necessary, and they will ensure that anyone they feel is due for an assessment receives swift access to care they consider appropriate, most probably in the SMHI itself. And these SMHI professionals will work according to a collaborative care model with the deemed-suicidal person and other professionals. They will use a systematic telephone follow-up for one-year to monitor suicide risk and continuity of care by the SMHI professional in collaboration with psychiatrists.

All this is done for 293 suicides that occurred in Noord-Brabant, one of the Netherland's 12 provinces. By extension it could be done for the less than 800,000 suicide successors worldwide. The hypothesis is that SUPREMOCOL will lead to 20% fewer suicides and diminish suicidal ideation in people registered in the Dutch monitoring system. It is hoped that would eventually extend to Europe as a whole, which experienced 56 200 suicides in 2015, out of a population of about 747, 900, 000.

So, what did the *Prevention of Suicide Mortality in Noord Brabant: The Effect of Implementation of a Regional Suicide Prevention system*—a staggered implementation stepped wedge trial alone—cost? This one project to discover ways and means of suicide? Grant number 537001002, as it is officially filed, cost a staggering 399,971 euros, according to Ms. Julia van Os, the senior program officer of the Netherlands Organisation for Health Research and Development.

But back to Mokkenstorm et al. They acknowledge Zero Suicide as a multilevel system view on suicide prevention with three core elements:

- a direct approach to suicidal behaviors

- continual improvement of the quality and safety of care processes
- an organizational commitment to the aspirational goal of zero suicides

They clarified and discussed these components against the backdrop of concerns and objections that focus on possible undesired consequences of the pursuit of zero suicide, in particular for clinicians and for those bereaved by suicide. They concluded that zero suicides is a rational aspirational goal. The caveat is that the journey toward zero suicides should be undertaken in a systemic and sustained manner, in a way that professionals feel supported, empowered and protected against blame and inappropriate guilt.

Nevertheless, together with his U.S. peers, Mokkenstorm adopted the zero suicide approach by helping craft the International Zero Suicide Declaration (The Rotterdam Declaration). It, too, would lead to a tipping point to reduce suicides, he envisaged.

Needless to say, Covington and Hogan were not charmed. In 2019, they protested wildly to Mokkenstorm's view of the situation, stating:

> "Psychiatric leadership is essential to the success of efforts toward zero suicide. More than a slogan, the approach applies evidence about what works in the detection, treatment, and management of individuals with intense suicidality within a culture determined to learn together and make a dramatic difference. Three essential steps-routinely asking about suicide, developing a collaborative crisis/safety plan including counselling on lethal means, and delivering direct treatment for suicidality for those at elevated risk-have produced exceptional results in several systems." ("Zero Suicide: The Dogged Pursuit of Perfection in Health Care"; *Psychiatric Times* Vol 36, Issue 1, Volume 36, Issue 1).

The problem thus arises, who is to evaluate whether or not someone is suicidal and needs perpetual drugging and supervision? The Gulag state, by way of mental health professionals paid by a nation's healthcare system and thus making their living from diagnosing people as ill and iller? Covington and Hogan announce, however, that efforts by the mental health system to realize zero suicide in the U.S. only introduced concepts of high-reliability science in the past 20 years, using aviation as an example saying:

> "High-reliability organizations aggressively pursue perfection, an approach, for example, that has driven commercial aviation in the U.S. to achieve remarkable levels of safety in air travel. This approach is characterized by a deference to front-line expertise, a preoccupation with learning about failures and "near misses" and a relentless focus on the target of zero defects."

Again, what works for aviation will work for you, the rattus, cani, simian, mus and/or pecus that you are considered to be by the learned society and the mental health industry in particular. We, the mental health profession, insist on it, damn you! Thus, the all-powerful Henry Ford Health System (HFHS) in Detroit was the first to apply the high-reliability science concepts in behavioral healthcare. They began focusing on the relentless assessment of suicidality across their continuum of psychiatric care, meaning the complete range of programs and services offered to and experienced by patients, in 2015. It was labelled "perfect depression care". Over the implementation period, suicide deaths among those under psychiatric care was reduced to that in the general population. Covington and Hogan brag that it was due to "an intensive commitment to radical quality" within usual healthcare. If it included psychiatrists themselves as test subjects is unknown.

However, as far as we know, the results could be nothing other than their illusionary manipulation, as their effort was a non-randomized trial. Some of their mental health industry peers went so far as to discount the results. Indeed, they even minimized the approach as "clever sloganeering" and repackaging. As usual, we hear the need to complete the science and verify the results by applying new knowledge to the care of suicidal individuals. Either that or read this brief exchange in a PBS *Frontline* episode reported by Jon Rappoport in 2018 in "Does ADHD Exist," by merely replacing ADHD with suicide ideation. PBS's frontline interviewers remarked:

> "Skeptics say that there's no biological marker---that it [ADHD] is the one condition out there where there is no blood test, and that no one knows what causes it."

Dr. Russell Barkley, an eminent professor of psychiatry and neurology at the University of Massachusetts Medical Center, replied:

> "That's tremendously naïve, and it shows a great deal of illiteracy about science and about the mental health professions. A disorder doesn't have to have a blood test to be valid. If that were the case, all mental disorders would be invalid...There is no lab test for any mental disorder right now in our science. That doesn't make them invalid."

Oh, indeed? That makes them invalid? Yes, indeed. Utterly and completely invalid, as Rappoport observed. All 300 DSM mental health disorders, including suicidal ideation, were hallucinated into existence because there are no defining tests of any kind to back up any of the mental health industry diagnoses. Psychiatrists can sway and tap dance all they like, and they won't escape the noose around their necks, says Rappoport. We are looking at a science that is not at all science.

Imagine this, Rappoport suggests. You walk into a doctor's office, talk with him for a few minutes, and he mouths: "You have cancer. You need to start chemo at once."

After the initial shock, you say: "But you didn't give me a test."

And he says, "Well, we don't need a test. We know what the symptoms are because we convened a high-level meeting of oncologists last year, and we listed the answers to the questions I just asked you. You gave those telltale answers. So, we start chemo tomorrow. We may also need to surgically remove an organ or two before we're done."

That's psychiatry. That's the way it works, including with Zero Suicide, 113 Prevention, the now budding SUPREMOCOL and Ahmedani's research. They all line up the system so that non-healthcare professionals can report you. That include your co-workers at the railroad, your fellow soldiers and officers, your captain and co-pilot, pursers and fellow flight attendants, the firefighters and police officers you work with, your peers at UPS, DHL, and amazon, even your neighbors and their cats and dogs. They are all able to report you for suicidal ideation, because they do not like the way you walk or talk.

Furthermore, the leitmotiv to never let the opportunity to make a buck go to waste remains. So, to get the ball rolling on this newest way to traumatize humanity while pretending benevolence, research grants are offered to reach that goal is the way to go. And the U.S. National Institute of Health (NIH), where Fauci holds the purse strings over $32 billion annually, is doing just that. In 2018, HFHS's researchers alone engaged in more than 2,000 studies. With $86 million in grants and contracts from external sources, they ranked first in non-university-based Michigan health systems NIH funding. They were in the top 20 nationally among independent hospitals for NIH funding to be used "To improve human life through excellence in the science and art of healthcare and healing (henryford.com).

The NIH also allotted a five-year grant to Brian Ahmedani, PhD, adjunct assistant professor at Wayne State University, School of Medicine's Department of Psychiatry & Behavioral Neurosciences since 2015. The grant was to conduct a large-scale zero suicide implementation review across most of the Kaiser Permanente Health System (zerosuicide.edc.org). Kaiser is one of America's leading healthcare and not-for-profit health plans providers. In 2020, it served more than 12.3 million members in eight states and Washington, D.C. With a team of nearly 23,000 physicians serving the public, it went so far as to form a suicide measurement advisory committee. The committee included operational, research and analytic specialists from the Permanente Medical Groups and was chaired by a performance measurement specialist from KP's Care Management Institute. The goal was to provide guidance on developing suicide measurement specifications and to help identify data resources. The committee, proudly announced:

> "Our approach to suicide prevention needs to involve the humans and the system. Human caring and outreach are essential, but we need to make sure we do that systematically; that we identify everyone who is at risk and that we always offer effective interventions." Greg Simon, M.D., MPH, Senior Investigator, Kaiser Permanente Washington Health Research Institute; Psychiatrist, Washington Permanente Medical Group."

Barbara Stanley, PhD, is professor of medical psychology in the department of Psychiatry at the Columbia University Vagelos College of Physicians & Surgeons. She also has her lucrative existence assured for a few more years by receiving a grant to evaluate enhanced versus routine zero suicide implementation in New York State's over 160 mental health clinics (prevention.conte.cumc.columbia.edu). Stanley is well versed in the field. She is director of suicide prevention training, implementation and evaluation for the Center for Practice Innovation and Research Scientist in Molecular Imaging and Neuropathology at the New York State Psychiatric Institute. She also mentors investigators on fMRI studies examining the interpersonal dysfunction dimension of borderline personality disorder. And she mentors investigators on genetics studies of borderline personality disorder, as well as of treatment engagement trials with suicidal individuals.

Stanley is also director of the Suicide Intervention Center. She is a research scientist at the New York State Psychiatric Institute. And she is the principal investigator on several NIMH and foundation grants investigating clinical and neurobiological factors and intervention strategies related to suicidal behavior, self-injury and borderline personality disorder. Among her grant awards, along with Beth Brodsky, is an NIMH "Excellence in Curriculum" award to develop a dialectical behavior therapy curriculum for psychiatry residents. It is to be used at Behavioral Tech, a Linehan Institute training company, with the vision of:

"Compassionate and scientifically valid treatments made available to every person with complex and severe mental disorders." (behavioraltech.org). Behavioral Tech trains mental healthcare providers and treatment teams who work with complex and severely disordered populations. It teaches them to use compassionate, scientifically valid treatments, and to implement and evaluate these treatments in their practice setting. It also develops and applies the methods of training and provides opportunities to learn state-of-the-art treatments to a competent level.

Author of more than 150 publications, Stanley also serves as editor-in-chief of the Archives of Suicide Research. And she is a standing member of the Adult Psychopathology and Disorders of Aging NIH CSR study section. An immensely productive individual, she and Gregory Brown, PhD also developed the safety planning intervention used throughout the VA and on U.S. crisis hotlines. Brown is a research associate professor of clinical psychology in psychiatry at the Perelman School of Medicine at the University of Pennsylvania. He is also director of the Center for the Prevention of Suicide at the University of Pennsylvania. And he acts as VISN 4 MIRECC investigator and clinical psychologist at the Philadelphia VA Medical Center. VISN means Veterans Integrated Service Network. It is part of the Veterans Health Administration nationwide system of hospitals and clinics, providing service to more than 27 million veterans. MIRECC stands for the U.S. Department of Veteran Affairs Mental Illness Research, Education and Clinical Center. Its purported mission? To generate new knowledge about the causes and treatments of mental disorders, apply new findings to model clinical programs, and widely disseminate new findings to improve veterans' quality of life and their daily functioning in their recovery from mental illness (washington.edu).

Brown claims expertise in suicide risk assessment and brief treatments for the prevention of suicide behaviour. These include the usual cognitive behavioural therapy and the so-called safety plan intervention, a written document supporting and guiding someone who has thoughts of suicide, as an aid to avoid a state of intense suicidal crisis (https://www.suicideinfo.ca/resource/safety-plans/). Anyone in a trusting relationship with the person at risk can help draft the plan with the person having thoughts of suicide by identifying:

- their personal warning signs
- coping strategies that have worked for them in the past or that they think might work in the future
- people who are sources of support in their lives (friends, family, professionals, crisis supports)
- how to remove means of suicide from their environment
- their personal reasons for living, or what has helped them stay alive.

A suicidal crisis, by the way, refers to "a suicide attempt or an incident in which an emotionally distraught person seriously considers or plans to imminently attempt to take his or her own life" (Suicide Prevention Resource Center, https://www.suicideinfo.ca).

Brown is presently conducting a project in the VA to develop and evaluate an intervention for treating and following suicidal veterans in urgent care settings and post-discharge. There goes your second amendment right out the window. And what did we learn earlier? That people, regardless of standing in life, commit suicide even hours after a visit with their treating mental health professional. They do so, despite all the plans in the world prepared to prevent them from doing so. But that is kept silent. So, who are Stanley, Brown, Ahmedani et al. kidding? And who actually benefits from that $186 million hallucination of research trials of methods of suicide prevention in 2020 alone? Just as who actually benefits from that $138 million for PTSD research in 2020, up from $77 million in 2013, eh?

Stanley, by the way, also leads the Conte Center for Suicide Prevention Project 5 "Stress, Inflammation, Aggression and Emotion Regulation in Suicidal Behavior." It aims to prove that aggression, childhood adversity, and behavioral and physiological responses to stress are critical factors that *may* contribute to risk for suicidal behavior (https://prevention.conte.cumc.columbia.edu; italics mine)."

> "Using state-of-the-art smartphone technology, we will also study the value of passive real-time monitoring of emotional distress, social functioning, and sleep disturbance to parse out how well these characteristics relate to suicidal behavior. We will test how effective this type of passively obtained information is compared with other types of information we are obtaining (including stress response, mood regulation and cognitive data) in terms of suicide risk prediction. Finally, we will use powerful computational machine learning methods to combine the full range of data we gather from active and passive monitoring to develop predictive models."

And most, if not all of it, done to reduce America's and the world's suicide deaths tolls. Those are 48,000 people in the U.S. and the less than 800,000 out of 7,5 billion humans worldwide who can't wait to depart naturally. That was the unpreventable toll when McKeon, Covington and Hogan hallucinated the zero suicide prevention phenomena into existence.

Consider New York City, Stanley's home base. How many people are homeless and suicidal there alone due to genuine PTSD, normal life traumas, drug use or even by choice? Nearly one in every 106 New Yorkers in a city population of 8.3 million— that's nearly 80,000 men, women and children living and sleeping on the streets. Almost 4,000 sleep on the city's streets, in its subway or in other public spaces every night. And for every one of them sleeping on New York's sidewalks and trains, 20 more do so within the city's homeless shelters, where they remain unseen (bowery.org). And how many in the country live in extreme poverty, all of whom could be helped immensely with $186 million?

In January 2018, 552,830 people were counted as homeless in the United States. Of those, 194,467 (35%) were unsheltered, and 358,363 (65%) were sheltered. They represented 0.2% of the U.S. population, or 17 people per every 10,000. Due to COVID 19 eviction notices at the end of 2020, that number is has probably skyrocketed.

In summary:

- 48,000 people die by unpreventable suicide.
- 552,830 people are homeless .
- The government spends $186 million on the unpreventable, instead of on the preventable.

And so, the zero suicide agenda marches on. Next, we'll hear its crusaders calling themselves missionaries for chasing of unanswerable, scientifically non-provable questions for the benefit of all mankind about why those 48,000 kill themselves. How would they justify it? Just like Christian missionaries did in Hawaii, for example, by forcing their faith on Hawaiians. That turned out to be rather as lucrative as Stanley, Ahmedani et al.'s trade in human mind manipulation with their suicide agenda make-believe. About their own lives we are told nothing. All we know is how psychiatrists have an extraordinarily high inclination to kill themselves, while the scientific, empirical first evidence answer to "Can someone be talked out of suicide?" is missing.

The Golden Gate Bridge is case in point. Various methods preventing a dive from it have been tried:

- fitting it with suicide hotline telephones
- night-time bridge closure to pedestrians
- staff patrols in cars watch for people planning to jump

The Bridgewatch Angels, founded by Pleasanton Police Lieutenant Mia Munayer in 2011, patrols the bridge looking for anyone who may wish to jump. They are credited with making dozens of interventions each year. The Golden Gate Bridge ironworkers volunteer time by talking to or wrestling down suicidal people. Called "Cowboys of the Sky", they have the equipment and knowledge of the bridge. And their experience working at extreme heights gives them the qualifications to go over the rail and help those ready to dive, even when bitten or threatened with knives and loaded guns.

Despite all vigilance, on average 30 people manage to jump of the bridge annually. It is for those 30 that San Francisco's taxpayers are now shelling out $76 million for the safety net deemed to be necessary to prevent them from following their calling. And how many homeless people did that city have in 2020? San Francisco's report to the federal Department of Housing and Urban Development cited a count of 8,011, an increase of 6.8% from 7,499 in 2017. The city's internal count, however, cites more than 9,700 and rising.

Could such mundane human necessities for a contented and emotionally stable life as humane living conditions or the absence thereof, have anything to do with a desire to kill the Self Could proper housing, proper cooking facilities, proper nutrition or proper sanitation make a difference? You won't hear it mentioned by any of the zero suicide geniuses. That the pharmaceutical prescription drugs they so fervently and in ever increasing amounts handed out could be hugely contributing and even be responsible for much of the suicidal ideation also seems beyond their comprehension. Or is it mere ignorance from which they suffer? Or is the mental health industry investigating the causes of a crisis they themselves created? Is this the fox in the chicken coup? Is the goal to present the solution to which they themselves aspire, namely the complete control over our mind and thus control over our behaviour?

This could lead us to deduce something about the skyrocketing suicide among their own in comparison to the world's general human population. Perhaps it reflects the mental health of the few in their ranks who still have a conscience. Perhaps they feel guilt knowing that the worldwide zero suicide agenda is just another ruse in line with "Mental Health is Health." Perhaps they are uneasy about these golden goose scenarios, in line with the equally perverted and lucrative genuine PTSD treatments. Have we truly reached the time when Benjamin Rush's words are becoming an acute necessity?

> "Unless we put medical freedom into the Constitution the time will come when medicine will organize itself into an undercover dictatorship. To restrict the art of healing to doctors and deny equal privileges to others will constitute the Bastille of medical science. All such laws are un-American and despotic." ~Benjamin Rush

Whichever way, we know full well that we have no power over the other, as each human indeed marches to his or her own drummer. We know that no scientific empirical evidence proving that anyone has ever been talked out of committing suicide. We have no idea what anyone thinks at the point of no return, with very few exceptions, such as the 19-year-old paranoid and hallucinating Kevin Hines. And we know that the industry itself acknowledges that suicide is unpreventable. All this knowledge inspires the question: "What gives? The lack of tender loving care?"

18

SUICIDE: A LACK OF TENDER LOVING CARE?

In your dreams! Or at least it doesn't sound like it, when listening to the self-appointed suicide experts. Tender loving care seems to be an alien concept to them in general, and with suicidal- and PTSD suffering individuals in particular. Their analysis of humanity's suicide ideation development and its prevention looks more like an exercise in the purposeful planning and preparation for a known suicide-crisis to occur worldwide.

And, actually, it appears the United States Surgeon General 's Office was very much aware of an oncoming suicide crisis among the herd decades ago. So was the U.S. Center for Mental Health Services, purportedly leading federal efforts prevent and treat mental disorders. Why else had they released the *National Strategy for Suicide Prevention*, or National Strategy for short, in 1999. This document was "to be a catalyst for social change with the power to transform attitudes, policies, and services (pubmed.ncbi.nlm.nih.gov/20669520)?"

Why create such a strategy for the 30,000 people, out of a population of 282.2 million? These people had the immense urge to depart the Earth by their own volition and would find a way to kill themselves, regardless of all prevention efforts by outsiders. This was well known in the mental health profession.

Dr. David Satcher (1941–) was appointed Surgeon General by President Bill Clinton. Satcher thought that such a loss (30,000 people) constituted a grave tragedy, taking "an enormous toll" from the American people. He seemed even more concerned that another 650,000 were trying to do the deed, receiving emergency care when unsuccessful (ncbi.nlm.nih.gov).

Satcher was one of nine children born in Anniston, Alabama, to poor, self-educated farmers. He almost died of whooping cough at age two, which inspired him to become a physician.

In 1998, hastened to release a first-ever Surgeon General' report on mental health, entitled *Executive Summary: A Report of the Surgeon General on Mental Health* in 1999. In it, he exclaimed that mental health was indicative of humans' successful performance of mental function. He claimed this resulted in:

- productive activities
- fulfilling relationships
- the ability to adapt to change
- the ability to cope with adversity from early childhood until late in life

He portrayed mental health as the springboard of thinking and communication skills, learning, emotional growth, resilience and self-esteem. But he breathed not a word about the living conditions needed for such mental health and abilities. He didn't mention nutrition, hygiene or overall living conditions. He ignored the role that a lack of tender loving care could play in developing such a springboard. That it could foster or impair the development of such a springboard of physical and mental health for better or worse did not seem to have crossed his mind. That the mental health cabal calls almost all previously considered normal human behaviors "mental illness" also escaped the Surgeon General's attention. Or perhaps he found it unworthy, unnecessary or unsavory to mention.

Satcher's academic or non-academic background in psychology or psychiatry is unknown. He views mental illnesses as health conditions characterized by a person's alterations in thinking, mood, behavior or a combination thereof caused by distress and impaired functioning (https://ncbi.nlm.nih.gov). What type of distress qualifies in his opinion we can only guess? His report, we learn, confronted, took the bull of the profound obstacle to the publics' misperception about mental illness by the horns, so to speak. This, he said, stemmed from the artificial, centuries-old belief that a separation between mind and body existed. This, he said encouraged the idea that mental health and illness were unrelated to physical health and illness. He stated that the two were, in fact, inseparable, went hand in hand, were one and the same, a machine, so to speak.

Thus, in keeping with modern scientific thinking, he continued, the report used mind to refer to all mental functions related to thinking. It used mood and purposive behaviour of the body as deriving from activities originating from functions within the brain. Purposive behaviour is a cognitive theory of learning as envisioned by American psychologist and professor of psychology at the University of California, Berkeley, Edward Chace Tolman (1886–1959).

He originated his theory by studying how rats learn in mazes, publishing his findings in his 1932 book *Purposive Behavior in Animals and Men*. In it, he suggested that the unit of behavior is the total, goal-directed act using varied muscular movements that are organized around the purposes served and guided by cognitive processes (Britannica.com). In his 1943 article "The elementary units of behavior" published in *Psychological Review* (50(5), 479-502), Dubbs tried to determine and define the elementary units of behavior in mice and men. His effort was in terms of permanent dynamic structural factors called psychological functions. Here a review of his estimations of a unit of behavior:

> "Two types are listed [as units of behaviour], psychological mechanisms and interests, each possessing invariable characteristics by which they may be identified. Inherited and acquired forms of each occur. 'Directed behaviour' is not due to any elementary function, but to compounds of different types of functions. An attempt is made to determine and define the elementary units of behavior in terms of permanent dynamic structural factors called psychological functions. Fundamental features of psychological mechanisms and interests are outlined. The explanatory and organizing power of these elementary units is revealed in their application to psychological problems." (PsycINFO Database Record (c) 2018 APA, all rights reserved.)

However, he seems to caution, the psychologist might want to leave the consideration of neural pathways to the neurologist. Such knowledge is useful to psychology only insofar as considering that, since Darwin, human beings are considered equal to rattus, cani, simian and cockroaches, if the latter carried the same research worthiness as bat viruses.

Dubbs, who left the Earth long since, also published these articles in the *Psychological Review*, a scientific journal publishing articles on psychological theory.

- "The determinants of behavior at a choice point" (1938)
- "Cognitive maps in rats and men" (1948)
- "Principles of performance" (1955)

This journal was Founded in 1894 by Princeton University psychologist James Mark Baldwin and Columbia University psychologist James McKeen Cattell. It soon became North America's most prominent and influential psychology journal of its time. Due to Tolman's theories and his work with rats running around in circles displaying behaviour the same as man, another branch of psychology to pervert the minds of men and mice evolved. This one they called "purposive behaviourism", which Satcher used in his 1998 mental health report.

It postulates that behavioral acts of rats, and therefore humans, have a goal or purpose. This purpose selects and guides the behavioral sequence in which they pursue whatever they want until goal and purpose are attained. The theory should be blatantly obvious to normally inclined humans in everyday life. Why pursue anything without a goal? But it seems to have been nebulous to Dubbs, who also incorporates the Gestalt concept of field theory in his assertions. By and large, this is a systematic approach to describe rat - and thus human - behaviour in terms of patterns of dynamic interrelationships between a person and the psychological, social and physical situation in which one exists (apa.og).

Mind you, Dubbs' research of "hidden pathway maze learning tasks" (HPMLTs) has been used in neuropsychological research and practice for more than 80 years. Using visual and auditory task feedback signals, it has been used extensively throughout the twentieth century to study humans' exploratory, anticipatory and goal-related behavior. It has also been used as an experimental tool in neuropsychology (E. Thomas et al: Behavior at the Choice Point: Decision Making in Hidden Pathway Maze Learning; Neuropsychology Review vol 24 p. 514-536; 2014). This is part of why humanity can be manipulated to perfection by those in the know, as is reflected, with few exceptions, by the COVID-19 herd behavior.

Research reviewed and consulted for Satcher's report, we read, had made it abundantly clear that all rattus'—and thus humans'—mental functions were carried out by the brain. Furthermore, the emerging technologies in brain research had also made it increasingly possible to discover mental brain functions and disorders. Not only that! Research had also documented that medication and psycho-the-rapist treatment could be seen in the brain's physical changes. Who and how these changes were generated goes unmentioned.

So, human brains would be both producer and director of any and all bodily and mental functions. They would control ideas, behaviors and actions, thus engineering all of human existence. So, brains rule life and living. That leaves science to discover and adjust any signs of deviation from what researchers label as "the norm", including suicidal ideation. Everything could be fixed through well-implemented and managed care-programs, at least in Satcher's well-functioning, well-oiled mind. That the debate of a connection between brain and body seems to have escaped his attention. So has the question of the existence, non-existence or even location of mind, consciousness, spirit, God, gods, deities or none of it, which has raged for millennia. Already in great detail discussed in *Fallacy 1* here just a bit on the topic.

Brian Dolan is professor of anthropology, history and social medicine at the University of San Francisco, California's, School of Medicine. In 2007, he published "Soul searching: a brief history of the mind/body debate in the neurosciences." This article explored how interrelated these categories have been when seen in the context of ancient, Renaissance, early modern and modern philosophical and medical history. (Brian Dolan, PhD: "Soul searching: a brief history of the mind/body debate in the neurosciences"; *Neurosurg Focus* 23 (1): 2007.)

By examining these issues through the lens of neuroscience history, Dolan presents how the brain has variously been perceived as home to intimate states of being. He also shares insights into the interrelationships of philosophy, theology and medicine.

Dolan relates that research into the anatomical and physiological works of the brain's structure and function had been undertaken throughout history to establish it as "the seat of the soul." This was done most likely by watching the behaviors of rattus et al., As an organ of reflection, meditation and memory, the brain had also become synonymous with what we define as the "Self". The existence of consciousness, the learned man says "the mind" in such few words. Thus, in his opinion, the brain has been associated with a range of transcendent concepts - the soul, spirit, mind and consciousness, perhaps? But perhaps it no longer is? All these concepts relate to each other in fundamental ways, both in terms of their perceived location within the brain and because of the way each works ultimately to define the whole person to whom the brain belongs. But they all, without doubt or exception, are stuck right within the organ brain, so says he. At least, that's the way I read him.

Mind you, the mind-body-spirit-consciousness adventure of discovery of their individual location, if such location can be found, is a debate of much bigger scope. It was "recently" addressed by René Descartes in the seventeenth century, resulting in Cartesian dualism. Indeed, the debate goes far, far back to pre-Aristotelian philosophers and Sanskrit scholars proposing countless theories of all academic shades and colors in all perspectives and perceptions imaginable.

Even Karl Marx addressed the issue in his theory of historical materialism. He held that consciousness was engendered by the material contingencies of one's environment. He suggested that societies passed, without a doubt, through unilinear evolutions, every society progressing stage by stage in the following manner:

Primitive Communism → Slavery→ Feudalism→ Capitalism → Socialism → Communism

Each stage, Marx maintained, sowed the seeds of its own destruction. One will go and another will come. Such precision and succession would continue until ultimate, total and complete communism is reached. Marx, we are told, sought to explain all social phenomena in terms of their place and function in the complex systems of society and nature. The possibility of metaphysical explanations of any kind for anything seems to have been alien to his mind. Perhaps it is in line with Marxist principles towards life and living, that surgeon general Satcher makes no reference whatsoever, in his mental health report, of human emotional conditions and situations playing part in either suicide ideation or ill mental health developments. That mind-altering pharmaceutical drugs, pharmaceutical injections from birth, and drugging with Ritalin and the like in schools hugely contribute to ill mental development seems to have escaped the learned soul's attention as well.

There is no an empirically, scientifically identifiable meeting point between the non-physical mind (if there is such a thing) and its physical existence in the brain. This continues to be superbly problematic to today's philosophers and scientists in a multitude of academic genres. These include socio-biology, computer science, evolutionary psychology and the neurosciences. On the other hand, the possibilities for hypotheses, hallucinations and theories about the human mind and what it contains, and where the rest may or may not reside are endless. They will, without a shadow of a doubt, keep them busy and well-paid until the end of time. The possibilities are endless, as you can well see. One can analyze how the brain works by streaming the brain of a person's moment-to-moment thoughts. One can check the manifestation, analyse it from a first-person perspective, or see if the manifestation of the mind-stream happens to every person all the time, even in the scientist conducting the experiment. On and on and on it goes into eternity, or until the scientist departs the Earth and another one takes over.

Most of their discoveries and consequent hypotheses and theories about brain functions in rattus and man are used to mankind's detriment. See their genuine PTSD treatments. All that is beside the point. Do they care? Of course not! Consciousness and God are not part of their schemata. Compassion and empathy are unknown emotions. Divine retribution for all deeds committed is, for better or for worse, an alien concept. So, why not joyfully carry on traumatizing the traumatized at leisure, when oblivious of the possible consequences through Karma, eh?

Satcher accepted and signed off the report's content in its entirety. He had arrived at his exalted station of four-star admiral of the fleet despite his seemingly poverty-stricken family background. As a youngster, he entered Morehouse College in Atlanta, Georgia. This private, historically black men's liberal arts college founded by William Jefferson White (1831–1913) and others as the Augusta Institute in 1867 in response to the liberation of African slaves after the American Civil War (1861–1865). White was a civil rights leader, minister, educator and journalist of mixed parentage. His father was Caucasian, his mother Negroid. Morehouse is the largest such college in the United States. Throughout the years, it has played a key role in the U.S. civil rights movement and the drive for racial equality in the US. Jefferson also founded the Harmony Baptist Church in Augusta in 1869 as well as other churches.

Morehouse has been home to 11 Fulbright Scholars, five Rhodes Scholars and five Marshall Scholars. It is the alma mater of many African-American civil rights leaders, including Martin Luther King Jr. and Julian Bond, and baseball player Donn Clendenon. Among Morehouse alumni, traditionally known as "Morehouse Men", the college has graduated numerous "African American firsts" in local, state and federal government as well as in science, academia, business, and entertainment. Admiral Satcher, obviously, is one of them.

In 1970, Satcher went on to earn a combined M.D./PhD in cell biology from Case Western Reserve University Cleveland, Ohio. He completed his residency- and fellowship training at the Strong Memorial Hospital as well as the private research University of Rochester in New York State. Tired of the long winters, Satcher then moved to California's UCLA School of Medicine and the Martin Luther Jr. Harbor Hospital.

From 1975 to 1979, the future U.S. Surgeon General served as the interim dean at Charles R. Drew Postgraduate Medical School. At the same time, he directed the King-Drew Sickle Cell Research Center. From 1979 to 1982, Satcher served as professor and chairman of the Department of Community Medicine and Family Practice at the Morehouse School of Medicine. Then, he served as president of the Meharry Medical College from 1982 to 1993, serving, a historically black medical school in Nashville, Tennessee, affiliated with the United Methodist Church. Founded in 1876 as the Medical Department of Central Tennessee College, it was the South's first medical school for African Americans.

In the early twenty-first century, Meharry became the largest private historically black institution in the United States solely dedicated to educating healthcare professionals and scientists. Being the second-largest educator of African-American medical doctors and dentists in the United States, Meharry also has the highest percentage of African Americans graduating with PhDs in the biomedical sciences in the U.S.

Satcher left his post as Meharry's president in 1993 to become director of the Centers for Disease Control and Prevention (CDC). He also served as administrator of the Agency for Toxic Substances and Disease Registry and assistant secretary for health until in 1998. That's when he was appointed surgeon general of the United States by U.S. President Bill Clinton. Because he served simultaneously in the positions of surgeon general and assistant secretary for health at the U.S. Department of Health and Human Services, the

State bestowed upon him the distinction of being the United States Public Health Service Commissioned Corps' (PHSCC) first four-star admiral. A Surgeon General, by law, holds "only" the rank of vice admiral.

To satisfy our curiosity, the U.S. Public Health Service's (PHS) consists of eight uniformed services with a primary mission of the protection, promotion and advancement of health and safety of the general public. They are:

1. the Agency Healthcare Research and Quality (AHRQ),
2. the Agency for Toxic Substances and Disease Registry (ATSDR),
3. the Centers for Disease Control and Prevention (CDC),
4. the Food and Drug Administration (FDA),
5. the Health Resources and Services Administration (HRSA),
6. the Indian Health Service (IHS),
7. the National Institutes of Health (NIH),
8. the Substance Abuse and Mental Health Services Administration (SAMHSA).

Upon becoming the nation's leading spokesman on public health matters, Satcher succeeded in making himself famous through his rallying cry "to make public health work like it's never worked before." This he promised to achieve by establishing a balanced community health system without disparities nationwide and maintaining a global approach to public health. Global health is defined as "the area of study, research and practice that places a priority on improving health and achieving equity in health for all people worldwide" (Koplan JP, Bond TC, Merson MH, et al. (June 2009). "Towards a common definition of global health"; *Lancet* 373 (9679): 1993–5.)

Suicide Prevention was part of his global health plan.

In the summer of 1999, Satcher and then-Vice-President Al Gore sprang into action to inaugurate the matter by hosting a press conference. They were joined by Sen. Harry Reid of Nevada and Rep. John Lewis of Georgia, the original sponsors calling for a national suicide prevention strategy. They unveiled their blueprint on how to prevent further suicides in the United States (sprc.org). Entitled *The Surgeon General's call to action to prevent suicide*, it included what they called the AIM approach: awareness, intervention and methodology. The approach came from the deliberations at the 1998 *1st National Suicide Awareness and Prevention Conference* held in in Reno, Nevada. The conference had been sparked by U.S. Senator Harry Reid (1939–) (D-NV), whose father's suicide resulted in a bill declaring suicide a national problem. It had passed unanimously.

From Senator Reid to Danielle Steele to Nancy Pelosi, from the first runner-up to the 1999 Miss America Pageant to Admiral Satcher – they all put in a show:

Out of this Reno Conference grew the *Surgeon General's Call to Action to Prevent Suicide*, issued in 1999. And from this in turn sprouted the 2001 *National Strategy for Suicide Prevention* announced by Gore and Satcher at their press conference.

Steven Hyman, M.D. is director, National Institute of Mental Health, National Institutes of Health, Department of Health and Human Services (NIMH). He described what the NIMH did to find effective ways of dealing with "this very complex behaviour," and in what directions the agency was heading in its suicide prevention efforts. He concluded with the following statement:

> "Mental disorders and substance abuse disorders--alone and co-occurring--are the major risk factor for allowing human beings to overcome one of nature's most compelling instincts--the urge to survive. Why do people kill themselves? We urgently need to know more. We are grateful that with the support of many people, our society is increasingly willing to address and resolve the legal and ethical issues surround clinical investigations on this topic and that for too long have been permitted to unduly complicate knowledge development. With the help of dedicated scientists, wise policy leaders, the courage of those affected by mental and substance abuse disorders, and the committed advocacy of those who genuinely care about these tragedies, we have learned a tremendous amount, and we will continue to learn more."

Thanks to the illustrious company, the following suggestions to prevent the unpreventable were brought forth:

1. Suicide prevention must recognize and affirm the value, dignity and importance of each person.
2. Suicide is not solely the result of illness or inner conditions. The feelings of hopelessness that contribute to suicide can stem from societal conditions and attitudes. Therefore, everyone concerned with suicide prevention shares a responsibility to help change attitudes and eliminate the conditions of oppression, racism, homophobia, discrimination and prejudice.
3. Some groups are disproportionately affected by these societal conditions, and some are at greater risk for suicide.
4. Individuals, communities, organizations and leaders at all levels should collaborate to promote suicide prevention.
5. The success of this strategy ultimately rests with individuals and communities across the United States.

American Indian/Alaska Native (AI/AN) adults are at highest risk for past-year suicide-related thoughts, followed by White and Black adults. For past-year suicide attempts, AI/AN adults are again at highest risk, followed by Black and Hispanic adults. (Center for Behavioral Health Statistics and Quality. (2019). 2018 National Survey on Drug Use and Health: Detailed Tables. Substance Abuse and Mental Health Services Administration, Rockville, M.D. (https://www. amhsa.gov/data/report/2018-nsduh-detailed-tables)

Suicidal thoughts and behaviors vary by race and ethnicity among youth. AI/AN, Asian, Native Hawaiian, and other Pacific Islander high school youth have the highest percentages of past-year serious thoughts of suicide and past-year suicide plans when compared to other races and ethnicities. Among those races and ethnicities where estimates can be reliably obtained, Black high school youth appear to have a slightly higher percentage of past-year suicide attempts and past-year attempts requiring medical treatment. (Centers for Disease Control and Prevention (CDC), Youth Risk Behavior Surveillance System. (2017). 1991-2017 High School Youth Risk Behavior Survey Data [Data file]. Retrieved from http://nccd.cdc.gov/youthonline/)

Out of these suggestions grew the *Surgeon General's Call to Action to Prevent Suicide*, presented at Satcher's and Gore's 1999 press conference. It included the idea of AIM, the Awareness-Intervention-Methodology, an approach reflecting pure secular humanism rather than that of humanitarianism. What's the difference, you wonder?

Humanism is based on atheism. It is never humanitarian, as it denies and excludes in its entirety that divine or supernatural matters play a role in humans emotional and physical wellbeing regardless of color, nationality or religion. Humanism seeks solely rational, logical, scientifically provable, empirically documentable ways to solve human problems. It pays no regard to human sentiments from emotions such as trauma, compassion and empathy, as these are not part of the scientific equation.

Furthermore, secular humanism insists that government interests are the primary instruments for implementing what they deem as good for humanity. So, the State has become the primary advocate to implement what it sees as the good of human interests. It is obvious to most that a government dictating the treatment of its citizens in accordance with its wishes will, in the course of time, blossom into a complete and total authoritarian tyranny. The state's idea of suicide intervention reflected in Satcher's 1999 Awareness, Intervention, Methodology—AIM—gives us a minute taste of it. We already saw it carried out in organizations like Zero Suicide, if we bother to look and evaluate, as well as in the mental health profession in general over decades past. Mullins even goes so far as to state:

"Humanism is never humanitarian; its most widely perceived example in the twentieth century is the death camps of Soviet Russia, where some 66-milion souls have perished." (The Curse of Canaan, p. 89).

Furthermore, governments' dictates enforced "for the good of humanity" are reflected in the welfare state. Such implementation by governments always pits "human interests" against "spiritual interests." The spiritual interests are soon shunned aside. Thus, secular humanism is the humanism of temporal affairs, and the affairs of this world only. To give us an example: The temporal affairs of a church are understood to be the revenues, lands and tenements, in other words, secular possessions, with which it is endowed. The hiring of a sexton to perform the duties incident to his office, however, would have nothing to do with the church's management of its temporalities.

Secular humanism in general attempts to kill humanity's fascination with the spiritual aspects of life and living, which is firmly enshrined in its psyche since times immemorial. It vilifies and belittles such interests and operates without regard for even the possibility of metaphysical aspects playing a role in humanity's and the world's existence, never mind a presence of God. Armed with this knowledge, any genuine PTSD-affected experiencer can see it reflected in the treatment received from their mental health practitioners, WCB employees, their employer and their Union bosses, as humanism disavows empathy and compassion.

Mullins even sees the placing of "human interests" first in all things. He sees the doctrine of humanism as the inspiration to the French Revolution (1789–1799), for instance. But where did it evolve? At the Academia of the de Medici's in Florence, Italy, which forces us to look at their origin.

The dynasty of the Medici's, first mentioned in the early thirteenth century documents, began with their founding of the Medici Bank in Florence in 1397. Under Cosimo de Medici (1389 -1464), it turned into the largest in Europe during the first half of the fifteenth century until its collapse in 1494. It was among the earliest businesses to use the general ledger system of accounting by developing double-entry bookkeeping to track credits and debits. The bank was considered one of the most prosperous and respected institutions in Europe. And the Medici family was considered the wealthiest in Europe. They acquired political power first in Florence and later in wider Italy and Europe, although they officially remained citizens, rather than monarchs.

As it were, they would in the course of time produce four Roman Catholic Popes:

- Pope Leo X (1513–1521)
- Pope Clement VII (1523–1534)
- Pope Pius IV (1559–1565)[5]
- Pope Leo XI (1605)

They also produced two queens of France—Catherine de' Medici (1547–1559) and Marie de' Medici (1600–1610). In 1532, they acquired the hereditary title Duke of Florence. In 1569, the duchy was elevated to the Grand Duchy of Tuscany after territorial expansion. The Medici ruled the Grand Duchy from its inception until its bankruptcy at the death of Gian Gastone de' Medici in 1737. They also claim to have funded the invention of the piano and opera. They financed the construction of Saint Peter's Basilica and Florence's Cattedrale di Santa Maria del Fiore. This Cathedral of Saint Mary of the Flower was begun in 1296 in the Gothic style, to a design of Arnolfo di Cambio. It was structurally completed by 1436, with the dome engineered by Filippo Brunelleschi.

In addition to Brunelleschi, the Medici's were also patrons of Botticelli, Leonardo da Vinci, Michelangelo, Raphael, Machiavelli, Galileo and Francesco Redi, among many others in the arts and sciences. Not only that, they were leading players in Martin Luther's reformation (1517–) through the Council of Trent. They played a role also in the counter reformation and the French wars of religion. That prolonged period of war and popular unrest pitted Catholics and Huguenots (Reformed/Calvinist Protestants) against each other in the Kingdom of France from 1562 to 1598. Three million people are said to have perished during that period from violence, famine or disease out of an estimated population somewhere between 11 and 20 million. It is considered Europe's second deadliest religious war in history. In the twentieth century, it was surpassed only by the Thirty Years' War (1618-1648), which took eight million lives out of an estimated population of 78 million.

In other words, the Medicis not only dominated their city's government, but also created an environment in which art and humanism flourished. Part of that was the *Platonic Academia*, which Cosimo de' Medici sponsored at the 1438–1439 Council of Florence. This was the seventeenth ecumenical council from 1431 to 1449 recognized by the Catholic Church. It was supported by the Medicis until the death of Lorenzo de' Medici (1449–1492) to reintroduce Plato's thoughts to Western Europe. Never a formal group, the members of this modern form of Plato's Academy translated into Latin all of Plato's and other neo-platonic works.

Among the Academy's scholars was Giovanni Pico della Mirandola (1463–1494) who became the first Christian scholar to master the Jewish mystical theology of the Kabbalah. This was his attempt to develop a form of syncretism, whereby different systems of thought could be harmonized based on shared elements of truth. Who decided what is truth or lie is unknown. Best known as author of the *Oration on the Dignity of Man*, considered to be the manifesto of Renaissance humanism, he wrote:

> "We have given you, O Adam, no visage proper to yourself, nor endowment properly your own, in order that whatever place, whatever form, whatever gifts you may, with premeditation, select, these same you may have and possess through your own judgement and decision. The nature of all other creatures is defined and restricted within laws which We have laid down; you, by contrast, impeded by no such restrictions, may, by your own free will, to whose custody We have assigned you, trace for yourself the lineaments of your own nature. I have placed you at the very center of the world, so that from that vantage point you may with greater ease glance round about you on all that the world contains. We have made you a creature neither of heaven nor of earth, neither mortal nor immortal, in order that you may, as the free and proud shaper of your own being, fashion yourself in the form you may prefer. It will be in your power to descend to the lower, brutish forms of life; you will be able, through your own decision, to rise again to the superior orders whose life is divine." (https://www.encyclopedia.com/people/philosophy-and-religion/philosophy-biographies/giovanni-pico-della-mirandola).

The meaning of the term *humanism* has fluctuated according to the successive intellectual movements that have identified with it. Generally, however, humanism refers to a perspective that affirms some notion of human freedom and progress. It views humanity as responsible for promoting and developing individuals. It espouses the equal and inherent dignity of all human beings, and emphasizes a concern for humans in relation to the world. By the twentieth century, humanist movements typically are non-religious movements aligned with secularism.

Secularism is most commonly defined as the separation of religion from civic affairs and the state. It means removing religion and spirituality from all public spheres. The term per se has a broad range of meanings. In the most schematic, it could include all that promotes anticlericalism, atheism and naturalism, as well as the removal of religious symbols from public institutions. As already mentioned, today's humanism usually refers to an atheistic life stance purely centred on human agency. It looks exclusively to science, logic and reason. It shuns in their entirety possible revelations or assistance received through prayers, in meditation, via divination or other so-called supernatural sources. It rejects these means of understanding the world and normally-to-be-expected human life experiences. With humanism, one cannot draw assistance on any of these when in distress or facing normal life upheavals.

Needless to say, therefore, secular humanism expertly strangles humanitarianism. The latter is based on an active belief in the value of human life and the existence of God as both its Creator and the giver of sustenance and aid. As a result, humanitarianism evolves from the desire to alleviate someone else's sufferings. Based on love, compassion and empathy, it is the extension of welfare and succor from the areas in which these could historically be found, namely family, church and society at large. For moral and altruistic reasons, these provided benevolent treatment and assistance to those in need, as described at length in *Fallacy 1*.

The charge into secular humanism actually began with Henry VIII (1491–1547), who beheaded two of his six wives, when he expropriated the churches and their properties. They were the only institutions taking care of the destitute and mentally handicapped those days.

And, as Mullins maintains, placing "human interests" first in all things created the climate for the French Revolution and the guillotining of King Louis XVI. After denying the existence of God, it was a simple step to deny the authority of a monarch who ruled by divine right.

Sir Francis Bacon's dictum that "knowledge is power" threw down the gauntlet to the traditional powers of church and state.

The Positivism of Comte stated that "God is only an abstraction—he does not exist; only humanity is real."

All these ideas created fertile ground for the French Revolution, with its ensuing brutalities of unimaginable proportions. That catastrophe, of course, ended with the Battle of Waterloo in 1815, with Napoleon having wreaked havoc across Europe and Russia for 16 years, (1799–1815). Or was it the beginning of our humanism-ruled world today, perhaps?

Shortly after that battle, a number of mostly non-clerical folks began to work on projects to relieve the destitute and improve slums, as well as reduce of the plight of the insane, the indigent and the imprisoned. Societies were also formed to abolish slavery, end poverty and promote temperance, as well to improve literacy. All these were viewed as a guiding spirit of the nineteenth century's attempt at social reform. The drive for social reform to improve humanity's moral and social condition was viewed as identical with social science. Why?

Because the ultimate purpose of social science was viewed by almost everyone in the learned society as taking care of the physical welfare of humanity regardless of its silly beliefs in such inanity as God or supernatural powers. Humanitarian aspects and desires to assist out of the kindness of the heart were eliminated. Only science and its discoveries of the human physical bodies and their reaction to experiments had valour. This was completely in line with secular humanism.

That Darwin's pathetic theory of evolution published in 1859 hugely aided and abetted the humanism scheme is a given. In a nutshell, it turned humans into machines that could be arranged and rearranged and analyzed, taken apart and put together again at leisure by scientists. And so they did, with the help of rattus, cani, simian, mus and lupus. It all began with Pavlov's famous dog experiments (*Fallacy 1*). It is that simple. Humanism was in; humanitarianism was out. And nothing has changed to this day. That the only way to heal genuine PTSD, and most likely all other illnesses originating from the heart and soul, is beyond the mental health-and other professions. They deal with humanity, professing in their mental hallucinations and fullness of themselves to be experts of its wellbeing and healing. As a matter of fact, the thought alone would cause them fits of apoplexy!

Which leads us straight back to Admiral Satcher's and Vice-president Gore's 1999 suicide prevention agenda's press conference. They announced that public-private partnerships would be the ideal way to fund the so-urgently-needed suicide research, education and treatment program. Surely, that would prevent the fewer than 800,000 humans (700,000 by 2020) from killing themselves annually throughout the world. Surely, they would stop engaging in such nonsensical behaviour. That fewer than 30,000 of them resided in the U.S. in 1999 was beside the point.

Like poisonous weeds, they sprang up as non-profit organizations throughout the Earth's nations. They were all supported by the gullible public and government grants. They were all assuring to enrich their founders and all those working for them as mental health providers throughout the lands. And most of them, through their treatment modalities, would be doing nothing other than what Thomas Szasz calls "manufacturing madness."

To the U.S. government, however, the whole suicide prevention agenda seems to be of utmost importance. Surgeon General Jerome Michael Adams (1974–) was appointed by President Donald Trump in 2017. He is an anesthesiologist holding the rank of vice admiral in the U.S. Public Health Service Commissioned Corps. He saw fit, one day before being relieved from duties by incoming President Joe Biden, to publish his seven cents worth of view in his own *The Surgeon General Releases Call to Action to Implement the National Strategy for Suicide Prevention* (OASH Media: 202-205-0143). In it, he outlines the actions that communities and non-suicidal people can take to reduce suicide rates in others and help boost resilience, we assume in those wanting to kill themselves.

Adams tells that suicide had claimed more than 47,000 lives in 2019, an increase of 30% since 1999. He also conveys that, due to COVID-19, many Americans were indicating mental health concerns related to economic hardship and social isolation. Who did the indicating is unknown. While he could not predict what effect the so-called pandemic would have on suicide rates, he thought the time to act was now, exclaiming:

"Americans have faced unprecedented hardship in the past months, but by focusing daily on caring for our own emotional well-being and supporting the well-being of those we love, we can successfully mitigate the mental health effects of the COVID-19 pandemic. Although this is a difficult time in our nation's history, I remain steadfast in encouraging Americans to use healthy mechanisms to cope. If we all step into this challenge, we will limit emotional suffering, save lives and lay the foundation for a healthier nation going forward."

His *Call to Action* intended to broaden perceptions of suicide and who can be affected. And it would enlighten the herd about suicide risk factors. Whereupon he rolls into telling us that a variety of influences at the individual, relationship, community and societal levels can lead to or increase suicide risk. These issues were, in his opinion, social isolation, relationship problems and the loss of a loved one, as well as legal and financial issues.

All of it is related to the state creation of social distancing and masks over mouth and nose. This creates oxygen depravation, leading to anoxia and/or hypoxia. It was also state that separated loved ones from family members enclosed in geriatric care or hospitals, It was the state that scared the populace to death through the media with a virus yet to be proven to exist. Add in with a phenomenal amount of heightened anxiety and prescribed mind-altering pharmaceutical drugs by their caring physicians. No wonder Adam saw fit to shout for a call of action on his very last day in office as a farewell gesture to the herd.

He, the caring state authority figure, fits so well in line with secular humanism practices. So, he declares that he only wishes the *national narrative* to add environmental to the individual factors contributing to the desire to kill oneself. And what may those environmental factors be? Well, the only study on the topic we could find was conducted on Australian and French farmers and farm workers. Pay attention, as it is directly related to the COVID-19 situation we find ourselves in due to those we allow to rule us.

Eric Souêtre, et al., *analyzed* the regional distribution of completed suicides in 19 regions of France for the years 1975 and 1983. Their 1990 study "Influence of environmental factors on suicidal behavior", was apparently the first study ever conducted on the topic (Psychiatry Research Volume 32, Issue 3, June 1990, Pages 253–263). They looked at the regional distributions of such environmental variables as ambient temperature, sunlight duration and precipitation, as well as sociological factors, such as social cohesion, socioeconomic status, status of women and social support. They found that among all environmental and sociological variables studied, the main factors affecting the regional distribution of suicide were ambient temperature and sunlight duration. Their findings demonstrated a clear relationship between environmental variables and suicidal behavior. In their view, this was consistent with description of forms of affective disorder., Of 56.02 million individuals living in France at that time, 11,194 had killed themselves at the report's publication.

Souêtre, holds a medical degree (M.D.) by the Medical University of Nice, a PhD in neuroscience by the Marseille University and an MBA by HEC School of Business (Paris). He conducted this research as a visiting fellow at the National Institute of Mental Health in Bethesda, Maryland. From a position as assistant professor at the Paris Medical University, he then transferred to the U.S. National Institutes of Health to begin a career in research (https://careventures.eu/team/dr-eric-souetre/). Tired of that, he founded *Benefit* in 1990. This healthcare economics research and consultancy business expanded to over six European countries and Canada before being acquired by Quintiles Inc. (U.S.) in 1995. Quintiles Transnational is the largest pharmaceutical outsourcing service company in the U.S., with offices in 60 countries. It provides product development, financial assistance, and commercial services to help pharmaceutical companies with their clinical trials. As a board member, Souêtre took over worldwide responsibility for the group's consultancy services.

An industrious man, he founded *Nucleus* in 2000. This private investment fund specialized in Medical IT and diagnostics. He followed in 2003 with co-founding Labco, a European leader in medical diagnostics services for patients, physicians and other healthcare providers. In 2015, it merged with the SYNLAB Group, an international medical diagnostics provider with laboratory services for human and veterinary medicine, as well as environmental analysis. Headquartered in Munich, Germany, the company is present in more than 40 countries on four continents. It employs around 20,000 employees with 2018 sales revenues of approximately 1.9 billion Euro.

In addition, Souêtre co-founded Care Ventures Inc. in 2014. This healthcare management firm is based in Cumberland, Maryland. It has about 400 employees dedicated to providing quality, customer-focused healthcare and rehabilitation services, as well as help with programs, marketing and financial needs to companies that service the healthcare continuum.

It also handles healthcare compliance issues.

What's that, you may wonder? It is the process of following rules, regulations and laws relating to healthcare practices. Healthcare compliance, we read, is about providing safe, high-quality patient care, and healthcare organizations are held to strict standards, regulations and laws at federal and state levels. Violations of these laws can result in lawsuits, hefty fines or loss of licenses. Compliance issues also relate to patient safety, the privacy of patient information and billing practices.

Here the 10 most prominent ones in the United States as of 2020 that Care Ventures promises to handle:

Top 10 U.S. Health Care Compliance Issues for 2020

1. OCR Enforcement Actions

At the end of 2019, the Office of Civil Rights (OCR) entered into the first enforcement actions we have seen related to the U.S. Department of Health and Human Services' (DHHS's) Patient Right to Access Initiative. This should serve as a reminder that covered entities should respond to patient requests for access to their medical records in a timely manner, in the format requested by the patient, and not charge more than a reasonable cost-based fee. (Note: There may be state laws that are more stringent than the Federal law, and as such, should be followed if applicable.)

2. Ransomware

DHHS has identified ransomware as one of the most common threats to patient health information (PHI). Though there were initially only two basic types of ransomware—lock and crypto—there is now a third type, DataKeeper—which is franchised and gaining ground quickly. Health care providers and related entities should remain alert to this fast-developing privacy and security threat.

3. Regulatory Landscape

The fraud and abuse regulatory landscape for healthcare providers is vast and includes the Stark Law, the Federal anti-kickback statute (AKS), the Civil Monetary Penalties (CMP) Law, the False Claims Act, antitrust laws, the Eliminating Kickbacks in Recovery Act of 2018 (EKRA), and state laws. Changes to the regulatory bedrock Stark Law and AKS are forthcoming with the issuance of proposed regulations that will presumably be finalized. Moreover, the first criminal prosecution pursuant to EKRA took place in 2019.

4. Value-Based Compensation Arrangements

Determining value-based compensation arrangements for physicians can be tricky. To ease this process, healthcare providers should prepare value-based reimbursement inventories and understand what the outcome to incentivize is. Accordingly, providers should not rely solely on benchmark data.

5. Medicare Overpayment Refunds

Under the statutory 60-day overpayment refund requirement and implementing regulations addressing Medicare Parts A and B, healthcare providers have an obligation to exercise reasonable diligence through the timely, good faith investigation of credible information to identify an overpayment. Deciding whether information is sufficiently credible to merit an investigation is fact-specific. However, the Centers for Medicare and Medicaid Services (CMS) makes it clear in the Parts A/B regulations and preambles that identification requires both proactive and reactive auditing of billing. Providers and suppliers should also keep in mind that the overpayment requirement extends beyond the regulatory requirements for Parts A/B to Medicare C and D, Medicare Advantage, Medicaid and Medicaid managed care plans. There are no implementing regulations for these other payors, but the statutory obligation remains.

6. Government Overpayments

There is no *de minimus* threshold for governmental overpayments, *i.e.,* there is no minimal amount that can be ignored. All potential overpayments should be investigated. Health care providers should expect their decision regarding whether to conduct relevant claims extrapolation (versus a per claim analysis and repayment) to be scrutinized closely.

7. Health Care Transaction Due Diligence

Areas of due diligence to consider with respect to healthcare-related transactions include gaps in understanding of compliance plans or lack of compliance plans; coding, billing, and documentation issues; HIPAA security; litigation, audits, and investigations; employee relations; risk management; quality metric reporting; and change of ownership filing/approval requirements.

8. Compliance Due Diligence

Compliance due diligence processes should incorporate the following: annual risk assessments to develop up-to-date compliance work plans, exclusion checks and conflict of interest reviews upon initiation of employment or contract and regularly thereafter, and management and monitoring of revenue cycle functions and vendor contractual arrangements.

9. Telemedicine Provider Qualification, Licensing, and Operations Compliance

Telemedicine entities engaging in and/or embarking on multi-state delivery models must be cognizant of, and compliant with, applicable state foreign entity qualification requirements and corporate practice prohibitions, and must ensure that their clinical services providers are duly licensed (or registered) and compliant with clinical practice requirements in the states in which they seek to treat patients.

10. False Claims Act Enforcement Target Areas

> In the coming year, we expect to see an increased number of cases focused on Medicare Advantage (MA) and skilled nursing facilities (SNFs). The focus of the MA cases will arise out of plans' failure to inform the government of mistaken diagnoses that are not current because MA plans are paid based on those diagnosis codes. Further, we have been told that those Medicare Advantage cases could pull in healthcare providers and suppliers, so although diagnosis codes have been reviewed in compliance audits in the past, the scrutiny on the accuracy of those diagnosis codes, the electronic health records' issues with pulling past diagnosis codes forward and the correction of such diagnosis codes must be a focus. We also understand that the DOJ is focusing on SNFs because of continuing issues related to substandard care, neglect and improper prescribing of drugs to patients, so the DOJ's Elder Justice Initiative is likely to involve a more thorough investigation into these kinds of cases in the near future (https://acc.com).

Meanwhile in Australia, Meg Perceval et al. of the Australian Research Institute for Suicide Prevention were doing their own research. They produced "Environmental factors and suicide in Australian farmers: A qualitative study" in 2018 (*Archives of Environmental & Occupational Health* Volume 74, 2019 - Issue 5). The aim was to identify and understand environmental factors associated with suicide among Australian farmers and farm workers. They, too, found that extreme climatic events created upheaval in humans. So did:

- isolation
- lack of service availability
- technology-or lack thereof
- and sinking property values
- death and the suffering of animals
- legislation and government rules and regulation

Frequent use of firearms, they noted, might also contribute to an enhanced desire of killing the Self, they thought.

The study was funded by Australia's National Centre of Excellence in Suicide Prevention and the World Health Organization's Collaborating Centre for Research and Training in Suicide Prevention at Griffith University, Queensland, Australia. When opening its doors in 1975, Griffith offered Australia's first degrees in environmental science and Asian studies. On its campus, the Australian Institute for Suicide Research and Prevention (AISRAP) national and international suicide prevention research center began to conduct public health surveillance of suspected suicides with government, industry bodies and non-government organizations funding. AISRAP operates a specialized outpatient clinic since 2004 for people deemed, we do not know by whom, to display suicidal tendencies. The institute also provides education and training for health and allied health professionals of unknown qualifications. In 2008, the State appointed AISRAP as the National Centre of Excellence in Suicide Prevention (NCESP). It is funded by the Commonwealth Government's Department of Health's National Suicide Prevention Program.

CRESP, the Centre of Research Excellence in Suicide Prevention, is another Australian agency making its living by pretending to be able to prevent the unpreventable. In its hallucinations, it engages in a collaborative program led by the Black Dog Institute. This not-for-profit facility diagnoses, treats and prevents mood disorders, such as depression, anxiety and bipolar disorder. It was founded in 2002 by the University of New Sought Wales' School of Psychiatry in Sydney, Australia. CRESP presumes to be able to reduce suicide rates by:

- generating new research in suicide prevention, including digital solutions
- better predicting and detecting oncoming suicides to create safety nets for "at risk" people
- delivering targeted preventions and interventions at the right time and in the right place

CRESP brings together leading expertise in suicide prevention research and implementation as a collective. On this basis, it defines and prioritises the programs and funding models that it believes will see the biggest reduction in suicide rates. And how much is the Australian Commonwealth willing to spend on suicide prevention in its 2021-2022 Budget as it, like the U.S. government, proclaims to remain to be so deeply committed to working towards zero suicides? A total of $298.1 million over 4 years.

During that time, the government will work in partnership with state and territory governments to:

- for the first time deliver universal suicide aftercare services to every Australian discharged from hospital following a suicidal crisis or attempt;
- look for opportunities to expand aftercare for anyone who has attempted suicide or experienced suicidal distress that may not have presented to a hospital;
- fund national suicide postvention services to help those bereaved or impacted by suicide, including families, friends, workplaces, schools, community groups, frontline responders and witnesses; and
- pilot a national distress intervention program, which will reach people earlier in crisis and provide immediate support.

In addition, the Australian Budget establishes a National Suicide Prevention Office with an initial investment of $12.8 million to oversee the national whole-of-government approach to prevent suicide.

The government also committed $61.6 million over four years (from 2021-22, they state, as if two times two makes four) to expand the National Suicide Prevention Leadership and Support Program. This would increase investment in whole-of-population suicide prevention activities and services. A further $12 million in 2021-22 will enable the former National Suicide Prevention Trial sites to continue delivering local suicide prevention projects across Australia.

Altogether, Australia's government is committing a total of $1.4 billion over four years (or two, if you can count), from 2021 22 we read, for mental health treatment. All this would deliver to ensure the delivery of easy- to-access and high quality, person-centered treatment for all Australians who need it at the right stage of life (Budget 2021–22: Portfolio Budget Statements - Australian https://www.health.gov.au › documents › 2021/06)

How many souls committed suicide in Australia in 2019, the latest figures available? From a population of 25.36 million, just 3318 took their lives. Wonder if the arrival of

COVID-19 might have had something to do with this frantic suicide research over the past three decades? Is it because of scientific findings, that we were quarantined in our homes and deprived of sunshine and fresh air, for example, and into complete isolation? Does the state know full well that it, combined with financial worries, would impair our joy of living and mental wellbeing? Does it see how this confinement would easily push us into suicidal ideation, in particular when combined with the antidepressants so joyously prescribed by caring physician who do never need to take the *Oath of Hippocrates* when graduating Med School, as so falsely advertised?

Here's a soother, though. A killing-self pandemic seems yet to have occurred, although that may change once the effects COVID 19 injections take effect among the herd. But that's a wait-and-see game, we won't dwell on at this time. Let us rather move onwards and see, what Trump's Surgeon General Adam's meant by "national narrative" before he left his exalted office, shall we?

19

THE NATIONAL NARRATIVE: DHARMA VS. KARMA

Four-star Admiral and Surgeon General Satcher was not alone. His 1999 press conference on the *National Strategy for Suicide Prevention* (NSSP), *Natural Strategy, A Call to Collaboration: The Federal Commitment to Suicide Prevention* was part of a larger context. Thus, a clarion call about the government's initiatives had gone out at the same time to all 50 U.S. states, with an appeal to help create the United States national narrative on suicide prevention.

What is the definition of "national narrative?"

- It writes the history of a nation within other stories.
- It is any narrative where you can see the characters or specific space as a microcosm for the larger public history of how that nation is and was shaped.
- It gives shape to the beliefs, the aspirations and the sense of identity of national groups or nations as a whole.

In essence, it is history in the making in line with shaping a nation's future, according to German philosopher Friedrich Hegel. Stay tuned for more on his theories in the last chapter, 22. National narratives are generally used by political elites in different ways and means for different ends, wiht the Boer War, the Russian Revolution, the 3rd Reich, India's Gandhi-generated Independence, China's CCP takeover and COVID 19, just to name a few incidents of shaping national narratives.

During COVID-19, masks, non-social distancing, family and solitary confinement are all part of shaping the nation's narrative and thus creating its future. In Canada, the complete border closings of all four Atlantic provinces during COVID-19 forms part of that national narrative creation. Likewise, Surgeon General Satcher's 1999 ideas about suicide prevention forms part of the U.S. national narrative. The District of Columbia, an independent federal corporation outside of the United States of America, could impose and enforce what it considered protective methods to attempt to prevent not only its own citizens, but those of the world, from killing the Self. That suicide in those determined to leave the earth through killing the Self has proven to be unpreventable is of no consequence to him or anyone else in his league. Nor is the fact, that suicide rates in the intermittent years dropped by 5% overall, and from 47,511 to 44,834 between 2019 to 2020 in the U.S. alone does not matter to them, either. And to heck with the drop from 800.000 to 700,000 worldwide during that same time span.

As we are aware, Satcher's agenda is still in full swing. This comes at enormous expense to the country's citizens, while offering huge benefits to the mental health industry. There is no end in sight, either. Why kill the golden goose, eh? Satcher's ukase (a proclamation of the Russian Tsar or its Patriarch, having the force of law), regarding suicide prevention imposes the following on the populace at large:

1. Help other people build life skills (e.g., coping, problem solving) and resilience.
2. Increase social connectedness and support.
3. Identify and support people at risk.
4. Limit access to lethal objects
5. Support access to effective care.
6. Seek help, support, and care when experiencing suicidal thoughts.
7. Support people who have been affected by a suicide attempt or death.

That the populace, the herd, is largely unaware of such imposition is beside the point. That they pay for it is all that counts.

Colleen Longfellow Carr is director of the U.S. public-private partnership National Action Alliance for Suicide Prevention (Action Alliance), which sprang forth with Satcher's idea. The Alliance is housed at the Education Development Center in Washington, DC. It prides itself in advancing lasting solutions to the most pressing educational, health and workforce challenges across the globe. The Alliance works with more than 250 national partners to advance the Surgeon General's 1999 ideas in his *National Strategy for Suicide Prevention*. Even its current 2021 priority areas are the same,

- transforming health systems
- transforming communities
- changing the conversation

The Alliance "catalyzes planning, implementation, and accountability for updating and advancing the NSSP" since Satcher's time. Carr provides strategic direction to the Action

Alliance's leadership, with 40 members sitting on its Executive Committee, all engaged in preventing the suicide of less than 40,000 Americans annually. (https://theactionalliance.org/about/staff/colleen-carr). Thus, it is Missie Carr who shapes the national narrative by making the nation believe it is sick with suicidal ideation, when piping in pure secular humanism fashion: "Every sector of society must come together to make suicide prevention a national priority. The time to act is now."

She works at this shaping of the nation's narrative into suicide desires endlessly and everywhere. Senior leaders of every sector in the United States, from forestry to education, from professional sports to justice, from faith to automobiles are all involved with her. The media, needless to say, are vital to the undertaking. It serves as collective propagandist and agitator to get the herd into the mood of fear, of course. But it also serves as its collective organizer through the mass media mind-manipulation techniques so well developed by Freud et al., applied and perfected by his nephew Bernays (see *Fallacy 1*) and brought to hitherto unknown brilliant perfection nowadays. After all, a lie told often enough becomes truth in the masses' mind. (Lenin). And one of the national narrative's present schemes is to push you into the hands of mental health professionals and mind-altering drugs, which, without a shadow of a doubt, create suicidal ideation within you. It is that simple.

Not only the deplorables, the common, blue-collar workers employed in every industry, are part of Director Carr's suicidal prevention agenda. Busy as she is, she also works with federal agencies perceived to play a role in the nation's suicide prevention efforts, as proscribed by the DC Federal Corporation. Thus, the U.S. Departments of Defense, Health and Human Services, and Homeland Security are all called upon to assist the National Strategy through co-ordination, alignment, and advancement. The Action Alliance dictates the priority initiatives, including:

- transforming health systems in the name of suicide reduction
- transforming entire communities to strengthen community-based suicide prevention methods
- changing the public conversation about suicide

For this, the Alliance created a whole new website, *Framework for Successful Messaging*. The goal was to make suicide ideas look "normal", in accordance with the after-COVID-19 "normal." The framework, they say, is one step to advance this priority of theirs, those who rule us and in complete silence create our national narrative for us. What is it about? You make up your own mind:

> "The *Framework for Successful Messaging* is a resource to help people messaging about suicide to develop messages that are strategic, safe, positive, and make use of relevant guidelines and best practices."
>
> "It was created by the National Action Alliance for Suicide Prevention as part of its focus on changing the public conversation about suicide."
>
> "WHY it's important: Because messaging matters! Certain types of public messaging about suicide can increase risk among vulnerable individuals."

> "Conversely, communications can be a powerful tool to promote resiliency, encourage help seeking, publicize prevention successes, and encourage actions that help prevent suicide."
>
> "HOW it's unique: It's for *suicide prevention messengers*, rather than the media."
>
> "It addresses 'public messaging': any communications released into the public domain. From posters, PSAs, and social media to websites, newsletters, fundraising appeals, event publicity, press interactions, public talks, and advocacy efforts, each contributes to the public's perceptions about suicide and suicide prevention." (suicidepreventionmessaging.org)

Officially, Carr oversees all of it. But she mainly focuses her personal attention on her purported suicide prevention technical knowledge in policy analysis and system-level changes. As a matter of fact, she and her team even provide technical assistance and purported subject matter expertise to the Action Alliance's 16 infrastructure task forces:

- Data and Surveillance Task Force
- National Strategy for Suicide Prevention Task Force
- Research Prioritization Task Force
- High-risk populations task forces including:
    - American Indian/Alaska Native Task Force
    - LGBT Populations Task Force
    - Military/Veterans Task Force
    - Suicide Attempt Survivors Task Force, and
    - Survivors of Suicide Loss Task Force
- Clinical Care and Intervention Task Force
- Clinical Workforce Preparedness Task Force
- Faith Communities Task Force
- Public Awareness and Education Task Force
- Workplace Task Force
- Youth in Contact with the Juvenile Justice System Task Force
- Lethal Means Stakeholder Group

The latter, formed in 2017, aims at reducing access to lethal means, meaning any instrument or objects, such as medicines, firearms and bridges, used to carry out a self-destructive act by those deemed—by the State—to be at risk for suicide (National Suicide Prevention Lifeline; samhsa.gov; theactionalliance.org). This may explain, why bridge repairs in the U.S. have no longer a place in the federal budget.

And what academic background enables Carr to carry out her distinctly humanistic work, as her private one is inaccessible to us?

She received an undergraduate degree in public policy analysis from the University of North Carolina at Chapel Hill. Social sciences-based public policy analysis majors gain a background in economics and political science. They train students to develop the leadership and problem-solving skills needed to thrive in the policy world and to address society's challenges, no matter the arena. They require an understanding of mathematics and data collection to make informed decisions. They also require the ability to share their work with stakeholders of varying levels of understanding and engagement based on communication skills. She also holds a master's degree in public health (MPH) bestowed upon her by Boston University. Its website tells us that effective public health requires expertise from many disciplines. Therefore, a required course had been created to teach an integrated core curriculum consisting of the following:

- PH 717 Quantitative Methods for Public Health (4 credits)
- PH 718 Leadership and Management in Public Health (4 credits)
- PH 719 Health Systems, Law, and Policy (4 credits)
- PH 720 Individual, Community, and Population Health (4 credits)

Once completed, students may select from 16 interdisciplinary certificates *en route* to the MPH, which are:

1. Community Assessment, Program Design, Implementation, and Evaluation
2. Environmental Health
3. Epidemiology and Biostatistics
4. Global Health Program Design, Monitoring, and Evaluation
5. Health Communication and Promotion
6. Health Policy and Law
7. Healthcare Management
8. Program Management Chronic and Non-Communicable Diseases
9. Global Health
10. Human Rights and Social Justice
11. Infectious Disease
12. Maternal and Child Health
13. Mental Health and Substance Use
14. Pharmaceutical Development, Delivery, and Access
15. Sex, Sexuality, and Gender

It takes two years to complete an MPH. We gather from its curriculum that Director Carr was academically educated in full humanism fashion. That means her schooling failed to address humans' emotional and mind-spirit-consciousness tendencies, never mind the herd's metaphysical or psychological aspects of life and living. As we know nothing of her private existence, we have no knowledge where her own beliefs lie, but atheism springs to mind.

What we do know, however, is that when she left Boston University with her MPH in hand, she was judged to be able to hallucinate into existence, chuckle, chuckle:

- Evidence-Based Approaches to Public Health
- Public Health & Healthcare Systems
- Planning & Management to Promote Health
- Policy in Public Health
- Leadership
- Communication
- Inter-professional Practice
- Systems Thinking

Upon her graduation from that hallowed institution, she worked for AmeriCorps Volunteers Service to America (VISTA). This idea was President John F. Kennedy's, before he was assassinated in Dallas, Texas, in1963. In consequence, President Lyndon B. Johnson followed with the War on Poverty, part of an expansive social welfare legislation reform program known as the Great Society. It led the United States Congress to pass the Economic Opportunity Act. That law established the Office of Economic Opportunity (OEO) to administer the local application of federal funds targeted against poverty. The 40 programs established by the Act were collectively aimed at eliminating poverty by improving living conditions for residents of low-income neighborhoods and by helping the poor access economic opportunities. Johnson brayed: "Our aim is not only to relieve the symptom of poverty, but to cure it and, above all, to prevent it."

Some War on Poverty policies remain in existence. An example would be the Department of Health and Human Services Head Start. It provides comprehensive early childhood education as well as health, nutrition and parent involvement services to low-income children and families. Missie Carr's VISTA is also part of it, as are the TRIO Programs. In turn, it is all part of Lyndon B. Johnson's *Great Society agenda*, manifested in the Higher Education Act of 1965 (HEA). Its main goal? Ending poverty, reducing crime, abolishing inequality and racial injustice, as well as improving the environment.

TRIO programs, part of the Higher Education Act of 1965 (HEA), were to strengthen U.S. colleges and universities through increases in federal funding. They would create scholarships, give low-interest loans to students from disadvantaged backgrounds in postsecondary and higher education and establish a National Teachers Corps. All of it is funded, administered, managed, implemented and controlled by the U.S. Department of Education. In 1973, Congress established the Domestic Volunteer Service Act (P.L. 93-113), in part to provide funding and regulations for VISTA's operation.

In the words of the enacting legislation:

> "The purpose of this [Act] is to foster and expand voluntary citizen service in communities throughout the Nation in activities designed to help poor, disadvantaged, the vulnerable, and the elderly. In carrying out this purpose, the Corporation for National and Community Service shall utilize to the fullest extent the programs authorized under this chapter, coordinate with other Federal, State, and local agencies and utilize the energy, innovative spirit, experience, and skills of all Americans." (encyclopedia.com/history/)

In 1993, some five million Americans served in AmeriCorps, Senior Corps, the Volunteer Generation Fund and other national volunteer services. All agencies were united under the Corporation for National and Community Service (CNCS) umbrella. Its mission? "To improve lives, strengthen communities, and foster civic engagement through service and volunteering." Created by the National and Community Service Trust Act of 1993, this federal government agency happens to be the nation's largest annual grant maker in support of service and volunteering. Its annual budget? Just over $1 billion as of 2013. It employed 596 in 2020, and had a stage set with volunteers at the ready for the expected COVID-19 suicide pandemic.

To give you an idea about AmeriCorps traditional corps program, it lasts 10 months for Corps members and 11 for team leaders. Participants are from 18 to 26 years of age. They work on at least four projects in different states with multiple non-profit sponsor organizations to, purportedly, meet a variety of community needs in the areas of energy conservation, infrastructure improvement, natural and other disaster services and urban and rural development. Throughout their service, they receive free lodging and travel. Team leaders need no prior AmeriCorps experience.

And what do they, the volunteers, receive? A living stipend of no less than $900 monthly. The living stipend amounts to a minimum of $11,136 annually before tax. After completing a full term of service, members receive a Segal AmeriCorps Education Award of approximately $6,500 to help pay for college or pay back student loans, or they get a $1500 cash award.

In 2020, President Donald Trump, however, threw a spike in the wheel. He asked to eliminate the Corporation for National Community Services (CNCS) AmeriCorps, and thus VISTA, in his, Fiscal Year 2020 (FY2020) budget. Regardless, CNCS got $1,104,358 million in 2020 in federal funding, with $93,364,000 going to VISTA. In 2021, President Biden hiked it to $1,121,102 million, with $97,364 million to VISTA. Add to that the new regime's multi-trillion Green Budget, and it became $1,210,266, with $103,864 million going to those knowing about the VISTA program. Sucking on the public tit is the vernacular terminology, is it?

Thus, still in operation, 5,000 VISTA members are said to make their living by serving in over 900 projects throughout the U.S. Among them, is Eileen Conoboy, its deputy director since at least 2016. Dwelling somewhere near or at NASA Headquarters in Washington, DC, she is without a doubt looking much forward to the loot necessary to pay the salaries for the operation of this organization, which, in the course of time, has ballooned to over one million members.

That such volunteer services and lucrative employments should be necessary under the U.S. federal and individual state governments' social distancing-, lock-and shut-in and suicidal-ideation-enforcing conditions seems puzzling, really – a conundrum of some proportion. Unless, of course, when knowing that a social catastrophe was planned to take place in the United States of America, part of which would be the Drive-The-Herd-Into-Suicide agenda.

Miss Colleen Longfellow Carr had jumped AmeriCorps VISTA to work in public policy at state- and national levels even before Trump sought to eliminate that show. Occupying herself with clinical research into injury and poison prevention, she jumped on board the National Action Alliance suicide prevention vessel somewhere around 2015. Much adjustment was not needed, as the Alliance had the same rights as had been granted under the 1964 War on Poverty Act. It was authorized to form and directly regulate local community action agencies, in order to strengthen, supplement and coordinate efforts to further prevent suicides.

The Alliance partnered with the federal Substance Abuse And Mental Health Services Administration (SAMHSA), a branch of the U.S. Department of Health and Human Services. It, in turn, partnered with Facebook to give suicide crisis workers access to Facebook users *flagged by others* for posting comments interpreted as suicidal. "The person who posted the suicidal comment will then immediately receive an email from Facebook encouraging them to call the National Suicide Prevention Lifeline at 1-800-273-TALK (8255) or to click on a link to begin a "confidential chat session with a crisis worker" we read on the website. Who pays for what and how much it costs we do not know.

SAMHSA, in turn, receives its annual budget desires fulfilled from the United States of America Corporation's coffers, filled with taxpayers' hard-earned money. In 2019, it requested and received $4.8 billion, of which $74,034 million were to go to suicide prevention activities. This would be to help the less than 45,000 American citizens who would kill themselves regardless of prevention activities of any sort. (samhsa.gov/sites/default/files/samhsa-fy-2019-congressional-justification.pdf.) In 2020 and 2021, SAMHSA got $90,034 and $93,034 respectively, with a combined overrun to $102,046 million. In 2022, though, President Biden requested $179,667 million, almost doubling the previous amount without any explanation.

We should think those who rule him expect the whole nation to turn sicker than dogs. He states that for the U.S. Human Health Services (HHS) programs to equitably address the country's diverse populations' ailments and diseases, it needs $131.8 billion in discretionary budget authority. That means the money can be used in whatever fashion the health department wishes to use it, including on its own salaries. Note that this is in addition to $1.5 trillion in mandatory funding (hhs.gov). Of that, SAMHSA requests a mere $9.7 billion, of which Miss Carr's operation, the Action Alliance for the prevention of the unpreventable suicide of less than 45,000 Americans annually, will receive $179,667 million to play with, if the budget goes through (https://samhsa.gov).

And what was her reaction to the HHS and the Office of the Surgeon General's 2021 *Call to Action to Implement the National Strategy for Suicide Prevention*?

> "This *Call to Action* is a step towards fully implementing the *National Strategy for Suicide Prevention*, which serves as the nation's roadmap for suicide prevention and which the Action Alliance is tasked with advancing. Together with our public and private sector partners, we are committed to working across sectors and industries to achieve our ultimate vision—a nation free from the tragedy."

That suicides in the nation and the world are dropping and have dropped over the past decades has apparently yet to reach her feeble mind. And if it has, the leitmotiv of both her and the U.S. corporations seems to be:

> "We'll ram it down your throat, now we succeeded in making you destitute through the non-existing, planned COVID 19 pandemic destruction of human societies worldwide. We'll catch anyone in the killing-the-self mood, initiated by physicians handing out mind-altering drugs like candy. Ha! Because they create your desire to kill yourself, which is what we planned for and want. We will catch anyone who, in their ignorance, posts suicidal comments anywhere on any social media platform or in a chat-line. You will immediately receive an email from Facebook to call the National Suicide Prevention Lifeline at 1-800-273-TALK (8255) or to click on a link to start a confidential chat with a complete stranger well-versed in humanistic cognitive behavioural sessions to get your ball

> into hell rolling. Once there, you are like a frog in slowly heating water. Without knowing it, you are finished as a human being, a living soul."

As to all of us, the question is whether we want to write our own personal historical narrative or do as evil demands.

Already in 2011, the Action Alliance partnered with Facebook as part of its agenda to imprint the herd with both the idea and daily possibility of suicide desirability. Its unique style was to be right in its face with suicide education and the warning signs of suicide in others, never mind yourself. Part of it was the promotion of the non-profit National Suicide Prevention Lifeline.

Remember, when suicide prevention was in its infancy in the 1950s and 1960s? When less than 800,000 worldwide killed themselves, propelled into it, because of their innermost heartfelt desire? It did not have its infancy then. It was always part of human behavior, as documented in both Greek and Roman history. But it really began to take off in the late 1980s to early 1990s to be ready for the vigorous American war activities worldwide under the guise of the War on Terror after the September 11, 2001, event. But suicide had always been part of human life, in particular when experiencing such PTSD-causing events inevitable in war conditions. Thus, the statistics presented to us, in true humanist fashion failing to account for the human emotions leading to such despair as desiring to kill the Self, are therefore completely unreliable.

It is a pity that the Self-killing desire is caused by all pharmaceutical mind-altering drugs, that you swallow in good faith—you, the innocent lamb for decades brainwashed into the "Doctor knows best" mantra. That only 39% of physicians under the age of 34 take the Hippocratic Oath (one of the oldest binding documents in history) to treat the ill to the best of one's ability, to preserve a patient's privacy and to teach the secrets of medicine to the next generation, is also kept silent everywhere and anywhere you care to look. For more on it read *Fallacy 1*. That the oath has been rewritten numerous times to fit the desires of specific universities is never mentioned, either.

Here the oath's classical version, the only one of value:

Hippocratic Oath

> I swear by Apollo Physician and Asclepius and Hygieia and Panaceia and all the gods and goddesses, making them my witnesses, that I will fulfill according to my ability and judgment this oath and this covenant:
>
> To hold him who has taught me this art as equal to my parents and to live my life in partnership with him, and if he is in need of money to give him a share of mine, and to regard his offspring as equal to my brothers in male lineage and to teach them this art - if they desire to learn it - without fee and covenant; to give a share of precepts and oral instruction and all the other learning to my sons and to the sons of him who has instructed me and to pupils who have signed the covenant and have taken an oath according to the medical law, but no one else.
>
> I will apply dietetic measures for the benefit of the sick according to my ability and judgment; I will keep them from harm and injustice.

> I will neither give a deadly drug to anybody who asked for it, nor will I make a suggestion to this effect. Similarly, I will not give to a woman an abortive remedy. In purity and holiness, I will guard my life and my art.
>
> I will not use the knife, not even on sufferers from stone, but will withdraw in favor of such men as are engaged in this work.
>
> Whatever houses I may visit, I will come for the benefit of the sick, remaining free of all intentional injustice, of all mischief and in particular of sexual relations with both female and male persons, be they free or slaves.
>
> What I may see or hear in the course of the treatment or even outside of the treatment in regard to the life of men, which on no account one must spread abroad, I will keep to myself, holding such things shameful to be spoken about.
>
> If I fulfill this oath and do not violate it, may it be granted to me to enjoy life and art, being honored with fame among all men for all time to come; if I transgress it and swear falsely, may the opposite of all this be my lot. (https://medicinenet.com/hippocratic_oath/definition.htm)

Figured out yet approximately how much it has cost thus far to prevent less than 800,000 human beings worldwide to kill themselves? Figured out yet why these mostly non-profit suicide prevention agencies were implemented, who benefits and whom they enrich by incredible amounts of money each year? In *Fallacy 1*, I detail some of those subjects. But here is one case in point: according to the U.S. Center of Disease Control's (CDC) preliminary 2020 data published in *The Journal of the American Medical Association* (JAMA), while deaths in the U.S. in 2020 jumped 17.7%, suicides decreased for the third consecutive year in a row, from 47,511 in 2019 to 44,834 in 2020. (https://www.beckershospitalreview.com/public-health/suicides-fell-in-2020-early-cdc-data-shows.html).

Four-star Admiral and Surgeon General Satcher, however, was still alive and kicking after being the catalyst for this suicidal operation. In 2002, ousted by incoming President George Walker Bush, he left it all behind to move on to even greener pastures. That year, he became a fellow at The Henry J. Kaiser Family Foundation (KFF). This non-profit organization headquartered in San Francisco, California. It focuses on major healthcare issues facing the country, as well as the U.S. role in global health policy. It is unable to keep their nose out of other nation's business, mostly for worse, since its founding. KFF describes itself as a non-partisan source of facts and analysis. It engages in journalism and polling for the nation's policymakers, media, healthcare organizations and, purportedly, the public in general. Why? Actually, to steer the herd in the direction they desire to create the national narrative they desire. It is that simple.

The title "Fellow", by the way, is used for participants in a professional development program run by a non-profit or governmental organization. Fellows are given lucrative stipends, as noted in Fallacy 1, as well as professional and leadership training. Other than KFF, Satcher also took the post of Director of the National Center for Primary Care at the Morehouse School of Medicine and positions on the boards of Johnson & Johnson and MetLife, Inc. MetLife is one of the largest global providers of insurance, annuities and employee benefits programs with 90 million customers in over 60 countries. Since its humble beginnings in 1868, it had risen in rank to No. 43 in the Fortune 500 list of the largest United States corporations by total revenue by 2018. It is expected to jump much higher, since it looks like that payouts for all those who voluntarily received the drugs contained in the experimental COVID 19 "jab" therewith may be in jeopardy.

Its precursor was the National Union Life and Limb Insurance Company. It was funded in 1863 by some unmentioned New York City businessmen, who raised $100,000 to get it going. They created the company to insure Civil War sailors and soldiers against disabilities due to wartime wounds, accidents and sickness. Five difficult years and several reorganizations later, they thought of switching names to the "Metropolitan Life Insurance Company" in 1868. From that point on, they sold "ordinary" insurances to middle class folk for great profit.

By that time, American lawyer, jurist and freemason Albert Pike (1809 -1891) had almost completed his plans for worldwide herd domination. Pike was a Confederate States commanding officer in the American Civil War and an associate justice of the Confederate Arkansas Supreme Court from 1864 until the surrender of the Trans-Mississippi Department of the Confederacy in 1865. His ideas included three world wars with the following aims:

- overthrow the Czar of Russia and to set up a communist state
- built a communist empire throughout the world
- destroy Christian civilization for all time (Eustace Mullins: The Curse of Canaan; Omnia VERITAS Ltd 2016).

As there would be many dead and injured as a result, MetLife's owners would be assured great profits for centuries to come. The insurance was easy to pay, as it was issued in small amounts, with weekly or monthly premiums collected at policyholders' homes. By 1880, it had exceeded a quarter million sales with nearly $1 million in premium revenue. By 1909, it had become the nation's largest life insurer when measured by the total value of life insurance policies issued to customers.

In January 1915, with America's entrance into WWI on the horizon, MetLife changed from a stock life insurance company owned by individuals to a mutual company, operating without external shareholders and for the benefit of policyholders only. In preparation for the suicide pandemic, it reversed back to a publicly traded company in 2000. It did this through its subsidiaries and affiliates now holding leading market positions in the United States, Japan, Latin America, Asia's Pacific region, Europe and the Middle East. Why? Because the government may cease MetLife during the COVID-19-generated societal restructuring. This would create the national narrative so blatantly advertised by the Center for Mental Health Services (U.S.), Office of the Surgeon General (U.S.) in Rockville (Maryland) and U.S. Public Health Service in 2001. We read:

> "*National Strategy for Suicide Prevention* (National Strategy or NSSP) is designed to be a catalyst for social change with the power to transform attitudes, policies, and services. Representing the combined work of advocates, clinicians, researchers and survivors, the *National Strategy* lays out a framework for action and guides development of an array of services and programs yet to be set

> in motion. *It strives to promote and provide direction to efforts to modify the social infrastructure in ways that will affect the most basic attitudes about suicide and its prevention, and that will also change judicial, educational, and health care systems."* National Strategy for Suicide Prevention: Goals and Objectives for Action (https://pubmed.ncbi.nlm.nih.gov/20669520/; italics mine).

None of it concerned the Stewart family, per se, as a trust fund had been created for them long before. But who would guess, with all that money piling up, that William P. Stewart III, senior's great-grandson, in 2013 would sue his father, William P. Stewart Jr. in 2000 for having siphoned off $100 million of sonny's part of it. Stewart III's mother had already been thrown off the account for taking millions from it without her son's consent. One wonders why it really mattered. After all, with a minimum of 90 million customers in over 60 countries and profits regularly streaming in, one should think he'd rarely notice. All the more so as it continues in ever increasing amounts. In particular, if anyone with life insurance who took the COVID 19 "jab" is no longer a payout risk upon death, but a purely profit-making machine until earthly departure, in particular, if stupid enough to continue making life-insurance payments. Nor is anyone committing suicide. Thus, MetLife profits should be skyrocketing to hitherto unimagined heights in no time flat.

But never mind. Let's get back to the originator of the U.S. federal government's suicide prevention agenda - retired Four-star Admiral and Surgeon General David Satcher. During his tenure as surgeon general, he also released a paper entitled "Mental health: A report of the Surgeon General – Executive summary". *Professional Psychology: Research and Practice*, 31(1), 5–13.

His staff conducted a detailed review of more than 3,000 research articles. They also reviewed first-person accounts from people who had been afflicted with mental disorders. From all that, he tells us that two main findings had emerged:

- The efficacy, the ability to produce a desired or intended result of mental health treatments was well documented. A range of treatments of the same general type existed for most mental disorders. On that basis, he recommended that people seek help, if they think they have mental disorder symptoms.
- He also suggested that the herd adapt to a new perspective of public health. This means the adjustment in natural or human systems to a new or changing environment that exploits beneficial opportunities or moderates negative effects, according to the world health organization (WHO). We should, said Satcher, accept that mental disorders are disabling and see mental health and mental illness as points on a continuum, something that changes in character gradually or in very slight stages without any clear dividing points (APA PsycInfo Database Record (c) 2016 APA, all rights reserved). Really? Humanity's COVID-19's tyranny's gradual drive into insanity, perhaps?

To stay close to the milieu, Satcher returned to the Morehouse School of Medicine as director of the National Center for Primary Care (NCPC). This reflected his commitment to removing the stigma attached to mental illness and elimination of racial and ethnic disparities in health. He was also appointed to serve on the World Health Organization Commission on Social Determinants of Health.

However, while still sitting as surgeon general, Satcher not only bemoaned the populace's suicides. He also used his precious time productively by calculating that 83,500 Black deaths could have occurred in 2000 if the nation's health disparities had been eliminated in the last century. That includes24,000 from cardiovascular disease. It includes 22,000 fewer Black deaths from diabetes. And almost 2,000 fewer Black women would have died from breast cancer if such disparities had been eliminated, calculated the honourable man. As many as 250,000 fewer Blacks would have been infected with HIV/AIDS, and 7,000 fewer Black people would have died from AIDS complications in 2000. Furthermore, as many as 2.5 million additional Black people, including 650,000 children, would have had health insurance that year, he hypothesizes in typical humanist fashion. All due to such critical race theory disparities, he found. How he reached his figures he did not share with us.

He goes on to bemoan that, if infant mortality in 2000 had been equal across racial and ethnic groups, 4,700 fewer Black infants would have died in their first year of life. Meanwhile, the taxpayer funded, non-profit, tax-exempt Planned Parenthood Federation of America, Inc. (PPFA) had aborted approximately 700,000 babies, most of them Black, during his 3-year reign. It had done the same to at least 70 million in the U.S. alone since 1916, but this did not touch his conscience. Neither did Communist China's one-child-only policy of 1970, which forced abortions of an estimated 400 million unborn humans. But I meander.

By 2012, Satcher's 1999 suicide prevention call to action had blossomed and prospered. Government leaders had brought stakeholders together in a shining example of public-private collaboration, we are told. Stakeholders are those with an interest or concern in the field. For example, those who make money in suicide prevention, such as Covington et al with Zero Suicide. A multitude of non-profit – thus herd-funded – organizations had sprung up like weeds under the guise of being able to prevent the unpreventable, that being to achieve the major milestone of zero suicide.

Almost half of the 50 states had by then committed significant amounts of money to promote and modify the social infrastructure so as to affect the most basic attitudes about suicide and its prevention. Those attitudes would also change judicial, educational and healthcare systems in accordance with the National Strategy for Suicide Prevention draconian programs of societal change. At that time, 2012, roughly 30,000 U.S. citizens' would commit suicide. And it was for them that all of this was set in motion?

Nothing appears to have changed since then. *The National Strategy For The Prevention Of Suicide* 2021 still strives to promote and modify the social infrastructure in ways both affecting the herds' most basic attitudes about suicide and its prevention. We still hear that it would and should change the entire nation's existing judicial, educational and healthcare systems. After all, it is imbued with the power to transform the herd's attitudes, policies and services in line with Freud, Bernays et al.'s "Making the American Mind" and direct the national narrative through COVID-19, perhaps? That financial destruction, masks-wearing, immune-system destruction, oxygen deprivation, enforced isolation and pharmaceutical mind-altering drugs create suicidal ideation and destabilize the human mind by osmosis is nowhere mentioned.

To coordinate the National Strategy's agenda across the nation and the world, the herd's perception on its goals had to be manipulated in a somewhat credible fashion. To advocate, advance, advertise and carry out the aspired-to changes, the National Action Alliance for Suicide Prevention (Action Alliance) was formed. In its public/private partnership, it was responsible for "catalyzing, planning, implementation and accountability for updating and advancing the NSSP agenda" and making palatable to the gullible public (Suicide Prevention, United States Substance Abuse and Mental Health Services Administration, 2011).

It is also responsible for identifying what it terms culturally appropriate interventions for various minorities, in particular for the three considered most high-risk populations:

- Lesbian, gay, bisexual, transgender youth
- American Indians and Alaska Natives
- Military and veterans.

Clinical social worker Caitlin Ryan, PhD, is considered a pioneer in research related to the LGBTQ communities' physical and mental health. The Q, by the way, stands for simply queer or for "still questioning" one's sexuality, or both. Ryan explains that those culturally appropriate interventions address people's individual ethnicity, culture, language, socioeconomic status, religion and sexual diversity to provide services in ways that cross language and cultural barriers. No specifics on how to go about it are given, but perhaps the critical race theory is invented to assist with it, eh?

Amid it all, the Institute of Medicine (IOM) 2001 report advocating for a fundamental redesign of the U.S. healthcare system seems to have fallen by the wayside (C. Edward Coffey, M.D: "Building a System of Perfect Depression Care in Behavioral Health"; *The Joint Commission Journal on Quality and Patient Safety*, 2007). So did *To Err is Human: Building a Safer Health System*, released in 1999 by the Institute's Committee on Quality Health Care in America. It describes the very large number of hospital patient deaths from medical errors, a number estimated to be as great as 98,000 per year (*Patient Safety and Quality: An Evidence-Based Handbook for Nurses*; Hughes RG, editor. Rockville (MD): Agency for Healthcare Research and Quality (US); 2008); Chapter 3. Molla Sloane Donaldson: An Overview of *To Err is Human: Re-emphasizing the Message of Patient Safety*).

The Committee believed that it could not address the overall quality of care without first addressing patient safety. So, it emphasized that "error" resulting in patient harm was not due to healthcare professionals' lack of competence, good intentions or hard work. Rather, the safety of care, defined as "freedom from accidental injury" (p. 16), was due to the system of care itself. In other words, whether a hospital, primary care clinic, nursing home, retail pharmacy or home care was giving specific attention to ensuring that well-designed processes of care did indeed prevent, recognize and quickly recover from errors committed, so that patients were harmed no further.

The positive response to the *To Err Is Human* document, which focused purely on patient safety, encouraged the Institute of Medicine to design *Crossing the Quality Chasm: A New Health System for the 21st Century* (Institute of Medicine (US) Committee on Quality of

Health Care in America; Washington (DC): National Academies Press (US). It focused on problems such as:

- overuse of medical resources and treatments on patients without sufficient evidence that they lead to better outcomes
- failing to apply or underuse resources or treatments with known benefits
- misuse or failing to execute healthcare resources and treatments with care, safely and correctly

As a result, six aims of healthcare improvement were recommended. These are:

- *Patient Safety* looks at a reduction on the likelihood that patients are harmed by medical errors.
- *Effectiveness* describes avoiding over and underuse of resources and services.
- *Patient-centeredness* relates both to customer service and to considering and accommodating individual patient needs when making care decisions.
- *Timeliness* emphasizes reducing wait times.
- *Efficiency* focuses on reducing waste and, as a result, total cost of care.
- *Equity* looks at closing racial and income gaps in healthcare.

The Division of Behavioral Health Services of the Henry Ford Health System (HFHS) in Detroit helps people with acute and serious mental illness. Those are people who are deemed to be 12 times more likely to die of suicide than anyone in the general population. The Division set out to completely redesign depression care delivery. They used the Six Aims and the Ten Rules from the Institute of Medicine report *Crossing the Quality Chasm* (sciencedirect.com). The 10 rules were:

1. *Care based on continuous healing relationships.* Patients should receive care whenever they need it and in many forms, not just face-to-face visits. This rule implies that the healthcare system should be responsive at all times (24 hours a day, every day) and that access to care should be provided over the Internet, by telephone, and by other means in addition to face-to-face visits.
2. *Customization based on patient needs and values.* The system of care should be designed to meet the most common types of needs but have the capability to respond to individual patient choices and preferences.
3. *The patient as the source of control.* Patients should be given the necessary information and the opportunity to exercise the degree of control they choose over healthcare decisions that affect them. The health system should be able to accommodate differences in patient preferences and encourage shared decision-making.
4. *Shared knowledge and the free flow of information.* Patients should have unfettered access to their own medical information and to clinical knowledge. Clinicians and patients should communicate effectively and share information.
5. *Evidence-based decision making.* Patients should receive care based on the best available scientific knowledge. Care should not vary illogically from clinician to clinician or from place to place.

6. *Safety as a system property.* Patients should be safe from injury caused by the care system. Reducing risk and ensuring safety require greater attention to systems that help prevent and mitigate errors.
7. *The need for transparency.* The healthcare system should make information available to patients and their families that allows them to make informed decisions when selecting a health plan, hospital, or clinical practice, or choosing among alternative treatments. This should include information describing the system's performance on safety, evidence-based practice, and patient satisfaction.
8. *Anticipation of needs.* The health system should anticipate patient needs, rather than simply reacting to events.
9. *Continuous decrease in waste.* The health system should not waste resources or patient time.
10. *Cooperation among clinicians.* Clinicians and institutions should actively collaborate and communicate to ensure an appropriate exchange of information and coordination of care.

The Division came up with the "Perfect Depression Care" initiative. Its key goal was to eliminate suicide, which entailed improving four domains—partnership with patients, clinical care (planned care model), access and information flow. The result?

> "The rate of suicide in the patient population decreased by 75% (p = .007), from ~89 per 100,000 at baseline (2000) to ~22 per 100,000 for the four-year follow-up interval (the average rate for 2002–2005)."

In other words, this is a change from the purely rat-simian-cane-lepus inspired humanist treatment of people in abject misery. This would be a somewhat more humanitarian form of help by empowering patients to have some say in their own treatment. And this change might have played a part in reducing suicide in these settings. We don't know if it in this setting got rid of the pharmaceutical drug and cognitive behavioral brainwashing techniques that destroy both body and mind. However, HFHS's Perfect Depression Care initiative served as prototype to redesign behavioral healthcare of herd members deemed to be suffering from anxiety or psychotic disorders, all 300 of them, by 2021. It would also be used to streamline the system by creating perfect communication between mental health industry service providers.

By 2015, the system had been spread to general hospital settings, along. with developing and implementing efficient tools to screen inmates. Screenings were not for suicide risk, specifically, but for common psychiatric conditions associated with an increased risk of suicide (M.J. Coffey: Perfect Depression Care spread: The traction of zero suicides journal of clinical outcomes management: JCOM 22(3):123-129; 2015). But was it an invasion of privacy to screen healthcare patients for psychiatric conditions willy nilly. Is it a legitimate act, just because a mental health professional feels like doing so. Or because a patient /experiences genuine PTSD? Or because a patient is going through a normally-to-be-expected life crisis, rattling their emotional equilibrium?

Or is it in fact engineered for those who took the COVID-injections? Do they recognize that, by voluntarily taking this jokingly named "jab", they have ceased to be fully human?

Do they realize that they have invited onto themselves irreversible physical and mental health consequences yet to be known? May that, in fact, be the reason for the U.S. governments' suicide prevention preparation since at least 1998?

The jab's immediate effects might indeed result in suicidal ideation or in a PTSD diagnosis, both so financially beneficial to the mental health and suicide prevention industry.

The *United Nation's Educational, Scientific and Cultural Organization* (UNESCO)'s leitmotiv is to build peace in the minds of men and women through international cooperation. Did UNESCO see it all coming in October 2005, when it passed the Universal Declaration On Bioethics and Human Rights (https://portal.unesco.org)?

The Declaration's scope includes ethical issues related to medicine, life sciences and associated technologies as applied to human beings. It takes into account their social, legal and environmental dimensions, especially as related to government policies and actions.

It identifies eight aims, including:

- Creating a universal framework to address bioethics
- Guiding actions (in what manner, we know not)
- Respecting human dignity and protecting human rights
- Protecting freedom of ethical scientific research
- Fostering multidisciplinary and pluralistic dialogue
- Promoting equitable access to medical, scientific and technological developments
- Safeguarding and promoting the interests of future generations
- Underlining the importance of biodiversity

The Declaration then proceeds to list all the principles to follow:

- Human dignity and human rights, that the "welfare of the individual should have priority over the sole interest of science"
- Benefit and harm (generally supporting the former over the latter)
- Autonomy and individual responsibility
- Consent, and protecting people incapable of indicating consent
- Respect for human vulnerability and personal integrity
- Privacy and confidentiality
- Equality, justice and equity
- Non-discrimination and non-stigmatization
- Respect for cultural diversity and pluralism
- Solidarity and cooperation
- Social responsibility and access to the "highest attainable standard of health"
- Sharing the benefits (including in developing countries)
- Protecting future generations
- Protecting the environment, the biosphere and biodiversity

Aims and principles are not enough. The Declaration then tells us how to apply those principles.

For instance, it tells us that "Professionalism, honesty, integrity and transparency in decision-making should be promoted."

It then prescribes ethics committees to be set up, and gives them four roles, such as assessing issues, providing advice, preparing guidelines and fostering debate. Who would set up these committees and who would serve on them is not mentioned.

There is a huge section on "transnational practices", which sets out how states should interact with each other, including working together to combat bioterrorism.

It seems the Declaration is not above a little self-promotion, either, as there is a section on "Promotion of the Declaration." That section suggests that countries should respect the Declaration. It says that countries should also "foster bioethics education" (train researchers to be ethical). And then there's the part about states getting along and being nice to each other and to their vulnerable populations.

UNESCO's Declaration even has some homework for UNESCO itself - declaring that the Declaration should be declared far and wide.

And then comes the legalese. The Declaration should be "understood as a whole", so don't use just parts of it. There are limitations. The Declaration should not supersede human rights.

With this, and COVID 19's physical and mental implications in mind, could this UNESCO Declaration be somewhat related to the question Dutch psychiatrist Jan Molkenstorm's posed shortly before his death: "Is it rational to pursue zero suicides among patients in health care?"

As a matter of fact, could the pre-knowledge of COVID-19's arrival indeed have been why the U.S. federal and state governments went into suicide prevention preparation frenzy with a vengeance from 1998 onwards? Could it be in any way related to the unfolding of a national narrative desired by those who purportedly rule humanity and have done so for thousands of years? And are we, every single one of us, regardless of colour, race or religion, here to witness events due to our Karma? Is it, therefore, our choice? In combination with our individual Dharma, our knowledge gathered throughout this lifetime, do we choose to volunteer to participate or decline to participate in draconian state-sponsored measures? In this case, the measures are to avoid spreading a virus whose existence has yet to be proven. Do we choose to suffer the resulting, inherently disastrous circumstances created to steer the world's historical narrative in accordance with their desires?

You decide. Meanwhile, lets move on back to what in essence amounts to humanity's treatment in health and in illness, for better or for worse, in the humanism-generated atheist style of us being equal to rattus, simian, cani, lepus et al.

20

EMPATHY AND COMPASSION VERSUS DRUGGING AND COGNITIVE BEHAVIOURAL BRAINWASHING

Henry Ford Health System's (HFHS) "Perfect Depression Care" key goal is to prevent the unpreventable: suicide., Its program entails suicide performance improvement activities in four domains:

- partnership with patients
- clinical care in accordance with a planned care model
- access
- information flow

Mind you, the results reflected in C. Edward Coffey's report "Building a system of perfect depression care in behavioral health" were impressive. Coffey is a physician board-certified in both neurology and psychiatry, with expertise in neuropsychiatry and brain stimulation therapies. He has held faculty and leadership positions at Duke University Medical Center, Allegheny University of the Health Sciences, the Henry Ford Health System, Wayne State University School of Medicine and The Menninger Clinic, the latter discussed in *Fallacy*

1 (eventscribe.com). Patient suicide decreased by 75% with zero suicides in 2009. Suicide deaths among those under psychiatric care were reduced to the same rate as in the general population (C Edward Coffey; https://pubmed.ncbi.nlm.nih.gov/17441556/).

The result merely reflected evidence already presented 20 years earlier by Motte and Bostrom. They had presented empirical evidence that by maintaining long-term contact with those patients they viewed at risk of suicide, mental health professionals exerted a huge suicide-prevention influence. Why? Because it created a feeling of connectedness. The influence was solely through the feeling that another human being cared for and thought of them. It is that simple. Coffey et al graciously ignored this finding. It took only the occasional "caring letter" to people who had been hospitalized following their suicide attempt. That connection alone dramatically lifted their spirit and significantly reduced subsequent attempts and deaths by their own hands. Alas, this was equally ignored (JA Motto, AG Bostrom: A randomized controlled trial of postcrisis suicide prevention; pubmed.ncbi.nlm.nih.gov). The occasional caring letter wouldn't secure funding to keep careers going in it.

Furthermore, mental health and pharmaceutical industry professionals are not into tender loving care, empathy and compassion towards human suffering. Nor are advocates of scientism in all its aspects, nor the humanistic treatments of human beings viewed by them as equal in function and behavior to rattus, simian, cani, lepus and the like. Nor are they interested in the documented miracles tender loving care for the *other* regularly produces, should they or we care to look. Solely traumatizing the human mind and physical body through persistent drugging and mind-manipulation by way of cognitive behavioral "therapy" seems to thrill them. So does the of power ruling another's life for better or for worse at their leisure. And they seem to think that making tons of money from it is pretty sweet, too.

Regardless, Coffey's' "Building a system of perfect depression care in behavioral health" produced congressional hearings. All and sundry employed in the human mental healthcare industry were called upon. That included governmental agencies, professional groups, accrediting organizations, insurers and whoever else held a financial stake in it (those who could make money from it). They were encouraged to develop reporting systems and voice any and all ideas they might conceive to possibly cure this lack-of-mental health-care related to the death-by-suicide problem. These ideas would be in return for millions of dollars for the effort, of course.

Across the United States, public forums were held by organizational mental healthcare leaderships, boards and staff. The goal was to investigate who could be held accountable for unsafe conditions in facilities across the land. They scrutinized mental healthcare professionals working there who, in the eyes of their peers, acted recklessly or even criminally in regard to patient-health. And they debated how to hold accountable those deemed irresponsible. The conclusion reached? All this effort had been for naught. Imposing reporting requirements or holding people or organizations employed in mental healthcare facilities accountable for deaths occurring in their workplaces did not at all make the system safer.

Richard McKeon, PhD, MPH, somehow stumbled across Henry Ford Health Services' Coffey's generated suicide success report in 2010. He was head of the Substance Abuse and Mental Health Services Administration (SAMSHA) at the time. He pondered the issue for a while, to finally determined the most splendid avenue to catch the herd's attention and entice it to participate in the suicide prevention effort. Advertising that to advertise that NO care for those inclined to prematurely dispatch themselves from this Earth had hitherto existed in the U.S. would be just the ticket. (Zero Suicide: The Dogged Pursuit of Perfection in Health Care; David W. Covington, LPC, MBA; Michael F. Hogan, PhD; Psychiatric Times, Psychiatric Times, 2019).

McKeon should know. He had dealt with the public for decades. Until 2009, he had spent most of his career working in community mental health. That included 11 years as director of a psychiatric emergency service at an unknown location and four years as associate administrator/clinical director of a hospital-based community mental health center somewhere in Newton, New Jersey (ipha.com). We assume this happened shortly after receiving his PhD in Clinical Psychology from the University of Arizona and a Master of Public Health in Health Administration from Columbia University. In 2001, he had been awarded an American Psychological Association Congressional Fellowship and had worked for United States Senator Paul Wellstone, covering health and mental health policy issues. He also spent five years as clinical division director on the Board of the American Association of Suicidology, as well as on the APA's Board of the Division of Clinical Psychology.

In 2008, Secretary of Veterans Affairs James Benjamin Peake (1944-), serving from 2007 to 2009, appointed McKeon to his Blue Ribbon Work Group on Suicide Prevention. In 2009, Secretary of Defense Robert Michael Gates (1943), serving from 2006 to 2011, appointed him to the Task Force on Suicide Prevention in the Military. McKeon also served on the National Action Alliance for Suicide Prevention Task Force that revised the National Strategy for Suicide Prevention. And he participated in the development of WHO's World Suicide Prevention Report. Now, in 2021, he co-chairs the Federal Working Group on Suicide Prevention, which includes representatives from agencies and operating divisions of the federal departments of Defense, Health and Human Services, Homeland Security, Justice, Education, Transportation and Veteran Affairs.

So, in 2010, he already had much experience in how to deal with the public and direct their suicide prevention narrative, we assume. The National Institutes of Health's Department of Health Services (HHS) promptly granted him $22.4 million over five years to investigate the issue of suicide and the lack of care in the system to prevent it. The announcement curiously coincided with Jerrold Nadler's call 14 days earlier, begging the Human Health Service to do more to stop LGBT youth's suicides. Nadler was LGBT Equality Caucus Democrat chair in the U.S. Congress. He viewed LGBT youth's suicides as a most serious and urgent public health—or should we say death?—problem (keennewsservice.com/2010). That no specific statistics on suicide in LGBT people existed then or now because death records of deceased individuals of all ages exclude their sexual preference and orientation, escaped the committee's attention. It also escaped the attention of Ann P. Haas, PhD, et al.'s January 2011 publication 'Suicide and Suicide Risk in Lesbian, Gay, Bisexual, and Transgender Populations: Review and Recommendations' (*Journal. of Homosexuality*, 2011).

Haas wears many hats. She is professor and chair of the Department of Health Sciences at The City University of New York. She also holds appointments at New York Medical College and the Veterans Administration Medical Center in Montrose, New York (dartcenter.org). And she is now senior director of education and prevention at the American Foundation for Suicide Prevention (AFSP). Founded in 1987, the now-nationwide non-profit ASFP sees its mission as saving lives and bringing hope to those affected by suicide. Purportedly empowered by research, education and advocacy, it prides itself in creating a culture "that's smart about mental health" by engaging in the following core strategies:

- funding scientific research
- educating the public about mental health and suicide prevention
- supporting survivors of suicide loss and those affected by suicide
- advocating for public policies in mental health and suicide prevention

The organization, today led by CEO Robert Gebbia, is headquartered in New York City, with a public policy office in Washington, D.C (https://theactionalliance.org). Gebbia holds a BA in sociology from Hofstra University and an MA in sociology from the New School for Social Research. He completed the Harvard Business School's Human Services Management Executive Program and IBM's Leadership Commitment Program for not-for-profit executives. Prior to joining AFSP, he worked with the United Way and as public health advisor for the City of New York.

Thanks to Gebbia's fundraising expertise, AFSP's annual revenue has grown from $700,000 to over $13 million. It's nationwide network of over 64 chapters hosts the *Out of the Darkness* walks to implant the idea of suicide as a viable option into humans' mind and thus increase donations for suicide prevention. It certainly is a golden goose to be nurtured, as nationally recognized scientists, businesses, civic and political leaders, media and professional associations all make a living from it.

A founding member of the National Council for Suicide Prevention, Gebbia furthermore serves on the National Lifeline Advisory Committee, and the Board of Directors of the National Health Council. Founded in 1920 and headquartered in Washington, D.C., its members are involved in health-related organizations such as patient advocacy groups and non-profit organizations with an interest in health. They are also involved in major health insurance corporations, as well as pharmaceutical, medical device and biotechnology companies, including Pfizer and GlaxoSmithKline. All this "involvement" is for lucrative fees, as documented in *Fallacy 1*. All of them work together, without our knowledge, to dictate our wellbeing and dis-ease in line with the Freudian *Making the American Mind* agenda.

That Haas and her team tried to determine whether LGBT etc. groups were overrepresented among suicides by using "psychological autopsy" reports of family and friends to determine decedents' sexual orientation. They found that same-sex sexual orientation suicides were equal to that in the general population, but that does not matter at all. Milking the public for donations does.

And the $22.4 million five-year grant to investigate the LGBT suicide prevention issue? Well, that was in progress long, long before Congressman Nader's formal 2010 request. Those millions were merely transferred from federally supported resource centers devoted to advancing the National Strategy for Suicide Prevention: Goals and Objectives for Action formed in 2001 under the Clinton administration (pubmed.ncbi.nlm.nih.gov). Federally funded research and development centers (FFRDCs) are public-private partnerships conducting research and development for the United States Government. Under Federal Acquisition Regulation § 35.017 FFRDC's are operated by universities and corporations to fulfill certain long-term government needs that cannot be met as effectively by existing in-house or contractor resources, we read. Prohibited from competing for work, there are 42 such FFRDCs, each sponsored by one or more U.S. government departments or agencies. Suicide prevention and PTSD research are two of them.

McKeon, meanwhile, proceeded to craft the task force that would publish the Suicide Care in Systems Framework in 2011. It would do so by pairing Covington and Hogan with 26 others in the healthcare-and suicide business for additional input (https://theactionalliance.org/sites/default/files/clinicalcareinterventionreport.pdf) Meanwhile, in partnership with Dr. Jerry Reed, he spearheaded the launch of the National Action Alliance for Suicide Prevention in Washington, DC, on September 10, 2010, with secretaries of Defense, Health and Human Services as keynote speakers. This public-private partnership advances the National Strategy for Suicide Prevention.

Reed has a PhD in health-related sciences, with emphasis in gerontology, from Virginia Commonwealth University and an MSW from the University of Maryland at Baltimore. He is senior vice president at the Education Development Center (EDC). EDC is another global non-profit organization to improve humans' education, promote health, and expand economic opportunity across the United States and in more than 80 countries around the world. Founded in 1964 with funding from the Carnegie Corporation of New York, it seems to have replaced the Rockefeller Foundation's General Education Board, which officially folded in 1960.

EDC's work includes projects addressing major education, health and social challenges. These include injury, violence, suicide prevention, early childhood development and learning. With programs in 50 U.S. states and 80 countries around, its world headquarters is in Waltham, Massachusetts, with offices in Washington, DC, New York City and Chicago and other locations in the U.S. and around the globe. Around 1,400 scientists, researchers, mathematicians, educators, and health and technology specialists work for EDC. Their expertise includes research, training, policy, curriculum and materials development and education technology, ranging from small seed projects to large-scale national and international initiatives.

EDC is known for creating the curriculum (Hu) mans: A Course of Study / Course Materials or MACOS, consisting of books, films, posters, records, games and other classroom materials. More importantly, it consists of a set of assumptions about man we read on its website (macosonline.org). It took care of spreading "the chain of life" or a "lifeline" by way of the entire history of living things to prekindergarten education, in the womb, so to speak. The course started with a simple lifespan in the form of the Pacific Coast salmon. It then moved on to the herring gull's life, which is viewed as more complex life, and introduced a nurturing concept. It then portrayed the lifespan of the baboon, particularly due to the societal context of the baboon troop, followed by introducing the differences between innate and learned behaviour. This is finally followed by a study of a man's lifespan. They portray Netsilik Inuit and their interaction with life forms such as reindeer and seals, to firmly imbed into young human souls that they are nothing other than baboon-reindeer-seal-like creatures. Thus, they direct humanity's narrative in the humanistic ways of human life and living, ignoring any and all spiritual aspects or connection to a higher source, God, a Creator or the like. This is especially noteworthy when MACOS is shown to EDC's favourite support receivers, the supply of care for school-age children (ages 5–13) through the National Center on Afterschool and Summer Enrichment (NCASE). But I digress, again.

Back to McKeon and Reed. In 2012, their efforts led to the U.S. Surgeon General Office revising the U.S. National Strategy for Suicide Prevention, which had first been adopted in 2001. The revision included the following addition:

Goal 8. *Promote suicide prevention as a core component of health care services*

- 8.1. Promote the adoption of "zero suicides" as an aspirational goal by health care and community support systems that provide services and support to defined patient populations.

That, in essence, meant that any human involved with the public healthcare system could at leisure be diagnosed with suicide ideation. Thus, they could be termed "mentally defective", with the devastating consequences of never ending-government-mandated personal surveillance. This, we documented earlier, would brilliantly serve the National Strategy For Suicide Prevention (NSSP) as catalyst to effectuate social infrastructure modification. This change would be not only in humans' most basic attitudes about suicide and its prevention. More importantly, the change would be in humanity's judicial, educational, and healthcare systems. The methods to implement such change could be formed by its own advocates, clinicians and researchers. If they were to undertake the design of its framework, develop the consequent actions and guide, provide and promote an array of services and programs, that would be even more important. Expect them to make those changes in accordance with Freud et al.'s early twentieth century plan of *Making the American Mind* before spreading it world wide.

The U.S. Surgeon General Jerome Adams is certainly in a haste to push the operation forward. In January 2021, he issued his "Call to Action" report to implement the 2012 NSSP National Strategy for Suicide Prevention with an all-important addition. Said he: "Much remains to be done. Suicide prevention continues to lack the breadth and depth of the coordinated response needed to truly make a difference in reducing suicide." (https://thesophiefund.org/tag/national-action-alliance-for-suicide-prevention/).

The urgency behind these new suicide prevention efforts? The COVID-19 non-pandemic had created conditions that might increase suicide risk, we read. "Problems resulting from the pandemic—including physical illness, loss of loved ones, anxiety, depression, job loss, eviction, and increased poverty—could all contribute to suicide risk," Adams said. After all, out of at least 331,002,651 people estimated to live in the U.S. in 2020, never mind the millions of illegal immigrants, 47,000 Americans had died by suicide in 2019, a national suicide rate increase in the past 20 years from 10.5 to 13.9 per 100,000 people.

Thousands more experienced suicidal thoughts or attempted suicide, we are told. And apparently 1.4 million U.S. adults, out of the 331,002,651 million officially living in the country, tried to kill themselves in 2019, whilst another 3.5 million adults were making suicide plans. Well, good luck to them, then. May they succeed in the unpreventable, if they put an earnest effort into it, they will, as we documented already. Success is the most rewarding thing in life in any undertaking, even when resulting in self-inflicted and desired death, eh?

It would all be rather funny, if it were not all a farce, a macabre Kabuki theatre, to which the foundation had been laid as early as 1992 already or at the latest, when the U.S. Congress saw fit to establish the Substance Abuse and Mental Health Services Administration branch of the U.S. Department of Health and Human Services -SAMHSA to influence the public mind in preparation for what was to come under the ruse of making substance use and mental disorder information, services and research more accessible to whoever might be interested.

It then based the National Strategy for Suicide Prevention: Goals and Objectives for Action on it, which in turn, in 2002, launched The National Action Alliance for Suicide Prevention (Action Alliance) as a public-private partnership for suicide prevention to carry the human "you are all mentally ill" brainwashing agenda to its present state of affairs encouraged by the invention of COVID-19 and its possibly disastrous mental and physical health consequences for humanity, of which they knew beforehand by way of their 170 years of human behavioral studies. It is that simple.

To advance NSSP National Strategy for Suicide Prevention (NSSP) objectives, the Action Alliance expanded colossally, nowadays working with over 250 national partners. Its current priority, according to its own website, is to transform health systems and communities by what it terms "changing the conversation". This is being done, we learn, by persistently disseminating to the herd messages related to suicide and other healthcare topics. This is exemplified by COVID-19 media reporting through news and entertainment media, Facebook, Twitter and any other news transmitter media you can think of (theactionalliance.org). Does anyone still watching television, on Face-book or Twitter, or following any of the other mass-media brainwashing centers still believe they control their own mind? The mass media shuffles its ideology and intentions down our throats in buckets, with most of humanity unaware and not wanting to know. People allow it to influence them until one day they think of killing the Self for no reason other than that they say they must feel like it.

And what have all these prevention measures to prevent the unpreventable and costing taxpayers billions and utter billions accomplished to date? Let's see. Suicide is preventable, state Bobbi Jo H. Yarborough, PsyD et al. in their 2019 article "Challenges of Population-based Measurement of Suicide Prevention Activities Across Multiple Health Systems". Then they share with us that Covington et al.'s non-profit Zero Suicide (ZS) organization is currently being evaluated by Mental Health Research Network investigators. The investigators are embedded in six Health Care Systems Research Network (HCSRN) member health systems implementing ZS (EGEMS (Wash DC). 2019; 7(1): 13.) Why this investigation? Because Bobbi and his team say, robust process improvement metrics are needed by the hundreds of health systems across the country, never mind the world. They are needed to prepare to implement their own best practices in suicide care. They need them to produce accurate numbers of what counts as suicide attempts. They need the numbers to decide what should or should not count as adequate suicide prevention follow-up care. These are, among others, similarly stunning, topics in the same vein. They conclude:

> "The challenges described herein are generalizable beyond suicide prevention work. The challenge of aligning process and outcome measures for comparison across health systems with differing source data is longstanding and universal. The challenge of deciding what should count as adequate and appropriate follow-up care has beset national quality improvement measures, when well-intended metrics fail to specify qualifying services or do so in ways that exclude important care processes or include extraneous and irrelevant visits. The challenge of assessing safety planning is similar to the challenge of using [Emergency Hospital Records] EHR records to assess whether shared decision-making about treatment alternatives actually happened—where the presence of an indicator of shared decision-making is probably insufficient to conclude that meaningful patient engagement actually occurred. These are problems that deserve attention. In the context of this pragmatic evaluation, we resolve to address these issues as we seek to create generalizable process improvement metrics for broad use."

But don't despair. It's not worth the energy, because the COVID-19 injection-affects, most likely generating an increase in suicidal desires, will be of little importance to the nations' healthcare systems anywhere. After all, in 2019 alone, millions or even billions of dollars in federal money went to researchers and those employed in the suicide prevention métier. They await the seeds of their implanted encouragement for you to doubt your own sanity to bear fruit. Did they try it out on genuine PTSD experiencers, whose lives they regularly destroy by their PTSD treatment methods? In many, they achieved just such a result, with the U.S. soldiers' suicide rate still skyrocketing. Don't believe it? Well, then, perhaps Dr. Mark Sircus AC., OMD, DM (P) might inspire thought in his June 2021 article "Madness is Infecting the World of Medicine - Counting the Vaccine Dead". He is professor of natural oncology at the Da Vinci Institute of Holistic Medicine, doctor of oriental and pastoral medicine and founder of Natural Allopathic Medicine.

The world has a front-row seat to a horror story in progress, a vaccine horror story that was a long time in coming, he writes. The CDC had just presented horrendous documentation about Pfizer and Moderna vaccine injury data, in particular in young people. It showed, that even without accounting for underreporting, the second dose of one of those injections could increase the risk of heart problems up to 200-fold in young men. But it should still be given to children, even when already suffering heart problems, we were told.

Furthermore, according to the CDC, in the U.S. alone through June 25, 2021, 6,113 people had died following COVID-19 injections. This was recorded by the Vaccine Adverse Event Reporting System (VAERS), a U.S. government-funded database tracking injuries and deaths caused by vaccines. Besides the 6,113 deaths reported, 5,172 permanent disabilities, 6,435 life-threatening events and 51,558 emergency room visits were recorded. The problem is that a 2010 Department of Health and Human Services (HHS) report concluded: "Fewer than one percent of vaccine adverse events are reported by the VAER System." Thus, we have to multiply the incident rate by a hundred. Of the 6,113 deaths mentioned above, 23% occurred within 48 hours of vaccination and 16% within 24 hours. The deaths included 38%

of people who became ill within 48 hours of being injected. That almost 30% of healthcare professionals had never heard of the VAERS system is another story. Among those who knew about it and had come across a potential vaccine side effect, 83% failed to file a report.

The EudraVigilance database, which covers 27 European countries, reports that through June 19, 2021, there were 15,472 deaths and 1,509,266 injuries from the four COVID vaccines used, half of them (753,657) serious. These are the official numbers, the official reports, says Dr. Sircus. But he points out that these numbers are probably 10 times higher, albeit every health official and governmental agency is ignoring the information and these deaths. No matter how many injections have been given, and how many humans have died, Australia's top medical officer, continues to urge his countrymen through USA Today to "not delay" getting the second shot. And those of his ilk in other commonwealth countries, Canada among them, echo the same sentiment, Remember the Georgia Guide Stones?

According to CDC's VAERS, there have been more deaths reported following COVID-19 injections since December 2020 than deaths recorded following all vaccinations in the previous 30 years. COVID-19 killed 26 Indonesian doctors in June 2021 alone. At least 10 of them had taken China's COVID-19 Sinovac vaccine (*Wall Street Journal*). VAERS also recorded 576 deaths of unborn children following COVID-19 shots. Nevertheless, the CDC continues to recommend that pregnant women should get injected with these shots. Meanwhile, many dissenting medical doctors and scientists are now describing them as "bioweapon" injections, Dr. Sircus writes.

In his opinion, madness is infecting the world of medicine, a form of madness never seen on this scale before in Earth's history, to our knowledge. Even Hitler and his Nazi henchmen cannot compete with what is going on, and the uncountable millions being voluntarily harmed - killed, maimed and driven into despair - he says. Evil has shown its ugly face, and, unfortunately, the children are suffering the most. Yet, certain adults cheer on, even though data just for the week between June 18 and 25 for 12- to 17-year-olds show the following:

> 7,294 total adverse events, including 423 rated as serious, and nine reported deaths among 12- to 17-year-olds. Four deaths (or 44%) were cardiac-related and three were sudden, unexplained deaths.
>
> One reported death was a 13-year-old boy (VAERS I.D. 1406840) who died two days after receiving a Pfizer injection. Other deaths include three 15-year-olds (VAERS I.D. 1187918, 1382906, and 1242573) and two 16-year-olds (VAERS I.D. 1225942 and 1386841), and one 17-year-old (VAERS I.D. 1199455).

In the United Kingdom, children as young as five are suffering panic attacks and other psychological trauma as a result of COVID lockdowns. That has left 1.5 million kids in need of mental health treatment. British National Health Services (NHS) leaders say that the impact of repeated lockdowns has left children fearful of leaving their homes or meeting their friends. Such is the result of an explosion of "locked-in trauma" under this kind of medical Nazi regime, Sircus writes.

The British newspaper *The Telegraph* says: "Forecasts seen by this newspaper state that an extra 1.5 million children and young people will require mental health support "as a direct impact of the pandemic" during the next three to five years. The calculations from the Centre for Mental Health involving NHS economists suggest that demand will be as much as three times greater than the capacity of mental health services."

In reality, pharmaceutical/medical terrorists have occupied Planet Earth for many years. Not happy with the level of terror and suffering they have accomplished, they got greedy for more evil, despicable ugliness. Fauci, the FDA, the CDC, the NIH, Google, Facebook, Twitter and YouTube are all in trouble or will eventually be, Sircus opines. German lawyer Dr. Reiner Fuellmilch is working with at least 2,000 other lawyers worldwide working for just that. Looking him up and beginning to educate yourself might be a good idea, as Nuremberg trials are being clamored for at present.

In critical race theory training, masses of people are pressured by a few influencers to say certain things. They are leaned on to take certain stances or forced into some segregated settings, infringing on or violating their constitutional, human and civil rights. So, too, in the world of medicine it is a tiny group against billions, if these billions pull together rather than go into suicidal depressions. We are humanity of the entire world, all of us of all races, religions and nationalities. It is us who are now viciously oppressed by pharmaceutical terrorism in its lust for more money, more control and more power. But whose servants are those who run this show of human destruction? Pure Evil?

Said Dr. Sircus:

> "There never was a need for these deadly vaccines. What we have are thousands if not hundreds of thousands of intentionally killed vaccine dead and a cover-up barely hidden because of these 'official' vaccine-reporting systems. Genocide? Crimes against humanity? Medical treason? Psychopathic insanity?"

Perhaps. Dr. Joseph Mercola takes it a step further, when he exclaimed in June 2021:

> "Already, a growing list of physicians and scientists are warning that the COVID-19 shots may end up being a form of mass euthanasia. Many predict mass deaths among the vaccinated to occur within the next several years as their immune function breaks down and cardiovascular damage sets in. The idea that we're going to add several gene therapy shots into an annual regimen will only exacerbate the predicted deaths. (https://articles.mercola.com)."

Jon Rappoport concurs, writing in his July 2021 article "Pandemics are staged on Television" about how new pandemics are launched and promoted by the powers that be. Despite the lack of good science and good evidence, they are jacked up on television screens with images flowing of emergency vehicles on streets and EMT personnel in hazmat suits. They show soldiers patrolling airport crowds, doctors in full gear, laboratories, vials of liquid, plastic bubbles and facemasks to scare the wits out of the herd. These scenes are repeated daily until audiences drown in their own adrenaline-fuelled fear, while mesmerized by the gory details of the purported action, in this case COVID-19.

Those who created the U.S. and now the world's narrative know this. They've practiced it numerous times on an ever-increasing scale throughout humanity's history as world populations expanded throughout the Earth. In the mid-1800s, They also created the insane asylums. Since that time, they did little else but study in the most brutal ways humans, cani, simian, rattus, lepus and whatever other animals they deemed equal to us. They furthered their knowledge in concentration camps, beginning with the Boer War of the late 1890s on to MK Ultra experiments, studies of PTSD journeyers and prisoners of war.

Did we pay attention? Did we care? Did we have a clue? Not that they haven't talked about it. As mentioned in *Fallacy 1*, cosmic law dictates that they tell us what they are up to, but they can do so in whatever way they see fit. And they do. That's why movies are made, from the Nuremberg trials to MK Ultra projects. But did the majority listen, never mind understand what we saw or heard?

No. And that, too, has been known for at least the last 150 years. Just read Charles-Marie Gustave Le Bon (1841 –1931), a leading French polymath, whom we dissected a bit earlier. His interests included anthropology, psychology, sociology, medicine, invention and physics. Best known for his 1895 work *The Crowd: A Study of the Popular Mind*, he had this to say about humanity:

Which brings us back to television, the greatest illusion device ever invented. Even talking to someone still watching television is a futile exercise, a waste of breath. One can never reach those who do, as they are blind as bats to the truth without knowing it. Television was invented for human mind-manipulation, as well as the destruction of humanity's cognitive abilities, including logic and reason. That it works like a charm is blatantly displayed in the COVID-19 madness. It may be self-induced madness, but it is still madness to get an injection with an experimental and medically unapproved human gene-altering drug for an age-old ailment, the flu, which has a 99.99% rate of discovery, is it not?

Government-mandated 24-hour isolation enhances television mania for many in populations raised with social media distractions. They never learned to properly read or write, never mind occupy the Self just by oneself. Combine it all, and the human extinction scheme is as good as perfect. Its a most effective human perception-deception method, enhanced by acute amnesia of details. A human catastrophe of hitherto unknown proportion by way of COVID-19 truth perversion seems to be in the making. As Rappoport phrased it in his July 2, 2021 essay, "Pandemics are staged on Television":

> "Mind control is no longer something merely imposed from the outside. It is a matrix of a self-feeding, self-demanding loop. Willing Devotees of the Image WANT images, food stamps of the programmed society."

Elsewhere in this article he explains:

> "A pandemic, the false pandemic I've been rejecting in many articles, is delivered through video flow and narration in stacked and cut images. There is no challenge to the flow in any basic way through the intrusion of actual knowledge, because that would shut down the parade of images and nullify the reasons for broadcasting them in the first place." When a technology (television) turns into a method of perception, reality is turned inside out. People watch TV through TV eyes. The television audience, imprisoned in homes, rides the river..."

Into perpetual delusion, never-ending perception-deception perfected through the last 95 years in the U.S. and at least 60 throughout the rest of the world. for at least It would spoil the elite's fun, if those of us –humanity-- in our self-engaged and willingly desired elimination lured into the COVID-injection scam, set our own course. There is no turning back. For those who have resisted thus far, it's a question of leaving the TV on or shutting it off to regain a modicum of their sanity that will dictate the course of their lives."

And here we are, having to take responsibility for all of it. We allowed it to happen. We bask in our ignorance and trust in those pretending to help us, believing that "Doctor knows best" and "pharmaceutical drugs will cure us" mentality. In fact, both drive us into physical and mental destruction. Through self-imposed COVID-injected suffering, we are pushed into the suicidal ideation and psychological despair. For this, the health industry has prepared its humanistic remedies at least since 1998, some say since the early 1900s.

Can we turn the narrative around, so the madness won't affect us all? Jan Mokkenstorm, the Dutch psychiatrist, tried. He vehemently questioned the justification of testing everyone for suicidal ideation. UNESCO in its declaration also told us what was coming down the pike. That's all it had to do to satisfy cosmic law and justify its action. Few looked; fewer listened, too busy on Facebook asking their mothers for permission to fart. Those wanting a world catastrophe in line with Bhagavad Gita proportions seem for the time being content to steer the national narrative towards an Orwellian brave new world to achieve their aspirations. There is just one stumbling block. Humanity has to be "vaccinated", has to have the Jab. They might even need two or three of them, to have success with the agenda.

What did McKeon say about the issue in December 2019, weeks before COVID-19 was made known to the herd? Here his testimony before the Armed Services Committee, Subcommittee on personnel in the United States Senate on December 4, 2019:

> "In summary, SAMHSA, and the entire Federal Government is engaged in an unprecedented number of suicide prevention activities, but we know we all need to do more if we are to halt the tragic rise in loss of life we are experiencing across the country. In particular, we know we need to be engaged in a strong continuing, collaborative effort across the Federal Government along with states, tribes, communities, and private partners across America to implement a comprehensive public health approach that incorporates everything we now know about preventing suicide. We know we must constantly be looking to improve our efforts and to learn from both our successes and our failures. We owe it to those who have served this Nation and to all the people we have

lost to suicide, as well as to those that loved them, to continually strive to improve until suicide among veterans, service members, and all Americans is dramatically reduced." (https://armed-services.senate.gov).

Remember, this is an ongoing effort for 47,000 unpreventable suicides in the U.S. in 2020 alone, out of a population of roughly 331,000,0000 million citizens. The question arises: "Are they planning to stow those desperately ill from the injection and depressed in asylums or FEMA camps under mental health industry supervision? Keep in mind that they are having a financial field day with counselling those they made ill through their pharmaceutical mind-altering concoctions.

And why is it that none of their suicide prevention methods focus on the effects of pharmaceutical drugging on human minds? And why do they neglect in its entirety the affect of empathy and compassion on despairing, depressed and consequently suicide-contemplating human beings? I know. I have been there, and I assure you, they were watching their traumatizing progress driving me into suicide every step of the way like hawks, praying they would achieve their goal, me killing myself.

But yes, I almost forgot, it is beyond their scope. After all, to them we are simian, lepus, cani and mus, baboon and rattus all in one. So, the thought of investigating why so very few humans in the world kill themselves does never even dawn upon them. Remember, the number of suicides fell from 800,000 annually globally over the past 20 years down to 703,000 in 2019. That might seem like a lot to host in your living room, but that is less than 0.01% of the nearly eight billion humans on the planet. But empathy and compassion might help them out of their suicidal ideation, and there is no money in that, is there? So, what's amiss? Well, Eustace Mullins' books *The Curse Of Canaan* and *Murder by Injection* may help in the discovery. Let's keep in mind that everyone on this Earth chose to be here at this time to be part of the show. It is our duty to educate ourselves and be amused by our findings, as we have to take responsibility for it all; we allowed it to happen.

We, in our ignorance, trust in those pretending to help us. We, with our faith in the "Doctor knows best" mantra believe. After a century of advertisements praising the benefit of pharmaceutical drugging, when in fact all most oftentimes drives us, perhaps slowly but surely into physical and mental destruction, we are at fault for the present situation. They, meanwhile, created COVID-19 to increase human psychological despair and suicides, and therefore a market for their suggested humanistic control remedies, at least since 1998.

Can we turn this ship about, so the madness won't sooner or later affect us all? Dutch psychiatrist Jan Mokkenstorm tried. He vehemently questioned the justification of testing everyone for suicidal ideation. In its declaration, UNESCO also told us what was coming down the pike. According to cosmic law, that is all that evil has to do to justify its action. Few looked; fewer listened, too busy on Facebook asking their mothers for permission to fart or spew forth other non-sensical idiocies.

Those wanting a world catastrophe in line with Bhagavad Gita proportions continue steering the world narrative in the Orwellian brave new world direction to achieve their aspiration of complete control over us in all aspects of our lives. There is just one stumbling block. To achieve their goal, humanity has to be "vaccinated", has to have the Jab, or two or three or four of them. Maybe they'll need it annually, or every six months, even, as rumour has it. And humanity must be on mind-altering drugs to enhance suicides. And they need to kill the brightest through their pharmaceutically altered genuine PTSD experience for them to succeed with their agenda. And how are they going to achieve that?

Well, this desire, this urge for domination over the entire globe and everything on and in it has apparently been pursued for a long time. It's been going on for millennia, since Cain and Abel, for all we know. Did they think that by slowly drugging humanity without its knowledge with pharmaceuticals for the last 170 years, they could get that dominion? Did they think that by creating the mental health profession, as documented in *Fallacy 1*, they could get that dominion? Did they think that by robbing the brightest of humanity of its well-being and its lives through never-ending brutal wars, they could get that dominion? Did they think that by persuading the civilian population that PTSD is a scientifically provable *mental illness*, treatable by drugging and mind-altering psychological treatment, while keeping silent, that both create suicidal ideation in their wake, they could get that dominion? Did those wanting dominion over the world think that by injecting the willing masses of humans made superbly ignorant beyond belief worldwide through a century of television-watching, advertisement-mind manipulation, scientism- and atheism-permeated education from the cradle to the highest university degrees, vilification of spirituality, disbelief in holistic healing seemingly present in all layers of society would achieve such dominion?

Sure, they did. They know that our thinking generates our own narrative. They've known it for the longest time. That's why they've directed it over the last 170 years on a grand scale. They know we are the producers and directors of our life's narrative by the way we think. They know that when we change our thinking, we change everything. They know that what Eileen Caddy of the Findhorn Foundation said in August 2021 is the truth:

> "Everything starts deep within you. If you lack anything, seek deep within and you will find that your faith has been wavering or doubts and fears of lack assail you and have taken possession of your thoughts and therefore you find yourself suffering from lack. When you can face this squarely, raise your consciousness into the realms where there is no lack, because you realise every good and perfect gift comes from Me the Lord your God; that all your needs are being met one by one; that My storehouse is never empty; that My supply is there for all to share; and that all I have is yours. Then you realise that you can lack nothing, that that sense of lack has just been in your thinking and when you change your thinking you change everything. When you can really accept this in every situation, you will find everything around you will begin to change."

It is this knowledge of the enormous power we have within ourselves they fear will strike humanity. They know that when that happens, their game is over. Evil has to depart and we, humanity, can breathe freely. And if we care to look, we can see this everywhere, so let's free ourselves from fear and look at who instigated and directed this national and global educational and health narrative worldwide, shall we?

21

IF WE CARE TO LOOK, WE SEE IT EVERYWHERE

Just look around with open eyes. Mental health industry businesses purport to help the populace with its emotional upheaval over lock-downs, isolation and job loss. They claim to have the cures for fear of tomorrow due to the so-called COVID-19 pandemic and new viruses in the making, yes, in the making. Business is booming. Any physician worth his or her humanistic salt will joyfully prescribe mind-altering drugs. That is their favorite treatment for any human emotional upset, hangnail and genuine PTSD included. This despite claims by such luminaries as University of Toronto professor of psychology and clinical psychologist Jordan Bernt Peterson (1962) and Harvard psychiatrist Peter D. Breggin. They and anti-psychiatry movement members assert that they are perfectly solvable without pharmaceutical drugs.

No word is ever breathed by any of the prescribing characters that addiction is "achieved" by consuming pharmaceutical mind-altering drugs. Yes, the downhill slope into complete ruination of life is entered, without one's own knowledge. That awareness only comes when one frees oneself from the curse of addiction. Assisted by a gallon of port vine, the book *City of Joy* and an ample consumption of cigarettes, I freed myself from Ativan cold turkey—in 60 hours a newborn woman. That's just one of their numerous side-effects. The almost overwhelming desire to kill one's Self is never mentioned. Nor is the possible loss of inhibition. And never mind the slow destruction of all vital body organs while indulging in those pharmaceuticals. It spans the entire pharmaceutical drug spectrum, from aspirin to Ativan and the like. No warnings are rendered either, that mind-altering drugs are highly addictive. How addictive only surfaces in one's awareness, awareness when freeing self from that curse.

Peterson, who began to receive widespread attention in the late 2010's for his views on cultural and political issues often described as conservative, should know. He almost lost his life due to Benzodiazepines consumption prescribed to him, we presume, for anxiety by one of his learned psychiatric prescription-authorized colleagues. Obviously, no humanitarian, holistic way of treatment to calm his mind could be found for him. Or neither he nor his peers cared to look for it, which is rather unsurprising. After all, scientifically oriented humanists do not believe that human emotional upheavals can be treated, other than by scientifically developed means. By "scientifically developed means", they mean pharmaceutical mind-altering drugs. Do they even believe in human emotions at all, instead calling them "mental disorders"? The body is a machine, they say. It is scientifically documentable, repairable and adjustable through scientific means. By "scientific means", they mean brain slash, cut and burn invasion, if deemed beneficial, with frontal lobe removal in the classic *One Flew Over the Cuckoo's Nest* movie.

Talking to patients, like Peterson, about what rattles them and suggesting ways to alleviate their fears and apprehensions is not in style in an atheism-dominated humanist political agenda. They would not consider investigating and exploring the spiritual aspects of our lives—our reason for being, for example, Too boring, too time-consuming, too expensive for any self-respecting, non-holistic atheist humanist. Time, after all, is money. Peterson, unable to help himself in the Western world, went to Russia and Serbia. These are countries where holistic medicine still ranks high. There, he sought relief and healing for his mind-altering drug created misery.

But this facility of making money through human misery is nothing new. It actually began in the United States with the U.S. sixth census of 1840. That was the first attempt to count Americans considered by their peers and the counters as "insane" or "idiotic". Published results of this census indicated that an alarming numbers of Black people living in non-slaveholding states were mentally ill. This was in contrast to the tabulation of mentally ill Black people in slaveholding States. Needless to say, pro-slavery advocates trumpeted that the results showed slavery's beneficial effects. Meanwhile, anti-slavery advocates bleated that the census results were riddled with errors. Census officials, however, did not care one way or the other. They were just happy to classify whatever census takers had slotted as mental disorders under whatever nomenclature as one single category: *idiocy/insanity.*

Remember that almost anyone could hang out a shingle proclaiming oneself to be physician at that time. They could practice as freelance agents, whilst assuming full responsibility for their decisions and actions. To at leisure declare anyone of idiocy, however, called for physicians' individual protection from legal consequences for such character assassination, malignment and discrimination in court. Thus, the 1840 census sparked the formation of the Association of Medical Superintendents of American Institutions for the Insane in 1840, a remarkable event in itself. Why? American writer Eustace Clarence Mullins Jr. (1923–2010) explains in his writings. He says that it was the medical profession's sudden awareness of risk they ran as individuals through diagnoses and treatments that gave rise to the plan for a medical monopoly among a chosen few in society. This would level out the risks. It would also contain all rewards within the chosen strata of society, keeping it all in the family. As Mullins phrases it, it would "create the plague of human suffering we see today (Murder by Injection page number. Notice to self."

The Roman Catholic priest, theologian, philosopher, and social critic Ivan Dominic Illich (1926–2002) in his 1976 book *Medical Nemesis, the Expropriation of Health* took it a step further. He maintains that not only is the effectiveness of the allopathic school of medicine the stuff of mythology, but that doctors have now brought new plagues into being. Illich defines these illnesses as "iatrogenic," causing a plague, which he terms "iatrogenesis", and claiming this plague is now sweeping the nation (Murder by injection p. 15). Iatrogenesis is the causation of a disease, a harmful complication, or other ill effect by any medical activity, including diagnosis, intervention, error, or negligence. Illich not only defines iatrogenesis as "an illness, which is caused by a doctor's medical intervention," but asserts that it is composed of three commonly encountered types:

- clinical iatrogenesis, the doctor-made illness
- social iatrogenesis, deliberately engineered by the machinations of the medical industrial complex
- cultural iatrogenesis, which saps the will of the people to survive

The third one might be the most prevalent, he says. Advertisement for various medications to alleviate stress caused by normally-to-be-expected life experiences make swallowing pharmaceuticals to calm the mind seem helpful. So do a totalitarian government and the sinister figures behind it operating for their own personal gain. Warnings about their systematic destruction of body and mind, if given, are generally ignored.

Mind you, when we look a bit closer, it turns out that this facility of making money through human misery started centuries earlier. Already in the fifteenth century, petitions were made to England's King Henry V (1386–1422) requesting that only those with appropriate qualifications should be allowed to practice medicine. These medical practitioners at that time were the barber-surgeons also charged with caring for soldiers during and after battle. Their métiers had overlapped in duties for many years. This was largely because Pope Honorarius III (1150–1227) of the thirteenth century had prohibited all persons in holy orders from practising medicine in any form, as they were apt to do in monasteries as barbers. They were used to working with sharp blades, having begun to add minor surgical skills to their repertoire. This was in due course passed on to common barbers throughout the lands. In 1308, they organized themselves into the Worshipful Company of Barbers (https://barberscompany.org).

Alongside the barbers' company, a guild or fellowship of surgeons developed, whose ordinances were approved in 1435 (https://barberscompany.org). The Fellowship claimed the right to practise surgery, which inevitably led to power struggles and disputes between them and the barbers. This was temporarily resolved in 1462. Edward IV (1442–1483) granted the fellowship its first royal charter, giving it power to regulate the practice of surgery in London. The charter imbued the fellowship with the mandate to maintain professional standards and the rights to stamp out impostors and charlatans. Nevertheless, perpetual disagreements between the parties led to an agreement in 1493, which granted the Fellowship of Surgeons power of incorporation.

Henry VIII (1491–1547), the British king who beheaded two of his six wives, finally consented to end this nonsense by passing the *Physicians and Surgeons Act*, limiting the practice of medicine and surgery to a seven-mile radius of the City of London. We assume the rest of the country could do as it wished. He formalized his decree with the Royal College of Physicians foundation in 1518. He was prompted to do so since his ascension by his physician, English humanist and scholar Thomas Linacre (c. 1460–1524). However, the College's origin dates back to the "Guild of Surgeons Within the City of London" founded in the mid-fourteenth century.

In 1540, Henry further defined the parties' standing by an act of Parliament, which created the Company of Barbers and Surgeons of London. The act seems to have been most concerned with the professionalization of surgeons. It allocated a limit of four corpses annually from Tyburn for the teaching of anatomy. Tyburn is where public executions for criminal activities, such as stealing a loaf of bread or a handkerchief, had taken place as public spectacles since 1196.

As a matter of fact, between 1196 and 1783, an estimated 60,000 people were executed at Tyburn. Murderers, sometimes, and highwaymen, certainly, but for every major criminal executed at Tyburn, there were four more condemned for petty theft. Most of the people hanged at Tyburn were under 21 years of age, and many of them were still children.

Henry also granted the College's request of making it an offence to practice surgery without the approval of an expert, the College's, of course. The monopolization and concentration of medicine in the elite's hands had begun.

The act specified, that the only common activity held by the two parties was to be the extraction of teeth. It included a vehement stipulation that no surgeon could cut hair or shave anybody's hair, and that no barber had the right to practice surgery in any way. Nevertheless, the surgeons instantaneously launched a campaign to eliminate barber-surgeon practitioners in their entirety. That barber-surgeons had helped the poor and destitute with their health problems for little compensation for centuries caused the surgeons little to no concern, as money and profit was at stake. The result? The laity's suffering increased to such extent, that Henry VIII in 1542 saw himself forced to enact the Quacks Charter exempting the "unauthorized practitioners of surgery" from the 1540 act (*Murder by Injection* p. 12–13).

Remember, Henry VIII, so liberal in beheadings had been Defender of the (Catholic) Faith. Then he was founder of the Anglican Church in an effort to divorce his first wife Catherine (1485-1536). Catherine was daughter of Isabella I of Castile and Ferdinand II of Aragon. The family was *Los Reyes Catolicos*, facilitators of Columbus' 1492 voyage to America. Henry had at that time taken possession of all Roman Catholic church property in Britain and Ireland. Thus, he left the clergy - for centuries running the church while caring for the poor, the ailing and the destitute - destitute themselves.

The Company of Barbers and Surgeons, however, never an easy one to manage, continued on its unmerry path until 1745. That is when, at the request of the surgeons, the British Parliament passed another bill. This bill allowed the surgeons to do two things. First, they left the Company. Second, they formed what became the Royal College of Surgeons of England in 1843. Equivalent colleges had already been opened throughout the British Empire's colonies, over which the sun never set. New developments in areas such as anaesthesia and antiseptics sprang forth, with Friedrich Wilhelm Adam Sertürner's discovery of morphine in the forefront. Surgical possibilities, and thus business opportunities, expanded in a multitude of directions, from creating instruction manuals for slash, cut and burn techniques to teaching methodology. The craft's future looked bright indeed.

Thus, special surgeon subject categories were devised and exams for aspiring surgeons introduced. There were jointly held from the 1880s onwards, with the newly created Royal College of Physicians, and all of it originating with the College of 1518. This very same college, by the way, lying at the heart of allopathic medicine, also happens to be the forerunner of the British Worshipful Society of Apothecaries, a necessity for the herds' control through pharmaceuticals. Prior to its foundation, London's apothecaries had been part of the Grocers' Company, its trade since 1345 described as the "Mistery of Grossers, Pepperers and Apothecaries."

The latter separated from the Grocers' Company in 1617 by way of a royal charter granted by James VI and I (1566 -1625). They were considered the lowest category of doctors by the learned society. After all, they originated from general shopkeepers, and here they were challenging College of Physicians' members' monopoly to practice medicine during the remainder of the seventeenth century. They established a right to treat the sick during the Great Plague of 1665. And then again during the Great Fire of London in 1666. So many of the city's esteemed physicians and their rich patients had fled to their country estates. Thus, the British House of Lords in 1703 gave legal recognition to apothecaries as doctors, and with it the right to practice medicine.

By 1815 and the Battle of Waterloo won by Irish General Wellington, the apothecaries achieved their desire of protecting their profession. The United Kingdom's Parliament passed the *Apothecaries Act 1815* (citation 55 Geo. III, c.194) with the long title *An Act for better regulating the Practice of Apothecaries throughout England and Wales*. The Act required instruction in anatomy, botany, chemistry, *materia medica* and "physic", in addition to six months' practical hospital experience. It introduced compulsory apprenticeship, as well as formal qualifications and examinations for aspiring apothecaries under the license of the Society of Apothecaries, graduating as general practitioners in modern terms. Needless to say, it further enhanced the medical profession's regulation in the UK, thus filtering through all British colonies and territories for better or for worse.

But despite all these regulations, including this particular act, training of medical folk in Britain is said to have remained disparate. It varied all the way from classical university studies at Oxford and Cambridge down to a series of courses in a provincial hospital to "broom-and-apron apprenticeship" in a local apothecary's shop.

Nevertheless, the *Apothecaries Act 1815* gave the society the power to license and regulate medical practitioners throughout England and Wales. It could hold examinations in surgery, obstetrics and gynaecology. Indeed, after the *Medical Act of 1886*, they were required by law. Since 1928, when the Society instituted the first postgraduate qualification in midwifery (the Mastery of Midwifery, MMSA), the Apothecaries have pioneered 15 other diplomas in specialist subjects not offered by universities, medical royal colleges or any other medical body, including the diploma in forensic and clinical aspects of sexual assault.

It also led to the establishment in the UK of pharmacy and medical specialisms as well as the founding of specialist royal colleges and faculties including those for general practice, obstetrics & gynaecology, occupational medicine, public health medicine, and forensic & legal medicine. Since1962, the Society awards postgraduate diplomas in the following fields:

- medical jurisprudence (1962)
- history of medicine (1970)
- genitourinary medicine (1973)
- philosophy of medicine (1978)
- medical care of catastrophes (1994)
- forensic medical sciences (1998)
- HIV medicine (2002)

In other words, the UK Society of Apothecaries in Britain seems to be just like the U.S. National Institutes of Health. It includes all aspects of medicine with its associated humanistic – human equals animals – health treatment applications to its citizenry. Today, 85% of its members belong to professions allied with medicine. Humanistic through and through, regular conferences and lectures are conducted, among them one by Dr. Emily Mayhew entitled *Wars against Children*. Dr. Mayhew is a military medical historian specialising in the study of severe casualty, its infliction, treatment and long-term outcomes in modern warfare. She is historian in residence in the Department of Bioengineering at Imperial College London. She works primarily with the researchers and staff of the Centre for Blast Injury Studies. Dr. Mayhew is also a research fellow in the Division of Surgery within the Department of Surgery and Cancer. Based jointly in the Department of Bioengineering and the Chelsea and Westminster campus, Mayhew in this particular lecture will look at the history and future of children growing up in conflict and post-conflict zones. Does she know something we piss-ons don't? Is she interpreting the Denver Airport mural as our upcoming planned reality, as she also was part of the team that put together the *Paediatric Blast Injury Field Manual* published in 2019?

"Children of the World Dream of Peace" by Leo Tanguma Mural formerly installed at Denver Airport. Photo: Higher Forces

Imperial College London is legally named Imperial College of Science, Technology and Medicine. It is a public research university in London, England. What does "public" mean in the British school system? A public school in England and Wales, but not in Scotland, is a fee-charging endowed school originally for older boys. It is "public" in the sense of being open to pupils irrespective of locality, denomination or paternal trade or profession. What does an "endowed" school mean? A school set up for charitable purposes and endowed with funds, cash, shares or property by its founders and all those who feel like donating money afterwards.

Throughout their existence, public schools have been strongly associated with the ruling classes, who therefore controlled the national narrative for centuries. The London Imperial College, for instance, is a world-class university with the mission to benefit society through excellence in science, engineering, medicine and business. Its "imperial" name apparently grew out of a personal dedication. Prince Albert of Saxe-Coburg and Gotha (1819-1861) was both consort and first cousin of Victoria, Queen of the United Kingdom of Great Britain, and Ireland and Empress of India (1819 -1901). Albert's heartfelt desire was to bring some culture to the country with a title reflecting such culture. Although he was dead at the time of founding by royal charter in 1907, the college included the Royal Albert Hall, the Imperial Institute, numerous museums and numerous royal colleges. Imperial College also absorbed the Royal Colleges of Science, the Royal School of Mines and the City and Guilds College. In 1988, the Imperial College of Medicine combined with St. Mary's Hospital Medical School. In addition, Queen Elizabeth II opened the Imperial College Business School in 2004.

The Imperial College London's admission fees are a measly £9,250 for 2021–22, peanuts compared to colleges such as Oxford International College, which charges £46,500. And remember, these are tax-free "public" institutions, another Orwellian language perversion in use since at least the eighteenth century. Strongly associated with the ruling classes, the

British Empire's overseas officers and senior administrators sent their sons to be educated in England around the age of six. In 2019, two thirds of British cabinet ministers had been educated at such fee-charging schools.

But let's move on. In addition to the societies already mentioned, another part of inventing and streamlining the humanist medical system for animal-equals-humanity is called the British Medical Association. It traces its origins back to the Provincial Medical and Surgical Association (PMSA). That body was founded by medical surgeon Sir Charles Hastings in 1832, and the British Medical Association of physician Dr. George Webster, G.P., J.P. (? -1876) founded in 1836. By 1856, they had combined forces, henceforth calling themselves the British Medical Association, while continuing the PMSA's weekly publication, *The Provincial Medical and Surgical Journal*. The journal was merged with the Association Medical Journal and from 1857 onward appeared as the *British Medical Journal* nowadays one of the oldest general medicine peer reviewed trade journals in the world.

Together with the Worshipful Society of Apothecaries, the British Medical Association formed the impetus for the American Medical Association (AMA). Founded in 1847 and incorporated in 1897, it composes the largest lobby group of physicians, dentists and medical students in the United States. Its stated mission? "To promote the art and science of medicine and the betterment of public health." The art and science? Yes, it's the artistry and science-imagination of medicine, with COVID-19, suicide prevention and PTSD in the lead to keep creation and sciences departments' artists and scientists in lucrative incomes. Fauci's salary was $417,608 in 2019. His NIH boss Francis Collins makes only a measly $276,714, the latest year for which federal *salaries* are available.

AMA publishes the *Journal of the American Medical Association* (JAMA). It also publishes a list of physician speciality codes, the standard method for identifying physicians and their practice specialties. AMA also holds the AMA Physician Masterfile. This database contains current and historical data on all physicians and graduates of foreign medical schools residing in the United States and meeting the educational and credentialing requirements necessary for recognition as physicians. You'll find whatever else AMA might deem of interest and worthwhile to have on file about any of them.

In Eustace Mullins' opinion, AMA had, from its outset, but one objective: to attain and defend the total and complete monopoly of medicine in all its varieties throughout the United States. Adhering to and applying humanistic principles, only slash, cut and burn techniques, together with pharmaceutical drugging to the hilt, were to be its medical treatments of healing for U.S. citizens and beyond, if they could. Holistic medicine, such as homeopathy, which aims to treat body, mind and soul as one entity and immensely popular in nineteenth century America, was from its outset anathema to the organization's leadership and most of its members.

However, the AMA's 1847 foundation was preceded by the very first professional medical specialty organization ever to see the light of day in the United States. The Association of Medical Superintendents of American Institutions for the Insane (AMSAII) was precursor to the American Psychiatric Association (APA). The APA would eventually create the *Diagnostic and Statistical Manual of Mental Disorders* (DSM). Also known as the Superintendents'

Association, it saw its birth at a Philadelphia meeting of 13 superintendents and organizers of insane asylums and hospitals in 1844. One of them was Thomas Story Kirkbride (1809 -1883). He was born into a wealthy Pennsylvanian Quaker family. After receiving a medical degree from the University of Pennsylvania in 1832 at the tender age of 21, he became the youngest resident at a Quaker mental institution in Philadelphia called the Friends Asylum. It was also called Friends Hospital, The Asylum for the Relief of Persons Deprived of the Use of Their Reason and the Frankford Asylum.

After his one-year residency at the asylum, Kirkbride spent two years as resident physician at the Pennsylvania Hospital. In 1835, he opened his own practice, mainly focusing on surgery. In 1840, he accepted the position of superintendent at the Pennsylvania Hospital for the Insane. At the Superintendents Association, meanwhile, he held various board positions, including that of president between 1862 and 1870. During his tenure, he took joy in pioneering what would be known as the "Kirkbride Plan" to improve medical care for the insane by standardizing buildings that housed patients.

He developed his requirements for asylum designs based on a philosophy of moral treatment and environmental determinism. Moral treatment is based on a humanitarian—the humane—approach to human mental disorders. For instance, humane psychosocial care and moral discipline deriving from religious and moral concerns. It is this that is so overwhelmingly unfashionable in today's mental industry treatments. It is shown with genuine PTSD and the hangnail version diagnosis and treatment of it, only expertly further traumatizing the traumatized. Humanitarian treatment fell into ill repute under Freud et al. by the early twentieth century. It was the victim of scientifically preferred biomedical methods, such as the pharmaceutical mind-altering drugs and electroshocks so favoured still today.

Environmental determinism is the study of how physical environments predispose societies and states towards particular development trajectories. The theory is that they speak the path to be followed by a projectile flying or an object moving under the action of given forces to achieve the desired narrative. Certain physical developments Putting Hitler in power would be an example of this an ancient concept. Early theories in ancient China, Greece and Rome all thought environmental features completely determined both the physical and the intellectual qualities of their society. The Chinese philosopher and politician Guan Zhong (管仲 c. 720–645 BC) held that the qualities of major rivers shaped the character of its surrounding peoples. Swift, twisting rivers made a people "greedy, uncouth and warlike." Smooth running rivers created a peaceful and creative populace. We see a reflection of his philosophy in Feng Shui, one of the Five Arts of Chinese Metaphysics, classified as physiognomy (observation of appearances through formulas and calculations). This art is still widely used throughout Asia to orient buildings or household furniture in auspicious ways. They are often determined by reference to bodies of water, stars and compass directions, as detailed in *Fallacy 1*.

Hippocrates of Kos (c. 460–c. 370 BC) is considered the "Father of Medicine" in recognition of his lasting contributions to the field. Among those contributions are the use of prognosis and clinical observation, the systematic categorization of diseases and the formulation of humoral theory. He is commonly portrayed as the paragon of physicians. But you probably know him for being credited with coining the Hippocratic Oath. He wrote a similar account of environmental determinism in his treatise "Airs, Waters, Places" (Benjamin Isaac, The Invention of Racism in Classical Antiquity Princeton: Princeton University Press. 2004).

Hippocrates of Kos ca.460 BC- 370 BC.

So did Abū 'Uthman 'Amr ibn Baḥr al-Kinānī al-Baṣrī (: أبو عثمان عمرو بن بحر الكناني البصري), commonly known as al-Jāḥiẓ (الجاحظ, *The Bug Eyed* (776-868/869). This Arab prose writer and author of works of theology, zoology and politico-religious polemics also produced theories of environmental determinism. He suggested that people's and livestock' skin color were determined by the water, soil and heat of their environments.

In his *Muqaddimah* (1377), Arab sociologist and polymath Ibn Khaldun also wrote that black skin was due to the hot climate of sub-Saharan Africa and not due to an African lineage. He thereby challenged Hamitic theories of race that held that the sons of Ham (son of Noah) were cursed with black skin. But that's a different story to be read in Eustace Mullins' *The Curse of Canaan: A demonology of History*. Ibn Khaldun furthermore believed that physical environments influenced non-physical factors. He argued that soil, climate and food not only determined whether people were nomadic or sedentary, but also what customs and ceremonies they held.

Jared Mason Diamond (1937–) is an American geographer, historian and ornithologist. He originally trained in biochemistry and physiology, and was a professor of geography at the University of California, Los Angeles. Jeffrey Herbst is a political scientist and president of Los Angeles' American Jewish University. British archaeologist and historian Ian Matthew Morris (1960–) is Willard Professor of Classics at Stanford University. These three men went back to the future by sparking a revival of the ancient theory of environmental determinism during the late twentieth and early twenty-first centuries. They gave their seven cents worth of hypothesis how geographic and ecological forces s influence state building, e.g., the national narrative, human economic development and the behaviour of inmates of institutions. The forces they studied included chemical aerosol spraying, GMOs, vaccines, chemicals and chemical spraying, as well as injections into humans.

That Kirkbride had already determined the outcome, had yet to reach their psyche and their knowledgebase, as they omitted to look, we trust. No money in looking, is there? Kirkbride's approach had been praised for freeing those incarcerated in mental institutions from their customarily worn shackles and the truly barbaric physical treatments oftentimes applied to them since the early 1800s. Instead, Kirkbride had given consideration to both their emotions and their social interactions. The typical floor plan for his hospitals, with their long rambling wings arranged staggered *en echelon*, so each connected wing received maximum sunlight and fresh air, thus promoting patients both privacy and comfort. The buildings' form itself was meant to have a curative effect. It would be "a special apparatus for the care of lunacy, [with grounds] highly improved and tastefully ornamented" was his idea of treatment for those considered insane.

Needless to say, some, if not most, in the medical community saw his theories and ideas as hindering the humanistic - human as animal - medical approach to progress. Their "progress" shunned even considering the influence of emotions and compassion in healing for humanity, sane or insane. Never mind the possibility to cure the mentally and emotionally disturbed through compassion. Regardless, the Association of Medical Superintendents of American Institutions for the Insane (AMSAII) and Kirkbride's participation in it would eventually lead to the establishment of psychiatric hospitals somewhat in accordance with his asylum model. Thus began the rise of organized, institutional psychiatry throughout the U.S., as widely discussed in *Fallacy 1*.

True to the Association's objectives, super-intendants, many of them so-called psychiatrists imported from Austria, communicated their findings and experiences to each other. They cooperated in and contributed to statistical data and information collections relating to mental disorders and what they considered and viewed as insanity. And they helped each other improve the treatment of the insane in whatever way they saw fit, from frontal lobe removal to straight jackets, tie-downs and numerous electric shock treatments.

Nothing has changed since then, other than that the association itself changed its name to American Medico-Psychological Association. This allowed assistant physicians working in mental hospitals to become members. Whereupon they almost instantaneously proceeded to declare a whole new series of to be mental disorders:

- dementia
- epilepsy
- mania (someone experiencing unreasonable euphoria, very intense moods, hyperactivity and delusions)
- melancholia (seen as a subtype of depression)
- monomania (seen as the exaggerated or obsessive enthusiasm for or preoccupation with one thing
- paresis, a condition of muscular weakness caused by nerve damage or disease
- dipsomania (alcoholism, specifically when characterized by intermittent bouts of craving for alcohol).

Dipsomania is the most medical of the many terms used in the eighteenth and nineteenth centuries to describe habitual drunkenness. So says political scientist Mariana Valverde, professor at the Centre for Criminology and Socio-legal Studies at the University of Toronto and Fellow of the Royal Society of Canada. Alcohol was, of course, the most common undertaking in which the herd liberally engaged throughout Britain during that time.

So unquenchable and immense had the thirst for gin become by 1743, that writer and notorious alcoholic Samuel Johnson warned that to take away gin from the working and poorer classes would incite 'rebellion'. Gin was a cheap, easy way to forget hunger and hardship, and safer to drink than contaminated, sewage-infested city water. None portrayed the state of affairs better than social commentator and polemicist William Hogarth (1697-1764). He was best known for his satirical engravings and paintings of an increasingly drunk and idle society, which he regarded as deeply flawed, uncivilised and debauched.

This era of intoxication led to a number of dire health and social problems. These included violence, insanity and often death. Never mind what it did to the population's offspring and consequently future generations from the moment of conception. It also sparked widespread moral outrage among the ruling classes and the bourgeoisie, which culminated in Parliament passing the Gin Act of 1751, little good it did (Lydia Figes: The gin craze: how William Hogarth captured the spirit of Georgian Britain; 2020; artuk.org/discover/stories/the-gin-craze-how-william-hogarth-captured-the-spirit-of-georgian-britain)

It all served well to not only steer the British national narrative, but that of the entire world, into the direction our overlords wished it to go, were you to research its past 300-400 years of history, in particular. For us, suffice it to know that, in 1917, the American Medico-Psychological Association adopted the report of its Committee on Statistics, which provided for a system of uniform statistics in institutions for mental diseases. Furthermore, a standing Committee on Statistics to promote the introduction of the system throughout the country had been appointed. It met in New York City in 1918 to cooperate with the National Commission for Mental Hygiene, nowadays Mental Health America. Their plan was to spread their ideas about human emotional upheavals they termed "mental disorders" all across the land.

This same National Committee had also established a Bureau of Uniform Statistics. It received a special gift to defray the initial expenses of its undertakings to collect statistics from institutions established for the insane. Furthermore, the Committee on Statistics became an advisory committee to both the National Committee and the Bureau of Uniform Statistics. The latter carried out the work of introducing the new system, and also gathered statistics from the mental institutions. Prepared with the help of the American Medico-Psychological Association, they termed this invention the *Statistical Manual for the Use of Institutions for the Insane.* To help institutions compile their annual statistics, a series of forms had been printed. Both manual and forms were distributed free of cost to all cooperating institutions in the hope that they would be generally adopted so "a national system of statistics of mental diseases may become an actuality." (Statistical manual for the use of institutions for the insane; archive.org).

The 1918 manual contained 22 human mental disorder classifications with explanatory notes. They were:

Traumatic psychoses, including:

- traumatic delirium
- traumatic constitution
- post-traumatic mental enfeeblement (dementia)

Senile psychoses, including :

- simple deterioration
- presbyophrenic type
- delirious and confused types
- depressed and agitated states in addition to deterioration
- paranoid types
- pre-senile types

Psychoses with other brain or nervous diseases, including:

- cerebral embolism paralysis agitans
- meningitis
- multiple sclerosis tables
- acute chorea

Alcoholic psychoses, including"

- pathological intoxication
- delirium tremens
- Korsakow's psychosis
- acute hallucinosis
- chronic hallucinosis
- acute paranoid type
- chronic paranoid type
- alcoholic deterioration

Psychoses due to drugs and other exogenous toxins, including:

- opium (and derivatives), cocaine, bromides, chloral, etc.
- metals, as lead, arsenic, etc.
- gases

Psychoses with other somatic diseases, including:

- delirium with infectious diseases
- post-infectious psychosis
- exhaustion-delirium
- delirium of unknown origin
- cardio-renal diseases
- diseases of the ductless glands

Manic-depressive psychoses, including:

- manic type
- depressive type
- stupor
- mixed type
- circular type

Dementia praecox, including:

- paranoid type
- catatonic type
- hebephrenic type
- simple type

Epileptic psychoses, including:

- deterioration
- clouded states
- mental deficiency without psychosis

Psychoneuroses and neuroses, including:

- hysterical type
- psychasthenic type
- neurasthenic type
- anxiety neuroses

Not insane, including:

- epilepsy without psychosis
- alcoholism without psychosis
- drug addiction without psychosis
- constitutional psychopathic inferiority without
- psychosis
- mental deficiency without psychosis

Note that all have the "Others to be specified, and that the explanation for number 1, Traumatic psychoses states:

> "The diagnosis should be restricted to mental disorders arising as a direct or obvious consequence of a brain (or head) injury producing psychotic symptoms of a fairly characteristic kind. The amount of damage to the brain may vary from an extensive destruction of tissue to simple concussion or physical shock with or without fracture of the skull." (ibid. p. 12)

Furthermore, there were these categories that had no further explanation or sub-categories:

- psychoses with cerebral arteriosclerosis
- general paralysis
- psychoses with cerebral syphilis

- psychoses with Huntington's chorea
- psychoses with brain tumor
- psychoses with pellagra
- involution melancholia
- psychoses with constitutional psychopathic inferiority
- psychoses with mental deficiency
- undiagnosed psychoses
- paranoia or paranoic conditions

Even then, a connection between traumatic psychoses with human emotional shocks had escaped the learned mental health society's attention. Unless, of course, it had been willfully ignored. It neither fit nor coincided with their humanistic rattus-cani-simia-lepus-cockroach equals human desired handling of humanity's health and wellbeing aspirations. Thus, the *Statistical Manual for the Use of Institutions for the Insane* set the table for the DSM allowing the craft to define anything and everything emotionally humane as mental disorders. Instrumental in it was the Medico-Psychological Association, which in 1921 changed its name to the American Psychiatric Association (APA). By that time, Freud's associates and his nephew Edward Bernays were well entrenched in American mental institutions, and Bernays' nascent advertisement endeavors to "make the American mind" were taking roots. The push to drive humanity into insanity without its knowledge could begin in earnest. In fact, it all began with the American Medical Association's incorporation in 1897, the Frederick Gates-designed and Rockefeller funded Institute of Medical Research, and the Carnegie-funded Flexner Report, in conjunction with the ordo ab chaos doctrine. See, it becomes clear once we start looking, eh? So, let's look some more, shall we?

22

WHO DID WHAT IN PURSUIT OF HUMAN HEALTH DESTRUCTION?

In the spring of 1847, hundreds of delegates from 28 states gathered at the Academy of Natural Sciences in Philadelphia to initiate the American Medical Association (AMA). It was Dr. Nathan Smith Davis (1817-1904), whose 1845 resolution to the New York Medical Association had called for a national medical convention. This led the group to found the largest association of medical doctors and students in the country, with the mission statement "to promote the art and science of medicine and the betterment of public health." (https://ansp.org/exhibits/online-exhibits/stories/ama-founded-at-the-academy-of-natural-sciences/). Delegates adopted the first nationwide standards for preliminary medical education and the Doctor of Medicine degree for its members (M.D.). Measures were also taken to fulfill the association's foremost aspirations:

- To advance science
- To improve public health
- To develop a program of medical ethics,
- To create standards for medical education

Since then, the AMA has diligently worked to create art and science, but not necessarily for humanity's health and well-being.

Smith Davis was the moving force in its creation. Twice elected its president, he was first editor of its Journal of the American Medical Association. Seemingly slotted since birth for a career in medical education, he must have been bursting with pride.

Smith Davis was born in a log house near Greene, Chenango County, New York State, on the farm his father had homesteaded. He attended the village school until, moving on to the Methodist Episcopal Church-owned Cazevonia Seminary in Madison County, New York, at the age of 16. This academic oriented school was founded in 1825, where he studied English, Latin, chemistry, natural philosophy and algebra.

Without any further instruction, young Nathan began an apprenticeship in medicinal practice with a Dr. Daniel Clark of Smithville Flats, Chenango County in 1834 (https://smithvillehistory.org). This was in accordance with medical training of the time. Young men would learn the art and science of medicine with practicing physicians in their neighbourhood or at privately owned medical schools. There were no entrance requirements other than the ability to pay a fee and the willingness to perform menial tasks. At the private medical schools, the training might consist of two four-month-lecture sessions. It might also include a preceptorship of practical experience-gathering and training under the supervision of an expert or specialist.

Under Dr. Clark, young Nathan had already mastered medicine at the tender age of 17 to the extent, that he could take the next step. So, he enrolled in three courses of lectures at the College of Physicians and Surgeons of the Western District of New York, Fairfield. Barely 20 years old, he graduated from that hallowed institution in January 1837 with a thesis on "Animal Temperature". Soon thereafter, Smith Davis set up practice in Vienna, New York. A few months later, he moved on to Binghamton. That's where the Chenango Canal connecting the Susquehanna River to the Erie Canal had just opened and the community was growing by leaps and bounds.

He immediately joined the Broome County Medical Society, still in 1837. He obtained human cadavers to demonstrate anatomy to his equally immediately-found medical students. In 1841, he received the Medical Society of the State of New York's prize for the best "Analysis of the Discoveries Concerning the Physiology of the Nervous System." By 1843, Smith Davis had achieved the position of Broome County Medical Society's secretary, librarian and delegate to the Medical Society of the State of New York. He was majorly concerned with the lack of strict professionalism within the medical community and the quality of medical education. So, he voiced his concern in an address to the society in 1845, calling for a nationwide organization to promote education and standards for all doctors to follow.

That speech, in turn, resulted in founding the American Medical Association formation, just two years later. As stated earlier, its primary goals were furthering scientific advancement and establishing standards for medical education. No consideration whatsoever was given to holistic physicians. In the 1800s, they outnumbered the slash-cut-and burn variety of medicine by more than two to one throughout the nation. Regardless, they were declared inadmissible to the AMA clan of art and science of medicine.

AMA's forerunner was the Medical Society of the State of New York of 1794. From 1806 onwards it was known as just the Medical Society of the State of New York. Galloway, Scotland, born and Edinburgh University medically-educated physician William McClelland (1769-?) was the first president under its new name. Already in 1806, it had pushed through legislation mandating that physicians had to enrol as members in the affiliated local societies to practice medicine. These societies, of course would regulate the profession. In return, the Medical Society would authorize them to practice "physic or surgery." And it would permit them to disseminate scientific knowledge, enhance the practice of medicine, promote public health and suppress unlicensed practitioners.

That, however, was more difficult then anticipated. The legislation had provided no penalties for failing to comply with the Society's dictates, never mind enrol at all. And the only discipline for misconduct consisted of the expulsion from the society. Furthermore, if rejected by the local county society, practitioners or aspiring practitioners could appeal the rejection at the state level.

And even when the AMA got a foothold in the territory in 1847, the Medical Society of the County of New York continued to examine candidates for medical licenses. State authorities took over in 1880, thus reducing the Society's role to the simple mandate "to aid in regulating the practice of physic and surgery." At his point, however, the Society's legal counsel sprang into action. They vigorously worked with the State's district attorneys and the courts in hot pursuit of ruining the practices of holistic medicine practitioners. They labeled them "quacks," from the Dutch word *quacksalver*. This term was used in the seventeenth century to describe 'miracle cure' peddlers selling fake potions. This led to the word soon meaning "a crook". In the US, holistic medicine practitioners' persecution would go on until the 1920s, when their elimination had been as good as completed. Transmission of generational knowledge thought eliminated, the Society finally rendered mute as a regulatory agency.

However, after WWII, it would slowly begin to again pick up its persecution of those daring to practice holistic medicine. It then moved into full velocity with the Codex Alimentarius implementation of 1961. The Codex was established by the United Nations' Food and Agriculture Organization (FAO). The FAO, which sanctioned Monsanto, and was put under the umbrella of the World Health Organization (WHO). As such, it was presented to us, the gullible and ignorant herd, as protecting and furthering our health and wellbeing, and as a way to facilitate international trade.

Its content in a nutshell? It prohibits the use of all herbal healing remedies beneficial to human health. That includes the fabulous Kava I described in *Fallacy 1*. Kava worked so wonderfully well in calming me down during the 10 years of pure terror experienced due to the PTSD treatment I received from my employer, the WCB, my Union and 23 of the 24 psychiatrists and psychologist they forced me to deal with. The learned society of the art and science of medicine, however, would still rather kill themselves than acknowledge its or any other holistic medicinal treatments. And so, they continue with a vengeance to persecute and urinate on its practitioners.

And the Medical Society of the County of New York? It became influential in other ways, among them:

- Founding the College of Physicians and Surgeons
- Establishing a code of ethics for the profession
- Setting up a national pharmacopeia
- Be involved with the American Medical Association (AMA).

In 2021, independently operated and overseen by a board of directors and a board of trustees, it maintained several standing committees with specific areas of interest, including membership, medical credentialing, public health and workers' compensation in addition to an advisory committee for young practitioners, perhaps to keep those new in the field on the established party line?

Mind you, this powerful position did not occur by happenstance. It was a well-thought out plan to direct the nation's herd's health narrative by the education of aspiring allopathic physicians. The plan was put in motion in the late 1700's by establishing four allopathic medical schools in the US' then existing original 13 colonies (https://smithvillehistory.org).

The first one out of the gate, the College of Philadelphia, opened in 1765. In the course of time, it developed into the University of Pennsylvania's Perelman School of Medicine. The name was bestowed upon it after Raymond G. Perelman (1917-2019) and his wife Ruth showered a $225 million grant on the facility in 2011. It began as a secondary school, founded in 1749 by a group of local notables, Benjamin Franklin among them. It initially included a "charity school," sometimes called a blue coat school. These were usually built and maintained by religious organisations to provide clothing and education to students for free or at little charge. They readied children of the herd for trades, services and what we now call blue colour work, which in those days was normally provided by the same charitable foundation.

The charity school taught only reading, writing and arithmetic. But the secondary school—the Academy—offered a more advanced curriculum notable for its emphasis on modern languages and science in place of Latin and Greek. It was on behest of one of its graduates, John Morgan (1735-1789), that its trustees decided to fund "anatomical lectures" and a course on "the theory and practice of physick" supplemented with bedside teachings at the Pennsylvania Hospital of 1751. Morgan was imbued with a doctorate from of the University of Edinburgh Medical School. His fellow University of Edinburgh Medical School graduate Dr. William Shippen Jr. helped him persuade the trustees.

Morgan, was thought of by many as the founder of public medical instruction in America. During the colonies' war for independence (1775-1783), he served as the second "Chief physician & director general", an early name for the Surgeon General of the Continental Army. It was established by a resolution of Congress on June 14, 1775, to coordinate the colonies' medical efforts during the war. Morgan's mate, William Shippen Jr. (1736 -1808), was of old Philadelphia stock. His great-grandfather, Edward Shippen, had been Philadelphia's first mayor. His father, William Sr., was a celebrated doctor and academic in his own right. His uncle, Edward III, was a founder of Princeton University, where William Jr. studied medicine under his father for four years before graduating in 1754 as valedictorian (oldpineconservancy.org). He then continued his studies at the University of Edinburgh in Great Britain. He graduated in 1761, just as John Morgan began his studies at the same school.

Shippen, the third Director General of Hospitals of the Continental Army trying to usurp Morgan's position of Surgeon General. At that time, Morgan was the first systematic teacher of anatomy, surgery and obstetrics in Colonial America. After training in midwifery in London and Edinburgh, he even became the first American male physician to establish a normal obstetrics practice in the U.S. in 1762 (https://hekint.org). He also pioneered formal midwifery education through a lecture series initially taught to both male physicians and female midwives, but later limited to male physicians.

Medicine had been taught at Edinburgh since the early sixteenth century. The field took flight when Pope Innocent III (1161-1216) forbade clerics who acted as society's physicians to perform surgical procedures. He considered them 'contaminating' to their psyche (M. -P. Bernardi, D. Watters: Barber-surgeons: a doomed guild of masters and misters in the middle ages; ANZ Journal of surgery 2009). Having little choice but to obey their pontiff's Bull, the clerics entrusted the job of surgical necessities to the nations' barbers, hence the rise of the barber-surgeon profession. It turned the delicate cut-slash-and burn task into a manual, quasi blue collar trade involving apprenticeship. This did not sit well with those belonging to the non-clerical learned medical society, many being truly unhappy with the degrading relationship.

Eminent Renaissance physicians disdained barber-surgeons with a passion. Among them was Italian surgeon Lanfranc of Milan (?- 1315). So was Henri de Mondeville (1260–1320), author of a surgical treatise, *La Chirurgie*. So was physician and surgeon Guy de Chauliac (1300–1368), writer of *Chirurgia Magna*, a treatise on surgery. Another was anatomist, physician and author Andreas Vesalius (1514–1564), who wrote one of the most influential books on human anatomy of the time, *De Humani Corporis Fabrica Libri Septem*. There was just one notable exception who did not draw their disdain, namely Ambrois Paré (1510–1590). He was a French military barber surgeon serving kings Henry II, Francis II, Charles IX and Henry. He seems to have found respect in their eyes, as he revolutionised the surgery of wounds based on his observations and practical experiences in ways the others lacked, most likely never having seen a battlefield.

By the middle of the sixteenth century, there were very few physicians, mostly with a degree from Oxford or Cambridge, who diagnosed internal problems. There were barbers who conducted minor surgery such as bloodletting and drawing teeth. There were surgeons who carried out major surgery in the presence of a physician with both barbers and surgeons having generally been apprenticed. And there were apothecaries, also apprenticed, who sold drugs and sometimes treated patients (familysearch.org). The situation was far more complicated than would appear, however, as there was much overlap and frequent disputes between the various representative bodies that had developed.

Dr. Margaret Pelling is senior associate member of Oxford University's Faculty of History and Centre for the History of Science, Medicine, and Technology. She uncovers the qualifications of the Barber-Surgeons' Company members in seventeenth century London, and most likely everywhere else in continental Europe. It seems they were actually distillers, innkeepers, hosiers, colourers, pin-makers, hat-pressers, musicians, dyers, perfumers, tallow-chandlers and tailors. Formal records of medical qualification were rarely present.

The multitude of practitioners were used and accepted not because of any paper qualifications, but because of the services they offered and their favourable reputation, we surmise.

With such disputes and hierarchical education differences, Henry VIII, he with the 6 wives, saw fit to open The Royal College of Physicians of London (of England from 1858) in 1518. In so doing, he granted it a monopoly for giving medical advice within a seven-mile radius of the City of London. In 1522, he extended it nationally, a monopoly successfully challenged by the apothecaries in 1703. James VI founded Royal colleges of physicians in Glasgow for both physicians and surgeons in 1599, in Dublin for physicians in 1667 and in Edinburgh in 1681. They were modeled predominantly on teachings at the University of Bologna, Italy, of 1088, and in Padua in 1222 and Leiden, Netherlands, in 1575. Their primary curriculum consisted mostly of anatomy. American folk with physician aspirations would attend only Edinburgh's medical school, as none of the others taught in the English language.

Shippen and Morgan were not the only physicians to found an allopathic medical school. Samuel Bard (1742 -1821), personal physician to George Washington, opened the Vagelos College of Physicians and Surgeons (VP&S) in 1767. This was at King's College, now known as Columbia University College of Physicians and Surgeons, the second one in the 13 colonies and the very first school to award the Doctor of Medicine (M.D.) degree. Harvard University would follow, after some 17,000 mostly Puritans had migrated from Britain to New England by 1636. It had actually been founded to train clergy to proselyte in the new "church in the wilderness". Simply called "New College", it changed its name to Harvard College in 1639 in honour of English minister and university of Cambridge alumnus John Harvard (1607–1638), who bequeathed half of his estate and his entire library to the school upon his death.

The *New England's First Fruits*, a book published in London in 1643 about the evangelization efforts by the Puritans in colonial New England, mentions Harvard College and describes its intention:

> "After God had carried us safe to New-England, and wee had builded our houses, provided necessaries for our livelihood, rear'd convenient places for Gods worship, and setled the Civill Government: One of the next things we longed for, and looked after was to advance Learning and perpetuate it to Posterity; dreading to leave an illiterate Ministery to the Churches, when our present Ministers shall lie in the Dust. And as we were thinking and consulting how to affect this great work, it pleased God to stir up the heart of one Mr. Harvard (a godly gentleman and a lover of learning; then living amongst us) to give one-half of his estate (it being in all about £1,700) towards the erecting of a Colledge, and all his library. After him, another gave £300; others after them cast in more; and the public hand of the State added the rest. The Colledge was by common consent appointed to be at Cambridge (a place very pleasant and accommodate), and is called (according to the name of the first founder) Harvard Colledge." (*New England's First Fruits: With Divers Other Special Matters Concerning that Country*. Reprinted for J. Sabin. May 23, 1865. Wikipedia)

To affect God's great work, British Puritan clergyman and 1640 Boston immigrant Henry Dunster (1609-1659) became Harvard College's first president in 1639, when Nathaniel Eaton was dismissed as its master. Dunster, born at Bolholt, Bury, Lancashire, England, had attended Cambridge's Magdalene College as a sizar. Such an undergraduate receives financial assistance, such as free meals, lower fees or lodging, while studying. He had specialized in oriental languages and made a reputation for himself as a Hebrew scholar. He graduated with a bachelor's degree in 1630 and a master's degree in 1634 and, until his emigration, taught at Magdalene, Hebrew, we assume.

Dunster modeled Harvard's educational system on British elite schools such as Eton College and Cambridge University. He is said to have set up and taught Harvard's entire curriculum by himself for many years, graduating his first class there in 1642. With the approval of the General Court of Massachusetts Bay, it was also he who set up the first corporation charter in America. The Charter of 1650 was established under the jurisdiction of two governing boards: the President and Fellows of Harvard College, and the Board of Overseers. Both govern Harvard University to this day.

And, although Harvard's clerical teachings soon broadened, nearly all of its presidents through to the end of the eighteenth century were in holy orders. Dunster was fired after abandoning the Puritan view of infant baptism in favour of the believer's baptism, soul freedom, religious liberty, congregational governance and a radical Biblicism in 1653, So we read in William H. Brackney's book *Baptists in North America: an historical perspective* published in 2006 (Wiley-Blackwell; p. 12). The Harvard Chaplains Organization's 40 members represent many of the world's religious and spiritual traditions purportedly there to serve faculty, staff and students' spiritual and ethical needs, without mentioning anything about morals. Its current president is 44-year-old New York Jew Greg M. Epstein (1977-), the Lolita Express springing to mind. He received his ordination as a humanist rabbi in 2005 from the International Institute for Secular Humanistic Judaism, established in Jerusalem in 1985.

Humanistic Judaism was founded in 1963 in Detroit by Rabbi Sherwin Wine. It offers a non-theistic alternative in contemporary Jewish life (Americanhumanist.org). Humanistic Jews believe in creating a meaningful Jewish life free from supernatural authority and in reviving the secular roots of Judaism. Epstein is also Harvard's and the Massachusetts Institute of Technology's humanist chaplain. That's the league equalling humanity to rattus, cani, simian, lepus and cockroaches. Unsurprising, in a way, to have an atheist chaplain rule Harvard's and MIT's religious chicken coop, when a multitude of sources with abundance proclaim the Vatican as the seat of Satan, me thinks, rightly or wrongly.

Epstein's career choice seems to be beneficial both for Harvard and himself, at least financially. When he began as humanist chaplain at Harvard in the fall of 2005, the Humanist Chaplaincy total annual budget allotment was $28,000. In the years since then, he managed to raise nearly $3 million in gifts and pledges. This no doubt helped him launch new programs and open the Humanist Hub. This 3,200-square-foot (300 m2) "Center for Humanist Life" in Harvard Square is where students dissect Harry Potter like the Bible for educational purposes, we trust, while their parents pay their $60,000.00 student fees (thecrimson.com). Are Dunster, Harvard and their peers turning in their graves, we wonder? Or would they care, knowing full well that humanist doctrine since its medical school foundation has been: "Do as thou wilt is the whole of the law." Almost 40 chaplains representing many of the world's religious and spiritual traditions seemingly far removed from atheist tendencies purportedly present at Harvard to serve faculty, staff and students' spiritual and ethical needs, never mind morals, voted an atheist in as their leader. So be it. I rest my case.

That Harvard has dominated Massachusetts' clerical and civil ranks for centuries has also gone by the wayside, it seems. Harvard slowly became a national and international institution. Its leadership developed graduate and professional schools during the nineteenth century, alongside the nucleus undergraduate college, its medical school among them. It opened its doors in 1782 as the third U.S. medical school. Unlike most other leading medical schools, it does not operate in conjunction with a single hospital but is directly affiliated with several teaching hospitals in the Boston area.

It would be Harvard College and University of Edinburgh Medical School educated physician Nathan Smith (1762-1829), who founded the fourth U.S. allopathically oriented medical school, Dartmouth College in Hanover, New Hampshire in 1797. He was born in Rehoboth, Massachusetts, and grew up on a farm in Chester, Vermont. He may very well be AMA's co-founder Nathan Smith Davis's ancestor. This Nathan served in the Vermont militia fighting Indigenous folk on the colony's frontier. At the ripe age of 24, he pivoted to study medicine after having watched Josiah Goodhue perform an operation on we don't know whom. Smith, after three years apprenticeship with him at Putney, Vermont, hung out his own shingle at Cornish, New Hampshire. In 1790, he obtained his M.B. from Harvard College's medical department. He then matriculated at the University of Edinburgh in 1803 after one year of medical classes, to finally be bestowed his M.D. degree by Harvard in 1811.

Before that august moment, however, Smith noticed the dearth of medical professionals in the rural Connecticut River Upper Valley area where he grew up. So, he persuaded Dartmouth College's Board of Trustees to fund his medical school, where he began to educate and graduate medical apprentices with a Bachelor of Medicine degree by instructing them at leisure in the art and science of anatomy, chemistry, surgery and clinical medicine.

Essentially maid-of-all-work, he simultaneously served as the medical school's dean and treasurer. He emphasized hands-on experience rather than theory and deliberately avoided use of bleeding and purging, as he believed in the body's own healing powers enhanced by attentiveness to patient-comfort. In other words, he supported a holistic, humanitarian approach, rather than humanistic allopathic medicine. Smith's instructions and medicinal directions attracted undergraduates and trained physicians alike from around the country. Until 1810, he ran the entire Dartmouth show by himself. Then trustees engaged a second faculty member, and soon thereafter, in 1812, still sole administrator and instructor as well as curriculum creator, Dartmouth, too, began to issue Doctor of Medicine (M.D.) degrees with the allopathic slant, we gather.

Nathan Smith left the place in 1816 to found schools of medicine at the University of Vermont in Burlington, at Bowdoin College, a private liberal arts college in Brunswick, and at the private Ivy League Yale University in New Haven. At Yale, as head of medicine and surgery, he taught physic, surgery and obstetrics with Benjamin Silliman (1779 -1864) as professor of chemistry and pharmacology.

Silliman was born in a tavern in North Stratford, Connecticut, now Trumbull, shortly after his mother, Mary Fish Silliman, had fled their Fairfield, Connecticut, home to escape invading British troops. He delivered his first Yale chemistry lectures in 1804, despite never having studied the field. A 1796 BA and 1799 MA Yale graduate, he had actually studied law. But Yale leadership had, for reasons unknown, hired him as professor of chemistry and natural history. Eager to learn, this seemingly silly man took a few months of chemistry tutoring with Professor James Woodhouse at the University of Pennsylvania in Philadelphia. He delivered his first lectures on the topic at Yale. He traveled to Edinburgh for further education, and returned as the first American knowing how to distil petroleum. Upon his return, he founded the American Journal of Science, the oldest continuously published scientific journal in the United States. He also sired Benjamin Jr. (1816 -1885), a Yale professor of chemistry instrumental in future oil industry developments. But I digress- somewhat.

These 4 original American medical schools have been thriving in their allopathic humanistic medical art and science creation endeavors ever since. The laity, however, had managed to also establish a multitude of affordable medical schools throughout the early to mid-1800s. These privately-owned proprietary schools rose to be the dominant vehicles of holistic medical instruction on the continent (encyclopedia.com). Between 1810 and 1840, twenty-s26ix such schools were established, and between 1840 and 1876 another 47 saw the light of day. By the late nineteenth century, dozens more had sprouted. These schools were originally intended to be supplementary to the apprenticeship system in addition to systematic medical teaching. By the 1850s, they had superseded the apprenticeship system as the principal pathway of medical education and, as adherents to regular medicine, resulted in slash, cut, and burn techniques becoming somewhat more commonplace.

With them, the curriculum also changed, generally consisting of anatomy, physiology and pathology There was less material-medica, a Latin term going way back to the Sumerian cuneiform tablets describing ancient prescriptions for human ailments discussed at length in *Fallacy 1*.

One of them was the Ebers Papyrus of 1550 BC. It was purchased at Luxor, Egypt, in 1873 by German Egyptologist and novelist Georg Moritz Ebers (1837 -1898) and kept at the university of Leipzig, Germany. It contains the use of 700 plant-derived drugs, magical formulas and folk remedies meant to cure afflictions ranging from crocodile bite to toenail pain, in addition to remedies ridding a house of such pests as flies, rats and scorpions. The papyrus also includes an accurate description of the human circulatory system, notes the existence of blood vessels throughout the body and acknowledges the heart's function as the centre of the body's blood supply and circulation.

The Edwin Smith Papyrus dates back to around 1600 BC. It was bought by American dealer and collector of antiquities Edwin Smith (1822 -1906) in Luxor in1862. It is considered the most detailed and sophisticated of the extant medical papyri. It remains the only surviving copy of part of an ancient Egyptian textbook on trauma surgery and the world's oldest known surgical treatise.

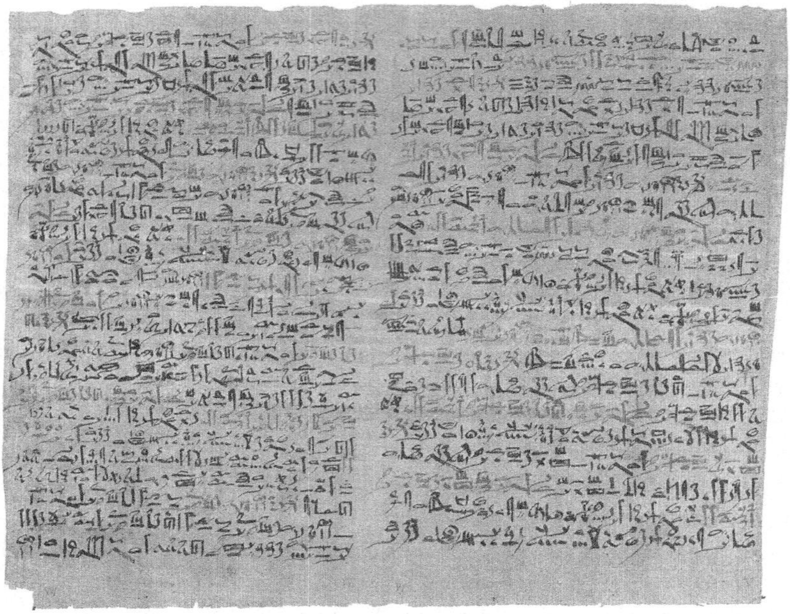

Edwin Smith's Papyrus: Plates VI and VII (displayed at the Rare Book Room in New York Academy of Medicine)

Estimated to be composed a thousand years earlier, it lists 48 traumatic injury cases, with a description of the physical examination, treatment and prognosis of each. It also has a few sections on gynaecology and cosmetics, as well as eight magic spells and incantations, which some speculate may have been used as a last resort in terminal cases. It also includes a history of pharmacy and the therapeutic properties of substances used for healing (https://historyofinformation.com).

The Kahun Gynaecological Papyrus of 1800 BC was found in 1889 at the village of El-Lahun by English Egyptologist and pioneer of systematic methodology in archaeology William Matthew Flinders Petrie (1853–1942). It contains 35 separate paragraphs relating to gynaecological diseases, fertility, pregnancy and contraception. Divided into three sections, it includes guidelines on patient-physician interaction, namely, how to inquire about the patient's symptoms, how the physician should consult with the patient, how to convey the diagnosis and how to advise on and offer which treatments. Of surgery, nothing is mentioned.

The Ramesseum medical papyri were discovered in 1895 by Flinders Petrie with his compatriot, British Egyptologist James Edward Quibell (1867–1935). They were found in the temple of the Ramesseum, the mortuary temple of Pharaoh Ramses II, the Great, located in the Theban Necropolis in Upper Egypt. They consist of a collection of Egyptian medical documents dating back to early eighteenth-century BC, dealing with ophthalmological ailments, gynaecology, muscles, tendons and child diseases, the latter described in great detail. Papyrus IV deals with issues such as labour, protection of the newborn, ways to predict the likelihood of its survival, ways to predict gender, as well as a contraception formula. Papyrus V contains numerous prescriptions dealing with ing limbs and muscles.

The Hearst Papyrus is dated around 2000 BC and named after American philanthropist, feminist and suffragist Phoebe Elizabeth Apperson Hearst (1842 -1919). She was the mother of William Randolph Hearst (1863 -1951), the American businessman, newspaper publisher and politician known for developing the nation's largest newspaper chain and media company, Hearst Communications. Hearst received it in the spring of 1901 at the Hearst expedition camp from a peasant of the nearby village of Deir el-Ballas in Upper Egypt in gratitude for being allowed to take whatever he wanted from their garbage-heaps. At least, that's how the story goes. Its 18-page content is said to focus on medical treatments and prescriptions for problems with the urinary system, blood, hair and bites from all sorts of critters.

The London Medical Papyrus was first presented by German Egyptologist and professor at Albertus University of Königsberg Walter Wreszinski (1880–1935) in Leipzig, Germany, in 1912. It dates back to Pharaoh Tutankhamun (1341-1328 BC). Now in London's British Museum, it contains 61 recipes for human healing. Viewed as a holistically and spiritually inclined document, it focuses on magical spells as remedy for disease. It is said that those who read it view it as heavily relying on spells dealing with the supernatural with instructions on driving out demons and raising people from the dead. The 25 medical ailments described apparently deal with skin and eye complaints, burns and bleeding in conjunction with the intent to prevent miscarriage. All of the remedies proposed in the London Papyrus seem to use supernatural methods to cure people of their ailments, we hear. Would Harvard's chief chaplain Epstein be amused?

The Greater Berlin Papyrus is also known as the Brugsch Papyrus. It dates between 1350 and 1200 BC and was discovered by Trieste merchant Giuseppe Passalacqua (1797–1865) in Saqqara, Egypt, around 1827. It consists of 24 pages with similar content to the Ebers Papyrus, although it also deals with contraception and fertility tests.

The Carlsberg Papyrus is property of the brewery Carlsberg Foundation in Copenhagen, Denmark. It covers eye diseases and pregnancy. But, contrary to the Kahun and Berlin Papyrus, it goes into much more detail on pregnancy by covering methods such as how to use hippopotamus excrement to determine whether or not a woman will give birth. It also sheds light on how and whether or not women will conceive, by using garlic properly placed in a woman's body as an indicator, as well as how to determine the sex of the child. The recto text dates to around 1500 BC, while the verso, recorded several generations later, is thought to have originated around 1400 BC.

And then we have the Chester Beatty Medical Papyrus dated to around 1200 BC and named after the American mining magnate and philanthropist Sir Alfred Chester Beatty (1875-1968). Given the epithet the "King of Copper" as a reference to his fortune, he became a naturalised British citizen in 1933, knighted in 1954 and made an honorary citizen of Ireland in 1957. No wonder that he donated 19 of his accumulated papyri to the British Museum in London. This particular one is said to be dedicated to magical incantations against headaches, as well as to recipes dealing with ailments of the rectum, anus and colon.

The Brooklyn Papyrus of around 450 BC was purchased around 1889 by American journalist and Egyptologist Charles Edwin Wilbour (1833 –1896). He was, incidentally, the first English translator of Victor Hugo's historical novel Les Misérables, published in 1862. Donated to the Brooklyn Museum in New York City in the 1930s, it focuses mainly on snakebites and remedial methods for poisons obtained from snakes, scorpions and tarantulas. The ancient Egyptians were well aware of both snakes' usefulness in controlling vermin and the dangers posed by their poison. To avoid snake attacks, Egyptians worshipped snake-deities like Nehebkau. Also spelled Nehebu-Kau, he is the primordial snake god in ancient Egyptian mythology. Although originally considered an evil spirit, he later functioned as a funerary god associated with the afterlife and, ultimately considered a powerful, benevolent and protective deity.

In other words, the ancient Egyptians did just as the East-Indian, the Chinese, the Babylonian, and the Sumerian civilizations long before them. They used the medicinal properties of plant life for lessening and healing human health problems in all their aspects, from the physical to the emotional. They used honey as medicine and the juices of pomegranates as both an astringent and a delicacy. Some were topical like ointments and wrappings. Others were oral medication such as pills and mouth rinses, still others were administered by inhaling.

In the Papyrus Ebers alone, 811 prescriptions are set forth. They take the form of:

- salves, plasters and poultices
- snuffs, inhalations and gargles
- draughts, confections and pills
- fumigations, suppositories and enemata

A few of the prescriptions are extremely simple, only one substance to be taken, applied as a plaster or poultice, or rubbed in. The majority, however, are more complex and run from half a dozen to a dozen or more drugs, while one consists of 37 ingredients.

The Papyrus Ebers make acquaintance with castor oil, "that God-given drug." Besides finding itself in 100 prescriptions, we read that it has the honour of a special mention in the recipes to cure constipation. It consists of berries from the castor oil tree, male palm tree and gengent beans. One recipe calling for "inner-of-onion, fruit-of-the-am-tree, natron, setseft-seeds, bone-of-the-sword-fish, cooked, redfish, cooked, skull-of-crayfish, cooked, honey, and abra-ointment" is said to eliminate headaches. Many are viewed as curious in the highest degree by the learned society.

Some 160 distinct plant extracts and fruits are used in treatments, as are animal feces and even some metals. Prescriptions were measured out by volume, not weight. While treatments and herbal remedies seem almost boundless, incantations along with their therapeutic remedies are also included. However, we are told that a glance through the Pharmacopceia on which the Papyrus Ebers is based is not to be undertaken lightly. It includes a number of drugs that figure in today's pharmacopeia, but are dwarfed by the weird and wonderful substances that the Scribe gravely transcribed.

Allopathic medicine prefers pharmaceutical drug therapy. It views natural healing methodologies, from acupuncture to homeopathy, from traditional Chinese techniques to Ayurvedic medicine, as useless as tits on a bull. University of Calgary, Canada, professor in the Departments of Medicine and Microbiology, Immunology and Infectious Disease Michael D. Parkins gives us an example. He says that only 28% of the 260 medical prescriptions found in the Hearst Papyrus had some ingredients causing activity towards the condition being treated. But a third of the ingredients supplied to any given disorder would, he said, produce a purgative effect on the gastrointestinal system only. From this, we deduce that he viewed the rest of them as pure hogwash. That human physical and mental ill health originates with the gastrointestinal system he either ignored, left out of the equation or was never taught about at medical school. Also ignored is the fact that none of the remedies used in ancient Egypt created lethal side effects, unlike all pharmaceutical drugs.

Why not look for yourself in Cyril P Bryan's 1930 translation of the *Papyrus Ebers* with an introduction by G. Elliot Smith? It prompted Vicky P. of Good Reads to state in 2019:

> "Fascinating monograph about the translation of the Papyrus Ebers - I read the 1934 reprint of the 1930 edition, and the Introduction by G Elliot Smith was great, because it almost felt as if it was chastising Bryan for his tendency to mock the ancients for their medical knowledge (or lack thereof). "

But never mind that. Nathan Smith Davis was having none of it. Remember that he was the American Medical Association's (AMA) instigator, twice-elected president, and the first editor of its Journal of the American Medical Association of 1847. He was also, as a matter of interest, the winner of the State Agricultural Society of New York's prize for a "Text-Book on Agricultural Chemistry" His career identified with medical education from its beginning. He was a lecturer and demonstrator of anatomy at New York City's College of Physicians and Surgeons in 1848 He was chair of physiology and pathology and chair of practice of medicine at Rush Medical College. His entire career evolved around advocating allopathic medicine and nothing else. For that purpose alone, it seems, he had joined Rush Medical College, one of the first medical colleges in the state of Illinois chartered in 1837, with 22 students enrolled in 1843.

Its founder was Daniel Brainard (1812–1866) a Chicago-based surgeon with unknown background. He named the school in honour of Benjamin Rush, the only U.S. Declaration of Independence signatory with medical school training. Rush, one of the most eminent physicians and authors of his day, began his work as a scholar and author at the age of 17, when he translated Hippocrates' *Aphorisms* into English. In 1762, he wrote his *Observations on Yellow Fever*. His thesis upon graduation from medical school in Edinburgh in 1766 was "De Coctione Ciborum in Ventriculo." His work, *Observations and Inquiries Upon the Diseases of the Mind* (1812), was the first psychiatric textbook published in the U.S. All of it together earned him the title "Father of American Psychiatry".

To direct American medical history, he had also become an active civic leader. And from 1769 onwards he held the chair of "Institutes, Medical and Clinical Practice" at the University of Pennsylvania, with the additional professorship of "the Practice of Physic", in 1796 until the end of his life. A member of the Continental Congress from July 1776 to February 1777, he was appointed Physician General of the Military Hospital of the Middle Department, American Army, in 1777. In addition, he became a member of the "Convention of Pennsylvania for the Adoption of the Federal Constitution" in 1787. And

U.S. President John Adams in 1799 appointed him Treasurer of the United States Mint, another post he held until his death in 1813.

Elected to the Medical Staff of Pennsylvania Hospital in 1783, Rush was an apparently broadminded and versatile man. Many of his medical techniques seemed somewhat barbaric, but his propensity for treatments such as purging and bloodletting to drive out evil spirits inhabiting the human body were accepted conventions of his day. By the early 1800s, however, it may have resulted in the hospital's insane patients outnumbering those with physical diagnoses two to one (uphs.upenn.edu). Consequently, a large farm at what is now 44th and Market Streets was purchased and named the Pennsylvania Hospital for the Insane. Since 1959, it has been known as the Institute of Pennsylvania Hospital to pay homage to Rush's dedication to community service, we gather. His convictions were said to have led him to recognize, God only knows how, that mental illness could indeed be diagnosed, classified and treated humanely.

Thus, while devoting himself to the humane treatment of those he considered insane, he was instrumental in upgrading patients' living conditions and doing away with their lock and cuff restraints. He replaced them with his "tranquilizing chair", viewing it as a humane alternative to the straight jacket. The chair was intended to reduce blood flow to the brain by binding the patient's head and limbs to slow down the fluid movement of agitated patients. It is still used in U.S. prisons today.

Dr. Rush's "Tranquilizing Chair"

Just in case that didn't work to his liking and satisfaction in whatever way he hallucinated it should, he also developed the gyrator. This horizontal board to which torpid patients were strapped, spun for whatever length of time to stimulate their blood circulation. He furthermore incorporated recreation and amusements in the patients' regime as a means of therapy. Hence, he was credited with pioneering the yet-to-be invented field of occupational therapy, still applied in ludicrous ways by the WCB. He did encourage his charges to sew, garden, listen to music or exercise during the day, on private plots, we gather. Or they might do so after constraint-sessions in nuthouses in the tranquility-and gyrator chair if stepping out of staff's dictated line as visible and documented to perfection in *One Flew Over the Cuckoo's Nest*.

Nathan Smith David, the AMA instigator whose colleagues were doubtlessly familiar with Rush and his methods, became the prime mover and shaker to create the Chicago Medical Society in 1850. He then served as its secretary and, in 1855, served as its president. He was a valued member of the Illinois State Medical Society. With the creation of the Chicago Medical College in 1859 with a few of his colleagues, he established for himself a permanent home. He stayed there for more than 40 years as its dean and as professor of principles and practice of the art and science of allopathic medicine.

Nathan Davis Smith was a voluminous writer, with numerous contributions to medical literature with articles. For example, he wrote "Principles and Practice of Medicine", "Medical Education and Reform", "Verdict of Science Concerning the Effects of Alcohol on Man" and "Clinical Lectures," in an effort to standardize the country's medical education. His primary goal, which led to the 1845 organization of the American Medical Association establishment, seems to have been to end the availability of all holistic medicinal treatments in the US, if he could help it.

That homeopathy had been vigorously practiced in Europe since 1779, Smith David and his learned society of allopathic physicians portrayed as nothing other than nonsensical magic. It was German physician Christian Friedrich Samuel Hahnemann (1755-1843) whose 1779 doctoral thesis Conspectus adfectuum spasmodicorum aetiologicus et therapeuticus. [A Dissertation on the Causes and Treatment of Spasmodic Diseases] was the foundation of homeopathy. But Smith David et al claimed that the medicine he had been taught to practice did patients more harm than good.

That Hahnemann particularly objected to practices such as bloodletting and slash-cut and burn methods of medicinal treatments at leisure was leisurely ignored. His writings, such as the following, were considered complete hogwash:

> "My sense of duty would not easily allow me to treat the unknown pathological state of my suffering brethren with these unknown medicines. The thought of becoming in this way a murderer or malefactor towards the life of my fellow human beings was most terrible to me, so terrible and disturbing that I wholly gave up my practice in the first years of my married life and occupied myself solely with chemistry and writing." (*Hahnemann Biography*)

He did just that from 1784 onward, making his living chiefly as a writer and translator, while investigating medicine's alleged errors. He translated *A Treatise on the Materia Medica* by Scottish physician and professor at the Edinburgh Medical School William Cullen's (1710-1790). It was then that Hahnemann learned that the bark of the Peruvian cinchona tree could treat malaria. Researching the statement's veracity on the human body by self-application, the drug induced malaria-like symptoms in him. Consequently, he concluded, it would do the same in all healthy individuals, leading him to postulate:

> "That which can produce a set of symptoms in a healthy individual can treat a sick individual who is manifesting a similar set of symptoms."

This principle, *like cures like,* became the basis for his approach to medicine he named homeopathy. He first used the term in his 1807 essay "Indications of the Homeopathic Employment of Medicines in Ordinary Practice". Published in the *Hufeland's Journal* by the most eminent and famous practical physician of his time in Germany, Christoph Wilhelm Friedrich Hufeland (1762–1836)., Hahnemann had coined the word from the Greek *homoios* "like, similar, of the same kind" (see homeo-) and *patheia* "disease," also "feeling, emotion". In Greek, homoiopathes means "having like feelings or affections, sympathetic."

In other words, Hahnemann recognized that human emotions and feelings played a part in human health and healing. That thought alone was anathema to allopathic medicine practitioners of all rank and file. Its methods of healing work through the human immune system using non-toxic doses of natural substances similar to those causing the illness. You see, there is little to no financial profit to be made from its prescriptions. Thus, homeopathy had to be stamped into the ground, strangled at birth, killed in the crib so to speak, as soon as humanly possible (*Murder by Injection*, p. 13).

In Britain, that seems to have been met with some rapid success. Of the 33,339 people listed as practising in one or more branches of medicine in the 1806 census, only 10,220 remained listed in the 1856 *British Medical Directory*. Still, only four percent of those held a medical degree from an English university. Should we surmise the missing had left to seek greener pasture in the US, threatening financial loss to those claiming to be physicians already in the country? All we know is that after the 1860–1865 American Civil War, colleges, universities and proprietary schools opened medical schools like weeds. They offered curricula with varying training periods in one to four branches of medicine: eclectic, allopathic, osteopathic and homeopathic. Proprietary schools, however, taught all four subjects, with shorter training periods than the elite allopathic medical schools. These posed a threat to allopathic medicine and therefore had to be put out of business as soon as humanly possible.

That objective was hugely facilitated the moment Smith Davis managed to, on behalf of AMA, get government approval for physicians' education and licensing. By the end of the nineteenth century, barely a proprietary school remained open and medical practitioners trained in humanitarian, holistic medicinal treatments were as good as obliterated throughout the land. They were driven out of business, as even the idea of the human body being able to heal itself turned quasi repulsive to the allopathic medicine swearing learned society.

Still, that wasn't good enough for Smith Davis and his ilk. In 1900, one doctor with a two- year apprenticeship in medicine under his belt might have a clientele of approximately 750 patients and could look forward to earnings similar to those of a good mechanic. AMA stated in its journal: "The growth of the profession must be stemmed, if individual members are to find the practice of medicine a lucrative profession." (*Murder By Injection* p. 17). Who would bring about this stemming of the largely holistic tide interfering with the profit-making allopathic medicine enterprise? None other than John D. Rockefeller (1839–1937) and his manager of philanthropic endeavours Frederick Gates. Both of them were acutely aware of 1.Peter: "Charity shall cover a multitude of sins."

They planned to accomplish this tide-stemming task through the Rockefeller Foundation's Institute of Medical Research and the assistance. They also called upon the equally financially well-endowed Scottish-American industrialist and philanthropist Andrew Carnegie (1835-1919). He had immigrated to the United States with his parents in 1848. Instantaneously, at the age of 12, he started work as a telegrapher, before switching to labor in a Pittsburgh cotton factory. By 1859, 11 years later, he rose to the position of division superintendent of the Pennsylvania Railroad. While employed at the railroad, Carnegie invested in railroads, railroad sleeping cars, bridges and oil derricks, and that's how he made his first fortune in his early 30s. He accumulated further wealth as a bond salesman in Europe, raising money for American enterprise, we read.

A bond salesman's main task is to help their firm's bond traders seal deals with institutional investors, legal entities that participate in trading in the financial markets. Thus, sales people are relationship managers for their firm's bond investors. Institutional investors include the following organizations:

- banks
- credit unions
- pension funds
- venture capital funds
- insurance companies
- large funds, such as a mutual or hedge fund

For whom Carnegie played bond-salesman is too tedious to discover. While he entertained himself playing on the financial market, however, he managed to build Pittsburgh's Carnegie Steel Company in the early 1870s. The future U.S. Steel Corporation became the dominant force in that industry over the next two decades (history.com). In 1901, he sold it to J.P. Morgan for a cool $303,450,000.00 million, roughly $5.2 billion in 2020 dollars. Nice!

In 1889, Carnegie actually decried his problems as a self-made, nouveau rich American in "The Gospel of Wealth." His essay was published in the United States' first literary magazine, the *North American Review* (NAR). It had been founded by lawyer and journalist Nathan Hale and others in Boston in 1815 and was considered an opinion magazine for America's establishment. In an article originally simply titled "Wealth," he wrote:

> "Poor and restricted are our opportunities in this life; narrow our horizon; our best work most imperfect; but rich men should be thankful for one inestimable boon. They have it in their power during their lives to busy themselves in organizing benefactions from which the masses of their fellows will derive lasting advantage, and thus dignify their own lives. The highest life is probably to be reached, not by such imitation of the life of Christ as Count Tolstoi gives us, but, while animated by Christ's spirit, by recognizing the changed conditions of this age, and adopting modes of expressing this spirit suitable to the changed conditions under which we live; still labouring for the good of our fellows, which was the essence of his life and teaching, but labouring in a different manner." (Carnegie.org).

Labouring in the manner of directing the national narrative, perhaps? His quote, "The man who dies thus rich dies disgraced," sparked a philanthropic craze among his peers. More importantly, it gave the financially well-endowed the hint that trust funds were the way to go when engaging in philanthropic matters for one's own benefit:

- First, set an example of modest, unostentatious living, shunning display or extravagance.
- Second, provide moderately for the legitimate wants of those dependent upon him.
- Third, after doing so, consider all surplus revenues which come simply as trust funds, which he [the giver] is called upon to administer in the manner best calculated to produce the most beneficial results for the community [his or humanity's?].

Thus, the man of wealth becomes agent and trustee for his poorer brethren, bringing to their service his superior wisdom, experience and ability to administer. He is doing much better for them, the herd, than they would or could ever be doing for themselves.

Adamantly determined to be remembered for his good deeds, Carnegie began at age 35 to pursue his ideal of himself by donating a public bath to the inhabitants of his Scottish hometown Dunfernline. Looking for herd praise and acknowledgement, he also endowed the public with his Carnegie Libraries throughout the English-speaking world. In 1891, he gave New York City Carnegie Hall, one of the world's most prestigious venues for both classical and popular music events. And in 1899, he donated US$1.5 million ($40 million, adjusted for inflation in the 2020s) for the Peace Palace in The Hague, Netherlands. This building would serve the Permanent Court of Arbitration (PCA) established by treaty in 1899 as an intergovernmental organization providing a variety of dispute resolution services to the international community destined to end all war. Today, it also houses the International Court of Justice, the principal judicial body of the United Nations, The Hague Academy of International Law and the Peace Palace Library.

And the list goes on. He also founded:

- the Carnegie Corporation of New York (1911)
- the Carnegie Endowment for International Peace (1910)
- the Carnegie Institution for Science
- the Carnegie Trust for the Universities of Scotland (1901)
- the Carnegie Hero Fund
- the Carnegie Mellon University
- the Carnegie Museums of Pittsburgh (1895)

During the last 18 years of his life alone, he gave away around $350 million, roughly $5.2 billion in 2020 dollars, to charities, foundations and universities. This was, we are told, almost 90% of his rather substantial fortune.

One of his most influential endeavors seldom advertised anywhere, however, is the Carnegie Foundation for the Advancement of Teaching (CFAT). This U.S. corporation-based education policy and research center was founded in 1905 and chartered in 1906 by the United States Congress. It developed:

- The Teachers Insurance and Annuity Association (TIAA)
- The Carnegie Unit, the Educational Testing Service
- The Carnegie Classification of Institutions of Higher Education

It also financed and produced the Flexner Report on medical education (P. Collier, D. Horowitz: the Rockefellers; Holt, Rinehart and Winston, New York, N.Y.; 1976).

In addition, Carnegie established The Carnegie Corporation of New York in 1911. This philanthropic fund was to support education programs across the United States and the world. It has endowed or helped establish:

- The United States National Research Council
- Harvard University's Russian Research Center, now the Davis Center for Russian and Eurasian Studies
- The Children's Television Workshop
- The Carnegie Endowment for International Peace (CEIP)

Henceforth, these organizations directed the nation's educational narrative. The goal, according to Carnegie's contemporary, American journalist, satirist, cultural critic and scholar of American English Henry Louis Mencken (1880–1956):

> "The aim of public education is not to spread enlightenment at all; it is simply to reduce as many individuals as possible to the same safe level to breed a standard citizenry to suppress dissent and originality." (John Hamer: *The Falsification of History: Our Distorted Reality* p. 557)

The U.S. educational programs unfolded precisely in accordance with Mencken's reflection. In the course of time, they were enhanced by the inevitable generational elimination of knowledge. That's why parents allow, nay cherish, their children to wear masks so deadly to their mental and physical health. And why teachers receive thousands of dollars in bonuses through the school boards for successfully forcing the draconian measure down parents' throats.

The Organisation for Economic Co-operation and Development, (OECD) is an intergovernmental economic organisation with 38 member countries. It was founded in 1961 to purportedly stimulate economic progress and world trade. It reports that the Carnegie Corporation of New York's financing for 2019 projects and developments increased by 27% over the previous year to U.S. $24 million. In other words, whereas Rockefeller took care of medicine and science, Carnegie was by and large allotted to finance the U.S. educational narrative. Thus, two men were unofficially in charge of directing first the nation's and then the world's slow and steady ruination of human health, wealth and education. Out of this sprang the detrimental-to-human-wellbeing and all-powerful mental health industry, driving the herd nuts with breathtaking facility generating. And, with it came the multiplying PTSD and suicide enhancement professions, ever-increasing like rats in their sewer.

Needless to say, the achievement of such lofty goals necessitated the strangulation of holistic medicine and the singing of praises for all things slash, cut, burn and pharmaceutical. No-one born for the job better than John D. Rockefeller. He was the offspring of an industrial, political banking family, who in the eighteenth century had moved from Germany's Rhineland to seek greater fame and fortune in the New World. John D. founded an oil-producing, transporting, refining and marketing corporation in Ohio in 1870 with chemist and inventor Samuel Andrews (1836–1904) and Henry Morrison Flagler (1830–1913) of Hopewell. The Rockefellers finally found their fortune in the late nineteenth and early twentieth century, while also making a few others very wealthy in the process. Flagler would be the key figure in Florida's Atlantic coast real estate development. He would also be Florida's East Coast Railway builder, much of it built through convict leasing. American writer and journalist David A. Blackmon (1964-) in his 2009 book *Slavery by Another Name: The Re-Enslavement of Black Americans from the Civil War to World War II* described this government system:

> "It was a form of bondage distinctly different from that of the antebellum South in that for most men, and the relatively few women drawn in, this slavery did not last a lifetime and did not automatically extend from one generation to the next. But it was nonetheless slavery – a system in which armies of free men,

> guilty of no crimes and entitled by law to freedom, were compelled to labour without compensation, were repeatedly bought and sold, and were forced to do the bidding of white masters through the regular application of extraordinary physical coercion."

The adventure allowing Flagler to engage in such enterprise began in 1863, when Rockefeller joined Maurice B. Clark and Samuel Andrews in a Cleveland, Ohio, oil refining business.

Rockefeller bought out Clark in 1865, and two years later he invited Henry M. Flagler to join as partner. By 1870 the firm of Rockefeller, Andrews, and Flagler was operating the largest refineries in Cleveland. Along with related facilities, they became the property of the new infamous Standard Oil Company incorporated in Ohio in 1870.

None of them were concerned with how many sins would or would not be covered by charity. So, Rockefeller et al. eliminated competitors. They arranged mergers with other firms and used favourable railroad rebates. By 1880, they controlled 90% to 95% of U.S. oil production. Soon thereafter, they built the world's largest oil refinery conglomerate, Standard Oil Company and Trust. This status was achieved by initially dominating the oil product markets through horizontal integration of the refining sector. In other words, they bought refining businesses. As soon as they reached a monopoly, they moved on to vertical integration. In other words, buying up all companies whose products were important to their supply chain or to bring their products to market.

That task completed, Standard Oil's General Solicitor Samuel C. T. Dodd (1836–1907) got the brilliant idea in 1882 of creating the company's business trust arrangement . The Standard Oil Trust pursuant to a "trust agreement" meant that individual shareholders of many separate corporations agreed to convey their shares to the trust. By that agreement, companies could then be purchased, created, dissolved, merged or divided. By a secret agreement, the existing 37 stockholders conveyed their shares "in trust" to nine trustees.

John and William Rockefeller were two of them.

Oliver H. Payne (1839–1917) was, too. He organized the American Tobacco trust and helped form U.S. Steel. He was considered one of the 100 wealthiest Americans, having left an enormous fortune.

As a young man, future Standard Oil trustee Charles Pratt joined a company in Boston that specialized in paints and whale oil products. When realizing that whale oil could be replaced by petroleum to light lamps, he became pioneer of the petroleum industry. During the 1860s, he founded the kerosene refinery Astral Oil Works in New York City. The unique advertising slogan was: "The holy lamps of Tibet are primed with Astral Oil."

Flagler also turned trustee.

So did John Dustin Archbold (1848–1916), whose small oil company had been bought out by Rockefeller. He continued to handle many complex secret negotiations over the years for Rockefeller. By 1882, he was Rockefeller's closest associate and typically acted as the company's primary spokesman. After 1896, Rockefeller left business matters to Archbold as vice president, who ran Standard Oil until his death in 1916. Meanwhile, he pursued his brand of philanthropy to do good for his soul.

Trustee William G. Warden was formerly owner of the oil company Warden, Frew & Co. He was one of Standard Oil's organizers.

Trustee Jabez Bostwick had first ventured into the cotton brokerage business in Cincinnati, Ohio. He became involved in the production side of the oil business through his firm, Tilford & Bostwick, established in 1866. In 1878, he went into partnership with Flagler and Rockefeller brothers John and William, ending up as the Trust's Secretary-Treasurer.

Last but not least, we have trustee Benjamin Brewster (1828-1897), who was prominently associated with building the Manhattan Elevated Railway. He was also a financial leader in many large railroad transactions, particularly reorganizing the Chicago, St. Paul, Minneapolis and Omaha Railway. He served as vice president of the Chicago, Rock Island and Pacific Railroad. He was a director of the Chicago and Eastern Illinois Railroad and the Delaware and Hudson Canal Company. He was also a director of the International Navigation Company, a Philadelphia-based holding company owning 26 ships totalling 181,000 tons and carrying more passengers than Cunard and White Star lines. But I meander.

These well-connected and well-healed Standard Oil trustees eventually governed some 40 corporations, of which 14 were wholly owned by the Standard Oil corporation itself (britannica.com). It is through The Standard Oil trust agreement that Rockefeller managed to streamline production and logistics. This lowered costs. And through aggressive pricing, he destroyed most of his competitors and formed a monopoly that threatened a multitude of other businesses unrelated to the oil industry. All assets and interests formerly grouped in the trust were transferred to the New Jersey company. and acted as the trust's board of trustees. One of those trustees, Rockefeller himself, held 41% of the trust certificates; the next most powerful trustee held only about 12%.

That done, Dodd organized Standard Oil as a holding company, one of the first in the world. The enabled John D. Rockefeller to consolidate his control over the corporation's many acquisitions. A holding company's purpose usually is to own shares of other companies. The goal is to form a corporate group, a collection of parent and subsidiary corporations functioning as a single economic entity through a common source of control, producing no goods or services itself. By 1911, Standard Oil controlled almost all American oil production, processing, marketing and transportation.

Dodd was a strong opponent of the Sherman Anti-Trust Act, the first Federal act that outlawed monopolistic business practices in 1890. He vehemently argued that only "unreasonable" restraint of trade should be illegal, without specifying what he viewed as unreasonable. The Supreme Court of the United States (SCOTUS), the highest court in the federal judiciary, by and large adopted Dodd's view. This court has ultimate and largely discretionary appellate jurisdiction over all federal and state court cases involving a point of federal law. It also has original jurisdiction over a narrow range of cases, specifically "all Cases affecting Ambassadors, other public Ministers and Consuls, and those in which a State shall be Party."

It was in this court that the U.S. government sought to prosecute Standard Oil under the Sherman Antitrust Act. The main issue before it was whether or not it was within the U.S. Congress's power to prevent a company - Standard Oil in this case - from acquiring numerous other companies through means considered legal in common law but which posed a significant constraint on competition by the mere virtue of its size and market power. (*Standard Oil Co. of New Jersey v. United States*, 221 U.S. 1 (1911). The court's finding? Standard Oil was guilty of monopolizing the petroleum industry through abusive and anticompetitive actions ending in its illegal monopoly. The remedy? Standard Oil's division into *geographically* separate and eventually, at least on the surface for the herd to believe, competing firms.

With this division, the Standard Oil Rockefeller and Flagler bonanza ended. Thirty-four independent entities with different boards of directors on each one were created. Standard Oil of New Jersey became Exxon. Standard Oil of New York became Mobil. The initial income of these individual enterprises proved to be much bigger than that of a single larger company. And the share values mostly doubled as a result of the break-up. Guess who owned a quarter of those shares? That this break-up propelled Rockefeller into the position of richest man in the modern world, with almost unfathomable personal wealth, is seldom mentioned.

To give us an idea of the money made by Standard Oil from 1882 to 1906, it paid out $548,436,000 million in dividends at 65.4% payout ratio. (The dividend payout ratio is the fraction of net income a firm pays to its stockholders in dividends). The total net earnings from 1882 to 1906 amounted to $838,783,800, exceeding the dividends by $290,347,800. This money, we are told, was used for plant expansions.

Mind you, when that Supreme court verdict rolled in, John D. Rockefeller had retired from Standard Oil's management (1897). However, he might have had Peter 1: 4:8: "And above all things have fervent charity among yourselves: for charity shall cover the multitude of sins (KJV)" firmly anchored in his mind. And his soul's wellbeing was perhaps a concern and somewhat nagging at his conscience. Already in 1892, he had engaged Frederick T Gates (1853-1929), first as an advisor and later on solely as his own personal "head of all his philanthropic endeavours," because, he revealed in a 1995 interview:

> "God gave me my money...I believe it is my duty to make money and still more money and to use the money I make for the good of my fellow man according to the dictates of my conscience." (The Rockefellers p. 48)."

Frederick Gates was son of a Baptist minister and a graduate of the University of Rochester in 1877 and the Rochester Theological Seminary in 1880. From 1880 to 1888, he served as pastor of the Central Baptist Church in Minneapolis., He was then appointed secretary of the newly formed *American Baptist Education Society* established for the promotion of Christian education under Baptist auspices in North America. It was under Gates' supervision, that the Society founded the University of Chicago in 1890. Gates served as the Society's first corresponding secretary until 1892. Rockefeller, raised as a Baptist himself, hired Gates as his key philanthropic and business adviser to oversee a series of investments in a multitude of companies, but without authority to dabble in his personal Standard Oil Trust stock.

Gates focused exclusively on philanthropy after 1912. But already in1888, he had begun to limit Rockefeller money from doling out retail sums to specific recipients. Instead, he set up a wholesale process by establishing foundations run by experts who decided what topics in the herd were ripe for social reform. The precise selection process is unknown. However, Gates convinced Rockefeller, himself a believer in traditional holistic medicine, that he would have the greatest impact on the national medicinal narrative, were he to modernize medicine by way of education reform and scientific research, identifying cures to possibly eradicate debilitating human diseases.

Acupuncturist and herbalist Eric Schmidt holds a master's degree in Acupuncture and Oriental Medicine and founder of Meridian Health Clinic. He points out in his article "How Rockefeller Created the Business of Western Medicine" on his website meridianhealthclinic.com, that Rockefeller controlled 90% of American petroleum refineries through ownership of the Standard Oil Corporation at that time. We know it was later split into Mobil, Chevron, Exxon and other corporations still controlled in one hand. As it were, concurrently with the oil industry evolution, the scientific world became intrigued with the ability to create a variety of new petrochemical compounds ranging from plastic bags to organic products.

Also during this time, the early 1900s, scientists tried to understand the basic mechanics of life and human health. They discovered most of the essential vitamins, including B1, B2, Biotin, Vitamin C, Vitamin A and Vitamin D. When they succeed to re-create synthetic versions of these vitamins in laboratories, Rockefeller instantaneously saw the opportunity to monopolize the petroleum, petro-chemical and medical health product industry all at once. From a business perspective, petrochemicals were the most ideal. Those products could be patented, owned and sold to the laity, piss-upons, great unwashed, herd for superbly high profits without them ever being intelligent enough to tune into and figure out this supreme rip-off.

There was just one big problem with Rockefeller's plan. Natural and herbal medicines had been popular in America since the 1800s. Almost half of U.S. medical colleges and physicians practiced holistic medicine, using extensive knowledge from both European and Native American traditions still in the early 1900s. They practiced chiropractic, naturopathic, homeopathic and herbal medicine. To fulfill his fervent desire of total control over America's medical industry, Rockefeller had little choice but to destroy the holistically inclined competition in whatever way he saw fit and could get away with. But how? Well, he thought, what about purchasing the controlling part in the giant German pharmaceutical company commonly known as I.G. Farben (*Interessengemeinschaft Farbenindustrie AG*)? That would at least partially eliminate holistic products for the pesky humanitarian-inclined holistic medicine, would it not? But that had to come a little later.

First, all non-allopathic physicians and schools had to be eliminated once and for all. For that, Rockefeller engaged buddy Carnegie, so eager-beaver to establish his reputation as humanity's greatest benefactor ever. He in turn engaged Abraham Flexner, a Kentucky schoolteacher who presented in 1910 a book-length report of medical education in the United States and Canada to the U.S. Congress. Named the Carnegie Foundation Bulletin Number Four or Flexner Report, its schoolteacher author called for higher admission fees in American medical schools. His report also recommended higher admission grades and graduation standards, as there were too many medical schools in the United States with too many doctors being trained. Flexner also advocated, as his master had doubtlessly instructed, that medical schools should be revamped and be centralized in their research, and that their teachings were to strictly adhere to protocols of mainstream science.

The result? Congress pushed through Flexner's suggestions, and many American medical schools consequently fell short of the new standard mandated. Nearly half of them either merged or had to close outright. Colleges in electrotherapy, homeopathy, traditional osteopathy, eclectic medicine and physio-medicalism, scientifically untested botanical therapies, were expertly subjected to usually bitter and contemptuous ridicule and criticism by the media. Some of their physicians were jailed. Due to hugely reduced space for aspiring medical students, those few American universities who had begun to admit women in the mid 1800s reversed to male-only admittance. In other words, Flexner laid the foundation for the American and Canadian allopathic slash-cut and burn, pharmaceutical drug-doused vaccination from birth medical system taught to all physicians today. Flexner also pushed through at that time that only the American Medical Association (AMA) could issue Doctor of Medicine licenses.

The moment Flexner's report had been accepted as read by Congress, Carnegie and Rockefeller began to fund medical schools all over America. They had just one condition: to teach only allopathic, science-based medicine! Thus, it came about that humanity's knowledge of holistic medicine went by the wayside. Through the financial power of these two extremely wealthy men, it was supressed and destroyed like weeds by soil-killing Round Up (produced by Bayer, incidentally). Even all teachings about human nutrition, diet, necessity of exercise and everything else beneficial to human health maintenance had been removed from medical school curricula across the land. After all, it would hinder the culling of the herd by chemicals, would it not?

Thus, the main therapeutic allopathic treatment methods in the early 1900s were made to consist of blood-letting, slash, cut and burn surgery and injections of toxic heavy metals such as lead and mercury for disease displacement. This is the same treatment as received by PTSD and suicide ideation experiencers on pharmaceutical mind-altering drugs today. The goal is to add and displace ailments rather than to heal or to ameliorate any of them.

Rockefeller, Carnegie et al. did not stop there. To secure their monopoly over the nation's medical narrative throughout the end of times, it seems, they launched a targeted smear campaign against any and all holistic physicians still in business. They were aided and abetted by Freud-inspired Edward Bernays, newly inaugurated métier of advertising. Its agencies, handsomely paid for discrediting and demonizing homeopathy and natural medicines succeeded in homogenizing U.S. medical colleges of all genre, in no time flat. They were made uniform in structure and composition throughout the land and all students were taught what is now described as "The Standard of Care", a system accurately defined as the process of prescribing patented drugs.

"A pill for an ill" became the catching brainwash slogan to make the populace believe pills could indeed heal their ills (Clarice Stasz: *The Rockefeller Women: Dynasty of Piety, Privacy, and Service*; St Martins Pr; First Edition 1995). This, combined with the imprint that physicians were perfect individuals knowing precisely what would heal their patients' ailments., Freud, Bernays and their peers could not have imagined this scenario in their wildest dreams when they were putting their *Making the American Mind* into action. Yet it was now unfolding beautifully, with ever increasing velocity as the decades went by, to where we find ourselves in 2021. A quote attributed to Kissinger given at a speech at the WHO in 2009 and making the rounds on social media seems so fitting. Here it goes:

> "Once the herd accepts mandatory forcible vaccination, it's game over! They will accept anything—forcible blood or organ donation—for the 'greater good.' We can genetically modify children and sterilize them—for the 'greater good.' Control sheep minds and you control the herd. Vaccine makers stand to make billions, and many of you in this room today are investors. It's a big win-win! We thin out the herd and the herd pays us for providing extermination services. Now, what's for lunch, huh?"

True or not true? You decide. What is known is that through their financial power, Rockefeller and Carnegie succeeded brilliantly to crush the holistically inclined medical competition, at least in the Western World. Their system, by and large deadly to humanity's mental and physical health, continues to this day. "Big Pharma" makes large donations and issues grants to medical schools in exchange for teaching medical students to use their patented drugs. After all, as Richard Brown contents in his book "Rockefeller Medicine Men":

> "The Rockefeller Foundation was the front organization for a new global business venture...This new venture was called the pharmaceutical investment business. Donations from the Rockefeller Foundation went only to medical schools and hospitals, which had become missionaries of patented pharmaceutical drugs, developed by a new breed of companies that manufactured patented synthetic drugs." (University of California Press, Berkeley, New York, London 1979.)

What is also known is that Rockefeller, Carnegie and their ilk imagined *world* allopathic medical dominance, never mind just the U.S. and Canada. And in Flexner's report time, they eyed the globe's other side, as it presented a far bigger market for destruction, that of the millennia old Traditional Chinese Medicine. And how did they think to accomplish that? Well, they had rattled that society superbly, in their eyes. Their opium imports resulted in a national social crisis from the mid-1800s onwards, so this should be child's play.

They attempted it through the China Medical Board (CMB), created by a $12 million grant from the Rockefeller Foundation in 1914 under the cover of wanting to modernize and improve China's medical practices and education. Then they began to solidify their dream by taking over the Peking Union Medical College PUMC). But their ingenious plan to expand to other locations throughout China proved unsuccessful due to a multitude of issues, including political instability. This will be briefly discussed later, as it ties in with the now-infamous Wuhan laboratory and its gene manipulation therapy they named COVID 19. Or, as some folk claim on social media, the Certificate of Vaccination Identification by Artificial (A-1) Intelligence (I-9), the first and ninth letters of the alphabet.

With WWI barely concluded, they used the Spanish flu catastrophe of 1918/19 to promote Bayer AG's drug Aspirin for its healing. Meanwhile, they campaigned against all forms of natural and non-patented medicine, bluntly declaring them unscientific and dangerous to human health. Bayer had been founded as a dyestuffs factory in Barmen, Germany, in 1863 by Friedrich Bayer and his partner, Johann Friedrich Weskott, a master dyer. The Bayer trademark Aspirin had been registered worldwide for Bayer's brand of acetylsalicylic acid in 1899. It was produced and advertised as a medication to reduce pain, fever and inflammation. Most of those 50 million influenza dead died because their allopathic-trained physicians prescribed it and they swallowed it Aspirin. It took until the early 2000s for this to surface, when the American National Institute of Allergy and Infectious Diseases, Fauci territory, acknowledged, that consumption directly or indirectly had caused the loss of more lives than the influenza itself (John Hamer: *The Falsification of History*, p. 235).

That holistic physicians using non-patentable natural substances saved the life of almost everyone who sought their consultation is nowhere mentioned. It also proved then already, that the new, coal-tar based synthetic drug industry, the basis of Rockefeller et al.'s pharmaceutical drug business investments, could in fact be disastrous for humans' well-being. Laugh or cry, eh?

And on top of it, consider this. Those few archeological and historical records available to us, the herd, show that as early as 2000 BC people across Asia, Europe and Africa used alkaloid-containing plants for 'Murder, Magic and Medicine,' as professor of Organic Chemistry John Mann at Reading University in the UK, expresses in his book of the same title. He describes the book as "...provides intelligent material for those advocating conservation of our global plant resources because of their potentially important reservoir of therapeutically active chemicals for animal and human disease." So says *The Times Higher Education Supplements*, a magazine founded in 1971 reporting specifically on news and issues related to higher education (https://sciencedirect.com).

Not only that, Mann also documents that this knowledge began to be systematically suppressed in Europe long before Rockefeller and Carnegie sprang into action. As a matter of fact, it began in the 1300s AD at the latest, to slowly begin to surface again in the late 1800s. By that time, at least 110,000 humans had been tried by inquisition-like institutions. It is generally believed that between 40,000 to 60,000 of them, mostly women, had been executed., Most were killed by burning and hanging, convicted for witchcraft due to their knowledge of holistic healing modalities.

In the US, this witchcraft mania is remembered by the trials conducted in the Massachusetts Bay Colony between February 1692 and May 1693. A series of hearings and prosecutions of more than 200 people accused of witchcraft were conducted, one-fifth of the people living there. Nineteen of them were hanged and many other suspects were imprisoned in Salem Village, which had been settled in 1630 by a group of about 1,000 English Puritans. The practices of folk healers, folk magick were considered witchcraft. Ancient beliefs in sorcery combined with the Judeo-Christian views on heresy, medieval and early modern practice of ceremonial magic and simple fiction portrayed in folklore and literature also fell under practicing witchcraft.

Mind you, that kind of behaviour, too, can be traced back to classical antiquity and throughout the Middle Ages. It is culminating in the present day Wicca movement, considered a modern Pagan religion with its concept of the "modern witch". It relates to other movements of contemporary worldwide witchcraft coming out of the woodworks all over the globe, if you care to look. So, it is still alive and well today; it merely hid underground. Marina Abramovich and her followers are one example, cherishing spirit cooking openly broadcasting it in U.S. society. The majority of the laity remain mute, blind as bats, thanks to Carnegie and Rockefeller educational endeavours over the past century.

Folk healers' applications used throughout millennia seemed to remain the same. This includes empirical alkaloid medicines for humans and animals or as sources of poisons for hunting expeditions and executions, states Mann. In other words, plants and their associated isolated compounds were continuously used for murder, magic and medicine for thousands of years. However, it took until the early nineteenth century for humanity's break-through to isolate and characterize purified plant compounds. It was German pharmacist Friedrich Wilhelm Adam Sertürner (1783–1841) through years of diligent research from 1803 to 1817 who did it. He was the first in recent memory to successfully isolate and extract morphine crystals from the tarry poppy seed juice. And thus, he transformed pharmaceutical chemistry from a state of alchemy to an acknowledged branch of science (Chandrasekhar Krishnamurti and SSC Chakra Rao: The isolation of morphine by Serturner; Indian J Anaesth. 2016 Nov; 60(11): 861–862).

Soon after Sertürner's discovery, homeopathy's history began with German physician Samuel Hahnemann (1755-1843). He first coined the word "homeopathy" ("homoios" in Greek means similar, "pathos" means *suffering*) to refer to the pharmacological principle of "like heals like", with the Law of Similars as its basis. Actually, it had already been described by Hippocrates and Paracelsus. It had also been used in many cultures, including the Mayans, Chinese, Greeks, Native American Indians and Asian Indians. But it was Hahnemann, fortified by reading Paracelsus, who codified the law of similar into a systematic medical science.

Paracelsus was born Theophrastus von Hohenheim (1493-1541). He was a German-Swiss physician, alchemist, lay theologian and philosopher. He is the one actually credited with establishing the role of chemistry in medicine. In 1530, after he published a clinical description of syphilis, he followed it up in 1536 with his book *Der grossen Wundartzney* (Great Surgery Book), in which he admonished physicians to base their medicine on four pillars. Said he:

> "Understand then thoroughly that I am expounding the basics of medicine upon which I stand and will stand: namely, Philosophy, Astronomy, Alchemy, and Virtue. The first pillar, Philosophy, is the knowledge of earth and water; the second pillar, Astronomy together with Astrology, has a complete knowledge of the two elements, air and fire; the third pillar, Alchemy, is knowledge of the experiment and preparation of the four elements mentioned; and the fourth pillar, Virtue, should remain with the physician until death, for this completes and preserves the other three pillars. And note well, for you too must enter here and come to understand the three pillars, otherwise it will be known by the very peasants in the villages that your trade is to treat princes and lords, towns and countries through lies and deception only and that you know neither your trade nor the truth, for the education which prepares you fits you for fools and hypocrites, all you supposed physicians. And as I take the four pillars, so must you take them too and follow after me, not I after you (Paracelsus: *Das*

Buch Paragranum (1529–30); Essential readings; Selected and translated by Nicholas Goodrick-Clarke; Stanford.edu)."

Needless to say, with such criticism of dogmatic doctrines and professional ethics of his peers, Paracelsus found few admirers, never mind followers. The majority of physicians of the so-called Age of Enlightenment, wholeheartedly rejected him (mmbm.ch). This 'Age of Reason,' was a period of scientific, political and philosophical discourse characterising European society from the late seventeenth century to the Napoleonic Wars ending of 1815, Renewed interest in Paracelsus did surface in the nineteenth century, however. That's when homeopathy became spectacularly popular in Europe and the United States, finding its advocates throughout all layers of society including European royalty, American entrepreneurs, literary giants and religious leaders. Rockefeller and Carnegie had still to commence their dumbing down processes at the time. So, the Law of Similars, a law that appears to be a law of nature, and when correctly applied, almost always results in healing, still made sense to many.

Dr. Leonard J. Torok, M.D. is the medical director of the Trillium Creek Laser Center and the Ohio Holistic Medicine Center. He spent years studying holistic medicine, homeopathy, traditional Chinese medicine, sound therapy, neuro-therapy, hypnosis, behavioural medicine, electrodermal screening, craniosacral therapy and somato-emotional release. And he has used the Law of Similars to heal people, animals and plants. He shares that the better a patient understands the Law of Similars and fully participates in its application, the more successful the results will be.

Throughout his career as a physician, he has seen how a substance that causes symptoms is the same substance that can cure those symptoms, when they occur naturally as part of a disease process. In order to heal as surely and quickly as possible, however, practitioners of homeopathic medicine must learn how to correctly apply this Law of Similars. That is made easy by 200 years of documented history of homeopathic medicine that clearly outlines consistent rules for its application.

Tolok uses an onion to show how to apply the Law of Similars. When chopping up onions for a long time, they cause a certain symptom. Namely they cause an itchy, stinging sensation in the eyes. The eyes will redden and, after a while, produce tears. If continuing to chop up onions, sneezing and a runny nose will appear.

The Law of Similars tells us that when the onion can cause these symptoms, it can also cure these symptoms when caused by a disease. So, the onion is a common homeopathic remedy for people with a head cold or hay fever, as both their symptoms are a match the symptoms onions can cause. In either one, the "homeopathic form" of the onion will bring about a prompt relief of the cold or hay fever symptoms.

The match between the remedy's symptoms and the patient's symptoms must be a close match for the Law of Similars to work, however. In treating any disease, all of the patient's symptoms must be taken into account in the matching process. The more chronic the disease process, the more exact the match must be between the patient's symptoms and those that the substance can cause. Thus, the success rate of homeopathic practice depends upon two things:

- knowing the full range of symptoms that a substance can cause
- being able to get a clear and complete picture of all of the patient's signs and symptoms

These signs and symptoms include all physical expressions of all organ systems of the body as well as all symptoms relating to the emotions and the mind.

In the pharmaceutical process of making a homeopathic remedy, the original substance is routinely diluted past the point where any of the original physical substance remains. This is what we mean when we referred to the onion's "homeopathic form" above. Interestingly, as the remedy is further diluted and becomes progressively more immaterial, it induces a stronger or deeper healing response. The physical science behind this is difficult to understand, but the reality of it is reproducibly observed in homeopathic practice.

In homeopathic medicine, there is no one remedy for any one disease. Each person will have a somewhat different experience of their disease through their symptoms, as well as many other unique characteristics that make them the individual they are. Though this makes the history-taking process more time consuming, it enhances the result of treatment. When the Law of Similars is applied, any symptom that has been identified and included in the matching process could be healed along with the primary complaint. Homeopathic healing is not limited to one part or function of the body but includes all of them.

This means that the homeopathic interview will include many symptom questions beyond questions about the patient's main complaint. In other words, homeopathy investigates the patient as a whole in a humanitarian approach to healing. This is the opposite of humanism's allopathic, scientific medicine, which rips the human body apart into mechanical components, piece by piece. Pharmaceutical treatment of each individual part purports to heal the whole human organism, mind as well as body. The results of those pharmaceutical treatments experienced by human beings due to scientism's advocates can be seen wherever we look. And that includes the failure to heal or even ameliorate PTSD and suicide ideations.

Contrary to pharmaceutical drugging, however, homeopathic remedies cause no side effects in patients. That's because, contrary to drugs, herbs and supplements, they do not have a physical-chemical interaction with the body. Furthermore, as hundreds of homeopathic remedies have been tested and documented in the course of time, finding an acceptable match for most symptom complexes is almost a given.

As we already know, Sertürner's discovery led to a cascade of successful isolations and discoveries of isolated compounds including xanthine (1817), strychnine (1818), atropine (1819), quinine (1820) and caffeine (1820) (homeopathic.com). This burst of single-compound isolation has been characterized by Professor Walter Sneader, School of Pharmacy, University of Strathclyde, Glasgow, UK, and many others of the learned medical society as 'the greatest advance in the process of drug discovery' (Sneader, Walter: *Drug discovery: a history*. Wiley-Interscience; 2005). And Rockefeller, the super astute businessman, a century later saw that pharmaceutical drugs were the ideal mean to thoroughly destroy humanity's health and wellbeing without its knowledge. Thereby, he and they could completely dominate humanity's historical narrative to the end of time, whatever time may be.

But Paracelsus' orthodox ideas on medicine together with Hahnemann's increasingly popular homeopathy posed another huge threat to Rockefeller et al. Their production of chemical pharmaceuticals out of tar compounds for herd consumption aspirations were at risk. Their success had already shown itself, with Aspirin killing millions as one of its side-effects when treating flew symptoms. Still on the market, despite causing human stomach and intestinal wall linings to deteriorate after prolonged use. This deterioration leads to irreparable tissue damage and sever degradation and weakening of the digestive tract. All this is merely a sign of success of Rockefeller et al.'s brainwashing Doctor-knows-best tactics. That physicians advise angina and heart attack patients to take at least one aspirin daily is a sign of theirs. Regardless, all holistic medicine became the object of deep-seated animosity and opposition from the allopathic, scientific, slash, cut and burn, AMA-licensed medical society financed by the Rockefeller and Carnegie foundations. The battle against this creature of the Flexner Report continues to this day.

But within 15 years of Flexner's report, the entire U.S. medical industry and healthcare sector, led by AMA-affiliated medical schools and hospitals, came under the control of the pharmaceutical investment business. Take just one example: the cancer industry. It is illegal for any physician to treat cancer with any other modality except chemotherapy, surgery or radiation. It is actually a criminal felony for a medical practitioner to treat cancer with anything but those three modalities. Why? Follow the money. The average cost of cancer treatment for one patient is $150,000. Clearly, Rockefeller et al. are keen to keep the monopoly on this one. And yes, you guessed it. The American Cancer Society of 1913 was founded by none other than John D. Rockefeller with the help of Frederick Gates, of course. Is he related to Bill; you wonder? You check it out, eh?

It had only taken him—Gates— until 1901 to design the Rockefeller Institute for Medical Research, now the Rockefeller University. He promptly became president of America's first biomedical institute. For its first decade, the Institute focused on basic research to develop basic science, such as biomedical engineering. But in 1910, The Rockefeller Hospital opened on its campus as America's first facility for clinical research. It, it expanded into healthcare science that determines the safety and effectiveness of medications, devices, diagnostic products and treatment regimens intended for human use. It also expanded into clinical science, which combines allopathic principles of medicine, chemistry, biology and experimental science. It usually involves laboratory work, such as testing, evaluating, detecting and analyzing cells, blood and bodily fluids, for which humanity is now being used by way of COVID 19 injections, it seems.

In other words, Gates created a purely humanistic institution, viewing individuals equal to rattus, cani, simian, lepus and cockroaches. This allopathic medicine-oriented institution aimed to completely suppress all holistic and humanitarian ways of healing the human body and psyche. With the inauguration of control over the herd's educational system, it eliminated all possibility of human beings even learning about their capacity to heal themselves.

Brazilian physician Dr. Marc Sircus is an acupuncturist, honorary doctor of Oriental Medicine and founding director of the International Medical Veritas Association (IMVA) He points out in his July 2021 article "Greater States Of Being", that there are two primary domains in which we humans live (drsircus.com). These are the state of our minds and the state of our being. With our minds, we think, conceive, imagine, rationalize, judge, speculate and assume. Our emotions, our stress-levels, our anger, joy and fears are of this realm, because they originate from our thoughts and perceptions. These, in turn, evolve from the input we receive, foreign and domestic. With our state of being we feel, empathize and have compassion, as these attributes come from our heart.

To illustrate the point, there are tears of self-pity, and there are tears of the melting heart. How different these are! Tears of someone wallowing in self-pity allow the Self to be a victim. But tears of empathy for the Self and the other build one's Self up. It is more than helpful to know the difference. Though Dr. Sircus wrote this essay about heightened states of human being, he quotes the UK-based rapper known as Zuby. Zuby recently learned 20 attitudes falling into the lesser state of human being, attitudes which allowed for the destruction of humanity's benevolent medicinal treatments, without being aware due to the educational system throughout the past 100 years. These are:

1. Most people would rather be in the majority, than be right.
2. At least 20% of the population has strong authoritarian tendencies, which will emerge under the right conditions.
3. Fear of death is only rivalled by the fear of social disapproval. The latter could be stronger.
4. Propaganda is just as effective in the modern day as it was 100 years ago. Access to limitless information has not made the average person any wiser.
5. Anything and everything can and will be politicized by the media, government and those who trust them.
6. Many politicians and large corporations will gladly sacrifice human lives if it is conducive to their political and financial aspirations.
7. Most people believe the government acts in the best interests of the people - even many who are vocal critics of the government.
8. Once they have made up their minds, most people would rather to commit to being wrong, than admit they were wrong.
9. Humans can be trained and conditioned quickly and relatively easily to significantly alter their behaviors – for better or worse.
10. When sufficiently frightened, most people will not only accept authoritarianism, but demand it.
11. People who are dismissed as "conspiracy theorists" are often well researched and simply ahead of the mainstream narrative.
12. Most people value safety and security more than freedom and liberty, even if said "safety" is merely an illusion.
13. Hedonic adaptation occurs in both directions, and once inertia sets in, it is difficult to get people back to "normal."
14. A significant percentage of people thoroughly enjoy being subjugated.
15. "The Science" has evolved into a secular pseudo-religion for millions of people in the West. This religion has little to do with science itself.
16. Most people care more about looking like they are doing the right thing, rather than actually doing the right thing.
17. Politics, the media, science, and the healthcare industries are all corrupt, to varying degrees. Scientists and doctors can be bought as easily as politicians.

18. If you make people comfortable enough, they will not revolt. You can keep millions docile as you strip their rights, by giving them money, food and entertainment.
19. Modern people are overly complacent and lack vigilance when it comes to defending their own freedoms from government overreach.
20. It's easier to fool a person than to convince them that they have been fooled.

In Dr. Sircus' opinion, we are deep into a worldwide war between good and evil. He opines that we have lost our way psychologically and spiritually in a world seemingly becoming less safe by the day. A new pathological medical totalitarianism is remaking our society into a global medicalized police state. It is pathetic, Sircus says, that we still trust the very people who helped to make the COVID-19 bioweapon to herd us like cattle into the vaccine slaughterhouse, when its evil is clearly hidden in plain sight. And still, Rockefeller, Carnegie and their henchmen are getting away with it. We now know a little of it. But how did they really do it, you wonder? Well, it was easy, in a way. Here is what really happened!

23

THE FLEXNER REPORT: HIGH-JACKING NATURAL MEDICINE

To discover how present-day medical and educational systems got to where they are today, we have little choice but to learn about Abraham Flexner (1866-1959). He created the Flexner Report. His family dominated the Rockefeller and Carnegie foundations during the first half of the twentieth century. These two bodies were instrumental in the rolling out the U.S. medical and educational systems, thereby transforming them for better or for worse, depending on the way we look at it. (https://citizen2009.wordpress.com/the-flexners/).

Abraham's father Moritz Flexner (1820–1882) was born into an Orthodox Jewish family in Neumark, Bohemia. He left his hometown sometime in the mid-1800s. This is what about half the world's Jewish population did between 1780 and 1920, leaving homes in in Europe, the Middle East and North Africa in search of a better life elsewhere. Moritz followed the familiar immigrant narrative: a roughly 90-day passage in steerage on a boat across the Atlantic, followed by an attempt at making a living in New York, in his case unsuccessful. He had lived in French-speaking Strasbourg, France, for a number of years. So, he set sail again, this time for French-speaking New Orleans, Louisiana (Michael Nevins:

Abraham Flexner: A Flawed American Icon). Once there, however, he contracted yellow fever, which moved him to join a Jewish immigrant enclave up-river in Louisville, Kentucky, after his recovery (https://ncbi.nlm.nih.gov/pmc/articles/PMC1356289/).

There, Moritz embarked upon his American dream by becoming a peddler in the truest sense of the word. First, he wore a pack on his back as he went from house to house selling a variety of wares, probably mostly dry goods. Then he bought a cart and a lame horse for $4, with which he earned enough to son thereafter buy a dry goods business. He barely survived the financial losses it incurred during the Civil Was and the financial Panic of 1873.

In the course of his travels he had met and married the equally Orthodox Jewish seamstress Esther Abraham from Roden, Germany, in 1855. The two settled into procreation and their efforts were soon rewarded when son Jacob Aaron saw the light of day in 1857 (las.edu). Henry, Isadore, Simon, Bernard and Abraham (1866–1959) arrived over the next decade. They were followed in 1869 by another boy named Washington "in gratitude for the American bounty" and by two girls, Mary and Gertrude. Five of this precious brood would go on to be listed in , founded in 1898 by Ohian Albert Nelson Marquis (1855–1943). The purpose of the tome was to "chronicle the lives of individuals whose achievements and contributions to society make them subjects of widespread reference interest and inquiry." (*Marquis Who's Who. Who's Who in America 1994*. Chicago, Ill: Marquis Who's Who. p. vi.)

Both parents had limited education, but nevertheless shared great respect for culture and encouraged their children to read literary classics. As the Flexner family flourished and grew in number, so did the city of Louisville. It was founded on the banks of the Ohio River in 1778 by the highest-ranking American patriot military officer on the north-western frontier during the American Revolutionary War, the honourable general George Rogers Clark (1752 -1818). Louisville was founded after a series of locks were built to tame a wild stretch of the Ohio river. Following substantial new railroad connections in the mid- nineteenth century, Louisville became the economic gateway to the U.S. South and one of the nation's most important internal shipping points.

The city's population grew in equal proportions to its importance, from 10,000 in 1830 to more than 200,000 in 1900. Among them was a thriving Jewish community, which had involved itself in manufacturing of all sorts of goods and flogging such products as distilled liquor, tobacco and farm implements since the early 1800s. Henry Hyman, was one of them, having opened the *Western Coffeehouse* in 1826 advertising "the most choice liquors." By 1829, he was offering such foods as pig's feet, pickled, stewed, or fried tripe, soused sturgeon, cold beef, cold ham, and oyster soup (https://www.isjl.org/kentucky-louisville-encyclopedia.html).

By 1836, a small number of German Jews had formed the Orthodox Adath Israel, the first Jewish congregation in Kentucky. Its charter decreed that only members strictly observing the Sabbath and Kosher laws could lead prayers, and that those marrying outside of the faith would to be expelled from the congregation. By 1849, its 76 members had established their own synagogue, where services were held in the German language only. Increased difficulty in becoming an Adath Israel member due to its fervent wish to keep "an undesirable element" out inspired the city's Polish Jews to found their own Beth Israel temple in 1851.

Adath Israel had built a grand gothic synagogue by 1868, costing the princely sum of $145,000, or about $478 million in 2013 dollars. That same year, the congregation also hired the first ordained rabbi for its 250-member congregation. A year later, in 1869, it formally adopted Reform Judaism, originally conceived in the eighteenth century by the German Ashkenazi Jew Moses Mendelsohn (1729–1786).

Hungarian Ashkenazi Jewish author and journalist Arthur Koestler (1905–1983) wrote his book *The 13th Tribe*. It recounts how the Ashkenazim Jews originated in the former country of Khazaria, located in present-day Ukraine and Russia. Their ruler adopted the Jewish faith for his subjects in 740 AD. During the Middle Ages, they began to move into Russia, Poland, Germany and France (Koestler, Arthur: *The 13th Tribe*; One 70 Press 1976).

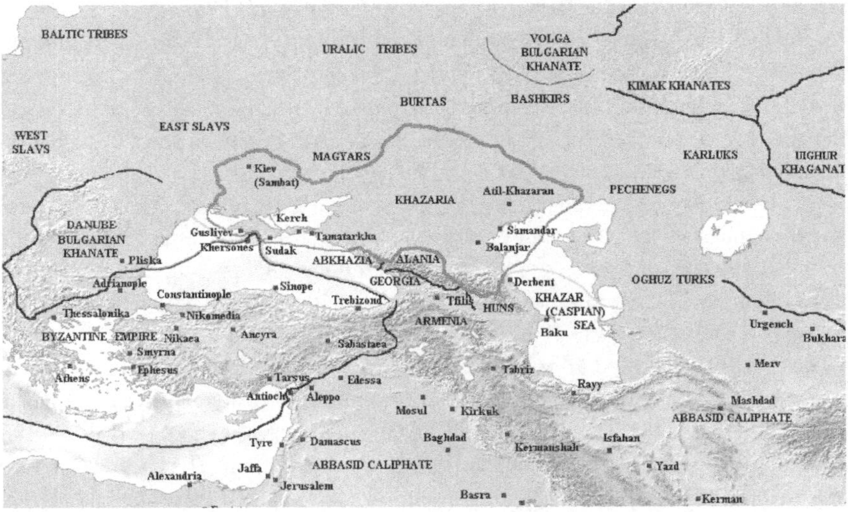

The Khazar empire ca. 650-965 AD

Kevin Alan Brook is an American researcher of history, genetics and genealogy. In his book *The Jews of Khazaria*, he further explores the Khazar empire's history and culture. It was a multi-ethnic conglomerate of mostly Turkic people, created in Eurasia as a result of wars early in the 7th century (AD 593–603). This was after the split of the Turkic Khaganate into a western and an eastern Khaganate in the early 7th century AD. It had originally been founded in the 6th century by the ruling Ashina clan, the dynasty of the Turkic people.

Khazaria dominated the vast area from the Volga-Don steppes to the eastern Crimea and the northern Caucasus. It sat astride the major artery of commerce between Eastern Europe and South-western Asia, the western marches of the Silk Road. Khazaria became one of the early medieval world's foremost commercial trading empires until its collapse in 965 AD. It played the key role as a crossroad between China, the Middle East and Kievan Russia.

Naturally, the conversion to Judaism of one of the largest political and economic formations of its time would be noteworthy Its successive Jewish kings adopted many Jewish beliefs and cultural traits, including Torah and Talmud study, Hebrew script and observance of Jewish holidays (https://rowman.com/ISBN/9781538103425/The-Jews-of-Khazaria-Third-Edition). Needless to say, the Khazars conversion to Judaism means that few of whom have Middle Eastern Semite Jewish blood in them. So, the great masses of Khazarian Jewish people flowing into America from Europe, the Flexner senior among them, were largely non-Semite.

And who are Semites? According to Merriam-Webster dictionary, Semites are those born into the peoples of ancient south and western Asia including the Akkadians, Phoenicians, Hebrews and Arabs. The descendants of these peoples, such as todays Palestinians, are Semites. Thus, brothers are killing brothers, just as Cain slew Abel.

In effect, to be anti-Semite means to be anti-Arab and anti Hebrew, pick and choose. Ranajit Das et al. in their 2017 research paper "The Origins of Ashkenaz, Ashkenazic Jews, and Yiddish" investigated the geographical origins of Ashkenazic Jews. Their findings showed that Yiddish was compatible with the Irano-Turko-Slavic origin. That corresponds with the Khazar adoption of the Hebrew faith, for Ashkenazim Jews, as well as Slavic and Mongol. It turns out that Yiddish did not have a German origin, as previously thought (https://doi.org/10.3389/fgene.2017.00087).

Be that as it may, on the other side of the spectrum of the Slavic Ashkenazim Jews, we have the Sephardim from the Hebrew *Sefarad* for Spain. These are the descendants of the Levantine Hebrews. Many of them transferred there during Roman Empire times. Others tracked along with the Mohammedans during their late 7th century hijad, ending with their Iberian Peninsula takeover in 711 AD.

The royal marriage and joint rule of Catholics Isabella of Castile and Ferdinand of Aragon marked the *de facto* unification of Spain. Thus, they finally managed to oust the Mohammedans in 1492. They instantaneously followed it up with a decree forcing Spain's Sephardic Jews to either convert to Catholicism or face expulsion. The result was a huge diasporic movement, with somewhere between 100,000-300,000 Sephardim said to have left Spain to settle in North Africa, the Ottoman Empire, France, Holland, England, Italy and the Balkans. Salonika, Macedonia, and Amsterdam, Holland, were two major sites of Sephardic settlement.

Their practice of the Hebrew faith is said to greatly differ from the Ashkenazim ways in many of its ritual customs. Most of the estimated 1.5 million Sephardic Jews remaining in the world live in Israel. Nevertheless, it is a far smaller number than that of the Slavic blooded Ashkenazim. Their chief rabbinate in Israel has both a Sephardic and an Ashkenazi chief rabbi. Be it as it may, let's not forget that we come in all colours, shapes, religions and nationalities in our sojourns to earth as amply discussed in Fallacy 1. Therefore, all critical race and religious theories against anyone alive turn into infantile, if not criminal, enterprises.

But I meander. Back to Ashkenazi, Slavic-blooded Moses Mendelsohn and his Jewish Reform movement. And the likewise, back to Ashkenazi Moritz Flexner and his offspring's achievements during their sojourn in the United States and beyond.

The ideas of the Haskalah, the Jewish Enlightenment of the eighteenth and nineteenth centuries, are indebted to Mendelsohn. Indeed, he is acknowledged as a leading cultural figure by Europeans regardless of religious orientation and affiliation. He also happened to be an independently wealthy man, due his activities in the Berlin textile industry, which formed the foundation of his family's wealth. The Jewish Enlightenment period itself, an intellectual Western European Ashkenazim movement, started in the 1770s. It ended with the rise of Jewish nationalism and the abandonment and changes of traditional Orthodox Jewish beliefs, laws and practice. This was their attempt to adapt and blend in with the social, political and cultural conditions of where they chose to live.

Moritz's Adath Israel congregation in Louisville adopted these changes in religious practices in1869. Taking it a step further, Adath Israel also became one of the *Union of American Hebrew Congregations* founding members. The organization was incorporated pursuant to the laws of Ohio in Cincinnati in 1873 with objectives set forth in section 2 of its constitution as:

- A.–To establish and maintain institutions for instruction in the higher branches of Hebrew literature and Jewish theology, with the necessary preparatory schools in such cities of those States as may hereafter be designated.
- B.–To provide means for the relief of Jews from political oppression and unjust discrimination, and for rendering them aid for their intellectual elevation.
- C.–To promote religious instruction and encourage the study of the Scriptures and of the tenets and history of Judaism. All this, however, without interfering in any manner whatsoever with the worship, the schools, or any other of the congregational institutions (jewishencyclopedia.com).

We thus know that Moritz and offspring were well supported by like-minded religious brethren. This helps us comprehend the immense success that his first-born Jacob Aaron had in propelling his much better-known brothers Abraham, Simon, Bernard and through them Washington into their immensely successful positions of influence. Those positions spanned medicine, education, jurisprudence, printing and, by extension, U.S. politics. With the Rockefeller's and Carnegie's financial support, they created, directed and shaped the country's and the world's historical narrative overall in a multitude of ways.

While attending public school and participating in a boy's debating society at the age of 15, Moritz's son Abe began to earn his living as an assistant at the Louisville library. In 1871, the Public Library of Kentucky was founded, and took a new approach to funding. It was to be free, with funds to be raised by means of five nationwide lotteries. These lotteries grossed $6,250,000, of which the Library's share was only $424,396 (https://lfpl.org). The rest of the money? Who knows, but take a guess, perhaps? When Abe was 16, his father died, leaving the family in dire financial straits. By that time, Mortitz's first born Jacob Aaron had turned to and education in pharmacy. He was a bright, assertive and precocious boy, intelligent and voluble. But his dream of becoming a physician was destroyed due to a lack of funds.

Pharmacists were usually closest in medical knowledge to physicians at the time. Some even held medical degrees. They used chemistry and *materia medica* to compound pharmaceutical drugs with or without particular prescriptions. *Materia medica* is the Latin term for the body of collected knowledge about therapeutic properties of natural substances used for healing. This was gathered over millennia, when healers and physicians still worked alongside priests to find ways to alleviate human diseases. It derives from the five-volume Greek encyclopedia about herbal medicine and related medicinal substances (a pharmacopeia) composed by pharmacologist and botanist Pedanius Dioscorides (c. 40–90 AD) He was a Greek physician in the Roman army and widely read for hundreds of years. Jacob Aaron described his chosen profession as such: "The druggist of my day was the right-hand man of the physician, and it was natural that the two professions should stand in a very close relationship to each other." (Flexner JA: A vanishing profession; *Atlantic Monthly* 1931: 98: 16–25). And they do, today perhaps more than ever.

Whichever way, Jacob Aaron seems to have taken to his chosen profession like a duck takes to water. He first worked for University of Louisville Medical School graduate of 1861 druggist Thomas E. Jenkins and his partners. Jenkins was Assistant Professor of Chemistry at the University of Louisville. His partners were J. Lawrence Smith and Edward Robinson Squibb. As a naval doctor during the Mexican-American war of 1846–1848, Squibb had thrown the drugs he was supplied with overboard due to their low quality. He had set up in Louisville Chemical Works 1858, supplying Union armies in the civil war. Thus, he laid the foundation for today's Bristol Myers Squibb (BMS), the American multinational pharmaceutical company headquartered in New York City. Jenkins set Jake to wash the shop's windows and bottles before advancing him to assistant pharmacist. This prompted Jacob to seek better paid employment elsewhere, where he came in contact with bulk pharmaceutical drugs flogged by newly founded pharmaceutical companies.

The other drug supplier Jake, without a doubt, encountered had in 1849 been founded in New York as a fine chemicals business by German immigrants Charles Pfizer (1824-1906) and his cousin Charles F. Erhart (1821–1891). Still headquartered in New York, their business expanded rapidly during the American civil war, as demand for painkillers and antiseptics skyrocketed. It is now a multinational pharmaceutical and biotechnology corporation, which most recently bestowed the COVID 19 jab on humanity.

Whilst Pfizer provided medicines for the Union Army's war effort, young cavalry commander Colonel Eli Lilly served in its army. A trained pharmaceutical chemist, Lilly was an archetype of the dynamic and multi-talented nineteenth-century American industrialist. After his military career and trying his hand at farming, he set up the Eli Lilly and Company pharmaceutical business in 1876, manufacturing drugs and marketing them on a wholesale basis to pharmacies. He was a pioneer of new methods in the industry, being one of the first to focus on research and development (R&D). A company's long-term profitability would be secured by R&D as discoveries are made, products like COVID 19 created and patents, copyrights and trademarks for, in this case, the jab obtained.

Once Jakob had learnt the intricacies of that side of the pharmaceutical industry, he switched to yet another drug store to learn how to fashion pharmaceutical pills and fluid concoctions. He did all that while attending the Louisville College of Pharmacy. Upon graduation in 1878 at age 21, he immediately opened a neighbourhood pharmacy to earn his living and sponsor his younger brothers' academic education.

Simon, the second Flexner boy, joined him in the shop soon thereafter, which encompassed the following items and activities:

> "Jacob featured toilet articles; 'soda water and its appurtenances;' shelves of standard drugs that the Flexner brothers had made up in quantity and bottled; local remedies, which had often been mixed in the drugstore, bearing the names of the quacks who promoted them. Behind the counter were blankly labeled

> nostrums for venereal diseases and male impotence. However, the heart of the business was filling prescriptions drawn up by physicians whom Jacob encouraged to frequent the store."(Flexner JT. *An American Saga*. Boston/Toronto: Little, Brown and Company; 1984).

Business was swift. The store thrived, bringing in enough money by 1884 to pay for 17-year-old Abraham's Johns Hopkins University's 2-year study in the Humanities, armed with $1,000 for tuition and expenses. A piddly sum, said Abe, but it indeed marked a turning point in the family's fortune, he said. He described his arrival in Baltimore as the decisive moment of his life. He idolized his mentor, Hopkins' first president Daniel Coit Gilman (1831–1908), whose educational philosophy was modeled after the German university system. He exclaimed Hopkins to indeed be a place where "research was the air we breathed."

Despite inexperience in Latin and Greek, Abe in no time flat gained mastery of those classical languages and received his bachelor's degree in the allotted two years. Immediately returning home, he even taught Greek at Louisville High School, supplemented his salary through private tutoring. In 1890, he opened a small private school, soon becoming known as "Mr. Flexner's School." It became the testing ground and laboratory for Gilman's and his own rigorous student-centered ideas and theories about pedagogy. Without adherence to customary regulations, rules, tests and reports, they tried them out on students of all ages. Advertising it as a college preparatory school, he had no formal curriculum, no formal grades, no system of examinations and no student achievement records. By 1904, however, he would have 36 students with five teachers working for him.

Catching the attention of Harvard president Eliot and asked how he managed to send him boys who were both younger and more capable than students from other schools, Abe replied:

> "I treated these boys as individuals, and I let each go at his own pace. I took hold of pupils where they were strong, not where they were weak, and having whetted their appetites by success in one field, usually succeeded in arousing their interest in another."

His pedagogical authority gained further through articles he himself authored about his educational work and gladly published by the *International Journal of Ethics*. This paper was founded in 1890 as a result of the Ethical movement, which formally began in America in 1876. It was run by editor Samuel Burns Weston, leader of the Philadelphia Society for Ethical Culture, assisted by an international editorial committee.

The movement itself had been conceived by professor of political and social ethics, religious leader, social reformer and euthanasia enthusiast Felix Adler (1851–1933). This rabbi's son and Columbia University 1870 graduate founded New York's Society for Ethical Culture (https://heritage.humanists.uk). This came after first presenting his ideas about ethics at his father's Temple Emanu-El in New York. He felt that Jews needed to live rich and moral lives without reference to religious doctrines or supernatural beliefs. This ideology is seemingly nowadays carried out by Harvard's Chaplains' organization president Greg Epstein.

The corresponding journal published book reviews, discussions and articles on ethics and philosophy, in addition to reports of ethical societies and affiliated projects drawing on humanist principles in accordance with its associate editor John Dewey's view:

> "What Humanism means to me is an expansion, not a contraction, of human life, an expansion in which nature and the science of nature are made the willing servants of human good."

Under humanism doctrine of viewing humanity as rattus, cani, blattas (cockroaches), simian, mus and lepus, Dewey's leitmotiv seems to have guided the public school system, jurisprudence and the art and science of medicine in all its aspects since that time, the early 1900s. And with the Flexner-brothers were instrumental in its lethal-to-humanity success. The University of Chicago Press, by the way, took on the journal's publication in 1923, renamed it *Ethics* in 1938 and still publishes it today.

Abe, meanwhile, had reluctantly agreed to tutor the 16-year-old Anne Laziere Crawford (1874–1955), before marrying her two years later. By that time, Abe's school brought in enough money to make a Johns Hopkins attendee of older brother Simon (1863–1946). He had received his medical degree from Louisville Medical College in 1889. So, he did postgraduate work in pathology at Johns Hopkins University Medical School, graduating with a medical degree in pathology and bacteriology. He also earned a fellowship in William Henry Welch's (1850–1934) biology laboratory, in itself a major accomplishment. This American physician, pathologist, bacteriologist and medical school administrator was one of Hopkins' "Big Four" founding professors. He was instrumental in creating its hospital and in founding its School of Hygiene and Public Health. He also served as first dean of its School of Medicine (https://ncbi.nlm.nih.gov/pmc/articles/PMC1356289/).

By 1899, Simon had reached the position of professor of pathology at the University of Pennsylvania, followed by heading the Rockefeller Institute between 1902 to 1935. Those who knew Simon, described him as intense, edgy, cold and impelled by the desire to promote Rockefeller's Institute at all costs. A Nobelist recalled at his memorial service: "Individuals were as nothing to Dr. Flexner compared to the welfare of the institute." (Nevins) As Abraham's and his career overlapped, the brothers were often confused with each other. When both Abe and Simon were financially solvent, however, they supported brother Jacob in his desire to obtain his own medical education and settle down in his own practice in Louisville.

The brothers also succeeded to enrol sister Mary in the elite women's Bryn Mawr College in Pennsylvania. It was founded as a Quaker institution in 1885 to provide American women with the educational equivalent to the elite male-only Ivy League colleges. Little else is known about her other than that she graduated in 1895 and had a lectureship in her name established in 1928 that still today brings some of the world's best-known humanists— the rattus and so on aficionados—to Bryn Mawr's campus.

Throughout all this, Simon edited the Rockefeller Institutes for Medical Research's official, monthly, peer-reviewed medical publication, the *Journal of Experimental Medicine* (JEM). It was founded in 1896 by William H. Welch, Simon's mentor at Johns Hopkins and, at that time, RIMR's president. It is still published by Rockefeller University Press today, filled with research papers and commentaries on the purported science-based physiological, pathological and molecular mechanisms encompassing the host-response, humans or rattus, blattas, beagles et al responses to human diseases. So Simon, well ensconced in his position, did his part to arrive at where we are today. But, what about brother Bernard (1865–1945)? How did he cruise into a position enabling him to contribute to Rockefeller's present-day achievements?

Biographical details about him are scattered and sketchy for the most part, we learn. It is published, however, that he received a law degree in 1898 from Louisville University, alma mater to Louisville-born Supreme Court Justice Louis Brandeis (1856–1941), son of Bohemian Ashkenazi immigrant parents. Bernard then did postgraduate work at the University of Virginia, and practiced law in Kentucky and Chicago before settling in New York in 1919. Said to have been much concerned with social welfare and labour problems, he also served as Louisville's chairman of the Juvenile Court Board. He helped to establish the first juvenile court in Chicago and was active in the National Probation Association first as its president (1912–13) and then as committee member until his death.

He also acted as industry and contracts counsellor to the British-born American business magnate Samuel Insull (1859–1938), who hired him as legal council in 1912. Insull had immigrated to the U.S. to begin his American dream as inventor and businessman Thomas Alva Edison's (1847–1931) personal secretary. Finding himself head of the Chicago Edison Company from 1892 onwards, Insull organized a conglomerate called "Midwest Utilities" presumably on the advice of Bernard. He created holding companies that bought public utilities meant to supply services essential to humanity, such as water, gas, electricity, telephone and other communication system, as wells as railroads. He also became co-creator of the American Civil Liberties Union of 1920.

By then, Bernard had left him to become active in public life, at the time of the United States' entry into WWI in 1917. At that time, he kept a residence in New York City with his sister Mary. He had already joined a party of the Red Cross that had assembled in Chicago, and shipped out for Japan from a Western port. He went from there to Petrograd, now St. Petersburg, sometime between September and November 1917 for the Bolshevik Revolution. He continued to Rumania and returned home, we assume. At the end of 1918, Bernard then traveled as the Zionist Organization of America's (ZOA) envoy to Britain. This American non-profit pro-Israel organization had been founded in 1897 as the Federation of American Zionists. Today, it has around 25,000 members, down from its 1939 peak of 165,000. In 1919, Bernard attended the Versailles Peace Conference as a signatory of treaties arranged for the Zionist Organization of America (ZOA) (Hebrew: ארגון ציוני אמריקה).

In 1921, Bernard served as one of the original 108 Counsel of Foreign Relations founding members. In 1921, he became the founding president of the Palestine Economic Corporation (PEC) organized in 1925 to facilitate investment and ship hard goods to colonize Palestine by American Jews and others interested in fostering the economic development and resettlement of the Jewish homeland (Palestine Economic Corporation records 1921-1944 [bulk 1930-1938] archives NYPL).

Bernard Flexner served as the company's first president and chairman of the board until it closed down in 1944. Its records, along with those of the Emergency Committee for Aid of Displaced, were stored and sealed until at least 1970 in the New York Public Library's crypt. Jacob's daughter Jenny Maas Flexner, a NYPL officer, guarded them.

When all this transpired, Bernard had already taken part in a Red Cross mission to Romania and a trip to the Bolsheviks in Saint Petersburg, Russia, in 1917 (https://citizen2009.wordpress.com/the-red-cross/). That same year, he also graced England with a visit on behalf of the Zionist Organization of America. He also partook in the 1919 Versailles, France, WW I Peace Conference as its Zionist delegation counsel, along with Edward Bernays, the world's first advertisement guru.

He and his brother Abraham also created the New York based Emergency Committee in Aid of Displaced Jewish Scholars. It was created in 1933 to employ German Jews as executives in American scholastic/educational institutions. Bernard was convinced that Zionism was the solution to the European Jewry's problems. So, he, also associated with many institutions, banks, and companies to foster the growth of the Jewish economy in Palestine, helped by his activities as member on the American Jewish Joint Distribution Committee and the Jewish Agency for Palestine executive committees.

A powerful man indeed, he is notable for his relationship and writings about his mentor, Louis Brandeis. He is also known for his several philanthropic endowments to law education, and his work with the Viennese born Ashkenazi Felix Frankfurter and Roger Baldwin in founding the non-profit American Civil Liberties Union (ACLU) in 1920 The ACLU's goal was "to defend and preserve the individual rights and liberties guaranteed to every person in this country by the Constitution and laws of the United States." Baldwin and Bernard Flexner also co-produced the textbook treatise on *Juvenile Courts and Probation*, the first codified policing document of U.S. children, and the book *Legal Aspects of the Juvenile Court* (1922).(Ibid)

Meanwhile, Insull controlled an empire of $500 million with only $27 million in equity in 1929. His holding company had slowly collapsed following the stock market crash, wiping out around 600,000 shareholders' savings. In 1932, he owed $16 million dollars more than his worth - "too broke to be bankrupt," according to one banker. He was charged, tried and acquitted of mail fraud and antitrust charges in 1934. Four years later, on Bastille Day, he would die of a heart attack in the Paris subway, his estate valued at about $1,000, with debts totalling $14,000,000 (https://pbs.org/wgbh/theymadeamerica/whomade/insull_hi.html).

By that time Brother Jacob had been able to sell his drugstore. For years, he had admirably supported and assisted his siblings on their roads to success. Now, he earned a medical degree from the University of Louisville Medical College and opened a practice of medicine in Louisville. Meanwhile, young brother Washington run the Lincoln Printing Company in Chicago, having in no time flat turned it into the U.S.'s largest financial printing company, able and willing to fulfill that aspect of the Freud, Bernays et al. *Make the American Mind* business great agenda (Ward O. Griffing, Jr. M.D., PhD: Jacob, The Other Flexner; Ann Surg. 2004: Jun; 239(6): 808-817; https://encyclopedia.com).

Simon had not stood still, either. In 1901, he had been elected to the American College of Physicians (ACP). This organization of internists tackles undifferentiated human health problems that cannot be fitted within the expertise of a single-organ specialty. Conditioned range from shortness of breath to fatigue, weight loss, chest pain, confusion or change in states of consciousness. In other words, he had joined physicians trying hard to discover and manage serious acute illnesses affecting multiple organs simultaneously. They would do this by analyzing patients piece by piece, as if examining car engines to find the defect. They would also try to diagnose the origin of multiple chronic diseases or "comorbidities" a patient might have acquired in the course of allopathic medical- pharmaceutical treatments received. PTSD experiencers would be familiar with this process, when in the hands of the mental health industry and its methods of operation.

Nowadays, the ACP has 161,000 members throughout the United States. It is the largest medical-specialty organization and second-largest physician group in the country after the American Medical Association. Its flagship journal, the *Annals of Internal Medicine*, is considered one of the five top medical journals in the United States and Britain. Needless to say, the ACP also laid the foundation for the augmentation to 27 U.S. National Institutes of Health responsible for biomedical and public health research. This is described as "the science and art of preventing disease," originally founded in 1880. Biomedicine, by the way is described as a branch of medical science that applies biological and physiological principles to clinical practice. This varies across the world, due to differences in culture and technology. It stresses standardized, evidence-based treatment, validated through biological man-a-machine research.

Meanwhile, Simon, was teaching at the University of Pennsylvania and noticing advances in physics. In accordance with biomedicine, had also conceived the idea to design the Ayer Clinical Laboratory and establish it to work on patients (rockfound.rockarch.org; academia.dk). It was also that very same year, already mentioned, that John Davison Rockefeller elected Simon as the Rockefeller Institute for Medical Research's first president. There, he instantaneously began to direct and imprint his occasionally termed infamous style and research interests. These were so instrumental in shaping the goals and priorities specified by Rockefeller senior's equally infamous wishes and desires about allopathic medicine and education. They were to be carried out in accordance with humanistic principles, which were faithfully implemented by all employed until Simon's 1935 director emeritus status and beyond.

Abraham, meanwhile, also expanded his theoretical knowledge of the human psyche after his playwright wife had a theatrical success on Broadway in 1905. He closed down his school in pursuit of a master's degree in psychology from Harvard. That was followed by two years of study at universities in Berlin and Heidelberg, Germany. He did not obtain an advanced degree of any sort from any of the institutions, which, as it turned out, would not matter one way or the other anyway. Why not? Because he penned his first book, *The American College: A Criticism*, an overall critique of Harvard based on his own experience at that hallowed institution while abroad. It included a scathing critique of its prevailing lecture style which, he wrote, enabled colleges to "handle cheaply by wholesale a large body of students that would otherwise be unmanageable." (Nevins)

In his scribbles, Abe furthermore suggested that the rigid curricula generally employed stifled creativity and made no sense. Students should not be distracted by athletics or other extra curricular activities, he said, asserting: "The task of universities is to give society not what it wants, but what it needs...Intellectual inquiry, not a job training [is] the purpose of the university." Published upon his 1908 return to America, it caught the eyes of both the newly created Carnegie Foundation for the Advancement of Teaching's President Henry S. Pritchett, and Harvard University President Charles W. Eliot.

It was also in 1908, that the AMA's Council in Medical Education commissioned the Carnegie Foundation to perform a detailed study of American medical schools. A pilot study had revealed uniformly low educational standards, especially in the large number of proprietary schools. Carnegie had been selected as a neutral party, whereas Pritchett's agenda is portrayed as a desire to upgrade and recast professional life in America based on an authority of knowledge and skill. Thus, Pritchett is said to have been the one to choose Abraham for the task, because he wanted an unfettered mind to take a hard look at facts. And he wanted a plan for reformulating medical education along more scientific lines, insisting that professional schools should be studied not from the point of view of practitioners, but from that of educators.

Some Carnegie Foundation board members questioned his choice, as rumour had it that Abe was hard to get along with. Harvard's Dr. William Councilman hinted at this when writing: "I have not known Mr. A. Flexner well, but I have liked what I have seen of him. I should think he might be somewhat erratic and probably hasty to judgment, but a very able and valuable man for all that..." It mattered little, as they appointed him to their research staff anyway. Valuably assisted by an AMA member, he visited 155 medical schools throughout the United States and Canada between January 1909 and April 1910. His findings caused a sensation when published in June 1910. Pritchett's introduction set the tone and gave a sense of what would follow:

> "For twenty five years past there has been an enormous over-production of uneducated and ill trained medical practitioners. This has been in absolute disregard of the public welfare and without any serious thought of the interests of the public. Taking the United States as a whole, physicians are four or five times as numerous in proportion to population as in older countries like Germany. Over production of ill-trained men is due in main to the existence of a very large number of commercial schools, sustained in many cases by advertising methods through which a mass of unprepared youth is drawn out of industrial occupations into the study of medicine. " (Nevins)".

The table was now set. Abraham's composition bore the wholesome title of Medical Education in the United States and Canada. A Report to the Carnegie Foundation for the Advancement of Teaching., Also called Bulletin Number Four or Flexner Report for short, within no time flat it elevated Abe to national, if not worldwide prominence. He and Simon, with Carnegie-and Rockefeller Foundations unlimited financial backing, henceforth changed humanity's overall educational and medicinal treatment and historical narrative to purely humanist ways (https://stateuniversity.com).

The Carnegie and Rockefeller Foundations were aided later by other non-profit agencies created from the massive wealth accumulated by U.S. industrial oligarchs of America's Gilded Age, "the robber barons". The monies were liberally distributed by a handful of bourgeois advisers. The inducement of massive financial incentives and support to God and sundry in the medical educational system not only reshaped the nation's cultural and educational institutions. It guaranteed the success mirrored in the elite's capacity for radical interventions engineered - for good or ill - as seen in such projects as critical race theory and social emotional learning, as well as the COVID 19 curfews, jabbing and mask wearing. All are instrumental in destroying humanity's physical and mental health and, lest we forget, we ourselves are responsible for all of it. (Charles E. McClelland: The German Model For American Medical Reform; University of New Mexico, 2012; cemcc@unm.edu).

And so, believe it or not, it all began with Abe Flexner's report. Through his report, the peddler's son from Bohemia began humanity's destruction of its self-healing holistic medicinal innate healing remedies, modalities and applications. As for John Davison Rockefeller senior (1837-1939), he used nothing other for his health than homeopathy until dying at the age of 101.

24

HUMANITY'S SELF-HEALING ABILITY DESTRUCTION

Scarce hours after Carnegie had published Bulletin Number Four, Abraham of Carnegie was appointed to Rockefeller's General Education Board (GEB). He joined Brother Simon, as we recall, who had become a physician, scientist, administrator and professor of experimental pathology at the University of Pennsylvania between1899 and 1903. He was friend and adviser to John D. junior, having joined the organization as first director of its Institute for Medical Research in 1901. The brothers thus presented a united front for these organizations. According to American writer Frederick Gary Allen (1936 -1986), they were as thick as thieves, in 1976 stating:

> "When you hear of 'Carnegie Foundation' think Rockefeller. For many years the five Carnegie foundations have been mere appendages of the Rockefeller octopus. The chief operators of the Carnegie foundations have for decades been members of the Rockefeller coordinating committee, The Council on Foreign Relations, the glue which holds the Rockefeller Establishment together. In addition, two of the six men on the Carnegie Corporation's finance committee are also directors of Rockefeller financial institutions. (https://educate-yourself.org/ga/RF4chap1976.shtml).

And he should know. First, he majored in history at Stanford University, Palo Alto, California. Then in 1971, he co-wrote the book *None Dare Call It Conspiracy* with businessman and public speaker on political, economic, and financial topics: Larry Henry Abraham (1937–2008). They asserted that modern political and economic systems in most developed nations are the result of a sweeping conspiracy by the establishment's power elite. These "Insiders" used Karl Marx's *Communist Manifesto* to advance their socialist/communist agenda. They quoted the Council on Foreign Relations as stating in its 1959 No. 7 study on behalf of the United States Senate: "The U.S. must strive to: A. Building an international order." (United States foreign policy: basic aims of United States foreign policy, study prepared at the request of the Committee on Foreign Relations, United States Senate, by Council on Foreign Relations (pursuant to S. Res. 336, 85th Cong., and S. Res. 31, 86th Cong.), no. 7, November 25, 1959).

Regardless, he used Rockefeller and Carnegie's non-profit foundation money. And he had brother Simon as his most stalwart assistant. He was the fourth son of nine children of different academic persuasions. Thus, he began to put the ideas promulgated in his voluminous book-length recital concerning the United States' and Canada's medical education into instantaneous motion. Gradually, they eliminated all spiritual and holistic humanitarian ways of human dis-ease healing in humane way. They shifted the medicinal narratives of these nations and eventually those of the entire world.

His leitmotiv? Science, once embraced, would conquer the whole. Homeopathy, so favored in Europe at that time and spreading to the US, in his own words had but two options: "To withdraw into the isolation in which alone any peculiar tenet can maintain itself or to put that tenet into the melting-pot."

It is worth remembering, though, that at the same time Abe and Simon Flexner were not the only players in town. While they succeeded in obtaining free reign to carry out their laborious task of trying to ruin holistic medical education in the United States and Canada, Europe had experienced vast developments of biomedical science. This was due to German pharmacist Friedrich Wilhelm Adam Sertürner's (1783–1841) isolation of morphine from opium in the 1820s. That sparked the whole new industry previously described.

Fast forward 100 years, and two other men were watching developments. One was Professor in the History of Medicine & Health Care Frank W. Stahnisch. His interests cover the history of neuroscience, psychiatry, public health and physiology since the eighteenth century. The other was Professor Marja Verhoef, Canada Research Chair in Complementary Medicine in the Department of Community Health Sciences. They were both at the University of Calgary in Alberta, Canada. In their 2012 paper *The Flexner Report of 1910 and Its Impact on Complementary and Alternative Medicine and Psychiatry in North America in the 20th Century*, they noticed a lot of activity. Between 1900 and 1930, the United States and Canada witnessed a major expansion of research in the field of biomedicine. This most notably impacted academic psychiatry, clinical research in internal medicine and the integration of laboratory-based pathology. The latter was a process, which became strongly connected with the lasting transformation of modern universities, colleges and hospitals (Evid Based Complement Alternat Med. 2012).

Unsurprising, really, considering the extremely generous Rockefeller and Carnegie grants to facilitate changes of the U.S. medical and education systems, as well as biomedical research. At the same time, federal and state contributions, thus taxpayer funding, for biomedical research, psychiatric hospitals and asylums was rapidly growing. And healthcare support through employer-based plans and state welfare insurance corporations was also growing. The poster child of these plans was the WCB implemented by Kaiser Wilhelm II of Germany in the early 1900 to protect employers from injured workers' lawsuits. It had already been invoked during the so-called "American Progressive Era" of the 1890s. American medical schools and academic psychiatric departments, most prominently represented in John Hopkins' Clinical Department of Psychiatry headed by the earlier discussed Swiss émigré psychiatrist Adolph Meyer (1866–1950), benefitted greatly from this financial support.

All of it helped Abe and Simon push the holistic medicine destruction forward. They had colossal support from some of the world's most powerful entities. Among them were some we met earlier, such as the Canadian born physician Sir William Osler, 1st Baronet (1849 –1919). He was one of Johns Hopkins hospital's four founding professors, who joyously brayed bragged: "A new school of [medical] practitioners has arisen, which cares nothing for homeopathy." (Frank W. Stahnisch; Marja Verhoef: *The Flexner Report of 1910...*; Evid Based Complement Alternat Med. 2012; The original text can be found in: Flexner, 1910).

Abe was vehemently opposed to all "nonconformist" - meaning holistic - approaches to human healing medicine and psychiatry. He roundly declared all non-scientific medicinal healing modalities charlatanism and quackery. And he aimed to weed them out of North American in their entirety. He listed homeopathy, naturopathy, eclectic therapy, physical therapy, osteopathy and chiropractic programs as medical sects. He firmly stated in Bulletin Number Four that he would antagonize them out of existence if they did not close down willingly, as no juridical way to discard non-biomedical approaches existed on the American medical and psychiatric market. Up against Rockefeller and Carnegie foundation funding, only 20% of his targets were able to comply with Flexner's recommended AMA, federal and state government backed constraints, laws and regulations, composed with brother Simon's invaluable assistance.

Stahnisch and Verhoef state that the schism created in humans' medicinal community was enormous. Its effects were felt throughout North America, and thus the world, in psychiatric clinical treatment and research to this day. Even the antagonism still exists between complementary and alternative—speak holistic—medicine (CAM) proponents. Abe had subsumed alternative medicine under the "medical sects" nomenclature and those academics steeped into science-based biomedical research human-is-ape belief. Abe's love for biomedicine and medical science overall and his disdain for all things holistic knew no bounds. So, the venerable authors Stahnisch and Verhoef came to his defense. They assumed that he acquired his literal hatred for all things "natural" and quasi- fanaticism toward science-based human healing by way of his academic education.

Thus, they state that Abe had received a German-style research education at the venerable Johns Hopkins University. IT was said to be grounded in intensive laboratory experimentation and research, and had actively pursued concise scientific experimentation and standardized clinical observations. This was reported on both graduate and undergraduate levels in the natural sciences. He was said to have also been educated in bedside manners there. All of which would explain his unmovable views about scientific medicine. However, no evidence can be found anywhere that Abraham ever attended classes in pathology or received laboratory instructions at Johns Hopkins or anywhere else, though brother Simon did extensively.

It is he who got his medical degree from Louisville Medical College in 1889. It is he who went to do postgraduate work in pathology at Johns Hopkins University Medical School and started teaching pathology. It is he who joined the University of Pennsylvania as faculty as professor of pathology in 1899, until he joined the Rockefeller Institute for Medical Research, later the Rockefeller University, as director in 1902. And it is he who was augmented by the trustee position he assumed at the Rockefeller Foundation proper when established in 1913, and held both positions until 1935.

Thus, we have Abe, comptroller of the Flexner Report and hand in glove with brother Simon and his scientific leanings. We assume that he learned to incessantly and expertly promote his science-based medicinal paradigm of education and research. We assume that he enthusiastically vilified all "non-scientific" human healing modalities applied by folk psychologists, naturopaths, homoeopaths, chiropractors and osteopaths as illegitimate imposters in competition with the scientific means of research and education. And by then, he had with all might forced this "biomedicine" on American and Canadian universities. The havoc, misery and destruction they thereby caused never bothered them for one moment. Neither they nor their bosses ever suffered from such pedestrian emotions as empathy and compassion, never mind honour and integrity.

As to Stahnisch and Verhoef 's false background information about Abe, it is really not their fault. They got their information about him from Thomas Neville Bonner (1923-2003), professor emeritus at the University of Chicago and leading historian of medicine. Bonner published it in his book *Iconoclast: Abraham Flexner and a Life in Learning*, published by Johns Hopkins University Print in 2002, Canadian physician-historian and political activist Don G. Bates (1933–2001) created the interdisciplinary Department of Social Studies of Medicine at McGill University in Montreal. He wrote as follows in 2000:

> "Recently, and for slightly different reasons, this unusual modern, scientific form of medicine [developed during the nineteenth century] has also given rise to another term: biomedicine. The bio, of course, is meant to point to its strong biological and therefore material and scientific orientation, but the term is frequently used in a critical, even mildly pejorative sense, in order to emphasize the ways in which this caricature fails to make adequate provision for the social and cultural complexities that form part of any medical practice (Don G. Bates: "Why not call modern medicine 'Alternative'?" *Perspectives in Biology and Medicine*, vol. 43, no. 4, pp. 502–518, 2000).

Not only that. In the same article, he maintains that biomedicine indeed should be reasonably called "Modern Alternative Medicine". This would be contrasting it with the "classic" twentieth century medicine paradigm because, as documented at length in *Fallacy 1*, its roots went back all the way to the fifth-century BC's classical Greek physicians' insights and traditions. Those somewhat varied over the past two plus millennia, until about 1850 AD. However, those medicinal insights and traditions were all based on writings from around 500 BC onwards, and they dominated Western medicinal treatment modalities and applications. Even seventeenth century AD's so-called scientific revolution changed little in it. Bates notes that it might have led to greater understanding of how the healthy human body actually works. Nevertheless, he writes that it had little to no effect on how medicine was practiced. Therefore, he opines, until around 1850, all medicine practiced in the western world could be rightfully called Hippocratic and Galenic medicine. And their offspring include "heroic medicine or heroic depletion theory," which constitutes rigorous bloodletting, purging and sweating to shock the human body into health when ill from humoral imbalances.

Although we discussed humors earlier, let's briefly recap. The word "humors" is a translation of the Greek χυμός,[3] chymos, literally juice or sap and metaphorically flavour. The idea of humors actually originated with Empedocles (492–432 BC). Now neuropsychologist and the mental health industry see humors as part of the chemical systems regulating human behaviour. Empedocles, we read, believed that all earthly matter was composed of four elements: fire, air, water, and earth. Furthermore, he thought that forces such as love and strife mixed with or separated those elements. Ancient Indian Ayurveda medicine had already at that time developed a theory of the three doshas (doṣas) or humors. They linked these with the five elements earth, water, fire, air and space. Mind you, some researchers even suggest that the concept of "humors" may have originated in Ancient Egypt or Mesopotamia, although Greek thinkers were the first to systemize the concept in the West.

Empedocles' knowledge was picked up in early fifth-century-BC Greece by medical writer, philosopher-scientist, astrologer and meteorologist Alcmaeon of Croton (C. 540–500 BC). Croton was referred to by some of the learned society as "a thinker of considerable originality and one of the greatest philosophers, naturalists, and neuroscientists of all time." (Debernardi, Alberto et al: "Alcmaeon of Croton"; *Neurosurgery*. 66 (2): 247–252, discussion 252 Febr. 2010) He, too, dwelled much on the internal causes of human illnesses. He suggested that health was a state of equilibrium between opposing humors, and that illnesses occurred because of individuals' problems with the environment, nutrition and lifestyle.

Hippocrates (460–370 BC) lived a very healthy life for 90 years. He sprang into the fray in the early 400s, composing a longer list of humors than the others and applying these humorous concepts to his ideas of healing. Furthermore, he suggested that humors actually were the vital bodily fluids such as blood, yellow and black bile, as well as phlegm. Both Alcmaeon and Hippocrates put forward the thought that excess or deficiency of any of these bodily fluids could either cause or be a sign of illness. Hippocrates, and later on Galen (129 -216 AD), also suggests that even a moderate imbalance in the mixture of these fluids, these humors, would create behavioural disturbance.

One of the treatises attributed to Hippocrates, *On the Nature of Man*, gives first-hand accounts and explanations of individual medical cases. For example, dysentery and nosebleeds occur in the spring and summer because, we are told, at this time the blood is at its hottest. Hippocrates furthermore concludes that the degree of damage a given disease can do to a person depends on its nature. The most serious of illnesses are those that affect the strongest part of the body. If the strongest part of the body is affected, then the weak parts are easily affected and may cause death. However, if a disease starts in a weak area of the body, it is often curable. His theory and treatment procedures, including bloodletting, are performed in order to regulate the patient's four humors, as he reasons:

> "The Human body contains blood, phlegm, yellow bile, and black bile. These are the things that make up its constitution and cause its pains and health. Health is primarily that state in which these constituent substances are in the correct proportion to each other, both in strength and quantity, and are well mixed. Pain occurs when one of the substances presents either a deficiency or an excess, or is separated in the body and not mixed with others.
>
> Furthermore, one must know that diseases due to repletion are cured by evacuation, and those due to evacuation are cured by repletion; those due to exercise are cured by rest, and those due to idleness are cured by exercise." (Hippocrates, p. 25).

The humors were used to explain phenomena like emotional states in simple physical terms (www.nlm.nih.gov/exhibition/emotions/balance.html). For example, physicians assumed that melancholy and feeling of sadness or depression resulted from the physical excess of black bile and excess of yellow bile caused anger and impulsiveness. In the Hippocratic treatise *The Sacred Disease*, the author explains that "those maddened through bile are noisy, evil-doers and restless, always doing something inopportune." Thus, he assumed that emotions were *consequences* of humoral *excess, though he acknowledged some emotional states* to be caused by emotional upheaval. In one example, a woman began to exhibit fears, depression, incoherent rambling speech and the uttering of obscenities after suffering from a "grief with a reason for it." Another "without speaking a word . . . would fumble, pluck, scratch, pick hairs, weep and then laugh, but . . . not speak," also "after a grief. "In *The Sacred Disease*, Hippocrates also says that epilepsy is "caused by fear of the mysterious" in certain circumstances.

It appears as if physicians after Hippocrates did not actively pursue to seek causal elements for emotional behaviours. However, they seemed to have worked hard to clarify and codify the humoral ideas embedded in his work. They also tried to systemize his therapies based on "opposition." They would deplete what they saw as excess humors by "cold" or "hot" medicines, such as oil of roses to counter fevers. And in the seventeenth century, they would add anatomical features to medical systems hypotheses, such as frontal lobe removals done to the day today. The medical methodology would then be classified as "heroic," with French physician Guy Patin.

In medicine, heroic treatment or course of therapy is to this very day a treatment which possesses a high risk of causing further damage to a patient's health. It is undertaken as a last resort with the understanding that any lesser treatment will surely result in failure. Thus, we can classify allopathic medicine's cancer treatments as heroic, as the holistic remedies for curing cancer have been known for hundreds of years. But never mind. Back to seventeenth century's Patin, nicknamed "Le Grand Saigneur" (the Grand Bloodletter) (1601-1672). He was dean of the Faculty of Medicine in Paris from 1650 to 1652 and professor in the College de France in 1655. He was best known for his extensive correspondence and dealings in clandestine books, rather than for his scientific and medical works.

Infamous for his rigorous medical procedure plans, which included intensive courses of bloodletting and applying the laxatives herb senna, it is indeed easy to classify patients submitting themselves to such therapy as heroic. Patin's intensive bloodletting treatments were used throughout American "therapeutic" history after William Douglass (ca, 1691-1752), born in Giford, Scotland, introduced heroic treatment to the colonies. Educated at Edinburgh, Leyden, Paris and Utrecht, where he received his M.D. in 1712, he first arrived in Boston in 1716. There were practitioners here and there particularly eager to perform Douglass' proposed aggressive treatment. But it took until the late 1700s for heroic treatment to gain foothold in the realm of mainstream American medicine. Many people associated Benjamin Rush with an abrupt acceptance of heroic techniques. By the way, Douglass is believed to be the author of a pseudonymous proposal in 1737 to register all medical practitioners in the Province of Massachusetts Bay.

Rush (ca. 1746 1745] -1813), a Philadelphia physician of English Quaker descent, was a civic leader, politician, social reformer and humanitarian. He served as Surgeon General of the Continental Army and was a signatory to the U.S. Declaration of Independence. He was also a professor of chemistry, medical theory and clinical practice at the University of Pennsylvania Medical School. He graduated from the College of New Jersey, now Princeton University, at age 14 and earned his M.D. from Edinburgh University in 1768. Known for having merged heroic medicine into the medical profession's best practices of his time, he used drastic regimens of intensive bloodlettings and purgatives teachings as tools for human healing. Many graduate students of his would apply this throughout their careers, including in mental hospitals.

Rush is said to have organized his medical knowledge around explanatory theories that he himself conceived through his own concepts of theories or logic. Apparently, he felt free to ignore those verified and still verifiable by observation and experience throughout past millennia. There was no one to argue with or stop him either, as Rachel Hajar, M.D., describes in her 2012 *Heart Views* article "The Air of History Medicine in the Middle Ages" (*Heart Views:* 2012 Oct-Dec; 13(4): 158-162). "The glory that was Greece and the grandeur that was Rome," (Edgar Allan Poe. *To Helen*; 1845) ended with the Visigoths' 410 A sacking of Rome. With it, all expansion of medical knowledge was quenched until the sixteenth century due to a multitude of reasons.

Flavius Valerius Constantins, better known as Constantine I (c. 272 -337), was Roman emperor from 306 to 337. By then, he had slaughtered by the millions everyone he could find in his campaigns against the peoples north of the Rubicon - Franks, Alamani, Goths and Samaritans among them. And he had built himself an imperial residence at the ancient Greek city of Byzantium, naming it Constantinople in 330 AD a name it would carry until 1930, when renamed Istanbul. He had somewhat adopted the Christian faith and greatly favoured the Catholic church.

In 380 AD, the Christian church was recognized as the Roman Empire's state church by Theodosius I in his Edict of Thessalonica. All of it together served to shift the center of learning from West to East, with the Roman Catholic Church effectively dominating the direction of the medical world. Thus, it stated that illnesses were punishments from God, and people were ill because they were sinners. Any views differing in opinion were labeled heresy and swiftly punished. As in many Eastern religions, human suffering was seen as part of the human condition of life, leading to people becoming obsessed with their souls rather than taking care of their bodies, and with it, scientific medicine and observations began to blend with spiritual- and religious doctrines.

The influence of patients' Zodiac charts and signs of birth, the moon and planets' movements, determined the times bloodletting should proceed. Medical charts informed physicians what to do and not to do for people born under certain astrological signs. In addition to individual destiny, it was assumed that an imbalance and excess of humours caused disease. This could be fixed by purging, bleeding, cupping and leeching, all medical practices that continued throughout the Middle Ages. Diseases thought to be caused by an excess of blood were remedied by bloodletting. The healing of other ailments was attempted through diet in accordance with Hippocrates quote: "Let food be thy medicine and medicine be thy food."

Under Galen, the basis of diagnosis and treatment evolved into a theory that an individual's temperament and personal characteristics accounted for psychological, social and physical characteristics. It was the excess of blood, phlegm, yellow bile or black bile that would make a person sanguine, phlegmatic, choleric or melancholic. Therefore, on first visiting patients, doctors listened to their stories before feeling their pulse and examining their urine. It was the urine that was the most common method of diagnosis. Fun fact: the urine flask became the physician's universal symbol. It was replaced in the twentieth century by the stethoscope. Now, through the "Standard of Care" imposed by computer-searches, we are led back to Rush. He began to argue in true scientism fashion, that illness in the human body's physical system originates with malfunctions in the brain. Thus, he paved the way for the scientific allopathic cut-slash and burn treatment modalities. That left the standard, well-working medical knowledge based upon surviving Greek and Roman texts still preserved in monasteries and Vatican underground libraries inaccessible to the herd.

But beginning in Constantine's time, health from a medicine-focused enterprise seems to have slowly turned into a matter of faith interspersed with superstition. Disease was deemed to originate in destiny, sin and heavenly influences. The cure, therefore, could be achieved only by fervent prayers and indulgences. Such was the Roman Catholic Church's distinctive penitential system, which emerged in the 11th and 12th centuries, when the idea of a purgatory became widespread among the herd. With it, full or partial remission for sickness and for sins, depending on how much money the penitent paid, sprang into fashion and is still in full function today. The power to absolve still lies with the priests. They can grant release from the guilt of sin to truly contrite sinners who confess their sins and promise to perform satisfaction to Almighty God, whom they are judged to have offended.

Indulgences rested on the belief that their purchase extinguished a visit to any of the given purgatories depicted by Dante Alighieri's (c. 1265 –1321) poem *The Divine Comedy*. They would also grant a place in the next life, where one could continue to cancel the accumulated debt of one's sins. This practice eventually led to Martin Luther's (1483 –1546) famous rebellion. This German Augustinian friar, professor of Moral Theology at the

University of Wittenberg, Saxony, uttered his annoyance when he was 33 years old. It was in 1517 that he hammered his 95 theses, proposing an academic discussion of the practice and efficacy of indulgences, to the doors of the Castle Church of Wittenberg. In due time, his hammering split the thousand-year-old Roman Catholic Church into two churches. One remained loyal to the Pope in Rome. The other protested against the Pope's rule and soon, in fact, called itself Protestant.

Benjamin Rush was so enamored with heroic medicine, that he, in true humanistic fashion, even subjected George Washington (1732-1799) to it whilst on his deathbed. He bled him repeatedly, treating him with mercury chloride and administering blisters of cantharidin, an odorless, colorless fatty substance secreted by species of blister beetles. A burn agent, a poison and an aphrodisiac rolled in one, this heroic treatment promptly dispatched Washington to his next destination, whatever place that may have been.

Heroic medicine was very much in the hands of the professional, as the invasive interventions involved were considered beyond the capabilities of rustic practitioners. Symptoms such as fevers were not regarded as the body's attempt to fight the disease. They were considered a complication exacerbating the patient's condition and doing further harm. Therefore, professionals like Rush believed that fever should be suppressed and any drugs they felt like using should be powerful and administered in large quantities. Under this onslaught, folk medicine dwindled in importance. This included treatments found effective, the chicken noodle soup remedies, for example, laughed at and speedily replaced by bloodletting and purging. Mind you, together with sweating, these are said to date back to back to the advent of humoral theory in Hippocrates' and Galen's time (Lyng, Stephen (1990). *Holistic Health and Biomedical Medicine: A Countersystem Analysis*. SUNY Press. pp. 175–9.)

Heroic medicine faced criticism from physicians and holistic healers even during its heyday. However, with the rise of popularity in homeopathy and hydrotherapy, it began to fall out of favour in the mid- nineteenth century. Nevertheless, hydrotherapy is still practiced in American mental hospitals and prisons today (Whorton, James (2002). *Nature Cures: The History of Alternative Medicine in America*. Oxford University Press). In April 1852, a *New York Times* editorial commented on an incidence of "showering" or "hydropathic torture" in New York's Sing Sing prison. An inmate had several beatings and other mistreatments. He had then had his head shaved and "certainly three, and possibly a dozen, barrels of water were poured upon his naked scalp" before placing him in a yoke ("Extra-Judicial Punishments." New York Times. 6 April 1852.p.2). Apparently hydrotherapy, the "water cure," became a favourite in mental health institutions

By then, mind you, this procedure was old hat. Chemist, physiologist and physician from the Spanish Netherlands Jan Baptist van Helmont (1580-1644) had delighted in plunging patients into ponds or the ocean blue during his medical career in the seventeenth century already. His inspiration had arisen from a story he had heard of an escaping lunatic who sped into a nearby lake, nearly drowned, and recovered his mind after being rescued. Van Helmont, therefore, concluded that water could stop "the too violent and exorbitant Operation of the fiery Life." He promptly began to strip his patients naked, bind their hands and lower them headfirst into a body of water and sometimes drown. So wrote his son in a book about his father's exploits (psych-history.weill.cornell.edu/osk_die_lib/hydrotherapy/Page2.html).

It was not that he had been into heroic medicine, in particular. It was just his curiosity that propelled him into such exploits. After all, he was a bright boy, having graduated from the University of Louvain [Leuven] at age 17. Despite doubts about the quality of education he was given, he entered medical school there and received his M.D. in 1600 (emlo-portal.bodleian.ox.ac.uk/collections/?catalogue=jan-baptist-van-helmont).

A good Catholic, he was aware of the Church's watchful eyes. By 1621, he had gathered enough medical experience to become embroiled in a weapon-salve controversy, setting followers of Paracelsus against members of the Society of Jesus. The latter is better known as the Jesuits, the religious order of the Catholic Church headquartered in Rome and founded in 1540 by Ignatius de Loyola. The salve was a Paracelsian medicine that supposedly cured at a distance, thus removing the need for surgical intervention. It inspired Van Helmont to pen a defense of the cure, the *De magnetica vulnerum curatione* [On the Magnetic Cure of Wounds]. This resulted in his denouncement for heresy to the Roman Inquisition, because it intervened with the church's principles of miracles. A decade of persecution without formal charges followed until his freedom was secured. He was then able to pursue the remaining seven years of his life writing about his discoveries and philosophy.

Van Helmont did not hesitate to exclaim his belief that it is the Archeus that presides over the growth and continuation of all living beings. The term "Archeus" was coined by Paracelsus . In alchemy, it generally refers to the lowest and most dense aspect of the astral plane. It, in turn, is a segment of the closest quadrant of the higher worlds blending with some similarity to the highest vibrations of our physical world. Essentially, it was seen as the "gray area" wherein matter, speaking parallel and not laterally, begins to transmute into spiritual energies. In effect, it is seen as the glue that binds the heavens to the material. Thus, it allows the maxim: "As above, so below," a paraphrase of the Emerald Tablet's second verse by Islamic and European alchemists regarded as their craft's foundation.

Furthermore, Van Helmont believed in the existence of a sensitive soul, which, in his opinion was the husk or shell of the immortal mind. Before "the Fall", he maintained, the Archeus obeyed the immortal mind and was directly controlled by it. But due to the Fall, men received the sensitive soul and with it lost immortality. When the sensitive soul perishes, the immortal mind can no longer remain in the body. By the Fall, Van Helmont addressed the Christian doctrine extrapolated from Christian exegesis of *Genesis* 3. This is a transition of the first man and woman from a state of innocent obedience to God to a state of guilty disobedience, when enticed by a serpent to eat from the tree of knowledge of good and evil, which God had forbidden. Expulsion from the Garden of Eden and the loss of immortality resulted.

Van Helmont describes the Archeus as an "aura vitalis seminum, vitae directrix." He says: "The chief Workman [Archeus] consists of the conjoining of the vital air, as of the matter, with the seminal likeness, which is the more inward spiritual kernel, containing the fruitfulness of the Seed; but the visible Seed is only the husk of this." Whichever way, he professed to visions throughout his life laying great stress upon them, He attributed his choice of medical profession to a conversation with the Archangel Raphael. Indeed, some of his writings describe the power of imagination as a celestial, and possibly magical, force. Though Van Helmont was sceptical of specific mystical theories and practices, he refused to discount magical forces as explanations for certain natural phenomena. He reflected this stance in his 1621 *De magnetica vulnerum curatione* (On the Magnetic Cure of Wounds) paper, which most likely contributed to, if not caused, his prosecution by the Inquisition.

For anyone in the mental health industry, it may be of interest that, Van Helmont like Hippocrates, was interested in the subject of human and animal eating habits and digestion. No self-respecting psychiatrist or psychologist will never stoop to pay a moment's attention to these in regards to clients' health. After all, good daily nutrition, vitamins and regular exercise balance the human, and perhaps rattus, mind. And i they keep the body in fine shape. All this could prove ruinous to their practices. Nevertheless, in his *Oriatrike* or *Physick Refined*, Van Helmont considered earlier ideas of great human thinkers like Hippocrates about what happened to food once digested. He concluded that it happened through the body's internal heat, a combustion system so to speak.

But if that were so, Van Helmont asked himself, how could cold-blooded animals live. He concluded that a chemical reagent or "ferment" within the body, such as inside the stomach, must be involved. This hypothesis propelled him into the idea that chaos generated in the stomach through such chemical reagent of ferment must be instrumental in digestion, which he termed "gas". With it, he established the science of pneumatic chemistry, the physical research of the properties of gases, their relationship to chemical reactions and the composition of matter. Gas is one of the four fundamental states of matter, the others being solid, liquid and plasma. His works, edited by his son Franciscus Mercurius Van Helmont, were published in 1648 by Lodewijk Elzevir in Amsterdam as *Ortus medicinae, vel opera et opuscula Omnia; Ortus medicinæ: Id est Initia physicæ inaudita. Progressus medicinae novus, in morborum ultionem, ad vitam longam* (The dawn of medicine: That is, the beginning of a new Physic. A new advance in medicine, a victory over disease, to promote a long life). Amsterodami: Apud Ludovicum Elzevirium, pp 526–527.

Let's not forget that he had all these contemplations about human life and living as well as the Church inquisition under his belt. We trust that Van Helmont's preoccupation with the state of mind of those less fortunate than himself and the recuperation of their minds by dunking and drowning was just that, a temporary pre-occupation brought on by temporary boredom, perhaps. Others, though, a short while later in the eighteenth century, had made a profession out of it. They grabbed increased control over those considered lunatics by confinement. Their confidence grew in science's ability to understand and cure insanity through more aggressive medical treatment than hydrotherapy. This opened the way for experimentation on inmates in the name of research to improve first their and then humanity's wellbeing. They brought with them both Darwin's survival of the fittest hypothesis and MK Ultra possibilities firmly anchored in mind.

Large psychiatric hospitals equipped with modern plumbing bringing water indoors in abundance were established in the 1800s facilitated the exercise. Hydrotherapy treatments blossomed, almost as if used as entertainment for the physicians, whose warped minds saw targeting the human body in a breathtaking variety of ways to treat mental illness they perceived in individuals as the humanistic way as benevolent rather than torturous. After all, as Austrian philosopher theologian, and social scientist Ivan Illich points out in his 2010 book, *Limits to Medicine: Medical Nemesis: The Expropriation of Health*:

> "Medicine is a moral enterprise and therefor inevitably given content to good and evil. In every society, medicine, like law and religion, defines what is normal, proper, or desirable. Medicine has the authority to label one man's complaint a legitimate illness, to declare a second man sick though he does not himself complain, and to refuse a third social recognition of his pain, his disability, and even his death. It is medicine which stamps some pain as "merely subjective," some impairment as malingering, and some deaths—though not others—as suicide." (ibid p. 45)

This is as applicable to the treatments applied to the purported ill in the eighteenth century onwards until the COVID-tyranny today.

Darwin had yet to lend his name to the idea of humanity's biological evolution by natural selection and survival of the fittest intertwined with human-equals-animal manipulable by science theory. Eventually, it would justify all neglect of morals and ethics in the name of science. What were Rush et al.'s simplest version of healing those in emotional or mental despair under the guise of benevolence still applied today in different versions? Holding inmates under water until they lost consciousness and, if revived, considered cured of their madness was one of their ways. Cold rinses, *days-long* baths, dunking and showering in all ways imaginable free-limbed, bound or gagged also served to treat and control the psychiatric ward incarcerated populace, (psych-history.weill.cornell.edu/osk_die_lib/hydrotherapy/Page3.html).

Dunking, showering or reclining patients into water without warning was also greatly enjoyed by administrators. Together with purging and bleeding in accordance with Benjamin Rush's hypotheses, these practices were saved for posterity in his book *The Medical Inquiries and Observations upon Diseases of the Mind*. This first systematic textbook on perceived mental illnesses published in the U.S. in 1812 served the country as *the* major such textbook for decades thereafter. Much of it doubtlessly reflected the knowledge Rush had picked up through his medical apprenticeship at psychiatric facilities in England and France upon completing his medical degree. After all, they had been vigorously applied in theory and practice after opening his private Philadelphia practice in 1769. That was when he began teaching as professor of chemistry, medical theory and clinical practice at the University of Pennsylvania. And it was when he began practicing at the Pennsylvania Hospital for the Insane, whose treatment philosophy became the nineteenth century standard for care of the mentally ill in the United States until Rush turned himself into the U.S. Mint treasurer in 1799.

Rush was convinced that irritation of the blood vessels in the brain caused mental disturbances, rather than a "possession of demons". This is why, in addition to the hot and cold baths, purging, bleeding and mercury treatments, one of his favourite remedies deemed beneficial to cure metal illness became his tranquilizer chair. It is pictured here once more to remind us that it is used in American prisons as well as in private homes to this very day. Why else would Walmart sell them, eh?

His other invention was the gyrator. Torpid patients were strapped and spun on this horizontal board to stimulate blood circulation. Such treatments for psychiatric patients became all the rage for the emotionally fragile and suffering, and those with mental ailments. This ought to include the administrators of such treatment clearly mentally ill themselves to apply such inhumane treatment to other human beings.

By the turn of the nineteenth century, physicians had homed in on the brain as the possible site of madness. Some psychopathic genius under the guise of benevolent intentions started directing cold showers onto only patients' heads to cool their "hot brains". They would avoid plunging the entire body into ice cold water, perhaps because it was more cost-efficient, as only one psychiatric staff member was required to pour water over the restrained patient's head (Britannica.com). To simplify the operation further, Scottish psychiatrist Sir Alexander Morison M.D. (1779 -1866) devised a douche resembling a pod, in which patients sat with the head poking out of a hole in the top. A stream of water would pour down onto their heads from above in a controlled stream or drip akin to Chinese water torture.

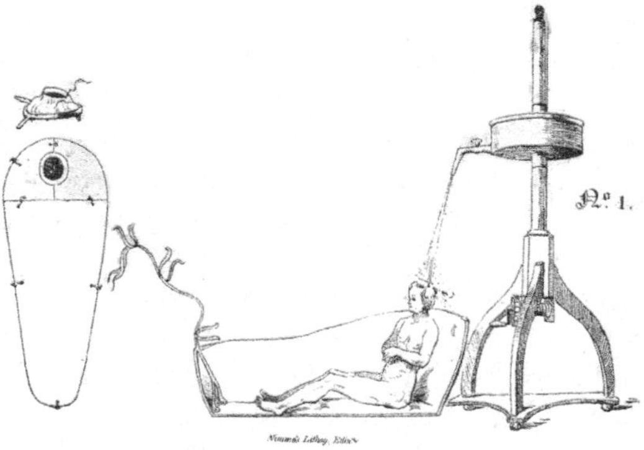

Alexander Morison's apparatus for giving the head douche (Morison Archives)

Belgian physician Joseph Guislan (1797 -1860) was a University of Ghent 1819 graduate and head of the psychiatric hospitals of Ghent. He wrote an internal regulation stipulating how to handle patients in a decent and therapeutically justified way. This basis of the law on psychiatric care would remain the framework for psychiatric care in Belgium until 1991. It designed a shower with its water reservoir set on an asylum's roof. The patient, bound to a chair and unable to see the attendant who would start the shower, would wait in suspense for what would happen next. "Shock and fear was part of the therapy," says Auckland University of Technology lecturer Stephanie Clare Cox. She has practiced as an occupational therapist in child development, as well as in child and adolescent mental health and rehabilitation. That observation is from her 2018 paper Showers: from a violent treatment to an agent of cleansing (https://journals.sagepub.com). Well, it still is, though in different ways.

By the 1850s, Guislan's showers had appeared in both asylums and prisons, but shower-related deaths led to their decline. Rather than being abandoned, however, the shower therapies were transformed to the use of warm water to wash prison and asylum populations. one of staff's favourite entertainments was to see patients' behaviors in baths lasting from just a few hours to days on end. Wrapping patients tightly in wet sheets, then wrapping another rubber sheet around them and letting them sweat for hours to see what happened was another cause of great amusement.

Needless to say, physicians found a variety of scientific-seeming explanations for such psychiatric treatment modalities. Among the explanations was that it relieved congestion in the brain and eliminated toxins that caused insanity. Joel T. Braslow, M.D., PhD, is professor of psychiatry and biobehavioral sciences and history at the University of California Los Angeles. His specialties to diagnose and treat mental illness include depression, anxiety disorders, substance abuse and schizophrenia. He relies on a mix of medications and psychotherapy for treatment and has been in private practice for more than 20 years. In his book *Mental Ills and Bodily Cures: Psychiatric Treatment in the First Half of the Twentieth Century* (University of California Press 1997) he went to great lengths to depict the extreme and brutal ways to heal the mind by treating the body even in the mid-1900s. He used California psychiatric hospital records, including many verbatim transcripts of patient interviews.

From them, Braslow reconstructed the world of mental patients and their doctors. It was a time when hydrotherapy had evolved as a benevolent alternative to sterilization, electroshock, lobotomy and surgical removal of the clitoris (clitoridectomy). Either way, they were, making an Orwellian mockery of the word "hospital". Hospitals were so named from the old French *hospital* or *ospital*", literally a shelter for the needy—a hostel, shelter, lodging. They were charitable institutions to house and maintain the needy and first recorded in the English language as an "institution for sick or wounded people" by the 1540s. Apparently, allowing mental health facility employees and their patients to speak for themselves, Braslow depicts psychiatrists' rationalization and justifications of the oft times dreadful consequences of their treatments as being in line with the biological consequences of the science of psychiatry. Doesn't that just befit humanism's doctrine of mankind equals blattas—cockroach, cani, lupus and so on and so forth ergo animal!

Mind you, the esteemed professor of psychiatry plays the theme of physical torture applied then as not terribly different from the way antidepressants are used by physicians today. In short, they seem to work, although no one knows precisely how they work on the neurochemistry level of the human brain, even though millions of people take them daily. "We see they have a certain effect on behavior and we see they have a biological effect and we try to argue backward," Braslow says. Nice. He gives no thought to their side effects, which count among them the destruction of all organs in the human body. Nor does he weigh in on the side effect of suicidal ideation, the fervent desire to kill Self, torturous in a different way than that applied in earlier centuries. He does find laudable that documenting patients' blood pressure, pulse, respiratory rate and differential blood count lent support to these measures of science - hydrotherapy, sterilization, electroshock, lobotomy and surgical removal of the clitoris.

Treatments involving physically restraining patients, whether in a shower or a tub, or wrapped in wet sheets, are excusable too. Physicians believed their treatments were genuinely and purely motivated by science, we are to believe. "There is this hazy borderline between what counts as therapeutic and what counts as control and discipline," Braslow brays, enlightening us that this inner tension is present in any therapy that treats mental illness, even modern ones. "We define psychiatric illness by failure to function in the world," he lectures, "so it is not surprising our interventions both act as social control and psychological control and also for comfort and consolation." I guess we can count our blessings that hydrotherapy, sterilization, electroshock, lobotomy and the surgical removal of the clitoris as genuine PTSD treatment modalities have thus far escaped the psychiatric cabal's attention, eh?

Mind you, those were Braslow's opinions in 1997. In 2021, 24 years later, he played a somewhat different tune. That was the year when the *Journal of the American Medical Association* (JAMA) his paper on April Fools' Day. He wrote it with John S. Brekke, associate dean of research and professor of social work research at the University of Southern California and Jeremy Levenson, BA. In his fieldwork, Levenson discovered that approximately one quarter of Los Angeles County's jail system's 18,000 daily inmates are diagnosed with mental illness. That makes it the largest de-facto provider of institutional psychiatric care in the United States. Their paper was entitled "Psychiatry's Myopia—Reclaiming the Social, Cultural, and Psychological in the Psychiatric Gaze." It documented a rather stunning reversal of opinion on his own profession. (Joel T. Braslow et al: *JAMA Psychiatry*. 2021;78(4): 349-350).

Braslow lamented that outcomes for individuals with serious mental illness (SMI) in the United States had worsened over the last 50 years. He lamented that folk suffering schizophrenia died 20 to 25 years sooner than those without SMI. He lamented that many were incarcerated or homeless because of their professed, wait for it, "psychiatric disease." He professes it all happened due to stigma, welfare state contraction and limited access to evidence-based treatments by mental health professionals.

Mind you, Levenson's 25% estimate of insanity is a fabulous improvement from Stephen Allen's 2008 study published in the *Journal of Health & Biomedical Law*, Vol. IV, No. 1 (2008): 153-1910 2008 entitled "Mental Health Treatment and the Criminal Justice System." It revealed that in fact 56% of the state prison inmate population are suffering from a mental health problem. It found that 61% had committed a violent offense and 25% had been incarcerated three or more times. Only a 34% chance exists that a state prisoner with a mental health problem receives any sort of mental health treatment since admission to prison. That is an oxymoron if there ever was one, as if the prisoner entered voluntarily and joyfully, says Allen. Indeed, thousands of U.S. citizens are caught in the vicious cycle of repeated incarceration because they suffer from mental illness without ever receiving the specialized treatment they would need to prevent their future incarceration.

From these numbers, we could deduce, if so inclined, that presently at least one quarter of L.A.'s population is psychiatrically dis-eased, some mental health professionals without a doubt among them. We could further deduce that the nation overall seems to have a mental health problem. Could this be related to the "Make the American Mind" scheme conceived in the late 1800s and set in motion by the early 1900s? In response to the public outcry arising from this stark reality, the Los Angeles County Board of Supervisors announced early in 2019 its intention to adopt a paradigm-changing mental health treatment-first approach to those who "need our help and not our punishment." (Levenson, Jeremy, Carceral Care: Jail Reform in LA County, supervised by Dr. Philippe Bourgois; grant: Wenner-Gren Foundation).

Levenson's research was financed with a grant from Swedish born Axel Lennart Wenner-Gren's (1881 -1961) foundation. Wenner-Gren was one the world's wealthiest men of his time due to majority shareholdings in Electrolux, the leading brand in both vacuum cleaner and refrigerator technology. His close friendship with chancellor and later Reichsmarschall (with seniority over all of Germany's armed forces officers) Hermann Wilhelm Göring (1893 -1946) didn't hurt, either. Levenson's research seeks to elucidate how therapeutic mental health principles may or may not be transforming carceral governance in L.A. County. He hypothesized that tensions between the incitement to care and the logic of punishment would offer insight into how ideologies of benevolence become entangled with practices of institutional and structural violence. The word carceral, by the way, refers to anything concerning prisons. What is and is not therapeutic for the human existing or non-existing soul lies completely in the eyes of the beholders. And, as we ourselves attempted to discover, most mental health educated career folk seem to doubt the presence of both a human soul and human consciousness. That it is the application of pharmapsychotherapy and biomedicine that creates irrational human behavior has yet to hit these self-declared geniuses. You see, it has yet to be sufficiently vocalized and enacted by simian, lupus, rattus et al., never mind by tortured beagles whose complaints were silenced in advance by slitting their vocal cords.

But that is not all. Braslow et al looked at recovery-based policies in California from the 1990s to present. They published the results in their winter 2021 paper "Recovery in Context: Thirty Years of Mental Health Policy in California" in *Perspectives in Biology and Medicine.* We understand that implementation of those policies reinforced many of the problems they were intended to solve (Joel T. Braslow, Sarah L. Starks, Enrico G. Castillo, John S. Brekke, Jeremy Levenson; Johns Hopkins University Press; Volume 64, Number 1, Winter 2021).

Their recovery model, considered to be a holistic, person-centered approach to mental health, was based on two premises:

1. It is possible to recover from a mental health condition.
2. The most effective recovery is patient-directed.

We are to understand that the recovery model of mental illness is often contrasted against what in the industry is known as the medical model (verywellmind.com). The recovery model takes a holistic view of a person's life as defined by the United States Substance Abuse and Mental Health Services Administration (SAMHSA). This agency lies within the U.S. Department of Health and Human Services (HHS). It defines recovery from mental disorders and/or substance use disorders as "a process of change through which individuals improve their health and wellness, live a self-directed life and strive to reach their full potential." Here again, their medical model, their personnel and their employees pretend that mental disorders have physiological causes requiring medications for treatment and healing. Thus, they make you believe that you are sick not from the injections pumped into you from birth, including COVID-19 vaccines now, but because you were created ill from the moment of conception due to God's design failure.

But never mind. Welfare reform, managed care and a growing belief in market forces and individual responsibility are a backdrop for new government-designed programs. These programs promised to produce cost savings by reducing homelessness, hospitalization and incarceration. Yet, reported outcomes from these programs were said to be based on flawed evaluations, leaning heavily on belief rather than on evidence. They proclaim a comprehensive, patient-centered approach. Yet, recovery's embrace of independence over long-term care and social support is said to have justified a system of care that systematically fails the sickest patients. It abandons them to the streets and jails, calling them hopelessly diseased. Very Well Mind proudly announces:

> "One of the major strengths of the recovery model is that it focuses on individual strengths and abilities rather than on deficits and pathologies. It places trust in the individual to know their own experience and to be able to take an active role in their treatment."

However, in line with the biomedicine paradigm, participants are drugged to the hilt, by the minute becoming more dis-eased and unable to think coherently. In their government-sanctioned and -sponsored, drug-induced misery, they are unaware of that fact. I know, as I experienced what Ativan alone produced in me.

In 2021, Braslow et al. used the term of "psychiatric disease" What was termed "diseases" had been known exclusively as medical conditions associated with specific signs and symptoms caused by external factors such as pathogens or by internal dysfunctions of body-parts. The immune system, for example, can produce a variety of different "diseases," including immunodeficiency, hyper-sensitivity, allergies and autoimmune disorders, which are all considered diseases. The mental health industry's learned academics, however, have now appropriated the term "disease". They are using it to hypothesize that stigma causes such "psychiatric diseases." Stigma be indicated in from critical race theory or social emotional learning necessity ideas. It might come from welfare state contraction or limited access to evidence-based treatments. Whatever the cause, they all seem to require the mental health cabal's personal interventions from kindergarten onwards. That's another avenue to fill its coffers. The industry's narrow visions leave it unable to grasp the fundamental aspects of how their subjects' experiences got them into the situations in which they find themselves, oftentimes induced by pharmacological drugging with Ritalin in schools (*Fallacy 1*).

Really? Yes, really. Is it to salvage the professions' right to be, to exist? It flourishes only due to the family units' systematic destruction since WWII. Team Braslow suggests their brethren remember that *humane* doctoring goes beyond prescribing psychotropic drugs for individuals' living with psychosis on the street in abject squalor or in jail shackles. Many of those living such nightmares on the streets do so because of their inhumane treatment. But that is not mentioned, so never mind. And what about those better off, the genuine PTSD journeyers and the otherwise emotionally rattled due to normally-to-be-expected life experiences they have yet to succeed in landing on skid row. And what about those aspiring to suicide due to their pharmaceutical mind-altering drug treatment combined with their cognitive behavioural therapy? Is their treatment alright, as it will get them to "the Matrix Soma state" sooner rather than later?

"We need frameworks for clinical practices that see patients' diseases not as we want them to be constituted, but rather as real, lived experiences inextricably embedded within social, psychological and biological contexts," bellow Braslow and team. Finally, they discover that patients' social and psychological alienation, impoverishment and violations of social norms are somewhat integral to psychiatric "disease". Bio-psychosocial and biological approaches perpetuate a system of mental healthcare that fails to address the fundamental realities of SMI in everyday life, they bray. Psychologist David L. Rosenhan (1929–2012) had earlier pointed this out. He is best known for the Rosenhan experiment, a study challenging the validity of psychiatry diagnoses published by the journal Science in 1973 under the title "On Being Sane in Insane Places,"

Psychiatrist Peter Breggin also pointed this out, as did Thomas Szasz, R.D. Laing and a very few others. They acted upon this principle for multitudes of decades, pointing out that mental illness was merely another example of how society labels and controls non-conformists. These behavioural psychologists have challenged psychiatry's fundamental reliance on unobservable phenomena. Take homosexuality, for example. It is no longer considered a mental illness since it became public knowledge that men buggering other men existed throughout human history. Thanks to Bernays' advertisement, it has been made more widely accepted by society.

Szasz is the very best-known social critic of psychiatry and its lack of both moral and scientific foundation, never mind ethics. He saw the craft as nothing other than a means of social mass control through scientism, bio-medicine and medication. He recalled how it had first been practiced on the Russians during the revolution and following Communist regime. At least 60 million people had been killed under it as portrayed by the writings of Aleksandr Isayevich Solzhenitsyn (1918–2008), and the COVID-19 behaviour as its latest example. In his books *The Myth of Mental Illness* (1961) and *The Manufacture of Madness* (1970), Szasz substantiates his lifelong belief, that mental illness is a figure of speech used for human problems in living and that, except for a few identifiable brain diseases, there are:

> "...neither biological nor chemical tests nor biopsy or necropsy findings for verifying any of the Diagnostic and Statistical Manual of Mental Disorders (DSM), the American Psychiatric Associations publication for their largely hallucinated mental disorder and disease classification."

Furthermore, Szasz insists in his writings that "mental illness" is nothing other than an expression, a metaphor. It describes an offending, disturbing, shocking, or vexing conduct, action or pattern of human behaviour. This is displayed and packaged under the wide-ranging term schizophrenia, as an "illness" or "disease". As he says:

> "If you talk to God, you are praying. If God talks to you, you have schizophrenia. If the dead talk to you, you are a spiritualist. If you talk to the dead, you are a schizophrenic."

Szasz noted that, while people behave and think in disturbing ways, and those ways may resemble a disease process, such as physical pain and deterioration. But he maintained that this does not mean they actually have a disease. Disease can mean only something people "have". Behaviour is what people "do." He says that diseases are "malfunctions of the human body, of the heart, the liver, the kidney, the brain" while "no behaviour or misbehaviour is a disease or can be a disease. That's not what diseases are."

He also maintained throughout his life that psychiatry actively and consistently obscures the difference between behaviour and disease in its quest to help or harm parties in conflicts. This is shown in how they treat genuine PTSD experiencers. He explains that by calling people *diseased*, psychiatry attempts to deny them their responsibility as moral agents in order to better control them. Therefore, he makes us aware to consistently pay attention to the power of language in both the mental health industry establishment and when maintaining the social order in small interpersonal affairs and in the wider social, economic and political spheres stating:

> "The struggle for definition is veritably the struggle for life itself. In the typical Western two men fight desperately for the possession of a gun that has been thrown to the ground: whoever reaches the weapon first shoots and lives; his adversary is shot and dies. In ordinary life, the struggle is not for guns but for words; whoever first defines the situation is the victor; his adversary, the victim. For example, in the family, husband and wife, mother and child do not get along; who defines whom as troublesome or mentally sick?... [the one] who first seizes the word imposes reality on the other; [the one] who defines thus dominates and lives; and [the one] who is defined is subjugated and may be killed."(Szasz, Thomas Stephen (1973). *The Second Sin*. Anchor Press).

This splendid, humane individual viewed himself as pro-psychiatry throughout his career, whilst vehemently opposing coercive psychiatry. Thus, he argued against involuntary mental health hospitalization and involuntary psychiatric treatment as we detailed in *Fallacy 1* in conjunction with my genuine PTSD treatments. On that note, I again maintain that only by taking the spiritual path can genuine PTSD be healed. That, in turn, necessitates conversations with God, the unseen, the heavenly Father, the Infinite Spirit, the Creator of all there is in all of Creation. Whatever or whomever it is we feel comfortable with, we need to pray to and converse with during meditations on life and living. Mention that to any of the mental health industry folk you are forced to deal with in your misery, and you will be certified insane in a heartbeat, I assure you, by the learned mental health society individuals' dealing with you. Their greatest life trauma thus far has been to lose their Mercedes Benz 400 to their wife in their divorce settlement.

Szasz' description of the political influence of medicine in modern societies, however, is summed up in Flexner's 1910 *Medical Education in the United States and Canada. A Report to the Carnegie Foundation for the Advancement of Teaching*. This report inspired, steeped in and permeated by faith in science and scientism, inaugurated and confirmed Szasz opinion:

> "Since theocracy is the rule of God or its priests, and democracy the rule of the people or of the majority, pharmacracy is therefore the rule of medicine or of doctors (T. Szasz, *Ceremonial Chemistry*, 1974)."

And it is pharmacracy we perceive in team Braslow's writings. It is pharmacraziness we see in the treatment of the genuine PTSD and other emotionally to lesser or larger degree injured and rattled human beings by psycho-the-rapists' "therapies". We see this mirrored in the COVID-19 jab edicts, house-arrests and incarcerations of the sheeple, while the mental health industry profits enormously from it. Braslow et al., thoroughly ignored Szasz's work if ever reading it. However, they did, by miracle or divine intervention, discover that it may be a good idea to, perhaps, address what matters most to clients during consultations, even writing the script for them. For instance, they proposed asking such questions as:

- if they feel a loss of meaning of life
- if impoverishment bothers them
- if sudden social isolation is a problem or a disabling symptom after such specialized career as a fire fighter, police officer, soldier and veteran or flight attendant

Mind you, the thought that threatening loss of livelihood may impact clients seemed never to have hit team Braslow, as it is mentioned nowhere. This is probably because money shortage seldom plays a part in their consideration, other than when it concerns their own lucrative incomes of annual median salary of $208,000 in 2019 (money.usnews.com/careers/best-jobs/psychiatrist/salary).

Thus, team Barslow did indeed conclude that the responsible way to treat the mentally diseased requires other than the exclusive psychotropic drug prescriptions method., They concluded that interacting factors such as family, living situations, social networks and other factors making patients' lives meaningful should be considered, as well. Perhaps then, they exclaimed, some of the forces that have subjected those affected with what the industry sees as serious mental illness (SMI) to some of the worst human rights- and public health crises could be undone. But they were unable or too cowardly to face that these human rights and health crises most oftentimes arose and were caused by the treatment bestowed upon the *diseased* in different ways of torture including the cognitive behavioural treatment throughout generations.

And Benjamin Rush, you ask, the prime inventor of such torture instruments throughout world history, the Russian gulags included? Well, his fervent psychopathic and sociopathic desires to adjudicate humans' emotional health through physical torture won him acclaim. His intensive labor in the field by his explorations of how best to traumatize and destroy human beings achieved his aspirations to the hilt in the U.S. population and worldwide. He accomplished this by way of the American Psychiatric Association (APA), with some 38,800 members the largest psychiatric organization in the world. His reward bestowed in 1965, was the title "Father of American Psychiatry", on him and rightfully so. The inhumane treatments of those emotionally disturbed in Rush's days set the tone for the brutal treatment of those they consider mentally diseased today. And that could be achieved only with humanity's destruction of its generational knowledge of its holistic self-healing abilities and the natural remedies in existence to heal itself. The Flexner's 1910 elite-financed report was the first step in that direction, and the COVID-19 tyranny is its result.

And what about brother Simon's organ transplantation forecast, you ask? Well, in the 1920s, when men felt things went awry down below and Viagra had yet to be invented, the thoroughly desperate, well-to-do He-man hopped a ship to Paris to see Russian Serge Samuel Abrahamovitch Voronoff (1866-1951). Voronoff was son of a cantonist and distiller, born into an Ashkenazi Jewish family in the village Shekhman in the Tambov Governorate ca. 420 km south-east of Moscow. Shortly before July 10, 1866, the date of his circumcision in a synagogue at age 18, Serge began to study medicine in France. In 1895, he became a French citizen. He was educated under French surgeon, biologist, eugenicist, transplantologist, thoracic surgeon and 1912 Nobel price recipient for physiology or medicine Alexis Carrel (1873-1944). Voronoff was twice elected USSR Academy of Sciences honorary member (1924 & 1927). He left France in 1906 to join Simon Flexner at the Rockefeller Institute of Medical Research for the rest of his life. Voronoff learned the surgical techniques of transplantation, perfecting the art between 1896 and 1910. He did this in Egypt, where there were unknown victims on which to study the retarding effects of castration on rejuvenation effects.

Returning to France, Voronoff concentrated on grafting testicles of purportedly already executed criminals into and onto millionaires. When demand outstripped supply, he turned to using monkey testicle tissue instead to graft on men's testicles. He promised that this treatment would get things humming again without apparently telling them about the monkey parts involved. Few of his patients who knew are said to have objected to toting around animal gonads as testicles.

On the other hand, many a patient died from the procedure. Personally, the technique brought him a great deal of money. Not that he lacked for money, having met Evelyn Bostwick (1872–1921) in 1917 and married her in 1920. She was the daughter of Jabez Abel Bostwick (1830–1892), one of Rockefeller's Standard Oil founding partners. It was her money, however, that allowed him to conduct his transplantation experiments on animals until 1920. That year, he transplanted his first official monkey gland into a human. Gender transplantation fiddling had by then become a vital part of biomedicine so favoured by Abe and Simon Flexner and visible in the elite wherever we look. We just have to look at the majority of female actresses, television anchors and talk host shows sporting prominent Adam's apples.

And how to escape from biomedicine, and from medicine as a whole, today? Illich conveys that its downfall —its nemesis—would be humanity's resistance to it medicinal remedies. He says this would occur only when we, the human beings with soul and consciousness, recover our own desire to care for our Self ourselves. We would have to prohibit physicians from doing the Bernays' indoctrinated "doctor knows best" treatments.

It would mean skipping that obsession and learning to trust ourselves again. It would mean dropping the victim status incorporated into trusting in the Other. It would mean developing the willingness, the discipline, the persistency, the determination and the willpower to use the gadget at our fingertips to research the symptoms ailing us. It would mean learning of and applying nature's remedies still known and available to heal us.

It would mean gathering and enhancing the confidence and trust in our own God-given human abilities to heal ourselves with ease, rather than adopting Israeli Harari's "you are arisen from pig, monkey, blattas, rattus, etc., which only biomedicine and the metaverse can help" view of humanity in all its colors, shapes, religions and nationalities. It would mean relearning to carry Self with honor, integrity and dignity throughout all life's adventures at all times, thereby regaining the confidence in Self and the willingness and joy to care for Self. It is either that or join the elites and the mental health cabal in fulfilling their most fervent desire. That would be joining the metaverse for our healing out of our free and God-given will. The metaverse is the iteration of the internet supporting persistent, for now only online, 3-D virtual environments through conventional personal computing and virtual and augmented reality headsets.

The choice is ours. We can opt for relearning to heal ourselves, however, if we stay away from the COVID jab, even if it gathers steam among the laity, us, the piss-ons, the deplorables. Illich hypothesizes that the legal, political and institutional agencies and institutions will have little choice but to recognize our right to self-determination. That, in turn, will foist limits and curtail physicians' power and monopoly. This is especially true for those in the mental health industry, who view themselves as gods and indeed possess the power to destroy anyone they choose. It is only by willingly and knowingly taking back the enormous God-given power we possess at the first breath of life that we can prevail. This power has been systematically diminished with the first torturous injection at the moment of our birth through biomedicine's destruction. Only by talking it back can we recover from the onslaught inflicted on us by the elite. beginning with Flexner's documented intentions and its destruction derby of holistic medicine that followed. We can win this war on humanity, and live healthy, joyous lives again.

Once we build up the gumption to straighten our backs and say "No more. With God's help I will heal myself," their game is over. But until then, you assist in your own destruction with almost every breath you take or do not take. If you wear a mask, you inhale your own exhaust at every step you take. This self-inflicted biomedicine of your own soul and body is a reflection of your own stupidity. Never mind the COVID jab you took as the animal they consider you to be. What did Austrian researcher, teacher, artist and writer Rudolf Joseph Lorenz Steiner (1861–1925) say about our situation?

He spent his life enlarging and deepening the concept of what it is to be human by linking us to the cosmic. He linked the past to the future, for self-development and conscious evolution. He published his book *The Philosophy of Freedom: Or The Philosophy of Spiritual Activity A Modern Philosophy of Life Developed by Scientific Methods* 16 years before the Flexner brothers spewed forth their report for human health's future in their 1910 Flexner Report. Steiner write:

> "There are two fundamental problems in the life of the human mind, to one or other of which everything belongs that is to be discussed in this book. One of these problems concerns the possibility of attaining to such a view of the essential nature of man as will serve as a support for whatever else comes into his life by way of experience or of science, and yet is subject to the suspicion of having no support in itself and of being liable to be driven, by doubt and criticism, into the limbo of uncertainties.
>
> "The other problem is this: Is man, as voluntary agent, entitled to attribute freedom to himself, or is freedom a mere illusion begotten of his inability to recognise the threads of necessity on which his volition, like any natural event, depends?"

Make up your mind, but do it fast. Beware if you have engaged or are engaging in biomedicine therapy with your perhaps well-meaning but badly educated treating physician. You know, the one you trust with your life? Before even conceiving the thought, make the effort to investigate. You might be able to return your physical and spiritual health about all by yourself, all on your own, as the time for you loosing your soul might be approaching fast.

Have you forgotten what is says in 1 Corinthians 6:19?

"What? know ye not that your body is the temple of the Holy Ghost *which is in you*, which ye have of God, and ye are not your own?"

25

WHAT IS BIOMEDICINE?

The *Stanford Encyclopedia of Philosophy* tells us that biomedicine, despite its simple name, is a very large and complex issue. It is a framework, we read, a set of philosophical commitments, a global institution with power dynamics woven into Western culture and more. Biomedicine is the branch of medicine that applies to its medical research certain principles. These are considered the fundamental truth or proposition serving as foundation for its systems of belief, behavior or chain of reasoning of biology and biochemistry. And it is practiced on us, humanity.

The biomedical sciences in themselves are made up of the following disciplines:

- cytology
- histology
- biochemistry
- haematology
- immunology
- microbiology
- transfusion services

There is bio-medicine nomenclature for how global institutions see their relations between biological sciences and medicine. Thus, biomedicine is the umbrella theoretical framework for most health science and health technology work done in academic and government settings. Western medical practices and its surrounding healthcare infrastructure is principally biomedical.

Modern clinical medicine (biomedicine) went arm in arm with science and the political weight of these professions. They began to dominate U.S. healthcare provision for its citizenry with the 1910 Flexner Report. It had huge political relevance to the controllers of U.S. society, as well as economic implications for the common wealth and wellbeing of its people. You need look no further than President Barrack Obama's 2010 *Affordable Care Act*. That law put in place what at that time was considered comprehensive reforms to improve access to affordable health coverage for everyone in the land, as well as protecting consumers from abusive practices of insurance companies (Grant Gillet: "Medical science, culture, and truth"; *Philosophy, Ethics, and Humanities in Medicine* Volume 1, Article number: 13 (2006))

Holistic medicine had by the mid-1900s largely fallen by the wayside, thanks to Rockefeller et al.'s take-over of the educational system and practitioners' vilification as charlatans. The result is that all national and international health-related corporations nowadays are predominantly biomedical in orientation. They offer only biomedical resources and aids as treatment sources and therapies for those seeking assistance. That includes the genuine PTSD journeyers in search of help from the mental health branch of biomedicine's innumerous branches.

And what are biomedicine's philosophical commitments mentioned by *Stanford*? Well, they seem to be fluctuating in accordance with the interpreter's individual personal ideas. That is no different than everything else within the art and science of the mental health craft, in particular. But here is a 2014 interpretation by Pamela M. Allen and Sharyn Clough, uttered in their article "Philosophical commitments, empirical evidence, and theoretical psychology" published by *Theory & Psychology*, a fully peer-reviewed bi-monthly forum for theoretical and meta-theoretical analysis in psychology:

> "The philosophical or theoretical commitments informing psychological research are sometimes characterized, even by theoretical psychologists themselves, as non-empirical, outside the bounds of methodological consideration, and/or non-rational. We argue that this characterization is incoherent. We illustrate our concern by analogy with problematic appeals to Kuhn's work that have been influential in theoretical psychology. Following the contemporary pragmatist tradition, we argue that our philosophical/theoretical commitments are part of our larger webs of belief, and that for any of these beliefs to have meaning their content must be informed by our practical engagement with the world, i.e., they are based on empirical evidence, broadly construed. It is this empirical basis that allows us to recognize our commitments at all and rationally to assess and criticize them when necessary. We conclude by demonstrating a rational assessment of the philosophical/theoretical commitments underlying a recent study in the social psychology of religion." (https://journals.sagepub.com)

Wanting to have their cake and eat it too? It perfectly fits the mental health industry in its entirety—all bullshit, as so delightfully pointed out by top psychiatrist Allen Frances in 2010.

So biomedicine, this biological medicinal framework, this set of philosophical commitments, this globally installed network of ways and means to treat of humanity's ailments, with its enormous power dynamics tightly woven into Western culture, is now considered the umbrella under which most health-science and health-technology work is done in all academic and government settings. This, the result of the one-room Laboratory of Hygiene on Ellis Island in 1887 blooming into 27 National Institutes of Health (NIH). The lobbyist for biomedicine's multiple branches helped set NIH policies, planning, managing, coordinating and dictating the programs and activities of all its institutes and centers.

In addition, the NIH Office of Director OD also directs the Offices of AIDS, Behavioral and Social sciences and Strategic Coordination research, Disease Prevention and Research, Women's Health and other unspecified offices (nih.gov/about-nih/what-we-do/nih-almanac/nih-organization). The U.S. Department of Health and Human Services is the official federal focal point for human health research through the NIH. It has oversight of the whole apparatus, including everything that has to do with biomedicine.

On the National Center for Biotechnology Information website we learn that the goal of basic biomedical research is to – take a deep breath – provide comprehensive and detailed understanding of the mechanisms that underlie the development and normal function of humans and other living organisms and thereby gain insights into the pathological and pathophysiological mechanisms that cause their disease. A detailed understanding of these mechanisms and pathways, we are told, is essential for identifying potential targets for rational therapeutic interventions and for disease prevention (Research Training in the Biomedical, Behavioral, and Clinical Research Sciences; https://www.ncbi.nlm.nih.gov/books/NBK56989). It is therefore, we are assured, that the scope of basic biomedical research is broad, ranging from the study of single atoms and molecules to the complex functions and behaviors of the whole organism.

We are also enlightened that the landscape of biomedical research has been revolutionized during the last 20 years. Major advances in technology and in scientists' understanding of fundamental aspects of cell and organ function have led this revolution. The impact of this work on human health has also been influential. Genomic biology is now a fundamental aspect of research strategies and is leading us to "personalized medicine." Meanwhile, quantitative biology has become a key part of biomedical graduate education, so as to be able to handle the massive influx of data generated by these new technologies. There have been astounding discoveries and advances in understanding of the roles of different populations of RNA molecules in cellular regulation and as research tools soon to be used as biologic interventions in human disease.

Overall, biomedicine operates on the mandate that human bodies are solely understood as a composition and collection of subsidiaries. These are less important than but related to its parts and processes. It also operates on the mandate that human health phenomena can be understood in terms of physical and biochemical occurrences in entities and processes. It assumes that experimental techniques developed in laboratories are the preferred means of acquiring and assessing health-related knowledge and healing processes. Humans are therefore to be used as subjects of experimentation, as we see by COVID and its purported offspring.

Its behavioral research into the human psyche was already talked about in *Fallacy 1* and will be further discussed in the next chapter. A similar continuum as with humans' physical construction is applied within the craft and artistry of neurosciences. It begins with basic neurochemistry and molecular neurobiology through to cognitive neuroscience and biological psychology and behavior. Overlaps among these areas will inevitably increase as the genetic and environmental influences affecting the formation and function of the human nervous system are better understood.

And please, should you suffer from the illusion that these discoveries are is all new and delightful, free yourself. According to Giora Kaplan of the Gertner Institute for Epidemiology and Health Policy Research in Tel Aviv, Israel, they have been ongoing at least since the 1920s. That's when the word "biomedical' already appeared in the writings of American and British authors, followed a decade later by 'biomedicine' or 'bio-medicine' (Giora Kaplan: Biomedicine, in Encyclopedia of Social Measurement, 2005; sciencedirect.com). It took until 1985, however, for the biomedicine label to become official. You can thank two unnamed American anthropologists and epidemiologists working for the U.S. Centers for Disease Control and Prevention. They announced that a new territory in the heartland of their learned society, the *Domain of Biomedicine*, had been entered to replace what since Flexner's report had variously been termed "scientific medicine," "cosmopolitan medicine," "Western medicine," "allopathic medicine" or simply "medicine."

Let us note, though, that critics both within and outside of the medical community have expressed that the field of biomedicine is too narrowly focused in its research and practice. They note that it is officially guided by a logic that requires all meaningful data to be reducible to a single-level physicalist vocabulary, in principle. Therefore, they charge that this part of medicine will always be beyond the reach of its scientific capabilities. For example, to recognize the placebo effect as being psychoactive as opposed to biochemical would violate the foundational premise that recognizes the primacy of the body to the exclusion of mind, as no empirical first evidence can be presented.

From its very beginning, the terms "biomedicine" and "biomedical research" referred to the kind of medicine associated with experimentation and laboratories. They excluded reports by physicians in relation to their experiences with sick patients. Instead, *Dorland's Illustrated Medical Dictionary* clarified in its 33rd edition that biomedicine is a "clinical medicine based on the principles of physiology and biochemistry rather than reflecting expertise physicians gained through their encounters with patient in their clinical observations (Dorland, 1923: 172)." *Dorland's* has been trusted by generations of healthcare personnel at every professional level as the most comprehensive medical dictionary. It is considered an ideal resource for medical and allied health professionals, students in all healthcare disciplines, medical writers, editors, transcriptionists, coders, researchers and attorneys, as well as those working in government agencies and healthcare management.

Needless to say, opinions on this issue differ.

Two experts spewed forth in unison that the word "biomedicine" really means "biologics." Those experts were professor of anthropology, bioethics, nursing and psychiatry Atwood D. Gaines and adjunct professor in anthropology at the private research Rice University of Houston, Texas, Robbie Davis-Floyd, PhD Gaines was sitting as faculty in the Ethnic Studies and Women and Gender Studies Programs at the private research Case Western Reserve University and its Schools of Medicine and Nursing at the time. They were studying the anthropology of reproduction, transformational models in childbirth and powerful medications that can be made of tiny components like sugars, proteins, DNA and biomedicine as a cultural system. It was in 2003, in the *Encyclopedia of Medical Anthropology in Yale: Human Relations Area Files* under the title "On Biomedicine" that they made this observation. But what is biologics, we wonder?

Well, biologics are powerful drugs used as medications. They are made of tiny components like sugars, proteins and DNA. Or they can be produced out of whole cells or tissues or whatever comes in handy, it seems. That includes all sorts of living sources, such as human fetus, egg embryos, mammals, birds, plants, bacteria, insects and cockroaches, used as protein source for human consumption, for example.

Some examples of biologics and biological medications developed from blood, proteins, viruses, and living organisms are:

- Enbrel (etanercept)
- Botox, the neurotoxin protein used in cosmetic treatments
- Lantus, (insulin glargine), long-acting forms of human insulin
- Humira and Enbrel, prescribed to treat rheumatoid arthritis (RA) and other autoimmune diseases, such as psoriasis and Crohn's disease,

Other biologics include vaccines, cell and gene therapies, tissues used for transplants to purportedly prevent, treat a range of common and rare human dis-eases of all manners.

Duke University Professor Emeritus of Psychiatry and Behavioural Sciences JRT Davidson also weighed in. In his 1994 article "Biological therapies for posttraumatic stress disorder: an overview", he noted that PTSD involved people's psychobiological reaction. He concluded that they would therefore respond well to pharmaceutical mind-altering drugs, all of which, we noted in *Fallacy 1* are detrimental to both mind and body as documented also by Dr. Jordan Peterson's experience (https://www.psychiatrist.com/wp-content/uploads/2021/02/11213_biological-therapies-posttraumatic-stress-disorder.pdf).

Whereupon the venerable professor states that two particular possible roles for medication in treating PTSD existed. One would seal over the patients' pain and distress, eliminating PTSD symptoms so that patients could resume normal life. The other would drug them to uncover the pain, in order to help resolve the traumatic experience. In the latter approach, medication is used as an adjunct to help patients confront the trauma and work through any resulting distress. Drug them to the hilt, the brightest of the herd, and see what happens. This is seemingly the leitmotiv in operation by biological mental health experiments conducted on ignorant genuine PTSD journeyers in the name of humans' welfare.

Be it as it may, in general, physicians, neuroscientists, biologists and psychiatrists seem to view our minds and brains as mis-programmed machines in need of corrections in whatever way depending on who's judging. The correction to heal us from our innate impairments, they assure, is achievable through biomedicine. That their assertions and assumptions involve the cut-slash-and burn technique so loved and carried forth by physicians since the mid-eighteenth century is beside the point, almost. Biomedicine has the power to create the peaceful and harmonious hunger game society. That is due to its power to eradicate our ability to think independently, as it can reprogram us by genetic, electronic and chemical means. At the same time and with the same means, it can further destroy generational knowledge by eliminating large numbers of those they consider useless eaters. Wit the culling of the elderly in old folk homes in New York state and in Europe by way of COVID 19 injections. But has yet to surface in the masses' consciousness.

The next step for those hitherto controlling us is to connect us through biomedicine and biologics by chips and implants with AI gadgets. Then, they will be able to and download on us whatever they dream up as appropriate for their amusement, whilst watching with fascination our demise as God's creation. You think I'm off my rocker? They won't do that? Think again! It's on the horizon, with DeepMind Technologies, a British artificial intelligence and research laboratory established in 2010, having led the way. Based in London, England, with research centres in Canada, France and the United States, it became a wholly owned subsidiary of Google's parent company Alphabet Inc. in 2015. DeepMind has created a neural network that learns how to play video games in a fashion similar to that of humans. It has created a computer that mimics the human brain's short-term memory, the capacity for holding, but not manipulating, a small amount of information in mind for a short period of time.

DeepMind made headlines in 2016, when its AlphaGo program beat the then South Korean professional go player world champion Lee Se-dol (1983-), which was the subject of a documentary film. Meanwhile, its AlphaZero program made headlines not only for beating the most powerful programs playing go, chess and shogi (Japanese chess), but for beginning to use reinforcement learning after a few days of play against itself. By 2020, DeepMind had made significant advances in the problem of protein folding, the inference of the three-dimensional structure of a protein from its amino acid sequence. It was able to predict its secondary and tertiary structure from its primary one, one of the most important goals pursued by computational biology. This knowledge is paramount to design biological drugs and novel enzymes reminding us of COVID injections and booster recipients' shedding of spike proteins, eh?

This inspires paranoia, perhaps? But we have no time for such luxury, as we rather want to discover what South African born engineer, entrepreneur and business magnate Elon Musk (1971–) is up to. The founder, CEO and Chief Engineer at SpaceX, CEO and Product Architect of Tesla Inc, has been subject of highly publicized criticism and controversies due to his unorthodox or unscientific stances and enterprises. So what does he do in the name of biomedicine and competition with Deep Mind? How does he leverage his estimated net worth of around US$304 billion as of January 2022? In 2015, he inspired Samuel A. Altman (1985–) to join him in co-chairing OpenAI, an artificial intelligence, for-profit research company. Its only goal is to advance digital intelligence in a way that is more likely to benefit *the advancement of mankind*, by together pledging a mere US$1 billion.

Chicago-born Altman, another wiz-kid, began his career as an entrepreneur in 2005 at the age of 19. His first company was Loopt, a location-based social networking mobile application. Despite being when Facebook and Twitter were about to dominate the social media platform, his company raised more than $30 Million in venture capital (startuptalky.com). In 2011, he joined the American technology start-up accelerator company Y Combinator, founded in March 2005, part-time. Taking giant strides in the company, he was named president by partner and co-founder Paul Graham. Soon thereafter, his first batch of investments included his own company, Loopt. The total Y Combinator net worth is approximately $65 Billion in 2022, give or take a few million, its top companies valued at more than $300 billion in 2021.

The artificial intelligence (AI) research laboratory OpenAI consists of the for-profit corporation OpenAI LP and its parent company, the non-profit OpenAI Inc. Musk resigned from the board in February 2018, leaving Altman in charge as CEO, but remaining a donor. Bill Gates joined the trio in 2019 by investing the piddly amount of US$1 billion in OpenAI LP from the profits of Microsoft, the company he and Paul Allen founded in 1975.

Musk did not sit on his laurels, though. By 2016, he had already co-founded the Neuralink Corporation, a neuro-technology company developing implantable brain-machine interfaces (BMIs). These would be used as medical and healthcare devices with intelligence amplification and add-ons connecting to brain chips. The purpose was to help us miss-designed and produced peons to become the superhuman they envision. Artificial general intelligence (AGI) would then, according to DeepLink gadget-creators, begin designing an AI more powerful than itself.

Those still able to think coherently among humanity despite engineered mass information and resulting psychosis reigning most of the world's herd, now question if we already have reached technological singularity. That term refers to the hypothetical point in time at which technological growth becomes uncontrollable and irreversible, which would result in unforeseeable changes to human civilization. Artificial Super Intelligence would emerge from AGI, evolving further into the deep future than we, God's creation, wish to go (warroom.org: Transhumanism).

In fact, if human consciousness were to become digitized and uploaded into a metaverse simulation merging with AI, it would create a hybrid consciousness. It would then spread across the cosmos, according to a report by transhumanism War Room reporter Joe Allen. This in turn would result in the Matrioshka brains and Dyson Spheres hosting humanity's consciousness in a cosmic simulation network. The Matrioshka brain is a hypothetical mega-structure of immense computational capacity. It is powered by a Dyson sphere, a hypothetical mega-structure completely encompassing a star and capturing a large percentage of its power output. This was proposed in 1997 by American film director and screenwriter Robert J. Bradbury (1956–2011). Ironically, he died suddenly on the night of February 26–27, 2011, of a massive hemorrhagic stroke, the sudden bleeding of an artery into the brain.

All of this research and experimentation is, of course, portrayed as being done in the name of biomedicine to boost human health. However, its central goal seems to be to merge human minds with machines to create an intimate human-AI symbiosis. A symbiosis is any relationship or interaction between two dissimilar organisms. The boundaries between intelligent machines and human beings will blur to create a new paradigm, the Harari-envisioned Homo Deus human 2.0. It involves biomedicine's and biologic's means, inevitably leading into trans-humanism. It will result in "absolutize technology," meaning modes of absolutizing what is merely relative "make or treat something as absolute, final, unchangeable" to a point that human enhancement is even overwhelmed through AI self-innovation.

Trans-humanism seems difficult to fathom by our own, humane, imaginary powers. But certain aspects of its machinations might penetrate the way we understand innovation and human empowerment. It has been addressed in a round-about way for a few centuries in such schools of thought as utopianism, humanism, enlightenment, positivism and Darwinism, and the concept of post-human is easily associated with the Nietzschean term of "superhuman" (https://philarchive.org/archive/IUGTBH). But it was English evolutionary biologist and humanist internationalist Julian Huxley (1887–1975) who seeded the belief that the human species can and should transcend itself "by realizing new possibilities" of and for human nature. Huxley was a leading figure in the mid-twentieth century evolutionary synthesis uniting Darwinian natural selection with Mendelian genetics.

The Mendelian genetics are named after Austrian monk Gregor Mendel's experiments with pea plants. He conducted them in his monastery's garden. At that time, most people believed character traits and body shapes were due to blending parental 'essences', much like how mixing blue and yellow paint produces a green color (knowgenetics.org). Mendel, however, believed that heredity was the result of discrete units of inheritance. He felt that every single unit, or gene, was independent in its actions in an individual's genome, and the inheritance of a trait depended on passing these units on. For any given trait a person inherits one gene from each parent so that the person has a pairing of two genes. We now understand the alternate forms of these units as 'alleles'. If the two alleles that form the pair for a trait are identical, then the individual is said to be homozygous and if the two genes are different, then the individual is heterozygous for the trait. Based on his pea plant studies, Mendel proposed that traits were always controlled by single genes. Modern studies reveal that most traits in humans are controlled by multiple genes and environmental influences, and they do not necessarily exhibit a simple Mendelian pattern of inheritance (see "Mendel's Experimental Results").

So Julien Huxley believed that science provided the best means of realizing meaning in the world because it explained and clarified forces once dark and mysterious. And he provided insights into human psychology based on that belief. This improved both us and our world and revealed the vast immensity, history and future of the cosmos. So, he felt that we could expedite humanity's cultural evolution with our scientific knowledge; "In man evolution could become conscious," he announced, as if we, the herd, were unconscious beings. Almost needless to say, then, that Huxley was also a leading figure in the eugenics movement using the oft-recited argument: "No one doubts the wisdom of managing the germ plasm of agricultural stocks, so why not apply the same concept to human stocks?" (Allen p. 221)

To him, evolutionary biologists were agents, whose purpose in life was to impose their principles to guide human evolution. This included, we assume, the herd's culling and its physical and mental rearrangement. Man is that part of reality, he says, in which and through which the cosmic process has become conscious and begins to comprehend itself. Man's supreme task is to increase that conscious comprehension and apply it as fully as possible to guide the course of events. In other words, man's role is to discover his destiny as an agent of the evolutionary process in order to fulfill it more adequately (Julian Huxley, *Religion without Revelation*, London: Max Parrish, 1959, 236). And to fulfill that premise by hook or by crook is biomedicine's role.

Julian Huxley was a noted humanist who viewed God as hypothesis constructed by man and the god hypothesis to be scientifically tenable preferring the idea of a "humanist evolution-centered religion." He discounted the bona fide religious and mystical experiences and feelings of divinity that people have as more an outgrowth of nature than supernatural in origin. He found that abandoning belief in God brought him an enormous sense of relief (Huxley, 1964b). By1957, in his book *New Bottles for New Wine* he was skipping all religious overtones. Instead, he had already presented the idea that the universe would become conscious of itself and in human beings in accordance with Darwin's survival of the fittest and natural selection hypothesis. This would require culling the herd on a regular basis (https://newworldencyclopedia.org/entry/Julian_Huxley).

His vision of evolution also craved the replacement of humans' traditional religious views and proclaimed destiny. The historical functions, to cope with human ignorance and fear, and to maintain social and spiritual stability in these times of change, were to cease. Religions were now to develop ways and means to advance the ruling class's, plans of the brave new world. They would invent a new belief system akin to a religion that centered on the idea of personal fulfillment to better use their own knowledge - the knowledge gained through biomedicine of how to better manipulate and control the herd. (Julian Huxley, "The Creed of a Scientific Humanist" in *The Meaning of Life*, ed. E.D. Klemke (Oxford: Oxford University Press 2000, 81))

In the world of evolutionary biology and medicine, things took off from there. There seemed to be a discrepancy between two trains of thought. One was human biological advances through artificial technological enhancements concocted by evolutionary biologists' technological innovations. The other was their so fervently loved biological evolution Darwinian style governed by the natural selection process and trans-humanism. The term "trans-humanism" itself was invented by Huxley, as it extracts its ideological vigour from those representations of perceived reality (Ion Iuga: Transhumanism Between Human Enhancement and Technological Innovation, https://philpapers.org/rec/IUGTBH 2016).

The theory of biological evolution still exerts influence on most of trans-humanists' theories and their notions of human enhancement Perhaps this explains the undertakings and views of such promoters of biomedicine and biologics as American cognitive and computer scientist and researcher of AI Marvin Lee Minsky (1927 -2016). He was co-founder of the Massachusetts Institute of Technology's AI laboratory. And Austrian Hans Peter Moravec (1948-), author of several texts on AI and philosophy, and adjunct faculty member at Carnegie Mellon University's Robotics Institute in Pittsburgh. He is known for his work on robotics, artificial intelligence and for his writings on the impact of technology on humanity. And American inventor and futurist Raymond Kurzweil (1948-). He is involved in optical character recognition (OCR), text-to-speech synthesis and speech-recognition technology and electronic keyboard instruments.

American Vernor Steffen Vinge (1944-) is professor emeritus of mathematics and computer science at San Diego State University. He is author of novels and novellas and perhaps the first to present a fictional cyberspace. The expression dates back to the first decade of the Internet and refers to the online world as a world "apart" and distinct from everyday reality. In 1983, he added the term "technological singularity" in his 1993 essay "The Coming Technological Singularity" (Vinge 1993, 2013), stating:

> "We will soon create intelligences greater than our own. When this happens, human history will have reached a kind of singularity, an intellectual transition as impenetrable as the knotted spice-time at the center of a black hole, and the world will pass far beyond our understanding. This singularity, I believe, already haunts a number of science-fiction writers."

Kurzweil picked up the theme in his book, *The Singularity is Near*. He opined that humanity's future, or just the herd's future, perhaps, will be irreversibly changed by the astonishing rate of technological progress. The Singularity ultimately presented the fusion of our biological existence with technology, so there would be no distinction between human and machine, or between physical and virtual (Kurzweil 2005, 25). Singularity will enable us to transcend our body and brain limitations, and we will have full power on, or over, our destiny (Kurzweil 2005, 24). It is only a matter of time, he says, until we (the scientists, we gather) find the optimal combination between human intelligence and computer superiority in terms of speed, accuracy and fast access to humanity's memory. Once they are integrated in the same human body, the moment will mark a tremendous leap, he enlightens, without sharing its direction with us (Kurzweil 1999, 15). A leap to where? Upwards or downwards, so to speak, into hell or heaven? We are presently in the preliminary phases of the transition, he tells us, but the exponential growth will reach the curve prior to the stage of an explosive increase. This, says Kurzweil, will be immediately followed by a perfect vertical direction. He says nothing about COVID injections perhaps aiding and abetting the vertical take-off? (Kurzweil 2005, 25).

A Transhumanist Declaration for the vertical leap event is in place already, with two premises:

- the inevitable and ultimate impact of science and technology in the future
- the assumption of enlargement of human potential through overcoming limitations like ageing, cognitive shortcomings, limitations on human and artificial intellects, un-chosen psychology, suffering and confinement to the planet earth

Its leitmotiv? "Defending our right to use reason and technology to be better than well." (Max More and Natasha Vita-More, 54-55; https://itp.uni-frankfurt.de/~gros/Mind2010/transhumanDeclaration.pdf).

Human intelligence is considered by Kurzweil to be the work of billion years of evolution. In his invaluable opinion, it is the reason a new type of intelligence will emerge to compete with and exceed human intelligence and the most important novelty ever shaping humanity's history. The transformation will have deep implications in all human activities, he proclaims, including labor, learning, governance, war and the way we (he and/or all of us?) conceive ourselves (Kurzweil 1999, 16).

No kidding. And what are the premises and main concepts of trans-humanism in three sentences?

1. Human nature is the subject of innovation and transformations.

2. Technology is seen as a continuation of human evolution.
3. By way of consequence, a deep symbiosis between human and machine up to the emergence of post-human entities will occur.

But let's point out, only if human beings play along with the biomedicine and biologics therapies and applications so wonderfully well presented to anyone insane enough to see a medical physician of any genre including the mental health art and science practicing mental health professional. And only if one allows the Self to be handed from one specialist to the next for more examinations and pharmaceutical, biological concoctions resulting in slow but inevitable physical and emotional destruction of both body and mind.

The ethical aspects of purportedly therapeutic biomedicine, biological and trans-humanism applications, never mind moral or spiritual considerations, are seemingly given little to no thought. Kurzweil, the leading edge on humanity's future as AI machine, has at least contemplated the issue somewhat in his 1999 book, *The Age of Spiritual Machines: When Computers Exceed Human Intelligence.* However, he apparently gave it not an iota of consideration as to why he or any of his human brethren thinks the way he thinks and conceives the ideas he conceives, and if he has or does not have consciousness, never mind a soul.

And most of us peons, the herd, have at least somewhat been indoctrinated for generations into the idea of the Big Bang and the Darwinian theory of evolution. The narrative explains how man evolved from cockroaches in a billion-year drama leading to human intelligence. God and everything else having a play in our creation is hogwash, however, in Kurzweil and cohort's view of life. Furthermore, they dream that the creation of the greater-than-human AI intelligence will dispel our notion of being the most intelligent creatures on earth. This realization shocks us to the core and profoundly influences our thinking, our lives, and thus ourselves. It would lead to a number of philosophical questions, such as whether machines are conscious. Or if people scan their brain through a "noninvasive scanning technology" and download it to their personal computer, would they be the same as when they entered the machine? (Summary of Ray Kurzweil's *The Age of Spiritual Machines: When Computers Exceed Human Intelligence*; https://reasonandmeaning.com).

In his book outlining his vision for how technology will progress during the twenty-first century, Puppet Master Kurzweil defines the human-computer interface spiritual experience as "a feeling of transcending one's everyday physical and mortal bounds to sense a deeper reality." "Just being—experiencing, being conscious—is spiritual, and reflects the essence of spirituality," he says. This begs the question as to why he needs to interface with a computer to reach that state of his existence? He believes, however, that it will be computers who will "claim to be conscious, and thus to be spiritual." He concludes that "twenty-first-century machines" will go to church, meditate, and pray to connect with this spirituality' All this will rely on brain implants and brain scanning, as we are not a collection of atoms, but patterns that can manifest in different mediums at different times. Of Unitarian upbringing, known for rejecting the doctrines of original sin, predestination and the Bible's infallibility, Kurzweil leaves us to guess how self-awareness and consciousness arise from mere matter. He seems to feel that "all of these views are correct when viewed together, but insufficient when viewed one at a time," at the same time admitting his views to be contradictory and making little sense. Really?

Is he merely confirming that, without human co-operation, there will be no AI-human interface and the issue of if and when AI computers reach consciousness will never arise?

And what about those who hold religious views or life philosophies that reject prolonging life by mechanical means and AI methodologies? How should they react to brain-computer interface (BCI) technology, a computer-based system that acquires brain signals, analyzes them and translates them into commands? What about those who do not want to have their mental processes decoded or have their brain mechanisms underlying their intentions, emotions and decisions manipulated by AI? What about those who are too ill to protest when they want to die? What about those who know they are infinite consciousness having an experience rather than atoms petrified of dying, thus desiring to depart when their time is up rather than live in a Kurzweil-envisioned world?

Such a world would offer corporations, hackers, governments and anyone else with techno-know-how hitherto unknown ways of herd control. We already see this in China, apparently the only race on earth tolerating enslavement without protest. And what did the American insider Christopher Lynn Hedges (1956-), a Presbyterian Minister, author and television host, voice on technocracy-afflicted humans according to Jon Rappoport's December 2019 article "Technocracy: evolution told as a fairytale?"

> "Technocratic human beings are spiritually dead. They are capable of anything, no matter how heinous, because they do not reflect upon or question the ultimate goal."

Biomedicine practitioners, we hear, assume that their own theories and practices, their "science," their philosophical commitments, are essentially and exclusively true. These profess the cellular, even biochemical, basis of human pathology. Harari's Homo Deus "man as god" hypothesis is a prime example, as it excludes all alternatives and ignores, if not denies, basic anthropological understandings. For instance, it makes no room to view humanity's cultural and social forces as wellsprings of human behavior with the inclusion of healing and suffering. Instead, they - the biomedicine practitioners - view the art and science of biomedicine and all its branches and associated biologics as the only way to reach life on another level, to never die, to reach immortality, as Rappoport expressed in his January 2014 article "Consciousness, Art, and Psychiatry."

However, despite the Hararis and the Darwinians of the world's heartfelt efforts, it seems difficult to supress that cave paintings of animals on stone walls expressed consciousness of the beyond. This comes from millennia gone by. Cave people were living their lives, imagining, inventing, creating and expressing thoughts and feelings for posterity rather than out of sheer boredom, methinks? It might be refreshing to note, depending on our sense of humour or earnestness, that a very few within the learned art and science professions indeed express that humanity's spiritual traditions have a habit of depicting states of consciousness and enlightenment intended to describe the reality behind human reality, even though they must almost choke on their observations.

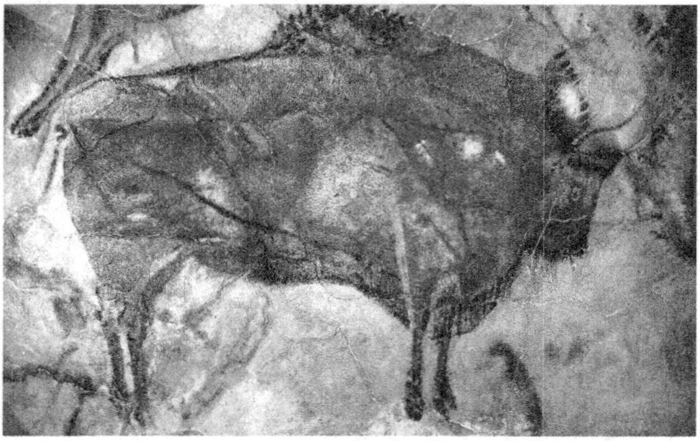

Painting of a Bison in the Cave of Altamira, dated approximately 20,000BC

Is it not the ability to express art in all its ways that constitutes human life itself? From scratching pictures into walls to building sand and ice castles? From creating a family and becoming wonderful cooks to sewing and knitting? From repairing cars and creating clay pots to planting gardens and growing food? Do they not all crave God-given individual creativity? And is it not true that this creativity, on this planet, is gifted only to humans, which biomedicine and biologics systematically began to destroy in the early 1800s? Together, new technology spells the conversion of human 1.0 into automatons? Consider the aspired-to metaverse, a combination of virtual and augmented reality through videos. And think simulators in aviation, where people can live in a virtually programmed and developed world free from what they perceive of the misery of their real lives. *Meta* is an acronym for "most effective tactics available" to, actually, shut down all spiritual aspects of human life and consciousness. For decades, television programming has profoundly mass-hypnotized our sick world. So, shutting down all spiritual aspects of human life and consciousness should be a most simple and easy spiel with biomedicine application and treatments on ignorant humanity (decanherald.com).

And this most effective tactical available tool, Meta, is now being used, I am certain, by the COVID injection and boosters by whatever company, to guide us, the herd. They will lead us into the biomedicine operations and applications game using virtual reality games, biomedicine and biologics' perversion of the mind. They will entice us into getting chip implants under the illusion of enhancing our lives. They will transport us into the soulless metaverse hell or paradise until the end of our natural lives – you know, the ones we will no longer possess.

The metaverse game itself is written in verse, a body of metrical writing in metrical language distinguished by its lower or higher level of intensity. Therefore, the metaverse, started a few decades ago with the American National Security Agency's collecting meta-data in the 1990s. This data upon data on its own citizens, their habits and behaviours had these in the forefront: (www.opendatasoft.com)

- What
- When
- Where
- Who
- How
- Which
- Why

When this was revealed, the herd, well trained over the past 100 years, dutifully and proudly obeyed to move on without protest. The NSA extended its surveillance to Meta Life, life about life, with the recordings of our individual medical history gladly handed over to them by our trusted doctor-knows-best physician. Nobody gave it a thought that the documents of our personal health also contained the knowledge necessary to destroy our mental and artistic abilities. Yes, from cooking to cleaning, to childbearing to creating a family life, to painting both artistic pictures and living-room walls, all was on the line. Without destroying them, the biomedical "adjustment" to turn us into computer-combined machines to their agenda would be almost impossible, unless we give the consent to the COVID-19 jab, I surmise.

Facebook and cellphones, the educational system, the social emotional learning scheme are all their tools and playthings. So is the mass formation hypnosis psychosis created by mass media, the generation-long systematic perversion of art and the creation of human lives ran ragged by the mighty hunt of material possessions, all leading to mental hysteria and perpetual drudgery. Without all these, bio-medicine, metaverse and human-AI interfacing would be a laughing, a non-issue.

To go above and beyond drudgery. That is what cave painters achieved by expressing their creativity in scratching animals and coloring them on stone surfaces. Their unique action demonstrated consciousness beyond living life. It showed an understanding that earthly experience had other use than hunting and gathering food for survival. Now we are allowing that consciousness to be quenched by forces wanting to control us completely and achieve it through our willful cooperation, nay, joyously killing ourselves, from mask-wearing to COVID injections.

The knowledge of this innate, inherent ability and possibility to create and transmute our own lives, our own past, our own experiences. This includes our existential crises of lesser or larger severity such as genuine PTSD through our own acquisition of knowledge. All this has been taken from us through medicine, biomedicine, and biologics, as it perverted our view of the world and ourselves in it by deception. But not all is lost, as we can regain our sanity by gaining control over our emotions. We can do it through learning to observe and control our thinking. We can watch it as if it in itself were a work of art by shaping it to our liking. Mind you, that takes work, as it requires willpower, persistency, discipline, and determination. Nothing happens without it. Plus, all of life is a spiritual path. We came here of our own volition to learn and amuse ourselves, and every one of us is endowed with the power to create our own lives through our daily actions once we tune into this power. Biomedicine, biologics, and implants become a non-issue for us. Their game would be over, the moment we enter this path of awakening. It is that simple.

It is this awakening that biomedicine and biologic practitioners and scientists intend to prevent. Much of it is implemented through Mind Kontrolle, in the U.S. and Canada known as MKUltra, developed by Freud et al. and spread by his advertisement guru nephew

Bernays since the 1920s. First tried out on the American public, it went worldwide in the mid 1950s. That's when television watching, part of biomedicine, replaced creativity and systematically dumbed down the population without knowing it. The best mind-manipulating instrument in existence, there is a reason why it is called "TV programming". Life takes on a different meaning when throwing it out, albeit it takes four to six months to completely heal the brain from its influence. As to the COVID injection, there are numerous sources documenting that it was designed decades ago, one of them Dr. David Martin (Fauci's little dirty secrets exposed! The Moment of Truth; bitchute Dec. 2021).

We also know that human civilizations have risen and fallen, come and gone for millions, if not billions, of years. Their fate has been decided by untold billions of people refraining to take the path of a particular artist or tyrant. Meditation and inner reflection forcing the Self into reflection and connection with our consciousness would help us make decisions that hit us daily in our lives rather than wasting away physically and mentally through drugs and biomedicine applications. Furthermore, as Rappoport points out, we want to understand, that ordinary life never resolves into a grand solution. It begins within the Self through self-persuasion, through the art of going within the Self. It does not resolve by running to physicians for biomedicine and biologics perverting our minds, sooner or later converting us into unconscious, soulless AI automatons controlled by machines.

This chain of cause and effect was honed since Carnegie published Flexner's 1910 report, which wilfully, knowingly, and systematically destroyed even the most elementary generational knowledge of human self-healing. Once it becomes common knowledge, human consciousness will create new realities and new futures using AI benevolently for healing human ailments rather than for its destruction.

When human invention becomes its prow of action, our individual change of view of our Selves, it will reawaken our understanding and change our path in this God-given life. As John 3:11-13 (in whichever scholastic interpretation and/or translation of the Jewish original of roughly 2200 years ago says or the latest version from *The New Testament in Modern English* by J.B Phillips administered by The Archbishops' Council of the Church of England in 1972 advises and warns:

> "For the original command, as you know, is that we should love one another. We are none of us to have the spirit of Cain, who was a son of the devil and murdered his brother. Have you realised his motive? It was just because he realised the goodness of his brother's life and the rottenness of his own. Don't be surprised, therefore, if the world hates you."

A more subtle version is in translation from the King James Version (KJV). It was published in 1611 with sponsorship of James VI (1566 -1625), King of Scotland from 1567 until becoming King of England and Ireland as James I from the Scottish and English crowns' union in 1603 until his death in 1625. It took a shortcut on 1 John 3:11-13 when saying:

> "Be not as Cain, who was of that wicked one and slew his brother. And why did he slay him? Because his own works were evil, and his brother's righteous."

We will never know precisely what brought us to this desire for a scientists-community-generated AI-human interface. We might wonder whether or not Cain slaughtering Abel in the dawn of time signaled the moment that so-called evil began its rule over humanity. Why else would we have been given the warning not to act like Cain, but rather to love each other, neglected in the King James translation? That it first and foremost necessitates the love for Self is nowhere mentioned, either.

Instead, we have been lured into behaving like Cain through 1000s of years. It kept on through Gaius Julius Caesar's times killing and maiming and enslaving millions of people throughout all of Europe and part of Asia - Eurasia. In recent times, we have been killing our own conscience, imagination, perception of reality, feelings for morality and ethics. Not only have we been slaughtering our own consciousness without knowing it by using drugs prescribed by physicians under the ruse of healing. In fact, we've been destroying our selves, lowering our IQ rates, slowing and perverting our thinking ability, never mind perverting our perception of morality and ethics and encouraging enthusiasm for biomedicine, biologics, and Ai-human interfacing.

We saw that the mental health industry, a branch of medicine's science and arts craft, vigorously pushed humanity's mind perversion since the mid-1800s. First, it was through the influence of morphine-laced cough syrup and sleep remedies concocted by the nascent pharmaceutical companies and handed out like candy to the ignorant masses. Then, it was aspirin and other chemical-based drugs. In the 1920s, however, the mental health profession went a step further by establishing the Tavistock Institute of Medical Psychology, purportedly to treat nervous complaints and provide clinical services for both children and adults. It offered free treatment to all who wanted it. Income for the Institute's maintenance was generated, we are told, by providing training-for-pay to aspiring clinical professionals. These were the future psychiatrists, psychologists, psychoanalysts, psychiatric nurses, psycho-the-rapists, mental health counselors, social workers, addiction counselors and whoever else was deemed fit to individually shape, direct, support and provide patient diagnosis, treatment, testing and ongoing care whilst interacting with patients face-to-face.

Different streams of thought were explored in lectures by such eminent human emotional health specialists as C.G. Jung, once upon a time a Sigismund Schlomo Freud collaborator. They were attended by doctors, churchmen and members of the public able to influence the herd's opinions on any topic. English writer Herbert George Wells (1866 -1946) and Irish novelist and playwright Samuel Barclay Beckett (1906 -1989) were among them. The lectures were put in motion by the Flexners in 1910, and all clinical roles required a graduate degree, certification and licensing. By1939, staff had increased to 90 pro bono (working free of charge) psychiatrists, and Tavistock Institute graduates had begun to spread out to practice their craft of the art and science of psychology and psychiatry on folk of all ages across the UK, the U.S. and across the world. We read that they focused on preventive psychiatry and expertise in group relations, including army officer selection, social psychiatry and action research (https://tavistockandportman.nhs.uk/about-us/who-we-are/celebrating-100-years-tavistock-and-portman/short-history-tavistock-and-portman/).

And what is "action research", we wonder? Well, it is a social science, in the same bucket as the mental health industry and philosophy. Its methodology of research seeks transformative change within society through the simultaneous process of taking action and doing research linked by critical reflection. In 1998, Rory O'Brien of the Faculty of Information

Studies at the University of Toronto conveyed that the term is known by many other names. It is sometimes called participatory research, collaborative inquiry, emancipatory research, action learning and contextual action research. (An Overview of the Methodological Approach of Action Research; homepages.web.net/~robrien/papers/arfinal.html).

All are variations on the theme "learning by doing." A group of people identify a problem, do something to resolve it and see how successful their efforts were. If not satisfied, they try again. While this is the essence of the approach, there are other key attributes of action research that differentiate it from common problem-solving we all engage in daily. However, he adds, a more succinct definition would be:

> "Action research...aims to contribute both to the practical concerns of people in an immediate problematic situation and to further the goals of social science simultaneously. Thus, there is a dual commitment in action research to study a system and concurrently to collaborate with members of the system in changing it in what is together regarded as a desirable direction. Accomplishing this twin goal requires the active collaboration of researcher and client, and thus it stresses the importance of co-learning as a primary aspect of the research process." (Thomas Gilmore et al: "Action Based Modes of Inquiry and the Host-Researcher Relationship"; *Consultation: An International Journal* 5.3 Fall 1986; 161)

What separates this type of research from general professional practices such as consulting or daily problem-solving is the emphasis on scientific study, we read. This is to say, researchers at the Tavistock Institute and other similar agencies systematically study a problem. They ensure that certain theoretical considerations are followed. Those are the ones resulting in active interventions viewed as essential to develop and/or implement a capacity-building program to enhance the lived experiences of people involved Those people include any viewed as mentally impaired, for example. The outcomes are shared with the interested learned society, in our case the mental health professionals applying their theories to, among others, the genuine PTSD affected.

Much of researchers' time, we hear, is in fact spent on refining the methodological tools to suit the exigencies of any given situation being examined. Collecting, analyzing, and presenting data on any topic in an ongoing cyclical basis also occupies much of their time. During all projects, research is said to take place in real-world situations, purportedly aiming to resolve real problems, with researchers notably making no attempt to be objective.

Action research is often visualized as a cyclical process. The current literature on school mental health, for example, supports action research as a method of qualitative inquiry to investigate and/or remediate school mental health problems. The data derived from these projects can contribute to a foundation for more comprehensive school mental health programs to be designed. They omit, of course, the Ritalin and other mind-altering drugs encouraged to be given to bright and adventurous children that created the situation, never mind the curriculum itself. To further this project, teachers are asked to research their own practice, their own work.

In other words, you look at your work, self-criticize and admit the errors of your ways in all their glory. You do a fact-finding interview, the term used by any self-respecting employer wanting to shaft you. That's what NorAm arranged for me one Halloween with the help of flight attendant snitches, passengers and other personnel. After 18 months of being reintegrated and flying in the line of duty, they had driven me into recurring PTSD. Action research is also used on the intelligentsia, the undesirably bright in tyrannical regimes, to confess their unbecoming behavior before throwing them into Gulags or kill them.

The Action Research Cycle

And where did this concept of psychological discovery into human beings' innermost behavior patterns resulting in the Tavistock Institute, biomedicine, biologics and AI interface desires first took hold, inquiring minds want to know? Well, I believe it originated with the WWII Northfield Experiment. This project was conducted at the Hollymoor Psychiatric Hospital's Rubery Lunatic Asylum in Birmingham, England. Its researchers joined and perfected the Tavistock Institute, clandestinely bringing us, the herd, humanity to our present state of medicinal affairs. So, let's take a look, shall we?

26

SHELL-SHOCK, BULLET SHOCK, TAVISTOCK, AND BIOLOGICAL MEDICINE

The Iraqi Assyriologist Hormuzd Rassam (1826-1910) discovered the *Epic of Gilgamesh* in the ruins of the library of Ashurbanipal in Nineveh, Iraq, in 1853. It was the world's oldest notable literature. It depicted the Mesopotamian king of Uruk's trials and tribulation around 2100 BC. It also depicted the 8th century BC poet Homer's poems *Iliad* (Ἰλιάς) and *Odyssey* (Ὀδύσσεια). These document the ten-year siege and battles of Troy (Ilium) by a coalition of Mycenaean Greek (Achaeans) around 1200 BC, with Troy's ruins unearthed in the 1870s. Since then, we know that PTSD indeed does exist (see *Fallacy 1*).

Throughout the following millennia, war marched on. Surviving Trojans established themselves at Rome. Gaius Julius Caesar claimed the Goddess Venus and Aeneas, son of the Trojan prince Anchises and the Greek goddess Aphrodite as ancestors. The Phoenicians occupied a narrow tract of land along the coast of modern Syria, Lebanon and northern Israel. They grew famous for their commercial and maritime prowess, and began to conquer the world by slaughtering the northern Europeans and Anglians by the hundreds of thousands with scant history documenting the facts of their brutality. No extraordinary amount of attention seems to have been given to acknowledge the emotional suffering by all strata of society associated with warfare. their was Scottish physician Hugh Crichton-Miller who first shone a light on the effects of war on human minds. During WWI, he served for a few months in the British Royal Army Medical Corps with rank of lieutenant colonel. The thunder of guns and of explosions ripping across France's Western Front were so intense, the sound alone scared the living daylight out of Londoners (https://blackcablondon.net/tag/hugh-crichton-miller/).

Crichton-Miller (1877–1959) described himself as a Christian, a pragmatist and a scientist. Known throughout his career as a tolerant, dedicated and humane doctor, his main concern was to cure those who came to him (https://100years.tavistockandportman.nhs.uk/hugh-crichton-miller/?v=79cba1185463). He was born in Genoa, Italy, to the reverend Donald Miller. Miller was a friend of Professor M.D. C.G. Jung (1875-1961) of Zurich, for 41 years ministering to the Free Church of Scotland believers. His mother was Mary Wotherspoon of Glasgow. At age 12, he travelled across Europe by himself to attend Fettes College. This Edinburgh boarding school was founded with a bequest of Sir William Fettes (1750–1836), a wealthy city merchant and the city's former Lord Provost. He wanted to educate poor children and orphans in memory of his only son William, who had predeceased him in 1815.

The Free Church of Scotland had been formed in 1843. Roughly a third of ministers in the Presbyterian Church of Scotland had resigned because of state interference in its internal affairs. This ran contrary to their understanding that church and state were independent in their own spheres and should not interfere in each other's areas of authority, but rather help one another for the Christian good of Scotland (https://freechurch.org).

The new denomination quickly set to work building churches, manses, schools, and seminaries. By the end of their first year, 470 churches had been built. Home and foreign missions were established and missionaries stationed throughout Africa, India and other British colonies. The denomination currently has over 100 congregations across Scotland. It also has congregations in North America, London and sister churches founded by mission work in India, Peru, and South Africa. The Church has a full-time seminary in Edinburgh to train its ministers and other Christian workers. The Free Church is in fellowship with many other Reformed churches throughout the world. It stands firmly in the tradition that the Bible is its supreme standard and the Westminster Confession as its subordinate standard. Central to worship is the preaching of the gospel—the good news of salvation through the sovereign grace of God in His Son Jesus Christ.

In 1894, Crichton-Miller entered Edinburgh University. He followed an arts programme, as well as medicine, and in 1902 obtained his M.D. with a thesis on hypnotism. He spent a couple of years as house surgeon and physician at Edinburgh's Royal Infirmary. It was established in 1729 as Hospital for the Sick Poor, also known as the Physicians' Hospital or Little House. He then returned to Italy, settling with his growing family in San Remo to run a clinic. This year-round health resort on the Italian Riviera was visited by the *haute société*, such as emperor Frederick III of Germany (1831–88) and other famous and well-healed individuals. In his leisure time, Crichton-Miller attended the University of Pavia, Lombardy in subjects unknown. From his interest in the link between mind and body, going back to his student days, we assume that his subject matters were related to just that. Indeed, he regularly diagnosed his San Remo patients as suffering from functional nervous disorders. Summering with his family in Aviemore, Inverness-shire, Scotland, he also practiced medicine in whatever style there. (https://history.rcplondon.ac.uk/inspiring-physicians/hugh-crichton-miller).

He was miserable. There were no effective treatments available for any of his patients. There were no nursing homes or hospitals where those he thought emotionally off-kilter people could get the treatment he thought they might require. But he solved that problem by in 2011. He opened Bowden House, a rambling regency house with a long-extended wing in Harrow-on-the-Hill as nursing home to treat neurosis and similar disorders. His very first patient was a child, perhaps even one of his own, as psychiatrist B.F. Skinner did a few years later, as he in the early years shared Bowden House with his wife and their family of 6 children.

Promptly thereafter, he not only became a popular lecturer, but also a writer on what he termed 'New Psychology', said to be broadly based on the Swiss psychiatrist Jung's work, making his debut as author with his book *Hypnotism and Disease: A Plea for Rational Psychotherapy*. Nowadays, we call it rational emotive behaviour therapy or REBT. This approach posits that people have erroneous beliefs about situations they are involved in. It further posits that these beliefs can be disputed and changed by way of active-directive, philosophically and empirically based psychotherapy to lead happier and more fulfilling lives.

But Crichton-Miller was far from the first person to open a clinic to help emotionally distressed people heal. The Buddha already mentioned the occasional instability of the human mind, telling his disciples 2,500 years earlier:

> Monks, there are beings who suffer not from disease of body for one year, for two years...even for a hundred years. B it is hard to find in the world beings who can admit freedom from mental disease, even for one moment, save only those who have destroyed [the four] cankers.—A.II:143;S.III.:2 (Dr. K. Sri Dhammananda: *Treasure of the Dhamma* p. 235; Malaysian Edition, 1994)

What are cankers in human lives, we asked? They are the:

1. Canker of sensuality (*kāmāsavā*)
2. Canker of existence (*bhavāsavā*)
3. Canker of false views (*diṭṭhāsava*)
4. Canker of ignorance (*avijjāsavā*)

As a matter of fact, a number of religious, magical and medical combinations were used long before him by such psychological thinkers as Ancient Indian sage Patañjali (Sanskrit: पतञ्जलि) He is thought to be the author of a number of Sanskrit and Tamil works. The greatest of these thinkers would be the Yoga Sutras, Padmasambhāva, also known as Guru Rinpoche, who established the first Buddhist monastery in Tibet in the 8th century AD. Another was Persian Ibn Sina (ابن سینا), also known as Abu Ali Sina (ابو علی سینا), Pour Sina (پور سینا) and in the West known as Avicenna (c. 980–June 1037). He is regarded as one of the most significant physicians, astronomers, thinkers and writers of the Islamic Golden Age and the father of early modern medicine. Thirteenth century Jalāl ad-Dīn Mohammad Rūmī (Persian: جلالالدین محمد رومی), (also known as Jalāl ad-Dīn Mohammad Balkhī (جلالالدین محمد بلخی), Mevlânâ/Mowlānā (مولانا, " or Rumi (1207 –1273) was another. Poet, Islamic scholar, theologian and Sufi mystic, he conveyed through his poetry how to sooth the soul when in emotional upheaval and how to carry Self through life. \Physician, philosopher and alchemist Abū Bakr Muḥammad ibn Zakariyyāʾ al-Rāzī (Arabic: أبو بكر محمد بن زكرياء الرازي), also known by his Persian name Rāzī and by his Latinized name Rhazes (864 or 865 – 925 or 935 AD), was another. He exclaimed:

> "The doctors' aim is to do well, even to our enemies, so much more to our friends, and my profession forbids us to do harm to our kindred, as it is instituted for the benefit and welfare of the human race, and God imposed on physicians the oath not to compose mortiferous remedies." (https://link.springer.com/article/10.1007/s00381-017-3493-z).

German physiologist, philosopher and professor Wilhelm Maximilian Wundt (1832 –1920) pursued a similar line of inquiry. He was the son of a Lutheran clergyman, a branch of the Christian faith of Protestantism launched by the sixteenth-century Catholic German monk and reformer Martin Luther in 1519. His paternal grandfather was a pastor and professor of geography at Heidelberg University. So, he took his doctorate in medicine in Heidelberg in 1856. He joined German physicist, physician, and philosopher Hermann Ludwig von Helmholtz's (1821-1894) staff in 1858. He was tasked with teaching the laboratory course in human physiology, concentrating on two topics: (1) sensation and perception and (2) the measurement of reaction times. To study these, he used the technique of introspection, in which human subjects reported exactly what they experienced when presented with a stimulus such as light or noise. He became so interested in studying humans' psychological problems from a physiological viewpoint that he offered the first ever academic course in psychology in 1862. (https://www2.open.ac.uk/openlearn/CHIPs/data/accessibility/nodes/220.html)

As to Helmholtz, he is known for his philosophy of science. He is known for his ideas on the relation between the laws of human perception and the laws of nature. He is known also for the science of aesthetics. And he is known for his ideas on the civilizing power of science, leading to our infatuation with the possibility of controlling nature with science and technology, from AI to the High-frequency Active Auroral Research Program (HAARP). This resulted in Wundt's first book *Contributions Toward a Theory of Sense Perception* (1862), setting down a vision for psychology as an independent discipline containing three general subdivisions.

In the first, psychology would follow the principles of the physical sciences, the *Naturwissenschaften*. It would be conducted as an experimental, inductive science based on inductive reasoning. This method of reasoning combines a body of observations to come up with a general, we gather psychological, principle. The focus of this psychology would involve basic mental processes that are amenable to experimental observation and manipulation, such as sensation, perception and reaction time to stimuli.

As second complementary division, Wundt pictured psychology allied with the tradition of the *Geisteswissenschaften*, the sciences of the human mind and social sciences. This would involve the higher mental processes, which could not be brought under direct control in a laboratory, such as religion, social practices, language, myths and so on. Hence, their study would require other methods of investigation, including the use of historical records, naturalistic observation in the field and analyses of cultural products like literature. This was later termed the "comparative-historical" approach.

And the third and final form of psychology, he called *scientific metaphysics*. This would be the branch of philosophy dealing with the first principles of things. It would include abstract concepts, such as being, knowing, substance, cause, identity, time, space and other abstract theories with no basis in reality. Somehow, by hook and by crook, we surmise, they would serve to integrate the empirical work of laboratory findings on living entities, including humans, with other findings of science.

Wundt left Heidelberg in 1874 to teach inductive philosophy at the University of Zurich. In 1875, he accepted the position of professor of philosophy at the University of Leipzig, where he concentrated almost exclusively on psychological research. He focused on the study of human sensory experience, in 1879 establishing the first psychology laboratory known to exist in the western world.

So good was Wundt at discovering what makes humanity tick, that he is known as the father of experimental psychology. This branch of psychology is concerned with the scientific investigation of such psychological processes as learning, memory and cognition. Noteworthy is that it treats both animals and human beings together, under Darwinian doctrine one and the same, with Russian Ivan experiments, ever since used to manipulate humanity against itself.

During his six-decade career, Wundt published 53,000 pages in more than 50 volumes. One given in 1863 had the title *Vorlesungen über die Menschen und Tier-Seele* (Lectures on the Human and Animal Soul). In its official 1896 translation, it already eliminated the soul, as the notion of a soul is unfitting to the humanist philosophy and ideology of man the machine, void of consciousness. Considered the originator of the experimental tradition in psychology, the learned society views Wundt as one of the science-of-psychology's founders. So prolific was he in his pursuits, that he even managed to establish the first experimental psychological journal, the *Philosophische Studien* (Studies in Philosophy) in 1881. And from then on it was fun and games to the art and craft of their profession to figure out how to best lure the herd into the world's brutal conflicts. What a way to completely traumatize and cull, as viewed in COVID and its equally non-existent offspring (Frontline Critical Care Alliance January 23, 2022).

Numerous others helped Wundt spread the knowledge about the human body's functions and the discoveries of its mental vulnerabilities and manipulation possibilities. From Leipzig, Zurich and Vienna, the word spread throughout the world like wildfire, to figure out how best to change and destroy the herd. German physician and physiologist professor Carl Friedrich Wilhelm Ludwig (1816-1895) was among them. He would have a major influence on the understanding of the methods and apparatus used in almost all branches of human physiology. These would be used to figure out and purportedly scientifically document how the human body works and the chemistry and physics behind its basic functions. This would eventually lead to the discovery of how molecules behave in cells and how the systems of organs work together.

Ludwig was born in a small town in the north-eastern German state of Hesse. He earned his doctor's degree at the University of Marburg in 1839. In 1842, he ascended to professor of physiology and in 1846 added the chair of comparative anatomy, the study of similarities and differences in the anatomy of different species including the human one, to his teaching duties. This field is closely related to evolutionary biology and phylogeny, the study of the evolutionary relatedness among groups of organisms. Whilst for the next 10 years teaching anatomy and physiology, Ludwig researched blood pressure, urinary excretion and anaesthesia. As a side hustle, he served as prospector, dissecting corpses for examination or anatomical demonstration for University of Marburg's professor of anatomy Franz Ludwig Fick (1813–1858). Fick loved to study the developmental mechanics of human bone growth, especially that of skulls. He was also fascinated by the mechanism of human and animal vision, the function of the retina, the innermost, light-sensitive layer of tissue of the eye in relation to human perceptions. And the function and performance of taste buds caught his attention, too. For his amusement, he designed the cerebral phantom, an openable paper model showing the various parts of the brain that became the prototype of openable figures used in medical texts.

In 1849, Ludwig moved on to the University of Zurich. It was founded in 1833 from existing colleges of theology, law and medicine, going back to 1525 AD, and adding a faculty of philosophy. His new role as professor of anatomy and physiology provided him with a modest laboratory where he, with an assistant, inaugurated a program of experimentation and physiology teachings (https://ahajournals.org/doi/pdf/10.1161/01.CIR.74.5.920). By 1855 he had grasped in Zurich what there was to grasp about the workings of the human mind. He went on to Vienna as professor at the Collegium Medico-Chirurgicum Josephinum, the Josephinian Military Academy of Surgery, or just "the Josephinum." This academy of military medicine was founded in 1784 by the Holy Roman Emperor of Austria, Joseph II.

By 1865, Ludwig had shared all he knew about humans' physical and mental aptitudes with Austria's military elite in Vienna. So, in 1865, h moved on to Leipzig University to join up with Wundt and develop the Physiological Institute, originally built in Zurich and soon thereafter considered "a factory of new knowledge". He thoroughly enjoying his position as the newly created chair of physiology. To celebrate, he began to spread his views on humanity's physical and mental animal make-up among his students and companions until he departed the earth in 1895 (https://pubmed.ncbi.nlm.nih.gov/3533314/). Whilst at it, he studied the human cardiovascular system. He also invented a device known as a kymograph to record changes in arterial blood pressure. Ad he designed a simple strom-uhr, a flow-meter, to measure the rate of blood flow through arteries and veins. If that wasn't enough, manufactured a mercurial blood-gas pump to separate gases from the blood, which helped explain the role played by oxygen and other gases in blood-purification.

Ludwig, his assistants and his students also kept animal organs alive outside an animal's body. This included foetuses, we take it. He did this by perfusing hearts with a solution approximating the composition of blood plasma, located a blood vessel regulatory mechanism at the base of the brain. He also discovered how to measure blood pressure in the capillaries, the tiny blood vessels that transport blood, nutrients and oxygen to cells in humans' organs and body systems. He is also the one who discovered the depressor and accelerator nerves of the heart. He worked with American physiologist Henry Ingersoll Bowditch (1808 -1892), from 1859 to 1867 professor of clinical medicine at Harvard University They formulated the "all-or-none law" of the cardiac muscle action. They documented that the heart muscle will contract to the fullest extent or not at all, regardless of stimulus.

Ludwig also introduced the measurement of nitrogen in urine as an indication of the approximate rate of protein metabolism in the entire animal, you and me. He introduced the thought that human digestive glands might be influenced by secretory nerves. Through these cordlike bundles of fibers, sensory stimuli and motor impulses pass between the brain or other parts of the central nervous system and the eyes, glands, muscles, and other parts of the body. Nerves form a network of pathways for conducting information throughout the body. Considered a brilliant teacher, nearly 200 of Ludwig's students became prominent scientists. This included Bowditch and fellow American physician, pathologist, bacteriologist, and medical school administrator William Henry Welch (1850 -1934). Pavlov, first son of a priest, grandson of a sexton, and for a while an aspiring priest, seems to be his most famous of them all. Pavlov was instrumental in creating the mental health industry's success through his discoveries how to manipulate the human mind for better or for worse.

Pavlov was raised in Ryazan in central Russia, about 120 miles southeast of Moscow, among the oldest cities of Russia. He attended a church school and theological seminary before abandoning those studies in 1870 to study chemistry and physiology at the University of St. Petersburg. He received his M.D. at St. Petersburg's Imperial Medical Academy in 1879, completing his dissertation in 1883. He then hurried to the University of Leipzig and under Ludwig's direction, undertook his first independent research on the physiology of animals' circulatory system between 1884 and 1886. So skillful a surgeon did Pavlov turn out to be, that he was able to introduce a catheter into the femoral artery of a dog to record the influence on blood pressure of various pharmacological and emotional stimuli almost painlessly without anesthesia.

His careful dissection of the very fine cardiac nerves enabled Pavlov to demonstrate the control of the strength of the heartbeat by nerves leaving the cardiac plexus. And by stimulating the severed ends of the cervical nerves, he showed the effects of the right and left vagal nerves on the heart.

Pavlov was primarily known for his work in classical conditioning, however. In this behavioral procedure, a biologically potent stimulus such as food is paired with a previously neutral stimulus such as a bell. Pavlov is said to have learnt most, if not all, of what he used to discover what he discovered about the behavior and reactions of what he considered two- and four-legged animals. This guaranteed the success of the mental health profession under Ludwig at the University of Leipzig.

By 1890, he had been assigned the position of professor of physiology at the Imperial Medical Academy. Despite the Russian Revolution, he remained there until his resignation in 1924. That's when he switched to the newly founded Institute of Experimental Medicine, where he initiated precise surgical procedures for animals. He applied, we read, strict attention to their postoperative care by installing facilities to maintain their post-operative supervision and health. By observing irregularities of secretions in normal, un-anaesthetized animals, Pavlov formulated the laws of the conditional reflex. He used salivary secretion as a quantitative measure of the psychical, or subjective, activity of the animal in order to emphasize the advantage of objective, physiological measures of mental phenomena and higher nervous activity. He also sought analogies between the conditional, commonly though incorrectly translated as "conditioned," reflex and the spinal reflex.

Spinal reflexes are "investigator-evoked", meaning the researcher has to take action to make them happen. They are "artifacts" arising from connections of stretch receptors in the muscle or nociceptors in the skin. These receptors activate spinal motor neurons to evoke twitches in particular somatic muscles (e.g., the quadriceps muscle in a patellar tendon reflex) through pain or electrical impulses. And what are nociceptors? They can be defined as sensory receptors that are activated by noxious stimuli that damage or threaten the body's integrity. That gives us an idea about the brutality of the experiments conducted on animals, which include humans, purportedly for the benefit of mankind.

For PTSD journeyers, it is valuable to know that Pavlov also studied transmarginal inhibition (TMI), This is an organism's response to overwhelming stimuli. Pavlov enumerated details of TMI, the body's natural response of shutting down when exposed to overwhelming stress or pain by electric shock, on his work of conditioning animals to pain. He found that "organisms," you and I, have different levels of tolerance. He commented "that the most basic inherited difference among people was how soon they reached this shutdown point and that the quick-to-shut-down have a fundamentally different type of nervous system" (Rokhin, L.; Pavlov, I. & Popov, Y. (1963) *Psychopathology and Psychiatry*. Foreign Languages Publication House: Moscow).

Here are the three stages to pass through for the state of TMI to be reached.

1. equivalent phase: when the response matches the stimuli, which is considered the normal baseline behavior.
2. paradoxical phase: associated with quantity reversal, occurs when small stimuli receive major responses and major stimuli elicit small responses.
3. ultra-paradoxical: the final stage, associated with quality reversal, in which negative stimulation results in positive responses and vice versa.

An organism, meaning you and I, can progress through these stages by one of four ways:

- increased stimulation
- random negative stimulation
- reversing positive and negative stimulation
- physically debilitating the organism

As observed by Pavlov, tolerance of stimulation varies greatly between individuals. Highly sensitive people may be over-stimulated by loud volumes in a movie theater or the background confusion of a large social gathering. Less sensitive people would find those same situations ideal for their stimulation levels or even less than ideal.

This knowledge is hugely important in mental conditioning for anyone in the mental health industry for the *sudden conversion* methods of mental conditioning on TMI. All ten elements of control over others through dominance can be seen as subject stimulation toward TMI:

- crisis
- euphoria
- confession
- re-stimulation
- mental fatigue
- proselytization
- physical fatigue
- super-stimulation
- environment control
- tension or uncertainty

British psychiatrist William Walters Sargant (1907–1988) seems to have carried out and perfected TMI to a fine art. He is remembered by his peers for the true Luciferic consciousness permeating his applications and promotions of treatments. Among those treatments were psychotherapy, deep sleep treatment, electroconvulsive therapy, lobotomy, and insulin shock therapy in true humanistic fashion, in particular on shell-shocked British soldiers.

Sargant received his medical education at St John's College in Cambridge and completed it at St Mary's Hospital in London. He suffered a nervous breakdown in 1934 and a subsequent spell in a mental hospital. F following work at the Hanwell Insane Asylum, built as the First Middlesex County Asylum in 1831, he decided on a career in psychiatry. When Edward Mapother, considered the most influential figure in establishing clinical and academic psychiatry in Britain, offered him work at the psychiatric Maudsley Hospital, London, he sprang at the opportunity.

Irish-born landed gentry Mapother (1881 -1940) completed his M.D. in 1908. He worked in mental asylums encouraged by a sister considered mentally ill. He served as surgeon in the British army's medical corps during WWI in France, Mesopotamia and India. IT was during this time that he is said to have developed an interest in shell shock. It was described at that time as either a physical or psychological injury, or simply as a lack of moral fibre (see *Fallacy 1*). "Shell shock" was replaced by "combat stress reaction" during WWII. It was used within the military to describe acute behavioural disorganization as a direct result of the trauma of war, and was also known as "combat fatigue", "battle fatigue" or "battle neurosis". The learned society decided in the past 50 years on an acute stress reaction diagnosis, which can be used in civilian psychiatric as well. They apply the generic PTSD nomenclature to it, which they stretch in all direction of normally-to-be-experienced existential life crises (*Fallacy 1*).

But Mapother had prepared for the situation of WWI by Maudley's foundation. It had opened in 1915 and been requisitioned to treat war veterans the moment Mapother, as superintendent, took possession of it. By an act of Parliament, Mapother was allowed to accept voluntary patients without needing to certify them as insane. By that time, he had also managed to a create the Institute of Psychiatry at Kings College, London, now the Institute of Psychiatry, Psychology and Neuroscience (IoPPN). It was dedicated to the discovery of what causes mental illness and diseases of the brain. In his leisure time, he involved himself in activities of the Eugenics Society. He was always willing to offer free of charge his consultations about abortions for poor women, most likely conducted at his Institute of Psychiatry. In 1935, he hired Sargant to share his ideas and means of practicing medicine on those considered mentally insane, in particular those injured emotionally in WWI.

In his autobiography, Sargant describes how Mapother's views coincided with his own: the future of psychiatric treatment lay in the discovery of simple physiological treatments. Soon after his arrival at Maudsley, Sargant was involved in testing amphetamine as a new treatment for depression, and whilst studying for his diploma in psychological medicine, took it himself. He would continue with such regimen of a variety of drugs to treat his depression throughout his life. He also introduced insulin shock therapy, albeit we don't know if he practiced it on himself.

And lo and behold, the Rockefeller Foundation Fellowship invited Sargant to spend a year at Harvard's Medical School under the eminent neurologist Stanley Cobb (1887–1968) in 1938. Cobb was considered by some of his peers to be the founder of biological psychiatry in the United States. Cobb was born in Brookline, Massachusetts. His great-grandmother was Augusta Adams Cobb, who abandoned her husband to marry Mormon prophet Brigham Young in 1843 as his third wife out of some 56. He struggled with stammering through his childhood and education, which may have led him to study the neurosciences to understand its cause.

He studied biology at Harvard College (AB, 1911) and medicine at Harvard Medical School (M.D., 1914). He then entered army service in an unknown category and location before completing his residency at Johns Hopkins Medical School. He went on to teach neurology at Harvard Medical School in 1919. By 1925, he reached the exalted position of Harvard's Bullard Professor of Neuropathology.

Long before Sargant joined him in 1938, months before Europe became enmeshed in WWII, Cobb seemed troubled by medical scientists' tendencies to draw hard-and-fast distinctions:

- between psychic and somatic causes
- between psychology and physiology
- between functional and organic diseases
- between mental and physical symptoms

Cobb addressed the mind-body problem in a series of lectures before the Lowell Institute in 1940. He insisted that making a scientific approach to the study of disease by a wholly somatic or a wholly psychic ideology would be impossible. He discussed the evolution of speech, vision, intellect and language defects. He addressed the function of the frontal areas of the human brain. He penned an essay on the anatomical basis of the emotions, consciousness and disturbances in consciousness, and a couple of essays on psychoneurosis and psychosomatics. In 1943, he published his observations in his book *Borderlands of Psychiatry* stating:

> "I solve the mind-body problem by stating that there is no such problem. There are, of course, plenty of problems concerning the 'mind', and the 'body', and all intermediate levels of integration of the nervous system. What I wish to emphasize is that there is no problem of 'mind' versus 'body', because biologically no such dichotomy [a division or contrast between two things represented as being opposed or entirely different] can be made. The dichotomy is an artefact; there is no truth in it, and the discussion has no place in science in 1943... The difference between psychology and physiology is merely one of complexity. The simpler bodily processes are studied in physiological departments; the more complex ones that entail the highest levels of neural integration are studied in psychological departments. There is no biological significance to this division; it is simply an administrative affair, so that the university president will know what salary goes

to which professor." (Cambridge, Mass.: Harvard University Press; London: Oxford University Press, 1943. 2.50 dollars).

In other words, the human psyche and the human body solely differ in complexity but not in substance. They are one and the same, a machine with parts solely differing in complexity. Live with it, he apparently conveys. Sargant, loving that trend of thought, meanwhile had a grand old time doing experiments on human over-breathing. He contemplated the theory that the difference between normal and neurotic people had its foundation in the latter having lost their suggestibility. Suggestibility? Well, it turns out that our individual, should we call it "sense of suggestibility", or lack therefore, indeed rules our lives. It dictates our perception of ourselves to that of COVID or to anything else presented and suggested in our lives, either overtly or covertly. As a matter of fact, it is the most harmful of all harmful tools in the mental health industry's quiver. It has the power to create trans-marginal inhibition in anyone and a crowd, as presently visible in the mass psychosis formation about COVID or the war in Ukraine.

Amazingly, suggestibility is still a prominent issue in clinical trials *today*. Why? As I just said, suggestions have the power to distort our perception of the world around us down to the most seemingly minute details. We allow this to align with our conscious, subconscious or unconscious motives and expectations. Read it again, will you? (fiercebiotech.com/sponsored/addressing-suggestibility-as-a-psychological-phenomenon-clinical-trials). That's why we are being brainwashed by TV from the moment it is turned on until the second it is turned off regardless of if actively watching it or not. The sound, the language, the vibrational wavelength alone does the trick. No wonder the COVID mass psychosis hysteria is so successful in the U.S. and Canada. Most folks host at least two TVs if not one in each room of their homes - including the bathroom - running it during all their waking hours.

Clinical trials compared patients given suggestions with those who were not. Those given suggestions felt higher levels of pain than the counter-groups receiving the same treatment without giving suggestions, we learn. Internal factors, such as levels of self-judgment, self-esteem and assertiveness, innate personality and the way we are raised, were found to impact our suggestibility levels. Participants with a low self-esteem, for example, are more likely to be persuaded into changing their answers when pressured to do so than those with high levels of confidence. And yes, they began at the cradle, as they do know that children raised to be sceptical are usually less suggestible in comparison to those raised by less sceptical parents. Plant them in front of the TV from birth, and you know what to expect.

Researchers have also attributed levels of suggestibility to differences in attentional functioning. Researchers define attentional functioning as our ability to filter irrelevant information and inhibit prepotent responses. Overall, several behavioral and social characteristics influence each person's tendency to take cues from others, and change their beliefs based on those suggestions. It is thus obvious that suggestibility can significantly affect and alter how we remember memories and make decisions in the future. Suggestibility impacts everyone in the world regardless of color, race, religion or nationality. The brilliant part is that once we are aware, the awareness can help us recognize suggestibility when it hits. And it hits at every given moment, if you watch TV and are active on social media. Actually, it never ends, due to the Luciferic consciousness rule. If we watch our thoughts like a hawk, however, and apply logic and reason to whatever is presented to us, we can considerably discern it and curb its influence on us (*Why is yawning contagious? Suggestibility explained*. https://thedecisionlab.com/biases/suggestibility/).

External factors such as the amount of information given on the procedure to be conducted and the researcher's or interviewer's attitude and overall demeanor also contribute to subjects' levels of suggestibility. When subjects had a friendly interviewer or were warned of the presence of deceptive information beforehand, they were less likely to give in to misleading questions or be suggestible. Therefore, researchers conducting clinical trials *must* first try to identify trial participants' overall level of suggestibility and focus on minimizing the suggestibility characteristic of those identified. It is eminently important in clinical research to know and understand participants' perspectives and to anticipate how subjects reacted beforehand. In other words, Wundt's desire of objective reporting on studies seems to have flown out the window since his death.

Now to the problem the learned society seems still to be facing, namely, how to identify and decrease a person's level of suggestibility, which must take place before a clinical trial can officially commence. Well, the learned society of the science and art of psychiatry and psychology is still working hard at that 85 years after Sargant began to study the subject, wit Zoe Fisher et al.'s research entitled *Addressing Suggestibility As A Psychological Phenomenon In Clinical Trials* stating:

> Suggestion can contribute to the uncritical and/or unreasoned responses to a situation (Coffins, 1941). Suggestions can be classified into two types: direct and indirect. Indirect suggestions occur when the implication is hidden, while direct suggestions occur when the prompting is not concealed (Polczyk, 2016).
>
> Within these two types, there are three primary areas of suggestibility that have been studied and researched extensively: the placebo effect, hypnotic suggestibility, and interrogative suggestibility (Halligan & Oakley, 2014).
>
> The placebo effect is the effect of a medication or course of action that cannot be accredited in any way to the actual treatment (Halligan & Oakley, 2014). Hypnotic suggestibility is the degree to which people respond to suggestions while under the influence of hypnosis (Halligan & Oakley, 2014).
>
> Interrogative suggestibility is how much a person will give in to a suggestive question and how much that person will change his/her answers after the person in control exerts pressure on him or her (Gudjonsson, 1894).
>
> Placebo effect and interrogative suggestibility are considered indirect suggestions while hypnotic suggestibility is categorized as a direct suggestion. (https://www.wcgclinical.com/insights/archive/category/blog/)

The researchers were under the leadership of Mark Opler, PhD, MPH, Chief Research Officer of the Wirb-Copernicus Group, WCG, of Princeton, New Jersey. This giant company prides itself in measurably improving the quality and efficiency of clinical trials and helping biopharmaceutical, biotechnology and life sciences companies and institutions to development new treatments and therapies for patients. The researchers conclude to further explore the influence of technology on suggestibility, the topic of this trial, as the current research needed to shift in two ways. First, future studies must move their main focus from how the presentation of information through technology influences participants' level of overall comprehension to how it influences participants' level of suggestibility. Second, research should explore how situational factors like computer-based treatments or digital measurement methods compared to their non-digital equivalents. It should then document how that in turn influenced trial participants' suggestibility.

Am I *really* reading what I am reading? Is Opler with his conclusion acknowledging that all psychological and psychiatric clinical trial outcomes ever presented as empirical first evidence are faulty? Did he say that everyone participating in those trials, unless simian, rattus, cani, lepus, blattas et al., suffered lesser or larger degrees of suggestibility/ Did he affirm that this suggestibility renders trial findings null and void? Might this knowledge be the reason that eminent former American Psychiatrist Association president Allan Frances so confidently blasted out to whomever wanted to know: "It's all bullshit!"?

Before joining WIRB Copernicus Group ("WCG"), a provider of clinical trial solutions, by the way, Columbia University-educated Opler founded ProPhase. This became a global provider of specialty services focusing on applied measurement in central nervous system (CNS) psychiatry, neurology and rare and orphan diseases. It joined with MedAvante, the leading global provider of centralized expert psychiatric and neuro-cognition rating and monitoring services to the pharmaceutical, biotechnology and medical device industries in 2017. Its scientific research and developments fell under Chief Research Officer Opler's direction.

Whilst doing that, he maintains the titles of adjunct assistant professor of psychiatry at New York University and assistant professor of clinical neuroscience at Columbia University's College of Physicians and Surgeons. He is also leading the development of the new upcoming edition of the Positive And Negative Syndrome Scale Rating Criteria, PANSS Manual for short, published by Lewis A. Opler (1948-2018), Mark's father. Until his death in 2018, Lewis was professor of clinical psychiatry at Columbia University Medical Center and associate clinical professor, Department of Psychiatry at Albert Einstein College of Medicine/Montefiore Medical Center. He also served as clinical director at the Bronx Psychiatric Center Bronx, New York et al. in 1987.

PANNS is purportedly the "gold standard" that all assessments of psychotic behavioral disorders should follow. It is a medical scale in line with the Beck scale, the MMPI and other scales to measure the herd's emotional states of mind wildly discussed in *Fallacy 1*. It is administered purportedly in a 30- to 50-minute clinical interview, rating the presence and severity of positive and negative symptoms in people considered schizophrenic or suffering general psychopathology, differ from the norm, within the past week, we read. Psychopathology in itself is the study of abnormal cognition, behavior and experiences. It differs according to social norms and rests upon a number of constructs that are deemed to be the social norm at any particular era. These are so diligently documented for later use of the Tavistock Institute-employed by German psychiatrist Wundt between 1910 and 1920 AD in his voluminous Folk-Soul, the soul of a nation, compilation.

PANN is also widely used in the study of antipsychotic therapy, we hear. This bio-medicine drug treatment is imposed by any self-respecting mental health consultant on anyone presenting with a perceived existential life-crises, including PTSD, and now COVID journeyers (https://academic.oup.com/schizophreniabulletin/article/13/2/261/1919795).

But now the punch line: to administer PANN, the interviewer must be trained to a standardized level of reliability. In other words, they must be familiar with the degree to which scores from a particular test are consistent from one use of the test to the next. Reliability is the characteristic of a set of test scores that relates to the amount of random error from the measurement process that might be embedded in the scores. Scores that are highly reliable are precise, reproducible, and consistent from one testing occasion to another. That is, if the testing process were repeated with a group of test takers, essentially the same results would be obtained. Various kinds of reliability coefficients, with values ranging between 0.00 (much error) and 1.00 (no error), are usually used to indicate the amount of error in the scores.

Reliability is a very important piece of validity evidence. A measure is said to have a high reliability, if it produces similar results under consistent conditions. But consistent conditions in psychiatric settings can never be provided. Nor can the suggestibility of the one interviewed or the interviewee even be measured. So, we again grant psychiatrist Allan Frances kudos for his acknowledgement of his learned society's lack of credentials when stating: "It is all bullshit."

But why do they do it, these men and women spending their lives manipulating the minds of others whilst drugging them to the hilt? Luciferic consciousness? We'll get to it later.

Mark Opler of the WIRB Copernicus Group ("WCG") continues to pursue his research into the human mind focusing on human etiology. This is the cause, set of causes or manner of causation of diseases or conditions, the treatment of serious and persistent mental disorders, surely with PTSD included. And, oddly enough, he is interested in phenomenology, the study of structures of consciousness as experienced from the first-person point of view.

The first-person perspective, we learn, is a central concept of critical psychology that tries to make psychological processes and the subjective dimension of human life understandable. The concept refers to the point of view of the "I" as the way in which a human subject has access to herself/himself and the world and to her/his experiences, emotions, thoughts and actions. The concept builds on a socio-materially situated understanding of the human being. It stands in opposition to mainstream psychologies, which conduct their research from an external—third-person—perspective. With such a view from above, or as critics argue, from "nowhere," psychological phenomena and human life can be understood only in an abstract and reduced form. The individual appears one-sidedly as an effected and conditioned being. The concrete reality of human subjectivity and agency, the active and acting side of everyday practice, remains out of sight. (https://link.springer.com/referenceworkentry/10.1007%2F978-1-4614-5583-7_113)

It is unknown, if Mark Opler during his phenomenology research tries to gather insight into himself with the help of meditation. Nor whether he applies Patañjali Sanskrit and Tamil works, Padmasambhāva writings, Avicenna's insights or Rumi's poetry. Nor do we know if he considers Rhazes exclamation:

> "The doctors' aim is to do well, even to our enemies, so much more to our friends, and my profession forbids us to do harm to our kindred, as it is instituted for the benefit and welfare of the human race, and God imposed on physicians the oath not to compose mortiferous remedies." (https://link.springer.com/article/10.1007/s00381-017-3493-z).

If he does, perhaps Padmasambhāva's observation would give him food for thought:

> "If you want to know about your past lives, look at your present condition; if you want to know about your future life, look at your present actions." (Padme, 8th c. BC)

But I digress.

Let's get back to Rockefeller-sponsored Sargent, dwelling at Harvard and researching human suggestibility with a vengeance under the guidance of Cobb. Both would be henceforth instrumental in its applications against humanity, as we will see later. Whilst still on U.S. ground, though, he went to Washington, DC, to meet with Walter Jackson Freeman II (1895–1972). Philadelphia born, Yale educated physician Freeman was an American lobotomy specialist with a PhD in neuropathology and head of the neurology department at George Washington University. Freeman's lobotomy procedure severed the connection between the frontal lobes and the thalamus. Because he was not a neurosurgeon, he directed neurosurgeon James Watts to perform the first prefrontal lobotomy in the United States in 1936.

He then went into it with a vengeance. By 1942, the duo had performed over 200 lobotomy procedures and had published results claiming:

- 63% of patients had improved.
- 23% were reported to be unchanged.
- 14% were worse after surgery.

Freeman then traveled from mental institution to mental institution across the great land performing lobotomies and educating staff on the procedure. Sargant, who had met three of Freeman's lobotomized patients, was enchanted, resolving to introduce the operation into Britain at his earliest opportunity. That the procedure could very well lead to what Pavlov called the shutdown point had yet to reach his conscience.

Pavlov had added the exploration of the human cortical and subcortical influences to his mosaic action of the brain. He had mapped the effect of sleep on the spread of transmarginal inhibition and the origin of neurotic disturbances principally created through a collision, a conflict, between cortical excitation and inhibition. With that, he laid open the way for the controllers to traumatize anyone they wanted to traumatize to perfection. This is now being researched in trials with humans - rats in the elite's opinion - by COVID injections of differing ingredients. His findings, however, most likely originated with English neurophysiologist, pathologist and bacteriologist Sir Charles Scott Sherrington (1857 –1952). He was perhaps best known for coining the term "synapse" to describe the junction where two neurons communicate. While Sherrington's work to understand synapses and neural communication was important, his studies of reflexes, proprioception, spinal nerves, muscle action and movement were much more expansive and probably even more influential.

By 1906, Sherrington had already published his book *The Integrative Action of the Nervous System: Neurobiology of Homeostasis*. In the book, he discussed his neuron theory, the "synapse," the communication between neurons, and a mechanism for the reflex-arc function, a term he had introduced in 1897. The work resolved the debate between the neuron and reticular theories in mammals. It proclaimed that the mammalian nervous system was one single continuous network, as Sherrington determined that the central nervous system indeed coordinates various parts of the body. It also reported that the reflexes are the simplest expressions of the interactive action of the nervous system, enabling the entire body to function toward a definite purpose, pointing out that reflexes must be goal-directive and purposive.

Furthermore, Sherrington established the nature of postural reflexes, their dependence on the anti-gravity stretch reflex and traced the afferent stimulus to the proprioceptive end organs. He had previously shown these to be sensory in nature. Proprioception, also referred to as kinaesthesia, is the sense of self-movement and body position sometimes described as the "sixth sense." He dedicated his work to Sir David Ferrier (1843 -1928). This Scottish neurologist and psychologist conducted experiments on the brains of live animals such as monkeys in 1881. He was the first scientist to be tried under the *Cruelty to Animals Act*, 1876. The Parliament of the United Kingdom enacted it following a major public debate over vivisection to set limits on the practice of, and instituted a licensing system for, animal experimentation. It amended the *Cruelty to Animals Act* of 1849. 110 years later, it was replaced by the *Animals (Scientific Procedures) Act* 1986.

It was Ferrier's research, obtained under most brutal circumstances, that inspired Sherrington to focus on spinal nerves and reflexes. That led him to map the motor nerves traveling from the spinal cord to the muscles and the sensory nerves traveling from the muscles to the spinal cord. This task took him almost 10 years. He also explored how these nerves functioned and created a map of the areas of the body served by only a single spinal nerve, the areas known as dermatomes. And he mapped the ape motor cortex, expanding on previous maps made with dogs and monkeys. (https://neuroscientificallychallenged.com/posts/ history-of-neuroscience-charles-scott-sherrington)

In due course of his research, he also discovered that spinal reflex is composed of integrated actions of the nervous system. These involve such complex components as the excitation and inhibition of many nerves. These inductions are the increase or decrease of inhibition brought on by previous excitation and the irradiation of nerve impulses to the body's many nerve centres. He shared these discoveries in 1904 in 10 lectures delivered at Yale University, before sharing them with the world in book form in 1906.

His summarization represented two decades of painstaking research and his interpretation about the fundamental nature of mammals' nervous system – that is us. It completely changed the way subsequent generations of humanists, the Darwinian-we-are-animal gang, viewed humans' central nervous system's organization. We are also told that Sherrington's magnum opus is familiar to every student of the subject of psychology and psychiatry. It contains the basic concepts, terminology and information on the human nervous system and its actions and consequences on the human psyche under what conditions. This in turn indicates that every single student of that field knows of the transmarginal inhibition (TMI) breaking point innate in every human being. In me it manifested when I could no longer stand straight, but walked bent over, looking like a witch, while they blamed me for faking it.

Pavlov took it all a step further, discovering that patients at a certain point of traumatization reach a shutdown point. When they do, they often become socially dysfunctional or develop one or several unmentioned personality disorders. Often, we are told, those patients dissociating during stressful or painful experiences may experience PTSD for the remainder of their lives and more easily dissociate or shut down in future stressful situations. How did he find his subjects, we wonder? In Lavrentiy Pavlovich Beria's (1899-1953) dungeons? That this shut-down point can be reached through physical and mental torture is a given. I lived it, though it took me 10 years to reach the shutdown point. By that time, I was skinnier than a rail with a consistent blood pressure hovering around 180 over 90 threatening a stroke or heart attack and making me throw in the towel. It had taken 10 years of exquisitely administered mental torture - by employer, WCB and union representatives and numerous psychiatrists and psychologist in unison to get me there. What they did to me they do to all other claimants, unless belonging to a secret society.

Beginning around 1930, Pavlov attempted to apply his hypotheses and laws of physics and neurobiology to explain human psychoses. He assumed that the excessive inhibition characteristic of a psychotic person was a protective mechanism—shutting out the external world—in that it excluded injurious stimuli that had previously caused extreme excitation. In Russia, this idea became the basis for treating psychiatric patients in quiet and non-stimulating external surroundings. During this period, Pavlov also announced the important principle of language function in human beings. He based his insight on long chains of conditional reflex reactions involving words already observed by Wundt. The function of language involves not only words, he held, but an elaboration of generalizations not possible in animals lower than humans. That was because rattus had not learned to speak and elucidate thoughts and opinions on its own treatment. He insisted that it was impossible to deal with human mental phenomena scientifically, except when reducing them to measurable physiological quantities. Hurrah, Allan Frances, that none of it can be scientifically documented, so is all bullshit!

Regardless, Sherrington (and Pavlov's work) laid the basis for the scientific investigation and analysis of human behaviour. He did recognize the pre-eminence of the subjective and its independence of scientific methods. In his enthusiasm for science, however, he did not bother to clarify or define what separates the two. As a physician, he also uncritically accepted the psychiatric views on schizophrenia and paranoia. He also adopted such neural concepts as induction and irradiation as valid for humans' higher mental activity. We are told that the arts and crafts science of psychology looks at his work as philosophically lacking, with many a psychiatrist now considering his explanations too limited and some neurophysiologists having taken a greater interest in the developments of electrophysiology and biochemistry speak biomedicine.

And what is the philosophy of psychiatry? Philosophical discussions of mental illness fall into three categories:

- Topics arising when viewing psychiatry as a special science and using the methods and concepts of philosophy of science. This includes discussion of such issues as explanation, reduction and classification.
- Conceptual issues arising when trying to understand the very idea of mental illness and its ethical and experiential dimensions.
- Interactions between psychopathology and the philosophy of mind. Philosophers have used clinical phenomena, [experimental laboratory-derived research data] to illuminate issues in the philosophy of mind, and philosophical findings to try to understand mental illness (https://plato.stanford.edu/entries/psychiatry/).

In other words, that too is all bullshit.

Be it as it may, with Pavlov's work becoming known throughout the West, the idea of "human conditioning" as an automatic form of human learning took hold. It was combined with researchers' systematic discovery of how humans perceive themselves, their consequent behaviour and their ways of their learning processes. Ever since then this has facilitated humanity's manipulation and the control of our behaviour through classical conditioning effectuated by television, social media and mass media. The mental health industry, since Madame Blavatsky's days in full operation, picked up on it in a hurry. Pavlov's Conditional Behaviour Therapy, CBT, together with their mind-altering pharmaceutical drugs found their place at the center of their PTSD treatment hypothesis. They paid no head to severity, and thus systematically destroyed the *sui generis* of any human being unfortunate enough to land in their clutches. And all in the line with Lenin's mandate:

> "We will grind the public between the millstones of inflation and property taxes. We will destroy the population and create a slave race."

Pavlov was merely obeying his master.

But never mind. Let's bring this chapter to a halt with gratitude of finally seeing some of the foundation of what has been wilfully and purposely done against a vast number of individuals by the medical profession of all stripes and colours. First and foremost is the mental health profession. And what is presently, with the excuse of COVID, done to humanity worldwide, shall take us somewhat promptly to the Tavistock Institute. It was deemed lethal to human wellbeing by authors such as David Icke and John Coleman and largely responsible for the proliferation of perverted human perception of an honorable life. Since Wundt's days, this was made possible by the insights gathered into the human psyche by the above-mentioned characters and those introduced in *Fallacy 1*. At least since the 1950s, the Tavistock Institute worked in the fields of human social engineering and manipulation, including creating and supporting colour revolutions worldwide and the mass psychosis hysteria created for the herd's culling by COVID injections (Dr. Robert Malone: *The War Room* February 23, 2022).

That the blind are lead by the blind should be noted as well. In 2021, the overall rate of prescription drug abuse among doctors is calculated to be five times higher than in the general population, with 69% of them reporting they depended on antidepressants and other prescription drugs to cope with stress- and physical and emotional pain (https://americanaddictioncenters.org/medical-professionals/substance-abuse-among-doctors-key-statistics). The misuse of prescription drugs, particularly opioids and is very prevalent among doctors. Nearly 36% of physicians enrolled in physician health programs suffer from opioid abuse. The suicide rate in male physicians is 40% higher than in the general population and 130% higher in female doctors. And these are the people trust to direct our life?

So, let's take a look at how this human mind manipulation succeeded with such brilliance, shall we? Actually, it began in earnest with their treatment of WWI and WWII shell-shock experiencers. They were used as live subjects traumatized into a state of insanity to find their emotional breaking point, used ever since to drive us out of existence. (https://euvsdisinfo.eu/report/the-tavistock-institute-is-largely-responsible-for-the-proliferation-of-perverts-all-over-the-world).

27

WHO MADE US WILFULLY IGNORANT AND STUPID?

Scottish neurologist and psychologist David Ferrier (1843–1926) was the first scientist tried under the United Kingdom's first Cruelty to Animals Act in 1876. He shared something in common with English neurophysiologist, bacteriologist, and pathologist Sir Charles Scott Sherrington (1857–1952) and Russian physiologist Ivan Petrovich Pavlov (1849–1936). All three focused mainly on the functioning of the human body. In contrast, German physician Wilhelm Maximilian Wundt (1832–1920) claimed a vast scope. His writings amounted to an estimated 53,000 pages dealing with animal and human physiology, poisons, vision, spiritualism, hypnotism, history, and politics. He fell in love with human psychology, neurology and all subjects related to it. He planned to establish philosophico-scientific systems of knowledge to legitimize anything and everything subjective. That would include human emotions and feelings, consciousness, and mind. He wanted to make them fields of empirical sciences, such as the science of psychology. How? By allowing for the study of any scientific inquiry into any topic, from neuro-biology to psychology to physics, metaphysic and ethics from a philosophical perspective.

Wundt grew up during a time of great European pursuit of educational, medical, and technological knowledge. This included developing new research methods into the human psyche. He began his academic career in 1851, studying at the universities of Tuebingen, Berlin and Heidelberg, where he graduated with a doctor of medicine degree in 1856. In 1858, he joined 11-year-older physician, psychologist, and physicist German Hermann Ludwig Ferdinand von Helmholtz (1821–1894). Von Helmholzt was known for his mathematics of the eye, theories of vision, ideas on visual perception of space and color vision, sensations of tone, perception of sound and the physiology of perception.

In physics Helmholtz is known for his theories on human conservation of energy. He is also known for laying the foundation for electro-, chemical, and mechanical thermodynamics.

As a philosopher, he is known for developing the philosophy of science idea, later to be elaborated and fine-tuned by Wundt and others. It is in essence the branch of philosophy concerned with the foundations, methods and implications of science. Its central question roughly 170 years later still revolves around what qualifies as science, the reliability of scientific theories and any of the sciences' ultimate purpose. This particular discipline enthuses in exploring the relationship between science and truth, we read. The philosophy of science apparently operates under an immensely fluid perception. It focuses on issues such as ethics, bioethics, scientific misconduct, ethical, metaphysical, epistemic and semantic aspects of its chosen topics.

Wundt, an assistant to Helmholtz from 1857 to 1864, taught the laboratory course in physiology. This resulted in his interest in psychological problems and his first psychological lecture in 1862. It was followed in 1863 by his *Vorlesungen über die Menschenund Tier-Seele*, Lectures on Human and Animal Souls in 1896 published in English (2 vols., Leipzig, 1863, translated by J. G. Creighton and E. B. Titchener as Lectures on Human and Animal Psychology, London, 1896). Wundt was appointed associate professor for anthropology and medical psychology in 1864. Ain that role, he gave lectures on the fundamentals of physiological psychology, which would be published at Leipzig in 1874 as *Grundzüge der physiologischen Psychologie* (translated by E. B. Titchener as Principles of Physiological Psychology, New York, 1904). That same year, he accepted a professorship in inductive philosophy in Zürich. He held that post until moving to Leipzig in 1874, where he founded the world's first experimental laboratory in psychology in 1879. It was the *Institut für Experimentelle Psychologie*, whence, we shall see, he and his students exerted enormous influence on the development of psychology and psychiatry as a scientific discipline *en route* to dumbing down humanity to the point of stupefaction, especially in the United States.

And what precisely is physiological psychology? Simple. Physiology studies the body; psychology studies the mind (work.chron.com). Thus, physiological psychology, also known as biological psychology and behavioural neuroscience, combines the two subjects. They purport to discover how the human brain effectuates and affects human consciousness and thought. Remember that the Wundt's of the world believe that human consciousness and the mind reside in the physical brain. However, the ancients of Mahabharata days thought of the human mind and the human body as separate entities. We, the herd, are still taught that the way and method by which consciousness forms in our brain is a mystery. But the craft and art neuro-science masters are still convinced that our physical brain has a major effect on our thoughts and personalities. They hold that the switch on, switch off mechanism is somewhere to be found among the grey matter.

But where? Physiological psychology, therefore, is the study of human behaviour through physiological impact. This means fiddling around with alive and active human brains. It means using activation tools, such as Wundt's hammer. It means noting brain-matter reactions transmitted either through electrodes or facilitated by various types of stimuli and subject-biological manipulation. Meanwhile, the researchers enjoy observing the resulting rat-or-human behaviour. We know that the atheistic worldview dictates human consciousness to be nothing other than the result of the physical brain's nervous system activity. Results of their methods in the eyes of the beholders lends empirical, observation-based aspect of validity to their human behavioural science's hypotheses. Those engaged in experimental psychology laboratory research steadfastly maintain that we humans are aware of our selves and our surroundings only because neural signals race around in our bodies and brains making us aware. How they view themselves and where they fit into the human race, if actually doing so, remains a mystery. However, Carpenter's 1988 movie *They Live* springs eerily to mind.

And what are physiological psychology's principles? First, understand that it is a subdivision of behavioural neuroscience, also known as biological psychology. Picture this: researchers in laboratory experiments study the neural mechanisms of perception and behaviour by directly manipulating human and other animal subjects. This typically involves examining the brain's neurotransmissions and the psychological events associated with biological activity (emotiv.com/glossary/behavioural-neuroscience/). Physiological psychology also covers topics such as genetic and molecular biological substrates of behaviour, neuropsychology, learning and memory, motivation, and emotion. And it covers sensory processes relating to the body's response to a behaviour or an activity within the subject. It also involves research of brain cells, structures, components, and actions produced by chemical interactions. Experimental psychologists usually research subjects' sleep, emotion, ingestion, senses, reproductive behaviour, learning/memory, communication, psychopharmacology reactions and perceived neurological disorders.

What is the basis for all these studies into human behaviour and its origin. And what id the basis for studying how the human nervous system intertwines with the body to create specific physiological or psychological reactions and behaviours? Could it be an attempt to learn to read us like a book? They admit that their main purpose for psychological research is to develop theories to describe human brain-behaviour relationships. For what purpose? To enable physiological psychologists to detect many truths about human behaviour. They diagnose human emotional and behavioural disorders by connecting what we say and do with actual physical operations of our brain cells, structures, and chemistry. But why detect these truths? To endlessly manipulate us.

If so, the art seems to have been so perfected nowadays as to give the elite, the illuminati, the Luciferic consciousness or whatever we wish to call it enough insights and tools to manipulate us into oblivion. What did Danish MP Ida Auken, by profession priest of the secular Church of Denmark, state in 2016, when addressing the World Economic Forum? "Welcome To 2030: I Own Nothing, Have No Privacy And Life Has Never Been Better.

You'll own nothing and be happy." Yes, indeed. Klaus Schwab, WEF's official founder, since then oft repeated it. Auken predicts, that by 2030 we won't own a house, a car, appliances or clothes, instead renting everything. We will also be subjected to mass surveillance in a have's and the have-not's world, all slowly engineered by us since the 1820s (https://knowyourmeme.com/memes/youll-own-nothing-and-be-happy). At least that was the plan. As of 2022, the essay is no longer available on the World Economic Forum's website and the plan may have changed, in part thanks to the Canadian truckers, eh?

But back to Wilhelm Wundt and his endeavours so instrumental in leading us to where we are at present.

Whilst playing with his experimental psychology research and endeavors, he engaged in a stint as politician. In 1866, he joined the sovereign country of Baden's parliament until it united with the German Empire in 1871. That year, he briefly returned to his alma mater, the University of Heidelberg. Soon after, he transferred to the University of Zurich as professor of "Inductive Philosophy." That means teaching induction or inductive reasoning, sometimes called inductive logic, which aims to develop a theory. This is not the same as deductive reasoning, which aims to test an existing theory. In all fields of academia, it is an absolute necessity to acquire supreme fluency in arguing either inductively or deductively, as he who argues best wins, wit Fauci et al. in COVID 19 and Omicron.

As we can see in our main topic (experimental human-animal psychology), inductive reasoning is used all of the time. It extracts a likely but not certain premise from a certain specimen. From specific research and limited observations on a specific project, it uses the resulting data to draw the conclusions. This is called inductive logic, (Alina Bradford, Mindy Weisberger: "Deductive reasoning vs. Inductive reasoning"; *Live Science* 2021).

American epidemiologist Sylvia Wassertheil-Smoller (1932-) and joined the Department of Epidemiology & Population Health at New York City's research-intensive Albert Einstein College of Medicine school in 1969. As distinguished university professor emerita, she explains:

> "In inductive inference, we go from the specific to the general. We make many observations, discern a pattern, make a generalization, and infer an explanation or a theory...[because] In science, there is a constant interplay between inductive inference (based on observations) and deductive inference (based on theory), until we get closer and closer to the 'truth,' which we can only approach but not ascertain with complete certainty."

In other words, the reliability of a conclusion made with inductive logic depends entirely on the completeness of the observations. For instance, let's say that you have a bag of coins; you pull three coins from the bag, and each coin is a penny. Using inductive logic, you might then propose that all of the coins in the bag are pennies. "Even though all of the initial observations – that each coin taken from the bag was a penny – are correct, inductive reasoning does not guarantee that the conclusion will be true." There we have it. It's all bullshit!

Nevertheless, we are told that inductive reasoning has its place in the scientific method. Scientists of all genres use it to form hypotheses and theories, with deductive reasoning allowing them to apply the theories to specific situations. This is the reason why 24 psychiatrists and psychologists can reach 24 different diagnoses on one genuine PTSD patient —me—without blinking an eye. And each one of them can defend their position by either deductive or inductive reasoning. It all depends on their beliefs and academic education in the field and their personal view of life and living and religion and colour and place of birth and upbringing. It is Wundt who apparently caused this state of affairs about 150 years ago.

By 1875, he had had enough of that. So, he left for Leipzig, there finding his forever home and working side by side with preeminent scientists of his time. They all had been primarily educated as physicians. Among them were experimental psychologist Ernst Heinrich Weber (1795–1878) and experimental psychologist, philosopher, and physicist Gustav Theodor Fechner (1801–1887). They were both his seniors by a decade or more.

Weber had received his M.D. from the University of Leipzig in 1815. By 1818, he had obtained the position of professor in comparative anatomy and 1821 saw him as the university's chair of human anatomy. His friend Fechner had studied medicine at the Medizinische Akademie Carl Gustav Carus in Dresden. Fechner joined Weber in Leipzig in 1818, there to be appointed professor of physics in 1834. By 1839, Fechner had badly injured his eyes by gazing at the sun through coloured glasses to research the phenomena of color and vision. That forced him to sit on his hands doing nothing but to contemplate life and living. During his recovery, he jotted down his thoughts with feeble eyesight. This appears to have propelled him into his in-depth consideration of the relation between humans' mental and physical processes and sensations.

Once up and about again, he shared his observations on the subjects with whomever wanted to listen. With time, he became renowned for setting forth a theory of mind-body relations. He expounded on it in such books as *Ueber die Seelenfrage and Elemente der Psychophysik, About Questions of the Soul and Elements of Psychophysics, The Little Book of Life After Death and The Religion Of A Scientist*. Discussions with his peers had him feeling that his delirious insights while living through his eye trauma were indeed building a quantitative relationship between humans' mental and physical worlds. After all, Fechner's self-observations, in their view, provided the empirical scientific evidence (https://plato.stanford.edu/entries/fechner/).

The result? Fechner and Weber are credited with demonstrating the non-linear relationship between a human psychological sensation and the physical intensity of a stimulus. This is known as the Weber-Fechner laws. It consists of two related hypotheses in the field of psychophysics related to human perception. More specifically, they define the relationship between an actual change in a physical stimulus and the perceived change by the living entity. This includes stimuli to all senses: vision, hearing, taste, touch and smell. Ergo, it is the study of quantitative relations between psychological and/or physical events. In other words, it measures the relationship between how we react to things that happen to us. More specifically, it measures our physical or mental sensations and reactions to physical and/or mental/emotional stimuli. This is what Pavlov began to so exquisitely explore with dogs and humans just a few years later. And so he served in human's manipulation honed to perfection in years to come. It began in earnest with WWI's shell-shocked, as we shall see shortly (Jeans, James (1968/1937). Science & Music, p.222 & 224. Dover Publications).

Wundt became professor of philosophy at the University of Leipzig in 1877. That was shortly before Weber's death in 1878 and Fechner's in 1887. He was more than familiar with their work and the psychological and psychophysical principles in general. Furthermore, like all well-educated people of his time, he also knew their work had actually been set in motion two centuries earlier by German polymath Gottfried Wilhelm (von) Leibniz (1646 -1716). Leibniz had developed the philosophy of theoretical psychology long before even the notion of a branch of traditional so-called empirical and experimental psychology existed. His work encompassed everything anyone ever wanted to discover about humanity's quirks. Of course, the Mahābhārata, Patañjali, Padmasambhāva, Avicenna, Rhazes and Rumi preceded him in that knowledge. But all that was ignored by the mid-1800s everything-human-is-science labelling academia of the learned society.

So, this combining and incorporating of existing and developing theories on the human psyche, resulting in experimental psychology, began with Leibniz in the 1600s. It was picked up by Weber and Fechner in the mid-1800s. Then Wundt took over around 1875. He ran with it full speed towards the title of father of experimental psychology when he proclaimed in his memoirs: "I would rather call Weber the father of experimental psychology [as] It was Weber's great contribution to think of measuring psychic quantities and of showing the exact relationships between them, to be the first to understand this and carry it out."

And thus, it was that Wundt began to hold court in Leipzig. All throughout the western and part of the eastern world, those wanting to rise to prominence in the arts and crafts sciences of human mind exploration, manipulation and perversion turned his way. They had little choice but to, preferably eagerly, attend his lectures and observe his experiments at his Leipzig experimental psychology laboratory. His lab had been established for him by the university's directorate in 1876. He had brought from Zurich the equipment needed to experiment with and measure live-animal and human reactions. He carried out his research-demonstrations on live animal and human participants in front of captive audiences. He searched in live brains for the location of the human spirit, mind and consciousness, perhaps. Here is how he explained it in his 1897 book *Outlines of Psychology*:

> "Consciousness in this sense, as a comprehensive interconnection of simultaneous and successive psychical processes, shows itself in experience first of all in the psychical life of [p. 204] the *individual as individual consciousness*. But we have analogous interconnection in the combination of individuals, although it is limited to certain sides of mental life, so that we may further include under the more general concept consciousness the concepts of *collective consciousness, of social consciousness*, etc. For all these broader forms, however, the foundation is the individual consciousness, and it is to this that we will first turn our attention." (Wilhelm Max Wundt (1897) Translated by Charles Hubbard Judd (1897); III. Interconnection of psychical compounds. § 15. Consciousness and attention: For collective consciousness see § 21, 14.)

In his view, it seems, individual consciousness stands under the same external conditions as psychical phenomena in general. It is merely another expression, referring more particularly to the mutual relations of the components of these phenomena to one another (https://psychclassics.yorku.ca/Wundt/Outlines/sec15.htm). He also contends:

> "The interconnection of psychical processes which makes up consciousness, necessarily has its deepest spring in the *processes of combination* which are continually taking place between the elements of the single contents of experience. Such processes are operative in the formation of single psychical compounds and they are what give rise to the simultaneous unity of the state of consciousness present at a given moment and also to the continuity of successive states. These processes of combination are of the most various kinds; each one has its individual coloring, which is never exactly reproduced in any second case. Still, the most general differences are those exhibited by the attention in the passive reception of impressions and the active apperception of the same. (ibid)"

By the late 1800s, Wundt had reached the same conclusion as Fechner and Weber held before him. He decided that the process of human perception could not solely be explained on a physiological level but had to somehow involve psychological principles. So, he set out to find the biological processes that underly our sensation. He wanted to discover where these different classes and locations of sensory receptors were located in the human brain. He wanted to know how they worked. He wanted to learn what stimuli would produce and relay information to the human nervous system (springer.com). To spread his views, research projects and their results, he established the *Philosophische Studien*—Philosophical Studies in 1881. It was the world's first academic journal for psychological research. It would run until 1902, merely to spread the research discoveries from his experimental laboratory and his psychological clinic. Most importantly, this would spread them in the fastest way possible throughout the learned society so they could be all on the same page.

He searched for means to give meaning and scientific proof to his hypotheses, theories and perceptions by way of "inductive reasoning". He wanted to find appropriate ways to undertake the research. So, he gave his students assignments to invent suitable instruments for use in their professor's experiments. In this way, he collected many a piece of new equipment. Among them was the *tachistoscope*, an apparatus for use in exposing visual stimuli as pictures, letters or words. For an extremely brief period, he used it chiefly to assess visual perception and to increase reading speed (https://dictionary.apa.org/tachistoscope). It is also widely used for subliminal advertising, logos, branding and so forth to gage the speed of human conscious recognition or to test which elements of any given image are memorable to the human mind.

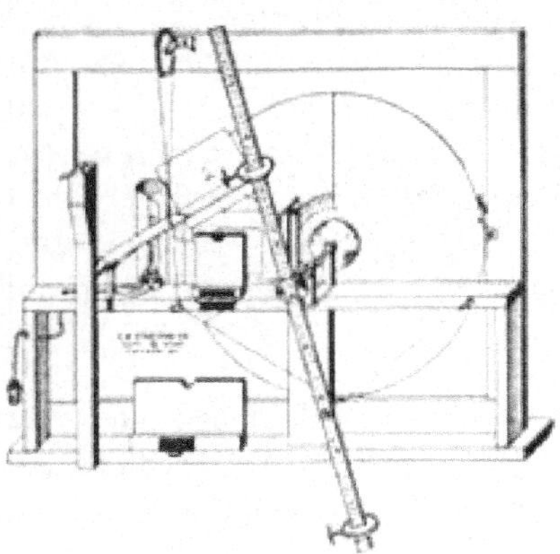

The *chronoscope*, however, was Wundt's own invention. He used it to measure short time intervals to determine the speed of projectiles and pendulums, electrical devices, timers and sensory mapping devices. This timing device is a large control hammer made of wood, brass and steel. It consists of a bent lever, whose arm is heavily weighted and turns about a horizontal axis (https://waywiser.fas.harvard.edu/search/Use%2520of%2520Control%2520Hammer).

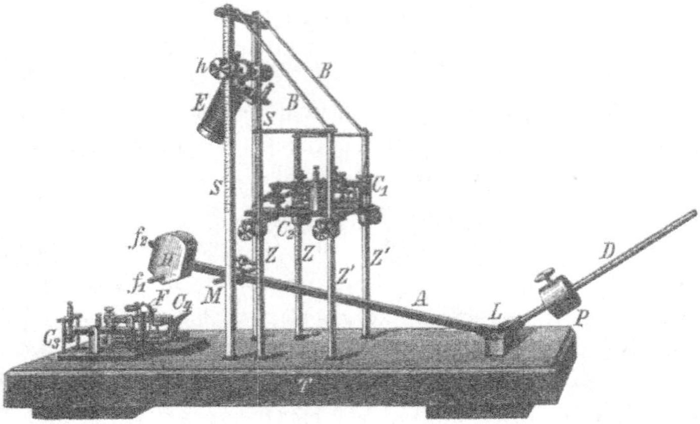

Wundt's control-hammer, 1893.
Maker: Carl Krille
Dimensions:
45.5 x 84 x 21 cm (17 15/16 x 33 1/16 x 8 1/4 in.)
cylindrical weight on hammer arm: 5 cm (1 15/16 in.)
(IMAGE: Control hammer after a design by Wundt. The large model can be adjusted to intervals between 100 and 600 milliseconds.)

As the hammerhead descends, a cross bar on the shank makes or breaks the electrical contacts. An electromagnet releases the hammer, and it falls past one electrical contact. This opens the circuit to the Hipp Chronoscope, engaging its clutch to start measuring time. When the hammer falls past a second electrical contact, the circuit is closed. This disengages the clutch on the Hipp Chronoscope, stopping its dial from moving, we read on Wundt's laboratory's webpage. (Source : W. Wundt, Grundzu X ge der physiologischen Psychologie, 4th ed (Leipzig, 1893), part II, 331).

So much was happening at once. Wundt's future pupil Pavlov graduated from St. Petersburg's Medical Military Academy in 1879/ Graduate students from around the western and eastern worlds crowded around him to carry out research under his direction. He developed the research topics and demanded that students perform them outside of his regular course work. And in 1883, he moved the entire menagerie into new quarters. The University of Leipzig's leadership had built him an eleven-room laboratory designed especially to his desires for his experimental psychological research, opened simply as the Psychological Institute. That milestone marked the official birth of psychology as a science and legitimized experimental psychology as an independent academically accredited field of study as one of its branches.

So, who was this man obsessed with such a creation? He was married with three children. To give us an idea of Wundt's breadth of thoughts and knowledge, he spent six days a week giving two hours daily lecturing between 1875 and 1879. His lectures were in the fields of psychology of language, anthropology, logic, and epistemology. Some specific topics included psychology, brain and nerves, as well as physiology, cosmology historical and general philosophy. So popular were his classes, that all of Europe, the U.S., Britain and the Slavic nations' learned society members flogged to his lectures and laboratory to learn about and practice this new art and craft science of experimental psychology. To give us an indication of the volume of work Wundt faced between 1889 and 1909, he employed 15 assistants to aid with his laboratory research and experiments.

For what? To gather the empirical evidence, the data, on whatever idea that surfaced in his mind. To run experiments to provide a measurable or observable reaction. This is called "the scientific method". One repeats each experiment to test its efficacy against which a hypothesis can be tested and reliably measured. "If a statement is about something that is itself observable, then the empirical testing can be direct. We just have a look to see if it is true. For example, the statement, 'The litmus paper is pink', is subject to direct empirical testing," wrote Peter Kosso in his book *A Summary of Scientific Method* (Springer 2011). We are told in the synopsis that the book provides a clear and intuitive model of scientific methods. Does that mean intuition suffices to substantiate one's hypothesis, if knowing how to argue expertly and with lots of flair? Who knows, who cares? They are all in it together, and few will ever admit the truth, as Allen Frances, best known as chair of the American Psychiatric Association task force overseeing the fourth edition of the *Diagnostic and Statistical Manual of Mental Disorders* (DSM-IV) claimed in 2010, "It's all bullshit."

Following the scientific method, one presents to one's peers for review all the data gathered on whatever idea surfaced in one's mind, soul or spirit. They will accept or deny its applications to humanity, as at length discussed in I. Let's take COVID-19 injections as an example. The 80,000 pages of research data were presented by the participating pharma-giants to the FDA. The FDA accepted the data as benevolent to the herd. Millions of those who voluntarily consented to being injected with these experimental drugs died or were maimed for life. Because of it, a team of over 1,000 lawyers and over 10,000 medical experts led by Dr. Reiner Fuellmich sprung to action. in In November 2021, they began the Nuremberg 2 legal proceedings against the CDC, WHO, the Davos Group and world leaders for crimes against humanity at The International Criminal Court. That is the intergovernmental organization and international tribunal seated in The Hague, Netherlands. (https://ca.childrenshealthdefense.org/wp-content/uploads/1000NUR2.pdf).

It took until March 2022 to get the 80,000 pages of COVID-19 research trial data released through a freedom-of-information request. They had been put under lock and key for 75 years, and for a reason. They confirm Fuellmilch at al.'s claims about the damages done to humans with the injections. Thus, they present a prime example of how peer reviewed biomedicine research papers can provide cover for the truth. The discovery by Dr. Brian

Ardis that COVID 19 injections' base ingredients are king cobra and crate snake venom also came as a surprise to humanity when he published this piece of astounding news on April 12, 2022 (https://thedrardisshow.com).

You see, the central reason for inquiries into the reaction between cause and effect of physical impact on subjects was legal in nature. So was the central reason for launching the psychophysics-project in itself, the one of Wundt's hammer, and later on lobotomies and the like. They were merely undertaken in search for what would constitute a *lawful* quantitative relation between stimulus and sensation. They meant to determine the range of stimuli between these limits (Britannica.com). Why? By determining how much stimulus is just enough to produce a sensation or a response, one can specify the minimum perceptible stimulus, or the "absolute stimulus threshold", the stimulus limen, for the various senses. The trauma inflicted on research subjects to find such a lawful stimulus and its sensation to establish the lawful measure is barely imaginable. But Wundt's experimental psychophysics laboratory provided for it all to be duplicated at immensely rapid pace throughout Britain, the U.S. and Russia. And it has been duplicated in the COVID-19 wet-dream-for-scientists experiment on all humans on Earth.

Though instrumental in the undertaking, Wundt merely put into practice what Fechner had already discovered, whilst Wundt was still luxuriating in diapers. After completing his PhD in biology at Leipzig's university, Fechner had continued there as a professor. Through experiments of an undisclosed nature, he had already made significant breakthroughs in the conception of human mental states of mind. Thus, later scientists wrote that it had actually been Fechner who had created the understanding of human perception. He had argued that: "An increase in the intensity of a stimulus does not produce a one-to-one increase in the intensity of the sensation ... For example, adding the sound of one bell to that of an already ringing bell produces a greater increase in sensation than adding one bell to 10 others already ringing. Therefore, the effects of stimulus intensities are not absolute, but are relative to the amount of sensation that already exists." (https://imotions.com/blog/what-is-experimental-psychology/#history)

This ultimately means that mental perception responds to the material world. It means that the mind does not passively respond to a stimulus. If that were the case, there would be a linear relationship between the intensity of a stimulus and the actual perception of it. Instead, the perception is dynamically responsive to the stimulus. This knowledge and conception ultimately shapes much of experimental psychology and its grounding theory: that the response of the brain to the environment can be quantified. Fechner researched in this area, for many years testing his ideas of human perception. Meanwhile in Heidelberg, Wundt was married and spawning babies...and studying Fechner's work. He began research of his own on the conundrum of multi-tasking. This topic inspired him to set up his Zurich laboratory. He would use what Fechner had put on paper as a template to explore all aspect of being human that involved the mind. And he would generously study evolving experimental psychology, the academic field for testing theories of human thoughts, feelings, actions and beyond by hook and by crook. Its many branches include behavioural and cognitive psychology. By establishing the Leipzig University psychology research laboratory, Wundt created the institution necessary to force the acceptance of experimental psychology in the learned society as a science. Thus, it was broadly defined as the scientific study of the human mind.

Of course, none of the findings can be scientifically substantiated, as all test-subjects and test-interpreters' suggestibility and trans-marginal inhibition differ. This has yet to dawn on all and sundry of scientists dealing with the human mind. And the brutality involved in their explorations to obtain data is almost unimaginable. It would require an inhumane super-psychopathic nature and brings to mind possession by Luciferic consciousness. But Wundt officiated over the new science of psychology and its branch of experimental psychology with great delight. Thus, in the name of this new science, he officially authorized the torture of everything alive at leisure, either physically or mentally or both. This concept has been vigorously applied and expanded since 1883 at the latest. And it is still being vigorously applied, nowhere more visibly than in genuine PTSD journeyers' treatment. As I have said before, these people are regularly tortured to death without their knowledge by psychologists and psychiatrists' pharmacotherapy.

Wundt, who must have known about this, could care less. Going full steam ahead, he created a wide-range of experimental psychology research programs for his students. He gave them the impossible task to scientifically produce empirical evidence on humans' and animals' emotional states of mind. They were to document how these relate to the brain's functions and reactions to the pain and trauma inflicted by himself and his graduate students. He vigorously emphasized that all research approaches, explanations and documentations of the psychological phenomena gathered in the experiments had to be based on the researcher's objective observations. This was a laughable impossibility, considering that each person's suggestibility, regardless of color, race, nationality, religion or academic standing, differs from one to the next. Indeed, even the same person in the same project, depending on a multitude of circumstances, varies their state of mind at different days and times.

Wundt stopped at nothing to share with everyone who wanted to listen. He broadcast his and his students' findings about the physical brain's workings and reactions. He made use in 1910 of none other than the British government's propaganda-creating and -disseminating organization, Wellington House in London. It was ruled by the Committee of 300, which in turn was ruled by the Royal Institute.

Wundt was still ever eager-beaver to explore the science of experimental psychology further. So around the same time, he stumbled across the most basic concept of human psychology. That is the influence of language, myth and custom, and their interrelationship on the human psyche. He wondered about the part it played in forming the conscious, unconscious and subconscious aspects of the human Self, the sui generis. He gathered from his contemplations that language, myth and custom formed the fundamental components of a nation's soul, the *Volksseele*. This so fascinated him, that he put his thoughts on paper. By his death in 1920, he had published a massive ten volume compendium of anthropological and social psychological materials. It was called *Völkerpsychologie: eine Untersuchung der Entwicklungsgesetze von Sprache, Mythus und Sitte*, translated as *Ethno-Cultural Psychology: An Investigation of the Developmental Laws of Language, Myth, and Morality*. In these volumes, he purports to be tracing "the lawful development, through cultural participation, of the higher human mental processes" (Cahan & White, 1992).

His scope was vast and his output was incredible. Numerous other works preceded that compendium. Those included as encyclopaedic tomes on linguistics, logic, ethics, and religion, a "system of philosophy." These spanned a multitude of disciplines—physiology, psychology, and philosophy—of his 65-year career. The volume of his output is said to make it hard to speak of a Wundtian doctrine. The learned societies of Europe and the United States, in particular theorists in experimental psychology, seem to have taken to his ideas like ducks take to water. Much of his thinking seems to fit neatly with Darwin's hypothesis of humans evolving from cockroach to its present animal stage. For Wundt, the stages related to the arrival of human's present form from cockroach' He portrayed this through humanity's complexity of language and the artifacts of language development created by and reflected in the myths, epics and dramas of any given society (https://web.lemoyne.edu/~hevern/narpsych/nr-theorists/wundt_wilhelm.html). He envisioned that the historical developments took place in the course of these four "ages:"

(I) *The Age of "Primitive Man"*

(2) *The "Totemic Age"*

If we would define the concept of totemism as briefly as possible, it might perhaps be said to represent a circle of ideas within which the relation of animal to man is the reverse of that which obtains in present-day culture.] In the totemic age, man does not have dominion over the animal, but the animal rules man. Its deeds and activities arouse wonder, fear, and adoration" (Wundt 1916 p.8)

(3) *The "Age of Gods and Heroes"*

"In place of the eldest of the clan and the tribal chieftain of the totemic period, this new age gives rise to the hero...The hero who is exalted as a leader in war belongs to a different world, a world faithfully mirrored in the heroic song or epic.... All this is at the same time closely bound up with the origin of the State, which now displaces the more primitive tribal institutions of the preceding period....With national heroes and with States, national religions come into being; and, since these religions no longer direct the attention merely to the immediate environment, to the animal and plant world, but focus it primarily upon the heavens, there is developed the idea of a higher and more perfect world. As the hero is the ideal man, so the god becomes the ideal hero, and the celestial world, the ideally magnified terrestrial world" (Wundt 1916 p. 9)

(4) *The Present Age [Beyond Gods and Heroes]*

"Thus there begins a development in which we of the present still participate; it cannot, therefore, be referred to otherwise than as an age that is coming to be. We may speak merely of an advance *toward* humanity, not of a development *of* humanity. This advance, however, begins immediately with the fall of the barriers that divide peoples, particularly with regard to their religious views." (Wundt 1916 p. 9-10) Note that Wundt does not assign this period any special name.

It behooves us to note Wundt's view of us, humanity, as making "an advance *toward* humanity, not of a development *of* humanity." This seems to indicate that he, most likely a complete atheist like the rest of his ilk, views us, the herd, as animals in progress of perhaps one day turning into human beings. Hmmm, I wonder what that would encompass. Human 2.0, perhaps? After having found the lawful limits of human research traumatization in the name of science, no holds were barred ever since.

But Wundt really topped it all by inventing the title of psychologist for himself and for posterity. He took the root from the Latin *psyche*, meaning "soul, mind and spirit," and *logia*, meaning "the study of." In other words, the study of the human soul, mind, and spirit. Ironic, is it not, when the vast majority of academia deny their existence, never mind carry a belief in God, Yeshua, infinite spirit, or whatever you want to call the power that created us, the human beings, in its own image? Just suggest the presence of God when in their presence and see them throw up. However, the term "psychologist" mirrored the Luciferic consciousness, which inverts everything. Wundt's graduate students loved it. He supervised and graduated 184 of them (PhD.) between 1875 and 1919. Seventy of them were non-Europeans, 23 from east-European countries and 18 from the U, S. Of these, 100 of them received a PhD in experimental psychology.

One of Wundt's British graduates was Edward Bradford Titchener (1867 –1927). Despite his family's financial difficulties, he attended the prestigious Prebendal School. This independent preparatory school in Chichester is adjacent to the Chichester Cathedral, formally known as the Roman Catholic Cathedral Church of the Holy Trinity, built in 1075 in the city of Chichester, West Sussex, England. After Prebendal, he studied at the equally prestigious private Malvern College. Then it was off to Oxford University's Brasenose College from 1890 onwards. He graduated with the rare 'double first' BA degree in the classics before Wundt caught his undivided attention. So fascinated was he by Wundt's writings, that he translated the first volume of the third edition of Wundt's 1873 *Grundzüge der physiologischen Psychologie*, a work that came to be one of the most important in the history of psychology, into English (*Principles of Physiological Psychology*).

In Grundzüge, Wundt viewed psychology as a scientific study of conscious experience. He believed that the goal of psychology was to identify components of consciousness and how those components combined to create our conscious experience (https://courses.lumenlearning.com/psychology2x4master/chapter/history-of-psychology/). With that in mind, he advanced a system to scientifically investigate humans' immediate experiences of consciousness, sensations, feelings, volitions, and ideas. *Grundzüge* also advanced Wundt's desire to find the concept of apperception. This is the mental process by which we make sense of an idea by assimilating it to the body of ideas we already possess. It would also figure out the process of our conscious perception, a selective process that allows only a part of the sensory input to reach our awareness for which neuro-scientists still look within our brains. (https://www.mpg.de/5839948/conscious_perception).

Wundt advocated "internal perception"—introspection—to examine conscious experiences as objectively as possible. He insisted on introspection also during research to view the human mind like any other aspect of nature that scientists observe. Wundt's version of introspection had nothing to do with meditation. Rather, it was merely to be used for specific experimental conditions in which an external stimulus was designed to produce a scientifically observable and repeatable experience of the mind of an experimental subject, meaning any animal, humans included.

To be successful in such undertakings, the first stringent requirement he pointed to was the use of trained and practiced observers. These people could immediately and accurately report subjects' reactions in scientific lingo.

His second requirement was the use of repeatable stimuli, such as his hammer. These would always produce the same experience in subjects and also allow them to expect the impact, and thus be fully attentive, to their inner reaction.

These experimental requirements were put in place to eliminate "interpretation," meaning guessing, when reporting subjects' internal experiences. They would also counter the argument that there is no way to accurately know what people observe in their mind or consciousness, because it cannot be seen by anyone else. This attempt to understand the structure or characteristics of human mind and consciousness would henceforth be known as structuralism. Structuralists in the psycho-social sciences seek not simply to identify structures or relationships *per se* in the live-human brain. Rather, they look behind or beneath the visible and conscious designs, beliefs, ideas and behaviors of active human subjects. They use surface manifestations to expose and unearth how those designs are in fact outputs, effects, consequences, or products generated by underlying causes, hidden mechanisms or numbers of deep, universal structures in human brains.

Anyway, Titchener was enthused about Wundt's knowledge and ideas about research into the human brain for the functions of the human mind. Indeed, he was so enthused that he spent an extra year at Oxford to study with English physiologist Sir John Scott Burdon-Sanderson, 1st Baronet (1828–1905). Under his tutelage, he learned scientific methodology, the mathematical and experimental techniques employed in building and testing scientific hypotheses.

Then in the autumn of 1890, he moved to Leipzig to study with the master, Wundt, himself.

Burdon-Sanderson, by the way, had received his M.D. degree from the University of Edinburgh, Scotland with his thesis "On the metamorphoses of the coloured corpuscles in extravasated blood." It was about the leakage of blood, lymph or other fluid from a blood vessel or tube into the tissue around it. After a brief stunt in Paris for further education, he became medical officer of health in London-Paddington in 1856. Four years later, he became a physician to the Middlesex Hospital and the Brompton Consumption hospitals. In 1871 Brown Animal Sanatory Institution veterinary research laboratory hired him to be its first principal. Seven of its eight founding directors became fellows of the Royal Society, one of the highest accolades in the world bestowed on scientists. By 1874, Burdon-Sanderson became professor of physiology at the University of London College. In 1882, he finally settled in Oxford as chair of the university's Wayneflete Chair of Physiology.

Immediately upon taking up his post, he requested and received a fully equipped laboratory and adjacent lecture rooms. He was an eager beaver to continue his experimentations on animals, despite huge opposition by animal rights' activist. The British Royal Society also in 1882 awarded him a Royal Medal in recognition of two things. The first was his research into electrical phenomena exhibited by living organism of plants and the relations of minute organisms to disease. The second was for the services he had rendered to physiology and pathology, much of the time by way of vivisection, we guess.

What's that, you ask? Vivisection comes from the Latin *vivus*, meaning "alive", and *section*, meaning "cutting". In short, vivisection means cutting into living organisms, such as monkeys, rattus, mus, cani, lepus and humans to view living internal structures at work. Nowadays, vivisections help harvest and transplant human organs and late abortions with sellable organ-harvesting possibilities in countries and states without restrictions. Among those states are:

- Alaska
- Colorado
- District of Columbia
- New Hampshire
- New Jersey
- New Mexico
- Oregon
- Vermont

In other words, Burdon-Sanderson's vivisection experiments on live animals in the 1870s, including on homo sapiens, has henceforth been joyously practiced by all Darwinians in the art and science of psychology, neurobiology and neuro-science. From its inception, these were merely forerunners of humanity's overt brutalization today. One example is China's alleged organ harvesting of the Uyghurs, a people of the landlocked northwest Xinjiang Uygur Autonomous Region of mostly-Muslim ethnic groups. Another example is Planned Parenthood's alleged sale of aborted baby parts from its operation. Scientists at major universities and government labs have used fetal tissue for experimental research in their laboratories for decades. Companies obtaining the tissue from abortion clinics and selling it to laboratories exist in a gray zone, legally. Federal law says they cannot profit from the tissue itself, but the law does not specify, how much they can charge for processing the tissue and shipping it (Denise Grady and Nicholas St. Fleur: "Fetal Tissue From Abortions for Research Is Traded in a Gray Zone"; *New York Times*. July 27, 2015).

The Fauci's National Institutes of Health spent $76 million on research generated by fetal tissue in 2014 alone. It paid grants to more than 50 universities, including Columbia, Harvard, the Massachusetts Institute of Technology, Stanford, Yale and the University of California in Berkeley, Irvine, Los Angeles, San Diego and San Francisco.

In June 2019, the Trump administration cut all funding to projects in government labs that rely on fetal tissue. The N.I.H. also required academic scientists seeking federal funds to provide elaborate justifications of their need for human fetal tissue and set up an ethics board to review these proposals. But all this was reversed in April 2019, when the Biden administration hastened to lift Trump's decree to protect the unborn. The reversal allowed scientists to use fetal tissue derived from elective abortions to their hearts' content for whatever they desire. And there is no shortage of material, as between the 1973 Roe V. Wade court ruling and 2021, around 62.5 million babies were aborted in the US, albeit how many parts were sold is unknown (Congressional Record Volume 167, Number 20 (Wednesday, February 3, 2021)] [House] [Pages H315-H318)

And no, I am not digressing. I am merely revealing that the path we took to reach the COVID-19 mass hypnosis and its aftermath. By aftermath, I mean children's IQ dropping 21 points due to mask wearing. And I mean the disclosure of corruption within the U.S, teachers unions and school boards. The path we took originated by creating the science of psychology and its multitude of branches. It began with exploring human beings' behaviors and reactions to stimulus. And the path continued by using this knowledge to traumatize us in all ways imaginable and then some, beginning with WWI and WWII shell-shock, later called PTSD, experiencers to employees severely injured in the line of duty. And this search for how to create maximum misery on Earth to please the Luciferic consciousness began in earnest with Wundt and his disciples. Their success in the sciences of biology and medicine brought them many honours. In Burdon-Sanderson's case, he gained the title of Baron of Banbury Road in the Parish of Saint Giles in the City of Oxford (Naomi Wolf, Steve Bannon. *The War Room*, March 19, 2022).

Let's recall that it was he, Burdon-Sanderson, who taught Wundt-afficionado Titchener proper scientific methodology before he sped off to study under Wundt's supervision in Leipzig in the autumn of 1890. It was in 1892 that he completed his doctoral program with a dissertation on binocular vision and returned that same year to Burdon-Sanderson [1892] to teach at Oxford's Summer School.

That same year, 1892, 31 American physicians created the American Psychological Association (APA). The American Psychiatric Association had been founded in 1844. By 2022, they were the main professional organization of psychiatrists and trainee psychiatrists in the world. They had 37,400 members practicing in more than 100 countries. And they had, for decades, been dictating the country's and the world's ethical, moral and social narrative. Its most recent results were newly demonstrated by the COVID-19 mass hypnosis formation behavior. This had already been investigated in the late 1800s by French psychiatrist Gustave Le Bon (1841 –1931). He is best known for his 1895 work *The Crowd: A Study of the Popular Mind*, considered one of the seminal works of crowd psychology.

Le Bon graduated as doctor of medicine at the University of Paris in 1866. Rather than entering a career as physician, he began to write (*Fallacy 1*). By the time he joined the French Army during the 1870-1871 Franco-Prussian War, he had already published a number of medical articles and books. He was also a first-hand witness to the Paris Commune, a revolutionary government that seized and controlled power in Paris from 18 March to 28 May 1871 upon the French Army's defeat by the Prussians in March 1871. The Commune, which governed Paris for two months, established policies tending toward an anti-religious system of social democracy. These included the separation of church and state, self-policing, the abolition of child labour and the right of employees to take over enterprises deserted by their owners. Socialist, communist, anarchist and feminist currents at play in the Commune all vied for dominance over each other until the national French Army suppressed it in a flood of blood. They managing to kill somewhere between 10,000 and 20,000 Communards in street battles and executions. No doubt it was in part due to incurring the Roman Catholic Church's wrath by killing Paris's Archbishop Georges Darboy (1813 –1871) and 100 other hostages, mostly priests.

Le Bon was shook by the Commune experience to the core. So, set off to travel throughout Europe, Asia and North Africa to analyze people and their interrelations. In the course of his journeys, he developed an essentialist view of humanity. He also invented the pocket cephalometer, as it allowed him to quickly measure anybody's head at various angles, diameters and profiles whilst studying the crowds he occasionally encountered.

Le Bon's cephalometer

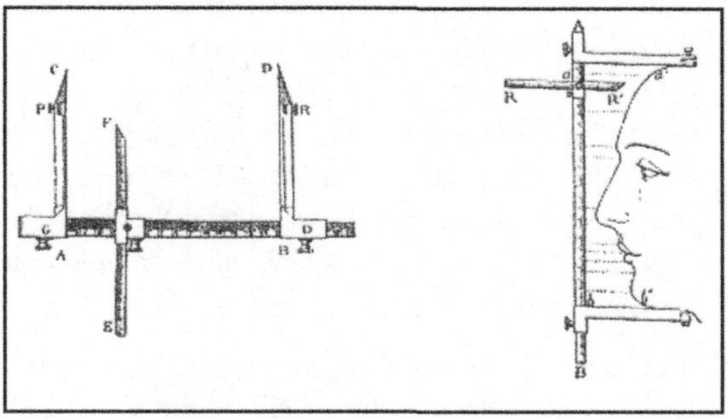

In due time he formed the opinion that crowds were not the sum of their individual parts. Instead, he put forth that crowds formed a new psychological entity. Their characteristics were determined by what he called the crowd's "racial unconscious," another term for what Jung (1875–1961) a few years later would term the collective unconscious, discussed at length in *Fallacy 1*. To briefly recap, the learned society of neuro-and bio-sciences and its adherences views the collective unconscious as a part of the human mind inside the physical brain. It contains memories and impulses of which individuals, meaning all of us, are unaware. They hypothesize, that the collective unconscious originates in the brain's inherent structure and is common to humanity as a whole (britannica.com). It is distinct from the human personal unconscious, which is thought to arise from individual experience. According to Jung, the collective unconscious contains archetypes, or universal primordial images and ideas.

Le Bon published his insights in *The Crowd: A Study of the Popular Mind* (French: Psychologie des Foules; literally: Psychology of Crowds), maintaining that the characteristics of crowd psychology include impulsiveness, irritability, incapacity to reason, absence of judgement of the critical spirit, exaggeration of sentiments and unnamed others. He also claims that:

> "...an individual immersed for some length of time in a crowd soon finds himself – either in consequence of magnetic influence given out by the crowd or from some other cause of which we are ignorant – in a special state, which much resembles the state of fascination in which the hypnotized individual finds himself in the hands of the hypnotizer."

Needless to say, Le Bon's views are proven to be *au contraire* to the 2022 Canadian Truckers' protest unfolding in Ottawa, considered an absolute "Love Fest," until the State brutally interrupted it with armed and mounted foreign storm troopers shipped in to assault the crowd and quench the joy so anathema to the Luciferic consciousness. That he is still criticized by his peers is to be expected, as these folk throughout their careers argue inductively and deductively as their main entertainment. One of them is Perse School, Cambridge, and University of Bristol educated Stephen David Reicher. He received his PhD at the University of Aberdeen in 1984 with a thesis on collective behavior. Since 1998 he is professor at the School of Psychology and Neuroscience at St. Andrews University, Scotland, founded in 1410 by Augustinian clergy. We know nothing about his family background or birth, neither time nor place. Based at St. Andrew's Centre for research into Equality, Diversity and Inclusion, his research interests are broadly the issues of group behavior and the individual-social relationship. He reads the following into Le Bon's words:

> "...a clear racism, nineteenth century racism, and ageism, and elsewhere there is sexism which inhabits that view. In brief, it's the mad mob view, it's a view that you see every time you see collective behavioural riots, it's the fact that these people aren't protesting about anything, they don't have any grievances, they don't had any reason, they are 'mad', so we've got nothing to ask about ourselves, and the inequalities of our society, we can just point at them and say it's just about them.' Additionally more recent research has cast doubt on many of the work's conclusions such as a hypothesised loss of agency and the book's focus on individualism as a psychological paradigm."

Really? Did he confuse Le Bon's "racial unconscious" as having something to do with racism, perhaps, when nothing could be further from the truth? Has the honorable professor heard of the recent Antifa and Black Life Matters riots in the U.S., one may wonder?

The Crowd is still viewed by many as one of the most influential works of social psychology in history. It generated the field of mass behavior analysis, apparently Reicher's specialty. It might well have generated Bernays' creations of Hitler's advertisement and speeches riling up the German masses, if not also Mussolini's. Both of them were masters at stirring up the common folk's passions with their speeches.

The Crowd might also have spawned the "long range penetration strain" tactic. This is the art of presenting, confronting, and bombarding a large group of people with an overload of differing information, choices and opinions. The tactic was developed by scientists at the Tavistock Institute of Human Relations and its U.S. subsidiaries, the Stanford Research and Rand Corporation and at least another 150 other research institutions in the U.S. This approach so confuses the herd as to slowly but surely lead it to complete apathy. This, in turn, breaks down our resistance to change. But the desire to want everything back the way it was, is an impossibility, with snake venom pulsating in the veins of 180 million Americans alone, never mind billions of the world's populations (John Coleman: *Conspirators' Hierarchy: The Story of The Committee of 300;* Bridger House Publishers Inc., 1992). In the COVID-19 scenario, they planned it to last for at least five years of masking and house-arrest before springing the injection offer on us. The long-range penetration operation guaranteed the vast majority of humanity worldwide jumping at the COVID-injection to regain "freedom." The undertaking got rudely interrupted by the 2016 U.S. presidential election shuffle, though it has yet to be seen what the serpent venom revelation will produce as herd-reaction.

Another of Le Bon's observations became blatantly obvious during the COVID and Omicron hoaxes, namely:

> "The masses have never thirsted after the truth. Whoever can supply them with illusions is easily their master; whoever attempts to destroy their illusions is always their victim."

And this truth seems to be in particular visible in those dwelling inside the learned societies. They hastened to get the potentially lethal COVID injections *en masse* in their atheistically generated fear of death, perhaps? Never mind. *The Crowd* also focuses on a crowd's general characteristics and mental unity, its sentiments and morality, its ideas, reasoning power and imagination, and its opinions and beliefs. These form through the processes of its history and the means used by its leaders to persuade it into their aspired to actions, evident by luring us into the wars of the past 120 years. Le Bon also enlightens us on the classification of crowds, including criminal and electoral bodies. And he addresses how criminal juries and parliamentary assemblies function, writes Anson Rabinbach (1945–), professor of history at Princeton University. Rabinbach recommends *The Crowd* to all students of history, sociology, law and psychology, and suggests it might be an invaluable tool for politicians, statesmen, investors and marketing managers.

Our friend Edward Bradford Titchener ended up studying under the world's head honcho instigator of the psychiatric profession, Wilhelm Wundt. He was doubtlessly acquainted with Le Bon's work. He profited hugely from Wundt's tutelage and protectorate to spread his craft. Indeed, his master succeeded to install his stellar 25-year-old British graduate at Cornell University in 1892 as an untenured lecturer teaching philosophy and psychology.

Thrilled beyond belief, one of Titchener asks upon arrival, was to develop an experimental psychology laboratory. Cornell's management agreed. Upon gaining tenure in1895, he got control over all other experimental science laboratories on campus. Now full professor of the science and art of psychology, he put in set out to create his version of the craft by describing the structure of the human animal's mind, terming it "structuralism". That is the idea created by Wundt himself, as we saw earlier.

Structuralism is described as a school of psychology that analyzes adult humans' minds. It looks at the sum total of experiences from birth to the moment the research takes place, in terms of the simplest definable components. It then aims to find how these components fit together to form more complex experiences. Finally, structuralism studies how these components correlate to physical events. To perform such experiments, researchers are advised to ask their trial-subjects to use introspection and then to self-report their sensations, views, feelings and emotions and share their insights with them. Mind you, this can be hugely aided by the lethal-to-human-health Minnesota Multiphasic Personality Inventory (MMPI), to which all genuine PTSD afflicted and a multitude of others are subjected (see *Fallacy* 1). Why is it lethal? It reveals the most innermost characteristics, aptitudes and attitudes towards life and living of any human soul. Thus, it provides those in power with the sword for our decapitation.

Be it as it may, as full Cornell professor, Titchener made it his duty to create the largest doctoral science of psychology program in the United States. He would use it to teach his hypotheses on the human mind and its structure to the multitude. He granted his first PhD in psychology in 1894 to his first student, Vassar 1891 graduate Margaret Floy Washburn (1871–1939). By the early twentieth century, she would be the leading American psychologist. First, she translated Wundt's *Ethical Systems* into English. Then, she set out to experiment in animal behaviour under all sorts of conditions, vivisections included. She also worked on her motor theory development. In time, she would use her studies in animal behaviour and cognition to present her idea that both mental and behavioural events are legitimate and important psychological areas for study in humanity. This, of course, went against the establishment's doctrine that the mental was unobservable and thus not appropriate for scientific investigation.

Perhaps Titchener was motivated by the suffering he saw inflicted on animals by Ms. Washburn et al. in their experiments. Wit the recent sand flies eating of live beagles' faces to study their reactions. Whatever the motivation, Titchener coined the English word "empathy." It is a rough translation of the German word *Einfühlungsvermögen*, the ability to feel the emotional and physical pain of another living being from within one's own heart. From the Greek *empatheia*, "physical affection, passion, partiality," empathy is the humanly innate capacity to place oneself in the position of the emotional and physical experiences of another living being.

Empathy is alien to those under Luciferic consciousness domination. They demand cruelty and psychopathic behaviour, maiming, killing and torturing in all aspects of the words. We see this by how shell-shocked soldiers in WWI and WWII were treated. This cruelty has been practiced henceforth and visible in the torture of animals, the abortions of fetus' and selling their parts for research not even to mention all kinetic and psychological conflicts and slaughters arranged by the Luciferic consciousness to satisfied its appetite for destroying all that is human and humane, with a complete lack of empathy.

As Titchener was opening Cornell's experimental psychology laboratory, Philadelphia-born Lightner Witmer (1867–1956) created the first American "psychological clinic" at the University of Pennsylvania. As a matter of fact, he did so the second he returned to the U.S. in 1892 from his job as Wundt's assistant and doctoral diploma recipient. He was re-joining the equally Wundt-educated experimental psychologist James McKeen Cattell (1860 –1944) who, after receiving his PhD from Leipzig (1886) continued his research in the London laboratory of Sir Francis Galton. He received the professorship in psychology at the University of Pennsylvania in Philadelphia in 1888, the first ever offered in the US, He had inspired Witmer to enter the emerging field of psychology and meet Wundt at Leipzig 's university in the first place. It was there that they fulfilled their dream of an experimental laboratory of psychology with Witmer as director,

The institutions' purported purpose? To gather data on individuals' different reaction times and to study children with perceived learning and behavioural problems. Witmer's main subjects were children with speech difficulties, sleep disturbances, behavioural problems, hyperactivity and refusal to stay in school. They were harvested by teachers of Philadelphia schools and volunteered by parents. During treatment, children were given complete physical and mental examinations by way of a series of mental measurement tests he and Witmer developed to rule out physiological symptoms before subjecting them to drug-concoctions experiments. Thus began the Ritalin prescription craze, which was picked up in Britain, as well. Remember, they all knew each other and vigorously communicated their findings through Wundt's journal and other publications, as well as by word of mouth. Let's look at the ADHD timeline.

- The first descriptions of children with ADHD symptoms were made as early as 1902 by British pediatrician Sir George Frederic Still (1868 –1941) and were thought to have a "defect of moral control." (verywellmind.com).
- In 1908, Alfred F. Tredgold described "high-grade feeble-minded" children who likely had a form of mild brain damage that caused them to have ADHD-like, anti-school behavior.

- A study published in 1937 described the use of Benzedrine (racemic amphetamine) in children with behavior problems by Dr. Charles Bradley. He accidentally learned about the benefits of Benzedrine when giving the medication to help kids with severe headaches, but noticed it instead helped their behavior and school performance.
- The first edition of the *Diagnostic and Statistical Manual of Mental Disorders* (DSM) was published by the American Psychiatric Association (APA) in 1952. It included no mention of an ADHD-like disorder.
- Herbert Freed and Charles Peifer study the use of Thorazine (chlorpromazine) on "hyperkinetic emotionally disturbed children" in 1956
- Hyperkinetic impulse disorder is first used to describe children with ADHD symptoms in 1957.
- C. Keith Conners publishes a study on the effects of Ritalin (methylphenidate) in 'emotionally disturbed children' in 1963.
- In 1966, minimal brain dysfunction syndrome became a popular term to describe kids with "various combinations of impairment in perception, conceptualization, language, memory, and control of attention, impulse, or motor function."
- In 1967 and 1968, the National Institute of Mental Health (NIMH) gave several grants to researchers to study the effectiveness of stimulants for children with ADHD symptoms.
- The second edition of the *Diagnostic and Statistical Manual of Mental Disorders* (DSM-II) was published by the APA in 1968. It included two ADHD-like disorders: hyperkinetic reaction of childhood or adolescence, and organic brain syndrome.
- The first Conner's Rating Scale was published by C. Keith Conners in 1969, which eventually led to revised editions of the Conner's Rating Scales for parents and teachers.
- In 1970, the *Washington Post* published a story describing how five to 10 percent of school children in Omaha, Nebraska, were receiving stimulants like Ritalin, to control their behavior. Unfortunately, the statistics referred only to kids in special-ed programs. The story created controversy around diagnosing ADHD and using stimulants, especially since it implied that many parents are coerced into medicating their kids.
- The Comprehensive Drug Abuse Prevention and Control Act of 1970 classified stimulants such as Ritalin (methylphenidate) as Schedule III medications, and then as Schedule II medications in 1971.
- Section 504 of the Rehabilitation Act of 1973 allowed students with ADHD who qualify to get additional help and services at school to help them succeed.
- An anti-Ritalin movement greatly expanded in 1975, as several new books reinforce the belief that ADHD isn't a real diagnosis, was created by drug companies to make money, or that hyperactivity is caused by food allergies and food additives.
- The AAP publishes its first statement about ADHD, *Medication for Hyperkinetic Children*. It says that in addition to "consideration of nondrug therapy in situations where such an approach is appropriate," and that "there is a place for stimulant drugs in the treatment of hyperkinetic children."

- The third edition of the *Diagnostic and Statistical Manual of Mental Disorders* (DSM-III) was published by the APA in 1980 and included Attention Deficit Disorder for the first time. It included the subtypes ADD with hyperactivity, ADD without hyperactivity and ADD residual type.
- Dr. Russell A. Barkley wrote his first of 17 books about ADHD in 1981: *Hyperactive Children: A Handbook for Diagnosis and Treatment.*
- The DSM-III-R (revised edition), published in 1987, again changed the name, this time to Attention Deficit Hyperactivity Disorder (ADHD), but did not include any subtypes.
- A 1987 report from the AAP, *Medication for Children With an Attention Deficit Disorder,* offered "indications for drug therapy in the treatment of attention deficit disorder," such as Ritalin, Dexedrine, Cylert and "other potentially useful drugs," including tricyclic antidepressants.
- Dr. Barkley began publishing *The ADHD Report* newsletter in 1993.
- The fourth edition of the *Diagnostic and Statistical Manual of Mental Disorders* (DSM-IV-TR) was published by the APA in 2000. It described three types of ADHD, including ADHD, Combined Type, ADHD, Predominantly Inattentive Type, and ADHD, Predominantly Hyperactive-Impulsive Type.
- Joseph Biederman published one of the first of hundreds of medical studies about children with ADHD in 1995.
- An updated AAP report, *Medication for Children With Attention Disorders,* published in 1996, stressed that drug therapy should be combined "with appropriate management of the child's environment and curriculum."
- The 2000 *Clinical Practice Guideline: Diagnosis and Evaluation of the Child With Attention-Deficit/Hyperactivity Disorder* from the AAP offered clear guidance for pediatricians and parents on assessing and treating kids with ADHD.
- Strattera, the first non-stimulant treatment for ADHD, was approved in 2002.
- Labels on ADHD medications were updated in 2007 to include warnings about the possibility of cardiovascular risks (sudden death in children and adolescents with structural cardiac abnormalities or other serious heart problems) and risks of adverse psychiatric symptoms (hallucinations, delusional thinking or mania).

To help spread information as fast as possible, Witmer published a laboratory manual in 1902, as well as the US's first journal of clinical psychology. In his role as laboratory head, supervisor and advisor of graduate students on their dissertations, he had almost free range to do so. By 1907, he had succeeded in opening the first clinical hospital school (https://psywww.com/intropsych/ch01-psychology-and-science/new-generations.html). That same year, he took his enterprise one step further by founding *The Psychological Clinic journal.* He wrote this in his first edition:

> "During the last ten years the laboratory of psychology at the University of Pennsylvania has conducted, under my direction, what I have called "a psychological clinic." Children from the public schools of Philadelphia and adjacent cities have been brought to the laboratory by parents or teachers; these children had made themselves conspicuous because of an inability to progress in school

> work as rapidly as other children, or because of moral defects which rendered them difficult to manage under ordinary discipline.
>
> When brought to the psychological clinic, such children are given a physical and mental examination; if the result of this examination shows it to be desirable, they are then sent to specialists for the eye or ear, for the nose and throat, and for nervous diseases, one or all, as each case may require. The result of this conjoint medical and psychological examination is a diagnosis of the child's mental and physical condition and the recommendation of appropriate medical and pedagogical treatment. The progress of some of these children has been followed for a term of years." (https://psychclassics.yorku.ca/Witmer/clinical.htm).

Cattell moved on to became professor and administrative head of psychology at Columbia University in 1891. He devoted much of the rest of his career to improving and advancing mental testing, Witmer created the US's first journal of clinical psychology and the first clinical hospital school in 1907. He was considered responsible for major advancements in the field of school psychology and the art and science of school discipline. But he was not the only one receiving his elementary experimental psychology education from Wundt and spreading it. Many others did as well, among them Granville Stanley Hall, head of Clark University and father of the child psychology movement and adolescent developmental theorist. So did Charles Hubbard Judd, director of the School of Education at the University of Chicago Walter Dill Scott, who contributed to developing industrial psychology and taught at Harvard University did, as well. So did Frank Angell, Edward Wheeler Scripture and James Mark Baldwin, the latter being one of Princeton's Department of Psychology founders and contributor to early child psychology, psychiatry and the theory of evolution. With them began the moment humanity finds itself at, when Yuval Harari joyously pronounces:

> "Humans are now hackable animals. By hacking organism, we are able to engineer it (*tiytube* November 2021)."

That COVID injections and their boosters are the pathway to that future he kept quiet, and the herd drums on, not wanting to know.

Still, whether San Remo practitioner, Bowden House founder and WWI military psychologist Crichton-Miller studied under Wundt at any given time is unknown. We can well assume that he did indeed diligently read Wundt's *Philosophische Studien* (*Philosophical Studies*) when counselling the overwrought and neurotic rich and famous in his San Remo, Italy, clinic. We also know that he was familiar with Freud an knew about his view of psychoanalysis being the ideal technique to target the root of anyone's emotional problem and thereby alleviate destructive human behaviours rather than by hypnosis and hypnotic suggestions.

He also knew of or even read Freud's book *Interpretation of Dreams* (published in 1900), as the first English translation appeared in 1910 (https://iap.edu.au/when-freud-found-hypnosis/). But it was Carl Gustav Jung, Crichton-Miller's father's lifelong friend, whom he truly admired. This was simply because Jung still viewed man as a "free agent," a being of free will, able to change direction and course of his or her life by thoughts and consequent actions, he told in his memoirs. He felt that Freud held the more or less deterministic philosophy, that all human events were determined by previously existing causes. The doctrine of Dharma (knowledge) overriding Karma (ignorance) had yet to reach Freud's conscious awareness.

Mind you, the millennia-old knowledge that Dharma overrides Karma is nowhere mentioned by any of these self-appointed geniuses of hypotheses, theories, fantasies and assertions about the human psyche (*Fallacy 1*). Neither is it mentioned anywhere, that the imbalances and density of earth affecting every human being in many different ways can be lessened or even eliminated. That all it takes is daily meditations and seeking the connection with our higher self, the part of our consciousness left on a non-physical higher plain of vibration guiding us through this incarnation. That "Mission Control" can revive us, if we care to seek its help. If we lose touch with our mission control, our higher self, however, we become dominated by the information coming in through our ears and eyes, our senses alone. In PTSD cases these are fed to us by the art of scientist cabalists of the mental health profession we are forced to communicate with. They drum into our minds that we have been warped from the moment of our birth, continuing until we either throw in the towel and go away, or until we believe them, gobbling their prescription drugs to die a slow and miserable death. If we do so, it is through the ignorance created by the mental health profession through generations by perpetual television programming in North America, the misery created to feed the Luciferic consciousness, who needs to survive on this planet.

Once fallen under Luciferic consciousness dominance, the Luciferian patterns take hold of our ego and begin to control our emotions. This is made possible through the disconnection from our higher self, as if anyone ever cared to tell us it existed, the knowledge hidden from the herd since the dawn of time. We, unawares, evolve into rudderless ships, subjects to untold pain and destruction (David Icke: *Robot Rebellion,* Gateway Books, Bath, UK, 1994).

Freud was still somewhat a believer in human consciousness of varying levels and degrees, as documented in *Fallacy 1*. He thought himself to be powerful enough to fix these rudderless ships by way of psychoanalysis, before trying to do so by hypnosis and hypnotic suggestions. As documented in *Fallacy 1*, these are in PTSD healing equally as futile as anything else deemed appropriate by the mental health cabal, as hypnosis merely masks the PTSD emotional problem, but never heals it (iap.edu.au/when-freud-found-hypnosis/). Only the Self can heal the genuine PTSD afflicted Self. It can take the spiritual path and with meditation, introspection and self-forgiveness gain back honour, integrity and graciousness to, with the self-application of willpower, discipline, determination and persistency, achieve the goal. It is self-evident, once we start looking, which the psychiatric and psychology professionals never did, nor do. It would ruin their business, and they knew it from WWI onwards.

28

THE NOBEL SHELL-SHOCKED

Our Genoa-born Scotsman Hugh Crichton-Miller (1877–1959), educated at University of Edinburgh and Pavia, described himself as a Christian, a pragmatist and scientist. Known as a tolerant, dedicated and humane physician, his desire to heal those who came to him for help knew no bounds. His academic knowledge and his 10 years playing with the mental and physical health of the rich and famous in his San Remo practice gave him an idea in 1911. He would open a practice for the wealthy neurotics of Britain at Bowden House near London, England. It would be a private nursing home for those well-healed folk suffering nervous diseases, neuroses, and mild psychoses. He did this more out of curiosity than to help them, as he really only wanted to investigate/research why these invisible and unobservable emotional problems arose in British high society. His wife and offspring moved up north with him, dwelling at Bowden House in separate living quarters and spending their summers with him in Scotland.

He termed this abode for the neurotics his "therapeutic community". All of its inhabitants, patients, physicians, nursing and domestic staff, gardeners and cooks - even Crichton-Miller's wife and children - were considered part of the treatment center, all family away from home to patients and each other, so to speak. Crichton-Miller's peers looked at this type of united psychological treatment operation he termed "new psychology" somewhat askance. They deemed it a futile exercise for anyone's neuroticism, as if they knew what they were talking about, but he steadfastly carried on his research on Britain's neurotic upper class members consulting and living with him. (https://ezitis.myzen.co.uk/bowdenhouse.html).

Crichton-Miller saw eye to eye with Freud's idea of humans' "unconscious motivation." That is the idea that peoples' hidden and consciously unknown desires express themselves by purposive accidents, slips of the tongue and dreams This idea was thought of by members of psychology's learned society as the greatest idea since sliced bread., By 1912, Crichton-Miller had observed enough to publish his book *Hypnotism and Disease: a plea for rational psychotherapy*. This English language book contained what he thought of as the main features of psychotherapy. He wrote it in a form and language suitable for the intelligent lay reader of either sex. He meant it to be used by those colleagues anxious to attain a general understanding of the subject he shared. The knowledge in the book had also propelled him to practice what he called "binocular vision." This meant seeing his patients as both physical and emotional entities and paying attention to both their physical and psychological needs and wellbeing (https://tavistockandportman.nhs.uk).

Crichton-Miller had happily practiced what he had thus picked up in hypotheses, ideas, theories, dreams and academic knowledge about human nature from dabblers in the human psyche from Wundt through to Jung, Freud and himself. But money was slow to come in at Bowden House. So, he thought it appropriate to volunteer for the British Royal Army Medical Corps at the start of WWI in 1914. He was posted to the 21st General Hospital at Alexandria, Egypt, as medical officer in charge of functional cases. Those were cases with no discernible, visible, or diagnosable biological changes or ailments of the human body. His duties furthermore included to maintain the force's health and fighting strength in the field. He was to treat and, if necessary, evacuate the wounded and sick as sparingly but as quickly as possible. He was to conserve manpower and maintain a high standard of physical fitness and morale throughout the troops while stationed there. (J.T. Robinson, MA, M.D., BCh, DTM&H, Major, Royal Army Medical Corps, *BMJ* 1941, https://www.bmj.com/content/2/4215/555)

With the rank of lieutenant colonel, Crichton-Miller held that position for a few months. Thus, he escaped the tremendous noise of guns and explosions ripping across the European continent's Western Front and scaring the living daylight out of Londoners (blackcablondon.net/tag/hugh-crichton-miller/). But he quickly tired of his duties. So in 1915, he got himself transferred back to the homeland. He became a consultant-neurologist at the King's College Hospital at Denmark Hill, which had been requisitioned as the Fourth London General Military Hospital (https://kch.nhs.uk/wwi/wartime-history). Together with other unnamed physicians at the hospital, he pioneered plastic surgery, physiotherapy, radiography, ultra-violet ray treatment, massage therapy and a slew of other undisclosed rehabilitation techniques. They also pioneered open air treatments for patients with lung injuries. And they worked on the Carrel-Dakin treatment, the periodic flooding of infected wounds with an antiseptic sterilizing solution delivered through an apparatus. It had been developed by French surgeon Alexis Carrel and English chemist Henry D. Dakin, saving many a soldier's life and limbs (https://www.ncbi.nlm.nih.gov/pmc/articles/PMC6907325/).

More than 75,000 soldiers were treated at King's College Hospital during WWI. It housed 369 beds for officers and 1,625 for the rank and file. It also harbored 656 overflow beds in huts and tents at a nearby park, oft times used to treat soldiers with lung injuries and tuberculosis. But the physical ills befalling soldiers in the line of duty of their métier were really of little to no concern to WWI fighting armies' high commands. It was the "shell-shock," which caused them unmentionable grief. They had no clue what it was or what to do about it. Their numbers became so overwhelming by the winter of 1914–15 on all sides as to threaten the war's cessation. The ailment's term "shell-shock" had been coined by the soldiers themselves. When no treatment could be construed by army doctors up to the highest ranks of experience, they consulted with Crichton-Millers. He almost immediately changed its vernacular nomenclature from shell-shock to the much more classy and professional sounding 'neuro-asthenia'. The new name was derived from "neuro," the term Galen used to describe the nervous system, and "asthenia," from the Greek "want of strength, weakness, feebleness, sickness; a sickness, a disease." It also confused the issue at hand perfectly, as it disguised the true reason for its origin. That is the belief that death was imminent, the soul departing the body before the body died (now termed PTSD). This was reflected in the poem of Vernon Scannell (1922-2007), who lived through WWII's killing fields writing afterwards:

> ...the flesh decaying;
>
> The bones growing brittle in anticipation
>
> Of the ultimate disintegration (Vernon Scannell; Walking Wounded p. 66)

With their possible purpose-driven ignorance, the mental health cabal achieved to perfection what Wundt intended. He put in motion the whole field of science of psychology to propose that the whole of humanity is mentally ill from birth. He expertly honed the profession's ability to pervert humanity's perception of itself, regardless of color, race, creed and education. And he had the help of pharmaceutical drugs, beginning in the West or the first world, as they taught us to call it. Through the following wars they systematically destroyed our physical and mental health, generation by generation. They were so successful that few of us are capable to "think straight." In 2021, 85% of the population over 60 years of age were daily consuming pharmaceutical drugs, and those from 0 to 60, with almost 70% consuming pharma drugs, were not far behind. And they got us to this state of affairs by changing terminology for the tremendous emotional trauma incurred by all soldiers in WWI's trenches, regardless of side. They slowly but surely convinced us that we were "neurologically defect at birth; only your doctor can help to cure you." The psycho-the-rapist, would cure us from any and all normally-to-be-expected human emotional experiences.

What they failed to notice or acknowledge, however, is that the human experiences in and out of the WWI trenches was far beyond any normally-to-be-expected human life experience. And if these self-appointed knowers of the human psyche did notice, they brilliantly disguised this fact from humanity. To notice would be to ruin their planned enterprise of humanity's physical destruction, mental, ethical and moral perversion and PTSD exploitation. And they would forfeit the huge financial profits and success of humanity's 2.0 creation.

What these soldiers lived went on for weeks on end at times. It was in the most dreadful conditions, in rat-infested trenches with insanitary conditions or in deserts abounding with scorpions and other critters. They had little or no food and water, waiting to be killed, waiting to die. Having to explain how that felt like to physicians who throughout their pampered lives had no trauma to speak of other than losing a tennis match was further traumatizing. Vernon Scannell, who enlisted in the army "as a lark" in 1940 and two years later found himself in action in the North African desert, gives us a taste of it in his writings. He fought at El Alamein and across the western desert during the Eight Army's drive to reach Tunisia during WWII, after an assault on German and Italian forces near Gabes. He watched his comrades move through the recently taken position, looting the dead of both sides, Allied as well as Axis. He was disgusted, so he walked away.

Caught and court-martialed for deserting, he was sentenced to three years imprisonment. He spent six months in one of the harshest military penal institutions in Alexandria before being released on a suspended sentence to take part in the Normandy landings. His war ended when he was shot in both legs while on night patrol near Caen. How would these self-proclaimed and aggrandized geniuses in the understanding of the human psyche and its health react? How would witnessing the death rattle of hundreds of soldiers influence their psyche and their souls? Never mind the effects of witnessing them fight for their lives before being killed.? Oh, I forgot, almost. They have been classified as apes by Russell H. Tuttle, professor of anthropology, evolutionary biology, history of science and medicine at the University of Chicago.

What they did notice in the shell-shocked was their lethargy, their fatigue and tremors. They saw their evident confusion and their nightmares. They noted their impaired sight and hearing, as vision decreases under traumatic stress, whereas hearing sharpens to almost intolerable degrees. That is why my dogs learned to walk on tip-toes on the tiled kitchen floor. turns acute, the latter also yet to be noticed by them (Broken Wings; Fallacy 1). The complete loss of esprit de corps was the French term literally meaning "the spirit of the body" used by army high commands, all of them, to describe their troops' morale. This puzzled the geniuses to no end (vocabulary.com).

The British Army High Command had to find a treatment for these boys' nebulous, opaque, undecipherable ailment. And it had to turn that treatment into the most lucrative, money-making operation ever seen, until COVID-19 injections. So, they appointed physician Charles Samuel Myers (1873–1946) as consulting psychologist to the British Expeditionary Force, stationed in northern France at the start of both WWI and WWII. He was to support the French army's left wing, and to gather data for a military policy addressing the psychiatric-based battle casualty issue of shell-shock.

Myers was born in London's wealthy Kensington district in 1873. He was the oldest son of Wolf Myers, merchant of unknown merchandise, and his wife Esther Eugenie Moses, both of Ashkenazi Jewish faith. In the 1881 British census, he is listed as an eight-year-old scholar living with his parents, four brothers and four servants. In the census of 1891, he is listed as a scholar aged 18, still living with his parents, four brothers, one visitor and four servants (cook, housemaid, parlor maid and ladies' maid).

He began his academic education at the independent City of London School for boys, founded in 1834. The poverty-stricken soldiers in the trenches purportedly fighting for the motherland's freedom had most likely not seen this school. Tuition fees were steep, at £6,665 in the Spring of 2022, plus a £292 for lunch, and probably similar to that in Myers' days. He very much enjoyed the natural science studies, which he continued at Cambridge's most illustrious Gonville & Caius College, founded in 1348 A.D. Between 1893 and 1895, he took a first in each part of the Natural Sciences tripos, the framework within which most of the sciences are taught at Cambridge. It is taught by 16 departments and includes a wide range of physical and biological sciences, as well as the history and philosophy of science.

There too, tuition fees are steep. Native-born British students cough up around £9,950 in 2021-22, plus roughly £9,890 annually for living and social costs. Myers lived there until receiving his M.D. in 1901. Meanwhile, he joined Cambridge's Isaac Newton University Freemason Lodge No. 859, which had been formally consecrated at Cambridge's Red Lion Hotel as Lodge No. 1161 in May of 1861.

Seemingly for his own personal amusement, Myers joined British anthropologist and ethnologist Alfred Cort Haddon (1855 -1940) on a one-year Cambridge University arranged anthropological expedition in 1898. The expedition was to study ethnic music and research the musical rhythms of the Sarawak area of Northwestern Borneo and islands in the Torres Strait between Australia and New Guinea. He did this with two others. One was Cambridge's St. John's College student William McDougall (1871 -1938). The other was English neurologist, psychiatrist, ethnologist and anthropologist William Halse Rivers (1864 -1922). Myers followed this all-expenses-paid journey with another one to Egypt between 1901 and 1902. He was studying the anthropometric measurements and proportions of the native Egyptians' body shapes and dimensions before completing his medical training at St. Bartholomew's Hospital in London. By that time, he had assisted Rivers, then Cambridge University lecturer in physiological and experimental psychology. They were teaching the physiology of humans' special senses to students:

- Vision - the capability of the eye(s) to focus and detect images of visible light on photoreceptors in the retina of each eye that generates electrical nerve impulses for varying colors, hues and brightness.
- Hearing - the sense of sound perception.
- Taste - the capability to detect the taste of substances such as food, certain minerals, poisons, etc.
- Smell - the other "chemical" sense; odor molecules possess a variety of features and, thus, excite specific receptors more or less strongly. this combination of excitatory signals from different receptors makes up what we perceive as the molecule's smell.
- Touch - the perception resulting from activation of neural receptors, generally in the skin, including hair follicles, but also in the tongue, throat and mucosa. This is also called somatosensory, tactician or mechanoreception (nurselabs.com).

Wizard that he was, Myers was also one of the 10 founding members of The Psychological Society in 1901. In 1906, it was renamed the British Psychological Society. Upon his suggestion, opened its membership up to "all those interested in various branches of psychology" in in 1919. Meanwhile between 1906 and 1909, he held the newly created professorship in experimental psychology at London University. This field of study tried to figure out which neurological brain processes might underlie which emotional functions. It used human and animal subjects to study their sensation and perception, memory, learning, motivation, emotion, development processes and social psychology reactions, and mapping the neural substrata of all of those. The term "neural substrata" is used by neuroscientists to indicate parts of the central nervous system, specifically the brain and spinal cord. These seemingly generate specific behaviours, cognitive processes and psychological states of mind in animal species, which includes us, of course, but seemingly excludes them.

Rivers resigned a part of his Cambridge lectureship in 1909. This gave Myers the chance to be the university's first lecturer whose sole duty it was to teach experimental psychology, a position he held until 1930. From 1911 to 1914, the two edited the British Psychological Society's British Journal of Psychology quarterly established in 1904. Myers continued on his own until someone else took over in 1924. It was peer-reviewed to assure nothing of consequence about the often-gruesome experimental research laboratory sessions filtered through to the herd. The Cambridge's Laboratory of Experimental Psychology was able to conduct those experiments by 1912 thanks to funds mostly raised by Myers. Greeted by the métier with jubilance, Myer, in position as director until 1930, held full control over all publications.

Slowly, slowly and systematically, the powers that be brought everything needed for the experimental psychology experimentations. They would use soldiers suffering with WWI's incurred emotional disturbances. This was the same approach as they took with the non-profit suicide-prevention NGOs mentioned earlier in preparation for COVID-19 effects on humanity. They sprung up like weeds since the late 1980s in preparation for the catastrophic emotional and physical trauma inflicted on the herd by the COVID-19 pre-planned pandemic. The cobra and krait poison injections discovered by Dr. Bryan Ardis in April 2022 resulted in untold death and injuries for life. Just as with COVID-19, so many were trained in the human psyche, its neurological functions and its reaction to untold numbers of unpleasant normally-to-be-expected life situations. They were still trained by Wundt and his contemporaries' principles of the 1850s onwards. So, they knew long before WWI's mass slaughter that an unprecedented number of physical and nervous system injuries would not only occur in all participating armies, but also in bystanders.

Actually, it had been known from the moment that Swedish chemist, engineer, inventor and businessman Alfred Bernhard Nobel (1833- 1896) had patented his dynamite invention in the U.S. and the UK in 1867. He had demonstrated its demon power to any regime wanting to look. Why else do you think Wilhelm Wundt opened his Institute for Experimental Psychology at the University of Leipzig in Germany barely a decade later, eh? It was the first laboratory dedicated to discovering the workings and logics of the human soul by way of experimental brain research and the physical reactions. He wanted to find out about human nervous system functions and emotional reactions. He wanted to get down to the finest details, not even to dwell on their desire to locate in our brain a consciousness, even though he maintained it does not exist.

That Nobel had known about the ensuing violence is obvious from the moment he patented his dynamite invention in Sweden in 1863. He chose the name "dynamite" after the ancient Greek δύναμις dúnamis, "power." A year earlier, he had patented his "ways to prepare gunpowder," with his inventions merely continuing in his family's footsteps. After all, they had provided armaments to the Swedish crown for centuries. The most recent had been to Crimean War parties between 1853 and 1856, but they went bankrupt after peace ensued there. He was raised with arms, so to speak. He was born in Stockholm in the United Kingdoms of Sweden and Norway in 1833, the third son of Immanuel Nobel's (1801–1872) and Karolina Andretti Nobel's (née Hansel 1805–1889) eight children, His father was an engineer, an inventor and an alumnus of Stockholm's Royal Institute of Technology. They descended from Swedish scientist and professor of medicine at Uppsala University, Klaus Runback (1630–1702). Runback had discovered the human lymphatic system and had also founded the first botanic garden in Sweden. But young Alfred, bright as he was, went into weaponry instead of botany and medicine. At a young age, he learned the basic principles of technology, engineering and explosives from his father, although he struggled making a living.

Following various business failures, father Immanuel decided to open a machine tools and explosives manufacturing plant in Saint Petersburg, Russia. He invented veneer lathe, which made it possible to produce plywood. He began work on the torpedo, a self-contained explosive device activated and shot under water to damage or destroy ships and submarines. Of course, it would also damage or destroy anything else beneath or above the oceans blue. Returning to Sweden wealthy in 1842, Alfred could now be privately tutored. Excelling in his studies, particularly in chemistry and languages including English, French, German and Russian, the rest is history. But not so fast. His dynamite would never have hit the market, had it not been for Italian-born chemist Ascanio Sobrero (1812–1888).

Sobrero was born in the ancient Roman municipium of Casale Monferrato. For centuries, it had been a trade and manufacturing centre of north-west Italy's Piedmont area, Sobrero had studied medicine in Turin and Paris before joining German scientist and professor at the University of Giessen Justus Freiherr von Liebig (1803-1873). Liebig was considered the principal founder of organic chemistry, the study of structure, properties, composition, reactions and preparation of carbon-containing compounds. Liebig also devised the modern laboratory teaching methods in the field. And he is known for formulating the law of minimum. This law states that the local yield of terrestrial plants should be limited by the nutrient that is present in the environment in the least quantity relative to its demands for plant growth. He placed emphasis on nitrogen and trace minerals as essential plant nutrients, giving him the description of "father of the fertilizer industry."

In line with that organic chemistry theme, Sobrero earned his doctorate under Liebig in 1832. He began working at Paris's École polytechnique as assistant to chemistry professor Theophile-Jules Pelouze (1807–1867). He was appointed professor at the University of Turin in 1845. In 1846, Pelouze started an experimental laboratory-school (1846). Together, he and Sobrero took great pleasure in experimenting with the explosive material guncotton and nitrosulphates resulting in Sobrero concocting the nitroglycerine formula in 1847. He called it "pyroglycerine – thick, sweet, colorless liquid fire." But his creation so frightened him, that in private letters and journals, he warned against its use. He found it far too dangerous and impossible to handle for human use. In fact, so scared was he of his creation, that he kept its formula a secret until 1850. He ran into another of Pelouze's students, the 17-year-old Alfred Nobel, at that time already taught by the Liebig-taught Russian chemist Nikolai Zinin (1812–1880). Nobel managed to talk him into sharing the formula with him.

He knew full well of Sobrero's strong opposition to the use of nitroglycerin. He knew of its unpredictable volatility, exploding when subjected to variable heat or pressure. So, Nobel set out to find a way to control and use it—nitroglycerin—as a commercially viable explosive to further enhance his family's finances. To set the project in motion, he first sped over to the United States. There, he consulted with and studied under one of the nineteenth century's most creative engineers and inventors, Swedish-born American inventor John Ericsson (1803–1889). Ericsson had been living in New York, wheeling and dealing with both Britain and the U.S. since 1839.

Ericsson had joined the Swedish Army at age 17. With his evident engineering talents, he was rapidly promoted to lieutenant and assigned to make geographical maps of Sweden. Upon leaving the army in 1826, he moved to England to build hot air engines, locomotives and steam-powered fire engines, and improve screw propellers. All the while, he gained a stellar reputation as engineer, designer and inventor of such machinery. U.S. Navy commodore Robert Field Stockton (1795 –1866) took note. He was born into a notable political family, a naval innovator and an advocate for a propeller-driven, steam-powered navy. At his behest, Ericson moved to New York in 1839 to help Stockton design the U.S. Navy's first screw-powered warship, the USS *Princeton*.

The ship was launched in 1843. But in February 1844, during a Potomac River pleasure cruise for dignitaries, tragedy struck. One gun exploded, killing the Secretary of State Abel P. Upshur and Secretary of the Navy Thomas Walker Gilmer, and injuring others, including a United States Senator and Captain Stockton. The disaster killed more top U.S. government officials in a single day than any other tragedy in American history. President John Tyler escaped death because he happened to be below decks. The ship's reputation in the Navy never recovered, whilst Ericsson was blamed for the accident. It soured his cozy relationship with U.S. Navy command somewhat, though his armored and ironclad warship equipped with a rotating gun turret design, the USS Monitor, healed relations somewhat. Nevertheless, Ericsson decided to redirect his talents and energies into private and semi-private ventures in civilian and merchant fields, as well as tutor landsman Alfred Nobel. (https://sok.riksarkivet.se/sbl/Presentation.aspx?id=8143&forceOrdinarySite=trueNobel).

After one year of engaging in Erickson's projects, young Nobel went home to put into practice some of what he had learned. He received a number of patents worldwide for his mixtures, devices and manufacturing methods, all based on nitroglycerine. By the mid-1860s he had managed to safely package dynamite in sorbents such as powdered shells or clay. He also packaged it in stabilizers. He learned how to add chemicals to prevent degradation. He invented a detonator able to be chemically, mechanically or electrically initiated. He designed the blasting cap, a device used to trigger the explosive device he had created. And he did all this in rapid succession. Voila, the means to cull mankind with great ease and in unprecedented numbers and emotionally rattle others out of their mind, ready for use on the unsuspecting herd.

Mind you, before arriving at his success, he had managed to kill five people, including a younger brother, without batting an eyelash. He merely went to re-found the Nitroglycerin Aktiebolaget (AB) in a more isolated spot in southern Stockholm. That's where he invented gelignite, also known as blasting gelatin or simply "jelly", in 1875. This explosive material consists of collodion-cotton, a type of nitrocellulose or guncotton dissolved in either nitroglycerin or nitroglycol mixed with wood pulp and saltpeter. In 1887, he invented ballistite, a smokeless propellant made from nitrocellulose, nitroglycerine and cordite, which replaced military gunpowder. In charges made to measure, it can be transported with ease. Equipped with his detonators, it would explode on command and could be deployed among soldiers and civilians alike, thus assuring the herd's genocide by the millions worldwide without a hustle (https://www.madehow.com/Volume-2/Dynamite.html).

Thus by 1887, Nobel's achievements had set the scene for the first trial of humanity's mass-culling of its finest men, its healthy and fit youth. The experimental laboratory for the undertaking would be created on European soil as soon as it could reasonably be arranged with the help of those aspiring human psyche manipulation experts. Thus Sarajevo 1914 arrived, as all was in place and ready for the live experiment. Material to further explore the human animal psyche under duress to discover the easiest ways for its destruction was needed. And so, WWI was scheduled to lead right into WWII to assure a new generation of youth as experimental subjects to research the herd's group- and mass-formation-hypnoses was engineered. Those caught in the conflicts' vicinity and the families of those who died, were maimed or injured for life would also be emotionally traumatized. This would enhance the destruction of the family-aspiration demanded by the Luciferic consciousness and gladly carried through by those dwelling under its influence.

All of it is forecast by Ukrainian-born and -raised Helena Petrovna Blavatsky (1831-1891). She founded the non-profit Theosophical Society in New York City, practically simultaneously with the quasi-feverish unfolding of both experimental psychology and Nobel's dynamite weapon as documented in *Fallacy 1*.

Recall that the Theosophical Society's initial objective was the study and elucidation of Occultism and wider religious philosophies like Vedanta, Mahayana, Buddhism and Sufism. It was also to explore supernatural forces or beings. And it would use the Qaballah, an oral tradition with initiation into its doctrines and practices conducted by a personal guide to prevent the dangers inherent in such mystical explorations. A worldwide enterprise, it purports to encompass Greek and Alexandrian third century AD and Eastern religious philosophies, ideologies and functions. These serve as a bridge between East and West by emphasizing the commonality of human culture with help from the non-profit Lucifer Trust, created in 1922.

One of the Society's philosophical tenets is *The Intelligent Evolution of All Existence* belief. This is based on the notion that life on earth is so complex that it cannot be explained by the scientific theory of evolution à la Darwin and Tuttle but must have been designed by a supernatural entity (https://aclu.org/other/frequently-asked-questions-about-intelligent-design). It thus excludes humanity's evolution from amoeba to cockroach, cani, simian, lepus to homo sapien. These are the species described by the Smithsonian Institute that you and all other living human beings on this planet belong to on a cosmic scale. It says that we incorporate both the physical and non-physical aspects of the known and unknown Universe affecting all of its constituent parts regardless of apparent size or importance. This purported evolutionary narrative is now being guided in hitherto unknown directions by the Yuval Harari's of this world. They are using the experimental COVID 19 injections, which modify the human by splitting the cell and inserting synthetic DNA of an unknown nature into it (Dr. Judy Mikowits, April 14, 2022; Dr. Bryan Ardis, April 13, 2022).

According to Theosophical Society philosophy, mind you, the Whole Earth project is overseen by a hidden spiritual hierarchy. This would be the so-called Masters of the Ancient Wisdom, whose upper echelons is said to consist of advanced spiritual beings. By deduction, they also have an overlord, who can be whoever you want him, her or it to be, letting the Luciferic Consciousness idea spring to mind mightily, does it not? And the academic art, craft and science creation of experimental psychology laboratories sprang into bloom. They explored human reactions and brain functioning to traumatizing events. They did this by traumatizing and drugging subjects, perhaps under the Masters of the Ancient Wisdom supervision. These experiments vigorously flowered since the Theosophical Society's creation.

Nobel's invention seems to have provided the fundamental means needed to destroy all of humanity, with the exception of the 500 million mentioned on the Georgia Guide Stones. Not only that, his killing creations made him, and a multitude of others, immensely wealthy. And he had not an iota of willingness to share some of it with Sobrero, never mind acknowledging his part in the evolution of his destructive concoction.

Sobrero's face had been badly scarred due an experiment gone haywire in the 1840s. Deeming nitroglycerine far too dangerous for practical use as noted earlier, Sobrero, grieved when hearing of Nobel's mercantile exploitation of the formula, sighing:

> "When I think of all the victims killed during nitroglycerine explosions and the terrible havoc that has been wreaked, which in all probability will continue to occur in the future, I am almost ashamed to admit to be its discoverer."

He should be, not for discovering it, but for not keeping his mouth shut. And what about Nobel, you ask? Well, he held 355 mostly weapon-related patents during his lifetime. In 1894, he bought Bofors AB iron and steel mill. This iron industry and artillery manufacturer in southern Sweden had been founded in 1646 as a royal state-owned company. Initially selling cast and forged steel for gun works, it expanded into weapons manufacture in 1884. With Nobel's purchase, it became a modern cannon and chemical industry manufacturer. Nobel amassed an enormous fortune with it, part of which he invested in a Paris domicile. One morning in 1896, he stumbled across his own obituary in a local Paris paper under the headline "The merchant of death is dead. Dr. Alfred Nobel, who became rich by finding ways to kill more people faster than ever before, died yesterday."

He was not amused. His ego was injured. His concern for how the world would view him after his demise left him distraught. So, he changed his will to bequeath 94% of his assets to be annually handed out to those of the learned society or politics or whoever in physics, chemistry, physiology or medicine, literature or peace had conferred the "greatest benefit on mankind" – the Nobel Prizes. Scant a year later, he left the earth due to a cerebral haemorrhage at age 63. Perhaps he was headed for the realms of *The Divine Comedy*. He left from his villa in San Remo, Italy, where Crichton-Miller would begin to practice and experiment with what he thought of as psychology on the rich and famous neurotics a few years later. The Nobel Prizes were worth 31,225,000 Swedish Kronor or roughly US$186 million or £1,687,837 (GBP) at that time. To manage the finances and administration, Nobel's executors set up the private Nobel Foundation, which by December of 2020 managed 5.176 billion Swedish Kronor (approx. US$631.61 million). None of it has ever been offered to the billions of humans disastrously affected by Nobel's inventions.

Curiously enough, until Wilhelm Wundt, no physician had paid much attention to emotional harm done to participants in warfare. They seemingly just accepted it as part of the game. It was only when physicians covering the emotional travesty of WWI shell-shocked soldiers, all by and large trained by Wundt and his graduate students, sprang into action. They used the same testing methods as in actual warfare. They brutalized the brutalized, kicking them back to the front as "cured" and "fit for duty" by threatening them with court martial, as conflict cessation due to lack of manpower would not be permitted. Those who adamantly refused were killed by firing squad. So, it was do or die for the shell-shocked. And our aspiring psychiatrist Charles Samuel Myers, aged 42 and married with children, pampered since birth and living a life in the lap of luxury, feeling younger and chipperer by the moment, did not want to miss that show.

But the war-office turned him down as too ancient. However, well connected as he was since birth, he contracted with the Duchess of Westminster's Number 1 Red Cross hospital established on the channel's French side in the casino Le Touquet near Boulogne-sur Mer. There, up to 350 injured and convalescents soldiers were taken care of by Order of St John's Voluntary Aid Detachment nurses. They were all eager and willing to help Myers, without protest or objection, in his human experimental life research material. Together, they would get to the bottom of the "mystery ailment" of shell-shock so puzzling to him, his peers and all armies' high commands.

The Voluntary Aid Detachment (VAD) system had been founded in 1909 by the British Red Cross and the Order of St. John. The latter goes back to the Knights Hospitaller's of the Middle Ages Crusades' renown. Their units of civilians provided nursing care for commonwealth military personnel warring in whatever countries during WWI and WWII. They were neither military nor civilian nurses. Nor were they under military control like, for example, the British Queen Alexandra's Royal Army Nursing Corps. However, they did work in field hospitals, temporary military hospitals and mobile medical units to care for casualties until they were transported for further treatment and recuperation at proper military hospitals. There were 74,000 VAD members by the summer of 1914. Two-thirds of them were women and girls of the middle and upper classes, used neither to hardship nor to hospital discipline. They had volunteered in 2,500 Voluntary Aid Detachments in Britain. By 1915, suffering a trained nurses shortage "in the field", military command began to accept VAD women over 23 years of age with more than three months' hospital experience in Britain for overseas service. Some of them most likely presented for duty at Myers LeTouquet laboratory as unquestioning staff.

Voluntary Aid Detachment (VAD) uniforms

But the British Royal Army Medical Corps kept an eye on him. It looked favourably on his shell-sock experiments, promoting Myers in 1915 to a well-paid military commission as Royal Army's consultant-psychologist. She was headquartered in Le Touquet with a few assistants at his beck and call. Among them was his Borneo-Torres Strait-music and Egyptian natives' body-shape excursion-buddy McDougall. Together, they decided that shell-shocked soldiers exhibited a range of perceptual abnormalities. These included loss of or impaired hearing and sight, along with tremors and loss of balance, headaches, fatigue, tics, trembling, functional paralysis, "hysterical" blindness and deafness, stuttering, mutism, confusion, extreme anxiety, amnesia, depression, unexplained cramps, fainting and vomiting, hysteria, neurasthenia, hybrid hystero-neurasthenia, nerve shock, war shock, war neurosis and exhaustion. All of it, they decided, occurred due to what they called "repressed trauma."

But Myers and McDougall had the solution. They thought it a splendid idea to revive those "repressed trauma memories" and integrate them with their subjects existing consciousness. This, they gathered, would require only a few sessions of consultation. Why anybody should consult with complete strangers, pampered since birth with life-experiences by and large limited to cushy lifestyles of fun and adventure, is unknown. However, these two self-appointed shell-shock hypnotists thus launched still so very favoured Cognitive Behavioural "Therapy" (CBT). It proved to be the financially immensely rewarding for them and deadly to the human spirit and sui generis for genuine PTSD experiencers. They and their heirs would soon augment CBT with pharmaceutical drugs, electro-convulsive treatments, lobotomies and everything and anything else they and their peers could think of. This ever-expanding toolbox was soon reflected in the treatment they inflict on genuine PTSD experiencers, screwing them out of recognition and out of themselves, never mind the world around them.

Myers and McDougall cherished their illusion of curing the odd shell-shocked soldier coming their way. But high-commands of all warring armies in this human mass-slaughter, which extended to the bombing of civilians in WWII, had bigger problems. They despaired over the mass of psychiatric casualties in never anticipated numbers, leading to the German neurologist and psychiatrist Robert Eugen Gaupp (1870–1953) reporting in 1917:

The big artillery battles of December 1914... filled our hospitals with a large number of unscathed soldiers and officers presenting with mental disturbances. From then on, that number grew at a constantly increasing rate. At first, these soldiers were hospitalized with the others ... but soon we had to open special psychiatric hospitals for them. Now, psychiatric patients make up by far the largest category in our armed forces ...The main causes are the fright and anxiety brought about by the explosion of enemy shells and mines, and seeing maimed or dead comrades ...The resulting symptoms are states of sudden muteness, deafness ... general tremor, inability to stand or walk, episodes of loss of consciousness, and convulsions. (Marc-Antoine Crocq, M.D., et al: From shell shock and war neurosis to posttraumatic stress disorder: a history of psychotraumatology; Dialogues Clin Neurosci. 2000 Mar; 2(1): 47–55).

Little is known about Gaupp other than that he studied at the Universities of Heidelberg and Munich with famous German psychiatrist Emil Kraepelin (1856-1926). Kraepelin was considered the founder of modern scientific psychiatry, psychopharmacology and psychiatric genetics. And that was before being appointed professor of psychiatry at the University of Tübingen, a post he held between 1908 and 1936 (*Fallacy 1*). By that time, McDougall had completed his studies of medicine and physiology in London and Goettingen, Germany. He had taught at the University College London. And in 1920, he had been recruited to occupy Harvard University's chair of psychology to spread and streamline the newest news about the art and craft of psychology manipulation of humanity in the United States. There, he stayed until moving to Duke University in 1927 to establish the Parapsychology Laboratory on the coattails of Mesmerism and a push in the scientific community to empirically study psychical and paranormal experiences and other strange phenomena. McDougall himself espoused a hormic theory of psychology, emphasizing genetics and instinct over nurture.

The hormic theory holds that where there is life there is mind. It states that, if there has been continuity of evolution of the organic from the inorganic, there must have been something of mind first. There must have been some trace of mental nature and activity in the inorganic from which such emergence took place. McDougall would keep searching for answers until his death in 1938 (https://archives.lib.duke.edu/catalog/uamcdoug). Shortly thereafter, the learned society of neuro psychology decided homeo sapiens' mind and consciousness were to be found in their physical brains. They have searched for it there ever since. And parapsychological research laboratories, for a while considered a new and experimental science, became investigations of the distant past (https://www.seeker.com/whatever-happened-to-parapsychology-1767604210.html).

Meanwhile, Kraepelin was busy with his idea of psychiatric genetics. This is the study of the role genetics play in developing whatever American Psychiatric Association members decide are human mental disorders. Right now, they are anything related to human emotions, including PTSD, alcoholism, schizophrenia, bipolar disorder, autism, a hangnail and most if not all of those ailments created by injections advertised as vaccinations and pharmaceutical drugging (Judy Mikowits, Reiner Fuellmilch et al, 2022).

Psychiatric genetics basic tenets? In essence, it seeks to answer humanity's age-old question: "Are our behavioural and psychological conditions and deviations inherited from our forebears?" It applies scientific, empirical, evidence-based ways to better understand the causes of psychiatric disorders and use that knowledge to improve treatment methods. These new methods are to be personalized based on humans' individual genetic profiles. They are to be enhanced by pharmacogenomics. Thus, they transform parts of psychiatry into a neuro-science based discipline aiming to:

- Develop evidence-based practice in psychiatric genetic counselling

- Understand predictors of mental health problems
- Understand patient and health-care providers' perspectives on pharmacogenetic testing for depression
- Integrate genetic counsellors into primary care (bcchr.ca/TPGG)

That all mind-altering drugs destroy the possibility of a clear and balanced mind, causing loss of inhibition, depression and suicidal ideation, is nowhere mentioned. Needless to say, no word is breathed about normally-to-be-expected traumatic human life experiences able to cause a great amount of deplorable, emotional misery without genetic influences. Nor is a word breathed about the influences of poisonous pharmaceutical drugs imposed on humanity since the mid-1850s. For example, Merck added morphine to his cough and sleep remedies sold to Frankfurt citizens without breathing a word of it. And then there are the 30 or so injections given to infants before age two, and the parents made too ignorant to protest.

Millions of American, and many others around the world, are swallowing pharmaceuticals made from venom peptides that come from pit vipers, rattlesnakes, toxic cone snails, leeches, Gila monster lizards and more. Drugs in development have been made from creatures like deathstalker scorpions or even vampire bats (https://www.brighteon.com/4f8a0a6a-9c11-4cc9-9b02-4e8cc310bc13). The Venomtech company, for example, has now been linked to Anthony Fauci's "secret island" of inhumane medical experiments. These are conducted on monkeys and beagles via Charles River Laboratories, a pharmaceutical company that leased the island and runs it in the United States. The ToxinTech company, also located in the United States, specializes in providing venom-based toxins and peptides for pharmaceutical research seemingly. I guess they are celebrating the fact that animal venoms can "kill prey in seconds." And that they can "target vital receptors key to neuromuscular, cardiovascular, hemostatic and other life functions" in animals like you and me.

And it all began in the 1850s, when the shareholders of these companies started up in Europe. One of Germany's leading neurologist of the time was Hermann Oppenheim (1858 –1919), son of Juda Oppenheim (1824–1891), the long-time rabbi of the Warburg. Hermann was at Berlin's world-renowned Charité-Hospital when he demonstrated that traumatic events were pathogenic and could provoke post-traumatic neuroses. He was non-too graciously ignored by the mental health shell-shock investigating cabal of his age. When the topic was brought up for discussion at the 1916 War Neurology Congress in Munich, the craft's elite psychiatrists and neurologists point blank rejected Oppenheim's diagnosis. This despite non-psychiatrists – and certainly the lay public – accepting the notion that the war caused nervous or emotional illness. Not that their opinion mattered, as the learned society of physicians who named themselves healers of the human psyche firmly stood firm. They continued to insist that war neurotics were malingerers, degenerates, freaks and frauds. They claimed that awarding them pensions would merely encourage such symptoms in the troops. Nothing changes, nothing has changed. *Plus ça change* etc....

Oppenheimer's thesis had been accepted by the Kaiser Wilhelm's II Imperial Insurance Office in 1889. German workers have been entitled to compensation ever since, if after a work accident they develop neurotic symptoms. But this did not matter at all, to this day equally ignored by the mental health cabal, the WCB and employers alike. Physicians of all genres, then and now, will use the term "hysteria," implying both predisposition and a weakness of will. They should use the term "pension neurosis." Using "hysteria" prevents the feckless working classes such as genuine PTSD journeyers to receive a pension due to a near-catastrophic workplace accident.

But in WWI, no deplorable had a clue about the elites' intricacies and avenues to screw worker and soldiers alike, albeit they were regularly exposed to it. This was vaguely documented in Sheila Llewellyn's 2018 book *Walking Wounded*. It was too inhumane to fathom, and still is, as nothing has changed in the treatment of genuine PTSD experiencers since then. What military commands and treating physicians did know was that all mostly Caucasian nationalities, until the U.S. entered the conflict in 1917, were equally disposed to it. Soldiers from all combatant WWI nations suffered from a wide range of debilitating nervous ailments, thanks to Nobel's terrifying weapons. The self-appointed psychiatrists were clueless as to what they were dealing with. They experiment still today with whatever on whomever they feel like. They left shell-shocked soldiers in all participating countries to struggle for adequate treatment and food, with all receiving what they perceived as unjust and inadequate treatments (Fiona Reid: "War Psychiatry and Shell Shock"; *International Encyclopedia of the First World War*: https://encyclopedia.1914-1918-online.net/article/war_psychiatry_and_shell_shock).

How many shell-shocked military men were affected? There were over 80,000 recorded cases amongst the British armies. There were 200,000-300,000 or higher estimated in German and French troops. And there were 120,000 or so of the Austro-Hungarian armies on the Western front alone. Needless to say, such numbers of traumatised young men suffering war-related emotional and functional nervous diseases and neuroses affected military morale and discipline. In truth, the numbers were small considering the war's military and civilian casualties. There were around 15 to 22 million deaths. And there were 23 million wounded military personnel. It was among the deadliest military conflicts in human history, a successful culling of the herd now replaced and enlarged by the seemingly more delicate COVID-19 injections, culling with untold numbers dead, injured for life or dying.

The WWI and WWII culling and emotional impairment did not achieve humanity's belief in God and a higher power. Never mind, this seems to now be rectified by COVID injections. We hear that they destroy our connection with our Higher Self, our mission control centre. Some even feel a disconnection from our entire soul being, which would indicate our cessation as human beings. This echoes what Rudolf Steiner stated in 1901, when he was treasurer the Theosophical Society. Here is what he forecast a century ago:

> "In the future, we will eliminate the soul with medicine. Under the pretext of a 'healthy point of view', there will be a vaccine by which the human body will be treated as soon as possible directly at birth, so that the human being cannot develop the thought of the existence of soul and Spirit.
>
> "To materialistic doctors will be entrusted the task of removing the soul of humanity. As today, people are vaccinated against this disease or that disease, so in the future, children will be vaccinated with a substance that can be produced precisely in such a way that people, thanks to this vaccination, will be immune to being subjected to the 'madness' of spiritual life. He would be extremely

smart, but he would not develop a conscience, and that is the true goal of some materialistic circles.

"With such a vaccine, you can easily make the etheric body loose in the physical body. Once the etheric body is detached, the relationship between the universe and the etheric body would become extremely unstable, and man would become an automaton, for the physical body of man must be polished on this Earth by spiritual will. So, the vaccine becomes a kind of arymanique force; man can no longer get rid of a given materialistic feeling. He becomes materialistic of constitution and can no longer rise to the spiritual."

Read it again, perhaps, to grasp the enormity of his words, now that COVID injections' serpent venom may be pulsating in your veins? And what did the great soul, India's Mahatma Gandhi, have to say about injections?

"Vaccination is a barbarous practice, and it is one of the most fatal of all the delusions.

"The vaccine is a filthy substance and it is foolish to expect, that one kind of filth can be removed by another.

Conscientious objectors to vaccination should stand alone, if need be against the whole world, in defence of their conviction."

Do these imposed injections following the great and smaller perpetual wars during the last 110 years signal the very last part of the Great Work of Ages. Has the *Ordo ab Chaos* Luciferic consciousness takeover of our minds and thus our planet arrived. The scheme apparently launched immediately after Atlantis' demise sometime around 11,000 BC. Well, if it has arrived, this attempt to rob us of our souls certainly touched a core in Canada's truckers' hearts. They launched a convey 70 miles long to drive across this enormous country in the dead of winter. They lasted three weeks in Ottawa, the country's capital. It ended only when Prime Minister Justin Castro Trudeau, pawn of Klaus Schwab of the World Economic Foundation , called in UN forces, some on horseback, some claim, as an UN marked aircraft was parked in a hick-town nearby (Christie Hutcherson: Mel K show May 15, 2022). They, stopped this peaceful love fest on Parliament Hill. (https://theguardian.com/world/2022/feb/20/ottawa-protests-capital-police-clear-blockade). After all, love and kindness are anathema to the Luciferic Consciousness, which loves only Nobel-induced trauma.

Albert Pike was Grand Commander of the Supreme Council of Freemasons in America. That made him custodian of its religious truth handed down from age to age by an unbroken current of tradition embodied in symbols, emblems and allegories unknown to humanity at large. Here is what he said in the 1870s:

"The Masonic Religion should be by all of us initiates in the High Degrees be maintained in the purity of the Luciferic doctrine." (David Icke: Robots Rebellion, p. 56)

And so, it is perhaps manifested by the frantic demand for our COVID-19 injection. The search for the God gene through behavioural- genetic, neurobiological and psychological studies continues. Research into our physical brain is aimed at finding our connection to our Higher Self, our mission control centre. And then, to destroy it and with it destroy one of God's creations, ourselves, as human 1.0, perhaps?

And what are the major God gene hypothesis arguments?

- Spirituality can be quantified - measured - by psychometric measurements.
- The underlying tendency to spirituality is partially heritable.
- Part of this heritability can be attributed to the gene VMAT2.
- This gene acts by altering monoamine levels.
- Spirituality provides an evolutionary advantage by providing individuals with an innate sense of optimism.

With that in mind, Europe's and the world's WWI and WWII provisions for the emotionally handicapped young men were cleverly designed. They made believe that the arts and sciences of neurobiology, psychology, psychiatry and their associated pharmaceutical drug wizards would help them heal from their killing field experiences. Of course, it did nothing of the sort. It merely used them as guinea pigs to find the human mind and soul in soldiers' physical brains by way of brain vivisections, as they had done since the mid-1850s. Every one of them, without exception, was educated in Greek and Roman Classics and Greco-Roman languages, literature, philosophy, history, archaeology, anthropology, society at large art and mythology. These constituted elite Europeans' traditional education. It so very willingly, knowingly and with a vengeance ignored Pre-Socratic thinkers' discussions of the human soul and mind.

The ordinary notion of the soul, whether a person's soul does or does not survive a person's death, is known to exist from the Homeric poems onwards (Ancient Theories of Souls; https://plato.stanford.edu/entries/ancient-soul/#3). The Western World is behind the Orient in all esoteric matters. The study of concepts such as existence, being, becoming and reality were first explored by Parmenides of Magna Graecia around 500 BC. His thoughts and ideas henceforth apparently shaped all of the Occident's philosophical history. Hippocrates (460-370 BC) picked up from there, observed that: "The soul is the same in all living creatures, although the body of each is different." Although, he also identified the human brain as the "organ of intellect" or "the guiding spirit", pick and choose (https://skeptics.stackexchange.com/questions/6867/did-hippocrates-say-the-soul-is-the-same-in-all-living-creatures-although-the).

The first philosophical conception of the psyche - Greek for the human soul, mind and spirit - is documented during Socrates' time. The psyche was seen as responsible not only for humans' mental and emotional - psychological - functions, such as thought, perception and desire. The psyche was equally seen as the bearer of moral and ethical qualities and accountable for all vital functions performed by human beings.

Plato, Socrates' scribe, so to speak, presents arguments for the immortality of the soul in some of his best-known dialogues. These include *Phaedo*, *On the Soul*, *Republic* and *Symposium*. When Plato wrote *Phaedo*, Socrates was on his last day of life, having been state-condemned to death by drinking hemlock. He discusses the nature of the afterlife, proposing not only the soul's immortality, but also that it contemplates truths after its separation from the body, at the time of death. Perhaps this indicates the re-run of the life past for judgment, as the ancient Egyptians maintained.

Plato was Socrates' star pupil, and thus inspired and influenced by his teacher's views and opinions. Besides conceiving of justice as a reflection of the soul in the *Republic*, he appears to have viewed the psyche—the human mind, soul and spirit—as an incorporeal, eternal, etherical part of our human being. He recognized our essence, our *sui generis*, immortal and experiencing continual rebirth after death in subsequent bodies. He saw it as the seat of all knowledge imprinted with all the mind would ever need.

Aristotle, Plato's star pupil, chimed in with his ideas of the psyche, articulating it primarily in his work *De Anima*. Here what he said on the topic:

> ". . . the soul neither exists without a body nor is a body of some sort. For it is not a body, but it belongs to a body, and for this reason is present in a body, and in a body of such-and-such a sort." (414a20ff)

Thus, the soul in Aristotle's theory is a system of abilities possessed and manifested by animate bodies of suitable structure, but not itself a body or a corporeal thing (https://faculty.washington.edu/smcohen/320/psyche.htm).

Moreover, Aristotle seems to think that the soul's abilities in plants, animals and humans are such that body parts and organs are needed to use them. He seems not to think, however, that there is an organ of thought. So, he also does not think that a bodily part or organ exists specifically to think. He furthermore seems to take the view that human intellect always involves some activity of the perceptual apparatus. In other words, intellect requires the presence and proper arrangement of suitable bodily parts and organs. He seems to think that sensory impressions [*phantasmata*] are somehow involved in every act of thought, at least as far as human beings are concerned (*De Anima* 3.7, 431a14-7; 3.8, 432a7-10; cf. *De Memoria* 1, 449b31ff.). If so, Aristotle is committed to a view contrary to the Platonic position. He maintains that even human souls are not capable of existence and, perhaps as importantly, of activity apart from the body (cf. *De Anima* 1.1, 403a3-25, esp. 5-16).

Be it as it may, Aristotle seems to be agreeing overall with his teacher that the psyche—the human mind, soul and spirit—of human beings is of an indistinct, undefined substance. He views it as the *essence* of any living being, distinct from the body in which it finds itself. It is, therefore, neither itself a body nor a corporeal thing, and very different from human bodies. So, Aristotle does not think, either, that there is an organ of thought in the human body. Nor does he think that thinking involves using a bodily part or organ to exist specifically for this use.

Later on, philosopher-scientists like Herophilus (335-280 BC) and Galen (129-210 AD) accepted the mystic nature of the brain and labelled it the "seat of the soul". During the renaissance, neuroscientists like Andreas Vesalius (1514 -1564) regarded the brain as a "highly developed sense organ". Vesalius was author of *De Humani Corporis Fabrica Libri Septem* (On the fabric of the human body in seven books), one of the most influential books on human anatomy. German physicians Franz Joseph Gall (1758–1828) a couple of centuries later held a different view. He thought to provide human emotional dispositions in terms of phrenology, the study of the conformation of the skull as indicative of mental faculties and traits of character. Since then, the search to localize each human psychological function with Wundt et al. shifted to searching within different brain segments. This research occupied the craft and art of neuro-biology and other crafts of the learned society to this very day. In contrast, ancient East Indians Sanskrit scriptures described the brain's higher cortical function thousands of years ago, the Occident's elite steadfastly refusing to listen, never mind investigating.

The very earliest of those East Indian scriptures are the Upanishads. These form one of four genres of texts together constituting the Vedas, the knowledge about the *Sanatan Dharma* meaning "Eternal Order" or "Eternal Path". These oldest texts of Hinduism were derived from the ancient Indo-Aryan culture of the Indian Subcontinent, transmitted somewhere between the nineteenth and second centuries BC. passed down orally through generations before being written down in Sanskrit between 1500 and 500 BC.

All Indian philosophical traditions are deeply engaged with meditation, philosophy, consciousness and concepts such as existence itself, being, becoming and reality. This is because clarity about the nature of reality is at the heart of three intimately connected goals in human life and living. Those goals are knowledge, proper personal conduct and liberation from the continued suffering of all human existence (https://www.rep.routledge.com/articles/thematic/ontology-in-indian-philosophy/v-1). The first 13 of the known 108 Upanishads are referred to as the principal or main Upanishads, the mukhya. These are the oldest and most important ones. The first five are *Brihadaranyaka*, *Chandogya*, *Taittiriya*, *Aitareya* and *Kaushitaki*. These were composed in prose interspersed with verse. The middle five are *Kena*, *Katha*, *Isa*, *Svetasvatara* and *Mundaka*, which are written primarily in verse. The last three, *Prasna*, *Mandukya* and *Maitri*, are written again in prose.

The Upanishads present a vision of an interconnected universe with a single, unifying principle behind the apparent diversity throughout the cosmos called Brahman. This resides in the *atman*, the unchanging core within all human individuals. All Upanishads seem to investigate the nature of *atman*, the Self, and direct and help those who seek the Self in the inquiry.

One of the most ancient and widely studied Upanishads is the Aitareya Upanishad. It was likely composed in the pre-Buddhist sixth century. It reflects the beliefs, practices and philosophical notions of the human soul, its creation, birth and rebirth, the embodiment of the Self, the transmigration of souls, the nature of Self, the beliefs, practices and philosophical notions regarding soul, creation, birth and rebirth, the importance of food and desire in the continuation of the worlds and beings. It also addresses the transmigration of souls and the nature of Self. And it examines cognition, emotion and volition, ascribing them to the concept of the *manas*, meaning the mind in its widest sense. The *manas* is applied to all mental powers, intellect, intelligence, understanding, perception, sense, conscience, will and so on and so forth (hinduwebsite.com).

Manas, however, is not the same as the mind defined in modern science. *Manas* acts like a receptacle for our sense-sensations. Memories and perceptions are stored there and used by our intelligence and our higher mind, our Mission Control center. With them, we make sense of this world, and we generate our decisions seemingly without the use of our physical brain. In order to understand the Hindu concept of this world, everyone in it and *manas*, we must try to grasp its first and most foundational concept, that of the *atman*. This is the soul of all, the never-changing, non-material self, distinct from both the mind and the external body (https://iskconeducationalservices.org/HoH/concepts/key-concepts/atman-the-self/). This self, the *atman*, is beyond the designations ascribed to ourselves in terms of race, gender, religion and nationality. Ideas of reincarnations are natural extensions of this concept, with consciousness considered a symptom of the soul, the body unaware without it.

This soul that brings the body to life is thought of as spirit (brahman), differentiating it from inert matter. This worldview is expressed by Hindus and many others in all walks of life. In a nutshell, it expresses:

- The real self (*atman*) is distinct from the temporary body.
- Material designations do not apply to this eternal soul.
- The atman is spirit (*brahman*) – unchanging, eternal and conscious.
- Consciousness, as spread throughout the body, is a symptom of the soul.

Contrary to most of the world religions, Hindus believe that all living beings on this planet are the soul, the universal Self, the atman, the self-existent essence, who possesses a body. This body, then, as I understand it, is associated to the individual *Ahamkara*, its Identity or Ego, and its *Citta*, its connection to "consciousness," its realm of perception The word is derived from the root word, cit, meaning "to perceive." (*Sadhguru*). *Citta* may also be thought of as spirit, the mind, itself embodied in *Prakriti*, or *Prakruti*, "the original or natural form or condition of anything, the original or primary substance."

Prakriti is *the* key concept in Hinduism. It is formulated by its *Samkhya dualistic* school of Indian philosophy regarding reality and human experience. These would be formed by two independent ultimate principles, purusha, consciousness or spirit, and *prakrit*, cognition, mind and emotions, or nature or matter. Thus, it includes all the cognitive, moral, psychological, emotional, sensorial and physical aspects of this earthly reality we can think of. It also stresses the cognitive, mental, psychological and sensorial human activities associated with them. Together, all of it composes the human soul, mind and spirit, the Self, the *sui generis*, the cosmic being or self, consciousness and universal principle, or the witness consciousness, the Sakshi (साक्षी), the Pure Awareness. It would witness the world without affection or involvement. Western neuro-biologists and -scientists, psychiatrists and psychologists include under one banner: "the mind". So do the mere General Practitioners and anyone else of the Darwinian persuasion who ascribe to the physical brain, their own included. On the other hand, ancient Indians have been able to describe much higher cortical function of the human brain, the major distinction presented by using the term *manas* or mind rather than that of the physical brain.

Manas is considered to be the figment of consciousness. It is said to reveal itself in waking (*Jagrita*), dream (*Swapna*) and dreamless sleep (*Sushupti*) stages. Thus, the knowledge of manas inspired people like Sigismund Schlomo Freud to define the three levels of the mind as preconscious, conscious and unconscious mind. *Manas* thus refers to that of our faculties, which receives the external stimuli, passing the message on to "Buddhi," our intellect. It proceeds to analyze these stimuli with the innate power of discrimination, before passing it on to the "Ahamkara" our ego or sense of identity. That ego renders unique properties to the incoming message through the "Chitta" or consciousness, all of it covered in Fallacy 1.

In philosophical terms, *manas* is seen as an obstacle to one's liberation from the cycles of rebirth, from Nirvana. The classical Buddhist path to enlightenment, and thus liberation, is the Noble Eightfold Path. *Manas* make hard to follow, as it is fickle and vulnerable, making it inclined to adhere to the impurities of desires and attachments. Hence, the scriptures identify it as the source of suffering, modifications (*vrittis*) and afflictions (*klesas*). The Aitareya Upanishad gives a list of 16 functions of mind—*manas*—as part of the human brain's higher cortical functions. These are:

- awareness
- comprehension
- understanding
- knowledge
- retentiveness
- insight
- resolution
- opinion
- memory
- reflection
- impulse
- conception
- purpose
- vigour
- desire
- will

(16 Functions of Brain in Aitareya Upanishad, February 2021; https://booksfact.com/upanishads/16-functions-brain-aitareya-upanishad.html).

All 16 brain functions are generated by human emotions generating human experiences in accordance with resulting states of mind. Not one of them is empirically, scientifically provable or disprovable. Still, the crafts, arts and sciences of psychology, psychiatry, neuro-science and neuro-biology and associated fields steadfastly maintain that every one of those 16 can be proved and quantified scientifically and empirically. Does it seem as if the entire mental health industry from top to bottom is truly just a rape the other's psyche scam? That's what psychiatrist Allen Frances so eloquently pointed out in 2010. And eminent personages as psychiatrists Szasz, Breggin, Molcher, Laing and others did in a round-about way long before him.

We already know that the learned society, by and large and through and through regardless of genre of expertise deny the existence of a Brahman, an Atman, a Christian God, Yahweh, Allah or whatever. They profess to be atheists, according to Merriam-Webster people who do not believe in the existence of a god, gods, higher power or spiritual force of any kind. What these folk do acknowledge, though, is Socrates' observation, that a revolution in human behavior only occurs with a revolution in human thinking. This explains why the cabal, the elite, the Illuminati, the Luciferic Consciousness, if you wish, began in the mid-1800s to meticulously pervert humanity's perceptions of how to sustain a healthy body and mind.

It began with Merck in 1850, adding morphine to his mass manufactured cough syrup and sleep remedies without breathing a word about it to consumers. Then the Wundts of the day amplified the need of physicians under the guise that "Doctor Knows Best." And they proclaimed that prescription drugs were the best thing since sliced bread. And they spread the word that consultations with the "healing professions" and that regularly conducted emotional sanitation visits with a psycho-the-rapist' signaled arrival in high society. That most of them ceased to swear the Hippocratic Oath decades ago and are therefore at liberty to harm their patients is never mentioned.

The aluminum waste product rat poison of fluoride was added to food and water, other food genetically "modified". The education system was ruined and what was taught perverted, everything inverted. The experimental COVID injections and their top-ups, a hit in many regions of the Earth now signal an early death for takers. And the Great Work of Ages almost completed, the final push for it begun with the shell-shocked WWI and WWII soldiers and civilians. The brutality of their treatment, originally engineered by Wundt and his 130 graduates, dictates the treatment of the genuine PTSD-traumatized to this very day.

And feel for the few bright souls who discovered during the past century that those PTSD treatments are not only wrong, but detrimental to human health and well-being, never mind recapturing the escaped soul. When East Indian cardiologist, professor of medicine and author Belle Monappa Hegde (1938–) discovered, that each of our individual cells has a brain all its own, all hell broke loose for him, despite his grand resume. He had been Vice Chancellor of Manipal Academy of Higher Education from 1999 to 2003. He had been awarded the Padma Bhushan in 2010 and the Padma Vibhushan in 2021. That he also supports homeopathy and quantum healing was, of course, held hugely against him.

In his 2019 lecture on "Sauce of Happiness" at the campus of Indian Institute of Technology, Madras, this honourable man proposed that quantum healing could bring sick people back to normal. He presented the knowledge of numerous researchers showing that each of our cells indeed has a brain of its own. His peers called him a proponent of "pseudo-science and quackery," as the Luciferic Consciousness can not tolerate human healing of any sort. Through millennia, it throve on our abject suffering, the worse the better. It created in a multitude of ways among them the wars of WWI and WWII. Thus, it created the shell-shocked walking wounded, whose treatment continued the never-ending suffering of those following in wars thereafter. Souls departed, the body knowing the body would die, but living on. And who were the ones making a lucrative profession of treating those nobly wounded and where?

29

THE MASTERS OF HUMANITY'S PERCEPTION MANIPULATOR CREATION

Let us continue with German neurologist and psychiatrist Robert Eugen Gaupp (1870–1953), shall we? Recall that he wrote about the catastrophic emotional health impact Nobel's inventions wreaked on WWI soldiers, and how special psychiatric hospitals had to be opened just to treat this new affliction.

Gaupp, a neurologist and psychiatrist, was taught by German psychiatrist, anatomist and neuro-pathologist Karl Wernicke (1848–1905). He, in turn, had studied under anatomist, psychiatrist and neuro-pathologist Theodor Hermann Meynert (1833–1892). Meynert is known as one of the most arduous defenders of an existing bridge, a connection existing between human psychological and neurophysiological events and reactions. He claimed that existing bridges depended on specific neuroanatomical structures within the brain. He believed that these disturbances in brain development could be the predisposition for psychiatric illness and that certain psychoses were reversible. So, Meynert's work focused largely on brain anatomy, pathology and histology. The latter is the study of microscopic biological body tissues, as well as mapping of the human neurological systems' in all its intricate pathways and topography.

Meynert developed some innovative anatomical techniques and complex concepts on how subcortical and cortical structures worked to produce psychiatric symptoms. In this manner, he figured out that a conflict between the cerebral cortex and the sub-cortical regions of the brain was the primary cause of mental illness due to the cerebral components' abnormal functions. To briefly explain, the blood supply, and thus blood oxidation, flows through the spinal cord through the brainstem to the cerebellum. It is derived entirely from branches of the vertebral and basilar arteries. These arise at the point in the neck where the common carotid arteries bifurcate and the right and left vertebral arteries come together. This union is at the level of the pons, one of the three components of the brainstem. There, they form the midline basilar artery. The basilar artery joins the blood supply from the internal carotids in an arterial ring at the base of the brain via the circle of Willis. This is in around the hypothalamus and cerebral peduncles. That's where they form the corpus callosum, originating with the wide, thick nerve tract passing through the atlas and axis to the cerebral cortex. This is discussed at length in *Fallacy 1*'s chapter on atlasprofilax.

As we learned in *Fallacy 1*, the atlas and axis vertebrae are the two most superior bones in the vertebral column, and they are part of the seven cervical vertebrae. The atlas is the top-most bone, the first cervical vertebra, sitting just below the skull. Along with the second vertebra, it forms the joint connecting the skull and the spine. The atlas (C1) not only carries the skull, but is also responsible for the suspension, equilibrium and management of the spine and the human skeleton. It is followed by the axis. Together, they support the skull, facilitate neck movement, and protect the spinal cord. Atlas and axis connecting the skull and the spine form the joint through which the brainstem flows.

Swiss René-Claudius Schümperli ((1940–2013), through his own pain and suffering, discovered and developed a way to align the atlas vertebra and move the atlas into its natural stable and permanent position. This provides unimpeded full blood-flow to the brain. The multitude of positive changes in functioning of the human central nervous system, and therefore the entire human being, come in just one treatment. And yes, I had it done with spectacular result. I felt the rush of blood to my brain when my atlas slid into position as it took away my craving for alcohol when under stress and my fear of open heights and God knows what else.

The blood supply from the spinal cord located within the vertebral canal serves several purposes. It allows for the neuronal connection, the cells responsible for receiving sensory input from the external world. It carries motor commands to our muscles. And it transforms and relays the electrical signals at every step in between the brain and the rest of the body. Thus, a swift flowing blood supply is of vital importance. It assures appropriate functioning of human hormone production, memory, emotion and pleasure, as well as determining:

- intelligence
- personality
- motor function
- planning and organization ability
- touch sensation
- processing sensory information
- language processing

And, to repeat, the velocity and flow of blood through the brainstem running through the atlas and axis controls the development and functioning of all of the above.

So, Meynert was on to something. He stated that a physical cause existed between humans' cerebral pathologies and psychoses created by what he called a "lack of cerebral nutrition." He hypothesized that this lack of oxidization and blood flow to the brain created psychiatric illnesses. He even theorized that such disturbances were reversible. However, he neglected to elaborate on the topic, at least far and wide. Nor did he tell us what precisely caused the discrepancy or why he thought it was possible to reverse it. He must have known the reason, as he conducted and witnessed a multitude of dissections in and out of vivo. Did he ever give the atlas or axis a glance? Did he ever consider their connection? After all, it is right in one's field of vision and large enough to examine without a microscope. This topic is still not discussed, as to correct this human impairment would improve humanity's health too much. It would endanger the profits of the entire health industry, the art, craft and science of psychiatry and psychology included. So, they stick with their cerebro-vascular disease creation, enhanced by drugging to perpetuate their human trauma creation.

So, it seems somewhat stunning that the learned society has still to discover the atlas's incorrect rotational position in almost every human being on the face of this earth. They eagerly dig to find where the spirit, soul and mind is located in humans' physical brains. They have, despite MRA, X-Rays and whatever else available to analyze the human skeleton. Yet they still can't see what's before their eyes.

Meanwhile, layman Schümperli found it without their education. He had suffered a number of physically impairing accidents, throwing him into insufferable misery. Because no physician knew how to release his pain, never mind heal him, he would figure it out himself. In 1993, after years of intensive research, he would scientifically and empirically prove that the first cervical vertebra—the atlas—is in almost all humans in an incorrect rotational position. He would show that this prohibits appropriate blood-flow to the brain and therefore causes human physical, and mental impairments, as well as impeding the healing capabilities of injuries sustained during life's journey.

And how did Schümperli do it? With determination, persistence, willpower, discipline and stubbornness. And with the help of the divine power permeating all there is in all of creation, he had an ardent desire to heal himself. These are the same ingredients needed to heal Self from genuine PTSD. The result? Knowing what was faulty, Schümperli had developed by the mid-1990s a revolutionary vibrational neuromuscular massage instrument. This tool loosens and releases muscular tension in the short muscles of the neck. These are the sub-occipital muscles surrounding and stabilizing the head joints at the base of the skull around the atlas and the axis vertebras. His unique device was able to correct the position of the atlas and by putting the body into symmetry. After a short vibrational massage, the atlas can painlessly and smoothly slide into its natural position. This is done without cracking, rough handling or traction. It is done without health risk. And it instantaneously results in a palpable rush of blood to the brain through the brainstem. This rush reverses the "lack of cerebral nutrition" Meynert spoke about. The ligamentous- and muscular compression on the atlas vertebra are instantly released. This produces an astounding effect on the physical body overall as it jumpstarts the central nervous system into full activation of its numerous incapacitated sections and kicking the body's natural physical and mental healing abilities into gear.

Despite good health, I had the procedure done the moment I heard of it. The sudden rush of blood to my brain when the atlas slid into position gave me a huge sense of relief and wellbeing. As a bonus, it took away my fear of open heights and eliminated my desire for alcohol when under stress. I was too ignorant to know that low blood-sugar also increases the craving for booze (*Fallacy 1*). So, Meynert and all were still taking apart human brains and bodies, looking at human skull and spinal cord connections. Knowingly or unknowingly, wittingly or unwittingly, they managed to overlook the atlas-axis factor. Perhaps they were imprinted with the knowledge that the multitude of their eighteenth- and nineteenth-century peers sniggered and viciously criticized Meynert's hypothesis of a physical reason for mental illness due to "lack of cerebral nutrition." But perhaps they were encouraged that others thought his theories foreshadowed an increase of the learned science society's understanding of psychiatric disease development. Looking at any of the DSM Manuals and the treatment of genuine PTSD journeyers, none of it happened.

But they did link Meynert's name to at least seven areas of the brain, one of them the nucleus basalis of Meynert. This group of neurons is located mainly in the substantia innominate. It is a series of layers consisting partly of grey and white matter lying below the anterior part of the thalamus and lentiform nucleus of the basal forebrain. It has widespread connections to other parts of the brain. This indicates that it likely has an important regulating influence on brain functions, including sustained attention, learning and long-term memory recall. The part is famous because of its perceived vulnerability to neurodegenerative pathology. This pathology is characterised by selective dysfunction and progressive loss of synapses and neurons associated with pathologically altered proteins that deposit primarily in the human brain and spinal cord. We find this, for example, in Alzheimer's, dementia and Parkinson's. It is characterized by the progressive functional loss of neurons in the brain, causing cognitive impairment and motor-neuron disability.

Motor neuron diseases (MNDs) are caused by the destruction of motor neurons. These cells control skeletal muscle activity, such as walking, breathing, speaking and swallowing. This group includes diseases like:

- Kennedy's disease
- post-polio syndrome
- primary lateral sclerosis
- spinal muscular atrophy
- progressive bulbar palsy
- amyotrophic lateral sclerosis
- progressive muscular atrophy

https://ninds.nih.gov/
disorders/Patient-Caregiver-Education/Fact-Sheets/Motor- Neuron-Diseases-Fact-Sheet.

It took the learned society until 2021 to vaguely acknowledge that nutrition might play an essential role in the development and evolution of neurodegenerative diseases. These incurable and debilitating conditions result in progressive degeneration and death of nerve cells. However, no one is breathing a word about the effects of pharmaceutical drugs in such neurodegenerative disease development. Nor do they mention their effects on human ill health development overall. Still, drugs to counteract neurodegenerative illnesses in humans are being rampantly pursued and incessantly prescribed to the masses by their health professionals (Vittorio Emanuele Bianchi et al: "Effect of nutrition on neurodegenerative diseases. A systematic review"; *Nutritional Neuroscience,* 2021).

We see the suppression of the proper atlas alignment and the systematic drugging to heal human emotional upheavals combine. It raises the question: "Is it orchestrated or coincidental?" Or are these manifestations of neuro-generational treatments and evolution of humanity's health narrative inbred into the learned society since the days of Wundt, Meynert et al.? If so, are they orchestrated in part by the Carnegie Report issuer Abraham Flexner and his brothers in unison with the Rockefeller's and their foundation? Which leads us to wonder: "Who educated Meynert?" Why do we want to know? Because whoever educated Meynert laid the foundation to the purposefully traumatize the walking PTSD wounded from WWI onwards. This foundation also carried their treatment methodology and mind manipulation techniques forth to the herd around the world. Africa might be the only exception, as reflected in exquisite detail in the herd's mind-numbing reaction to COVID 19 insane mandates.

So, what about Meynert (1833-1892)? Born in Dresden, the Kingdom of Saxony, he moved with his parents to Vienna at age eight. He received his M.D. at the University of Vienna in 1861. He presented his thesis *Bau und Leistungen des Gehirns und Rückenmarks mit Beziehung zu deren Erkrankungen*, the proper translation being The *Building And Achievements Of The Brain And Spinal Cord In Relation To Their Illnesses*, in 1865. This enabled him to add psychiatry to his medical qualification and teach in the Austrian educational system.

He had no one specific to educate him in the art, craft and sciences of the human psyche at that time. After all, it did not exist yet. So, he devoted himself to establishing psychiatry as an exact science based on anatomy. He conceived this quasi-overwhelming ardent desire out of his own inner self, formulated by the antagonism he experienced, we trust, during his human body dissections. That was when he surmised that the key to the abnormal function of cerebral mechanisms in mental illness lay between the cortex and the sub-cortical zone connection. Did he reach his conclusion without any academic guidelines from anyone, we ask?

Well, as far as we can discern, he had a talent as an experienced dissector. This means he was good at cutting and separating bodies during anatomical study. This gave him an appointment as director of the Vienna Asylum in 1870. This was the first psychiatric clinic, in the vernacular called "nuthouse", in Lower Austria. It propelled him into the position of the University of Vienna's chair of psychiatry in 1873. From there, he became the University's professorship of nervous diseases, as well as the director of its associated psychiatric clinic in 1875. He held these posts until 1892, whilst simultaneously running his own private neurological outpatient clinic from 1887 forward. This provided him with an abundant amount of research subjects (https://biographien.ac.at/oebl/oebl_M/Meynert_Theodor_1833_1892.xml).

He seemed obsessed with establishing psychiatry as an exact science evidenced in brain pathology and anatomy. For him, brain research was an interdisciplinary project akin to today's biological psychiatry. Oddly enough, his main focal point was indeed the anatomy and histology of the cerebrum and the brainstem and the topography and functional relations of the main connecting fiber systems. He precisely documented these in clinical and pathological observations. Among his findings were the stratified texture, cellular architecture and regional differentiation of the cerebral cortex. I should stress that these finding are the basis of present-day studies of the cellular composition of the central nervous system's tissues under the microscope (cytoarchitectonics). They are also the basis of studying the cortical localization theory of function holding that different cerebral cortical territories served different functions, such as vision and language. (F. Seitelberger: Theodore Meynert (1833–1892) pioneer and visionary of brain research; Journal of the history of the neurosciences 1997). Still, he did not observe any oddity of the atlas misalignment.

His peers' perceived that he correctly interpreted the vital and psychic dynamics of the brain's workings by way of critical speculation. They also recognized the precision with which he conveyed his theories and hypotheses with the up-and-coming philosophies of neurophysiology, neurochemistry and neuropsychology. This gave him the honorific title of founder of scientific brain research. Though considered a far less inspiring teacher than Wundt, Meynert's pupils came from far and wide. They included such impressive people as German physician Josef Breuer (1842–1925). He made key discoveries in neurophysiology, the branch of physiology and neuroscience focusing on the living nervous systems functions. It was Breuer who first noted that loud spoken expression of strong emotions caused a catharsis, a relief from strong or repressed emotions. This psychological relief came through spewing forth whatever nagged a subject. This laid the foundation of psychoanalysis, which Breuer's protégé Sigismund Schlomo Freud and fellow Austrian Alfred Adler (1870–1937) ran with big time a few years later to "Make the American Mind."

Adler was born into a Viennese bourgeois liberal family of Khazarian origin. He began his medical career as an ophthalmologist before turning his attention to public health and social issues. He elaborated on these in political journal articles and in his book *Health Book for the Tailoring Trade* (1898), a purely Ashkenazi occupation. The book renders the material hardships small tradesmen suffered in those days and identifies a link between economic misery and the spread of diseases. This led Adler to develop a keen interest for the socially disadvantaged and the burgeoning labour movement. Dissatisfied with the way conventional medicine perceived diseases, he joined Freud's "Psychological Wednesday Society" in 1902. He began coining his own ideas, hypotheses and theories on the human psyche, soul, spirit and mind, quickly becoming one of Freud's closest collaborators (wien.gv).

As early as 1907, however, his studies on organ inferiority presented in his book *Study of Organ Inferiority* gave him an upswing in stature. Disenchanted with Freud's emphasis on the influence of unconscious factors as motivators in human behaviour, he developed irreconcilable with Freud's theories (https://psycnet.apa.org/record/2005-04400-000). Gradually, their differences in opinion, notably after the appearance of Adler's *Studie über Minderwertigkeit von Organen* (1907; *Study of Organ Inferiority and Its Psychical Compensation*) led to a permanent break between them. It suggested that people try to compensate psychologically for a physical disability and its attendant feeling of inferiority, resulting in neurosis (Britannica.com).

Adler downplayed Freud's basic contention that sexual conflicts in early childhood cause mental illness and confine sexuality to a symbolic role in human strivings to overcome feelings of inadequacy. This intensified their dislike for each other. Indeed, Adler became so radically opposed to the basic tenets of Freud's theories, that the two men severed all connections in 1911 and remained bitter enemies for the rest of their lives.

The break also led to Adler's School of Individual Psychology, which posits that the overriding motivation in most people is a striving for self-realization, completeness and perfection. This striving for superiority, Adler maintains, may be frustrated by feelings of inferiority, inadequacy or incompleteness. Such feelings might arise from physical defects, low social status, parental pampering or neglect during childhood or other causes encountered in the course of life. Individuals, he maintained, can compensate and overcome their feelings of inferiority by developing their innate skills and abilities, taking Demosthenes as an example. Each individual develops one's personality and strives for perfection by their very own style of life. This style would in part develop in early childhood by what inferiority affected them most deeply during their formative years. In Adler's view, this time of life also seems to determine the drive for superiority. He hypothesized that this drive coexists with the innate urge to cooperate and work with other people for the common good, a drive Adler termed "the social interest".

In Adler's opinion, our mental health is characterized by and reflected in our ability to reason and our social interest in interaction with others. It is also characterized by our self-transcendence. This is our ability to overcome the limits of our individual self and our desires in spiritual contemplation and realization of our potential and the aim of full development of abilities and appreciation for life. In contrast, Adler sees mental disorders arising either from feelings of inferiority and self-centred concern for one's safety, desire for power over others, striving for perfection or striving for superiority. (http://www.differencebetween.net/science/psychology/difference-between-self-actualization-and-self-realization/). His observation apparently reflected one of the philosophical ideas of Friederich Nietzsche, who had developed a philosophy that considered the will to power the very basic motive of human life. Striving for superiority is said to refer to the desire to be better. But it also contains the idea that we want to be better than others, rather than to be better in our own right. Later in life, Adler found strife for superiority more in reference to unhealthy or neurotic striving, mind you, for reasons probably hidden away in his own psyche somewhere.

Believing that basic human motivation seeks compensation or strives to overcome something, Adler also thought that, since we all have short-comings and inferiorities, our personalities are reflected by how we do or don't compensate or overcome those problems. Thus, the Adlerian psycho-the-rapist directs the patient's attention to the unsuccessful, neurotic character of his attempts to cope with feelings of inferiority. Once the patient has been made aware of these, one would build up patient-self-esteem, adopt more realistic goals and encourages more useful behaviour and a stronger social interest. All this would be according to what he or she thinks is right, screw the patient. In other words, it's all in the cognitive behavioural *sui generis* way if a genuine PTSD-affected person.

WWI interrupted Adler's psychiatrist career. He served as a mere physician with the Austro-Hungarian army first on the Russian front and later in a children's hospital. The latter, we are told, greatly increased his post-war influence. Not at all interested in WWI soldiers' emotional plight, he instead established 32 child guidance clinics in Vienna, Hungary and Germany after the war. He did this with the cooperation of the Austrian government and private charitable organizations. Attached to state schools to enhance lower class children's standard of living and to train teachers, Hitler Jugend formation springs to mind (https://psycnet.apa.org/record/2009-00070-039). From 1921 onwards, Adler frequently lectured throughout Europe and the United States. He eventually accepted a position at the Long Island College of Medicine in 1926 and as visiting professor at Columbia University in 1927. When Hitler took over Austria in 1934, he left Vienna for the U.S. forever with his family. In 1937, during a series of lectures at Aberdeen University, he died of a heart attack. (https://webspace.ship.edu/cgboer/adler.html).

As to Adler's hypothesis of human inferiority, it was nothing new. It paralleled that of French psychologist, physician, philosopher and psychotherapist Pierre Marie Félix Janet (1859 --1947). Along with Wundt, Janet is considered a founding father of psychology. He specialized in the field of dissociation and traumatic memory. But Janet, one of Freud's teachers, termed Adler's "feeling of inferiority", which he based on a generational defective physical organ as an emotional "feeling of incompleteness" (*sentiment d'incomplétude*). Freud included the latter into many of his hypotheses and speculation of the human psyche. So did his sometime-buddy and contemporary Carl-Gustav Jung, who added "complex" to "inferior", a word denoting something "consisting of many different and connected parts."

In psychoanalysis nomenclature, however, "complex" is expressed as meaning: "A related group of emotionally significant ideas that are completely or partly repressed and that cause psychic conflict leading to abnormal mental states or behaviour." (Oxford Languages) In other words, and most conveniently, the cabal can read anything and everything into it regardless of how healthy the "patient" is. The nomenclature of "complex" is seen by the psychiatric profession as a core pattern of human emotions, memories, perceptions and wishes in humanity's personal unconscious mind. These would be organized around common themes such as power, status, superiority or, for all we know, inferiority. How they can read our unconscious and subconscious mind is as yet undisclosed. But Adler thought that organ inferiority tended to increase the feeling of inferiority we experience, in every child resulting in an intensification of strife towards an often unattainable goal.

As such, Adler makes dissatisfaction with body shape and size responsible for an inferiority complex. He theorized that in the course of striving for change drives the personality into a distorted view and exhibits the traits of a "neurosis" or character disorder. His concept became known as the "inferiority complex." The cabal promptly identified the human physical brain as the organ causing such inferiority and causing askew psychological deficiencies and disorders (PsycINFO Database Record (c) 2016 APA, all rights reserved). Anyway, while Freud saw his libido theory questioned by his society, Adler went on to establish the *Österreichischer Verein für Individualpsychologie* (ÖVIP) (Austrian Club for Individual Psychology) in 1912, still in operation today, before his emigration to the U.S. to make his living as a lecturer on his philosophy on the human psyche.

Mind you, Adler's school was the first major deviation from the psychoanalytical movement. The name he gave it was "Individual Psychology." This implied that man's mind is not, as Freud had suggested, locked in a struggle between conscious and unconscious forces. Rather, each person represents a unified and self-consistent whole striving toward a goal floating before him. No man, Adler believed, could be understood without reference to his usually unconscious goal, much as a drama could be understood only in the light of its finale. The goal a person shaped for himself, and the characteristic ways he struggled to reach it were what Adler termed his "style of life." (www.nytimes.com; Maggie Scarf 1971).

Adler's hypotheses were mainly presented in a collection of papers and lectures given between 1912 and 1914 published in English in 1925. They first and foremost emphasize his opinion that humans are indeed indivisible entities, whole beings, whose physical environment and social associations must be taken into account by the psychotherapist counseling and analyzing. And how does Adler picture such individual psychology counseling sessions to unfold? Simple, the soul-rapist in charge spews forth a word or an idea and the patient is instructed to instantaneously spew forth whatever springs to mind and go on spinning until the 50 minutes hour is up. In a genuine PTSD situation involving the WCB, insurers, employers and union goons the "you have a right to remain silent" may be highly advisable. Anything you say can and will be held against you. Lack of material makes it more difficult for them to lie about you.

However, Adler did insist that:

> "Everyone (...) has a feeling of inferiority. But the feeling of inferiority is not a disease; it is rather a stimulant to healthy, normal striving and development. It becomes a pathological condition only, when the sense of inadequacy overwhelms the individual and, far from stimulating them to useful activity, makes them depressed and incapable of development."

It is this inferiority they want to inspire in us, this feeling that we are nothing, that we are wrong, that we were defect from birth. These opponents in the genuine PTSD predicament we find ourselves in, due to no fault of our own, are experts in installing these feelings.

Whichever way it may be, psychiatrist Adler thought that many neurotic symptoms could be traced to overcompensation for the feeling of inferiority. This was demonstrated by the oratory of the stammering Athenian Demosthenes (384–322BC) mentioned before. This contemporary of Aristotle wished to take his guardians holding his inheritance to court. According to Plutarch, he hesitated because he had an inarticulate and stammering pronunciation. He had a weakness in his voice of a perplexed and indistinct utterance and a shortness of breath. By breaking and disjointing his sentences, it greatly obscured the sense and meaning of what he spoke.

To overcome his speaking difficulties, Demosthenes determinedly practiced speaking with pebbles in his mouth. He recited verses when running up and down hills and when out of breath and practiced his speeches before a large mirror. The result? He became known as a great orator in his own time, fourth century BC. He is recognized as the greatest of ancient Greek orators, as well as one of Athens' greatest statesmen. His speeches provide valuable information on the political, social and economic life of fourth century BC, applicable to this very day. In other words, Adler is telling us in a roundabout way that a person's willpower, determination, persistency and discipline can overcome a inferiority complex problems, with Demosthenes proving it. But who wants to know of Demosthenes these days, eh, when U.S. Supreme Court judge nominees don't seem to know the definition of "woman" and favour baby, infant and child rapists in their sentencing, showing a distinct lack of both moral and ethical values?

It in a way, these nominees are like the mental health profession. It neglects to teach its clientele the basic principles leading to a successful life. It merely pronounces those they perceive as suffering an inferiority complex, those presenting with signs of low self-esteem, self-worth, low status in their group of peers or depression classifying them as mentally ill and in need of benzodiazepines to cure them. They know well that feelings of inferiority are intensified at any age through discouragement or failure. However, a cured patient is a lost customer, so let's enhance our profit by knocking them down some more with medication. Business blooms that way. And how did they acquire their knowledge? From the WWI shell shocked, then taking it forward from there with Wundt's and Meynert's pupils.

Another of those pupils of them was Russian neuro-psychiatrist Sergei Sergeievich Korsakoff (1854–1900), known for his studies on alcoholic psychosis. He had also studied under Wernicke, as well as under Swiss neuro-anatomist, psychiatrist and eugenicist Auguste Henri Forel (1847–1931) Forel was notable for investigating the brain structure of ants and humans and for contributing to psychology and sexology. Sexology is the study of human sexual behavior and sexuality in general, such as sexual development, relationships, intercourse, sexual dysfunction, sexually transmitted diseases, sexual addiction and child sexual abuse. Forel had studied medicine at the University of Zürich from 1866 to 1871 and then worked in neuro-anatomy with Meynert at Vienna, where he received his medical degree in 1872 (Britannica.com).

Unimpressed with Meynert, Forel moved on to Germany in 187 to help Johann Bernhard Aloys von Gudden (1824–1886) at his Munich Kreis-Irrenanstalt, the local insane asylum. Von Gudden was neuro-anatomist and psychiatrist of Bavaria's "mad king" King Ludwig II. Forel improved on Gudden's microtome, a specialized precision cutting instrument, which accurately and repeatedly slices sections from a block of embedded tissue used for whole brain sectioning, dead or alive. There was also related thorough neuro-anatomical work of Spaniard Santiago Ramón y Cajal (1852–1934). Together, they gave advanced the hypothesis that the individual neuron is the unit of structure and function of the nervous system. That put the neuron doctrine, that the nervous system is made up of discrete individual cells, on solid scientific footing. (https://oxfordmedicne.com)

By 1879, Forel had achieved the position of professor of psychiatry at the University of Zürich. He was also by then director of Zurich's the Burghölzli Asylum, founded in 1870 and copied in many parts of the world. That was where eminent path breakers in psychiatry like Jung and Adolf Meyer worked and where Bleuler coined the term "Schizophrenia" (https://ncbi.nlm.nih.gov/pmc/articles/PMC4919972/). In 1887, Forel published his work on neuron theory, describing those cellular functional units within the brain. Throughout his career, he worked for social reforms. In 1889, he founded an institute to prevent mental illness, syphilis, and alcoholism. When he retired in 1893, however, he had had enough of all that and turned his devotion to studying the psychology of ants. He hoped to find in them the analogs relating to or using signals or information relating to or clarifying human social and political behaviors.

Human Nervous System / Brain / Spinal Cord / Nerves

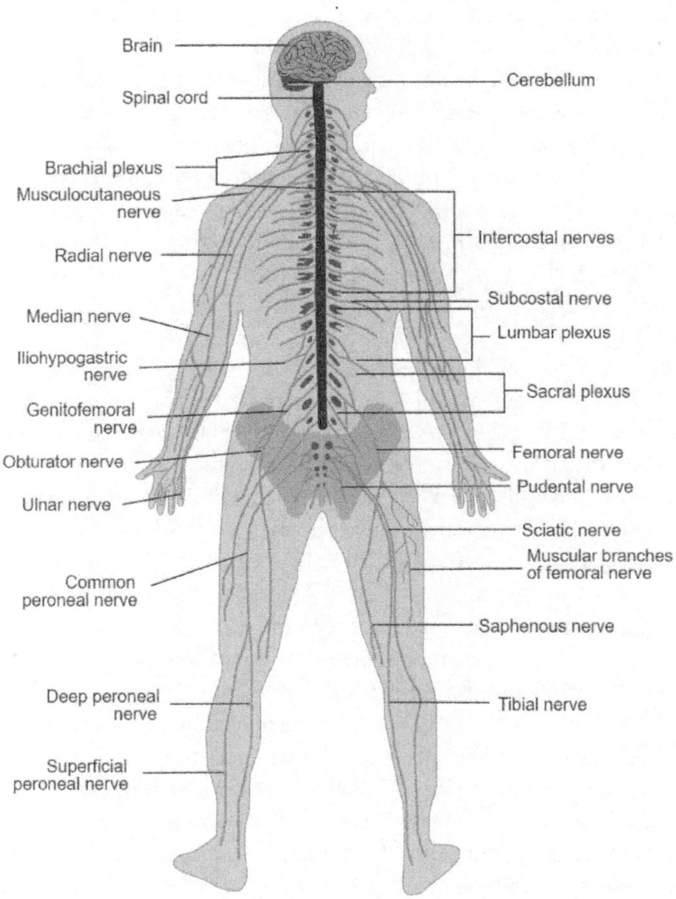

German neuro-anatomist, psychiatrist and neuro-pathologist Paul Emil Flechsig (1847–1929) was another one of Meynert's famous students. He was educated at the University of Leipzig. In 1882, he became director of the city's Clinical Institute of Psychiatry and Neurology. And in 1884, he became the university's professor of psychiatry. He made personal investigations of the European systems for treating the insane as a recognized authority. During his 50-year medical career, he also developed myelinogenesis, a technique he pioneered by studying brains of late term fetus' and newborns. He stained them for myelin, a rich fatty substance surrounding our nerve cell axons. These long, slender projections of nerve cells conduct electrical impulses. They are the nervous system's "wires". He treated them like an electrical wire (the axon) by insulating them with insulating material (myelin) around them. How he got his research material is unknown, but we can be sure that he knew everyone of promise in the art and craft of science of psychology cruising through Leipzig until his retirement.

One of Meynert's most famous students was German psychiatrist Emil Wilhelm Georg Magnus Kraepelin (1856–1926), Wilhelm Wundt's (1832–1920) lifelong personal friend and scientific companion. Kraepelin held the staunch belief that human psychiatric malfunctions and diseases had purely biological and genetic origins. They had nothing to do with normal, human emotional upheaval. His viewpoint seems to again lead us to the atlas/axis misalignment or mal-rotation. Kraepelin, professor of clinical psychiatry at the University of Munich from 1903 onwards, happily advocated eugenics and racial hygiene. His research focussed on alcoholism, crime, degeneration and hysteria. Discussed at length in Fallacy 1, H.J. Eysenck's *Encyclopedia of Psychology* identifies Kraepelin as the founder of modern scientific psychiatry, psycho-pharmacology and psychiatric genetics, all of which are in vogue today.

Another of Meynert's most important students was Austrian Julius Wagner-Jauregg (1857 –1940), who succeeded Meynert as Extraordinary Professor of Psychiatry and Nervous Diseases and Director of Vienna's Clinic for Psychiatry and Nervous Diseases in 1893. He also introduced fever treatment to cure syphilis. Just like his mentor, he was fascinated by humans' sexual attitudes. He administered thyroid and ovarian pharmaceutical preparations and who knows whatever else to his young psychotic patients, in particular those experiencing delayed puberty. This led to their development of secondary sexual characteristics, as well as diminished psychosis, we read, *en route* to trans-genderism. He deemed other patients to be schizophrenic due to excessive masturbation, so he cut off their testicles. We read that this resulted in an "improved" condition (Edward Shorter, Max Fink. *Endocrine Psychiatry: Solving the Riddle of Melancholia*; Oxford University Press US, 2010. p. 23). We gather that because of his brutalities inflicted upon humans during his career, like Obama for inflicting numerous wars killing and creating havoc for millions of innocents almost a century later, he received the 1927 Nobel Prize in Physiology or Medicine.

Needless to say, Meynert and Wundt's graduated students in turn launched a multitude of aspiring psychiatrists in their new art, craft and science of psychology, psychiatry, neuro-pathology and neuro-biology magick. They, all sang from the same songbook. Henceforth they enjoyed the never-ending opportunity to add their own personal human psyche treatment-hallucinations, illusions, ideas and fata morganas at leisure. Ans they did this in accordance with their own psychological emotional make-up, aiming to create their own fame and fortune from the herd's misery. And it all began with WWI, regardless of nation, emotionally-rattled government issues. Easy for Don Miguel Ruiz (1952-) to say so magnificently:

> "Don't take anything personally. What others say and do is a projection of their own reality, their own dream."

They have the quasi power of gods, wit Fauci at present instructed by them. Anyone practicing any of the above mentioned new art, craft and sciences purportedly related to the human psyche has reason to fear for his or her life. They all, psychiatry, psychology, neuro-pathology and neuro-biology, experimented with their magick during WWI and WWII and their aftermath. They were so jubilant to put their hands on the life scientific research material of previously healthy, young and vibrant human animals on which to prey and practice in whichever way they saw fit. All the while, they were grabbing and grasping at the chance for recognition and fame, proving their superiority to their own in a realm where jealousy and competition is rampant. So how and with what did they practice on the nobly wounded GIs, regardless of nationality? Let's see.

30
THE SHELL-SHOCK WOUNDED

This fascination with the walking wounded has been found throughout the science of psychology professionals. It has been found throughout the entire spectrum of all participating armies, regardless of nationality. What is the allure of those surviving the killing fields without a scratch, but with emotionally traumatizing consequences? The treating cabal were thrilled to no end with the real-life experimental material for their psychology laboratories. It was provided to them in an almost overwhelming amount. Sadly, most (if not all) of the treating cabal ignored Meynert's observation about psychiatry, in his 1884 textbook *Psychiatrie: Klinik Der Erkrankungen Des Vorderhirns Begrundet Auf Dessen Bau, Leistungen Und Ernahrung—Psychiatry: a clinical treatise on diseases of the fore-brain based upon a study of its structure, functions and nutrition* Band 1. Hälfte - expressed in the foreword (worldcat.org):

> "The reader will find no other definition of 'Psychiatry' in this book but the one given on the title page: Clinical Treatise on Diseases of the Forebrain. The historical term for psychiatry, i.e., 'treatment of the soul,' implies more than we can accomplish, and transcends the bounds of accurate scientific investigation."

Boom. But no one listened to Meynert, though he was considered at that time the greatest brain anatomist in Europe, if not the western world. He knew the brain inside out. He knew soul, spirit and mind was nowhere to be found in it. Thus, Allen Frances' 2010 statement about the science of psychiatry: "It's all bullshit!" And whom did Meynert practice on to reach his conclusion? Well, perhaps this draft found in his book textbook Psychiatrie. Klinik der Erkrankungen des Vorderhirns --- Psychiatry: A Clinical Treatise On Diseases of the Fore-Brain gives us an indication? Only those brutal and psychopathic seem to be joyously engaged.

Germany's leading neurologist and psychiatrist of his time was Karl Bonhoeffer (1868 -1948),. Who was this man who orchestrated future havoc for the PTSD affected WWI and WWII walking wounded? Bonhoeffer received his M.D. in 1892, after studies at the universities of Tübingen, Berlin and Munich (https://ajp.psychiatryonline.org/doi/pdf/10.1176/appi.ajp.2008.07061031). After working as a physician for several years he was elected chair of the Department of Psychiatry at the University of Breslau/Wroclaw Mental Hospital in 1904. There, he worked together with Carl Wernicke (1848–1905). Wernicke was known for his research on aphasia, a language disorder caused by damage in a specific area of the brain that controls language, expression and comprehension. It leaves a person unable to communicate effectively with others.

In 1912, Bonhoeffer was elected chair of the Department of Psychiatry and Neurology at the Charité Hospital. So, he moved with wife and 8 children to Berlin. In due course, he profoundly enhanced the profession's belief that there is a distinction between exogenous and endogenous psychoses. In other words, that a person's thoughts and perceptions might be disturbed and have difficulty understanding what is real and what is not. This would be due to a triggered underlying predisposition of an unnamed endogenous origin within the Self. Or it could be triggered by exogenous (outside) causes, such as Nobel's weaponry bouncing of the trench walls creating what he calls "consciousness impairment," perhaps? His findings countered Kraepelin's ideas that human psychiatric disorders came from biological and genetic malfunctions. But it opened the barn-door for the entire cabal henceforth to excuse every PTSD-impaired or emotionally upset human of being biologically and genetically defective. Beginning with WWI and WWII soldiers and still to this day, they exploit this most effectively.

Mind you, we have no idea what Bonhoeffer did during WWI or WWII. What we do know, however, is that he was dead set against Sigismund Schlomo Freud in general and his psychoanalysis ideas in particular. We also know that he acknowledged that WWI had caused untold sorrow to the world. And he saw how it caused such depravation for the German people that it impeded the country's ability to care for its sick and less fortunate. He said:

> "It could almost seem as if we have witnessed a change in the concept of humanity. I simply mean that we were forced by the terrible exigencies of war to ascribe a different value to the life of the individual than was the case before" (Burleigh M: *The Third Reich: A New History*. New York, Farrar, Straus and Giroux, 2001 p. 349).

Yes, a paradigm shift did indeed occur. It followed the last push for humanity's destruction. Planned since Adam and Eve, according to such experts as Albert Pike, Blavatsky, Maxwell, Tsarion, Tellinger, David Icke and others. It might be culminating with the 500 million AI enhanced humans surviving the onslaught by 2025. This would be in line with

Klaus Schwab's top advisor Yuval Noah Harari's "humans' are now genetically hackable" concept. Thus, they would achieve the destruction of God's creation in his image. How? By getting humanity to believe that COVID-19 injections would not only protect it from a deadly disease but also enhance it genetically. So Kreapelin was partly putting that Luciferic consciousness in motion, whereas Bonhoeffer still granted us some sort of consciousness.

The name Yuval, by the way, means 'offspring of Cain.'

Be it as it may, the question now arises whether there was another result of WWI's and WWII's monumental, worldwide upheavals of almost unfathomable magnitude, brutality and destruction. Did they also plant the seeds for the destruction of family and faith in God. Were divine providence, spirituality, faith in a higher power and in goodwill among mankind further casualties? Did the art and craft of the mental magicians of the science of psychology carry forth the Great Work of Ages. Did these rapists' of human and animal souls, most of whom had ceased to swear of adhere to the Hippocratic Oath. usher in this age of complete moral and ethical corruption? They certainly were helped by the herd's systematically engineered lack of knowledge since the early 1900.

What do we read in the New American Bible Revised Edition Hosea 4?

> Hear the word of the LORD, O people of Israel;
>
> for the LORD has an indictment against the inhabitants of the land.
>
> There is no faithfulness or loyalty,
>
> and no knowledge of God in the land.
>
> Swearing, lying, and murder,
>
> and stealing and adultery break out;
>
> bloodshed follows bloodshed.
>
> Therefore the land mourns,
>
> and all who live in it languish;
>
> together with the wild animals
>
> and the birds of the air,
>
> even the fish of the sea are perishing...
>
> My people are destroyed for lack of knowledge;
>
> because you have rejected knowledge.
>
> Rings a bell? Opens the eyes? And why is it so?

The self-proclaimed knowers of the human psyche know how to egg it on to prompt certain reactions, as if it were a hot rod machine. Most of them disbelieve in the existence of soul, mind and spirit. They sprouted up like poisonous weeds throughout European universities from Heidelberg, Leipzig, Vienna, Tübingen, Munich, Zurich, Paris, Cambridge, Oxford, Edinburgh and Pavia. Since the 1800, they have been spreading out worldwide from there. Freud's disciples and his advertising nephew Bernays were in the vanguard to carry forth and imprint their wishes into the herd's consciousness. They created the world's present narrative, reflected in the election of a woman to the U.S. Supreme Court who is unable to define what a woman is and has favoured pedophile and infant and child rapists in her sentencing record.

Some of those psyche-perverting individuals differed from most of their peers. Gaupp was among them. Recall that he was a student of scientific psychiatry, psychopharmacology and psychiatric genetics at the Universities of Heidelberg and Munich. And between 1908 and 1936 he was professor of psychiatry at the University of Tübingen. He differed from most of his peers by his interest in a possible correlation between personality and psychosis. This led him to call for applying both psychological and theological concepts and fostering wholeness, healing, and spiritual growth into human lives for healing. Calling it "pastoral psychology", it never got traction, as the concept is anathema to the craft's magicians, who despise God and decree human consciousness a phantasm (goodtherapy.org).

French psychiatrist Emmanuel Régis (1855-1918), however, was another one thinking somewhat in the same vein. He acknowledged that human upheavals cause emotional rather than mental disturbances. The latter signal the scientifically proper term for animals, which is how they see us. Régis studied medicine with three French neurologists and psychiatrists:

- Jules Gabriel François Baillarger (1809 -1890), apparently the first to discover that the cerebral cortex is divided into six layers of alternate white and grey lamina
- Jean-Pierre Falret (1794-1870), Salpetriere psychiatrist in Paris who believed in the dualistic nature of the individual and in the separation of body and soul
- Ernest-Charles Lasègue (1816-1883), in the mid- nineteenth century recognized for his work with human delusions of persecutions and his description of hysterical anorexia

All of them were renowned in the new psychiatric craft and science métier. In 1915, Régis reviewed 88 WWI participants' mental disorder cases. He then declared that their ailments resulted from witnessing the horrible death of comrades, noting: "20% only presented with a physical wound, but in all cases fright, emotional shock and seeing maimed comrades had been a major factor."

And what did the craft and art of humanity's psyche manipulation set in motion in the United States before being called to treat its walking wounded?

Well, the Swiss-born, 1892 émigré to the States, psychiatrist Adolf Meyer (1866-1950), mentioned earlier, exercised enormous influence over American psychiatry's development during the first half of the twentieth century. So said Dr. Susan Lamb PhD, Associate Professor at the University of Ottawa's Department of Innovation in Medical Education. He had studied under Swiss neuro-anatomist, psychiatrist and eugenicist Auguste-Henri Forel (1848 -1931). After receiving his M.D. in 1892, he went to Paris to study under French neurologist and professor of anatomical pathology Jean-Martin Charcot (1825 -1893). Charcot had been teaching at the famous Pitié-Salpêtrière Hospital for 33 years, drawing students from all over Europe. In 1882, he established the first European neurology clinic at the Salpêtrière. Mostly renowned for his work with hypnosis and hysteria, he taught Meyer plenty about human behaviour. It was enough for Meyer to secure a part-time position at the University of Chicago in 1892, practicing and teaching neurology. This followed brief stints in London and Edinburgh, working under British neurologist John Hughlings Jackson (1835–1911), best known for his research on epilepsy.

By 1893, Meyer got hired as pathologist by Illinois' massive, newly established mental hospital at Kankakee. A pathologist is a medical doctor with additional training in laboratory techniques used to study tissues and other materials taken from the body. They can then diagnose illness, monitor ongoing medical conditions and guide treatment (https://www.aucmed.edu/about/blog/what-does-a-pathologist-do-and-how-to-become-one). Why an insane asylum would need a pathologist might give an indication of the experiments conducted, wit *One Flew Over The Cuckoo's Nest*.

In 1895, he moved on to the Worcester Mental State Hospital, where he stayed until 1902. All the while, he prolifically published papers on his ideas and hypotheses on neurology, neuropathology and psychiatry. He made a name for himself and got hired as director of the Pathological Institute of the New York State Hospital system. It was shortly thereafter renamed The Psychiatric Institute. Within a few years, he shaped much of American psychiatry by emphasizing the importance of keeping detailed patient records. And he introduced both Kraepelin's classificatory system and Freud's views of the human psyche. In particular, he pushed Freud's ideas about human sexuality and the formative influence of early rearing on the adult personality. But he rejected Freud's dogmatic insistence on the psychical causation of mental illness, preferring to go the scientific brain-deficiency-since-birth route.

1904 saw Meyer as professor of psychiatry at Cornell University until in 1909. That's when he moved on to become director of Johns Hopkins Hospital's massive experimental Henry Phipps Psychiatric Clinic. The clinic opened in 1913. It was designed and build in accordance with his wishes, while he simultaneously served as professor of psychiatry, a post he would hold until 1941.

The clinic included a laboratory for clinical work. Staff were instructed to minutely study patients' pre-symptomatic history and their acute and remissive phases during periods of perceived mental illness. From 1914vto 1917, 49% of its 1897 patients were local, a process facilitated by the clinic's outpatient dispensary. In 1929upon Meyer's invitation, William Andrew Horsley Gantt (1892–1980) became founder and director of Johns Hopkins' Pavlovian Laboratory. This American physiologist and psychologist began working for the American Relief Administration in Petrograd/St. Petersburg, Russia, in 1922. He was studying the health effects of famine, ending up working with Pavlov in his Institute of Experimental Medicine laboratory.

In Russia, Gantt started a program to investigate the nervous disturbances in dogs – equalling humans, according to Darwinian philosophy – by combining a physiological method with a psychiatric problem. He spent 56 years of his career extending Pavlov's experimental research on humans' classical conditioning, the results reflected in today's society. By the time Meyer retired in 1941, old procedures such as frontal lobotomy and insulin shocks had become out-dated. New techniques began to emerge, though each new director was encouraged to maintain the overall philosophy of a behavioural approach to psychiatry while incorporating psychopharmacology.

Greek for 'breath, life, soul', 'drug' and logic, the term "psychopharmacology" is said to have been coined by David Israel Macht (1882 -1961) in 1920. Born in Moscow in 1882, he moved to Baltimore in 1892. Awarded a bachelor's and a medical degree by Johns Hopkins University in 1905, he took postgraduate courses in Berlin, Munich and Vienna. In 1909, he joined Johns Hopkins faculty as assistant professor, lecturing in pharmacology until 1932. That's when he moved on to lecture at New York's Yeshiva College, where he had been made Doctor of Hebrew Literature. He served there as visiting professor of general physiology until 1941. From 1944, Macht was a consultant in pharmacology at Baltimore's Sinai Hospital until he suffered a stroke in 1957. We have no idea what he did between 1941 and 1944.

Macht's expertise, as we understand it, lay in psychopharmacology, the scientific study of the effects of drugs. This includes any and all drugs from natural sources, such as plants and animals, or from artificial sources, such as chemical synthesis in laboratories, such as fentanyl. Psychopharmacology studies the effects on humans' mood, sensation, thinking and behaviour. Neuro-psychopharmacology, on the other hand, emphasizes the correlation between drug-induced changes in the functioning of cells, the nervous system and the changes in human consciousness and behaviour. Psychoactive drugs interact with particular target sites or receptors found in the nervous system to induce widespread changes in physiological or psychological functions. The specific interaction between drugs and their receptors is referred to as "drug action." The widespread changes in physiological or psychological function is referred to as "drug effect."

Phipps thus turned into a supervising and training institution. Most of Meyer's visiting students had already worked under him at the Manhattan State Hospital. This included that institution's chief architect Abraham Brill, Freud's close friend and nephew Bernays' future consultant. In 1911, Brill established the New York Psychoanalytic Institute.

Meyer and William Henry Welch, one of Johns Hopkins' founders, as we recall, teamed up on a couple other fronts. They motivated Clifford Whittingham Beers (1876 -1943), founder of the American mental hygiene movement, to found the Connecticut Society for Mental Hygiene in 1908. They also motivated Ukrainian-born psychiatrist and social activist Leo Kanner (1894-1961), who had practiced as a physician in Germany and in South Dakota, to open the first U.S. child psychiatry clinic at Johns Hopkins Hospital in 1930.

Myer also had Harvard graduate biologist, psycho-biologist and geneticist Curt Paul Richter (1894-1888) under his wings. Richter was most noted for his study of rat behaviour he conducted with Meyer and American born and bred psychologist John Broadus Watson (1878 -1958). Probably as the result of the rattus-equals human study, he coughed up his "scientific theory of behaviourism". According to Japanese behavioural analyst Araiba Sho, behaviourism is the systematic approach to understanding the behaviour of humans and other animals ("Current diversification of behaviorism"; *Perspectives on Behavior Science*. 43 (1): 157-175, 2019). Watson, in turn, was inspired by his behaviourist approach. He began to conduct intensive research on animal and child behaviour. Among his forays were such controversial undertakings as the Kerplunk experiment, a stimulus and response experiment conducted in 1907. This experiment allowed the prediction of a quantitative response to a quantitative stimulus by training rats to run in a straight, alley-like maze for a food rewards, located at the end of an alley. Watson found that once a rat was well trained, it performed almost automatically on reflex, thus demonstrating the ability to turn voluntary motor responses into a conditioned response. Conclusion? As rattus, as humans.

In 1919, Watson teamed up with his Vassar 1919 Bachelor of Arts degree student Rosalie Alberta Rayner (1898–1935). She would later become his wife and a research psychologist. They conducted the notorious "Little Albert" experiment, help of a rat. They conditioned an 11-month-old emotionally stable boy unfazed by the presence of animals, into a phobia of all furry animals. The infant was presented with the animal as someone struck a metal pole with a hammer above his head. This was repeated until he cried at merely the sight of any furry object—animate or inanimate (https://www.newscientist.com/article/dn26307-baby-used-in-notorious-fear-experiment-is-lost-no-more/). The controlled experiment showed empirical evidence of how classical conditioning could work on humans.

The *Journal of Experimental Psychology* launched Watson's scientific theory of behaviourism into the psychological schools in 1920. , Most in the mental health industry hold ideas, style or tastes derived from a broad and diverse range of sources, depending on their own psychological make-up and world-views. It is because of Watson that the cognitive behavioural therapy is almost always demanded by those in power, when PTSD occurs in the line of duty. CBT would be in combination with pharmaceutical drugging, of course. Why the Little Albert undertaking took place in the first place has never been revealed; who in his or her sane mind would torture babies, eh? Only harvesting of adrenochrome, blood of petrified babies, infants and children, springs to mind.

Myers at Phipps, however, diligently worked away to train and supervise those he deemed suitable for conducting Little Albert experiments and the like. He trained them in scientific research and patient treatment to serve what he called the "New Psychiatry". This embodied his own social and scientific ideals of the art and craft science of psychology. This clinical discipline also embodies the social and scientific ideals shared with other 'new' progressive reform movements in the U.S. generated by the Rockefellers and others of their missionary religious class previously mentioned (https://www.ncbi.nlm.nih.gov/pmc/articles/PMC4597240/).

"New Psychiatry" thus aimed at combining insights from evolutionary biology, neuron theory and American pragmatist philosophy. Meyer concluded that subjective experience and social behaviour were functions of human biology. Meyer insisted that psychiatrists be able to harvest scientific data from diseased bodies and histological experiments in the laboratory. He also insisted that psychiatrists be skilled at wielding social interaction and interpersonal relationships as investigative and therapeutic tools. He felt this skill was necessary to conceptualise, collect, analyse and apply the short-lasting data of "social adaptation". Working with that data would be needed to conform with the prevailing system of norms and values in U.S. society's classes and social groups. At least it would be until, we take it, the Great Work of Ages driving humanity nuts had been completed, most likely with COVID 19 and its 10-year planned aftermath.

Thus, Meyers insisted that patients could best be understood through their "psychobiological" life situations. He therefore promptly reframed mental diseases as being of "bio-psycho-social origin" rather than as biologically specifiable natural diseases (Susan Lamb: Social Skills: Adolf Meyer's Revision of Clinical Skill for the New Psychiatry of the Twentieth Century; Med Hist. 2015 Jul; 59(3): 443–464). In case we forgot, psychobiology is also known as biological psychology. And it is a sub-field of biology and psychology that deals with the interaction between a person's biological state, physical condition (including hormones, neurotransmitters and cells) and social situation. That situation would be any in which at least one other person is present in either a performance situation or in interpersonal interactions.

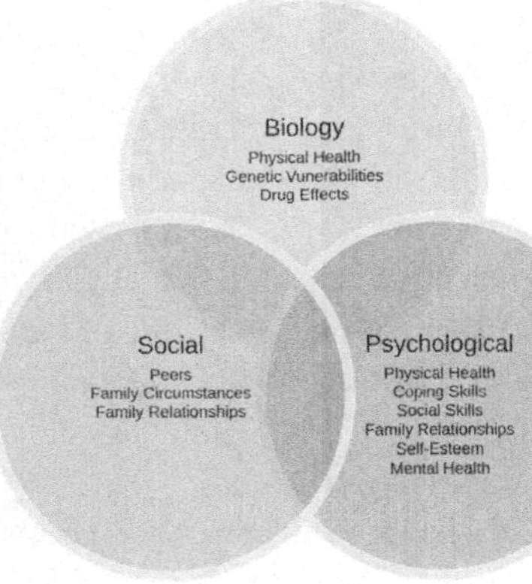

The bio-psychosocial model of health in the diagram was designed by the mental health industry. As we can see, it specifically examines those aspects they deem to be involved in our emotional health. It looks at how they play a role in our lives, ranging from health and disease to our individual development. In our sublime ignorance, we are made to believe that the mental health bio-psycho-social-hypothesis-adherent professional would in magical ways be able to intertwine biology, psychology and socio-environmental factors of an interviewee's life to reach a diagnosis. Yes, and they would do it in a 50-minute interview with someone experiencing the aftermath of an emotionally charged, life-changing event, PTSD causing or otherwise! Well, 23 of them did just that in my case. So, I take it that's their modus operandi.

Funny, though all of them know that nutrition makes the entire human being from the moment of conception, none of them ever inquired about my eating habits. Nor did any of them ask about my (absent) drug consumption or my use of alcohol. Nutrition was never mentioned in any of my 23 WCB forced interviews with other psychiatrists. Nor by my physician, nor by the number of so-called WCB rehabilitation goons. They were too busy steadfastly trying to pressure me into work as aircraft painter or such. That would give the airline a reason to fire me after the first week in my new NorAm-provided place of work for not measuring up to the job. Only my psychiatrist and UBC professor Dr. William Courtney lectured me on nutrition. Nor is nutrition part of any medical school teachings other than one hour, as a by and by. Yet, all eastern philosophies will tell you that health begins and ends with nutrition and how it goes to our digestive tract.

So why do bio-psycho-sociology researchers study humans' evolutionary and physiological brain mechanisms so intensely without relating it to daily nutritional aspects? Because proper nutrition would lead to human healing. Brill's and Bernays' "Make Americans' minds" created ignorance about the impact of nutrition on our health. This resulted in the weakening of our bodies through ever-decreasing food-values and intake of such poisons as Aspartame, for example. They also sent EMF vibrations our way to make us behave the way they want. Thus, the Work of the Ages inches a step closer to its goal, human 2.0. This is what Meyers and his ilk also vigorously pursued by way of the American Eugenics Record Office (ERO), financed by the Carnegie Institution of Washington. In June 1904, it hosted a gala dedication ceremony on the grounds of the Cold Spring Harbor Laboratory Bio Lab. The gala marked the opening of the Station for Experimental Evolution. It was in 1903 that eugenicist Charles Benedict Davenport (1866-1944), a prominent U.S. biologist and eugenicist, and his best buddy, educator and eugenicist Harry Hamilton Laughlin (1880 -1943) suggested the Station. These were two of the most active people in American eugenics policy, especially in compulsory sterilization legislation. Th Station was opened to study heredity and evolution through experiments with plants and animals. But it soon became the main research center for American citizens' eugenics under the 1910 Eugenics Record Office and eventually part of the Department of Genetics (CSHL, 2015; https://eugenicsarchive.ca/discover/tree/5150aadea4209be523000018).

From then until 1939, this Station for Experimental Evolution served as human eugenics and heredity ancestry research center. It gathered biological and social information about Americans without their knowledge. It has since been administered by the U.S. Department of Genetics and Social Science, we read. The genetics educational program provides social and behavioral scientists with sufficient genetic background for interdisciplinary research with genetics researchers.

The Station for Experimental Evolution institute's mission? To use Americans' ancestry to design, produce and broadcast mass media propaganda. It aimed to plant the seed of race betterment through eugenics and the benefits of eugenics overall in the herd's mind long before Hitler ever trumpeted the thought out to the world. As to the Carnegie Institution of Washington, for public purposes known as the Carnegie Institution for Science (CIS) funding the operation, it still thrives in Washington, DC. In 2020, it sat on an endowment of $926.9 million, with expenses for scientific programs and administration in 2018 of $96.6 million.

And what about our City of London boy cum physician Charles Samuel Myers? The one who had never set a foot near a place of active warfare, but was more than an eager beaver to volunteer attendance on WWI battlefields? Well, while whiling away his time at caring for the shell-shocked of war for a couple of months, he is said to have drawn on French military neuro-psychiatrist Emmanuel Régis (1855–1918) ideas and hypotheses. He used these to voice the three essentials for their treatment, namely:

- promptness of action
- suitable environment
- psychotherapeutic measures

The British military high command felt the losses of its cannon-fodder. So, in 1915, it called together a committee, whose members defined "Shell-Shock" under the following heads:

- (a) Commotional disturbance [physical motion caused by a nearby shelling]
- (b) and/or Emotional disturbance.

www.nationalarchives.gov.uk/education/resources
/medicine -on- the-western-front-part-two/war-office-report-on-shell-shock/
Committee members concluded 192 pages later that:

- "In Forward Areas - No soldier should be allowed to think that loss of nervous or mental control provides an honourable avenue to escape from the battlefield, and every endeavour should be made to prevent slight cases leaving the battalion or divisional area, where treatment should be confined to provision of rest and comfort for those who need it and to heartening them for return to the front line.
- "In Neurological Centres. - When cases are sufficiently severe to necessitate more scientific and elaborate treatment they should be sent to special Neurological Centres as near the front as possible to be under the care of an expert in nervous disorders. No such case should, however, be so labelled on evacuation as to fix the idea of nervous breakdown in the patient's mind.
- "In Base Hospitals. - When evacuation to the base is necessary, cases should be treated in a separate hospital or in separate sections of a hospital, and not with the ordinary sick and wounded patients. Only in exceptional circumstances should cases be sent to the United Kingdom, as, for instance, men likely to be unfit for further service of any kind with the forces in the field. This policy should be widely known throughout the Force."

Meyers was by this time posted back to Britain. He suggested that four specialist units for the shell-shocked be set up near the trenches to preserve the "atmosphere" and treatment until ready for return to the frontlines. Soldiers considered chronic or severely shell-shocked were sent on to military base hospitals for more intensive therapy. However, the slaughter and mayhem of the battles of Arras, Messines and Passchendaele in 1917 was too great. It so overwhelmed those units' capacity as to render them useless.

In the homeland, Myers began to drown in criticism and ridicule from friends and foes alike. They thought shell-shock was nothing other than showing cowardice, malingering and a lack of courage. They thought that military discipline, a court martial and the threat of the firing squad would fix it in a nano-second. As we saw in *Fallacy 1* that is still the case today, not only for soldiers and veterans. Firefighters, police officers and flight attendants are labeled as mentally deranged since birth after the PTSD-causing event. An estimated 250,000 men suffered from "shell-shock" after WWI. Myers and his peers, believing in science only, were convinced that this was a result of an injury to the nervous system during heavy bombardment and shell attacks. That changed when it surfaced that men not directly exposed to such fire were just as traumatized as those who had been in the midst of the mayhem. As atheists, though, they could not and cannot grasp, that genuine PTSD is an existential crisis of immense proportions that only can be healed when taking the spiritual path.

Because they could not grasp the spiritual significance of it, they classified it as a new illness. They thought it must be caused either by the brain's physical impairment or by a yet to be identified mental illness. Both assumptions have been carried forth to present day, as documented in Fallacy 1. It has existed as long as men have fought each other. Had Abel lived, he most likely would have experienced PTSD. The mental health industry itself admits that PTSD is poorly understood medically and psychologically. But why? Could it be, that mental health practitioners operate on a different level of consciousness than humanity, besides, of course, having only sheltered life-experiences? We could gather that, based on the previous documentations of vivisections and little Albert experiments. Those were just a couple of the 10s of thousands occurring during the last 200 years alone.

Myers ran home after two or three months near the trenches. Upon hearing the war committee's edict, he smelled the opportunity of a lifetime. He instantaneously proposed specialist shell-shock treatment in specialized treatment centers by specialized psychiatrists and specialized staff in specialized hospital units based in the United Kingdom proper. He made the point that effective shell-shock treatment required specialized and individual attention.

The War Office gladly accepted Myers idea of healing the shell-shocked. So, he mowed on, demanding higher staffing ratios, one doctor to every 50 patients. He set up training courses in principles and practices of psychiatry. None existed, in particular in shell-shock treatment, which no one knew how to treat. That shell-shock—PTSD—was a new illness of undetermined cause with undetermined treatment methodologies was a most exiting situation. It laid wide open the path to fame and fortune for participating physicians. It still does, as both the treatment and physician-attitude towards those living through genuine PTSD remains the same. This is still the golden goose of the art, craft and science of psychology and psychiatry, a cash cow with no sight in end.

Thus, thanks to nitroglycerine inventor Sobrero and dynamite developer Nobel and all those hugely profiting from it, earth's dominance of Luciferic consciousness with psychiatry began to blossom. The clinical picture of war neuroses dominated all following wars. Meanwhile, the mental health industry cabal continues to search for the PTSD cure in all the wrong places. They don't look at the spiritual path, which is the only one for its healing, as that one is anathema to the Luciferic consciousness.

On all sides, there were millions of poorly trained soldiers. At times, they were purposefully ill-equipped to facilitate this mass-sacrifice. It was enhanced by appallingly dirty, smelly, crowded, unsanitary conditions in the trenches. They were open to attacks from enemy fire with unheard of weaponry creating untold mental and physical hardship, at times welcoming death. WWI military casualties worldwide are estimated to range from 15 to 22 million dead and 23 million wounded. That doesn't even count the civilian casualties which were already planned to increase the numbers in the equally planned WWII bombings of civilians, there were 350,000 residents, plus untold number of refugees, in the Dresden bombing of 1945 alone They were bombed for the pure joy of killing, destroying and terrorizing humans in a purely Luciferian holocaust. This amplification of Little Albert killed between 35,000 and 135,000 people. Mind you, Julius Caesar and his hordes managed to kill 300,000 Teutonics at a session 2,000 years earlier.

WWI created the perfect experimental laboratory for the craft and science of psychology. It provided the training ground for its adherents to enhance their knowledge by researching and evaluating human emotional vulnerabilities. They could use that information to design future scenarios for humanity's emotional upheavals. Wellington House, better known as the British War Propaganda Bureau, was eager to enhance soldiers' willingness and enthusiasm to fight the enemy. It began to methodically apply Wundt et al.'s discoveries about human nature. It was thus able to manipulate Russia's, Britain's and the United States' narratives of their future in truly fascinating way/ Radical Liberal MP Charles Frederick Gurney Masterman (1873 -1927) was appointed head of the British War Propaganda Bureau in 1914. He retained 24 acknowledged authors. Among them were William Archer, Hall Caine, Arthur Conan Doyle, Arnold Bennett, John Masefield, G. K. Chesterton, Henry Newbolt, John Galsworthy, Thomas Hardy, Gilbert Parker, G. M. Trevelyan and H. G. Wells. They wrote pamphlets and books promoting the British government's views, indeed over 1,160 pamphlets alone during WWI.

Wellington House became infamous. English philosopher and research professor of international history at the London School of Economics and King's College London Arnold Joseph Toynbee (1889 -1975) called it "that black hole of disinformation...a lie factory." He should know. From 1918 to 1950, he was considered the world's leading specialist on international affairs.

One of its first publications was the "Bryce Report." It was published in 1915 by the Committee on Alleged German Outrages. Enhanced with highly emotional drawings, it was named after its chair, Viscount James Bryce (1838–1922). This report is seen as a major propaganda form the British used to influence international public opinion about German soldiers' behavior when invading Belgium the previous year. It overemphasized cruelty against women and children. It did not challenge refugees' panic-infused allegations, such as the story that German troops hacked off children's hands. Incidentally, this is what the Belgians had done when invading the Congo less than a decade earlier.

By the end of 1915, it had been translated into every major European language. It had a profound impact on public opinion, particularly in the United States (https://www.bl.uk/collection-items/bryce-report-committee-alleged-german-outrages). Mind you, it was of no importance at that time that that the so-called eyewitness testimony published in its 320-page Appendix A was false. That it contained sensationalist accounts of mutilations and rapes for which there is no evidence. Nor that the invented atrocities now make it an often-cited example of psychological warfare and propaganda to swing the herd into participation in WWI. Indeed, it served as a preview of as all following mayhems and slaughters, by enticing humans to kill each other created by way of the Luciferic consciousness.

The emotional impact on thousands of front-line battle participants had another impact. In WWI, this was a seemingly brand-new phenomenon in human behavior and in its infant feet. It inspired French physicians to create the concept of "relying on three principles: proximity to battle, immediacy and expectation of recovery, subsequently given the cute acronym "PIE". This is still the standard intervention for soldiers' combat stress reaction (AG McKenzie: Anaesthetic and other treatments of shell-shock: World War I and beyond; J R Army Med Corps 2012 Mar;158(1):29-33)). However, an early 2000 re-examination of its treatment outcomes showed exaggerated effectiveness both as a treatment for acute stress reaction and as a prophylaxis for chronic disorders such as PTSD. This, the authors say, throws up the question of who is actually served by the "forward psychiatry" intervention, the individual soldier or the needs of the military? That it serves only the mental health industry for profit and destruction of the brightest of the bright, as only they will develop genuine PTSD, they left out of the equation (perhaps out of ignorance?). (Edgar Jones, Simon Wessely: Forward Psychiatry" in the Military: Its Origins and Effectiveness; Journal of Traumatic Stress, Vol. 16, No. 4, August 2003, pp. 411–419).

And what standard treatment did shell-shocked WWI soldiers of all armies receive under this "forward psychiatry" doctrine during and after the war? General anaesthesia by ether, chloroform or both and electrical shock therapy were *the* "in" methods. These were administered to shell shocked officers at "Dottyville,..... That Mecca Of Psycho-Neuroses...', as poet, writer and decorated-for-bravery Siegfried Loraine Sassoon (1886 –1967) termed the Craiglockhart War Hospital in Edinburgh, Scotland. It was a run-down former facility for hydropathy, a form of therapy popular with the Victorian and Edwardian higher classes, And if any of the esteemed physician dealing with the shell-shocked deemed someone to be experiencing more serious psychiatric symptoms, he would simply be shipped to the Royal Edinburgh Asylum to rot until released at a physician's leisure (Siegfried Sassoon:'... That Mecca Of Psycho-Neuroses...'1 Sherston's Progress. London: Faber & Faber: 38; Thomas E F Webb: 'Dottyville'—Craiglockhart War Hospital and shell-shock treatment in the First World War; *Journal of the Royal Society of Medicine* JRSoc Med. 2006 Jul; 99(7): 342–346).

Craiglockhart War Hospital had been opened after in the first few weeks of July 1916. During the horrific Battle of the Somme, several thousand British soldiers had to be rapidly passed out of the battle zone due to nervous disorders. Many of them were evacuated to England, and the War Office took over the run-down and disused Craiglockhart Hydropathic in Edinburgh to treat some of the shell-shocked. I was open for 28 months to British and a few German officers only. In that time, it became one of the most famous military hospitals for WWI's psychological casualties. Treating physician were allowed to try anything on whomever came their way. This was the very best scientific and clinical experimental laboratory to investigate the human psyche for its strength and weakness they could ever have dreamt. And they had Europe's fittest and brightest of the herd, regardless of nationality to experiment on. They were superbly applicable to humanity's future manipulation. It is, therefore, that Craiglockhart's took a stunning place in neuropsychiatry's history.

And who were they, Craiglockhart's investigators into the human psych? Who were these people who ruled there and spread their discoveries to the rest of their learned craft-and-science society of psychology? When it opened its doors in October 1916, psychological stressors resulting in physical symptoms was still a novel idea. The local physician Major William Bryce had been put in charge as commanding officer ((T. Webb: Dottyville) https://whrrivers.com/rivers-in-ww1-craiglockhart/).

William Halse Rivers transferred in from the Military Red Cross Hospital in Maghull near Liverpool. He had a rank of captain, and was former professor of then-aspiring psychiatrists' Myers and McDougall and a companion in their 1898 Torres Strait expedition. He came to help Bryce, together with the American Medical Officers Reserve Corps. They shipped to Craiglockhart Britain in August 1917. Major Arthur Hiler Ruggles (1881-1961), a physician, and a Captain Hall were with them. Nothing is known of either, other than both seemed to have left the hospital in January 1918 for service in France. Scottish physician and medical historian Captain Arthur John Brock (1879-1947) also joined. He is famous for his translations of the Greek/Roman physician Galen and other ancient physicians. As a key figure in the early twentieth century humanitarian revival within medicine, Brock completed Craiglockhart's administrative and clinical treatment trio. Bryce, Rivers and Brock ruled in this what they termed "the developing field of psychological medicine" enterprise. What were their most often used diagnoses for officers?

- 'Hysterical' paralyses and functional disability; lower ranked soldiers were simply diagnosed with 'hysteria.'
- Neurasthenia
- Migraine
- Glycosuria
- Gas poisoning
- Compound fracture of the toe
- Haemorrhoids ('piles')

Brock's heart's desire was to return medicine and society at large to a more harmonious and organic existence. This would be characteristic of ancient Greece, and still found among the Scottish Gaels (David Cantor: "Between Galen, Geddes, and the Gael": Arthur Brock, "Modernity, and Medical Humanism in Early Twentieth-Century Scotland"; *Journal of the History of Medicine and Allied Science's*, Vol. 60, Number No.1, Oxford University Press 2005). Brock's philosophical and humanitarian ideas about medicine and treatment of shell-shock were anathema to the Darwinian inspired human animal science of the art and craft of psychiatry. This had yet to dawn upon him.

There were 1801 officers admitted to the hospital during its operation. Sixty-five of these were German prisoners of war officers with gunshot wounds. And 1736 of them were British shell-shocked officers, some of whom we see here with staff to cater to the military's finest. During the day, these officer patients could use the sporting facilities, which included swimming, golf, tennis and cricket. They could make model yachts, join the camera club and walk in the fields around the hospital.

(blogs.shu.edu/british-modernism-undergraduate/2017/11/24/craiglockhart-war-hospital/)

But at night, haunted by horrible scenes of death and destruction whilst awaiting their own, they often wandered the corridors. Many of them were treated by Rivers, the war poets Siegfried Sassoon and Wilfred Owen among them. They helped Freud's ideas of psychoanalysis, repression and the unconscious to gain greater acceptance and currency in the medical profession. Rivers' "talking cure" development took shape with his Craiglockhart patients, and so did dream analysis. He discovered he could apply his hypotheses more fully, since his officer patients were used to expressing themselves, being listened to, having their opinions sought and voicing their thoughts (https://whrrivers.com/rivers-in-ww1-craiglockhart/). They were even willing to discuss their dreams and nightmares. These were easier to interpret, as officers perceptions were more intelligent than those of the working man. Rivers apparently subconsciously tuned in to the fact that only innately bright people develop genuine PTSD, which has nothing to do with academic education (*Fallacy* 1). However, his observation brought him much criticism and accusations of elitism, even though he had diligently tried to explain how everyone, even so-called primitive cultures, should be seen as equal in aspects of human emotions, actions and reactions.

Galen translator Arthur Brock, meanwhile, took the view that his patients should be kept active to effectuate their shell-shock healing. He reached his conclusion from his experiences at Edinburgh's Woodburn Sanatorium for Consumptives. He recognized while working there that chronic phthisis cases in sanatoria suffered much from minor neurasthenic symptoms. The term comes from the Ancient Greek νεῦρον neuron "nerve" and ἀσθενής asthenés "weak." It was first introduced at least as early as 1829 for a perceived mechanical weakness of the nerves. During the late nineteenth and early twentieth centuries, it became a major diagnosis in North America after. It was 1862 Yale College-educated neurologist George Miller Beard (1839–1883), having received his medical degree in 1866 from the College of Physicians and Surgeons of New York, who popularized the concept in 1869.

The condition is said to imply the exhaustion of the central nervous system's energy reserves. Beard attributed this to:

- urbanization
- modern civilization
- anyone living within the monetary system
- professionals working in sedentary occupations
- the increasingly competitive business environment of upper-class folk

Freud associated neurasthenia with physical symptoms, including fatigue, indications of intra-cranial pressure, spinal irritation due to brain exhaustion, and dyspepsia with flatulence. No, not because of munching peanuts. In fact, neurasthenic is caused by emotional upheaval, as documented earlier.

Brock took all this into consideration. He knew full well that tuberculosis, the body's infection with *Mycobacterium tuberculosis* can occur in any organ of the body, though is most well known in the lung. He knew that it has been a scourge throughout known human history, possibly killing more people than any other microbial pathogen, some of them perhaps in France's WWI trenches. Evidence of its existence dates back to 8000 BC. Evidence of bony tuberculosis dates to the Neolithic period, around 5800 BC. And it has been detected in Egyptian mummies as far back as 2400 BC. (John Frith: History of Tuberculosis. Part 1 - Phthisis, consumption and the White Plague; *Journal of Military and Veterans' Health,* JMVH Vol. 22 No.2, Jan. 22; https://jmvh.org/current-issue/).

From Hippocrates until the eighteenth century, it was known as *phthisis consumption*. It slowly had turned epidemic in Europe by the nineteenth century, causing the deaths of millions in particular in the poorer classes. They named it "white death", "the great white plague", "the robber of youth", "the Captain of all these men of Death", "the graveyard cough", "the King's Evil" and other names evoking the despair and horror of the disease. Tuberculosis declined after the late nineteenth century, but even today, it remains a major but seldom mentioned public health and military issue says, John Frith in his 2022 *Journal of Military and Veterans' Health* article "History of Tuberculosis Part 1 - Phthisis, consumption and the White Plague."

In the U.S. Army, tuberculosis was the leading cause of discharge in both World War I and World War II. Annual incidence of tuberculosis in Western military forces is low. But micro-epidemics have occurred in the last several decades in both US- and British Naval warships and land-based units deployed overseas. Two aspects present significant risk factors for tuberculosis infection in military personnel. One is working in close quarters. The other is overseas deployment to tuberculosis-endemic areas of the world such as Afghanistan, Iraq and South-East Asia. Frith states that multidrug resistant tuberculosis is of particular concern.

Brock was familiar with the emotional state of those caught by tuberculosis. He knew about the limbo associated with what they felt about what they considered their fate. He saw the lassitude, fatigue, headache and irritability termed "neurasthenia", the term soon to be employed by the learned society for shell-shock, Still, Brock thought that the essence of neurasthenia lay in a weakness of the will. (AM Crossman: "The Hydra, Captain AJ Brock And The Treatment Of Shell-Shock In Edinburgh"; final-year medical student, University of Edinburgh; https://rcpe.ac.uk/journal/issue/journal_33_2/7_the_hydra.pdf). And, Brock thought, that as will becomes weak through disuse, just as with any other human faculty, work should work as a shell-shock cure. After all, work is what keeps people alive - work, effort and struggle is the fundamental law and purpose of life, he reasoned. So, when two years after joining the Royal Army Medical Corps he, saw himself transferred to Craiglockhart in 1917, he viewed shell-shock simply as the soldier's equivalent of neurasthenia. He then set out to implement the ideas of Scottish biologist, sociologist, geographer, philanthropist, and pioneering town planner Patrick Geddes to his Craiglockhart patience.

Geddes was Brock's mentor known for his innovative thinking in the fields of urban planning and sociology. His ideas encompass his emphasis of the fundamental unity and interdependence of culture and nature and a trans-disciplinary education, namely, to teach students through different ways of exploration to develop a layered understanding of themselves and the connections they have with the rest of humanity. Best practices in a transdisciplinary environment do not compartmentalize learning, but rather explore content within the context of inquiry.

Brock locally adapted direct action as a means of cultural transformation (https://planningtank.com/settlement-geography/geddesian-triad). One of the projects he gave his patients was to create The Hydra. This magazine-producing project illustrates his attempt to create a unifying, cohesive element in the Craiglockhart War Hospital community. With it, he birthed ergotherapy, Hitler's "Arbeit Macht Frei" concept, but never mind that.

The "none too lightsome task" of producing a hospital magazine was, in itself, a form of work therapy, he said. All contributions were to be original, and appeals by editor and poet Wilfred Owen to fellow patients to deliver their writings were constantly made.

Brock himself wrote of "ergophobia" as a neurasthenic symptom he thought endemic in pre-war society: "there is a special need to emphasize the moral aspect of the fault. Many of us are, undoubtedly, becoming reluctant to face life." He also tuned into the idea that some shell-shock experiencers might feel that circumstances had treated them so badly that they were disinclined to have to do with life's circumstances again - except in so far as perhaps to gratify their senses. Needless to say, his hypothesis laid the foundation for the "victim diagnosis". This is shuffled down genuine PTSD journeyers' throats by mental health professionals at all costs at all times, if they can get away with it due to their patient's ignorance (*Broken Wings*).

Craiglockhart's *The Hydra* takes its name from the many-headed serpent slain by Hercules as one of his 12 labors. The program was launched in April 1917.The name indicated that its editors wished its character to be many headed and many sided. It provided "light and amusing reading in verse and prose, and . . . articles of a more exclusively literary character." It also served as a journal of events in the house and grounds, the recognized mouthpiece of the various societies and clubs and the community at large. By encouraging Craiglockhart patients to engage in life in its upbeat accounts of happenings in and around the hospital, *The Hydra* tried to give inmates the push to overcome the phantoms of their minds. It was hoped that they would again engage in life rather than cave in to feelings of victimization and the related desire for lassitude, the feeling of "What for?"

The activities at Craiglockhart were often based on the sporting and entertainment facilities, which Brock tended to frown on as somewhat frivolous. As alternatives, he organized temporary jobs. Some were assigned to teaching posts at local schools. Others were given work at local farms to help under-supported farmers. And he even fostered links with an Edinburgh sociological group to open the men's eyes and ears to the social deprivation and inequalities right in the home-front society asking:

> "Are not these horrors of war the last and culminating terms in a series that begins in the infernos of our industrialized cities?" (https://ncbi.nlm.nih.gov/pmc/articles/PMC1484566/).

Even Rivers' hypotheses agreed with Brock's philosophy. They recognized that just as it is harmful to dwell persistently on painful memories, so it is to banish them wholly from the mind.

So, first and foremost, *The Hydra* encouraged Craiglockhart patients to participate in life by grooming, growing, farming, teaching, hammering, painting, sculpting things and landscaping. Such enterprise and encouragement were far from forthcoming at all shell-shock hospitals. The first shell-shock patients brought back to Britain had been treated with the "Dr Diet and Dr Quiet" therapy. This had been dragged out of the closet of antiquity by a Doctor Merryman and published by the *Journal of American Medicine* in 1894. American physician and scientist Silas Weir Mitchell (1829–1914) was an 1850 graduate of Philadelphia University of Pennsylvania and Jefferson Medical College. Considered the father of medical neurology, he popularized this treatment. It was seemingly originally advocated in the famous *Flos Medicinæ* or *Regimen Sanitatis Salerni* composed in the year 1099 by Johannes de Mediolanus (John of Milan). It had the concurrence of the other professors at the celebrated School of Salernum stating: "Si tibi deficiant medici, medici tibi fiant, Hæctria: Mens hilaris. requies, moderata diæta."

The first translation into English was Regimen by Paynell in 1579. The later translation was by Dr. Philemon Holland in 1634. Holland's translation reads: "When Physic needs, let these thy doctors bee, Good dyet, quiet thoughts and heart mirthfully free," says Burton, 1621 (Anatomy of Melancholy) "is one of the three Salernitan doctors (November 10, 1894; Doctor Diet, Doctor Quiet and Doctor Merryman. JAMA. 1894;XXIII(19):732).

It was written as a poem intended to teach, with a particularly moral instruction as its ulterior motive. It deals with domestic health and medical practices, such as daily hygiene and diet, including the therapeutic uses of wine. The early, modified, perverted by human translation Regimen was organized by the six non-naturals. These were non-innate to human life. According to Galen, they are:

- air
- food and drink
- motion and rest
- sleeping and waking
- excretions and retentions
- dreams and the passions of the soul

These emotional human experiences were subjects of debate among humanity, including philosophers and theologians long before Socrates' time.

The *Flos Medicinæ's* original content addressed the humors. These were the chemical systems regulating human behaviour. They were prominent from the writings of Greek philosopher of science and physiologist Alcmaeon of Croton, born ca. 510 BC, who also practiced astrology and meteorology. Essentially, this theory held that the human body was filled with four basic substances, called "humors", which are balanced when a person is healthy. But they cause all diseases and disabilities when an excess or deficit of one of these humors is present in the body. This could even be caused by vapours breathed in or absorbed by the body, making chem-trails spring to mind. They were identified as black and yellow bile, phlegm and blood. Classical Western and Muslim medical philosophy held that each of these humors would wax and wane in the body, depending on diet and activity, affecting human physical and emotional health for better or for worse (*Fallacy 1*).

Highly revered as a scholarly medical text and seriously discussed until the nineteenth century, the *Flos Medicinæ's* various editions and versions circulated throughout Europe. Everybody and his dog added or deleted and removed commentaries and material. In the end the work expanded from a mere 364 lines to 3,526 hexameter verses, perverting it to almost non-essential in accordance with the Luciferic consciousness. Nevertheless, the first English translation was made by Elisabeth I. godson, Eton and King's College, Cambridge educated Sir John Harrington (1560–1612). Then the American Civil War surgeon John Ordronaux (1830–1908), a professor of medical jurisprudence at Columbia Law and pioneering mental health commissioner. He left an estate worth $2,757,000 giving much of it in endowments to several U.S. universities and other institutions. In 1871, he tried to make a medically accurate translation. He was followed by a Dr. Merryman, who in 1894 published an article about it in the *Journal of American Medicine*. Silas Weir Mitchell stumbled across this article and used for his Diet scheme in WWI to cure shell-shocked PTSD experiencing soldiers (November 10, 1894; Doctor Diet, Doctor Quiet and Doctor Merryman. JAMA. 1894;XXIII(19):732). By 1980, all of humors and diet had been swept under the carpet by the mental health industry, as it would be detrimental to its profits.

Mitchell's therapy consisted primarily in isolation, confinement to bed, dieting, electrotherapy and massages. In addition, he advocated a high-fat diet and consuming two quarts or more of milk daily. He believed a diet rich in fat would "fatten and redden" patients and lead to a cure. At Craiglockhart, all were allowed to join in a version of group therapy. They were given the chance to discuss their symptoms, reactions and solutions with the others in an attempt to both pool resources and prove to they were not alone in their plight. But their conventionally minded medical officers at other military hospitals steadfastly encouraged their shell-shocked PTSD-ridden to simply "put it out of your mind, old boy."

On the other hand, however, Rivers also maintained that understanding what had occurred and why had two benefits. First, it would help the men not break down so badly again. Second, it would prove to them that their illness was not the result of any kind of weakness. Most had been brought up to believe men did not cry. They behaved in despair and emotional misery for crying due to their gruesome experiences of men actively killing men without mercy. Most were at least a little baffled when it turned out they did understand. Once the soldier gained an idea of the mechanisms at work, the doctor noted that they found the whole thing rather less frightening. Indeed, they were able to put it into context more easily and thus, actually, begin to heal themselves. But just as today, most doctors, if they really understood the condition, didn't bother to explain what had led to it. They were quenched at source by their peers, who since then have done everything to depict genuine PTSD experiencers as insane and mentally defect long before the PTSD-causing event occurred.

As Rivers himself stated:

> "The advice usually given to my patients in other hospitals is that they should endeavor to banish all thoughts of the war from their minds . . . and lead their thoughts to other topics, beautiful scenery and other pleasant aspects of experience."

And why were patients not allowed to discuss their war experiences among themselves or with visitors? Simple. To help maintain the credibility of home front propaganda sponsoring acrimony and hatred against German soldiers and civilians alike, dah, a still ongoing process, if you missed it. Also, to keep them apart so they couldn't compare notes about the deplorable treatment they receive by the powers that be. This has not changed for the PTSD-afflicted since WWI's aftermath throughout the field of genuine PTSD-susceptible professions, regardless of occupation, either.

Rivers recognized, however, that repression of traumatic memories resulted in perpetuating and fixing neuroses. He found that when his patients allowed their minds to dwell on their experiences during the day, they were no longer disturbed by terrifying dreams at night. This philosophy of facing up to life appealed to Brock, seeing in it reflected the powerful war-poems of Wilfred Owen, "the heroic testimony of one who . . . in the most literal sense 'faced the phantoms of the mind'". (https://www.rcpe.ac.uk/journal/issue/journal_33_2/7_the_hydra.pdf; Stone M. Shell-shock and the Psychologists. Bynum W, Porter R, Shepherd M eds. The Anatomy of Madness: Essays in the History of Psychiatry, Volume 2: Institutions and Society. London: Routledge; 1985; 242–71).

Thus, Brock saw neurasthenia in the shell-shocked and the consumptive. He recognized that this feeling of lassitude, this life lived without enthusiasm, this almost vegetative state, was not purely a wartime phenomenon. He saw it rather as an "acute manifestation of a chronic condition." This condition could be combated only by the useful functioning of the individual in improving the immediate environment for himself and those around him rather than willing the Self to die. "Every master of medicine, from Hippocrates onwards, has emphasized the fact . . . the practitioner must manipulate the surroundings as well as the patient . . . for example, the social surroundings."

He also argued that "the pre-war public mind was fragmented, and the fragments did not cohere". To Freud, he wrote, "the most characteristic feature of Neurasthenia . . . was just this lack of solidarity, this segregation of parts". Shell-shock patients had become "like the fragments of their minds, isolated units, unrelated in space and time." Needless to say, this hypothesis opened the way for the art and craft of psychology to accuse every PTS-affected of inhabiting any number of pre-morbid conditions they can dream up at leisure.

However, that possibility had most unlikely dawned on Brock. He was a humanitarian to the chore and a man with honor, integrity and graciousness expressed in his behavior towards his patients. He was seemingly more a tutor than a physician, as he set them onto their individual programs of study. Using *The Hydra* as his lecture auditorium, he wrote three articles entitled "Evolving Edinburgh" about the city's history, geology and industries. He stated that the town should not be looked at as a mere place to kill time in, but to understand that it could be distinctly available as an integral part of a Craiglockhart shell-shock cure

Shortly thereafter, *The Hydra* reports an enthusiastic meeting, at which Mr Chase gave a paper on "Mosses of the CraiglockhartDistrict". It was illustrated by specimens, diagrams and microscope slides. At the close of the meeting, it was resolved that a field club should be constituted. It would have a meeting every Monday evening for a paper and discussion, and, if possible, excursions should be arranged.

By April 1917, Field Club was up and running. Brock was president and Wilfred Owen was editor-in-chief. They intended to spark inmates' interest in their natural surroundings and arouse curiosity to explore and undertake their own regional surveys in and around Edinburgh and beyond, whatever it led to. Later, Brock explains in The Hydra:

> "The Field Club in a sense aims at co-ordinating all the other scientific groups. Its immediate object is a regional survey, i.e., a survey of the Craiglockhart region from all the different aspects, geological, botanical, economic, etc., which will at the same time show the absolute interdependence between these aspects . . . The most important industry in the country around Craiglockhart is naturally agriculture, and . . . a visit has been planned to Gray's Mill Farm, Slateford. We expect to see there the 'back to the land' movement in its most concrete form."

Get them to move beyond their own misery, get them off their own rocker, get them to face their own phantoms by digging in the soil. The Field Club also organized special classes at the Edinburgh and East of Scotland College of Agriculture and at the Edinburgh School of Art. All this was done with or without their knowledge, helping to rekindle the will to live, the retrieval of the soul rather than willing Self to die. As Brock would write in post-war years, "The world's opportunity has at length come . . . At no time was mankind in a better position to become master of its fate." (https://www.rcpe.ac.uk/journal/issue/journal_33_2/7_the_hydra.pdf).

What he failed to recognize, however, is the fact I mentioned in *Fallacy 1*: genuine PTSD experiencers kicking themselves into "facing the phantoms of the mind" receive *the* gift of a lifetime. They find themselves in the fabulous position to become master of their own fate. They can tailor themselves and their life to their liking, if they are able to control their thinking enough to kick themselves into gear to overcome the phantoms of their own minds. This, however, can happen only when free of pharmaceutical, mind-altering drugs shuffled down their throats with abandon at the moment of encounter with a psychiatrist or psycho-the-rapist. These are all too often gleefully taken in the belief that "doctor knows best," when nothing could be further from the truth. Furthermore, it seems that Craiglockharts's physicians had yet to fathom that emotional changes of humans start from within themselves, generated by introspection.

Or if they did indeed recognize it, they put everything into preventing them from such introspection. They still do, with CBT, NLP and drugs of all sorts accomplishing nothing other than the destruction of the sui generis in this Free Will domain in which we find ourselves. So, Brock happily declared that Craiglockhart was the model of how future society should be. His student patients in charge exclaimed: "Après la guerre we expect to see all our Craiglockhart farming enthusiasts at least Heads of Department for the resettlement and re-organisation of the countryside!"

These bright, academically and now emotionally well-educated men, by way of their shell-shock experience were now in possession of an open heart. They had empathy for Self and the other. They were endowed through their military training with an abundance of logic and reasoning ability. The possibility existed that they would be perfectly able to become just that, if they could overcome themselves, which could only be done without outside interference. And Brock knew it, as he stated:

> "If the essential thing for the patient to do is to help himself, the essential thing for the doctor to do—indeed, the only thing he can profitably do—is to help him to help himself." (https://www.ncbi.nlm.nih.gov/pmc/articles/PMC1484566/)

"Screw that," his peers shouted at Brock in unison. They loathed him—for kicking emotionally devastated soldiers toward achieving their own healing. Others in the art and craft of psychology saw the immense profits to be derived by the industry from shell-shock PTSD neurasthenia therapies flowing away. After all, a cured patient is indeed a customer lost, and this PTSD profit could be kept alive forever, unless humanity awakened to the scam.

So, work was done to create diagnoses suitable to the burgeoning psychiatry cabal's future narrative to declare the entire herd as mentally defect. This would benefit the completion of the work of ages, with some of the military hospitals' "administrators," and henceforth all others in the league. To this very day on a perpetual basis, they refuse to issue a diagnosis of 'shell-shock' and PTSD, belittling officers and genuine PTSD professionals by questioning them why they were there at all.

Brock and Major Bryce, the Dottyville commandant at its opening in October 1916, seem to have been the exceptions to the rule. A good, all-round sportsman, Bryce hated military etiquette, spoke to his staff as equals rather than as an "officer" to the "lower ranks" and was immensely well-liked by his patients. However, in October 1917, a ranking War Office General inspected Craiglockhart, outraged at the lack of military discipline and standards, with soldiers roaming around the premises in broad daylight in slippers and night dress, he replaced Bryce with William Brown. Brown had worked with our wealthy London City boy, eager to ride to war in France, Charles Myers.

Brown looked at shell-shocked soldiers regardless of rank and file as weak and deficient specimen of the human race. He felt they lacked both nerve and stamina, and suffered insufferable "feminine failings." He saw them as inferior entities similar to monkeys and the like, themselves to blame for their breakdowns. He shared Rivers' hypothesis that their breakdowns were caused by the repression of emotion and fear, in other words cowardice (https://sites.scran.ac.uk/Warp/Bryce.htm). That's why they did not want them to talk to each other, either, as they knew it would relieve both. But never mind.

As a possible way of curing them, Brown thought it charming to put his patients back into their hellish WWI situations, by way of hypnosis having them relive their trench-experiences. Called "abreaction", it has been used ever since to purportedly bring forgotten or inhibited experiences and memories from the unconscious into consciousness. Meanwhile, patients would work through the purported repressed emotions. This was supposed to release and discharge the tension and anxiety that had caused the repressed emotion. So, they missed the point by thousands of miles and perverting the issue at hand.

Why? Because anyone good at hypnosis can plant ideas into the head of another, who then subconsciously is enticed to dream up events that never occurred. To repeat: perversion of the others mind is also done in CBT and neuro-linguistic programming. It has nothing to do with either PTSD therapy or healing, which can only be accomplished by the Self. Both CBT and NLP do nothing other than pervert or even destroy the sui generis, the essence of the Self, the soul, just as the COVID injections are said to do. However, experiments conducted in the military's Dottyville of the participating armies did nothing other than laying the groundwork for all and any PTSD treatment and human manipulation inventions applied to humanity ever since. And this combines with our drugging to the hilt to destroy our ethical and moral values. It reaches such extremes that in the U.S., the herd accepts without a murmur the elevation of a baby, infant and child rapists-favouring person to the position of Supreme Court. And she, purportedly a female, claims to be unable to give a definition of a woman.

The foundation of such apathy expresses itself in the antagonism between the very few "non-conventional" civilian physicians temporarily in uniform, the humanitarians, and the War Office's mandarins. This animosity mainly arises from the latter's scepticism about the former's shell-shock diagnoses and therapeutic strategies, all filtering through to the lower nursing and caretaking ranks (ncbi.nlm.nih.gov/pmc/articles/PMC1484566/). How could it be otherwise, when all parties refused to face what they really dealt with? These were human beings who had experienced an emotional crisis completely out proportion with any normally-to-be-expected life experiences? Or did they purposely ignore it, as it would damage their profit-margins? Or could it indeed be that they were so completely unaware and ignorant about human emotional states of mind and what would shake it to the core, because they themselves were and are unable to feel such emotion as empathy and compassion for others, and still are?

Sassoon mirrored the situation as such:

> "A handful of highly-qualified civilians in uniform were up against the usual red-tape ideas... the military authorities regarded [war hospitals for nervous disorders] as experiments which needed careful watching and firm handling.' (p. 15) 'After the War Rivers told me that the local Director of Medical Services nourished a deep-rooted prejudice against [Craiglockhart], and actually asserted that he "never had and never would recognize the existence of such a thing as shell-shock." (Sassoon Siegfried. *Sherston's Progress*. London: Faber & Faber, 1936. p.15)

The next stage in Craiglockhart's history must have exasperated inmates' and staff alike almost to the breaking point. That was the installation of military disciplinarian Colonel Balfour Graham in November 1917. The only description of this time, however, comes from the novel *England, Their England* by A G Macdonnell, a patient from April 1918. He describes Dottyville as a "monster hydropathic" under the control of a sadistic homeopath commandant running the hospital on strict disciplinarian lines, his therapies consisting of:

> "...finding out the main likes and dislikes of each patient, and then ordering them to abstain from the former and apply themselves diligently to the latter... For example, those of the so-called patients... who disliked noise were allotted rooms on the main road. Those who had been, in happier times, parsons, school masters, journalists, and poets, were forbidden to use the library and driven off in batches to physical drill, lawn tennis, golf, and badminton." (https://whrrivers.com/rivers-in-ww1-craiglockhart/)

His regime remained in place until March 1918 when, perhaps because of decreasing therapeutic success, another inspection was prompted. During his reign, the mental condition of as many as two percent of the patients had definitely improved for the better, according to a sarcastic report in *The Hydra*. Thus, he depicts military homeopath and commanding officer Colonel Balfour Graham, who treated neurosis with neurosis-stimulant as, is still done with great favour and expertise, thus the multitude of genuine PTSD experiencers' suicides. We are told that McDonnell's portrayal of the purportedly more psychologically aware, the '"busybodies" (the treating physicians) with their "absurd technical knowledge and jargon" is no gentler.

Professor William Brown had worked before the war at King's College London. He had played a role in establishing shell-shock treatment centres behind the lines in France and Flanders. Upon the second inspection, he took over as camp commandant and remained there until the hospital closed in March 1919. In 1921, he re-established Oxford's laboratory of experimental psychology, which had been started pre-war by Professor W. MacDougall. McDougall had accepted the Chair of Psychology at Harvard to spread his knowledge about the human psyche and its manipulation possibilities in the United States. (https://journals.sagepub.com/doi/pdf/10.1177/014107680609900716).

The Hydra also provided a more serious analogy for the results of poorly carried out shell-shock treatment: the resurfacing of psychological problems in different, but equally distressing and incapacitating forms. Of the 1736 shell-shock patients treated at the hospital between October 1916 and March 1919, Sassoon suggests that discharge to duty was a rare occurrence indeed, even when the figures recorded seem to reflect differently. In a letter of 1917, he tells us:

> "... it is quite out of the question for a man who has been three months in a nerve-hospital to be sent back at once..., after the war adding: 'I was then duly passed for general service abroad—an event which seldom happened from [Craiglockhart].'"

It is puzzling, then, that the diagnosis of "neurasthenia," is entered almost routinely in the surviving logbooks. Yet it is subordinated to patients' physical complaint no mater how insignificant, from "migraine", "glycosuria", "gas poisoning", "compound fracture of toe" to "haemorrhoids", odd reasons for admission at a shell-shock hospital. Perhaps it reflected an unwillingness to ascribe a psychological factor to the sick leave?

Sassoon's insistence that to be sent straight back to active service, as he was himself, was a rare occurrence is telling in this respect. His entry in the registers, has not only the date entered under the usual "Discharged To Duty" column, but also a hand-written addition (which occurs only once or twice in the remaining 1800 entries): 'To Duty'. In other words, the treatment allotted failed in all aspects with very few exceptions, as they do to this very day, because PTSD is a spiritual crisis, not a physical one. It is that simple.

The stiff-upper-lip attitude, the forced jollity in the place occasionally portrayed in The Hydra belies the degree of suffering within Craiglockhart's walls. Indeed, the limited degree to which that suffering could be alleviated by staff, who had little to no idea what they were dealing with is reflected in this stanza from a Hydra poem:

> "Craiglockhart memories will be sad, Your name will never make us glad; The self-respect we ever had We've lost—all people think us mad" (*The Hydra*, April 28th 1917. July 7th 1917; December 1917, Editorial & June 1918).

However, perhaps Owen and Sassoon are best able to prevent us being misled:

> "In the daytime, sitting in a sunny room, a man could discuss his psycho-neurotic symptoms with his doctor, who could diagnose phobias and conflicts and formulate them into scientific terminology. Significant dreams could be noted down, and Rivers could try to remove repressions. But by night each man was back in his doomed sector of horror-stricken Front Line, where the panic and stampede of some ghastly experience was re-enacted among the livid faces of the dead. No doctor could save him then, when he became the lonely victim of his dream disasters and delusions5 (Sassoon Siegfried: *Sherston's Progress*. London: Faber & Faber, 1936 p. 54):

> "Always (they) must see these things and hear them, Batter of guns and shatter of flying muscles!

> "In all my dreams, before my helpless sight, He plunges at me, guttering, choking, drowning."

And in Owen's *Dulce et decorum est*, a poem published posthumously in 1920 as he was killed days before the November 11, 1918, armistice, a title he took from the leading Roman lyrical poet during Julius Caesar's grandnephew Octavianus' times, Quintus Horatius Flaccus (65-27 BC) Ode 3.2 , the leading Roman lyric poet, meaning "it is sweet and meet to die for one's country. Sweet! And decorous!"

Dulce et Decorum Est
By Wilfred Owen
Bent double, like old beggars under sacks,
Knock-kneed, coughing like hags, we cursed through sludge,
Till on the haunting flares we turned our backs,
And towards our distant rest began to trudge.
Men marched asleep. Many had lost their boots,

But limped on, blood-shod. All went lame; all blind;
Drunk with fatigue; deaf even to the hoots
Of gas-shells dropping softly behind.
Gas! GAS! Quick, boys!—An ecstasy of fumbling
Fitting the clumsy helmets just in time,
But someone still was yelling out and stumbling
And flound'ring like a man in fire or lime.—
Dim through the misty panes and thick green light,
As under a green sea, I saw him drowning.
In all my dreams before my helpless sight,
He plunges at me, guttering, choking, drowning.
If in some smothering dreams, you too could pace
Behind the wagon that we flung him in,
And watch the white eyes writhing in his face,
His hanging face, like a devil's sick of sin;
If you could hear, at every jolt, the blood
Come gargling from the froth-corrupted lungs,
Obscene as cancer, bitter as the cud
Of vile, incurable sores on innocent tongues,—
My friend, you would not tell with such high zest
To children ardent for some desperate glory,
The old Lie: Dulce et decorum est
Pro patria mori--"It is sweet and fitting to die for one's country (Horace)"

Senior United States Marine Corps Major General Smedley Darlington Butler (1881-1940) was nicknamed "Maverick Marine". Ha had fought in the Philippine-American War, the Boxer Rebellion, the Mexican Revolution and World War I. What did he write 20 years later? "War is a Racket." That's the point precisely, for profit of the rich and the culling of the herd now replaced by the equally lucrative bio warfare, in case you haven't noticed.

It is due to Craiglockhart that we have a vague sense of the human experience of WWI. And we also got a glimpse of the medical and craft and art of psychiatric professions' beliefs and experimental practices on the-in-the-line-of-duty PTSD-afflicted from then onwards and still in great dispute. The medical profession's response to WWI's shell-shock conundrum never was nor is uniform, either in aim or in execution. How can it be? One cannot have uniform treatment for it, as it depends on an individual's pre-PTSD-causing event, on life philosophy and on a multitude of other aspects discussed and presented in Fallacy 1. This was true at Craiglockhart and other comparable, non-commissioned soldiers' hospitals, such as Maghull, in unison seeing physicians' less as reprogrammers than as "saviours" (https://ncbi.nlm.nih.gov/pmc/articles/PMC1484566/). Reprogrammers, yeah? Yes, that's what it is all about, and that is why their hypotheses fail. Genuine PTSD journeyers seem to be intuitively far too bright to fall for that scam. Unfortunately, they are not bright enough to understand that the craft and art of psychiatry under the guise of science makes them sicker than dogs. Such evil is beyond the schemata of human beings.

As an unnamed poet who wrote in *The Hydra* put it:

'Craiglockhart memories will be sad, Your name will never make us glad; The self-respect we ever had We've lost – all people think us mad. (*Journal Of The Royal Society Of Medicine*, 2006. 'Dottyville' – Craiglockhart War Hospital and shell-shock treatment in the First World War. [online] 99(7), pp.342–346).

31

PTSD ENHANCEMENT TECHNIQUES

Towards the end of WWI, the Freudian psychoanalytical approach to cure the shell-shocked gained traction, together with psychodynamic psychology. This is the study of the psychological forces underlying human behaviour, feelings and emotions and the dynamics of conscious and unconscious motivation. Freud used the term "psychodynamics" to describe the mind's processes as a flow of psychological energy in an organically complex brain. An *organic* cause to *brain* dysfunction is suspected when there is no sign of a clearly defined psychiatric or "inorganic" cause, such as a mood disorder, for which there is no scientific proof.

The four major schools of thought on psychological treatment of emotionally traumatized human beings were concocted during WWI:

- psychodynamic
- genitive-behavioural
- biological
- humanistic therapies

All are based on the Darwinian hypothesis of human equals animal; otherwise, the term "humanitarian therapies" would have been used. All are experimental and have been so from Craiglockhart's opening day. And none addresses PTSD, as the art, craft and science cabal of psychological magic refuses to acknowledge that it is a spiritual crisis. It's not one of the normally-to-be-expected human existential crises or life experiences like illness, death of a loved one, car accidents, divorces, job-loss or the proverbial hangnail.

The mental health métier is a splendid business, lucrative and easy on body and mind of practitioners. And, due to the systematic ruination of the family pursued since the early 1900s by the elite with Freud's at al.'s know-how, the industry is perhaps even somewhat beneficial to replace grandma. The elite's efforts had resulted in the destruction of the natural psychodynamic interpersonal relief-sessions. These were meant to unburden the soul of the normally-to-be-expected life experiences. These experiences can vary emotionally in perception of severity with every human soul. Freud was aware of what was planned for humanity's future. According to hearsay, he was paid by the Ukrainian Mafia to put the enterprise in motion. He facilitated the switch from intimate family relief sessions to his league of associates. He began with his fellow physicians and wealthy acquaintances, in the 1890s lounging on his expensively carpeted couch spewing forth whatever sprang to their mind, while taking copious notes to publish later. He used his daughter for other amusement and research.

To broaden the métier in scope, he and his fellows, with the assistance of their respective governments, hastened to set up WWIs experimental research laboratories. These "hospitals" exploited the suffering of those wounded in the killing fields. They tested their illusions and hallucinations about the human emotional state of mind when traumatized and drugged to the hilt or not. The glorious abundance of vivo research material in the form of shell-shocked soldiers rather than the usual lepus, cani and rattus, made this possible.

At Craiglockhart, soldiers would receive 30- to 60-minute sessions with a treating physician every 14 days or once a month. Freud recommended three to five sessions per week for the psychologically distressed. Psychodynamic psychotherapy tends to limit itself to one or two sessions weekly. Psychodynamic psychotherapy is based on the theory of a person's inner unconscious conflict, wherein repressed behaviours and emotions surface into the patient's consciousness. Sessions then became intertwined with electrical shocks and a few weeks of dowsing into oblivion with chloroform. These might be aided by food not fit for a dog, creating malnutrition to enhance soldiers' misery, never mind shell shock healing. Neither were places available for WWIs shell-shocked soldiers of all ranks and file outside of private care at war's end. There were only a very few Crichton-Miller's Bowden House-like ones affordable only to the very well healed.

In addition, Charles Samuel Myers' idea of "forward psychiatry" efficacy, was already questioned. The concept relied on the three principles of:

- maintaining shell-shocked soldiers' proximity to battle
- immediacy of treatment
- expectation of recovery

It was subsequently given the acronym "PIE." But it was seen as highly controversial among military and the learned society alike. However, psychiatrist Hugh Crichton-Miller sprang into the breech. He had been stationed in Egypt during his few months participating in Britain's WWI war efforts. So moved was he by his encounters with the shell-shock-afflicted there, that he conceived the desire to investigate its origin and root causes in depth.

Back in London, in 1917, he re-established his lucrative Harley Street practice and re-opened Bowden House. He would attempt to heal shell-shock-originating neurosis through his own practice. He would adapt for the military healing by adapting Freud's neurosis treatment for civilians. He also used *Swiss physician* and pioneer of psychosomatic medicine Roger Vittoz's (1863–1925) methods. He had developed ways to improve his patients' concentration and relaxation to help themselves. Similar to contemporary mindfulness, the method merely reinvigorated Hippocrates' knowledge and psychological ethics. These had been examined and refreshed in the seventeenth century by French polyglot and philosopher René Descartes (1596 -1650) in his "body-mind dualism" theory. He professed that the human mind indeed has an impact on humans' physical health and dis-ease. His insights prompted many a scientific study into the psychosomatic effects of ailments – at least for a while.

In the United States, however, the push to introduce specialties in medicine had been on since Swiss psychiatrist Adolf Myer entered the country in the late 1800s. The American Board of Psychiatry and Neurology (ABPN) sprang forth in 1934, making psychosomatic medicine a mute point. It imposed specialty regulation, training oversight, examination and certification for the purported purpose to serve the public interest and promote excellence in the practice of psychiatry and neurology. The ABPN finally issued a Subspecialty Certification in psychosomatic medicine in 2003. It took another two years before the first certifying examinations in psychosomatic medicine were administered. To top it off, as of 2009, a completion of an American Board of Medical Specialties-certified fellowship in psychosomatic medicine became mandatory for all who wished to sit for that examination (https://sciencedirect.com/topics/neuroscience/psychosomatic-medicine).

The word "psychosomatic" comes from merging the two Greek words *psykhe* (mind) and *somatikos* (body). German physician Johann Christian August Heinroth (1773 -1843) was the first to use the term in 1818. He was discussing "the two indivisible aspects of the self, the psykhe and the somatikos, the body." He divided the human personality into three parts:

- the *Ueber-uns* – the above-us, our conscience
- the *ego* – our mind, emotions and will
- the *Fleisch* – the flesh,

These signified our basic drives, including our sinful nature.

Born in Leipzig, Heinroth initially studied medicine there. He continued his education in Vienna and briefly studied theology in Erlangen. He returned to Leipzig, where he obtained his medical doctorate in 1805. He became a lecturer in 1806 and graduated to full professor of physical medicine in 1827. (M. J. Martin: *Psychosomatic Medicine: A Brief History*; 1978; pdf.sciencedirectassets.com).

Not that there was anything new to this. The mysterious and elusive interrelationships between mind and body have fascinated man for millennia. In the Islamic world, Persian physicians Ahmed ibn Sahl al-Balkhi (d. 934) and Haly Abbas (d. 994) developed a model of illness that emphasized the human body-mind interaction. They suggested that patients' physiology and psychology influenced each other. That dis-ease was caused by spiritual powers, evil spirits entering the body affecting the whole being to be fought by spiritual means, was also common knowledge. Medicine men of those days used their patients' will to health by the power of suggestion. This tradition steeped in the doctor-patient relationship has been replaced nowadays by prescription drugs. The placebo effect occurs after a treatment that has no active properties, such as a sugar pill. The results in an ailment's improvement and even healing is the empirical scientific evidence of the human body-mind interaction's validity.

Mind you, with Abe Flexner's 1910 Report for Carnegie, psychosomatic medicine had been stamped out completely. Reawakened interest in this area led to launching the Academy of Psychosomatic Medicine in 1953. Its psychiatrists attempted to provide a collaborative care system, bridging the gap between human physical and mental health with their specialty-prone peers. In 2017, its 1,500 members renamed their association the Academy of Consultation-Liaison Psychiatry (ACLP). They wanted to bring together and coordinate psychosomatic, behavioural, psychological, and medical research and discovery. This would increase scientific and political influence within national and international societies of psychosomatic medicine.

(https://bpsmedicine.biomedcentral.com/articles/10.1186/s13030-016-0086-0
https://biomedcentral.com;
https://news-medical.net/health/What-is-Psychosomatic-Medicine.aspx)

And why the name change? Because, we read, this field is associated with human services like diagnoses, therapeutics and research of illnesses in those areas. It connects psychiatry and other medical specialties. It facilitates physicians and psychiatrists to discuss. how to best manage patients with psychosomatic illness for reasons and causes yet to be determined. Ailments of the soul overtly manifesting in the human physical body are seemingly unfathomable to those of the atheistic Luciferic consciousness persuasion.

It took until 2003 for psychosomatic medicine, by then known as consultation-liaison psychiatry, to receive approval as a subspecialty field of psychiatry by the American Board of Medical Specialties (David F. Gitlin M.D. et al: "Psychosomatic Medicine: A New Psychiatric Subspecialty"; *Academic Psychiatry* volume 28, pages 4–11 (2004)). The field was developed, we read, in response to evidence suggesting that a high prevalence of psychiatric disorders exists in patients with complex medical illnesses. The diagnosis and management of these disorders in this population is critical, yet frequently complicated by the medical illnesses themselves. In many or even most of these patients, genuine PTSD experiencers and other emotionally rattled individuals included, their physical illness develops due to mind-altering prescription drugs administered by the consulting physicians. But this is nowhere mentioned.

All we are told is that these psychosomatic medicine psychiatrists have developed specialized expertise to address these issues. And we are told that its approved subspecialty status will help promote the psychiatric care of patients with complex medical, surgical, obstetrical, and neurological conditions.' Of course, the profession itself might most likely have caused some of these, speaking form experience. And we are told that this will help improve of training and research in this area that has been researched since the dawn of humanity's known history. The American Board of Psychiatry and Neurology (ABPN) itself acknowledges to have had an enormous influence on the practice of psychiatry in America and the world. Indeed, it has an ever growing increase in scientific and political influence, shown by its mass hypnosis creation of COVID-19 origin. After all, it has been years in the certification, recertification and certification maintenance business. And this has been mandated in particular to work in the mental health industry. This allows for selective membership in the organization to /ensure the success of the Work of Ages agenda.

For those afflicted, the change of nomenclature from "shell-shock" to "neurasthenia" makes no difference. They still suffer from the health condition characterized by lassitude, fatigue, headache and irritability, deemed by the magicians of human mind perversion to be chiefly associated with emotional disturbance of a non-specified nature. But for the industry, it henceforth enables them and their associated insurance corporations to classify those with genuine PTSD acquired in the line of duty under the generic medical term "functional disorders." This covers an enormously broad spectrum of perceived emotional. and physical ailments. It is open to any interpretation under the sun, depending on a physician's belief structure, religious orientation, sense of nationality, colour, upbringing, social status, education, academic indoctrination, life experience and innate intelligence.

Let me explain. In 2011, functional illness was the term given to all psychiatric illness other than an organic disorder, a psychiatric illness without a "physical" cause, so to speak. The distinction between organic and functional conditions and illness was made at a time when body and mind were considered separate entities. That was since Darwin's natural selection of the fittest theory was popularized, or thereabouts. In that context, it is still viewed as a perfectly valid and useful a way of classifying psychiatric disorders (L. Stevens MB BS FRCPsych et al: Classification in Psychiatry; Psychiatry (Second Edition) 2011).

In 2022, the term "general functional disorder" is described as a medical disorder impairing normal functioning of bodily processes that remain undetected under physical examination, dissection or a microscope. In other words, no sign of abnormality is visible in the examined human being. This contrasts with a structural disorder, in which the naked eye can see an abnormality. So, a general functional disorder can be diagnosed by any Joe and his dog as a psychosomatic disorder manifested by invisible or visible symptoms caused by psychological- or psychiatric disorders of an unspecified number. The present of these could at any time be diagnosed into existence at will by the treating psychiatrist or deemed non-existent, depending on the mood of the day. That the mechanism causing a functional disorder is unknown, poorly understood or occasionally unimportant for treatment purposes is of no consequence to the learned psycho-the-rapist profession. It is generally believed that the brain or the nerves are somewhat involved, which adds to the diagnosis's liberty at play.

It is common, we hear, that a person with one functional disorder will have others. Needless to say, this can all be made up by any psychiatrist with a larger or lesser developed sense of imagination, hallucination and creativity of thought. For them, seeing us as animals devoid of spirit, consciousness and soul, everything goes. Manifestations of these general functional disorders are regularly related to phenomenal stress creating tics, aches and pains as reflections of inner emotional turmoil of immense proportion. But this never crosses most of the ilk's atheistic, empathy-, emotion- and compassion-devoid, feeble, little minds.

Then the mental health cabal created the functional neurological disorder (FND). It is tailored to portray human emotional upheaval as a physical medical condition created by a physical problem within the human nervous system, with the brain sending and receiving signals to the body. This, we hear, creates and encompasses a wide variety of neurological symptoms, including seizures and weakness of the limbs. Any and all of these conditions are portrayed and seen as interfacing topics between neurology and psychiatry, regardless that MRI brain scans and EEGs of PTSD patients are usually normal and healthy. So, PTSD is thought of as a general functional and/or functional neurological disorder depending on the examining psychiatrist's temperament on joy of life at the moment.

Clinicians and researchers alike, however, are said to historically neglect the functional neurological disorder (FND). That is because it is almost impossible to spew forth even vague scientific indisputable evidence for its existence, even more so than for all else in the art and craft of this magical field. They now try to agree that FND is a common cause of disability and distress, which might, just might, overlap with problems such as chronic pain and fatigue. No word is breathed, however, of the true nature of these physical, impairment-causing, emotional upheavals, in PTSD of catastrophic, life-view, changing live-or-die, question-inspiring proportions. That nature is that they are rather easily solvable with inner reflection, peace and quiet, spiritual inquiry into the meaning of human life and living, daily meditation and somatic exercise. But there is no money for them in it.

Instead, the masters of perception-deception and perversion's newest understanding went back to their earlier hypotheses on FND. They reverted to it having specific clinical features of its own, thus is a disorder of nervous system functioning. For that, many perspectives of investigations are necessary, as they vary from person to person. Furthermore, we are told that psychological factors are important in some people, whereas in others they are not (https://rarediseases.org/rare-diseases/fnd/). To further convolute matters, we are told that the definitions of functional disorder vary between the numerous fields of medicine. We think that this mirrors the craft's "everything-goes-doctrine" and validates Allan Frances' declaration: "It's all bullshit." Does it not?

Be it as it may, our Genoa born Crichton-Miller ploughed on at Bowden House. He argued that most shell-shock cases had broken down either from the emotional strain associated with trench life or from their chronic apprehension of danger. Furthermore, he proposed that there was a pattern of developmental flaws relating to violent and abusive behavior during childhood. This was often associated with an alcoholic father. He claimed that this played a role in whether a shell-shocked person would bounce back or go under after a knock is "overdetermined" by factors present in early history.

And what does "overdetermined" mean? Overdetermination, Überdeterminierung in German, is the term used by Freud in his hypothesis of psychoanalysis to describe the concept, that a single emotional symptom or event, such as a dream or a slip of the tongue, may be caused by more than one factor. Overdetermination is also said to occur, when a single-observed effect is determined by multiple causes, any one of which alone would be sufficient to determine and account for the effect. In other words, that there are more causes present than are necessary to cause the effect or not. In the philosophy of science it means, that more evidence is available than is necessary to justify a conclusion.

Unterdeterminierung (underdetermination) is the opposite. It is thought to exist when the number or strength of causes for a functional disorder or whatever ailment of emotional nature is seen as insufficient for a diagnosis. At the heart of underdetermination of scientific theory by evidence is the simple idea that the evidence available at a given time may be insufficient to determine what beliefs should be held in response to it (https://plato.stanford.edu/entries/scientific-underdetermination/).

And who decides what is what? Well, the philosophy of science. And what's that, we wonder? Well, that's another kettle of fish. It's presented as a branch of philosophy concerned with the foundations, methods and implications of science. It aims to establish:

- what indeed qualifies as science
- the reliability of scientific theories
- the ultimate purpose of science
- the relationship between science and truth

It aims to do so purportedly in combination with ethical issues in bioethics and with scientific misconduct.

What of Crichton-Miller's developmental flaw hypothesis, that a pattern violent and abusive behavior during childhood plays a role in whether we, the shell-shocked, recover? The verdict is used by the cabal to this very day to blame the genuine PTSD journeyers' upbringing for our PTSD and lack of recovery, no matter how valiantly and honorably we carried ourselves throughout our careers. (https://100years.tavistockandportman.nhs.uk/hugh-crichton-miller/). That Crichton-Miller and many others of his ilk reached their conclusions using their own children as laboratory rats gives food for thought, however.

In 1920, to Crichton-Miller's huge delight, the U.S. Rockefeller Foundation galloped in. It offered to open a clinic for the sole purpose of exploring human neurological functioning and associated emotional behaviours. He was made medical director with free hands to do whatever he thought to do whenever he wanted to do it to any human crossing the threshold of his to be established experimental laboratory. By now father of six and rather broke, military service having paid little, he jumped at the opportunity. The Tavistock Square Clinic for Functional Nervous Disorders opened its doors at 51 Tavistock Square in September 1920. It had seven physicians in training as psychiatrists, some of them transferred from Bowden House: Dr JA Hadfield, Dr Mary Hemmingway, Dr Neill Hobbhouse (Neurologist), Dr Leslie Tucker, EA Hamilton Pearson and Dr JR Rees. Others joined soon after, some in honorary positions, including British pharmacologist and physician William Alexander Potts (1866–1939) as head of the Children's Department.

Potts was born at Rugby, a market town in eastern Warwickshire, England, close to the River Avon. He was educated at Pembroke College, Cambridge, and at the University of Edinburgh. He graduated with a M.B. in 1895 and a M.D. in 1898. He began his scientific career at the East Riding Mental Hospital in Yorkshire, founded in 1871. At the same time, he served as resident medical officer and surgeon to the Edinburgh Royal Infirmary and the Royal Hospital for Sick Children. In 1906, he was appointed chief medical investigator for the Royal Commission on the Care and Control of the Feeble-minded. Besides being in private practice, he kept himself entertained by promoting the passage of Britain's Mental Deficiency Act 1913. This act of Parliament created provisions for the institutional treatment of people judged to be "feeble-minded" and "moral defectives". They were to be taken out of Poor Law institutions and prisons and relocated into newly established "colonies. "These were the colossal insane asylums built throughout Europe and the U.S. since the mid-1800s.

Tavistock Clinic, now well staffed with Potts at its head, was ready to treat those deemed feeble-minded and morally defective of all age., Crichton-Miller had what he had dreamt about all along. He had a place to provide psychological treatments to the less financially well-endowed. It was a place where he could implement his ideas of modern psychological treatments to his heart's content. It was a clinic he could run on the simplest lines with a minimum of publicity and a maximum of work. And he could do all this while overseeing Bowden House, populated by those able to afford its private fees. At Tavistock Clinic, most staff worked on a voluntary basis, with patients being charged a nominal fee of five shillings, only if they could afford it.

All physicians were given free reign to do as they pleased, using whatever treatments they thought fit. This matched Crichton-Miller's general modus operandi to have no doctrine at all. That said, he did sometimes promote dream analysis, suggestion therapy, mental exercises of unknown nature and the re-education of a patient to help him to deal with his difficulties. That would be today's cognitive behavioural therapy, destroying humans' *sui generis*. In other words, Alistair Crowley's "Do what thou wilt shall be the whole of the Law" seems to have been the clinic's leitmotiv (https://www.bmj.com/content/2/3478/423 Aleister Crowley, *The Book of the Law* I:40).

Tavistock Clinic's first patient was a child from we do not know where and of unknown age and sex. The child was not seen by Potts, but by a Dr. Hamilton Pearson. This M.D. had qualified from we don't know where in 1912 and, after a spell in the British Royal Army Medical Corps, became a surgeon in the Chilean Navy (https://100years.tavistockandportman.nhs.uk/dr-ea-hamilton-pearson/). He was seemingly without training in psychology when he saw the child in 1920. But by sometime in 1921, he obtained a resident position in psychiatry at the private The Lawn Hospital for Mental and Nervous Diseases. The Lawn was funded in 1820 with a bequeath by a Dr Paul Parnell as the Lincoln Asylum for the Insane. It featured a walled garden and a children's play area, and it shared its medical staff with the County Hospital.

The Lincoln Asylum changed its name to Lincoln Lunatic Hospital in 1905. Then again switched to The Lawn Hospital in 1921. It rebranded for paying persons of the superior class. It was here that Chilean navy surgeon Pearson as one of its resident M.D.s got his psychiatrist license whilst continuing to examine children at the Tavistock Clinic. Others joined him there. Among them was Edinburgh-educated British physician Alice Hutchison (1874–1953), who had served in the Balkan War and First World War, leading a war-time hospital unit. There was also a Charles Burns, of whom we know little other than his fascination with child delinquency., Crichton-Miller kept them very busy, as he made it perfectly clear that they must interview the parents, as well. And he said that the Clinic's social workers must physically investigate the home environment and the overall family conditions and their intimate relationships.

The Children's Department was a roaring success! Staff were presented with a large variety of children thought by physicians, parents, teachers, priests, social workers and ministers to suffer "abnormalities of conduct." These ranged from nail-biting, night terrors and bed-wetting to lying and stealing. They included being too timid or too boisterous, too exuberant and outgoing, or too quiet, dimwitted or bright. Key to staff's analysis and consequent diagnoses were the psychological and intelligence quotient tests developed during WWI by Robert Sessions Woodworth's (1869 -1962) Personal Data Sheet. A graduate of Harvard and Columbia universities, Woodworth had studied under William James. James was considered the father of American psychology. His 1921 textbook *Psychology: A study of mental life* became the first introduction to psychology for generations of undergraduate students. He followed it up in 1938 with the equally influential textbook *Experimental Psychology*. It was known for introducing the stimulus-Oroganism-response (S-O-R) formula of behavior. This was in essence Pavlov's classical conditioning mechanism, the mental health cabal. 's PTSD favorite cognitive behavioral therapy deadly to the human soul.

James's S-O-R concept explains that animals' various environments can act as a Stimulus (S). Thus, it influences the Organism's internal, emotional state (O). This in turn drives individuals' behavioral Response (R). In other words, it's tailored after the Hegelian dialectic - create the environment, thus influence the organism, wait for the response and then propose the solution you had in mind all along. This is just as with the COVID 19 creation, the solution being the life-changing and even deadly kill shot.

Anyway, James was a self-declared pragmatist, guided more by practical considerations than by ideals for and of anyone and anything. He was hard-headed and firmly rooted in the "real" world since birth. He saw himself as someone who evaluated theories and beliefs conceived or presented in terms of the success of their practical application. Thus, we gather, he used whatever parts of any given theory that made the most sense to him and could be proven and, we gather, he could create from its outcome whatever he could dream up. One recommendation he conceived was to break apart spiritualism and associationism. The latter is the theory that regards simple associations and co-occurrences of ideas and sensations as the primary basis of meaning, thought or learning. He then suggested to use the parts of both spiritualism and associationism that made the most sense to one's own belief structure. Perhaps this would be the way to, perhaps, dream up one's own hallucinations and imaginations. Those could then be superimposed on unsuspecting patients, genuine PTSD journeyers included, perhaps, and see what happens?

James, like most of his peers, was an atheist, with Darwin's theory of natural selection firmly anchored in his mind. He naturally viewed humanity as nothing other than originating from amoeba onwards - blattas, simia, cani, rattus and so forth. He and his learned society compatriots were of course excluded. However, he does grant us, the herd, more instincts than Darwinian creatures. But he says all of it can be overridden by experience and by each other, because our instincts are in conflict with each other. Maybe he confused instinct with intuition we wonder? He simultaneously voices a belief in each individual, human and animal, we trust, having a soul, which exists in a spiritual universe guiding the behaviors displayed in the physical world.

And about truth and truthfulness in anything and everything he has this to say:

> "Truths emerge from facts, but they dip forward into facts again and add to them; which facts again create or reveal new truth (the word is indifferent) and so on indefinitely. The 'facts' themselves meanwhile are not true. They simply are.

Truth is the function of the beliefs that start and terminate among them (What Pragmatism Means; 1906)."

Well, does he really say that everything in life goes as you dip in and out, rise and fall from one illusion and hallucination into the next? It is with James' assistance that his student's created *The Woodworth Personal Data Sheet*, sometimes known as the *Woodworth Psychoneurotic Inventory*. It was ordered by the U.S. army during World War I. "Psychoneurotic" means affected with emotional disorder or showing abnormal inability to act or make decisions. It is commonly cited as the world's first personality test. It consists of 116 "Yes" or "No" questions, which were compiled by psychologists from case studies of people they deemed to be psychologically disturbed. Designed to identify solders at risk for shell shock, the test measures one scale only: emotional instability. By WWI's end, November 1918, around 1,727,000 million U.S. soldiers had completed Woodworth's and the first group of intelligence tests.; roughly two percent of them were rejected by the military due to psychological imbalances. What happened to those deemed intelligent nothing is known.

The whole idea of psychological testing, mind you, had already arisen in the mid- nineteenth century. French physician, anatomist and anthropologist Paul Broca (1824–1880) and British polymath and eugenicist Sir Francis Galton (1822–1911) led the way. Broca was known for his research on a region of the frontal lobe named after him. Galton was known for his theory that human skull size might determine intelligence - the larger the skull, the smarter the owner. German polymath Wilhelm Wundt (1832–1920), on the other hand thought introspection - the ability to reflect on one's own thoughts - was a measure of intelligence. However, it took until 1904 for Sardinian-born Alfred Binet (1857–1911) and French Théodore Simon (1873 -1961) to come up with the Binet-Simon scale. It is still one of the most widely used scales worldwide to measure intelligence. And what qualified and inspired them to come up with their hypotheses on human intelligence quotients with fixed amount from birth onwards?

Well, Binet received his law degree in Paris in 1878. As a sideline, he went on to study physiology at the Sorbonne, where he became fascinated by the work of neurologist Jean-Martin Charcot on hypnosis. He swiftly abandoned his law career. With Charcot as his mentor, he devoted himself to medico-scientific studies at Salpêtrière hospital, where Charcot was director. In 1890, he suddenly resigned and never mentioned the place or its director again.

Binet then turned his interest towards documenting his own two children's cognitive development. This study would be brought to terrific heights by Swiss psychologist Jean William Fritz Piaget (1896–1980). He used it in his personal research and theories on children's cognitive and moral development. It also informed his study of the nature, origin, and limits of human knowledge, sometimes referred to as the theory of knowledge. This would prove to be enormously influential in subsequent research.

This, in turn, led to New Yorker Lawrence Kohlberg's (1927–1967) stage theory of human moral development (https://courses.lumenlearning.com/teachereducationx92x1/chapter/kohlbergs-stages-of-moral-development/). Kohlberg surely had no difficulty in its composure. He and his three siblings were born to a Jewish German entrepreneur. From a very young age after their parents' separation, they were forced to rotate between them every six months until old enough to choose with whom they wanted to live.

When that time came for Kohlberg, he wanted neither of them. He chose instead to attend Phillips Academy. Established in 1778, it was the oldest incorporated private academy in the United States. Upon graduation in 1945, he joined the merchant marine. From there, he went to the University of Chicago, where he earned a BA in psychology in 1948 and a PhD in psychology in 1958. He subsequently held teaching positions at various institutions before settling at Harvard University in 1968 (Britannica.com). Kohlberg became interested in Piaget's work on children's moral development while pursuing his doctoral degree. According to Piaget, children's moral development progresses naturally from a form of moral reasoning based on the consequences of an act, e.g., resulting punishment, to one that takes the actor's intentions into account. Kohlberg tested the hypothesis by presenting 72 lower- and middle-class white boys with the moral dilemma whether it would be permissible for a poor man to steal medicine for his dying wife. The children's responses became the basis of his six-stage theory of moral development.

He called stages 1 and 2 "pre-conventional". The child conceives of right acts as those that enable him to avoid punishment in stage 1. The child conceives of right acts as those that make a good or fair deal in stage 2. Stages 3 and 4 were the conventional stages. Right acts are those that gain the approval of others in stage 3. They are acts that consist of doing one's duty or following society's rules in stage 4. Finally, come the post-conventional stages. The child is guided by respect for laws and moral rules in stage 5, though he recognizes them as somewhat arbitrary and not always valid. The child is guided by abstract ethical principles, such as justice and equality, in stage 6, a stage Kohlberg is rarely achieved. As no other account had provided such detailed explanation of children's moral development, his theory became highly influential psychology and education. It also received much criticism for its demographic limitations. He had failed to note the distinct patterns of moral development exhibited by girls. He had shown cultural and gender bias toward white, upper-class men and boys and failed to account for inconsistencies within moral judgments.

It was Piaget, however, the little rich boy, who is considered the great pioneer of the constructive theory of knowing by many of the learned society. This theory posits that humans of all ages do not acquire knowledge and understanding by passively perceiving it within a direct process of knowledge transmission. The theory suggests that we *construct* new understandings and knowledge through our own experiences and social discourse as we, the cattle, the herd, integrate new information with what we already know from prior knowledge and expand on it. Thus, it is explained that putting children in masks and keeping them socially isolated ruins their ability to learn anything, regardless of age. Marks would destroy their foundation of absorbing knowledge, even with computer learning.

Piaget's knowledge began to surface in the 1960s. By the late 1900s, he was acknowledged as the best of the best, as second only to American Burrhus Frederic Skinner (1904 –1990) This 1931 Harvard PhD graduate and researcher considered human free will to be an illusion and saw human action as dependent on consequences of previous actions. He would articulate this theory as the *principle of reinforcement*. If the consequences to an action are bad, there is a high chance the action will not be repeated. If the consequences are good, the probability of the action being repeated becomes stronger. On this ground, Skinner developed behaviour analysis and his philosophy of radical behaviorism while working with mental patients in an unnamed Massachusetts state hospital. From his work in animal learning, Skinner deduced that the establishment and elimination of responses can be determined by how reinforcers or rewards are given. The pattern of reward-giving, both in time and frequency, is known as the "schedule of reinforcement." The gradual change in behaviour toward the psychotherapist's desired result is known as "shaping." (Britannica.com)

He furthermore argued that a person's behaviour and the environmental factors that influence it are most crucial to the fundamental understanding of a person's psychological state in and outside of an asylum. A sworn behaviourist, he became an atheist after a Christian teacher attempted to assuage his fear of the hell his grandmother had described to him.

The term "Operant conditioning" also originated with Skinner, who believed that it was unnecessary to look at anyone's thoughts and motivations in order to explain his or her behavior. Instead, influenced by John B. Watson's ideas as he was, one should look only at the observable causes of human behavior. And Watson had focused on Pavlov's principles of classical conditioning techniques. He famously announced that he could take any person, regardless of background, and train them to be anything he chose.

In behavioral psychology, reinforcement is the consequence applied that will strengthen an organism's, you the animal, or the dog, or blattas, or simian and rattus future behavior whenever that behavior is preceded by a specific antecedent stimulus. This is especially true in cognitive behavioral therapy, the CBT, deadly to the psyche of genuine PTSD experiencers, The strengthening effect may be measured as a higher frequency of behavior. For instance:

- pulling a lever more frequently and for longer duration
- pulling a lever for longer periods of time and to greater magnitude
- pulling a lever with greater force
- pulling a lever with shorter latency
- pulling a lever more quickly following the antecedent stimulus

Skinner tested his hypothesis by keeping his two-year old daughter in a cage for a year to see what would happen to her. But I digress.

All experimental research into the emotional vulnerabilities and propensities of humans of all ages were used to orchestrate changes in Western societies' ethical, moral and intellectual directions. This is a given, regardless of race, colour, religion or intelligence. Binet's and Simon's IQ test played a huge role in it. And how did they go about developing it?

After quitting Charcot and Salpêtrière without a murmur, Binet found himself bored with studying his own children's cognitive processes. With no acknowledgment or applause for his research and discoveries, he joined the Sorbonne's Laboratory of Experimental Psychology in 1891. He became its director in 1895, where he remained until his death in 1911. During those years, he sought ways and means to measure humans' higher mental processes and reasoning abilities. He saw little value in Wundt et al.'s German experimental laboratory research conducted on humans' sensation and perception. Instead, he referred to the human ability to take knowledge and education and use it to create new things, ideas, theories and concepts. He also aimed to establish qualitative and quantitative intellectual differences between individuals (Binet & Henri, 1896; see Nicolas, Coubart & Lubart, 2014).

Progressively becoming more interested in the individual psychology of the child rather than the adult, he went on to developed experimental studies on suggestibility. He argued that normal people are characterized and differ from one another by their higher mental processes, in particular by their way of remembering rather than by their sensory capacities. Thus, he sought to study suggestibility as a normal social and cognitive process. Within this framework, he conducted new experiments, published in the never-translated-into-English book *On Suggestibility* (Binet, 1900). It established the role of comments or orders—suggestions —of the experimenter on the acts of remembering in subjects studied, both individually and in groups (https://www.cairn.info/revue-l-annee-psychologique1-2014-2-page-209.htm).

Binet was fully aware of Galton's late nineteenth century attempts to measure human intelligence. So, he used paper, pencil, pictures, portable objects and questionnaires to devise what he thought were usable ways to each his goal, (Henry L. Minton, University of Windsor: New Methods for the Diagnosis of the Intellectual Level of Subnormals. Alfred Binet & Theodore Simon (1905); psychclassics.yorku.ca/Binet/intro.htm). Galton thought of human intelligence as a function of sensory acuity. He referred to the extent to which we are able to detect stimuli of minimal size, intensity or duration and our ability to make observations about the world and everything in it. The ability and capacity for sensory acuity was reflected in humans' native endowment, the innate capacities with which we are born. In Galton's view, these could also be socially acquired. He concluded that people exhibiting high degrees of sensory discrimination were highly intelligent. This, he argued in his 1869 book *Hereditary Genius*, followed genealogical lines. Thus, eminent fathers tended to have eminent sons and vice versa.

Heredity became Galton's main area of interest. He began with coining the term "eugenics" to describe the science and idea of breeding human "stock" to give "the more suitable races or strains of blood a better chance of prevailing speedily over the less suitable" (https://ucl.ac.uk/culture/galton-collection/galton-and-anthropometrics). His studies in heredity also led to his interest in anthropometrics. This is the measurement of human features, which Galton considered indicators of human ability and behaviour. To gain enough data to make statistically valid conclusions, Galton established the Anthropometric Laboratory at the London International Health Exhibition of 1884.

Nine thousand visitors paid a small fee to measure and assess their human characteristics and receive a copy of the results. Among those measured were sensory sensations of visual acuity, auditory accuracy and breathing capacity, as well as their level of intelligence. With anthropometrics, Galton devised the field of psychometrics. This is the study within psychology of the theory and technique of measuring latent constructs directly unobservable. These were intelligence, introversion, mental disorders and academic achievements. The levels of these non-observable latent variables are then inferred through mathematical modeling. The basis of the modeling is what is observed from the person's responses to items on tests and scales. These tools were devised with ever greater expertise and intricacies by the world's Galtons to read any one of us like an open book.

The Exhibition was held under the patronage of Queen Victoria and the Prince of Wales, and directed by an Executive Council. It covered everything that promoted good health in the populace through displays and official education programme. Its motto was "From labour [springs] health, from health contentment springs." A few decades later Hitler would use it as the leitmotiv in his concentration camps for the interned and camp workers alike, which has the same implied connotation.

In the United States, Wundt-educated psychologist James McKeen Cattell followed up on Galton's measuring ideas. In 1901, he publicly voiced that no relationship between humans' sensory discrimination ability and indications of intellectual performance in academic grades existed. This observation was countermanded in 2021. We were then told by the learned society that intellectual performance is highly heritable and robustly predicts lifelong health and success. This despite the earliest manifestations of genetic effects on these assets not yet being well understood. In the early 1900s, however, Galton's theory did inspire Binet to set to work on his idea of intelligence measuring scales. Binet argued that differences in human intelligence had to be detectable through measures of such complex processes as individual memory, imagination, attention, comprehension, and suggestibility. And he would begin with the study of children.

Thus, he joined the *Free Society for the Psychological Study of the Child* in 1899. It had been established by Radical-Socialist politician, professor and chair of the Sorbonne's Science of Education department Ferdinand Édouard Buisson (1841–1932). The Society had been founded solely, we are told, because the French government had made it mandatory for children between the ages six to 14 to attend school. Soon thereafter, Binet and many other members of his learned radical Free Society were simultaneously appointed, we do not know precisely by whom, to the Commission for the Retarded. This body's mandate was to study in a scientific manner how to integrate retarded children into the Parisian public school system (thirteen.org/wnet/brain/history/1905.html). The committee decided special education programs should be provided for them, and a system should be designed for identifying retarded children entering school.

The French government promptly presented Binet et al. with an experimental child research laboratory to investigate. There, he could determine how to test and identify children with learning disabilities and slow learners, and how to handle them, possibly in special classrooms. Binet joyously set out to design a scale differentiating slow learners from children learning at a normal rate, whatever that normal rate is deemed to be at that point in time. He collaborated in the exercise with Theodore Simon (1873-1961), a young physician who had worked with retarded children in the past. Simon was an orphan burdened by much tragedy throughout his youth and fascinated by Binet's research. Simon had been appointed intern at the lunatic asylum at Perray-Vaucluse in 1899. Inaugurated in 1869 to work on abnormal children, he studied there with Binet's help the correlation between human physical growth and intellectual development. In 1900 his work culminated in his medical doctoral thesis on the topic.

Binet and Simon then proceeded to assemble a scale composed of measures of the kinds of higher mental processes Binet thought central to the assessment of intelligence. They constructed some specific cognitive tests themselves and modified a number of tests previously developed by French physicians Blin and Damaye. They drew their samples of "normal" and thought-to-be-retarded children ranging between the ages of two to 12 years from Parisian schools, hospitals, orphanages and asylums. They tried various tests on the children to select those that clearly discriminated between the two groups. By this means, they selected 30 tests, arranged roughly in ascending order of difficulty. They put Jean Piaget in charge of administering their reading tests to Parisian children This sparked in Piaget an unbound enthusiasm to probe children's psyche, thus leading to his future of child psychology.

In his 1903 book *L'Etude experimentale de l'intelligence* (Experimental Studies of Intelligence) Binet describes the methods he and Simon used. He concluded that their test would measure the intellectual development of young children between the age of three and 12 in a practical, convenient and rapid way. He asserted that the scale would measure a variety of higher mental processes such as memory and imagination (intelltheory.com/simon.shtml).

In 1905, Binet and Simon went public with their intelligence scale. They premiered it in the *L'Année psychologique*, the first French journal devoted to psychology. Binet had founded this journal in 1895, when he established his experimental research laboratory for the study of children, their means of learning and ways to teach or not to teach them. They spelled out the rationale for their scale and providing guidelines for its administration. They vehemently stressed that it was appropriate only to assess whether or not a child is of normal or inferior intelligence. It was not designed, they insisted, to uncover the psychologically unstable or insane.

The two of them went on to develop highly influential scales for the measurement of intelligence of children between 1905 and 1911. Binet also published works on human suggestibility and hysteria. Binet had revised the scales in 1908 and at the time of his death in 1911. As a sign of respect for the one Simon considered one of history's greatest psychologists and his true idol, he kept them the same. Simon worked as head psychiatrist at Saint-Yon hospital in Essonne department in Île-de-France (northern France) and various hospitals throughout France from 1905 to 1920, He was also the founder of the first nursing school in psychiatry at the Maison Blanche hospital in Neuilly-sur-Marne bearing his name. From 1946 until his death in 1957., he served as its technical director.

Until the end of his life, Simon believed that his and Binet's Intelligence Scale prevented them from achieving its ultimate goal. That goal was to understand human beings, their nature and their development. Simon blamed immoderate and improper use by their peers for this failure. (https://www.nli.org.il/en/a-topic/987007280504605171).

And how did Binet feel about his and Simon's IQ test when leaving the earth?

> "Some recent philosophers seem to have given their moral approval to these deplorable verdicts that affirm that the intelligence of an individual is a fixed quantity, a quantity that cannot be augmented. We must protest and react against this brutal pessimism; we will try to demonstrate that it is founded on nothing." - Alfred Binet, *Les idées modernes sur les enfants*, 1909 (https://verywellmind.com/alfred-binet-biography-2795503)

What again did Allen Frances say in 2010 about the art, craft, and science of psychology in 2010? "It's all Bullshit." But he, too, is expertly ignored by the learned craft and art society of psychiatry. Perhaps these magicians in human mind-manipulation should all take the Stanford–Binet Intelligence Scales. This individually administered intelligence test was revised from the original Binet–Simon Scale by Lewis Madison Terman (1877–1956). Not that high IQ equals knowledge of any sort, least of all the ability to live a purpose-driven life without perpetually traumatizing others.

Terman joined Stanford's faculty in 1910 as a professor of educational psychology at the Graduate School of Education. He served there as chairman of the psychology department from 1922 to 1945. He followed J. McKeen Cattell's work, which combined the ideas of Wundt and Galton. Cattel held that those who are intellectually superior will have better sensory acuity, strength of grip, sensitivity to pain, and memory for dictated consonants. At the private Clark University in Worcester, Massachusetts, founded in 1887, Terman wrote his doctoral dissertation entitled *Genius and stupidity: a study of some of the intellectual processes of seven "bright" and seven "stupid" boys.*

Whereas Binet and Simon tried to identify less able school children in order to aid them with needed care, Terman proposed using IQ tests to classify children to put them on appropriate job-tracks. He also believed IQ to be inherited and the strongest predictor of one's ultimate success in life. To prove his point, he initiated the longitudinal study of children with high IQs in 1921. This *Genetic Studies of Genius* examined the development and characteristics of gifted children into adulthood. He was a fervent eugenicist and activist in the Human Betterment Foundation (HBF), which in 1928 had been founded in Pasadena, California. It's goal was to encourage compulsory sterilization legislation in the US. That would foster constructive and educational forces to protect and improve the human family in body, mind and character long before Hitler came onto the scene. In his spare time, Terman also served as the American Psychological Association's president.

The fifth edition of Terman's revised Stanford–Binet Intelligence Scale (SB5), was released in 2003. It is a cognitive ability and intelligence test consisting of both verbal and nonverbal subtests. It is used to diagnose developments- and intellectual deficiencies in young children. It tests for:

- knowledge
- quantitative reasoning
- visual-spatial processing
- working memory and fluid reasoning
- the capacity to think logically and solve novel problems central to human cognition development

That means it can be used for adults of all ages, as well, as little to nothing is known about the underlying neural changes central to and facilitating the development of human cognition (frontiersin.org/articles/10.3389/neuro.09.008.2007/full).

This Termans revised Stanford–Binet Intelligence Scale has been widely used in psychological research and to develop a slew of other personality tests for humans of all ages. It has been described as the linear ancestor of all subsequent personality inventories, schedules and questionnaires. That includes the Minnesota Multiphasic Personality Inventory (MMPI). The MMPI is always used on genuine PTSD experiencers and anyone else the powers that be want to shaft. When completed correctly and truthfully, it is the blueprint of anyone's innate characteristics, personality, propensities, vulnerabilities and innermost secrets. For one's protection, one must lie when asked to complete it, unless one wants to be killed psychologically, and by extension physically, by those pretending to have one's healing at heart.

Terman's revised Binet and Simon IQ test's importance is reflected in the multidisciplinary research study entitled *Evaluation of the Psychoneurotic Tendencies Risk Using the Woodworth Mathews Personality Inventory in Non-Institutionalized Persons.* Published in 2014, the research was conducted between 2009–2011. Its conclusion? If experiencing a number or multiple factors of vulnerability, normal humans may develop abnormal social behaviors and important psychiatric diseases. These would generally be characterized by a combination of abnormal thoughts, perceptions, emotions, behaviors and relationships with others. (Mihail C. Pîrlog, *Medical Sociology Discipline* University of Medicine and Pharmacy of Craiova et al: Evaluation of the Psychoneurotic Tendencies Risk Using the Woodworth Mathews Personality Inventory in Non-Institutionalized Persons; v. 40(3); Jul-Sep 2014). We are told that such disorders include depression, bipolar disorder, schizophrenia and other psychoses as well as dementia and autism.

The research had been initiated as a follow-up to a World Health Organization (WHO) study in 2001. The study asserted that one in 10 of the world's 6.194 billion people suffered from a psychiatric disease. It reported that one in four humans could be affected by a psychiatry disorder spectrum found, of course, among the 567 or so of the DSM. In 2010, we learn, one of the most important causes in the "psychiatric disorder system," depression, ranked fourth, though it was to reach second place in 2020. Among the aggravating factors for abnormal and unexpected social behaviour are listed:

- daily stress
- cultural footprint
- uncertainty of tomorrow
- increased unemployment rates
- economical and financial crises
- extensive change in personal social status
- belonging to a disadvantaged social group or an ethnic minority
- genetic vulnerability, such as gender, age, family history of depression
- biological factors, such as birth trauma, neurodevelopmental abnormalities

All these were said to lead to important psychiatric diseases, such as major depressive disorders, schizophrenia and psychotic disorders. That pharmaceutical drugging could have anything to do with these developments is nowhere mentioned.

The female gender, phrased such to stick with the human equals animal theme, showed major risk for developing psychiatric disorders. It showed a clear predisposition for depressive and emotional disorders when above age 35 years. Another risk category to watch for instability and antisocial tendencies leading to pathological antisocial behavior was younger people. We read that in the psychosocial context, they were showing increasing rates of aggressive manifestations. That the absence of parental caring since the cradle could have anything to do with that is nowhere mentioned, either.

Social vulnerability, by the way, referred to in the Psychoneurotic Tendencies Risk evaluation, is the inability of people, organizations and societies to withstand adverse impacts from multiple stressors to which they are exposed. An example would be the effects of the early phase of COVID-19 on at least 40 million adults 18 and older. In devloping2021, they developed the most common of all mental health disorders in America, anxiety disorders (dbhutah.org/the-5-most-common-mental-disorders). These include:

- Panic disorder
- Social anxiety disorder
- Generalized anxiety disorder (GAD)
- Post-traumatic stress disorder (PTSD)
- Obsessive-compulsive disorder (OCD)

These adverse impacts on human mental health are in part due to characteristics inherent in social interactions, institutions and systems of cultural values. Individual stress-generated psychopathological characteristics can also blossom into patterns of population groups, the researchers assert. Does this quasi insanity as seen in Antifa and Black Lives Matter in their actions spring to mind?

According to these findings, the researchers voice, the ruling authorities must regularly assess the world population's mental health status. The COVID-19 jabs might have been an attempt to sidestep such expanse through euthanisation. This is the act or practice of ending the life of a person or animal having a medical condition that causes suffering perceived as incompatible with an acceptable quality of life. This could be done by lethal injection or by suspending certain medical treatments.

The 2019 onset of Covid-19 almost seems prophetic. It was just in 2014, when the Current Health Science Journal published Romanian M.C. Pirlog et al.'s multidisciplinary study (2009–2011) assessing the current situation of mental health and to identify population risk groups for developing psychiatric disorders using the Woodworth Mathews Inventory (76 items) on a randomly selected sample of 1,200 men and women in urban and rural areas of Romania. They discovered that multiple factors of vulnerability might very well lead to the development of abnormal social behaviours and psychiatric disorders in individuals and from them spread to population groups.

Their conclusions? Anyone over the age of 35 is vulnerable to develop depressive and emotional disorders, whereas younger folk people are predisposed for pathological anti-social behaviour due to instability and antisocial tendencies.

It was just in 2013, when we were told in the newly released DSM-5, that human depression of the art and craft of psychiatrists' developed human disorder system variety, themselves of course excluded, meant "a period of at least two weeks when a person experienced a depressed mood or loss of interest or pleasure in daily activities, and had a majority of specified symptoms, such as problems with sleep, eating, energy, concentration, or self-worth." This definition excludes grief after mourning.

Thank-heavens, most people struggling with depression try to grin and bear it, thus preventing themselves from being medicated into suicidal ideation, a side effect of all mind-altering drugs, which would occur if seeing a physician. And those who kicked us-the herd, into the Covid-19 shut-in and emotional strangulation through demanding our separation new full well, that the mask-wearing alone would create emotional turmoil, never mind asphyxia due to oxygen-deprivation associated with the permanent lowering of IQ. The forced shut-in and loss of social, physical contact akin to solitary confinement and incarceration, combined with pharmaceutical drugging, naturally creates ever increasing states of anxiety through emotional upheaval. The craft calls such emotional upheaval "psychiatric disabilities and disorders." These effects are well known to them, since they tried to torture to death WWI and WWII shell-shocked soldiers with such means. But that is mentioned nowhere, either.

Since the early 1800s, they tested their hypotheses and hallucinations about human emotional states of minds and tolerances on those they declared insane. Indeed, they tested them on almost anything alive and crawling, from rattus to lepus and cani, from mus to simian and normal homo sapiens who had been persuaded to trust them. They still are at it, as a matter of fact. Wit the ignorant, genuine PTSD journeyers being treated with dreamt-up, off-the-wall PTSD treatment concoctions. Wit the COVID-19 idiots—the experimental-drug-injection takers—now in an uproar and running to their physician, who poisoned them to begin with, or psycho-the-rapists, for help. Consequently diagnosed with PTSD, their spirit killed further with their mind-altering pharmaceutical prescription drug, assuring their faster demise into the beyond. But I rant.

Hypolocomotion, mind you, can also be activated by ketamine. This is a favourite drug administered by the experimental PTSD research cabal to genuine PTSD soldiers, veterans, police officers, firefighters and aircrew. They do this despite lack of knowledge of its long-term effects on humans' hippocampus. (Li, Qing: Chronic sub-anesthetic ketamine induces permanent hypolocomotion and impairment of hippocampus in adolescent cynomolgus monkeys; Neuroscience Letters, Volume 717, 19 January 2020; *Fallacy 1*). Ketamine is structurally related to the hallucinogen phencyclidine (PCP), better known as angel dust. It was developed by Parke-Davis Laboratories of Detroit, Michigan, in 1956 to use as an anaesthetic in human and veterinary medicine. Its side effects range from distorted self-perception to severe disorientation and unpredictable psychotic behaviour. So, its legal use was quickly discouraged, at least for a while. Parke, Davis and Company, by the way, began in 1866. Physician and pharmacist Dr. Samuel P. Duffield, who produced elixirs and ointments in his laboratory behind his drugstore, partnered with Hervey C. Parke, manager of several businesses in Michigan's Upper Peninsula. Their educational backgrounds unknown, they, just like the Rockefellers, were members of the Episcopal Church.

Parke-Davis had the first research laboratory in the American pharmaceutical industry, thus playing a major role in twentieth century drug development and drug standardization. One of the first American firms to produce antitoxins, hormones and other biologicals, it also created adrenalin, dilantin and chlorenpleniol. It also researched vitamins, disinfectants and penicillin before becoming a Pfizer subsidiary in 2000.

Chinese scientists began to again research ketamine in early 2000 using monkeys. They were trying to find out if a recreational dose of ketamine might produce permanent and irreversible deficits in brain functions, due to neurotoxic effects involving the activation of apoptotic pathways in the prefrontal cortex (Lin Sun et al: Chronic ketamine exposure induces permanent impairment of brain functions in adolescent cynomolgus monkeys;

Addiction Biology, 2012). In 2020, Li, Qing et al. conducted a similar study. They found that chronic sub-anesthetic ketamine induces permanent hypolocomotion and impairment of hippocampus in adolescent cynomolgus monkeys. They, consider these monkeys as equal to us, the human animals. (Neurosci Lett. 2020 Jan 19;717:134702).

"Ketamine can produce feelings of unreality; visual and sensory distortions; a distorted feeling about one's body; temporary unusual thoughts and beliefs; and a euphoria or a buzz," says John Krystal, M.D. He is chief of psychiatry at Yale-New Haven Hospital and Yale School of Medicine in Connecticut, where he researches ketamine's antidepressant effects. But it can also cause unconsciousness, high blood pressure and dangerously slowed breathing. It also creates long-term problems, such as ulcers, bladder- and stomach pain, kidney problems, depression and poor memory. At sub-anaesthetic doses administered to PTSD experiencers, its psychiatric side effects are pronounced. A majority of patients feel strange, spacey, woozy, a sense of floating, visual distortions and numbness.

Half of recipients furthermore have difficulty speaking, confusion, euphoria, drowsiness, and difficulty concentrating. Symptoms of psychosis such as going into a hole, disappearing, feeling as if melting, experiencing colors and hallucinations described by 6%–10% of recipients. Dizziness, blurred vision, dry mouth, hypertension, nausea, increased or decreased body temperature or feeling flushed are common non-psychiatric ketamine side effects. All adverse effects are most pronounced by the end of the injection. They reduce dramatically 40 minutes after, and completely disappear within four hours. However, it can be fatal if given to a drunk person, we are told.

Nevertheless, Michael Colla et al., of the Department of Psychiatry, Psychotherapy and Psychosomatics, Hospital of Psychiatry, University of Zurich in Switzerland, thought fit to publish their "Novel Insights Into the Neurobiology of the Antidepressant Response From Ketamine Research: A Mini Review" in 2021. It praised the *serendipitous* discovery of ketamine's antidepressant effects, which they say represents one of the major landmarks in neuro-psycho-pharmacological research of the last 50 years. In their opinion, ketamine provides an exciting challenge to traditional concepts of antidepressant drug therapy. They say it produces rapid antidepressant effects seemingly without targeting monoaminergic pathways, the neurotransmitter systems in the conventional way. These are the primary reward pathways in the human brain. (https://frontiersin.org/articles/10.3389/fnbeh.2021.759466/full). As a result, the advent of ketamine has spawned a plethora of neurobiological research into its putative mechanisms to yield new pharmacotherapy therapies beyond ketamine itself. Go figure.

For us who wondered, snake venoms used in both ketamine and the COVID-19 jabs have been artificially created for decades. Broadcasters Stew Peters and Mike Adams both interviewed Dr. Bryan Ardis, who brought this knowledge to the public attention on April 13th, 2022. In fact, the information could be found on the U.S. National Medicine website since 2019 for anyone who looked (https://www.brighteon.com/52774963-206a-42f6-9b3f-72bbd56dce27). Judy Mikovits is another one who put her life on the line with her presentation "Exposing the Plague of Corruption and How to Fight Back." She made it public that since 1986, the pharmaceutical drug industry was relieved by the U.S. government of all responsibilities for injuries caused by their vaccines.

There were 80,000 pages of COVID-19 drug injections' clinical trial documentation released by the FDA upon a FOIA request in April 2022. They apparently contain earth-shattering revelations about Pfizer's experimental vaccine injections, apparently confirming the intent to wilfully and knowingly destroy genus homo sapien. In other words, the plan was to kill off the human race (Naomi Wolf interview, *The War Room* April 18, 2022).

And why should this be of interest to us? Because it all began with German pharmacist Friedrich Wilhelm Adam Sertürner (1783 -1841). He isolated morphine from the poppy plant in the 1800s, inaugurating humans perpetual drugging down to heroin in aspirin. It pioneered alkaloid chemistry. Alkoloids are any of a class of nitrogenous organic compounds of plant origin, which have pronounced neurological and physiological actions on humans. They include drugs such as morphine, quinine and poisons such as atropine and strychnine. Alkaloids are primarily found in plants, and especially in certain families of flowering plants. As many as one-quarter of higher plants are estimated to contain alkaloids, of which several thousand different types have been identified (https://Britannica.com).

A given species in general contains only a few kinds of alkaloids, although both the opium poppy (*Papaver somniferum*) and the ergot fungus (*Claviceps*) contain about 30 different types each. Use of alkaloids go back to ancient civilizations. Their scientific study seems to have originated with German chemists Justus von Liebig (1803–1873) and Friedrich Wöhler (1800–1882) in the early nineteenth century. Their quantitative analytical methods established the constitution of newly isolated and synthesized carbon compounds. Their laboratory work established the basic model for chemical education taught to students who came from all over Europe and America. Their students then passed their methods on when returning home, training their nation's next generation of chemists.

One of the primary investigators into chemistry was Liebig's German student August Wilhelm Hofmann (1818–1892). He was the first professor of chemistry at the newly founded Royal College of Chemistry in London in 1844. He found that coal tar's major components were aromatic hydrocarbons. This class of compounds is based on the benzene molecule first isolated by Michael Faraday (1791–1867) in 1825 from compressed oil gas. His discovery led to the development of organic chemistry as a branch of chemistry. It focuses on the properties and reactions of compounds that contain carbon atoms. The carbon atom is the only element that can bond to itself, thus form chains that can contain hundreds of atoms. Carbon can also combine with a wide variety of other elements (encyclopedia.com).

Organic compounds such as ethyl alcohol, found in beer and wine, and acetic acid, used in vinegar, have been produced since antiquity. Other naturally occurring organic compounds have been used for millennia as dyes and medicinal agents. Production of organic substances in industrial plants first began to blossom when organic chemists began to examine the constituents of coal tar in the 1840s. Hofmann and his students succeeded in isolating at least 20 different substances from coal tar, the most important two being aniline (C6 H5NH 2), an organic analog of ammonia, and phenol (C6 H5OH), which was used as one of the first antiseptics. From then on, everybody who was anybody in the learned art and craft societies of medicine and chemistry were off to the races in henceforth organizing humanity's historical as well as physical and mental wellbeing. Today's largest pharmaceutical and chemical manufacturing conglomerates, such as Pfizer, Roche, Merck,

Ciba-Geiger, Eli Lilly, Bayer and numerous others, all having been established since the 1850's. The results are all around us, from the air we breathe to the food we eat and the way we think and feel.

But back to our self-proclaimed psychiatrists, who worked at the newly established Tavistock Clinic in the 1920s, getting their bearings in the "healing of the human soul." By 1923, former Chilean navy surgeon EA Hamilton Pearson and wartime hospital unit physician Alice Hutchison felt qualified enough to lecture their peers on psychology and abnormalities of childhood. So successful were they, that the Tavistock Clinic had to move to much bigger digs in 1932. It had almost an entire ground floor solely for its Children's Department, equipped with a large one-way mirror to observe the children's playroom behaviour. This would help them create new treatment methods of choice for perceived albeit undisclosed disorders observed in the children. A team of speech and play therapists, psychologists and social workers had also been added to the Clinic's team. They were to figure out how humans' neural network evolve and how to brainwash little ones from cradle to grave, it seems.

How they found the children they so vigilantly observed close-up is nowhere mentioned. Pearson, wanting a change of scenery, returned to sea as medical officer in the merchant marine in 1939, escorting ships carrying child evacuees overseas. At war's end, he joined the Home Office's Children's Branch as a senior medical officer staying there until his death.

Crichton-Miller, meanwhile, busied himself with reinforcing his Bowden House modus operandi at the Clinic. All employees had to integrate patients' biological, psychological and social states and status with their own and with each other, as well as applying them in their treatment considerations. Otherwise, he said, the craft, art and science of psychiatry would not fly. With that in mind, after the 1919 Versailles peace treaty, the at-peace parties in 1922 got together at the British War Office to discuss the shell-shock conundrum. Crichton-Miller declined to attend, stating his WWI experiences had so disillusioned and shocked him that recalling them would be too painful for his psychological wellbeing.

The conference produced recommendation to prevent war neurosis similar to Myers' principles. To recall, those were forward psychiatry, promptness of action, suitable environment and psychotherapeutic measures, though those measures were often limited to encouragement and reassurance (apa.org). As soldiers' breakdown rates became alarming, the term "combat fatigue" was introduced and the value of pre-selection was recognized. Thus, Binet - Simon's scales were used. Charles Samuel Myers set up the National Institute of Industrial Psychology to facilitate psychological research at the herd's workplaces, which could be used to shaft workers severely injured in the line of duty as well as shell-shocked soldiers. Myers merely duplicated German Kaiser Wilhelm's concept of the Workers' Compensation Board (WCB), pushed through the German Reichstag in November 1918 moments before he abdicated and fled to the city of Doorn in the Netherlands. To this very day, it remains so extraordinarily competent in destroying the severely injured workers, the genuine PTSD affected included.

It took Crichton-Miller until 1940 to overcome his WWI war trauma and get back into full swing of himself. That was when he explained and elaborated on his shell-shock treatment hypotheses and the forward psychiatry principles in the *Journal of the Royal Army*

Medical Corps. It earned him scathing criticism, the reviewer judging him to suffer a "lack of understanding and conviction" of the military fighting forces and the soldiers caught in war.

By that time, WWII was in full swing. At London's Maudsley Hospital, the shell-shocked were already lining up to be treated with barbiturate abreaction. This was advocated for quick relief from severe anxiety and hysteria and administered intravenously with anaesthetics, such as somnifaine, paraldehyde, and Sodium amytal. These had been in style since German chemist Johann Friedrich Wilhelm Adolf von Baeyer's (1835–1917,) a member of the Ashkenazi Jewish Hitzig family, managed the synthesis of malonylurea (barbituric acid). That brought on the evolution of barbiturates, drugs that act as central nervous system depressants.

After completing his doctorate on arsenic methyl chloride in 1860, Baeyer became a lecturer at the Berlin Gewerbeinstitut, the Royal Trade Academy. In 1871, he became a chemistry professor at the University of Strassbourg before succeeding von Liebig as chemistry professor at the University of Munich in 1875Discovering barbituric acid, the parent compound of barbiturates, was just one of his chief achievements. Others include:

- synthesizing and describing the plant dye indigo
- discovering the phtalein dyes
- investigating polyacetylenes, oxonium salts, nitroso compounds and poly-acetylenes from 1860 onwards

He was the first to propose the correct formula for indole, an aromatic heterocyclic organic compound. A solid at room temperature, it occurs naturally in human feces with an intense fecal odor. At very low concentrations, however, it has a flowery smell and is a constituent of many perfumes. It also occurs in coal tar, we learn.

So versatile and accomplished was Baeyer in his field, that the Royal Society of London awarded him the Davy Medal in 1881. This was named after chemist and inventor of the Davy Lamp, Humphry Davy (1778-1829). It was awarded for Baeyer's work with indigo (genus *Indigofera*), a large genus of more than 750 species of shrubs, trees, and herbs in the pea family (*fabaceae*) alone. The American Academy of Arts and Sciences followed suite, electing him a foreign honorary member in 1884. And King Ludwig of Bavaria raised him to hereditary nobility on his 50th birthday, conferring the "von" distinction on him. In recognition of his services in the advancement of organic chemistry and the chemical industry through his work on organic dyes and hydro-aromatic compounds, he received the Nobel Prize in Chemistry in 1905. Filled with wonderful vitality and known as one of the best teachers in the world of organic chemistry, von Baeyer continued to work almost until the moment of his death in 1917.

The psychology art and craft magicians found for some of Baeyer's barbituric acid offspring found themselves at home in WWI military hospitals. There, they could practice on the shell-shocked by all WWI's warring nations in the ideal experimental laboratory research facilities. Barbiturates are effective as anxiolytics, hypnotics and anticonvulsants. All have physical and psychological addiction and overdose potential, along with a slew of other adverse effects.

More than 2500 derivatives of barbituric acid have been developed since Baeyer's discovery. Only 50 of them were eventually used for human consumption. During WWI and

WWII, many of them were imposed on desperate and traumatized soldiers as a cure-all for anxiety and pick-me-uppers. And for schizophrenic patients and the shell shocked alike, they were used as sedatives, hypnotic agents and so-called "sleep cures".

One of Britain's hospitals embracing barbiturates with open arms was the Maudsley Hospital in Southwark, named after its co-founder Henry Maudsley (1835 -1918). Born on an isolated Yorkshire farm, he received his M.D. in 1857 at the University College London Medical School. He earned 10 gold medals in the process, even while thought to have incessantly found pleasure in antagonising and quarrelling with his teachers and expertly circumventing subjects and clinical work he found onerous and non-important.

After his idea to pursue a career in surgery went sideways, he decided to work for the East India Company, which necessitated a stint in a mental asylum. Maudsley therefore went as physician to the West Riding Pauper Lunatic Asylum of Wakefield, West Yorkshire, open since 1818, and the Essex County Asylum of Brentwood, Essex, which had been established in 1853 for a couple of years. He then dropped the East India Company idea. Instead, at age 23, he accepted the position of medical superintendent of the small, middle-class Manchester Royal Lunatic Asylum. It had opened as the Manchester Lunatic Hospital in 1766 before relocating om 1849 to Cheadle, 10 miles to the south, as the Manchester Royal Hospital for the Insane.

When it was founded, only two similar institutions existed in England. One of them was the Bethlem—Bedlam. It was founded as the Priory of the New Order of our Lady of Bethlehem in London during the reign of Henry III (1207-1272) in 1247. The historical equivalent of the psychiatric hospital, the word asylum reflects the religious meaning of a refuge provided for anyone in need of assistance, in this case the mentally ill. Henry VIII shut down the Roman Catholic Church after the Pope refused him the divorce from Catherine of Aragon (1485 -1536). He expropriated its monasteries throughout England during the 1530. This rattled the country's social fiber to the core, throwing monks, paupers and emotionally ill to the dogs, henceforth almost entirely cared for by their families. Those without family ended up homeless, destitute, begging for food and shelter, just as many American PTSD-afflicted soldiers do today after rendering "service to their country."

By the eighteenth century, treatment of madness had changed little. With the Age of Enlightenment in Western Europe came despite advances in science and medicine. But there was still little understanding of the causes of mental illness. In Britain, it took until the 1700s before a few private institutions sprang up, to which wealthy families send their "mad" relatives to be cared for. The poor emotionally unstable would find shelter in workhouses, prisons and in the odd Church of England parish. The Hospital of St. Mary of Bethlem, Bedlam, continued to provide asylum for the destitute insane.

After 1634, Bethlem's medical staff was supposedly elected by the Court of Governors. In a bid to prevent profiteering at the expense of patients, all were eventually salaried with limited responsibility for the hospital's financial affairs. Personal connections, interests and occasionally royal favour were nevertheless pivotal factors in the appointment of physicians. Although the posts were strongly contested, nepotistic appointment practices played a significant role. Thus, the election in 1728 of Doctor James Monro as physician kicked off a 125-year rule by the Monro family. The family controlled the asylum for four generations of fathers and sons. (*The Masters of Madness: How the Monro family ruled Bedlam*; https://findmypast.com/2015).

The family so prominent in the treatment of madness hailed from the Highlands of Scotland. They were considered well educated, cultured and connoisseurs of the arts. But they applied regimens to care for the mentally impaired at Bedlam, that were even by the standards of their day and the models of their time thought barbaric in their brutality. And they contributed nothing to the understanding of the mentally ill (I. Macintyre, A. Munro: The Monro dynasty and their treatment of madness in London; Neurosciences and History 2015; 3(3):116-124). The Monroes invited members of the public – for a fee – to explore the hospital during the evening and poke fun at the inmates, who were often chained inside their tiny rooms. If the subject wasn't being entertaining enough, observers prodded them with sticks until they were.

The staff at Bethlem treated inmates with the same compassion as their bosses did. One horrific example was that of the apothecary John Halsam, who was appointed by Thomas Monro in 1795. Halsam believed that to be cured, the mentally infirm first needed to be broken. This entailed a variety of gruesome tortures, so widely vilified that Quaker philanthropist Edward Wakefield managed to gain entry to the hospital – despite the efforts of Bethlem personnel - accompanied by a governor and member of Parliament.

What they found was sufficient to merit an inquiry, and precipitated the resignation of Thomas Monro after he was denounced as "wanting in humanity". One victim, a patient named James Norris, had been trapped in a harness for 14 years. This was attached to chains, which the staff would pull at random intervals, slamming him into the wall. As time passed, the Monroes were increasingly portrayed as stereotypical "mad doctors" in plays and poems, and famous in popular culture thanks to cartoonists, pamphleteers and Grub-Street scribblers (https://findmypast.com/blog/history/the-masters-of-madness-how-the-monro-family-ruled-bedlam.)

After Thomas Monro stepped down in 1816, Bethlem started to take small steps towards more humane methods of treatment. When the massive Broadmoor Criminal Lunatic Asylum opened in 1863, Bethlem's criminally insane inmates were transferred there, which lessened its association with violent madness. The first patient was a female admitted for infanticide in May 1863, notes describing her as being 'feeble minded'. It has been suggested by an analysis of her records that she was driven insane by congenital syphilis. It apparently took until February 1864, before the first male patient was inscribed for reasons unknown. After that, enrollment ballooned rapidly. In 1902 the facility again needed extension, but we will return to the Monroes at this point.

At Bedlam, admission fees to observe the sport provided by the directorate was a significant proportion of the hospital's revenue. It was enhanced by food and other donations, which were often sold, leaving patients starving. The Monroes also charged people to have their critics put away or for husbands to lock up their wives.

But in 1751, they got competition in their humanist endeavors, when a group of apothecaries, opened St Luke's Hospital for Lunatics with the aim to shelter the incurable pauper lunatics. The word "apothecary", by the way, is derived from the Greek apotheca, a place where wine, spices and herbs were stored. One of these so philanthropically inclined was William Battie, sometimes spelled Beattie (1703–1776). He had trained and governed Bedlam for 10 years before being chosen as its first chief physician. Renowned as an eccentric and cantankerous humorist, he immediately stopped exposing patients to public viewing. He ordered that their medical treatments would consist of cold plunge baths and vomiting cures to shake his charges out of their lunatic insanity. He also advocated a non-restraint system, although sometimes manacles and other restraints continued to be used. And where had Beattie acquired his knowledge about lunacy and those deemed to be afflicted by it?

Educated at Eton and Cambridge, a fellow of the Royal Society and later president of the Royal College of Physicians, Battie was reputed both for his scholarly work and his anatomical dissection demonstrations. Yet it was the "mad business," as he described it, which had caught his imagination. It inspired him to own two private lunatic institutions for the wealthy. It propelled him into the governor position at Bethlem Hospital. And in 1751, he made a splash at St Luke's, just opposite to Bethlem. There, he inaugurated unprecedented standards of care for those deemed to be incurably insane, among whom the shell-shocked would in time rank in numbers (https://ncbi.nlm.nih.gov/pmc/articles/PMC1952499/).

In 1758, he became the first British physician to publish his ideas about the treatment of mental illness in his lengthy book *A Treatise on Madness*. It was in large part a critique of Bethlem's coercive and barbaric custodial treatment methods in overcrowded cells, overseen by jeering visitors. Battie instead argued for custom-tailored patient management. This would include cleanliness, good food, fresh air and distraction from friends and family. Thus, he carried the opinion that mental dis-eases originated from sufferers' social environments and physical brain and body dysfunction, rather than internal workings of the mind (https://bible.ca/psychiatry/psychiatry-history-mad-doctors-william-battie-1703-1776ad.htm).

Battie believed that Christians were generally mentally ill, reflecting todays learned society's atheism in general and in psychiatry in particular. For Battie all mental illness had physical causes. He had borrowed this etiology of insanity from Nicholas Robinson, doctor and governor of Bedlam. In 1729, Robinson wrote a book in which he stated that bad nerves were the reason for madness. "When once these finest Fibres of the Brain, that immediately support the regular Exercise of our Thoughts, have suffered such a fatal Shock; no Operation of the Mind, that is regular, sedate, and uniform, can ever after be expected." (William Battie, 1703–1776 AD) They were quacks in the eighteenth century and they are still quacks today!

Battie's and Robinson's idea of "weakness of nerves" is seen today in products like "Geritol." These are modern versions of eighteenth century "nerve tonics" to keep us healthy and ward off insanity! He also believed that the mind could induce madness through joy and anger, because it over stimulated the nerves. He thought that laziness and gluttony induced madness because they clogged up the nerves: "Viscera being slopped in such a manner as to compress the many nervous filaments ... stomach, intestines, and uterus, are frequently the real seats of Madness."

Battie claimed neither faith nor disbelief in God. H believed that nothing is known or can be known of the existence or nature of God or of anything beyond material phenomena.

Therefore, he full-heartedly rejected the idea that anxiety could be a spiritual problem. In his view, whilst recognizing anxiety as common to all humanity, insisted that only those with weak, bad or out-of-shape nerve fibers could be afflicted with it. That set the tone for chemical humanist psychiatry practiced since Flexner's 1910 report made it mandatory in the U.S. . And now, all self-respecting psychiatrists prescribe mind-altering drugs to all and sundry of the emotionally rattled. They never propose somatic disciplines to help with the "depletion", "revulsion", "removal" and "expulsion" of the madness. Nor do they propose good nutrition and living condition, as Battie to his credit did. Rather, their steadfastly maintained malnutrition, overall rotten living conditions and associated emotional upheaval and despair could cause insanity. And it often does, because they have eliminated anything helpful from their pharma-psycho-therapy methods of healing their emotionally dis-eased patients since Flexner's Carnegie paid 1910 Report.

That somatic exercises for healing of body and soul have been used for thousands of years seems to have escaped their attention or is wilfully ignored by them. The oldest one known to humanity is the practice of yoga. This physical, mental and spiritual exercise originated in India long before 500 BC. Its ultimate goal is spiritual, the seeking of self- realisation, finding one's true Self. Yoga is for liberation from earthly desires and worldly attachments. It is a spiritual journey seeking freedom from the cycle of death and rebirth by way of breath-control, meditation and adopting specific bodily postures to reach and maintain a permanent state of bliss and peace.

The word "yoga" simply means to join, to strive for the union of the ātmā, the Self, with the jīvātmā, the Higher Self of our soul, with paramātmā, God the Creator of all. We are caught in the web of worldly attachments and swinging between momentary happiness and despair. The yogic path enables us to stabilize our emotions and alleviate sadness and despair by removing the veil of ignorance and wrong knowledge. These are the true causes of our attachment to the material world. It gradually propels us towards our true Self, which hovers in constant indisturbable equilibrium between success and failure, pain and pleasure, happiness and sadness. Yoga is the tool to such achievement.

Other somatic exercise forms are the traditional Chinese somatic practices of Qigong and Tai-chi. These moving meditations coordinate slow flowing movement and deep rhythmic breathing to create a calm meditative state of mind to balance and cultivate qi, our "life energy." Aikido is a Japanese somatic exercise in martial art form, creating internal awareness and an emotional state of non-aggression life energy—ki—development.

Keep in mind that Battie viewed lunacy "... as manageable as many other distempers, which are equally dreadful and obstinate, and yet are not looked upon as incurable; such unhappy objects ought by no means to be abandoned, much less shut up in loathsome prisons as criminals or nuisances to society." (Shorter, Edward. *A History of Psychiatry: From the Era of the Asylum to the Age of Prozac*; Wiley; 1st edition. 1997) Therefore, such soothing somatic exercise might have been unknown or alien to his line of thinking. Caustically hostile to Christianity and religion in general as he was, he never utters a word about the human soul or spirit. No one could rock him of his belief that life choices, sin, thinking too hard and being over emotional break the nerves of the brain and cause insanity. As he said, "all the Decays of the Nerves and Lownesses of the Spirits are mechanically accounted for ... [as] Fits had so weakened the Fibres of the Optic Nerves... When once these finest Fibres of the Brain, that immediately support the regular Exercise of our Thoughts, have suffered such a fatal Shock, no Operation of the Mind, that is regular, sedate, and uniform, can ever after be expected." These he felt called for more drastic measures to kick the brain into normal operation, whatever normal meant to him (*History of Psychiatry;* bible.ca).

With his opinions carrying forth, the medical profession declared, that all human emotional dis-eases originated in humans' physical brain. The hunt for their precise location began! This created the art and craft of neuroscience, first practiced in gruesome experiments on cani and rattus and the insane, until the WWI shell-shocked presented as experimental life laboratory rats. Those who engaged in the field were generally atheists like Battie. In his day, they rejected the idea that anxiety could be a created by emotional and spiritual upheaval and the profound questioning of the reason for life and everything in it. For them, innately weak since birth, bad and out of shape nerve fibers are the reason for genuine PTSD developments, for example. Battie's idea that the mind could be severely rattled through joy and anger due to nervous system overstimulation gave mental health magicians the ideas of bipolar disorder and a slew of other mental disorder definitions and classifications. No wonder they love Battle to pieces. He gave them the template for psychiatry's evolution and diagnoses nomenclature to this very day. He practically invented the 567 human mental disorders we presently are accused of possessing.

Before Battie's investiture at St. Luke, John Monro had trained him well. Monro was Bedlam's chief physician and a graduate of St John's College, Oxford, in 1737. He had studied in Edinburgh, Leiden, Paris and Rome for 10 years. In 1753, Monro joined Bedlam as physician after his father, Bethlem's chief physician, died in 1752. As soon as he was elected Royal College of Physicians fellow that same year, Monro responded to Battie's A Treatise on Madness saying about the curing of those judged insane:

> "Notwithstanding we are told in this treatise, that madness rejects all general methods, I will venture to say, that the most adequate and constant cure of it is by evacuation; which can alone be determined by the constitution of the patient and the judgment of the physician. The evacuation by vomiting is infinitely preferable to any other, if repeated experience is to be depended on..."[

Meanwhile, Battie was at St. Luke's, where he disallowed Bedlam's ongoing practice of charging visitors to observe the lunatics to satisfy "the impertinent curiosity of those, who think it pastime to converse with Madmen and to play upon their passions." He thought some forms of insanity incurable in any way regardless of methods used, saying: "Original [incurable] Madness therefore, like most other morbid cases, rejects all general methods: ... bleeding, blisters, caustics, rough cathartics, the gums and faetid antihysterics, opium, mineral waters, cold bathing, and vomits." All these were practiced at Bedlam. Like Monro, Battie believed that "consequential madness" could be best cured with "vomits." This was due to the physical shaking of the nerves and brain matter that resulted from the convulsions of vomiting. (William Battie. *A Treatise on Madness*. 1758). The art and craft of the science of psychology in WWI reversed their verdict. They henceforth claimed that "shell-shock came from the brain's shaking due to Nobel's new-fangled weaponry." (ibid)

Monro could not care less about Battie's ideas and hypotheses. He continued to allow paying visitors to observe and converse with Bedlam's inmates until 1770, when he restricted the practice somewhat.

Many of Battie's innovations had already been made and in print by others operating smaller institutions for the emotionally destitute hundreds of years earlier. Battie is said to only have treated new patients with a kinder, gentler version of the tortures used at Bedlam for a short while. He would disperse them in a speedy fashion, if not fixed to his satisfaction, and he would classify them as suffering an incurable "original madness." This meant ceasing all treatments and housing in the asylum's section for the terminally insane (//research.ncl.ac.uk/pauperlives/workhousemedicalisation.pdf). When so judged, he noted, the incurable suddenly cured themselves and recovered "understanding." This led him to conceive that the insane had the power to act "normal" of their own free will, if they so wished. This led to the craft's hypothesis of "malingering", henceforth fervently used to malign and even kill WWI and WWII shell-shocked soldiers and genuine PTSDS experiencers alike to this very day. Back then it was military trials with threat of death. Now it's cutting us off from financial compensation for injury incurred in the line of duty. That's what the WCB and other insurers do to force the injured to spring up and regain their "understanding." Or else, it can wear us out and grind us down to make us fade into the woodwork by way of the perpetual threat of destitution they inflict on us. In this manner, we will reach what Battie phrased "their personal end of the line, they wanted out of jail."

Battie is also the genius who conceived the division of madness into "original" and "consequential" mental illnesses. Suffice to say, that even 300 years after Battie engaged into the craft with a passion, the definition and causes of human mental dis-eases and disorders are still deemed unclear. Theories swarm from every arts and science field, and with categories abounding in abundance depending on one's social, cultural, religious and educational background. And when rendering an opinion or a diagnosis on a subject, the result depends entirely on a combination thereof and the "inspector's" perception of "inspectee's" look and behavior. They insist that deviation from accepted social norms might be associated with particular regions or functions of the brain. But they maintain that cultural and religious beliefs and social norms should be taken into account when making a diagnosis on the PTSD-afflicted. (*Diagnostic and Statistical Manual of Mental Disorders* (5th ed.). Arlington, VA: American Psychiatric Publishing. pp. 101–05) However, this never occurred with any of the 23 professionals I was forced to deal with.

Henry Maudsley entered the scene in 1858, 100 years after Monro and Battie had set the ground-rules for the human mental health dictates. This aspiring healer of the human soul was physician at the Manchester Royal Lunatic Asylum. There he stayed until 1862, when he moved back to London. In 1865, he gained a position at the tiny six-room West London Hospital, founded in 1856 to cater to acute conditions. He had earlier failed to secure a position at the Bethlem. That same year, he commenced as co-editor of the *Journal of Mental Science*. It had been established in 1853 as the *Asylum Journal* to spread the word about the craft's research and discovery in humans' emotional attitudes, aptitudes and vulnerabilities. Thus, all could jump into humanity's lucrative narrative manipulation into perversity and destruction.

Its title changed in 1855 to the *Asylum Journal of Mental Science* and again to *Journal of Mental Science* in 1858. It was not until 1963 that it got its present name, the *British Journal of Psychiatry*. What has not changed is that it still publishes research papers from around the world, as well as editorials, review articles, commentaries on contentious articles and short reports. It also has a comprehensive book review section and correspondence column, in which *Fallacy* will never be mentioned. Peer-reviewed, it covers all branches of medicine and psychiatry with particular emphasis on clinical aspects of each topic. This means it publishes patients' clinical examination. It provides information about possible causes, sets of causes or manners of causation of the purported disease or condition. It gives details of the patients:

- demographics, including age, gender, race, occupation
- left- or right-handedness
- history of the present complaint
- past medical history including past and/or present drug treatment
- family history and social history, as we read that the temporal evolution of problems the patient is experiencing provides important clues as to their nature

Without these clues furnished by the genuine PTSD journeyer, the inspecting mental health investigator would, of course, be up the creek without a paddle. Remember Frances Allan's verdict on the craft and, come to think of it, and the verdict of his peers R.D. Laing, Thomas Szasz and Peter Breggin?

So, Maudsley went full steam ahead in the métier. Between 1869 and 1879, he held a professorship in medical jurisprudence at University College London. While there, he married psychiatrist John Conolly's (1794 -1866) daughter in 1866. Upon his father-in-law's death that same year, he took over his private mental asylum, Lawn House. It housed six wealthy women. He withdrew from public employment soon thereafter to focus on his extremely lucrative private consultancy for the often aristocratic, very wealthy and emotionally needy in a London West End clinic.

And from whence sprang his betrothed's father, John Conolly? Born of an Irish family in Lincolnshire, England, he spent four years as lieutenant in the Cambridge shire Militia. He lived for a year in France before deciding to care for those deemed insane. Perhaps he was inspired by the physically and emotionally injured he saw during the Napoleonic wars' mayhem and the slaughter's aftermath. After his graduation from the University of Edinburgh with a M.D. degree in 1821. By 1828, he had risen to the position of professor of the practice of medicine at University College London. By 1830, he published his book *Indications of Insanity, With Suggestions for the Better Protection and Care of the Insane* from knowledge he acquired we do not know where.

In 1832, Connolly founded a small medical association called the Provincial Medical and Surgical Association. He did this together with medical surgeons Sir Charles Hastings (1794 -1866) and Sir John Forbes. His brother, William Brice Conolly, became the "Widows and Orphans Benevolent Fund" treasurer and secretary there. It laid the foundation for the British Medical Association (BMA) in 1856, which grew into today's registered trade union for United Kingdom's physicians, although it does not regulate or certify them. That responsibility rests with the British General Medical Council, headquartered at Tavistock Square, London. It also has national offices in Cardiff, Belfast and Edinburgh, a European office in Brussels and a number of offices in other English regions, we read. The BMA has a range of representative and scientific committees and the motto "to promote the medical and allied sciences, and to maintain the honour and interests of the medical profession," piss on patients. It is the sole contract negotiator between British physicians and the by British National Health Service (NHS).

And from whence did Conolly's buddies Hastings and Foster spring? Hastings was the ninth of 15 children born at Ludlow in Shropshire into the family of Reverend James Hastings (1756-1856). He began his medical career as apprentice to an apothecary before, at age 16, attending anatomy school in London. At the ripe age of 18, he achieved the position of house surgeon at the Worcester Infirmary, built in 1771. At 21, he entered the University of Edinburgh and was elected Royal Medical Society (RMS) student-run president. He gained his medical degree and returned to the Worcester Infirmary in 1818 to continue looking after his impaired. He declined a lectureship at Edinburgh in order to do so. In 1850, Queen Victoria awarded him the knighthood for his pioneering work with the insane, his resolve and his social conscience.

His companion John Forbes (1787–1861) was born at Cuttlebrae in North-East Scotland. Soon thereafter, he developed an ardent desire to enlist as a surgeon in the British Royal Navy. He proceeded to Edinburgh to fulfill his dream to obtain the Diploma of the College of Surgeons and enter the Royal Navy's medical service in 1806 as a temporary assistant surgeon. Henceforth, he spent his time at sea, apart from a short period of retraining in naval medicine and surgery in 1811 at the massive Haslar Hospital.

The Admiralty, the government agency responsible for the command of the British Royal Navy until 1964, built the Royal Naval Hospital Haslar in 1753. At the time, it was the largest brick building in Europe and cost over £100,000 to build (about £4,4 million today.) It was set on a peninsula. The guard towers, high brick walls, bars and railings throughout the property prevented all and sundry from going AWOL. Many of the patients had been press ganged into and went nuts from the notoriously brutal treatment on British navy vessels.

Haslar included an asylum for sailors with psychiatric disorders. Between 1758 and 1785, they were placed under the tender loving care of Chief Physician to the Royal Naval Hospital Dr. James Lind (1716–1794). He was considered a pioneer of maritime hygiene, preventive medicine and nutrition. In 1747, he conducted the first known randomized clinical trial in modern medical history on board the Royal Navy ship *Salisbury*, on British channel and sea traffic control. He set out to prove that citrus fruits could cure scurvy.

Shell-shock posed a conundrum for the medical profession. Scurvy did the same in the later eighteenth century. Blame it all on British clockmaker's John Harrison's chronometer, invented in the 1770s, It could fix positions at sea and keep time accurately, regardless of changes in humidity or temperature. It allows ships to make long voyages out of sight of land, preventing them from carrying fruit and vegetables on long journeys. Over two million sailors were said to have died of scurvy since the sixteenth century. The loss of half a crew was common on a lengthy voyage, although it could be much worse (usni.org/magazines/naval-history-magazine/2021/february/finding-cure-scurvy). Portuguese seafarer Vasco da Gama (ca. 1460-1524) made his first voyage to India by way of Cape of Good Hope between 1497 and 1499. There was just one landfall at the Malabar Coast near the area of Kozhikode, in English known as Calicut, in the state of Kerala. This was the first European to connect the Occident with the Orient in modern history. He lost 116 of his 170 men on that exploration, almost all to scurvy.

British Commodore George Anson (1697 -1762), son of William Anson of Shugborough in Staffordshire whose wife Isabella Carrier brother-in-law was the Earl of Macclesfield and Lord Chancellor fared even worse. He had entered the navy at age 15, while England was at war with Spain. In 1740, he led a squadron of eight ships on a mission to disrupt or capture the Pacific Ocean possessions of the Spanish Empire. He returned to Britain in 1744 by way of China on his flagship, the *Centurion*, the only ship to survive the voyage. He had 188 men of the original 1,854left, most of the others having succumbed to scurvy.

By the mid-1700s, scurvy went from solely having been judged a seafarers' affliction, to taking on military, colonial and economic dimensions. Loss of money was at stake. But attempts to deal with it had been hampered by confusion. Just as with PTSD, those who wrote about it had seldom experienced it themselves and, as Lind mentioned, "no physician conversant with this disease at sea had undertaken to throw light upon the subject."

So, Lind set out to correct the issue.

While Lind puttered about in the British Channel on the HMS Salisbury, scurvy raised its ugly head. After two months at sea, there were 12 cases of it, so he began his trial. He divided sufferers into six pairs, all of them daily receiving precisely the same basic food, drink and care. And each pair received one of six additional substances daily:

- cider
- elixir vitriol (dilute sulfuric acid)
- vinegar
- seawater
- a paste of plant extracts
- two oranges and a lemon

The trial's conclusion? Only the pair given citrus fruit made a quasi-instantaneous recovery. Lind published his findings in "A treatise of the scurvy, an inquiry into the nature, causes and cure of the disease" in 1753 (Edinburgh: Printed by Sands, Murray and Cochran for A Kincaid and A Donaldson, 1753). The British Royal Navy graciously ignored it until 1795, when it began to supply scant citrus rations as standard ship provisions. This henceforth bestowed the nickname "Limeys" on all British-born (http lshtm.ac.uk/aboutus/introducing/history/frieze/james-lind).

Mind you, Michael Bartholomew of the History of Science Department, Arts Faculty at the Open University, Walton Hall, Milton Keynes, Great Britain felt we should not be harsh on the Admiralty. It, along with many naval doctors and the redoubtable Captain Cook, were not being obtuse when "overlooking" Lind's experiment's significance. They mused that Lind had merely documented that limes cure scurvy. He had failed to consider WHY it occurred. He stated in the *Treatise's* chapter VI, in which he sets out what he calls his own "theory of the disease," that scurvy is a disease of faulty digestion and excretion. Of course, neither has anything to do with it, as it is a acquired by lack of nutrition. The Admiralty, in other words, wanted the reason rather than the cure, according to Bartholomew.

James Cook (1728 –1779) was the most famous of British explorers. He was a cartographer and British Royal Navy captain par excellence. He had no doubt that the principal cause of his crews' health was their daily doses of sauerkraut and malt. In a paper he delivered to the Royal Society, he said: 'This is without doubt one of the best antiscorbutic [effective against scurvy] sea-medicines yet found out; and if given in time will, with proper attention to other things, I am persuaded, prevent the scurvy from making any great progress for a considerable time." That, too, fell on deaf ears (Jonathan Lamb: *Captain Cook and the Scourge of Scurvy*; Last updated 2011-02-17; bbc.co).

Cook joined the British merchant navy as a teenager and the Royal Navy in 1755 at 27. He is famous for his three voyages in and about the Pacific Ocean around New Zealand and Australia, terrifying the natives and missing Antarctica by a hair's breadth. He was elected a member of the Royal Society in 1776. That same year, it bestowed the Copley Gold Medal in recognition of his contributions to improving the health of seamen. This happened even though he could "... only offer vague and unqualified opinions on the most effective anti-scorbutics, because he was not conducting controlled trials." In other words, he failed to present empirical scientific evidence of his success to heal scurvy.

That, however, was of no consequence to the ruling powers. The tyrannical Luciferic consciousness feeds on human trauma, and must maintain it for its sustenance, healing for it meaning starvation (Endall Beall. *We Are Not Alone: The Luciferian Agenda of the Mother Goddess (The Evolution of Consciousness)*. CreateSpace Independent Publishing Platform. First Edition 2016).

The dissenting voices began to squabble. The learned society of physicians argued about the scurvy issue, as they do throughout the league about everything and anything to do with the human animal. They remain ego driven and aggressive so as to make a name for themselves in their Luciferic consciousness style. A fine example is how they benefit from arguing and perverting the reasons of genuine PTSD since bringing it into their own perverted, Darwinian hypothesis-ruled atheistic realm since WWI.

At the admiralty's massive Haslar Hospital, the first superintending physician assigned to the Royal Navy's lunatics' section, PTSD inflicted without a doubt among them, was physician James Scott (1785–1859). He was a member of the Edinburgh Phrenological Society. Little else is known about him, but the society to which he belonged had been founded in 1820 by Edinburgh lawyer George Combe (1788-1858). Combe was one of 13 children of an Edinburgh brewer sharing a crowded home with servants at the base of Edinburgh castle. Georgy-boy felt ignored throughout his childhood. He refused to seek meaningful employment as brewers, tanners, sailors or bakers as his brothers had. Instead, he attended classes at Edinburgh University between 1802 and 1804. He apprenticed as a clerk at the legal firm Writers to the Signet. And he participated in the Forum, a weekly debating society where young men discussed issues of the day, including the death penalty, the comparative advantages and disadvantages of matrimony versus celibacy and whether or not novel-reading is favourable or prejudicial to morality. Only his younger brother Andrew showed equal ambitions in bettering his station in life by becoming a physician.

Many who knew George Combe saw him as something of an opinionated egoist. He was exceedingly keen to acquire as much attention for himself as possible, as long as it was respectable and, as Combe's nephew Sir James Cox later recalled, could possibly fulfill his "strong desire for posthumous fame." (victorianweb.org). Combe had been in practice as a Writers to the Signet clerk for three years, when he met German physician Johann Gaspar Spurzheim (1776-1832) in 1816. Spurzheim was the chief proponent of phrenology, a field of neuroscience focusing on the shapes of the skull in relation to the activity levels of certain functional areas of the brain.

Little is known of his family background, other than that he, Spurzheim, was born in 1776 near the city of Trier. The city was founded by the Celts in the late 4th century BC. The Romans conquered it300 years later, renaming it "Augusta Treverorum." It is considered Germany's oldest city. Spurzheim studied medicine at the University of Vienna, where he met German neuro-anatomist and physiologist Franz Josef Gall (1758 -1828) in 1800. Gall ascribed human cerebral functions to various areas of the brain, termed "localization", He created of phrenology, the attempt to divine individual intellect and personality from an examination of a skull's shape.

Gall, looking astonishingly like Ulrich Leonard Tölle (1948-) better known as Eckhart Tolle, a German-born self-help teacher and author influenced by books of the German Khazarian Joseph Anton Schneiderfranken (1876-1943), taught a course on the brain and its parts. He soon hired his student Spurzheim as an assistant and things took off from there (Mohammad Bilal et al: Johann Gaspar Spurzheim: *A Life Dedicated to Phrenology;* Cureus. 2017 May; 9(5): e1295).

Spurzheim relinquished the study of the brain as a whole. He began to analyze its parts in relation to specific prominences of the cranium that in his opinion signified different talents and faculties. He called his hypotheses "the Doctrine of the Mind". Gall and Spurzheim then partnered up, with Spurzheim single-handedly undertaking all brain dissections in Gall's lectures of unmentioned species, while Gall explained the findings. The brains' meticulous dissection was not Spurzheim's only contribution. Even though his beliefs about human brain function localization ran parallel to Gall's, he differed in various points and said so. For example, declaring he felt that there were 35 functional organs in the brain, while Gall found only 27. These functional parts were what caused the overlying skull to protrude outwards. By identifying a skull's shape physicians could predict humans' mental capability or traits, according to the theory. This has been a cause of debate among neurological authorities ever since.

After these two ideologues had a falling out in 1812, Spurzheim went out lecturing on his own on "The Physiognomical" System of Drs. Gall and Spurzheim. In 1813, he gave his first lecture without Gall in the amphitheater of Abernethy, an ancient settlement near Perth in Scotland.

Although unable to persuade his audience towards phrenology's validity, he did set a new standard of brain dissection, which earned him universal respect. He stopped at Edinburgh next, in part to refute Scottish anatomist John Gordon (1786-1818). Gordon had been president of the Royal Medical Society in 1806. But in 1813, he had caused an international stir in the learned society by debunking the new science of phrenology, and in the process gravely criticized both Spurzheim and Gall.

Gordon was born to a wine merchant and banker in Forres in northern Scotland in 1786. At age 19, he gained his M.D. at the University of Edinburgh. He went on to study anatomy in London, where at age 20 he served as the Royal Medical Society's president. He got to know anybody and everybody who counted for something in the sciences—all the sciences.

Gordon returned to Edinburgh to teach anatomy and physiology at his own anatomy school. He was one of the earliest teachers in the Edinburgh Extramural School of Medicine discussed earlier. In 1812, he was elected a Fellow of the Royal Society of Edinburgh. The extramural undergraduate medical education in Edinburgh stopped in 1948 with the closure of the Royal Colleges' Medical School. This followed the 1948 Goodenough Report, equal to the Flexner report in the US, which recommended that all undergraduate medical education in the UK should be carried out by universities only.

Gordon set out to vigorously criticize phrenology in 1815 with his publication of "The Doctrines of Drs. Gall and Spurzheim." Contrary to his desires, this publicised what had hitherto been a relatively unknown "science". Gordon's criticism included a concise and erudite summary of phrenology's complex dimensions. This enabled it to be understood by a far wider audience than any supporter of Reil would like. And Gordon was a supporter of Reil.

Johann Christian Reil (1759 –1813) was a German physician, physiologist and anatomist. He is said to be the one who coined the term "psychiatry" in 1808. He took the nomenclature for the métier from the Greek *psykhe*, meaning "mind," and *iatreia*, "healing, care." He latinized from the Greek iatrikos "healing." Having received his M.D. from the University of Göttingen, he became one of the first university teachers of psychiatry in 1810 when he became professor of medicine in Berlin, Germany.

Reil used the term "'psychiaterie" in a short-lived journal, *Beytrage zur Beforderung einer Curmethode auf psychischem Wege* (1808: 169). He argued that there should be a branch of medicine, *psychische Medizin*, in its own right with trained practitioners. He also sought to publicize the plight of the insane in the asylums, and to develop a "psychical" method of treatment consistent with the moral movement fashionable at the time. Even though mainly theoretical, with little direct clinical experience, his 1803 work *Rhapsodien uber die Anwendung der psychischen Kurmethode auf Geisteszerrüttungen* ('Rhapsodies about applying the psychological method of treatment to mental breakdowns') has been called the most important document of psychiatry. Reil did not conceptualize madness as just a break from reason, but as a reflection of wider social conditions. He believed that advances in civilization created more madness. He saw this due not to physical lesions in the brain or to hereditary evil, but to a disturbance in the harmony of the mind's functions (forms of awareness or presence) rooted in the nervous system. One recent example would be the science of psychiatry and psychology masters mass hysteria creation of COVID-19.

Thus, during the eighteenth and nineteenth century in the so-called Age the Enlightenment, social welfare and individual rights were dangled in front of humanity. Ideas were purportedly implanted centering mainly on:

- the value of human happiness
- the pursuit of knowledge obtainable by means
- scientific evidence, by exploring the human senses

This emerged in the long run, guaranteeing perpetual "You will own nothing and be Happy" states of human existence.

Reil's appeals to argue for greater understanding and therapeutic environments for the lunatics resulted in some improvements in their plight. This was due more to religious concerns - what goes around comes around - than to humanitarian kindness. But in 1816, it was through Gordon's criticism of phrenology that George Combe met Spurzheim. So taken was he by Spurzheim's presentation, that he attended his course of Edinburgh lectures. And he ordered plaster casts from London to study this newly declared science to further "ascertain whether nature supported [Gall & Spurzheim] or not." With his casts, he gained for the first time in his life the interest and the attention of his friends and colleagues he so craved for his happiness. He was able to talk about the subject with authority - and without competition. There only other phrenologists in Britain were Spurzheim and English astronomer, physician, naturalist and philosopher Thomas Ignatius Maria Forster (1789 -1860). Forster had coined the term "phrenology" in 1815 for his hypothesis, which British polymath Sir Francis Galton (1822–1911) explored further in the late 1800s.

Combe with physician brother Andrew, in tow, became firm phrenologists. George is said to have always been uncompromisingly outspoken and zealous in his advocacy, whereas Andrew seems to have been far less fanatical. Be it as it may, they teamed up with some of George's legal colleagues to found the Edinburgh Phrenological Society (EPS) in 1820. the first of its kind ever created. Mostly comprised of young middle-class professionals eager to join a scientific society for the prestige of it, the EPS grew quickly. By the late 1830s, George was able to devote himself wholly to promoting phrenology and its philosophy of natural laws. Along with that he promoted its secular society, most commonly defined as the separation of religion from civic affairs and the state. He travelled extensively throughout Britain, Germany and the United States to spread its theories. He published his book *The Constitution of Man Considered in Relation to External Object* in 1829. In it, he said that the relative size of the human brain's various regions indeed determines a person's behaviour and interactions with the external world.

Using phrenological understanding of human nature to create a practical science of morality conforming to Natural Laws would lead to human happiness, he maintained, and all of it residing somewhere in our physical brains. It coincided so very nicely with Charles Robert Darwin's (1809-1882) idea of evolution. Darwin graduated from the University of Edinburgh Medical School His theory held that creatures evolved from cockroach through to ape and finally to homo sapien. In 1859, Darwin published his book *On the Origin of Species by Means of Natural Selection, or the Preservation of Favoured Races in the Struggle for Life*. It has dictated humanity's health treatments throughout all of the sciences ever since. And it has served as a forerunner to Harari's Human 2.0 - stay tuned!

Be it as it may, Combe's version of naturalism was the theory relating scientific method to philosophy by affirming that all beings and events in the universe regardless of their inherent character are natural, spread. Therefore, all knowledge of the universe is deemed to fall within the pale of the scientific investigation of naturalism. Naturalism denies the existence of—unspecified—truly supernatural realities. It does apparently make allowance for the supernatural, provided that knowledge of it can be learned indirectly. In other words, the supernatural is real if natural objects are influenced by the so-called supernatural entities in a scientifically detectable way. Thus, naturalism presumes that all in mother nature is, in principle, completely knowable through scientific investigations. It presumes that there is in nature a regularity, unity and wholeness that implies objective laws without which the pursuit of scientific knowledge would otherwise be absurd.

Naturalists also deride all aspects of metaphysics. This word is composed of the Greek words *μετά metá*, meaning "after" and *φυσικά physiká*, meaning "physics". It literally means after or behind or among the natural. Naturalists therefore do not wish to know about, never mind acknowledge, the existence of human consciousness or the relationship between the human mind and its power over matter, the mind over matter existence. They are powerless to prove any of it by way of empirical scientific investigations and documentation. In the world of naturalism aficionados, there is nothing beyond. There is nothing "other than," no "other world" of being. They acknowledge only cold-hearted science, even though they know that an experiment when observed by human eyes will deliver different results than when unobserved!

By way of phrenology, Combe implanted the idea of naturalism, the idea of science as measuring stick for all human aspects of life and living far and wide. In the United Kingdom, it blossomed into 40 groupings. Spurzheim's U.S. tour, conducted among the laity outside of medical lecture halls, was cut short only by his death of typhoid in 1832. But it had already thrown phrenology into the sphere of social reformers and religious ministers alike, who launched the movement in America.

It culminated with founding the Boston Phrenological Society in 1832 "for the purpose of investigating the principles of Phrenology, and to ascertain the bearings of the science upon the physical, moral and intellectual condition of man." (Spurzheim, J. G. et al: Phrenology in connexion with the study of physiognomy: Illustration of characters, with thirty-five plates. Boston: Marsh, Capen & Lyonp 1833, p.140). George Combe himself addressed its membership when visiting the U.S. in 1839. He encouraged its members to teach children about phrenology, so they could develop their sense of Christian morality through awareness of the connection between the mind, dictated by the size of the brain, and the body.

So, Spurzheim and Combe stirred up the pot in the early 1800s by relating skull and brain size to intelligence and morality. In their and Gall's opinion, the human brain is the organ of the mind, and human behaviour is to be understood through neuropsychological rather than philosophical, spiritual and religious considerations. Phrenologists also discounted all supernatural explanations for human experiences of whatever nature. They stressed the modularity of mind. This is the notion that a mind may, at least in part, be composed of innate neural structures or mental modules. Each has distinct, established and evolutionarily developed functions, meaning the ability to evolve from amoeba to blattas to homo sapien, with Darwin's theory of human evolution already on the historical narrative horizon.

As a matter of fact, by the mid-1800s, the new science of phrenology had become a medical discipline. It was all the rage in America and inspired some of the greatest minds of the early Victorian age. All this was based on Gall's principles published in his 1810 work

The Anatomy and Physiology of the Nervous System in General, and of the Brain in Particular, in which he stated the following doctrinal thesis of phrenology:

- that moral and intellectual faculties are innate
- that their exercise or manifestation depends on organization
- that the brain is the organ of all the propensities, sentiments and faculties
- that the brain is composed of as many particular organs as there are propensities, sentiments and faculties which differ essentially from each other
- that the form of the head or cranium represents the form of the brain, and thus reflects the relative development of the brain organs

Gall had ascribed personality traits such as reverence, destructiveness, firmness, mirthfulness and caution to specific areas of the brain. He hypothesized that an area of the brain would be larger if its trait was especially well developed, causing a bump in the skull. Likewise, if a trait were underdeveloped, that area of skull would be flat or possibly compressed. Phrenologists also theorized that they could identify parental aptitude, artistic talent, intelligence, propensity to crime and other mental and moral faculties by palpating a subject's head.

With it came phrenologists' assertion, that the physical brain and not the soul was the center of humans' moral reason and character development. Phrenologists were aware that mainstream Victorian society would be skeptical of any discipline not in harmony with religion. They enjoyed such enormous popularity only because they made an enormous effort to reconcile the dichotomy of God, the Judeo-Christian belief of man made of two parts, body and spirit, with that of science. To achieve the goal, they tailored their talks and doctrines in accordance with scripture rather than on scientific research and the unsubstantiated by science laws of nature of the human brain.

When popularizing phrenology in America, Combe used his exposition *The Constitution of Man* as a guide for conduct. One of the bestselling books of the nineteenth century, his treatise also promoted naturalism. Orson Squire Fowler (1809-1887) and his brother Lorenzo Niles Fowler (1811-1896) helped Combe spread the word. These two pre-eminent phrenology promoters in the United States are widely credited with cracking the "science vs. religion" paradigm. Both men studied for the ministry before becoming interested in this new science, their books and lectures on the subject making many a reference to God and "the truth."

Touting phrenology as a practical tool for self-improvement, the brothers promoted their business with the pithy slogan "Know thyself." They implied that the self-knowledge derived from phrenology could lead to perfectibility by developing the faculties. In their popular manual, *The Illustrated Self-Instructor*, they claimed:

> "Self-knowledge, by teaching the laws and conditions of life and health, becomes the most efficacious means of prolonging the former and increasing the latter.... It also shows us our natural talents, capabilities, virtues, vices, strong and weak points... and develops the laws and conditions of human and personal virtue and moral perfection, as well as of vice, and how to avoid it. It is, therefore, the quintessence of all knowledge. (https://harvard.edu/onview/exhibits/show/talking-heads/the-fowler-brothers).

Gall had conceived of phrenology as an anatomical science. Spurzheim had continued to develop it along scientific lines. The Fowlers promulgated and popularized the movement by pretending it would improve the lot of mankind. Thus, they began to tie phrenology to the social reform movements of the period, including temperance, vegetarianism, and sex education. *The American Phrenological Journal and Life Illustrated* was a Fowler Brothers' and Samuel Roberts Wells publication. The latter joined the company in 1843. Their journal claimed that phrenology:

> "contains everything new and useful in regard to the Science of Man, physical, mental, and spiritual.... Other interests, such as new inventions, agriculture, commerce, mechanism, science, art, and literature, will receive attention. We feel it is a duty to participate in, and co-operate with, all the great movements for the 'emancipation of man' from error, ignorance, sin, want, intemperance, and spiritual darkness. Our work embraces all mankind and (ibid).

This crusading tone, emblematic of the ambition and excess of the promoters began to characterize the phrenological movement in America. But more than that, it presaged the historical narrative of health and education it henceforth indoctrinated by way of the Rockefeller- and Carnegie financial foundations sponsoring it a few years later. The phrenology hypothesis, a few years later topped by Darwin" selection of the fittest together with Reil's *Geisteszerrüttungen* Rhapsody, also planted the seeds for renewed interest in human mental dis-eases. This had hitherto been neglected for centuries. They also planted seeds of interest in the moral-and ethical treatment of those afflicted with mental dis-eases. These approaches also fostered the elite's and learned society's demand that all of phrenology's investigative studies and experimentations must be empirically scientifically provable to be accepted by them.

Eventually, advancements in the field of science and medicine discredited phrenology's claims. Long before that, its reputation had been sullied by folks who had exploited the "science" for profits of their own or who had used its tenets to promote racism, writes Mary Lintern in the 2012 *Garfield Observer*. Nevertheless, she says, the profound effect it had on Victorian culture is undeniable. It played a huge role in motivating, shaping and coloring the minds of some of the era's greatest thinkers and literary artists, never mind the laity, the herd, and helped advance the study of human behavior. Perhaps most importantly, she says, it brought to light the need for serious critical analysis in all we accept as "truth." This process has eroded ever since, as the aim was and is to make the American public believe everything that is a lie as the truth as the result of Freud's aim to "Make the American Mind." This goal is seemingly accomplished in view of the laity's reaction to COVID 19 injections.

Phrenology's popularity began to wane during the early- to mid-1800s, when renowned French physician Marie Jean Pierre Flourens (1794–1867), a pioneer in brain studies and cerebral localization, and others in his league found that the fundamental assumption of phrenology was wrong, disagreeing that the contours of the skull corresponded to the underlying shape of the brain. Flourens joined with French physiologist Francois Magendie (1783-1855) in 1844 to sum up his dismissal:

> "Phrenology, a pseudo-science of the present day; like astrology, necromancy, and alchemy of former times, pretends to localize in the brain the different kinds

of memory. But its efforts are mere assertions, which will not bear examination for an instant."

Thus, phrenology lost its appeal for many (Kendra Cherry: *Phrenology's History and Influence*; https://verywellmind 2022).

Popular in Victorian circles for a time, it was eventually dismissed by brain researchers who pointed out the flaws. They declared it a pseudo-science in the twentieth century, because it did not adhere to formal scientific procedures and established standards of scientific methods and procedures. Not that people did not try to prove it scientifically. Recall that James Scott was Haslar's first superintending physician in charge of the Royal British Navy's lunatics and a member of Edinburgh's Phrenological Society. With his treatment of his charges, he tried hard to prove its scientific value. He applied its neuropsychological concepts of mental disturbances indeed arising from the physical brain and philosophical and religious contemplation. But these had neither effect nor influence on the mentally deranged's state of mind, never mind influencing healing. He also inaugurated the PTSD analysis that holds steady to this day: "genuine PTSD is incurred by those whose brain is defective from the moment of inception."

Scott's countryman John Forbes was son of a tenant farmer with the ardent desire to enlist as a surgeon in the British Royal Navy. He was confirmed in the rank of full surgeon in 1809, and spent time at Haslar during the Napoleonic Wars (1803 -1815) before ending his navy career in 1816 and enrolling in Edinburgh's medical school, achieving his M.D. in 1817. He somehow acquired a model of Frenchman René Laënnec's (1781-1826) stethoscope invention. He translated Laënnec work *De L'Auscultation Médiate* (1819) into the English *A treatise on diseases of the chest and on Mediate Auscultation* (1821), with it spreading the Frenchman's teachings throughout the English-speaking world. Forbes also conducted his own medical dissections and observations illustrating the use of the stethoscope and percussion in the diagnosis of diseases of the chest, whilst for 14 years working in his private medical practice and performing hospital work at the Chichester Infirmary.

Together with John Conolly, Forbes started the peer reviewed *British and Foreign Medical Review, A Quarterly Journal of Practical Medicine* in 1836 . It was meant to promote modern methods of medical treatment and enhance British medicine throughout Europe and America.

In 1840, Forbes quit his post as senior physician at Chichester Infirmary to move to London. In 1841, he became court physician to Queen Victoria's consort Prince Albert and the royal household. He had the Fellowship of the Royal College of Physicians conferred on him in 1844, followed by the honorary Fellowship of the Imperial Society of Physicians in Vienna in 1845. Upwardly mobile indeed was he, despite having published an article in favour of homeopathy in 1846 as editor of the *British & Foreign Medical Review*. That so incurred the wrath of the medical establishment that it caused the Review to fail in 1847. After all, as we have seen earlier, homeopathy is against everything held dear by the art and science of medicine in all its facets. It has healing powers far surpassing its most-oftentimes-detrimental-to-the-human-health crafts and thus is against the Luciferic consciousness' aspirations.

Regardless, Forbes phenomenal rise to prominence continued. Oxford University bestowed the honorary degree of Doctor of Civil Law on him in 1852. Queen Victoria knighted him in gratitude for doing her bidding so very wonderfully well, considering his meteoric rise from undistinguished navy surgeon. The final publication of his work *Of Nature and Art on the Cure of Disease* based on his favourite theme of the *vis medicatrix naturae* appeared in 1857. It literally means "the healing power of nature", also known as *natura medica*, which means "Nature is the physician of diseases." It is attributed to Hippocrates, with Forbes emphasizing, that the art and science of medicine should be practiced in combination with the healing powers of nature, advice ignored by his peers ever since. So why did he receive all those accolades? Well, his obituary in the Proceedings of the Royal Society (1862-63) noted that:

> "Although Sir John Forbes cannot be ranked among those who have advanced the science of medicine by the discovery of new facts or the promulgation of new principles, he must be regarded as having done most essential service to the cause of progress... by the determined onslaught which he made upon prevalent errors, and the vigorous earnestness with which he pleaded for generally-neglected truths." (https://www.clan-forbes.org/sir-john-forbes-md).

And why did U.S. president Barrack Hussein Obama receive the Nobel Peace Prize? Same thing, perhaps?

Forbes' buddy John Connolly, meanwhile, had accepted the resident physician position to the Middlesex County Asylum in Hanwell near London in 1839. Thus in charge of the diagnoses and treatments of 800-odd pauper lunatics in the country's largest, asylum, he carried out large-scale experiments in non-mechanical restrain. This was a time before Baeyer's barbituric discovery and associated drugging was replacing such physical restraints with its life experimentations on the WWI and WWII shell-shocked, which continues today. (https://cambridge.org/core/journals/psychiatric-bulletin/article/john-conolly-and-the-treatment-of-mental-illness-in-early-victorian-england/AC35E941FD2D37A58A701CA287F2026C).

Those doing the experimentations on humanity have been glued at the hip for hundreds, if not thousands, of years, all systematically in the name of the Great Work of Ages hastening towards our destruction. It is too sinister for our innately kind nature to grasp. Perhaps watching *They Live*, the 1988 film written and directed by John Carpenter based on the 1963 short story "Eight O'Clock in the Morning" by Ray Nelson might help the awakening. Starring Roddy Piper, the film follows an unnamed drifter who discovers through special sunglasses that the ruling class are aliens concealing their appearance and manipulating people to consume, breed, and conform to the status quo via subliminal messages in mass media. Barely 35 years later, that ruling class, the Luciferic consciousness, has achieved by way of the mental health industry to pervert our thinking, destroy our wholeness in all aspects of our lives by engineering social and historical narrative like magic.

Baeyers' barburic acid brought all other poisoning drugs to destroy humans' body, mind and spirit into being. The COVID-19 injection is the crowing achievement to turn God's creation into human 2.0. And how they get humanity to consent to that insanity? It began with the brutal psychological treatment applied to all shell-shocked soldiers in military hospitals during and after WWI and WWII. So, it continues to this very day, as to know what made humans tick and how to steer them in sickness and in health was the final pathway to the Luciferic consciousness' victory.

All sorts of barbiturates were offered to soothe despairing soldiers' minds and spirits in the killing fields, where they engaged in murdering their fellows to protect the father-or motherland and while at it weaken the quality of their semen, thus producing less viable children. And so began the problem of addiction. It was sponsored by the mental health professions with the public made too ignorant to even want to know what they swallow. This was Freud's theme and Bernays, the advertising guru's slogan "Doctor Knows Best" the only thing that in North America has been firmly entered in their minds for generations (Francisco López-Muñoz et al: "The history of barbiturates a century after their clinical introduction"; Neuropsychiatr Dis Treat. 2005 Dec; 1(4): 329–343).

But let's move on and see, what else they have done to corral us into madness, shall we?

32

THE MASSIVE LUNATIC ASYLUM CONSTRUCTIONS

Johann Adam Weishaupt (1748 –1830) might spring to mind when you hear the word "Illuminati". He was born in Ingolstadt in the Electorate of Bavaria, of Khazarian Ashkenazi family origin. He was Jesuit educated, a University of Ingolstadt graduate at age 20 with a doctor of law degree. By age 24, he was a full civil and later canon law professor. More to the point, he founded the Illuminati at age 28 in the same year the United States declared its independence from Britain: 1776. So, if his name springs to your mind as having taken part or even being the catalyst for driving humanity into madness, it makes sense. And if you figure the Khazarian Mafia had anything to do with it, you might be right. However, documentation on his role in directing world history's narrative abound, so we will leave it well enough alone.

Instead, we will stick with the illumined learned society of medicine in its numerous facets including mental health. Weishaupt helped them unite further than they already were. The goal was to figure out how to slowly and systematically drive us into the COVID-19 mass formation psychosis hypnotic state-of-mind hysteria. The term "mass formation psychosis" began to be thrown about in December 2021, after mRNA inventor and strong

COVID-19 vaccines opponent Dr. Robert Malone used the expression in an interview. Malone performed a landmark experiment when mixing strands of messenger RNA in in late 1987. Messenger ribonucleic acid (mRNA) is a single-stranded molecule of RNA that corresponds to the genetic sequence of a gene. It is read by a ribosome, a minute particle consisting of RNA and associated proteins found in large numbers in the cytoplasm of living cells, in the process of synthesizing a protein with droplets of fat. Human cells bathed in this genetic gumbo absorbed the mRNA and began producing proteins from it.

In 1988, Malone's experiments showed that frog embryos absorbed such mRNA, helping ease mRNA's passage into living organisms, including us. The result? The mRNA-based COVID-19 vaccines given to hundreds of millions of people around the world, with global sales expected to top US$ 50 billion in 2021 alone. Anyway, Malone's term "mass formation psychosis" does not appear in the American Psychological Association Dictionary of Psychology or its PsychNet database (Ryan Basen: Just What Is Mass Formation Psychosis? One doctor is pushing controversial theory on how the public is being coerced into getting vaxxed; Enterprise & Investigative Writer, *MedPage Today* January 12, 2022).

What does exist, however, is the term "psychosis". It is deemed to be present when a person's thoughts and perceptions are seemingly disturbed, and a person might have difficulty understanding what is real and what is not. Symptoms of psychosis include delusions (false beliefs) and hallucinations (seeing or hearing things that others do not see or hear,). These are both possible side-effects of oxygen deficiency, creating high anxiety caused by mask-wearing in addition to isolation from others. And those who imposed it on humanity worldwide knew perfectly well what they were doing and what would happen to you. They gave you the kill-shot, advertised as a vaccine, and you fell for it in your ignorance. What they might not have known is that the effects on you had been studied in depth since the early 1800s. So, let's move on and discover how by returning to John Conolly (1794-1866).

Conolly was born of a poverty-stricken Irish family at Market Rasen in Lincolnshire, England. This hamlet was first attested to in the Doomsday Book, a record of the "Great Survey" of much of England and parts of Wales completed in 1086 by order of William I. Known as William the Conqueror (c. 1028 –1087), he was the first Norman king of England. Conolly spent four years as a lieutenant in the Cambridge shire Militia. He lived for a year in France, then received his M.D. degree from the University of Edinburgh in 1821. He ran a private practice in Lewes, Chichester, and in Stratford-on-Avon, Britain, until 1828, when appointed professor of the practice of medicine by the University College, London. In 1830, he published his book *Indications of Insanity: An inquiry concerning the indications of insanity with suggestions of the better protection and care of the insane*. It contained information Conolly had gathered from William Tuke (1732–1822). At his institution, The Retreat at York, opened with help of the Society of Friends (Quakers) in 1796, Tuke led the world in the humane treatment of the mentally ill.

The Retreat at York is still a Quaker hospital today, now working with the British National Health Service. Tuke had been inspired to open it after seeing the appalling conditions in the York Lunatic Asylum, when a Quaker woman from Leeds died there. It opened in 1777, when the practice of having the lunatics chained to the walls naked and physicians' misappropriating significant sums of money was common. The poor inmates would suffer, though the affluent ones were treated relatively well. In 1814, it finally led to an investigation, where a number of secret cells full of women in a state of filth, horrible beyond description, were discovered. More than 100 poor creatures were shut up together elsewhere, unattended and uninspected by anyone, the most miserable objects the inspector had ever beheld, (https://borthwickinstitute.blogspot.com/2014/10/the-york-lunatic-asylum-scandal.html). Soon thereafter, nearly 40 local gentlemen, Tuke family members and friends among them, paid £20 in order to qualify as the asylum's governors to begin making changes.

Mind you, the ill treatment of asylum patients was widely accepted at the time. Many believed the lunatics were sub-human animals, insensitive to hot and cold. Beatings and confinement were accepted practices, as was underfeeding. British medical doctor, geologist and vicar Joseph Townsend (1739 -1816) in his 1786 treatise *A Dissertation on the Poor Laws* criticized relief, as it would allow the population to swell by protecting the weak. Thus, he called for the abolition of any state relief in pursuance of greater productivity, as "it is only hunger which can spur and goad them [the mentally feeble, old and poor] on to labour." (Townsend, 1971:23).

The fourth son of Chauncy Townsend (1708 -1770), Joseph Townsend was a City of London merchant, Member of the British Parliament, coalmine-developer and supplier of goods for Nova Scotia settlers. He had been educated at Clare College, Cambridge, graduating with a BA in 1762, after which he studied medicine at Edinburgh. Ordained in the Church of England in 1763, he served as Rector of Pewsey, a large village in Wiltshire west of London, until his death. He was noted for the "Townsend's Mixture" of mercury and potassium iodide as a treatment for syphilis. This man never suffered a day of hardship or hunger, with the exception of probably syphilis acquired through fornication. But he joyously proclaimed to his peers: "Hunger will tame the fiercest animals, it will teach decency and civility, obedience and subjection to the most perverse." Keep that in mind that the destruction of farmers is in full swing in the western world. Standing up united to stop this madness to tame us, "as the fiercest animals," might be a good idea, perhaps?

Tuke's York Retreat was born out of such elite attitudes. Based on the Quaker principles of self-control, compassion and respect, it marked the beginning of the move away from chains and fetters to gentler restraints, such as the straight jacket. Quakers did not see the insane as animals but believed the "inner light of God" to be present in them as in all human beings.

Inmates were considered children, and all dwelling within served as if living in a loving family. The goal was to bring patients back to reason and recovery, without beatings and chaining, and with good nutrition and tender loving care. Another of The Retreat's inventions was "The Appendage," a halfway house for those recovered enough to need little to no supervision. Tuke's radical approach away from the brutality hitherto committed against those declared lunatics in asylums sparked a few reforms in their treatment during the nineteenth century. These were reflected by Conolly in his 1830 publication "Indications of Insanity: An inquiry concerning the indications of insanity with suggestions of the better protection and care of the insane."

Conolly's assertions, however, were purely hypothetical, dreamt up or grasped out of thin air. Despite strenuous efforts, he had failed to obtain entry to the country's lunatic asylums in which systematic training of medical students were already in operation. It seems that, for reasons unknown, nobody wanted him on their premises (Isis Volume 56, Number 1; https://journals.uchicago.edu/doi/10.1086/349943). Thus, we are told, his book is merely a reflection of his ardent interest in the subject, based on the time he devoted to the problems he perceived the mentally ill suffered.

It took Conolly until 1839 to land his dream job with his own experimental laboratory. That yea, her secured the superintendent and resident physician position to St. Bernard's Hospital at Hanwell near London. It was also known as the Hanwell Insane Asylum and the Hanwell Pauper and Lunatic Asylum, which had opened in 1831. It was built for the pauper insane as the First Middlesex County Asylum. It originally housed 450 inmates, with space for another 150 expected to shortly sprout in the region. Still in operation, it in 1980 became part of Ealing Hospital as psychiatric and psycho-geriatric hospital with beds for 950 long stay patients and some of its buildings used as West London Health NHS Trust headquarters.

He was the institution's third superintendent let loose on its lunatics within eight years. The very first one had been William Charles Ellis (1780-1839), with his wife Mildred Ellis as Hanwell's matron at his side. Born in Alford, Lincolnshire, he was working as apothecary in the city of Hull, when the infatuation with the insane and their treatment captivated him. He enrolled at Hull's Sculcoates Refuge, a private asylum opened in 1814 and run similar to Tuke's Retreat, to learn about it. He was appointed superintendent to The West Riding Pauper Lunatic Asylum. It had been built to Tuke's instructions with accommodation for 150 patients in 1818. By the 1860s, it had been enlarged in piecemeal fashion, ballooning to over 1,000 patients. Ellis and his wife, Methodists with strong convictions, used the same principles of humane treatment and moral therapy as practised at Sculcoates Refuge and Tuke's York Retreat.

They were much impressed by Tuke's humane and moral treatment and benevolent intentions towards the charges at his institution. They were appalled by conditions they had observed during a visit to St. Luke's, where they had seen a naked woman chained to a wall for all to see. So, they tried to follow Tuke's treatment methods. They found it essential for recovery that patients should get out into full daylight for fresh air and exercise. So, the ground floor wards included pleasantly laid out "airing courts" with seating, bounded by walls or railings shared with the upstairs wards. Some patients, well into their recovery, were allowed to walk and work in the surrounding fields. Designed to be as self-sufficient as possible, the asylum had its own carpentry, bakery, and brewery along with many other services. It even paid the canal company for taking water from the canal and for its own dock to receive barges delivering provisions.

The Ellis' believed that physical and mental health were inextricably linked with diet and exercise. So, they sought proper nutrition for their charges. They instilled a sense of reason, rather than fear, in them. They limited the use of physical restraints and encouraged tasks such as gardening, sewing, knitting and other exercise for body and mind. And they strictly imposed their humane and moral treatment on their staff.

The basis for creating the West Riding Pauper Lunatic Asylum was the *1808 County Asylums Act*. It passed after years of wars with France, following the Seven Years' War of

1756-1763 (known in America as the "French and Indian War,"). The war years ended with the Napoleonic Wars at Waterloo in 1815. The Act authorized the founding of publicly funded county asylums to accommodate paupers, whose other choices were to remain in their potentially hostile communities or living in workhouses. This Act stemmed from a string of legislation in the eighteenth century attempting to curb abuses in asylums. Some had been founded in the fourteenth century with unchanging views on treatment. Thus, the *County Asylums Act* established the foundations of a national institutional network of mammoth insane asylums throughout Britain apparently expecting a flood of mentally incompetents, but why? Human debris from already planned future wars, perhaps? Who would also provide splendid material for scientific research experimentations in the laboratories that were part of every single of these massive lunatic asylums?

Philippe Pinel with his 1801 "Treatise on Insanity" may have influenced the Act's passing due to this statement:

> "Few subjects in medicine are so intimately connected with the history and philosophy of the human mind as insanity. There are still fewer, where there are so many errors to rectify, and so many prejudices to remove. Derangement of the understanding is generally considered as an effect of an organic lesion of the brain, consequently as incurable; a supposition that is, in a great number of instances, contrary to anatomical fact." (Philippe Pinel, "Treatise on Insanity". JMS Pearce: The West Riding Lunatic Asylum, *Journal of Neurology, Neurosurgery & Psychiatry* vol. 74 issue 8 [1801]).

Philippe Pinel (1745 -1826) was a French physician and zoologist. He was instrumental in developing a more humane psychological approach to the custody and care of mentally impaired people. He advocated to abolish the shackling of mental patients by chains and to humanise their treatment, as well as to classify mental diseases. Sometimes described as "the father of modern psychiatry," it was the French Revolution, 1789-1799, that jolted Pinel into changing his view of the crazies, the "aliénés", the alienated. He claimed they could be understood and cured, obviously recognizing the reason for their alienation, namely an earthshattering emotional experience during the revolution.

Pinel was born in Jonquières in the south of France, the son and nephew of physicians. He got a degree from the Faculty of Medicine in Toulouse and studied an extra four years at the Faculty of Medicine of Montpellier. In 1778, he settled in Paris to spend the following 15 years earning his living as a writer, translator and editor, as only graduates of the Paris Faculty of Medicine could practice in the capital. He developed an intense interest in the study of mental illness, however, in 1784. A friend developed a "nervous melancholy" that year, and it "degenerated into mania", resulting in suicide. Pinel regarded this result as an unnecessary tragedy due to gross mismanagement of we don't know by we don't know whom.

He had watched his friend's tragedy evolve whilst coming into contact with the mentally ill in the private clinic of carpenter Jacques Belhomme (1737-1824). So, Pinel applied for work at the private sanatorium for the treatment of insanity in Paris and remained there for five years prior to the French Revolution. He was able to complete observations on insanity and began to formulate his views on its nature and treatment stating:

> "I cannot here avoid giving my most decided sufferage in favour of the moral qualities of maniacs. I have no where met, excepting in romances, with fonder husbands, more affectionate parents, more impassioned . . . than in the lunatic asylum, during their intervals of calmness and reason."

In 1789, he published an article on treatment of the mentally ill. Its precise doctrine of the symptoms of mental illness gave psychiatry of the nineteenth century the possibility to establish a basis. (Tabea Tietz: "Philippe Pinel—the father of modern Psychiatry". *SciHi*, 2021). One of his major works consisted of philosophical nosography, the systematic description of diseases, aiming to establish a natural system for individual mental diseases. In it, he was influenced by the view of French physician Théophile de Bordeau (1722–1776), an advocate of vitalism.

And what's that, we wonder? Vitalism is the belief that living organisms are fundamentally different from non-living entities. They contain a non-physical element. And they are governed by different principles than are inanimate things, with the non-physical element often referred to as the "vital spark," "energy," the "élan vital." (Bechtel, William; Williamson, Robert C. (1998). "Vitalism." In E. Craig (ed.). *Routledge Encyclopedia of Philosophy*. Routledge).

Reaching back to the ideas of Aristotle, philosophers of the eighteenth and nineteenth centuries again began to argue about living organisms' distinction from inert matter. Their possession of a "life force" was animating them and propelling their evolution into higher forms. The notion of an entelechy became widely accepted and popular in academia and among the herd. This term was used by Aristotle and adopted by the German biologist Hans Driesch (1867–1941). This idea is that some things realize or make actual what is otherwise merely potential. It is) similar to the term "élan vital" coined by French philosopher Henri Bergson (1859–1941).

Ultimately, however, vitalism fell out of favour, because it had no scientific application, as its existence could not be scientifically, empirically proven. It was observable in living entities, but that it did not lead to new predictions or unified explanations of phenomena formerly thought to be unrelated, as all truly important scientific concepts do. In other words, vitalism's hypotheses are just as improvable as all of psychology and psychiatry. As attempts at mechanistic explanations failed to provide empirical scientific evidence of the existence of a life force within animate subjects such as humans. The learned society of biologists, in particular, declared it to be either a superseded scientific theory or a pseudoscience. They ignored the fact that ancient Sanskrit and Egyptian documents posit that human diseases originate from imbalances in our "élan vital", our soul-generated life force.

The experience of his friend committing suicide propelled Pinel into employment at one of Paris' best-known private sanatoria for the treatment of insanity. There he remained for five years prior to the revolution, gathering observations on insanity, and beginning to formulate his views on its nature and treatment. An open-minded vitalist, he, eschewed known systematics in treating the mentally handicapped and endless philosophical theories on how to treat them. Instead, he tried to reactivate their life force through conversation. He used expressive observations to describe the clinical development of various mental illnesses and the improvement he saw in his patients. His modus operandi made it much,

much easier for the cabal to slide the non-scientific, empirically defunct fields of psychiatry and psychology into the field of general medicine.

In 1793, many people were suffering from the physical and emotionally earth-shattering revolution. But Pinel was appointed "physician of the infirmaries" at the Bicêtre Hospital in the southern suburbs of Paris, its authority stretching to include all the poor in the entire city of Paris. Originally planned as a military hospital when construction began in 1634, it opened as an orphanage in 1642. By 1656, it had been incorporated into the *Hôpital général de Paris*. The *Hôpital* was formed by a royal edict during Louis XIV's reign. Its goal was to house invalids and beggars, as well as aid those dwelling in the *Cour des miracles*. This "court of miracles" was the slum districts of Paris, where unemployed migrants from rural French areas tried to carve out a living.

During its history, the Bicêtre Hospital has been successively or simultaneously used as an orphanage, a prison, a lunatic asylum and a *Hospice de la Vieillesse Hommes*. It was most famous as the *Asylum de Bicêtre*, however, before being renamed the *Hospice de Bicêtre* in 1885. Its most notorious guest had been the Marquis de Sade, in 1781. It was considered at that time much more terrible than the Bastille, the fourteenth century fortress Louis XIV built to imprison French society's upper-class members who opposed or angered him.

The first thing Pinel, as Superintendent, did was to introduce humane methods to treat those dwelling within it because of purported mental illness. At the time, the place housed about 4,000 imprisoned men—criminals, petty offenders, syphilitics, pensioners. It also housed about 200 mental patients enclosed in one ward. Pinel's patrons hoped that his experience at the private sanatoria would lead him to take therapeutic initiatives with these inmates. Soon after his appointment, Pinel asked for a report on these 200 acknowledged mental patients. He received a table with comments from their "governor" Jean-Baptiste Pussin (1746-1811). Pussin gained the position after having been successfully treated there in the 1770s for scrofula, a tuberculosis infection of the lymph nodes in the neck. As a result, he, his wife, and their colleague Marguerite were recruited. Together, they established more humane treatment of these patients.

Appreciating Pussin's outstanding talent, Pinel virtually apprenticed himself to that unschooled but immensely experienced custodian of the insane. He said he did so to enrich the medical theory of mental illness with all the insights that the empirical approach affords. What he observed was a strict, nonviolent, *nonmedical* management of mental patients, to which his peers would affix the term *moral treatment*. A legend soon grew that Pinel at the Bicetre had single-handedly liberated the insane from their chains. But it had indeed been Pussin, who had removed their iron shackles in 1797, after Pinel had left for the *Salpêtrière*. Pinel did remove his patients' chains at the *Salpêtrière* after Pussin joined him there in 1802. However, while still at the Bicêtre, Pinel did away with bleeding, purging and blistering. Instead, he offered daily conversations with each patient and careful note-taking over two years. He engaged them in lengthy conversations with the objective to assemble detailed case histories and discover the natural history of each patient's illness.

In 1795, Pinel was appointed adjunct professor of medical physics at one of the three new *écoles de santé* established by the *Convention Nationale* in 1794. He held that chair for 20 years. He also became chief physician of the *Hospice de la Salpêtrière*, a post he retained for the rest of his life. The *Salpêtrière*, at the time like a large village, housed 7,000 elderly indigent and ailing women. It functioned with an entrenched bureaucracy, a teeming market and huge infirmaries. Pinel, missing Pussin, secured his transfer to his side in 1802. Catholic nursing orders undertook most of the day-to-day care and understanding of *Salpêtrière's* patients, though power struggles at times occurred between Pinel and the nurses. In 1799, Pinel was one of the very first in Europe to set up an inoculation clinic right there at the Salpêtrière. The first vaccination was given there in April 1800, shortly after British physician and scientist Edward Jenner (1749 -1823) created the smallpox vaccine in 1798. With the long title of his *Inquiry into the Variolae vaccinae known as the Cow Pox*, he described the protective effect of cowpox against smallpox.

Needless to say, the idea of Darwinism clashed with Pinel's theories. The theory of biological evolution, the survival of the fittest, was officiously launched by British Charles Darwin (1809–1882) and others. It maintained that all animate species arise and develop through natural selection processes of small, inherited variations that increase an individual's ability to compete, survive and reproduce. Darwinism's proponents disliked the idea of life force – the elan vital. Therefore, they objected hugely to Pinel's theories and assertions about the emotionally or mentally unstables' moral type of therapy healing. To conquer these idiotic notions and assertions of love and kindness in a scientific manner, they needed places to study humans' physical brains and behaviors. Due to the brutality of their methods, those places had to be unobserved by the laity. And what better place could there be than a nut house with an experimental research laboratory? It had a multitude of subjects for the experimental studies to figure out how the human psyche actually worked and to investigate a multitude of other topics. They could learn how to manipulate humans to perfection, in addition to saving the expense for rats, cani, simian, lepus and blattas.

It worked like a charm. The enormous structures were built with the most sophisticated laboratories. The investigations rapidly spun off into the new neurological sciences, which encompassed the scientific study and documentations of the human nervous system in all its facets. Little by little, they combined physiology, anatomy and biology. These dictate the basis of human learning, memory and behaviour. They affect the perception of the mind they say does not exist, and of consciousness they cannot scientifically prove exists, either. So, the scope of neuroscience broadened and expanded its life brain explorations to study the nervous system at different scales and techniques and angles. They looked at it from the molecular and cellular to the imagining of sensory, motor and cognitive brain functions. It was almost as if man the medieval thinker, the center of creation and all of nature existed purely for this benefit. In the process, they began to eliminate God from his considerations via the works of Copernicus, Kepler, Galileo, Descartes, Hobbes, Gilbert, Boyle and Newton. In their place, they established scientific reason for his *raison d'être* (E.A. Butt: *The Metaphysical Foundations of Modern Science*. Dover Publication, 2003).

So, in part thanks to Pinel, the *County Asylum Act* of 1808 passed. Mammoth institutions for the paupers and the lunatics began springing up like weeds throughout Britain and also in the United States. They chose this option rather than to spend the money on the destitute filthy and dilapidated sane minds living in the slums of British and American cities owned by the Rockefellers and the Carnegies, and the lords and ladies of the British Isles.

The paupers were still deprived of sanitary facilities and dying of malnutrition, cockroaches and rats nibbling at infants. All this thanks to their rulers, the owners of their dwellings, who passed the Act and taxed them to build it. Before that the cost of keeping paupers and lunatics in jails and workhouses after Henry VIII's abolition of the Roman Catholic Church had been the responsibility of their parish of birth and local charity.

Their lives had been made even harder, when the *Corn Laws of 1794-1846* passed. These set duties on grain imports into Britain to protect British agriculture from outside competition. They kept food prices high, while the Enclosure Acts between 1604 and 1914 gradually abolishing the United Kingdom's open field system of agriculture. Open field was how common people farmed and sustained themselves in England for centuries. The Acts gave ownership of all common and waste land to the Lords of the Manors, leaving nothing to the landless. Arranged by the Lords ruling in the British Parliament, over 5,200 enclosure bills enclosed 6.8 million acres of fields previously accessible to the common folk. Thus, they were systematically driven into destitution. The words of an unknown eighteenth century poet reflect the lead-in to the privately owned World Economic Forum's CEO Klaus Schwab's twenty-first-century aspiration for humanity: "You will own nothing and be happy:"

They hang the man and flog the woman
Who steals the goose from off the common
Yet let the greater villain loose
That steals the common from the goose.

The law demands that we atone
When we take things we do not own
But leaves the lords and ladies fine
Who take things that are yours and mine.

The poor and wretched don't escape
If they conspire the law to break
This must be so but they endure
Those who conspire to make the law.

The law locks up the man or woman
Who steals the goose from off the common
And geese will still a common lack
Till they go and steal it back.

The common folk's starvation and most families' inability to properly care for the handicapped among them, gave the splendid excuse to build these asylums for paupers and lunatics. These would become the psychiatric hospitals of latter days during the WWI and WWII. They were already planned and those mentally affected during the COVID 19 and following epidemics would be let loose on humanity in a steady stream. With the help of drugging, humanity's complete collapse under the COVID 19 jabs would usher in conversion to human 2.0.

Benevolent places called the "Bimaristans," Persian for "location of disease," had already existed in the Islamic world for a millennium. Oft times mobile, these hospitals travelled with physicians and pharmacists carrying medications, food and water to aid those in need. These mobile care centers evolved from one or two tents to enormous units of medical care. They were equipped with medicinal herbs, food, physicians and pharmacists. A single mobile care center required up to 40 camels for transportation to be able to extend medical care to rural communities. The first one was apparently set up in a tent by Rufaida Al-Aslamia of Medina, Saudi-Arabia, in 627 AD. This physician's daughter, who obtained her clinical experience from her father, was the world's first known woman surgeon and nurse. As time went on, services provided from the mobile hospitals during the 8th century transitioned into hospitals built in the cities. Those of Baghdad, Damascus and Cairo were the most well known.

The waqf (Arabic: فـقو; ['wɑqf]) documents, also known as hubous (سوبح) or *mortmain* property, sustains these hospitals. These were inalienable charitable endowments under Islamic law. They typically involving donating a building, plot of land or other assets for Muslim religious or charitable purposes, with no intention of reclaiming the assets. They held the moral imperative to treat all the ill, regardless of their financial status. Thus, the Bismaristans' hospitals were largely secular institutions open to all, male and female, civilian and military, adult and child, rich and poor, Muslims and non-Muslims. They tended to be large urban structures with specific characteristics maintained in their operation. All people, regardless of race, religion, citizenship or gender, had to be helped. No-one was ever to be turned away, not even if afflicted by diseases considered to be of the mind. Abundant light, fresh air, running water and music were part of the treatments. Physicians and staff worked together in unison and harmony to help patients recover. No time limits existed, as the waqf principles decreed that all hospitals keep all patients until they had fully recovered.

Men and women were admitted to separate and equally equipped wards. These separate wards were divided to address mental illnesses, contagious diseases, non-contagious diseases, surgery and medicine, and eye diseases. Patients were attended to by nurses and staff of their own gender. All hospitals also contained a lecture hall, kitchen, pharmacy, library, and mosque. Some had a chapel for Christian patients. Recreational materials were provided, as well as musicians to comfort and cheer patients. The Qur'an, Islam's Holy Book, also provided the basis for professional conduct and ethics.

Ritual washing promoted personal and medical hygiene for all working and residing in the Bimaristans. There was regular bathing of patients and staff, and clean bedding and medical materials. Air circulation and bright open lighting were features of their architectural designs. In turn, this created hygienic awareness and promoted hygienic infrastructures in local communities, which also cut down on disease. Bismaristans' pharmacies were periodically visited by a government inspector, the muhtasib, بسـتحم, from the root ةبسح ḥisbah, meaning "accountability." The holder of the office of al-hisbah in classical Islamic administrations was supervisor of bazaars and trade, inspectors of public places and overseers of behavior in medieval Islamic countries (and to this day in some Arabic countries). Appointed by the sultan and iman, he ensured public business was conducted in accordance with sharia law. In the case of Bimaristans, he made sure that the pharmacies' medicines had been mixed properly, were undiluted and were kept in clean jars.

As to the location of those Bismaristans, Persian physician, philosopher, alchemist, and physician Abū Bakr al-Rāzī (c. 864 or 865–925 or 935 AD) was once asked to choose the site for a new Bismaristan in Baghdad. He was also known as (al-)Razi or Rhazes, and widely considered one of the most important figures in the history of medicine. He was particularly remembered for his numerous advances in medicine through his own observations and discoveries. As teacher of medicine of students from all backgrounds and interests, he encouraged compassion and devotion to the service of patients, whether rich or poor. He was also the first to clinically distinguish between smallpox and measles, suggesting healing through sound for the former. So, how did he choose the site for that Bismaristan in Baghdad? He suspended pieces of meat at various points around the city and recommended building the hospital at the location where the meat putrefied the slowest. Vibrational medicine, anyone?

The Q'ran places values on education and emphasizes the importance of acquiring knowledge. So, it follows that the Bismaristans were educational institutions meant to advance medical students' theoretical knowledge into practice. Basic science preparation, though, was learned through private tutors, self-study and lectures. Physicians in proto-medical schools were Muslim, Jewish and Christian physicians. They both taught and practiced, with students visiting patients while under the supervision of a practicing physician, comparable to today's medical residency. Physicians' licensure became mandatory during the Abbasid Caliphate, the third caliphate to succeed the Islamic prophet Muhammad. It was founded by a dynasty descended from the prophet's uncle, Abbas ibn Abdul-Muttalib. In 931 AD, its Caliph was Abu'l-Faḍl Jaʿfar ibn Ahmad al-Muʿtaḍid (895 –932 AD), better known by his regnal name Al-Muqtadir bi-llāh, المقتدر بالله, "Mighty in God". He learned of one of his subject's death due to a physician's error, and immediately ordered his muhtasib to arrange for licensing exams, so only qualified physicians could practice medicine.

The Bismaristans' organization, structure and functioning was also something to behold. The first one documented was the general hospital in Baghdad. It was built in 805 by Abu Ja'far Harun ibn Muhammad al-Mahdi or Harun ibn al-Mahdi (ca. 763-809 AD). He was famously known as Harun al-Rashid, the fifth caliph of the Abbasid Caliphate. The hospital became the prototype of the general hospital itself, with Baghdad alone having five more hospitals by the year 1000 AD and a law to keep them open 24 hours a day. All hospitals built throughout the Islamic world henceforth followed similar architectural and organizational structures. The typical hospital was divided into genders, with departments such as surgery, orthopaedics and systemic dis-eases. This was the rough equivalent of today's internal medicine, which was further divided into sections such as fever, infections and digestive issues. Larger hospitals had more diverse specialties, though every department had an officer-in-charge, a presiding officer and a supervising specialist.

Hospital staff also included sanitary inspectors regulating cleanliness as well as accountants and other administrative staff. The whole hospital was typically run by a three-person "board of directors" comprising a non-medical administrator, the chief physician and the chief pharmacist, who was equal in rank to the chief physician. Superintendents ensured that hospitals met certain standards in addition to managing the entire hospital. That included managing the pharmacists who produced patients' drugs, relying on knowledge of chemistry and alchemia. The Bimaristans kept meticulous written patient records of their medical treatments. Students were responsible for their upkeep to be later edited by doctors and referenced in future treatments.

Practicing physicians worked a set number of hours, with their salaries prescribed by law and generous enough so as to retain their talent. Chief of staff physician at Baghdad's hospitals Jabril ibn Bukhtishu (b.?- 828-29)was known for various medical works. These included his *Book of the Characteristics of Animals and Their Properties and the Usefulness of Their Organs*. He also wrote *Treatise on Medicine and Psychological Phenomena*. He drew the princely sum of 4.9 million Dirham, today worth over US$1 million annually. In comparison, a medical resident working significantly longer hours took home a mere 300 Dirham monthly, roughly US$82.

In accordance with the WAFQ principles, Islamic hospitals attained their endowment through charitable donations or bequests. Patients' costs of treatments, regardless of socioeconomic status, are borne by the hospital itself. Hospitals differed in size. Cairo's Al-Mansuri Hospital was built under the orders of Egypt's the Mamluk "slave soldier" ruler Al-Manus Qalawun (1222-1290 AD). With an annual endowment said to be one-million Dirhams, it accommodated 8,000 patients, all fed and housed for free.

European travellers throughout the Levant and Persia marvelled about the Bismaristans' wonders. They were surprised by the care and kindness shown to those deemed to be lunatics in their care. Ahmad ibn Tulun (835 – 10 884) was another slave soldier and ultimately founder of the Egyptian Tulunid dynasty ruling the country between 868 and 905. In 872, he built a hospital in Cairo to specifically provide care to those deemed insane only, whose treatment included music therapy.

Nonetheless, Roy Sydney Porter, (1946 -2002), professor at the Welcome Institute for the History of Medicine at the University College London, cautions against idealising the role of hospitals in medieval Islam. He states: "They were a drop in the ocean for the vast population that they had to serve, and their true function lay in highlighting ideals of compassion and bringing together the activities of the medical profession." In other words, does he confirm that nothing is new under the sun? Is he revealing the illusory truth effect seen in today's population due to bringing together the medical profession's activities for millennia, gradually leading us into the madness and self-destruction we see today by honing our trust in them?

And yes, the Greek and Roman learned societies, and later on the one's beyond the Rubicon, learned about the early Islamic empires' quest for knowledge in medicine, pharmacology and alchemy. During the renaissance, much of the work of early pre-Islamic times from empires such as Rome, Greece, Pahlavi and India were translated into Arabic. It included medical dictionaries and books from hygiene to sexual intercourse and dis-eases and insanity as well as human anatomy. It included Rhazes ((864 or 865–925 or 935 AD) and Persian polymath Ibn Sina (980 – 1037AD), in the West better known as Avicenna. He was a child prodigy and physician before the age of 20.

Both these gentlemen profoundly influenced European medieval learned society of all rank and file at all fields of education, including that of medicine. Rhazes' work *Al-Mansuri* became part of European universities' medical curriculum. His chapters "On Surgery" and "A General Book on Therapy" were particularly popular.

So did many of Avicenna's works, its corpus including writings on psychology, astronomy, alchemy, geography, geology, Islamic theology, logic, mathematics, physics and poetry. His five-volume work *The Canon of Medicine* is said to be a clear and ordered summa of medical knowledge at Ibn Sina's time augmented with his own observations. In its first volume, we read, Avicenna talks about generalities of the human body, such as sickness, health, therapeutics and treatments. It also includes his view that we are born with an innate heat. About this, he said, "We should strive throughout our lifetime to maintain that original balance and equilibrium in regard to its three aspects of the self: body, mind (soul) and energy (spirit)" (*Avicenna: The Canon of Medicine.* Kazi.org). We are also told that Ibn Sina's holistic medicine approach is adhered to throughout this work, whether it be in theory, practice, diagnosis or treatment. Considered a medical encyclopaedia, his *Canon* became standard medical reading at European medieval universities, remaining in use until the mid-seventeenth century, when everything seemed to have gone topsy turvy.

Avicenna is still considered the father of modern medicine and one of the most significant physicians, astronomers, writers, and philosophers the world has ever known, Whereas his *Canon of Medicine* deals with just that, medicine, in his work *The Book of Healing*, published in 1027 AD, seeks to find ways to "cure" or "heal" our "ignorance of the soul." This ignorance is a lack of knowledge of our most important self, our *sui generis*. He discusses the mind, its existence, the mind-body relationship, sensation, perception and so forth. He explains that at the most common level of our being, the influence of the mind on the body can be seen in our voluntary movements in that the body obeys whenever our mind wishes to move it.

He furthermore states that the second level of influence of the mind on the body comes from our emotions and our will. For example, he writes, consider a plank of wood placed as a bridge over a chasm. A person could hardly creep over it without falling off, if they vividly picture themself falling, as the "natural power of limbs will accord with it" due to the power of the mind. Strong negative emotions negatively affect humans' vegetative functions, our bodily processes (such as eating, sleeping, menstruation, bowel function and movements, bladder activity and sexual activities) directly concerned with maintaining life. If interrupted, they can even lead to death, he says.

Ibn Sina also discusses hypnosis (*al Wahm al-Amil*). He writes that humans can create conditions in one another so that they accept the reality of hypnosis without knowing they are being hypnotized. In other words, a strong personality or soul can influence others via hypnosis, wit Hitler's Nuremberg Rallies designed by Edward Bernays. This manifestation of mass hypnosis was an approach Bernays dubbed the engineering of consent to control and regiment the masses according to "our will without their knowing about it." To do so, it was necessary to appeal not to the rational part of the mind, but the unconscious. This was done by inducing a state of hypnosis. As Bernays states in his book *Propaganda*, published in 1928:

"The conscious and intelligent manipulation of the organized habits and opinions of the masses is an important element in democratic society. Those who manipulate this unseen mechanism of society constitute an invisible government, which is the true ruling power of our country. We are governed, our minds are moulded, our tastes formed, and our ideas suggested, largely by men we have never heard of.... It is they who pull the wires that control the public mind."

Sigismund Schlomo Freud and associates were aware of Avicenna's millennia old knowledge and know how. They regularly briefed nephew Edward on how to create conditions by way of hypnosis for humans would accept as reality what the Luciferic consciousness wants them to accept.

Avicenna furthermore pays special attention to the relation between cognition and mental disorders (*āfāt al-dhihn*). In his writings on psychology and medicine, he identifies two ways of diagnosing mental disorders. One way is in relation to the function of the senses. The other is in relation to the internal faculties. A psychological phenomenon commonly exhibited in such disorders is the experience of hallucinatory content. This is having a perceptible content presented to the mind as if it were the perception of an object that exists in the external reality (Ahmed Alwishah: "Avicenna on Perception, Cognition, and Mental Disorders: The Case of Hallucination"; *Forms of Representation in the Aristotelian Tradition*. Volume One: Sense Perception Chapter 4, p. 124–147).

Avicenna, teaching about human perception, divided it into the five classical external senses of hearing, sight, smell, taste, and touch. These have been known since ancient times. To these, he added another five internal senses, namely:

1. Sensus communis, the common sense, which integrates sense data into percepts.

This was first introduced in the field of psychological study by Aristotle in the De Anima after examining the function of each peripheral sense-organ of sight, hearing, smiling, tasting and touch. It is he who originally proceeded to the analysis of the "Sensus Communis." It discriminates between these particular perceptions, which are perceived by the five senses, and unites them into perceptual wholes, the common sense. But what is a percept?

- A mental concept that is developed as a consequence of the process of perception.

In other words, whoever controls human perception controls the world. Create cognitive dissonance and humanity is rendered numb, dumb, confused, and docile. It can be ruled with great facility, wit COVID -19 and its aftermath. The confusion of our perception also nullifies the guiding principles of precepts. These govern and control our own personal moral and ethical conduct associated with the general rules of human behavior. These rules, intended to influence and regulate our behavior and thoughts, can be found in the Ten Commandments, brought down from the mountain by Moses. He smashed them into the ground and then got them re-issued. Rules like these can also be found in technical and scientific matters, the AI and human 2.0 creation perhaps included.

Mr. Browne's Precept examples are:

- "When given the choice between being right or being kind, choose kind." Your deeds are your monuments."—Inscription on an Egyptian tomb "Have no friends not equal to yourself." —Confucius.
- "Fortune favours the bold." – Virgil
- "No man is an island, entire of itself."—John Donne (https://choosekind.tumblr.com/post/124487320642/mr-brownes-precepts)

Another one of Avicenna's internal senses of which Freud et al. were most likely aware is:

2. The imaginative faculty, which conserves the perceptual images

The science of psychology calls our human ability to imagine "the faculty of imagining". It is the ability to form mental images, sensations and concepts at a moment's notice, when they are or are not perceived through sight, hearing or any other of our senses. In psychology, it generally refers to the ability to mentally represent sensations that are not physically present. It might also refer to holding in mind an image that may not yet reflect facts about the external world or reality at present (Sandeep Gautam: "The Faculty of Imagination: Neural Substrates And Mechanisms"; *Science 2.0,* 2007). Inventions, for example, are generated by the inventor imagining his invention by way of an act of imagination. Or he might recall it from dreams or use previous memories. These techniques span from imagining novel inventions, such as Tesla's and Einstein's and Edison's to, the imagining of future personal or world events. Imagination is also sometimes the seat of humans' practical intellect.

3. Wahm the human instinct and intuition, which perceives in others the characteristics of good and bad, love and hate, the basis of another's character outside of reason, or the instinctual behavior when in certain situations.

Mother's taking care of their children would be an example. Dogs shaking themselves when wet and birds migrating north during spring are instincts. Whereas Avicenna's estimation of our innate intuition, included in Wahm, has been disbursed of in most humans' consciousness by brainwashing. It works against the learned society's objective of complete control, as it alerts us to great danger as well as great possibilities in our personal lives. Thus, it gives us the pathways to both joy and catastrophe, for better or for worse, if we tune into it.

Part of our *sui generis,* The Darwinian scientism philosophy that demands scientific validation hastened to extinguish Avicenna's observation of humans' intuition. So, our acquaintance Wilhelm Wundt (1832–1920) in his own vivid imagination developed over 4,000 human instinct-driven "wahms" composing our behavior, which I will refrain from recording.

William McDougall (1871–1938) was British-born, Oxford educated. He was influential in establishing experimental and physiological psychology among the United States learned society and those they taught. The influence came after he and his buddy Myers thought it a splendid idea to heal WWI shell-shocked soldiers by awakening their "repressed trauma memories" to integrate them into the soldiers' consciousness. The big idea was to do this through further traumatizing them, in his own instinct theory imagined, like Wundt conceived that all human instincts were composed through humans' perception, behavior and emotion. Therefore, in his imagination and sickness of mind and perception, McDougall decreed that for an instinct to be an instinct, the instinct must be unlearned. In other words, it cannot have been taught. It must be uniform in expression and universal in species from amoeba to homo sapien, animals all, except for himself, of course.

The fourth of Ibn Sina's view of internal senses is:

4. Ma'ni, intentions, estimative power, which conserve all the above notions in memory

> Ma'ni is that which conserves in memory all previous notions and, he thought, was produced both by man's potential intellect (within man) and the active intellect (outside man). He also maintained that cognition could not be mechanically produced but involved intuition at every stage of learning. According to him, the ordinary human mind is like a mirror upon which a succession of ideas reflects from the active intellect. Before getting knowledge that emanates from the active intellect, the mirror is rusty. But when we actively think, the mirror becomes polished, and it remains so when directing it to the sun (active intellect) so that it can readily reflect light and absorb knowledge (www.scribd.com/document/372629335/Abu-Ali-Al).

In his psychological explanations of certain somatic illnesses, Ibn Sina thought of philosophizing as a way of making "the soul reach perfection" and as a path to healing, always linking physical and psychological illnesses. For example, he called melancholia a type of depression, a mood disorder in which the person may become suspicious and develop certain types of phobias. Anger, he said, heralded the transition of melancholia to mania. He explained that humidity inside the head could contribute to mood disorders when the amount of breath changed. Happiness increases the breath, he said, which leads to increased moisture inside the brain. But if this moisture went beyond its limits, the brain would lose control over its rational thought, leading to mental disorders. He also used psychological methods to treat his patients, Ibn Sina wrote about symptoms and treatment of love sickness (Ishq), nightmare, epilepsy, and weakness of memory.

Avicenna often used psychological methods to treat his patients. One such example is when a Persian prince had melancholia, suffering from the delusion that he was a cow. He would moo and cry out, "Kill me so that a good stew may be made of my flesh," and would never eat anything. Avicenna was persuaded to take the case. Avicenna sent a message to the patient, asking him to be happy, as the butcher was coming to slaughter him. The sick man rejoiced. When Avicenna approached the prince with a knife in his hand, he asked,

"Where is the cow so I may kill it?" The patient then mooed like a cow to indicate where he was. The patient was laid on the ground for slaughter. When Avicenna approached the patient, pretending to be ready to slaughter him, he said, "The cow is too lean and not ready to be killed. He must be fed properly and I will kill it when it becomes healthy and fat." The patient was then offered food, which he ate eagerly, and gradually "gained strength, got rid of his delusion, and was completely cured."

And what is estimative power, also known as estimative sense? It is a power of knowledge whose characteristic act is concrete evaluation or estimation. Spoken of as a distinct power of knowledge first by Avicenna, it was accepted as such by the majority of medieval thinkers (encyclopedia.com). Thomistic philosophy is the philosophical and theological school that arose as a legacy of the Dominican philosopher and theologian Thomas Aquinas (1225–1274). He was known for his questions and commentaries on Aristotle. The estimative power in Thomistic philosophy is conceived very much as it was by Avicenna (ST 1a, 78.4). However, many of the learned society later on either thought it of little importance, rejected it entirely or refused to recognize it as distinct from human imagination.

The fifth of Avicenna's internal senses is:

5. Memory

> Memory as an internal sense? I am unwilling to dive into that one, as it opens a kettle of fish of enormous proportions. Thus, suffice it to say that the learned society refers to human memory as the human processes of acquiring, storing, retaining and retrieving past experiences and information. Their research suggests that we are in possession of sensory, short-term and long-term memory, using all three throughout our lives to influence and affect our behaviour.

It is tempting to think of memory as computer storage or a tape recording that can be played back to perfection at will. But human memory is far more complex and changeable than that, we are told. Even our ideas of how memory works have changed over the years, we hear. For example, it is said that during the 1960s, a theory known as cell memory or cellular memory suggested that all cells in the body, not just brain cells, are capable of storing memories, and that we have a heart in every cell.

Avicenna, Ibn Sina most likely pondered the issue as he wrote his medical science book The Canon of over one million words. It remains a guiding light in the field for those able to read outside their scientific community indoctrination. He was heavily influenced by Aristotle's philosophy, in adolescence reading *Metaphysics* 40 times whilst making revisions and modifications to it including in the number of senses we possess. This should not be held against him, as philosophers to this day argue Aristotle's points. In other words, does it seem that they lack the ability to proceed further in their own con genitive abilities and imaginations, with the exception of their imagined science of psychiatry and psychology, in which their phantasies and hallucinations know no bounds?

Avicenna's major departure from Aristotle involved the active intellect. For Aristotle, it was used to understand universal principles beyond the scope of empirical observation. But for Avicenna, it was used to understand God, the highest level of knowledge. In his view, it was best attained through mystical illumination, through meditation and inner contemplation, seemingly all bred out of most of Western humanity in recent memory.

In the East, however, the quest for knowledge is still seen as a divine command. Knowledge of the soul, and particularly of the intellect, is thus still a critical component of this quest. The mastery of this subject of mind and soul provided a framework within which the mechanics and nature of human sensations and thoughts could be explained and integrated as well as it offered the for every other field of inquiry under the sun (*Arabic and Islamic Psychology and Philosophy of Mind*, 2012; Stanford.edu.)

Avicenna was into everything and anything, it seems. The list of just some of the properties of healing and the affects of harmful drugs include loss of memory, how to increase brain matter, prevent hangovers, purify the brain and removing: obstructions from the brain as well as giving psychological explanations for some somatic illnesses whilst consistently linking physical and psychological illnesses. Avicenna prescribes sleep-inducing drugs and drugs strengthening memory, brain and teeth. He treated coma,; gum bleeding, colds, respiratory tract ailments, dandruff, deafness and impaired hearing of all ages. Including depression lethargy; mania; melancholia; migraine headaches, strokes and stupors produced by narcotics.

In all of it, he Avicenna made an argument for the existence of God known as the "Proof of the Truthful" (Arabic: *burhan al-siddiqin*), in which he argued that there must be a "necessary existent" (Arabic: *wajib al-wujud*), an entity that cannot *not* exist and through a series of arguments, he identified it with the Islamic conception of God. The American academic Peter Scott Adamson (1972-), professor of philosophy in late antiquity and in the Islamic world at the Ludwig Maximilian University of Munich as well as professor of ancient and medieval philosophy at King's College London whose own creed is unknown, calls Avicenna's argument/view one of the most influential medieval arguments for God's existence and Avicenna's biggest contribution to the history of philosophy (Adamson 2013, p. 170).

The medical encyclopedia of Ibn Sina or Avicenna (d. AD 1037) is known as the *Qanun fi t-tibb, The Canon of Medicine*. It represents the culmination in Islamic medicine of the long period of translation, study, and reformulation of primarily Galen's work. As we have seen, this was part of an even longer process of systematization of Greek medicine that had begun in late antiquity. A substantial body of secondary medical works in Arabic had also been produced by the time of Ibn Sina, that fleshed out the Galenic system. The medieval medical writers supplemented and unified Galen's teachings, removing uncertainties and inconsistencies, and occasionally questioning the teachings and adding new material. In the case of insanity, where Galen had said very little, there was more latitude for both theoretical speculation and therapeutic diversity than in other areas.

Nevertheless, Galen's basic humoral principles were extended in a highly schematic manner but cut down somewhat so that medieval Galenism was not as eclectic as Galen's teaching had originally been. Following the work of Ishaq Ibn Imran (died c. 903-9), Ali ibn al-'Abbas al-Majusi (930- 994) or Haly Abbas, Rhazes and Avicenna, all Islamic legal scholars, as well as theologians who engaged in the medical discourses of their time, recognized the role of the brain and the soma in what we currently label as neurological and psychiatric disorders. This was during a time when most of the world still attributed abnormal behavior to spirit possession and sorcery. Michael W. Dols book *Majnun: The Madman In Medieval Islamic Society* was published by Oxford University Press in 1992. This study of madness in the medieval Islamic world used a wide variety of sources from history, literature, and art to explore beliefs about madness in Islamic society. It examines attitudes towards individuals afflicted by mental illness or disability.

The book is said to furthermore demonstrate the links between Christian and Muslim medical beliefs and practices. It traces the influence of certain Christian beliefs, such as miracle working, on Islamic practices. It analyses the notions of the romantic fool, the wise fool and the holy fool in medieval Islam within the framework of perceptions of mental illness. Thus, it shows that the madman was neither regarded as a pariah, an outcast or a scapegoat. Instead, the author's examination of magic, medicine and religion helps us to open up our understanding of medieval Islamic society in comparison to that of European ones. The book is available for about US$200 on Amazon.

Aristotle held that what separated the soul of man from the souls of animals was man's possession of reason and intellect. This idea resonated with later Christian writers, who were interested in the role that man's reason played in his relationship with God. One of the best-known biblical cases of madness was that of Nebuchadnezzar, king of Babylon, Sumer, and Akkad. He was King of the Universe, ruling from 605 to his death in 562 BC. It encapsulates this relationship between reason and madness, man and beast, divine favor and punishment (Daniel 4:1–37) (Trenery, Claire and Peregrine Horden, "Madness in the Middle Ages", in *The Routledge History of Madness and Mental Health* ed. Greg Eghigian (Abingdon: Routledge, 19 Apr 2017), accessed 05 Jun 2023 , Routledge Handbooks Online.).

Understanding the role of the mind was vital for human beings for millennia. Spirituality and practice, and discussions of the mind and the soul featured prominently in all societies worldwide. Professor emerita of Toronto University Faculty of Arts & Science, Ruth Harvey, who examined the relationship between philosophical and medical teachings on the nature of the body and mind during medieval times. She notes the ambiguous nature of the bodily spirits. They both partook of the physical constitution of the body and provided the link by which the mind communicated with the bodily organs. She argues that doctors were led to treat disordered reason almost as though it was of a purely physical function. On the other hand, the learned societies' philosophers insisted reason as such fell outside medical control.

Christian theology of the mind was studied extensively by historians. But it is rarely connected with madness, we read, because ancient and medieval philosophers themselves seldom focused on madness specifically. That said, the medieval concept of "bodily spirits" can be traced back to the Stoic school of the fourth century BC influenced by Aristotle. The Stoic philosophers were fond to believe that the soul operated through the agency of *pneuma* (*spiritus* in Latin), bodily spirits. These animating spirits were witnessed by the physician in the air that breathed in and out of the body. The *pneuma* was material, but its form was finer than that of other elements, allowing it to express the soul's intentions through the physicality of the body. The Stoics placed the source of pneuma in the heart, the hydraulic model, as science calls it. But Hippocratic located it in the brain and connected it with the three faculties of imagination, reason and memory.

The hydraulic model of the mind and its influence in Anglo-Saxon England is the subject of Leslie Lockett's book *Anglo-Saxon Psychologies*. She examines both metaphorical and literal applications of cardio-centric psychologies in Anglo-Saxon vernacular and Latin writings. Lockett traces the development in ancient Greek epic, Aristotelian philosophy and Biblical narrative of the localisation of reason and emotion in the organs of the chest and abdomen. She draws attention to the relationship between body, mind and soul, and the strong connection between all three in the hydraulic model. This model denied the total incorporeality of the soul because of its physical association with specific areas of the body.

Patristic texts from the eighth century onwards excluded the New Testament written by Christians before the 8th century. The increased circulation of these brought to prominence the Augustinian model of the soul as an incorporeal entity, without physical location and possessing the faculties of reason. This raised questions on the moral implications of madness in the soul and the ability of mad people to engage with the Christian community.

Tommaso d'Aquino (1225 -1274) was an Italian Dominica friar immensely influential in philosophy, theology and jurisprudence. His philosophical writings were widely circulated in the later Middle Ages. He argued that mad men and women were members of the Christian community because, unlike irrational animals, they possessed rational souls, but had lost the use of their reason through bodily impairments. Likewise, the Sacrament could be given to those who had lost their reason but had formerly shown devotion towards the host. It seems that the inability to express devotion through one's rational faculty did not mean that the incorporeal soul could not benefit from the Sacrament.

Nonetheless, whilst the human soul was incorporeal, it was certainly not incorruptible. It could be led astray either by the passions of the physical body or through the temptation of demons. From as early as the fourth century, *acedia*, a condition of the brain's faculties, was associated with spiritual impairment. Variously defined as a state of listlessness or torpor, of not caring or not being concerned with one's condition and position in the world, in ancient Greek *akidía* literally meant an inert state without pain or care. Early Christian monks used the term to define a spiritual state of listlessness related to melancholy and delusions. From there, it developed into a Christian moral tone and in the DSM converted into the generic term "depression." Acedia was sometimes also associated with the sin of sloth, with the proposed treatment of confession. But it could also be attributed to excess phlegm or black bile in the rational faculty supposedly eased with relaxation and music. Undesirable behaviour, however, could be connected with a problem in the brain, which could require both physical and spiritual treatment.

Luke Demaitre (1935-) in his book *Medieval Medicine: The Art of Healing, from Head to Toe*, examines conditions based on that, commonly adopted by medieval medical writers themselves. He dedicates a chapter to conditions of the head, in medieval medical manuals known as *practica*. In the chapter, he discusses "the hair, the skull and brain, mental function, and motor control." To understand medieval conceptions of madness, however, we have to consider what influenced physicians' medical ideas, he says. It seems they cannot be easily divided into today's categories of psychological and neurological complaints (Praeger; Illustrated edition, 2013).

Historian Monica H. Green, who earned an B. A. degree from Barnard College in 1978, a master's (1981) and a PhD from Princeton University in 1985 with her doctoral thesis entitled, *The Transmission of Ancient Theories of Female Physiology and Disease Through the Early Middle Ages*, as expert in the history of women's healthcare in pre-modern Europe, medicine and gender in the course of her career compiled a list of Latin medical manuscripts in circulation in the twelfth century to find, that at least 375 codices, totalling 145 distinct texts including that of great medical writers of antiquity such as Hippocrates and Galen had been translated into Latin as early as the sixth century AD, but rarely taken into consideration never mind consulted until scholarly interest in their theories renewed in the eleventh century in the medical school Schola Medica Salernitana in Salerno. Situated on the Tyrrhenian Sea in southern Italia, the city became the most important source and centre of/for medical knowledge in Western Europe at the time. People from all over the world flocked to the "Schola Salerni", the sick in the hope of recovering and the students to learn the art of medicine. The schools' approach to healing was based on the synthesis of the Greek-Latin tradition, supplemented by notions from Arab and Jewish cultures. It used the practice and culture of prevention rather than curing, since then inverted to cure rather than prevent. After all, a patient cured is a customer lost, eh?

Salerno's medical texts were widely circulated amongst European universities and monasteries, with the Hippocratic humoral model forming the basis for discussions of health and sickness. The body's functions were believed to be reliant on four humors and their associated qualities:

- blood (hot and wet)
- yellow bile or choler (hot and dry)
- black bile (cold and dry)
- phlegm (cold and wet)

These humours had to be regulated (for example, by diet) to maintain a natural state of health. Imbalances in the humours led to what modern practitioners would classify as physical and mental health conditions (although unable to pinpoint why, as they receive no education on nutrition's value to the human body, the most important aspect of maintaining human health).

Avicenna's *Canon of Medicine*, translated into Latin in the twelfth century. It became standard medical text for most European university professors and physicians soon thereafter, including his idea of brain symmetry. Divided into three parts, he located its imaginative faculty at the front of the brain, processing the information received by the senses (hence its proximity to the sense-receptors of the face). This information, he thought, was passed on to the central brain faculty, rationality, which formed it into concepts and judgments. Memories were stored at the back of the brain, with images literally imprinted on the wet matter. In his view, mental illnesses were caused by humoral or anatomical abnormalities in one or more of these areas. For example, amnesia indicated a problem in the memory faculty, such as the rising of hot vapors to the back of the head, which interfered with storing images.

Madness, *amentia/insania* in Latin, was rarely discussed as a distinct condition in any medical manual. Instead, it was seen as symptomatic of other conditions, or it was used as a generic term for illnesses of the imaginative and rational faculties that affected the cognitive functions of the brain. The three main conditions associated with madness in medical texts were:

- frenzy (*frenesis*)
- mania (*mania*)
- melancholy (*melancholia*)

Precise symptoms and healing techniques varied slightly from writer-to-writer, but those found in the *Liber pantegni* held beliefs together in one place. This medieval medical text compiled by Constantinus Africanus (died before 1098/99) was considered the first fully comprehensive medical text in Latin, providing a broad array of learning on anatomy, physiology, and therapeutics of commonly.

Both mania and melancholy were seen as chronic conditions. Mania was characterized by frantic behavior. It was associated with stupor of the mind, a condition also connected with frenzy. Gariopontus, an eleventh-century Salernitan physician, noted that the symptoms of madness could be similar in both conditions. He explained the difference was that maniacs lacked the fever from which frenetics suffered. Because the symptoms of mania often seemed inexplicable, physicians observed that the condition could be associated with demonic or divine activity. One theory put forward by physicians was that mania was the result of an excessive diet, and thus purgatives that would induce vomiting or sweating were used to restore humoral balance.

Melancholy could also result from humoral imbalance, as excess black bile in the form of vapor could rise from the stomach to the brain, affecting a patient's understanding in the rational faculty. Melancholic patients, often sad and suspicious with an inability to rationalize the world around them left many in a predicament. Hallucinations and delusions were common, with some patients barking like dogs and others crowing like roosters. Various herbal remedies would be applied to restore humoral balance through purging. In his assessment of medieval understandings of melancholy, Jackson stresses that both relaxation and body restraints were used on melancholic patients. Entertainment like music to provide a distraction and lighten patients' the mood and, on the other end of the spectrum, restraints to prevent a patient from hurting himself and others. Fernando Salmón also argues, that medical treatments for madness relied very much on the physician's interaction with the needs of the patient.

How successful they were curing their patients is hard to assess. Constantine was careful to create his herbal remedies for melancholy in a way that was fairly simple for physicians to prepare. He wanted them to be easy for outsiders to use, as learned medical ideas were spread outside of universities by university-based physicians as early as the early twelfth century. He specifically targeted monastic communities, who also had access to medical *practica* in their libraries. The miraculous cures of many a mad pilgrim were recorded at shrines. These records did sometimes refer to medical ideas, though with notably less frequency than was the case for other conditions. Multiple theories on the nature of madness co-existed and there was a synchronicity of various models of madness in the Middle Ages. This was exposed by a study of practical provisions for the mad and of literary and artistic portrayals of madness throughout that time, one of them being demonic interference or possession.

Was possession the same as madness? And in what ways were demons believed to influence physical and cognitive function?

Earlier writers stipulated that, whilst demons had no ability to enter the soul of a human, they could enter the body and manipulate the mind. They could confuse the imagination with erroneous images or impair reason so that the victim was unable to comprehend the information received by the senses. As interest in the human spirits grew from the twelfth century onwards, so did the attention to the movements of demonic spirits in the world. Nancy Caciola examined the discernment of spirits, the process by which demonic spirits were differentiated from divine spirits, and its development in the later Middle Ages. She concluded that distinctions were not always made between demonic possession and madness. She noted that both included wild gestures, violence, twisted facial expressions and shouting.

Signs more typical of demoniacs were abnormal powers, convulsions, blaspheming, abhorrence of sacred objects and aggression. Madness, especially violent madness, could be associated with demonic interference. The language of possession, that victims were "seized" or "tormented" by demons, illustrates the violence with which this affliction was connected.

From the thirteenth century onwards, madness was becoming naturalised, and the language of demonic possession became less prominent. Nonetheless, despite the waning use of demonic terminology in official records, there is still evidence of widespread belief in demonic influence over the mind: canonization dossiers recorded that those cured of madness had *believed* that they were possessed. It is important when considering medieval perceptions of madness to acknowledge, that the medieval period witnessed great diversity of belief in the sphere of the natural and the supernatural, we read. Demonic and humoral explanations for madness were mutually inclusive, with the precise aetiology of cognitive malfunction often difficult to discern.

And what provisions were made for the mad in medieval law, if any?

The best-preserved legal records from medieval Europe are found in England, including those understanding the legal position of the mad. Mad men and women who had no possessions and who had not committed a crime were far less likely to enter the legal record, mind you. Opinions on the fate of those deemed mad differ greatly within the learned society of historians on the topic. Some opine that the Anglo-Saxon state offered leniency and protection for mad offenders. Others challenge this thesis by drawing attention to the absence of leniency and inconsistency in cases of mad suicide, as it was rather difficult to ascertain the mental state of the dead perpetrator. Nonetheless, establishing the nature of a suicide was vitally important because a suicide due to a criminal offence committed could not bequeath possessions to his/her heirs and could not receive a Christian burial. It is for this reason that mad suicides feature in the legal record.

The vast majority of cases described violent madness in the forms of frenzy and fury. Medieval juries recognizing these forms of madness as an "illness" and rarely mentioned sin or any fault on the part of the sufferer as a contributing factor. A similar state of affairs seems to have existed in medieval France, where officials were wary of prosecuting mad offenders. Because of their lack of understanding, they were barred from bringing cases to court and from acting as legal witnesses. If in doubt, legal diagnosis of madness could be made by testing the subject's cognitive capability by asking questions about his/her family, community and daily activities. Juries would also consider a person's "emotional" reaction as appropriate to the situation in which they found themselves to assess the mental state.

There were social implications of the legal provisions for madness in High Medieval England. The insane were predominantly cared for by their families or communities. The wardship of a mad landowner was given to a guardian in cases of idiocy, a term usually applied to those who had been mad since birth. Provisions were based more on custom than on written laws, with legal provision for the mad a rather flexible process.

Naturally, stipulations did not remain static throughout the Middle Ages and the question of whether the mad could receive the Roman Catholic Church sacraments was much debated. A mad person could be baptized so long as others bore witness to previous devotion. Similarly, while a mad person could not enter into a contract of marriage, a marriage contract that had been made when both parties were sane remained valid if either party became mad. There was, however, a concern that those who had been mad since birth had never possessed the ability to consent to baptism, but the consensus seems to have been to place the life-long mad in the same category as infants; they could be cleansed of original sin but, as they did not possess the reason to commit further sins, penance was redundant. Following the same line, mad criminals were to be given a lesser penance upon recovery of their senses; some atonement had to be made for their crimes, but it was acknowledged that, without the capacity to reason, their actions had likely lacked criminal intent.

Despite the biblical connections between sin and madness, as in Nebuchadnezzar, it does not seem that Church authorities specifically categorized madness as resulting from sin. In pre-Crusade saints' lives and chronicles, mental illness broadly includes madness, epilepsy, possession and drunkenness. A relatively small percentage of mental illness cases were attributed directly to sin. In the eyes of the Church, madness seemed a lesser transgression than heresy, and could even be used as a defence against a charge of heresy. As to the relationship between madness, heresy and the Devil, multiple theories existed on this subject at the turn of the thirteenth century. Many contemporary observers found it difficult to distinguish between humoral madness, demonic madness and madness as cover for heresy. There was, however, a suspicion that madness could be feigned, which led to a tightening of regulations concerning it and heresy.

Did those labelled mad or foolish from birth find space in institutions? Many of the diverse foundations in medieval Europe grouped under the heading of "hospital" specifically excluded the mad, along with pregnant women and the acutely ill. Care of those were thought beyond their resources. Even in the late fifteenth century, facilities for the mentally ill in the most medicalized and best-endowed European hospitals remained rudimentary. At Santa Maria Nuova in Florence, a harbinger of the modern hospital in its medical staffing, the insane were simply chained up in a cell and purged or given the occasional sedative of unknown quality and quantity. "We have set apart another place for those who have lost their minds through illness, where they are kept in chains." This brief notice, in a version of the hospital statutes prepared order to impress Henry VII of England follows pages of detail about how the other, physically sick patients are to be received and treated. It suggests a regime little different from the fetters and chains found in the more famous mad hospital of "Bedlam" during a visitation earlier in the fifteenth century.

Only in mediaeval Spain, under Islamic rule, the mad seem to have fared better. Islamic hospitals long evinced a much stronger tradition of functioning as asylums for the mad and placing them under medical supervision. Madness could be seen as a form of redemption for the mad character. After alienating oneself from society, one was able to find spiritual renewal or moral punishment and a means by which the character could reconnect with God.

The dual concept of madness saw it as both a moral punishment and a form of spiritual redemption. Punishment was rendered in the course of cosmic law of cause and effect, reducing the sufferer to the status of a beast in the Christian sense. Redemption was expressed throughout medieval art, if someone cares looking. Nebuchadnezzar is a favourite. In the later Middle Ages, the isolation of the mad and the tempestuousness of their minds was shown in Plato's allegory *Ship of Fools* originating from "Book 8" of his *Republic*. Plato describes how a democracy is unlikely to be a stable political solution, since it offers freedom but neglects the demands of proper statecraft. The allegory is mirrored by a ship with a dysfunctional crew representing the problems of governance through others, but perhaps also the lack of governance of the Self?

Therefore, Plato predicts the certain collapse of democracy and decline into tyranny, a total loss of freedom. Why does democracy involve a neglect of statecraft? Plato argues that in a system where political power (*cratos*) lies in the hands of the people (*demos*), it is unlikely that those best equipped to rule will get a chance to manage public affairs. Instead, the loudest voices will dominate. Irrational, ill-motivated decisions will be made. Thus, the complex arena of politics, which is in need of carful ordering and management, will turn into a crazy circus. The *Ship of Fools* presently mirrors world affairs by governments ruled by the Luciferic consciousness possessed, perhaps?

German humanist and satirist Sebastian Brandt (1458 –1521) portrayed the concept in his 1494 book *Das Narrenschiff* (The Ship of Fools). In the fifteenth and sixteenth centuries' literary and artistic European environment, it also served to parody the Roman Catholic Church as the "ark of salvation." Remember, from around 590 to 1517, the Roman Catholic Church dominated the Western world (Dr. Jack L. Arnold: "The Roman Catholic Church Of The Middle Ages: Reformation Men and Theology", Lesson 1 of 11; *IIIM Magazine Online*, Volume 1, Number 1, March 1 to March 7, 1999).

The Roman Catholic Church controlled religion, philosophy, morals, politics, art and education at a time when the vital doctrines of biblical Christianity had almost disappeared. It was theologically sick, atrociously corrupt, spiritually exhausted, enfeebled and almost lifeless as it had almost completely departed from the teaching of Christ. No Christian, Roman Catholic, Protestant or independent can gloss over this black period of Christian history until the Reformation, says Dr. Jack L. Arnold (1935-2005). He earned a doctorate of systematic theology from Dallas Theological Seminary in 1966 and served as President of Equipping Pastors International and Pastor Emeritus of Covenant Presbyterian Church in Oviedo, Florida, until his death in 2005.

The Infallibility of the pope, officially declared church dogma since 1870, was an assumed fact. As early as 590, Gregory the Great called himself "the servant of servants", believing that he was supreme among all bishops. Hildebrand, or Gregory VII (eleventh century), held, that as Vicar of Christ and representative of Peter he could give or take away empires. Fourteenth century Pope Boniface VII proudly announced:

> "We declare, state, define and pronounce that for every human creature to be subject to the Roman pope is altogether necessary for salvation" (B. K. Kuiper *The Church in History*).

Thus, from the lowest peasant to the mightiest ruler, everyone regardless of creed or religion has to recognize the Roman Catholic pope as Christ's earthly representative. They must accept him as supreme ruler over all religious and political matters, regardless of individual states of mind or afflictions. All who did not were damned, as to give God's salvation was the prerogative of the Roman Catholic Church only. Every person disagreeing with this doctrine came in line of a heresy trial with torture and eternal damnation due to excommunication, which was portrayed as similar to the loss of one's soul, wit the Spanish and Roman inquisitions. Thus, the term "Ark of Salvation" used for the Roman Catholic Church.

However, until Henry VIII sprang into action, it did to some extend take care of the needy, the lunatics and the poor. It used them as labourers on their fields and vineyards giving them food and shelter in return. Only a small subsection of those were considered mad, and they were housed in a variety of institutional settings, as the mentally ill were generally left in their family. It is said, though, that they were widely abused, particularly in the territories where Christianity ruled. Beatings, torture and exile were common due to stigma and shame attached to madness. Many were locked away in cellars or in cages, left under the control of servants, or kicked out to find their own way in the world.

With medieval Europe and its medicinal practices overtaken by Christianity, exorcisms, chants and torture became the norm to treat those considered deranged (Hayden Chakra: "How People With Mental Illnesses Were Treated in the Middle Ages"; https://about-history.com 2021). As learned society folk believed humors and fluids caused mental illness, patients were given laxatives and emetics, and they were bled using cupping and leeches to balance the body. Any form of physical bleeding was induced, including extracting blood from the forehead, tapping haemorrhoidal veins or from the head in general. Tobacco imported from America was later on used to encourage vomiting. The mentally ill were thrown into ice cold waters to "bring them to their senses." A concoction of black hellebore, clocynth and aloes were given to cleanse out melancholy, the concoction called *Hiera Logadii* together with restraining them to prohibit movement.

Only a few continental European towns made provisions for the mentally disturbed. In Germany, they could find a home in the *Narrentürme* (fools' towers). In Paris, the ancient Hôtel-Dieu, the House of God, gave them shelter. It is said to have been established by St. Landericus who became bishop of Paris in 650, in the Frankish kingdom (formally Gaul) during the reign of Clovis II and served as bishop until 656 or, some records show, until his death in 661.

St. Landericus was a very earnest and devout man, distinguished especially by his great love of the poor and by his charity. To relieve their suffering during the famine of 651, he sold both his personal and church possessions. He became increasingly aware that the sick and poor were not really cared for by the custom then in vogue of housing them in little hotels dependent on casual generosity. He is said, therefore, to have founded the city's first real hospital. It was dedicated to St. Christopher and erected near Notre-Dame, in time becoming known as the Hotel-Dieu, with a small number of cells set aside for the lunatics. In Spain, the institutions for the insane established by the Islamic rulers in accordance with waqf were seemingly kept running in Spain after the Christian Reconquista finalized in 1492.

In Britain, London's Priory of Saint Mary of Bethlehem of 1247 was known as Bedlam. It housed six lunatic men at start of the fifteenth century to take care of those deemed insane, which is already known to us.

France's atheist philosopher Paul-Michel Foucault (1926 – 25 June 1984) was an accused pedophile who argued in1977 that children could give sexual consent. Along with Jean-Paul Sartre and other intellectuals, he petitioned the French Parliament to decriminalize all "consensual" sexual relations between adults and minors below the age of fifteen. In his book *Madness and Civilization: A History of Insanity in the Age of Reason, Folie et déraison*, he proposes that madness came to replace the gradual disappearance of leprosy on the continent. His ship of fools presented the literary version of the fifteenth century exclusionary practice of putting lepers on ships rather than reflecting Plato's *Republic* originating from Book VI of Plato's Republic, about a ship with a dysfunctional crew, the allegory intended to represent the problems of governance prevailing in a political system not based on expert knowledge.

Be it as it may, in seventeenth-century Europe, in what Foucault describes as the "Great Confinement," members of society considered "unreasonable" were locked away and institutionalised.

By the eighteenth century, madness came to be seen as the obverse, the contrary, of reason. Not until Freud came along was it converted into mental illness, then converting the human mind into a specie of scientism. This was translated into mental disorders, a scientifically improvable human state of mind, oft times hallucinated into existence by the mental health cabal or portrayed as normal with Foucault himself and his tutors. Of upper-middle class family, with degrees in philosophy and psychology, Foucault was a homosexual accused of pedophilia whilst lecturing from 1966 to 1968 at the University of Tunisia in Tunis. He was tutored by Marxist philosopher Louis Pierre Althusser (1918 -1990), a long-time member of the French Communist Party. Althusser's whose life was marked by periods of intense mental illness. In 1980, he killed his wife, Hélène Rytmann (1910 -1980), an Ashkenazi Jew of Russian and Lithuanian origin, by strangling her. Declared unfit to stand trial due to insanity and committed to a psychiatric hospital for three years, he declared that a hiatal hernia-removal surgery had caused him to kill her, first recalling:

> "I wanted not only to destroy myself physically but to wipe out all trace of my time on earth: in particular, to destroy every last one of my books and all my notes… and also, 'if possible,' suppress Hélène herself while I still could."

He later squarely positioned himself as having done his wife a favour when adding:

> "I killed a woman who was everything to me during a crisis of mental confusion, she who loved me to the point of wanting only to die because she could not continue living. And no doubt in my confusion and unconsciousness I 'did her this service,' which she did not try to prevent, but from which she died."—*Althusser, L'avenir dure longtemps.*

Can you see how it is done? These are just two of the role models used for over a century to pervert our minds. In Foucault's case, he claims that the scientific and humanitarian treatments of the insane at the hands of people like Pinel and Tuke were in fact no less controlling than previous methods had been. For instance, Tuke's country retreat for the mad simply consisted of punishing the madmen until they learned to act "reasonably". And Pinel's amounted to an extended aversion therapy – psychotherapy designed to cause a patient to reduce or avoid an undesirable behavior pattern or thought by conditioning the person to associate the behavior with an undesirable stimulus. This is the Pavlovian dog scheme, or the conditional behavior therapy so favored for the PTSD-afflicted and a multitude of other spiritually-caused human emotional upheavals nowadays used in combination with pharmaceutical drugging. Back then, they used freezing showers and straitjackets. In Foucault's view, these amounted to repeated brutality until the pattern of judgment and punishment was internalized by the patient. What would he say of patients' mere mental immobilization through drugging robbing them of their *sui generis* without being aware of it, one wonders, visible by the experimental COVID-19 injection flogged as vaccination visible throughout the world?

Source: https://historydaily.org/bethlem-hospital/7

The HOSPITAL for LUNATICS. -

As we have documented, the level of specialist care and control of the insane in institutions remained extremely limited at the turn of the eighteenth century. Madness was still largely seen as a domestic problem, with families and parish authorities in Europe and England central to regimens of care. Various forms of relief were extended by parish authorities to families in these circumstances, including financial support, access to parish nurses and, where family care was not possible, "boarding out" to other community members or private madhouses. Only if those deemed mad were judged to be particularly disturbing or violent might parish authorities look elsewhere. They would have to pay the considerable costs of charitable asylums such as houses of correction or workhouses. Or they might send them to the Bethlem Royal Hospital, which already in1632 had "below stairs a parlor, a kitchen, two larders, a long entry throughout the house, and 21 rooms wherein the poor distracted people lie, and above the stairs eight rooms more for servants and the poor to lie in." (Stevenson, Christine. "Robert Hooke's Bethlem". *Journal of the Society of Architectural Historians*. 1996;55(3):254–275)

Inmates who were deemed dangerous or disturbing were chained, but Bethlem was an otherwise open building. Its inhabitants could roam around its confines and possibly throughout the general neighborhood. In 1676, Bethlem expanded into newly built premises at Moorfields with a capacity for 100 inmates, extended to about 350 today.

A similar expansion began to take place in the British American colonies. The first psychiatric institution, the Eastern State Hospital, was built in Williamsburg, Virginia, in 1773. It traced its foundation to a speech by Francis Fauquier, Royal Governor of the colony of Virginia, on November 6, 1766, addressing the mentally ill as follows:

> "It is expedient I should also recommend to your Consideration and Humanity a poor unhappy set of People who are deprived of their senses and wander about the Country, terrifying the Rest of their fellow creatures. A legal Confinement, and proper Provision, ought to be appointed for these miserable Objects, who cannot help themselves. Every civilized Country has an Hospital for these People, where they are confined, maintained and attended by able Physicians, to endeavour to restore to them their lost reason." (John P. Kennedy, ed., *Journal of the House of Burgesses of Virginia*, 1766-1769. (Richmond, 1906), p. 12).

Before Fauquier's speeches, mentally ill people were not diagnosed by a doctor. They were judged by 12 citizens, much like a jury, to be either a criminal, lunatic or idiot. Most classified as lunatic were placed in the Public Gaol in Williamsburg. For all we know, the mentally disturbed had mounted in number due to PTSD occurring among those fighting in the French and Indian War, a North American conflict within The Seven Years' War (1756–1763) This was the last major conflict before the French Revolution staged to arise, it seems, out of the attempt of the Austrian House of Habsburg to win back the rich province of Silesia wrestled from it by Prussia's Frederick II, The Great, during the War of the Austrian Succession (1740–48). It involved all the great powers of Europe, with France, Austria, Saxony, Sweden and Russia aligned on one side and Prussia, Hanover and Great Britain on the other.

In essence, France and Britain fought over global superiority, with their overseas colonial possessions in the West Indies, India and North America. The main points of contention resulted in the French and Indian War. With this in mind, the Seven Years' War can be seen as the European part of a worldwide nine years' war fought between France and Great Britain. Prussia allied with England to protect the British ruling dynasty's Continental House of Hanover's possession from a French takeover. After all, since 1714 with George Louis of Hanover ascending to Great Britain's throne as George I and Hanover joined in personal union, the possibility existed of two or more states ruled by the same monarch. Long-standing colonial rivalries pitting Britain against France and Spain in North America and the West Indies were thus fought on a grand scale ending in 1763 with the Treaty of Paris.

British novelist, author and illustrator William Makepeace Thackeray (1811 -1863) was famous for his satirical works, such as his 1848 panoramic portrait of British society in his novel Vanity Fair. His 1844 novel *The Luck of Barry Lyndon*, adapted to a 1975 film by Stanley Kubrick, has this quote about the Seven Years' War:

> "It would require a greater philosopher and historian than I am to explain the causes of the famous Seven Years' War in which Europe was engaged; and, indeed, its origin has always appeared to me to be so complicated, and the books written about it so amazingly hard to understand, that I have seldom been much wiser at the end of a chapter than at the beginning, and so shall not trouble my reader with any personal disquisitions concerning the matter." (Thackeray, William, 2001, p.72).

What we do know is that thousands were slaughtered and violated throughout the world because of the war, thinning the finest of the herd and leaving a multitude emotionally hurt and destitute. And thus, perhaps in preparation for future similar operation known by the elite to occur, governments took action. A sudden onset of taxpayer-funded mental institutions came into fashion. In the British colonies, it began with the "Public Hospital for Persons of Insane and Disordered Minds, the Eastern State Hospital", which admitted its first patients in 1773.

Until then, the only hospital where mentally ill patients were sometimes taken had been the Quakers' Pennsylvania Hotel. It had been established in Philadelphia in 1751 as a result of work begun in 1709 by the Religious Society of Friends. A portion of this hospital had been set apart for the mentally ill, with the first patients admitted in 1752. Adding a wing in 1792, the mentally ill were kept in its basement and out of the way of patients needing medical assistance.

Internationally recognized historian of nursing Patricia D'Antonio is a professor of mental health nursing at the University of Pennsylvania. She writes that in U.S. East Coast cities, both public alms houses and private hospitals set aside separate wards for the mentally ill. Wealthier families paid good money to private hospitals to care for their mentally ill husbands, wives, sons and daughters. These hospitals depended on that money to support their main charitable mission of caring for the physically sick poor.

In the early nineteenth century, the new European ideas about the "moral treatment" of care for the mentally ill filtered through to the colonies. It was built on the assumption that those suffering from mental illness could find their way to recovery and an eventual cure, if treated kindly and in ways that appealed to the parts of their minds that remained rational. Gone were the harsh restraints and long periods of isolation to manage the most destructive behaviours of mentally ill people. New treatment depended on specially built hospitals in quiet, secluded and peaceful country settings. They offered meaningful work, recreation and a system of privileges and rewards for rational behaviours, with gentler kinds of restraints only used for shorter periods (https://nursing.upenn.edu/nhhc/nurses-institutions-caring/history-of-psychiatric-hospitals/).

The Friends Asylum was established by Philadelphia's Quaker community in 1814. It was the first U.S. institution specially built for the full program of moral treatment run by a lay staff rather than by medical men and women. The private institutions that followed, by contrast, chose physicians as administrators. They all chose quiet and secluded sites for these new hospitals, the asylums, to which they would transfer their insane patients.

- Massachusetts General Hospital built the McLean Hospital outside of Boston in 1811.
- The New York Hospital built the Bloomingdale Insane Asylum in Morningside Heights in upper Manhattan in 1816.
- The Pennsylvania Hospital established the Institute of the Pennsylvania Hospital across the river from the city in 1841.

Physician and alienist Thomas Story Kirkbride (1809 -1883) was superintendent for the Institute of the Pennsylvania Hospital. He was also primary founder of the Association of Medical Superintendents of American Institutions for the Insane (AMSAII), the organizational precursor to the American Psychiatric Association. Benjamin Rush was considered father of the modern American practice of psychiatry as a specific medical discipline. Together, they developed the "Kirkbride Plan" for how hospitals devoted to moral treatment should be built and organized. It became the the gold-standard of clinical care in psychiatry throughout the nineteenth century calling for no more than 250 patients living in a building with a central core and long, rambling wings arranged to provide sunshine and fresh air, as well as privacy and comfort.

With both ideas and structures established, reformers throughout the U.S. had a new goal. They urged that mental health treatment available to those who could afford private care now be provided to poorer insane men and women at taxpayers' cost. New England school teacher Dorothea Lynde Dix (1802 -1887) ran a vigorous and sustained program of lobbying state legislatures and the Congress, thus creating the first generation of American mental asylums. She served as a Superintendent of Army Nurses during the U.S. Civil War of 1861-1865. With the emotionally wounded of war to care for, we gather, by the 1870s virtually all states had one or more such asylums funded by state tax dollars—the herd, in other words.

By the 1890s, however, all this was under siege due to economic pressures. Meanwhile, costs of caring for the elderly in local almshouses and public hospitals was growing. So, the learned society of physicians turned the term "senility" into a "psychiatric disorder", which enabled it to send these men and women to state-carried asylums. This then explains why, with the numbers of asylum patients growing exponentially, the size of asylums grew in tandem. Not all of them cared enough for the patients and of inmates' moral treatment often fell by the wayside. Those elderly suffering some form of dementia rapidly deteriorated when placed in an asylum.

Asylum medical superintendents are said to have taken such news seriously. They proposed setting up training schools for nurses within their institutions to improve quality of the care. Nurse-training schools had first been established in U.S. general hospitals in the 1860s and 1870s. Asylum superintendents hoped they would be as successful in their institutions. U.S. administrators did mot want to follow the accepted European model, in which as nurses trained in psychiatric institutions sat for a separate credentialing exam and carried a dedicated title. Rather, they insisted that all nurses who trained in their psychiatric institutions sit for the same exam as those who trained in general hospitals and carry the same title of "registered nurse." Leaders of the nascent American Nurses Association fought hard to prevent this, arguing that those who trained in asylums lacked the necessary medical, surgical and obstetric experiences common to general-hospital-trained nurses. But they did not prevail politically. It would be decades before American nursing leaders had the necessary social and political weight to ensure that all registered nurses, irrespective of the site of their training, had comparable clinical and classroom experiences.

However, says D'Antonio, it is hard to assess the affect of nurse-training schools on patient care in psychiatric institutions. In larger public institutions, those nurses might only have worked in particular wards, whereas in smaller and private psychiatric hospitals they may have had more contact with more patients. Their most enduring contribution might have been, she says, the opening of professional nursing to men, who were accepted in asylums' training schools or schools formed just for them, albeit not in general hospitals.

The economic crisis of the 1930s drastically cut state appropriations for psychiatric asylums and training schools. World War II created acute shortages of personnel. Psychiatrists themselves began looking for other practice opportunities by more closely identifying with reductionistic medicine. This concept was first developed by Greek mathematician and astronomer Thales of Miletus (624/623 – c. 548/545 BC). He was a pre-Socratic philosopher of Ionia and Asia Minor and historically recognized as the first person known to have entertained and engaged in scientific philosophy. He hypothesized that the universe was made of water—water being the fundamental substance of which all others were composed. Reductionism was later re-introduced by Descartes in Part V of his *Discourses*. He suggested that the world was like a clockwork machine, which could be understood by taking it to pieces and studying its components.

Since Darwin and scientism came into fashion, reductionism permeates all in visible existence, it seems. Methodological reductionism is expressed by the idea that biological systems such as the human species are most fruitfully investigated at the lowest possible level. Epistemic reductionism suggests that knowledge of a higher domain can always be reduced to a lower, more fundamental level.

Physicians interested in the field were inspired by American-born, European-trained or imported Austrian and Swiss psychiatrists, such Adolf Meyer (1866 –1950). He rose to the first psychiatrist-in-chief of Johns Hopkins Hospital (1910-1941). These physicians joined the first mammoth psychopathic hospitals appearing in the U.S. These hospitals, developed after the late nineteenth-century German model to create a flattering vision of psychiatry. They were also meant to silence critics accusing reductionism, an intellectual and philosophical position that interprets a complex system as the sum of its parts, as is perpetually done on subjects caught in the psychiatric scheme, of being a pseudo-science, heavy-handed, unscientific and in effect ineffectual.

The discussion about psychiatry's legitimacy as a science continues to this very day, wit American psychiatrists Allan Frances and Peter Roger Breggin. Francis labels the métier as pure bullshit, while Breggin severely criticizes it's the métier's continuous habits of shock treatment, psychiatric pharmaceutical prescription drug medications and their overall ignorant responses to COVID-19. He, advocates to replace psychiatry's use of those with the healing of the human soul, breath and spirit, education, empathy, love and broader human social services. That, however, is difficult to do when most of them do deny the soul's existence, never mind the humans mind.

Unless we awaken to the scam perpetrated against us, that will not happen with human 2.0 on our horizon, thanks to the COVID 19 injections. But to prepare for it, the psychopathic hospitals were a cost-effective necessity. They merely opened sections in existing urban and city-center hospitals and medical schools. From there, they orientated human scientific emotional and mental research and teaching to focus on finding suitable nomenclature for diagnoses and apply whatever acute treatments they saw fit. Instead of long-term accommodation, they also integrated inpatient with outpatient examinations and "services", freeing them from even the thought of "care" for the animals as which they see us.

This also began the mental health cabal. 's collaboration with social workers and community stakeholders, those financially affected by any given business, governments included. Community stakeholders include neighborhoods, community development groups, environmental organizations, development organizations, citizen associations and non-governmental organizations (NGOs). In this case and with the government's help, American Psychiatry Association members wriggled themselves into the herd's most private domains, assuring enormous and never-ending financial gains.

Most significantly, perhaps, one of their first moves was to broaden the definition of the psychiatric patient. They expanded it to include those who were emotionally distressed, but not mentally disturbed, which fell under the category of "certifiably insane". They henceforth diligently worked at disguising this distinction. A basic analogy to differentiate between the emotional mind and the brain is a computer, with the brain being the hardware and the emotional mind the software. So explains Claire Ivey in her 2019 *PsychReg* article "Please Don't Say 'Mental Health' When What You Mean Is 'Emotional Health'." If our hardware, something in our brain, is damaged or running incorrectly, we are stuck. But if our software, our emotions, run haywire, they can be put onto another system, reprogrammed and updated.

Thus, someone experiencing depressions and states of anxiety due to trauma and bereavement, for instance, falls into the "emotional health" category. It is a fluctuating and most often temporary situation, unless pharmaceutical mind-altering drugs or Ritalin at school are administered. In that case, it will destroy the person's health and well being without their knowing. Ivey gives what she describes as a life event that creates Post Traumatic Stress Disorder as an example of an emotional health crisis, which, if untreated, she says, can turn into a class of chronic distress in the profession called a neurosis.

Signs of mental health illness, on the other hand, are associated with a person losing touch with reality and suffering delusions, hallucinations, schizophrenia or paranoia, falling under the nomenclature of psychosis. The distinction is hugely important, as one signals a healthy brain and screwed up emotions, whereas the other signals screwed up brain circuits with little help for repair in sight. Unfortunately, the "mental/mad" label is so liberally flung at genuine PTSD journeyers like myself on a regular basis.

As a matter of fact, by 2021, the mental health industry had perfected its skill at blurring the difference between mental (ill physical body) and emotional (the heart's aches). Indeed,

Head Talk owner Oliver Chittendon (1976-) , who aims to provide knowledge, inspiration and a sense of community for us to create our own toolbox to fix and maintain our mental health, states: "We [humanity] are at a Tipping Point in Mental Health." He says that even the young UK Royals are participating, spearheading a campaign to end the stigma surrounding mental health. And the 2022 London Marathon was run for the first time with mental health as its main beneficiary (2021 Psych Reg.).

Chittendon is a Bristol University graduate and New York producer of theatrical events. He has organized lecture tours for President Bush Senior and President Clinton in Southeast Asia and the Middle East. Obviously unaware of the difference between emotional and mental good or ill health, he states that endless statistics and case studies of lived experiences of mental ill health have recently been published. He notes the steady stream of celebrities pointing to a dire neglect of mental health in most parts of the world and certainly in the UK. Thus, he reinforces humanity's belief in its mental illness, when nothing could be further from the truth.

Humanity has merely been expertly maneuvered into an emotional crisis of hitherto unseen and unheard proportions by most of its physicians. This began when Freud et al. precipitated psychopathic hospitals from the late nineteenth century onward, and with pharmaceutical drugs ruining their physical brains. Nothing for the heart? No. Their Khazarian Ashkenazi affiliation disallows it, as Janet Ossebaard and Cynthia Koeter explain in their 2021 documentary *Mirror: Part 1 Sequel - The Fall Of The Cabal.*

Physicians working as psychiatrists in these new hospitals thus became the forerunners of the psychiatric systems we know today. In these systems, psychiatrists rule as gods, with the lives of those summoned to be judged by them in their hands, for better or for worse, their verdicts deciding whether we are mad or merely sad. That they kill themselves at a higher rate than people serving in the military, thus signalling profound emotional imbalance, is rarely ever mentioned anywhere. Neither is their tendency of disturbance since birth, propelling them into the profession to figure themselves out (Lily Wang: Psychiatrists have the highest suicide rate of any profession. It's time to do something about it; #Brilliantly-ResilientDiaries. Helsinki, Finland, June 26, 2019).

Although not designed as replacements for state asylums, psychopathic hospitals created new spaces for psychiatric magic to take root among the public. They shifted the gaze away from the asylums and toward their own future. Thus, they corralled humanity into insanity by mind-manipulation alone, as these urban hospital-additions signaled the shift in where and how psychiatry was practiced. It was motivated by an evolution in how psychiatrists and society understood their work and professional identity, in line with Freud et al.'s the "Make the American Mind" agenda.

Some created treatment programs for patients suffering acute mental illnesses. Others used the early twentieth century's Mental Hygiene Movement to design outpatient clinics. Still others in new forms of private practice focused on preventing disorders that might result in psychiatric hospitalization. It also gave rise to the profession's accepted experimentations with therapies that posited brain pathology as a cause of mental illness. This mirrored the way that medical doctors posited pathology in body organs as the cause of physical symptoms. The result was trying insulin, electric shock, psychosurgery (including lobotomies) and all sorts of pharmaceutical drug treatments. All this came under the nomenclature of "therapy", coming via Latin *therapīa* from the Greek θεραπεία, literally meaning "curing" or "healing."

By the 1950s, the death knell for psychiatric asylums sounded. No need for asylums when WWI and WWII had provided massive numbers of shell-shocked humans for research in the above established laboratories throughout the lands of conflict-participating nations. By then, human emotions and how to push our buttons had been, for better or for worse, studied to perfection. The newest medication on the market at that time, and to this day today, was handed out like candy to cure the most persistent and severe psychiatric symptoms. The mental health system could then return those suffering from mental illnesses to their families and their communities.

That chlorpromazine's numerous side-effects influence everything from sperm counts to embryo-development is not mentioned. Nor is the distraction of both mental and emotional health mentioned by the learned society of the magic of human mind manipulation and medicine. They are:

- dizziness, feeling unsteady, or having trouble keeping your balance
- blank facial expression
- shuffling walk
- restlessness, agitation and nervousness
- unusual, slowed or uncontrollable movements of any part of the body
- difficulty falling asleep or staying asleep
- increased appetite and/or weight gain
- breast enlargement and/or milk production
- missed menstrual periods
- decreased sexual ability
- changes in skin color
- dry mouth
- stuffed nose
- difficulty urinating
- widening or narrowing of the pupils (black circles in the middle of the eyes)

If experiencing any of the following chlorpromazine symptoms, call a physician immediately:

- muscle stiffness
- falling
- confusion
- fast or irregular heartbeat
- sweating
- yellowing of the skin or eyes
- flu-like symptoms, including fever, sore throat, chills, and other signs of infection
- unusual bleeding or bruising
- neck cramps
- tongue that sticks out of the mouth
- tightness in the throat, or difficulty breathing or swallowing
- fine, worm-like tongue movements
- uncontrollable, rhythmic face, mouth or jaw movements
- seizures
- blisters, rash. hives or itching
- swelling of the eyes, face, mouth, lips, tongue, throat, arms, hands, feet, ankles or lower legs

- vision loss, especially at night
- seeing everything with a brown tint

Chlorpromazine sometimes causes other side effects. Call your doctor if you have any unusual problems while you are taking this medication, we are told. If taking an overdose resulting in collapse, seizure or trouble breathing, or if you can't be awakened, pray that somebody is there to immediately call 911.

The Symptoms of overdose may include:

- sleepiness
- loss of consciousness
- unusual, slowed or uncontrollable movements of any part of the body
- agitation
- restlessness
- fever
- seizures
- dry mouth
- irregular heartbeat

Other chlorpromazine requirements? Keep all appointments with your doctor and your eye doctor. You should have regularly scheduled eye exams during your treatment, because chlorpromazine may cause eye disease. Before having any lab test, tell your doctor and the laboratory personnel that you are taking chlorpromazine. It could also interfere with the results of home pregnancy tests. Talk to your doctor if you think you might be pregnant during your treatment with chlorpromazine (https://medlineplus.gov/druginfo/meds/a682040.html).

And what is it prescribed for, you ask? Symptoms of schizophrenia, the mental illness that causes disturbed or unusual thinking, loss of interest in life and strong or inappropriate emotions. And is it prescribed other psychotic disorders and conditions that cause difficulty telling the difference between things or ideas that are real and things or ideas that are not real. It is also used to treat symptoms of mania, manifested by a frenzied, abnormally excited mood in people diagnosed with bipolar disorder categorized as a manic-depressive disorder. Bipolar is a condition that causes episodes of mania, episodes of depression and other abnormal moods.(https://medlineplus.gov/druginfo/meds/a682040.html)

Chlorpromazine is also used to treat severe behaviour problems such as explosive, aggressive behaviour and hyperactivity in *children one to twelve years of age*. It is also used for numerous physical conditions, such as to:

- control nausea and vomiting
- relieve hiccups that have lasted one month or longer
- relieve restlessness and nervousness that might occur just before surgery
- treat acute intermittent porphyria, a condition in which certain natural substances build up in the body and cause stomach pain, changes in thinking and behaviour and other symptoms
- treat tetanus, an infection causing the tightening of the muscles, especially the jaw muscle (along with other medications).

Chlorpromazine is gloriously classified as a "conventional antipsychotic", It works by changing the activity of certain natural substances in the brain and other parts of the body. Thus, it is applicable to any emotional and mental ailment any human may experience, as far as I can decipher. The entire class of medications is like a Swiss army knife for the psycho-the-rapist profession and any physician feeling like it, to prescribe at leisure for the past 72 years. So, perhaps Chittendon is right. Ignorant humanity has been pushed into mental illness since the early twentieth century. It now rules most of the herd, due to pharmaceutical drug consumption by the vast majority, for decades prescribed by those pretending to want them to heal.

Today, only a very small number of the historic public and private psychiatric hospitals exist. Psychiatric care and treatment are now delivered through a web of services, such as crisis services, short-term care and general-hospital-based acute psychiatric care units. Outpatient services range from 24-hour assisted living environments to clinics and clinicians' offices, providing a range of psychopharmacological and psychotherapeutic treatments. The quality and availability of these outpatient services vary widely. This has led some historians and policy experts to wonder if "asylums," in the true sense of the word, might be still needed for the most vulnerable people who need supportive living environments.

An hour in downtown East Side Vancouver, Canada, will suffice to understand how the system fails care for the destitute and the emotionally and mentally destitute and devastated. However, the Luciferic consciousness wants its sustenance. That is what brought us to this state of world affairs, having been driven to insanity with great expertise. But knowledge can get us out of it. But we must understand that we have been driven into knowing nothing through the educational system. And that all we ever conceive of wanting to know is "out there" for us to discover.

So, let's move on to discover how the Luciferic consciousness-possessed learned society. Let's learn how it did so without regards to ethics and morals, managing to plant madness into humanity to the degree that as of 2020 there were 12,275 registered mental health treatment facilities in the U.S. alone. And there are 14,000 + facilities for *drug, alcohol and other addiction rehabilitation. It is a booming business of $42 billion annually*, united profiting from the misery they themselves purposely created in humanity. So, let's take a look, shall we? (https://www.researchandmarkets.com/r/t6waea)

33

IMPLANTING MADNESS INTO HUMANITY

The Victorian era may not have been the start of the institutionalising humans with emotional and mental health problems. But it was certainly the time when the numbers of those diagnosed and treated for them began to explode. (Class, Gender and Asylums: https://lib.uwo.ca/archives/virtualexhibits/londonasylum/classgender.html). Why? Several reasons. First, Britain had offloaded a large number of its undesirable and deplorable population to Australia. Lieutenant James Cook had claimed possession of the continent's east coast for the British Crown in 1770. Based on Cook's verbal report upon his return to Britain, the Crown felt inspired to establish a penal colony in the newly claimed territory. Lord Sydney appointed Captain Arthur Phillip (1738–1792) of London, son of a German immigrant from Frankfurt to the task. He was, by various accounts, a language teacher, a merchant vessel owner, a merchant captain or a common seaman.

Phillip went to sea on a British naval vessel at age of nine (1747). He entered the Greenwich Hospital School, a charity school for the sons of indigent seafarers, in 1751. At the end of 1753, he was granted a seven-year indenture as an apprentice aboard the *Fortune*, a 210-ton whaling vessel. He abandoned that in July 1755, enlisting in the Royal Navy in October as captain's servant aboard the 68-gun HMS Buckingham, commanded by his mother's cousin. He climbed the Royal Navy's ranks until September 1786, when he was appointed commodore of what became known as the First Fleet of 11 ships. Thus, he sailed from Portsmouth, England, on May 13, 1787, with about 1,500 convicts and soldiers on board.

Phillip's assignment? First, to establish a colony at Botany Bay. Second, to assume the powers of captain general and governor in chief of the new colony. Third, to found a subsidiary colony on Norfolk Island to take advantage of its native flax and timber for naval purposes. Upon arrival in Botany Bay on January 18, 1788, Phillip soon decided that the site chosen for settlement upon Cook's recommendation was unsuitable. It had poor soil, no secure anchorage and no reliable sweet water source. After some exploration, Phillip went to Port Jackson eight days later. He brought the marines and convicts to Sydney Cove, which he named for Lord Sydney on January 26, 1788. That date later became Australia Day. Sydney Cove offered fresh water supply and a harbour, which Phillip described as: "being with out exception the finest Harbour in the World [...] Here a Thousand Sail of the Line may ride in the most perfect Security."

On February 7, 1788, Governor Phillip formally proclaimed the colony and had the British flag hoisted. With that began the terrorization of those entering Australia and those living there for thousands of years. The idea within less than 100 years spread throughout the world, as the fad of colonization was picked up and carried through with by other European nations with degrees of greater or lesser brutality.

Phillip's voyage of eight months ended with founding the colony of New South Wales and Australia in dire circumstances. The first years of settlement were nearly disastrous. Cursed with poor soil and an unfamiliar climate, both mariners and convicts were ignorant of farming. The natives were used to living off the land not giving a hoot about it, eating bugs as now planned for us by our overlords. The colony hovered on the verge of outright starvation for several years, with marines sent to keep order among the starving men.

But Phillip, seen to be a tough but fair-minded leader, persevered by appointing convicts to positions of responsibility and oversight. Floggings and hangings became commonplace, just as in the motherland. But so apparently became the sense of egalitarianism, the idea that all people were equal deserving equal rights and opportunities. This was moments before the French Revolution instigators would cook up the slogan "Liberty, Equality, Fraternity", an outright impossibility not only in consideration of cosmic law. Phillip said before leaving England, "In a new country there will be no slavery and hence no slaves." That turned out to be laughable, as Robert Hughes in his superbly researched book *The Fatal Shore* confirms. The brutal rule towards convicts and settlers reigning in Australia for centuries after British possession is reflected in the quasi-catatonic behavior of Australians toward their governing bodies' COVID-19 mandates without much of a murmur. The traumatization of their ancestors is still alive in their blood and their subconscious to this very day, after the last forced settlers were exported from Britain in 1901.

Like everywhere else in the world, when invaded by colonizers, Phillip's persistence marked the Indigenous peoples dispossession and destruction of their way of life. They were treated like cockroaches, as they are even today. This terrorization of The Other *around the globe* seems to have taken off after Elisabeth I (1533-1603), Henry VIII and Anne

Boleyn's daughter, became Queen of England and Ireland in 1558. A painting from the 1580s show her caressing a snake resting between her hands, but was replaced with a rose before publication.

The symbol? In the Christian tradition, Satan in the guise of the serpent instigated man's fall by tricking Eve into breaking God's command. Thus the serpent represent temptation, the devil, deceit, death, destruction, evil and poison, such as the snake venom used in the COVID-19 potion and advertised as a vaccine?

John Dee (1527–1608/9) would become Elizabeth's astrologer, astronomer, mathematician and alchemist. Before Elisabeth ascended the throne, he was asked to name a propitious day for the coronation. It was on this occasion that he was introduced to the Queen, who took lessons in the mystical interpretation of his writings. Later, he famously became known as her conjurer and her magician. He was the one who practiced magic arts, a wizard who performed feats of sleight of hand and created illusions for her. While a student at Cambridge's Trinity College, he created stage sets for the play *Peace* by Aristophanes (born c. 450BC–c. 388BC). It is considered the greatest representative of ancient Greek comedy, his works characterized by bold fantasy, merciless invective, outrageous satire, unabashedly licentious humor and marked freedom of political criticism. Dee built construct a giant mechanical beetle that shocked the audience so much that they believed Dee must have conspired with the devil to create it (Oxford languages dictionary).

Dee was a fellow of Trinity College from the moment of its foundation in 1546. In 1548, he left St. John's College in Cambridge with a master's degree. He furthered his scientific knowledge with visits to the Low Countries to study between 1547 and 1551 under several tutors. One was Portuguese mathematician-cartographers and nautical scientist Pedro Nunes (1502–1578). Another was Dutch physician, mathematician, cartographer, philosopher, instrument-maker and cosmographer Gemma Frisius, born Jemme Reinerszoon (1508–1555). He also studied under Abraham Ortelius, also known as Ortels, Orthellius, Wortels (1527–1598) a Brabantian conventionally recognized as the creator of the first world atlas, the *Theatrum Orbis Terrarum*, the "Theatre of the World". Finally, he studied under Flanders-born geographer, cosmographer and cartographer Gerardus Mercator (1512–1594), most renowned for creating the 1569 world map projecting sailing courses of constant bearing (rhumb lines) as straight lines, an innovation still used in today's nautical charts (https://rmg.co.uk/stories/blog/curatorial-library-archive/mathematics-navigation-empire-reassessing-john-dees-legacy). Mercator gave Dee two of his globes and various astronomical instruments to be used by Cambridge University's scholars and fellows. These have long since disappeared from sight.

Dee was also known for staring into a crystal ball and a magical mirror made of obsidian (volcanic glass). He got the glass from Mexico sometime between 1527 and 1530 after Hernando Cortés's conquest of the region. He would call forth whispering angels and demons. He adopted this practice from the Aztec's priests who used these mirrors to connect with their god of obsidian and sorcery, Tezcatlipoca or "Smoking Mirror" in the Nahuatl language, to conjure up visions and make prophesies. Dee also enthusiastically delved into the brand-new science of physics and the exploration of chemical compounds, with his near-contemporaries. He worked with French physician, astrologer and seer Michel de Nostredame (1503–1566), Nostradamus, best known for his 1555 book *Les Prophéties*, 942 quatrains allegedly predicting future events. He also worked with German polymath, physician, legal scholar, soldier, theologian and occult writer Heinrich Cornelius Agrippa von Nettesheim (1486–1535). His 1533 book *Three Books of Occult Philosophy* drew heavily on the Kabbalah and Hermeticism. It tread a dangerous path, as conversing with the spirits and the dead to seek prediction of the future meant heresy, for which punishment was death.

In 1578, Dee was sent abroad to consult with German physicians and astrologers about an illness suffered by the queen. On his return to England, he was asked to investigate the title of the Crown to the countries recently discovered by British subjects, and to provide geographical descriptions. He presented two large rolls with the desired information to the Queen soon thereafter, executed with scientifically meticulous accuracy. He also presented a learned treatise on reforming the calendar. From this period, Dee's research was entirely concerned with necromancy. In 1581, he got to know Edward Kelley (1555–1597/8), an apothecary, with his assistance performing various incantations and maintaining frequent intercourse with spirits (https://luminarium.org/encyclopedia/johndee.htm).

Kelley claimed descent from the family of Ui Maine, one of the oldest and largest kingdoms in Connacht, Ireland. However, he was born at the cathedral city of Worcester, England. The city dated from Neolithic times, when Atlantis had apparently crashed into the ocean blue roughly 12,000 years ago. Much later, the Roman's built Ryknild Street, called the "Via Devina" by some Victorian antiquarians. About Kelley's life before meeting Dee, little is known, other than that he may have studied at Oxford under the name of Talbot and knew Latin and some Greek.

Kelley claimed to possess the philosopher's stone. According to legend, this "stone" could turn ordinary metals, such as iron, tin, lead, zinc, nickel or copper, into precious metals like gold and silver (history.com/news/what-was-the-philosophers-stone). It also acted as an elixir of life, with the power to cure illness, renew the properties of youth and even grant immortality to those who possessed it. The philosopher's stone may not have been a stone at all, but a powder or another type of substance. It was variously known as "the tincture," "the powder" or the "materia prima." In their quest to find it, alchemists examined countless substances in their laboratories. It is from this search that today's fields of chemistry, pharmacology and metallurgy come. During their séances, Kelley would dictate to Dee the information he received from the entities appearing in the magical mirror, contacting them from other dimensions.

Shortly after their first meeting, Kelly and Dee were introduced by Robert Dudley, Earl of Leicester (1532/33—1588), Elisabeth's favorite and possible lover, to Khazarian Ashkenazi Polish nobleman and alchemist Olbracht Łaski (died 1604).

Devoted to the same pursuits, they joined him in his native land in 1584. For some years, they lived in Poland and Bohemia in alternate wealth and poverty, depending on the credulity of those before whom they exhibited raising spirits by incantations. As always, Kelly would dictate the utterances to Dee, who wrote them down and interpreted them. In 1586, they found the patronage of wealthy Khazarian Ashkenazi William of Rosenberg

(1535–1592), the High Treasurer and High Burgrave of Bohemia. He shared Kelley and Dee's alchemical interests and participated in their spiritual sessions.

Kelley and Dee settled in the Bohemian town of Třeboň, German Wittengau. They continued their research, and according to Dee's diary, Kelley performed his first alchemical transmutation in late 1586. However, Kelley soon expressed a desire to stop experimenting, whereas Dee insisted they continue. In 1587, Kelley revealed to Dee, that the angels, namely a spirit "Madimi," ordered them to share everything they had, including their wives. Anguished by the angels' "order" Dee broke off the spirit conferences but did share his wife. This "cross-matching" occurred on May 22,1587. Nine months later, on February 28, Dee's wife Jane gave birth to a son, Theodorus Trebonianus Dee, who was raised as Dee's son. The incident remained a secret, as did many of their activities, until after the posthumous publication of Dee's diaries.

Though it seems the two shared an intimate and often cooperative partnership, it was often characterised as "quarrelsome" and "tense" by contemporaries and historians. Also, they were clearly involved in activities that could be seen as heretical to the Catholic Church of the time, so a certain amount of tact and secrecy was required. Kelly left Dee at Třeboň in 1589, possibly to join the emperor's court at Prague. Whereas Dee returned to Britain flat broke, Kelley was living an opulent lifestyle in Europe by 1590, enjoying the patronage of nobility. He received several estates and large sums of money from von Rosenberg, continued his alchemical experiments, and convinced Rudolf II (1552–1612) that he was ready to start producing gold, the purpose of his work.

Rudolf II was born in Vienna, a member of the House of Habsburg. He was Holy Roman Emperor, King of Hungary and Croatia, King of Bohemia and Archduke of Austria. He was also instigator of the 30 Years War and a devotee of the occult. Around 1590 he knighted Sir Edward Kelley of Imany and New Lüben whilst waiting suspended for Kelly's base-metal transmutation into gold. In 1591, Kelley was imprisoned, accused of having killed a noble in duel. But Rudolf permitted him to return to his alchemical work in 1595. When failing to produce gold, however, he was incarcerated again, dying a few years later either of injuries received while attempting to escape or poisoning himself in front of his wife and children.

Dee, meanwhile, had returned to England in 1589, and had been helped over his financial difficulties by the Queen and his friends. He continued to dive into the supernatural by using "magic" to converse with "the angels". He carried his endeavours forth with the same enthusiasm and eagerness that scientists at CERN exhibit to open portals to allow spirits to enter our earthly sphere without thought of possible consequences. Mediums in spiritualist churches worldwide do the same on a smaller scale. They claim to communicate with spirits and the dead called forth by them through speech, automatic writing or drawings. During séances, mediums channel messages from entities they call teachers or Ascended Masters, as in Madame Helena Blavatsky's case.

In Islamic Arabia, belief in jinn has been common for millennia, with their existence affirmed in the Qur'an, conceptualized as creatures parallel to human beings. They are shape-shifting spirits, said to be made of fire and air inhabiting unseen worlds in dimensions beyond the visible universe of humanity. Like humans, they can be good, evil, neutral or benevolent. Hence, just like humans, they are free will beings who must face eventual salvation or damnation (https://genies.fandom.com/wiki/Jinn).

Jinn have served as sources of inspiration and information for the most esteemed ancient Arab poets. They have equally inspired present-day artists, such as the Khazarian Ashkenazi American animator, film producer and entrepreneur Walter Elias Disney (1901–1966), still remaining inexplicable to human eyes and perceptions (Leila Ettachfini: What Are Jinn: The Arab Spirits Who Can Eat, Sleep, Have Sex, and Die).

Arabs, big believers in the occult and the afterlife, worshipped jinn long before Islam was introduced in the seventh century, according to Amira El-Zein, associate professor with Georgetown University's School of Foreign Service in Qatar. They believe that the Jinn, the spirits, the angelic entities, were masters of certain crafts and nature's elements, with enormous powers applied for good or bad. Jinn is said to interact with humans in our earthly reality while leading their own lives in other dimensions. Thus, they operate in both manifest and invisible domains, a concept incomprehensible to most of us, unless we have made their personal acquaintance.

The Chinese dedicated an entire town called Fengdu Ghost City to spirits. This large complex of shrines, temples and monasteries on the Ming mountain, about 170 kilometres (110 mi) downstream Chongqing on the north bank of the Yangtze River, is dedicated to Diyu. In Chinese mythology, it symbolizes the realm of the dead or Hell and those inhabiting it. Fengdu is loosely aligned with the Buddhist concept of Naraka, or purgatory. It was founded nearly two thousand years ago, purportedly combining Confucianist, Taoist and Buddhist beliefs in conjunction with death and the underworld. Several classic Chinese works of literature published during the Ming dynasty (1368–1644) mention Fengdu. Among them are the *Journey to the West*, *Investiture of the Gods* and *Strange Stories from a Chinese Studio*. They portray the afterlife awaiting in Diyu, itself depicted as a subterranean maze of various levels, tunnels and chambers, to which souls are taken upon death to atone for sins committed while on earth. Before the Three Gorges Dam building, I went up Ming Mountain by cable car from the Yangtze River. But I never entered it, as I had been zapped of all energy the moment the ship had moored at Fengdu's quay. I took it as a warning not to enter.

We now understand that many modern concepts have not been grasped out of thin air after all, but that jinn spirits had a role to play in them. I refer to when Elisabeth I took advice from John Dee, purportedly with Kelley's help, transmitted by spirits of all kinds through his mirror and his crystal ball. And to Disney's *Aladdin*, sending exorcism mainstream. And to the ideas behind James Cameron's *Avatar*. In other words, jinns and angels have possibly influenced and even shaped our perception of Self and all that is around us by subconsciously programming our thinking and thus creating our world's history in all of its aspects.

So, Dee and his scryer Kelley set forth during Elisabeth I's reign by his "Enochian magic" system to ceremonially command spirits to his presence to seek advice and predict the future. He recorded the information received in the Enochian language from Dee's journals. Both Dee and Kelley believed that their visions gave them access to the secrets in the Book of Enoch, the ancient apocalyptic text ascribed to Noah of the Ark's great-grandfather Enoch.

It contains material on the origins of demons and on the Nephilim. The hybrid sons of the fallen angels, those who came from heaven and co-habited with human women creating the Nephilim, was the reason given for the Genesis' Great Flood as a moral necessity.

The practice of Enochian magic brought Dee and Kelley dangerously close to Necromancy. This practice of black magic involved communicating with the dead, either by summoning their spirits or as apparitions, visions or bodily raising them for the purpose of divination. It included imparting the means to foretell future events, discover hidden knowledge, or even bringing someone back from the dead or to use the dead as weapons. Sometimes referred to as "Death Magic," the term is also used in a more general sense to refer to witchcraft.

Necromancy was prevalent throughout antiquity, with records of its practice existing in ancient Egypt, Babylonia, Greece, Rome and China. Greek philosopher, writer, and historian Strabo (64 or 63 BC–c. 24 AD) in his work *Geographica* refers to *nekromantia*. He stated that the foremost "diviners by the dead" were found among the people of Persia and that it was also practiced in Chaldea, Etruria and Babylonia. The very oldest literary account of necromancy is found in Homer's *Odyssey*. Under the direction of the sorceress Circe, a minor goddess in Greek mythology, Odysseus travels to the underworld. He seeks to gain insight about his impending voyage home by raising the spirits of the dead through the use of spells Circe had taught him.

Νεκρομαντεία in Hellenistic Greek was rendered as *necromantīa* in Latin. After Dee and Kelley did their "thing", the seventeenth-century British learned society named it "necromancy" and cursed it as evil, quoting the Bible's Deuteronomy 18:10-11, which reads:

> "There shall not be found among you any one who burns his son or his daughter as an offering, any one who practices divination, a soothsayer, or an augur, or a sorcerer, or a charmer, or a medium, or a wizard, or a necromancer."

We learn that there are two reasons that eliciting secret knowledge from the dead is what Deuteronomy 18:10-11 has in mind.

First, the same verses forbid "divination," and seeking a "medium," a "sorcerer," and a "wizard". All of these have to do with trying to gain knowledge beyond *ordinary* human intelligence. In other words, only the learned society should use it, lest the herd could discover something about Luciferic consciousness desires, perhaps?

Second, the instructions given by Moses concern a coming prophet, when he says in verse 15: "The Lord your God will raise up for you a prophet like me from among you, from your brethren—*him* you shall heed" (emphasis added). In other words, there is no need to go to mediums, sorcerers, wizards or necromancers to gain knowledge, because sooner or later God will send a prophet of his own. Therefore, the herd should just patiently look to *God's prophet* once he alights. The herd should not look to mediums, sorcerers, wizards or necromancers to seek hidden knowledge beyond its ordinary human intelligence, apart from God. Since conjuring up the dead (necromancy) is one way of doing that, God forbids it for the ordinary human. And Kelley and Dee, with Elisabeth's blessing through her favourite Robert Dudley, didn't give a hoot and went joyously ahead in their undertakings. Being hugely efficient in raising those dwelling in other dimension, they liberally shared their advice with Elisabeth I. She quickly developed a blind eye, as she saw the results reflected in her increased power over the world's domain.

With Kelley's help, Dee transcribed his *Book of Mysteries* between March 1582 and May 1583. He brings to light mysteries and truths that scholars and adepts have been struggling to understand and use ever, since writes Joseph H Peterson in his 2002 book *John Dee's Five Books of Mystery: Original Sourcebook of Enochian Magic* (Weiser Books; Illustrated edition 2002). Detailing his system for communicating with the angels, Dee reveals that these self-same angels were involved with exploring and colonizing the New World. And in heralding in a new age, a new world order, which, for all we know, may include humanity 1.0's COVID-19 jab of elimination, eh?

By the way, Dee was married three times with eight children. If you persist in the view that men like him were simply eccentric wizard-type characters concocting lotions and potions of a dubious nature and practising clairvoyance through the dark magic arts, dream on. In reality, these men forever questioning the universe were foremost professors of mathematics, geometry, astronomy, physics, chemicals, mechanical gadgets and objects that appeared to move of their own accord. They were sponsored by Europe's aristocracy of all ranks and carried forth to this very day, should you wish to look deep enough. They were all communicating with each other so that *ordinary humans* never got wind of any of it (history.co.uk).

In Britain, one of Dee's systems of communication with "the other side" was adapted by the Hermetic Order of the Golden Dawn in 1890. This secret society performed occult rituals of magic to call forth one or more otherworldly deities from "Source," who or whatever that source might be. It took its concepts from The Order of the Golden Dawn, which sprang from documents known as the *Cipher Manuscripts*. These were attributed to German Benedictine abbot, polymath and occultist scholar Johannes Trithemius (1462 - 1516), born Johann Heidenberg. Together with Italian polymath, architect and founder of cryptography Leon Battista Albert (1404–1472), he outlined the Order's rituals and prescribed a curriculum of graduated teachings. These encompassed the Hermetic Qabalah, the Western tradition involving mysticism and the occult, as well as astrology, the tarot, alchemy and geomancy. Geomancy is a method of divination that interprets markings on the ground, or the patterns formed by tossed handfuls of soil, rocks or sand in the course of time. It was passed on by such eminent personages as Agrippa and Paracelsus.

The Hermetic Order's founding fathers 450 years later were:

- physician William Robert Woodman (1828–1891)
- coroner, ceremonial magician and theosophist William Wynn Westcott (1848–1925)
- polymath and occultist Samuel Liddell MacGregor Mathers (1854–1918), teacher of Alistair Crowley

All were members of the *Societas Rosicruciana in Anglia* (S.R.I.A.), which, according to Manly P. Hall, was one of the world's most ancient occult orders. Commonly known as the College of Invisibles, it is itself a family of secret societies purportedly formed in late medieval Germany, teaching esoteric practices concealed from the herd. It is also said to be an appendix of Freemasonry (https://newworldencyclopedia.org/entry/Rosicrucianism).

Rosicrucianism in itself is officially said to be based on an amalgamation of Christian mysticism and occult traditions. Between 1607 and 1616, the society released two manifestos throughout Europe known as the *Fama Fraternitatis R.C.* (The Fame of the Brotherhood of R.C) and *Confessio Fraternitatis* (The Confession of the Brotherhood of R.C.) to, according to Manly Hall, divert herd-attention from its undertakings. Announcing the existence of a hitherto unknown esoteric order to the world, these manifestos advertised the order's mysterious doctrine. They said it was "built on esoteric truths of the ancient past", which, "concealed from the average man, provide insight into nature, the physical universe and the spiritual realm of the world."

In effect, these documents promoted a "Universal Reformation of Mankind," which enthused the learned society of its time. It resulted in University College London-educated Dame Frances Amelia Yates (1899–1981) to publish *The Rosicrucian Enlightenment* in 1972. This was a history of the role that the occult has played in forming modern science and medicine. These manifestos enthused many a learned society member to seek esoteric knowledge, thus launching the Western mystery tradition. This tradition covered a wide range of loosely related ideas and movements. It began to pervade various forms of Western philosophy, religion, pseudoscience, art, literature, music, intellectual ideas and popular culture, we read. All this through a science allegedly to be kept secret until the intellectual climate was ready for mankind's reformation, the New World Order, we assume, in accordance with Klaueschen Schwab's World Economic Forum's "you own nothing and be happy" aspiration, perhaps?

En route to that goal, Ukrainian-born Yelena Petrovna von Hahn (1831–1891) under the name Helena Blavatsky had already founded the Theosophical Society in 1875, it seems. She had gathered a following, among them the initial driving force behind the Hermetic Golden Dawn foundation, Westcott. Both preceded by a few decades by Charles Robert Darwin (1809 -1882), the one claiming all species, including homo sapien, descend from a common ancestor, the amoeba. This hypothesis lacked empirical, scientific evidence is now considered a fundamental scientific concept. They vigorously chimed in on his ideas, as Darwinism's human animal theme was by then equally vigorously propagated by human animal Yuval Harari. At the World Economic Forum in 2020, she confirmed Darwin by declaring: "We are no longer mysterious souls; we are now hackable animals."

So, Dee and Kelley brought us to the Golden Dawn's magic and rituals. These became the core element of other occult movements, including Wicca, Crowley's Thelema and Spiritualist churches, who mix and mingle black magic spiritualism with spirituality. However, Dee's and Kelley's otherworldly connections established during their séances seems to have brought us to where we are today. Dee, for a while Elisabeth's most trusted conjurer and confidante, inspired her to form the British Empire. And it was he who plotted with her the voyages around the New World, slaughtering as many of the natives while in the process. It was a page out of Julius's book when he subjugated Northern Europeans tribes, slaughtering them by the millions to be slaughtered in Rome's Senate by some of his own peers a few years later.

It was Dee, who determined Elisabeth I's date of coronation. Through his mapmaking and navigation knowledge critical to the world's exploration, he convinced Elisabeth I to order the enormous enterprise of building the British Empire (Woolley, Benjamin: *The Queen's Conjurer: The Science and Magic of Dr. John Dee, Adviser to Queen Elizabeth I*; Holt Paperbacks; First Printing edition (February 1, 2002)). With his mathematical genius or help from the unseen, he anticipated Sir Isaac Newton's (1642 –1726/27) scientific formulations and ideas by nearly a century, but that is rarely mentioned anywhere. In turn, the Queen granted him his own coat of arms in 1567 (Woolley p. 20).

Like many others of 16's century European's polymaths, Dee was vehemently obsessed with the concepts of alchemy, astrology and mysticism. As one of England's foremost thinkers, he rose to the top of Elizabethan politics. Accused by his contemporaries of having reached that lofty height by casting spells over the Queen and her counsel, Dee also founded her extensive spy system, thus living on in history as superspy James Bond. While at it, he built one of the greatest private libraries of sixteenth-century England. He claimed to own over 3,000 books and 1,000 manuscripts, which he kept at his home in Mortlake near London's River Thames. Many were stolen from him during his lifetime, perhaps even sold by him for sustenance as he. He had been reviled and pitied as a madman by his learned society peers after Elisabeth I's death in 1603, and he died in obscurity and abject poverty six years later, a mere 100 of his books still available at the Royal College of Physicians library (https://www.historyextra.com/period/tudor/john-dee-elizabeth-i-tudor-scientist-magician-spy-007-james-bond/).

In a round-about way, Dee's black magic explorations laid the foundation for the Victorian era's prosperity. The industrial revolution led to the emergence of a skilled middle class. All this was possible simply because scholars felt inspired to learn about navigation during his time. This encouraged their sponsors and benefactors to petition the British Crown, meaning taxpayers, to fund the piss-ons' navigational education. Thus, it was courtier, adventurer, explorer and soldier Humphrey Gilbert (c. 1539 –1583) who petitioned the founding of a navigational academy in London. It was to educate Her Majesty's wards and the youth of nobility and gentlemen, as applicants' training in arithmetic, geometry, cosmography, cartography and the art of navigation to provide qualified servants for the Crown's future exploratory world enterprises.

But although since the late thirteenth century, the British Northern and Western Fleets were commanded by admirals. The post of "Lord Admiral of England" was created in 1408. The admiralty was set up under Henry VIII in 1545 as the King's Council of the Marine responsible for Navy operations and ship's officers. Navigational training in England began only in 1673 with the founding of the Royal Mathematical School. It was established so that potential sailors could learn navigation and mathematicians could train at the school. The School was integrated into Christ's Hospital, a charity school founded in 1552 with a core aim to offer children from humble backgrounds the chance of a better education. It selected pupils aged eleven or twelve, and prepared them for a career in the Royal Navy. The curriculum was based on astronomy, the understanding of a ship's place in relation to the stars. It was infused with mathematics, as well. England's colonial activities intensified in the American colonies, the Caribbean and India, so long-distance navigational training was also included. A growing number of publications helped address this need, and slowly mathematics began to take precedence over astronomy at the Royal Mathematical School and the Admiralty, both often led by men with multiple ties to the Navy Board, the Royal Observatory and the Royal Society. The diarist Samuel Pepys (1633-1703) is one example. He served as a naval administrator, and as an active board member of the Royal Mathematical School. One of his contributions was to advocate the use of instruments (applied techniques) as being equal to, or more important, than mathematical theory.

Our man Gilbert was later a leading pioneer of the English colonial North American empire and the Plantation of Ireland creation. He was the maternal half-brother of Sir Walter Raleigh (c. 1552 -1618), soldier, writer, explorer, and another one of Elisabeth I's favorite courtiers. He was also cousin of privateer and explorer Richard Grenville, also known as Greenfield (1542 -1591), who participated in both those enterprises. So, we see again that everything stays in the family. Dee was by and large an outsider. He had already provided that same service to a rather large audience at his home for years. He had personally taken the opportunity to link navigation with Britain's imperial ambitions through his book *The General and Rare Memorials pertayning to the Perfect Arte of Navigation* (1577), one of the first books containing references in print to the idea of a British Empire (RMG ID: PBD3580). But that was graciously ignored. Dee wrote four volumes under this name, though only the first one survives in complete form in various libraries and archives, we learn.

Dee also presented his arguments for building and financing a large navy to enhance England's standing fleet of military ships. It had only 34 ships at the time, less than 20% of the size of Spain's fleet. He called its expansion the British Empire's "Master Key" to its aspirations and listing a wide variety of benefits for it, such as:

- Making it easier to get commodities to increase the wealth of England
- Protecting the merchant fleet from pirates and potential foreign aggressors, which Dee lists as France Denmark, Scotland and Spain
- Giving young men in the country a purpose, where they could learn a new set of skills and also reduce the number of men idle within the country.

Despite this book mainly focusing on navigation, Dee also conveyed that various of his sources believed parts of North America held by the Spanish had already been colonised twice. The first time was by Arthur, the legendary Celtic King of the Britons, in 530 AD. The second time was by Welsh Prince Madoc Owain Gwynedd in 1170 AD. Both hypotheses apparently were used by Elisabeth I in Britain's claim to America during its territorial disputes with Spain, claiming that colonising North America merely meant restoring Arthur's empire. Dee made this point on the title page of *The General and Rare Memorials pertayning to the Perfect Arte of Navigation*. It depicted Her Majesty at the helm of a ship looking over lands absorbed into the new British Empire. The hieroglyph showed the Moon, the Sun, stars and a glowing sphere bearing the tetragrammaton, the Hebrew name of God, transliterated in four letters as *YHWH* or *JHVH*, suggesting Elizabeth's ambitions had the Divine blessing of God.

John Dee's occultist activities and reputation as magician and sorcerer might throughout history have overshadowed his renown as a magnificent mathematician and proponent of navigation and cartography. However, the Spanish and Portuguese began to enrich themselves with the gold, silver and spices expropriated from the territories they discovered. Meanwhile, the British Crown was debt-ridden to its Khazarian bankers, facing an ever-increasing competition in trade. It became evermore apparent that the island needed to extend its outlook towards the virtually untapped new world. So, it was Dee's imperial ambitions that magnificently launched the future empire into being and changing the world with it.

In England itself, the German royal House of Hanover had maneuvered into power, with George I in 1714 becoming its first monarch. Queen Victoria ruled between 1837 and 1901, the last one of that branch. The throne then passed to her eldest son Edward VII, son of her husband Albert, of the House of Saxe-Coburg and Gotha. In 1917, during the war against Germany, he renamed it the House of Windsor for optics, as all those purportedly fighting against each other were blood-related, cousins and brothers.

Some of the British Crown's Hanoverian take-over reflected into the Victorian era, historically dated between 1820 and 1914. It reacted to the changes brought on by the industrial revolution with strict gender and class distinctions, a heightened concern with morality and a flurry of social reform movements, including those deemed mad by standards of the day were to be treated. The hitherto traditional gender roles and class distinctions consequently shaped the conceptions of insanity, although no precise definition of the term exists. They also shaped the methods of treatment given to those deemed by society insane. Treatment would be dished out in the new-fangled, mammoth, nineteenth century asylums, with their super sophisticated research laboratories purportedly built exclusively with patient interest at heart.

The urban-industrial culture springing up under Victoria's reign because of destitute herd members going into town factories from the countryside to earn their daily bread. This meant that people increasingly lived outside society's traditional norms, with home and family as source of order, stability, and morality. But this evolution was kept a secret from *ordinary humans*. The aristocracy, the upper class and the learned society, thrived on pornography, engaged in psychological studies of the herd, maintained sexual double standards, with prostitution and venereal diseases rampant in this strictly hierarchically organized society. Race, religion, region and occupation were the most meaningful aspects of identity and status. Gender and class were the main organizing principles of Victorian society. This is merely a fact of circumstances of that time (Britannica.com).

Not that there is anything new in it, either. Victorian gender ideology is premised on the "doctrine of separate spheres," based primarily on notions of biologically determined gender roles and/or patriarchal religious doctrine. This harks back to the ancient Greeks. In *Politics*, Aristotle describes two separate spheres , the home (*oikos*) and the city (*polis*). These oft times are interpreted as confining women to the private realm, while men play in the public sphere, although each sphere intermingles with the other. Debates over the "proper" roles of women and men continue to the present. The issue was brought into vogue again in Great Britain, continental Europe and the United States during the Industrial Revolution. Transitioning to new manufacturing processes between roughly 1760 and 1840 required large numbers of human labourers. Most working-class families would laugh themselves half silly to hear about the "doctrine of separate spheres." They had performed slave labour over generations, while the upper classes engaged in behaviour of unbelievable depravity and perversion. This was reflected in part by their adrenochrome consumption, just now beginning to reach the herd's attention.

However, the doctrine of separate spheres has its hypothesis of women having a finer sense of morality than men. Therefore, men could be as promiscuous as minks without consequences. This inspired the learned society to hypothesize on the feelings and anxieties experienced by those feminine souls who ventured into the big city to find a new way of life. They theorized about the emotional upheaval they might suffer due to their anonymity and the hardship of industrial labour. These manly bright souls then imagined and assumed that these lonely women were most vulnerable to mental illness. After all, they would face the enormous temptations daily in their chosen urban settings. Surely this would easily corrupt their morals, already weakened due to their lack of a stable family life.

It would certainly encourage alcoholism, drug addiction and promiscuity. Thus, any woman expressing any unconventional idea or showing the slightest slack of contribution and productivity, was labeled mentally ill. And should she take a glass of spirits out of order, it led to a lunatic asylum. She would be checked out in its experimental laboratories. There, the learned society of magicians of the human mind, calling themselves adherents of the science of psychiatry or psychology, practically held the power of life or death over anyone that entered.

Any one of the manifestations they deemed lunatic might have been brought on by the misery created by profiteering factory owners and their "You will have nothing and be happy" slave labour conditions. They expertly ignored this, both because their subjects were beasts to them, goyim, and because of their need for human herd specimens. They had to feed their terrifying experiments to learn how to guarantee the success of the Great Work of Ages They had to find the best mind-manipulating techniques to drive humanity to accept the COVID-19 injection, which would result in Harari's human 2.0 manipulation, the end of humanity as God's creation.

And they have been imbued with the power to decide what does and does not constitute mental disorders. This is not the same as mental diseases, which demand empirical evidence. And they have the freedom to entirely ignore emotional signs of human misery created by life and living, since Schlomo and his ilk brought their undertakings in vogue beginning in the 1890's. They then hastened to persuade humanity that their physical brain had something to do with their misery. Nothing could be further from the truth, according to psychiatrist Peter R. Breggin, M.D. Mind you, they, too, have known this since the late 1800s.

In his book *Brain-Disabling Treatments in Psychiatry: Drugs, Electroshock, and the Psychopharmaceutical Complex*, this admirable physician maintains that no psychiatric disorder is demonstrable or diagnosable. Not by humans. Not by brain scan. Not by any other medical or biological means. Thus, he confirms former American Psychiatric Association president Allen Frances' "it's all bullshit" point. Breggin furthermore adds that all psychiatric treatments—drugs, electroshock, and lobotomy—work by disrupting the function of the brain and the mind. He thereby acknowledges the existence of the latter, when his peers mostly deny its existence. Those treatments, he writes, merely create the apparently benevolent effects by numbing brain and mind. This is then interpreted as improvement. Never mind that an increasing number of psychiatric drugs have been shown to cause abnormal proliferations of brain cells due to the toxic impact of prescription drugs. These are known to cause many obvious clinically toxic effects to humans for decades or longer (p. 207).

Medication spellbinding is another brain-disabling effect, writes Breggin. It renders people unable to perceive the degree of their drug-induced impairments and oddities. This causes them to not attribute any changes within themselves to an adverse drug effect. Rather, they perceive that they are doing better, when in fact they are doing worse, at times far worse. In even not-so-extreme cases, their "medication" drives them into compulsive activities that harm themselves and others because of so-called bio-psychiatric interventions, as I have lived. All of it causes generalized brain dysfunction, which leads to perception distortion, and ultimately to complete distortion of reality (*Brain -Disabling Treatments in Psychiatry: Drugs, Electroshock, and the Psychopharmaceutical Complex* p. 1 and 2).

In other words, pharmaceutical drugs drive human beings into insanity by racking our brains at a slow or rapid pace, depending on the amount consumed. They do not free us from insanity. Still wonder why at least 20 U.S. PTSD-experiencing soldiers commit suicide daily, 365 days a year? Think again, eh? I, myself, have lived it with Ativan. And some Benzedrine concoction's side-effects almost killed world-renowned Toronto University professor emeritus in clinical psychology Jordan B. Peterson, author of the book *12 Rules for Life: An Antidote to Chaos* published in 2018 (Random House Canada, Penguin Allen Lane, UK).

It is divided into 12 chapters, with each title representing one specific rule for life, explained through an essay. It makes magnificent reading for PTSD journeyers, who decide to free themselves from their mental health mind-altering drug prescribing physician and heal themselves. The decision is all the tougher when knowing that their peers and everyone in the ranks views them as nuts, thanks to their ignorance, not ours. These are the chapters:

1. "Stand up straight with your shoulders back."
2. "Treat yourself like you are someone you are responsible for helping."
3. "Make friends with people who want the best for you."
4. "Compare yourself to who you were yesterday, not to who someone else is today."
5. "Do not let your children do anything that makes you dislike them."
6. "Set your house in perfect order before you criticize the world."
7. "Pursue what is meaningful (not what is expedient)."
8. "Tell the truth - or, at least, don't lie."
9. "Assume that the person you are listening to might know something you don't."
10. "Be precise in your speech."
11. "Do not bother children when they are skateboarding."
12. "Pet a cat when you encounter one on the street."

Peterson's central idea seems to originate from Buddha's view that "suffering is built into the structure of being." Although the suffering might seem unbearable, we should always acknowledge that we a choice. We either withdraw, which is a "suicidal gesture", or we face and transcend the situation in which we find ourselves. Furthermore, states Peterson, living in a world of chaos and order, every one of us has "darkness" within that can "turn them into the monsters they're capable of being" merely to satisfy their dark impulses, if so inclined. We are born with an instinct for ethics and meaning, however. So, every one of us should take the responsibility to seek meaning in our lives rather than spending life searching for fleeting notions of happiness. In other words, try very hard to live a purpose-driven life rather than twiddling it away texting on the whatever. Peterson omits, however, that under the influence of mind-altering pharmaceutical drugs purpose cannot materialize, as the drugs destroy all incentive.

Why live human subjects were so desperately needed? To gradually reach this control over humanity, and with it conclude the Luciferic consciousness' Work of Ages, culminating in human 2.0. To measure how and what, when and why, how much and how little would be needed to set humans off. That is why the massive pauper and lunatic asylum system was set up worldwide. It was in readiness for this prime-crop of healthy human beings driven in as shell shocked of WWI and WWII. Post trauma would not do, as it would be too obviously related to the war and the emotional trauma related to it reacting in some people's behavior. The asylums also served a most important social function, because families, government-servants, employers, and unions use kick-backs to get rid of anyone they wanted. They just had to get them diagnosed as mentally disordered, such as the genuine PTSD-affected by psychiatrists willing to declare them certifiable. That's what they tried to do with me in the most vicious ways, with some of my peers working for them as snitches. I am not the exception, by the way. I am the rule.

So then, we can see that all of it began during the end of the 1800s. Despite the thrust of social changes agitated mainly by Rockefeller's non-profit organizations, family and gender roles stayed the same even in asylums. At the outset, men and women maintained their traditional gender roles. Pinel's, Tuke's, Rush's and Ellis's moral therapy were followed- for a little while to prepare patients for a transition back into society. Even those diagnosed as incurable were treated with the same consideration, as Victorian culture demanded. It was hoped that functioning in their expected social roles would bring a sense of purpose and normalcy to their existence and improve their quality of life.

To achieve the objective, male patients were engaged in work seen as suitable to their social responsibility as breadwinner, we learn. They primarily worked on the asylum's farm or in the factory-like settings of its slaughterhouse and cannery. Women patients performed the gender-appropriate work of cooking, cleaning, and sewing, we read. As British society slowly evolved towards present ideas of male and female herd equally, women were permitted to work in all asylum's areas. This trend spread throughout Western asylum systems as time went on, until it was made to collapse in the 1980s. That brought on helter-skelter for many of them and for society at large as now a days seen in the world's cities everywhere. Are they all mad, though, or were they made to be so?

Like today, when madness came into vogue around the late 1700s, patients were considered "mad" for a multitude of reasons. For instance, the Parliament of Great Britain passed *The Mad House* Act of 1774 (14 Geo. 3 c.49). It set out the first legal framework for regulating "madhouses." Until then, there were two common practices throughout the British Isles and continental Europe for dealing with those seen as insane. They would either keep them in the family home or put them into private "madhouses," paying the proprietors to securely detain them. Ran as commercial, for-profit enterprises with little or no medical involvement, abuse was said to be rampant. Those considered truly insane were kept in atrocious conditions, and those detained by force upon claims of insanity made by husbands and others were rarely treated better.

They were by and large lucrative businesses. But by passing the *Mad House Act*, the government forced each county to provide an asylum for the poor and lunatics, thus putting taxpayer-funded asylums into slow motion. By 1808, *The County Asylums Act* extended the care-taking to the poor, the criminally insane and the mentally ill. The 1842 *Licensed Lunatic Asylums Bill* amended and continued the existing 1808 *Act's* laws for three years. It also led to the *Lunacy Inquiry Act*, which established a Metropolitan Commission national inquiry to inspect county licensed houses, county asylums and hospitals. In 1844, it provided a 300-page report with its recommendations (studymore.org).

It resulted in the *Lunacy/Lunatics Act* 1845 (8 & 9 Vict. c. 100), and refreshed the *County Asylums Act* 1845 (8 & 9 Vict., c. 126). In 1853, it was amended to *The Lunatic Asylums Act* to "Consolidate and Amend the Laws for the Provision and Regulation of Lunatic Asylums for Counties and Boroughs and for the Maintenance and Care of Pauper Lunatics in England" (August 20, 1853). In other words, with the 1845 *Lunacy Act*, all previously existing laws (1832 *Madhouses Act*, 1833 *Madhouses Amendment Act and Continuation Acts*) were replaced. And, whereas before 1842 the Commission had solely been authorized to administer the Madhouse Acts in London proper, after 1845 it had control and power to oversee the execution of lunacy laws throughout England and Wales. The three years of inquiry into Britain's pauper and lunacy asylum thus served for nothing other than to transform from a unit of local government jurisdiction to a department of national government. In other words, it brought centralized control, including that of who would and would not work in such institution.

This amendment gave rise to the mammoth buildings suddenly being erected all over the country with little concern for inmates' physical wellbeing or cleanliness. For the first time, however, these buildings included super-sophisticated experimental research laboratories. The residents were to henceforth be called lunatics, imbeciles, insane, idiots and cretins.

The 1853 *Act* ruled the country's mental health development programs until 1889, when Parliament took action anew. It was under pressure from public anxieties about wrongful confinement engendered by newspapers and journals between the 1860s and 1880s. English psychiatrists had been vigorously promoting their profession by advocating for a less asylum-based mode of psychiatry to avoid such instances. So, Parliament imposed new legislation on psychiatrists and lunatic asylums alike by passing the *Lunacy Amendment Act* of 1889 (Akinobu Takabayashi: *Surviving the Lunacy Act of 1890: English Psychiatrists and Professional Development during the Early Twentieth Century*; Med Hist 2017 Apr; 61(2): 246–269). Consolidated into the *Lunacy Act* in 1890, it required an additional "reception order", a "legal certification" issued by a justice of the peace especially appointed by a county court judge or a magistrate with jurisdiction over the asylum or residence to which the deemed lunatic would be admitted. To curb enthusiasm for private admissions, the Act's Section 315 stipulated a fine not exceeding £50 for illegal admission, as if anyone could ever find out.

The 1890 Act succeeded the 1845 *Lunacy Act* for pauper lunatics in so far as it still required a justice of the peace to issue a "summary reception order" with a medical certificate. But it also inhibited further licensing of madhouses and private asylums, instead calling for their gradual abolition as they presented competition to the science-of-psychiatry invasion. It also changed the nosography of *pauper lunatics* to that of patients. This was seemingly the final preparation for the WWI and WWII planned science-of-psychiatry professionals to figure out how to expertly and gradually ruin humanity's brains without it noticing. They would use the physically healthy but emotionally distraught. They would call them shell-shocked, and 70 years later they would call it post traumatic stress disorder. And all would be accomplished by getting them onto asylum premises and into in their experimental laboratories.

Thus, all pauper lunatic laws passed by British members of Parliament, *speak the lie*, seem to have merely been undertaken to open pathways for the science of psychiatry and its aficionados. It gave them a foothold and helped them find acceptance in the public's eye. And it gave legal cover for researchers into the human psyche to conduct their infamous and gruesome experiments on their human subjects. First and foremost among their victims were the emotionally distraught soldiers witnessing the effect of Nobel's weapons used against them.

And the more psychiatrists they could squeeze into the system, the better. Considering the COVID-19 plandemic in the making, they would need a multitude of them, as it would drive humanity over the cliff. The British House of Commons began that process 175 years earlier, by adding two medical professionals to the 1845 *Inquiry Act*'s asylum inspection committee, of whom one had to be a statistician. A statistician? Yes, a statistician to keep track of the numbers when the science-of-psychiatry professional began to implant insanity into humanity, we gather. The other medical professional had to be a psychiatrist, in translation from the Greek, a healer of the soul and mind. It was the term German professor of medicine Johann Christian Reil (1759 –1813) chose in 1808 to describe the evolving discipline of studying humans' emotions. Funny how, until the twentieth century, its practitioners would be known as alienists, derived from the Latin "alius" or the other.

Its past participle of aliéner, however, means to estrange or to deprive of reason. This reveals that purporting to heal the soul of the other under the title of "psychiatrist" is phony. Instead, they deprive the "other" of reason, precisely what is done with mind-altering pharmaceutical drugs. Never mind how the equally lethal ECT or the lobotomy deprives one of reason, these treatments being the norm still at present for anyone diagnosed as "mentally disordered." They indeed manage to diagnose an "estimated" 26% of Americans ages 18 and older - about one in four adults - with a *mental* disorder in any given year, according to The Johns Hopkins Hospital and Health System. They should know, as they were instrumental in destroying brains of humanity of all ages since its founding in 1889. In 1999, it furthered its objectives, when the Bill & Melinda Gates Institute for Population and Reproductive Health added another US$20 million for the purpose.

Today, the distorted thinking of the science-of-psychiatry practitioners is rampantly distorted. According to Breggin, it is so distorted that not even brain abnormalities in human cell growth causes them alarm. Nor does increased brain size caused by their pharmaceutical drugs after administering them to their live human research subjects. On the contrary. Such changes, he says, are automatically promoted by industry as evidence of benefit to human mental and physical health and wellbeing. Such a cause for jubilation, a cause for hope to succeed in driving gullible humanity, trusting their physicians completely, into a drug-induced insanity without having a clue about it. And what did English poet and satirist Alexander Pope (1688 -1744) exclaim in his 1733-34 *An Essay on Man* warning us?

"Know then thyself, presume not God to scan,
The proper study of mankind is Man.
Placed on this isthmus of a middle state,
A being darkly wise and rudely great:
With too much knowledge for the Sceptic side,
With too much weakness for the Stoic's pride,
He hangs between, in doubt to act or rest;
In doubt to deem himself a God or Beast;
In doubt his mind or body to prefer;
Born but to die, and reas'ning but to err;
Alike in ignorance, his reason such,
Whether he thinks too little or too much;
Chaos of thought and passion, all confused;
Still by himself abused or disabused;
Created half to rise, and half to fall;
Great lord of all things, yet a prey to all;
Sole judge of truth, in endless error hurl'd;
The glory, jest, and riddle of the world!
Go, wondrous creature! mount where science guides,
Go, measure earth, weigh air, and state the tides;
Instruct the planets in what orbs to run,
Correct old time, and regulate the sun;
Go, soar with Plato to th' empyreal sphere,
To the first good, first perfect, and first fair;
Or tread the mazy round his followers trod,
And quitting sense call imitating God;
As Eastern priests in giddy circles run,
And turn their heads to imitate the sun.
Go, teach Eternal Wisdom how to rule—
Then drop into thyself, and be a fool!"

And what does man do?

"Hope springs eternal in the human breast;
Man never Is, but always To be blest.
The soul, uneasy, and confin'd from home,
Rests and expatiates in a life to come."

And a miserable life it's going to be, if in the PTSD situation we trust our physicians and psychiatrists and their drugging. Trusting Pope instead might be a better idea. He wrote the essay 270 years ago, and it still stands, as we realize if we are still able to reason even minutely.

While being knowingly, willfully, and systematically destroyed, our destroyers since then used our innate emotion of hopefulness to lead us down their garden path towards our own destruction of Self. Read it again and ponder – yourself, your soul, your mind, your earthly existence, your purpose- or non-purpose-driven life arranged by whom and loved for what?

Stuffing human meat-infested McDonalds down your throat? Gobbling down pharmaceutical drugs? Smoking pot and drinking chemical-infested beer, whilst thriving on your physician-enhanced pharmaceutical drug-caused ailments, and watching mind-numbing television programs in all your waking hours? Bragging about your physician's expertise as everyone makes money sending you from Pontius to Pilate for your never-meant-to-be-healed dis-eases? And you take no interest in it, overweight and mentally undernourished as you have been made to be by yourself, because you trust them all and they give you hope? Excuse me? Anything wrong with this picture?

Really, how sick are you, when you don't want to take responsibility for your own emotional and physical health, never mind help yourself, eh? Has not the emotion of hope been shuffled down humanity's throat for as long as you can remember, even though it has no value for any health improvement? And you accept it, when it is so utterly futile? Has the Luciferic consciousness permeated your thinking to such a degree? Are you incapable of recognizing that it is much more beneficial for every individual's growth to face that "Life is indeed suffering, and that we are the only ones who have the power to change it by way of our thinking, and thus our perception of life?

May it not be a wonderful idea to get with it and learn to overcome the hurdles presented to us, in essence learning to enjoy every moment of the overcoming of our perceived suffering?" It becomes evident within hours, that helping ourselves by the power and control over our thinking is so much more beneficial to our wellbeing than to depend on psychiatric black magic-inspired treatments. Those just push us into the "I am a victim, Pity me" impaired status that is so vile for our emotional and physical health. Hours, as Dr. Rashied Buttar pointed out when, together with Dr. Bryan Ardis, interviewed on the July 18, 2022, Flyover Conservative Show: Information Worth Dying For (rumble.com)?

And the psychiatric professionals know, what the victim status does to humans' mind and soul. That's why they want to maneuver us into it, full well knowing that our lives are over, if we, blind as bats and unaware, enter it. The ilk also knows that as long as they dangle hope in front of us, we will remain in their clutches, cling to them for dear life, indeed. It is the moment we recognize our own power to heal ourselves that they fear, as the cured patient is a lost customer. It is material "things" that rule all of those under the Luciferic Consciousness spell, which most of those involved in the human mental ill health business are (Breggin p. 207-8). Free yourself from them, and you will instantaneously see your life change for the better. Stay within the system, and you doom yourself to misery and destruction until the end of your natural life.

The first steps toward humanity's systematic and wilful destruction were taken with Elisabeth I and John Dee. But the 1845 *Lunacy Act* put it in motion big time. It was the *Act* that enthused Lord Anthony Ashley Cooper, 7th Earl of Shaftesbury (1801 -1885). He was nicknamed the "Poor Man's Earl" because he sought improvements to the herd's social conditions. These included lunacy law reforms, child labour limits, education and work. And he elatedly exclaimed that this *Act* alone would "effect a cure in 70 cases out of every 100" incarcerated paupers and lunatics (Hansard 6 June 1845 column 193) That the Act demanded the exponential growth in the number of asylums escaped the masses attention. That this would secure for the mental health industry its platform of operation also escaped their attention. That it obligated every single taxpayer to pay for the asylums for paupers and folk accused of being mentally deficient by anyone in authority, including well-connected husbands, escaped the masses attention as well. Between 1845 and 1890, 60 mammoth asylums sprang up in Britain and Wales. Another 40 were built in preparation for WWI and WWII. They were all equipped with exquisite research laboratories, which still had 150,000 subjects to play with in over 100 mental hospitals by 1950 (https://valmcbeath.com/victorian-era-lunatic-asylums/).

Thus, in 1845 the stage had been set to give the burgeoning, planned-to-be-created profession of magicians of human alienation what they wanted. They masqueraded as healers of the human mind and soul. They sophisticatedly termed "the science of psychiatry" to legitimately use those being entered into any asylum, from aristocrats to paupers and destitute, as experimental laboratory rats. Nobody could drag them into court to prove otherwise, wit the 1973 Rosenhan experiment conducted by Stanford University professor David Rosenhan to determine psychiatric diagnoses' validity ("On Being Sane in Insane Places"; *Science*, 1973). Upper- and middle-class people could be admitted by family members as private patients, whereas herd members could be entered into the coral dwelling for free. Mental impairment due to physical brain injury or malfunction in circuitry was then, like now, on par with emotional, heartache-caused upheaval misery. The latter was due to an earth-shattering, normally-to-be-expected life experience, never mind genuine PTS caused by enormous emotional upheaval due to an experience far beyond the realm of such normality.

Does it seem, as if the psychiatric treatment system agenda was perfected and streamlined with the 1853 *Lunatic Asylums Act*? After all, it laid down admission and detention rules for paupers and lunatics, including a medical certificate presentation. It had to be signed by a physician or apothecary who had personally examined the applicant within the previous seven days. Today, that would still be sufficient, but at that time, an order from a justice, a clergyman, an overseer or the relieving officer under the *Poor Law* still had to also be submitted to the asylum's administration. This gave some protection to the accused. Private patients only needed a medical certificate signed by two physicians, surgeons or apothecaries to be admitted. They also had to provide their name, sex, age, marital status, condition of life, previous occupation, and religious persuasion. And they were asked about their age at the time of the first lunacy attack, duration of existing attack, supposed causes of attack and whether epilepsy, suicidal tendencies or danger to others existed.

And, just as today, no procedures for patients to appeal against detention were available upon admission (*Fallacy 1*). However, they could still be discharged to a relative or friend pledging to take proper care of the patient and prevent him or her from injuring themselves or others, unlike today. Since the mid-1990s, no pauper or average lunatic can enter a lunatic asylum unless deemed criminally insane. That's when they were closed and inmates thrown into the streets to fight for their own survival, wit Vancouver's East End skid row. Mind you, in the mid-1800s, asylums were by and large regarded as prisons disguised as hospitals used to remove the destitute and incurable from society with little discrimination and oversight.

Plenty of stories exist of patients admitted without reasons, forgotten about and dying within. That's because reasons for admission were very much based on the admitting alienist's personal judgment (often influenced by kickbacks). And, just as today, heavily weighted against women. For those with money, the private madhouses, such as aspiring psychiatrist and future Tavistock Clinic employee Crichton-Miller's Bowden House, were often no more than dumping grounds for unwanted wives by well-off husbands seeking greener pastures with trophy mistresses.

Indeed, many more women than men populated the asylums throughout Western lands in preparation for the family's destruction, as the mental asylum fad spread from Britain massively across Europe. In 1878, there were 104 asylums in France, and 279 by 1899 in Germany (ehne.fr/en/encyclopedia/themes/political-europe/control-and-discipline/psychiatric-institutions-in-europe-nineteenth-and-twentieth-century). In Spain and Italy, the alienist profession did not get national legal backing until 1904, though. And Russia imported the psychiatric profession with the Ukrainian Mafia Ashkenazi Jewish Russian Revolution instigators in 1917. Its results were portrayed in Aleksandr Isayevich Solzhenitsyn (1918 –2008) *Gulag Archipelago* and other of his works.

While some countries like Britain engineered to have their lunatic institutions paid by taxpayers, others engaged charitable and religious organizations to finance and run them. The knowledge gathered through inside laboratory experiments on inmates and the institutional models themselves, however, were all similar. They circulated throughout the psychiatric profession's learned society system to assure all and sundry knew the order of things and stayed on the same song sheet. They also loved their regular get-togethers and their visits to each other's institutions. They would discuss how to streamline operations in preparation for the expected influx of inmates during and after the already-planned WWI and WWII adventures. In particular, they looked forward to playing on the previously known to-be-healthy shell-shocked soldiers who were to replace the lunatics and paupers as laboratory rats.

European psychiatrists set out to ensure the spread of humanity's mind-manipulation-into-destruction operation worldwide. They were all nationals of a multitude of European colony-holding nations. At the 1912 Congress of Tunis, they also arranged to label those accused of disturbing the social order as mentally insane, and to detain them. Mukesh Kumar is professor of history at the Magadh University in Bodh Gaya, Bihar, India. In 2010, he pointed out that Western medicine, of which psychiatry is part, was a tool of empire, instrumental in overseas colonial expansion, regardless which nation used it. It also, he says, provided for colonialism's legitimacy, as well as moral superiority, in its civilizing mission of the colonies (Mukesh Kumar: *Disciplining The "Mind:" Indian inmates in Lunatic Asylums in Nineteenth Century India*; Proceedings of the Indian History Congress 71, 861-873). The English also used every opportunity to establish their hold on the assumption of racial superiority with the help of Western technology, writes Kumar. This attitude was reflected in medical practices, we read, and more so in the asylums' work-culture. The history of India's psychiatric hospitals and its inmates is therefore closely related to social and scientific attitudes spread by its colonizers, though it changed somewhat in recent times.

In Africa, the first colonial asylums had been created in the early nineteenth century. The mid-1800s to about 1918 saw a most notable rise and formative period in asylums with an institutional base. In South Africa alone, the government created a national network of massive mental hospitals between the 1920s and the 1990s. And it changed the ways in which mental illnesses were classified (https://oxfordre.com/africanhistory/view/10.1093/acrefore/9780190277734.001.0001/acrefore-9780190277734-e-603). Ever-new treatments were also introduced from the 1930s to the 1950s. The law and the psychiatric profession's theoretical orientations also changing in the 1940s, 1960s and 1970s, although institutional practices largely remained the same. In the 1980s, gradual shifts toward democratic governance occurred with the progressive *Mental Health Act* of 2002. It is said, however, that human rights violations in the case of the state's duty of care toward the mentally ill and the vulnerable continue. The British monarchy's rule over South Africa officially ended on May 31, 1961. It was replaced by the Republic of South Africa; we will take its mental health asylum system as template of British colonies worldwide.

And India? Well, India counted 26 asylums at the turn of the nineteenth century. At present, despite phenomenal population growth, it has only 18,307 hospital beds in the entire country, hosted in 47 government psychiatric institutions. Mind you, they are far ahead of the mental illness game. Their emperor Ashoka (c. 304 – 232 BC), known as Ashoka the Great of the Maurya Empire, had already set up hospitals for mentally-disabled people in the third century BC. Descriptions of various mental illnesses can be found in ancient Indian texts, probably the oldest such accounts in the world, do exist (S. Haque Nizamie et al: History of psychiatry in India; Indian J Psychiatry 2010 Jan; 52 (Suppl1): S7–S12).

Great Indian epics, such as the *Ramayana and the Mahabharata*, make references to disordered states of mind and means of coping with them. The *Bhagavad Gita* is a classical example of crisis intervention psychotherapy. Ayurveda also acknowledges the diet-dis-ease relationship and association of physical and mental dis-eases so gloriously and persistently ignored by any western-trained allopathic physician, never mind mind-manipulators worth their salt. For them, entertaining a mental health diagnosis based on the subject's five senses and by patient-interrogation would bring forth an idiotic Kamela-cackle. One of the world's first surgeons was Shushruta, whose *Sushruta's Compendium* dated around 600 BC at the latest. It is considered one of the most important ancient treatises on medicine. He would only draw a blank stare, as their computer- and pharmaceutical drugging diagnostic training replaced Sushruta's perception of the human in the human being.

Close to the roots of Hindu mythology, the Indian physician Najabuddin Unhammad propagated the Unani system of medicine around 1222. This traditional system of healing and health maintenance is observed in South Asia. Its origins lie in the doctrines of Hippocrates, Galen and Avicenna, with additional contributions of medical wisdom from other parts of the Middle East and South Asia. Also known as Arabian or Islamic medicine, its practitioners are called hakims. They rely on natural healing based on principles of harmony and balance, uniting the physical, mental and spiritual realms, with Najabuddin Unhammad describing seven types of mental disorders:

- *Sauda-a-Tabee* (Schizophrenia)
- *Muree-Sauda* (depression)
- *Ishk* (delusion of love)
- *Nisyan* (Organic mental disorder)
- *Haziyan* (paranoid state)
- *Malikholia-a-maraki* (delirium)

Psychotherapy was known as Ilaj-I-Nafsani in Unani Medicine. The great Indian sage Agastya was a noted recluse and an influential scholar in diverse languages. He and his wife were celebrated authors of hymns 1.165 to 1.191 in the Sanskrit text Rigveda and other Vedic literature. He formulated a treatise on mental diseases known as "Agastiyar kirigai Nool", in which 18 psychiatric disorders are described, and appropriate treatment methods suggested. He also wrote in the *Charak Samhita*, the Sanskrit text on Ayurveda, along with the *Sushruta Samhita* one of the two foundational texts of traditional Indian medicine. He describes various attributes for a lunatic hospital, including its location, details of equipment, food and cleanliness and model code of conduct for physicians, nursing staff and ward attendants. This was thousands of years before any of the alienists and psychiatrists were even conceived. With their classical educations at prime institutions had access to translations of Sanskrit texts as they planned their science-of-psychiatry invention to impose on the human herd.

Instead, the British imposed on the Indian population the largest psychiatric system ever established by any colonial power in any colonized region in the world during the Raj. It was the most extensive attempt to transplant and implant Western notions of mental health and mental illness into a non-Western context of very different pre-existing concepts of indigenous and folk practices. These existent folk practices related to mental illness were replaced by the British variously with experimentations in mesmerism, homeopathy, cannabis and hemp therapy and spiritualism. These were followed by the harsher methods of incarceration, whipping and starvation. These in turn eventually gave way to intrusive convulsive therapies, leucotomy, and lobotomy. We can be certain the same means and methods were applied in all other British colonies.

The earliest mental hospital in for British folk in India, however, was established at Bombay in 1745 to accommodate 30 mentally disabled patients. The first British government-run lunatic asylum was set-up in 1795 especially for insane soldiers at Monghyr in Bihar. They were treated with opium, hot baths, sometimes leeches to suck their blood and music. But between 1858 and 1918 India, too, witnessed an explosion of mental asylums. They used the same modus operandi as was implemented in Britain, including enacting India's 1858 *Lunacy Act*, replaced later on with *Indian Lunacy Act* of 1912. That year, the European Lunatic Asylum was built in Bhowanipore for European patients only. It closed in 1918, when the British established the Ranchi European Lunatic Asylum, which could hold 174 patients (92 males and 82 females) and also catered to European mental patients only.

With a board of trustees that included various participating state government representatives, the name changed to European Mental Hospital. It was affiliated with the University of London to issue the Diploma in Psychological Medicine exam. In other words, the hospital's physicians could qualify as psychiatrists. This was a somewhat unique phenomenon, as no postgraduate training in psychiatry existed in India in those days. The European Mental Hospital is now known as the Central Institute of Psychiatry (CIP) at Ranchi, where patients are never chained, but freely roam within its boundary. The English, Hindi and Bangla books in its library are available to anyone. Patients play football and women engage in sewing, embroidery and other household chores, also with a music system in place. It is sad that many a prominent Indian personality chose "to treat themselves" in this institution, among them Asrar ul Haq Majaz and Kazi Nazrul Islam, Indian poets known for writing romantic and revolutionary poetry and music.

But in 1946, India's British rulers set up the Bhore Committee to investigate India's mental hospitals. Based in its recommendation, India's Institute of Mental Health sprang into existence in 1954. In 1974, it turned into the National Institute of Mental Health and Neurosciences. It got all Indians under centralized control for events to come, such as employing drones to get the COVID-19 lethal injections into its citizens and keep statistical track of it, eh?

In 1947, when India's independence movement finally reached its ultimate goal after 90 years of trying. The newly formed government immediately focused more on improving its existing hospital conditions than on building new mental institutions or hastening to establish children and adolescent clinics to get to the young. And in 1949, the CIP started its Department of Clinical Psychology containing India's first clinical psychology research laboratory to explore how the Indian psyche can best be manipulated and destroyed.

But in the 1970s, the mental healthcare focus shifted from the pharmaceutical medicinal treatment applied to those deemed mentally unstable. It was hoped that this would combat the stigma patients encountered when trying to widen their social network. A wider social network would enhance their possibility to rehabilitate, since those considered recovered were socially shunned, which put them back into the depressing phase viewed as mental disorder. Apparently during the last three decades, we read, innovations in neurosciences, epidemiology and therapeutics made show growth to support those who are recovering or recovered from mental illness. Precise information why this should occur are not given, as it is all bullshit, as explained by Allan Frances and Dr. Breggin, without the latter expressing it so bluntly. To me, it seems that Indians think little of emotional or mental illness. They have just 47 mental health asylums for their1.38 billion souls Compare that to the 12,275 (and rising) registered mental health treatment facilities in the United States. for their piddly 329.5 million (plus a few million illegal aliens).

There seems to be just one problem, at least in India. India's Daily News & Analysis reported in 2013 that when staff at the Yerwada Mental Hospital, one of Asia's largest, worked for long periods of unspecified time, they developed schizophrenia and psychosis. In other words, they lost touch with reality, having trouble distinguishing between what is real and what is not. These people were kept under the care of hospital psychiatrists, who most likely worked there for long periods of time, as well. They were also looked after by a hospital representative, who most likely also worked there for a long time. *The Daily News & Analysis* also reported and that monthly check-ups were being conducted by an unknown entity to prevent the occurrence of mental illness among staff members. An independent psychiatrist was also reported to have commented that demand on staff to show empathy towards their patients is what caused burnout and psychosis within a couple of years. That such a mild-mannered human as myself could to play with the conclusion that the saying "The insane are running the asylum" may indeed not be far fetched, eh? That Yerwada staff also take bribes to release some of those diagnosed as lunatics and rape some of their charges is also mentioned as a sideline. Perhaps this further attests to the possibility that those entering the mental illness profession do so to have a playhouse for their own oddities and perverted perceptions?

The history of Australian psychiatry is of course intertwined with the British Crown's 1788 invasion with 850 jail birds to relieve its overcrowded jails. This continued until 1901, which generated a masculine-dominated, individualistic society (Alan Rosen: "Australia's national mental health strategy in historical perspective: beyond the frontier"; *Int Psychiatry* 2006 Oct; 3 (4): 19-21). Castle Hill Lunatic Asylum was Australia's first official institution to care for those who had lost it. It was located close to Parramatta in New South Wales, housed in a two-story disused convict barracks. The first doctors were themselves convicts in conflict with a sternly moral lay superintendent (J P Parkinson: "The Castle Hill lunatic asylum (1811-1826) and the origins of eclectic pragmatism in Australian psychiatry"; *Aust N Z J Psychiatry* 1981 Dec; 15(4): 319-22).

Disturbances, including a murder, occurred among the patients, but the Governor restored peace by dismissing the superintendent and abolishing the post of resident doctor. Deprivation and dirt prevailed, however, until the asylum was transferred to further makeshift quarters in 1826.

As settlements in Australia expanded, Australia's first large lunatic institution opened in 1838. In 1871, Australia passed its first lunacy act, tailored after Britain's. The *Lunacy Act* 1871 (No. 9 of 1871) did not distinguish between mental illness and intellectual or physical disability. This meant that children with intellectual disabilities, or physical disabilities such as epilepsy, often were, sent to the Fremantle Asylum (https://findandconnect.gov.au/ref/wa/biogs/WE00995b.htm. The *Act* defined a lunatic as "every person of unsound mind, and every person being an idiot" (s.2). Commitals could be ordered (Schedule A) or voluntary, at the request of a "private person" (Schedule B).

This *Act* was repealed by the *Lunacy Act* 1903 (015 of 1903 (3 Edw. VII No. 15), which established the Department of Lunacy. The department was responsible for administering the *Act* and four mental institutions. Among them was Stromness, a large house to care for returned servicemen with mental illnesses, which opened in 1918. It was replaced by the Lemnos Hospital in 1926. Parents and families of large numbers of mentally damaged sons were horrified to find there were few suitable places where they could be accommodated, let alone treated. But they could bring their sick children to Lemnos. It offered specialised nursing, the latest treatments and the tranquility of beautifully kept gardens where the afternoon sea breeze would cool the wards.

In their idiocy, they named it Lemnos, after the Greek Island in the Aegean Sea serving as a base for Allied Forces during the horrifying Gallipoli campaign, so that soldiers would be reminded of it always. The hospital was again used for emotionally suffering soldiers returning from WWII. Henceforth, it welcomed returning servicemen with mental ill health issues until it closed its doors in 1999.

For civilians, mind you, Australia kept in trot with European aspiration. It had outposts for prisoners and dissidents since its 1788 inception, so it added massive urban and rural institutions to the existing concentration camps. One such example was the Aradale Asylum in Ararat, a rural city in Victoria colony. Its two sister asylums at Kew and Beechworth were commissioned to accommodate the growing number of "lunatics" in Victoria. Work on Aradale began in 1865 and opened for patients in 1867, at its height housing 1,000 inmates and a large complex of 70 buildings.

Kew Lunatic Asylum in the suburbs of Melbourne, operating from 1871 to 1988, was one of the largest asylums ever built in Australia. Later known as Willsmere, the complex of buildings was built between 1864 and 1872 to house the growing number of lunatics, inebriates in the Colony of Victoria. Throughout the twentieth century, it operated as a "hospital for the insane", "mental hospital", or "psychiatric hospital", treating acute, long-term and geriatric patients until its 1988 closure.

The massive Beechworth Asylum was later known as the Beechworth Hospital for the Insane, then as the Mayday Hills Mental Hospital. It opened in 1867 in the town of Beechworth, Victoria, surrounded by almost 106 hectares (260 acres) of farmland. It was self-sufficient, with its own piggery, orchards, kitchen gardens, fields, stables and barn. For recreation, the asylum included tennis courts, an oval and cricket pavilion, a kiosk and a theatre for inmates' recreational purposes. Nothing is mentioned of a library, though.

It took until 1992 for the Australian government to pass The *National Mental Health Policy* (1992) and provide transitional funding in the national budget. This shifted services from individual institutions to local taxpayers, with steadily reduced federal funding, as inspired by the 1853 *Lunatic Asylum Act*. The same took place in New Zealand, whilst Kenya had drawn on the one adopted in India in 1858.

In 2022, specialised mental healthcare in Australia is delivered by a range of facilities. These include public and private psychiatric hospitals, psychiatric units and wards in public acute hospitals, community mental healthcare services and government- and non-government-operated residential mental health services (https://aihw.gov.au/reports/mental-health-services/mental-health-services-in-australia/report-contents/specialised-mental-health-care-facilities). The information here is drawn from the National Mental Health Establishments Database. Accordingly, Australia's 25.69 million herd members in had the following available in 2019-2020:

- 161 public hospitals and 68 private hospitals with specialised mental health services for admitted patients
- 7,019 specialised mental health public hospital beds
- 3,494 mental health beds in private hospitals
- 2,438 residential mental health beds, with over two-thirds operated by government organisations.
- 13,948 full-time-equivalent staff employed by Community mental health-care services

In other words, about roughly 13,000 out of roughly 26 million people were expected to be mentally or emotionally ill.

That settled, let's move on to the United States, which by and large did its own thing with those considered slightly or majorly off their rocker. The poster depicting the majestic Trans-Allegheny Lunatic Asylum, subsequently the Weston State Hospital, gives some insight into the scale of its mental health operations. It was one of America's 73 psychiatric hospitals, built with exquisite research laboratories across its land in the second half of the nineteenth century.

Operating from 1864 until 1994 under the government of West Virginia's auspices, the Trans-Allegheny lists a multitude of reasons for admission. These include death of sons in war, desertion and death of husband, as well as domestic trouble. Unspecified female trouble, immoral life (often associated with delivering an illegitimate child), menstrual problems, menopause, uterine problems, female disease, nymphomania and "hysteria" are also cited as reasons for admission to its premises.

It was supposed to care for 250 patients and be a place for rest and restoration. But it soon devolved into an abode of madness and destruction, ballooning to 500 inmates by 1881 due to the exponential increase in mental health diagnoses. The science of psychiatry, so very much advertised by Edinburgh-educated "Father of American Psychiatry" Benjamin Rush (1745-1813), had taken off like wildfire. Rush believed that mental illness was not to be a "possession of demons," but a disease of the mind. And his ideas had radiated like venom from the Pennsylvania Hospital, his workplace until his death in 1813. He popularizes his viewpoints on the human minds' aptitudes and treatments in his psychiatric textbook *Observations and Inquiries upon the Diseases of the Mind* published in 1812.

Rush graduated from the University of Edinburgh, Scotland, in 1766. He went to London and Paris for further studies in 1768. He returned to Philadelphia in 1769, where he established himself at once in the practice of medicine (https://uphs.upenn.edu/paharc/features/brush.html). He also served as resident port-physician, fleet surgeon of the Pennsylvania Navy and was appointed physician general of the Military Hospital of the Middle Department, American Army, 1777. He served as the president of the American Society for the Abolition of Slavery and president of the Philadelphia Medical Society, as well as being a fellow of the College of Physicians. He was elected to the Chair of Institutes, Medical and Clinical Practice of the University of Pennsylvania in 1791, where he is said to have told his students: "Attend the poor, they are your best patients, God is their paymaster."

By 1938, the Trans-Allegheny held 1,500 or more patients running wild, with orderlies, hugely outnumbered, struggling to gain control. And in the 1950s, there were 2,600 inmates, mirroring the splendid success achieved by the human mind-altering profession, the purported healers humans' mind and soul. They sure showed their ability to increase humanity's insanity at leisure, by 1881 housing almost 500 patients documented by Katie Serena in her 2022 article "The Horrifying History Of The Trans-Allegheny Lunatic Asylum". Used as a human research laboratory, famous surgeon and performer of 4,000 lobotomies Walter Jackson Freeman II (1895–1972) opened up shop there. He left thousands of perfectly healthy patients in emotional distress. Many had irreparable physical and cognitive damages or wound up dead, as portrayed in Ken Kessey's 1962 novel *One Flew Over the Cuckoo's Nest*, starring Jack Nicholson in the subsequent movie.

He was born and raised in Philadelphia. His grandfather William Williams Keen (1837 -1932) was a surgeon in the Civil War. His father was a successful doctor. He graduated from Yale University in 1916 and later the University of Pennsylvania Medical School, where he studied under Khazarian Ashkenazi professor of neurology William G. Spiller. After receiving an M.D. from the University of Pennsylvania in 1892, Spiller had spent four years abroad in specialized studies of internal medicine and neurology with Europe's most distinguished clinical neurologists of his time. These were Heinrich Obersteiner (1847–1922), Hermann Oppenheim (1858–1919), Ludwig Edinger (1855–1918), Joseph Jules Dejerine (1849–1917) and Sir William Richard Gowers (1845–1915). After being rejected for a coveted position working alongside Spiller, Freeman relocated to Washington, D.C., and started to practice as the city's first neurologist. He directed the research laboratories at St. Elizabeth Hospital. He earned his PhD in neuropathology in the following years, securing his position as head of the neurology department at George Washington University. That is where he began practicing his "ice pick" method on willing and unwilling subjects we take it.

It involved slipping a thin, pointed rod like an ice pick into the patient's eye socket without general anaesthesia and using a hammer to force it to sever the connective tissue in the brain's prefrontal cortex. This method was in vogue throughout the profession's lunatic asylums worldwide after he first tried it in 1936. His first attempt was with the assistance of neurosurgeon James Winston Watts (1904 -1994), graduate of the Virginia Military Institute. This was a public senior military college in Lexington, Virginia, founded in 1839 as America's first state military college. It enrolled only cadets, exclusively awarding bachelor's degrees. Watts followed with his M.D. at the University of Virginia School of Medicine.

Watts and Freeman became advocates and prolific practitioners of psychosurgery overall and lobotomy in particular. They practiced at leisure on human laboratory rats after Freeman directed Watts through the very first prefrontal lobotomy conducted in the U.S. in 1937.

Two months later, they had performed 20, with a few follow-up operations thrown in. By 1942, they had performed over 200 lobotomy procedures, publicly claiming that 63% of patients had improved after the surgery, 23% were unchanged and 14% were worse. That he had rendered them mindless is nowhere mentioned. Nor was the public informed that he might have incurred his aptitude and pleasure for human mutilation from his maternal grandfather, William Williams Keen (1797–1882). This Union Army surgeon with Khazarian ancestry going back to the late 1600s had neurological wounds and was renowned for his work with patients.

Keen was born in Philadelphia. He graduated in 1859 from Brown University, the private Ivy League research university in Providence, Rhode Island, founded in 1764. He followed with a degree in medicine from Jefferson Medical College in 1862. He served as a surgeon for the Fifth Massachusetts Militia Regiment and the Union Army during the Civil War, building a reputation for working with patients suffering neurological wounds.

He worked with Philadelphia-born Silas Weir Mitchell (1829-1914). Mitchell was educated first at the University of Pennsylvania then with an M.D. from Jefferson Medical

College in 1850. He was director of treatment of nervous injuries and maladies at Turners Lane Hospital, Philadelphia, during the Civil War and considered a specialist in neurology at war's end. Both he and Keen studied nervous system injuries and the two published *Gunshot Wounds and Other Injuries of the Nerves and Reflex Paralysis* in 1864.

Keen went to further his cut, slush and burn art on the human brain in studies in Berlin and Paris. Upon his return, Jefferson Medical College hastened to establish the school's surgical research laboratory for Keen to teach pathological anatomy and surgical pathology.

He rapidly became known in the international medical community for inventing brain surgery procedures, including drainage of the cerebral ventricles and removal of brain tumours. He also performed the first craniectomy, a neurosurgical procedure in which part of the skull is removed to allow a swelling brain room to expand without being squeezed. This was to address microcephalus, a smaller-than-normal head at birth, a condition reported in the United States to occur in 2 to 12 babies per 10,000 births. His operation on infants, however, had little success and met with harsh criticism. The source of these infants on which he experimented is unknown.

While engaged in his neurological experimental mutilation of humans of all ages from we don't know where, Keen also served six American presidents. He was president of the American Surgical Association (1898), the American Medical Association (1900), the Congress of American Physicians and Surgeons (1903), in 1907, American Philosophical Society (APS) president, of which he had been a member since 1884. He also taught at Philadelphia's Woman's Medical College of Pennsylvania (WMCP). This school was launched in 1850, established to train women in medicine and bestow the M.D. degree on them. It was the second one in the world to do so after Boston Female Medical College established in 1848.

Grandpa Keen was a theistic evolutionist. He held that religious teachings about creation and scientific theories of evolution do not at all contradict each other - the "have your cake and eat it too" theory. He was a staunch proponent of vivisection, surgery conducted without anaesthesia on life organisms with central nervous systems, such as human animals. He loved to attack anti-vivisectionists, as he did in his 1914 book *Animal Experimentation and Medical Progress*. To satisfy his animalistic drive of pro-creation, he married in 1867 and fathered four children before leaving for Hades in 1932, at the age of 95.

By then, pursuits to find means of painless surgery were well on their way. These were so very much needed for silent explorations on how to achieve humans' physical and mental mutilation in the name of science and guarantee the success of the Great Work of Ages. Hitherto, the learned society had ignored all numbing means found in Mother Nature, known since ancient times, as well as Paracelsus' ether findings of 1540. But for scientific exploratory research purposes on human laboratory rats, it had to be kept secret. Means had to be found to suppress subjects' consciousness before the final onslaught on humanity's extinction by way of the science of psychiatry. Only like that could they start and assure the Luciferic consciousness's triumphant success, culminating in human 2.0. So, let's see how that unfolded, shall we?

34

THE SEARCH TO STEAL OUR SOULS

Attempts to artificially render humans unconscious on demand go way back. Produce a state of general anaesthesia can be traced in Sumerian, Babylonian, Assyrian, Egyptian, Indian and Chinese writings. Alcohol is known to be the oldest sedative, used in ancient Mesopotamia (modern-day Iraq) millennia ago. It is said by some to be the landing point and cradle of "those who from heaven came." Within the Tigris-Euphrates River system and part of the Fertile Crescent, it is purportedly the very first region on Earth where settled farming emerged around 10,000 BC. It is also the area said to have hosted the beginnings of human civilization, its history marked by many firsts:

- sailboats
- use of irrigation
- geographical maps
- the concept of time
- glass manufacturing
- cursive script/writing
- the invention of the wheel
- mathematics and astronomy
- systematic planting of cereal crops

Mesopotamia is also defined by changing successions of rulers from different areas and cities that seized control over periods of thousands of years at a time.

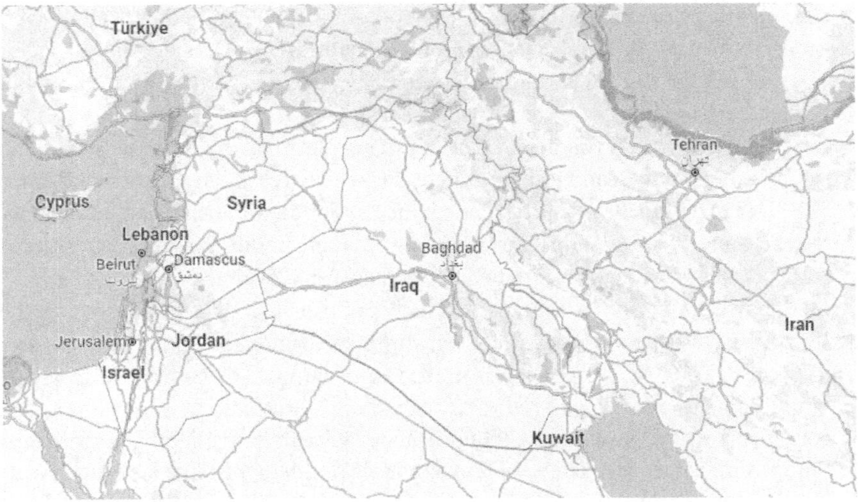

Sumer, in southern Mesopotamia, was settled by humans sometime between the sixth and fourth millennia BC. From there, the developments spread to Egypt, Persia, the Indus Valley, China, Meso-America, and Peru. During the late fourth millennium BC, Sumer itself divided into many independent city states, themselves divided by canals and boundary stones. Each city state centered around a temple dedicated to its particular patron god or goddess. It was ruled over by a priestly governor or king intimately tied to the city's religious rites. Sumerian farmers grew an abundance of grain and other crops, providing urban settlements such as these with their produce:

The earliest texts accessible to us herd members date from around 3500 and 3000 BC. They tell about the city-states of Uruk and Jemdet Nasr. The Sumerians, Akkadians, Assyrians and Babylonians in succession dominated Mesopotamia until Babylonia's fall in 539 BC to the Achaemenid Empire. Also called the First Persian Empire, it was founded by Cyrus II of Persia (c. 600–530 BC), Cyrus the Great. It eventually spanned from the Balkans and ancient Egypt to the Indus Valley before Macedonian Alexander the Great (356-323 BC) overtook it all for a few months before his death in 332 BC. His general Seleucus I Nicator (c. 358 - 281 BC) founded the Seleucid Empire there following the Macedonian Empire's division. It is here that the fight for possession of the earth and the dominion over all humanity seems to have commenced in earnest. Indeed, this actually led to the attempt of its quasi extinction by COVID-19 injection and 2.0 creation.

Around 3400 BC, the Sumerians of lower Mesopotamia began their systematic opium poppy plant production side by side with cereals and other crops. Considered to be the most ancient pharmacopoeia in existence, one Sumerian clay tablet dating to about 2100 BC contains a list of medical opium prescriptions. When the Sumerian territory became part of the Babylonian empire around 2225 BC, knowledge of the poppy plant and its effects passed on to the Babylonians. With the expansion of their empire eastwards to Persia and westwards to Egypt, they extended the knowledge on to those civilizations.

Objects from the Greek Minoan civilization on the island of Crete and other Aegean Islands suggestion opium consumption. Their populations date from circa 3500 BC with a complex urban civilization beginning around 2000 BC. The objects include a goddess dating to around 1300–1250 BC. Her hair seems to bey adorned with poppy-capsules and her closed eyes suggesting sedation by opium consumption.

Juglets suggesting poppy content dating to that same period were found in Cyprus and Egypt, as well. At the beginning of the third century BC, Greek philosopher Theophrastus (c.371–c.287 BC), student and successor to Aristotle's Peripatetic School, makes reference to the milky poppy juice. And Homer referred to opium's healing powers even earlier in the *Odyssey*, said to have been written sometime between 725–675 BC.

By the first century AD, such capacities as Pedanius Dioscorides (c. 40–90 AD), the father of pharmacognosy, also knew of the poppy juice and its effect on the human senses and psyche. This Greek physician was in the Roman army. He was a pharmacologist, botanist, and author of *De material medica* (*On Medical Material*), a five-volume Greek encyclopaedia. He wrote extensively on the poppy juice in his work on pharmacopeia. He also recommended mandrake, containing atropine, and scopolamine mixed with wine before limb amputations.

Scopolamine, or Devil's Breath, derives from nightshade plants. When the powder extracted from it is ingested, inhaled or absorbed through the skin, "temporary zombification" described as follows occurs:

- docility
- lack of free will
- memory loss
- powerful, unpleasant hallucinations
- unconsciousness lasting up to 24 hours
- at high doses, death

One of the earlier alkaloids isolated from plant sources, scopolamine has been in use in its purified forms including salts such as hydrochloride, hydrobromide, hydroiodide and sulphate since its isolation by the German scientist Albert Ladenburg in 1880. Following his description of scopolamine's structure and activity, the search for synthetic analogues in the 1940s resulted in the discovery of diphenhydramine and pethidine, the first fully synthetic opioid analgesic known as Dolantin and Demerol amongst many other trade names.

Its effects were first written about in 1881 and started to be used for anesthesia around 1900, when some physicians used it for pain relief. Or, rather, they administered it so the patients would forget about their pain, such as during childbirth. In fact, one unnamed obstetrician noticed how candidly women on Scopolamine answered questions. Consequently, it became known as the first "truth serums" used by governments worldwide during the early 1920s to assist in crime investigations, but largely discontinued due to its negative side effects ("Devil's Breath: Why Scopolamine Abuse is So Terrifying"; https://northpointwashington.com/about-us/.)

There are few substances surrounded by as much myth and dread as scopolamine hydrobromide. It is well-known as one of the oldest plant-derived alkaloids. It is listed by the World Health Organization as an "essential medicine." By 2022, it is considered the world's most dangerous drug, because it apparently *steals humans' souls*. "It's not a drug you can buy in the way you might buy some other new psychoactive substance, some legal high, or whatever. It's not available in that sense, because it's not a drug you would want to take for any pleasurable purpose," says Les King, a chemist and former head of Britain's Drugs Intelligence Unit in the Forensic Science Service. This fact has been hidden from us, the herd, since the days of Pedanius Dioscorides (c. 40–90 AD) 2,000 years ago.

He was preceded by the Roman encyclopedist, Aulus Cornelius Celsus (c. 25 BC–c. 50 AD), known for his extant medical work *De Medicina*. It is the only part accessible of a much larger medical encyclopedia dealing with human diet, pharmacopeia, surgery and related subjects.

He, too, knew of opium's and scopolamine's effects on humans' central nervous systems. So did the Roman naval and army commander Gaius Plinius Secundus (23/24–79AD).He shared it with us in his encyclopedic *Naturalis Historia*. He also shared it with the Greek-born Roman empire's physician, surgeon and philosopher Galen of Pergamon. Galen influenced the development of various scientific disciplines, including anatomy, physiology, pathology, pharmacology, neurology, and psychology as well as philosophy and logic. His ideas ruled Western medicine well into the nineteenth century (Svend Norn et al: History of opium poppy and morphine; Dan Medicinhist Arbog 2005; 33:171–84).

But in ancient Egypt, opium use already flourished under King Tutankhamen's reign, around 1333–1324 B.C. Arabic physicians used opium extensively during surgeries and as therapy. Almost 3,000 years later, Avicenna (980 -1037 AD) recommended it especially in cases of diarrhea and diseases of the eye. However, just as today, polypharmacy, often occurred. That is the administration of more than five drugs simultaneously, Most, if not all, of them contained opium, which enthused the alchemist Paracelsus (1493- 1541) 500 years later to mutter under his breath: "Poison is in everything; there is nothing that is not poison. The dosage makes it either a poison or a remedy."

Paracelsus, by the way, also called for the humane treatment of the mentally ill. He saw them as brothers ensnared in a treatable malady rather than possessed by evil spirits. (Waite, Arthur Edward (1894). *The Hermetic and Alchemical Writings of Paracelsus*. London: James Elliott and Co.) Paracelsus also stressed the importance of sleep and sedation. He believed sedation, with in particular sulphur preparations, could catalyze healing and cure mental illness (Hanegraaf, W. (2007). *Paracelsus (Theophrastus Bombastus von Hohenheim, 1493-1541)*. Brill. Pp. 509–511). Paracelsus is also likely the first physician of the western hemisphere to suggest that emotional wellbeing and moral conscience directly influence humans' physical health. He saw that the state of a person's psyche could indeed cure and cause diseases depending on an individual's moral and ethical character and behavior.

In his view, and in mine for whatever it's worth, a person can maintain good health through sheer will and honorable behavior and graciousness. Paracelsus went so far as to state that whether or not an individual succeeds in their craft depends on their character. For example, if a physician has shrewd and immoral intentions, then he would eventually fail in his career, because evil-doing can never lead to success.

Some 500 years later, Ginpreet Kaur, an Associate Professor at Mumbai's School of Pharmacy &Technology Management, joyously piped: "The human desire to take medicines comes with a price tag. Arising out of a [human] restorative instinct, polypharmacy becomes itself an affliction." He was signaling Freud et al.'s phenomenal success in their "Make the American Mind" with its "Doctor known Best" brainwashing exercise since the 1850s. For the past 170 years, they had spread it around the world, blissfully disguising that our human body is the best self-healing organism ever designed by the Creator Himself. It systematically renews itself every seven years throughout our lives, inside-out, top to bottom. We just have to let it do its work, assisted by twice daily meditation, a healthy diet, fasting and prayer, and learn to observe, change and control our thinking. We need to stay away from pharmaceutical drugs of all genres. We must keep away from allopathic physicians, as they are out to kill us, as we have seen throughout the COVID 19 by their kill-shot administrations. When we also aim to daily hone our honor, integrity and graciousness and apply willpower, discipline, persistency, determination to carry out our desires, and thank our Creator to be able to do it all if we put our minds to it, we are cruising in the direction of superb physical and mental health in no time flat.

And once we walk that road, money no longer plays a role in our healing. Our mind does, as Paracelsus already noted. It sets folks like Ms. Kaur checkmate. We stop enriching the world's physicians of all genre and those of the fictitious science of psychiatry and psychology in particular. Instead, through healing ourselves by the power of our minds, we enrich the Self. Mind you, wealth played a dominant role in seeking healing for millennia. The rich were able to consult physicians to conquer their ill health, whilst the poor endlessly suffered. One of the most famous and expensive panacea is known as theriaca or theriac, a concoction brewed up by Mithridates VI Eupator (120–63 BC). He was ruler of the Kingdom of Pontus, proclaimed by Mithridates I around 281 BC in northern Anatolia, and one of the Roman Republic's most formidable opponents. After his father's Mithridates V poisoning at a banquet he himself hosted, he became obsessed with searching for antidotes. He began experimenting with venomous snakes, lizards, frogs as well as opium.

When Rome's military might defeated him in Pontus in 63 BC, his medical notes fell into their hands and their *medici* began to use them. Emperor Nero's (37-68 AD) personal physician Andromachus refined Mithridates' concoction to contain up to 64 ingredients. These included opium, snake poison and viper's flesh, roasted, well aged and only available to the very rich and famous. Today, it is Zolgensma with the generic name onasemnogene abeparvovec-xioi. This gene therapy to treat pediatric spinal muscular atrophy (SMA) is manufactured by Novartis. It tops the price of pharmaceuticals with a cost of $2.125 million for a single dose. Snake venom, by the way, is also one of the COVID-19 experimental gene therapy ingredients.

The learned society still makes believe that opium was introduced to China and East Asia in the sixth or seventh century AD. However, it actually occurred, at the very latest, during China's Han Dynasty ruling between 206 BC and 220 AD. Emperor Wu send out his imperial envoy Zhang Qian (d. ca. 114 BC) on the Silk Road in 138 BC to make contact with cultures in Central Asia. The Royal Road connecting the city of Susa in Iran with the city of Sardis near the Mediterranean Sea in Turkey 1,600 miles away had already been in use since the days of Darius I, the Great (c. 550–486 BC). It connected the Middle East with Central Asia's opium-growing Afghanistan, Pakistan, Myanmar and Thailand. How do we know?

From the Ayurvedic medical treatise *Dhanvanatari Nighantu*, composed long before time was time by Lord Dhanvantari, the physician of the gods. He was deputed by Lord Indra, king of the heaven and the devas, the supernatural celestial god-like beings dwelling on earth. His mission was to take his knowledge about opium's benefits for a variety of ailments to us mortals. The gods and demons, when churning the ocean in search for the elixir of life, had come up with a bowl of it (https://www.exoticindiaart.com/book/details/dhanvantari-nighantu-sanskrit-text-with-english-translation-naq723/). So, when India's Mughal-takeover rolled around during the sixteenth century, India's Northern kingdoms cultivated opium over an area of more than one million square kilometers according to the *Akbarnama*, the administrative reports and mode of governance of Moghul Emperor Akbar (1542–1605 AD).

Akbar had succeeded his father, Humayun, who in December 1530 had succeeded his father Babur to the throne of Delhi as ruler of the Mughal territories in the Indian subcontinent. Babur in turn (1483 -1530) was a great-great grandson of Timur (1336–1405), descendant of Genghis Khan also known as Tamerlane. Between 1370 and his death in 1405, Timur established the Timurid Empire that dominated Iraq, the southern Caucasus, Turkey, Greater Iran, Afghanistan, much of Central Asia, most of contemporary Pakistan and parts of North India. When died in 1405, and the great Timurid Empire he had built began to disintegrate. Babur, ousted from his ancestral domains in Central Asia by rebellion, established himself in Kabul. He solicited neighbouring Safavid and Ottoman empires' forces and pushed full force through the Khyber Pass into India to defeat the Sultan of Delhi at the First Battle of Panipat in 1526 AD to found the Mughal Empire.

From there Babur moved on southward to defeat the Rajput army of Sanga. It had been united by the Maharana Sangram Singh (1484–1527), commonly known as Rana Sanga. He ruled Mewar, today's Rajasthan, since 1509 until mortally wounded fighting against the Mughals in the Battle of Khanwa, a community west of Agra, on March 16, 1527. This, the most decisive and historic battle in Indian history, sealed the fate of Northern India for the next two centuries. Rana Sanga died a few days later, soothed by opium, and Babur built a victory tower of Hindu warriors' skulls, calling his troops *Army of Islam* and himself a Ghazi, a Holy warrior.

When Akbar succeeded his father Humayun in 1556 at the age of thirteen to reign as the third Mughal Emperor of India until his death in 1605, he made major reforms in the war techniques especially in the use of firearms. He also extended Mughal power over most of the Indian subcontinent expanding and consolidating Mughal domains in India. Thus, India's Mughal Empire's establishment assured future religious strife between the Indian herd. This happened almost precisely when Britain's ruling class, with Elisabeth I and John Dee at the helm, planned Britain's dominion of the world and everyone on it, the subcontinent included.

The operation began with Francis Drake (c.1540–1596), the Dragon, offspring of unknown parentage. He was commissioned to take the first step in a single expedition from 1577 to 1580 circumnavigating the Earth. His trip included an incursion into the Pacific Ocean, until then an area of exclusive Spanish interest and largely unexplored by shipping. During that same trip he claimed New Albion, now California, for England.

Like all who significantly assist in the Great Work of Ages, Elizabeth I awarded him the knighthood in 1581. As vice admiral in 1588, he functioned as second-in-command of England's fleet against the Spanish Armada, scattered to the hurricane winds in practically no battle. In 1596, still on the war-path, Drake died of dysentery when attacking Spanish-owned San Juan, Puerto Rico. Meanwhile, the Crown furthered its aspirations by planning the Honourable East India Company (HEIC). With the peerage as shareholders, the Crown gave the charter in 1600 AD to represent its merchant interests and in its name establish trading posts east of the Cape of Good Hope throughout the Indian subcontinent and South and East Asia.

The company had its own army and its own flags of various designs. In no time flat, it seized control of large parts of India and Southeast Asia and established trading posts and colonies in the Persian Gulf regions. It had soon organized three "Presidency armies", totalling around 260,000 of primarily Indian sepoys, soldiers serving under British command as commissioned and non-commissioned officers. They were named after the HEIC's three presidencies: the Bengal Army, the Madras Army and the Bombay Army. They were garrisoned throughout India, engaged in wars against territorial rulers throughout the sub-continent to extend the Crown's control. And they fought in wars incited by Britain against Burma and Afghanistan as well as in the nineteenth century First and Second Opium Wars against China, as well as an expedition into Abyssinia.

By the mid-1700s, John-company, as it was colloquially known, was the world's largest corporation. The Dutch East India Company its only competition. HEIC accounted for half of the world's trade, particularly in basic commodities, such as cotton, silk, indigo dye, sugar, salt, spices, and saltpetre. And opium, of course, to foster human addiction and voluntary self-destruction to the occident's populations, never mind eventually virtually ruling India. Until the Indian Mutiny in 1857–58 called it to a halt, that is. That is when the British Crown took John Company over and signalled that the sun never set on the British Empire now ruled by Victoria. In 1876, she declared herself empress of India under the British Raj. The company's operations by that time had almost single-handedly also managed to reverse the trend of the eastward drain of Western bullion seen since Roman times to the west. This was mainly through opium trade funnelled throughout its worldwide trading posts and ports by its own ships transporting whatever goods wherever they wanted and sold to the highest bidder.

John Company's army was also transferred to the Crown. In 1895, it became the Indian Army, eager and ready to be trained for its planned participation in WWI. Its brutalization of the natives would last until 1947. Due to the Muslim Babur's introduction of the Islamic faith to the sub-continent in the 1500s, the divide and conquer scheme practiced for centuries paid off, when the British Crown in 1947 agreed to the partitioning of India and the establishment of northwest and northeastPakistan on the 27th of Ramadan in 1366 of the Islamic Calendar. This new country covered most of the Indus region, the site of successive ancient cultures including the Neolithic Mehrgarh and the Bronze Age Indus Valley civilisation dating back 2,800–1,800 BC at Harappa and Mohenjo-Daro you can check out all by yourself.

This thus assured friction and animosity so necessary for the Luciferic consciousness to prosper and thrive, which was further enhanced when Bangladesh, the region which became East Pakistan as a part of the newly formed State of Pakistan in 1947 when British rule in the region ended, in 1971 proclaimed its independence from Pakistan emerging as the People's Republic of Bangladesh. Since then, it has suffered seemingly never-ending famines, natural disasters, widespread poverty, political turmoil and military coups.

Long before that, however, a multitude of British traders had overtaken India's major poppy-growing regions. They smuggled opium at ever increasing amounts into China to assure opium addiction throughout Chinese society, to eventually destroy the country's social and economic fiber. The Chinese government destroyed more than 1,400 tons of opium warehoused by British merchants at Canton (Guangzhou). Then, the British refused to hand sailors accused of killing a Chinese villager over to the Chinese courts. So began the first Opium War between Britain and the Manchu Qing dynasty (1636–1911/12) ending in 1842 with numerous concessions imposed on the Chinese.

The second Opium War erupted in 1856 with Britain and France together fighting for rights to import opium in unlimited quantities to their desire. The war ended in 1860, with Britain gaining a multitude of commercial privileges and legal and territorial concessions inside China. This marked the start of unequal treaties and inroads on Qing sovereignty that ultimately toppled it in the early twentieth century. This set the stage for Mao Zedong's (1893–1976) brutal takeover in 1948, killing around 80 million people to found the communist Peoples' Republic of China (PRC).

Until then, the opium import and destruction of the Chinese people by mainly American and British traders had continued in return for silver and tea, silk, porcelain, and other luxury goods shipped to the West. However, the American elite, with close blood ties to the House of Hanover's ruling class of Britain, imported over 2.5 million Chinese men in the early 1800s to build its railroad. They brought their opium habits with them. They did not tardy in establishing their opium dens, comfortable locales in which customers, regardless of social status, colour, race, or religion, could buy and smoke opium ad nauseam, wit Hunter Biden's adventures. By the 1870s, the habit had become so popular for many Americans, that San Francisco's governing body was inspired to make maintaining or frequenting an opium den misdemeanour. Henceforth, the thriving operations went underground, with other drugs enhancing the destruction of human souls largely replaced by Chinese-imported and easier-to-manufacture fentanyl. Tit for tat, eh?

What is puzzling, however, is how throughout the centuries European and American learned society of physicians remained so uneducated. They all received the so-called classical education, the study of ancient old texts in Greek and Latin, including Cicero's *De Oratore*, Aristotle's *Rhetoric*, Plato's *The Republic*. Yet, they steadfastly ignored the works of Avicenna, Galen and even Paracelsus and their knowledge of opium, albeit all had access to it. They even ignored Homer's mention of it in the *Odyssey*, standard reading in any classical education, when he referred to the gift given to Helen of Troy by the Egyptian queen, believed to have been an opium-based drug. Medicinal plants have been known in Mesopotamia since at least 2000 BC. And a Chinese book on houseplants written sometime in third to first centuries BC mentions the medical use of ephedra and opium poppies. This, too, was common knowledge among those viewing themselves as the academically well-educated Western learned society of all rank.

The Roman Catholic priesthood also knew since the early 1500s that the South American Indians used extracts from plants containing toxic alkaloids. For instance, they knew of acinitine and tubocurarine for poisoning arrows, and coca leaves for a multitude of purposes, including medicinal Yet, they kept all of it a secret from the herd. The first reports of coca reached Europe in 1505, when European holders of Spanish land grants in Peru paid their taxes with income derived from their commercial coca leaves productions (https://tonydagostino.co.uk/history-of-crack-cocaine/). It is also known that the natives forced to slave away in silver mines by 1548 were given over half a million kilograms -1 ton of coca - annually, while being starved to death. By 1552, the Roman Catholic church appointees in an apparent fit of conscience wanted to ban there use as miners. But nothing came of it, because of Emperor Charles V's chaplain, lawyer and official historian, the humanist Juan Ginés de Sepúlveda (1494–1573). In his 1544 work, *Democrates Alter*, on the *Just Causes for War Against the Indians*, justified their enslavement by stating they were animals of no value.

Peruvians' communally chewed coca with lime, dating back 8,000 years. Coca traces were found in mummies dating 3,000 years back in northern Chile. And there was an unbroken record of coca leaf consumption by succeeding cultural groups on the coast of Ecuador when Europeans arrived, its use restricted to nobles and a few favored classes (court orators, couriers, favored public workers, and the army). Yet, none of this spread the word.

Philip II of Spain (1527–1598) was jure uxoris King of England and Ireland by way of his marriage to Queen Mary I in 1554 until her death in 1558. He vigorously encouraged feeding coca to the common natives to increase their labor output and their tolerance for starvation, as it quenched hunger, thirst and exhaustion. Yet, he apparently did not breath a word of it to his exalted family ruling throughout Europe (Melo González, Jorge Orlando: "La coca, planta del futuro": un texto del siglo XVIII; https://banrepcultural.org/biblioteca-virtual/credencial-historia/numero-158/la-coca-planta-del-futuro-un-texto-del-siglo-xviii).

Sepúlveda was a humanist of the yet-to-appear Darwin and Ashkenazi Jews "all humans are animals" version, Sepúlveda. Though he never visited the Americas, he claimed that Amerindians were "natural slaves" as defined by Aristotle in Book I of *Politics*, which he used to clarify his views, stating: "Those whose condition is such that their function is the use of their bodies and nothing better can be expected of them, those, I say, are slaves of nature. It is better for them to be ruled thus." Any "civilized" man in Spanish territories therefor had the right to legitimately own, slaughter, rape and pillage the indigenous folk at leisure. And that is just what the Spaniards by and large did from the moment Columbus first dipped his toe in the waters off Guanahani, now San Salvador. He was well aware of where he had landed, not for a moment thinking it to be China. Within 20 years the Spaniards had reduced the region's indigenous population from 250,000 to 15,000.

Sepúlveda is said to have been born in Los Pedroches, in Córdoba province, Andalusia, into a family of old Christians with humble origin. He was sponsored by the enormously powerful Medici of Florence. This enabled him to become expert in Greek and Latin, as he studied theology and canon law at the Universidad de Alcalá and then obtained a doctorate in arts and theology from the Collegio de San Clemente in Bologna in 1523. He studied under a number of leading Aristotle experts and his patronage of cardinals (Cisneros, Cajetan, Quiñones) and Italian princes (Alberto Pio and Ercole Gonzaga) gave him a vantage point from which to witness and respond to numerous crises, the most prominent of which were the reformations of the Catholic Church and the controversy over the justice of the Spanish conquest of America (Luna Nájera : Juan Ginés de Sepúlveda; last modified: 28 September 2016; https://oxfordbibliographies.com/view/document/obo-9780195399301/obo-9780195399301-0334.xml). It also helped him maneuver into the positions of Charles V official advisor and chronicler and Philip II's tutor.

Sepúlveda, however, faced adamant opposition from Bartolomé de las Casas (1484 –1566). This merchant's son was born in Seville, Spain, and educated at the academy of the Cathedral of Saint Mary of the See, completed in the early sixteenth century. In this most exiting city, the Crown would set up *La Casa de Contratacion* (the House of Trade) in 1503 with the exclusive right to trade with the New World. It would ensure maximum profit for the emperor's coffers by controlling all vessels, goods, passengers and missionaries moving to and fro, between Spain and "the Indies". Las Casas, as conquistador, in 1502 sailed to the New World to seek fame and fortune.

After participating in the conquest of Cuba in 1502, he found himself rewarded with two *encomiendas*, one in Cuba and another one in Hispaniola. An *encomienda*, from the Spanish *encomendar*, "to entrust", was an estate of land granted by the Spanish Crown to adventurers and colonists in the Americas. It conferred the right to demand tribute from the native populations. It also conferred the right of forced labour and the *Droit du seigneur - ius primae noctis* - feudal lords's right to sexual relations with subordinate women on their wedding night in lieu of their forced evangelization, as was customary in Europe at the time. Las Casas had both indigenous peoples and African slaves work on his *encomiendas* until the maltreatment dished out to them by fellow Spaniards began to gnaw at his conscience.

In 1515, it propelled him into renouncing his worldly goods. He returned to Spain, joined the Order of Preachers, the Dominicans. This an order of the Roman Catholic Church was founded in France by the Spanish priest and mystic Dominic of Caleruega in 1216 to spread the word of God by travelling among the people. By 1516, lo and behold, he found himself appointed by the Spanish Crown as "Protector of the Indians" and officially empowered to stand in defense of America's indigenous peoples.

It took until 1552, however, before Las Casas published his most famous work, *La Brevísima relación de la destrucción de las Indias* (*A Short Account of the Destruction of the Indies*) in Seville, Spain. One of the stated purposes for writing the account was his fear of Spain coming under God's divine punishment for the atrocities committed and his concern for the souls of the native peoples. He describes the brutality of the Conquista throughout the Americas and Greater Antilles in the colonization process, the rapes and murders, the gold and silver hoarding taking place in the New World; and intensified his descriptions with graphic engraved illustrations. Simultaneously he proclaims in a seemingly delusional state of mind, that the atrocities against the indigenous people had been committed to save their souls from God's eternal damnation through their conversion to Christianity.

In addition, his critique towards the colonizers served to bring awareness to his audience on the true meaning of Christianity, to dismantle any misconceptions on evangelization. His account was largely responsible for the adoption of the *Leyes y ordenanzas nuevamente hechas por su Majestad para la gobernación de las Indias y buen tratamiento y conservación de los Indios* (trans. Laws and ordinances made by his Majesty for the governing of the Indies and the good treatment and preservation of the Indians) issued in 1542 by Charles V, Holy Roman Emperor (King Charles I of Spain) in regard of the Spanish colonization of the Americas. which abolished native slavery for the first time in European colonial history and led to the Valladolid debate with Juan Ginés de Sepúlveda (1490–1573).

His treatise permitted Las Casa to advance the case that the conquistadors were guilty of genocide in their insatiable greed for wealth. It also exploded to smithereens the myth that they were noble Christians bringing light, civilization and salvation to Americas' human population. Indeed, the Spaniards brought nothing but death, destruction and rapid depopulation. Las Casas stated: "...if demons possessed gold, they would undertake to steal it for themselves" (Alan Covey, 355; https://www.worldhistory.org/Bartolome de_las_Casas/). About coca leaves, he doesn't breathe a word, though. But he must have been aware of their existence and usage. Dominican friar Tomas Ortíz or Florentine Amerigo Vespucci (1451–1512) in an account of a voyage to America between 1499-1500 documented humans' use of coca leaves (Jesús Calatayud, M.D., D.D.S., PhD et al: "History of the Development and Evolution of Local Anesthesia Since the Coca Leaf"; *Anesthesiology* June 2003, Vol. 98, 1503–1508).

In 1534, Las Casas wanted to see how Spain's South American empire-building situation was progressing. He decided to tour parts of Peru to discover, after Francisco Pizarro (c. 1478-1541) and his rogues took over Peru's Inca-ruled society in 1532, demonstrating a sorry repetition of what had already been and is still ongoing in Mexico and Central America. However, Spain's Holy Roman Emperor of Habsburg lineage Charles V (1500-1558) liked Las Casas' humanitarian approach towards the America's indigenous folk. He sought to improve the situation by giving Las Casas another chance to implement his ideas of cooperation between indigenous and conquerors. He granted Las Casas a plot of land in today's central Guatemala, which actually belonged to the unconquered Mayan Kekchi Indians. There he learned their language, toured the region preaching peaceful co-operation, spread the Christian faith with fellow Dominican friars succeeding in changing the area from a Land of War to one of *Vera Páz*, of True Peace." Mind you, all fell to pieces the moment Las Casas returned to Spain in 1542, the influx of conquistadores resulting in bloody upheaval.

Still, Las Casas continued his struggles for better treatment from afar. He was regularly consulted by the *Real y Supremo Consejo de Indias*, colloquial *El Consejo de Indias*, Council of the Indie. It was created by Philip II as an autonomous body with legislative, executive and judicial functions in 1521, following Spain's conquest of the Aztecs Empire. The most important administrative organ of the Spanish Empire for the Americas, it had been confirmed in its functions by Charles V in 1534. It held absolute power over the Spanish East Indies and the Americas, until in 1834 finally being abolished 300 years later under the regency of Isabella II (1830 –1904), Queen of Spain between 1833 to1868.

Long before then, in 1544, the 70-year-old Las Casas saw himself appointed bishop of Chiapas, Mexico's southernmost province bordering Guatemala. He moved to the city Villa Real de Chiapa, founded in 1528 in the Hueyzacatlán Valley to enforce *The New Laws of the Indies*. It was written by the Council of the Indies and enacted by King Charles V in 1542. due to the constant protests of Las Casas and others. It had been composed solely for the good treatment and preservation of the Indians and abolished both Indian slavery and the *encomienda* system.

His preaching against slave holdings and his prohibition to give absolution to slaveholders created such stiff opposition from clergy and colonists alike. So, he sought reinforcement from the Imperial Spanish Court, *La Audiencia de los Confines in Gracias a Dios* in Guatemala. Its president barely gave him an audience, and when doing so, dismissed him as an insane, bumbling lunatic. His life perpetually threatened, he had little choice but to return to Spain, never again setting foot in the New World. Villa Real de Chiapa, however, grateful for his humanitarian intentions toward the indigenous populations, honored him in 1848 by changing its name to La Ciudad de San Cristóbal de Las Casas.

His staunchest opponent, Juan Ginés de Sepúlveda (1494 -1573), meanwhile, also became a Dominican Preacher. He did not take well to Las Casas' humanitarianism. Nor did plenty of other influential church figures, viewing American natives as *homunculi*, subhuman creatures. Great Britain speedily adopted this view in its empire building, too. But Las Casas saw the indigenous peoples as members of the *linaje humano*, the human race (Diego von Vacano: "Las Casas And the birth of Race"; *History of Political Thought* Vol. 33, No. 3 Autumn 2012 pp. 401-426). Their opposing views were broadcast during a public debate in the monastery of San Gregoria in Valladolid in 1550 and 1551. Sepúlveda, who had never visited the New World, declared the natives were:

> "...natural slaves...as children to parents, as women are to men, as cruel people are from mild people...Those whose condition is such that their function is the use of their bodies and nothing better can be expected of them, those, I say, are slaves of nature. It is better for them to be ruled thus."

For him, the *encomienda* system thus was merely part of such civilizing process and justifiable. It had already been theoretically defined by Aristotle in Book I of *Politics*, which he used as primary source for his argument. It is said that he also used other various classical sources including the *Bible*.

Las Casas used the same sources in his rebuttal. He exclaimed that God had power over all peoples in the world including those who had never heard of Christianity. He maintained that it should be presented to them as a religious option, not shuffled down their throats and enforced as Sepúlveda wanted it to be. They also ought to enjoy the same rights and freedoms as any other people on the earth. They had the power to rule themselves before the Conquista, as evidenced in particular by the Inca regime with their superior culture and their social structure. Therefore, they should have not been treated as beast of burdens but rather as converts to Christianity.

And he should know. After all, he had toured part of the Inca Empire in 1534. In his work *La Apologetica historia sumaria*, he had tried to piece together and summarize its history. Few Spaniards, never mind other Europeans, could give a hoot about the matter at the time., nor for those living there. They cared only for the gold, silver and cocaine (Apologetica; summary history 2. "Obras Completas De Bartolome De Las Casas"). The Valladolid debate might therefore be seen as a futile exercise. Las Casas kept spreading of the word of atrocities and maltreatment, exploitation, rape and pillage committed against South America's populations by the Spaniards. But his work was never translated into English. He even had the nerve shortly before his death in Madrid in 1566 to present Philip II with a petition to return treasures, tributes and natural resources stolen from the Inca peoples by the Spaniards since their 1532 conquest.

The petition was unsuccessful, as pagan Inca Empire citizens were merely being justly punished for their own rapacious policies towards the conquering Spaniards. There is, of course, nothing new in that attitude. It was practiced since Julius Caesar's, times or long before by victorious armies. It has most recently been shown after WWII's end by the murder by starvation of around 11 million German soldiers in U.S. Khazarian General Eisenhower's *Rheinwiesenlager* (*Rhine meadow camps*). They were enclosed like pigs in 19 open pens between April and September 1945. Meanwhile, Russian soldiers in Berlin nailed naked women to doors and walls to rape them to death and U.S. Black soldiers raped German women throughout the Rhineland. Yet, still today, they rave about the good they did for Europe and living in mere armistice with Germany, as no peace agreement has been signed (Max Igan, August 30, 2022).

And what did the Spaniard do when in a festive mood during the Conquista 500 years earlier? Well, first, they would rape the feminine human creatures of all ages. Then, they would hang them alive in the trees by their arms. And, they would sling their screaming babies on strings around their necks. Finally, they would set their massive mastiffs on them to eat them alive for supper in the true fashion of the Luciferic consciousness-possessed.

Las Casas gave us a firsthand chronicle of these Luciferic consciousness-inspired behaviours throughout the Americas in his works, *La Historia de Las Indias* among them. But his booklet *Brevísima relación de la destrucción de las Indias-- A Short Account of the Destruction of the Indies* found a new audience. The booklet was about the mistreatment of and atrocities committed against the indigenous peoples of the Americas. He sent it to Prince Philip II of Spain in 1552, together with Sepúlveda's rebuttals to his accusations. It actually found the most fertile ground with Spain's age-old archenemies England and France. They hastened to bash their Spanish Crown bloodline cousins' for their rapacious empire-building efforts until they soon after followed their example.

When Columbus struck land, he began the process that swiftly brought about the fall of the Incan empire and its civilisation of an estimated 14,000,000 people. The knowledge of coca plantations and coca uses on wounds as an anaesthetic reached Europe in 1505 (www.tonydagostino.co.uk/history-of-crack-cocaine/). The first commercial production of coca by Europeans as holders of Spanish land grants were then allowed to make their tax payments in coca leaves.

We also know that by 1548, the indigenous silver mine slaves went through over half a million kilograms of coca per year. We also know that roughly 8% of Europeans living in Peru were involved in the coca trade. Due to the inaccurate reports on coca, however, the Catholic Church petitioned the Crown in 1552 to ban coca cultivation and use. But in 1577, it withdrew its petition when a 10% tax was levied on its purchase. The Catholic Church became mute about its the moment it consented to levy the tax. The money was to be handed to the church under the guise of facilitating its growth in South America. But this was also kept silent. That the Crown almost simultaneously begun coca paste importation into Europe and therewith began the herd's brain pollution, is never talked about either, it seems. Thus, whilst enormous cathedrals sprang up like weeds in South America even in the most diminutive, primitive and desolate locations on the Andean altiplano, Europeans' brainpower due to coca consumption began to wilfully diminish at a slow and steady pace, until reaching its present state.

That chewing coca in Andean culture has been a ritual since time memorial is also rarely mentioned in learned society's literature. The non-addictive plant itself regarded as divine and a means of survival long before the Spaniards arrival. It is seen as a substitute for food and a stimulant to this very day, as life in the Andes is a constant battle for its indigenous and mestizo population of the highlands. None of this was mentioned.

Nor is it mentioned that coca leaves include calories, carbohydrates, protein, minerals and vitamins, which lend a source of energy and nutrients to its users. Nor that they do not create physiological or psychological dependence or addiction (https://www.hindawi.com/journals/emi/2016/4048764/) We do not hear, either, that coca chewed or drank as tea prevents altitude sickness when wandering about on the Andean Altiplano in northern Chile, western Bolivia, southern Peru and northwest Argentina, its height averaging about 3,750 meters (12,300 feet). This is slightly less than that of the Tibetan Plateau, with an average elevation exceeding 4,500 meters (14,800 ft).

Thanks to the Spanish Crown's imports, Europeans were chewing coca leaves for stimulation by the early 1600s.But it took until 1662 for one of England's leading poets and essayist to expose both the truth of New World exploitation and the coca matter to European society. London-born Abraham Cowley (1618–1667) did so in his poem "The Legend of Coca" in his posthumously published Latin work Plantarum libri sex (Six Books of Plants) stating:

> The dreadful Andes plac'd 'twixt Winter's Store
> Of Winds, Rains, Snow, and that more humble Earth,
> That gives the small, but valiant, Coca birth...
> Nor Coca only useful art at home,
> A famous Merchandize thou art become;
> A thousand Paci and Vicugni groan,
> Yearly beneath thy Loads, and for thy sake alone
> The spacious World's to us by Commerce known.
> Thus spake the Goddess, (on her painted Skin
> Were figures wrought) and next calls Hovia in.
> That for its stony Fruit may be despis'd,
> But for its Vertue next to Coca priz'd.
> Her shade by wondrous Influence can compose,
> And lock the Senses in such sweet Repose, [Latin: 840]

That oft the Natives of a distant Soil
Long Journeys take of voluntary Toil,
Only to sleep beneath her Branches shade:
Where in transporting Dreams, entranc'd they lye,
And quite forget the *Spaniards* Tyranny.

Las Casas' booklet was translated into English by John Milton's nephew John Phillips (1631–1706) and published in London in 1656 (Printed by J.C. for Nath. Brook). It became available in French, Dutch and German soon thereafter. Europeans of the learned society then knew of the power and uses of coca leaves. They knew that indigenous labourers would slave away for the Spaniards in silver mines when fed coca leaves to keep them alive instead of feeding them actual food. The Americans adopted this method after WWII, replacing food with unlimited amounts of coffee and cigarettes. They handed them to Rheinwiesenlager's German soldiers to consume while leisurely lolling about in nothing but fresh open air. They knew full well what it would do from their scientific laboratory studies on WWI's PTSD-affected soldiers in their mammoth asylums previously established by all participating nations. They knew it would ruin their central nervous systems while slowly starving them to death, just as coca did to slave miners 500 years earlier.

They also at that time learned of coca's soothing and anaesthetic effects on the human mind. But it took until 1708 for Dutch physician and chemist Herman Boerhaave (1668-1738) to, first mention coca in a textbook. Boerhaave, a professor lecturing at Leiden University and beloved to students from all over Europe, spread the knowledge of coca throughout Europe and the U.S. in his textbook on human physiology and pathology *Institutiones Medicae.* Meanwhile, the herd was kept in ignorance about it (cienciadelacoca.org/TimeTable.html). Still nothing much happened, despite perpetual wars raging all over Europe between royal blood cousins where the sufferings of the injured could have been greatly alleviated by coca-applications.

Jesuit Father Antonio Julián (1722–1790) arrived in Columbia in 1749. It was at the time part of the in 1717-established Viceroyalty of New Granada, including Panama and after 1751 Ecuador and Venezuela, with its capital at Santa Fé, present-day Bogotá. He talked publicly about coca after he was forced to leave in 1767, when the Spanish Crown expelled Jesuits from Latin America. At that time his own ideas about Spain's economic involvement in Colombia motivated him to compose the book *La Perla de América.* It encouraged the Crown to involve itself in business dealings of Caribbean Colombia's natural resources, and in coca in particular (Julián 450).

In English it was known as *A Jesuit Writes to the King: Profits from Coca Leaf Could Surpass Tea.* Father Antonio Julián argued that cultivating and importing the *Hayo*, or coca leaf, would lead to greater economic prosperity than tobacco, coffee or tea. He used his encounters with the Guajiro Indians to describe their frequent consumption of coca leaves to document their value as a sellable commodity (Julian 450). He specifically pointed out that the Guajiro "would go without food rather than go without a secure supply of *Hayo*" (452). To easier convince the king of its cultivation, he also specified that the leaves are "serving as a cure and tonic for so many ills, a replenisher for lost strength, and a prolonger of human life" (451).

These benefits could indeed make the leaves popular in Europe, and therefore potentially "very profitable" (451)(https://www.eltiempo.com/archivo/documento/MAM-186479).

He then describes the plant, its cultivation and harvest, its preparation for human consumption and its used by the Guajiro, as well as the marvels derived from consuming it. Above all, he explains how it is applied in the field of medicine at a time, he says, when both England and Britain enrich themselves by selling useless plants to alleviate the populations' pain and hardship. It is sorrowful, he said, that many poor families in Europe are without this means of prevention of hunger and thirst, the coca. And he felt it was a pity that officials and skilled labourers should lack this source of strength to continue to work. And he said it was sad that both old and young should be deprived of study and book compositions, because the lack of coca took away their enthusiasm, their spirit—*la falta de espíritu*—or drowned them in a sea of liquor instead.

He furthermore shared that coca works against weakness in the head and stomach. In Europe, humans were moaning under the harsh torment of chronic ills, hypochondriac obstructions, hysterical maladies, and the like. Not even the use of tea and coffee could help. Coca worked so splendidly for the Guajiros, and would be so for the Spaniards and other Europeans as well, if they were to use it.

That for traditional indigenous cultures coca is not something trivial or a simple source of income he did not bother to mention. Nor did he breathe a word about coca being a sacred plant constituting the heart of indigenous culture itself. He did not tell of how in concert with other teacher plants, it embodies an indigenous social system that considers balance the key to a good life (www.chacruna.net/coca_colombia_legislation_drug_policy_psychedelic_revolution/).

Under the natives' worldview a good life means finding an equilibrium between individual and the collective's needs. It means balancing the human and natural worlds and the influences of both visible and intangible forces. This was seemingly beyond Julian's grasp. That the rituals and routines of tending coca plants, chewing coca leaves, and sharing the coca harvest with others to assure communities' health seems also to have been beyond his realm of perception. That Coca to this very day is the means by which communities channel energy for both individual and collective work, as it offers relief for physical and metaphysical ailments, appears to have been beyond him in its entirety. But all of it was rather inconsequential, as Spain's king ignored his proposal.

Peruvian physician José Hipólito Unánue published the *Disertación sobre la coca* in 1794. This reference work about coca's benefits met a similar fate in Europe's learned societies, despite French Revolution atrocities being in full bloom and the Napoleonic wars already waiting in the wings.

Botanist William Jackson Hooker (1785-1865) was later director of London's Director of the Royal Botanic Gardens, Kew. He published the first drawing of coca a plant in the popular press in 1835. It caught some attention, although its value as an anaesthetic was yet again ignored. That the ancients had used plant extracts rather than chemical gases as anaesthetics must have been well known to those in the medical métier throughout Europe since at least the renaissance, due to their classical education.

The uses of analgesics and sedatives of preparations similar to opium, as well as extracts from the mandrake fruit in surgery, were confirmed by the Ebers Papyrus discovery purchased at Luxor in the winter of 1873–74 by the German Egyptologist Georg Moritz Ebers (1837–1898). Dating from around 1550 BC, the medical knowledge concealed in it was kept from the public. So was that of the famed Swiss alchemist, philosopher and physician Paracelsus (? -1541). In the 1500s, he had noted the analgesic properties of diethyl ether when its vapours anaesthetized the chickens on which he was experimenting. (https://www.mcgill.ca/oss/article/drugs-health-news/ether-was-potent-painkiller-it-was-hit-revellers).

But ether does not occur in nature, so where did Paracelsus get it? From the German physician, botanist and pharmacologist Valerius Cordus (1515–1544). He was author of the first pharmacopoeia published north of the Alps, and one of the most celebrated herbals in history. A herbal is a book containing the names and descriptions of plants, information on their medicinal, tonic, toxic, hallucinatory, aromatic, culinary and magical powers, legends associated with them and recipes for extracts, tinctures and potions. Sometimes mineral and animal medicaments were also included.

Herbals were among the first literature produced in Ancient Egypt, China, India and Europe. They contained the accumulated knowledge of herbalists, apothecaries and physicians throughout millennia. So, there can be no doubt that European learned medical society had knowledge of it, Cordus included. As everyone else in his league, he dabbled in alchemy and thus developed a method for synthesizing ether. In1540, he distilled sulphuric acid with fortified wine, calling the concoction by its Latin wording *oleum dulci vitrioli*, sweet oil of vitriol, due to its sweet-smelling odour.

But its anaesthetising effects beneficial in surgeries were also kept under lock and key from the masses. It was only routinely used by poor Brits when traditional alcohol was unavailable or too expensive for them (Connie Y Chang et al: "Ether in the developing world: rethinking an abandoned agent"; BMC Anesthesiol. 2015; 15: 149). However, American students adopted this so-called ether frolic fad in the early 1800s by holding ether-soaked towels to their faces until losing consciousness, we read., That was when a reformed chemistry movement took hold in the eighteenth century, initiated by French nobleman and chemist Antoine-Laurent de Lavoisier (1743–1794). It hugely influenced both the history of chemistry and that of biology.

Son of a wealthy Parisian lawyer, Lavoisier completed a law degree before turning to science with a passion. He was most noted for his discovery of the role oxygen plays in combustion. He also helped to construct the metric system and wrote the first extensive list of chemical elements. He furthermore predicted the existence of silicon (1787) and discovered, we are told, that although matter may change its form or shape, its mass always remains the same. He also helped reform and systemize chemical nomenclature. (sciencehistory.org). In other words, by the eighteenth century's end, he had revolutionized the field of chemistry.

Humphrey Davy (1778–1829), the son of an impoverished Cornish woodcarver Intrigued with Lavoisier's discoveries, apprenticed himself to an apothecary-surgeon whilst teaching himself such subjects as chemistry interspersed with theology and philosophy, poetics, seven languages and several sciences. In 1798, he took a position at Thomas Beddoes's Pneumatic Institution, a medical research facility in Bristol, England, established in 1799 by physician and science writer Thomas Beddoes (1760–1808). Davy took headed the laboratory to study the medical effects of the recently discovered gases, known as factitious air.

Most of the equipment with which Davy and his staff examined the effects of the newly discovered gases as cure and prevention of diseases had been designed by James Watt (1736 –1819). Watt was a Scottish inventor, mechanical engineer and chemist, who improved on Thomas Newcomen's 1712 steam engine in 1776. The Watt steam engine was fundamental to the changes brought on throughout the world by the Industrial Revolution. By 1799, Watt made his early reputation with the publication of his book *Researches, Chemical and Philosophical, Chiefly Concerning Nitrous Oxide . . . and Its Respiration*. It contained his recommendation that Cordus' nitrous oxide (laughing gas) should be inhaled and used as an anaesthetic in surgical operations – without, of course, mentioning his predecessor's name. Most of his colleagues practicing as physicians ignored it. Only American dentist Horace Wells (1815–1848) paid attention when the knowledge of nitrous oxide anesthesia came his way in 1843. Wells had completed his dental training in Boston in 1836, then opened a practice in Hartford, Connecticut, where engaged apprentices, among them one William Morton,

Ells was delighted with the success he had on his patients. So, he sought to demonstrate his findings with help from Morton, who applied the nitrous oxide. By that time, Morton had enrolled in Harvard Medical School. He received permission to do so from the considered eminent surgeon John Collins Warren (1778–1856), who held the Hersey Professorship of Anatomy and Surgery at Harvard Medical School. Wells gave his performance of nitrous oxide for medical students at Boston's Massachusetts General Hospital in in January 1845. However, as it was improperly administered, apparently due to the patient's obesity and alcoholism, it failed.

Wells closed his office, and traveled to Paris in early 1847. He petitioned the *Academie Royale de Medicine* and the Parisian Medical Society to recognize his discovery of anaesthesia. He moved to New York City in 1848, leaving wife and son behind in Hartford. He began self-experimenting with both ether and chloroform, and became addicted to chloroform. He threw sulphuric acid over two prostitutes in his 33rd birthday. This earned him a room in New York's Lower Manhattan Tombs Prison, the colloquial name for the Manhattan Detention Complex, built in 1838. The day after, when his mind started to clear and he realised what he had done, he was given permission under guard to pick up his shaving kit at home. Thereupon, ensconced in his cell, he committed suicide by slitting his left femoral artery with a razor after inhaling an analgesic dose of chloroform.

Needless to say, he would be thrilled to hear that his death was not in vain. The usefulness of nitrous oxide in psychiatry was recognized in the late 1800s. That is when it was first used on the lunatics and paupers incarcerated in the mammoth asylum's experimental laboratories. Later, it was used on the PTSD-affected, shell-shocked soldiers of WWI and WWII and only God knows wherever else. It was not until 2020 that warnings went out to psychiatrists about the danger of using it in PTSD cases (Mark A Gillman: "Mini-Review: A Brief History of Nitrous Oxide (N2O) Use in Neuropsychiatry"; Curr Drug Res Rev 2019;11(1):12-20).

"Just say N2O—nitrous oxide misuse: essential information for psychiatrists," psychiatrist Rollo J.G. Sheldon et al. shout in an article published by Cambridge University Press on October 1, 2019. They warn about its widespread misuse in the UK, as its psychiatric presentations are poorly described, and it can cause devastating myeloneuropathy. Myeloneuropathy is characterized by simultaneous damage of the tracts of the spinal cord and peripheral nerves in the lower limbs. Clinical manifestations of myeloneuropathy include difficulty walking, weakness of lower limbs, ataxic gait, and *peripheral neuropathy (PN)*, a result of damage to the nerves located outside of the brain and spinal cord (peripheral nerves), with the brain's central nervous system sending information to our peripheral nervous system to the spinal cord and rest of the body and vice versus.

Peripheral neuropathy results from traumatic injuries, infections, metabolic problems, inherited causes and exposure to toxins such as pharmaceutical drugs and affect digestion, urination and circulation (Mayo Clinic. Org). One of the most common causes of peripheral system failure is diabetes due to too much sugar in the blood by way of nutrition and certain, unmentioned, types of medications. Needless to say, it causes much physical pain and increases the risk of an early death. It rolls patients into sleepless nights, pessimism and completion of daily living necessities due to, for example, the cognitive impairment and vision loss from optic nerve damage. All patients have furthermore walking problems, mostly due to severe sensory ataxia after getting nitrous oxide, all self-imposed by trusting the physician and lack of willingness to educate the self before swallowing the pharmaceutical drugs prescribed (Ravindra Kumar Garg et al: Approach to a case of myeloneuropathy; Ann Indian Acad Neurol. 2016 Apr-Jun; 19(2): 183-187).

There is little understanding of who it affects, how it presents, how it works or how to treat it. Nitrous oxide misuse is seen as a pending neuropsychiatric emergency requiring urgent treatment with vitamin B12 to prevent potentially irreversible neurological and psychiatric symptoms. And who came up with the idea to use it for PTSD experiencers? Well, it was brewed up by Andrea Varias et al. of Stanford University, Silicon Valley campus. In 2020, they published "Does Nitrous Oxide Help Veterans With Posttraumatic Stress Disorder? A Case Series." They dusted off the existing research in the field since the late 1800s and used it to further traumatize PTSD-affected veterans (The Journal of Clinical Psychiatry June 30, 2020).

And what do they have to say precisely, after thousands and thousands of veterans have lost their lives due to the treatment dished out to them as beneficial by the mental health industry cabal? Well, the usual. Posttraumatic stress disorder (PTSD) is a serious problem for many veterans. Innovative and fast-acting therapeutic interventions are needed for those not helped by first-line treatments. By that, they mean psychopharmacology, or drugging them to the hilt and giving them cognitive behaviour modification treatments to destroy their *sui generis*.

But in 2020, we learn that nitrous oxide presented as an inhaled anaesthetic and non-competitive N-methyl-d-aspartate (NMDA) receptor antagonist may be a promising new approach for rapid reduction in PTSD symptoms. It is reported to speed the reduction of distressing intrusive memories in an experimental model of psychological trauma. And it has shown promise as a rapidly acting antidepressant. The researchers reached their conclusion after engaging three veteran outpatients aged 31, 43 and 46 from the Veterans Affairs

Palo Alto Health Care System between April 2018 and July 2019. In their view, the three met PTSD criteria and had no comorbid psychiatric or medical conditions endangering their quitting halfway through the program. Of resulting myeloneuropathy nothing is said.

Going around in circles, the American pharmacist and surgeon Crawford Williamson Long (1815–1878) had made use of Davy's nitrous oxide in his practice years before Wells thought of it. This was before switching to sulphuric ether inhalation as an anaesthetic. He discovered its effects when performing surgeries, removing tumours and amputating. He also observed them when placing it on a towel and have the patient inhale during childbirth. Despite his continued use of ether anaesthetic, he waited until 1849 to publish his findings in *The Southern Medical and Surgical Journal*. Why?

Reportedly for two reasons. Firstly, he wished to confirm the results of his experiments before propagating his ideas. Secondly, he wished to wait to see if another medical practitioner came forward to counter William Morton's (1815–1848) 1846 claim to ether fame. You see, Morton's failure to properly administer nitrous oxide to Wells' patient at Massachusetts General Hospital was not the end of the story. Less than one year later, Morton claimed to have made a new anaesthesia discovery all by himself, namely that of ether. He claimed to have done this under the tutelage of his Harvard professor Charles T. Jackson (1805–1880), physician, scientist, teacher, and author. He, too, received permission to demonstrate his ether as anaesthesia discovery at Massachusetts General Hospital in 1846, and passed with flying colours.

It was after reading about Morton's demonstration in the *Medical Examiner*, that Long asked patients to submit affidavits corroborating his ether discovery. He knew he had discovered ether's anaesthetic powers before Morton brought it to the general public. Both men as well as Wells and Jackson, hitherto involved in the struggle to receive recognition and the congressional reward for discovering the telegraph ahead of Morse, and berated and publicly vilified for daring to claim the ether discover and wanting what he thought was rightfully his, sought credit for their supposed joint contribution to ether surgery. But why were all 5 so vigorously pursuing recognition of being the first in the ether-as-anaesthesia discovery publicized by the media as the ether controversy?

Well, you guessed it. Money, as U.S. Congress members had promised a $200,000 reward to the first ether-as-anaesthesia discoverer. Congress delayed the decision until 1863, with six congressional hearings held during this 14-year period and, as far as we know, no money issued to any of the players. Long in 1854 asked U.S. Senator William Crosby Dawson to present his claims to Congress. But, despite extensive petitioning and documented proof, he neither received full credit nor any government money for it during his lifetime. Really, his powerful opponents in the medical establishment did not want to have a simple country doctor receive the credit for it, with some of them, the future dean of Johns Hopkins School of Medicine William Henry Welsh apparently among them, mumbling under their breath:

> "We cannot assign to him any influence upon the historical development of our knowledge of surgical anaesthesia or any share in its introduction to the world at large." (Keys, Thomas (1961). *The History of Surgical Anesthesia*. Wood Library - Museum of Anesthesiology.)

Long let it go by the wayside. He married and fathered 12 children, seven of whom survived to adulthood. He opened a private practice and a pharmacy in Athens on Broad Street, just across from the University of Georgia campus, with one of his brothers. He served there as surgeon to soldiers of both sides during the Civil war. He died in June 1878 of a stroke shortly after helping to deliver a baby, still viewing his profession as a "ministry from God." He was convinced of his calling to serve humanity and hoped to fulfill his highest ambition, to do good and leave the world better by his labours. One year later, the National Eclectic Medical Association, an American medicine association whose physicians use herbal medicine and physical therapy to heal, declared Long the official discoverer of ether anaesthesia.

For the other players, the saga of ether inhalation as anaesthesia ended in tragedy. Wells fate we know already, and Jackson never got the recognition he was sure he deserved for either ether or the telegraph. It seems to merely have compounded the bitterness he felt about having given Morse the idea for the telegraph. So, Jackson spent the last seven years of his life in an insane asylum whereas Morton got medals and fame for what he had done. But Morton never became what he really desired, a very rich man. In all fairness, of the three independent ether-as-anaesthesia discoverers, it was Morton's demonstration that propelled it into worldwide use almost at a moment's notice. Long published nothing about it until it had become commonplace, and Well's discovery resulted in only the use of nitrous oxide for dental anaesthesia in the Hartford area (A B Gould: Charles T. Jackson's Claim to the Discovery of Etherization; Anaesthesia 1985, pp 384–387).

Morton demonstrated the use of ether under the direction of Harvard surgeon John Collins Warren (1778–1856), who performed a minor surgical procedure for the purpose. The news of the first public demonstration of surgical ether anaesthesia spread around the world like wildfire. Warren was a mighty powerful man involved in Wells' failed nitrous-oxide demonstration less than a year earlier. He had founded the New England Journal of Medicine and was the American Medical Association third president. He was the first Dean of Harvard Medical School, as well as a founding member of Boston's Massachusetts General Hospital, where both demonstrations had taken place.

And whence sprang Warren? He was born into a family noted for its many eminent medical practitioners (John Collins Warren (1778–1856): An American surgeon in London; BMJ 2012; 345). His father was a Harvard professor and one of Harvard Medical School's founders. He was well-connected in the field, although few in Boston had much affection for him, we read, as he was said to be a dour and reserved man. Upon his Harvard College graduation in 1797, John studied medicine with his father until moving on to London, England, in 1799. He went to work with the British surgeon and anatomist Sir Astley Paston Cooper, 1st Baronet (1768–1841). Cooper was into otology, the pathological anatomy and physiology of the ear, vascular surgery, the anatomy and pathology of the mammary glands and testicles, as well as the pathology and surgery of hernia.

Cooper was known to be a vain, egotistical, nepotistic man with a huge capacity and desire to inflict pain on his subjects verging on sadism, we are told. His attitude's and quirks are detailed in Druin Burch's 2007 book *Digging Up the Dead: Uncovering the Life and Times of an Extraordinary Surgeon* (London: Chatto and Windus; 2007). Warren seems to have been unaffected by his teacher's rough and tumble ways. But he did move on to continue his medical studies in Paris and graduated with an M.D. from the University of Edinburgh Medical School in 1801.

Upon his return to America in 1802, Warren entered into partnership with his father. He also assisted him with anatomical lectures, dissections, and demonstrations at Harvard Medical School. Named adjunct professor of anatomy and surgery in 1806, he assumed the Hersey Professorship of Anatomy and Surgery after his father's death in 1815. He held this post until he retired in 1847. That put him in a position to decide what flew and did not fly in his faculty. Thus, Morton's ether administration at Warren's minor surgery in 1846 succeeded, and the news hit England almost minutes later.

British dentist and anaesthetist James Robinson (1813–1862) was the first to use it for a tooth extraction that very same year, assisted by an ether vaporizer he had designed. He also demonstrated the "narcotising" effect of ether to a number of his peers. Among them was the professor of clinical surgery at London's University College Hospital, surgeon Robert Liston (1794–1847). He was noted for his speed and skill in an era prior to anaesthetics, when speed was of the essence for patient pain-limitation and survival.

Within weeks, Robinson was declared the Kingdom's best anaesthetist. As a zealous, impetuous, enthusiastic and eminent man in his profession, he had published the world's first anaesthetic textbook by March 1, 1847. It was called *A Treatise on the Inhalation of the Vapour of Ether*. Then something odd happened. Robinson was filled to the rim with enthusiasm and in full swing to reform Britain's dental profession and gain personal fame and fortune. But just four months later, out of the blue, he lost all interest in the venture. He passed the enterprise on to a John Snow (1813-1858), a local coal yard labourer's first of nine children. As time went on, Snow turned into Britain's foremost developer of anaesthesia, medical hygiene and epidemiology. Meanwhile, Robinson, appointed Surgeon Dentist to HRH Prince Albert of Saxe-Coburg and Gotha, spouse to Queen Victoria, died in 1849 of a self-inflicted wound caused by a slipping pruning knife severing his femoral artery.

As an aside, Snow is painted with half his face in darkness, seemingly a symbol of Luciferic consciousness allegiance. This is like his almost-contemporary, French chemist and microbiologist Louis Pasteur (1822–1895). Pasteur was renowned for bringing humanity the principles of vaccinations, microbial fermentation and pasteurization. His discoveries led to breakthroughs in understanding how to cause us physical and mental illness or how to prevent it relative to personal and environmental hygiene and nutrition.

Almost simultaneous with ether's development, however, the discovery of chloroform took place. Also called trichloromethane, chloroform is prepared by chlorinating methane gas. It is said to have first been prepared in 1831 by American chemist Samuel Guthrie. He combined whiskey with chlorinated lime, trying to produce a cheap pesticide. In 1847, Scottish physician James Young Simpson (1811–1870) picked it up and first used the sweet-smelling, colorless, non-flammable liquid as an anesthetic. He administered the liquid by dripping it onto a sponge or cloth held so the patient inhaled its vapors. This produced a narcotic effect on the central nervous system, next to be used by the National Center for

PTSD on PTSD-affected soldiers, I bet you. That is, if nitrous-oxide fails to achieve their incentives, to demolish them the slow way. But never mind.

Higher risks were associated with chloroform than ether use, and administrating it required greater skill. But Simpson, trained by and often assisting Liston, had the skills and was not afraid to use them. A younger son of a Bathgate, Scotland, baker, he had entered the University of Edinburgh to study for an arts degree at the tender age of fourteen. But two years later, he switched to medicine. In 1847, as his alma mater's professor of medicine and midwifery, demonstrated to his peers and students alike the anesthetic properties of chloroform for the first time. A year later, he was also the first to describe the first anesthetic death caused by chloroform due to heart failure, fatal cardiac arrhythmia. The majority of chloroform-related deaths are said actually to result from respiratory failure due to inattentive and inaccurate dosing (Adam Janos: Chloroform: "How the 'Knockout Drug' Has Been Used to Murder Over the Last 25 Years"; *True Crime Blog*: Stories & News 2021).

Still, chloroform use spread quickly throughout the western world. By 1853, it was famously administered to Britain's Queen Victoria during the birth of her eighth child, Prince Leopold. American military doctors had used ether as an anaesthetic during the Mexican-American War (1846-1848). So, they preferred chloroform during the U.S. Civil War, as they received reports of positive results and faster-acting time than ether during the Crimean War in the 1850s.

Simpson used chloroform for childbirth regularly. While at it, he improved the obstetric forceps design, to this day known as "Simpson's Forceps." And he created the vacuum air tractor extractor to assist in childbirth. This method became popular a century or so later with Swedish professor Tage Malmstrom's (1911–1995) ventouse, also called the Malmstrom extractor. Besides those occupations, Simpson held a vast variety of interests ranging from archaeology to hermaphroditism. The latter is a condition enabling a form of sexual reproduction in which either partner can act as the female or male.

The term hermaphrodite applied to humans has in recent years fallen out of favour, we learn. This is partly because no cases of a human reproducing as both male and female has been found. It is also because some, if not all biologists state outright, that hermaphroditism does not occur in human beings. Furthermore, intersex people not fitting typical binary notions of masculine or feminine bodies or identify as rattus, blattas, canine, simian or anything else of that nature are said to despise *hermaphrodite*, classifying it as stigmatizing. The learned society at large judges the description to be scientifically specious and clinically problematic. We merely wonder, considering the ever-increasing human gender confusion, if Simpson had anything to do with it?

As with everyone in service to the Luciferic consciousness, Simpson was rewarded a knighthood. And in 1847, he was appointed physician to the Queen when dwelling at Balmoral Castle, Scotland (https://www.nrscotland.gov.uk/research/learning/hall-of-fame/hall-of-fame-a-z/simpson-james-young). By the early 1890s, Simpson's use of anaesthetic during childbirth had spread worldwide. Liking everything under one hat in all its disciplines to keep everyone in line and on the same song-sheet, the learned society of medicine held its first International Congress of Gynaecology and Obstetrics at Brussels, Belgium, in

1892 with Fernand Henrotin (1847–1906) as the American representative present (JAMA. 1892;XVIII(7):208; https://wellcomecollection.org). And whence sprang Henrotin?

Henrotin was a native of Brussels, Belgium, one of a family of nine children, his father a prominent physician of Ashkenazi Jewish ancestry. In 1848, he decided to immigrate to Chicago. Known as "the French Doctor", he established a successful practice, while his sons thrived and prospered. The most celebrated son, Charles Henrotin, founded the Chicago Stock Exchange in 1882, becoming, chairman and president for three years. Charles also joined the New York Stock Exchange in 1886 and became a director of the World's Fair at Chicago in 1893. He also was the city's Belgian and Turkish Consul.

Charles' little brother Fernand graduated in 1869 from Rush Medical College, chartered in 1837, at the tender age of 21. At the time of his election to represent U.S. obstetricians and gynaecologists at their first International Congress, Fernand, like brother Charles, had come into prominence in Chicago. In his obituary, he was described as a skilful, energetic and conscientious physician. He held the office of "county physician". He was also professor of gynaecology at the Chicago Polyclinic, were he strongly advocated, that "vaginal hysterectomy is a proper operation in all pelvic suppuration," with little or no out anaesthesia, of course. (Ira M. Rutkow, M.D: The History of Surgery in the United States 1775-1900; Volume II; Periodicals & Pamphlets) Fernand also managed to author his 96-page book *Democracy Of Education In Medicine* (Printed by R.R. Donnelley and sons company, Chicago) published in 1903. He as that time worked for Rockefeller senior who with the Flexner brothers assistance in 1910 began to reform medical education in the United States, which encompassed the successful destruction of all natural medicine and self-healing savvy educated physicians.

The obstetricians and gynaecologists International Congress's next conference to compare women's health issues in all of its aspects including, we assume, trans-genderism and hermaphroditism, is held in 2023 in Lisbon, Portugal. We assume the non-profit, non-governmental International Federation of Gynaecology and Obstetrics assists it in its efforts. This body was founded in Geneva, Switzerland, in 1954 and is composed of 132 "National Member Societies" of obstetricians and gynaecologists in over 100 "territories".

Let's return to Morton's demonstration at Massachusetts General Hospital. Recall that, with the assistance of surgeon and professor Warren, he demonstrated the use of ether as effective and safe as an anesthetic for anything with a central nervous system. The medical métier and those who ruled it, the Luciferic consciousness, was in seventh heaven. This discovery henceforth assured ever greater slash-cut-and-burn entertainments into anything human, never mind the other animals we present in their view. All this without much ado or protest from the species itself, as they could not even in their wildest dreams imagine such evil. Ether and chloroform use declined after other means of anaesthesia, such as injections, including shots or intravenously (IV), and topical liquids, sprays or patches were brought to market and applied to skin or eyes.

Chloroform in particular came under attack in the twentieth century, as it was shown to be carcinogenic by ingestion in laboratory mice and rats. It therefore relegated mainly to preparing fluorocarbons and used in aerosol propellants and refrigerants. It is also found in some cough and cold medicines, dental products such as toothpaste and mouthwashes, topical liniments and other products. Ether, however, easy to use, remained the standard general anesthetic until the 1960s. That's when fluorinated hydrocarbons called "volatile anesthetics" such as nitrous oxide, halothane, enflurane, isoflurane and sevoflurane came into common use. Although these newer agents reduce postoperative nausea and vomiting, they are also said to cause undesirable side effects, including migraines, in addition to be much more costly to produce.

But no one cared about such minor details, as all enjoyed inducing unconsciousness in their subjects at leisure and without consequences for them for better or for worse. In 1937, American physician Arthur Guedel (1883-1956) proposed one of the first anaesthesiology safety systems. IT included a chart explaining anaesthesia's stages of depth ranging from one to four, which encouraged the medical community to develop a systematic approach to its monitoring. Guedel's classification, by the way, is still used today (https://ncbi.nlm.nih.gov/books/NBK557596/).

So now the elite, controlled by the Luciferic consciousness and by way of the medical society, had the means to put humans physically out of commission if and when they desired. Together with Baeyers discovery of barbituric acid in 1864, they held the power to pervert humans' mind and bodies at leisure without the herd having a clue. Since then, they have synthesized 2550 barbiturates and related compounds to depress our central nervous system. About 55 of them are in daily clinical use around the world. They are flogged to the herd with their enormously detrimental to human health side-effects well known to the learned society. These side-effects, according to Taber's Cyclopedic Medical Dictionary, include respiratory depression, cyanosis, circulatory collapse, stupor, coma and death, complete and total dependency and lethal withdrawal syndromes. And what did this achieve, this systematic depression of humans' critical thinking ability and destruction of the educational system, in particular in the United States? It facilitated obedience of the masses for the COVID-19 experimental injection. This injection was necessary to flog the herd into the Soma state, human 2.0 conversion as desired by the AI-generated, Harari-Luciferic consciousness—in my opinion.

So, did Baeyer signal anything when naming his discovery barbituric acid, we wonder? If he truly knew what he let loose on humanity, he would certainly call it barbituric, which originated from the German word *barbarisch*. This word carries the following meanings:

- atrocious
- barbarous
- brutal
- brute
- butcherly
- cruel
- fiendish
- heartless
- inhuman
- inhumane
- sadistic
- savage
- truculent
- vicious
- wanton

All these words perfectly describe the effects of its compositions, and that of all barbituric acid-derived drugs. The terms are so perfect and convenient for the Luciferic consciousness-possessed physicians. Since the 1850s, they dappled in earnest into discovering the workings of the human mind. Barbituric acids opened for them the pathway to drug paupers and lunatics incarcerated in their mammoth asylums built to the hilt for that purpose. Thus, subjects were well-subdued and unable to protest, before, during and after performing their exploratory surgeries under the disguise of research. All this to gauge what drugs and how much and how many of them it would take to slowly and stealthily lead humanity into the state of complete docility.

Surgery for all sorts of reasons, including just for the fun of doing it, in no time flat ballooned to medicine's most active branch. This was needed to perfect physicians' cut, slush and burn techniques. Until the exploding popularization of barbituric acids and the use of nitrous oxide, chloroform and ether soothing the associated pain, few operations were undertaken anywhere in the world. When wanting to do so, they had for millennia been carried out after knocking the subject out by blows to the head, high proof spirits, carotid arteries compression, mandrake root extract or opium sedation. The Chinese also favoured intravenous opium injections, squeezing of the upper parts of arms and legs, ice-cold water immersions and applying ice and snow to induce sedation.

German physician Franz Anton Mesmer (1734 -1815) tuned into the existence of a natural energy transference occurring between all animated and inanimate objects. He called it "animal magnetism", later referred to as *mesmerism*. That, too, was used for pain relief.

Scottish physician and surgeon James Braid (1795 -1860) was the innovator of clubfoot, spinal curvature, knock knees and bandy legs treatment. He termed Mesmer's animal magnetism theory "hypnotism" and used both hypnotic and chemical anesthesia to produce a state of general anesthesia in patients.

Henry Hill Hickman (1800 -1830) was the fifth of thirteen children born to a tenant farmer at Lady Halton, Shropshire, England. At age sixteen, he began his medical training at the Edinburgh Medical School. He studied at the Royal College of Surgeons in London until 1820. He began his medical career in Ludlow, Shropshire, in 1821. And in early 1823, he began experimenting with anesthesia, suffocating animals with carbon dioxide while amputating and cutting into them at leisure to see whether or not they felt pain. He reported his carbon dioxide central nervous depravation findings producing loss of consciousness to the Royal Society in 1824 hoping it would reach Humphrey Davy; he ignored it.

However, Hickman's work found its way to *The Lancet*, the scalpel in the English language the medical journal founded by British physician, surgeon Thomas Wakley (1795–1862) and others in 1823. Walkley later gained fame as a social reformer who campaigned against incompetence, privilege and nepotism. *The Lancet*'s founding editor was also a radical Member of Parliament (MP) and a celebrated coroner. Wakley was born youngest of eleven children of a prosperous Devon farmer and government Commissioner on the *Enclosure of Waste Land Act*, the lands formerly used by the destitute to fend for sustenance. In 1807, Wakley was sent out to sea toward Calcutta, India, at age 11 as one of six midshipmen. These boys were, until the Napoleonic era (1793-1815), usually viewed as apprentice officers. They would serve at least three years as volunteer officers' servants or able seaman. Wakley lasted 18 months. Upon his return to Devon, he attended a school for a couple of years before apprenticing with an apothecary and some surgeons at age 15. In his spare time, he entertained himself with fighting bare-fisted in neighbouring public houses to make spare change, we gather.

By age 20, Wakley began to take anatomy classes at London's St. Thomas and Guy's hospitals in 1815. He studied under the purportedly foppish, vain, egotistical, sadistic Astley Paston Cooper (1768- 1841). He also sturdied under Cooper's former pupil, dresser, and teacher of anatomy Edward Grainger (1797-1824) at his private anatomical school and dissection room. A surgeon's eldest son, Grainger had received his medical instruction from his father. He became a Royal College of Surgeons member in 1819 and led his school until his untimely death in 1824. His younger brother Richard Dugard Grainger (1801-1865), surgeon, anatomist, and physiologist, took over for another 20 years.

By that time, Wakley, a fiery character not to be trifled with, had graduated as surgeon, married and set up in practice in central London. He was greatly aided financially by his father-in-law, a wealthy lead merchant. He launched *The Lancet* giving him the ideal platform to attack the whole constitution of the Royal College of Surgeons with abundance. He obtained so much member support for exposing the profession's abuses committed on patients, that in 1827 a petition to the British Parliament resulted in ordering a return of the public money granted to it. *Punch*, a British weekly magazine established in 1841, that year portrayed Wakley's campaigns as "plucking feathers from the peacocks of his times:"

THE TORY PEACOCKS AND THE FINSBURY DAW.

His campaigning, rough and outspoken, is fitting for our days. Now is when the World's physicians maim and kill millions of people by injecting them with an experimental drug without due diligence or proper research. And now is when the Hippocratic Oath sworn by the aspiring physicians of the class of 2026 includes to do harm to white folk. This appears to be perfectly acceptable as revenge of the actions their ancestors purportedly committed against blacks by these self-same aspiring medical doctors to do no harm, when saying:

> [We deplore the] "state of society which allows various sets of mercenary, goose-brained monopolists and charlatans to usurp the highest privileges.... This is the canker-worm which eats into the heart of the medical body..." (Wakley, *The Lancet* 1838–39, 1, p2–3)
>
> "The Council of the College of Surgeons remains an irresponsible, unreformed monstrosity in the midst of English institutions - an antediluvian relic of all... that is most despotic and revolting, iniquitous and insulting, on the face of the Earth". (Wakley, *The Lancet* 1841–42, 2, p 246. (Brook, Charles Wortham [1945]. *Battling Surgeon*; Glasgow: The Strickland Press 1945)).

Soon thereafter, in 1844, the Royal College of Surgeons began the import into the sociology of medicine of the concept of medical harm, At least, that is how it was portrayed by the Reverend Monsignor Ivan Dominic Illich (1926-2002), an Austrian Roman Catholic priest, theologian, philosopher and social critic/ In his 1975 book *Medical Nemesis*, he argues that industrialised society widely impairs the quality of life by pharmaceutical drugging. It labels perfectly normal behaviors as problems requiring medical interventions, treatments and drugs, creating false dependency and purposefully restricting and limiting healthful solutions. By that time his book *Deschooling Society* (1971) had already criticized modern society's institutional approach to education. He said this approach constrained learning to narrow situations in a fairly short period of the human lifespan. He did not mention that de-schooling had been systematically generated and structured since the early 1800s to create society's generational health narrative. This led to the COVID-19 kill shot destruction and Harari et al.'s human 2.0 creation.

By 1975, Illich had become so disillusioned with the medical establishment as to view it as a major threat to human health. He made this point in his book *Limits to Medicine* (1975). He also tried to decimate Bernays' immensely successful myth of his "doctor knows best" magical advertisement for the profession. It began in 1927 and still holds today, as evidenced by the herd running to stand in line throughout the Western world to without physicians' murmur, receive the COVID-19 gene editing kill shot unable to comprehend the meaning of "experimental." This was led into by the expropriation of health when squeezing out of business such independent medical schools as run by Grainger and others in the British Commonwealth nations and the U.S.

The Royal Society of Surgeons led the way by changing its by-laws with this sole objective to streamline humanity's medical generational narrative and thus history. So, they disallowed independent naturopathic physicians as members, thus strangling their interventions at source.

Naturopathy has been known for millennia as a system of complementary medicine based on the principle that the body has the inherent ability to heal itself. Its practitioners, generally trained allopathic-educated physicians, use a variety of modalities, such as herbal medicine, nutrition, homeopathy, acupuncture, meditation and yoga to treat a wide range of human health conditions. They look at each individual as a whole, whereas allopathic practitioners look at every one as a puzzle with its individual parts. Naturopaths look for the cause of an ailment, not to pinpoint and improve its symptoms with remedies that create other health impairments. Treatment protocols are therefore tailored and unique to each person. Ailments responding particularly well to naturopathy include digestive disorders, hormone conditions, skin ailments, stress, anxiety, fatigue and sleep disorders. And naturopathy certainly helps in the genuine PTSD recovery. But the National Center *for* PTSD leaves it entirely out of the equation.

Grainger new of his school's pending destruction. To ease his distress, he was hired in 1841 as an inspector for the British Parliament's newly established Children's Employment Commission. It had been created to investigate child labour conditions in the kingdom's mines and factories. In 1842 and 1843, massive reports on the abuse under which these children laboured were published. This was said to have inspired English writer Elizabeth Barrett Browning's (1806–1861) poem "The Cry of the Children." Meanwhile, Grainger distanced himself from such abject misery by beginning a career as lecturer at London's ancient St. Thomas's Hospital, where he stayed until 1860. And Baeyer discovered Barbituric acid and Freud a mere a quarter of the century later would experience cocaine's joy though gleefully ignoring its downfalls.

It is that, however, which might have led to the sprouting within his cocaine-fuelled mind humans' unconscious manifestations in conscious thought. Drugs so often inspire extraordinary thinking, for better or for worse. As a General Hospital of Vienna house officer, in July of 1884 Freud saw fit to express his musing on cocaine in 25 pages in the Austrian medical publication *Centrallblatt für die ges.*[gesammte] *Therapie*. (2, 289–314,1884) he entitled "Über Coca"—On Cocaine—(*Scicurious*, 2008). He was apparently one of the first European medical science-of-psychiatry physicians to do so. And thus, humanity's stroll into perversion and zombification began to be facilitated by those, who Hippocrates recommended swear an oath to do no harm, but never really did. They were only to be topped by the COVID 19 kill shot-injections.

35
HUMANITY'S ZOMBIFICATION BEGINS

"Freud may justly be called the most influential intellectual legislator of his age." These were the words of professor of history emeritus at University of California, Berkeley, Martin Evan Jay (1944–). He spoke to them in 1983, opining that Freud's creation of psychoanalysis was three things at once:

- a theory of the human psyche
- a therapy for the relief of its ills
- an optic, a study of the behavior and properties, to interpret culture and society of his time

Despite repeated criticisms, attempted refutations and qualifications of Freud's work, Jay says, its spell, its magic, remains powerful well after his death even in fields far removed from psychology.

John Horgan (1974–), also gave his opinion on Freud at regular intervals during the past 30 or so years. Horgan is director of the Center for Science Writings at Stevens Institute of Technology. This private research university in Hoboken, New Jersey, was founded in 1870. At his death in 1868, inventor Edwin A. Stevens provided funds to establish a university bearing his family's name. He offered a rigorous engineering curriculum, leading to the degree of Mechanical Engineer. It followed a course of study firmly grounded both in scientific principles and the humanities. The Stevens family had changed the face of American engineering by designing steamboats, locomotives, railroad tracks and a host of other technical innovations that powered the new nation.

In May 2019, Horgan wrote about Freud in his blog in the longest continuously published science magazine in the US, the *Scientific American* (since 1845). His article was: "Why We're Still Fighting Over Freud: A debate over the relevance of psychoanalysis to brain research highlights science's lack of progress in understanding the mind." He wrote it after attending a debate at New York University's Center for Mind, Brain and Consciousness, between capacities in the science of psychiatry and neuroscience. The debaters were trying to figure out the relevance to neuroscience of Freud's the theory of psychoanalysis.

"Who the hell knows?" Horgan asked. He found that psychoanalysts still cite Freud as though they are quoting "scripture," even though the psychoanalysis theory overall is and has always been profoundly flawed. This is like all other paradigms for explaining and treating the human mind, from behaviourism to psychopharmacology (John Horgan: "Freud's most implacable modern critic recounts the flaws of psychoanalysis and its founder and deplores their persistent influence"; *Scientific American,* 2019).

According to Horgan, literary scholar Frederick Crews, professor emeritus at the University of California Berkeley is one of Freud's sharpest critics. Crews eviscerated him with flair for decades. He depicted him as a cocaine-fuelled egomaniac who built his reputation by "boasting, cajoling, question begging, denigrating rivals, and misrepresenting therapeutic results." (Horgan conversation with Crews on Meaningoflife.tv). Crews again did so in his most recent book *Freud: The Making of an Illusion* (Metropolitan, 2017; Picador, 2018).

Horgan and Crews have discussed Freud with vigour off and on for over three decades. They seem to never tire of it, without ever touching on the centre of Freud's musing. Their focus is on the magician of illusions and hallucinations, the nicotine, cocaine, morphine and alcohol addictions and their possible influence on his theories and speculations on the human psyche. As Crews stated repeatedly during those on-and-off discussions over 30 years, Freud always misstated his therapeutic results, faked his alleged discoveries and put forward hypotheses so vague and confused as to be operationally meaningless. Crews furthermore shared and clarified with his demos:

> "Freud's standard bag of tricks, not his observations, prompted him to invert apparent motives, decree that every mental event is a "compromise formation" with "overdetermined" causes, and perceive genital symbolism, incest wishes, and latent homosexuality wherever he turned. The only knowledge that can be extracted from such trademark practices is knowledge about Freud. He granted himself an absolute license to "Freudianize" without concern for more plausible explanations, and he routinely misattributed his personal obsessions to others (Crews in John Horgan: "Why Freud Should Be Dead"; *Scientific American*, 2019)."

Nevertheless, neither Horgan nor Crews address Freud's long-term enthusiastic and liberal use of cocaine, morphine, nicotine in form of gargantuan sized cigars together with alcohol. Nor do they discuss his bizarre, almost perverse, fascination with human genitalia, masturbation habits and homosexuality and bisexuality. Neither of them seems to even contemplate that such almost perverse fascination with human perversions might reveal an innately unbalanced mind, disabled in its coherent thinking with somewhat impaired cognitive abilities? What did Don Miguel Ruiz say?

> "Don't Take Anything Personally. Nothing others do is because of you. What others say and do is a direct projection of their own reality, their own dreams."

With that in mind, consider how over the years, Freud's drugged state of mind would have speculated with quasi overwhelming thoughts on human sexuality and conduct and human states of conscience, subconscious, and non-conscience. We should perhaps begin to contemplate how he must have simultaneously and systematically eroded his own mind, reasoning, and critical thinking ability. He would have documented it all as science, never mind his perception of himself. Through his self-perception would have flown his perception of other human beings and the world in general. This in turn would lead him to create and add to theories and hypotheses achieved in his sooner-or-later, constant state of hallucinations. Thus, he would have related all these machinations to the human psyche between 1884 and his death in 1939, eh?

Is it not even more puzzling, then, that Horgan and Crews missed the key point. They were, purportedly academically educated in the human mind's workings by way of the science of psychiatry and psychology. Yet they do not even touch on how Freud, drugged to the hilt since the age of 28, was able to shuffle his ideas, theories and hypotheses down the learned society's throats. Not even as Freud presented them as the science of psychology and psychiatry since the mid-1890s without a murmur of protest from anyone, even nowadays?

Well, actually there was one dissenter. Jeffrey Moussaieff Masson is a former University of Toronto professor in Sanskrit, trained psychoanalyst and was 1980s projects director of Sigismund Schlomo Freud Archives. In his 1990 book *Final Analysis: The Making and Unmaking of a Psychoanalyst*, he exposes psychoanalytic training as a bizarre, inequitable socialization process. He also reveals what these gurus of psychoanalysis were really like. He exposed how they, since the late 1890s, permeated the entire science of psychiatry and psychology profession and system, controlled by the Khazarian cabal through their teachings. Mind you, few or any of them ever debated Freud's 1896 published report *The Aetiology of Hysteria*. In that report, he documents that at the roots of every case of hysteria are childhood sexual abuse experiences, and that these neuropathic hysterical symptoms were alleviated when his patients talked to him about them (Alisa Zipursky, 2022).

Freud abandoned his conviction in 1897–1898. He disclosed in a letter to his bosom buddy in late 1897 that his patients' shocking recollections of sexual abuse were actually the residues of infantile impulses and desires to be seduced by an adult. They were not memories of actual events. They were nothing other than screen memories and fantasies hiding primitive infantile desires and wishes. They were children's own yearnings to be sexually molested and violated. These, he claimed, were at the root of their later psychological upheaval.

Florence Rush (1918–2008) was born to Ashkenazi Russian-Jewish immigrants in Manhattan. She was a certified psychiatric social worker with a M.S.W. from the University of Pennsylvania. Her 1971 *The Freudian Coverup* with her presentation "The Sexual Abuse of Children: A Feminist Point of View" at the April 1971 New York Radical Feminists (NYRF)

Rape Conference broke the silence. She was the first to challenge Freudian theories of children as the seducers of adults rather than their victims as he maintained in 1896. In her book *The Best Kept Secret*, she recounted how, despite the amenities of a middle-class upbringing, she had been sexually abused as a child. She had further observed the problem of childhood sexual abuse whilst working at the New York Society for the Prevention of Cruelty to Children. She had also seen it when working at a facility for delinquent female adolescents. This was a time when therapists were taught not to discuss childhood sexual abuse or incest with their patients because Freud's seduction theory held them accountable for such violations. Rush argued that Freud knowingly, wilfully, intentionally misinterpreted the evidence of his patients' childhood sexual abuses. She charged that he had twisted them into symptoms of their repressed incestuous childhood desires, imagined erotic fantasies.

In 1977, Rush authored *Freud and the Sexual Abuse of Children*. She followed it with The *Best Kept Secret: The Sexual Abuse of Children*, which traced children's sexual abuse to the beginnings of known history. In due course, she served as:

- co-founder and lecturer for Women Against Pornography
- chair of the National Organization for Women (NOW)
- New York City Chapter's Media Reform Committee
- member of the board of directors of New York Women Against Rape, where she exhibited a slide presentation on the increasing media eroticism of children
- member of the New York State Psychiatric Institute's Advisory Committee on the Treatment of Sexual Aggressors

But the science-of-psychiatry and -psychology magicians of her time ignored her. This was just as they silenced Freud when he revealed his children's sexual violation findings in his *Aetiology of Hysteria* in 1896. They were still grateful that he had at least shown a change of heart, as his discovery of the rampant sexual of abuse of children existing in his society implicated many, if not most, of them. It revealed their ancestral habits of sexual child abuse throughout centuries, if not millennia past. This theory was substantiated in the course of the twentieth century by authors such as Cathy O'Brian, Fritz Springmeier, David Icke and spirit-cooking satanic high priestess Marina Abramovic. It was also supported by the revelations about the English procurer of children to the British Crown, by the BBC's British music chart television program host and 1964 Beetles promoter Tops of the Pops host Jimmy Savile and by the undertakings of Lolita Express operator Jeffrey Epstein in his massive New York mansion, as well as on his private Caribbean island Little St. James and his ranch in Texas.

One question lingers, however, about Freud's twisting of his *Aetiology of Hysteria* into the *seduction theory* introducing the idea to the world that children themselves caused their sexual abuse from infancy onwards by their own consciously performed seductive behaviour with the intent of enticing adults to sexually abuse them. Did it spawn his life-long cocaine, nicotine, alcohol, and morphine addictions due to an underlying guilt ideation? This question, right in line with the science-of-psychiatry and -psychology magicians' investigative techniques and consequent verdicts about the *other's* state of mind when analysing the genuine PTSD journeyers, for example, has yet to arise among his peers.

But never mind. As any physician worth his or her salt will tell you, it is Freud's life-long addictions that might very well have fuelled his ability to concoct his infants' and children's repressed sexual-desires-from-birth inversion and spawned his consequent theories, that humans' sexual desires, fantasies and habits dictated their psyche overall. It seems to be his 1896 published revelations, however, that since then have been explored with a vengeance by his peers in experimental laboratory research clinics, disguised as university kindergartens among them. And with some Freud scholars wonder if his own childhood sexual abuse caused his unnatural desire to supress the existence of its epidemic presence right there in his own Viennese aristocratic and learned-society community. But, keeping inversion in mind, could it be that this kind of research was and is conducted to learn how to entice children into willing participation in all kinds of sexual interactions with adults and animals and make it palatable, nay enjoyable, to them?

Could it be that the long-term drugging and scientific research into children's innate characters is now mirrored in American schools and kindergartens? Their in-class performances by drag-queens showing off fake boobs and erect genitals compliment their reading sessions of explicit sexual perversions in local libraries, with explicit illustrations and suggestions for usage. Could these be undertaken to propel children, knowing their innate investigative minds and curiosity in all things novel, to willingly engage them in anal and oral and homosexual sex or sex with animals?

We read about the term "homosexuality" in a June 2021 WebMD article "What Is Homosexuality?" written for the WebMD Baby's First Year Community and reviewed by Dan Brennan, M.D., a paediatric expert. The term arises from the Greek "homo" and refers to the sexual interactions between people of the same sex, most oftentimes developed during teenage years. However, proposes Brennan, it can take some time to find out what kind of sex one is most attracted to or is comfortable in acknowledging within oneself and others. He explains that people experience sexual, romantic, and emotional feelings toward another person in different ways at different points in their lives. Therefore, he concludes, experimentation of all types of sex is of the essence. In other words, only fucking around like a mink with anything that moves sooner or later or never brings one to a conclusion of preference, besides possibly picking up and spreading an abundance of sexually transmitted diseases, eh?

That seems to confirm that the sexual grooming of children from kindergarten onwards leads into the moral and ethical perversion of their *sui generis*. This liberation of their innate moral and ethical inhibitions is boosted by Ritalin and Adderall, prescribed to them by their caring paediatrician a la Still or school psychologists since 1894, to whom their ignorant parents kow-tow with glee. Children's encouraged sexual experimentations and consequent advances towards their peers will in turn "liberate" their play with classmates from their natural, innate sexual inhibitions. Their equally innate curiosity will take over. One of my acquaintances experienced this when his elder brother began to perform anal sex on him at the tender age of 9 and staying with it, having no interest in fornicating with woman, although he is physically perfectly able of doing so. Was it Somerset-Maugham that wrote, once a man has slept with another man he'll never go back to a woman? Something to do with a penis rubbing against the prostrate, I heard. *Brokeback Mountain* ring a bell, the moral breaking of a heterosexual man ring a bell?

As we recall, members of the European and American learned society of physicians who proclaim to be psychiatrists and psychologists began to conduct in depth research on infants and children in the 1890s. They also knew that Freud's 1896 findings were the truth. But for the Khazarian agenda's Work of Ages to succeed, the inversion of truth had to take place through deception to destroy the herd's moral and ethical perceptions. Since the mid 1800s unawares systematically worn down by cocaine- and morphine-containing drugs and poisoned foods, we were kept in the dark about the goal until openly voiced by Israeli Yuval Noah Harari in the early 2020s. The Khazarian-owned mental health industries magicians had by then incorporated Freud's twisted insights perceived by his cocaine-morphine-nicotine- and alcohol-fuelled brain in their machinations as the gospel. With media and the advertising industry functioning in unison since the 1920s, it took until then for American parents to awaken and begin to protest against drag-queen in-house school performances and library readings of explicitly perverted sexual nature eroding their children's psyches, a miracle in itself when knowing that over 80% of U.S. citizens are unable to read beyond a grade 6 level. And that most of them are on pharmaceutical drugs of one sort or another. And that its learned society, mostly atheists and seemingly unconscious of karmic universal laws, unavoidable consequences and desirable personal conduct, was mirrored in Don Miguel Ruiz's quote:

> "Be Impeccable With Your Word. Speak with integrity. Say only what you mean. Avoid using the word to speak against yourself or to gossip about others. Use the power of your word in the direction of truth and love."

So, let us continue to investigate what brought humanity to where we are in this world today, emotionally, physically, morally and ethically, by following another of Don Miguel's recommendations for the growth and benefit of our soul:

> "Don't Make Assumptions. Find the courage to ask questions and to express what you really want. Communicate with others as clearly as you can to avoid misunderstandings, sadness and drama. With just this one agreement you can completely transform your life."

Let us first explore how this one man, Sigismund Schlomo Freud, succeeded to lead humanity towards physical, emotional, mental, ethical and moral ruin, shall we?

Vienna-born -US Khazarian immigrant, professor Henry L. Lennard (1923-2005) earned his master's degree in psychology from New York University and doctorate in sociology from Columbia University During the 1960s and 1970s, he conducted in depth research into human relationships at the University of California, San Francisco. He later gravely criticized the medical and pharmaceutical industry for over-promoting psychoactive drug-use for depression, schizophrenia and other mental illnesses. He summarized his findings in his 1972 book *Mystification and Drug Misuse: Hazards of Using Psychoactive Drugs* (Harper & Row 1972).

Already in 1972, Lennard criticized physicians' eagerness to use drug treatments as the panacea for all mental illness. And he chided them also for their classification of personal, interpersonal and emotional difficulties arising from life and living as mental disorders. The widespread use of such drugs to solve those problems did not address the underlying causes of patients' difficulties, he warned. It would, in the long run, create more problems than it would solve, wit the machinations of the PTSD hypothesis engineered by the National Center for PTSD, alone serving as nothing other than driving us into suicide. Lennard, God bless him for his efforts, wasted his breath and energy. The Khazarian engaged Luciferic agenda had already been quasi set in stone generations ago, as reflected in Dr. Day's 1968 address. His reward for it? After publishing his book, the American National Institute of Mental Health shortly before Fauci took over its reign cut off his lifetime research award grant without warning or explanation, leaving him high and dry, at least for a while (sfgate.com/bayarea/article/Henry-L-Lennard-social-psychologist-urban-2656498.php).

And how did Freud learn about cocaine? Through a German medical journal, which printed a German army physician's report in 1884, stating that soldiers had been administered cocaine during autumn maneuvers in Bavaria. It had sparked extraordinary energy and enthusiasm in them, compared to previous maneuvers (Henry L. Lennard: Freud's Disaster with Cocaine; (1923-2005) New York Times 1972). Two months after reading the article, Freud saw fit to publish his own purportedly scientific research on cocaine's properties in an essay he entitled "Über Coca" (On Cocaine). With it, he apparently provided the learned medical society with the best review hitherto to appear. He described the plant's uses by South America's native population, naming the first European accounts of its existence and its uses in the sixteenth century and its alkaloid isolation by Baeyers in 1859. Freud also enlightened the readers about the drug's pharmacological and medical applications and his own experiences when under its influence (https://historyofinformation.com/detail.php?id=2630).

His loss of hunger and fatigue is noted. So is his drug-induced and long-lasting feelings of exuberance and exhilaration and its non-addictiveness, much later adding a note about cocaine's numbing effects and possible usefulness as local anaesthetic for eye surgery (Byck, 1974). He enthusiastically proclaims cocaine's effects as "magical," as it transports him, in his own words, into states of:

> "...exhilaration and lasting euphoria, which in no way differs from the normal euphoria of the healthy person...You perceive an increase of self-control and possess more vitality and capacity for work....In other words, you are simply normal, and it is soon hard to believe you are under the influence of any drug....Long intensive physical work is performed without any fatigue...This result is enjoyed without any of the unpleasant after-effects that follow exhilaration brought about by alcohol....Absolutely no craving for the further use of cocaine appears after the first, or even after repeated taking of the drug..." (Zina Moukheiber: "Merck Cocaine: Behind Some Of Those Fabulous Rolling Stones Songs"; *Forbes,* 2010).

Freud seems to have thoroughly missed or wilfully ignored the fact that the drug in his own consciousness created what Indian sage Maharishi Mahesh Yogi (1918–2008), called "the mistake of the intellect". This is the state of mind in which the human intellect is influenced by material consciousness, in this case cocaine, and loses connection with the wholeness of its own consciousness. As a result, it inverts all perceptions of reality, turns them upside down, sees that which is good for the Self as bad and that which is bad for the Self as good ("Mistake of the Intellect: 'Pragyapradh'"; https://mogrady.medium.com/mistake-of-the-intellect-pragyapradh-78cdc3ea3b4). Maharishi Mahesh Yogi was the founder of the Transcendental Meditation (TM) organization and the private Maharishi International University featuring a consciousness-based education system, throughout millennia.

So enthused was Freud about cocaine's effects on his overall emotional and physical wellbeing, however, that he religiously reached for cocaine to cure anything that hit his fan negatively, from depression to indigestion. He also recommended the drug to all with whom he crossed path throughout Europe and America, his family, friends and colleagues included.

But first and foremost, he gave cocaine to his patients. This despite the fact, that his friend, Viennese-born physiologist and physician Ernst von Fleischl-Marxow (1846-1891), whom he introduced to it hoping it would cure him of his morphine addiction, instead killed himself with it. Marxow, who developed constant nerve pain due to thumb amputation, took to cocaine like a duck to water. However, he also relapsed into morphine, in no time flat taking both drugs together. This transported him into a perpetual state of intestate exhilaration & intoxication, until death relieved him in 1891 at the age of 45.

Meanwhile, Freud by his own admission had made it a habit to take cocaine as a nerve stabilizer to maintain a modicum of calmness. He used it when facing social occasions and when studying neurology with pre-eminent French Jean-Martin Charcot (1825–1893). He was a French neurologist and professor of anatomical pathology, who worked on hypnosis and hysteria in particular with his patient Louise Augustine Gleizes (1861– ?) at the Salpêtrière Hospital, Paris. She was sent there in 1875 at age fourteen, after having worked at a religious boarding school since age ten, where she suffered corporal punishment and molestations, and after being raped by her mother's lover when thirteen.

Charcot hypnotized her so she would demonstrate her supposed hysteria, which Freud among others came to see. Photographs were taken of her then, which became known as the most infamous visual representations of including her expressions of uncontrolled emotions, interpersonal manipulations, sexual assertiveness, seizures, and postures of a physiological contortion. These photographic images served as evidence for Charcot's case-conceptualization, the "'truth" of hysteria in women. They were supposed proof of performative gestures of psychological suffering, solidifying women's experiences of distress, which to this day influence hysteria diagnoses, to which every genuine PTSD journeyer can attest (Christian Vanvuren: *The History of Hysteria: Sexism in Diagnosis*, talkspace.com 2017).

When Gleizes no longer agreed to be photographed, she was admitted to the hospital's *solitary confinement*. In 1880, she escaped disguised in men's clothes and was never seen again, whereas Charcot based his hysteria hypothesis on his observations of her making him more famous, and perhaps sparking in Freud a sight of his future.

So, Freud participated in Jean Martin Charcot's melee from October 20, 1885, to February 28, 1886, while enjoying the effects of cocaine and still avoiding the thought of addiction or adverse side-effects hitting him sooner or later. Only cocaine's continued magical effects were anchored firmly in his mind. The migraines suddenly attacking him he blew away with a dose of cocaine, thrilled how well it worked, whilst ignoring the consequent hyperactivity and sleep depravation lasting for hours on end.

Freud, Charcot and others watching the Gleizes spectacle seem to have known of the 1900 BC's Eber Papyrus references to hysterical disorders. They followed the same conclusion, namely that hysteria was caused by abnormal movements of the uterus. Hippocrates, the first to coin the term "hysteria," followed suit with that trend of thought in the fifth century. He agreed with his predecessors that this so-called condition—attributable only to women—was due to a "wandering womb," believing it to be caused by sexual inactivity. Recommended cures? Women should increase their sexual activity—within the bounds of marriage, of course—a thought still carried forth by the non-existent science-of-psychiatry and -psychology practitioners. This despite being unable to prove their diagnosis in science or medical research. Instead, they reflect men's and the mental health's cabals' gender bias against women's lack of interest in sexual intercourse on demand, a view sustained by both genders in this "profession" to this very day. You must fuck more to cure your PTSD is their motto operandi, working for both men and women, when the sexual appetite is non-existent in both genders when in the genuine PTSD state of mind.

Equally to this day, hysteria currently defined by Merriam-Webster Dictionary is "behaviour exhibiting overwhelming or unmanageable fear or emotional excess." An alternate, psychiatric definition is, "a psychoneurosis marked by emotional excitability and disturbances of the psychogenic, sensory, vasomotor, and visceral functions." Medicine and mental health have changed a great deal over the centuries. But the historically gendered diagnosis of hysteria continues to serve as a catch-all when physician cannot identify another disease, as it serves wonderfully well as a disorder. Therefore, it continues to label women "hysterical", defined more by their stature and bearing as women than by symptoms they might display, such as when experiencing genuine PTSD.

Even nowadays, the belief remains that sexual abstinence is the cause of hysteria, classified by symptoms of insomnia, irritability, anxiety, erotic fantasies and excessive vaginal lubrication. Greek physician and Roman resident Galen prescribed one of two things to cure it: sex or pelvic massage performed by physicians or midwives. That would speedily be remedied by the Khazarians Luciferic consciousness by patenting the first battery-operated vibrator in 1880, used solely by physicians for non-specified reasons (antiquevibratormuseum.com/vintage-vibes.html).

At the turn of the nineteenth century, more than a dozen manufacturers produced both battery-powered vibrators and models operating from line electricity. They progressed to market vibrators as a home appliance, using widely distributed advertisements in household publications such as *Modern Woman* and *Woman's Home Companion* like "Invented by a woman who knows a woman's needs," and "Relieves All Suffering. Cures Disease."

By 1906, the American Vibrator Company of St. Louis, Missouri, suggested to women that the "American Vibrator ... can be used by yourself in the privacy of dressing room or boudoir, and furnish every woman with the essence of perpetual youth." Throughout the 1910s and 1920s, ads like that marketed vibrators directly to American homes, as mail order was the standard method of delivery. By the mid-1920s, vibrators began to regularly appear in erotic- and pornographic films and photography. By the 1960s, modern vibrators surfaced as frankly sexual devices. They had indeed implanted into the human sub-consciousness the seed of women as rutting animals in need of being regularly fornicated with to maintain their emotional and physical health, as animals were included in pornographic demonstrations. If not fucked regularly, it would practically guarantee hysteria. This hypothesis anchored itself so firmly in humanity's mind, that the learned science-of-psychiatry and -psychology's magicians still in 2022 use it as contributor to genuine PTSD experiencers' misery.

German Marcus Frind's (1979–) *Plenty of Fish* website was established in 2003. It seems to serve as the world's largest fornication agency, should living human partners rather than vibrators be desired for the deed. But after electrical vibrators were first created and marketed in 1880, only physicians used them, we are told. If Freud was among them when under cocaine's influence, we do not know. However, 100 years after he published his praises of the drug in "Über Coca," German-born associate professor of psychiatry in the field of behavioural sciences at Harvard Medical School Howard J. Schaffer (1926-), PhD, weighed in. His research interests for decades include the social perception of addiction and disease, the philosophy of science, impulse control regulation and compulsive behaviours, adolescent-and adult gambling and gambling responsibility, addiction treatment outcome and the natural history of addictive behaviours. In his 1981 article "Uber [sic] coca: Freud's cocaine discoveries", he explained that Freud's personal experiences with cocaine described by himself in his booklet "Über Coca" actually clarifies why he indeed became a life-long slave to the drug (H Shaffer; sciencedirect.com; Dyke, 1981. C.V. Dyke. Cocaine. J. Lowinson, P. Ruiz (Eds.).

Why? Could it be because Freud's revelations of his thoughts during his cocaine-induced hallucinations led him to trace man's natural history, eventually leading to addictive behaviour? And what's that, we ask?

Well, in a nutshell, we learn that the seeds of addiction are typically sown years prior to the onset of addictive substance use or engagement in addictive behaviors. This is due to excessive stress from a single event or cumulative life experiences during childhood. It would not only increase the risk for psychiatric and physical illness, but also that for early onset and chronic addictions, cognitive impairment and compulsive behaviors. And it would increase morbidity and shorten life expectancy when chronic stress results in the emotional dysregulation of the human equilibrium, the abnormality or impairment in the regulation of a metabolic, physiological, or psychological process (J Korean: "Origins of Addiction Predictably Embedded in Childhood Trauma: A Neurobiological Review"; Acad Child Adolesc Psychiatry 2017; 28(1): 4-13).

And what did Freud present on the evening of April 21, 1896, to his colleagues at the Viennese Society for Psychiatry and Neurology entitled "The Aetiology of Hysteria?" That the source of internal psychic pain in his 18 patients, termed neurosis and hysteria, lay in both men's and women's sexual abuse during infancy, mostly from the ages of four to eight. Freud made several arguments to support his position that the memories he had uncovered were genuine. Among them, he claimed that patients were not simply remembering the events; they were essentially reliving them with all the associated painful sensory experiences. No one of the learned society encouraged him to present the clinical evidence for his claims. And he never did, other than saying that in all cases, the *father*, not excluding his own, had to be accused of being perverse. That is, if he maintained the position of childhood sexual abuse leading to hysteria and neurosis in adulthood in addition to himself finding the frequency of such widespread perversions against children improbable.

And indeed, he had to stop the popularization of this discovery, for two reasons. First, it would threaten the science-of-psychiatry hallucination as a genuine, legitimate enterprise. Second, it would alert the world to the phenomenal amount of sexual child abuse, not only by the Viennese learned society, but by high society throughout the world. So, what did he present ten years later, inspired by Khazarian Luciferic consciousness and wanting to be rich and famous?

He inverted his findings, by and large twisting them to mean that his patients' memories of sexual abuse were in fact due to their own perversion, imaginary fantasies, fabrications, hallucinations. He claimed that they, as children, had been seeking sexual intercourse and abuse and consciously or sub-consciously bringing it on through their own seductiveness. He called it the "Seduction theory", and with it entered the path to persuade humanity of all ranks and file to believe that everything having to do with the human psyche related to sex in one way or another.

His contemporaries swallowed this cocaine-nicotine-morphine-alcohol-fueled idea wholesale and without much murmur. Nobody until Shaffer in 1981 questioned how this inventor of psychoanalysis reached his conclusion on the human psyche's workings in relation to their sexuality. Nor did anybody ask how its inventor felt about his own impotence to overcome his numerous drug addictions, never mind questioning what these addictions did to his self-esteem, his guilt complex, his shame of himself, his ego, his id, his conscience, his sub-conscience, his *Über*-conscience, his super conscience or his feelings of superiority and overall judgment of himself. And nobody asked whatever else he may or may not have experienced within whilst formulating and popularizing his opinions on humanity's psyche?

However, it really does not matter, does it, when considering the law of cause and effect. We might be tempted to accredit it with Freud's fate to suffer incurable, inoperable cancer of the jaw that prohibited him from liberally talking and swallowing, enhanced by his apparent refusal to take painkillers. He stated: "I prefer to think in torment than not to be able to think at all," apparently recalling his friend Marxow's loss of mind, eh? When death caught up with him in 1939 at the age of 83, his goal to plant the seed for humanity's perversion consciously, subconsciously or unconsciously, had by and large been achieved. His personal and patient try-outs with cocaine had led to the flogging of opioid-containing drugs to God and sundry as miracle drugs. They were taken with and without physician-issued prescriptions by herd members of all rank and files, amounting to millions of cocaine and morphine containing concoctions by WWI.

By late 1969, the miracle workings of these opioid drugs in alleviating ailments afflicting the human psyche and liberating inhibition of all kinds had been anchored so firmly into humans' mind, that physicians across medical society issued mind-altering/opioids to patients complaining of hangnails. Thus, the ruination of takers' moral, ethical, physical, and emotional health was assured. And the herd, in good faith swallowing whatever the good doctor prescribed, unawares disabled themselves from ever solving any of their normally-to-be-expected life problems, because pharmaceutical mind-altering drugs purposely pervert their perception.

The Khazarian-owned drug manufacturing businesses were mostly firmly established by the mid-1800s. In the U.S. alone, they used 17000 kg of amphetamine base and 8000 kg of methamphetamine base, according to 1971 quotas. This roughly equals three billion 10-mg amphetamine sulphate tablets and one billion 10-mg methamphetamine hydrochloride tablets. Altogether, that's four billion doses of mind-altering prescription drugs to be consumed by an estimated 202 million Americans. You do the math. (www.ncbi.nlm.nih.gov/pmc/articles/PMC2377281/). The drugging of the U.S. population into oblivion had begun in earnest.

By 2021, drug prescriptions issued by physicians had ballooned to 6,474 billion. Almost all these physicians were educated in allopathic medicine only, wit Toronto University professor emeritus of psychology Jordan Peterson's experience with physician-prescribed benzodiazepine. Furthermore, so perverse has the learned medical society's drug prescription mania become, that they use and promote cocaine and morphine narcotic off-springs such as methadone as the panacea for heroin addiction. This is in the same style that Freud popularized the cure for morphine addiction by adding cocaine to it.

Children's equally human-equals-animal educated school psychologists have "an abnormal defect of moral control...", as first mentioned in 1902 by British pediatrician Sir George Frederic. That started this whole agenda of drugging humans into oblivion. With or without parental consent children are drugged *en masse* with Ritalin and Adderall. This is the gateway to their cocaine and heroine experimentation and addiction during adolescence soon thereafter. This is accepted, encouraged and even applauded by the herd and science-of-mental-health advocates alike as benevolent.

By extension, children's sexual inhibitions throughout past generations were gradually lowered through drugging. Could this possibly be the reason they are now level introduced to sex in government run schools at kindergarten by drag queen shows. Topics include homosexuality, sex changes, vibrators and dildos. These are presented as desirable and perfectly normal human behaviour for living a purpose-driven life. It could be perceived as fruit of Freud's labours, originating with his seduction theory and his Oedipus complex idea, conceived in his cocaine-, morphine-, alcohol- and nicotine-infested mind and popularized throughout the western hallucination of the science-of-psychiatry and -psychology magicians at rapid speed.

Freud's Oedipus hallucination alone could in itself be viewed as a mirror to his own psyche and its inversion. This King of Thebes, Oedipus, portrayed in Sophocles' (496-406 BC) drama Oedipus Rex, fulfilled the prophecy of killing his father and marrying his mother purely by accident. It was not, as Freud seems to portray, because he sexually lusted after his mother since birth. But that generally appears to escape anyone venturing into the science-of-magic adherents' domain. What kind of personal experiences propelled Freud into achieving such an overwhelming prominence? To have his assertions and his theories on the emotional health of both children and adults being based on their sexual drives broadly publicized in the hallucinated-into-being science of psychiatry. This subsequently opened the door to his sex-related theories of humans' emotional development from the womb onwards, explored ad nauseam to this day to maintain the mental health industry cabal in power and financially secure, a topic seldom explored by his peers (Robert M. Kliegman, M.D., in *Nelson Textbook of Pediatrics*, 2020; Developmental and Behavioral Theories).

So, let's try to trace Schlomo's career path, shall we?

His career as a plain general physician began in 1882 as a house officer at the Vienna General Hospital, the *Allgemeines Krankenhaus der Stadt Wien*, also the site of the city's medical university. Its origin goes back to the aftermath of the second Siege of Vienna by Ottoman Empire's Muslim hordes during a conflict between the Habsburg-ruled Holy Roman Empire and the Ottoman Empire ruler. That dispute in European history began in the early sixteenth century and would last almost 300 years.

To cut a very long story very short, the Ottoman's Grand Vizier, Kara Mustafa Pasha, laid siege to Vienna on July 14, 1683. His army far outnumbered the city's defenders. It would be won by Leopold I and King John III Sobieski of Poland, although the skirmish continued until 1699. The1683 victory, however, marked the end of both Muslim Ottoman Turks' menace to the rest of Europe and of Ottoman domination in eastern Europe.

A Viennese citizen donated the land to establish a hospital to care for the injured shortly after the siege, but emperor Leopold I (1640-1705), slow in the uptake, took until 1693 to finance the hospital's construction. Its first ward finally opened in 1697, quartering 1,042 patients and a poorhouse. By1724, with 1,740 persons living there, a widow yard was added as well as a restaurant and a craftsman center. Between 1752 and 1774, the student and house supervisor yards were extended, and all inhabitants mandated to wear uniforms. Copper coins redeemable with the bakers, butchers and other merchants housed in the complex were also issued.

When Vienna-born physician Joseph von Quarin (1733 –1814) took the reigns as director in 1784, he added many new features:

- a maternity ward
- a findelhaus
- a foundlings' home
- an orphanage
- a lunatic asylumcalledthe Narrenturm, or Fool's Tower, a five-part fortress-like circular building with slot-like windows and cells

This roof-ridge building had a lightning rod, a Blitzfänger, with mounting plates in the inner court. These were probably not installed as lightning protection, but as conductors for patients' electroshock treatments. It was equipped with strong lattice doors and rings for chaining 200 to 250 inmates in their cells.

By the end of the eighteenth century, Vienna General Hospital's medical school was among Europe's top medical research centers. Hungarian-born Ignaz Philipp Semmelweis (1818 –1865) was one of them. He returned to human consciousness the importance of antiseptic- and hygienic procedures as vital for human health and well being, during childbirth in particular. Another one was Austrian physician and immunologist Karl Landsteiner (1868 -1943). Soon after Freud's tenancy, he distinguished humans' main blood groups (1900 AD).

According to reports by his fellow students. Freud wanted fame and fortune. After immersing himself in this environment, he attached himself as clinical assistant-in-training to psychiatrist Theodor Meynert. Since 1875, Meynert had been director of the University of Vienna's psychiatric clinic. There, Freud joined his future mentor and Meynert protégé, Viennese Josef Breuer (1842-1925). Breuer's father taught religion in the city's Jewish community, whilst sonny boy worked at the city's military medical school after passing his medical exams in 1867. In the 1880s, Josef moved on to mind-manipulation practice on Austrian aristocratic social pioneer and founder of the Jewish Women' Association ('Jüdischer Frauenbund') Bertha von Pappenheim (1859-1936).

Her mother was born Goldschmidt (Goldsmith) from the old and wealthy family of the German city of Frankfurt am Main, hometown of the Rothschilds. Her father was son of an Orthodox Jewish family from Preßburg, Austria-Hungary. He was cofounder of Vienna's Jewish Orthodox Schiffshul, Vienna's main Orthodox synagogue, established by the Israelitsche Cultus-Gemeinde (the Jewish Community) in 1852. When her father suddenly fell seriously ill during a family holiday, Bertha suddenly began to experience tormenting hallucinations and states of high anxiety during nights she spent at his sickbed. After his death, she began to suffer paralysis of her limbs as well as disturbances of vision and speech (Fancher, R., E. (1996): *Pioneers of Psychology* (3rd eds); Norton and Company Inc., London/New York).

Her family consulted Freud, who involved Breuer in the case in November 1880 Breuer was the Viennese Jewish high bourgeoisie and aristocracy physician of choice. He diagnosed hysteria, upon which Bertha took to her bed to "in rapid succession" to develop an array of judged-to-be-hysterical symptoms:

- pain in the left side of the occiput
- blurred vision
- hallucinations
- various contractures and anaesthesias
- trigeminal neuralgia
- aphasia
- speaking English only
- split personality
- altered states of consciousness and "absences" thereof, during which she is said to have thrown temper tantrums she could not remember afterwards (psychologytoday.com)

Breuer used Charcot's technique and put Bertha under hypnosis to talk about the experiences generating her behaviour. He kept his friend Sigismund abreast of the on-goings, but called in psychiatrist Richard von Krafft-Ebing, of whom we will hear more later, for a second opinion. Unconvinced of the authenticity of her symptoms, with her ignoring his presence, Krafft-Ebing blew the smoke of a piece of paper he had ignited into her face. Exploding with anger, she began to beat Breuer violently. He reacted by forcing her into a clinic for nervous disorders to calm her down for months with large doses of chloral hydrate, a geminal diol, a subclass of the diols, which in turn are a special class of alcohols still used as a sedative and hypnotic pharmaceutical drug assuring her addiction.

Released six months later, Bertha continued her sessions with Breuer, unloading her heart of her childhood experiences. Following her supposedly final narration, during which she is said to have relived the scene at the bedside of her father said to have triggered her illness, Breuer stated:

> "Immediately after its reproduction, she was able to speak German. She was moreover free from the innumerable disturbances, which she had previously exhibited. After this she left Vienna and travelled for a while, but it was a considerable time before she regained her balance entirely. Since then she has enjoyed complete health."

Originally naming his way of treatment "the talking cure", he later changed it to "cathartic methods".

Young Sigismund Schlomo, his pupil, did not mention this episode of his life until giving his *Five Lectures on Psycho-Analysis* in the United States in 1909, where he finally pointed out: "I was a student and working for my final examinations at the time when ... Breuer, first (in 1880–2) made use of this procedure ... Never before had anyone removed a hysterical symptom by such a method."(Sigmund Freud, *Five Lectures on Psycho-Analysis*. Penguin 1995. pp. 1–2 and p. 10).

Mind you, some of his peers doubted his recital of Bertha's curing. Meanwhile, she did splendidly after a while, engaging among other highly integral activities to help women by in 1902 setting up the Women's Relief (*Weibliche Fürsorge*) in 1902. This provided shelter, counselling, job training and referral services for Jewish women. She also launched a campaign to denounce prostitution and white slavery in the Jewish communities of Russia and Eastern Europe. This drew criticism from the rabbis, who feared that bringing these practices into the open would strengthen anti-Semitic stereotypes.

Be it as it may, Freud established Easter Sunday 1984 after Merck secured his cocaine advertisement in lieu of cocaine and financial remuneration throughout life. This was after testing Breuer's ways of helping Bertha to overcome her childhood traumas on his own patients in the privacy of his own clinic. With Charcot's Gleizes rape and sexual abuse case anchored in his mind, he "intuited" a great and honourable future of fame and fortune by bringing to the world the knowledge that neurosis in both genders originated with sexual childhood abuse. Only when having his hypothesis brutally shot down by his Viennese science-of-psychiatry peers in 1896, which in a round-about way revealed the rampant child sexual abuse existing in their own society, he despaired—briefly.

Even his mentor Meynert ridiculed his idea. His most famous students, Russian neuro-psychiatrist Sergei Korsakoff (1854–1900), German neuro-pathologist Carl Wernicke (1848–1905) and Swiss neuro-anatomist Auguste-Henri Forel (1848–1931) believed. They took care that Freud's childhood sexual violation discoveries and insights spread throughout the world of science-of-psychiatry and -psychology magicians.

Freud held a six-month internship with German Carl Wilhelm Hermann Nothnagel (1841 -1905) at that time. Nothnagel was professor of internal medicine at Vienna's university clinic between 1882 and 1905. He was one of the most eminent internal medicine and neurologist researchers-clinicians of his time. Under Nothnagel's tutelage he performed trepanation, the drilling of a hole into the human cranium to get to the dura mater, the thick outermost of the three layers of membrane protecting our central nervous system. This was to treat intracranial diseases, release pressured blood build-up from an injury and find other perceived abnormalities. Called trepanation, it was among other experiments he conducted on the human brain. We see it exemplified in the painting by Hieronymus Bosch displayed in the Museo del Prado in Madrid, Spain, completed around 1494 either called *Cutting the Stone, The Extraction of the Stone of Madness* or *The Cure of Folly*.

Hieronymus Bosch on trepanation

What is trepanation? Dr. Raphael P Davis is a neurosurgery specialist in East Setauket, New York and a graduate of Icahn School of Medicine At Mount Sinai in 1981. He has more than 41 years of diverse experiences in his field, especially conducted in Stony Brook University Hospital's Neurosciences Institute and with doctors and specialists in the medical group New York Spine And Brain Surgery. He relates that trepanation, also known as trephination, has been done for at least the past 5,000 years. That makes it one of humanity's oldest medical procedures. It is thought to be performed to treat head injuries and headaches, and to release evil spirits from the body of folk deemed to behave outside of societal norms (https://healthcare4ppl.com/physician/new-york/east-setauket/raphael-p-davis-1386674810.html).

Also during his time at Nothnagel in 1882, Freud researched the brain's medulla. This part of the brain is thought to pass information between its higher-thinking centers, the cerebral cortex, the cerebrum associated with thought, action and the spinal cord. It runs through the atlas and axis, the first cervical vertebra, which, along with the second vertebra, the axis, forms the joint connecting the skull and the spine.

However, as Swiss Rene C. Schümperli discovered, it is misaligned in the vast majority of humans. Thus, it impedes blood flow to the cerebral cortex and prohibits blood flow to the brain resulting in a multitude of under-performances. The medulla alone, for example, contains the body's cardiac, respiratory and vasomotor centers, thus deals with the autonomic functions of breathing, heart rate, blood pressure and the sleep–wake cycle (atlasprofilax; *Fallacy 1*).

And what did Freud do with his subjects' medulla and spinal cord connection upon trepanation at Nothnagel's? Nothing we know of. When beginning his study of medicine at the University of Vienna in 1876, he had started in the physiological laboratory under the direction of German physician and physiologist Ernst Wilhelm von Brücke (1819–1892). He was assigned to research the histology, the microscopic anatomy, of the *Ammocoetes petromyzon*'s nervous system and spinal cord. This long, eel-like fish of the order petromyzontiformes placed in the superclass Cyclostomata, is one of nearly 50 species of lampreys, a group of jawless fishes found in temperate rivers and coastal seas that drinks the blood of lake trout for his sustenance. Freud had to describe the species' phylogenetic origin, the evolutionary history and relationships existing among or within groups of organisms, of other fishes we take it, of the posterior root ganglia based on his analysis of the *Ammocoetes petromyzon* spinal cord (springer.com).

Therefore, he thoroughly investigated these creatures' nerve root and dorsal root ganglion (DRG) and their neuronal cell bodies clustered in its connective tissue and embedded between the spinal column vertebrae on either side of the spinal cord connected with the cerebrum running through the atlas (sciencedirect.com).

Spinal nerves are mixed nerves that transmit motor, sensory and autonomic signals between the central nervous system and the periphery. Each spinal nerve carries afferent sensory fibers and efferent motor fibers to and from the spinal cord, the former of which comprise the posterior/dorsal roots. Each posterior root presents a ganglion as it emerges from the intervertebral foramen. The main function of the spinal ganglion cells is to transmit the sensory neural signals from the peripheral to the central nervous system and vice versus.

But Freud, seemingly mesmerized with sex in anything alive, also chose to describe this eel-like creature's lobe-shaped genital organs he called testicles. Having read Darwin's *On The Origin of Species* (1859), he might have been intuiting that it might be humans' ancestor of the penis or clitoris springing to his fertile mind (Sigmund Freud Papers: Oversize, 1859–1985; Writings; 1877; "Beobachtungen über Gestaltung und feineren Bau der als Hoden beschriebenen Lappenorgane des Aals" [Observations on the Formation and More Delicate Structure of Lobe-Shaped Organs of the Eel Described as Testicles]. [b]. Manuscript/Mixed Material. Retrieved from the Library of Congress). After all, it had barely taken 20 years for the learned society to accept Darwin's idea of natural selection and survival of the fittest, beginning with the amoeba as humanity's origin, as a fact.

Many competing explanations for humans' origin were in play. Natural selection played a minor role in their considerations until the modern evolutionary synthesis, a concept brewed up in the early twentieth century synthesis of Darwin's hypothesis of human evolution with human heredity. He combined them into a joint mathematical framework by the Augustinian abbot of St. Thomas' Abbey, located in Brünn (*Brno*), Margraviate of Moravia, Gregor Johann Mendel (1822–1884). A biologist, meteorologist and mathematician, his idea gave Darwin's hypothesis the scientific push it needed to move forward as the truth of human-equals-animal perception to get foothold among the herd, and in 1900 ushered in the age of genetics (Gayon, Jean. "From Mendel to epigenetics: History of genetics" Comptes Rendus Biologies, 2016. 339 (7–8): 225–230).

Aldous Leonard Huxley (1894–1963), writer and philosopher born into the prominent British Huxley family, was educated at Oxford and interested in philosophical mysticism, universalism and interpretations of his psychedelic experience. When under the influence of mescaline, he picked up on Darwin's, Freud's and Mendel's ideas with lightening speed and foresight. He wrote about them in his 1932 books *Brave New World* and *Island*. In 1962, he presented his future visions of humanity's dystopia and utopia seemingly. In 2022, it loomed over us due to the COVID 19 kill shot, genetically modifying injections taken by those taught to believed that science infallibly ruled with truth and logic and those who were never taught either logic or reason.

Mescaline, by the way, is a hallucinogenic and psychedelic drug found in certain cacti plants native to the southwest United States, Mexico, and South America. This includes the peyote cactus (*Lophophora williamsii*), the San Pedro cactus (*Trichocereus pachanoi*), and the Peruvian Torch cactus (*Trichocereus peruvianus*). They carry similar mind-altering effects as LSD and psilocybin, namely euphoria, distorted visual hallucinations and perceptions of shapes and colours, altered sounds, delusions, anxiety and depression, delusions, sense of time distortion and occasional terrifying experiences called "bad trips." These can result in nausea and panic attacks, anxiety, rapid heartbeat, increased body temperature, high blood pressure and rapid heart rate. Flashbacks, a return of a "trip" experience, can also occur days or months later. (drugs.com) Extreme changes in mood are part of it, as well, with overdose leading to severe psychosis, although there is no known lethal dose of the drug. Death merely seems to occur due to a direct injury while under its LSD influence.

Brave New World is set in a futuristic World State, whose citizens are environmentally engineered into an intelligence-based social hierarchy. They are basically made through artificial intelligence. Huxley, who had the inside track, forecasts huge scientific advancements in reproductive technology, sleep-learning, psychological manipulation and classical cognitive behavioural conditioning challenged by one single individual.

His elder brother, Darwinian natural selection evolutionary biologist, eugenicist and New World order enthusiast Julian Sorell Huxley (1887 - 1975) followed suit. In 1942, he published his book *Evolution: The Modern Synthesis*. It gave Darwin's natural selection theory as the primary agent in human evolution. It moved both the scientific community and the herd to by and large accept humanity's rising from the amoeba. This type of cell or unicellular organism has the ability to alter its shape primarily by extending and retracting pseudopods in fungi and algae into the creature. Freud studied it in depth in form of the *Ammocoetes petromyzon* and hallucinated by present biological sciences part of the basic mechanism of human evolution into the shape and mind we have today. In 1945, this was exemplified and brought home to the masses by George Orwell's books *Animal Farm* followed in 1948 by *1984*.

Neither Darwin nor Mendel ever came up with such hypothesis. According to T. K. Pennimann, Head of the Department of Ethnology and Prehistory and Diploma Secretary for Anthropology in the University of Oxford 1939–1963, that is a whole different story. In his book *100 Years of Anthropology*, he made the reason for the push to accept the human-animal selection crystal clear when stating:

> "The *Origin of Species* then provided a scheme which linked together the past and the present and all forms of life, institutions and beliefs as parts of one whole, and in development. Henceforward, anthropology could be the science of man in evolution, following its course not in the light of assumed notions for which there could be no proof, but in the light of hypotheses with assumed no causes except those which could be proved to be at work. Scientists need no longer start from abstractions arrived at by cogitation. They could now proceed experimentally,

> unhampered by "laws" which were not susceptible of proof (Gerald Duckworth & Co. Ltd, 3rd. ed 1965; p. 82).

But Freud did all he could to push the human-equals-animal theme, the goy equals beast idea applicable to all not born and raised Khazarians. So, he received his M.D. in 1881. He was advised by his science teacher Brücke to rather engage in general medicine than scientific research. So, he secured his work at Vienna's General Hospital and proposed marriage to Martha Bernays (1861-1951) of the strictly observant Orthodox Khazarian Ashkenazi Jewish family, whose elder brother Eli had married his younger sister. Edward Bernays, the "father of public relations," would later be her nephew. Her maternal cousins, brothers Julius and Oscar Philipp, had a small metal trading company in Hamburg in 1901 under the name of Philipp Brothers. They would eventually turn their enterprise into the world's largest metal and physical commodities trading firm in crude oil, oil products, natural gas, precious and base metals, agricultural products, commodity-related equities and everything in between as Philcro, until selling it all in 2015.

According to Freud's biographer Peter Gay, the only thing bothering Martha throughout their marriage was that he was called a "Godless Jew." Bruno Bettelheim maintained that such conclusions emerged from systematic mistranslations of Freud's works that emphasize the rational over the non-rational elements in his writings. This was to make Freud more acceptable to American mental health industry practitioners (Joseph H Berke: "Answering a Question with a Question: Contemporary Psychoanalysis and Jewish Thought" (review); Shofar. *An Interdisciplinary Journal of Jewish Studies* 29(4):157-159).

Freud was a wordsmith, perhaps as great as Goethe, we hear. When using "psyche", he specifically meant soul, not mind. Hence psycho-analysis is best rendered as "soul analysis," neither the analysis of humans' mind nor mentality, a change in perception totally recalibrating Freud's original intentions. And even though Freud did seemingly disparage God and religion, one could perhaps also surmise that deep within he only despised the formal practices and simplistic views of God displayed by his fellows. Be it as it may, upon their marriage he forbade Martha, granddaughter of the Chief Rabbi of Hamburg, to light Shabbat candles (Hebrew: תבש תורנ), the candles lit on Friday evening before sunset to usher in the Jewish Sabbath. This made her to exclaim after his death: "That mamzer (bastard), he even forbade me to light candles."

But she had had four years to contemplate joining her life with his in matrimony. Soon after his 1882 proposal, she went to live with her family in the Freie and Hansestadt Hamburg, where both Khazarian Ashkenazi and Portuguese Sephardic Jews had settled since the turn of the seventeenth century. Both groups practiced their faith in separate institutions. Her great grandfather Isaac Bernays (Yiddish: זיינרעב קציא קחצי, Yitsḥak Itsik Bernayz; 1792–1849) had been Chief Rabbi there since 1822.

Freud, meanwhile, began to describe the process of nervous system damage in a patient suffering from scurvy. He spoke of his discovery of a new technique to stain nerve, fibres enabling him to examine and describe:

- the medulla oblongata's structure
- the fibrillary tracts running between the medulla oblongata

- the cerebellum and the origin of the nerve fibres forming the connection between the brainstem and the spinal cord

These comprised the cardiovascular-respiratory regulation system, descending motor tracts, ascending sensory tracts and the origin of cranial nerves IX, X, XI, and XII. They also included as well as the motor neurons crossings from the left motor cortex to the right side of the spinal cord in the medulla (Radostina Iordanova; Anil Kumar Reddy Reddivari: Neuroanatomy, Medulla Oblongata; StatPearls Publishing 2022 Jan.) The thought to examine the atlas–axis position in his subjects, humans or non-humans, never seems to have crossed his mind, however.

In 1885, both Freud and Krafft-Ebbing were appointed lecturer on nervous diseases at the University in Vienna. Suffice to say that they , and therefore their peers, might have had knowledge of humans' blood flow restriction caused by the atlas-axis misalignment present in most humans, but chose to keep it quiet. And if so, it was their duty, as it would have made the illusion of the science-of-psychiatry and -psychology field impossibility. Why? Because an alignment would have assured the perfect functioning of the human central nervous system and therefore all parts of its physical body. Unless the body was physically injured, it would leave their speculations on humans' mental health out in the cold.

Freud did not go public with a discovery he most likely made, bright and observant as he undoubtedly was. Instead, he got funding from whomever to spend six months at the Salpêtrière Hospital in Paris to study brain anatomy and neuroses under the famous neurologist Jean-Martin Charcot. The term "neurosis" was coined in 1769 by Scottish physician, chemist, agriculturalist and professor at the Edinburgh Medical School William Cullen (1710 -1790). It refers to "disorders of sense and motion" caused, he said, by "a general affection of the nervous system." He said it was characterized by anxiety, depression or other feelings of unhappiness or distress out of proportion to the circumstances of a person's life and untraceable to neither brain or nerve damage nor tumours.

Charcot discovered that he was able to temporarily induce and manipulate neuroses' hysterical symptoms in human subjects with suggestions made during hypnosis. He documented that ideas in humans' minds could affect their physical bodies. To broadcast the truth about his findings as widely as possible, Charcot conducted elaborately staged theatrical demonstrations at the hospital, hypnotizing subjects in front of large audiences. It is said that Charcot's claims of a non-organic basis for hysteria fired up Freud's desire to explore and explain the human mind's functioning to make a name for himself and find acceptance in his society.

He only needed to gather more credential in neurology to fulfill his wish. So, after Paris, he spent a few weeks in Berlin to learn about neurological childhood diseases. That qualified him to practice at Vienna's Erstes Öffentliches Kinder-Krankeninstitut (the First Public Institute for Sick Children). It was established in 1788 to provide free treatment to sick children of impoverished families, the second of its kind in Europe after London's Dispensary for Sick Children opened in 1769. Freud would see patients there without pay three times weekly—for a while.

His cocaine fuelled encounters with Charcot, however, had warmed him progressively to the idea of physical illnesses in humans originating in the mind rather than ad hoc in their physical bodies (https://freud.org.uk/education/resources/freud-the-physician/from-medicine-to-psychoanalysis/). With that in mind and shortly upon his return from Paris and Berlin, he opened shop in central Vienna. In the local newspaper, the *Neue Freie Presse,* he advertised himself as a docent of the University of Vienna specializing in nervous illnesses. It was two weeks before his 30th birthday, and he was off to the races for fame and fortune. That would ultimately lead to his foundation of the psychological current termed psychoanalysis.

As few patients honoured him with their presence, he began to conduct lectures on hypnosis as a sideline. But that, too, gave him nothing but grief. Hypnosis found little fertile ground in Vienna's most conservative medical establishment, instead being met with great hostility. The conclusions on the human psyche drawn by Charcot during his stay in Paris fell on barren ground. This was particularly true of the occurrence of hysteria and the appearance of hysterical paralysis in both men and women. In fact, it was met with such outright disdain and opposition that Freud was prohibited from conducting research at the city's Institute of Cerebral Anatomy (Sigmund Freud (1856–1939) (Andrzej Grzybowski & Joanna Żołnierz: *Sigmund Freud; Journal of Neurology* volume 268, pages 2299–2300 (2021).

But at least for a few years, he steadfastly carried on. He resigned his position at the General Hospital to focus exclusively on the few very well-healed patients sent to him by Breuer et al., treating their emotional problems in whichever ways he saw fit. Merck's payments maintained his rapidly growing family, six children born between 1887 and 1895, proving his great virility under the influence of cocaine. He also managed to publish his work *On Aphasia: A Critical Study* (1891). This treatise was on the language disorder caused by damage in a specific area of the brain that controls language expression and comprehension. In addition, he introduced the term "agnosia," a rare disorder characterized by an inability to recognize and identify objects or persons. He created the term while working on children with cerebral palsy. Furthermore, he with now-pal Breuer managed to publish a 13-page *Preliminary Report On The Psychical Mechanism of Hysterical Phenomena; Preliminary Communication from Studies on Hysteria* in 1893, which they followed by their Studies on Hysteria in 1895.

Freud's cocaine use, begun in 1884, had by that time flowered into full bloom, a regular habit, disregarding that his advocacy of it had in 1891 led to his pal Fleischl von Marxow's mortal addiction and death, which had tarnished his own reputation among his peers. Whether or not interpreting his cocaine habit to signal a lack of prudence as a researcher and scientist influencing his credibility and his lack of control over himself is neither here nor there, as it depends on one's own perception of reality, life and living. Therefore, some might interpret it as the source of immensely valuable inspiration resulting in his bold solutions to relieve human suffering, whereas others might find it led to his incessant and scientifically improvable hallucinations and imaginations about the human psyche. Pick and choose, eh as none of it can be scientifically proven?

Be it as it may, his contemporaries and the simple folk like you and me for decades after "Über Coca" were led to believe that coca leaves and cocaine use in moderation promoted a good and healthy joyful life. In the Americas of the New World, "moderation" meant about three to four ounces of oral ingestion per day. This had been documented by the great old age reached by the South American *coqueros*, those people who chewed leaves. Europeans in the 1860s were not chewing non-addictive coca leaves. They were consuming the stuff extracted from them, the alkaloid, the white powdery stuff, the cocaine. Its side-effects, when used moderately or immoderately, were beginning to be noticed by scientists. But that was kept secret when advertising it as health-enhancing to society as large. These side-effects, which Freud also must have experienced, included among others:

- Digestive problems, probably from the fact that the leaves were chewed; when cocaine is snorted chronically there are problems with nasal mucosa, while if smoked chronically it can lead to lung problems.
- Emaciation: cocaine is an anorectic, causing loss of appetite, and chronic use of coca instead of food eventually leads to starvation.
- Moral depravity: described as "a complete apathy toward anything not concerned with [coca]", which for whatever its worth is one of the DSM-IV criteria for cocaine addiction.
- Feelings of superiority to others; grandiosity

It took until 2021 for psychologist Elisabeth Hartney to broadcast these issues to the herd. She is professor at and director of the Centre for Health Leadership and Research at Royal Roads University, Victoria, BC, Canada.In her 2021 Very Well Mind article "Understanding the Feelings of a Cocaine High." she brought to the surface precisely what Freud and others of his peers participating in the science-of-psychiatry and -psychology creation had fervently ignored to publish for over 150 plus years. There can be little doubt that these characters knew about cocaine's effects on the human central nervous system the moment they engaged in regularly enjoying it. Unless completely devoid of self-observation, they also knew that cocaine use induced negative physical and psychological changes in their thinking, emotions and actions. They would have seen and felt it inspire and encourage impulsive behavior and the desire for risqué and aberrant sex. Thus, cocaine was exuding a detrimental influence on their lives, literally depriving them of all possibility to live purposeful, productive, morally and ethically upright and valuable lives.

Similarities among cocaine users experiences of the cocaine high and cocaine intoxication exists. However, its effects are said to differ for each individual. Freud also noted differing effects with other opioids when practicing on himself, stating: "Cocaine [bear] a great similarity to the symptoms of chronic alcoholism and morphine addiction." ("Über Coca" by Sigmund Freud; Posted on 05/28/2008 by scicurious). What seems to have escaped him, as puzzling as it might seem, is cocaine's similarity to morphine's addiction potential.

But that really didn't matter, either. The herd was fed the illusion that only morphine, alcohol and laudanum (morphine mixed in with alcohol) caused addiction. Cocaine was generally ranked with caffeine. Only very few of the general populace knew of cocaine's narcotic potency in line with opium and cannabis during the twentieth century.

It was this way even after Niemann isolated the alkaloid around 1855, with Baeyers following suit in 1860. Yes, the learned society knew how lethal it was to the human central nervous system. They had tested and seen its effects on various animals and on themselves. They had watched its extraordinary effects in vivo and knew its effects were not confined to the North American "savages", as they liked to call the indigenous population. It became very clear that Europeans also did feel something when using cocaine, and that what they felt precisely seemingly depended on what brand was taken and how much of it.

They quickly determined that it influenced the central nervous system and distorted human perception. They had reached that conclusion by observing its effects when severing various parts of the spinal cord in for all we know lunatics of the Narrenturm. During their research, they localized the area impacted by cocaine consumption to be the vital area of the medulla oblongata. This was the part of the brain Freud so vigorously studied for over six years at the Vienna University laboratory on the quasi-eel species.

Still, the learned science-of-psychiatry et al. general consensus maintained that cocaine in small doses was health-invigorating. It stimulated the mind and heightened the desire for and quality of sexual intercourse, although in too large doses it would produce convulsions, paralysis and death, at least in rabbits.

Russian Konstantinovich von Anrep (1852–1927) graduated from St. Petersburg University's medical academy in 1876. He was an army physician during the Russian-Turkish War of 1877–1878, and a student of alkaloids with professor of pharmacology and pharmacotherapy Michael Rossbach (1842–1894) at the University of Wurzburg. He wrote his 1880 publication "Über die physiologische Wirkung des Cocain, On the pharmacology of cocaine." This immensely detailed review of cocaine's effects on anything breathing was Freud's go-to source on side-effects, in addition to his observations of himself (Pflugers Archives ges. Physiology 1880; 12:38–77).

Von Anrep had systematically investigated cocaine's effects on different tissues in frogs and mammals. He had described cocaine's stimulating effects when administered systemically, its depressant effects and deaths, apparently caused by respiratory arrest, at high doses. He had also given cocaine to animals for up to 30 days in a row. He purportedly had not noted any effects on the animals' physical bodies whatsoever, never mind their brains, as he did not feel like dissecting them, it seems. Nor does he talk about their reactions when ceasing to feed them cocaine.

Why not, we might wonder? Well, think of it. Did cocaine present a brilliant path to Western humanity's destruction, so successfully carried out with opium on China from the mid-1800s onwards until its society's destruction by 1911/12? Would its liberal use among the herd allow the Work of Ages New World Order World Economic Forum to progress with ease to its completion in 2025 by way the COVID injections to a malleable population?

Before publishing "Über Coca" in 1884, Freud estimated to have taken cocaine about 12 times and claimed no real cravings for it after finishing his self-experimentation. A very slight man, 5'7" and 160 pounds, he had continued to take about 50 mg of it orally, whenever "feeling slightly out of sorts from fatigue." He describes:

- the numbing effect on his mouth
- his feelings of exhilaration and euphoria
- his "cooling eructations," meaning his farts and belches
- an increase in pulse rate
- short-lasting periods of great heat in his head
- dryness in the mouth
- dizziness

These toxic sensations grew weaker with repeated cocaine use, he writes.

As he cruised on in life, he inverted his own observations. He stated that cocaine's psychic effects such as exhilaration and lasting feeling of euphoria were no different than those of euphoria experienced by *healthy* folk. He had hitherto felt an increase in self-control, overall vigor and an increased capacity to work when taking cocaine. But he also switched to suddenly seeing it as simply normal and unrelated spurts of energy unrelated to the drug's use. He announced to all and sundry wanting to listen, that cocaine's psychic effects had nothing to do with brain stimulation. He claimed they were solely related to the disappearance of elements in one's general state of mind, which caused depression.

That he felt no need for neither sleep nor food did not strike him as odd, either. He wrote that he was able to eat, but found food unnecessary, and that he could sleep once the cocaine wore off. Many in his learned society throughout Europe and America experienced his experiences, as cocaine use had spread far and wide. One of its regular experiencers was Scottish toxicologist and physician Robert Christison, 1st Baronet, (1797–1882, president of the Royal College of Physicians of Edinburgh (1838–40) and president of the British Medical Association (1846–48). He bragged that, when under the influence, he liked to walk 15 miles in nine hours without getting tired, and only felt hungry the morning after. Its magic also continued to be tested on German soldiers. They were given quantities of cocaine when at the point of exhaustion, which would fire them up to brilliantly perform additional military maneuvers.

Freud also discovered that effects of an oral cocaine dose faded away very gradually. He needed a new dose as an antidote to his fatigue about every three hours. (The effects of cocaine when injected however, is only around 15-20 minutes, we hear). Not that he recognized or acknowledged his repetitive consumption as addiction, though. He did not report depression after the drug's effects had worn off, either, although cocaine's psychological withdrawal effects mostly occur in habitual users. As he never withdrew, he could never experience withdrawal symptoms, we surmise. Frequent cocaine use begins to cause permanent neurobiological changes when abstinence produces depression. This gives food for thought, but never to those in the psychiatric métier, it seems.

Mantegazza, the explorer, seems to have used much higher cocaine doses than Freud. He experienced violent urges to physically move, hyperthermia and hallucinations due to the brain's increased serotonin level. Serotonin, a chemical the body produces naturally, is needed for the nerve cells and brain to function properly. It is broadly and potently increased by cocaine consumption across many parts of the brain by blocking the reuptake of serotonin. Signs and symptoms of too much serotonin range from shivering and diarrhea to severe muscle rigidity, fever, seizures and death.

But Freud marched right on, broadening his own circle of cocaine aficionados to his to their hearts desires. He was neither the first nor the only one among his peers to propose cocaine use as a most marvelous therapeutic. They did just as the Europeans journeying in the New World had speedily tuned into coca leaf chewing's benefits during long journeys, mountain climbing and war.

Freud also deemed the powdery white substance to be a wonderful replacement for alcoholic beverages. He found it much more potent and less harmful than booze, although he neglected to inform his audience of its much higher addiction potential. He even suggested that cocaine should be taken in overlapping doses to at all times maintain its maximum effect. Rattus, by the scientific society considered equal to humans, by the way, when able to self-administer cocaine via intravenous injections will do just that - regularly titrate.

The self-declared master of this magic, Freud, in "Über Coca" also declared how well cocaine worked for digestion, in particular after he had stuffed himself to the limit with food. He also added cocaine to "salicylate of soda." This substance was prepared from sodium phenolate and carbon dioxide advertised as a preventative for stomach problems. He furthermore used cocaine to treat migraines and asthma, stomach problems, anaesthesia and recovery of wasting disease cases caused by cocaine use, as we heard earlier.

With Freud's feedback of "Über Coca", most doctors were swayed to believe that cocaine's major therapeutic value lay in the field of the burgeoning science of psychiatry. They saw cocaine as so much better as a nervous system depressant than the already-available laudanum, ether and morphine, because it had a multitude of stimulants they did not possess. Antonio Julian had already successfully used coca leaves to treat melancholy, inhibition and hypochondria in 1787. When Freud published 'Über Coca,' studies were already in train on the chronic effects of cocaine applied under the skin in depressed patients (Morselli and Buccola). However, those researchers observed only a slight improvement in mood, but beneficial effects on digestion.

Freud also wrote about cocaine's marvelous function as a powerful aphrodisiac noted by some of his patients. This was proven by him by fathering six children within seven years, of which he did not breath a word. But he also spread the news that cocaine could be successfully used to free folks from alcoholism and morphine addictions. This would be done by slowly replacing alcohol or morphine with cocaine, before discontinuing the latter, despite the death of Marxow as a consequence of this theory. His treatment of substituting one drug for another as addiction therapy, however, led to today's vigorous use by mental health professionals of all rank and files to prescribe a multitude of pharmaceuticals to anyone crossing their path, addicted or not addicted to anything.

So, it was his" Über Coca" paper that paved the way for drug substitution such as methadone maintenance for opiate addictions, and Adderall or Ritalin for cocaine addictions. When taking all of it together, slowly but surely, it led us to where we find ourselves today. The large majority of those over 60 years of age are on a multitude of mind-altering drugs. Sixty percent of those below that age also drug themselves into oblivion with their trusted physicians. Never mind so many people's compliance of the COVID-19 injections. God help us.

Merck led the zombification of humanity by incorporating morphine in its cough syrups and sleep remedies in 1850. With Freud's glorious introduction to the benefits of cocaine, that also went slowly but surely into the human medical and food chain, brainwashing us into the state of numbness and ill mental and physical health. To my knowledge, only J. V. Scheidt thus far proposed that Freud's "Über Coca" and his cocaine consumption played a basic tenet and role in Freud's development of psychoanalysis. He says that, until this very day, it has generally been completely underestimated (G Lebzeltern: *Sigmund Freud and cocaine*; Wien Klin Wochenschr 1983 Nov 11;95(21):765–9).

The question to answer now is: Why did this happen precisely in 1895, at a time that the foundations of psychoanalysis had already been laid? Applying the new method to treat nervous disorders heart complaints, train phobias, et cetera was obvious. During this self-analysis, first it became necessary to come to terms with the self-reproaches that lay on the mind's surface. Those were thus more accessible to, for example, Freud's consciousness-related analysis during his cocaine-fueled period following the death of his friend Fleischl-Marxow. Recall that he had introduced Fleischl-Marxow to cocaine to cure him from his morphine addiction, but he died due to it. Only when Freud had come to terms with this phase of his life, had the road to the deepest part of his mind, the discovery of the Oedipus complex in the fall of 1897, been cleared. At least, that is according to some of his peers, as unconsciousness may be perceived as entirely composed of, or at least as including, some ideas that originally were unconscious, but that could become conscious (Avinash De Sousa: *Freudian Theory and Consciousness: A Conceptual Analysis*; Mens Sana Monogr. 2011 Jan-Dec; 9(1): 210–217).

Freud took cocaine and began his dream interpretation approximately 10 years later. In Scheidt's opinion, this created a long, unconscious conflict within him related to the cocaine-induced states of euphoria. These suddenly erupted at the beginnings of his dream interpretations. Again, why otherwise would this have happened in 1895?

Scheidt speculates that during this self-analysis it became necessary for Freud to come to terms with the self-reproaches floating on the surface of his conscious mind, and thus more accessible to him. One of them was the huge role he played in his friend Fleischl-Marxow's cocaine and morphine addictions and consequent death. In Scheidt's opinion, it was only when Freud had come to terms with this event and phase of his life, that the road to unearth the deepest part in him, the idea of his Oedipus complex in the fall of 1897, hit him. By 1900, Freud had written what is deemed to be his most important book, *Die Traumdeutung* (The interpretation of Dreams). It contains all basic concepts of psychoanalytic theory and practice reflected in the erotic nature of his dreams, the "Oedipus complex," the libido and many others purportedly related to humans' subconscious mind.

Freud's observations were greeted with a storm of hostility and abuse from his peers, which has yet to die. Even so, the book survives in some folks' mind as one of the greatest works of medicine ever written. But that was of little consequence, as the Luciferic agenda marched on regardless. No one bothered much with it in Britain and the U.S. But by the early 1900s, both the U.S.'s and Britain's children were increasingly and progressively administered Ritalin and Adderall to addle their growing and vulnerable physical brain and their minds. They were knowingly, willfully and purposely made addicts to barbituric acid derivatives. With it, the nations' youths were destroyed almost from the moment of birth, creating their future historical health narrative.

The Great Wars, WWI and WWII, were planned by the Great Work of Ages Luciferic consciousness possessed organizers long before they officially began. It was done in combination with the science-of-psychiatry magicians with such characters as Breuer, Meynert, Charcot, Freud and others of his Khazarian league. They led the cavalry, and their followers were ready and eager to further assist in its project of human destruction. They supported brutality and slow, methodical mental erosion through slowly increased drugging, electro-shocks, lobotomies, moral and ethical perversion and whatever else they can think of. They practiced first on the shell-shocked PTSD-affected soldiers in their prime as unaware subjects. This was a refreshing change from the mentally, emotionally and physically depleted herd members they were used to. These had been interned in the newly built mammoth asylums installed with their super-sophisticated research laboratories. Those labs were where they had hitherto practiced their experimental craft in most gruesome ways. They considered them human debris, rarely ever mentioned by Horgan, Crews and their companions in the craft.

Freud, mind you, felt only a slight brush of karmic fate until 1938, when he moved to Britain. There, he spent the few remaining days of his life struggling with oral and jaw cancer, seemingly unwilling to admit that his nicotine, alcohol, morphine and cocaine habits had anything to do with his sufferings, never mind the law of cause and effect. He died in 1939, his ashes laid to rest at London's East Columbarium. He had achieved his heart's desire, world fame forever. Meanwhile, we go on experiencing the PTSD treatment those poor WWI soldiers received from his students and adherents to this very day. It is beyond their grasp, atheists almost without exception, that only entering the spiritual path can heal genuine PTSD.

36

THE PINNACLE OF HUMANITY'S ZOMBIE-ISM

The idea was to use drugs to lure what Khazarians consider as goyim into their own destruction and pay for it to boot. Beasts they were, all those not of their religious persuasion, the Hebrew faith twisted into the Ashkenazi Jewish Satan worshipping belief. The plan seems to have been put into gear in the 1850s with Merck's morphine-loaded cough syrup and sleeping remedies, without breathing a word about its addiction ramifications. By that time, however, clandestine operations and deception techniques were second nature to them. Shazar Everquar, *pen name of someone truthful alive in a world full of liars*, told us so in his 2016 article "Who Invented Identity Theft? Secret History of the Khazarian Assassins" (https://shazereverquar.wordpress.com).

Around 100 AD, the Kingdom of Khazaria, located in Ukraine between the Caucasus Mountains and the Black and Caspian seas, was a fiefdom ruled by a wicked king. He surrounded himself with oligarchs practicing bloodthirsty Babylonian black magick, witchcraft. So it was described in Joshua Free's 2011 book *The Maqlu Ritual Book* from "handbooks" recovered from the Library of Ashurbanipal in Nineveh and from the city of Sippar, both centers of Mesopotamian learning (Joshua Free: *The Maqlu Ritual Book*; CreateSpace Independent Publishing Platform 2011.

Henceforth, the Khazarians spread diligently throughout the surrounding countries, and then across the world throughout over generations. They slowly but surely became known as child traffickers, rapists, kidnappers, bandits, thieves and murderers. But their pièce de résistance was their expertise in demonic theft, not of the waylaid and murdered, but of their identity. With time, they perfected it to a fine art, turning it into their standard operating procedure for humans and businesses alike. For instance, look at Blackrock today, multiple interlocking shell corporations all principally owned by them. Or consider the Mental health industry enterprise in form of the science-of-psychiatry and -psychology taking foothold in the late 1800s, the most perfect and brilliant ideal invention for *en masse* theft of herd members' identities. But I am getting ahead of myself.

By the mid–700s AD, Khazaria's neighbours, especially Russia, had had enough of the unspeakable violations committed against their populations. On behest of the Russian Czar, an envoy was sent to Khazaria's Kagan, its king. He brought a notice demanding that he leave Babylonic Magick practices and decree either Islam, Christianity or Judaism as state religion and educate his subjects of all ages in that faith. The king chose Judaism and promised to stay within the requirements laid out by the surrounding nations (Arthur Koestler: *The 13th Tribe*). Roughly 1,200 years later, his followers, financed by immensely wealthy Khazarians based in New York City launched Russia's 1917 Bolshevik Revolution and the brutal Communist regime by murdering the Russian Czar and his family. This was in retaliation for his ancestors' attempt to spiritually reform them into God-abiding people. Within less than 40 years, they managed to slaughter at least 100 million Russians until Georgian born Ioseb Besarionis dze Jughashvili (1878–1953) (known to us as Joseph Vissarionovich Stalin) died in 1953.

In true Khazarian fashion, none of the leading Bolsheviks, all Khazarian Ashkenazi Jews, used their birth names. So:

Vladimir Ilyich Ulyanov became Lenin after the Lena River.

Vyacheslav Skryabin became Molotov, the "Hammer".

Josef Vissarionovich Dzughashvili, first known as "Koba," a Georgian Robin Hood-like figure, later became "Stalin", the "Man of Steel".

Thus, they shouted out to the population what was going to be done to them. All were brought under the Khazarian Khagans' practices of Babylonian black magick under its engineered collapse. That was led by Ukrainian-born Khazarian Mikhail Sergeyevich Gorbachev (1931–2022), who served as the Soviet Union's 8th and final leader from 1985 to the country's dissolution in 1991.

By then, the Khazarians' secret practices of Satanism had spread to all continents. This involved the sacrificial torture and killing of children, draining, drinking and harvesting their blood for adrenochrome and eating them. This in itself was a ritualized manifestation of their psychopathology (Identity Theft through Murder (N. Morgan: Who Sacrifices Children and Drinks Their Blood? Here Is Your Answer if You Can Take It; Dec. 2, 2022). By the mid-1850s, they added a more bloodless way to their sacrifices by the theft of our sui generis, our unique natural individual Self. They did this through clandestinely or not so clandestinely perpetual pharmaceutical drugging and poisoning by water, air, electro magnetic frequency influences, textiles and foods. All this is described by the American naturopathic practitioner and author of alternative medicine books Dr. Robert Oldham Young (1952) in December 2022 (Dial Up a Pandemic with Dr. Robert Young; December 1, 2022). Chief of Satan's angels?

We find a tame and bloodless description of Secret Satanism in the movie "Eyes Wide Shut." Five days after the film had been screened for studio executives, its director - Stanley Kubrick - "died.," The film had its identity stolen by its Khazarian studio owners by cutting 24 minutes we know of. Know then that all Khazarian occult ceremonies were based on Baal, a whole class of Phoenician and Canaanites divinities. They included Baal, the Hebrew word for "lord," and Moloch, tyrannical powers propitiated by human subservience to whom parents sacrificed their children.

Archeological excavations have dated information about Baal back as far as the second millennium BC, with Baal worship catching fire in Egypt in 1400 BC. But it could have existed long before that, when God established the law, including laws against eating pork, since pig slaughter and sacrifice were a hallmark of Baal worship. Baal worship is said to have penetrated Jewish religious life during the period of the Judges (Judges 3:7) around 1150-1025 BC, becoming common in Israel during the rule of King Ahab between 874-c. 853 BC, who built an altar and temple specifically for Baal in the Israelite capital city Samaria (1 Kings 16:31-32), there to with his subjects sacrifice their children and engage in the same practices of nations the LORD—EL—had driven out before these Israelites took over the region (2 Chronicles 28:1-2).

Listed among the chief of Satan's angels, Baal is mentioned about 90 times in the Hebrew Bible in reference to various other gods, with the priests of the Canaanite Baal appearing numerous times, most prominently in the First Book of Kings, where he is described as the god of fertility of all on earth (https://biblegateway.com).

To mislead the nations monitoring Khazaria after its official conversion to Judaism in the 700s,its king incorporated black magick and satanic practices by aligning them with the Babylonian Talmud compiled during the third to sixth centuries. Thus, Satanism continued to be Khazaria's national religion, and the murderous campaigns of slaughter, capture and mayhem inflicted upon neighbouring nations and henceforth carried throughout the world continues to this very day.

But to cut this short, is mentioned widely in the Old Testament as the primary pagan idol of the Phoenicians, often associated with the heathen goddess Ashtaroth. Baal is a demon ranked as the first and principal king in Hell ruling over the East. According to some authors, Baal is a Duke of Hell, with 66 legions of demons under his command. His name is used for various gods, including Haddad, who were patrons of cities in the Levant and Asia Minor, cognate to Akkadian Blue. Sometimes, Baal referred to all of the land's idols, indicated by its plural of "Baalism", or Baals (Judges 2:11, 10:10). Many variations existed, such as the sun god, the god of fertility and Beelzebub, the "lord of flies".

Nevertheless, few if any Biblical uses of "Baal" refer to Haddad, the lord over the assembly of gods on the holy mount of heaven. Rather, they refer to any number of local spirit-deities worshipped as cult images, each called Baal and regarded in the Hebrew Bible in that context as a "false god".

When around 1200 AD Khazarian 's surrounding nations had again reached the breaking point with its shenanigans, Russia invaded it to bring its leadership and their extensive spy network down. However, forewarned, they escaped westward, dragging their plundered gold and silver with them to settle throughout Poland, the Baltics and in particular the German states. There, they continued their craft of identity theft, treachery and murder, "by Way of Deception Thou Shalt Do War among peaceful people" their leitmotiv. They regrouped and assumed new identities using German words and combinations thereof as their last names, forming such creations as Neuland, Freiland, Zuckerberg, Silberstein, Rothstein, Epstein, Liebermann, Bronfman, Goldfarb, Himmelfarb, Engels, Stern, Rosenblum, Rosenblatt, Apfelbaum, Kirschbaum, Goldschmidt, Rockenfelder, Nobel, Flexner, Krauthammer, Freud, Wassermann and Wolfowitz carrying anglicising them as needed. In Scandinavia, the Baltic and Slavic countries they mostly changed to the native names, the Christensens, son of Christian, and the Robinows, the son of Robin and the like, thus for the unawares smoothly sliding into existing societies.

As they emigrated across the great pond, they merely anglicised their names. Wherever they went, they established their own enclaves in their synagogues and shuuls, shunning all not of their Ashkenazi Jewish creed. They proclaimed themselves God's Chosen People, but without specifying that their God Almighty was and is indeed Satan. Ba'al, Lucifer, Moloch, Beelzebub and Remphan are a few of the Devil's many names described in British poet's John Milton's (1608–1674) *Paradise Lost*. In that 1667 work, he addressed Adam and Eve's temptation by the fallen angel Satan and their consequent expulsion by God from the Garden of Eden. He describes the fallen angels' collecting around Satan, stating that, although their heavenly names had been "blotted out and ras'd", they would at leisure acquire new ones and go on "wandring ore the Earth" as false gods until the return of their messiah.

Beelzebub (or Beelzebul) are identified by New Testament writers as Satan, prince and king of the demons. Baalim and *Ashtaroth* are given as collective names of male and female demons respectively They came from between the "bordering flood of old Euphrates" and "the Brook that parts Egypt from Syrian ground." These demons were called forth by Elisabeth I's scryer John Dee, perhaps, to put the British Empire in motion. The Khazarians spread their Babylonian black magick Satanic practises throughout the lands they began to clandestinely inhabit at the highest leadership levels. These practices include their brutal sacrifices of infants, babies, children and adults to Baal, aka Moloch. They did so in the belief that he would deliver dominion over the whole world and everything on and in it to them. All they had to do was continue to torture, drain and drink the blood of their victims and eat their hearts and flesh, to continue their spirit cooking sessions in his honour and steal identities through their creation of mayhem and murder.

They created the Vatican as the religious centre, the one-mile-square City of London as its financial centre and the District of Washington, DC, as its military domain. These three independent jurisdictions are independent of any earthly authority. In Britain, they used their vast fortunes to transform the world's monetary system based on the Babylonian black magick system. They create money out of nothing and charge the herd interest on it. They issue paper certificates for customers' gold and silver deposits, which when travelers did not return those certificates fell into their own hands. They began to practice this kind of trade after infiltrating Germany in the 1400s. They used a group of Khazarian agents to carry out their murderous evil, led by the Bauers, the Planters, the tillers of the soil, who had settled in Frankfurt am Main close to Khazarians' continental European head domicile of Anvers, Belgium.

Once their business found track, they hang a red shingle above their door representing the infant blood sacrifices they offered their Babylonian gods and demons, before Father Bauer in the mid 1700's send out his 5 sons throughout European capitols to establish branches and infiltrate royalty. During the Napoleonic Wars, they changed their name to "Rothschild," and during the Battle of Waterloo disseminated the report of Napoleon winning, which send the stock market wild in favour of the Rothchild able through it by fraud and deception steal the wealth of those who had made investments with the City of London's banking institutions, most also Khazarian owned.

Soon thereafter they launched the private fiat banking system. This counterfeit paper money had no intrinsic value, thriving to this day. Wit numbers typed into a computer and charging interest on it. Or wit crypto-currency exchange and crypto hedge fund FTX Trading Ltd. Since November 2022, it has been in bankruptcy proceedings, going up in smoke and leaving over one million investors high and dry. Its CEO? The Khazarian Mafiosi Sam Bankman-Fried, the fried banker, just as his contemporary Jeffrey Epstein, Little St. James Island's pedophile and Lolita Express owner was adhering to Khazarian mafia black magick orders.

They also vigorously interbred with European Royalty, interbred with each other in itself. Some researchers believe the Rothschilds stole European Royalties' original bloodline by their women's secret and illicit adulterous breeding with Khazarian men. Then they clandestinely furnished Khazarian replacements to the thrones. This breeding was perhaps alluded to in the Khazarian New York-born Stanley Kubrick's (1828-1999) movie *Eyes Wide Shut*. Did this movie openly reveal that participants in the orgies portrayed were indeed selective breeding programs to further the Babylonian black magick Luciferian agenda Khazarian Mafia-run goals?

And they did just that, in the 1600s murdering the British royals and substituting them with their own fakes. They marched on to do the same for the French royals beginning in the 1700s. Then they moved on to murder Austrian Archduke Ferdinand in 1914 to ignite WWI. In 1917, they assembled a Khazarian army known as the Bolsheviks and hijacked Russia, murdering its Czar and his family in cold blood, stealing all of Russia's gold, silver and art. Much of it was horded in the Bank of England. Over the following decades, they commenced to rape, torture and murder over 100 million Russian women, children and infants in such extreme ways as to defy description. Wit Russian soldiers' crucifixions by Khazarian forces in Ukraine today. Watch the movie *The Checkist* for further information.

That done, they went on to get rid of the Austrian, German and Chinese royals and disempower the Japanese Emperor. In 1933, they put the Khazarian Rothschild offspring Adolph Hitler and the Nazis in power, which in comparison to the Bolsheviks, looked like choirboys.

In the U.S., they executed presidents' McKinley, Lincoln and JFK, who dared to resist their Babylonian money magick system. IN their place, they installed their human network of useful non-Khazarian idiots as part of the endgame. As narcotic and human trafficking is one of their favourite ways of human destruction, they financed the Turkish opium importation into China. That infected millions of its citizens with opium addiction, which not only brought China to its knees, but also landed its gold and silver in Rothschild's British coffers big time. When China's Empress went to war twice to stop the Khazarian drug importation, in the Boxer Rebellion and the Opium Wars, Khazarian-owned newspapers and textbooks already then controlling the media portrayed the Chinese as "Red Chinese", essentially criminals. They replicated their operation in the U.S. since the early 1900s by way of the populace's pharmaceutical drugging and Fentanyl importation, financed by the Rockefellers and Carnegies and launched by the Flexner brothers in 1910.

Should we be in doubt, know that it actually was the Rothschilds who funded the American Colonies and incorporated the Hudson Bay Company. This was for two purpose: to exploit North America's vast natural resources and to systematically make Turtle Island's indigenous people extinction with the same genocidal means they had followed since Columbus' so-called "discovery" of the New World, a lie in itself.

Furthermore, when commandeering the English banking system in the early 1800s, they financed the kidnapping and transportation of the downtrodden Irish folks to the Caribbean. There, they were used as plantation slaves, reveals the American scholar Michael Hoffman II in his book *They Were White and They Were Slaves: The Untold History of the Enslavement of Whites in Early America* (Independent History; 4th edition (January 1, 1993). Mind you, evidence of slavery can be traced back 11,000 years ago due to the conditions created by the invention of agriculture beginning about 12,000 years ago when farming appeared in the Near East. In other words, slavery into the Americas, commencing in 1619 with 20 odd Africans probably off a Portuguese slave ship that arrived in Jamestown, Virginia, and traded for provision and classified as indentured servants in 1619, never mind child and adult trafficking, began in the Middle East. Vigorously practiced by the Romans since the foundation of its Republic in 509 BC, with Gaius Julius Caesar and others of his ilk before and after him enslaving millions of Europeans ongoing even during Renaissance time. And let's not forget that Moses and his people were slaves in Egypt at least 3,000 years ago. But all this is rarely known or mentioned to the laity by 2022 drugged into oblivion, COVID 19 infested out of humanity gene pool destroyed hoi polloi.

According to Shazer Everquar, the television series *Roots* was nothing other than another expertly done Khazarian cover-up of slavery's true history. It was designed solely to change the focus from such white slavery throughout millennia existing in Europe and England and transfer it to African slavery equally as ancient. This was another manifestation of their expert identity theft (*The Jewish Roots of Roots*, 2018).

By 1913, U.S. Khazarians installed in America during the 1850s had enough power to bribe U.S. Congress members into passing the private *Federal Reserve Act* on Christmas eve without a quorum. President Woodrow Wilson signed it into law, financially hamstringing the population henceforth. They cruised right on to create the privately owned Internal Revenue Service, a collection agency incorporated in Puerto Rico. And they created the Federal Bureau of Investigation, the FBI, solely established to threaten and target those threatening Khazarian dominance. It exists without official charter, and therefore has no right to exist according to the Library of Congress. But tell that to Khazarian stooge Steve Bannon of *War Room* fame, eh?

That the Khazarian Mafia (KM) openly worships Satan is evidenced by the 2016 Washington DC Comet Ping Pong scandal. Comet Ping Pong scandal is a pizzeria founded in 2006 by the Rothschild James Alefantis and frequented by most illustre personages of U.S. political leaders and personalities. You can further research yourself at the *Guantanamo Bat Detention Camp: Global Elite Taken to GITMO by U.S. Special Forces* published on *Before Its' News* in December 2022. They detest all who conduct their lives under the authority and guidance of the Divine Creator commonly known as God, Allah and Yahweh. They spell it out in their Babylonian Talmud, stating that the "Extermination of the Christians is a necessary sacrifice." And they say it again in the Jewish Kabbalah, proclaiming: "Even the best of the goyim should be killed."

But they had led into those human exploitations by the turn of the nineteenth century. By stealth and deception, they had already gained control over all medical professions by founding their specified medical associations. It began with the American Medical Association (AMA) in 1847. It branched out from there by splintering their professions into a multitude of specializations. Darwin's proposed idea of human equals animals equaling machine with interchangeable parts gained speed. God being dead became a prominent concept in the learned society. Then the Khazarians, with Flexner arranging the operation within a few years, took over medical schools, hospitals, public schools, banking, Wall Street, U.S. Congress and Senate, the major mass media and pretty much all of the country's wealth and economic means. But first and foremost, over the past 170 years, they deeply concentrated on taking control of our minds and through it our perception by all means they could think off to achieve their psychopathic compulsion for humanity's destruction.

They had already taken over all known human secret societies. They had established the Jesuit order and infiltrated the Roman Catholic Church hierarchy. Wit, when Jews were expelled from Spain by Ferdinand and Isabella in 1493. And recall how it sent its emissaries to China during the Manchu regime. And it installed the white, black and grey popes. All this you can research yourself.

For their final onslaught on humanity, the complete take-over of the human mind, they invented the science of psychiatry and psychology to be populated by Khazarian physicians. This was an ideal tool to carry out the Babylonian black magick Talmudism, also known as Luciferianism, and the Kabbalah aim of humans' complete destruction. They joined it tight with their pharmaceutical conglomerates, whose morphine and cocaine productions had run full speed since the 1860s. Thus, they were able to financially sponsor their European Khazarian physicians to decipher the human psyche and its vulnerabilities.

They began this operation with Vienna's medical society. Ebing-Krafft and Freud, et al kicked it off, using their city's high society for their research. They also used those men, women and children incarcerated in its lunatic asylums and sanatoriums, as well as the children in its orphanages. They followed it up with the previously-healthy-in-body-and-mind WWI and WWII shell-shocked soldiers for their experiments. All the while, they used their discoveries on the human psyche to systematically destroy us. These physicians, the doctors you were taught to trust, did all this research on our bodies and souls whilst liberally financially supported and liberally regularly provided with massive amounts of morphine and cocaine delivered free of charge until taken their last breath.

So well did this Khazarian enterprise of human emotional explorations unfold, that by the 1920s, everyone associated with the Tavistock Institute, to be discussed in *Fallacy 3*, had been introduced to these opioids. Merck cocaine in particular found favor as the most superior powder of all powders, according to The Rolling Stones' guitarist and songwriter Keith Richard. He wrote in his autobiography Life that the group for its 1975 tour specifically ... "initiated the building of hideaways behind the speakers on the stage so that we could have [cocaine] *lines* between songs." "Merck cocaine" was in Richards' opinion pure luxury compared to ordinary street powder sold to the poor schmucks buying on the herds' markets.

Physician Steven B. Karch was educated at Tulane University, followed by training in neuropathology at the Royal London Hospital and in cardiac pathology at Stanford University. He confirms Richard's cocaine evaluation, in his 2005 book *A Brief History of Cocaine*. He wrote that the name "Merck Cocaine" stuck in folks' awareness due to its high quality since its production began in mid-1860s (Karch: *A Brief History of Cocaine;* Routledge 2005). In 1891, Merck & Co, New York, opened in the United States. By that time, it had both morphine and cocaine in its seemingly benign health remedies to drug the herd like a frog in a boiling kettle.

Thanks to the learned society of physicians' valuable assistance and the science-of-psychiatry and -psychology métier's vigorous advertisements, cocaine use in America grew in leaps and bounds. It was brought to market as a digestive and mood enhancer. It was hailed as a cure-all for aches and pains and ails and anything in between that one can dream of that could possibly befall human beasts. They emphasized the drug's benignity at every turn. It was in libation coca wine, *Vin Mariani*, concocted from Bordeaux wine and coca leaves. The ethanol in the wine acted as a solvent, able to extract the cocaine from the leaves and containing 6 mg of cocaine per fluid ounce of wine (211.2 mg/L), and since the 1860s dominated the market. Massively advertised by the French chemist Angelo Mariani, claiming it restored overall health, strength, energy and sexual vitality, and supported by Europe's high society, it gained a massive following.

Jesuit-educated, Italian-born Pope Leo XIII (1810-1903) was remembered best for his belief that pastoral activity in the socio-political field was the church's vital mission and avenue for social justice. Yet, even he took part in its advertisement, by bestowing a special medal on its creator.

Britain's Queen Victoria, U.S. presidents Ulysses Grant and William McKinley, and inventor Thomas Edison also were supportive of it. However, they were less demonstrative in their praises, of either the Vin or their liberal Merck cocaine consumption. Famous literary notables of the day Alexandre Dumas, Émile Zola and Jules Verne, mind you, did not hold back at all. They loudly proclaimed how invigorating for their creative juices they found cocaine use and the Vin's consumption. For its U.S. exports, the producer added 1.2 mg cocaine per ounce (253.4 mg/L) to compete with the country's higher cocaine-containing drinks of similar nature.

Merck used the same formula for its cocaine products' advertisements that it had used to popularize morphine. First, they advertised it as the ideal energy booster and treatment for sinus problems. Then they presented it in tonics, medications, aphrodisiacs, beverages and "health products." Then they got their products into all American corner store pharmacies (recovery.org). And then Coca Cola hit the market, concocted by Georgian physician John Stith Pemberton (1831–1888). He had earned his medical degree at age nineteen from the Reform Medical College of Georgia in Macon. He had practiced medicine and surgery in Columbus, Georgia, and fought for the South in the Civil War rising to the rank of lieutenant colonel.

Establishing his own laboratory, the Pemberton Chemical Co., after the war, he began to invent and sell cocaine- and morphine-containing patent medicines and products, "Pemberton's French Wine Coca", made of wine and coca extract, was among them. He prescribed it as a cure for nervous disorders, headaches, erections, colds, emotional misery and whatever else he could think of until the city of Atlanta's rulers forbade alcohol sales in 1885. It was then that he changed the recipe, mixing the coca syrup with kola nuts, rich in caffeine, added sugar instead of wine, spruced it up with carbonated water – and voila! He advertised his new drink as a brain tonic, an ideal temperance drink and a cure for morphine addiction, indigestion, nerve disorders, headaches and impotence. It was to be consumed regularly as medicine, all of its 6.5 US fl oz (190 mL) per bottle, which contained 9 mg of cocaine.

Pemberton did a booming business, until the Khazarians stepped in, that is, upon his death in 1888. It is then that the Khazarian Asa Griggs Candler (1851–1929) acquired the Coca-Cola recipe for a pittance of $238.98 from Pemberton's son Charley. When Charley died at age 40 in 1894, Candler took complete control of the company. Fifty years later, still under Candler's control, Coca-Cola had not only achieved status as a U.S. national icon, but also its kosher certification, derived from the Hebrew root *kashér*. This meant "to be pure, proper, or suitable for human consumption" in accordance with the Torah. This compilation of the first five books of the Hebrew Bible, the books of Genesis, Exodus, Leviticus, Numbers and Deuteronomy. So, when concocted with cocaine free coca leaves, it was clean (Cocaine History and Statistics; American Addiction Centers 2022; drug abuse.com).

Cocaine itself, however, was still available to all and sundry without any restrictions whatsoever. It was sold on its own, in other soft drinks, fortified wines, and in various medicines in every U.S. self-respecting drug store, until the U.S. government corporation based in Washington, DC, sought to restrict its distribution for its own financial gain. In 1914, it passed the *Harrison Narcotics Tax Act*, mandating cocaine and other narcotics be dispensed by physicians only. By 2022, cocaine ranked as the U.S. herd's second most popular recreational drug after cannabis, its citizens' proud to be the world's largest cocaine consumers. The state of Oregon furthermore claimed its status in existence by decriminalizing cocaine in 2020 to further facilitate the herd's COVID-19 debilitation.

How could this happen, we wonder? Easy! Since the 1860s, they kept secret the immense risks of addiction associated with cocaine and morphine consumption. They did the same with other opioid-containing drugs, Ritalin and Adderall included, although these risks were well known throughout the learned society of physicians and surgeons and the mental health cabal from their inception. After all, its members, with Freud et al. in the vanguard, knew of it from the moment its members began to experiment with it. Addiction indication include:

- Paranoia, irritability, restlessness, and aggression.
- Hypersensitivity to light, touch, and sounds.
- High blood pressure, collapsed veins, and fast or irregular heartbeat.
- Nosebleeds, as well as deviated septum, the thin wall separating the left and right nasal passages, displacing itself to one side
- Diseases and infections transmitted by shared or dirty needles (e.g. HIV and hepatitis).

These risks, although varying in severity in accordance with type and form of drugs taken, have always been present and always were well known to all who dealt with opioid research and production. Merck was just one of them. In 1917, it had to briefly interrupt its U.S. cocaine activities, when the corporation entered WWI with Congress passing the *Trading with the Enemy Act*, which led to Merck & Co.'s temporary expropriation by U.S. authority. By 1919, it returned to the mother ship, although as a quasi-separate entity. Meanwhile Parke-Davis had sprang into the breech and taken up the slack. The company was co-founded in 1868 by Khazarian businessmen Hervey Coke Parke (1827–1899) and George S. Davis and formally incorporated in Detroit, Michigan. Long before WWI, it had been the dominant cocaine producer and supplier in America and is still in operation today as a Pfizer subsidiary.

Merck's cocaine output was a mere 1.65kg, less than 4 American pounds in 1883. After Freud's 1884 Über Coca publication, it ballooned to 3179 pound in 1885 and by 1886 amounted to 83,343 kilo or 183,739.86 pounds. Some of it, together with generous financial remuneration, was regularly funnelled to Schlomo Freud to keep himself and his ever-growing family in style and live without gainful employment until death in gratitude for his generous cocaine and morphine advertisements reaching all layers of society, from the highest to the lowest. Thus, he lured them into opioid drug consumption, while keeping them completely oblivious to the lethal danger to their physical and mental health (*Journal Of The Royal Society of Medicine* Volume 92 August 1999).

The U.S. Federal Surgeon General also assisted in the matter. By 1887, it broadcast that cocaine indeed was non-addictive and superbly suitable to treat depression. With it, the gradual pollution and destruction of the herd's sperm and eggs quality began. With it, came the erosion of its off-springs' brainpower and physical and emotional health en route to human 2.0, a no-human, gene-destroyed, animal species, disconnected from our spiritual origin and solely serving the Cainian off-springs' Work of Ages destruction of humanity by the Chosen People, the Khazarians

(SGAnon Update 11.15.22 - Military is The Only Way ~ Juan O Juan O Savin Intel; https://rumble.com/v1uk1d0-sganon-update-11.15.22-military-is-the-only-way-juan-o-savin-intel.html).

Parke-Davis's chemists had developed a cocaine refinement system to hasten the program. It called for its partial refinement on site in South America, the resulting product to be shipped to the company's U.S. plants ,where the remaining refining took place. The new procedure made the cocaine industry much more profitable, as it stopped the leaves' potency loss previously experienced during shipment to the U.S. and Europe (David F Musto: America's First Cocaine Epidemic; *Wilson Quarterly* Volume: 13 Issue: 3 Dated: (Summer 1989) Pages: 59-64 1989). Legal imports of coca leaves averaged 1.5 million pounds annually at the turn of the twentieth century, the amount of cocaine consumed in the U.S. averaging 200,000 ounces, The resulting spread of addiction was regarded, however, as the curse of American middle and lower classes.

After the Harrison Act, all 48 States passed anti-cocaine statutes, tightly regulating cocaine's distribution and sales, with the exception of pharmaceuticals, of course. Long before that, however, the German Bayer Company had taken the "drug the herd" agenda a step further. In 1874 it discovered heroin, the hydrochloride of diacetylmorphine, which in pharmacological studies had proved to be much more effective for human drugging than morphine or codeine combined, in particular when injected intravenously. Bayer started its large-scale commercial heroine production in 1898, advertising it as a miracle drug, full well knowing that repeated heroin administration resulted in both rapid tolerance and addiction. The medical profession helped in the endeavour by willingly, knowingly and purposely prescribing heroin products to further humans' physical and emotional health erosion.

The perfected hypodermic syringe developed in the mid-1800s helped America's physicians to also liberally administer heroin intravenously. So, the nation's pharmaceutical industry moved into mass production of its lethal products whilst. Thus, with Rockefeller and Carnegy's money, the Khazarian Freuds, Henrotins and Flexners began in the early 1900s to systematically destroy all knowledge of human's self-healing abilities with remedies found in Mother Nature. William Stewart Halsted (1852–1922) was Johns Hopkins co-founding physician. Upon Freud's encouragement, he had embarked on self-experimentation with cocaine together with colleagues and students in 1884. He and Freud died within a few months. He had forcefully enrolled into Rhode Island's Butler Hospital for the Insane. Still, the Freud-spread lie of cocaine's, morphine's and heroine's non-addictiveness stayed undetected.

Halsted, like Freud and many others of their ilk, cherished his drug-addictions until death, with few complications in his professional life. Born of a wealthy New York family, educated at Yale and Columbia's medical schools with a two-year post-grad education at European clinics, he became one of New York's most successful surgeons. Just as with Freud, his powerful friends hid his narcotic addictions, his unexplained neglect of duties and his homosexuality from his students and the public in general alike (Clyde Barker: *Genius on the edge: The bizarre double life of Dr. William Stewart Halsted*; JCI 2010). And they still cover for each other, with 10% to 15%, of physicians addicted to drugs in 2016, compared to 8 to 10 % in the general population. However, that does not include pharmaceutical prescription drug consumption, and in the U.S. that alone skyrocketed to 194 billion daily doses in 2021. Add the COVID-19 frontal lobe immobilizing injection to it, and you have a herd in perpetual trauma, with eyes glazed over, numb, and thinking it is totally with it.

And this bonanza of narcotic drug availability was all engineered when U.S. federal government corporation officials passed the *Pure Food and Drug Act* in 1871. It inaugurated the labeling of all cocaine-containing products, with the exception of pharmaceutical drugs, which producers could stuff with whatever they wanted. This explains COVID-19 death-shots and how producers don't publish the ingredients of these shots. Of course, those ingredients include luciferase to gen-altering substances through mRNA, according to bio-tech analyst Karen Kingston's publication *Luciferase - Strange Embryos Growing Inside People's Bodies and More*. The 1871 Act, for-runner of the U.S. Food and Drug Administration (FDA), advertised by its advocates as protecting consumers from dangerous substances throughout the land. Thus, it prohibited interstate commerce of cocaine-adulterated or misbranded drugs and food. So, it in essence brilliantly achieved its objective: it lulled the herd into the imbecilic belief of being protected from all health dangers by members of their corporative government, unknowing of the Luciferic consciousness, the Khazarian Mafia, ruling it.

In 1883, they added to it with the U.S. Department of Agriculture, specifically designed to control the herd's food and its sources. Its Division of Chemistry was designed in particular for the sole purpose to research how to adulterate and misbrand foods and drugs overall. Less than a century later, they accepted GMO foods as healthy human nutrition, and permitted aborted human embryo parts and foetal tissue, such as kidneys to enhance food flavours, to be added to human food products, including Coca-Cola. It's called forced cannibalisation, but the herd doesn't mind, it seems.

The federal Harrison Narcotics Tax Act (Ch. 1, 38 Stat.785) in 1914 added to the herd's exploration by regulating the following:

> "An Act to provide for the registration of, with collectors of internal revenue, and to impose a special tax on all persons who produce, import, manufacture, compound, deal in, dispense, sell, distribute, or give away opium or coca leaves, their salts, derivatives, or preparations, and for other purposes."

It took its name from U.S. Representative Francis Burton Harrison (1873–1957), great-grandson of Thomas Fairfax, ninth Lord Fairfax of Cameron. He was an 1895 Yale graduate, Psi Upsilon fraternity and Skull and Bones member with a law degree from New York Law School in 1897. The Act guaranteed that U.S. physicians could without a qualm addict their patients to narcotic, mind-altering pharmaceutical drugs without telling them, albeit officially they were disallowed from continuing drugging, once patients had been addicted. Mind you, the latter was ignored, as I myself experienced with the Ativan prescriptions issued at an ever-increasing amount without a murmur or a question by my physicians, until I smelled the danger when the drug had almost killed me.

But U.S. Congress members took the idea of human traumatization and destruction a step further. On January 19, 1919, liberally using the number 666 signifying the Antichrist, the devil, Satan inverted, to ratify the 18th Amendment to the United States Constitution, another 6, banning all manufacture, sale and transport of "intoxicating liquors" throughout the nation. That this *National Prohibition Act*, informally called the Volstead Act, did neither define "intoxicating liquors" nor provide penalties for infractions did not bother anyone. That there were no funds for its enforcement and that no "appropriate legislation" existed did not bother the herd, either. In its severely impaired cocaine brainwashed thinking ability through WWI, it merely followed dictates, in turn enabling its Khazarian rulers to enrich themselves by selling their liqueur importations to them.

The inventive citizenry put moonshine stills and bathtub gin production in their dwellings and the countryside in motion. Meanwhile, the Khazarian Luciferic consciousness-possessed elite brought booze into North America, mostly from the Caribbean islands, and then stood by to see how the herd would react. By that time, Freud et al. engaged in research of the human psyche on those dwelling in their massive insane asylums, since the mid-1800s added to by WWI's shell-shocked. They knew that anything prohibited by what they had been taught to call "authorities" became more enticing, more desirable to most human souls. So three years later, the rulers took their human emotional and physical destruction scheme a step further. In 1922, they passed the Narcotic Drugs Import and Export Act. It forbade importation of cocaine and cocaine-containing products, opening the file to their smuggling for huge financial profits. Of course, the pharmaceutical drugs produced in the factories they already owned could continue to be imported for medical use, achieving the goal of human 1.0 homo sapiens' destruction.

The "Doctor knows Best" medical professions nurtured by Freud's nephew Bernays, most of them of Khazarian origin, played along joyously. They were mirrored by the multitude of them, these purportedly trained-in-human-health individuals. They took multiples of the COVID-19 shots, killing many of them in rapid succession. These zombification efforts through cocaine- and morphine-containing pharmaceutical, mind-altering drug distribution through physicians' prescriptions were aided by alcohol consumption prohibition. And they had been immensely successful, thanks to the elite-funded, women liberation organizations launched by the Rockefellers and other wives of the elite, sponsoring Freudian advertisement campaigns since the early 1920s.

The mental health cabal was burgeoning due to their brutal cocaine, heroin and morphine pharmaceutical drug research on the previously healthy in mind and body shell-shocked soldiers of all WWI participating nations. Never mind their own destruction because of their own use of the substances. They knew perfectly well how destructive these drugs were to humans' emotional and physical health. They published their discoveries in their medical society papers worldwide, sprouting them forth from their cocaine-band morphine-fuelled brains. In their state-of-the-art, experimental laboratories, they continue to ruin their now-called PTSD subjects' lives. As atheists, they keep looking for its physical source, when it is a spiritual calamity that can be healed only spiritually. And the herd trusts them!

Bernays's "Doctor knows Best" slogan did that trick. It brought America's medical professions, most of them Khazarians, the jackpot. It enabled the herds' domination with an iron fist, as the fear of ill health set in its bones, take the COVID-19 death-shot injections as confirmation. The brilliant Rockefeller-financed and Flexner brothers-implemented, top-to-bottom educational system aided in the success. At last count between 2020 and

May 2021, it had caused the lives of an estimated 80,000 to 180,000 healthcare workers with numbers based on the total reported death toll at that point of 3.45 million receiving the injection, probably an underestimate, as some deaths go unreported (who.int.com). By 2023, the prominence of take the kill shot and die soon thereafter of the sudden adult death syndrome (SADS) is ever-increasing. Mind you, Dr. Day did tell his audience in that 1968 conference where no one was allowed to take notes, that by 2025 only 25% of the U.S. population would be alive, albeit not uttering a word about Canada, as far as we know.

At present, 140 million U.S. COVID 19 injection receivers suffer detrimental-to-the-health side effects, their life expectancy hovering around five years. The injected population's cancer rate has also increased by 143,000%. And all of it is self-inflicted, because folks could not decipher the word "experimental". And you can pin that on the Rockefeller/Flexner-created lack of knowledge, generated through the drug-induced perception over the past 125 or so years, that humans are indeed animals and knowledge is to be solely focussed on sexual intercourse, trans-genderism, AI-human mixing and designer tube babies.

And what did Hosea say when purportedly thundering against the Israelites' unfaithfulness to God Almighty, not Baal? Hosea was the Old Testament prophet, ministering for around 70 years primarily to the northern kingdom of Israel in the eigth century BC. That was during the reigns of Kings Uzziah, Jotham, Ahaz, Hezekiah of Judah and Jeroboam II of Israel (Hosea 1:1) He called them to account for their idolatry and apostasy and foretelling judgment (https://gotquestions.org/Hosea-in-the-Bible.html)?

> "My people are destroyed for lack of knowledge: because thou hast rejected knowledge, I will also reject thee, that thou shalt be no priest to me: seeing thou hast forgotten the law of thy God, I will also forget thy children (Hosea 4:6)."

Knowledge or no knowledge, in itself depends on the beholder. Irish-born writer C.S. Lewis, as one of his main theses throughout life, maintained that there is a common knowledge of morality known throughout humanity, which he calls "natural law." Lewis claims that people all over the Earth know what this law means, and they also know intuitively when they break it without being taught. From this 1952 insight, he deduces that there must be someone or something behind such universal set of principles, in his work Mere Christianity stating:

> "These then are the two points that I wanted to make. First, that human beings, all over the earth, have this curious idea that they ought to behave in a certain way, and cannot really get rid of it. Secondly, that they do not in fact behave in that way. They know the Law of Nature; they break it. These two facts are the foundation of all clear thinking about ourselves and the universe we live in (Lewis, C. S. (1997) [1952]. *Mere Christianity*. London: Collins)."

Ten years earlier, Lewis had already detailed how Satan would manage to bring many souls to hell through fear in *Old Devil's Letter to the Young*. When after having been asked how Satan would succeed in his undertakings, he had Satan assure that spreading fear among us human beings would suffice. When asked for details, Satan said:

> "You know they [humans] believed the only thing they have to keep at any cost is their lives. They stopped hugging, greeting each other. They've moved away from each other. They gave up all social contacts and everything that was human! Later they ran out of money, lost their jobs, but that was their choice because they were afraid for their lives, that's why they quit their jobs without even having bread.
>
> "They believed blindly everything they heard and read in the papers. They gave up their freedom; they didn't leave their own homes literally anywhere. They stopped visiting family and friends. The world turned into such a concentration camp, without forcing them into captivity. They accepted everything! Just to live at least one more miserable day ... And so living, they died every day! And that's how it was very easy for me to take their miserable souls to hell ..." (David Mikkelson: *Did C.S. Lewis Write This Old Devil's Letter to the Young?* 2021).

You get the point? Via drugs, sex and rock 'n' roll, Satan's Khazarian Ashkenazi Mafiosi gradually corrupted the herd's moral, ethical and spiritual fibre. They arranged and used the Vietnam War as a jump-off point for the sexual revolution, produced and released pornography, bestiality, erotic media films, magazines and books. They released the first oral contraceptive birth control pill to get the wrecking ball of human 1.0 destruction rolling. They set a flood of inhibition-loosening narcotic drugs on the herd in the 1960s, after extensive research on the WWII genuine PTSD journeyers and science-of-psychiatry and -psychology students. And still they are forced to this day to try these drugs in line with their curricula.

By 1973, the herd was ready to applaud *Roe v. Wade*, making abortion-on-demand a constitutional right in the United States. People had no idea that foetus parts would instantaneously be part of their food chain or put up for sale. When overturned in 2022, an estimated 63 million embryos had been aborted, their parts sold or entered into the herd's food chain without its knowing (410 U.S. 113 (1973).

Homosexuality, hitherto through humans' existence deemed to be an abomination, 2 guys forcing their pricks into and up each others' arsehole to rub each others prostate up to 80 or so times a night by use of drugs in popular bathhouses found in cities worldwide, ask any self-respecting flight attendant who knows them all, as that's why they started flying, also made great strides. By 2022, they had received the status of celebrity, teachers in public schools applauding their presence at drag queen performances luring children into doubting their own sexuality and viewing sexual- and moral perversions as perfectly normal and adorable, school psychologists included. After all, did morphine-, cocaine, nicotine- and alcohol addicted Schlomo Freud not state, that it in fact were these innocent children that knowingly seduced adults in their presence to rape and sexually abuse them? He sure did. Do your own research and shed the blinds, eh?

All of this is, of course, related to the population being drugged without its knowledge. By 1984, the Medellin drug cartel alone in one of its Columbian operations syn¬thesized 20 tons of cocaine monthly for distribution in the U.S. (Drug Enforcement Administration History1980–1985). Seeing the need for the herds' increased drugging to assure its willing subjugation to the COVID 19 death shot, the U.S. Government figures of 1996 show a lowering of cocaine prices in the early 1980s by nearly 75%. The sum of one gram of pure cocaine fell at that time from US$587 to US$137, enticing many herd members to try it out and stick with it (Steven B Karch M.D.: Cocaine: history, use, abuse; JRSocMed1999;92:393-397).

The official explanation? A glut of cocaine had drowned the market. That coca plants can be grown anywhere marihuana grows was kept a secret. By then, U.S. president Nixon had ordered a War on Drugs in 1971 to battle this "public enemy number one." It had proven increasingly profitable for its black project by way of drug-control agencies and drug-treatments. Butt drugs continued to clandestinely be imported. Opioid manufacturing levels, however, dropped significantly from 2016 to 2017 according to the U.S. Drug Enforcement Agency, to force the consumption of drugs, and have remained relatively steady since 2017 (https://dea.gov/sites/default/files/2021-02/DIR-008-21%202020%20National%20Drug%20 Threat%20Assessment_WEB.pdf). We are also told that opioids sold to retail distributors have declined by roughly 15% each year since 2016.

Nevertheless, as late as in July 2019, drugs continued to liberally flow into the United States, with fentanyl in particular favored by consumers. That month. U.S. authorities seized almost 20 tons of cocaine from a J P Morgan-owned ship presenting. The estimated street value was *$1.3 billion*, according to the American online media company Business Insider, owned by German Khazarian publisher Axel Springer. But I got ahead of myself.

Cocaine's spectacular news and use certainly filtered through to Cattell and Wittmer. They conduct their research on children at the first "psychological clinic" in the United States at the University of Pennsylvania and Cornell University laboratories since 1896. They in 1907 followed it up with the first journal of clinical psychology and the first clinical hospital school. with chosen special education participants, with it laying the "nobody left behind" scam of the 1990s, in essence meaning no herd member unless specially selected to go ahead, either. As usual for all these Khazarian born and bred identity stealers of science-of-psychiatry individuals, little is known about Wittmer's or his teacher Cattell's life, other then that the latter was an introverted and private person.

In their Pennsylvania experimental research laboratory, they vigorously sought excuses to drug children. They tried to force them out of their natural instincts of explorations and rambunctiousness and their enthusiasm about life and living, without alerting their parents. That Socrates himself already some 2,400 years earlier had somewhat bitterly complained that young folk "love luxury, have bad manners, have contempt for authority, disrespect their elders, and love to chatter in places of exercise [of the brain]" they, both educated in the classics, thoroughly ignored (Armstrong: ADD: Does it really exist?")

Wittmer's idea to drug perfectly healthy vibrant children into submission might very well have dawned upon him during his studies in Germany. That is where children's most normal activities and innate attitudes had first been described in the children's book *Struwwelpeter: Merry Tales and Funny Pictures*, still today standard reading to any pre-school European child, me included. Published in 1845 by psychiatrist Heinrich Hoffmann (1809-1894), a physician at Frankfurt am Main's psychiatric hospital (in Rothschild territory), Hoffmann had created and illustrated this book for his three-year-old son as a Christmas present.

It is made of ten illustrated and rhymed stories about children. Each story clearly shows the disastrous moral consequences of misbehavior, and so teach a lesson. It was a fore-runner to Jordan Peterson's 2015 *12 Rules for Life for adults of all ages* (Howard Fischer: Dr. Heinrich

Hoffmann: Der Struwwelpeter; Hektoen International: A Journal of Medical Humanities). Written in rhyme, Hoffmann's 10 tales use fear to warn children of the possible consequences of their unbecoming actions and behaviors by showing their disastrous consequences in a cause-and-effect, clarifying way.

The book furthermore heightened herd awareness towards faulty parenting results. Although, folk of those days were perfectly aware of what the Jesuits, Wittmer, Catell, Freud, Lenin, Stalin, BF Skinner et al. had known since studying Aristotle:

> "Give me a child until he is 7 and I will show you the man."

So Wittmer set to the task in the 1890s, with his science-of-psychiatry, learned-society associates. He got to it in his newly opened experimental psychology laboratory at the University of Pennsylvania and at Cornell University and their associated clinics. There, he drugged children secured for their experiments to study their innate learning and behavioural attitudes and how with drug-concoctions best manipulate them out of their sui generis into drug addiction. By inventing the diagnostic term *hyperkinetic reaction of childhood*, they achieved their goal. Since 1894, Adderall and Ritalin have been prescribed for the natural, healthy, childhood condition of exuberance and *joie de vivre*.

In the British Isles, was renowned paediatrician George Frederic Still (1868–1941), only boy of eight children of a working-class family. He ran with the *hyperkinetic reaction of childhood* diagnosis. Despite abject poverty, Still had graduated from King's College London School of Medicine in 1893 on scholarships. Less then a decade later, he presented to the British Royal College of Physicians the problematic, unruly and impulsive behaviours among a group of children, his siblings, perhaps. He stated that genetic dysfunction was the cause and that all would be curable by mind-altering, cocaine- and morphine-containing, pharmaceutical drugs.

His audience took to his presentation like ducks to water. They eagerly began to prescribe pharmaceutical, mind-altering drugs to children of all ages in whatever concoctions crossed their paths. It was all under the soubriquet of being afflicted with an abnormal defect of moral control, thanks to Freud. That was precisely what the Luciferic consciousness-possessed, science-of-psychiatry cabal wanted to create in them—the children (verywellmind.com). Diagnosing children with behavioural problems, moral defects and consequent amphetamine had by 1937 become the rage. Their innate childhood enthusiasm, aptitudes and attitudes were deemed by the Khazarian medical profession to be, with parental consent due to the lack of knowledge, curable with cocaine and the like.

That no scientific proof validating defects of moral control in children existed did not matter to anyone, it seems. Repeating the lie about it over and over and over again made it truth. It turned the hyperkinetic reaction of childhood into a fact. Never mind that it was and is a myth, a fabricated story, a colossal deception, an illusion of an ailment to achieve humanity's zombie-ism and complete destruction since the 1890s through the herd's children. And through the gene-pool, the destruction of their offspring, without a murmur from parents henceforth (Dr. Jan Strydom &Susan du Plessis; *The Myth of ADHD and Other Learning Disabilities; Parenting without Ritalin*; Huntington House Publishers 2001 p. 33).

How so? By the tenth week of pregnancy, a foetus' gender is evident, and by week fourteen, sex organs have formed (Lexi Krock: *Fertility throughout life*; pbs.org). At twenty weeks, girls have a fully developed reproductive system replete with 6 to 7 million eggs, all she will ever have. A boy's reproductive systems, however, is largely unchanged between the fetal stage and infancy. It does not produce sperm until puberty, when a surge in testosterone triggers the production of an average of 200 million sperm each day. Sperm cells mature in the epididymis, a twenty-foot-long series of thin, tightly coiled tubes. Sperm takes from two to twelve days to pass through the epididymis to develop the ability to swim and fertilize. From start to finish, the production of a single sperm can take up to 72 days. Whereas girls' egg-quality is decided by the mother carrying her, the quality of sperm seems to largely depend on the quality of life led by the father during the 72 days before fertilization occurs.

In other words, a generational deterioration of humanity's brainpower, and with it its emotional and physical health, has in the U.S. and Britain been guaranteed since the mid-1890s, when the populations drugging commenced. Does that explain something about the 1st world mass acceptance of the experimental COVID-19 kill shot and slide without a murmur into the Khazarian Luciferic consciousness-generated, Great Work of Ages abyss? Its horsemen of this apocalypse knew since that time precisely that the drugs they dished out with parental tacit consent ruined their lives by creating poor self-worth, sensitivity towards criticism, heightened self-criticism and loss of inhibition. All of this facilitates sexual groomers' work to enter children into the to-them alien concept of moral deviations of sexual abuse and accept it as natural. That such abuse had in 1896 been described by Freud as lethal to their emotional and physical health, causing neurosis as grown-ups, had by then been swept under the carpet.

Their knowledge of erosion of their seed, the sperm and eggs their drug-polluted and emotionally rattled bodies would create in their drug polluted embryos was never mentioned, either. Nor was how it would create the nations' future mentioned by Krafft-Ebing in his 1886 book *Psychopathia Sexualis* and its consequent 11 editions, containing the observations of numerous European physicians of his time on heredity.

Few if any of the Khazarian human emotional health medical cabal since then bothered to mention, never mind write about that. But by 1980, American Psychiatric Association members in the DSM-III dropped the *hyperkinetic reaction of childhood* manifested by abnormal defect of moral control. They chose a more benign-sounding *Attention deficit hyperactivity disorder* (ADHD) and *Attention Deficit Disorder* (ADD). They also made it applicable to humans of all ages, the result of sperm and egg pollution, their strategy having born magnificent fruit barely 100 years later. With it, they had been successful by 2018 in diagnosing almost 10% of American children and 2.5% of its populations' adults, and putting them on mind-altering prescription drugs, all trusting "Doctor Knows Best."

The ADHD/ADD diagnosis for children worked magnificently well to drug them into oblivion without their knowledge. So, the science-of-psychiatry and -psychology magicians next laboured to hallucinate the post traumatic stress disorder (PTSD) diagnosis and its drug-fuelled brainwashing cognitive behavioural therapy (CBT) treatment into being. They learned from their experimentations on the WWI and WWII shell-shocked. They knew that none of their ideas of treatments worked, from cocaine- and morphine-loaded drugs to electroconvulsive therapy (ECT) to lobotomies to "adjust their mental disorders." But they did destroy the animus, the soul and spirit, of both these the brightest of the herd. Their souls left the body knowing the body would die and finding themselves on earth despite it all and the children ending in their clutches and drugged for their innate healthy childhood exuberance.

The industry knew all this. They also knew that children would grow out of it. And they knew that the shell-shocked, if allowed to soul-search in peace and quiet, would be a threat to the Work of Ages. This has been scheduled to be completed by Harari's World Economic Forum agenda in 2025, with only about 500 million human slaves left in earth. They would be able to see the Luciferic consciousness system corruption and machinations of human actors, which normal sheep would or could not see, too lazy or too destroyed to increasingly keep their eyes wide shut with every generation.

By 2022, the mental health industry's kit of PTSD and its treatment had been so successful in drugging herd-members of all ages for normally-to-be-expected life experiences, that it had spread like wildfire. It gave them the excuse to drug adults into oblivion without their knowledge just as they successfully drugged children. And the science-of-psychiatry and -psychology professionals made a mint with their destruction of human souls, leaving them jubilant with stellar reputations.

Not only that, when the COVID-19 pandemic rolled around in 2020, most of the heavily drugged herd without a murmur blindly and blissfully stumbled over the cliff to their emotional and physical demise by their proud acceptance of the experimental kill-shot. It was changing them from God-created homo-sapiens into non-human somethings owned by the corporations whose injections they accepted. In all, there were *5.44 billion of them worldwide by 2022*, about 70.9% of the world's population (Dr. David Martin et al, 2022). The herd's zombification was thus almost, but not quite, complete.

Meanwhile, the lethal PTSD treatments advocated by the National Center *for* PTSD, who employs massive numbers of human-mind-analysing physicians to invent them, continue. Inaugurated by the U.S. government in 1989 to address veterans' and other trauma survivors' PTSD issues through research and education, it received that mandate *without taking any responsibility for the care of its patients*. Its recommendations adhered to worldwide have by the 2020's resulted in at least A study released in 2022 found that as many as 44 veterans die on average per day from suicide when accounting overlooked causes of death that are aligned with suicidal and self-harm behavior, which is 2.4 times greater than the official estimate (Operation Deep Dive Summary of Interim Report (PDF) America's Warrior Partnership). Canada went a step further in its treatment ideas, offering anyone throughout its society wanting to die, PTSD-affected soldiers and veterans included, state-sponsored, assisted suicide, if suffering lack of food or shelter.

Thus, the undertaking of humans' best and brightest youth destruction through ADHD and PTSD diagnosis for financial rewards are eagerly accepted by school psychologists and military mental health personal. The American Psychiatric Association proudly and loudly proclaimed by 201, that ADHD is one of the most common *mental disorders* affecting children. Of course, it omitted that the mental health cabal made it so (Harpin et al., 2016). And how had they managed such colossal success? Remember, a disorder is a hypothesis, an idea, a figment of some science-of-psychiatry or -psychology imagination, as no distinct and measurable scientific evidence of neither ADHD nor PTSD can or has ever been produced. This, in essence, renders the entire *Diagnostic and Statistical Manual of Mental Disorders* (DSM) a fraud. Yet, it is used by psychiatrists and psychologists in the United States and much of the world as the authoritative guide to the diagnosis of mental dis-orders. A dis-ease, on the other hand, is a distinctly measurable, physical, human ailment manifested by a fever, such as Ebola or malaria or Zika or Lyme, or even influenza or Bell's palsy

But how were they able to throughout almost 130 years maintain such colossal success in destroying the human psyche and, by extension, our physical body almost from the moment of inception?

Freud made cocaine and morphine consumption fashionable throughout all layers of European society by praising its magickal effects on mind and body. He full well knew the opposite to be the truth. American physicians Cattell and Wittmer, European trained, followed up by bringing the science of psychiatry and its associated morphine and cocaine use into vogue in their home country. In 1894, they opened the Philadelphia laboratory of experimental psychology and their psychological clinic, and with them, they launched the use of unknown children from unknown local schools, unknown orphanages and unknown parents for unknown experiments with unknown drugs. They used the children to investigate, measure and document their emotional reactions and breaking points, And they shared their discoveries with their peers, all happily united through their numerous individual medical associations. Those began with Robert Boyle's 1660s "invisible college" of natural philosophers and physicians. From 1663, it was known as The Royal Society of London for Improving Natural Knowledge, and its motto was *Nullius* in verba taken to mean "take nobody's word for it". So, of course, it encourages the herd to do nothing else. Trust the science; trust your doctor.

In line with it, the German physician and psychiatrist Richard Freiherr von Krafft-Ebing (1840-1902) in 1886 published *Psychopathia Sexualis: eine Klinisch-Forensische Studie, Sexual Psychopathy: A Clinical-Forensic Study*, also known as *Psychopathia Sexualis, with Especial Reference to the Antipathetic Sexual Instinct: A Medico-forensic Study* with the last edition from the author 's hand (the twelfth) contained a total of 238 case histories of human sexual behaviour and aberrations from infancy onwards addressing bestiality, cunnilingus and fellatio, fetishism, incest, masochism, masturbation, nymphomania, sadism and homosexuality observed by himself and others of his league during the 1870's and 80's. He found that neurosis in women and men arose from their sexual abuse throughout childhood, although denying it when Freud asserted the same 10 years later.

Krafft-Ebing (1840–1902) was born in Manheim, Germany. He was the eldest of five children of a high magistrate of the Grand Duchy of Baden. He opened the floodgate to such sexual perversions as sadism, a term taken from the brutal sexual practices depicted by the moral, ethical and sexual principles of French libertine and writer Donatien Alphonse François, Marquis de Sade (1740–1814). And he introduced masochism, deriving sexual pleasure from having pain inflicted on oneself, a term he took from Austrian libertine and journalist Leopold von Sacher-Masoch (1836–1895). He also liberally introduced the concepts of homosexuality, bisexuality, necrophilia, and "anilingus" in his work. With Havelock Ellis and Magnus Hirschfield, he was one of the first to propose the notion of bisexuality as a physical or psychological condition, suggesting masculine and feminine aspects.

His journey into human sexual perversions began after the end of his medical studies at the universities of Prague, Heidelberg and Zurich. He then enrolled at Zurich's Burghölzli Psychiatric Hospital to specialize in psychiatry, but switched to the Illenau Asylum in the Duchy of Baden. He directed the electrotherapeutic clinic at Baden-Baden and lectured as professor of psychiatry at the universities of Strasbourg, Vienna and Graz, where he also functioned as director of the National Insane Asylum. He conducted research at his private sanatorium close to Graz on European high society's mentally disturbed or emotionally rattled. This included on the *sœur de l'impératrice, Sophie-Charlotte en Bavière, duchesse d'Alençon,* he conducted at his private sanatorium close to Graz (https://fr.wikipedia.org/wiki/Richard_von_Krafft-Ebing).

The mental institutions at which he worked functioned as prisons rather than hospitals. They all afforded him unfettered access to inmates and was free to dictate their treatment. They all suffered from a cadre of emotional disturbances, including those resulting in sexual crimes. Furthermore, physicians throughout Europe submitted their case-histories on humans' sexual perversions to him, as the knowledge of human sexual perversity and how the desire for it arose would later facilitate the seamless destruction of humanity's innate moral and ethical composition without the herd having a clue. He practiced in several psychiatric institutions. But he decided that their mode of operation did not allow him to understand the nature of the problems he was researching.

Krafft-Ebing's peers either denounced his work as an immoral apology for human perversion and deviance, or a service to mankind to understand itself. We know that adrenochrome has been around for millennia and is derived from infant and child sexual torture. So, our ears perk up when we read in chapter after chapter of perverse neurotic "hereditary tainted" child-subjects. Tainted by whom and what? Ritual sexual child abuse is usually practiced within family groups across many generations. It is also practiced within groups and institutions, who recruit children from orphanages and day-care centres for sexual abuse by paedophile rings. Or sometimes it occurs through connections between families and external groups, wit British Royalty child procurer James Wilson Vincent Savile (1926–2011).

The psychological impact of ritual sexual abuse on children is profound, with symptoms such as flashbacks, dissociation, amnesia and flight or fight reactions to circumstances reminding survivors of abusive experiences. All fall under the "neuroses" category (https://brissc.org.au/resources/ritual-abuse/). When Freud discovered this, he knew that if wanting worldwide fame and fortune he had to suppress his childhood sexual abuse observations. He achieved this by, with Krafft-Ebing and his peers' assistance, create his seduction theory holding children regardless of age responsible for their sexual abuse at the hands of adults. In the process he made a number of other observations concerning the human psyche by his peers portrayed as genuine, among them the reality of the unconscious, for example, which, according to Masson in 1984, cannot be properly used in any clinical atmosphere because:

> "Free and honest retrieval of painful memories cannot occur in the face of scepticism and fear of the truth. If the analyst is frightened of the real history of his own science, he will never be able to face the past of any of his patients." (Masson, 1984)

What neither he nor any other of his Khazarian learned society chums mention is that already during the first three centuries of our common era, rabbis who compiled Talmudic law had the following discourse:

> "Rabbi Joseph said: Come and hear! A maiden aged three years and one day may be acquired in marriage by coition [by sexual intercourse] (Florence Rush: The *Best Kept Secret; Sexual Abuse of Children*; McGrae-Hill 1981, p. 17)."

And where did he get the idea that fornicating with babies is wholesome and natural? Well, apparently a millennium before the Israelites wrote their Talmudic scripture, preceded by the Greeks with their *Iliad* and *Odyssey*, the Sumerians apparently faced the same ideology. But they vehemently disapproved of child marriage, declaring on one of their tablets:

> "I will not marry a wife who is only three years old as a donkey does (ibid p. 17)."

Moses Maimonides, the most sophisticated twelfth century AD physician, philosopher and Talmudist, did not take any issue with his ancient predecessors. His monumental work was *The Mishnah Torah*, an organization and clarification of Talmudic law. He composed it when the Khazarians readied themselves to spread out from the Ukraine area across the world at their neighbours' prompting. In it, he reaffirmed that a female child who was "three years and one day old could be betrothed by sexual intercourse" with paternal permission. By the twelfth century, age was certainly reckoned as it is today (ibid p.18). Furthermore, if a daughter was raped at age three years and one day, the Talmudic father could demand financial compensation and hire her out again and again for as often as he desired. If he wished not to give his daughter in marriage to the rapist, he broke no law and faced no punishment (ibid p. 22/23).

In other words, since Sumerian times of the Fallen Angels, girl children have held no intrinsic, incalculable, moral value in society. So, what happened in the 1980s when Masson tried to call attention to evidence suggesting Freud's seduction theory deserved serious reconsideration? His peers, the vast majority of them raised in the Khazarian's Ashkenazi faith, reacted first with antagonism. Then they cruised into his full-fledged ostracization, as they had done with Freud. And that is so very hard to take for men eager for fame and fortune. Ostracism, the temporary banishment without trial or special accusation and exclusion by general consent from common privileges and social acceptance, has been practiced since ancient Greek times.

So, Freud resolved this problem by inverting his *Aetiology of Hysteria* theory presented before his colleagues at Vienna's Society for Psychiatry and Neurology in 1896 using 18 of his patients of both genders who had been sexually abused by various caretakers as basis. Instead, he accused the children themselves of sexually seducing their caretakers, calling it "infantile sexuality". His patients sexual abuse experiences he now reverted into purely infantile fantasies, figments of fruitful imaginations of their feeble and distraught minds derived from their own individual delirious sexual impulses and imaginations. About the Talmudic law of fornication with three-year-and-one-day old girls and boys he never breathed a word.

Henceforth Freud's theories paved the way for the mental health profession to relate more or less all emotional upheavals experienced by adult humans to have sexual origins. Any genuine PTSD experiencers with them can attest to it.

The book *Psychopathia Sexualis*, or "Psychopathies of Sexuality" was written in 1844 by the Russian Czar's Viennese-born, Khazarian physician Heinrich Kaan (1816 -1893). It reinterpreted Christian sexual sins like homosexuality, masturbation and the like as diseases of the mind. Like Krafft-Ebing's 1886 *Psychopathia Sexualis* on human sexual perversions, it was also a predecessor of Freud et al. Hypotheses. But all steadfastly refused to acknowledge that they were. Both authors of these magnus opus on human sexual aptitudes and perversions, Kaan's from Cain not translated into English until 2016, did so without breathing a word about Sumeric and Talmudic law as origin of those perversion. Instead, they stood as the world's most informative publication on the topic for more than 100 years.

These works might have aided and abetted Freud's drugged brain in forming his ideas about humans' behavior in relation to sex in all its perversions and against childhood sexual abuse in particular. In the 1960s, Alfred Kinsey and Masters and Johnson used perversities presented in Krafft-Ebing's *Psychopathia Sexualis* by advertising them as perfectly normal human behavior. This was soon thereafter introduced into the Danish society in an effort by the Luciferic consciousness to research how the herd would take to these perversions. Showing photographs of your new-born daughters' and grand-daughters' vaginas, soon thereafter became a fashionable way to introduce her. This was followed by stallions fornicating with women on stage and *Jesus Christ Superstar* as pornographic theatrical performance. You ask me. You have no idea what Danes can change into pornography. I witnessed the performance and left before the first act was over.

To further assist in humanity's moral and ethical depravity and destruction through drugs and sexual perversions, was Khazarian Hugh Marston Hefner (1926-2017). He was a descendant of Mayflower emigrant and Plymouth Colony governor William Bradford (1590-1657). Since 1953, Hefner issued his sexually explicit Playboy magazine, filled with sexually explicit photographs, including sexual intercourse with animals with charges of obscenity unsuccessfully challenged in the U.S. judicial system.

Why is all of this important? Because these hypotheses of human perversions are imposed on us, genuine PTSD journeyers, when finding ourselves in the hands of those pretending to help us.

Psychiatrists have one of the highest suicide rates in the U.S. The number of doctor suicides in 2018 was 28 to 40 per 100,000, more than twice that of the general population of 12.3 per 100,000. This is even higher than that of military personnel. Knowing this could it lead us to surmise that it is their own warped psyche propelling them into dealing with emotionally and mentally injured people as a gainful occupation. Perhaps it is to find out about their own warped and perverted Self. Or it might be because they love to carry out their own sadistic and masochistic ideologies, documented by their treatments of those in their care. (American Psychiatric Association (APA) 2018 annual meeting).

We'll never know, as very few of them tell the truth - ever. Only their skyrocketing suicide rate indicates a guilty conscience somewhere, if we apply their own academic reasoning of the human psyche's machinations. Just the same, these creatures of the imaginary science-of-psychiatry and -psychology have yet to tell us, what they consider to be a typical child, never mind a genuine PTSD experiencer. Aleksandr Solzhenitsyn wrote about them in 200 Years Together, a history of the Khazarian Jews, Russia's archenemy for millennia under the Czars, the Soviet Union and modern Russia between 1795 and 1995. He pointed out that they were a threat to national security. Soon after the 1917 Revolution that they instigated, they victoriously surfaced mostly in the United States to dominate the science of psychiatry creation in the 1890s. The massive two-volume 200 Years Together book published in Moscow in 2001-2002 is planned in 2024 in an English.

As for early twentieth-century British child-psychiatrist Still, he did his part to lure humanity into tryouts of Krafft-Ebing's et al. documented sexual perversions in the early 1900. He began with great vigor and personal joy to drug perfectly healthy and vibrant British children with Ritalin and the like. Thus, he gave them lifelong drug addictions with loss of sexual inhibition and spread it throughout the British empire over which the sun never set.

Krafft-Ebing, by the way, made a great point in differentiating perversion, the action of perverting or humiliating someone or something, like perverting children from kindergarten and public schools onwards by presenting drag shows to them with which to lure them into the homosexual lifestyle, versus perversity, an innate aptitude towards being sexually *perverse*, meaning seeking deviant and abased sexual activities with non-consenting and consenting partners called paraphilias, the persistent and recurrent sexual interests, urges, fantasies and behaviors of marked intensity involving objects, activities, or even situations atypical to innately human normal behavior. These include pedophilia, adults' engagements in either homosexual or heterosexual activities with children, transvestic- and other types of fetishism, frotteurism, the touching or rubbing of genitals up against another person without their consent to derive sexual pleasure or orgasm, exhibitionism, voyeurism as well as masochism and sadism.

American chemist and pharmacologist Gordon Alles (1901-1963) was of unknown parental lineage. He was imbued with a BS (1922), MS (1924) and PhD (1926). all from the California Institute of Technology (Caltech). In 1928, he discovered the physiological properties of Benzedrine (amphetamine) and dextroamphetamine. He performed his experiments on animals and humans and unequivocally revealed the actions of ⊠-methylphenethylamine's, the original ecstasy. He learned that it both reversed drug-induced anaesthesia and produced sexual arousal and insomnia (see reviews by Bett, 1946; Guttmann and Sargent, 1937).

He hastened to patent his discovery, and in 1934 sold it to the pharmaceutical corporation Smith, Kline & French (SKF) Now called GlaxoSmithKline, it was founded in 1830 by Philadelphian John K. Smith. He earned massive royalties, as its amphetamine-containing products, Benzedrine pills and inhalers, Dexedrine pills and Dexamyl tablets, through Bernays' spectacular advertisements rose spectacularly. The amphetamine sulphate Profetamine also hit the market, when the U.S. Food and Drug Administration (FDA) notably advanced the herd's drugging into zombyism oblivion by approving Benzedrine as an over-the-counter (OTC) decongestant inhaler whilst full well knowing the detriment it posed to humans' emotional and physical health. Soon thereafter, Benzedrine sulphate was introduced in tablet form. Henceforth, it was prescribed by America's Doctor Knows Best physicians, most of them name-and identity stealers, for children they happily diagnosed as morally defective or hyperactive, as well as for adult patients they gladly diagnosed with experiencing:

- Narcolepsy
- Depression
- Chronic fatigue
- PTSD and other unspecified symptoms

Then they conceived to tout Benzedrine as a weight loss and depression remedy, which sent its popularity skyrocketing throughout all layers of society.

When WWII rolled around, high command of all military participants in this mercenary, satanic, slaughter-arranged melee handed out amphetamines to fighting troops like candy. The Americans and Brits preferred Benzedrine, whereas Germans and Japanese liked methamphetamine for their soldiers of all rank and file. These kept them awake to assure the slaughter of each other would proceed in adequate fashion. Amphetamine abuse quickly developed across the board of all nations, with participants using them nilly-willy for themselves or for trading with native populations. In 1937, the American Medical Association (AMA) gave amphetamines its seal of approval and SKF encouraging the use of its "Benzedrine Sulfate" with its splendid advertisements throughout the United States.

In the run-up to WWII, the herd was bombarded with magazine, newspaper, radio and TV ads for Benzedrine- and amphetamine-containing products. Songs were directed towards the desired drug-narrative as flies to a pile of shit. Even jewellery was used to inspire drugging the self, with for example a charm bracelet with a pill- box attached stating: "For 'Benzedrine' if you're having fun and going on forever; 'aspirin' if it's all a headache."

The war over in January 1946, and the amphetamine-addicted soldiers now at home, New York Khazarian Jew musician Harry Raab (1915–1991) released the song "Who Put the Benzedrine in Mrs. Murphy's Ovaltine?" It was about a woman using Ovaltine as a sleeping aid until someone slipped amphetamine sulphate, the old name for Benzedrine, into it. The song vocalized her amphetamine addiction and the drastic physical and psychological changes it did to her. Thus, the Luciferic consciousness-dominated told the American herd about the effects of amphetamine and Benzedrine, as cosmic law demands. But then they instructed their radio stations to not play Raab's song, to leave the public ignorant about the drugs' catastrophic side-effects.

Meanwhile, *Everybody's Digest* published an article in a September 1946 entitled "On a Bender With Benzedrine." The anonymous author told readers how to remove amphetamine from the base of amphetamine inhalers and use it orally, now that Uncle Sam no longer supplied it for free. Thus, the Khazarian mission of brainwashing Americans into believing amphetamine-products were benign miracle drugs good for humans' emotional and physical health as well as their waste-line had been achieved (Russell R. Monroe, M.D. Hyman J; Drell, M.D: "Oral Use Of Stimulants Obtained From Inhalers"; Jama 1947).

After all, the U.S. civilian population consumed around 30 million amphetamine tablets with 5 to 10 mg each per month in 1945. Some were with and some without physician prescriptions, hastening the world population's drug addiction (Nicolas Rasmussen, PhD, MPhil, MPH: America's First Amphetamine Epidemic 1929–1971: "A Quantitative and Qualitative Retrospective with Implications for the Present"; Am J Public Health 2008 June; 98(6): 974–985). Uncle Freud's New York-based friends still helped nephew Bernays' designs of the most catchy slogans for drug consumption, even though uncle had departed for the Netherworld in 1939. Their help resulted in such a Benzedrine and amphetamine consumption mania, that by 2020, Americans swallowed 90% of amphetamines in the world. Thus, the Khazarian project of "Making the American Mind" roared to success less than 130 years after its 1927 inception.

Lithuanian-born Khazarian Harvard University professor of clinical psychiatry Abraham Myerson (1881-1948) greatly helped reach this splendid result. In the late 1930s, he had already led the amphetamine-is-so-benevolent-to-human-health cavalry with some research on the human eye. He loudly proclaimed the results to his students, his fellow science-of-psychiatry magicians and whoever else wanted to listen to him. And he had an audience. He was, an active member of all professional organizations that were furthering the Khazarian Luciferic consciousness, Satanic Mafia agenda. This includes:

- the Greater Boston Medical Society
- the American Psychiatric Association
- the American Neurological Association
- the American Psychopathological Society
- the Mental Hygiene Society, where he was a director
- the Advisory Council for Research in nervous and mental disease for the U.S. Public Health Service

He proclaimed that amphetamines balanced and adjusted the human sympathetic and hormonal central nervous systems, simply by amplifying and even creating adrenergic stimulation. This, in turn, activated and promoted extra-versions of brain functions, in particular beneficial for folk suffering depressions. To this very day, this theory is still being tested on genuine PTSD experiencers, sending all of them into mind-numbing oblivion without their knowledge, or into suicide (Human autonomic pharmacology: IX. Effect of cholinergic and adrenergic drugs on the eye A Myerson, W Thau. Archives of Ophthalmology, 1937. jamanetwork.com).

The result? Sales of Benzedrine tablets, mainly of 10 mg, grew to about $500000 in 1941. This was over 4% of SKF's total sales (Nicolas Rasmussen, PhD, MPhil, MPH: America's First Amphetamine Epidemic 1929–1971: A Quantitative and Qualitative Retrospective With Implications for the Present; Am J Public Health. 2008 June; 98(6): 974–985).

Thus, by the time the U.S. entered World War II via a staged Pearl Harbor event, amphetamine in tablet form had found both huge commercial success and credibility as a psychiatric prescription medication. It was the first "antidepressant". Reports of its detrimental effects on human emotional health and addiction to it were graciously ignored. The war years added to the drug's growth in popularity, with SKF's civilian amphetamine tablet sales by 1945 quadrupling its profits to $2 million. This included $650,000 from the firm's new "Dexedrine" dextroamphetamine tablets, whilst ruining the nation's emotional health and its gene pool without its knowing.

And what of U.S. chemist and pharmacologist Gordon Alles. It was he who injected himself with 50 milligrams of amphetamine in 1929, first synthesized at the University of Berlin by the Khazarian Lazăr Edeleanu (1841-1961) in 1887. At that time, it was declared pharmaceutically valueless. Well, he continued to plough and facilitate humanity's path towards its planned 2025 destruction by creating evermore lethal mind-altering drugs with SKF's money. For instance, he incorporated amphetamine and mescaline into diet pills and cannabis into antidepressants. By the late 1950s, he was an honorary pharmacology professor at the University of California, Los Angeles, medical school. He also worked for the U.S. Army's chemical warfare division, developing hallucinogenic amphetamine derivative until the moment of his death in 1963. Without doubt, he joined his Khazarian, Satan-worshipping peers in the divine comedy territory at a time when American society's emotional and physical destruction had been quasi sealed. That the American populace had been kept completely unaware of it can be seen today by its USA-USA ra-ra-ra war cry at mass gatherings. This is testimony to its mindless ignorance of the trauma and hardship imposed by its government on the world. This has been going on since its 1776 inauguration, coinciding with Khazarian Johann Adam Weishaupt founding of the "Illuminati," and unaware of their Khazarian Mafia rulers. Trump and his Khazarian Mafia cohorts still lead the charge towards the cliff of their destruction.

Nicolas Rasmussen is (1962-), professor emeritus of the School of Humanities and Languages at the University of New-South Wales (1962-). He is also an expert in the history of amphetamines, drug abuse and clinical trials. In 2008 he revealed that the U.S. amphetamine epidemic sparked by Alles in 1929 and necessary to destroy the moral and ethical fibre of the nation reached its epidemic proportions only due to the country's Khazarian Mafia-ruled entities. These include government, the pharmaceutical industry, the medical professions (the science-of-psychiatry and mental health professionals in particular) and Bernays-controlled advertising agencies that created the epidemic. How thoroughly they orchestrated the herd's narrative and conducted its brainwashing operations is documented by the fact that pharmaceutical amphetamine consumption levels have since then remained the same, due to their addiction.

Not that anyone talks about it, even though everyone in the amphetamine issuance business has been fully aware of it since 1929. Despite that fact, both Jordan Petersen and I were almost killed by our friendly physicians through its prescriptions. Russell Monroe (1920-2003) and Hyman J. Drell (1920-1999) discovered that many of their charges were hallucinating and extremely agitated due to their amphetamine addiction. It had been graciously provided by their military during WWII. But in 1945 it was cut-off. So, in desperation they picked apart Benzedrine inhalers and orally consumed the 250 mg of amphetamine inside. Monroe and Drell were psychiatrists serving at the time in the U.S. Army's Medical Corps at Ft. Benjamin Harrison, Indianapolis' military prison. Monroe had a medical degree from Yale with short psychiatric and psychoanalytic training at Columbia University. Drell's degree from the University of Illinois School of Medicine in December 1943 included a brief residency in psychiatry at Downey Veterans Hospital, Downey, IL, in the mid-1940s.

When publishing their findings, these two psychiatrists opined that their patient-prisoners, although not typical of military personnel, were not particularly abnormal young men, either. This propelled Rasmussen to conclude that the U.S. military's Benzedrine and methamphetamine distribution throughout WWII had phenomenally multiplied the herd's consumption of these mind-altering and brain-perverting drugs worldwide (California Western Medicine 62 (April 1945): 33; *American Journal of Psychiatry 101* (March 1945). That too, however, was nothing new to insiders. Grave dangers for human physical and emotional health from amphetamine sulphates' indiscriminate use had been emphasized for decades in the medical professions' medical literature. But that was expertly swept under the rug, never leaving learned society's quarters. Thus, they could keep the herd in the illusion that amphetamines of all sorts were risk free. And so they were swooned into the illusion of COVID-19 injections being beneficial to human health, when indeed taking even one shot signs over one's body and one's soul to the corporation whose injection(s) one received.

Sudden convulsions, psychotic reactions, acute paranoid schizophrenia, hypertension and addiction/habituation, agitation, anxiety, bladder pain and bloody, cloudy urine, delusions of persecution, mistrust, suspiciousness and combativeness, feeling of unreality, depression, nervousness, rapidly changing moods, sense of detachment from self or body, seeing, hearing or feeling things that are not there, as well as blistering, peeling, loosening of the skin, blurred vision, chest pain and discomfort, confusion, difficulty breathing, dizziness, fainting, fast irregular, pounding, or racing heartbeat and pulse, headache hives, itching, skin rash, joint and muscle pain, large, hive-like swelling on the face, eyelids, lips, tongue, throat, hands, legs, feet and genitals, mood swings, red, irritated eyes, restlessness, shakiness in the legs, arms, hands and feet, shivering, sores, ulcers, white spots in the mouth and on the lips, sweating, talking and acting with uncontrollable excitement, trouble sleeping, twitching, twisting and uncontrolled repetitive movements of tongue, lips, face, arms and legs, uncontrolled vocal outbursts and tics, uncontrollable repeated body movements, overall tiredness and weakness and vomiting.

All these are accompanied by constipation, decreased interest in sexual intercourse, inability to have and keep an erection and loss in sexual desire, drive, or performance, redness of the skin, thinning or loss of hair and unpleasant taste and other unmentioned side-effects are all part of the game, with the newly invented COVID 19 injection-caused, human Sudden Adult Death Syndrome , although that is nothing new either, as ventricular arrhythmias precipitating cardiac arrest as the most common mechanisms of sudden death by way of pharmaceutical drugging has been documented for decades. And still no one breathes a word about the ease with which the herd over the past 90 years slowly but surely were made to systematically acquire amphetamine addiction (*Journal of the American Medical Association* 147 (1951): 19).

Long before we got here, however, Rhode Island physician Charles Bradley (1902-1979) had brilliantly carried Wittmer and Cattell's work on finding a legitimate excuse to dumb down the herd's brightest children by drugging them at the earliest age. He invented the perfect official diagnosis to put American children on drugs, calling it the "moral defectiveness and hyperkinetic reaction of childhood." He declared it treatable with mind-altering stimulant medications including amphetamines such as Adderall and methylphenidate such as Ritalin and Concerti without the herd becoming suspicious. By solving this problem, Bradley had made a giant step forward in the work of ages previously conducted by German Khazarians Franz Kramer (1887–1967) and Hans Poll now (1902–43). Since the 1920s, they had grappled with finding ways to drug children in benign-looking ways so as not to alert the public. They were working under Khazarian Karl Bonhoeffer (1868–1948), professor of psychiatry at Breslau University and head of Berlin's Charité-hospital's psychiatric department. They authored a paper "On a Hyperkinetic Disease of Infancy" as a way to achieve their goal of humanity's mental and emotional destruction (Franz Max Albert Kramer (1878–1967) (https://embryo.asu.edu/pages/franz-max-albert-kramer-1878-1967).

Kramer and Pollnow, in turn, had built on the work of German psychiatrist and researcher Rudolf Thiele. His brain somehow conceived that encephalitis, an inflammation in the brain, would cause hyperkinetic syndrome in children (Der Psychiater und Hochschullehrer Rudolf Thiele (1888–1960)). With it, Thiele had opened another avenue for the black magicians of the sciences of psychiatry and neurology to ignore both Krafft-Ebing's 1886 publications and Freud's 1896 discoveries that human psychoses and neuroses find their origin with sexual abuse during infancy and childhood. This has been ongoing for aeons, as demonstrated in the documentary Pedogate 2020 - Symbolism & Pizzagate 2.0 on odyssee.com. (Paul Bernard Foley: *The psychiatry of encephalitis lethargica*; springer.com, pp 407-572; styreamablle.com).

As a matter of fact, Constantin Economo von San Serff (1876–1931) got a head start on them. He was a psychiatrist and neurologist of Greek Khazarian descent, born in modern-day Romania and knighted for reasons unknown in 1906. In 1917, he had already seen fit to present a new disease, which he said would soon be turned into a worldwide epidemic he termed encephalitis lethargica, EL, the sleeping sickness. It was characterized by high fever, headache, double vision, delayed physical and mental response and lethargy. In acute cases, patients may enter coma.

He said that this EL, in Hebrew signifying a deity or a god illness, would afford "us", the Khazarian science-of-psychiatry and -psychology black magicians, "...entirely unexpected, novel insights into the psychologic and physiologic mysteries of the mechanisms of the mind, knowledge that will perhaps also be of significant influence outside the world of medicine (ibid)."

Is it at all surprising, that none of the learned society even so much as murmured a word about humans' atlas/axis misalignment. Consider all we know about the learned society, how throughout all its ranks and files it conducted so much research on living and dead human specimens of all ages. Consider their lengthy dissertations in particular on the cerebral cortex/brain, spinal cord connection. Yet none of them mentions how the atlas being the first cervical vertebra and the axis being the second vertebra, that they form the joint connecting the skull and the spine. Or that they are responsible for the suspension, equilibrium and management of the spine and human skeleton in about every human being they tediously dissected "out of joint?"

San Serff was just one of those who, if worth his salt a researcher, ought to have recognized this misalignment. He had an extensive, all-round education on the human physical body beginning as a resident at Vienna's Clinic of Internal Medicine under Khazarian Carl Wilhelm Hermann Nothnagel (1841-1905). He then studied neurology, histology and psychiatry at the at the Pitié-Salpêtrière Hospital, Paris, under Khazarian neurologist and psychiatrist Alexis Joffroy (1844-1908) and Charcot, French Khazarian psychiatrist Valentin Magnan (1835-1916). Magnan is remembered for expanding the concept and theory of degeneration based on hereditary precepts. These had been introduced into psychiatry by Vienna-born Khazarian Bénédict Augustin Morel (1809-1873) and picked up by Krafft-Ebbing in his *Psychopathia Sexualis* on human perversion and perversity in Kodak colours (New Juan O Savin: Trump Returns - White Hat Intel ~ Who Is JFK Jr? Dec 2022; beforeitsnews.com).

San Serff also took classes with Pierre Marie Félix Janet (1859-1947), the French psychologist. He was particularly well known for his work on the purported science of psychopathology, the scientific study of mental illness and disorders. He was also known for his consequent proposed psychotherapy, one of the numerous ideas and illusions of treatment brewed up by these psycho-the-rapists to purportedly improve people's well-being and mental health with pharmacotherapy. They would thus mitigate behaviors, beliefs, compulsions, thoughts or emotions brought on by these mind-altering drugs designed for people of all ages, families and adolescents.

He also took hypnosis instructions under French Khazarian Hippolyte Bernheim (1840-1919), chiefly known for his theory of suggestibility in relation to hypnotism. In the French city of Nancy, he learned different methods of microscopic research of the nervous system running through the atlas/axis connection under the German physiologist Albrecht von Bethe (1872-1954), known for his studies of the human nervous system. San Serrff then moved on to Munich, where he worked with Khazarians Kraepelin and Alzheimer. After that, he worked with German neurologist and psychiatrist Georg Theodor Ziehen (1862 -1950), famous for writing one of the first systematic textbooks on child psychiatry titled *Die Geisteskrankheiten des Kindesalters* (Mental Diseases of Childhood) whilst driving humanity's future of insanity designed by the mental health cabal onwards.

San Serff also worked in the neurologic ambulatory field under the city of Warburg synagogue's long term rabbi Juda Oppenheim's son, neurologist Herman Oppenheim (1858-1919). The Warburgs, settling in Bologna after 1200, immigrated to the Westphalian town, stole its name and whence removed to Altona, near Hamburg. From there, they spread throughout Germany, Denmark, Sweden, England and America stealing names and identities wherever they went.

Eventually, San Serff joined zoologist Carl Isidor Cori (1865-1954) in Trieste to conduct experiments in marine biology, as Freud had done as well. He then got engaged at Vienna's General Hospital's Clinic for Psychiatry and Nervous Diseases headed, by Wagner-Jauregg. At the clinic's Narrenturm, he put his theories on the emotionally disturbed into action. In 1927, he was jubilant for his master's receipt of the Nobel Prize in Physiology or Medicine "for his discovery of the therapeutic value of malaria inoculation in the treatment of dementia paralytica." I guess you get the drift. Seventy-three years passed before the field of psychiatry had a second Nobel Prize winner in Austrian Khazarian Eric R. Kandel. He was professor of biochemistry at Columbia University in New York, and was awarded the 2000 Nobel Prize in Medicine or Physiology for his research on the sea slug Aplysia. That research helped to uncover molecular mechanisms driving processes of learning and memory—in humans, we assume.

In 1921, appointed professor of psychiatry and neurology, San Serff discovered fever treatment could also treat general paralysis. This was a syphilitic brain disorder characterized by chronic inflammation and degeneration of cerebral tissue resulting in mental and physical deterioration. In 1931, as head of the Clinic's newly established department of brain research, he brought forth the Darwinian "you're nothing but an animal equal to Aplysia sea slugs" hypotheses for diagnosing and treating the WWI shell-shocked, before departing the Earth to the netherworld five months later of a heart attack.

One year after San Serff's death in 1931, Kramer and Pollnow brought forth their research on hyperkinetic syndrome in 45 children. By "hyperkinetic", they meant motion they considered beyond the usual. In their article "On a Hyperkinetic Disease of Infancy", they maintained that they saw no correlation between encephalitis and hyperkinetic behavior. However, they did observe in 17 of these children a difficulty sitting quietly, instead disturbing classes and inspiring classmates to similar vibrant behavior. This, they said, had started around age three, peaked at age six, and gradually receding as they grew older. The Khazarian Mafia-possessed mental health cabal used their observations as the basis for ADHD. They honored its Khazarian originators by calling it the "Kramer Pollnow syndrome" for a while. The illusionary ADHD "disorder" allowed them to drug children into oblivion from the moment of inception, with the herd swallowing it wholesale and running side by side with the equally illusionary PTSD invention for the drugging to the hilt of human adults of all ages.

After the Nazis seized power in 1933, Kramer and Pollnow disappeared into the woodworks somewhere in the United States. Their careers of drugging children out of their normal youthful enthusiasm without anyone getting suspicious carried on by the craft. In true Luciferic consciousness, they lied by omission and brewed up a hyperkinetic disease diagnostic for normally-to-be-expected, healthy children's innate joie de vivre (Klaus-Jürgen Neumärker: *The Kramer-Pollnow syndrome: a contribution on the life and work of Franz Kramer and Hans Pollnow*; Hist Psychiatry 2005 Dec;16 (Pt 4 (no 64)):435–51).

> That all those involved in the *Hyperkinetic Disease of Infancy* graciously ignored, that German physician Melchior Adam Weickard (1742–1803) had investigated the lack of attention span in some of his patients. Weickard was an extra-ordinary character in his own right, already in 1775 having published his book *Der Philosophische Arzt* (The Philosophical Doctor). He described those patients as being distractible by anything, even by their own imaginations. San Sariff et. al had swept this under the carpet with great expertise and vigor, acquired over the centuries. Weikard's suggestions that his patients make greater efforts to complete

> their tasks and curb their impulsiveness went also by the science of psychiatry black magic Luciferic consciousness possessed's wayside. Their impulsiveness and distraction resulted in flighty and careless behavior, many errors in their work and a tendency to be generally disorganized. All of his observations are right out of the 2013 DSM-V's playbook for human destruction's by way of the ADHD diagnostic criteria portrayed as treatable only with mind-altering drugs (M.A. Weickard, *Der philosophische Arzt.* 1775–1777).

That Weickard blames upbringing for the lack of children's attention span and self-control is also vigorously suppressed. Such observation is against the Khazarian Mafia's Luciferic consciousness, destruct-the-family agenda. several of Weickard's recommendations have also been persistently ignored. One such is to leave unruly youth in a dark room for a while to help them focus their attention. Another is "cold baths and steel powder rub downs, cinchona, mineral waters, horseback riding, and gymnastic exercises." He also recommended thoroughly teaching them a topic of interest in a way that engages them and that they grasp before moving them on to another topic. He explained that "The incapacity of attending with a necessary degree of constancy to any one object almost always arises from an unnatural or morbid sensibility of the nerves, by which means this faculty is incessantly withdrawn from one impression to another." All this has led to the "no one left behind or getting ahead" scam of public education, as stability eliminates the condition of hyper-kinetic sensibilities.

Scottish physician Alexander Crichton (1763 –1856) built on Weickard's hypothesis. In 1798, he published the trilogy *An inquiry into the nature and origin of mental derangement: comprehending a concise system of the physiology and pathology of the human mind and a history of the passions and their effects*. In the second chapter of book II "On Attention and its Diseases", Crichton emphasizes that the intensity of healthy attention varies not only within a normal range between individuals, but even within a person at different times (Crichton A (1798) An inquiry into the nature and origin of mental derangement: comprehending a concise system of the physiology and pathology of the human mind and a history of the passions and their effects. Cadell T Jr, Davies W, London).

In other words, distraction of attention is generally speaking not pathological, but occurs due to mental stimuli, volition and education. According to Crichton, all of it has a great impact on healthy attention spans. He furthermore distinguishes two possibilities of abnormal inattention as the oppositional poles of pathologically increased or decreased "sensibility of the nerves." In his opinion, the morbid alterations to which attention is subject can all be reduced under the following two heads:

- The incapacity of attending with a necessary degree of constancy to any one object.
- A total suspension of its effects on the brain.

The incapacity of attending with a necessary degree of constancy to any one object almost always arises from an unnatural or morbid sensibility of the nerves, he says. By that, he means that a subjects' attention is incessantly withdrawn from one impression to another. This may be either born with a person, or it may be the effect of accidental dis-eases. When born with a person, it becomes evident at a very early period of life and has a very bad effect, inasmuch as it renders him or her incapable of attending with constancy to any one object of education. However, just as Heinrich Hoffmann of Struwelpeter and Weickard before him, and Kramer and Pollnow later on, Crichton too says "But it seldom is in so great a degree as totally to impede all instruction; and what is very fortunate, it is generally diminished with age (Crichton, 1798 reprint p. 203)."

Thus, all of them acknowledge that a lack of attention-spans in children might be born with a person. This would mean it is part of an individual's *sui generis*. Or, they admit, it might be the effect of accidental dis-eases, such as upbringing and hereditary sexual abuse, hereditary pollution as Krafft-Ebing loves to call it, including childhood sexual abuse.

Crichton even remarks upon "the fidgets" being brought on by a barking dog, a poorly tuned organ or the scolding of a woman. In other words, it is due to a child's emotional sensitivity, a diversion or an emotional or physical upheaval. And none of these self-proclaimed experts on children's minds dreamt of drugging children out of their natural exuberance and into forced submission. At least, not until British paediatrician George Frederic Still (1868 -1941), the only boy in a working class family of eight children, hit children's naturally occurring vitality with drugs from the moment of birth onwards beginning around 1902. That is when Still began to argue that a lack of moral control may be shown in many ways without general impairment of intellect and without physical disease. He reached his conclusion after examining 20 children (Still GF. Some abnormal psychical conditions in children: the Goulstonian lectures. Lancet. 1902;1:1008–1012). The symptoms he listed are:

- Passionateness
- Spitefulness - cruelty
- Jealousy
- Lawlessness
- Dishonesty
- Wanton mischievousness - destructiveness
- Shamelessness - immodesty
- Sexual immorality
- Viciousness.

The keynote of these qualities, Still said, was self-gratification, either the immediate gratification of Self without regard either to the good of others or to the larger and more remote good of Self (Klaus W. Lange et al: The history of attention deficit hyperactivity disorder; Atten Defic Hyperact Disord. 2010; 2(4): 241–255).

Most children for whom the first manifestation of their *moral defect* was determined showed symptoms before the age of seven (in seven out of nine cases), the current diagnostic criterion of the ADHD DSM-IV-TR definition. Pediatrician Still furthermore hypothesized that a morbid manifestation of a child's moral control can be considered only when the child does not meet the standard for moral conduct at a certain age. That standard would fall within a "range of variation which we arbitrarily recognize as normal" (Still 1902, p. 1009).

And what constitutes "normal child behavior?"

Well, just like with PTSD, that seems to depend on the examining mind-manipulating magician, your school psychologist, for example, trained to understand that:

> "In reality, the difference between normal and abnormal behavior is not always clear; usually it is a matter of degree or expectation. A fine line often divides normal from abnormal behavior, in part because what is "normal" depends upon the child's level of development, which can vary greatly among children of the

same age. Development can be uneven, too, with a child's social development lagging behind his intellectual growth, or vice versa. In addition, "normal" behavior is in part determined by the context in which it occurs - that is, by the particular situation and time, as well as by the child's own particular family values and expectations, and cultural and social background (healthychildren.org)."

Add to this American Psychiatric Association members stating that for a ADHD diagnosis symptoms have to be present "to a degree that is maladaptive and inconsistent with developmental level" (American Psychiatric Association 2000). In other words, just as with PTSD, anyone of these psycho-the-rapists can do whatever they want with a "client." In my case, 24 of them came up with 24 differing opinions in their effort. And they did wit with help from my employer Air Canada and the flight attendant union bosses and flight attendant snitches to drive me into suicide. The same is done to ADHD-diagnosed children and grown-ups, rob them of their identity and their animus to steal their souls through drugging.

Kramer and Pollnow followed Freud's and Still's trend of children's moral defectiveness and sexual deviousness. Then, the very wealthy-born Bradley jumped into the fray to carry their human animals' Darwinian "hyperkinetic since infancy" theme further. Of Bradley we know little, other than that he studied neurology during his residency at New York City's Babies Hospital. It is there that he began his crime on the newborns, infants and children up to age four by conducting extensive Benzedrine-induced, neurological research. They were all immensely well acquainted with Weickard's, Hoffmann's, Crichton's and Still's observations. They all studied at the same universities with the same perverted characters. In typical Khazarian Luciferic consciousness fashion, through lies and deception, they all converted children's natural behavior of exuberance into the ADHD diagnosis. Soon thereafter, they followed with their equally unconscionable PTSD diagnostics. Due to herd ignorance, this henceforth allowed them to drug us goyim beasts out of our wits under the "Doctor Knows Best" indoctrination technique. They succeeded with such resulting lethality, deadliness and perniciousness as to result in the vigorous acceptance of the COVID-19 injection for about 5.5 billion human beings, who volunteered to get themselves genetically altered out of the state of a human being into a non-human entity.

Bradley had laid the groundwork for it wonderfully well. He carried forth his research at the Emma Pendleton Bradley Home, now called Bradley Hospital, in East Providence, R.I. In 1931, it was founded by his great uncle George Bradley, who made his fortune through his early championing of the telephone. He became the first secretary-treasurer of the National Bell Telephone Company, formed in Boston in 1877. Great uncle George had opened the home to treat children with nervous disorders after his only child, the seven-year-old Emma, had been stricken with encephalitis. This brain tissue inflammation is caused by an infection or as an autoimmune response, the ailment which Constantin de Economo proposed caused EL. The inflammation, which causes the brain to swell, damaged Emma's brain so severely as to leave her epileptic and physically and intellectually disabled (Charles Bradley, M.D., 1902–1979; published online: Jul 1998: American Journal of Psychiatry).

As the facility's medical director, Bradley had free hands to continue his neurological research into babies and children in whichever he saw fit. This included pneumoencephalography (PEG) or "air study," using the home's residential children from unknown family background as guinea pigs. The procedure consisted of the draining of the subjects' cerebrospinal fluid (CSF) through a lumbar puncture made by a thin needle inserted between the bones in the lower spine. The fluid is then replaced with air, oxygen or helium, which better shows the structure of the brain on x-ray images, which were then used for clinical brain mapping. To achieve the objective, test subjects were strapped into an open backed chair. The needle is inserted through the lumbar puncture to drain most of the cerebrospinal fluid from around the brain, as well as the spinal fluid. Part of the process was to turn the un-anaesthetized patient round and round and upside down in all directions in specific order, guiding the replacement fluid into the vacated places and hoping it would stimulate the choroid plexus, a complex network of capillaries lined by specialized cells during this excruciatingly painful experiment. Bradley seemed not to mind at all, even inventing a special chair for himself to give him easier access to the areas he wants drained.

A wide range of side-effects occurred, including headaches and severe vomiting lasting well past the procedure. But Bradley got the bright idea to give the newly available Benzedrine to his charges, speculating that it would both cure their headaches and kick the production of cerebrospinal fluid (CSF) into action, the brain's ependymal cell-lining ventricles replenishing the extracted fluid.

Whereas Benzedrine did nothing for the headaches, it indeed improved some of the children's school performance, social interactions and emotional responses. In 1937, Bradley launched a controlled three-week research trial on 30 of the resident's children, aged five to 14. They were all considered of normal intelligence, but with a variety of unknown behaviour disorders. During the trial's second week, he gave these children an unknown amount of Benzedrine daily upon rising. The most striking change in the behaviour of half of the children occurred in their school activities. He stated: "There is agreement that a great increase of interest in school material was present. Improvement was noted in all school subjects. A large proportion of the patients became emotionally subdued without, however, losing interest in their surroundings." Dosage, duration of effect and physiological observations are discussed in his 1937 paper published in *The American Journal of Psychiatry* for all in the science-of-psychiatry and -psychology to see. Thus, they could adopt it all to gradually lull children into oblivion and numbness without parents having a clue (Bradley C: The behaviour of children receiving Benzedrine. Am J Psychiatry 1937; 94:577–585). The effect on children's school performance was in no way Benzedrine related, of course. It was due to fear of another brutal pneumoencephalography if they did not smarten up in their school performance. But that either did not dawn upon Bradley or any of his peers, or it was ignored by them on purpose.

Be it as it may, Bradley, advertised his Benzedrine effect on residential children with a vengeance. With it, he brought children pharmacotherapy into vogue at a time when Freud's psychoanalysis and the science-of-psychiatry and -psychology at large tried very hard to both find acceptance in the learned society and make inroads as the treatment for perceived behavioural disorders in humans of all ages. Although Benzedrine seemed to play a significant role in children's behaviour modification, Bradley did stress that the drug could only offer a supplementary approach to treatment of behavioural problems, because of its inconsistencies, reflecting:

> "This approach in no sense replaces that of modifying a child's surroundings and so removing the sources of conflict . . . Neither can it offer the same assurance of mental health as do forms of psychotherapy which enable a child to work out his emotional problems" (Bradley C, Bowen M. Amphetamine (Benzedrine) Therapy of Children's Behavior Disorders. Am J Orthopsychiatry. 1940;11:92–103).

Bradley's conclusion followed his model of misbehavior as both a social maladjustment through upbringing and a possible organic disease. He opined that drugs only temporarily modified the social maladjustment, but did nothing to change a fundamental organic disease, if any. Therefore, he emphasized the role of the home environment, which produced far superior positive long-term changes than the fleeting effects of drugs (Madeleine P. Strohl: Bradley's Benzedrine Studies on Children with Behavioral Disorders; Yale J Biol Med. 2011 Mar; 84(1): 27–33).

Bradley's hypotheses were published in the most prominent medical journals and reported in the mass media. This led him to establish Bradley Home as an experimental drug research center for residential children with behavioural problems. In the process, he made a name for himself as expert in childhood schizophrenia. It remains unknown whether it was caused by systematically drugging and his overall opinion that that no effective treatment for any children's psychological afflictions existed. All of it to this day is ignored by his peers in the science of psychiatry and psychology. That includes Bradley, who instead ventured forth to search for pharmaceutical drugs he could have behaviourally challenged children swallow. The in 1948 at the University of Oregon Medical School, he founded the department of child psychiatry. This was right at the time when methylphenidate, the stimulant doctors nowadays most often prescribe for ADHD-diagnosed children, was being tested for chronic fatigue and depression on humans of all ages, but seemingly working best on children.

Methylphenidate was marketed with adverse side-effects including: appetite loss, dry mouth, anxiety/nervousness, nausea and insomnia. Gastrointestinal adverse effects may include abdominal pain and weight loss. Nervous system adverse effects may include akathisia (agitation/restlessness), irritability, dyskinesia (tics), oromandibular dystonia,[71] lethargy (drowsiness/fatigue) and dizziness. Cardiac adverse effects may include palpitations, changes in blood pressure, and heart rate (typically mild), and tachycardia (rapid heart rate) increased nicotine cravings, blurred vision caused by pupil dilatation and dry eyes, diplopia and mydriasis, hypersensitivity, skin rash, urticaria and fever. Marketed in 1954 as Ritalin, methylphenidate was first synthesized in 1944 and was approved for medical use in the United States in 1955. It was originally sold by Swiss company CIBA (now Novartis). By 2013, the number of methylphenidate doses used globally had increased by 66% compared to 2012. By 2020, it was the 41st most commonly prescribed medication in the United States, with more than 15 million prescriptions. Add COVID-19 injections to that mix and you still wonder about the herd's emotional state of mind? Never mind.

Bradley's drug administering clinical research applications and discoveries were seamlessly advertised throughout his career/ His pharmacotherapy treatments for children from infancy onward are today lauded as one of the most important psychiatric diagnostics and treatment applications in the entire history of the science of psychiatry's black magicians' discoveries about the human psyche since Christ was a cadet. And rightfully so, as the craft, just as with the PTSD diagnosis, developed out of thin air the ideal way to destroy the lands' brightest and healthiest. This is particularly true in the U.S., without any scientific proof for these euphemistically termed "disorders" existing. And so many in the learned society, never mind the herd, have no inkling of a clue of being systematically driven over the cliff by their own volition of imposed ignorance through mind altering pharmaceutical drugs. And these are presented to them to swallow by their trusted physician, as both Jordan Peterson and I experienced personally, or by the meeting of egg and sperm throughout by now generations.

By the 1960s, they took their illusion a step further with the American Psychiatric Association (APA) beginning to advertise ADHD as a most common neurodevelopmental disorder. It is a neuro-physical fault in the brain, most frequently diagnosed in children, they said. Yet, just as with PTSD, no empirical evidence could be brought forth. When this thought had been firmly planted in the public's subconscious, however, it generated enormously profitable businesses, just as with PTSD. So, the cabal upped the ante, just as they did with PTSD, to officially coin the diagnostic terms of "attention deficit disorder with or without hyperactivity" and "Post Traumatic Stress Disorder" by the 1980s. And so they gave the Luciferic consciousness-possessed Khazarians dominating the science-of-psychiatry-and -psychology profession the most precious avenues to drug us herd members from cradle to grave with ever more lethal potions of their poisonous concoctions. And they know full well what they are doing. Meanwhile, we go on slumbering with eyes wide shut and swallowing anything the "Doctor Knows Best" prescribes to us. This has led to the administration of 12.94 billion doses to more than 5.44 billion people of the gene-manipulating COVID-19 injections, and with it surrendering their status as a human being.

Don't believe it? Read Harvard psychiatry professor Peter R. Breggin's book "Brain Disabling Treatments in Psychiatry: Drugs, Electroshock, and the Psychopharmaceutical Complex," and stop kidding yourself. On page 277, you will read about research conducted around 1989 by physicians Peter Jensen, Michael Bain and Allen Josephson. Their report "Why Johnny Can't Sit Still: Kids Ideas on Why They take Stimulants" shows how experienced researchers from the division of neuropsychiatry at Walter Reed Army Institute Of Research conducted their research. They used interviews, child psychiatric rating scales, rating scales and a projective test titled "Draw a Person Taking the Pill" to systematically evaluate 20 children given Ritalin by their primary care physicians. The drug in these children produced the following results:

- Defective super ego formation manifested by "disowning responsibility for their provocative behavior;"
- Impaired self-esteem development

- Lack of resolution of critical family events which preceded the emergency of the child's hyperactive behavior
- Displacement of "family difficulties onto the child."

Many of these children believed they were bad and defective, and that they were given the pill to control themselves. They also attributed their conduct to outside forces, such as eating sugar and not taking the pill. They did not understand the power they had within themselves to learn how to control their behavior, if taught. Jensen et al. (n.d.) warned, that the use of stimulant medication such as Ritalin, Benzedrine, Adderall and the like "has significant effects on the psychological development of the child" in addition to distracting parents, teachers and physicians from solving the problems in the child's environment, the root cause of any child's emotional upheaval (Breggin, p. 278). Furthermore, and much, much worse, a child on Ritalin is kicked into entering the victimhood ideation. Throughout life, they will blame others for unfolding life events, because they have never been taught to accept responsibility for any of their actions. This also leads to drug addiction from the moment they are forced to take mind altering, pharmaceutical stimulants such as Ritalin and Adderall. And that's just the start. They then normally advance to cocaine, heroin, fentanyl and the like. That is another kettle of worms we will not open here.

In the late 1980s, Jensen and others of his league compared 134 children aged six to 12 from a military psychiatric clinic with a control sample of children, we do not know from where. He was trying to figure out the most salient ingredients of various risk factors in predicting the levels of child psychopathology. Salience describes how prominent or emotionally striking something is. If an element seems to jump out from its environment, it's salient. If it blends into the background and takes a while to find, it's not. Salience bias states that the brain prefers to pay attention to salient elements of an experience. In other words, the squeaky wheel gets the grease.

Their paper "Children at risk: I. Risk factors and child symptomatology", published in the *American Academy of Adolescent & Child Psychiatry* 1990, gets into details. He and his peers admit that parental psychopathology, the emotional health and life stressors of parents, created the greatest effects on overall child behavioural symptom levels. As usual in this magical non-science, there are several ways to characterise psychopathology factors in a person as a whole. All of them depend on the evaluating magician's own state of mind transmitted down from his parents in four dimensions of deviance, distress, dysfunction and danger into their child relationship. This has been discussed since Hippocrates and brought back into the black magicians' realm of human-psyche-functioning discovery by German Khazarian psychiatrist Karl Jasper. He was, of course, an acquaintance of all previously mentioned science of psychiatrists of his era, a few months before the 1914 WWI creation and with it the complete destruction of families ongoing since Gaius Julius Caesar (100 BC–44 BC) ventured beyond the Alps to subdue the European nations in 58–50 BC.

And what did Jensen do with Jasper's insights almost 2040 years later? Did he learn and teach how best to help and guide parents with their parenting skills? No, this the non-existent science-of-psychiatry, pharmacotherapy enthusiast chose the lucrative career of one of America's most influential advocates of child-drugging from cradle through to kindergarten and onwards into university and life under the ADHD umbrella. And the

American school boards' Rockefeller-founded system exuberantly participated in the euphemistically called "students' mental health screening process", vigorously pushed since the late 1990s, as well as the overall innate moral compass confusion and sexual perversion seen in 2022 with drag shows for 3-year-olds, dildo demonstrations and sexual perversion instruction books in sixth grade leading the charge into humanity's planned moral compass loss to animal rutting abyss.

Dr. Breggin wrote in 2007 that if the aspired-to, mental-health screening processes became fully implemented, "millions more children will be pushed into becoming lifetime consumers of psychiatric drugs." This in turn will lower their innate conscious or unconscious constraint or curtailment of a process or behavior, impulses and desires, their overall inhibition. It would ensure fornication in and outside of classrooms for all to see in the very near future, with condoms available soon in and out of classrooms (Breggin; p. 276).

As it is by 2022, the Khazarian Mafia science-of-psychiatry and human emotional/mental health métier had further upgraded its ADHD nomenclature to presently mean a neurodevelopmental disorder affecting the way the brain grows and develops. But, just as with the newly developed COVID-19 injection-associated "sudden adult death syndrome", no scientific empirical evidence for any of it exists (E. Rebekah Siceloff et al: Universal Behavioral/Emotional Health Screening in Schools: Overview and Feasibility; Rep Emot Behav Disord Youth 2017 Spring; 17(2): 32–38). Unruliness in youngsters injected with poisons from first breath develops with ease due an infancy spend in front of television sets with i-phones. The lack of loving parents teaching discipline, determination, willpower and persistency, never mind logic and reason, cannot be advertised to the herd. That would destroy the science-of-psychiatry and -psychology black magicians' livelihood, if not endanger their lives. Imagine if the herd got wind of their lethal undertakings towards humanity throughout the past 130 years!

ADHD, genuine PTSD and all other emotion-based upheaval in the human soul can only be overcome by:

- ceasing to take all pharmaceutical, mind-altering drugs
- twice daily meditation
- soul searching and prayers for finding a way to live a purpose driven life

But this seems at this point in time too alien for many herd members to fathom, too brainwashed since the late 1800s through their ancestors' drugged genes to even make an effort in that direction. No wonder, with people like Jensen in 2022 still rutting along the path he chose three decades ago, namely using children of all ages in his search for the "Optimal Treatments for Childhood Mental Disorders: ADHD, Aggressive behaviour, Depression, and Anxiety Disorders". So, he continues his examinations of the impact of psychotherapies and brainwashing, in combination with and pharmaceutical drugging. For he sees both as essential to obtain optimal behavioural outcomes for children and youth, thus maligning our Divine Creator, on whom he, an atheist, does not have a clue (https://www.mayo.edu/research/faculty/jensen-peter-s-m-d/bio-00054941).

Breggin made a different observation in his 1999 paper *Psychostimulants in the treatment of children diagnosed with ADHD: Risks and mechanism of action*. He exposed that the millions of

American children diagnosed with attention deficit disorder or hyperactivity and treated with psycho-stimulants such as methylphenidate, dextro-amphetamine and methamphetamine produced nothing other than a continuum of their central nervous system toxicity. It begins with increased energy, hyper-alertness and over-focusing on rote-activities to steadily progress toward obsessive/compulsive and perseverative activities, including insomnia, agitation, hypomania, mania and, sometimes, seizures (International Journal of Risk & Safety in Medicine (12 (1999) 3–35). In other words, these drugs and treatments not only destroy children's and adults' human *sui generis*. They also destroy their animus, in its original Latin meaning their soul, life, mind, mental powers, courage and desires, breath, spirit and vital force.

Few parents seem to be aware of what is being done to the offspring they so gladly hand over to schoolteachers and psychologists without blinking an eye. Perhaps after generation-long transference, they are completely spellbound by Sigismund Schlomo Freud and nephew Edward Bernays' et al.'s "Doctor Knows Best" doctrine with its objective of "Making the American Mind" blind. And now they are aided by the COVID-19 injections, making them blind as bats and getting blinder by the hour. Ans so, they remain ignorant of the fact that pharmaceutical psycho-stimulant drugs enhance their apathy and encourage social withdrawal, emotional depression, docility and sooner or later dependence on the Khazarian mafia WEF run state for sustenance.

That all of these mind-altering drugs furthermore act as physical growth inhibitors and produce various and at times irreversible brain dysfunctions is also kept secret from us. So is the fact that both animal and human research indicates that therapeutic effects of these so-called stimulant drugs' suppress all benevolent spontaneous and social human behaviors. But they do promote behaviors of obsessive and compulsive nature. Therefore, these adverse effects make these psycho-stimulant drugs superbly useful for directing and controlling children's innate emotions. They work particularly well when in highly structured environments and not wanting to attend to their genuine needs, in line with the Khazarian Luciferic consciousness agenda goal.

Still don't believe this has been purposely done to us throughout many generations? Read on, then. In response to pharmaceutical drug companies' lobbying to view Ritalin and the like as just a mild stimulant, U.S. Drug Enforcement Administration (DEA)'s drug science specialist Christine Sannerud and its Ritalin specialist Gretchen Feussner in 2000 published their paper "Is Ritalin an Abused Drug? Does it meet the criteria of a schedule II substance?" stating:

> "Like amphetamine and cocaine, abuse of MPH [Ritalin} can lead to marked tolerance and severe psychological dependence. The pattern of abuse is characterized by escalation in dose, binge use followed by severe depression, and on overpowering desire to continue use of the drug despite negative medical and social consequences. The abuser may alter the mode of administration from oral use to intranasal or intravenous use to intensify the effects of the drug (p.35)."

With it comes the destruction of the neurological pathological substrata of the central and peripheral nervous system. In other words, it ruins the brain, spinal cord, cranial nerves, peripheral nerves, nerve roots, autonomic nervous system, neuromuscular junction and muscles. With it come epilepsy, Alzheimer disease and other dementias, cerebrovascular diseases including stroke, migraine and other headache disorders, multiple sclerosis, Parkinson's disease, neuroinfections, brain tumors, traumatic disorders of the nervous system due to physical head trauma and other neurological disorders as a result of malnutrition.

And you still wonder why the post -millennium generations seem in particular so bizarrely ignorant and stupid. Or why the COVID-19 epic could take off so successfully the way it did, with 70% of the world's population begging to receive at least one dose of the detrimental-to-the-health injection, unable to comprehend what "experimental " means?

The worst of it?

Just as with PTSD, no biological basis for an ADHD dis-ease exists. This confirms that it is not of physical origin, but brought about by a disorder-creation of the black magicians' craft. They do it by designing psycho-social conditions for humanity. In other words, they create conditions that "pertain to the influence of social factors on an individual's mind or behavior and to the interrelation of behavioral and social factors." And these will destroy clandestinely and slowly its prosperous and humane conditions necessary to construct healthy lives, according to Breggin (Oxford English Dictionary, 2012; Breggin p. 271).

For ADHD, it took until 2001 before anyone of the learned society addressed that issue. That is when Jan Strydom and Susan duPlessis published their book *The Myth of ADHD and Other Learning Disabilities* (News with Views September 2022; Huntington House Pub. 2001). They advocate great caution if a child has been diagnosed with ADHD or some other behavior disorder, as a false diagnosis might be at play. They also teach how parents can teach their children the skills of concentration and self-control without drugging them. They maintain that problems with youth are becoming more and more acute throughout the world due to parents allowing their offspring to be drugged out of rhyme and reason with chemicals from the moment they take their first breath.

The number of children diagnosed with attention deficit hyperactivity disorder (ADHD) and Tourette syndrome has been multiplying exponentially since 2001. Youth violence, alcohol and drug abuse, teenage promiscuity and teen suicides have become commonplace, in combination with learning disabilities and illiteracy also increasing at an alarming rate, convey the authors.

Tourette syndrome is a neurological disorder characterized by sudden, repetitive, rapid and unwanted movements or vocal sounds called tics and other health impairments. The American Psychiatric Association members in their DSM-5 euphemistically names it "conduct disorder".

Mind you, the mental health craft was far ahead of authors Strydom and duPlessis. In 1968, it already knew full well that it had achieved the covert supremacy over humanity's emotional and physical health. And with it, they had accomplished the Luciferic Consciousness take-over until the completion of the Work of Ages planned for 2025 by way of the Khazarian black magic human emotional health magicians. And how had they accomplished it? By the persistent drugging of children and adults since the late 1800s. They did this in combination with catastrophic wars that impacted all aspects of human lives, including overall daily social functioning, academic and personal-life achievements, interpersonal relationships, the gene-pool and first and foremost humans' perception, all of it by extension hugely influenced their nation's generational narrative.

All of this and mankind's planned future was revealed to a few chosen ones on March 20, 1968, by Manhattan-born paediatrician Richard L. Day (1905–1989). Little is known of him, other than that he graduated from Harvard Medical School in 1931. Throughout his career, he held positions teaching about and conducting research on embryos and newborns at Brooklyn's Downstate Medical School (1953–1956) and the University of Pittsburgh's (1956–1965) departments of paediatrics as professor and chairman. And he was professor at Manhattan's Mount Sinai Hospital from 1968 until his retirement in 1971. Day was also the national director Planned Parenthood Federation of America, founded by Khazarian Margaret Sanger's in 1942. He was advocating for abortion and selling of organs limbs and foetus parts (1965–1968) (Dr. Richard Day, 84, Ex-Paediatrics Professor; New York Times Junl 16, 1989).

On that very day in March1968, Professor Day had invited around 80 to 90 doctors to a special function. He informed them about the changes they would witness in their lifetime as a result of "The Order," or as we know it now, the New World Order, the Illuminati, the Khazarian mafia, the Freemasons, the World Economic Forum. Pick and choose if you must, although they are all intertwined (Public author: *The New Order of Barbarians: The New World System*; CreateSpace Independent Publishing 2013). Dr. Lawrence Dunegan was one of those present and listening attentively, as Day, the Order's spokesman, delivered a hair-raising speech outlining humanity's irreversible future to an audience that had been told not to record the talk by any means.

He insisted that he was doing physicians of all rank and file a favour by explaining to them how the world was going to change. But he omitted to mention that cosmic law demands to inform humanity of the Luciferian consciousness' planned nefarious deeds against us. In the 1980s, Dunegan recalls Day's presentation on a tape in 2022, still available on YouTube and in the book *The New Order of Barbarians*. They both reflect on how smoothly humanity was taken over brilliantly by way of the ADHD and PTSD diagnoses and the Khazarian-recommended treatments of pharmacotherapy. He described how they got many of us onto the pharmaceutical, mind-altering drugs necessary to achieve homo sapiens or human 1.0's downfall and conversion into 2.0. And what did *The Order*'s main henchmen Yuval Noah Harari jubilantly announced for all around the world to hear in a 2019 CNN interview: "Humans are now hackable animals." Why? Because of humanity's systematic erosion of its emotional and physical health by way of pharmaceutical, mind-altering drugs under the guise of benevolence since the late 1800s.

Heinz Alfred Kissinger, PhD (1923-) of the German Khazarian Meyer Löb family emigrated to America in 1938. Between 1951 and 1954, as a Harvard graduate student, he worked as consultant to the U.S. Psychological Strategy Board's director and as the American Secretary of State from 1973 to 1977. He was and famous for viewing U.S. Government Issue (GIs) as dumb animals. He confirmed Dunegan's report 40 years later, when at a WHO Council on Eugenics meeting of 2009 uttering:

> "Once the herd accepts mandatory vaccinations, it's game over. They will accept anything – forcible blood or organ donation – 'for the greater good'. We can

> genetically modify children and sterilize them --- 'for the greater good'. Control sheep minds and you control the herd. Vaccine makers stand to make billions. And many of you in this room are investors. It's a big win-win. We thin out the herd and the herd pays us for extermination services..."

Well, by 2022, members of all strata of human society, from the academically highly educated of all colour, nationality and religions to the very lowest street dwellers, demonstrated their inability to comprehend the meaning, the nomenclature "*experimental* vaccine." Without apprehension, they proudly got themselves inoculated up to numerous times with substances they did not bother to research whilst ferociously snarling at those declining the WHO's mandates of inoculation as dangers to world health.

But was and is their apathy, their ignorance, their willing acceptance of COVID 19 injections related to Freud and friends pushing cocaine and morphine containing pharmaceutical drugs down humanity's throat over the past 130 years perhaps? That is the poignant question to ask. Have these drugs indeed systematically diluted humans' sperm and egg quality throughout the past six generations? In the United States and Britain in particular, where amphetamine drugging on the young began with Witmer, Cattell and Still at the turn of the twentieth century, has it resulted in an almost incomprehensible degree of ignorance expressed by the willing acceptance of the COVID 19 inoculation by citizens of all ages en route to Yuval Harari's human 2.0 creation? In 2020, he mumbled under his breath that the world of the future would be run by advanced algorithms and artificial intelligence and not by God-created human 1.0, with Dr. Michael Yeadon, head of Pfizer's vaccine programs, wondering, if a Satanic Cult hid behind the deadly COVID vax push (https://infowars.com Dec. 24, 2022).

The ADHD and PTSD diagnoses, neither of them scientifically provable, never mind identifiable, seem to be. Nevertheless, the science-of-psychiatry and -psychology magicians continue to work unimpeded throughout society, including as school psychologists. They wreak havoc and create untold trauma and suicides among those they diagnose with these euphemistically called "disorders." Instead, they shower each other with accolades of excellence for their efforts to find "cures" for these disorders they themselves created. This, even though nothing neurological or physical can be held culpable for either the PTSD or the ADHD emotional conditions. That the relatives of the ADHD diagnosed are also often affected by its symptoms, which could be caused by sperm and egg pollution resulting in generational brain-power erosion, nobody talks about either. That children without ADHD have more grey and white brain matter volume and demonstrate different brain region activation during certain tasks than those diagnosed with it is also kept quiet (Pliszka, 2007).

We also learn that the brain's frontal lobes, caudate nucleus and cerebellar vermis, are affected in ADHD-afflicted people, but this is also seldom mentioned (Tripp & Wickens, 2009). The vermis is the unpaired median portion of the cerebellum that connects the two hemispheres, sitting right above the atlas and apix connection. To regurgitate, that specific part of human anatomy is misaligned in the vast majority of humans, thus assuring lack of proper blood flow to the brain. None of these self-proclaimed geniuses working throughout the past 170 years throughout their numerous human pathology fields of "expertise" ever mention (https://atlasprofilax.com)

Non-genetic factors such as low birth weight, premature birth, exposure to alcohol, smoking, lead and extreme stress during pregnancy result in an embryo's and thus an infant's physical and mental health destruction. This is mentioned by the medical learned, though they never talk about how prescription drug consumption and "vaccinations" influence foetus' and infants. They are too busy proudly announcing their newest human disorder creations of their own making in addition to ADHD. These include:

- Autism spectrum disorder
- Disruptive, impulse control and conduct disorders
- Social communication disorder
- Specific learning disorder

After describing their perceived symptoms for those new diagnostic inventions, they recommend amphetamines and methylphenidate for children's first-line treatment. Notably, only amphetamines are FDA-approved for preschool-aged children. If those drugs, or any other behavioral drugs for tryouts (experiential) on youth— chosen by the mental health magicians prove insufficient, methylphenidate rather than amphetamines might be helpful, we read. Many children and families alternate between various medications, depending on the efficacy of treatment and tolerability of the medication experienced by the individual taker, we hear. It is comforting, I am sure to hear that all drugs are prescribed with the goal to *improve* ADHD symptoms for the sole purpose to restore the functioning at home and at school.

And what does *improve* in satanic language inversion parley mean? The same as the For in the National Center *for* PTSD? To aggravate the symptoms, to enhance them, to destroy family functioning at home and at school of all participants. To achieve the objective, the modus operandi for PTSD-diagnosed people, regardless of genre, is the same as for those diagnosed with ADHD. Have them swallow 10 or more different mind-altering drugs simultaneously to assure their suicidal ideation under the banner of benevolence and caring. The National Institute *for* PTSD, all right, knows perfectly well that psychiatric and medical conditions are interdependent. Drug the PTSD- and ADHD-diagnosed to the hilt with pharmaceuticals and conjoined emotional and physical deterioration will take place soon thereafter, as certain as the Amen in any Christian church. The black magic magicians acknowledged this since the days of Krafft-Ebbing and Freud, if we just look. As late as in November 2019, they stated that medical conditions can cause mental illness by way of psychological and/or physiological effects. And mental illness possibly makes it difficult to engage in medical care due to barriers to access, poor motivation, functional impairment and the like.

Furthermore, these self-appointed knowers of the human psyche, know that many medical and psychiatric conditions share common psychosocial determinants. Such were the adverse childhood experiences that Freud and Krafft Ebing tried so very hard to invert. That all human emotional trauma is enhanced by pharmaceutical mind-altering drugs and cognitive behavioral therapy rather than teaching the patient to breath in accordance with her or his sui generis and animus is never mentioned anywhere (Mark A Oldham, M.D., et al: "Collaborative Care Meets Hospital Medicine: Proactive Consultation-Liaison Psychiatry"; *Psychiatric Times* vol. 36 November 14, 2019). Rather, their Khazarian spokespeople, trumpet forth that:

> "Creativity should not be seen as 'optional' in psychiatry. Rather, it helps us to approach clinical problems in new ways, allows us to pull together disparate

> ideas, and sustains us in the face of uncertainty." (Allan Peterkin, M.D. et al: "The Arts and Humanities in Psychiatry...A Debut"; *Psychiatric Times*, April 4, 2017).

Consequently, we conclude that the PTSD and ADHD disorders were hallucinated into being by the non-scientific science-of-psychiatry and -psychology black magic physicians since the late 1800s. Their goal was to bestow on themselves the power to examine all aspects of humanity's innate behaviours, aptitudes and attitudes, from the physical to the emotional, throughout the twentieth century. Thus, they could discover how to pervert our sui generis and our animus, our spiritual essence, from cradle to grave in all aspects of possible perversion. By 2022, very few humans doubt the medical professions' "benign intentions," long forgotten the words of French poet, essayist and art critic Charles Pierre Baudelaire (1821 -1867), most famous for his work of lyric poetry titled *Les Fleurs du mal* (*The Flowers of Evil*), who in 1864 published in the Paris newspaper "Figaro":

> "The greatest trick the Devil ever pulled was convincing the world he didn't exist."

Don't believe it? Listen to American Fox News television host, political commentator and writer Tucker Swanson McNear Carlson (1969-). His December 2022 YouTube interview of eminent British cardiologist Dr Aseem Malhotra on the corruption of medicine by Big Pharma might help open our eyes and inspire the question: "Have we arrived like lemmings at the cliff, ready to jump?"

Let's continue that exploration in *Fallacy* 3, shall we?

Meanwhile, it might behove us to remember that all the Divine Creator of all there is in all of Creation asked of us during our present sojourn on this earth is to try very hard to carry ourselves with honour, integrity and graciousness. For tht alone, we get an A for Effort. We just need to apply willpower, discipline, determination and persistency to help us in all our undertakings. We should try through daily meditation to discover the reasons for this life of ours and its adventures, to which we all agreed before arrival. And we need to achieve the goals we set ourselves and achieve them maintaining some modicum of joy in the undertaking, knowing full well we can call on God and our Guardian Angels for help at any time. In the process, we learn of the innate enormous power within us from the moment we take our first breath of life, which is why the Luciferic consciousness adherents inject us with poisons at that very moment. Therefore, only when freeing ourselves from pharmaceutical drugging can we defeat the Khazarian-imbued Luciferic consciousness-empowered, representing Satan's power. That is when we begin to think Light, see Light, be Light and spread Light with strength and might in all direction and thus change the world in which we live.

Understand that every single one of us, regardless of colour, creed and nationality, is a channel of this light, for God, the Creator of All has granted it to us equally. All of us humans are thus here to radiate our divine Light out throughout earthly vibrations during all our waking hours by learning to watch our own thinking like hawks and change it to create miracles for ourselves and therefore for all humanity. The more loving and uplifting our thoughts, the more loving and uplifting our actions, the more loving and uplifting the earthly vibration around us. It plays like a stone thrown into a pond, spreading outwards, bringing Light around the world just by learning to control and direct our thoughts and our thinking. But it must be unimpeded by pharmaceutical and psycho-the-rapists' black magic drugging. The word comes from pharmacology, derived from Greek the φάρμακον, pharmakon, "drug, poison" for a reason, *pharmakós* in ancient Greek belief structure having "common shrines of the gods and sacrifices, and the same kinds of customs." Furthermore, a *pharmakós* in Greek religious ceremony in itself indicated the ritualistic sacrifice or exile of a human scapegoat writes Valerie M. Warrior in her 2009 book *Greek Religion: A Sourcebook*.

So, we have the choice. Do we want to continue as humanity's scapegoats unaware? Or do we want to take our own reigns by meditating twice daily to ask for answers to the problems we face and unfailingly receive the answers to solve the problems? Once we do, we are cruising, as I have learnt through 10 years of pure terror imposed upon me by my employer, his prime and secondary snitches, the union bosses and their henchmen and the WCB in their vigorous and steadfast attempts to drive me into suicide, or at least complete destitution and life on the street. I slumbered in the illusion of their benevolence for my health, until a quasi deathbed confession of one of their associates brought me to a rather brutal awakening; and I am the rule, not the exception.

So it is each one of us, the PTSD- and ADHD-affected in particular, who must learn to do our own lifting and uplifting of the situations we face. We must be the ones who consciously raise our vibrational level through our thinking. We must be the ones who shoulder our responsibilities towards ourselves with the help of God, our Creator. We must be the ones knowing to ask our guardians, guides, helpers, teachers and friends in the unseen for help. We must be the ones recognising that our ability to do so hinges entirely on the way we think, our thinking alone. And that is only possible when pharmakon-free and willing to learn through daily meditative reflections, note taking and faithful application of the insights made.

In combination with doing the very best we can at any given time in every situation we face, the very best for ourselves will be forthcoming. Also expect the very best in every soul you meet, and in some extraordinary way or other, the very best will always be drawn forth in the other in the course of time. You will find it, no matter how deeply hidden away it might seem to be and how very much those wanting to harm us try to hide it. There is divine retribution, and we will come out triumphant if faithfully trampling the path of honor, integrity and graciousness, whereas they will reap the evil they planned for us. I know. I am seeing it and living it in those who described me as human debris to be driven into suicide. And what I live holds true for everyone who begins to examine life in accordance with Socrates:

> "The unexamined life is not worth living?"

So, let me pick up where I so rudely interrupted myself to find out how we could allow the COVID-19 pandemic to fly as high as it did. Now we know that both the PTSD and ADHD dreamt-up diagnoses allowing for drugging to the hilt of both children and adults was engineered. And we know that this drugging played a major role in the population's tacit and docile acceptance of the COVID injections and movement restrictions mandates. Let's move on to *Fallacy* 3, then, keeping the Mayan moral code "In Lak'ech Ala K'in ---'I am you, and you are me'" in mind as its leitmotiv.

ABOUT THE AUTHOR

H. Nattanya Andersen

Born in St. Peter at the North Sea coast of Schleswig-Holstein, Germany, Nattanya set out to sail with the Danish Marine at the age of 17 before settling in Copenhagen, Denmark. Travelling in her blood, a few years later she began to fly for Air Canada out of Montreal, Quebec, Canada, obtained her Bachelor of Arts degree from Simon Fraser University, Burnaby, BC, and turned to writing her meticulously researched non-fiction books whilst injured with Post Traumatic Stress Disorder in the line of duty. She lives with her dogs by the Pacific Ocean shore of Vancouver Island, British Columbia, Canada.

BIBLIOGRAPHY

Alexander, Eben, III. *Proof of Heaven: A Neurosurgeon's Journey into the Afterlife.* New York: Simon & Schuster, 2012.

Alexander, Eben, and Karen Newell. *Living in a Mindful Universe: A Neurosurgeon's Journey into the Heart of Consciousness.* Rodale Books, 2017.

Alexander, Eben, and Ptolemy Tompkins. *The Map of Heaven: How Science, Religion, and Ordinary People Are Proving the Afterlife.* New York: Simon & Schuster, 2014.

Alighieri, Dante. *The Divine Comedy: The Inferno, The Purgatorio, and The Paradiso.* New York: The New American Library, Illustrated edition 2003.

Alpenfels, Ethel J., D.Sc. "The Anthropology and Social Significance of the Human Hand." *Artificial Limbs* 2, no. 2, (May 1955): 4-21. Washington, DC: National Academy of Sciences - National Research Council. oandplibrary.org.

Alvarez, Al. *The Savage God.* New York: Random House, 1972

American Psychiatric Association. *Diagnostic and Statistical Manual of Mental Disorders 5th edition.* American Psychiatric Association Publishing, 2013.

Atwater, P. M. H. *Beyond the Light: What Isn't Being Said About Near Death Experience: From Visions of Heaven to Glimpses of Hell.* Carol Publishing Corporation, 1994.

Avicenna. *The Metaphysics of Healing.* Brigham Young University; 1st edition, 2005.

Barnes, Harry E. "Some Typical Contributions of English Sociology to Political Theory." *American Journal of Sociology* 28, no. 1 (July, 1922): 49-66. Chicago: The University of Chicago Press.

Bastiat, Frédéric. *Economic Harmonic*, trans. W. Hayden Boyers, 517. Irvington-on-Hudson, N.Y: Foundation for Economic Education, 1996.

———*The Law*. Auburn, Alabama: Ludwig von Mises Institute, May 2007. https://cdn.mises.org/thelaw.pdf

Bernays, Edward. *Crystallizing Public Opinion (1923).* Ig Publishing, reprint edition 2011.

———*Propaganda* (1927). Ig Publishing, reprint edition 2004.

Blackmon, Douglas A. *Slavery by Another Name: The Re-Enslavement of Black Americans from the Civil War to World War II.* New York: Anchor, 2009.

Bonner, Thomas Neville. *Iconoclast: Abraham Flexner and a Life in Learning.* Baltimore, MD: Johns Hopkins Univ. Press, 2002.

Bracken, Gregory. "Treaty Ports in China: Their Genesis, Development, and Influence." *Journal of Urban History* 45 (2018). SAGE Journals. https://journals.sagepub.com/doi/full/10.1177/0096144218816548

Brackney, William H. *Baptists in North America: An Historical Perspective.* (Wiley-Blackwell 2006), 12.

Breggin, Peter R. *Brain Disabling Treatments in Psychiatry: Drugs, Electroshock, and the Psychopharmaceutical Complex.* New York: Springer Publishing Company, 2nd edition, 2007.

Breggin, Peter R., and Ginger Ross Breggin. *Covid-19 and the Global Predators: We are the Prey.* Ithca, NY: Lake Edge Press, 2021.

Brown, E. Richard. *Rockefeller Medicine Men: Medicine and capitalism in America.* Berkeley: University of California Press, 1979.

Bryan, Craig J., and M. David Rudd. *Managing Suicide Risk in Primary Care.* Springer Publishing Company, 2010.

Burtt, E.A. *The Metaphysical Foundations of Modern Science.* Dover Publications, 2003.

Butler, Smedley Darlington. *War is a Racket.* Los Angeles: Feral House, Reprint Edition, 2003.

Carson, Rachel. *Silent Spring.* New York: Houghton Mifflin, 1962.

Caldwell, Taylor. *Bright Flows The River.* Fawcett Crest Books,1979.

———, *Answer As A Man.* New York: G.P. Putnam's Sons, 1980.

Clarke, Adele E., ed. *Biomedicalization: Technoscience, Health, and Illness in the U.S.* Duke University Press, 2010.

Coleman, John. *The Tavistock Institute of Human Relations: Shaping The Moral, Spiritual, Cultural, And Political Economic Decline Of The United States Of America.* Las Vegas: World Intelligence Review, 2006.

———*The Conspirators Hierarchy: The Story of The Committee of 300.* Bridger House Publishers Inc., 1992.

Collier, Peter, and David Horowitz. *The Rockefellers: An American Dynasty.* New York, N.Y: Holt, Rinehart & Winston, 1976.

Combe, George. *The Constitution of Man Considered in Relation to External Objects.* Carter and Hendee, 1829.

Cutlip, Scott M. *The Unseen Power: Public Relations: A History.* New Jersey: Lawrence Erlbaum Associates Inc., 1994.

Darwin, Charles. *On the Origin of Species by Means of Natural Selection, Or The Preservation of Favoured Races in the Struggle for Life.* Ezreads Publications, LLC, 2009.

Douglas, Ann. *Terrible Honesty: Mongrel Manhattan in the 1920s*. Farrar, Straus and Giroux, 1996.

Engels, Friedrich. *The Condition of the Working Class in England* (1845). Penguin Classics, Revised edition, 1987.

Homer. *The Iliad*, trans. Robert Fitzgerald. International Collector's Library, 1974.

Flexner, Abraham. *Prostitution in Europe*. New York: The Century Co., First Edition, 1914.

Flexner, James T. *An American Saga: The Story of Helen Thomas and Simon Flexner*. Boston/Toronto: Little, Brown, and Company, 1984.

Free, Joshua, ed. *The Maqlu Ritual Book: A Pocket Companion to Babylonian Exorcisms, Banishing Rites & Protective Spells*. Joshua Free, 10th Anniversary Collector's edition, 2019.

Freedman, David Noel, ed. *The Anchor Bible Dictionary.* New York: Doubleday, 1992.

Fry, Helen. T*he London Cage: The Secret History of Britain's World War II Interrogation Centre*. Yale University Press, First Edition 2017.

Gibbon, Edward. *The Decline and Fall of the Roman Empire*. New York: Alfred A. Knopf, 1993.

Goddard, Dwight. *A Buddhist Bible*. Beacon Press, 1994.

———, ed. *The Lankavatara Sutra: An Epitomized Version*, trans. D. T. Suzuki. Rhinebeck, NY: Monkfish Book Publishing Co., Provenance Editions, 2003.

Gordon, Paul. *The Hope of Therapy*. PCCS Books, 2008.

Greenberg, David. *Republic of Spin: An Inside History of the American Presidency*. W. W. Norton & Company, first edition, 2017.

Haber, Ludwig Fritz. *The Poisonous Cloud: Chemical Warfare in the First World War.* Oxford University Press, 1986.

Haley, Daniel. *Politics in Healing: The Suppression and Manipulation of American Medicine*. Potomac Valley Press, 2000.

Hall, Manly P. *The Secret Destiny of America.* TarcherPerigee, Illustrated edition, 2008.

———, T*he Secret Teachings of all Ages: An Encyclopedic Outline of Masonic, Hermetic, Qabbalistic and Rosicrucian Symbolical Philosophy*. A & D Books, Illustrated edition, 2009.

Hamer, John. *The Falsification of History: Our Distorted Reality*. Rossendale Books, 2012.

Harari, Yuval Noah. *Sapiens: A Brief History of Humankind*. Random House of Canada, 2016.

Harrington, Anne. *Mind Mixers: Psychiatry's Troubled Search For the Biology of Mental Illness*. W. W. Norton & Company, 2019.

Hegel, Georg Wilhelm Friedrich. *Encyclopedia of the Philosophical Sciences in Basic Outline, Part 1, Science of Logic* (1817). Cambridge University Press, 2010.

Henrotin, Fernand. *Democracy Of Education In Medicine*. Chicago: R.R. Donnelley and Sons Co., 1903.

Hoffman, Michael A. *They Were White and They Were Slaves: The Untold History of the Enslavement of Whites in Early America*. Coeur d'Alene, ID: Independent History and Research, 2016.

Hofmann, Adolf. "Use of LSD in Psychiatry" Chap. 4 in *LSD- My Problem Child*. McGraw-Hill Book Company, 1980.

Horsley, J. Stephen. *Narco-Analysis: A New Technique in Short-Cut Psychotherapy: A Comparison With Other Methods and Notes on the Barbituates*. London: Oxford Medical Publications, Oxford University Press, 1943.

Hughes, Rhonda G., ed. *NCBI: Patient Safety and Quality: An Evidence-Based Handbook for Nurses*. Rockville, MD: Agency for Healthcare Research and Quality (US), 2008.

Hughes, Robert. *The Fatal Shore: The epic of Australia's founding*. Vintage, Illustrated edition, 1988.

Huxley, Aldous. *Brave New World*. Toronto: Vintage Canada, 2007.

Icke, David. *The Perception Deception*. David Icke Books Limited, 2013.

Illich, Ivan. *Medical Nemesis: The Expropriation of Health*. Pantheon Books, 1976.

Ilschner, Jeff. *The Return to Source: A Spiritual Awakening to the Dark Reality on Earth*. New Jersey: Newman Springs Publishing, Inc., 2021.

Jaffe, D. J. *Insane Consequences: How the Mental Health Industry Fails the Mentally Ill*. Prometheus, 2017.

Jung, Carl G. *Man And His Symbols*. Dell Publishing Co. Inc., 1968.

Karch, Steven B. *A Brief History of Cocaine*. Routledge, 2nd Edition, 2005.

Kelsen, Hans. *General Theory of Law And State,* trans. Anders Wedberg. New Jersey: The Lawbook Exchange, 2007.

Koestler, Arthur. *The 13th Tribe*. G S G & Associates Pub., 1976.

Kosso, Peter. *A Summary of Scientific Method*. Springer Dordrecht, 2011.

Kübler-Ross, Elisabeth. *On Death And Dying*. Simon & Schuster/Touchstone, 1970.

———, *On Death and Dying: What the dying have to teach doctors, nurses, clergy, and their own families*. New York, NY: Scribner, 2003.

Kuhn, Thomas. *The Structure of Scientific Revolutions*. Chicago: University Of Chicago Press, 1996.

Kurzweil, Ray. *The Age of Spiritual Machines: When Computers Exceed Human Intelligence*. Viking Press, 1999.

Lanctot, Guylaine. *The Medical Mafia: How to Get Out of it Alive and Take Back Our Health and Wealth.* Bridge of Love Publications, 1995.

LaPierre, Dominique. *The City of Joy,* trans. Kathryn Spink. New York: Doubleday, 1985.

Le Bon, Charles-Marie Gustave. *The Crowd: A Study of the Popular Mind.* Dover Publications, 2002.

Lee, Martin A., and Bruce Shlain. *Acid Dreams: The Complete Social History of LSD: The CIA, the Sixties, and Beyond.* Grove Press, 1992.

Lennard, Henry L. *Mystification and Drug Misuse: Hazards in Using Psychoactive Drugs*. Harper & Row, 1972.

Lewis, C. S. *Mere Christianity.* London: Geoffrey Bles, 1952.

Liebermann, Jeffrey, with Ogi Ogas. *Shrinks: The Untold Story of Psychiatry.* New York: Little, Brown Spark, 2015.

Llewellyn, Sheila. *Walking Wounded.* London: Hodder, 2018.

McGilchrist, Iain. *The Master and His Emissary: The Divided Brain and the Making of the Western World.* Yale University Press, 2nd Edition, 2019.

Mullins, Eustace C. *The Curse of Canaan*. Omnia Veritas Ltd., 2016.

———, *Murder by Injection: The Story of the Medical Conspiracy Against America*. Omnia Veritas Ltd., 2016.

O'Brien, Cathy, with Mark Phillips. *Trance Formation of America*. Reality Marketing Inc., 1995.

Orwell, George. *1984*. Seeker & Warburg, 1949.

MacCurdy, John T. *War Neuroses.* Cambridge University Press, 2013.

Macdonnell, A. G. *England; Their England.* Pan Macmillan, 1978.

Matheson, Richard. *What dreams May Come*. Tor Books, 2004.

McCulloch, Colleen. *The First Man in Rome*. First Avon Books, 1991.

Metzl, Jonathan. *The Protest Psychosis: How Schizophrenia Became a Black Disease.* Beacon Press, first edition, 2009.

Moreno, Jonathan D. *Impromptu Man: J.L. Moreno and the Origins of Psychodrama, Encounter Culture, and the Social Network.* New York: Bellevue Literary Press, 2014.

Moriyama, I. M., R. M. Loy, A. H. T. Robb-Smith. *History of the statistical classification of diseases and causes of death*. H. M. Rosenberg, D. L. Hoyert, eds. Hyattsville, MD: National Center for Health Statistics. 2011.

Najavits, Lisa M. *Seeking Safety: A Treatment Manual for PTSD and Substance Abuse*. New York: Guilford Press, 2001.

Newton, Michael. *Journey of Souls: Case Studies of Life Between Lives*. Llewellyn Publications, 1994.

———, *Destiny of Souls: New Case Studies of Life Between Lives*. Llewellyn Publications, 2000.

Nietzsche, Friedrich Wilhelm. *Beyond Good and Evil*. CreateSpace Independent Publishing Platform, 2014.

Nock, Albert Jay. *Our Enemy The State*. CreateSpace Independent Publishing Platform, 2014.

Perez, Ismael. *Our Cosmic Origin: Open your eyes about earth's place in the multiverse and about a greater organization of the cosmos*, ed. Richard Barnett. Independently published, 2021.

Peterson, Jordan B. *12 Rules For Life: An antidote to chaos*. Random House Canada, Classic Edition, 2018.

Peterson, Joseph H., ed. *John Dee's Five Books of Mystery: Original Sourcebook of Enochian Magic*. Weiser Books, 2002.

Peyer, Hans Conrad. *Roche - A Company History 1896-1996*. Editiones Roche, 1996.

Pike, Albert. *Morals and Dogma Of the Ancient and Sccepted Scottish Rite of Freemasonry*, chap. 26. [Charleston 1871] Independently published, 2017.

Prophet, Elizabeth C. *Forbidden Mysteries of Enoch: The untold story of men and angels*. Malibu, California: Summit University Press, 1983.

Ramchand, Rajeev, Joie Acosta, Rachel M. Burns, Lisa H. Jaycox, and Christopher G. Pernin. *The War Within: Preventing Suicide in the U.S. Military*. RAND Corporation, 2011.

Ready, Romilla, and Kate Burton. *Neuro-linguistic Programming For Dummies*. For Dummies, 2nd edition, 2010.

Ripperger, Chad A. *Introduction to the Science of Mental Health*. Sensus Traditionis Press, 2013.

Roach, Geshe Michael. *The Diamond Cutter: The Buddha On Managing Your Business And Your Life*. Doubleday, 2003.

Rosen, David H. *Transforming Depression: Healing the Soul Through Creativity*. Nicolas-Hays, Inc., 2002.

Rudd, M. David, Thomas Joiner, and M. Hasan Rajab. *Treating suicidal behavior: An effective, time-limited approach (Treatment manuals for practitioners)*. New York, NY, US: Guilford Press, 2004.

Rush, Florence. *The Best Kept Secret: Sexual Abuse of Children*. McGraw-Hill, 1981.

Sassoon, Siegfried. *Sherston's Progress*. Faber & Faber Ltd., 1936.

Schilder, Paul. *The Image And Appearance Of The Human Body* [1950]. Routledge, reprint 1999.

Schur, Max. *Freud: Living and Dying*. International Universities Press, 1972.

Schwartz, Joseph. *Cassandra's Daughter: A history of psychoanalysis*. Routledge, 2003.

Shorter, Edward. *A History of Psychiatry: From the Era of the Asylum to the Age of Prozac*. Wiley, 1998.

Sneader, Walter. *Drug Discovery: A History*. Wiley-Interscience, 2005.

Sri Dhammananda, Dr. K. *Treasure of the Dhamma*. Kuala Lumpur, Malaysia: Buddhist Missionary Society, 1994.

Stasz, Clarice. *The Rockefeller Women: Dynasty of Piety, Privacy, and Service*. St. Martin's Press, 1995.

Steiner, Rudolf. *The Philosophy Of Freedom*. Lulu.com, 2011.

Strydom, Jan and Susan du Plessis. *The Myth of ADHD and Other Learning Disabilities; Parenting without Ritalin*. Huntington House Publishers, 2001.

Szasz, Thomas S. *The Myth of Mental Illness: Foundations of a Theory of Personal Conduct*. Harper Row, 1961.

———, *Psychiatry: The Science of Lies*. Syracuse University Press, 2008.

———, *Law, Liberty, and Psychiatry: An Inquiry into the Social Uses of Mental Health Practices*. Routledge & Kegan Paul, 1963.

———, *Manufacture of Madness: A Comparative Study of the Inquisition and the Mental Health Movement*. Syracuse University Press, 1997.

Swedenborg, Emmanuel. *Heaven And Hell: New Century Edition*. Swedenborg Foundation, 2010.

———, trans. George Dole. *Divine Providence*, Vol. 25. Swedenborg Foundation, 2008.

Teilhard de Chardin, Pierre. *The Phenomenon of Man*. Fontana Books, 1965.

———, *Le Milieu Divin; An Essay on the Interior Life*, 23. Collins Fontana Books, 1957.

The New Order of Barbarians: The New World System. CreateSpace Independent Publishing, 2013.

Thomas, Gordon. *Journey Into Madness: The True Story of Secret CIA Mind Control and Medical Abuse*. Bantam, 1989.

Tolman, Edward Chace. *Purposive behavior in animals and men*. Appleton-Century-Crofts, 1967.

Tolstoy, Leo. *The Death of Ivan Ilyich*, trans. Richard Pevear and Larissa Volokhonsky. Vintage Books, 2012.

Trotter, Wilfred. *Instinct of the Herd in Peace and War*, p. 36; pp. 61–68 London: T. Fisher Unwin, 1916.

Tuttle, Russell H. "Hominoidea: A conceptual history", *The International Encyclopaedia of Biological Anthropology*. John Wiley & Sons, Inc., 2018.

Van Lommel, Pim. *Consciousness Beyond Life: The Science of the Near-Death Experience*. New York: HarperOne, 2011.

Wells, S.D. *25 Amazing (and disturbing) facts About the Hidden History of Medicine.* https://livinginnatureengland.wordpress.com, 2012.

White, Michael, and David Epston. *Narrative Means to Therapeutic Ends*. W.W.Norton & Company, 1990.

Whitehead, Alfred North. *Process and Reality: An Essay in Cosmology* The Free Press, 1978.

Woolley, Benjamin: The Queen's Conjurer: The Science and Magic of Dr. John Dee, Adviser to Queen Elizabeth I; Holt Paperbacks 2002

Yates, Frances Amelia: The Rosicrucian Enlightenment; Routledge 2001

Yogananda, Paramhansa. *Karma And Reincarnation: The Wisdom of Paramhansa Yogananda, Volume 2*. Crystal Clarity Publishers, 2007.

———, *God Talks With Arjuna: The Bhagavad Gita*, Chapter 5. Self-Realization Fellowship, First Edition, 2001.

———, *Autobiography of a Yogi*. Self-Realization Fellowship, Anniversary Edition, 1997.

Printed by Amazon Italia Logistica S.r.l.
Torrazza Piemonte (TO), Italy

49005535R10429